The SAGE Handbook of
Public Relations

The SAGE Handbook of
Public Relations
Second Edition

Edited by
Robert L. Heath
University of Houston

Los Angeles | London | New Delhi
Singapore | Washington DC

For information:

SAGE Publications, Inc.
2455 Teller Road
Thousand Oaks, California 91320
E-mail: order@sagepub.com

SAGE Publications Ltd.
1 Oliver's Yard
55 City Road
London EC1Y 1SP
United Kingdom

SAGE Publications India Pvt. Ltd.
B 1/I 1 Mohan Cooperative Industrial Area
Mathura Road, New Delhi 110 044
India

SAGE Publications Asia-Pacific Pte. Ltd.
33 Pekin Street #02-01
Far East Square
Singapore 048763

Printed in the United States of America

Library of Congress Cataloging-in-Publication Data

The SAGE handbook of public relations / editor Robert L. Heath.
p. cm.
Rev. ed. of: Hand book of public relations. c2001.
Includes bibliographical references and index.
ISBN 978-1-4129-7780-7 (cloth)
ISBN 978-1-4129-7781-4 (pbk.)
1. Public relations. 2. Public relations–Handbooks, manuals, etc. I. Heath, Robert L. (Robert Lawrence), 1941- II. Handbook of public relations.

HD59.H267 2010
659.2—dc22 2010010659

This book is printed on acid-free paper.

10 11 12 13 14 10 9 8 7 6 5 4 3 2 1

Acquisitions Editor: Todd R. Armstrong
Editorial Assistant: Nathan Davidson
Production Editor: Eric Garner
Copy Editor: QuADS Prepress (P) Ltd.
Typesetter: C&M Digitals (P) Ltd.
Proofreader: Scott Oney
Indexer: Michael Ferreira
Cover Designer: Candice Harman
Marketing Manager: Helen Salmon

Contents

Preface

Robert L. Heath

Having edited several books, I have had the opportunity to reflect on the role of an editor. In that regard, this occasion brought to mind my joy and curiosity as a lad in Western Colorado (United States) watching freight trains pass. Some cars carried cattle, sheep, and wool to market. Some conveyed fruit, especially peaches and apples, to waiting customers who were not fortunate to know what "tree ripened" truly means. More cars in the later years of my youth—and especially today—carried coal. Ours was a rail line that began upriver a bit. It joined other lines at various terminuses. Different cars and their contents had different destinations. They were designed differently. Some were enclosed but constructed so as to allow air to flow to animals. Others were refrigerated to protect the produce. Coal cars were open. However different in design and content, they all had a common purpose: to carry goods to the market.

Chapters for an edited book are the same. Like those cars or the booths at an open market, they serve to deliver goods to various destinations and for various purposes or outcomes. The chapters are a part of a system of scholarship and best practice. As I opened and read each, it was like those rail cars. "What's inside and where is it going?" I hope readers have that same reaction.

Authors who craft the chapters make claims that rhetorically seek to attract attention to their ideas, convince others that they have good ones, and foster relationships with one another and their various readers in ways that advance the discipline. In this collective enterprise, voices propose, counter, support, and reject each other much as in a seminar. Is this a dialogue, a cacophony, a babel, or a symphony? Only readers can decide.

Whatever else we say about the process, however, it is a narrative of a field that struggles to give identity and substance to itself. It strives to be thoughtful, innovative, important, relevant, and useful. But, as was true of the railroad cars, not all chapters contain complementary contents, however useful each might be. Without reservation, we can note various ethics and societal, as well as agentic, purposes behind each of the chapters.

A key question in this volume is "What about our knowledge of public relations can help it to best serve society?" The flip side of that question is "What would society be like without public relations?" "Would it be better or worse if public relations had never been 'invented'?" Of course, we can't erase public relations from society, although numerous critics wish for that end. However, if the value of each profession is what it does to serve the individual and collective interests of members of society, we can then explore what it does to earn its keep. In raising the ante to a societal level, that question has been one of the major themes of the past decade. Before then, much of the work concentrated on making organizations more effective by using public relations. This past generation has in various ways argued that no organization can truly be successful for the long haul if it does not relate well to and advance the society that enfranchises it. Thus, instead of addressing, as once was the case, what is good for society, we have learned to reverse that equation: What is good for society is good for General Motors.

At one pole, the rationale for public relations is to serve only the interest of the organization or individual who sponsors, employs, or enacts it. The other end of that continuum features the service public relations provides to some or all of society. Thus, we are prone to ask, "Can society exist without public relations?" At a pragmatic level, we know that society created it. In the United States, for instance, its role is protected by the First Amendment: the right of natural and artificial citizens to speak and to hear, read, and view what others say. It is broadly protected and advanced as democratic, however undemocratic its enactment has been, is, and likely will be. Even more fundamental, or broader, we know that even the actions of organizations and publics as they enact their roles in society have communicative, and public relations, impact on the discourse of society. And, as such, we ask, "Does that make society better?" "Does it foster truly enlightened choices, actions, policies, and all that is necessary for a collectivity to function as well as possible?" And, we might add, the rationale for society is the collective management of risk—the maximization of rewards and the minimization of losses in a world of uncertainty and even chaos.

As such, we frequently focus narrowly on communication as the essence of public relations. Then, we too often address the processes of public relations, ignoring its role in creating and enacting meaning. Some writers even downplay the technical aspects of the discipline and elevate the strategic planning aspects. Can efforts to separate those realms of engagement go too far? Have they already gone too far? We also can mistakenly take our eye off the reality that what a person or organization does is communicative and can instead speak more loudly than its public relations discourse about its position on issues, relationship development, and role in society.

Those of us interested in issues, rhetoric, dialogue, and discourse continue to emphasize that information does not serve for much without interpretation and advocacy, however loud or subtle. We lose sight of the richness of dialogue if we only feature information and don't address how meaning is crafted, shared, and enacted in ways that relate to collective and competitive sense making of the information/facts and evaluations at play. We wordy animals craft the reality in which we live by fostering a web of shared and conflicting ideas, evaluations, identification, and policies.

Purpose of This Volume

Volumes such as this one play many roles. I base this observation on the history of the 2001 *Handbook of Public Relations.* It serves scholars. Some of the chapters are cited, some frequently so, as major state-of-the-discipline documents. For graduate students, this sort of volume puts before them a feast prepared by leading contributors to academic literature. Professionals, through academic coursework and professional reading, find answers to their everyday best practices challenges. For these reasons, it is nice to know that these volumes have an enduring status in the growth of discourse about public relations.

Volumes of this sort offer evidence of tensions—some quite serious, not only in origins but also of growth, in terms of what we study and why we do—and the conclusions that we draw from them. There is continuing evidence of media relations, journalism, and similar origins in this volume. One of the kinds of evidence of this is the concept of information as something that is shared—something that flows through systems. Some researchers feature media relations for better or for worse as a grounding for the discipline.

Others, especially those from speech communication, or the more modern term *communication studies*, orientation feature concepts such as meaning, discourse, dialogue, rhetoric, persuasion, sense making, cocreation, and voice—even narrative—as the intellectual foundations of the discipline. So rather than featuring the paradigm of information flowing (often through media), from one entity to another (or even occurring through interpersonal communication), the communication studies disciples embrace all those by bringing to bear more of an advocacy, interpretation, social construction, and shared meaning view of the rationale and product of the communication—including the meaningfulness of organizations' actions, their enactment of themselves. These folks even embrace and do not flinch at the term *persuasion* as a means for understanding how sentient beings make choices.

One of the major advances in this volume is the literature shift, from making organizations effective to making society effective. Increasingly, there are calls for more attention to implications of meaning making, such as anthropology would help explain, as the rationale and product of public relations communication. This line of analysis is particularly relevant to those who believe that some standard of excellence exists as the defining concept of organizations and organizational practices. The rhetorical tradition has eternally aspired to understand the implications and responsibilities of the good organization communicating, knowing well that such communication is not linear—one-way—but dialogic. The critical tradition does not object to that theme. Nevertheless, it worries that either the good or excellent organization concept, or the relationship perspective, can blind academics and practitioners alike to not see an encompassing ethic that champions the quality of discourse as natural and neutral rather than constructed by interested parties and, therefore, ideological and value laden. The question is also how the discourse brings to bear or obstructs a sense of higher value—the quality of humanity per se—as the essence, function, and outcome of organizational discourse. Critical views increasingly press us to be less committed to modern and Western interpretations of the excellent organization, and its self-interested effectiveness, and more focused on the fully functioning society.

Some researchers aggressively draw on other disciplines. Relationship management draws on interpersonal communication and all too often assumes that *relationship* is a code word for something that is good and enduring. In fact, the interpersonal communication scholars are motivated in their quest to understand and improve this context by the realization that most relationships do not endure and may not be positive.

Other researchers like to believe that they can learn from management theorists. In particular, there are those who believe that they can define and predict what aspects of management produce mutual benefits for the organizations. Such interests often commit to an efficiency of resources model but can opt for seeing management as a discipline of resource management. In that model, some convince others to allocate the stakes they hold in exchange for the productivity—including seemingly qualitative relationships—that results from organizational management policy development and enactment. This resource management includes strategic management through budgeting to achieve one set as opposed to other sets of outcomes. Yet another view is based on management as the science and art of comingling resources through participative and collaborative processes.

As a paradigm, relationship management must address the reality of opposing perspectives. As organizations (typically businesses) are advised to create positive (even mutually beneficial) relationships, those who challenge, oppose, and even seek to destroy such organizations, including businesses and industries, also engage in creating, building, maintaining, and repairing relationships with their various power constituencies. In addition, the relationships they foster may actually threaten the ones other organizations are trying to create. Thus, environmental groups ask followers to identify, or, perhaps, "bond," with them. Even terrorists recruit and build relationships that give them power, resource management, in opposition to other entities, power, and relationships that they seek to defeat and even destroy. Such dialectics suggest that we must necessarily be vigilant that seemingly promising paradigms do raise additional questions and threaten the certainty of our conclusions to the detriment of our field and society.

Researchers pressed with such challenges often resort to shifting definitions rather than revisiting theoretical foundations and paradigms. They may focus primarily on one-organization-one-stakeholder public relationships, which narrows the scope of research and theory. Similarly, the researchers' work features publics as nonorganizational and in need of relationship development. Public relations is not exclusively about working with "lay" publics but also with other organizations (intra-industry, interindustry, and nonprofit).

The dialogue in handbooks is rich. It's where the action is. We hear the voice of Platonist philosopher kings of society who believe that they can figure out what is best for others. We hear disciples of Aristotle who believe in the democracy of public advocacy where voices compete openly in the contest of ideas and interests. Aristotelian advocates realize that one must tolerate and respond to opposing ideas. And we hear the followers of Isocrates who advocate that all that is said and done must fit the paradigm of the universal good citizen. Each person and organization must labor for the good of all—the spirit of citizenship that privileges no interest but works for the collective interest of all. As internal organizational communication is studied to make organizations better places to work, one of the themes of external organizational communication and enactment—including public relations—is goaded by the incentive to make society a better place in which to live and work.

One of the products—both a means for advancement and a hindrance—is that different perspectives and worldviews offer different terminologies. One contested term is *advocacy* as a productive aspect of dialogue. Some interpret it as inherently agentic. They don't see it at the societal level as the essence of collaboration and participative decision making that operationalizes the paradigm of statement, counterstatement: act, react, and the lesson learned. Those who adhere to a model of sharing information and instrumentalizing publics can presume that if everyone just had the same information, the same facts, they would draw the same conclusions and harmony would prevail. The objective of some discussants is to see society as agency, not as the voice of individual or collective organizations. So is the role of public relations to make organizations successful or is it to make society effective in using organizations for the collective management of risk?

In this pursuit, various themes continue. Some see one or two theories as becoming so widely established that what remains to be done is just to fill gaps and polish concepts. Other theorists believe that we have merely begun the journey and might not even have the best grounding for future research. Perhaps, they argue, we have gone in many wrong directions that have merely been dead ends. Researchers wisely believe that paradigm shifts are inevitable and continual.

Plan of the Book

The book is designed to feature three parts. One has railcars loaded with leading theories and theoretical perspectives. Part 2 features contexts of practice, yet does not ignore theory. The third part delves into international themes, as both context and challenge. The book ends with reflections to help us monitor progress and see ways to set our directions anew.

Plan of the Editor

Each year, I see myself more and more as a narrativist. This worldview and self-realization guides my editorial choices. Well aware of robust controversies in the field, I have tried to assemble a cast that—through their collective voices—gives a fair, open, and honest representation of key themes. Rather than constraining authors, except for length, I have tried to help them articulate their ideas. Let the marketplace decide which carloads of ideas and voices are worth buying into and which are not.

As editor, and in collaboration with key people at Sage, I see this book as less a conventional "second edition" than an updating of the field's progress over the past decade. Although I hope that many of the chapters in the 2001 version continue to be popular, useful, and cited as we move forward, much of what is written here did not appear in 2001. Thus, I see this volume as a continuation—not a replacement but an extension—of the 2001 version.

By every standard, we are a young academic discipline. We have much to offer, but we must continually push the envelope and take ourselves neither too seriously nor for granted, as many other disciplines vie for our traditional territories. We are not alone in the discussion of themes that recur in this volume and in the 2001 version. At times, we are stigmatized in our efforts by the negative connotation associated with our contribution to various literatures, simply by attaching the concept public relations. That should be incentive enough to work harder and not be deterred.

Acknowledgments

The Editor wishes to acknowledge key persons whose insights and professional efforts helped add this work to the growing list of major works on public relations. The following were asked to share their comments on the 2001 version to make this current work a solid contribution to the discipline:

Anne Gregory (Leeds Metropolitan University)

Darren G. Lilleker (Bournemouth University)

Bonnie Neff (Valparaiso University)

Lan Ni (University of Maryland)

Gayle Pohl (University of Northern Iowa)

Steven Raucher (University of New Haven)

Alison Theaker (University of Worcester)

Katerina Tsetsura (The University of Oklahoma)

Brenda Wrigley (Syracuse University)

The Editor also thanks these colleagues at SAGE Publications: Todd Armstrong (Senior Acquisitions Editor), who spearheaded this project; Nathan Davidson (Editorial Assistant), who helped sort through thousands of editorial details; the Production Editor, Eric Garner, who made the book attractive to readers; and the Marketing Manager, Helen Salmon, who thought of many ways to attract readers' attention to the contributions collected here.

Finally, the Editor acknowledges the authors whose work sets the standard of the discipline. This is good company to keep.

—Robert L. Heath

University of Houston

PART I

Mind, Self, and Society

Robert L. Heath

In comparison to the 2001 *Handbook*, several themes emerge or take on new life in this volume. That edition was narrow in comparison to the array of thoughts featured here. It seemed relatively disinterested in a thorough discussion of meaning related to how and what we communicate in order to cocreate enactable collective sense making and interest alignment. It often took communication for granted rather than treating it as an explorable concept needing new insights.

Cobwebs of previous work linger and cling to us as we attempt to move forward. Some authors assert that an interest in "self-interest" of an organization is the driving and dysfunctional factor in theory building and research. Some of the researchers who focus on process argue that the symbolic critical interpretivists can only think about how argument can be made in defense of an organization. Others advocate another point of view—propositional discourse, the paradigm of sharing ideas, offers a superior approach to the message/meaning/reflective management/collaboration paradigm.

These entanglements suggest that three dominant paradigms press against one another with ever-increasing force. In their various ways, all three paradigms address a "management" theme but place their bets on different horses. These paradigms are definable as management adjustive, discourse engagement, and normative/critical/ethical.

The management paradigm can be limited to roots in systems theory, advanced through structural functionalism (structuration) and featuring a cybernetic-adjustive paradigm. That version can be modeled as rational market efficiency management systems seeking cybernetic adjustments in relation to other organizations and definable populations. At its extreme, we can call this the thermostatic paradigm of public relations. What makes sense, the mechanical engineers will tell us, for instrumentation that adjusts systems to one another or parts of one system to another (such as HVAC [heating, ventilation, and air-conditioning systems for homes and buildings] structures and functions), does well when designed as a tool and calibrated by sentient beings. As such, even within chaos, the system functions because it has structured a part of chaos to respond to a command/control management system based on cybernetic balance. For those, especially those with an extreme mind-set, in management (academics, consultants, or enactors) communication, this view of management can actually be trivial. In a curriculum meeting years ago, a senior management faculty member said, "All anyone needs to know about communication can be learned by 30 minutes of reading if the person reads slowly." The modern management era featured efficiency and rationality (as defined by one set of managers regardless of their discipline) as flow of information (sharing ideas and information) as input, processing/throughput, and output.

In the "real" world, this line of Western management thinking buoyed by the end of World War II and the new era of mass production mass consumption (the first started post–Civil War) saw management efficiency and rationality as the solution to prosperity. Then, the rational and efficient train hit the wall: The turbulence of the 1950s, 1960s, 1970s, and 1980s. Old management views were battered by a new reality that spawned an interest in the management of chaos. Corporate social responsibility and stakeholder approaches to management and communication became more important than systematic MBO (Management by Objectives) modeling. Critical interpretivism and theories relevant to discourse analysis and enactment gained currency. Relationship theory tended to thirst for solutions to the problems that most relationships fail to sustain themselves, need repair, are manipulative, or are forcefully truncated.

In this era, issues management (whether a dominant, parallel, or subordinate discipline to public relations) developed as the new management science. It rests on management processes (mission- and vision-driven strategic planning, policy, implementation/budgeting, and evaluation) as an adjustive process balancing threats and opportunities. This organizational requirement is brought to life by three other pillars: being a good organization (meeting or exceeding stakeholder CSR [corporate social responsibility] expectations), multidisciplinary issue monitoring (discovering others' thoughts and interests, power resources, stakes sought and held), and multidimensional communication—collaborative discourse. Here we can blend systems, discourse, and normative adjustment. In this fray, academics and professionals have worked to define the nature and role of public relations and to determine the value it adds to organizations (a management incentive) and to society (the rationale for its enfranchisement as an artificial citizen).

Since each of the chapters that follow explains key points relevant to the nature of public relations, its role in the performance of organizations and as a actor in society, there is little need to highlight individual contributions. Nor is it relevant for the editor to critique themes with which he disagrees. Let those chips fall where they may. Instead, I suggest that we examine various rich/provocative statements about these matters.

As I suggest in the title of this section, the themes variously and collectively address matters of *mind* (what theorists think they know and can report about the *ideation* of the reality of public relations as a social and organizational force), *self* (what can and is said about the *identity* of the persons practitioners enact with, against, on behalf of, and contrary to), and *society* (the complex of *relationships* by which interests and self-interests are enacted through structures, functions, and shared meanings in varying degrees of cooperation, competition, and collaboration). Broadly, a key theme is structures and functions in varying degrees of harmony and coordination as expressions of self- and mutual interest. Another key theme is the creation and enactment of shared meaning, socially constructed reality, through discourse that largely can be characterized as statement, counterstatement—act, counteract, and the lesson learned.

Such thoughts often, and the following chapters give evidence of that, are most positively considered in the sense of *democracy*, a term broadly used to suggest that society grows or fails to be productive to mutual benefit because of varying degrees of participative decision making. The point of agency, rather than the organization as organization, is the collectivity of organizations and various individuals as sentient. As an unabashed narrativist, I look to understand the roles (including public relations), character, persona, plots, themes, and dialogic tensions that become enactable society and hope that it is civil. In that drama, how does public relations as a discipline and profession add value?

As a precursor to the discussion that follows, I offer three provocative quotations as guidelines, for whatever benefit they may have for others who read, consider, and accept or reject ideas shared in this section. The first is George Herbert Mead's (1934) view of the dialectic of mind, self, and society:

> Our society is built up out of our social interests. Our social relations go to constitute the self. But when the immediate interests come in conflict with others we had not recognized, we tend to ignore the others and take into account only those which are immediate. The difficulty is to make ourselves recognize the other and wider interests, and then to bring them into some sort of rational relationship with the more immediate ones. (pp. 388–389)

This line of reasoning is fundamental to management, especially reflective management. It presumes shared meaning created by various voices in degrees of harmony and tension. These ideas can be (should be?) held dear by researchers and practitioners.

The second quotation addresses the powerful implications of a preposition, "between." Entities working to foster mutually beneficial relationships seek what Buber (1965) called an I–Thou relationship (see Hallahan, 2004). Beneficial relationships exhibit a workable and mutually beneficial balance of control, trust, and positive regard. Championing dialogue, Buber featured the preposition *between.* Derived from the Greek word *dialogos,* dialogue blends *logos* (word) and *dia* (through or across). The standard of dialogue set by Buber depends on whether societal participants have "in mind the other or others in their present and particular being and turn to them with the intention of establishing a living mutual relation between" (p. 19) themselves and the others. A narrow ridge exists between sets of competing and complementary interests.

In matters of interests and interconnections with stakeholders/stakeseekers, we must continue to consider the reality that organizations often work to meet the public relations challenges of interacting with and engaging other organizations (private sector and public sector—as well as nonprofit organizations/NGOs [nongovernmental organizations]). Interactivity and engagement between organizations is easier to conceptualize than is the case for nonorganized publics and audiences. In that mix, we are remiss to ignore markets, as we are to discount citizens and taxpayers as public sector publics. And we are likely to misunderstand the complexity of many challenges if we presume that any organization can and should symmetrically engage everyone equally and effectively.

We make that mistake greater when we assume either an absence of interests, conflicting and compatible, as we search for outcomes such as reputation, liking/dislike, support/opposition, conflict/accommodation, or agreement/disagreement. Rather than needing to be the same, it's sufficient and probable that harmony can result from alignment for mutual benefit. In such a mix of actors, plot, character, and themes, we can have drama, comedy, tragedy, farce, melodrama, and even absolute failure. Even then, as one public or organization may be disappointed and even outraged, another might be pleased by the narrative as it unfolds—at least for the moment. But plots take nuances.

The third quotation is by coprincipal founder of Hill and Knowlton, John W. Hill (1958), who advised us to understand management as the initial step toward appreciating the roles and challenges facing public relations professionals. He cautioned,

> It is not the work of public relations—let it always be emphasized—to outsmart the American public in helping management build profits. It is the job of public relations to help management find ways of identifying its own interests with the public interest—ways so clear

> that the profit earned by the company may be viewed as contributing to the progress of everybody in the American economy. (p. 21)

He added,

> Big companies, if they are properly managed, have a keen sense of public responsibility. They guide their policies in keeping with the public interest and make sure that each of their plants is a good neighbor in its respective community. (p. 39)

Realizing that public relations challenges extend to what organizations do or do not do, this section features robust discussions of the processes and messaging/meaning coconstruction that works variously well and badly to build relationships, resolve tensions, cocreate shared and enactable social constructions of reality, and align interests. As much as process matters, is it trumped by meanings shaped and enacted in varying degrees of harmony and discord?

References

Buber, M. (1965). *Between man and man* (R. G. Smith, Trans.). New York: Macmillan.

Hallahan, K. (2004). "Community" as a foundation for public relations theory and practice. In P. J. Kalbfleisch (Ed.), *Communication yearbook 24* (pp. 233–279). Mahwah, NJ: Lawrence Erlbaum.

Hill, J. W. (1958). *Corporate public relations: Arm of modern management.* New York: Harper.

Mead, G. H. (1934). *Mind, self, and society.* Chicago: University of Chicago Press.

CHAPTER 1

Public Relations in the Enactment of Civil Society

Maureen Taylor

This *Handbook* seeks to create and extend our knowledge about public relations theory and practice. Creating knowledge is a dynamic process in which fields of study expand and paradigms change when members of an academic or professional community ponder and work to answer difficult questions (Kuhn, 1970). In this tradition, many questions about public relations as a practice and as an academic discipline need to be examined as the field moves forward. One of the more interesting questions that comes up regularly asks, "What is the role of public relations in society?" Answers to this question will influence how people practice public relations, and the answers will also influence the way in which researchers theorize about public relations. This chapter seeks to provide one answer to this question by first exploring the role of public relations in society. The second section explores the concept of civil society as another way of thinking about a macro role for public relations in society. The final sections suggest research methods for studying a public relations approach to civil society and identify future directions for public relations research and practice.

Evolving Perspectives on Public Relations

One way to answer the question about societal roles for public relations is to consider where public relations research and practice have been and then anticipate where the theories and practices are heading. This type of macro and meta-analysis allows for a holistic framework to understand the discipline and the practice. Looking at the past, we see that practices associated with public relations have been traced back thousands of years (Kunczik, 1997). Kings, military leaders, and activists have communicated to publics through a variety of tactics. Yet the formal academic study of public relations is a relatively recent endeavor. Consider that the first academic journal dedicated to public relations research, *Public Relations Review*, was published in 1974. The academic study of public relations is less than 40 years old. We can learn a lot about our past by looking at the articles appearing in the early years of *Public Relations Review.* Early articles focused on very practical issues in conducting public relations such as media relations and agenda setting.

Botan and Taylor (2004) observed that previous public relations research has followed a functional approach. A functional approach to public relations focuses on

> techniques and production of strategic organizational messages. Research plays a role only insofar as it advances organizational goals. The major relationship of interest is between the public relations practitioner and the media with a corresponding emphasis on journalistic techniques and production skills. Research from a functional perspective has traditionally been concerned with business-oriented topics such as advertising, marketing, and media relations. Under this approach, researchers focus on the use of public relations as an instrument to accomplish specific organizational goals rather than on relationships. (pp. 650–651)

Public relations scholarship following a functional approach inquires about effective media relations, links to advertising, explaining public relations to clients, measuring impact of media placements, agenda setting, and strategic message design. A public relations practitioner or scholar who follows the functional approach might answer the question about public relations' role in society as "*public relations creates and disseminates information that helps the organization to accomplish its goals.*" This societal role of public relations would most likely be accepted without question from many professionals in business, government agencies, and the nonprofit community.

Botan and Taylor (2004) noted that recent public relations theory-driven research has followed a cocreational approach, whereby publics and groups are cocreators of meaning. In this approach, public relations is what

> makes it possible to agree to shared meanings, interpretations, and goals. This perspective is long term in its orientation and focuses on relationships among publics and organizations. Research is used to advance understanding and the perspective embraces theories that either explicitly share these values (e.g., relational approaches or community) or can be used to advance them. (p. 652)

The cocreational approach does not confine the study of public relations to the functional outputs of organizational communication such as news releases, Web sites, or advertisements. Instead, the cocreational approach studies formation of meaning through communication and as the development of relationships between groups and organizations. Communication allows both groups and organizations to negotiate and change relationships with others. The benefit of the cocreational approach is that "publics are not just a means to an end. Publics are not instrumentalized but instead are partners in the meaning-making process" (Botan & Taylor, 2004, p. 652).

Theories that fall under a cocreational approach include relational theory (Broom, Casey, & Ritchey, 1997; Ferguson, 1984; Ledingham & Bruning, 1998, 2000), dialogic theory (Kent & Taylor, 1998, 2002; Pearson, 1989), communitarism (Leeper, 1986), fully functioning society theory (FFST; Heath, 2006), and rhetorical theory. Based on symbolic interactionism, cocreational theories generally view communication, relationships, and coconstructed meaning as core assumptions of how public relations functions in society.

A public relations practitioner or scholar who follows the cocreational perspective might answer the question about public relations' role in society as "*public relations uses communication to help groups to negotiate meaning and build relationships.*" A defining value of the cocreational perspective is that publics are not treated as "economic variables" that merely buy, sell, or respond to organizational outputs. The cocreational perspective avoids segmenting publics into demographic or even psychographic categories to predict their behaviors. Rather, a cocreational perspective treats individuals or groups who share interpretations as partners that are necessary for decision making at different levels of society.

The functional approach and the cocreational approach are not irreconcilable. People need the information created and disseminated by all types of social actors to be able to make informed decisions. Information from diverse sources is a necessary component of modern democratic life. Likewise, the assumptions of cocreational theories point us to the rhetorical and symbolic nature of human knowledge and the role that communication plays in an informed citizenry. But information and communication for decision making require certain conditions to exist. To truly get at a fundamental understanding of the role of public relations in a society, we must go back one more step from these approaches. We need to examine which conditions must exist before individuals and organizations create the information that helps them and others make sense of their worlds. We need to understand that there are certain societal conditions that are prerequisites for either the functional or cocreational approaches to public relations to exist.

This chapter provides a third way for understanding the societal role of public relations. It argues that both a functional approach and a cocreational approach to public relations together contribute to a society where people, groups, and organizations have the desire and agency to make their community/society/world a better place to live. Information (from the functional approach) and rhetorical discourse and symbolic action (from the cocreational approach) are possible when they exist within a civil society. Thus, a third answer to the question posed in the beginning of this chapter is: "*Public relations' role in society is to create (and re-create) the conditions that enact civil society.*" The next part of this chapter explores civil society theory and positions public relations as one condition as that which makes civil society possible.

Public Relations Builds the Relationships That Build Social Capital

Civil Society Theory

Civic society theory had its roots in ancient Greece and Rome, and it evolved into the Enlightenment conception of *civil society* (Hauser, 1998). Both the ancient and Enlightenment epochs were characterized by a growing awareness of public deliberations and decision making. Hauser (1997) defined civil society as "the network of associations independent of the state whose members, through social interactions that balance conflict and consensus, seek to regulate themselves in ways consistent with a valuation of difference" (p. 277). In other words, civil society was not about having one common idea; it was about a tolerance of debating different ideas. Hauser (1998) traced the historical development of the concept of civil society and argued that civil society provides an alternative way of understanding the discursive nature of the public sphere. Hauser's essays provided a starting place for understanding a public relations approach to civil society because he placed civil society within a discursive community framework that requires rhetoric. Hauser viewed society not as one big public sphere but as multiple spheres or "nested arenas" (p. 21), where there is the accommodation of a diversity of views (p. 26).

Tolerance of different opinions is a central point of civil society because it is the "evolution of cooperation and trust among citizens" (Hadenius & Uggla, 1996, p. 1622). Civil society is a communicative process grounded in information, communication, and relationships. Civil society theory not only embodies cocreational assumptions about public relations but also accepts that functional practices of public relations are inherent in a fully functioning society (Heath, 2006).

Some social theorists, such as Habermas, have critiqued public relations as serving only elite interests, and there are indeed some examples of how public relations has been used to accomplish selfish, not society-driven goals. For instance, the Hill and Knowlton's Citizens for a Free Kuwait campaign provides an example of how traditional public relations tactics can obscure, not highlight, the truth. Yet Hauser's (1998) conceptualization of nested arenas confronts Habermas's and others' fears that civil society can be co-opted by elites. Co-optation is always a possibility, but it is not a foregone conclusion of a resource-driven society. Hauser correctly noted that "whether civil society embraces and lives in truth is fundamentally dependent on whether or not its members are informed and attentive to the truth" (p. 30). In other words, people must have information, and they must be interested and able to pursue what they believe to be right.

The conception of society enacted by nested arenas depends on several interrelated conditions. Taylor (2009) argued that civil society is a process grounded in rhetoric. For civil society to occur, there must *first* be someone or some group that feels safe to create discourse that positions their views within the larger societal framework. Successful discourse will draw on some commonly accepted values, beliefs, or experiences. *Second,* there must be some trusted channels to carry the messages. The channels can include face-to-face communication and print, electronic (radio and television), or even digital media. *Third,* there must be others in the society who are listening to and considering the arguments in the discourse. And *finally,* there must be some societal process or system that enables people to pursue the call of the discourse.

What people do when they encounter societal discourse is their choice. Boulding (1977) posited that one of three outcomes can happen when individuals and societies come in contact with messages. First, messages can produce no change in the current images that people hold. Individuals or society may ignore the content of the message and continue on with their lives. The second thing that can happen is that a message can provide additional information to individuals' and society's existing images. Here, people may begin to consider alternative views but do nothing with this new information. Third, in rare cases, some messages encourage revolutionary change in a person's or society's image of the world. Individuals or society might make a change in their lives, values, or behaviors based on this information. Images, however, are fairly resistant to change, and Boulding noted that this third option is the least likely outcome of messages.

A public relations approach to civil society builds on Boulding's (1977) conceptualization of images, knowledge, and change. Civil society is about informed choice and enlightened action. Enlightened action, however, does not necessarily mean that interactants sit down together to engage in rational discourse to discuss the images that shape their understanding of the world. Sometimes *symbolic action* is needed before the *discourse* becomes something that people can pay attention to. DeLuca and Peeples (2002) provided an illustration of how "image events" (p. 135) may create wedges in societal consciousness that prompt discussions of topics that have been ignored by the mainstream media and societal institutions.

DeLuca and Peeples (2002) described how activist organizations have used publicity not to corrupt the public sphere but, instead, to bring topics before the public so that they can be discussed. Their example of anti–World Trade Organization (WTO) activists showed how small groups can use publicity to gain access to the "public screen" through image and pseudo events. Tactics such as boycotts, protests, speeches, and even the threat of violence attracted media attention to the antiglobalization message. Media coverage of the threats and actions of antiglobalization activists brought the issue into the living rooms of Americans. What the activists could not do in their strategic communication, they accomplished with their symbolic action. The media coverage during the WTO meeting allowed activists to raise concerns about human rights, environmental protection, and multinational corporations in a national discussion (even if only for a few days).

Hauser's consideration of civil society fits nicely with other cocreational theories in public relations. One of the clearest links is to Heath's (2006) FFST. FFST identifies the premises of how rhetoric and public relations can help make society a better place to live. A fully functioning society posits that relationships among organizations and groups create social capital that makes communities stronger and better able to meet the needs of members. Civil society is a rhetorical process that creates the conditions for social capital to emerge as an outcome of the actions of different actors. The next section explores social capital as an outcome of public relations activities.

Social Capital as an Outcome of Relationships

There are many different types of capital. Ihlen (2007) introduced the work of Pierre Bourdieu to public relations scholars. Bourdieu (1986) identified economic capital, cultural capital, and social capital as forms of symbolic capital that can be drawn on by individuals and organizations. Coleman (1988) noted that social capital is less tangible than economic capital because it exists in relationships among people and groups. Social capital produces trust, provides information, and creates the norms of society. According to Coleman, social capital also establishes sanctions against those who violate the norms of society. Social capital, unlike private economic capital, creates a type of public good that benefits many members of a society. The benefit exists even for those who were not involved in an activity or relationship.

Nahapiet and Ghoshal (1998) argued that the concept of social capital emerged from community/neighborhood studies in the late 1960s. By the mid-1980s, social capital had become an accepted sociological concept that sought to explain the various relationships that are foundational for a society (Bourdieu, 1986; Coleman, 1988). Lewis (2005) has suggested that organizational communication scholars should study social capital to show how organizations contribute to society. The same can be true for public relations scholars—social capital is one way that public relations contributes to society. Civil society is a process grounded in rhetoric, and the outcome of civil society is a system of trusting and supportive interconnected organizations (social capital).

Enacting Civil Society

Taylor (2009) explicated a rhetorical public relations approach to civil society arguing that the heart of civil society is discourse. Discourse provides the nexus of civil society because it is the way that interested parties can participate in multiple and often competing public spheres. As participants in this discourse, Taylor identified seven civil society partners, including individuals, social cause groups, societal institutions, media, business organizations, governance, and international organizations. Table 1.1 explains each partner in greater depth. These seven partners create a foundation for civil society by representing different citizen interests. Partners develop their own networks of like-minded organizations to pursue common interests. Civil society exists when these partners have interrelated objectives. When the interests of two or more civil society partners converge, then there is a much greater opportunity for those groups to achieve their goals. An enduring civil society occurs in the intersection of all the seven partners' interests. It is the relationships and interconnections that make a community a good place to live. And, when these relationships and interconnections are missing, then civil society's potential is diminished.

Civil society partners may be known as sectors of society. There are three sectors that are considered in economic and political research. The first sector is the business community that creates economic capital. The second sector is the government that creates the conditions for economic

Table 1.1 Civil Society Partners

Citizens: The foundation of civil society is the public. Civil society is premised on an informed and empowered public. In a civil society, the public has the right and, more important, the desire to participate in local, regional, and national decisions. Moreover, the public feels safe when participating in all levels of community decision making. An appreciation of civil society begins in early education and continues throughout life. Unfortunately, in the public sphere, individual voices of citizens are not often heard. Thus, one of the best ways for citizens to articulate their needs is through participation in societal institutions.

Institutions: Societal institutions such as religious organizations, professional groups (associations of doctors, lawyers, educators), universities, unions, and political parties are necessary in a civil society. These institutions provide a means for citizens to articulate their needs. Legitimate institutions have the power to speak out on issues and because they are respected, their positions on issues are valued. In a civil society, institutions must operate at all levels of the society. Institutions gain influence when they cooperate with the media and provide information to the media that contributes to the public agenda.

Media: The value of an independent media to civil society is clear. They disseminate factual information that people use to make decisions. Moreover, because of the agenda-setting function of the media, they are opinion leaders on key topics. The media also serve as watchdogs to ensure that government officials and businesses are held accountable for their actions. The media are the nexus for communication between institutions, organizations, the government, and the public.

NGOs: Nongovernmental organizations (NGOs) work on behalf of issues, but they are not part of the formal governmental structure. NGOs are organized groups of individuals, some small and others quite large, that are not yet institutionalized. However, some NGOs will become institutionalized as their value to the society becomes clear.

INGOs: International organizations (INGOs) provide financial and human resources to help facilitate development. These international organizations fund local groups who work to achieve societal goals. INGOs are especially important during the initial stages of civil society because they work directly with indigenous organizations and provide important training and activating of local civil society leaders.

Business: The business community also has a role to play in the development of civil society. Business organizations have opinions on issues such as regulation, licensing, access to natural resources, price controls, immigration laws, and legal reform. Their voices must also be included in civil discussions. However, too much influence from businesses or corporations may inhibit civil society development.

Governance: Civil society exists apart from the state. However, governance—the local, regional, and national leaders and members of the bureaucracy that support government—need to be accountable to the aforementioned partners. Government leaders need to carefully monitor public opinion and be willing to adapt to changing public needs. In civil society, government understands important issues and resolves them in a manner that benefits members of the society.

and cultural capital. The third sector is the nonprofit or voluntary sector. This sector's function is to create social capital. Public relations helps all sectors accomplish their goals. The best way to demonstrate how public relations enacts civil society is to illustrate how different sectors engage in relationships that build or hinder the creation of social capital.

Governance and Social Capital. Most of the definitions of civil society place civil society outside the state. They do this for a good reason since civil society is supposed to be a watchdog or regulator of the state. Yet it is naive to believe that government has no role in the creation or destruction of social capital. Governments create tax policies and regulations that create the conditions for the formation of economic capital and social capital. To help foster social capital, some governments provide tax incentives for individuals and corporations to donate resources to religious organizations, societal institutions, and social cause groups.

Yet governments can also stop the formation of social capital through other policies. In China, two government policies inhibit the formation of social capital. First, the government has created government-organized NGOs (nongovernmental organizations). These organizations, known as GNGOs, have been initiated by the Chinese government and receive government subsidies. The people in the leadership positions are generally appointed by the government (He, 2008). Because of their quasi-independent, quasi-governmental status, GNGOs have the greatest access to the Chinese media. A recent study of media coverage of civil society topics showed that GNGOs are cited as sources in news stories more often than other types of NGOs in China by the government-controlled press (Yang & Taylor, 2009). A second policy that inhibits social capital creation in China is the government's policy of monitoring Internet searches. This policy diminishes the amount and type of information that people in China have for decision making.

Contributions of the First Sector. Corporations and businesses can also contribute to civil society when they support philanthropic activities or engage in activities that strengthen the communities in which they operate. The business sector is a foundation of civil society, and just like government, its actions can foster or diminish social capital.

On the positive side, many business organizations have corporate social responsibility (CSR) initiatives that create social capital by providing information or services to people who may not otherwise have access to such resources. CSR is much more than a philanthropic activity; it should be a process of organizational participation in ensuring the greater good of a community.

One example of this second sector social capital occurs when business leaders serve on community boards of directors. Such membership provides both tangible resources (money) and intangible resources (information, networking) to community groups. Corporate sponsorship of prosocial activities, such as Home Depot's support of Habitat for Humanity, and 9-Lives brand cat food support of the American Society for the Prevention of Cruelty to Animals (ASPCA), provides examples of how the second sector can contribute to social capital formation.

The public relations function then can help organizations engage their community on a daily basis. Through public relations research, engagement, and the creation of relationships among community members, organizations can better serve their communities and create social capital.

Contributions of the Third Sector. Nonprofit organizations use public relations to inform people about issues ranging from local topics (environmental, zoning, local government watchdog functions) to national (policy reforms) and global issues (climate change, human rights policies). Lewis (2005) noted that this civil society sector is the fastest growing sector across the globe. There are nearly 2 million registered nonprofits in the United States. That means that there is one nonprofit organization for every 100 adults in the United States. There are millions of other types of nonprofit groups sometimes called NGOs or community service organizations (CSOs) around the world. For civil society theorists, every time a CSO or social cause group communicates with members (either in person or online), there is the potential for creation of social capital. Public relations tactics maximize that social capital. Every news release, every public service announcement, and every community forum adds potential social capital.

One of the greatest challenges for civil society organizations is mobilizing people and resources. Freeman (1979) proposed that activist organizations need a variety of tangible and intangible mobilizing resources to accomplish their goals. Tangible resources are things that bring monetary resources into the organizations. Intangible resources bring awareness of the organization and its issues and help the organization reach new members. The Internet is a valuable resource because it provides information to a variety of publics and also links different groups together. It offers the opportunity to "transform sets of geographically dispersed aggrieved individuals into a densely connected aggrieved population, thus solving one key problem of mobilization" (Diani, 2000, p. 388). The Internet has the potential to provide both types of resources if certain societal conditions are met. For instance, government monitoring of the Internet and surveillance of Web searches does not promote civil society.

The Internet provides additional opportunities to maximize information sharing, collaboration, and meaning making. Every Web page and every social media tactic generated by nonprofit organizations has the potential to create social capital. The Internet as an advocacy tool is not a new topic for public relations scholars. As early as 1998, Coombs (1998) and Heath (1998) argued for the Internet's use as a tool for activists. The Internet has most often been used as a one-way communication tool, but it can also be a relationship-building tool where the organization engages the visitor in two-way communication. Internet features, including Listservs, Blogs, and discussion groups, enable communication and relationship building between dispersed people with similar interests.

How can we determine if civil society exists, what is its strength, and what factors may be contributing to or inhibiting it? There are a variety of research methodologies available for public relations researchers.

Measuring Civil Society

Civil society can be measured through a variety of qualitative, quantitative, and rhetorical methods. Sociologists were one of the first groups to study civil society and social capital created by professional, community, and organizational relationships. They attempted to measure social capital, connectiveness, and the relationships that link organizations in a system together. Topics of research included information sharing, cooperation and competition, network density, network evolution and decay, and reputation.

Political scientists such as Robert Putnam have used secondary data to measure civil society. Putnam (2000) obtained data from national trend studies to look at membership in voluntary associations. Social capital is created when people form relationships through activities such as Parent Teacher Associations (PTAs), cultural groups, professional associations, and recreational activities. The trend studies showed that people were no longer participating in voluntary groups and, thus, were no longer benefitting from shared information or coordinated activities. Putnam noted that as people stopped participating in voluntary associations, social capital in the United States diminished.

Communication scholars have studied social capital in a variety of ways. Organizational communication research has examined how relationships among individuals in a firm, relationships among departments, and relationships among members of a particular kind of industry build both economic and social capital. Because so much of today's communication is taking place in cyberspace, other researchers have also studied links between

Web sites to identify leaders in a network (Shumate, Fulk, & Monge, 2005). Other researchers have examined relationships among civil society organizations, media outlets, and international donors (Doerfel & Taylor, 2005; Taylor & Doerfel, 2003).

Taylor (2009) acknowledged the contributions of these scholarly areas and methodological approaches to studying civil society but concluded that these perspectives fail to account for "the idea that *meaning making and relationships* enact civil society. Civil society is not an outcome; it is a process grounded in rhetoric" (p. 83). The use of language to persuade and create shared understanding is at the heart of all aspects of civil society. Through symbolic action and discourse, individuals and organizations participate in Burke's "wrangle of the marketplace" of ideas. Thus, another way to study civil society is to look at the discourse (or symbolic actions) generated by civil society actors.

There is a long tradition of rhetorical studies in public relations. Scholars such as Bostdorff (1992), Elwood (1995), Crable and Vibbert (1995), Hearit (1994), Heath (1992), and Heath, Toth, and Waymer (2009) have applied rhetorical theory and methods to case studies of organizational discourse. Their work provides a framework for examining how corporations, government, and activists have participated in civil society. By looking at the discourse of advocacy, we can see civil society enacted. Civil society is a normative theory as well as a positive theory. Civil society is enacted by humans as individuals and organizational members and, thus, reflects all the baggage that accompanies human agency.

Critiquing Civil Society Practices

There have been some critiques of a public relations perspective of civil society, and that dialogue has provided a valuable opportunity for debate about what civil society is and is not. Dutta-Bergman (2005) has equated civil society efforts in the form of Western development aid with the continued domination of nations in the subaltern. Through case studies of U.S. interference with governments across the world, Dutta-Bergman warned that civil society efforts may not be so civil. That may be true, but it is also important to remember that not all voluntary associations are good and not all externally supported civil society efforts are bad. The interference of one government in the internal affairs of another country is clearly wrong, and when we view civil society as the creation of discourse in the marketplace of ideas, then we have "a rationale and method for critiquing instances of antidevelopment and imperialist messages and activities" (Taylor, 2009, p. 88). A public relations approach to civil society can actually diminish the imperialistic or self-serving intentions of elites.

Future Directions for Civil Society Theory

Recent research that embodies a cocreational perspective has helped shape the future of public relations research. Ferguson (1984) and Broom et al. (1997) explicated a relational approach to public relations, where the existence and strength of relationships become the focus of study. Civil society is premised on interorganizational relationships among the societal partners noted in Table 1.1. A public relations approach to civil society allows us to understand how cooperative relationships help shape, change, and sustain communities ranging from small collectives all the way up to the nation-state.

If we accept public relations as the use of communication to negotiate relationships among groups (Botan, 1992), then we should also accept that any group could engage in public relations communication to build or change relationships. The outcome of any communication and relationship-building activities is open to negotiation. Rhetoric provides the discourse and the images, whereas public relations provides the process through which discourses and images are shared, negotiated, contested, and possibly resolved. Taylor (2009) argued that *meaning making and relationships* enact civil society. The social capital that is created by shared meaning and relationships among civil society partners makes society a better place to live.

The purpose of this chapter was to provide a third way for understanding the societal role of public relations. The functional approach and a cocreational approach to public relations together create a society where people, groups, and organizations have the desire and agency to make their community/society/world a better place to live. Information (from the functional approach) and rhetorical discourse and symbolic action (from the cocreational approach) are possible when they exist within a civil society. One answer to the question posed at the beginning of this chapter is that public relations' role in society is to create (and re-create) the conditions that enact civil society.

References

Bostdorff, D. M. (1992). "The decision is yours" campaign: Planned Parenthood's characteristic argument of moral virtue. In E. L. Toth & R. L. Heath (Eds.), *Rhetorical and critical approaches to public relations* (pp. 301–314). Hillsdale, NJ: Lawrence Erlbaum.

Botan, C. (1992). International public relations: Critique and reformulation. *Public Relations Review, 18,* 149–159.

Botan, C. H., & Taylor, M. (2004). Public relations: The state of the field. *Journal of Communication, 54,* 645–661.

Boulding, K. D. (1977). *The image: Knowledge in life and society.* Ann Arbor: University of Michigan Press.

Bourdieu, P. (1986). The forms of capital. In J. G. Richardson (Ed.), *Handbook of theory and research for the sociology of education* (pp. 241–258). New York: Greenwood.

Broom, G. M., Casey, S., & Ritchey, J. (1997). Toward a concept and theory of organization–public relationships. *Journal of Public Relations Research, 9,* 83–98.

Coleman, J. S. (1988). Social capital in the creation of human capital. *American Journal of Sociology, 94,* 95–120.

Coombs, W. T. (1998). The Internet as potential equalizer: New leverage for confronting social irresponsibility. *Public Relations Review, 24,* 289–303.

Crable, R. E., & Vibbert, S. L. (1995). Mobil's epideictic advocacy: "Observations" of Prometheus bound. In W. N. Elwood (Ed.), *Public relations inquiry as rhetorical criticism: Case studies of corporate discourse and social influence* (pp. 27–46). Westport, CT: Praeger.

DeLuca, K. M., & Peeples, J. (2002). From public sphere to public screen: Democracy, activism and the "violence" of Seattle. *Critical Studies in Media Communication, 19,* 125–151.

Diani, M. (2000). Social movement networks virtual and real. *Information, Communication & Society, 3*(3), 386–401.

Doerfel, M. L., & Taylor, M. (2005). Network dynamics of interorganizational cooperation: The Croatian civil society movement. *Communication Monographs, 71,* 373–394.

Dutta-Bergman, M. (2005). Civil society and communication: Not so civil after all. *Journal of Public Relations Research, 17,* 267–289.

Elwood, W. N. (Ed.). (1995). *Public relations inquiry as rhetorical criticism.* Westport, CT: Praeger.

Ferguson, M. A. (1984, August). *Building theory in public relations: Interorganizational relationships as a public relations paradigm.* Paper presented at the annual meeting of AEJMC, Public Relations Division, Gainesville, FL.

Freeman, J. (1979). Resource mobilization and strategy. In M. N. Zald & J. M. McCarthy (Eds.), *The dynamics of social movements* (pp. 167–189). Cambridge, MA: Winthrop.

Hadenius, A., & Uggla, F. (1996). Making civil society work, promoting democratic development: What can states and donors do? *World Development, 24*(10), 1621–1639.

Hauser, G. (1997). On publics and public spheres: A response to Phillips. *Communication Monographs, 64,* 275–279.

Hauser, G. (1998). Civil society and the public sphere. *Philosophy and Rhetoric, 31,* 19–40.

He, Z. (2008). Institutional barriers to the development of civil society in China. In Y. Zheng & J. Fewsmith (Eds.), *China's opening society: The non-state sector and governance* (pp. 161–173). New York: Routledge.

Hearit, K. M. (1994). Apologies and public relations crises at Chrysler, Toshiba, and Volvo. *Public Relations Review, 20,* 113–125.

Heath, R. L. (1992). The wrangle in the marketplace: A rhetorical perspective of public relations. In

E. L. Toth & R. L. Heath (Eds.), *Rhetorical and critical approaches to public relations* (pp. 17–36). Hillsdale, NJ: Lawrence Erlbaum.

Heath, R. L. (1998). New communication technologies: An issues management point of view. *Public Relations Review, 24,* 273–288.

Heath, R. L. (2006). Onward into more fog: Thoughts on public relations' research directions. *Journal of Public Relations Research, 18,* 93–114.

Heath, R. L., Toth, E. L., & Waymer, D. (2009). *Rhetorical and critical approaches to public relations II.* Hillsdale, NJ: Lawrence Erlbaum.

Ihlen, O. (2007). Building on Bourdieu: A sociological grasp of public relations. *Public Relations Review, 33,* 269–274.

Kent, M. L., & Taylor, M. (1998). Building dialogic relationships through the World Wide Web. *Public Relations Review, 24,* 321–334.

Kent, M. L., & Taylor, M. (2002). Toward a dialogic theory of public relations. *Public Relations Review, 28,* 21–37.

Kuhn, T. (1970). *The structure of scientific revolutions.* Chicago: University of Chicago Press.

Kunczik, M. (1997). *Images of nations and international public relations.* Hillsdale, NJ: Lawrence Erlbaum.

Ledingham, J. A., & Bruning, S. D. (1998). Relationship management in public relations: Dimensions of an organization–public relationship. *Public Relations Review, 24,* 55–65.

Ledingham, J. A., & Bruning, S. D. (Eds.). (2000). *Public relations as relationship management: A relational approach to the study and practice of public relations.* Hillsdale, NJ: Lawrence Erlbaum.

Leeper, K. (1986). Public relations: Ethics and communitarianism. *Public Relations Review, 22,* 163–179.

Lewis, L. (2005). The civil society sector: A review of critical issues and research agenda for organizational communication scholars. *Management Communication Quarterly, 19,* 238–267.

Nahapiet, J., & Ghoshal, S. (1998). Social capital, intellectual capital, and the organizational advantage. *Academy of Management Review, 23,* 242–266.

Pearson, R. (1989). *A theory of public relations ethics.* Unpublished doctoral dissertation, Ohio University, Athens.

Putnam, R. (2000). *Bowling alone: The collapse and revival of American community.* New York: Simon & Schuster.

Shumate, M., Fulk, J., & Monge, P. R. (2005). Predictors of the international HIV/AIDS NGO network over time. *Human Communication Research, 31,* 482–510.

Taylor, M. (2009). Civil society as a rhetorical public relations process. In R. Heath, E. L. Toth, & D. Waymer (Eds.), *Rhetorical and critical approaches to public relations II* (pp. 76–91). Hillsdale, NJ: Lawrence Erlbaum.

Taylor, M., & Doerfel, M. L. (2003). Building interorganizational relationships that build nations. *Human Communication Research, 29,* 153–181.

Yang, A., & Taylor, M. (2009). *Relationship-building by Chinese ENGOs' Web sites: Education, not activation.* Unpublished manuscript.

CHAPTER 2

Strategic Management of Communication

Insights From the Contingency Theory of Strategic Conflict Management

Augustine Pang, Yan Jin, and Glen T. Cameron

It is never easy to question the canon in one's field and to offer a theoretical perspective that has emerged to be diametrically opposed to a theory that has dominated research in a field (Botan & Taylor, 2004), or what its much-esteemed founders argued to be normative theory (J. E. Grunig & Grunig, 1992). When DeFleur (1998) decried the lack of paradigmatic theoretical advances in communication, he certainly failed to address the enormous resistance one faces in querying existing premises to make that quantum leap of a paradigmatic shift in thinking.

The contingency theory of strategic conflict management, which began questioning excellence theory's positioning of symmetrical communication as normative theory on how organizations should be practicing public relations that was regarded as the most ethical and effective (L. A. Grunig, 1996), might have had its humble beginnings as an elaboration, qualification, and extension of the value of symmetry (Cameron, 1997; Cameron, Cropp, & Reber, 2001). Over more than a decade, however, it has come into its own and emerged as an empirically tested perspective that argued that the complexity in strategic communication could not be reduced to excellence theory's models of excellence. Cameron (1997) suggested that scholars move forward "from four or five models which place our practice in boxes" (p. 40).

The alternative view pioneered by contingency theory of how strategic communication ought to be practiced, so that communication could be examined through a continuum whereby organizations practice a variety of stances at a given time for a given public depending on the circumstance, instead of subscribing the practice to strait-laced models, was by no means an attempt of contingency theorists to set up excellence theory for a "straw man argument" (Yarbrough, Cameron, Sallot, & McWilliams, 1998, p. 53). Instead, its proponents argued that it was a "sense-making effort to ground a theory of accommodation in practitioner experience, to challenge certain aspects of the excellence theory" (p. 53).

It was, by all intents and purposes, an attempt to provide as realistic and grounded a description of how intuitive, nuanced, and textured public relations has been practiced (Cameron, Pang, & Jin, 2008; Cancel, Mitrook, & Cameron, 1999). This paradigmatic reconfiguration might have ruffled more feathers than was initially realized (Cameron, 1997); nonetheless, it was a necessity born out of a need to demonstrate the subtleties of communication management that a single model such as the two-way symmetry, though argued to be "real" (J. E. Grunig & Grunig, 1992, p. 320), was "too inflexible to be meaningful" (Yarbrough et al., 1998, p. 53).

For a paradigmatic shift to emerge, Kuhn (1996) suggested that it must satisfy three conditions. First, it must build on "pre-established theory" (p. 16). Second, it must receive the "assent of the relevant community" (p. 94) whose "knowledge of [the] shared paradigm can be assumed" (p. 20), and this same community must agree to commit to the "same rules and standards for scientific practice" (p. 11). Third, it must represent a "sign of maturity" in the development pattern of the field (p. 11). For the emerging paradigmatic thinking to take root and be accepted, Kuhn (1996) argued that the theory "must seem better than its competitors, but it need not, and in fact never does, explain all the facts with which it can be confronted" (pp. 17–18).

By all measures, contingency theory has satisfied most, if not all, of Kuhn's criteria. Its genesis was in the established work of excellence and grounded theory, and it has been systematically subjected to the same scientific rigor required of all empirical research. While the jury is still out on whether contingency theory would be considered a paradigmatic breakthrough, it is timely to consolidate the advances the theory has made in transforming the practice of strategic communication and record the ongoing dialogue the theory has offered to the field to continually challenge prevailing presumptions and presuppositions.

To that end, this chapter is divided into two main sections with several subsections. The first section argues that contingency theory has *informed* practice of strategic communication by changing mind-sets, identifying important factors in communication, unearthing new factors that affect communication, and demonstrating how stakeholders can estimate stances the organization is likely to take. In so doing, this section seeks to record the theory's explanatory powers in portraying how communication is managed between the organization and its diverse publics as an alternative perspective to excellence theory. The second section seeks to demonstrate how the theory can *transform* the practice of strategic communication, that is, what it means for practitioners, and what application value the theory offers to the practical world. A theory grounded in the practitioners' world adds rich layers of context to understanding how theory and practice can integrate (Pang, Cropp, & Cameron, 2006).

This chapter an offers an impetus for practitioners to view strategic communication as opportunities to engage in strategic thinking. Strategic thinking is the process by which the organization uses an occasion as a platform to showcase, reaffirm, reexamine, and reenact its mission, values, and operations (Lerbinger, 1997). This involves an examination of the organization's epistemology, hierarchy, and existence (Seeger, Sellnow, & Ulmer, 2003).

How Has Contingency Theory Informed Practice?

Changing Mind-Sets: From Models of Practice to Practicing Dynamic Stances

Much of the literature on effective strategic communication had been built on J. E. Grunig and Grunig's (1992) and J. E. Grunig and Hunt's (1984) excellence theory. Four models of excellence have been posited:

- *Press-agentry/publicity model:* Here, the organization is only interested in making its ethos and products known, even at the expense of half-truths.
- *Public information model:* Predominantly characterized by one-way transfer of information from the organization to the publics, the aim is to provide information in a journalistic form.
- *Two-way asymmetric model:* Instead of a rigid transference of information, the organization uses surveys and polls to gain insights needed to persuade the publics to accept its point of view.
- *Two-way symmetrical model:* Here, the organization is more amenable to developing a dialogue with the public. Communication flows both ways between the organization and the public, and both sides are prepared to change their stances, with the aims of resolving the crisis in a professional, ethical, and effective way.

The two-way symmetrical model has been positioned as a normative theory, which stated how organizations should be practicing strategic communication in what was regarded as the most ethical and effective manner (J. E. Grunig & Grunig, 1992; L. A. Grunig, 1996).

Contingency theory, however, saw a different reality. Cancel, Cameron, Sallot, and Mitrook (1997) argued that there were several reasons why the four models were inadequate to explain the reality of strategic communication. Methodological concerns aside, it was inherent in the practice of the two-way symmetrical model that the organization must engage in dialogue with the public, even though the public may be morally repugnant. This included "offering trade-offs" to a morally repugnant public, an exercise that could be viewed as "unethical" (p. 38).

Related literature also questioned the possibility and ethics of dialogue. There had been instances when the organization would not enter into any form of dialogue with a public because it was unduly unreasonable and unwilling to collaborate. Kelleher (2003) found that strategic communication could be proscribed by circumstances, such as collective bargaining. There were also limits to collaboration, argued Leichty (1997), particularly as collaboration required "two or more parties to cooperate in good faith: Collaboration is a 'relational strategy' and cannot be enacted without cooperation" (p. 55). Roper (2005) questioned the motive of open, collaborative negotiation and communication, and "at what price?" (p. 83).

Stoker and Tusinski (2006) also thought that the goals of symmetrical communication were commendable but reasoned that they are unreasonable in that symmetry may pose moral problems in strategic communication and may lead to "ethically questionable quid pro quo relationships" (p. 174). Holtzhausen, Petersen, and Tindall (2003) rejected the notion of symmetry as the normative strategic communication approach. In their study of South African practitioners, the authors found that the practitioners developed their practice that reflected a greater concern about the relationship between the organization and its publics based on larger economic, social, and political realities.

The move from the four models to a continuum began when Cameron and his colleagues found studies indicating that "unobtrusive control" (p. 33) might exist in the symmetrical and asymmetrical models. Symmetrical communication should be refined "along less rigorous lines of a continuum ranging from conflict to cooperation" (Hellweg, 1989, cited in Cancel et al., 1997, p. 33). Using the findings of Hellweg (1989), Murphy (1991), and Dozier, Grunig, and Grunig (1995), Cancel et al. (1997) argued that strategic communication was more accurately portrayed along a continuum. "This view is a more effective and realistic illustration of strategic communication and organization behavior than a conceptualization of four models" (p. 34). Moreover, because of the fluidity of the circumstances, which, in turn, may affect an organization's stance and strategies, a continuum would be far more grounded to reality that was able to "more accurately portray the variety of public relations stances available" (p. 34).

The continuum, argued Cancel et al. (1999), thus explained "an organization's possible wide range of stances taken toward an individual public, differing from the more proscriptive and mutually exclusive categorization" (p. 172) found in the four models.

Contingency theorists took the idea of continua further to propose one that emphasized a more realistic description of how strategic communication is practiced. They examined how organizations practiced a variety of strategic communication stances at one point in time, how those stances changed, sometimes almost instantaneously, and what influenced the change in stance (Cancel et al., 1997). Their reasoning was this: Because strategic communication, particularly conflict management, was so complex and subtle, understanding it from any of the four models, particularly the two-way symmetrical model, would be far too limiting and rigid. "Effective and ethical strategic communication is possible at a range of points on a continuum of accommodation" (p. 53), argued Yarbrough et al. (1998). Excellent strategic communication activity, including dealing with conflicts and crises, "cannot and should not be typified as a single model or even a hybrid model of practice" (Cameron et al., 2001, p. 245).

The organizational response to the strategic communication dilemma at hand, according to contingency theory, which has advocacy at one end of the continuum and accommodation at the other end, was thus, "It depends." The theory offered a matrix of 87 factors (see the appendix), arranged thematically, that the organization could draw on to determine its stance. Between advocacy, which means arguing for one's own case, and accommodation, which means giving in, was a wide range of operational stances that influenced strategic communication strategies, and these entailed "different degrees of advocacy and accommodation" (Cancel et al., 1997, p. 37). Along this continuum, the theory argued that any of the 87 factors, culled from strategic communication literature, excellence theory, observations, and grounded theory (Cameron, 1997, p. 31), could affect the location of an organization on that continuum "*at a given time* regarding *a given public*" (Cancel et al., 1999, p. 172; Yarbrough et al., 1998, p. 40).

Pure -- Pure

Advocacy   Accommodation

The theory sought to understand the dynamics within and without the organization that could affect an organization's stance. By understanding these dynamics, it elaborated specified conditions, factors, and forces that undergirded such a stance, so that strategic communication need not be viewed by artificially classifying into boxes of behavior. It aimed to "offer a structure for better understanding of the dynamics of accommodation as well as the efficacy and ethical implications of accommodation" (Yarbrough et al., 1998, p. 41) in strategic communication practice.

Identifying Important Factors That Influence Adoption of a Stance in Strategic Communication

If strategic communication is managed through the adoption of a stance or stances, there are factors that determine each stance and the movement of stance along the continuum. To move this beyond the conceptual level, Cancel et al. (1999) took it to the practitioners. In wide-ranging and extensive interviews with strategic communication professionals, the authors sought to understand how the practitioners managed conflict and whether the theory made sense to them. "In effect, we set out to see whether 'there is anything to the contingency theory' and if so, to see how the theory can be grounded in the words, experience and perspective of practitioners" (p. 172), the authors stated.

The first test of the theory found traction with practitioners' experiences. Besides establishing the participants' concurrence with contingency theory's assertion that a continuum of advocacy and accommodation was a "valid representation of their interactions and their corporations' interactions with external publics" (p. 176), further insights were shed on the relative influences of the 87 factors in positing the organization's position on the continuum, spawning the contingency terms and predisposing and situational variables.

Among the 87 variables, practitioners argued that there were some that featured more prominently than the others. There were factors that influenced the organization's position on the continuum *before* it interacted with a public; and there were variables that influenced the organization's position on the continuum *during* interaction with its publics. The former have been categorized as predisposing variables, and the latter, situational variables. Some of the well-supported predisposing factors that Cancel et al. (1999) found included (a) the size of the organization, (b) corporate culture, (c) business exposure, (d) strategic communication to the dominant coalition, (e) dominant coalition enlightenment, and (f) individual characteristics of key individuals, such as the CEO. These factors were supported in the conflict literature. For instance, organizational culture had been found to be a key factor in ensuring the formulation of a sound crisis plan and excellent crisis management (Marra, 1998). Situational variables were factors that were most likely to influence how an organization related to a public by effecting shifts from a predisposed accommodative or adversarial stance along the continuum during an interaction. Some of the supported situational factors included (a) urgency of the situation, (b) characteristics of the other public, (c) potential or obvious threats, and (d) potential costs or benefit for the organization from choosing the various stances (Cancel et al., 1999).

The classification of the factors into two categories was by no means an attempt to order the importance of one over the other in a given situation. The situational variables could determine the eventual degree of accommodation an organization takes by "effecting shifts from a predisposed accommodative or adversarial stance along the continuum during an interaction with the external public" (Yarbrough et al., 1998, p. 43). At the same time, an organization may not move from its predisposed stance if the situational variables are not compelling or powerful enough to influence the position or if the opportunity costs of the situational variables do not lead to any visible benefits (Cameron et al., 2001). Consequently, both predisposing and situational factors could move the organization toward increased accommodation or advocacy. What was important in determining where the organization situates on the continuum involved the "weighing of many factors found in the theory" (Yarbrough et al., 1998, p. 50). Notably, the factors explain movement either way along the continuum.

Even as contingency theorists were able to explain the complexity, the context, and even the conundrum of a dialogic process, they had yet to answer one of the central questions they posed in arguing why symmetrical communication could not be normative. The question was whether communication could still take place with a morally repugnant public. A broader casting of the question was whether other factors precluded or proscribed communication termed variously as dialogue, trade-offs, accommodation, or symmetrical communication.

In a subsequent test of the theory, Cameron et al. (2001) found that there were occasions when accommodation was not possible at all, due to moral, legal, and regulatory reasons. These were labeled proscriptive variables. Six such variables were identified: (1) when there was moral conviction that an accommodative or dialogic stance toward a public might be inherently unethical, (2) when there was a need to maintain moral neutrality in the face of contending publics, (3) when legal constraints curtailed accommodation, (4) when there were regulatory restraints, (5) when senior management prohibited an accommodative stance, and last, (6) when the issue became a jurisdictional concern within the organization, and resolution of the issue took on a constrained and complex process of negotiation. The proscriptive variables "did not necessarily drive increased or extreme advocacy, but did preclude compromise or even communication with a given public," argued Cameron et al. (2001, p. 253).

To show how contingency theory was a realistic description of the practitioners' world and why two-way symmetrical was impractical and inflexible, Yarbrough et al. (1998) applied it to how conflicts were managed by C. Richard Yarbrough, Managing Director–Communications of the 1996 Atlanta Committee for the Olympic Games (ACOG). Three episodes—one involving the moving of preliminary volleyball matches from one venue to another due to a conflict between gay activists and local politicians who had passed an antigay resolution, the second involving a conflict between the ACOG board of directors and the media concerning the disclosure of executive salaries, and the third involving a conflict between the ACOG and a minority minister over an Olympic sponsor—illustrated how textured the conflicts were and how dynamic changes in stance were affected on the continuum. For the second episode, for instance, even though the ACOG initially practiced an advocacy stance against the disclosure of salaries, it finally relented due to the influence of situational factors, particularly changes mandated by a higher authority, the International Olympic Council (IOC), that forced its hand to move to the end of the continuum toward accommodation. The study proved not just the "sophisticated process" of assessment and management of a given situation, but that effective, ethical public relations can be practiced "in a full range of places on the continuum from advocacy to accommodation" (p. 55).

Understanding Contingent Factors That Affect Stance and Unearthing New Factors

Shin, Cameron, and Cropp (2006) conducted a national survey of public relations practitioners on the perceived importance of contingent factors and the influence in their daily public relations practice. The practitioners agreed that contingency theory did reflect their reality, and organization-related characteristics were found to be most influential.

With more than 80 distinct factors identified in contingency theory, Cameron et al. (2001)

acknowledged that to manage them in "any useful way" (p. 247), parsimony was further needed. While the proscriptive variables had been found to limit dialogue and accommodation, further delineation of the relative influences of factors was needed. In the first test of contingency theory in the management of an international conflict, Zhang, Qiu, and Cameron (2004) examined how the United States and China resolved the crisis over the collision of a U.S. Navy reconnaissance plane with a Chinese fighter jet in the South China Sea in April 2001. The authors found further evidence that supported the dominant coalition's moral conviction as a key characteristic in precluding accommodation and proscribing dialogue.

Reber and Cameron (2003) further set out to test the construct of five thematic variables through scale building on 91 top public relations practitioners. The five thematic variables were (1) external threats, (2) external public characteristics, (3) organizational characteristics, (4) public relations department characteristics, and (5) dominant coalition characteristics. The authors found that the scales supported "the theoretical soundness of contingency and the previous qualitative testing of contingency constructs" (p. 443). Significantly, for each of the thematic variables, they discovered the attitudes of public relations practitioners toward each of the thematic variables that would affect the organizations' willingness to dialogue. Some of the key insights the authors found relating to the thematic variables included the following.

External Threats. Contrary to earlier study, government regulations would not impede dialogue with a public because they were "infrequent enough" (Reber & Cameron, 2003, p. 443). However, organizations would not engage in dialogue with a public if that legitimized its claims by talking to them. Threats, both internal and external as identified in the original contingency factor matrix, have been commonly used to describe the state a nation, organization, or individual endures during a crisis. Jin, Pang, and Cameron (2005) conceptually differentiated threats from "risk," "fear," and "conflict," which are the cause and the effect of crisis. They proposed the explication of the concept by expanding, cross-fertilizing, and integrating ideas from an interdisciplinary review of literature and enumerated the dimensionality of threats. A threat-appraisal model within the contingency theory framework is based on the cognitive, affective, and conative levels of threats. Two empirical tests were conducted to test this threat-appraisal model. Pang, Jin, and Cameron (2005) adapted this model to examine the fabric and faces of threat on an ongoing issue and how it can be communicated. The issuance of terror alerts by the Department of Homeland Security (DHS) was analyzed in terms of how the terrorism-related threat was appraised by the DHS and the conservative and liberal audiences. Findings showed a shared view by the DHS and the conservative audiences, while the liberal audiences thought otherwise. Though there appeared to be consensus in threat communication, more internal consistency within the DHS is needed to optimize its effectiveness.

Jin and Cameron (2007) conducted an online experiment on the effects of threat type and threat duration on public relations professionals' cognitive appraisal of threats, affective responses to threats, and the stances taken in threat-embedded crisis situations. After exposing 116 strategic communication professionals to four crisis situation scenarios, findings revealed the main effects of threat type on threat appraisal, emotional arousal, and qualified-rhetoric-mixed accommodations, and the main effects of threat duration across all threat consequences. Interactions of these two threat dimensions revealed that external and long-term threat combination led to higher situational demands appraisal and more intensive emotional arousal. This study further examined the relationship between cognitive appraisal, affective responses, and stances as key aspects of threat consequences. High cognition and stronger affect regarding threats were found to be related to more accommodating stances.

External Public Characteristics. The size, credibility, commitment, and power of the external public were attributes that an organization would consider in its willingness to engage in dialogue. Choi and Cameron (2005) sought to understand how multinational corporations (MNCs) practiced public relations in South Korea and what contingent factors affected their stances in conflict situations. The authors identified a new contingent variable that was added to the matrix when they found that most MNCs tended to use accommodative stances based on fear. They feared the Korean media's negative framing of issues toward MNCs that often caused them to move from advocacy to accommodation. At the same time, they also feared the cultural heritage of the Korean people, a concept based on *Cheong* where clear distinctions were made between those who were part of them and those who were not. "In Korean culture, We-ness that tends to clearly distinguish our-side from not our-side, and *Cheong* is usually given to our-side (e.g. Korean firms) seem to influence how Korean audiences interpret MNCs messages and behaviors" (p. 186). Cho and Cameron (2006) also uncovered another new contingent variable ("*Netizen*") in their study of how an entertainment company dealt with its promotion of public nudity in cell phones.

Jin and Cameron (2004) called for attention to the role of emotions as central to public relations theory building. Using an adapted appraisal model of emotion in public relations, crucial dimensions were added to the contingency theory that take into account emotional tone, weight, and temperature with regard to contingency factors. An emotion-laden contingency model is presented on a multidimensional plane, proposing that for a given public at a given time in a given public relations encounter, and across external and internal contingent factors, the public's emotional tone, temperature, and weight regarding encounter-related contingency factors will have strong effects on the public's stance toward the organization on the accommodation continuum.

Organizational Characteristics. Past negative experiences and the presence of in-house counsel were likely to affect the organization's willingness to dialogue. Jin (2010) examined the perceived crisis preparedness of a random sample of strategic communication practitioners as evidenced in their assessment of crisis situations and organizational resources. The main effects of organization size and practitioner role were evident on practitioner's perceived crisis preparedness in different crisis situations. Organization type was found to be effective only when it interplayed with either practitioner role or organization size.

Public Relations Department Characteristics. Public relations practitioners' membership in the dominant coalition would affect the organization's willingness to dialogue. The need for strategic communication practitioners to be represented in the dominant coalition and to be involved in the frontlines of conflict management was further emphasized in the study by Reber, Cropp, and Cameron (2003) in which the authors described the tension of a hostile takeover for Conrail Inc. by Norfolk Southern Corporation. While legal practitioners' involvement in a high-profile crisis was a given, the study found that the dynamism of a conflict necessitated conflicts to be fought not just on the legal front but on the public relations front as well. Where regulatory, legal, and jurisdictional constraints forbade dialogue and negotiations to move to a higher level, public persuasion through the use of strategic communication initiatives and ingenuity went a long way to assuage hostile opinion. When legal and public relations worked together, as did the practitioners at Norfolk Southern, much could be achieved. Where legal involvement was restricted, the authors argued that public relations could be viewed as a "constructive creator of antecedent conditions for alternative dispute resolution" (p. 19).

Dominant Coalition Characteristics. When public relations practitioners are represented in the dominant coalition, organizations are likely to practice symmetrical communication. The theory was also applied extensively to examine public relations practice in South Korea in various studies. In their survey, Shin, Park, and Cameron (2006) reinforced the earlier findings of Shin et al. (2006) that organizational variables such as the involvement of the dominant coalition played a dominant role in defining public relations practice. This in turn constrained public relations activities, most notably, in the release of negative information and in the handling of conflict situations. Pang et al. (2006) extended the theory further to understand how it could be used to explain conflict and practice in an intraorganizational setting. In their case study of a Fortune 500 organization, the authors found that within an organization, the most important public, and by extension, the greatest source of conflict for public relations practitioners, was the dominant coalition. A less enlightened dominant coalition, coupled with a conservative corporate culture, and lack of access and representation of public relations in the dominant coalition were found to be factors that impeded the effectiveness of practitioners.

Explicating Organizational Stances and Publics' Estimates of Organizational Stances

Thus far, stance in contingency theory has been operationalized as the position an organization takes in decision making, which is supposed to determine which strategy to employ. Yet within each stance, one can conceivably further delineate the nature of the stance.

Organizational Stance Movement. Jin and Cameron (2006) developed and tested a multiple-item scale for measuring stance. Within the stance of accommodation, they found two categories of stance:

1. Action-based accommodations:
   - To yield to the public's demands
   - To agree to follow what the public proposed
   - To accept the publics' propositions
   - To agree with the public on future action or procedure
   - To agree to try the solutions suggested by the public
2. Qualified-rhetoric-mixed accommodations:
   - To express regret or apologize to the public
   - To collaborate with the public in order to solve the problem at hand
   - To change one's own position toward that of the public
   - To make concessions with the public
   - To admit wrongdoing

Jin and Cameron (2007) further found that strategic communication professionals tended to take a stance of more qualified-rhetoric-mixed accommodations when exposed to external threat rather than internal threat. For the purpose of image polishing or repair, professionals tended to take more rhetoric-based stances such as admitting wrongdoing and expressing regrets to the publics or to qualify their stances by collaborating and making concessions with the publics or changing their positions toward the publics. Jin, Park, and Len-Ríos (2010) recently found that Duke University employed more action-based and qualified-rhetoric-mixed accommodations toward internal publics than toward external publics in its handling of the lacrosse scandal.

Pang, Jin, and Cameron (2007, 2008, 2009) further differentiated the qualified-rhetoric-mixed stance from the action-based stance. In the former, the organization is willing to express regret and apologize to the public, to collaborate with the public, to make concessions, or to admit wrongdoing. In the latter, the organization is willing to yield to the public's demands, accept the public's propositions, and agree to the public's suggestion for solution. The former, as the name suggests, contains more rhetoric or posturing by the organization and may or may not lead to action that supports the rhetoric. The latter promises concrete action by the organization, in accordance to the public's demands, to resolve the situation. Therefore, saying what one *is willing to do* is only tantamount to posturing, or a qualified-rhetoric-mixed stance. Saying what one *will do* is an indication of an action-based stance.

Stakeholders' Estimate of Organizational Stances. Besides understanding how the organization enacts its stance to a given public in a give situation, Hwang and Cameron (2008a, 2008b) further argued that stakeholders can estimate stances of organizations, which provides important perspective from publics' point of view. In terms of the power of an external public and the impact of their organizational stance estimate, Hwang and Cameron (2008a) found that the general audience for a global crisis can become a grassroots force in the ultimate fate of policy decisions. Using the North Korean nuclear crisis as a case study, the authors identified dominant coalition characteristics, external threat, and external public characteristics as overall strong predictors for public estimation about the government's stance. They further found that the general audience's perception of situational factors (external threat and external public characteristics) was a stronger predictor for the participants' stance estimation than perception of predisposing factors (dominant coalition characteristics).

Considering the importance of general public support of an organization during a crisis, Hwang and Cameron (2008b) also examined how perceived leadership style influences public expectation about an organization's stance in a crisis and the relationship between perceived severity of threat and the expected stance of the organization based on leadership perception. The results of the study strongly supported the main effects of leadership on public estimation about an organization's stance. In another experimental study, Hwang and Cameron (2009) found a main effect of perceived leadership and an interaction effect of perceived leadership and perceived severity of threats on the public's estimation of organizational crisis responses. The results indicate that the contingent theoretical argument explaining the dynamics of organizational factors and situational factors that determine the stance taken by public relations practices can also be applied when explaining the outside latent public's thought patterns predicting an organizational stance and message strategy. As the authors concluded, contingency theory offers predictive power not just for the practitioner but for the public passing judgment on the stance taken by an organization.

How Does Contingency Theory Transform Practice?

As a general rule, argued Broom (2006), theory construction is an arduous process. It typically begins with a concept "derived from practice and viewed by practitioners as important" (p. 142). Theory construction in an applied field such as strategic communication is made more difficult because it has to resonate with the reality of practitioners. Thus, a theory grounded in the practitioners' world often adds rich layers of context to understanding how theory and practice can integrate (Pang et al., 2006). Even though practitioners rely on their experience and instincts to deal with conflict situations, increasingly, as Heath and Coombs (2006) argued, accepted wisdom "seats-of-the-pants thinking" must be "guided by theory" (p. 197).

So how does contingency theory transform the practice of strategic communication? The operative phrase is "strategic management of communication."

First, contingency theory recommends the reprogramming of thinking on how strategic communication can take place, that is, through the adoption of stances along a continuum instead of adhering to a set model of communication (Pang, Jin, & Cameron, 2010). Instead of viewing communication during crises as the practice of models, with the two-way symmetrical model held as the ideal model, an organization can consider adopting stances, or positions, ranging from advocating its case to accommodating the case to its publics. A model of practice often locks the organization or practitioner into thinking that there is only a set way(s) of communicating when more often than not, conflict situations are "dynamic" (Seeger, 2006, p. 241). By changing the view that strategic communication can be practiced as the dynamic enactment of stances along a continuum, organizations and practitioners are better placed and in greater control to determine how they can manage situations most effectively. It liberates them to think outside of the box.

Second, the theory exhorts organizations to engage in strategic analyses before and as they embark on strategic communication (Pang et al., 2010). Cognizance of the predisposing, situational, and proscriptive variables as posited by contingency theory would help organizations understand the complex realities they are working in. If strategic communication is "most effective when it is part of the decision process itself" (Seeger, 2006, p. 236), before organizations or practitioners adopt a stance or position in communication, they have to consider how key factors affect their decisions. These factors are critical in reflecting the characteristics, intents, and motivations of the organization (predisposing factors) as well as the external constraints, demands, and realities of the crisis (situational factors). For example, where communication is not possible during a crisis, it may mean that the decision, based on overriding concerns of the organization (proscriptive factors), prevents it from doing so. Predisposing factors shed light on the decisions that need to be considered *before* organizations and practitioners enter into crisis communication; situational factors illuminate the decisions behind each stance movement *during* crisis communication; proscriptive factors set parameters on why crisis communication may sometimes be curtailed. By understanding the dynamic interactions and interrelations of these factors, organizations and practitioners are able to assess how and why their decisions have an impact on their actions.

Third, the theory calls for a strategic assessment of the nature of the publics and the multidimensionality of external threats (Pang et al., 2010). This is extrapolated against the interplay of factors internally to meet the external demands from the crises and publics. If management of publics is paramount, as Seeger (2006) argued, organizations and practitioners would want to take cognizance of the threat involved in the crisis, and the makeup and influence of the publics even as they seek to understand the interplay of factors at work before and as they embark on crisis communication. Thus, understanding the makeup of the organization, incorporating and institutionalizing the involvement of strategic communication practitioners, and recognizing the dominance of the top management collectively play key roles in deciding how the organization should evaluate the importance of publics. Top management may possess organizational dominance, but strategic communication practitioners possess greater expertise to advice the top management on the value of stakeholder relationships.

Fourth, while the criticality of the role of the dominant coalition in crises may have been well documented (see Marra, 1998; Pauchant & Mitroff, 1992; Ray, 1999), this is reinforced by the findings of the theory: The character and competence of dominant individuals in top management are among the most important determinants and constants in managing the unfolding events and the way the organization conducts its crisis communication campaigns, without which a strategic communication campaign would not have strategic impact among the cacophony of competing voices in the chaotic marketplace (Pang et al., 2010). So what kind of leaders are ideal for organizations? It does appear that leaders who are involved, open to change, proactive, altruistic, supportive of strategic communication, and in frequent contact with publics are better placed to lead.

Fifth, given the ambiguity and uncertainty sometimes inherent in a conflict situation (Seeger, 2006), organizations seek directions to help them negotiate through the minefields while understanding the options open to them. Strategic adoption of stances along the continuum affords organizations a framework to assess the motivations of their positions and grants them a preview of the likely outcomes of their actions (Pang et al., 2010). In addressing fluid situations, the organization is given the flexibility of assuming different stances to different publics during a crisis at a given point in time. Movement along the continuum is never meant to be static. In some situations, it may mean having to accommodate, while in others to accommodate on one level and advocate on another, as long as the stances assumed are not used, as Seeger (2006) argued, to "avoid disclosing uncomfortable information or closing off further communication" (p. 242), where possible. On some issues, strategic communication may eventuate on an accommodative note, while on other nonnegotiable issues such as those cited in the proscriptive factors, it may permanently situate on the advocacy mode. Strategic communication may not always be a "win-win" situation; neither must it be a situation where one party wins and the other loses. It is a dynamic process of dialogue and negotiation.

Conclusion

Contingency theory has been conceptualized, developed, modified, tested, and improved over the past 12 years. J. E. Grunig (2006) argued that when assessing a theory, one must examine if "it makes sense of reality (in the case of a positive, or explanatory, theory)" (p. 152). Contingency theory has thus far offered a perspective supported by empirical foundations. By J. E. Grunig's (2006) definition, it is a positive theory.

At the same time, one could argue that while contingency theory has triggered a paradigmatic movement in public relations thinking, having met Kuhn's (1996) criteria that first, it has attracted "an enduring group of adherents away from competing modes of scientific activity," and second, it is "sufficiently open-ended to leave all sorts of problems for the redefined group of practitioners to resolve" (p. 16), it is not a normative theory because it does not prescribe what ought to be. J. E. Grunig (2006) argued that scholars need to develop both positive and normative theories to understand how strategic communication is practiced and "to improve its practice—for the organization, the publics, and for society" (p. 152).

Heath and Coombs (2006) argued that theories are developed from best practices. Contingency theory was developed to reflect the reality of practice. And even as the insights of the theory are now used to inform practice, it actually operates in a continual cycle of how practice informs theory and how theory transforms practice. As the field evolves, so does the theory. The work is cut out for contingency theorists to continually reflect this reality.

Appendix: Contingency Factors

Internal Variables

Organization Characteristics

- ❐ Open or closed culture
- ❐ Dispersed widely geographically or centralized
- ❐ Level of technology the organization uses to produce its product or service
- ❐ Homogeneity or heterogeneity of officials involved
- ❐ Age of the organization/value placed on tradition
- ❐ Speed of growth in the knowledge level the organization uses
- ❐ Economic stability of the organization
- ❐ Existence or nonexistence of issues management officials or program
- ❐ Organization's past experiences with the public
- ❐ Distribution of decision-making power
- ❐ Formalization: number of roles or codes defining and limiting the job
- ❐ Stratification/hierarchy of positions
- ❐ Existence or influence of legal department
- ❐ Business exposure
- ❐ Corporate culture

Public Relations (PR) Department Characteristics

- ❐ Total number of practitioners and number of college degrees
- ❐ Type of past training: trained in PR or ex-journalists, marketing, etc.
- ❐ Location of PR department in hierarchy: independent or under marketing umbrella/experiencing encroachment of marketing/persuasive mentality
- ❐ Representation in the dominant coalition
- ❐ Experience level of PR practitioners in dealing with crises
- ❐ General communication competency of department
- ❐ Autonomy of department
- ❐ Physical placement of department in building (near CEO and other decision makers or not)
- ❐ Staff trained in research methods
- ❐ Amount of funding available for dealing with external publics

- ❐ Amount of time allowed to use dealing with external publics
- ❐ Gender: percentage of female upper-level staff/managers
- ❐ Potential of department to practice various models of public relations

Characteristics of Dominant Coalition (Top Management)

- ❐ Political values: conservative or liberal/open or closed to change
- ❐ Management style: domineering or laid-back
- ❐ General altruism level
- ❐ Support and understanding of PR
- ❐ Frequency of external contact with publics
- ❐ Departmental perception of the organization's external environment
- ❐ Calculation of potential rewards or losses using different strategies with external publics
- ❐ Degree of line manager involvement in external affairs

Internal Threats (How Much Is at Stake in the Situation)

- ❐ Economic loss or gain from implementing various stances
- ❐ Marring of employees' or stockholders' perceptions of the company
- ❐ Marring of the personal reputations of the company's decision makers

Individual Characteristics (Public Relations Practitioners, Domestic Coalition, and Line Managers)

- ❐ Training in diplomacy, marketing, journalism, engineering, etc.
- ❐ Personal ethics
- ❐ Tolerance or ability to deal with uncertainty
- ❐ Comfort level with conflict or dissonance
- ❐ Comfort level with change
- ❐ Ability to recognize potential and existing problems
- ❐ Extent of openness to innovation
- ❐ Extent to which individual can grasp other's worldview
- ❐ Personality: dogmatic, authoritarian
- ❐ Communication competency
- ❐ Cognitive complexity: ability to handle complex problems
- ❐ Predisposition toward negotiations

- ❒ Predisposition toward altruism
- ❒ How individuals receive, process, and use information and influence
- ❒ Familiarity with external public or its representative
- ❒ Like external public or its representative
- ❒ Gender: female versus male

Relationship Characteristics

- ❒ Level of trust between organization and external public
- ❒ Dependency of parties involved
- ❒ Ideological barriers between organization and public

External Variables

Threats

- ❒ Litigation
- ❒ Government regulation
- ❒ Potentially damaging publicity
- ❒ Scarring of company's reputation in business community and in the general public
- ❒ Legitimizing activists' claims

Industry Environment

- ❒ Changing (dynamic) or static
- ❒ Number of competitors/level of competition
- ❒ Richness or leanness of resources in the environment

General Political/Social Environment/External Culture

- ❒ Degree of political support of business
- ❒ Degree of social support of business

The External Public (Group, Individual, etc.)

- ❒ Size and/or number of members
- ❒ Degree of source credibility/powerful members or connections
- ❒ Past successes or failures of groups to evoke change
- ❒ Amount of advocacy practiced by the organization

- ❐ Level of commitment/involvement of members
- ❐ Whether the group has public relations counselors or not
- ❐ Public's perception of the group: reasonable or radical
- ❐ Level of media coverage the public has received in the past
- ❐ Whether representatives of the public know or like representatives of the organization
- ❐ Whether representatives of the organization know or like representatives from the public
- ❐ Public's willingness to dilute its cause/request/claim
- ❐ Moves and countermoves
- ❐ Relative power of the organization
- ❐ Relative power of the public

Issue Under Question

- ❐ Size
- ❐ Stake
- ❐ Complexity

References

Botan, C. H., & Taylor, M. (2004). Public relations: State of the field. *Journal of Communication, 54*(4), 645–661.

Broom, G. M. (2006). An open system approach to building theory in public relations. *Journal of Public Relations Research, 18*(2), 141–150.

Cameron, G. T. (1997). The contingency theory of conflict management in public relations. In *Proceedings of the conference on two-way communication* (pp. 27–48). Oslo, Norway: Norwegian Central Government Information Service.

Cameron, G. T., Cropp, F., & Reber, B. H. (2001). Getting past platitudes: Factors limiting accommodation in public relations. *Journal of Communication Management, 5*(3), 242–261.

Cameron, G. T., Pang, A., & Jin, Y. (2008). Contingency theory: Strategic management of conflict in public relations. In T. Hansen-Horn & B. Neff (Eds.), *Public relations: From theory to practice* (pp. 134–157). Boston: Pearson Allyn & Bacon.

Cancel, A. E., Cameron, G. T., Sallot, L. M., & Mitrook, M. A. (1997). It depends: A contingency theory of accommodation in public relations. *Journal of Public Relations Research, 9*(1), 31–63.

Cancel, A. E., Mitrook, M. A., & Cameron, G. T. (1999). Testing the contingency theory of accommodation in public relations. *Journal of Public Relations Research, 25,* 171–197.

Cho, S., & Cameron, G. T. (2006). Public nudity on cell phones: Managing conflict in crisis situations. *Public Relations Review, 32,* 199–201.

Choi, Y., & Cameron, G. T. (2005). Overcoming ethnocentrism: The role of identity in contingent practice of international public relations. *Journal of Public Relations Research, 17*(2), 171–189.

DeFleur, M. (1998). Where have all the milestones gone? The decline of significant research on the process and effects of mass communication. *Mass Communication and Society, 1*(1/2), 85–99.

Dozier, D. M., Grunig, L. A., & Grunig, J. E. (1995). *Manager's guide to excellence in public relations and communication management.* Mahwah, NJ: Lawrence Erlbaum.

Grunig, J. E. (2006). Furnishing the edifice: Ongoing research on public relations as strategic management function. *Journal of Public Relations Research, 18*(2), 151–176.

Grunig, J. E., & Grunig, L. A. (1992). Models of public relations and communications. In J. E. Grunig (Ed.), *Excellence in public relations and communication management* (pp. 285–326). Hillsdale, NJ: Lawrence Erlbaum.

Grunig, J. E., & Hunt, T. (1984). *Managing public relations.* New York: Holt.

Grunig, L. A. (1996). Public relations. In M. D. Salwen & D. W. Stacks (Eds.), *An integrated approach to communication theory and research* (pp. 459–477). Mahwah, NJ: Lawrence Erlbaum.

Heath, R. L., & Coombs, W. T. (2006). *Today's public relations: An introduction.* Thousand Oaks, CA: Sage.

Hellweg, S. A. (1989, May). *The application of Grunig's symmetry-asymmetry public relations models to internal communications systems.* Paper presented at the International Communication Association annual conference, San Francisco.

Holtzhausen, D. R., Petersen, B. K., & Tindall, N. T. J. (2003). Exploding the myth of the symmetrical/asymmetrical dichotomy: Public relations models in the new South Africa. *Journal of Public Relations Research, 15*(4), 305–341.

Hwang, S. W., & Cameron, G. T. (2008a). The elephant in the room is awake and takes things personally: The North Korean nuclear threat and the general public's estimation of American diplomacy. *Public Relations Review, 34,* 41–48.

Hwang, S. W., & Cameron, G. T. (2008b). Public's expectation about an organization's stance in crisis communication based on perceived leadership and perceived severity of threats. *Public Relations Review, 34,* 70–73.

Hwang, S. W., & Cameron, G. T. (2009). The estimation of a corporate crisis communication. *Public Relations Review, 35,* 136–138.

Jin, Y. (2010). The interplay of organization type, organization size and practitioner role on perceived crisis preparedness: A cognitive appraisal approach. *Journal of Contingencies and Crisis Management, 18*(1), 49–54.

Jin, Y., & Cameron, G. T. (2004). *Rediscovering emotion in public relations: An adapted appraisal model and an emotion laden contingency plane.* New Orleans, LA: International Communication Association.

Jin, Y., & Cameron, G. T. (2006). Scale development for measuring stance as degree of accommodation. *Public Relations Review, 32,* 423–425.

Jin, Y., & Cameron, G. T. (2007). The effects of threat type and duration on public relations practitioner's cognitive, affective, and conative responses in crisis situations. *Journal of Public Relations Research, 19*(3), 255–281.

Jin, Y., Pang, A., & Cameron, G. T. (2005). *Explicating threats: Towards a conceptual understanding of the faces and fabric of threat in an organizational crisis.* New York: International Communication Association.

Jin, Y., Park, S., & Len-Ríos, M. (2010). Strategic communication of hope and anger: A case of Duke University's conflict management with multiple publics. *Public Relations Review, 36*(1), 63–65.

Kelleher, T. (2003). PR and conflict: A theoretical review and case study of the 2001 University of Hawaii faculty strike. *Journal of Communication Management, 8*(2), 184–196.

Kuhn, T. S. (1996). *The structure of scientific revolutions* (3rd ed.). Chicago: University of Chicago Press.

Leichty, G. (1997). The limits of collaboration. *Public Relations Review, 23*(1), 47–58.

Lerbinger, O. (1997). *The crisis manager.* Mahwah, NJ: Lawrence Erlbaum.

Marra, F. J. (1998). Crisis communication plans: Poor predictors of excellent crisis public relations. *Public Relations Review, 24*(4), 461–484.

Murphy, P. (1991). The limits of symmetry: A game theory approach to symmetric and asymmetrical public relations. *Public Relations Research Annual, 3,* 115–131.

Pang, A., Cropp, F., & Cameron, G. T. (2006). Corporate crisis planning: Tensions, issues, and contradictions. *Journal of Communication Management, 10*(4), 371–389.

Pang, A., Jin, Y., & Cameron, G. T. (2006). Do we stand on common ground? A threat appraisal model for terror alerts issued by the Department of Homeland Security. *Journal of Contingencies and Crisis Management, 14*(2), 82–96.

Pang, A., Jin, Y., & Cameron, G. T. (2007). *Building an integrated crisis mapping (ICM) model: Organizational strategies for a publics-driven, emotion-based conceptualization in crisis communication.* Washington, DC: AEJMC.

Pang, A., Jin, Y., & Cameron, G. T. (2008, March). *Second stage development of the integrated crisis mapping (ICM) model in crisis communication: Organizational strategies for crises that require high and low organizational engagements.* Paper presented at the 11th International Public Relations Research Conference, Miami, FL.

Pang, A., Jin, Y., & Cameron, G. T. (2009, March). *Final stage development of the integrated crisis mapping (ICM) model in crisis communication: The myth of low engagement in crisis.* Paper presented at the 12th International Public Relations Research Conference, Miami, FL.

Pang, A., Jin, A., & Cameron, G. T. (2010). Contingency theory of strategic conflict management: Directions for the practice of crisis communication from a decade of theory development, discovery and dialogue. In W. T. Coombs & S. J. Holladay (Eds.), *Handbook of crisis communication* (pp. 527–549). Oxford, UK: Wiley-Blackwell.

Pauchant, T. C., & Mitroff, I. I. (1992). *Transforming the crisis-prone organization.* San Francisco: Jossey-Bass.

Ray, S. J. (1999). *Strategic communication in crisis management.* Westport, CT: Quorum Books.

Reber, B., & Cameron, G. T. (2003). Measuring contingencies: Using scales to measure public relations practitioner limits to accommodation. *Journalism and Mass Communication Quarterly, 80,* 431–446.

Reber, B. H., Cropp, F., & Cameron, G. T. (2003). Impossible odds: Contributions of legal counsel and public relations practitioners in a hostile bid for Conrail Inc. by Norfolk Southern Corporation. *Journal of Public Relations Research, 15*(1), 1–25.

Roper, J. (2005). Symmetrical communication: Excellent public relations or a strategy of hegemony. *Journal of Public Relations Research, 17*(1), 69–86.

Seeger, M. W. (2006). Best practices in crisis communications. *Journal of Applied Communication Research, 34*(3), 232–244.

Seeger, M. W., Sellnow, T. L., & Ulmer, R. R. (2003). *Communication and organizational crisis.* Westport, CT: Praegar.

Shin, J., Cameron, G. T., & Cropp, F. (2006). Occam's Razor in the contingency theory: A national survey on 86 contingent variables. *Public Relations Review, 32,* 282–286.

Shin, J., Park, J., & Cameron, G. T. (2006). Contingent factors: Modeling generic public relations practice in South Korea. *Public Relations Review, 32,* 184–185.

Stoker, K. L., & Tusinski, K. A. (2006). Reconsidering public relations' infatuation with dialogue: Why engagement and reconciliation can be more ethical than symmetry and reciprocity. *Journal of Mass Media Ethics, 21*(2/3), 156–176.

Yarbrough, C. R., Cameron, G. T., Sallot, L. M., & McWilliams, A. (1998). Tough calls to make: Contingency theory and the Centennial Olympic Games. *Journal of Communication Management, 3*(1), 39–56.

Zhang, J., Qui, Q., & Cameron, G. T. (2004). A contingency approach to the Sino-US conflict resolution. *Public Relations Review, 30,* 391–399.

CHAPTER 3

Seeing the Forest Through the Trees

The Behavioral, Strategic Management Paradigm in Public Relations and Its Future

Jeong-Nam Kim and Lan Ni

As it has developed into an academic discipline and a professional field, public relations experienced tremendous growth in its body of knowledge and theoretical foundation. It also has developed many complementary and competing theoretical approaches. Among them, the managerial approach, also called the behavioral, strategic management paradigm in public relations (J. E. Grunig, Ferrari, & França, 2009, p. 8), has advocated a full-participation approach to public relations (L. A. Grunig, J. E. Grunig, & Dozier, 2002). Different from the *interpretive, symbolic approach* to public relations, this *behavioral, strategic management approach* focuses on the participation of public relations executives in strategic decision making to help manage the behaviors of organizations (J. E. Grunig et al., 2009, p. 9). This approach aims to provide a theoretical foundation for achieving excellent public relations that is managerial, strategic, symmetrical, diverse, and ethical (L. A. Grunig et al., 2002, p. 306).

The Excellence project and the resulting excellence theory (Dozier, J. E. Grunig, & Grunig, 1995; J. E. Grunig, 1992; L. A. Grunig et al., 2002) have been reviewed comprehensively in J. E. Grunig (2001, 2006, 2009) and J. E. Grunig, J. E. Grunig, and Dozier (2006). The resulting conceptual, qualitative, and quantitative details of this theory are substantial enough to be considered a general theory of public relations (a forest) comprising many middle-range theories and conceptual models (trees).

In this chapter, we aim to review how these small or large conceptual trees have grown in the behavioral, strategic management forest. To see the future forest of the behavioral management

Authors' Note: The authors thank Dr. Larissa A. Grunig and Dr. James E. Grunig for their constructive comments and guidance in the development and revision of this chapter.

approach by glimpsing at the present trees, we first provide an updated overview of the behavioral, strategic management paradigm in public relations, starting with excellence theory. We then review the most recent developments of the theory and its components, as well as suggest directions for future research.

Excellence Theory

Funded by the International Association of Business Communicators (IABC) Research Foundation, the Excellence project began in 1985. It was conducted in response to the IABC's call for proposals to answer two questions: How do public relations functions make organizations more effective (the effectiveness question), and how should public relations functions be organized to help achieve such effectiveness (the excellence question)? The following sections report on answers to these two main questions that examine how public relations adds value to organizations and to society and the generic principles of excellent public relations.[1]

The Effectiveness Question: The Value of Public Relations

To show how public relations adds value to organizations and society, L. A. Grunig et al. (2002) began by examining what people mean by "effectiveness." After reviewing the literature in sociology and business management, they identified four major approaches to organizational effectiveness. Each approach has its own strengths and weaknesses. The goal-attainment approach focuses on whether the organization is effective in achieving its goals. However, it is sometimes difficult to handle the problem of multiple, conflicting, and constantly changing goals. The systems approach evaluates effectiveness by whether an organization can survive in the environment through obtaining necessary resources. However, this approach has its problems, including the failure to adequately define what is meant by the term *environment;* the failure to differentiate efficiency and effectiveness; and the focus on survival, an insufficient goal for an organization. The strategic constituencies approach focuses on more specific segments of the environment rather than the total environment and identifies those segments that are most important for organizational survival and success. This approach is also problematic due to the difficulty in determining the priority or "strategicness" of the constituencies. The competing values approach focuses on whether an organization can incorporate the competing values of its constituencies into organizational goals.

Based on the above, the Excellence team decided to combine the four major approaches. Researchers in the team concluded that organizations are effective when they choose and achieve goals that are important to their self-interest as well as to the interests of strategic constituencies in the environment—groups that might have competing values (J. E. Grunig et al., 2009, p. 26). Linking this to the public relations function, the value of public relations lies in helping organizations become more effective by scanning the organizational environment, identifying the strategic publics, reconciling organizational goals with the expectations of these publics, and building long-term, quality relationships with these publics to reduce costs and gain support.

Demonstrating the Value of Public Relations. Even though it is difficult or impossible to establish a monetary value for relationships created through the public relations function (for reasons, see J. E. Grunig et al., 2009; L. A. Grunig et al., 2002), it is possible to measure the quality of an organization's relationships with its publics. This, thereby, indirectly confirms that a public relations function has created value for an organization. In addition, public relations also has value to society by encouraging organizations to practice social responsibility and helping reduce societal conflicts. Public relations achieves this by helping organizations develop quality relationships with their publics and pushing organizations to take into account both the interests of publics and their self-interests (J. E. Grunig et al., 2009, p. 30).

Measuring the Value of Public Relations. The Excellence study developed an alternative method for measuring the value of public relations by using a cost-benefit technique called *compensating variation.* First developed by Hicks (1943), Huber (1980), and Thompson (1980) and later elaborated and adopted by the IABC Excellence research team (Ehling, 1992; L. A. Grunig et al., 2002), compensating variation provides a way of transforming nonmonetary values, such as the value of good relationships, into monetary values. Essentially, the following two questions are asked: (1) For a program beneficiary, what amount of money is one willing to pay so as to be equally well off with the program or with the payment, and (2) for a person made worse off by a program, what amount of money is one willing to pay to eliminate the effects so as to be equally well off without the program or with the payment? Although these are soft, comparative measures, they provided strong statistical evidence of the value of public relations and have strong statistical correlations with the characteristics of excellent public relations. This then showed that excellent public relations contributes more value than less excellent public relations.

The Excellence Question: Generic Principles of Excellent Public Relations

The generic principles describe the characteristics of excellent public relations at different levels (functional and program) and provide the internal and environmental context of the organization that increases the likelihood that the public relations function will be practiced in an excellent way. The characteristics can be placed into seven categories that represent major areas of study and practice in public relations, including empowerment of public relations, roles, models, and the organization of the public relations function (L. A. Grunig et al., 2002).

Empowerment of the Public Relations Function. These principles enjoin the empowerment of the public relations function as a distinctive and strategic managerial function if it is to play a role in making organizations effective. Three principles were proposed, tested, and supported:

1. The senior public relations executive is involved with the strategic management processes of the organization, and communication programs are developed for strategic publics identified as a part of this strategic management process.
2. The senior public relations executive is a member of the dominant coalition of the organization, or the senior public relations executive has a direct reporting relationship to senior managers who are part of the dominant coalition.
3. Diversity is embodied in all public relations roles.

Public Relations Roles. Extensive research suggests four major roles that communicators play in organizations—the manager, senior adviser (also known as the communication liaison), technician, and media relations (for a review, see Dozier, 1992; L. A. Grunig et al., 2002, chap. 6). The manager and technician roles are the most common of the four. Three principles about roles have been proposed and tested:

1. The public relations unit is headed by a manager rather than a technician.
2. The senior public relations executive, or others in the public relations unit, has the knowledge needed for the manager role, or the communication function will not have the potential to become a managerial function.
3. Both men and women have equal opportunity to occupy the managerial role in an excellent department.

The results of the Excellence study solidly supported the proposition that for the senior communicator in a public relations department, the distinction between the manager and technician role is a core factor in distinguishing excellent from less excellent departments. However, results also showed the vital supporting role of technical expertise to the management role. More than any other variable, the availability of knowledge about performing a managerial role distinguishes excellent departments from less excellent ones.

Organization of the Communication Function, Relationship to Other Functions, and Use of Consulting Firms. For public relations to be managed strategically and to serve a role in the overall strategic management of the organization, two theoretical principles were proposed, tested, and supported:

1. An organization must have an *integrated communication function.* An excellent public relations function integrates all public relations programs into a single department or provides a mechanism for coordinating programs managed by different departments.
2. In addition, the public relations function should not be integrated into another department whose primary responsibility is a management function other than communication. In other words, public relations should be a management function separate from other functions.

Models of Public Relations. The models of public relations were introduced originally as a way of understanding and explaining the behavior of public relations practitioners (J. E. Grunig, 1976). Four models were originally proposed (J. E. Grunig, 1984; J. E. Grunig & Hunt, 1984): the *press-agentry* model (to get publicity in any way possible), the *public information* model (to offer objective information on the organization but not volunteer negative information), the *two-way asymmetrical* model (organizations do research and listen to publics in an effort to determine how best to change the behavior of publics to benefit the organization), and the *two-way symmetrical* model (organizations do research to understand publics and to balance the interests of organizations with those of their publics).

Over the years, these public relations models have been researched and debated (for reviews, Grunig & L. A. Grunig, 1989, 1992; J. E. Grunig, 2001; L. A. Grunig et al., 2002, chap. 8). L. A. Grunig et al. (2002) summarized and concluded that the two-way symmetrical model still appears to be a normative ideal for public relations practice. Public relations professionals can use the power of their knowledge—if they have it and if society recognizes the value of public relations—to advocate a symmetrical approach to public relations. The attempts of two-way symmetrical public relations to balance the interests of the organization and its publics are based on research and use communication to manage conflict and cultivate relationships with strategic publics. As a result, two-way symmetrical communication produces better long-term relationships with publics than the other models of public relations. Symmetrical practitioners therefore have *mixed motives*—they are loyal to both their employers and the publics of their organizations.

Three specific propositions were based on the symmetrical model:

1. The public relations department and the dominant coalition share the worldview that the communication department should reflect the two-way symmetrical, or mixed-motive, model of public relations.
2. Communication programs developed for specific publics are based on the two-way symmetrical, mixed-motive model.
3. The senior public relations executive or others in the public relations unit must have

the knowledge needed for the two-way symmetrical model, or the communication function will not have the potential to practice that excellent model.

As a continuous development in theory and research, the Excellence project (L. A. Grunig et al., 2002) isolated three continuous variables or dimensions underlying the original four models. The three dimensions were (1) a continuum from a one-way to a two-way *direction* of communication (i.e., whether research is used to obtain feedback from the publics), (2) a continuum from an asymmetrical to a symmetrical *purpose* of public relations, and (3) two continua indicating the frequency of using mediated or interpersonal *techniques* or both, depending on the situation and public. The Excellence team also proposed, but did not measure or test, a fourth dimension that represented the extent to which public relations activities are *ethical*. These new variables seemed to explain why organizations with an excellent public relations function practiced the two-way symmetrical, two-way asymmetrical, and public information models at the same time. These organizations practiced these three models because they had a symmetrical purpose in mind, favored research (i.e., two-way communication), and used both mediated and interpersonal communication (J. E. Grunig et al., 2009). Excellent public relations can, therefore, be better described in terms of these underlying dimensions than in terms of the four discrete models themselves.

Characteristics of Individual Communication Programs. In addition to theorizing about and researching the characteristics of the overall public relations function, the Excellence study also examined ongoing programs that excellent communication departments devise to cultivate relationships with their key publics, such as media relations, community relations, or employee relations. The results provided strong support for the proposition that communication programs organized by excellent departments should be *managed strategically*, or are more likely to have strategic origins and less likely to have historical origins.

External Context for Excellence: Activism and the Environment. The Excellence study also examined characteristics of the organization and its environment to determine whether excellence in communication requires certain external and internal contexts. Excellence theory predicted that externally *a turbulent, complex environment with pressure from activist groups* stimulates organizations to develop an excellent public relations function. Results confirmed that activism pushes organizations toward excellent public relations, although activism does not guarantee it.

Internal Context of Excellence. Organizational characteristics—structure, culture, internal system of communication, treatment of men and women, and power of the dominant coalition—are reported to predict organizational behavior and public relations practice. Therefore, excellence theory included five theoretical propositions regarding the organizational context for excellent public relations:

1. Participative rather than authoritarian organizational cultures
2. A symmetrical system of internal communication
3. Organic rather than mechanical structures
4. Programs to equalize opportunities for men, women, and minorities
5. High job satisfaction among employees

The results demonstrated that excellent public relations will thrive most in an organization with an organic structure, a participative culture, and a symmetrical system of communication, and one in which opportunities exist for women and racio-ethnic minorities. These conditions alone cannot produce excellent public relations, but they do provide a hospitable environment.

Overview of the Behavioral, Strategic Management Approach to Public Relations

Having summarized the key theoretical structure and findings of excellence theory, we continue with the overall behavioral management approach to public relations as a broader context for excellence theory, or the general forest of theorizing. We mainly discuss three areas: the role of public relations in strategic management, the identification of publics, and relationship management.

The Role of Public Relations in Strategic Management

Public relations should participate in the strategic management of an organization, an essential condition for bringing excellence to public relations (J. E. Grunig, 1992; L. A. Grunig et al., 2002). J. E. Grunig and Repper (1992) suggested a three-stage model for strategic management of public relations: *stakeholder, public,* and *issues.* In L. A. Grunig et al. (2002), the *crisis* stage is added as the fourth stage. The complete model of strategic management of public relations illustrates the connection between central concepts such as management decisions, stakeholders, and publics, and relationship outcomes (L. A. Grunig et al., 2002, p. 145).

Stakeholder Stage. In this stage, behaviors of the organization or of a stakeholder have decisional or behavioral consequences on the other. Groups exist that have stakes needed by the organization to achieve its mission. Public relations practitioners should therefore perform environmental scanning to identify those stakeholders whose behaviors will influence the organization and who will be influenced by organizational behaviors. Practitioners should first make a list of people who are linked to the organization through (potential) consequences on each other, rank these stakeholders to indicate their impact on the organization or the organization's impact on them, and then plan ongoing communication programs beginning with the most important stakeholders.

In the stakeholder stage, the concept of *linkages* (Esman, 1972; J. E. Grunig & Hunt, 1984) is commonly used. The four major types of linkages are *enabling, functional, normative,* and *diffused.* Enabling linkages provide the authority and control the resources that enable the organization to exist. Functional linkages provide inputs and take outputs. Input linkages include employees, unions, and suppliers, whereas output linkages include consumers and industrial purchasers. Normative linkages refer to those groups that face similar problems or share similar values, such as associations. Diffused linkages are those that cannot clearly be identified by membership, but when the organization has done something that creates consequences, these linkages can organize to do something against the organization.

Public Stage. In the public stage, groups find that they can use their stakes to push for changes in the performance of the targeted organization or industry; these groups form to exercise their influence. As organizations enter the public stage, the consequences that organizations and stakeholders have on each other may become a problem; in other words, a public arises as it finds certain consequences to be problematic. In most cases, publics approach organizations hoping to get organizational acknowledgment of their concerns and proactive corrections to the problem.

Practitioners need to identify and segment publics to increase the possibility of achieving communication goals with these publics. Specifically, practitioners are advised to use focus groups to involve publics in the decision-making process. The situational theory of publics (e.g., J. E. Grunig, 1997) has been used extensively in this stage to strategically identify publics. The common types of publics include *hot-issue*, *single-issue*, *all-issue*, and *apathetic* publics. Regarding the evolution of different stages of publics for the same situation, publics can be classified as *nonpublics*, *latent*, *aware*, and *active* publics.

Issues Stage. Finally, in the issues stage publics arise and make issues out of problems that they believe need to be resolved in their interest. Practitioners should segment publics, use mass media and interpersonal communication, and engage in negotiation. If the issues are not handled well, they can evolve into crises.

Identification of Publics: The Situational Theory of Publics

To facilitate public relations in the strategic management process, environmental scanning and identification of publics, a key component of environmental scanning, are researched. In particular, the *situational theory of publics* (J. E. Grunig, 1997; J. E. Grunig & Hunt, 1984) has been developed and used extensively over the years. This theory has three independent variables: *problem recognition*, *constraint recognition*, and *level of involvement*. These three variables have repeatedly been shown to affect whether and to what extent an individual engages in communication behaviors, as reflected in the two dependent variables of *information seeking* and *information processing*. It is considered one of the most useful theories for understanding why publics communicate and when they are most likely to do so (Aldoory & Sha, 2007). This theory has been applied and tested in different contexts (for a review, see J. E. Grunig, 1997). It has also been extended with studies about antecedents of variables (Aldoory, 2001; Aldoory & Sha, 2007; Sha, 2006) as well as in different cultural contexts (Sriramesh, Moghan, & Wei, 2007; Tkalac, 2007).

Relationship Management

Since Ferguson's (1984) call for a shift in focus to relationships, much research has been conducted on this topic. The premise of the behavioral, strategic management approach to public relations is that the value of public relations lies in the relationships an organization develops with its publics. Many scholars of this approach have been influential in this stream of research. J. E. Grunig and Huang (2000) developed a three-staged model of relationship management, including the *antecedents*, *maintenance strategies* (more recently called *cultivation strategies*), and *outcomes* of relationships. Based on that model, specific measures for the quality of relationships (e.g., trust, control mutuality, commitment, satisfaction) were developed by Hon and Grunig (1999) and Huang (2001), and types of relationships (e.g., exchange, communal, covenantal) were explored by Hung (2005).

Future Research on the Behavioral, Strategic Management Approach to Public Relations

Based on the review of core ideas from the general theory of excellent public relations, we identify a set of research agendas featuring three areas—publics, relations, and management. Of course, the list is not meant to be complete and exhaustive. Instead, we identify a few topics for future development of the behavioral, strategic management approach and research problems that were not previously discussed (e.g., J. E. Grunig, 2006). Each of the suggested research problems has the potential to evolve into productive and promising programs of research in their own tree, thus thickening the forest of the behavioral, strategic management approach to public relations.

Publics

Defining publics—who they are and how they behave—is the foundational task in defining the academic field and practice of public relations. The term *publics* is often understood as a "primitive term" (vs. a scientific "derived term," Chaffee, 1991) that refers to a general population, a word used in opposition to private members or citizens with legal rights and obligations. James E. Grunig's situational theory of publics laid the groundwork for defining publics as a scientific concept that summarized and advanced earlier social thinkers' work on publics, such as that of Blumer (1948) and Dewey (1927). In recent work, J.-N. Kim and Grunig (in press-a) developed a more generalized situational theory, the *situational theory of problem solving* (STOPS). This generalized situational theory revisits the definition of publics and provides several new options in identifying publics for research and practice. We briefly highlight the new theory and its implications for describing and defining publics.

Situational Theory of Problem Solving. The situational theory of problem solving incorporates a new concept, *communicative action in problem solving* (CAPS), as its dependent variable (J.-N. Kim, Grunig, & Ni, 2010). CAPS is introduced as a more generalized concept for active communication behaviors. It consists of four subvariables—*information forwarding, sharing, forfending,* and *permitting*—in addition to the two dependent variables of the theory of publics, information seeking and *information attending* (originally termed *information processing*). Active communication behaviors could mean more than active consumption (seeking or attending) of information related to a problematic situation. According to CAPS, situation-specific communication behaviors span active selection and transmission of information regarding problematic situations. In this vein, as CAPS incorporates proactive and reactive information transmission and selection, it increases the conceptual power and validity of the situational theory.

In addition, to explain communicative action, STOPS refines the independent variables of the situational theory of publics: problem recognition, constraint recognition, involvement recognition, and *referent criterion.* Notably, problem recognition and referent criterion have been redefined, and involvement has been renamed. The situational theory of publics defines problem recognition as occurring when "people detect that something should be done about a situation and stop to think about what to do" (J. E. Grunig, 1997, p. 10). In contrast, the new theory conceptualizes problem recognition as "a perceptual state one experiences after the failure of preconscious problem solving" (J.-N. Kim & Grunig, in press-a, p. 12). Problem recognition is now conceptualized as detection of a perceptual-cognitive problem. It is defined as "one's perception that something is missing and that there is no immediately applicable solution to it" (J.-N. Kim & Grunig, in press-a, p. 12). In addition, separating the "stop to think" about a problematic situation from the previous definition of problem recognition, the current theory now includes a situation-specific motivation. Situational theorists note that a person may detect a problem but may not stop what he or she is doing to do something about it. The state of "stop to think about what to do" conceptually falls into a motivational dimension rather than a perceptual dimension. The new motivational variable mediates the effects of antecedent perceptual variables on communicative behaviors. In addition, STOPS redefines referent criterion as "any knowledge or subjective judgmental system that influences the way in which one approaches problem solving," which includes "decisional guidelines or decision rules perceived as relevant to a given problem" (J.-N. Kim & Grunig, in press-a, p. 15). Unlike the referent criterion conceptualized in the previous theory of publics, a referent criterion could be imported from prior problematic situations or could be one *improvised* at an early phase of a new problem-solving situation (see Figure 3.1).

Figure 3.1 Comparison of the Situational Theory of Publics and the Situational Theory of Problem Solving

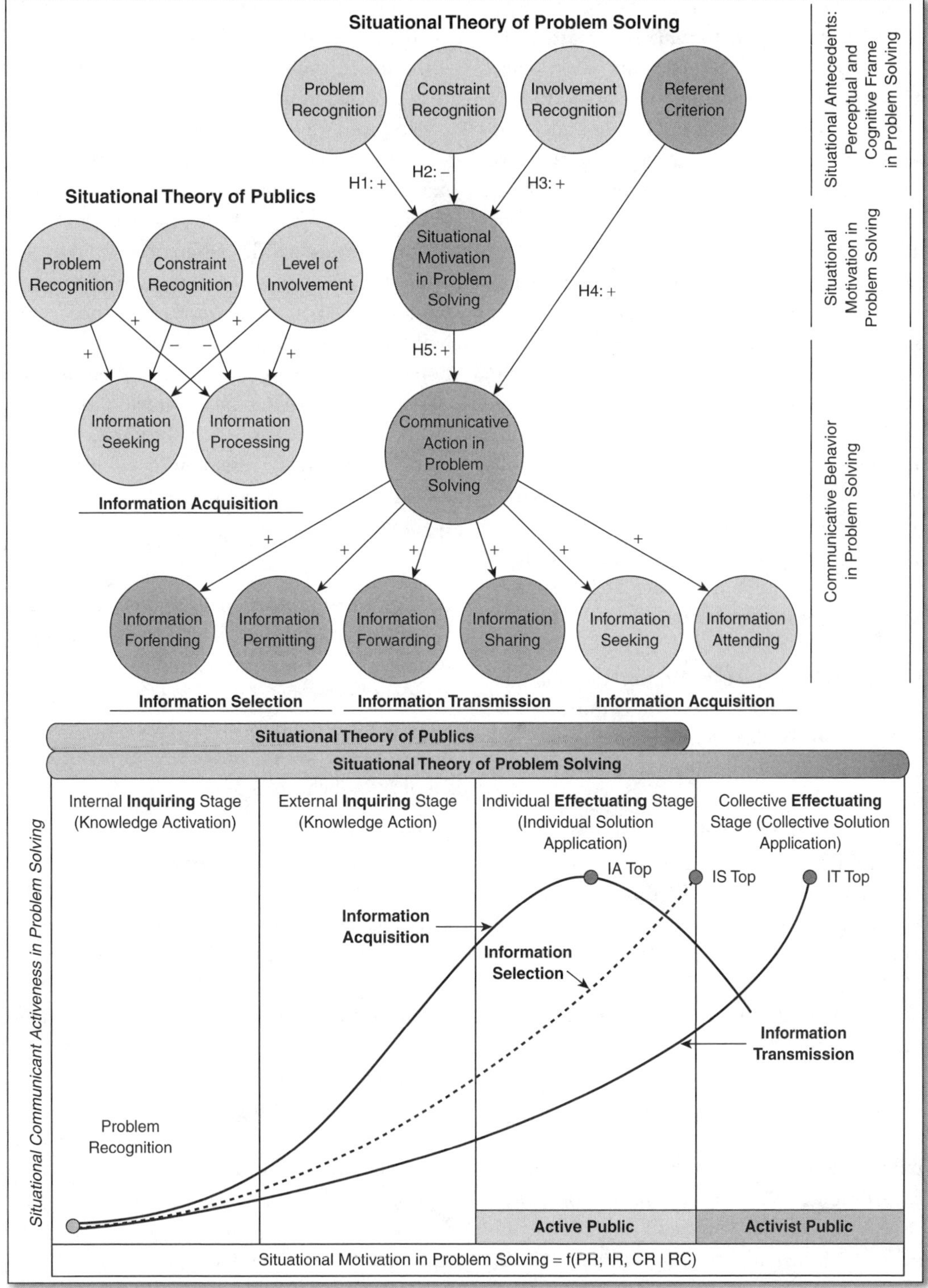

Source: J.-N. Kim and Grunig (in press-b).

The new STOPS and its subtheory, CAPS (J.-N. Kim, Grunig, & Ni, in press), generate implications for defining and identifying publics. A public and its members can now be described as *connected social actors*, rather than *individual economic actors,* who seek, select, and share information in their problem-solving process. Although J. E. Grunig and Hunt's (1984) original definition of a public conceives the dynamic, discursive, and interactive nature of a public, the situational theory of publics has variables only in information consumption. This, to some extent, has silenced how members of a public are communicatively active in selecting and exchanging information. Active information selection and sharing can reproduce similar perceptions in neighboring communicators and attract attention and resources necessary for problem resolution. In this regard, with its new variables, STOPS can better represent the nature of a public as a group of people who are active seekers, selectors, and sharers of information about a common problem.

Segmentation. The segmentation of publics is a necessary key step in strategic communication management. When defining any public relations problem, communicators need to map out the partner or subsegments in the population. In the process, they need to take into account constraints in material and time resources or constraints due to the lack of problem recognition of latent or nonpublics. Researchers and practitioners can benefit from the variety of segmentation methods and taxonomies of publics that capture the different aspects of public profiles (J.-N. Kim, Ni, & Sha, 2008). There are several proposed taxonomical frames of public segmentation, such as J. E. Grunig and Hunt's (1984) within-an-issue typology of publics (active, aware, latent, and nonpublic), J. E. Grunig's (1997) across-issues typology (all-issue, apathetic, hot-issue, and single-issue public), and Hallahan's typology (2000). Ni and Kim (2009) recently used and expanded additional segmentation of "aware" and "active" publics into eight types of subgroups using three problem-solving characteristics of a public: the *history* of problem solving, the extent of *activeness* in problem solving, and the *openness to approaches* in problem solving.

However, we still see much room for research here. *Publics* is one of the two key terms (i.e., *publics* and *relations*) that define our academic discipline and the field for practice. Thus, capturing various subtle differences in our key ground of research and practice is a critical line of new research. More research is needed to build additional theoretical frames and operational procedures (e.g., statistical methods) on classifying publics in public segmentation. In the future development of the behavioral, management perspective, researchers should make efforts to diversify the different taxonomies and typologies of publics.

Publics' Communication Behaviors. The strategic management approach to public relations requires that the public relations function have a clear understanding of how and why publics communicate among themselves. We therefore discuss below several important forms of communication behaviors of publics.

Word-of-Mouth Phenomena of Publics. The new situational theory and its communicative action model can broaden the understanding of public communicative behaviors. These behaviors should range from information acquisition to information selection and transmission within the social communicative networks of members of publics. Using the multidomain conception of communication behaviors, researchers and practitioners are able to conceptually describe who are the agents of information trafficking, to what extent they are filtering information, and to what extent their information yearning develops.

Figure 3.2 Three Problem-Solving Dimensions and Types of Publics

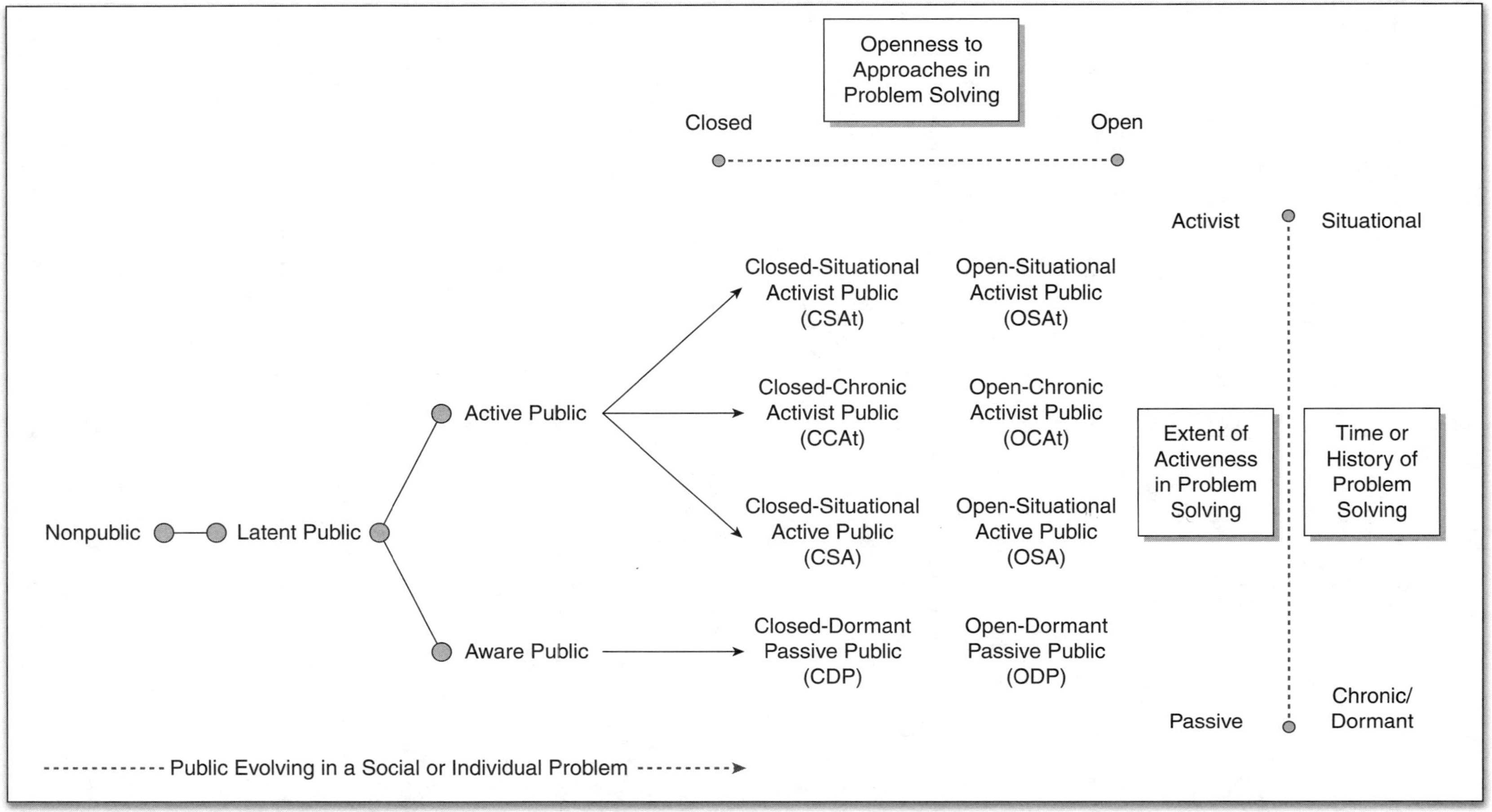

Openness to Approaches in Problem Solving
Closed
Open

Activist
Situational

Closed-Situational Activist Public (CSAt)
Open-Situational Activist Public (OSAt)

Active Public
Closed-Chronic Activist Public (CCAt)
Open-Chronic Activist Public (OCAt)

Extent of Activeness in Problem Solving
Time or History of Problem Solving

Nonpublic
Latent Public
Closed-Situational Active Public (CSA)
Open-Situational Active Public (OSA)

Aware Public
Closed-Dormant Passive Public (CDP)
Open-Dormant Passive Public (ODP)

Passive
Chronic/ Dormant

Public Evolving in a Social or Individual Problem

Source: Ni and Kim (2009, p. 221).

A recent study found that symmetrical communication efforts foster quality relationships with employees, which in turn increase positive communicative actions and decrease negative ones (J.-N. Kim & Rhee, in press). For example, when employees experience satisfactory interactions with their organization, they tend to talk positively about their organization ("positive megaphoning"). In contrast, unsatisfied employees are likely to talk about negative aspects—problems or controversies—to other publics ("negative megaphoning"). Moreover, during crisis periods, satisfied employees are more likely to defend their troubled organizations, whereas unsatisfied employees use these troubled periods as opportunities for punishing. Communicative actions are thus a way that micro-communicative actions result in macro-organizational consequences (e.g., on organizational effectiveness).

Finally, employees may be more or less engaged in voluntary information seeking, forwarding, and sharing about their organization's business or problems when they have satisfactory interactions with their management. For example, information circulation is analogous to blood circulation in a living organism: The individual members of an organization are information traffickers, and their information content (e.g., negative rumors, badmouthing, misinformation, disinformation, new trends, advocacy for management) could influence organizational health and its adaptiveness to environmental turbulence. At the center of the information circulation or trafficking, information behaviors (e.g., forfending, forwarding, seeking) of members of a public play the critical roles. In addition, such positive and negative aspects of communicative actions are word-of-mouth phenomena that applied communication researchers and practitioners have recently found intriguing and promising (Balter & Butman, 2005; Sernovitz, 2006). In this vein, we consider that the application of STOPS and CAPS to various types of publics, such as employees, consumers, and voters, will generate practical and theoretical knowledge for the behavioral, strategic management approach to public relations.

Digitalization and Online Communicative Actions. The Internet has created a virtual space for publics. Migration of offline activities, such as organizational and social procedures, into online communicative space reshapes not only how organizations operate (e.g., virtual team working, e-governance) but how publics behave (e.g., virtual communites, online activism). It is hard to estimate how and to what extent the digitalization of the social, political, and cultural process has reshaped public relations. The impacts of digitalization are multifaceted and intertwine across societal, organizational, and individual levels. We highlight several areas that offer further research.

Active publics are now conceptualized as active information seekers, forwarders, sharers, and selectors about a problem they are motivated to resolve. As they become active, publics use cyberspace as a tool for amplifying their problem perceptions and as leverage for empowering through identifying and connecting with fellow problem solvers. We coined a term, "cybercoping," to refer to such problem-solving efforts in cyberspaces among individual problem solvers and members of a public. STOPS conceptualizes active or activist publics as individuals or situational collectivities created by problem perception and problem-solving motivation. These individuals or groups then engage more in the cybercoping process. They seek, forward, share, and forfend information in virtual space for the purpose of problem solving. Not surprisingly, the Internet has transformed collective actions, as social media or Web 2.0 attract active and activist publics. It offers a better tool for publics to engage in social resistance and to exercise confrontational politics against problem-causing entities (Spears, Lea, Corneliussen,

Postmes, & Haar, 2002). In general, the ease with which people can protest online through digital or social media removes people's isolation and barriers to social aggregation (Postmes & Brunsting, 2002).

Another underexplored research area is that of Internet flamers as angry publics. *Flaming* refers to antisocial and antinormative computer-mediated communication (CMC) behaviors (Denegri-Knott & Taylor, 2005) that are abusive, offensive, or critical and that target other individuals or social objects (M. S. Kim & Raja, 1991, p. 7). Researchers previously studied flamers more as individuals with pathological personalities than as situational responses, or those who found the anonymous nature of CMC a chance to be unleashed from social norms (i.e., depersonalization effect, Kiesler, Siegel, & McGuire, 1984; Rock, 1973). Anonymity combined with situational causes—the asymmetrical organizational response—could turn ordinary but angry or frustrated (vs. psychopathic) citizens into flamers or evoke the use of *cyberviolence*. In such instances, unless organizations foster mutual interests with publics, the most likely results from the arrival and increasing availability of new digital and mobile media (e.g., Twitter, mobile phones) are malignant communicative actions, such as flaming, and deepening conflicts with more empowered publics than with the pre-Internet publics who lacked access to digital and virtual spaces.

In the behavioral, strategic management approach to public relations, one continuous challenge is how to advance prescriptive theories for activist public relations. For example, after Elliot's (1997) and Coombs's (1998) studies, there has been little follow-up research on how activist publics or groups can use the Internet and coalition-building tactics as an empowering strategy. From the framework of strategic activist public relations (J. E. Grunig & Grunig, 1996), we can argue that to fully use the pressure tactics and networking capacity of digital media, activist groups and their members should not only use Twitter, Facebook, Wikipedia, or other social media for channeling information about their causes but also diversify their online mobilization tactics.

Relatedly, this research on digital activism and online mobilization of publics and resources invites theoretical questions about publics and their sources of power. In the era of digitalization and virtualization, the sources of power and the tactics for mobilizing resources that are available to publics have undergone notable changes. (However, little research has actually been conducted on assessing the quantitative and qualitative impact of the Internet on activist publics and their "power" and "empowerment.") For example, Mintzberg (1983) identified the sources of power for insider influencers of an organization: "political will and skill," "privileged information" through gatekeeping and their central location, "access to influential" people, and "potential to exploit legitimate systems of influence" such as authority, ideology, and expertise (Mintzberg, 1983, pp. 183–187). However, there is still a gap in research on theorizing how (active and activist) publics could use digital and social media environments to enhance power and resources. We see a need for research on the source of power for publics (not organizations) beyond Mintzberg. In our review, we observe that the Internet has transformed publics in their problem-solving actions, either individual or collective. These actions in turn have had a "reverse influence" on transforming the social or digital media (Postmes & Brunsting, 2002). However, we found little theoretical attention to power and publics in digitalization or virtualization from the behavioral, strategic management approach to public relations. Researchers should thus invest more conceptualizing efforts of *strategic activist public relations* on the empowering process and create better procedures, especially in digital social media contexts. In the process, attention should also be directed to the existence of people without or with limited access to the digital world. For example, the elderly, the poor, and the politically constrained people in different parts of the world may still use few or none of the new electronic media.

Relations

Because organizations do not exist in a vacuum, they need to develop adaptive subsystems and procedures for dealing with changes from or to their environments. The interconnectivity between organizations and publics imposes opportunities and threats that require continuous, coordinated efforts of negotiation and collaboration. In other words, because organizations have relationships with *publics*, they need *public relations* to manage the constant process of negotiation and collaboration.

Research in the behavioral, strategic management approach to public relations has extended the relationship management literature in the following ways. Based on the three-staged model (J. E. Grunig & Huang, 2000), researchers have explored the three stages of (1) antecedents and mediators of relationships (H.-S. Kim, 2007), (2) relationship cultivation strategies (Rhee, 2007), and (3) outcomes of relationships (e.g., measurement of the quality of relationships, Huang, 2001; and types of relationships, Hung, 2005). Some studies have also explored the contribution of relationships to organizational effectiveness as reflected in organizational reputation (Yang, 2007) and achieving organizational strategies (Ni, 2006, 2009). However, more studies are needed to examine exactly how public relations practitioners can and should engage in the efforts of relationship building and cultivation. Ni and Wang (in press), for example, have explored how organizations should use relationship cultivation strategies to manage the anxiety and uncertainty of publics, and how such an effort leads to quality relationships. Following the studies on community relations (Rhee, 2007), employee relations (H.-S. Kim, 2007), and student-university relations (e.g., Ki & Hon, 2007), more research is also needed to examine the relationship management process and outcomes in different contexts or situations, or with different stakeholders. In particular, several interesting questions remain: How do organizations build and cultivate relationships with different constituencies? What kind of mediating process or variables would affect the nature and quality of relationships? Do and should organizations use the same strategies at different stages of the strategic management process, that is, the stakeholder stage, the publics stage, and the issues stage? Do and should organizations build and cultivate relationships when faced with different types of public relations problems?

Management

Public relations is defined as managing communication processes between organizations and their publics (J. E. Grunig & Hunt, 1984). We consider public relations as a *problem-solving process* in which *problems* arise out of *consequences* resulting either from the organization's behaviors or from the stakeholder's behaviors. As some individuals within a stakeholder group (or managers of an organization) recognize certain behavioral consequences as problematic, these individuals (or organizational managers) are motivated to address problematic states. Generally speaking, problem-solving efforts consist of two kinds of human acts: behavioral and communicative efforts. Public relations as communication management thus engages in communicative efforts of seeking, selecting, and sharing problem-relevant information from the problem-causing entities (e.g., organization) and for problem-solving opportunities (e.g., resource or power holders).

J. E. Grunig (2009; J. E. Grunig et al., 2009) identified two paradigms of public relations approaches: the *symbolic, interpretive paradigm* versus the behavioral, strategic management paradigm. In the symbolic, interpretive paradigm, public relations is used mainly to influence how publics interpret the organization's behaviors, whereas in the behavioral, strategic paradigm, public relations participates in choosing or managing an organization's decisions and behaviors.

The interpretive approach relies heavily on messaging to change or negotiate publics' interpretations of the organization's behaviors and uses only the press-agentry, public information, and two-way asymmetrical models to negotiate those interpretations. Communication is often one way, but can be frequently two way when the two-way asymmetrical model is used. However, interpretive public relations is not always limited to message dissemination. Research is often done to find out how the public is interpreting the organization's behavior and then is used to change the messages in an attempt to influence that interpretation. In other words, the negotiation in the two-way asymmetrical model comes from seeking to understand the public's interpretation before trying to change it. The purpose of the interpretive approach is thus to create favorable interpretations of an organization's behaviors to buffer those behaviors from public opposition or negative public behaviors—thus allowing the organization to behave the way it wants and still receive public approval of that behavior (Scott, 1987; Van den Bosch & van Riel, 1998).

In contrast, the strategic management approach thinks of communication more as dialogue and interaction than as messaging. Its purpose is to provide publics a voice in management decisions—bridging the gap between organizations and publics (Scott, 1987; Van den Bosch & van Riel, 1998). It provides management with valuable information from stakeholders and publics in the environment that helps it make more responsible decisions and choose behaviors that result in better relationships with publics. Thus, the two-way symmetrical model is the most important type of public relations used in the strategic management approach, although elements of the other models (such as mediated and interpersonal communication and two-way communication achieved through research) might also be used.

Institutionalizing Public Relations From a Buffering to a Bridging Function: The behavioral, strategic management approach to public relations maximizes its *coping potential* by influencing and revising behaviors that initially caused problems between the organization and publics. In this sense, public relations should manage the problem-solving processes by using communication efforts instrumentally for the purpose of *composing* and *revising decisions* and *behaviors.*

J. E. Grunig (2008, 2009), borrowing from organizational theorists' terminology, called the two paradigms of public relations *buffering* versus *bridging* functions (Scott, 1987; Van den Bosch & van Riel, 1998). In essence, the symbolic, interpretive paradigm sees organizational public relations as a buffering function. Such a function helps create enough impressions in the publics' minds to allow the organization to buffer itself from its environment so that the organization can act without being interrupted by publics. In buffering public relations, communication efforts are thus *tactical* and *technical* messaging efforts "to influence how publics interpret the organization" and crown interpretive concepts, such as reputation, brand, image, and identity, as the ultimate goals of public relations activities (J. E. Grunig, 2008, p. 9).

In sharp contrast, the behavioral, strategic management paradigm conceptualizes public relations as a bridging function. It bridges gaps of interests and stances on problems between an organization and its environment by communicating interactively and proactively (i.e., two way) and with balancing efforts for distinct interests (i.e., symmetrical communication management). In the short term, these efforts aim at adjusting individual interests and approaching problem resolution; in the long run, such communicative efforts and outcomes generate and incrementally enhance the nature and quality of relationships with publics.

Although the behavioral, strategic management perspective is clear on the conception of what public relations should be, more scholarly research is still necessary to better guide how public relations can become a strategic bridging function rather than a tactical buffering function. This is a research problem of institutionalizing public relations into the overall strategic management process so as to manage the communication process in guiding and aiding policy formation and the organizational decision-making process. Public relations researchers should ask and answer questions concerning the ways in which public relations can introduce itself to or become a member of the top management team, and how it can create opportunities to increase its contributions as a strategic counselor. Investigation of these questions is required to address the values that public relations creates for its hosting organization, and to determine the power strategies and adaptive tactics needed to enhance its power position in organizational charts, as well as in specific organizational designs and structures in terms of types of missions or businesses, size, history, and history of the organization.

Adaptive Management Structures and Strategies for Digitalization and Virtualization. One interesting field of research in organizational design and public relations is how the public relations function can adequately adapt to the changes of digitalization and virtualization in its internal and external environments—how to incorporate the changes due to publics' migration to cyberspace. Specifically, more research needs to be devoted to what kind of public relations structure and coordination designs for various communication units and staffs could lead to better adaptivenness to virtualization of public behaviors, and how and to what extent virtualization or digitalization will influence public relations strategies (e.g., Does digitalization require changes in Excellence principles? Does digitalization increase the need for a more symmetrical approach?). Some practitioners and educators claim that the behavioral, strategic management perspective is insufficient in the era of digital and social media (Phillips & Young, 2009). Some practitioners who diagnose fundamental changes in doing public relations in the Internet era even argue for a totally new conceptualization of public relations (Solis & Breakenridge, 2009).

It is obvious that many practitioners are now busy adopting digital technologies in their routine operations that go far beyond creating organizational Web sites or running an intranet. The so-called Web 2.0 technologies, such as creating blogs and interactive organizational social media sites, participating in interactive online communities, and using Twitter, are considered standard practices for most organizations. As they experience such a transition, practitioners and educators are questioning public relations researchers and theorists on how to communicate better and more effectively in the increasingly digitized and virtualized organizational working processes (e.g., virtual teams). They also question how organizations should respond to publics' adoption and adaptation to the digitized social environment (e.g., online collective actions). The public relations scholarly community should therefore look for adaptive structures and corresponding strategy building for publics who use the Internet, social media, blogs, and mobile communication as tools for their actions and problem solving.

As an initial response to such changes, J. E. Grunig (2009) noted that the changes of digitalization are substantial and important in a way that favors a more symmetrical approach, and the behavioral management public relations approach. He pointed out that many practitioners overestimate the necessary conceptual changes of thinking and doing public relations; they are typically "using new media in old ways" with an "illusion of controlling" the messages members of publics are exposed to as well as the cognitions, attitudes, and behaviors of message recipients (essentially following the same logic in the press-agentry, public information, and asymmetrical models of public relations). In an earlier phase of digitalization, for example, many practitioners attempted to use the Internet in a "one-way asymmetrical" way (Phillips, 2009) to spread messages for promoting their interests. These tactics ranged from spamming, a primitive tactic, to the more evolved tactic of creating blogs with favorable messages for their organizations. Notably, the Internet has evolved into maximizing two-way communicative interactions. However, using it as a one-way communication tool in an optimal message and communication design, in hopes of shaping and reshaping what publics think, believe, and do, is maladaptive (J. E. Grunig, 2009).

In the Web 2.0 era, it is more accurate to say that it is not that the Internet has changed how publics (users) behave but that publics (users) have changed the Internet to fit their needs and interests (e.g., the evolution from blogs to Twitter). The behavioral, strategic management perspective is growing in importance as J. E. Grunig (2009) predicted. This growth in importance stems from the inherent communication conception of digital and social media as a two-way interactive tool, the failing of the "illusion of control," and the fact that the symbolic, interpretive paradigm of public relations has difficulties in prescribing how public relations should be done in dealing with more capable and self-controlled publics in the digitalization era.

Finally, we found a lack of research on ethical considerations about organizational use of digital and social media. For example, some organizations create *flogs* (fake blogs) to deliver a favorable impression to their visitors, an online version of front group tactics called *astroturfing* (an artificial grassroots movement) to give favorable messages without disclosing the actual identity of those who posted positive messages or disguising their relationship with the promoted organization. In addition, some organizations use corporate social media Web sites as pseudosymmetrical communication—claiming that they make efforts for more spontaneous two-way communication with their publics, but being selective by removing or controlling posted opinions. Research into generating cases and developing guidelines for ethical cyber public relations is greatly needed but is currently sorely lacking.

Scope of Public Relations Management. In the behavioral, strategic management perspective, theorists have emphasized that the direction and nature of communication should be two way and symmetrical. The program of research on the situational theory of publics has found that the perceptions, cognitions, communication behaviors, and behaviors related with problematic situations are largely determined by publics rather than message senders. From these findings, situational theorists suggested that "creating a public" is very difficult, if not impossible (J. E. Grunig, 1997).

However, the public relations function is often requested to plan and program information campaigns, such as health or risk communication campaigns (e.g., H1N1 virus infection or pandemic prevention). In such instances, one communication goal is to create a public around the health issue or risk of interest. Whereas, in general, communication effectiveness in such campaigns is disappointingly low and falls short according to cost-benefit analysis, very often public relations managers still have to take responsibilities and initiatives, mainly for normative and ethical obligations. In other cases, such as fund-raising or marketing campaigns, the rationales are more about "survival" (J.-N. Kim, Ni, & Sha, 2008). Therefore, the behavioral, strategic management approach should conceptually embrace such types of public relations practices as well. However, caution needs to be exercised in judging and evaluating the effectiveness of such campaigns as a solution for public relations problems: for example, by not directly aiming at or assessing behavioral changes but aiming at problem perception.

In recent works, J.-N. Kim and Ni (2009) defined two common public relations situations, which by nature necessitate different public relations interventions and evaluation strategies. *Public-initiated public relations problems* typically start from a public's problem recognition and are found frequently in situations of conflict between an organization and publics. Hence, for public-initiated public relations problems, organizations need public relations efforts for communication programs to *decrease* stakeholders' and publics' *problem perception* and *(communicative) actions* regarding the problems—to "*de-create*" *a (possible) public.* In contrast, *organization-initiated public relations problems* usually start from an organization's problem recognition and often occur as nonconflict situations. Organization-initiated public relations problems occur when organizations encounter problems that discourage their efforts for achieving missions or goals. As examples, government health agencies have to plan campaigns for preventing pandemic diseases, or a university with a financial crisis will initiate fund-raising campaigns for more alumni and parents' gifts. For organization-initiated public relations problems, organizations attempt to increase problem perception, to install a new cognitive frame, and to foster communicative behaviors among stakeholders or a portion of a general population. This is often done using communicative tactics such as education or persuasion—to *create a(n) (aware) public* about the problem that the organizations experience or consider important (see Figure 3.3).

Such a typology of public relations problems is useful for integrating some forms of risk and health communications and for applying the body of knowledge available from the behavioral, strategic management paradigm. For example, for organization-initiated public relations problems practitioners can use segmentation tools and public typology to develop strategies and tactics, and use the nature and quality of relationships assessed to solicit more sympathy and *problem chain recognition* (J.-N. Kim, Shen, & Morgan, in press) regarding the problem (e.g., alumni with good relationships would perceive the school's financial trouble as more problematic than alumni with poor relationships). Notably, the realistic goal would be to create an aware public or increase the chances for inducing an already active public to engage in more (communicative) actions about the problem. Although it is still necessary to clearly understand the difficulties of creating a public, the scholarly community should conduct applied research to integrate organization-initiated public relations situations to develop more strategic procedures for improving communication efficacy.

Models of Public Relations. One of the key components in conceptualizing how public relations should be managed is the use of public relations models. The four models, especially the two-way symmetrical model, have consistently created much discussion and debate (for a review, see J. E. Grunig, 2001; L. A. Grunig et al., 2002). Researchers have been gradually shifting away from the four distinct models and adopting four dimensions of organizational communication behaviors that can better capture the nature and complexity of public relations practices. These dimensions include the direction (one way or two way), nature of

Figure 3.3 A Taxonomy of Types of PR Problems in the Strategic Management Context

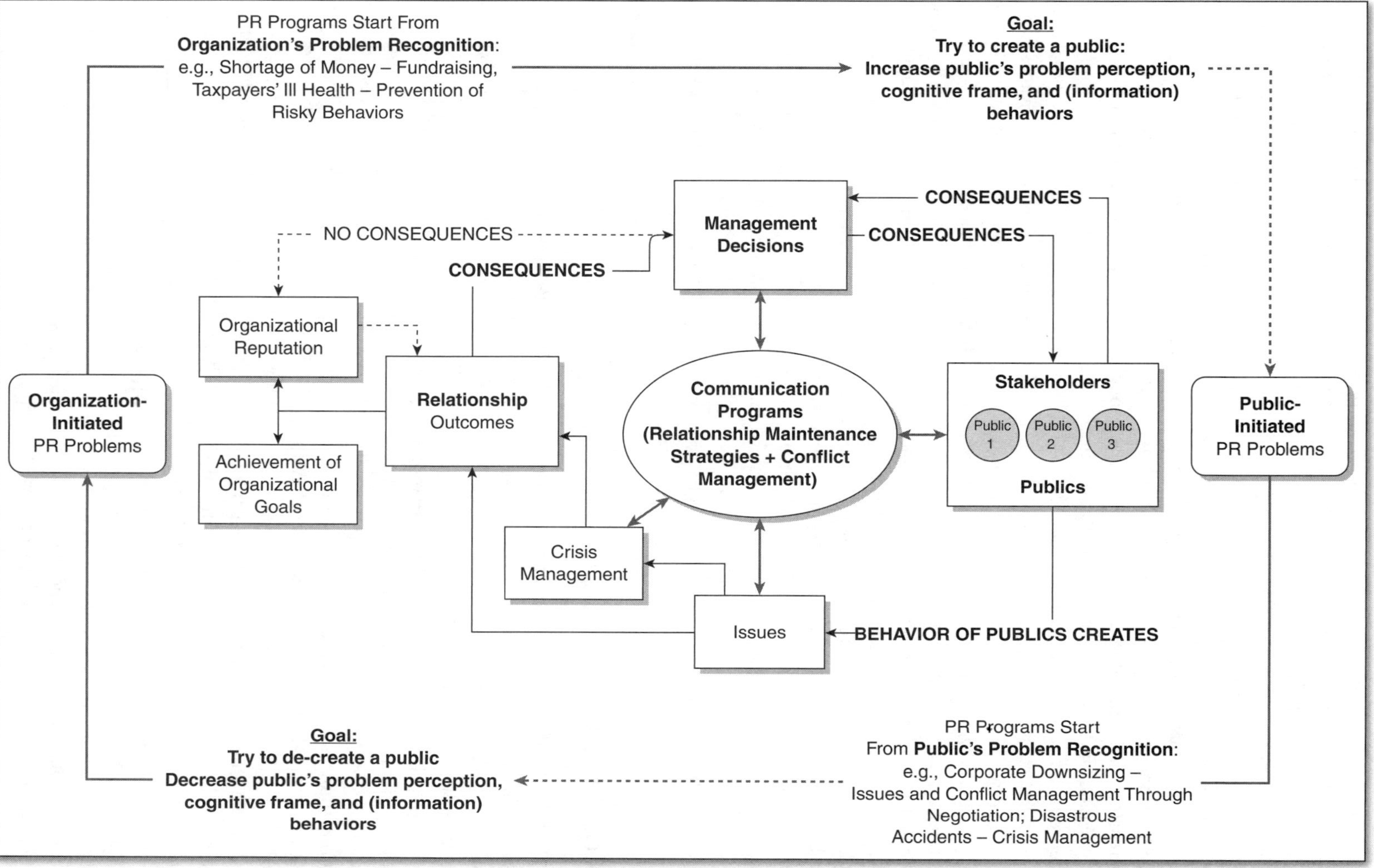

Source: Modified from L. A. Grunig et al. (2002, p. 145).

communication (symmetrical or asymmetrical), channel or media (interpersonal or mediated communication), and ethical nature (ethical or unethical). In recent years, Sha (2004, 2007, 2009) has contributed to the refined understanding of public relations models, especially the nature of symmetry as conceptualized together with the concept of conservation. More studies are needed not only to strengthen and refine the measurements of these dimensions but also to examine the relationship between different public relations practices and other important variables.

What we have discussed so far is in no way representative of the full scope of the behavioral, strategic management approach to public relations. For a full review of the major aspects and their current and future development, such as the globalization of public relations, inclusion of ethics, developing tools for strategic management, and application of theories to different contexts, see J. E. Grunig (2006). This review is based on the authors' perspective, which has guided our choice of the specific areas to discuss.

Conclusion

The behavioral, strategic management paradigm has its origin from the initial concept as explicated by J. E. Grunig (1966), which was a primitive term rather than a scientific derived term (Chaffee, 1991). Constructing the situational theory of publics, which is a descriptive and teleological theory, then enlivened the public relations community to define and identify publics clearly enough to conceptualize what they do as strategic communication management (J. E. Grunig, 2003). The behavioral paradigm then evolved further into other descriptive theories, such as the models of public relations approach, which describe how public relations is managed, and how and to what extent each approach results in different organization outcomes. From the descriptive models, behavioral management researchers tried to construct a prescriptive theory for how to better practice, educate, and counsel people who seek out public relations. The IABC Excellence study has analyzed and accumulated a vast number of theoretical building blocks and syntheses. As we mentioned at the beginning of this chapter, the conceptual building blocks and the resulting empirical findings are so significant that they now form a forest of a general theory of public relations. In the forest exist many growing trees of middle-range theories and conceptual models.

In this chapter, we reviewed how these small or large conceptual trees have grown in the behavioral, strategic management forest. Through this review, we hope to elucidate how the future forest of the behavioral management approach can grow even further. This challenge can best be overcome as more researchers and practitioners question how to develop and subscribe to more scientific concepts (vs. primitive concepts) and make efforts to conceptualize their working practice and processes beyond the *phenotypic surface* level to reach an underlying *genotypic crux.*

As a microevolution, we are experiencing more conceptual *speciation* (diversification) in theorizing about the antecedents, processes, and consequences of public relations; as a macroevolution, we are undertaking a paradigm shift from emphasizing *persuading* and *symbolic management* to the recognition of the importance of *communicating* and *behavioral management* in conceptualizing public relations. The behavioral, strategic management approach will assist and accelerate the evolutionary process of public relations from a mere occupation to a profession that creates value for its users (organizations or publics alike) and value for a society that recognizes the importance of mutual adaptation among its social actors.

Note

1. See L. A. Grunig et al. (2002) for details about the research team and the three books resulting from the Excellence project.

References

Aldoory, L. (2001). Making health communications meaningful for women: Factors that influence involvement and the situational theory of publics. *Journal of Public Relations Research, 13,* 163–185.

Aldoory, L., & Sha, B. L. (2007). Elaborations of the situational theory of publics for more effective application to public relations scholarship and practice. In E. L. Toth (Ed.), *The future of excellence in public relations and communication management* (pp. 339–355). Mahwah, NJ: Lawrence Erlbaum.

Balter, D., & Butman, J. (2005). *Grapevine.* New York: Portfolio.

Blumer, H. (1948). Public opinion and public opinion polling. *American Sociological Review, 13,* 542–554.

Chaffee, S. (1991). *Explication.* Newbury Park, CA: Sage.

Coombs, T. W. (1998). The Internet as potential equalizer: New leverage for confronting social irresponsibility. *Public Relations Review, 24,* 289–303.

Denegri-Knott, J., & Taylor, J. (2005). The labeling game: A conceptual exploration of deviance on the Internet. *Social Science Computer Review, 23,* 93–107.

Dewey, J. (1927). *The public and its problems.* New York: Henry Holt.

Dozier, D. M. (1992). The organizational roles of communications and public relations practitioners. In J. E. Grunig (Ed.), Excellence in public relations and communication management (pp. 327–356). Hillsdale, NJ: Lawrence Erlbaum.

Dozier, D. M., Grunig, L. A., & Grunig, J. E. (1995). *Manager's guide to excellence in public relations and communication management.* Mahwah, NJ: Lawrence Erlbaum.

Ehling, W. P. (1992). Estimating the value of public relations and communication to an organization. In J. E. Grunig (Ed.), *Excellence in public relations and communication management: Contributions to effective organizations* (pp. 617–638). Hillsdale, NJ: Lawrence Erlbaum.

Elliot, C. M. (1997). *Activism on the Internet and its ramifications for public relations.* Unpublished master's thesis, University of Maryland, College Park.

Esman, M. J. (1972). The elements of institution building. In J. W. Eaton (Ed.), *Institution building and development* (pp. 19–40). Beverly Hills, CA: Sage.

Ferguson, M. A. (1984, August). *Building theory in public relations: Interorganizational relationships as a public relations paradigm.* Paper presented to the Association for Education in Journalism and Mass Communication, Gainesville, FL.

Grunig, J. E. (1966). The role of information in economic decision making. *Journalism Monographs, 3.*

Grunig, J. E. (1976). Organizations and public relations: Testing a communication theory. *Journalism Monographs, 46.*

Grunig, J. E. (1984). Organizations, environments, and models of public relations. *Public Relations Research & Education, 1,* 6–29.

Grunig, J. E. (1992). *Excellence in public relations and communication management: Contributions to effective organizations.* Hillsdale, NJ: Lawrence Erlbaum.

Grunig, J. E. (1997). A situational theory of publics: Conceptual history, recent challenges and new research. In D. Moss, T. MacManus, & D. Verčič (Eds.), *Public relations research: An international perspective* (pp. 3–46). London: International Thomson Business Press.

Grunig, J. E. (2001). Two-way symmetrical public relations: Past, present, and future. In R. L. Heath (Ed.), *Handbook of public relations* (pp. 11–30). Thousand Oaks, CA: Sage.

Grunig, J. E. (2003). Constructing public relations theory and practice. In B. Dervin, S. Chaffee, & L. Foreman-Wernet (Eds.), *Communication, another kind of horse race: Essays honoring Richard F. Carter* (pp. 85–115). Cresskill, NJ: Hampton Press.

Grunig, J. E. (2006). Furnishing the edifice: Ongoing research on public relations as a strategic management function. *Journal of Public Relations Research, 18,* 151–176.

Grunig, J. E. (2008). Conceptualizing quantitative research in public relations. In B. van Ruler, A. T. Verčič, & D. Verčič (Eds.), *Public relations metrics: Research and evaluation* (pp. 88–119). New York: Routledge.

Grunig, J. E. (2009). Paradigms of global public relations in an age of digitalisation. *PRism, 6,* 1–19.

Grunig, J. E., Ferrari, M. A., & França, F. (2009). *Relações públicas: Teoria, contexto e relacionamentos* [Public relations: Theory, context, and relationships]. São Paulo, Brazil: Difusao Editora.

Grunig, J. E., & Grunig, L. A. (1989). Toward a theory of the public relations behavior of organizations: Review of a program of research. In J. E. Grunig & L. A. Grunig (Eds.), *Public relations research annual* (Vol. 1., pp. 27–66). Hillsdale, NJ: Lawrence Erlbaum.

Grunig, J. E., & Grunig, L. A. (1992). Models of public realations and communication. In J. E. Grunig (Ed.), *Excellence in public relations and communication management: Contributions to effective organizations* (pp. 285–325). Hillsdale, NJ: Lawrence Erlbaum.

Grunig, J. E., & Grunig, L. A. (1996, May). *Implications of symmetry for a theory of ethics and social responsibility in public relations.* Paper presented to the Public Relations Interest Group, International Communication Association, Chicago.

Grunig, J. E., Grunig, L. A., & Dozier, D. M. (2006). The excellence theory. In C. H. Botan & V. Hazleton (Eds.), *Public relations theory II* (pp. 21–62). Mahwah, NJ: Lawrence Erlbaum.

Grunig, J. E., & Huang, Y. H. (2000). From organizational effectiveness to relationship indicators: Antecedents of relationships, public relations strategies, and relationship outcomes. In J. A. Ledingham and S. D. Bruning (Eds.), *Public relations as relationship management: A relational approach to the study and practice of public relations* (pp. 23–53). Mahwah, NJ: Lawrence Erlbaum.

Grunig, J. E., & Hunt, T. (1984). *Managing public relations.* New York: Holt, Rinehart & Winston.

Grunig, J. E., & Repper, F. C. (1992). Strategic management, publics, and issues. In J. E. Grunig (Ed.), *Excellence in public relations and communication management* (pp. 31–64). Hillsdale, NJ: Lawrence Erlbaum.

Grunig, L. A., Grunig, J. E., & Dozier, D. M. (2002). *Excellent public relations and effective organizations: A study of communication management in three countries.* Mahwah, NJ: Lawrence Erlbaum.

Hallahan, K. (2000). Inactive publics: The forgotten publics in public relations. *Public Relations Review, 26,* 499–515.

Hicks, J. R. (1943). The four consumer surpluses. *Review of Economic Studies, 9,* 31–41.

Hon, L. C., & Grunig, J. E. (1999). *Guidelines for measuring relationships in public relations.* Gainesville, FL: Institute for Public Relations.

Huang, Y.-H. (2001). OPRA: A cross-cultural, multiple-item scale for measuring organization-public relationships. *Journal of Public Relations Research, 13,* 61–90.

Huber, G. P. (1980). *Managerial decision making.* Glenview, IL: Scott, Foresman.

Hung, C. J. F. (2005). Exploring types of organization-public relationships and their implications on relationship management in public relations. *Journal of Public Relations Research, 17,* 393–426.

Ki, E.-J., & Hon, L. C. (2007). Testing the linkages among the organization-public relationship and attitude and behavioral intentions. *Journal of Public Relations Research, 19,* 1–23.

Kiesler, S., Siegel, J., & McGuire, T. W. (1984). Social psychological aspects of computer-mediated communication. *American Psychologist, 39,* 1123–1134.

Kim, H.-S. (2007). A multilevel study of antecedents and a mediator of employee-organization relationships. *Journal of Public Relations Research, 19,* 167–197.

Kim, J.-N., & Grunig, J. E. (in press-a). Problem solving and communicative action: A situational theory of problem solving. *Journal of Communication.*

Kim, J.-N., & Grunig, J. E. (in press-b). *Situational theory of problem solving: Communicative, cognitive, and perceptive bases.* New York: Routledge.

Kim, J.-N., Grunig, J. E., & Ni, L. (2010). Reconceptualizing public's communicative action: Acquisition, selection, and transmission of information in problematic situations. *International Journal of Strategic Communication, 4(2),* 126–154.

Kim, J.-N., & Ni, L. (2009, March). *Creating a theory-driven strategic public relations procedure.* Paper presented to the 12th Annual International Public Relations Research Conference, Miami, FL.

Kim, J.-N., Ni, L., & Sha, B.-L. (2008). Breaking down the stakeholder environment: A review of approaches to the segmentation of publics. *Journalism & Mass Communication Quarterly, 85,* 751–768.

Kim, J.-N., & Rhee, Y. (in press). Employees as boundary spanners: Megaphoning and scouting effects in employee communication. *Journal of Public Relations Research.*

Kim, J.-N., Shen, H., & Morgan, S. (in press). Information behaviors and problem chain recognition effect: Applying situational theory of problem solving in organ donation issues. *Health Communication.*

Kim, M. S., & Raja, N. S. (1991, May). *Verbal aggression and self-disclosure on computer bulletin boards.* Paper presented at the Annual Meeting of the International Communication Association, Chicago.

Mintzberg, H. (1983). *Power in and around organizations.* Englewood Cliffs, NJ: Prentice Hall.

Ni, L. (2006). Relationships as organizational resources: Examining public relations impact through its connection with organizational strategies. *Public Relations Review, 32,* 276–281.

Ni, L. (2009). Strategic role of relationship building: Perceived links between employee-organization relationships and globalization strategies. *Journal of Public Relations Research, 21,* 100–120.

Ni, L., & Kim, J.-N. (2009). Classifying publics: Communication behaviors and problem-solving characteristics in controversial issues. *International Journal of Strategic Communication, 3*(4), 217–241.

Ni, L., & Wang, Q. (in press). Anxiety and uncertainty management in an intercultural setting: The impact on university-student relations. *Journal of Public Relations Research.*

Phillips, D. (2009, January 9). A Grunigian view of modern PR. *Leverwealth.* Retrieved March 2, 2010, from http://leverwealth.blogspot.com/2009/01/grunigian-view-of-modern-pr.html?disqus_reply=5552359#comment-5552359

Phillips, D., & Young, P. (2009). *Online public relations: A practical guide to developing an online strategy in the world of social media.* Philadelphia: Kogan Page.

Postmes, T., & Brunsting, S. (2002). Collective action in the age of the Internet: Mass communication and online mobilization. *Social Science Computer Review, 20,* 290–301.

Rhee, Y. (2007). Interpersonal communication as an element of symmetrical communication: A case study. In E. L. Toth (Ed.), *The future of excellence in public relations and communication management* (pp. 103–117). Mahwah, NJ: Lawrence Erlbaum.

Rock, P. (1973). *Deviant behavior.* London: Hutchinson University Library.

Scott, W. R. (1987). *Organizational, rational, natural, and open systems.* London: Prentice Hall.

Sernovitz, A. (2006). *Word of mouth marketing: How smart companies get people talking.* New York: Kaplan.

Sha, B.-L. (2004). Noether's theorem: The science of symmetry and the law of conservation. *Journal of Public Relations Research, 16,* 391–416.

Sha, B.-L. (2006). Cultural identity in the segmentation of publics: An emerging theory of intercultural public relations. *Journal of Public Relations Research, 18,* 45–65.

Sha, B.-L. (2007). Dimensions of public relations: Moving beyond traditional public relations models. In S. Duhe (Ed.), *New media and public relations* (pp. 3–25). New York: Peter Lang.

Sha, B.-L. (2009). Exploring the connection between organizational identity and public relations behaviors: How symmetry trumps conservation in engendering organizational identification. *Journal of Public Relations Research, 21,* 295–371.

Solis, B., & Breakenridge, D. (2009). *Putting the public back in public relations: How social media is reinventing the aging business of PR.* Upper Saddle River, NJ: Pearson Education.

Spears, R., Lea, M., Corneliussen, R. A., Postmes, T., & Haar, W. T. (2002). Computer-mediated communication as a channel for social resistance: The strategic side of SIDE. *Small Group Research, 33,* 555–574.

Sriramesh, K., Moghan, S., & Wei, D. L. K. (2007). The situational theory of publics in a different cultural setting: Consumer publics in Singapore. *Journal of Public Relations Research, 19,* 307–332.

Thompson, M. S. (1980). *Benefit-cost analysis for program evaluation.* Beverly Hills, CA: Sage.

Tkalac, A. (2007). The application of situational theory in Croatia. In E. L. Toth (Ed.), *The future of excellence in public relations and communication management: Challenges for the next generation* (pp. 527–543). Mahwah, NJ: Lawrence Erlbaum.

Van den Bosch, F. A. J., & van Riel, C. B. M. (1998). Buffering and bridging as environmental strategies of firms. *Business Strategy and the Environment, 7,* 24–31.

Yang, S.-U. (2007). An integrated model for organization-public relational outcomes, organizational reputation, and their antecedents. *Journal of Public Relations Research, 19,* 91–121.

CHAPTER 4

The Cursed Sisters

Public Relations and Rhetoric

Øyvind Ihlen

The rhetorical tradition offers public relations scholars, managers, and practitioners a resource that helps them understand organizational discourse, its effects, and its role in society. Rhetoric helps explain the ways in which organizations attempt to achieve specific political or economic goals, or build relationships with their stakeholders. Furthermore, in addition to offering down-to-earth practical advice, rhetoric also presents epistemological perspectives that temper theoretical tendencies toward naive realism and platonic notions of absolute truth. Rhetoric helps us understand how knowledge is generated and socially constructed through communication.

In recognition of the centrality of discourse, there has been a turn toward rhetoric in many academic disciplines. Scholars of philosophy, management, economics, law, political science, social psychology, history, anthropology, sociology, and literature have all drawn on rhetoric (Lucaites, Condit, & Caudill, 1999; Sillince & Suddaby, 2008). The application of rhetoric in public relations has also been championed, most notably by Heath (e.g., 1980, 1992, 2001, 2009). This chapter starts by giving a short overview of the rhetorical tradition before going on to discuss rhetoric in public relations. Particular attention is paid to epistemology, as this demonstrates why rhetoric should be included in the canon of public relations. It is proposed that the rhetorical tradition can still divulge crucial concepts and ways of thinking that illuminate public relations practice and help build theory. A call is also issued for more research on the rhetorical situations that organizations encounter and the archetypical ways in which they respond.

Classical Rhetoric

In everyday parlance, rhetoric is more often than not applied as a contrast to "substantial action" and "reality." Rhetoric is reserved for empty words and deception. Every rhetorician is happy to point out that this negative understanding of rhetoric is due to rhetorical theory that emphasizes only style and delivery and to argue that the ancient tradition is misrepresented. At the very least, it can quickly be pointed out that rhetoric is inescapable. Everyone uses rhetoric, not least the antirhetoricians.

The classic and best-known definition of rhetoric is given by Aristotle: "Let rhetoric be [defined as] an ability, in each [particular] case, to see the available means of persuasion" (Aristotle, trans. 1991, 1.2.1). According to this tradition, then, the normative aim of rhetoric is "persuasion" or "influence." Influence is defined as the capacity to affect the thoughts or actions of others by persuading or convincing them. This definition excludes force and material inducement, but allows for both rational and irrational processes. Although some use the terms *to persuade* and *to convince* interchangeably, there may, in fact, be a difference between them. To persuade somebody about *p* is to get him or her to believe *p*, but to convince somebody about *p* is to provide other sufficient reasons to believe that *p* is true or acceptable (Tranøy, 1986). Some argue that rhetoric should confess to its aim of influencing and changing people and that persuasion is thus the better definition (Andersen, 1995). Others, in contrast, stress that rhetoric involves both reason and emotion; that it attempts to convince *and* persuade (Corbett & Connors, 1999).

A particular concept touched on by most of the ancient theorists of rhetoric was that of *artistic* proofs in the form of *ethos, pathos,* and *logos*—that is, ethical appeal, emotional appeal, and appeal to reason. These proofs are linked to the rhetor, the audience, and the message, respectively. In a given discourse, "these are at all times coordinate [*sic*] and interact mutually, distinguishable but not separable from one another, although one may occasionally take precedence over the others" (Conley, 1990, p. 15).

Interestingly, the ancient rhetoricians treated emotions as epistemic, as a way of knowing. Today, logic and emotion are most often pitted against each other as intellectual and bodily processes, respectively. The ancients, however, saw feelings not only as subjectively real but also as objectively true (Andersen, 1995). In Latin, *sentire* means both to mean and to feel: "'I understand,' or 'I feel' or 'I see' are often equivalent to 'I know'" (Quintilian, trans. 1920/1996, 10.1.13). The purely logos-based rhetoric tends to ignore the fact that changing people's minds depends on at least two things: "the emotional intensity with which they cling to an opinion; and the degree to which their identities—their sense of themselves as integrated people—are wrapped up with that opinion" (Crowley & Hawhee, 1999, p. 153). Some use of pathos is thus indispensable for a rhetor.

Although classical rhetoric encompasses a range of other concepts, the notion of ethos, logos, and pathos are arguably the most well-known theoretical contribution. Rhetorical theory does not, however, end with the ancients. During the 20th century, a new form of rhetoric emerged.

New Rhetoric

The new rhetoric was largely driven by debates on epistemology. It was characterized by rhetorical scholars moving away from the aesthetic understanding of rhetoric that was so preoccupied with form, and from scientific understanding, with its modernist notion of objectivity. From the 1960s onward, the hegemony of the neotraditionalists was challenged (Booth, 1967; Fogarty, 1959). The luminaries of this movement included Kenneth Burke and Chaïm Perelman, and their respective books *Rhetoric of Motives* (Burke, 1950/1969) and *The New Rhetoric: A Treatise on Argumentation* (Perelman & Olbrechts-Tyteca, 1969) are widely held to be the two main texts on contemporary rhetorical theory (Gaonkar, 2001).

Some have argued that classical rhetoric—excluding the sophists (see Jarratt, 1991)—typically saw truth as something that the rhetor had arrived at previously and that rhetoric should merely help communicate this truth. Furthermore, there was a clearly defined relationship between the rhetor, the audience, and the world that was mediated by language. In modern rhetoric, however, there is no fully confident or generally accepted epistemological stance that articulates the relationship between the knower and the known (Lunsford & Ede, 1994; Ohmann, 1994), although a widespread position is that truth is inseparable from discourse, or the way in which we use language and interact. Rhetoric is not seen as something that decorates or disguises truth; rhetoric is a way of *creating* truth.

In 1967, Robert L. Scott (1999) argued that rhetoric is epistemic: It is a way of knowing. This so-called social-epistemic rhetoric understands rhetoric as constructing and modifying reality, social conditions, and relationships. Rhetoric is implicated in all human behavior and constructs social knowledge that is situated materially and historically. It is through rhetoric that ideas are accepted or rejected; truth is not discovered or unearthed and cannot be determined in any a priori way. Rhetorical interaction is involved when something is declared to be a fact, in the interpretation of that fact, and in how that fact is used to justify action. This also extends to discourse communities that try to deny that rhetoric plays a role, such as economics and branches of science that deal with "objective facts." All types of knowledge must rest on some kind of human consensus, and there is thus a need for rhetoric (Farrell, 1999; Moran & Ballif, 2000).

In a sense, then, truth can be conceived as being created moment by moment. This has brought about a renewed interest in the ancient sophistic tradition and its emphasis on contingency, or how something is probable rather than certain (e.g., Jarratt, 1991; Poulakos, 1999). Scott later regretted the use of the word "epistemic," as he saw no way of being certain. To him, rhetoric is *a* way of knowing or understanding, not *the* way. Most important, however, the positivist notion of the grand truth should be ignored (Scott, 1993).

Others have given this and related epistemological stances different labels, including *intersubjectivity*, *rhetorical subjectivism*, and *rhetorical relativism*. These stances can be shown to have a modern counterpart in what is alternately called *rhetorical objectivism*, *rhetorical dialectic*, or *critical rationalism*. The general view held by scholars taking the epistemological standpoint is that truth is discovered with the help of rhetoric. Attempts have been made to bridge this problematic dualism by placing the two positions on a continuum and by mixing them differently (Cherwitz & Hikins, 1999). The debate has clear parallels with the sociological discussion of social constructionism (Berger & Luckmann, 1966; Heide, 2009).

It is possible to argue that "reality" is a product of a synthesis between material structures and practices on one side and the use of symbols that reinforce or question those structures and practices on the other. The most radical version of the "rhetoric is epistemic" stance has little room for material existence. This leads to discussions of ontological matters, that is, thoughts of what exists, kinds of being, and the relationship between them. It is argued here that although material structures *do* exist, rhetoric is needed for the social mediation of this knowledge. It is not possible to communicate without rhetoric, and rhetoric is crucial for human understanding. In this sense, rhetoric is epistemic, but it seems most fruitful to comprehend it as having a dialectic relationship to the ontological.

Rhetoric and Organizations

Organizations define problems and their solutions and try to influence stakeholders' opinions and public policies to best suit their own interests and perspectives. Sometimes they succeed in this, and sometimes they do not. Sometimes the interest of an organization is shared by other parts of society, and sometimes it is not. These relatively banal observations notwithstanding, rhetoric is used by organizations in these instances regardless of the label appended to the communication activity, be it "lobbying" or "relationship management." The process by which organizations influence and are influenced by others involves persuasion. Unless an organization or its stakeholders uses force or material inducement, its power or influence is likely to be based on both rational and irrational processes. Ultimately, it rests on the agreement of the other party, in that the latter recognizes its own interest in complying with the wish of the rhetor. Such influence implies the presentation of arguments; that is, it involves rhetoric (Kennedy, 1991; Mayhew, 1997).

The rhetoric of modern organizations is different from the rhetoric of the ancient rhetor addressing an assembly. The first distinction is that the rhetors of today mostly represent organizations and are inseparable from those organizations (Crable, 1990). The practical consequences of this become especially evident during crises. For instance, when defending itself against charges of wrongdoing, the organizational hierarchy creates possibilities for denying or diffusing responsibility (Seeger, Sellnow, & Ulmer, 1998), resulting in the organization as a whole taking the blame, thereby absolving the individual. Alternatively, an individual may be made a scapegoat, thus deflecting blame away from the organization.

The second distinction is that modern rhetors have a variety of channels through which to convey their messages. This is reflected by the fact that the object of research on organizational rhetoric is not only speeches but also text in the broad sense. In the field of public relations research, it is the "public record" that is most often used as the unit of analysis, including rhetoric that is distributed via social media or the mass media (Toth, 1992).

Third, modern rhetors often reach mass audiences with which they have no direct contact. Unlike a physically present audience, a mass audience provides no immediate reaction. Furthermore, not only is the spatial dimension different, but also the audience is more diverse and may have widely differing values and multiple organizational identifications (Cheney, Christensen, Conrad, & Lair, 2004; Crable, 1990). This means that a strategy that is designed to communicate with one group of stakeholders can easily alienate another (Ice, 1991).

The fourth point is that rhetors are more or less agencies for organizations. They have become actors in the Hollywood sense: The "words we hear are someone else's: the understanding or emotions generated are controlled by forces off-stage. The actor in the Hollywood sense 'appears' and the actor in Burke's sense remains behind the scenes, not a part of the scene" (Crable, 1990, p. 123).

Taken together, such differences point to the need for a revamped rhetorical theory for organizations. Several attempts have been made in public relations to achieve this goal, as illustrated in the following.

Rhetoric in Public Relations Studies

Public relations pioneer Edward L. Bernays (1952) may well have been the first to mention rhetoric in conjunction with public relations. Nonetheless, an observer writing in 1970 noted the absence of any real exploration of the role of rhetoric in the early public relations literature (Knapp, 1970). Ten years later, however, Robert L. Heath (1980) published an article that laid the groundwork for much of the subsequent research on rhetoric and public relations. Heath proposed rhetoric to be the essence of an organization's relationship with its environment. One of the arguments that he has repeated since is that rhetoric affords public relations the possibility of ethical and pragmatic practice: "the good organization communicating well" (Heath, 2001, p. 39). With the help of rhetoric, organizations can achieve specific goals, such as legitimacy. Rhetoric can also help organizations focus on the different interpretations and zones of meaning of stakeholders (Heath, 1993). Rhetoric helps codefine and cocreate meaning. According to Heath, concurrence is the aim of the rhetorical process, and a clash of viewpoints strengthens the public opinion process. Based on these ideas, much effort has since been made to argue for the legitimacy and usefulness of a rhetorical approach to public relations (Heath, 2009; Toth, 2009).

Public relations scholars have suggested several analytical models for public relations based on the work of ancients such as Aristotle, Cicero, and Quintilian (Heath, 2009; Ihlen, 2002; Porter, 2010), Isocrates (Heath, 2009; Marsh, 2003; Porter, 2010), and new rhetoricians such as Toulmin (Skerlep, 2001), Bitzer (Heath, 2009; Ihlen, in press), and Burke and Perelman (Heath, 2009; Ihlen, 2004; Mickey, 1995). Although it would be wrong to claim that the rhetorical approach to public relations is flourishing, a considerable number of rhetorical concepts and cases have been analyzed in edited volumes such as *Rhetorical and Critical Approaches to Public Relations* (Toth & Heath, 1992), *Public Relations Inquiry as Rhetorical Criticism* (Elwood, 1995), *Corporate Advocacy: Rhetoric in the Information Age* (Hoover, 1997), *Power and Public Relations* (Courtright & Smudde, 2007), and *Rhetorical and Critical Approaches to Public Relations II* (Heath, Toth, & Waymer, 2009). The field has largely been dominated by U.S. scholars (Ihlen, 2008), although useful exceptions include the work by the U.K. scholar Jacquie L'Etang (1996, 1997, 2006).

Whereas some of the published rhetorical public relations studies have an intrinsic historical character that contributes little to theory building, there are also several that discuss particular rhetorical concepts. Authors have taken on enthymematic argumentation (Edwards, 2007), ethos (Bostdorff, 1992; Ihlen, 2009), paradoxes (German, 2007; Heath & Waymer, 2009), apologia (Hearit, 1995, 2001; Jerome, 2008), stasis theory (Marsh, 2006), metaphors (Zhang, 2007), model and antimodel arguments (Brand, 2007), employee recruitment strategies (Russell-Loretz, 2007), and strategies for high-tech industries (Baker, Conrad, Cudahy, & Willyard, 2009). Nevertheless, the best-developed line of rhetorical public relations research remains the studies of organizational self-defense and image restoration during or after crises (e.g., Benoit, 1995; Coombs, 1999, 2009; Hearit, 2006; Millar & Heath, 2003). Other rhetorical situations (Bitzer, 1968) are largely unexplored, a point that will be revisited later.

Scholars in the field of organizational communication have also made use of rhetoric (see Cheney et al., 2004, for an overview). These theorists have typically made a strong case for focusing on how reality is defined and created through the use of rhetoric, in line with the epistemological debate already touched on. Indeed, some propose that the use of rhetoric, or symbols, is the essence (if not the substance) of organizations. This means, they argue, that public relations practitioners should be taught to manage symbols rather than substance (Cheney & Dionisopoulos, 1989; Tompkins, 1987).

As indicated, the research streams of public relations and organizational communication can inform each other, despite their different foci on external and internal communication, respectively. Indeed, given that organizational rhetoric has both an internal and external audience, this traditional distinction often makes little sense (Cheney & Dionisopoulos, 1989). Others have similarly argued for the blurring of boundaries with other fields studying organizational rhetoric, such as propaganda analysis and social movement theory (Meisenbach & McMillian, 2006). Organizational scholars of various kinds have made great strides recently in bridging management and organizational rhetoric (e.g., Sillince & Suddaby, 2008), and public relations scholars are now following suit (e.g., Heath, in press), demonstrating the importance of external rhetoric.

Debates About Rhetorical Public Relations Studies

Various debates relating to orientation, ethics, epistemology, and ontology have emerged from the studies of public relations and rhetoric (Ihlen, 2008).

Scholars have argued that public relations should be studied like any other social activity (Ihlen & Verhoeven, 2009), and several authors have explicitly linked the rhetorical approach to the instrumental goals of organizations (e.g., Toth, 1992; Trujillo & Toth, 1987). Some authors, however, question this administrative approach and argue that it often underpins the research agenda even when a critical orientation is supposedly espoused. Thus, they contend, rhetorical public relations studies do not constitute an alternative paradigm to the dominant theories in the field (L'Etang, 1997, 2006; Porter, 2010). Others believe that these rhetorical studies have been *too* critical and that this explains why rhetoric is not a larger field of study within public relations (Toth, 1999).

Still, rhetorical public relations studies range from applied work that suggests strategies to help organizations survive crises (e.g., Coombs, 2009) to studies illustrating how public relations rhetoric works for particular ideologies (e.g., Crable & Vibbert, 1995; Holloway, 1995). This makes it difficult to argue that the rhetorical approach is one thing or the other in terms of the administrative versus critical perspectives. It is also recognized that public relations can play both a constructive and a destructive role in society (Heath, 2006).

A recurring issue for critics of rhetoric is its ethics, and whether persuasion can be considered a legitimate activity. This criticism echoes the traditional criticism of rhetoric (e.g., Plato, trans. 1960). Arguments for persuasion include the notion that practitioners are hired *precisely* to engage in persuasion on behalf of their organization or clients and that the field must address the issue of ethics in persuasion rather than denying its role altogether. Open and responsible dialogue is often suggested as the ethical ideal (Edgett, 2002; Kent & Taylor, 2002; Pfau & Wan, 2006; Porter, 2010).

Heath has argued that rhetoric is intrinsically ethical, as "rhetoric fosters truth as best as can be done; it serves to solve problems that confront the public" (Heath, 2007, p. 50) and "empowers participants to engage in dialogue" (Heath, 2001, p. 33). Heath's view is also reflected in the way in which he defines public relations, as "the management function that rhetorically adapts organizations to people's interests and people's interests to organizations by co-creating meaning and co-managing culture to achieve mutually beneficial relationships" (Heath, 2001, p. 36).

Although such normative definitions certainly have a place in a field that wants to be relevant for practice and to provide ethical guidance, much rhetoric and much of what goes on in public relations fails to live up to such standards. The rhetoric of public relations thus risks the conflation of the normative and the descriptive. Rhetoric and public relations may certainly have ideal forms, but unethical public relations thrives, as indicated by the number of front groups and public relations scandals that are covered in the mass media on a regular basis (Ihlen & Verhoeven, 2009). Another view is that neither public relations nor rhetoric is inherently ethical or unethical. Both disciplines, either alone or together, can be used ethically or unethically and for good or bad purposes.

A particular charge leveled against the rhetorical approach of Heath is its move away from perspectivism toward relativism (Cheney & Christensen, 2001). *The good organization, communicating well* is upheld as the ideal. "Well" in this context means not only adhering to norms such as "truthfulness" and "appropriateness for the situation" but also instructing, moving, and charming the audience. The ideal orator of Quintilian is dead, however, and modern rhetoric has an even less secure ontological and epistemological platform than its ancient counterpart (Lunsford & Ede, 1994). For what is really "good," and how is "good" determined? The solution that Heath suggests for this problem is that of relativism, or the idea that the "limit on any point of view is the counter statement that can gain more support" (Heath, 1997, p. 60). Relativism is regarded as a practical solution, as this may at least privilege "people in society to struggle in concert to reduce differences, to compromise and to have opinions challenged. That is the essence of the process of rhetoric" (p. 60). This has led to the criticism that Heath sometimes acknowledges reality to be socially constructed, yet at other times assumes that there is really one universal truth, that some "facts" are better than others. According to L'Etang (1997), the problem is that no hints are given as to how these two perspectives can be distinguished and why.

Heath's approach has also been subject to ontological criticism. Heath states that rhetoric is built on "dialogue to define and advance . . . interests within the limits of others' opinions about these matters" (Heath, 2001, p. 32). The underlying assumption is that "no entity can manipulate others forever, if at all" (Heath, 1993, p. 143). Public relations practitioners must thus advocate not only the needs of the organization but also the needs, concerns, and points of view of the public. Cheney and Christensen (2001) have criticized the ontological assumptions of this argument and the faith in a well-functioning "marketplace of ideas" in which the resource issue plays no role. A better metaphor may be a "supermarket of images in which large establishments offer their customers a limited number of brands promoted by a few social leviathans" (Sproule, 1988, p. 484). Not all arguments are guaranteed to be heard, nor is there a guarantee that the better arguments will prevail over the self-interested argument (Ihlen, 2002). Indeed, commentators on rhetoric and management have asserted that "rhetoric is a strategy of the powerful, a form of control" (Hartelius & Browning, 2008, p. 33).

Rhetorical Typologies of Public Relations Strategies

As already mentioned, the study of crises is by far the largest branch of rhetorical public relations studies (e.g., Millar & Heath, 2003). It has been demonstrated that organizations in crisis typically rely on different archetypical strategies ranging from the aggressive to the accommodative (Coombs, 2007). The rhetorical notion of *apologia*—or speech of self-defense—has been explored at length (e.g., Hearit, 2001), strongly linked to the writings of Perelman and Olbrechts-Tyteca (1969) and the notion of *disassociation*, or the separation of, for instance, the individual from the group.

Several other strategy typologies have been suggested. Cheney, in examining internal communication, argued that organizations "assist" in identification processes with their employees to induce cooperation or reduce the range of decisions to encompass only those alternatives that benefit the organization (Burke, 1950/1969, 1972; Cheney, 1983, 1991). At least three interesting strategies can be identified. The first is the use of common ground, whereby the rhetor puts emphasis on the humble origins that he or she shares with the audience. The second is antithesis, which is a strategy of congregation by segregation. The rhetor holds up an antithesis that suggests that the rhetor and his or her audience has a common enemy. The third is the device of the transcendent "we." This strategy often works on an unconscious level, as when an environmentalist identifies with a well-known activist and wants to partake in the same protest actions as this activist.

Ihlen (2009) suggested four archetypical ways in which corporations attempt to come across as credible environmental actors. Corporations will argue that (1) they make the world better with their product or the positive leadership that they offer; (2) they have cleaned up their own house by actions such as recycling or curbing emissions; (3) that others like them, such as the authorities or NGOs (nongovernmental organizations), approve of their environmental efforts; and (4) that they care about their stakeholders by, for instance, talking about the environmental challenges that they share with them.

It is posited here that the development of several more of these typologies would go some way toward establishing a rhetoric of public relations. Somewhat in line with this, Cheney et al. (2004) argued that rhetoric can be useful in the study of public relations strategies in four instances that relate to how organizations (1) *respond* to existing rhetorical situations, for instance, through crisis communication; (2) attempt to *anticipate* future rhetorical situations, for instance, through issues management processes; (3) attempt to *shape rhetorical situations*, for instance, through strategic definitions; and (4) try to *shape their own identities* (Cheney et al., 2004).

Here it is argued that future research should aim to develop typologies and a full-fledged rhetoric for the organizational activities described. However, avoiding the trap of "rhetoric-as-technique, rhetor-as-magician pole" remains a basic challenge (Conrad & Malphurs, 2008, p. 134). It is necessary to keep in mind the complex, dialectical relationships that exist between action, agency, and structure that help define rhetorical action. This could help avoid the reductionism that Burke, Perelman, and others warned against when they sought to revitalize the rhetorical tradition.

Conclusion

This chapter sets out why and how rhetoric is crucial for public relations, with particular emphasis on the epistemological perspective. In summary, it is argued that the epistemic and the ontological have a dialectic relationship. Rhetoric is seen as enacting and creating the environment, and facts as being conditioned by social agreement. At the same time, however, it is acknowledged that an environment exists and that humans must presuppose the existence of *something* that is true. The main implication is that a pluralism of perspectives should be invited, as truth with a capital "T" is impossible to achieve.

Adopting this perspective propels rhetoric to the forefront. However, some rhetorical scholars have argued that rhetoric should not be conceived of as a general all-encompassing epistemological theory because it has a normative ambition (Kock, 1997). Rhetoric strives to tell us how everything in an utterance should be in the context of the text, that is, the "opportune moment," or *kairós* (Sipiora & Baumlin, 2002). This is a reminder that scholars should also research whether public relations rhetoric has achieved what it set out to do. Still, here it is argued that such research endeavors should also be informed by a critical-analytical agenda. Public relations must be viewed within a wider cultural, economic, and political context (Ihlen & Verhoeven, 2009), and rhetorical theory could help analyze the symbolic strategies that organizations use. Creating new typologies of archetypical rhetorical strategies may be the first step toward a full-fledged rhetoric of public relations. The obvious conclusion here is that public relations needs its big sister: the *grand dame* of communication studies.

References

Andersen, Ø. (1995). *I retorikkens hage* [In the garden of rhetoric]. Oslo, Norway: Universitetsforlaget.

Aristotle. (1991). *On rhetoric: A theory of civic discourse* (G. A. Kennedy, Trans.). New York: Oxford University Press.

Baker, J. S., Conrad, C., Cudahy, C., & Willyard, J. (2009). The devil in disguise: Vioxx, drug saftey, and the FDA. In R. L. Heath, E. L. Toth, & D. Waymer (Eds.), *Rhetorical and critical approaches to public relations II* (pp. 170–194). New York: Routledge.

Benoit, W. L. (1995). *Accounts, excuses, and apologies: A theory of image restoration strategies.* New York: State University of New York Press.

Berger, P., & Luckmann, T. (1966). *The social construction of reality: A treatise in the sociology of knowledge.* London: Penguin Books.

Bernays, E. L. (1952). *Public relations.* Norman: University of Oklahoma Press.

Bitzer, L. F. (1968). The rhetorical situation. *Philosophy and Rhetoric, 1*(1), 1–14.

Booth, W. C. (1967). The revival of rhetoric. In M. Steinmann Jr. (Ed.), *New rhetorics* (pp. 1–15). New York: Scribner.

Bostdorff, D. M. (1992). "The decision is yours" campaign: Planned parenthood's characteristic argument of moral virtue. In E. L. Toth & R. L. Heath (Eds.), *Rhetorical and critical approaches to public relations* (pp. 301–314). Hillsdale, NJ: Lawrence Erlbaum.

Brand, J. D. (2007). Restoring investor confidence via model and antimodel advocacy by Merrill Lynch. In J. L. Courtright & P. M. Smudde (Eds.), *Power and public relations* (pp. 107–123). Cresskill, NJ: Hampton.

Burke, K. (1969). *A rhetoric of motives.* Berkeley: University of California Press. (Original work published 1950)

Burke, K. (1972). *Dramatism and development.* Barre, MA: Clark University Press.

Cheney, G. (1983). The rhetoric of identification and the study of organizational communication. *Quarterly Journal of Speech, 69,* 143–158.

Cheney, G. (1991). *Rhetoric in an organizational society: Managing multiple identities.* Columbia: University of South Carolina Press.

Cheney, G., & Christensen, L. T. (2001). Public relations as contested terrain: A critical response. In R. L. Heath (Ed.), *Handbook of public relations* (pp. 167–182). Thousand Oaks, CA: Sage.

Cheney, G., Christensen, L. T., Conrad, C., & Lair, D. J. (2004). Corporate rhetoric as organizational discourse. In D. Grant, C. Hardy, C. Oswick, & L. L. Putnam (Eds.), *The Sage handbook of organizational discourse* (pp. 79–103). London: Sage.

Cheney, G., & Dionisopoulos, G. N. (1989). Public relations? No, relations with publics: A rhetorical-organizational approach to contemporary corporate communications. In C. H. Botan & V. Hazleton Jr. (Eds.), *Public relations theory* (pp. 135–157). Hillsdale, NJ: Lawrence Erlbaum.

Cherwitz, R. A., & Hikins, J. W. (1999). Rhetorical perspectivism. In J. L. Lucaites, C. M. Condit, & S. Caudill (Eds.), *Contemporary rhetorical theory: A reader* (pp. 176–193). New York: Guilford Press.

Conley, T. M. (1990). *Rhetoric in the European tradition.* Chicago: University of Chicago Press.

Conrad, C., & Malphurs, R. (2008). Are we there yet? Are we there yet? *Management Communication Quarterly, 22*(1), 123–146.

Coombs, W. T. (1999). *Ongoing crisis communication: Planning, managing, and responding.* Thousand Oaks, CA: Sage.

Coombs, W. T. (2007). *Ongoing crisis communication: Planning, managing, and responding* (2nd ed.). Thousand Oaks, CA: Sage.

Coombs, W. T. (2009). Crisis, crisis communication, and rhetoric. In R. L. Heath, E. L. Toth, & D. Waymer (Eds.), *Rhetorical and critical approaches to public relations II* (pp. 237–252). New York: Routledge.

Corbett, E. P. J., & Connors, R. J. (1999). *Classical rhetoric for the modern student* (4th ed.). New York: Oxford University Press.

Courtright, J. L., & Smudde, P. M. (Eds.). (2007). *Power and public relations.* Cresskill, NJ: Hampton.

Crable, R. E. (1990). "Organizational rhetoric" as the fourth great system: Theoretical, critical, and pragmatic implications. *Journal of Applied Communication Research, 18*(2), 115–128.

Crable, R. E., & Vibbert, S. L. (1995). Mobil's epideictic advocacy: "Observations" of Prometheus bound. In W. N. Elwood (Ed.), *Public relations inquiry as rhetorical criticism: Case studies of corporate discourse and social influence* (pp. 27–46). Westport, CT: Praeger.

Crowley, S., & Hawhee, D. (1999). *Ancient rhetorics for contemporary students* (2nd ed.). Needham Heights, MA: Allyn & Bacon.

Edgett, R. (2002). Toward an ethical framework for advocacy in public relations. *Journal of Public Relations Research, 14*(1), 1–26.

Edwards, H. H. (2007). Avon calling—you! The influence of corporate sponsorship of the 3-day Walk for Breast Cancer. In J. L. Courtright & P. M. Smudde (Eds.), *Power and public relations* (pp. 39–58). Cresskill, NJ: Hampton.

Elwood, W. N. (Ed.). (1995). *Public relations inquiry as rhetorical criticism: Case studies of corporate discourse and influence.* Westport, CT: Praeger.

Farrell, T. B. (1999). Knowledge, consensus, and rhetorical theory. In J. L. Lucaites, C. M. Condit, & S. Caudill (Eds.), *Contemporary rhetorical theory: A reader* (pp. 140–152). New York: Guilford Press.

Fogarty, D. S. J. (1959). *Roots for a new rhetoric.* New York: Bureau of Publications, Teachers College, Columbia University.

Gaonkar, D. P. (2001). Contingency and probability. In T. O. Sloane (Ed.), *Encyclopedia of rhetoric* (pp. 151–166). New York: Oxford University Press.

German, K. M. (2007). Hillary Rodham Clinton and the rhetorical decpiction of family in "talking it over." In J. L. Courtright & P. M. Smudde (Eds.), *Power and public relations* (pp. 11–37). Cresskill, NJ: Hampton.

Hartelius, E. J., & Browning, L. D. (2008). The application of rhetorical theory in managerial research: A literature review. *Management Communication Quarterly, 22*(1), 13–39.

Hearit, K. M. (1995). From we didn't do it to it's not our fault: The use of apologia in public relations crisis. In W. N. Elwood (Ed.), *Public relations inquiry as rhetorical criticism* (pp. 117–131). Westport, CT: Praeger.

Hearit, K. M. (2001). Corporate apologia: When an organization speaks in defense of itself. In R. L. Heath

(Ed.), *Handbook of public relations* (pp. 501–511). Thousand Oaks, CA: Sage.

Hearit, K. M. (2006). *Crisis management by apology: Corporate response to allegations of wrongdoing.* Mahwah, NJ: Lawrence Erlbaum.

Heath, R. L. (1980). Corporate advocacy: An application of speech communication perspectives and skills and more. *Communication Education, 29,* 370–377.

Heath, R. L. (1992). The wrangle in the marketplace: A rhetorical perspective of public relations. In E. L. Toth & R. L. Heath (Eds.), *Rhetorical and critical approaches to public relations* (pp. 17–36). Hillsdale, NJ: Lawrence Erlbaum.

Heath, R. L. (1993). Toward a paradigm for the study and practice of public relations: A rhetorical approach to zones of meaning and organizational prerogative. *Public Relations Review, 19*(2), 141–155.

Heath, R. L. (1997). Legitimate "perspectives" in public relations practice: A rhetorical solution. *Australian Journal of Communication, 24*(2), 55–63.

Heath, R. L. (2001). A rhetorical enactment rationale for public relations: The good organization communicating well. In R. L. Heath (Ed.), *Handbook of public relations* (pp. 31–50). Thousand Oaks, CA: Sage.

Heath, R. L. (2006). Onward into more fog: Thoughts on public relations' research directions. *Journal of Public Relations Research, 18*(2), 93–114.

Heath, R. L. (2007). Management through advocacy: Reflection rather than domination. In E. L. Toth (Ed.), *The future of excellence in public relations and communication management: Challenges for the next generation* (pp. 41–65). Mahwah, NJ: Lawrence Erlbaum.

Heath, R. L. (2009). The rhetorical tradition: Wrangle in the marketplace. In R. L. Heath, E. L. Toth, & D. Waymer (Eds.), *Rhetorical and critical approaches to public relations II* (pp. 17–47). New York: Routledge.

Heath, R. L. (in press). External organizational rhetoric: Bridging management and socio-political discourse. *Management Communication Quarterly.*

Heath, R. L., Toth, E. L., & Waymer, D. (Eds.). (2009). *Rhetorical and critical approaches to public relations II.* New York: Routledge.

Heath, R. L., & Waymer, D. (2009). Activist public relations and the paradox of the positive. In R. L. Heath, E. L. Toth, & D. Waymer (Eds.), *Rhetorical and critical approaches to public relations II* (pp. 195–215). New York: Routledge.

Heide, M. (2009). On Berger: A social constructionist perspective on public relations and crisis communication. In Ø. Ihlen, B. van Ruler, & M. Fredriksson (Eds.), *Public relations and social theory: Key figures and concepts* (pp. 43–61). New York: Routledge.

Holloway, R. L. (1995). Philip Morris Magazine: An innovation in grass roots issue management. In W. N. Elwood (Ed.), *Public relations inquiry as rhetorical criticism: Case studies of corporate discourse and social influence* (pp. 135–156). Westport, CT: Praeger.

Hoover, J. D. (Ed.). (1997). *Corporate advocacy: Rhetoric in the information age.* Westport, CT: Greenwood.

Ice, R. (1991). Corporate publics and rhetorical strategies: The case of Union Carbide's Bhopal crisis. *Management Communication Quarterly, 4*(3), 341–362.

Ihlen, Ø. (2002). Rhetoric and resources: Notes for a new approach to public relations and issues management. *Journal of Public Affairs, 2*(4), 259–269.

Ihlen, Ø. (2004). Norwegian hydroelectric power: Testing a heuristic for analyzing symbolic strategies and resources. *Public Relations Review, 30*(2), 217–223.

Ihlen, Ø. (2008). Rhetorical theory of public relations. In W. Donsbach (Ed.), *The Blackwell international encyclopedia of communication* (pp. 4395–4397). Oxford, UK: Blackwell.

Ihlen, Ø. (2009). Good environmental citizens? The green rhetoric of corporate social responsibility. In R. L. Heath, E. L. Toth, & D. Waymer (Eds.), *Rhetorical and critical approaches to public relations II* (pp. 360–374). New York: Routledge.

Ihlen, Ø. (in press). Corporate social responsibility and the rhetorical situation. In J. Raupp, S. Jarolimek, & F. Schultz (Eds.), *Handbuch Corporate Social Responsibility: Kommunikationswissenschaftliche Grundlagen und methodische Zugaenge.* Wiesbaden, Germany: VS Verlag.

Ihlen, Ø., & Verhoeven, P. (2009). Conclusions on the domain, context, concepts, issues and empirical avenues of public relations. In Ø. Ihlen, B. van Ruler, & M. Fredriksson (Eds.), *Public relations and social theory: Key figures and concepts* (pp. 332–349). New York: Routledge.

Jarratt, S. C. (1991). *Rereading the Sophists: Classical rhetoric refigured.* Carbondale: Southern Illinois University Press.

Jerome, A. M. (2008). Toward prescription: Testing the rhetoric of atonement's applicability in the athletic arena. *Public Relations Review, 34*(2), 124–134.

Kennedy, G. A. (1991). *Introduction. In Aristotle, On rhetoric: A theory of civic discourse* (G. A. Kennedy, Trans., pp. 3–22). New York: Oxford University Press.

Kent, M. L., & Taylor, M. (2002). Toward a dialogic theory of public relations. *Public Relations Review, 28,* 21–37.

Knapp, M. L. (1970). Business rhetoric: Opportunity for research in speech. *Southern Speech Communication Journal, 35,* 244–255.

Kock, C. (1997). Retorikkens identitet som videnskab og uddannelse [The identity of rhetoric as a science and education]. *Rhetorica Scandinavica, 1*(1), 10–19.

L'Etang, J. (1996). Public relations and rhetoric. In J. L'Etang & M. Pieczka (Eds.), *Critical perspectives in public relations* (pp. 106–123). London: International Thomson Business Press.

L'Etang, J. (1997). Public relations and the rhetorical dilemma: Legitimate "perspectives," persuasion, or pandering? *Australian Journal of Communication, 24*(2), 33–53.

L'Etang, J. (2006). Public relations and rhetoric. In J. L'Etang & M. Pieczka (Eds.), *Public relations: Critical debates and contemporary practice* (pp. 359–371). Mahwah, NJ: Lawrence Erlbaum.

Lucaites, J. L., Condit, C. M., & Caudill, S. (1999). What can a "rhetoric" be? In J. L. Lucaites, C. M. Condit, & S. Caudill (Eds.), *Contemporary rhetorical theory: A reader* (pp. 19–24). New York: Guilford Press.

Lunsford, A. A., & Ede, L. S. (1994). On distinctions between classical and modern rhetoric. In T. Enos & S. C. Brown (Eds.), *Professing the new rhetorics: A sourcebook* (pp. 397–411). Upper Saddle River, NJ: Prentice Hall.

Marsh, C. (2003). Antecedents of two-way symmetry in classical Greek rhetoric: The rhetoric of Isocrates. *Public Relations Review, 29*(3), 351–367.

Marsh, C. (2006). The syllogism of apologia: Rhetorical stasis theory and crisis communication. *Public Relations Review, 32*(1), 41–46.

Mayhew, L. H. (1997). *The new public: Professional communication and the means of social influence.* Cambridge, UK: Cambridge University Press.

Meisenbach, R. J., & McMillian, J. J. (2006). Blurring the boundaries: Historical developments and future directions in organizational rhetoric. *Communication Yearbook, 30*(1), 86–123.

Mickey, T. J. (1995). *Sociodrama: An interpretive theory for the practice of public relations.* Lanham, MD: University Press of America.

Millar, D. P., & Heath, R. L. (Eds.). (2003). *Responding to crisis: A rhetorical approach to crisis communication.* Mahwah, NJ: Lawrence Erlbaum.

Moran, M. G., & Ballif, M. (Eds.). (2000). *Twentieth-century rhetorics and rhetoricians: Critical studies and sources.* Westport, CT: Greenwood.

Ohmann, R. (1994). In lieu of a new rhetoric. In T. Enos & S. C. Brown (Eds.), *Professing the new rhetorics: A sourcebook* (pp. 298–306). Upper Saddle River, NJ: Prentice Hall.

Perelman, C., & Olbrechts-Tyteca, L. (1969). *The new rhetoric: A treatise on argumentation* (J. Wilkinson & P. Weaver, Trans.). London: University of Notre Dame.

Pfau, M., & Wan, H.-H. (2006). Persuasion: An intrinsic function of public relations. In C. H. Botan & V. Hazleton Jr. (Eds.), *Public relations theory II* (pp. 101–136). Mahwah, NJ: Lawrence Erlbaum.

Plato. (1960). *Gorgias* (W. Hamilton, Trans.). London: Penguin Books.

Porter, L. (2010). Communicating for the good of the state: A post-symmetrical polemic on persuasion in ethical public relations. *Public Relations Review, 36*(2), 127–133.

Poulakos, J. (1999). Toward a sophistic definition of rhetoric. In J. L. Lucaites, C. M. Condit, & S. Caudill (Eds.), *Contemporary rhetorical theory: A reader* (pp. 25–34). New York: Guilford Press.

Quintilian. (1996). *Institutio oratoria: Books I–XII* (H. E. Butler, Trans.). Cambridge, MA: Harvard University Press. (Original work published 1920)

Russell-Loretz, T. A. (2007). Cross-media comparisons of employee recruitment messages between 1990 and 2000. In J. L. Courtright & P. M. Smudde (Eds.), *Power and public relations* (pp. 179–204). Cresskill, NJ: Hampton.

Scott, R. L. (1993). Rhetoric is epistemic: What difference does that make? In T. Enos & S. C. Brown (Eds.), *Defining the new rhetorics* (pp. 120–136). London: Sage.

Scott, R. L. (1999). On viewing rhetoric as epistemic. In J. L. Lucaites, C. M. Condit, & S. Caudill (Eds.), *Contemporary rhetorical theory: A reader* (pp. 131–139). New York: Guilford Press.

Seeger, M. W., Sellnow, T. L., & Ulmer, R. (1998). Communication, organization, and crisis. *Communication Yearbook, 21,* 231–275.

Sillince, J. A. A., & Suddaby, R. (2008). Organizational rhetoric: Bridging management and communication scholarship. *Management Communication Quarterly, 22*(1), 5–12.

Sipiora, P., & Baumlin, J. S. (Eds.). (2002). *Rhetoric and kairos: Essays in history, theory, and praxis.* Albany: State University of New York Press.

Skerlep, A. (2001). Re-evaluating the role of rhetoric in public relations theory and in strategies of corporate discourse. *Journal of Communication Management, 6*(2), 176–187.

Sproule, J. M. (1988). The new managerial rhetoric and the old criticism. *Quarterly Journal of Speech, 74,* 468–486.

Tompkins, P. K. (1987). Translating organizational theory: Symbolism over substance. In F. M. Jablin, L. L. Putnam, K. H. Roberts, & L. W. Porter (Eds.), *Handbook of organizational communication: An interdisciplinary perspective* (pp. 70–96). Newbury Park, CA: Sage.

Toth, E. L. (1992). The case for pluralistic studies of public relations: Rhetorical, critical, and systems perspectives. In E. L. Toth & R. L. Heath (Eds.), *Rhetorical and critical approaches to public relations* (pp. 3–16). Hillsdale, NJ: Lawrence Erlbaum.

Toth, E. L. (1999). Public relations and rhetoric: History, concepts, future. In D. Moss, D. Verčič, & G. Warnaby (Eds.), *Perspectives on public relations research* (pp. 121–144). London: Routledge.

Toth, E. L. (2009). The case for pluralistic studies of public relations: Rhetorical, critical and excellence perspectives. In R. L. Heath, E. L. Toth, & D. Waymer (Eds.), *Rhetorical and critical approaches to public relations II* (pp. 48–60). New York: Routledge.

Toth, E. L., & Heath, R. L. (Eds.). (1992). *Rhetorical and critical approaches to public relations.* Hillsdale, NJ: Lawrence Erlbaum.

Tranøy, K. E. (1986). *Vitenskapen: Samfunnsmakt og livsform* [Science: Society power and life form]. Oslo, Norway: Universitetsforlaget.

Trujillo, N., & Toth, E. L. (1987). Organizational perspectives for public relations research and practice. *Management Communication Quarterly, 1*(2), 199–231.

Zhang, J. (2007). Beyond anti-terrorism: Metaphors as message strategy of post-September-11 U.S. public diplomacy. *Public Relations Review, 33*(1), 31–39.

CHAPTER 5

Implications of Complexity Theory for Public Relations

Beyond Crisis

Dawn R. Gilpin and Priscilla Murphy

As the public relations field has matured, scholars have called for more careful reflection on the linkages between public relations research and larger bodies of theory to expand the scope of the discipline and situate it more effectively within an interdisciplinary, pluralistic framework (Bentele, 2007; Ihlen & van Ruler, 2007). We address that call here by extending prior applications of complexity theory in public relations beyond a nearly exclusive focus on crisis communication (Gilpin & Murphy, 2005, 2008, 2010; Goulielmos, 2005; Holtzhausen, 2004; Murphy, 2000, 2010; Paraskevas, 2006; Ulmer, Sellnow, & Seeger, 2007). Instead, in this chapter we consider the possible contribution of complexity-based thinking to public relations theory, as well as its implications for professional practice in areas such as media relations, stakeholder identification, issues management, and organizational reputation.

Complexity theories originated in the hard sciences, but because of their usefulness in modeling human social systems, social scientists have adopted the theories in disciplines as diverse as psychology and cognition (Maturana & Varela, 1980), sociology (Byrne, 1998; Chesters & Welsh, 2006), and public policy and political institutions (Byrne, 2001; Meek, De Ladurantey, & Newell, 2007). Complexity theories have proved particularly rewarding in the organizational realm (see Ashmos, Duchon, & McDaniel, 2000; Chiles, Meyer, & Hench, 2004; Dooley & Van de Ven, 1999; Mitleton-Kelly, 2003; van Uden, 2005), where scholars have focused primarily on areas of change and innovation, as well as on knowledge and learning (Chiles et al., 2004; Salem, 2002; Snowden, 2003).

In public relations as well, theories of complexity offer a useful framework for aspects of theory and practice that concern themselves with change and uncertainty. A complexity approach to public relations often requires rethinking traditional assumptions and prevailing practices, including the very ability of organizations to strategically analyze, plan, and shape public opinion. Ultimately, a complexity-based worldview will very likely entail the development of new methods, measures, and means of implementation.

Defining Complex Systems

According to Norwegian physicist Ingve Simonsen, attempting to define complexity is similar to a biologist's attempt to define life: "He will give you a list of characteristics. He probably won't give you a strict definition" (Cho, 2009, p. 406). Nonetheless, it is possible to distill theories about complexity into a few basic principles that most scholars would agree characterize complex systems. Complex systems are made up of *multiple interacting agents* (e.g., individuals, organizations, media sources) whose *local, recurrent, nonlinear, adaptable* relations bring about *fundamental change* to the system itself. Through these interactions, agents *self-organize* into identifiable patterns, although these patterns may be unpredictable. As a result, complex systems are *dynamic* and *unstable*, and all change is based on the system's own *history*; system features and evolution are therefore highly *contextual*. Complex systems also have *ill-defined and highly permeable boundaries*, so that there is no stable or clearly distinguishable "outside environment." Finally, complex systems are *irreducible:* Any attempt to break them into component parts causes unrecoverable loss of meaning. For these reasons, a complex system is said to be greater than the sum of its parts (Gilpin & Murphy, 2008).

Examples of complex systems abound in the natural and social world; they range from the patterns evolved by clouds, to interactions within anthills, to the irreversible chemical change of eggs into soufflés. In terms of human social systems, organizations represent the most accessible example. They are composed of numerous individuals whose ongoing interactions both construct and transform the nature of the organization. Actors who make up the organization also belong to other social groups that may overlap with the organization, or even be in direct conflict with the organization's stated direction or cultural influences. As the organization grows and changes, it may absorb more people, acquire businesses, move into new areas of business or geographic markets, or become involved in new issue domains, all of which alter its boundaries. Similar complex behaviors characterize a variety of other groups with which public relations engages: activist organizations, news media, or competitors in an evolving marketplace. Even from these brief examples, it is easy to see how a complex system could be defined social as one in which "many individual actors interact locally in an effort to adapt to their immediate situation. These local adaptations . . . accumulate to form large-scale patterns that affect the greater society, often in ways that could not have been anticipated" (Murphy, 2000, p. 450).

Complexity and Stakeholders

Given the emphasis on the relationship-building function of public relations in recent years (e.g., Broom, Casey, & Ritchey, 1997; Ledingham & Bruning, 2000), practitioners are increasingly called on to establish and maintain trust ties between organizations and a shifting multitude of stakeholders. At the same time, changes in the media landscape have altered the degree of control an organization can legitimately seek to exercise over its relationships, many of which are negotiated in publicly visible spaces of digital media. The messages and interactions that help build trusting relationships are rarely centralized, but "now spread across multiple partners, communities and individuals around the globe" (Arthur Page Society, 2007). Yet the loss of context that can occur in complex environments, when stakeholders may encounter messages outside the temporal or spatial circumstances in which they were formulated, can undermine the trust necessary to establish these relationships (Giddens, 1991).

The capacity of media to influence perceptions of time and place has long been a topic of interest to scholars. Years before the popular advent of the Internet and mobile technology, Meyrowitz (1989) argued that electronic media expand both our range of social experience and our perception of locality, shaping understanding of relative similarities and differences in ways quite distinct from abstract knowledge such as the kind learned in traditional classrooms. Mobile technologies have altered our understanding of time and space, allowing for instant textual, audio, and visual communication without much concern for geography. An organization can disseminate information to stakeholders no matter where they are located, in virtually any format and at virtually any time. At the same time, the information may be consumed not only instantly but also asynchronously in many ways: Both audiovisual and text-based materials are increasingly recorded and stored in a variety of digital formats, remaining accessible even for years after their initial issue, for consumption via television, online, or with a mobile device. Communication time becomes a paradox, both immediate and long-lasting, local and long-distance, building nonlinear temporal and spatial relations.

The current media landscape thus represents a complex system in which organizations and stakeholders seek to communicate and establish trust. The nonlinearity and uncertainty inherent in such a system, however, can confound efforts to build and maintain stable relationships. Although complex systems evolve over time through their own contextual history, the historical memory of a complex system resides within individual elements, such as accumulated personal experiences and opinions. An organization's relationships with its networks of stakeholders develop through accrued actions and communications that set the trajectory for future behavior. When stakeholder experiences with the organization differ widely due to the nonlinearity of the complex mediascape, it becomes difficult to foster a sense of shared culture and connection. Public relations practitioners may need to institute new ongoing organizational rituals in which internal and external stakeholders can participate rather than relying on linear historical communications and actions to build trust relationships.

Complexity and Strategic Planning\

Historical effects and nonlinear space-time relations in complex systems have practical implications for planning and prediction, activities that form the core of strategic public relations. The traditional process of analysis requires the analyst to break an observed phenomenon into fundamental parts to identify their traits and draw conclusions about the universal axioms governing their relationships (Gunter, 2008). The analytical method forms the basis for planning and strategy.

However, complex phenomena make it impossible to apply such linear methods. Instead, the exponential increase in information transmitted within and between individuals, groups, organizations, and institutions results in highly complex communication flows and cooperative ties (Nowotny, 2005). These dense, multidirectional, dynamic connections make causality itself difficult to establish. Complexity-based thinking approaches events quite differently: They are seen as highly *contextual* rather than universal, so there is no search for generalizable axioms; *holistic*, such that breaking them apart for analysis removes and distorts meaning; and *indeterminate*, or without a linear causal direction (Stacey, Griffin, & Shaw, 2000). As a result, the complexity approach to understanding phenomena "gives up predictability-in-principle" (Gunter, 2008, p. 7) and allows only a highly constrained degree of foresight and control (Gilpin & Murphy, 2010).

The instability of complex systems also poses increasingly serious problems for strategists who are interested in prediction. Boisot (2000) observed that "causal empiricism points to a world that is increasingly interconnected and in which the pace of technological change has been accelerating" (p. 114); this density and change indicate increasing complexity, and thus, increasing nonlinearity of cause and effect. Such a degree of speed and interconnectedness corresponds to classic physical models of turbulence, "and turbulence is a great enigma, even to scientists. It is something unknowable and unpredictable and uncontrollable" (Bryant, 2007, p. 128). Turbulence reflects a degree of instability that defies classic models of prediction, the same models on which social sciences and applied practices such as public relations rely.

Responding to a tightly coupled, nonlinear, and unstable communication environment, complexity offers a new paradigm for planning and prediction in public relations. The very nature of complexity theories, with their emphasis on context-dependent change through a large number of intervening variables, rules out the kind of predictable, generalizable results frequently considered a hallmark of valid research (Chaffee, 1996). External validity and reliability become problematic issues in complexity research, and processes of hypothesis testing and concept explication are also complicated. Some theorists argue that such "messiness" is desirable, a more accurate approach to studying a reality that is mutable and subject to sudden, unpredictable change (Latour, 2005; Law, 2004). For public relations practitioners, such a turbulent communication environment demands new modes of planning that allow for broader ranges of outcomes, adapt to both gradual and sudden change, and relinquish the idea of control.

The Complex Media Environment

Today's media can be seen as comprising a single complex system that encompasses a vast range of digital and nondigital, mass and personal communication. This system offers new opportunities for public relations practitioners to develop integrated strategies for monitoring and managing a broad communication context. However, it also means that information, rumor, and emotional responses can spread across media more quickly than ever before. Complexity theory can offer an approach to understanding this media environment for practitioners and scholars in search of new tools to help them navigate the turbulent mix of messages and stakeholders.

In fact, it is increasingly difficult to draw boundaries between digital media and traditional channels, treating them as separate systems, since digital media "integrate all known media into one converged multimedia system [with] an unlimited number of features" (Qvortrup, 2006, p. 350). Even traditional media, from print to broadcast, are migrating to digital formats. Multiple strands of messages and dialogue intertwine, disconnect, and recombine to form patterns across platforms and social contexts. These convergent environments can also be seen as complex communication systems constituting numerous actors, with the same traits of uncertainty, instability, unclear boundaries, and nonlinear consequences of change as described previously.

On the levels of both theory and practice, public relations needs to incorporate these new patterns of communication and interaction. Complexity can offer a useful framework for doing so, an alternative to views of digital media as ungated, bottom-up channels that counter the hierarchical gatekeeping modes of traditional media (Deibert, 1997). Instead, Qvortrup (2006) proposed approaching the Internet as a system for complexity management that makes it possible to navigate a densely interconnected global world of communication. This approach also shifts attention from the media themselves to underlying complex social processes from which new media forms emerge in response to new difficulties in complexity management, "creating an endless spiral of social-media complexity development dynamics" (p. 351). While nondeterministic views of media production and consumption are not new, complexity theories offer renewed potential for research on patterns of self-organizing communications rooted in social phenomena.

The public relations implications of the different approaches are significant: If digital media are viewed as distinct from "mainstream" media or social interaction, then scholars and practitioners risk missing important developments that may depend on complex interdependencies between multiple domains (Gilpin, 2010). These interactions may also be temporally nonlinear, requiring new monitoring techniques to identify these developments as they emerge. Some formulations of complexity invoked by social theorists refer to *convergent systems*, the result of self-organization by elements of complex systems into recognizable, orderly patterns (see Bryant, 2007). To remain effective in today's turbulent media landscape, public relations practitioners and scholars need to develop the ability to recognize these patterns across contexts, without drawing artificial boundaries between "online" and "offline" media and stakeholders.

Failure to understand how today's convergent media have compressed the amount of time required for dire consequences to take shape can prove costly. Social media and social networking sites have already proven to be vehicles for the rapid dissemination of information and rumor, often with unintended or unforeseen consequences. In such a system, seemingly minor problems can quickly spiral from "small, volitional beginnings" into major crisis situations, as "small events are carried forward, cumulate with other events, and . . . systematically construct an environment that is a rare combination of unexpected simultaneous failures" (Weick, 2001, p. 228).

For example, Johnson & Johnson were caught by surprise when scores of angry parents took offense at a Motrin ad campaign over a weekend in 2008, spreading their discontent and urging boycotts across blog communities and throughout Twitter (Evans, 2008). The protests quickly spread to national wire services and mainstream media (see Belkin, 2008; Johnson, 2008). However, Motrin executives were not monitoring online conversations over the weekend. By failing to be aware of the speed and reach of online social networks and their relationship to mainstream media, the company allowed the issue to reach crisis proportions within a significant stakeholder population and were forced to respond with expensive corrective measures to appease the affected publics (Esterline, 2009). A complexity-based approach that involved monitoring a full range of media to identify emergent patterns, and develop adaptive communication strategies before these patterns coalesced into crisis formations, might have helped the organization maintain and even strengthen its relationships with key stakeholders.

Implications for Public Relations Research and Practice

If the media can be seen as a convergent complex system, most of which is now available online, public relations scholars and practitioners are faced with both a simpler and more complex operating environment. Data for research are easily accessed through various online search engines, which call up results from traditional mass media as well as highly local or specialized publications and channels, social media, and other sites. Practitioners can use any of the myriad analytical tools available, many free of charge, to detect emerging issues and locate discussions of interest to their organization. It is easier than ever to segment stakeholders based on latent ties of shared interests and to automate the monitoring of public discussion in a vast range of media.

At the same time, the sheer quantity of channels and information makes it difficult to detect meaningful patterns, address key stakeholder groups, or develop effective communication strategies. Qvortrup (2006) argued that successful communication is a low-probability event in a highly complex environment, given the dense thicket of connections and information paths. Public relations practitioners are faced with many choices for communicating with stakeholders, but with a high degree of uncertainty about the relative effectiveness of the various options. Complexity theory suggests that the field needs to dedicate more attention to nonlinear communication strategies and outcomes in planning, execution, and evaluation. Furthermore, this complex environment raises the question of shifting boundaries, a topic of particular relevance in a public relations context.

Public relations has been described in the literature as a boundary-spanning role (Lauzen & Dozier, 1994; White & Dozier, 1992). Boundaries are "sites of ongoing negotiation" (Kreiner, Hollensbe, & Sheep, 2009, p. 706) between domains. Many nonphysical boundaries, such as identity groupings or role distinctions, are socially constructed, and once accepted they can become institutionalized and hegemonic (Zerubavel, 1993). Boundary studies in communication and related fields have proliferated in recent years, addressing topics ranging from media convergence (Deuze, 2007) to professional and personal roles (e.g., Ashforth, Kreiner, & Fugate, 2000; Kreiner et al., 2009), to organizational and personal identity (Giddens, 1991; Kreiner, Hollensbe, & Sheep, 2006). The boundary-spanning function of public relations therefore necessitates special attention to where boundaries are drawn and the ways in which they are negotiated by various actors.

The fluidity of boundaries characteristic of complex systems has implications for public relations practitioners as they seek to identify stakeholder groups and track issue domains and reputation. As networked organizations proliferate, it becomes increasingly difficult to distinguish the boundaries between "internal" and "external" communication. Organizations also "define the boundaries of their identity according to the parties involved in social relations" (Illia & Lurati, 2006, p. 298). Public relations practitioners may find themselves increasingly having to not only span boundaries but also constantly renegotiate the existence of various types of divisions inside and outside the organizations they represent.

The same complex patterns of multidirectional relations and communication described by Nowotny (2005) suggest new ways of conceiving of stakeholder groups. The need for more flexible tools for classifying complex stakeholder aggregations and relationships is already being felt, as evidenced by the academic literature. Recent scholarship has explored the nuances of stakeholder theories with regard to organizational identity (Illia & Lurati, 2006; Sha, 2009), issue arenas (Luoma-aho & Vos, 2009), and reputation (King & Whetten, 2008). Complexity theories situate these perspectives within a larger framework of dense interconnectedness, fluid boundaries, and uncertainty, which can highlight new avenues for research.

For example, a close relationship exists between role definitions and identity perceptions. Role definitions presuppose a shared sense of group identity, and in-group cultural perceptions are often overlooked by public relations practitioners in segmenting stakeholder groups (Sha, 2006). Some self-identities and roles are more clearly defined by group members than others. Ashforth et al. (2000) explained that sharper role boundary definitions may not only ease confusion related to blurring but also make transitioning between roles more drastic. Blurred boundaries are more difficult to maintain, but they facilitate transitions.

Public relations behaviors can influence the intensity of stakeholder identification with organizations (Sha, 2009), and news releases must express and negotiate multiple organizational identities as these change over time (Gilpin, 2008). Identities also form the basis for stakeholders' assessment of an organization's characteristics and actions and decisions made from within the organization (King & Whetten, 2008). From a public relations perspective, it can therefore be important to understand how both internal and external stakeholders perceive their group membership roles, and to what extent they identify with them, to develop and adapt effective strategies. At the same time, relationships with shifting categories of stakeholders require more complex communication and monitoring strategies. These strategies are particularly relevant in certain domains of public relations practice such as crises, issue, and reputation management.

Complexity and Crisis Emergence and Management

The lack of predictability and dense interconnectedness of complex systems make crises the natural first application of interest to public relations scholars and practitioners interested in exploring complexity. The physicist Stephen Eubank noted that "there are so many ways for a complex system to fail that it's impossible to prepare for them all" (cited in Cho, 2009, p. 407). It therefore comes as no surprise that crisis management has been the first frontier for complexity-based approaches in the communication literature (see, e.g., Bolton & Stolcis, 2008; Gilpin & Murphy, 2005, 2008; Murphy, 1996, 2000; Paraskevas, 2006; Ulmer, Sellnow, & Seeger, 2007).

These approaches depart considerably from traditional mainstream crisis management literature. Complexity-based approaches view crises not as external events that disrupt the organization but as emergent phenomena resulting primarily from causes endemic to the organization and its relationships with other actors. Most crises are deeply embedded in at least three different types of context. First, there is the context provided by history, in which expectations based on what has happened in the past channel the direction and interpretation of a current crisis. Second is the context provided by organizational culture, which selectively shapes crisis responses, even when it is clear to outsiders that these responses are suboptimal. The third type of crisis context is the media environment, in which current news about similar phenomena or industries creates a path along which the crises flow more easily into one interpretation than another. These contexts are dynamic, interdependent, and mutually influential. Given these interlocking contexts and the emergent nature of crisis, complexity approaches view transformation and renewal as the most desirable outcomes. This view differs sharply from classic approaches that see crises as punctuation marks in an otherwise stable organizational environment and seek normalization as the ideal objective.

The ability of contexts to compound a crisis once more raises questions about the effectiveness of planning, a cornerstone of mainstream crisis literature. A complexity view suggests that, rather than impose tight crisis planning parameters, with most crisis situations it may be more effective to understand the contexts in which they are embedded and then work with the multiple possibilities presented by those contexts (Gilpin & Murphy, 2008, 2010). Such a view emphasizes the role of contingency, uncertainty, and accident; the unexpected confluence of unrelated events; and the destabilizing influence of rapidly changing circumstances. This approach views crises as complex systems: environments composed of multiple actors, whose interactions are local and who may not be pursuing an overarching strategy but are merely attempting to hold their own or improve their immediate lot. In the networked world of complex systems, these manifold local interactions add up to larger patterns of diffusion and meaning, often in ways that the individuals involved could not have anticipated. Certain features of complexity theory—dependence on history, instability, nonlinearity, and self-organization—constrain the ability of organizations to exercise control over these patterns.

Traditionally, crisis experts have applied scientific management techniques for crisis anticipation and response, using advance preparation to gather and analyze information; disseminating information and monitoring audience reactions during the crisis; and revising formal crisis plans afterward (Fishman, 1999; O'Rourke, 1996; Smallman & Weir, 1999). These techniques attempt to mitigate the confusion and uncertainty of crisis by simplifying the decision environment and standardizing decision making. For similar reasons, the mainstream crisis literature frequently relies on cyclical models to identify discrete stages of crises—various permutations of before, during, and after the crisis event. Complexity theory acknowledges the nonlinearity and holistic nature of crises, which often have no clear start or end points, emerging instead from larger contextual patterns and relationships. Rather than seeking to pin down quantifiable aspects of crises, complexity theory approaches emphasize ongoing learning and sense making, and high tolerance for ambiguity (Gilpin & Murphy, 2010).

Authors are turning in increasing numbers to models of crisis description and management that favor complex combinations of errors and unintended consequences both inside and outside organizations involved in crises. Complexity offers a framework for understanding not only those crises precipitated by a single organization but also more diffuse crisis situations that emerge as a result of dense interconnectedness, ranging from food safety to beleaguered world financial markets, from terrorism to natural disasters (Gilpin & Murphy, 2010).

Issues and Issues Management

Like crises, issues are often characterized as having a linear life cycle. Issues, however, are nonlinear emergent phenomena characterized by multidirectional causality and nonsequential, often competing positions (Jaques, 2007). Issues management is one of those public relations functions that most expresses the boundary-spanning nature of the profession (Lauzen & Dozier, 1994), which makes it another natural terrain for a theoretical framework that emphasizes unstable, ill-defined boundaries. As scholars increasingly adopt a cocreational view of issues and publics, where fluid groupings of people and organizations constitute and reconstitute issue domains and positions within those domains, an understanding of issue emergence is central to public relations and other applied communication fields (Botan & Taylor, 2004).

Issue domains share numerous characteristics with complex systems, including a large number of elements that interact dynamically, and can thus produce nonlinear effects throughout the larger system: incompressibility, such that reducing the system in any way causes a fundamental loss of substance; self-organization, or the emergence of orderly patterns; history dependency; and the aforementioned shifting and uncertain boundaries. Complex systems are history dependent, meaning that at any given moment the system and its various subsystems are the product of their own unique past, and elements of that past influence the direction of future change (Gilpin & Murphy, 2008; McKelvey, 2003; Richardson & Cilliers, 2001). Relationships between organizations and stakeholders, and among the various actors who constitute and construct the issue domain, also develop dynamically over time. A complexity perspective on issues and issue management allows for a macroscale view of the issue domain as a holistic entity, focusing on the patterns of relationships within the domain rather than operating from the narrow perspective of a single organization.

With its emphasis on permeable boundaries and nonlinear change that can result from seemingly distant yet interconnected elements of a system, complexity theory urges a more inclusive view of issue domains than has been applied in the past. The traditional approach to issues focuses primarily on institutional actors such as organizations and policy-making bodies, the relationships among them, and how they negotiate conflict with other social actors (Coombs, 1992; Crable & Vibbert, 1985; Hallacher, 2005). By observing only institutional actors and those who interact with them regarding the issue, analysts neglect other segments of the population at large who may represent various pockets of opinions on the issue and influence its trends more indirectly. Approaching the issue domain as a complex system offers a broader landscape that includes individuals and groups who communicate about an issue through various types of media, thereby providing a more variegated picture of the issue network and its actors. This macroscale view can make it possible to identify patterns of aggregation that would otherwise go unnoticed and suggest new communication strategies for organizations involved in the issue.

Another advantage of the complexity approach to issue networks for communication research and practice is that it shifts the emphasis away from the system agents, or actors, to the relationships among them. This relational emphasis favors those who take an interest in the content of ties in addition to their structural implications. Despite some efforts and urging, little empirical work has been conducted to study the circulation of messages as well as social ties in issue domains (Curtin & Gaither, 2005; Elmer, 2006; Hellsten, 2003; Rogers, 2002). Complexity theories offer a conceptual structure in which to design and interpret studies of stakeholder segmentation around issues and issue positions, issue emergence and evolution, and message differentiation (Gilpin, 2009).

Reputation

In addition to reshaping perspectives on crisis and issues management, complexity theory can transform both the concept and the practice of the field known as "reputation management." Gotsi and Wilson (2001) referred to reputation as a stakeholder's overall evaluation over time, viewing it not as "a static element that can only be influenced and hence managed through impressive logos and well planned formal communication activities," but rather as a dynamic construct shaped by "all the ways in which a company projects its images: its behavior, communication and symbolism" (p. 29). Similarly, Deephouse (2000) emphasized reputation's cumulative nature as "a collective concept connecting the firm, media workers, stakeholders, sources of news about firms, and the readers of news" that "develops over time through a complex social process" (p. 1098). Both definitions highlight the instability of reputation as a social construct that is constantly negotiated by organizations and their stakeholders, remaining vulnerable to environmental factors that often defy organizational control.

This complexity-based approach to reputation conflicts with a great deal of what current practitioners say they do. Campbell, Herman, and Noble (2006) pointed out that, responding to management desires to control corporate environment, practitioners suggest that they can mold a client's reputation through strategic communication campaigns that generally involve the media (see Budd, 1993; Fombrun, 1996; Fombrun & Van Riel, 2004). However, the complexity-based conception of reputation as a precarious social construct increasingly conforms to the views expressed by public relations scholars who use other types of theories, including Berger (1999), Botan and Soto (1998), Campbell et al. (2006), Coombs and Holladay (2001), Hutton, Goodman, Alexander, and Genest (2001), Kiousis, Popescu, and Mitrook (2007), and Williams and Moffitt (1997). These and others have argued that, while public relations materials do influence news coverage to some extent, reputation generally has a life of its own and eludes organizations' attempts to herd it in directions of their own choosing. In the blunt language of Campbell et al. (2006), "'Reputation' is uncontrollable" (p. 193).

The same qualities that render reputation so hard to manage—its instability, multifariousness, and diffused locus of control—suggest that reputation can be conceptualized as a complex system. Like complex systems, reputations are cumulative and time based: They evolve and have a history. They often resist regulation by the professionals whose job it is to tend and shape them through media subsidies. Instead, reputations often take an unanticipated course as they accrete through the voices and views of multiple stakeholders—customers, media, employees, other companies—in a process involving as much chance as linear development according to plan. Like a complex system, over time reputations tend to acquire inconsistencies, inaccuracies, unintended associations, and other forms of cognitive noise. That untidy process of evolution can terminate in an abrupt reversal of fortune for a reputation, a change of direction that even the most skilled communication practitioners could not necessarily anticipate. Bromley (1993) captured the complex character of reputation by describing it as an unstable, though tightly coupled, web of relationships that are not amenable to public relations mitigation, "a widely spreading pattern of consequences and reactions—consequences that interact and produce further consequences, often of an unpredictable sort" (p. 7). Like a complex system, reputation responds to its own accumulated dissonances, acquiring associations over time that could just as easily transform it—for better or for worse—as guide it back into accustomed or intentional paths. We have applied complexity theory in a number of ways to explain the vagaries of individual and organizational reputation. For example, we have looked at the reversal of NASA's (National Aeronautics and Space Administration) reputation after the 1986 Challenger disaster (Gilpin & Murphy, 2008); the patterns of media coverage that preceded Martha Stewart's conviction for insider trading (Murphy, in press); and the mutual influence of Wal-Mart's press releases and media coverage of the company (Gilpin, 2007). However, much work remains to be done in exploring the complex interactions between multiple stakeholders' needs, current events (whether planned or unplanned), and even factors such as cultural values, as all these factors share the same arena in public attention, in which reputation is constructed and transformed.

Conclusion

Theorists in both natural and social sciences have suggested that complexity is one key to bridging the divide between their disciplines (Urry, 2003) and that we need "a deeper theoretical understanding of complexity, not as a mathematical, but as a social phenomenon" (Nowotny, 2005, p. 29). This chapter represents a step in that direction as we have sought to illustrate the implications of complexity theories for public relations research, theory, and practice. Those implications will be increasingly important as our communication environment continues to become more intricately and tightly linked, yet also more global. This paradox certainly affects those who study or practice public relations today. Complexity offers a framework for advances in conceptualizing stakeholders, studying the emergence of issues and crises, and tracking reputation across media and across national borders. This new perspective on research also suggests the need to develop new public relations practices focused on adapting to uncertainty. Crisis management has been the starting point for exploring complexity views of public relations, but the implications of these theories extend into every avenue of communication research and applied practice.

References

Arthur Page Society. (2007). *The authentic enterprise: Relationships, values and the evolution of corporate communications.* Retrieved August 12, 2009, from www.awpagesociety.com/images/uploads/2007AuthenticEnterprise.pdf

Ashforth, B. E., Kreiner, G. E., & Fugate, M. (2000). All in a day's work: Boundaries and micro role transitions. *Academy of Management Review, 25*(3), 472–491.

Ashmos, D. P., Duchon, D., & McDaniel, R. R., Jr. (2000). Organizational responses to complexity: The effect on organizational performance. *Journal of Organizational Change Management, 13*(6), 577–594.

Belkin, L. (2008, November 17). Moms and Motrin. *New York Times.* Retrieved December 10, 2008, from http://parenting.blogs.nytimes.com/2008/11/17/moms-and-motrin

Bentele, G. (2007). Applying sociology to public relations: A commentary. *Public Relations Review, 33*(3), 294–300.

Berger, B. K. (1999). The Halcion affair: Public relations and the construction of ideological world view. *Journal of Public Relations Research, 11*(3), 185–203.

Boisot, M. (2000). Is there a complexity beyond the reach of strategy? *Emergence, 2*(1), 114–134.

Bolton, M. J., & Stolcis, G. B. (2008). Overcoming failure of imagination in crisis management: The complex adaptive system. *Innovation Journal: The Public Sector Innovation Journal, 13*(3), article 4.

Botan, C. H., & Soto, F. (1998). A semiotic approach to the internal functioning of publics: Implications for strategic communication and public relations. *Public Relations Review, 24*(1), 21–44.

Botan, C. H., & Taylor, M. (2004). Public relations: State of the field. *Journal of Communication, 54*(4), 645–661.

Bromley, D. B. (1993). *Reputation, image and impression management.* New York: Wiley.

Broom, G. M., Casey, S., & Ritchey, J. (1997). Toward a concept and theory of organization-public relationships. *Journal of Public Relations Research, 9*(2), 83–98.

Bryant, A. (2007). Liquid modernity, complexity and turbulence. *Theory, Culture & Society, 24*(1), 127–135.

Budd, J. F. (1993). *CEO credibility: The management of reputation.* Lakeville, CT: Turtle.

Byrne, D. (1998). *Complexity theory and the social sciences: An introduction.* London: Routledge.

Byrne, D. (2001). Complexity science and transformations in social policy. *Social Issues, 1*(2). Retrieved February 24, 2010, from www.whb.co.uk/social issues/db.htm

Campbell, F. E., Herman, R. A., & Noble, D. (2006). Contradictions in "reputation management." *Journal of Communication Management, 10*(2), 191–196.

Chaffee, S. H. (1996). Thinking about theory. In M. B. Salwen & D. W. Stacks (Eds.), *An integrated approach to communication theory and research* (pp. 15–32). Mahwah, NJ: Lawrence Erlbaum.

Chesters, G., & Welsh, I. (2006). *Complexity and social movements: Multitudes at the edge of chaos.* New York: Routledge.

Chiles, T. H., Meyer, A. D., & Hench, T. J. (2004). Organizational emergence: The origin and transformation of Branson, Missouri's musical theatres. *Organization Science, 15*(5), 499–519.

Cho, A. (2009). Ourselves and our interactions: The ultimate physics problem? *Science, 325*(5939), 406–408.

Coombs, W. T. (1992). The failure of the task force on food assistance: A case study of the role of legitimacy in issue management. *Journal of Public Relations Research, 4*(2), 101–122.

Coombs, W. T., & Holladay, S. J. (2001). An extended examination of the crisis situations: A fusion of the relational management and symbolic approaches. *Journal of Public Relations Research, 13*(4), 321–340.

Crable, R. E., & Vibbert, S. L. (1985). Managing issues and influencing public policy. *Public Relations Review, 11*(2), 3–16.

Curtin, P. A., & Gaither, T. K. (2005). Privileging identity, difference, and power: The circuit of culture as a basis for public relations theory. *Journal of Public Relations Research, 17*(2), 91–115.

Deephouse, D. L. (2000). Media reputation as a strategic resource: An integration of mass communication and resource-based theories. *Journal of Management, 26*(6), 1091–1112.

Deibert, R. J. (1997). *Parchment, printing, and hypermedia.* New York: Columbia University Press.

Deuze, M. (2007). *Media work.* Cambridge, UK: Polity Press.

Dooley, K. J., & Van de Ven, A. H. (1999). Explaining complex organizational dynamics. *Organization Science, 10*(3), 358–372.

Elmer, G. (2006). Mapping the cyber-stakeholders: U.S. energy policy on the web. *Communication Review, 9,* 297–320.

Esterline, R. (2009). *Motrin moms: Case study.* Retrieved March 31, 2009, from http://crisiscomm .wordpress.com/2009/01/28/motrin-moms-case-stud

Evans, S. (2008). Motrin moms: Social media fail whale. *Mashable.* Retrieved November 21, 2008, from http://mashable.com/2008/11/16/motrin-moms

Fishman, D. (1999). ValuJet Flight 592: Crisis communication theory blended and extended. *Communication Quarterly, 47*(4), 345–375.

Fombrun, C. J. (1996). *Reputation: Realizing value from the corporate image.* Cambridge, MA: Harvard Business School Press.

Fombrun, C. J., & Van Riel, C. B. M. (2004). *Fame and fortune: How successful companies build winning reputations.* Upper Saddle River, NJ: Prentice Hall.

Giddens, A. (1991). Modernity and self-identity: Self and society in the late modern age. Stanford, CA: Stanford University Press.

Gilpin, D. R. (2007, May). *A complexity perspective on reputation: Wal-Mart and the media.* Paper presented at the International Communication Association conference, San Francisco.

Gilpin, D. R. (2008). Narrating the organizational self: Reframing the role of the news release. *Public Relations Review, 34*(1), 9–18.

Gilpin, D. R. (2009, May). *Issue identity as an emergent network property.* Paper presented at the

International Communication Association conference, Chicago.

Gilpin, D. R. (2010). Working the Twittersphere: Microblogging as professional identity construction for public relations practitioners. In Z. Papacharissi (Ed.), *The networked self: Identity, community and culture on social network sites.* New York: Routledge, pp., 232–250.

Gilpin, D. R., & Murphy, P. (2005). Reframing crisis management through complexity. In C. H. Botan & V. Hazleton (Eds.), *Public relations theory II* (pp. 375–392). Mahwah, NJ: Erlbaum.

Gilpin, D. R., & Murphy, P. (2008). *Crisis management in a complex world.* New York: Oxford University Press.

Gilpin, D. R., & Murphy, P. (2010). Complexity and crises: A new paradigm. In W. T. Coombs & S. Halladay (Eds.), *The handbook of crisis communication* (pp. 683–690). New York: Blackwell.

Gotsi, M., & Wilson, A. M. (2001). Corporate reputation: Seeking a definition. *Corporate Communications: An International Journal, 6*(1), 24–30.

Goulielmos, A. M. (2005). Complexity theory: A science where historical accidents matter. *Disaster Prevention and Management, 14*(4), 533–547.

Gunter, P. A. Y. (2008). Analysis and its discontents: Nonlinearity and the way things aren't. *Chaos, Solitons & Fractals, 20*(1), 5–9.

Hallacher, P. M. (2005). *Why policy issue networks matter.* Lanham, MD: Rowman & Littlefield.

Hellsten, I. (2003). Focus on metaphors: The case of "Frankenfood" on the web. *Journal of Computer-Mediated Communication, 8*(4), http://jcmc.indiana.edu/v018/issue4/hellsten.html

Holtzhausen, D. R. (2004, November). *Complexity, postmodern power and public relations.* Paper presented at the Convention of the National Communication Association, Chicago.

Hutton, J. G., Goodman, M. B., Alexander, J. B., & Genest, C. M. (2001). Reputation management: The new face of corporate public relations? *Public Relations Review, 27*(3), 247–261.

Ihlen, Ø., & van Ruler, B. (2007). How public relations works: Theoretical roots and public relations perspectives. *Public Relations Review, 33*(3), 243–248.

Illia, L., & Lurati, F. (2006). Stakeholder perspectives on organizational identity: Searching for a relationship approach. *Corporate Reputation Review, 8*(4), 293–307.

Jaques, T. (2007). Issue management and crisis management: An integrated, non-linear, relational construct. *Public Relations Review, 33*(2), 147–157.

Johnson, L. A. (2008, November 17). Slings and arrows: Online backlash ends Motrin ad. Retrieved January 15, 2009, from http://www.usatoday.com/money/economy/2008-11-17-4080031906_x.htm

King, B. G., & Whetten, D. A. (2008). Rethinking the relationship between reputation and legitimacy: A social actor conceptualization. *Corporate Reputation Review, 11*(3), 192–208.

Kiousis, S., Popescu, C., & Mitrook, M. (2007). Understanding influence on corporate reputation: An examination of public relations efforts, media coverage, public opinion, and financial performance from an agenda-building and agenda-setting perspective. *Journal of Public Relations Research, 19*(2), 147–165.

Kreiner, G. E., Hollensbe, E. C., & Sheep, M. L. (2006). On the edge of identity: Boundary dynamics at the interface of individual and organizational identities. *Human Relations, 59*(10), 1315–1341.

Kreiner, G. E., Hollensbe, E. C., & Sheep, M. L. (2009). Balancing borders and bridges: Negotiating the work-home interface via boundary work. *Academy of Management Journal, 52*(4), 704–730.

Latour, B. (2005). *Reassembling the social: An introduction to actor-network theory.* New York: Oxford University Press.

Lauzen, M. M., & Dozier, D. M. (1994). Issues management mediation of linkages between environmental complexity and management of the public relations function. *Journal of Public Relations Research, 6*(3), 163–184.

Law, J. (2004). *After method: Mess in social science research.* London: Routledge.

Ledingham, J. A., & Bruning, S. D. (Eds.). (2000). *Public relations as relationship management.* Mahwah, NJ: Lawrence Erlbaum Associates.

Luoma-aho, V., & Vos, M. (2009). Monitoring the complexities: Nuclear power and public opinion. *Public Relations Review, 35*(2), 120–122.

Maturana, H. R., & Varela, F. J. (1980). *Autopoiesis and cognition.* Dordrecht, The Netherlands: D. Reidel.

McKelvey, B. (2003). Emergent order in firms: Complexity science vs. the entanglement trap. In E. Mitleton-Kelly (Ed.), *Complex systems and evolutionary perspectives on organisations: The application of complexity theory to organisations* (pp. 99–125). New York: Pergamon Press.

Meek, J. W., De Ladurantey, J., & Newell, W. H. (2007). Complex systems, governance and policy administration consequences. *Emergence: Complexity & Organization, 9*(1/2), 24–36.

Meyrowitz, J. (1989). The generalized elsewhere. *Critical Studies in Mass Communication, 6*(3), 323–334.

Mitleton-Kelly, E. (2003). The principles of complexity and enabling infrastructures. In E. Mitleton-Kelly (Ed.), *Complex systems and evolutionary perspectives on organisations: The application of complexity theory to organisations* (pp. 205–219). New York: Pergamon Press.

Murphy, P. (in press). Chaos theory as a model for managing issues and crises. *Public Relations Review, 22*(2), 95–113.

Murphy, P. (2000). Symmetry, contingency, complexity: Accommodating uncertainty in public relations theory. *Public Relations Review, 26*(4), 447–462.

Murphy, P. (2010). The intractability of reputation: Media coverage as a complex system in the case of Martha Stewart. *Journal of Public Relations Research, 22*(2), 209–237.

Nowotny, H. (2005). The increase of complexity and its reduction: Emergent interfaces between the natural sciences, humanities, and social sciences. *Theory, Culture & Society, 22*(5), 15–31.

O'Rourke, R. J. (1996). Learning from crisis: When the dust settles. *Public Relations Strategist, 2*(2), 35–38.

Paraskevas, A. (2006). Crisis management or crisis response system? A complexity science approach. *Management Decision, 44*(7), 892–907.

Qvortrup, L. (2006). Understanding new digital media. *European Journal of Communication, 21*(3), 345–356.

Richardson, K. A., & Cilliers, P. (2001). What is complexity science? A view from different directions. *Emergence, 3*(1), 5–22.

Rogers, R. (2002). Operating issue networks on the web. *Science as Culture, 11*(2), 191–213.

Salem, P. (2002). Assessment, change, and complexity. *Management Communication Quarterly, 15*(3), 442–450.

Sha, B.-L. (2006). Cultural identity in the segmentation of publics: An emerging theory of intercultural public relations. *Journal of Public Relations Research, 18*(1), 45–65.

Sha, B.-L. (2009). Exploring the connection between organizational identity and public relations behaviors: How symmetry trumps conservation in engendering organizational identification. *Journal of Public Relations Research, 21*(3), 295–317.

Smallman, C., & Weir, D. (1999). Communication and cultural distortion during crises. *Disaster Prevention and Management, 8*(1), 33–41.

Snowden, D. J. (2003). Innovation as an objective of knowledge management: Part I. The landscape of management. *Knowledge Management Research & Practice, 1,* 113–119.

Stacey, R. D., Griffin, D., & Shaw, P. (2000). *Complexity and management.* London: Routledge.

Ulmer, R. R., Sellnow, T. L., & Seeger, M. W. (2007). *Effective crisis communication: Moving from crisis to opportunity.* Thousand Oaks, CA: Sage.

Urry, J. (2003). *Global complexity.* Cambridge, UK: Polity Press.

van Uden, J. (2005). Using complexity science in organization studies: A case for loose application. *Emergence: Complexity & Organization, 7*(1), 60–66.

Weick, K. E. (2001). *Making sense of the organization.* Oxford, UK: Blackwell.

White, J., & Dozier, D. M. (1992). Public relations and management decision making. In J. E. Grunig (Ed.), *Excellence in public relations and communication management* (pp. 91–108). Hillsdale, NJ: Erlbaum.

Williams, S. L., & Moffitt, M. A. (1997). Corporate image as an impression formation process: Prioritizing personal, organizational, and environmental audience factors. *Journal of Public Relations Research, 9*(4), 237–258.

Zerubavel, E. (1993). *The fine line: Making distinctions in everyday life.* Chicago: University of Chicago Press.

CHAPTER 6

Signs of the Times

Economic Sciences, Futures, and Public Relations

David McKie

Building on previous work on reducing insularity in public relations, this chapter extends earlier efforts in two distinct directions by drawing from two different disciplines. It identifies the contemporary time as one of exceptional turbulence, rapid change, and ongoing uncertainty. In addressing that volatility, it draws from ideas, methods, and research in the discipline of future studies. These are used to develop a more forward-looking public relations, to unsettle the field's attachment to outmoded linear thinking, and to question assumptions of business continuing as usual. The chapter also examines the field of economics to consider reputational change across time and to learn how to advance public relations as an applied practice.

Turbulence as the New Normality: Identifying Present and Future Characteristics

Signs of the times can be discerned in the recurring themes of books that engage in identifying characteristics of the present age. The two most common surface themes in public relations are the age of globalization and the digital age. Globalization emerges strongly from the 2001 version of the discipline's major benchmark, the *Handbook of Public Relations* (Heath, 2001). Heath (2001) devoted 64 pages, or the whole concluding section, "Globalizing Public Relations" (pp. 625–689), to considering corporate multinational, national, international, and regional (e.g., the European Union) dimensions of the phenomenon. His emphasis was reinforced by both editions of *The Global Public Relations Handbook* (Sriramesh & Verčič, 2003, 2009)—which turned the actuality of globalization into an intellectual project to address the diversity, nature, and scale of the process from diverse locations—and other books on *Global Public Relations* (Freitag & Stokes, 2009) and *International Public Relations* (Curtin & Gaither, 2007). All of them incorporate aspects of diversity as an integral part of globalization.

Alongside globalization, Heath's (2001) *Handbook* endorsed the digital age, albeit under the predigital age label of "Public Relations in

Cyberspace" (pp. 579–623), by devoting the complete 45 pages of the penultimate section to it. The digital age, in the more current terminology of the social media world, has subsequently increased in prominence from the level of specific skills in *The Public Relations Writer's Handbook: The Digital Age* (Aronson, Spetner, & Ames, 2007) and strategies in *Online Public Relations: A Practical Guide to Developing an Online Strategy in the World of Social Media* (Phillips & Young, 2009) to rejuvenation in *Putting the Public Back in Public Relations: How Social Media Is Reinventing the Aging Business of PR* (Solis & Breakenridge, 2009). However, despite Solis and Breakenridge's (2009) invocation of a paradigmatic break, few public relations books aimed for either depth of capture in any larger societal sense, or for grand strategic overview, but trained a rather restricted focus on one or two surface characteristics.

The difference is deeper than just globalization or "the current vogue for digital technology as the panacea" (Anderla, 2007, p. 14). The book's title, *The Age of Asymmetry and Paradox*, favored those two defining terms to accentuate injustices as "abysmal destitution" (p. 14) coexisting with an obesity epidemic to reflect an ambiguity typical of today's world. In the realm of finance, Greenspan's (2008) *The Age of Turbulence: Adventures in a New World* foregrounded both contemporary volatility and the risk of the unknown beyond just the economic aspects. In effect, his emphasis on turbulence encompassed globalization and the digital age but did so as aspects of a larger frame and not as age-defining aspects in themselves. In reaffirming Greenspan's turbulence, Kotler and Caslione's (2009) *Chaotics: The Business of Managing and Marketing in the Age of Turbulence* augmented it with the coinage "chaotics" to convey how the innovative and messy nature of the age interweaves with business as a whole: "Turbulence is the *new normality*, punctuated by periodic and intermittent spurts of prosperity and downturn—including extended downturns amounting to recession or even depression" (p. xii).

One former president and CEO of the Institute for the Future pulled together the age-identifying indicators through the acronym VUCA to present the environment as Volatile, Uncertain, Complex, and Ambiguous (Johansen, 2007, p. xix). The chapter augments VUCA to AVUCA (with a prefixed A to represent Asymmetry), to capture Anderla's (2007) insight that asymmetries, especially as inequalities, are a key dimension of the age. From this AVUCA-informed perspective, it seeks to develop a forward-looking public relations and begins by imagining a futurist scenario.

The scenario jumps two decades to invent benchmarks for public relations success in 2030. In the vision, 2030's high-point would be the 10th anniversary of the 2020 inauguration of the Nobel Prize for public relations. The event would simultaneously honor the sixth public relations woman laureate in the subject (a record in proportionate representation of numbers of female prizewinners across all fields). The year 2030 would also see this status reinforced by public recognition in the form of sales of thought-provoking public relations bestsellers. In the popular business and social sciences publishing sector, these had been overtaking the previous leading sales sector of student textbooks since the 2020s. In addition, in international classifications of scholarly publications, 2030 would see public relations add a new top-tier journal to make a total of three—all with demonstrated impacts on other disciplines. Furthermore, 2030 would confirm the establishment of a unique "public relations approach." This was first promoted in the controversial public relations Nobel Prize winners' speech of 2025 and has gradually been adopted by academics in other subjects to analyze business and social behavior. The year 2030 would also mark the 10th anniversary of the last public relations practitioner complaints about lacking a pathway to CEO positions and not being a natural part of senior executive teams in organizations.

Indeed, in 2030, public relations graduates would feature prominently, and in substantial numbers, among those identified as emerging leaders. They would be on track to join practitioners already occupying leadership positions and roles in corporate and not-for-profit organizations. These practitioners would complement the many participating at high levels in the traditional institutions of government that shape policy and strategy (i.e., strategy in the broadest sense, not just communication strategy). Moreover, by 2030, practitioner involvement would not just be as communication consultants but as full contributors to government action and decision making in war and peace, and in national emergencies, and in global crises. By 2030, research from public relations academics would be helping business and social enterprises succeed and would be highly visible in financial media for generating profits. In addition, with the widespread acceptance of communication as partially producing reality, public relations will not be seen as spinning reality but as openly constructing it, as less concerned with promoting organizational positions, and more with adding value to business with ethical values that maintain social trust and public reputation. Finally, in 2030, public relations has attracted respect because the field holds to a vision of justice that has widespread public support and because it has been seen to enact that vision in reducing inequality and poverty and promoting a more contented society across the globe.

Zeitgeist Bias (1): Seeing Contemporary Concentrations Through Former Futures

To realize this more ethical and purpose-driven vision will entail a steep learning curve. As an incentive, it is worth bearing in mind that scenarios usually come in threes and considering the options. For a dystopic one, imagine the field deteriorating in educational status—being downgraded to training courses with how-to manuals for literature—and losing social standing to the extent that it is unable to inspire trust or merit pathways to senior positions. The decline would be compounded by the lack of relevance of any field not undergoing radical remaking for AVUCA conditions. A third scenario normally tends to a middle-of-the-road narrative and would be close to the current business as usual path that is reliant on few significant professional and social changes.

The discipline of futures studies, as its name indicates, recommends a multiple futures approach to emphasize that the future is yet to be made. In bringing home the fact that we are shaping what will emerge by our present actions, it can teach public relations. In addition, despite being an even newer discipline, which is "not regulated" (Gordon, 2009, p. 4) and has no "agreed professional standards" (p. 4), future studies sets out to add value to society from the outset. The major attempt to justify future studies as a field, and to synthesize its various elements into a coherent framework, did not happen until Bell's (1996) *Foundations of Futures Studies: Vol. 1. History, Purposes, and Knowledge.* Nevertheless, Bell's emphasis on "purposes" is quickly clarified as "*to provide tools to empower both ordinary people and leaders to act so as to create better futures for themselves and their societies than they otherwise would be able to do*" (p. xxxiii).

Characterized by this larger social purpose, future studies also delivers other value that Gordon's (2009) *Future Savvy* subtitle spelled out as *Identifying Trends to Make Better Decisions, Manage Uncertainty, and Profit From Change.* Gordon examined a range of important biases that influence thought, and selected "The Zeitgeist Bias: Seeing Reality Through the Lens of Our Times" (p. 93) as a "very common" (p. 93) form of situational bias that deserves "particular attention" (p. 93). Taking the term from the German for "spirit of the times," Gordon used it to refer "to the full and often unconscious spectrum of intellectual views, analytical approaches, political and social concerns, and so on, that people in any era share" (p. 94).

He illustrated "the role zeitgeist plays in framing forecasts" (Gordon, 2009, p. 94) by examining a collection of forecasts, which were made a century earlier as a prelude to the 1893 Chicago Exposition. The forecasts, made by 74 famous—at least at the time—experts, were originally published in the

1890s and were subsequently republished as *Today Then: America's Best Minds Look 100 Years Into the Future on the Occasion of the 1893 World's Columbian Exposition* (Walter, 1992). In his retrospective analysis of these forecasts, which positioned railways as the Internet equivalent of their time, Gordon (2009) noted their successful predictions (e.g., trains capable of travelling at 100 miles per hour and Florida tourism outgrowing French Riviera tourism). Not surprisingly, after a century, the majority are mostly inaccurate, but what Gordon found "instructive" (p. 94) was that more than 50% of the forecasters were

> all handicapped in the same way—by the difficulty of seeing beyond the issues and preoccupations of nineteenth-century fin-de-siècle America. The authors singularly fail to capture the zeitgeist of 100 years later—the global, information-driven economy of the late twentieth century—which would have created a better forecast in principle even if some of the details were wrong. (pp. 94–95)

Taking contemporary U.S.—because other nations do not yet have the critical mass—textbooks as indicative of the state of public relations, the following analysis of three typical examples shows the field's neglect of the future and the influence of zeitgeist bias. The first striking feature is the absence in each of a chapter on the future. Indeed, Broom's (2009) 10th edition of *Cutlip & Center's Effective Public Relations* does not index "future" at all, and, of its 17 chapters, only one, "Historical Origins" (pp. 103–135), has any temporal focus. In 22 chapters, Lattimore, Baskin, Heiman, and Toth's (2007) *Public Relations: The Profession and the Practice* finds space for one on history, but none on futures, and omits any indexing of "future." The most attention comes in Wilcox and Cameron's (2010) 9th edition of *Public Relations: Strategies and Tactics*, which, while it did not index "future" either, at least allocated three of the chapter's 33 pages on "The Evolution of Public Relations" (pp. 39–71) to "Transformation of the Field: The Next 50 Years" (pp. 66–68).

Across all three books, a clear clustering of contemporary challenges merges into future challenges with technology, whether Broom's (2009) "digital age" (p. 131), Lattimore et al.'s (2007) "rich media" (p. 369), or Wilcox and Cameron's (2010) "Peek Into the Future" (p. 360) with "Social Media and Web 2.0" (p. 360). All cover similar issues. All are distinctly contemporary rather than futuristic and, at a time when businesses have already been advised to "go global or go home" (Cook, 2007), all three books put a heavy emphasis on aspects of globalization and culture. In effect, the textbooks align with the emphases in the *Handbook* (Heath, 2001) and the other books discussed earlier. Seitel's (2004) textbook did differ in having a whole chapter called "The Future" (pp. 509–540), but, in practice, it is simply summarizing the same present-day characteristics "with the communications revolution in full bloom, with convergence of communications technologies upon us, and with the world an eminently smaller sphere than ever before" (p. 509).

Zeitgeist Bias (2): Breadth of Vision, Methodological Matters, and Nonlinear Options

The zeitgeist bias of the convergence—not only in terms of content, but in terms of vision, methods, and linearity—emerges strongly in contrast to an earlier equivalent. Cantor and Burger's (1984) collection, *Experts in Action: Inside Public Relations*, devoted a section to "Where Public Relations Is Going" with a complete chapter on "Public Relations Faces the 21st Century" (Fiur, 1984). Over a quarter of a century ago, when Fiur (1984) considered the future, he took a very different approach. Instead of a relatively linear, and technologically oriented, future (singular), he set out futures plural through "four broad clusters of possibilities" (p. 381) that provide diverse examples of futures planning:

> 1. "The American Dream—in which our society is characterized by continuing growth and success" (p. 381) and was able to "overcome

> problems, maintain economic superiority, and prosper in social harmony." (p. 381)

Although his chapter later speaks of a growing global interdependence, Fiur's (1984) focus, as his title indicates, is U.S. society and contrasts starkly with the kind of global considerations that are now ubiquitous to suggest the more nationalist zeitgeist bias of a preglobalization era. Another immediate difference lies in the omission of technology as a key driving force and its replacement by other drivers. In the first scenario, three specific aspects (political, economic, and social) fall roughly under the first three categorizations of the four umbrella themes captured in the futurist acronym PEST (Political, Economic, Social, and Technological). PEST analyses deploy a framework of macro factors used in environment scanning for scenarios and strategic management. Fiur's other three scenarios also feature PEST without the technology dimension.

> 2. The American Disaster—a "hard-times" scenario, in which problems overwhelm us, causing economic hardship and social dislocation. (p. 381)

Scenario 2's most striking contrast is in envisioning a large, negative future outcome far from a projection of business as usual. Outside risk management, none of the textbooks allocate space for consideration of catastrophic developments at a time when "megacatastrophes" (Posner, 2004, p. v) could feasibly emerge from "global bioterrorism, abrupt global warming" (p. v).

> 3. The Disciplined Society—much like Orwell's 1984, in which we trade in our freedoms and accept controls to keep society running smoothly and ensure our comfort and security. (Fiur, 1984, p. 381)

Scenario 3 prefigures later 21st-century issues surrounding privacy (e.g., Facebook stalkers and Google's release of information to Chinese authorities), and the technologically enhanced "Big Brother" of the surveillance society. If the full PEST analysis is restored, this focus on politics, economics, and society could be productively integrated with the contemporary concentration on technology.

> 4. The Transformational Society—in which we adjust our values and priorities, focusing primarily on the individual. Fulfillment of human potential and quality of life are dominant. (Fiur, 1984, p. 381)

Scenario 4 sketches elements, in embryonic form, of the rising concerns identified in public relations' contributions to a fully functioning society (Heath, 2006). It is reassuring to find an optimistic option to set against the pessimistic dystopia of "The American Disaster"—an example of how multiple scenarios break linear patterns by giving options to show the future has different multiple possible pathways. However, their very divergence (e.g., disaster or transformation) raises issues around credibility. Fiur (1984) nailed his credibility colors to the mast of shaping forces: Each of the scenarios is "a legitimate candidate to represent our future because the seeds of each can be found in the events and trends that are visible today" (pp. 381–382). He selected five driving forces that differ from today in their boldness and breadth of future vision, but many, especially those based on hard demographic trends (e.g., aging), stay more relevant, and more useful, than the 100-year forecasts:

- Awareness of, and concern about, change itself. . . .
- The rejection of traditional structure and hierarchy, seen in the decentralization of organizations and avoidance of institutions in favour of the individual.
- The political movement away from party ideology and government process to issues and informal networks.
- The demographic shifts in age and income distribution, creating a larger and disproportionately affluent elderly population.

- Economic and social globalization, breaking down borders, superseding national interests and drawing together individuals everywhere around shared ideas and information. (p. 382)

Although Fiur's (1984) scenarios are not too far away from more recent scenarios (e.g., Kelly, 2005), accuracy is not the point: "A flexible and hedged view of the future that is 'somewhat correct' is obviously more useful to more people rather than a wrong prediction however singularly asserted" (Gordon, 2009, p. 24). If organizations can get things usefully right, then that can be enough to secure profits or save lives in health systems, especially when also illuminating "the unknown while shaking our assumptions" (p. 24) and "preparing us for a future that is inherently uncertain" (p. 24).

Adjusting for Futurist Bias and Adopting Futures Methods

Neither histories nor future stories are neutral. Both are designed to influence attitudes and actions, and, in looking forward, the main structural divide is between future-influencing groups and future-aligning groups. Both may use similar methods, both may be equally valid, and neither is inherently better or worse. It is useful to discriminate when assessing their validity because "future-influencing forecasts are far more prone to bias because of the self-interest in the project" (Gordon, 2009, p. 29). The future-influencing group aim to make their future happen by their actions, and by selecting, and assessing, forces and trends in favor of their agendas. They can vary from John F. Kennedy's vision of landing a man on the moon within a decade to Hitler's prediction of a 1,000-year *Reich*, but, in effect, they try to grow a groundswell and gather sufficient resources to bring their forecasts to fruition. Gordon (2009) usefully identified "three primary flags for indicating a future-influencing forecast" (p. 30). Flag 1 is publication because "a key component of future-influencing is getting the word out" (p. 30). Flag 2 is specifying "an external change agenda" (p. 31) whose "'signature' . . . is the broad call to action" (p. 31), and Flag 3 is "a forecast of extremes" (p. 31).

Toth's (2006) *The Future of Excellence in Public Relations and Communication Management* is a future-influencing example. Its publication, with the involvement of leading scholars, raises Flag 1. It reveals Flag 2 of its external agenda in the subtitle, *Challenges for the Next Generation*, which seeks to direct the research directions, and theoretical orientations, of future scholarship. It can, more arguably, be seen to raise Flag 3's forecast of extremes in presenting the future of "excellence," or outstanding work, in public relations as the equivalent of the future of the "Excellence Project" in public relations, and so narrowing the next generation of theory building to one tradition.

Future-aligning organizations, on the other hand, are less concerned with actively shaping the future than using "forecasts to determine the terrain of the future . . . to make earlier and better alignment" (Gordon, 2009, p. 26). Fiur's (1984) concentration on interpreting "the forces of change currently discernable in our environment" (p. 382) for how they "will shape the future of public relations" (p. 382) fits into the adaptive, future-aligning camp. This present chapter is a mix. It has the three-part, future-influencing agenda of breaking the field's backward-looking attachments to business as usual, of looking forward with less insularity, and of more active pursuing outside perspectives—aiming for what Gordon (2009) called the "distinct benefits" (p. 73) of "industry outsiders, who have less investment in the status quo and less to lose from change" (p. 73). The chapter is future aligning in seeking ways to find and understand key driving forces and trends and so anticipate how public relations will need to adapt. It concludes the future-aligning mode by assessing absences in public relation methods with a view to the augmentation of backward-oriented ones with forward-oriented ones.

The table of contents and index of the main methodology book in public relations, Stacks's (2002) *Primer of Public Relations Research*, reveal that it is remarkably short of futures methods.

Not only has the author excluded visioning and such innovations as prediction markets, but common forward-looking methodology—that is current in textbooks (e.g., classic Delphi studies, environmental scanning, and scenarios)—is missing. In fact, if public relations is to address future deficiencies, its methods have to be urgently supplemented with, at least, the latest *Futures Research Methodology Version 3.0* (Glenn & Gordon, 2009). With 39 peer-reviewed chapters by leaders in the field—more than 50% of the chapters were written either by the method's inventor or by researchers who contributed significantly to the evolution of the method—this is an essential tool. In this work, available on an easily accessed CD-ROM, Glenn and Gordon's (2009) contributors examine the origins, strengths, and weaknesses of a huge range of methods; consider appropriate—and evaluate some inappropriate—applications; weigh the factors involved in selecting methods; and speculate on possible future developments.

This is a good point to acknowledge the chapter's severe limitations in the significant area of futures work in public relations practice. There is much that escapes academic research, and, although much is confidential, I admit this is a substantial omission that undermines general statements about public relations. The size of the loss can be gauged through considering one method that has some of its techniques and findings in the public domain. Indeed worldwide CEO of Burson-Marsteller Mark Penn's future-oriented analytics could assist futures studies. Penn's (2007) *Microtrends* argued that "the most powerful forces in our society are the emerging, counterintuitive trends that are shaping tomorrow right before us" (p. xi) since "it takes only 1 percent of people making a dedicated choice—contrary to the mainstream's choice—to create a movement that can change the world" (p. xiv) and, in fact, if "Islamic terrorists were to convince just *one-tenth* of *1 percent* of America's populatio . . . they would have 300,000 soldiers of terror" (p. xv).

Penn's (2009) later account of bloggers would suggest that the profession must already, if not in a global way, be coming to terms with microtrends such as the growth of the paid bloggers: "Blogging is an important social and cultural movement that people care passionately about, and the number of people doing it for at least some income is approaching 1% of American adults," with the result that there are "almost as many people making their living as bloggers as there are lawyers," and the available research suggests that "we are a nation of over 20 million bloggers, with 1.7 million profiting from the work, and 452,000 of those using blogging as their primary source of income. That's almost 2 million Americans."

Learning From Economics (1): 2030 Revisited

If much can be learned from trends and the young field of future studies, what might public relations take from a mature field? Emulation is one answer: The earlier Utopian public relations scenario for 2030 virtually describes the status of current economics. In 2009, 40 years after its 1969 inauguration, Professor Elinor Ostrum became the first woman awarded the Nobel Prize in economic sciences. By 2009, economics had achieved all the other 2030 public relations scenario benchmarks. The year 2009 itself saw the publication of Levitt and Dubner's (2009) *SuperFreakonomics*, a follow-up to the same authors' international runaway bestseller *Freakonomics* (Levitt & Dubner, 2005). Written in an accessible style for general readers to illustrate the relevance of economics to everyday experiences, *Freakonomics* had "more than 4 million copies in print worldwide" (Fox, 2009) by fall 2009, while, on the scholarly side, a range of leading economics journals hold top-tier academic standing internationally.

By the time of his 1996 Nobel Prize, Gary Becker's (1976) advocacy—of "an economic approach in seeking to understand human behaviour" (p. 3), and his allied contention that "what most distinguishes economics as a discipline . . . is not its subject matter but its approach" (p. 5)—had become widely accepted. As for translating research into consultancy, Scholes and Merton (who later became Nobel laureates) were part of a long line of academics turned financial players, when, in the 1990s, they joined a huge hedge fund business called Long-Term Capital Management (LTCM). Social prominence has accrued to other economists, and their institutions, especially the Federal Reserve System (the Fed). In 2006, at the end of nearly three decades as Fed chairman, economist Greenspan was "feted as perhaps the greatest central banker ever" (Wessel & Taylor, 2009). *Time* magazine selected his successor, Ben Bernanke, as "Person of the Year 2009," and a book titled *In Fed We Trust: Ben Bernanke's War on the Great Panic: How the Federal Reserve Became the Fourth Branch of Government* (Wessel, 2009) implied near-divine status for the institution. In short, if law and medicine are the preferred role models for professionalism in public relations, then the economic sciences must be on the short list as a role model for disciplinary status and social recognition.

Despite its attainments and disciplinary maturity, economics has, periodically, sustained reputational damage. During the evolving 2007–2010 crisis, even Fed chairmen and the Fed itself were not immune—see the negative revisionism of Fleckenstein's (2008) *Greenspan's Bubbles: The Age of Ignorance at the Federal Reserve.* As for academic consultancy success, Scholes and Merton's LTCM lost "$4.4 million in the space of a few days" (Beinhocker, 2006, p. 381) and avoided bankruptcy only through a Fed-led bailout of $3.65 billion. Its near collapse diminished the credibility of academic economists in general, and Scholes and Merton in particular. Merton exacerbated the credibility loss by commenting on the $4.4 million loss that "according to our models this just could not happen" (cited in Beinhocker, 2006, p. 381) and Lewis (1999) called his article on LTCM "How the Eggheads Cracked" (p. 24).

Milton Friedman's monetarism, probably the most influential movement of the second half of the 20th century, attracted criticism and social stigma. His fellow Nobel laureate Joseph Stigler's (2007) "Bleakonomics" attacked the Friemanite movement's "belief in the perfection of market economies on models that assumed perfect information, perfect competition, perfect risk markets," which "were never based on solid empirical and theoretical foundations" and ignored academic explanations of "the limitations of markets—for instance, whenever information is imperfect, which is to say always." Friedman also came under fire for severing longstanding connections between political economy—traditional and Keynesian—and justice and social good. From a social activist perspective, Klein (2007) concluded that "when government after government embraced Friedman's advice . . . that it was a mistake to try 'to do good with other people's money'" (p. 353), it resulted in "the dismal reality of inequality, corruption and government degradation" (p. 353).

The Reputation Prize: Justice Issues, Economics, and Public Relations

Economists partially construct reality and influence the limits to what can be "realistically" done (e.g., for decades, there have not been enough funds to support low emission reduction targets and save the earth's ecological system, but trillions of dollars were immediately available to bail out firms too big to fail without endangering the global financial system). Enough economists have, however, kept their eyes on the prize, and not the Nobel Prize, but the prize of realizing a vision of a better world based on increasing resources and allocating them justly and rationally. Their aspirations and successes have earned respect. That respect acts as reputational capital.

Beinhocker (2006), for example, worked to restore social justice links by stressing the emancipation possibilities of economics. First, in the past, "economic evolution and growth [brought] with them unquestionable benefits. It is easy for rich Westerners to forget what life was like a mere eight generations ago, and is still like for over a third of the world's population" (pp. 451–452). Second, in the future, because while the "past two hundred years of explosive growth have freed billions from a Hobbesian existence of toil, hunger, and disease" (p. 452), the "next century could free billions more" (p. 452). Economics is seen as serving society, because the three "constructs of states, markets, and communities . . . together create the economic world" (p. 450) and "we can endeavor to ensure that these three elements work together to create wealth, societal capital, and opportunity" (p. 450). I interpret this "we" as a social "we"—rather than a community of economists—and read Beinhocker's (2006) emphasis on opportunity as widening the success of past economic growth to "free billions more" (p. 452) and increase fairness and justice in future economics.

However, Beinhocker's (2006) three "constructs of states, markets, and communities" extend the issues beyond economics. Communication, in general, partially constitutes—in Deetz's (1992) formulation "discursive practices are both 'in' organizations and productive of them" (pp. 5–6)—these constructs; public relations, in particular, has a significant role in their public visibility and credence. Indeed, as Ewen (1996) persuasively argued, for Bernays, and "for many others in the field" (p. 6), "public relations was about fashioning and projecting credible renditions of *reality* itself" (p. 6). An extreme recent example is how the public relations of the climate denial industry replaced scientific evidence of global warming with an alternative universe where human-instigated carbon emissions did not matter.

The constitution, or production, of realities issue goes to the heart of public relations. Instead of addressing it, and harnessing it appropriately, those defining the field overlook it, or, implicitly, deny it. Their preferred sense comes closer to discredited conduit theories of communication that make public relations resemble little more than a communication lubricant to "promote the exchange of influence and understanding" (Lattimore et al., 2007). In this process, public relations is an interested party in managing relations. In his commendably honest definition, Cameron positioned public relations as the "strategic management of competition and conflict for the benefit of one's own organization—and when possible—also for the mutual benefit of the organization and its various stakeholders" (Wilcox & Cameron, 2010, p. 7). The catch is "when possible," since, unlike purpose in futures studies, the "definition places the public relations professional first and foremost as an advocate for the employer or client, but acknowledges the importance of mutual benefit *when circumstances allow* [italics added]" (p. 7). In other words, the benefit to publics (other than their clients or organizations) and the larger society takes the form of a largely opportunistic by-product.

Learning From Economics (2): Self-Criticism, Importing Innovation, and Experimentation

So what can be learned about handling a bad reputation? Fortunately, for economics, the field contained contributors seeking a more justice-based, methodologically sophisticated, and socially relevant agenda: "It is not only businesspeople and journalists who are critical of the current state of economics; economists themselves are their own toughest critics" (Beinhocker, 2006, p. 22). Early self-criticism included Friedrich Hayek's (1974) Nobel lecture that observed the failure of economists to control inflation in the 1970s and saw their errors as "closely connected with their propensity to imitate as closely as possible the procedures of the brilliantly successful physical sciences" (see McKie, 2001, for an allied critique of public relations). The 2007–2010 crisis exposed further methodological shortcomings founded on mathematics drawn from physics through "the folly of the reliance by banks, insurance companies, and others" (Beinhocker, Davis, & Mendonca, 2009, p. 58) on the staples of traditional economics: "financial models that assumed economic rationality, linearity, equilibrium, and bell-curve distribution" (p. 58).

At the core of the field's unrealistic assumptions lies the model of *Homo economicus*, or "economic man," conceptualized as infinitely selfish and infinitely rational. It took the efforts of two generations of economists and, significantly—in terms of imported innovation—psychologists "to build a mountain of empirical and experimental evidence" (Beinhocker, 2006,

p. 119) against the economic man construct. However, behavioral economists moved mainstream with the 2002 Nobel Prize for Economics award that named psychologist Daniel Kahneman. Economic models of human behavior continue to advance dramatically as cognitive scientists, computer scientists, and psychologists combine to add evidence through new kinds of experiments. One example that gives a sense of the experiments, and how they are interpreted, is the "Ultimatum Game" (Wilkinson & Pickett, 2009), in which

> volunteers are randomly paired but remain anonymous to each other and do not meet. A known sum of money is given to the "proposer" who then divides it as he or she pleases with the "responder." All the responders do is merely accept or reject the offer. If rejected, neither partner gets anything, but if it is accepted, they each keep the shares of the money offered.
>
> They play this game only once . . . they know there isn't going to be a next time. In this situation, self-interested responders should accept any offer, however derisory, and self-interested proposers should offer the smallest possible amount, just enough to ensure that a responder accepts it. . . .
>
> In practice, the average offer made by people in developed societies is usually between 43 and 48 per cent, with 50 per cent as the most common offer. At direct cost to ourselves, we come close to sharing equally even with people we never meet and will never interact with again.
>
> Responders tend to reject offers below about 20 per cent. Rejected offers are money which the responder chooses to lose in order to punish the proposer and prevent them from making a mean offer. The human desire to punish even at some personal cost has been called "altruistic punishment," and it plays an important role in reinforcing co-operative behaviour. (pp. 199–200)

Across the world, researchers made thousands of experiments with the game. Their consistent findings undermine assumptions that people only care about the outcomes of economic transactions and their own gain or loss, without concern for justness. In fact, Akerlof and Shiller (2009) suggested that "considerations of fairness or social expectation trump . . . strictly economic concerns" (p. 20), and fairness is one of the five most important aspects of how the economy really works (p. 5). Fairness is increasingly important to practitioners too. Greenspan's (2008) midcrisis epilogue retained his commitment to a free-market faith by seeing "no alternative" (p. 529) to "global market capitalism" (p. 529) for achieving "material well-being" (p. 529). However, he immediately added the qualification that its "Achilles' heel is the widespread perception that its rewards are not justly distributed" (Greenspan, 2008, p. 529), and concluded that the fairness issue "sorely needs to be addressed" (p. 529).

Learning From Economics (3): Advancing Complexity and Widening Risk

These experimental methods merit emulation since a core theory of human behavior is as essential to public relations as it is to economics. Applied psychology is another area of shortfall in public relations. The gap, in terms of quantity and recency of citation, can be indicated by the references in the 26 chapters in Toth's (2006) *The Future of Excellence in Public Relations and Communication Management.* Alongside two chapters that cite three interpersonal communication textbooks and one persuasion book between them, only three of the rest cite psychological sources in their reference list. In the whole collection, no psychology articles or books referenced, with one 2004 exception, are published later than 1999.

Economists are actively addressing their other shortfalls through a substantial subdiscipline of complexity economics. Enhanced by work from anthropologists, biologists, cognitive scientists, computer scientists, evolutionary theorists, and physicists, its experimental methods include running software simulations (e.g., of buying behavior and stock market investing). Engagement with complexity sciences in public relations lags behind. Bowen's (2009) summary, for example, noted that, despite growth in complexity scholarship in complexity and risk, "communicating about risky issues has not been thoroughly researched through the theoretical frame of complexity or chaos theory" (p. 352) even though their application can "shed light on the uncertainties and social implications of communicating in a dynamic and ever-changing context" (p. 351).

Crisis and risk are the least insular, and most advanced, areas of public relations. For example, the field's one exception to making a substantive practical and theoretical engagement with complexity and uncertainty is *Crisis Management in a Complex World* (Gilpin & Murphy, 2008). It is not coincidental that their work and the *Handbook of Risk and Crisis Communication* (Heath & O'Hair, 2009) consciously address audiences external to public relations. One of the reasons that Gilpin and Murphy (2008) opted for crisis management over crisis communication, as their subject focus and title, is that management "also implies a comprehensive, strategic worldview that we believe is fundamental to understanding crisis" (p. 6).

Their complexity-based insight is equally relevant to how the whole of public relations might better engage with the whole contemporary environment by coming to terms with AVUCA to foster "the emergence of order from unstable conditions" (Gilpin & Murphy, 2008, p. 175). They imported from ethical anthropology, and from the social history of knowledge, as well as citing Daniel Kahneman, the psychologist awarded the 1992 Economics Nobel. In making recommendations to support agile and flexible responses through "improvisational fluency" (p. 172) and "adaptiveness" (p. 172), they draw from the futures toolkit. Gilpin and Murphy (2008) specified scenario planning as a process for assisting "managers to 'think different' and imagine a situation in great detail" (p. 168) and for "encouraging executives to leave behind assumptions that normally go unquestioned" (p. 169). In addition, they theorize a rationale for intensifying importations, inhibiting insularity, and attending to outside concerns because the "more turbulent and varied the environment, the greater the need to match environmental demands by keeping in play a range of possible responses" (Gilpin & Murphy, 2008, p. 172).

One final guideline from economics might be research findings that equality is the largest single factor in delivering a healthier, happier, and longer life. Wilkinson and Pickett's (2009) *The Spirit Level: Why More Equal Societies Almost Always Do Better* aggregated and analyzed empirical research on 23 rich countries. They found not only that inequality comes with significant costs from loss of community life, overall educational underperformance, increased violence, and poor workplace conditions, but that it is associated with poorer outcomes in relation to "lower life expectancy, higher rates of infant mortality, . . . AIDS and depression" (p. 81).

These findings gel with the "remarkable paradox that, at the pinnacle of human material and technical achievement, we find ourselves anxiety-ridden, prone to depression, worried about how others see us, unsure of our friendships, driven to consume and with little or no community life" (Wilkinson & Pickett, 2009, p. 3). Beinhocker (2006) was also prepared to entertain the radical doubt "that the real risk to humankind is not that we will fall off the growth curve, but rather we will stay on it" (p. 453), and simpatico economists have been active in happiness research (Layard, 2005). Others speculate about new limits to growth that are not just environmental. Accordingly, for Wilkinson and Pickett (2009), future human fulfillment "lies in improving the quality of social environment in our societies" (p. 265) with "a historic shift in the sources of human satisfaction from economic growth to a more sociable society" (p. 226). Public relations is well placed to align with, and to help enact, that transformation.

Conclusions

Contending that public relations is underprepared for engaging with new-normality turbulence or AVUCA futures, this chapter ends by reviewing its recommendations through Johansen's (2007) VUCA acronym (pp. 225–227) for how to respond to VUCA challenges. Johansen (2007) and the chapter overlap as follows: The V of volatility yields to vision—a compelling sense of where to go enables navigation in turbulence and public relations needs to redefine itself in a less process-oriented way, not so tied to narrowly partisan perspectives and with a more inspirational dimension; the U of uncertainty yields to understanding—public relations can draw from forward-looking methods and visioning techniques from futures studies to better anticipate what must be accepted as uncertainty and what might be made more comprehensible; the C of complexity yields to clarity—through seeking the simple rules underpinning complex behaviors and systems through complexity-based thinking and through experiments with real-world relevance; and A for ambiguity yields to agility—public relations can become more adaptable through accepting and working with paradox. Finally, the A of asymmetry does not yield to a neatly symmetric A word but involves imagining and enacting a justice agenda—a mature field can take a radical look at where it has come from, how it is performing, and, above all, how it can generate a more purpose-driven and egalitarian vision of where it ought to go.

References

Akerlof, G. A., & Shiller, R. J. (2009). *Animal spirits: How human psychology drives the economy, and why it matters for global capitalism.* Princeton, NJ: Princeton University Press.

Anderla, G. (with Dunning, A.). (2007). *The age of asymmetry and paradox: Essays in comparative economics and sociology.* Twickenham, UK: Athena.

Aronson, M., Spetner, D., & Ames, C. (2007). *The public relations writer's handbook: The digital age.* San Francisco: Jossey-Bass.

Becker, G. S. (1976). *The economic approach to human behavior.* Chicago: Chicago University Press.

Beinhocker, E. (2006). *The origin of wealth: Evolution, complexity, and the radical remaking of economics.* London: Random House.

Beinhocker, E., Davis, I., & Mendonca, L. (2009). The 10 trends you have to watch. *Harvard Business Review, 87*(7), 55–60.

Bell, W. (1996). *Foundations of futures studies: Human science for a new era: Vol. 1. History, purposes, and knowledge.* New Brunswick, NJ: Transaction.

Bowen, S. (2009). Ethical responsibility and guidelines for managing issues of risk and risk communication. In R. L. Heath & H. D. O'Hair (Eds.), *Handbook of risk and crisis communication* (pp. 343–363). New York: Routledge.

Broom, M. (2009). *Cutlip & Center's effective public relations* (10th ed.). Upper Saddle River, NJ: Prentice Hall.

Cantor, B., & Burger, C. (Eds.). (1984). *Experts in action: Inside public relations.* New York: Longman.

Cook, F. (2007, Winter). It's a small world after all: Multiculturalism, authenticity, connectedness among trends to watch in next 50 years. *Public Relations Strategist.* Retrieved September 19, 2009, from www.prsa.org/Intelligence/TheStrategist/Articles/view/6K-010710/102

Curtin, P. A., & Gaither, T. K. (2007). *International public relations: Negotiating culture, identity, and power.* Thousand Oaks, CA: Sage.

Deetz, S. (1992). *Democracy in an age of corporate colonization: Developments in communication and the politics of everyday life.* New York: State University of New York Press.

Ewen, S. (1996). *PR! A social history of spin.* New York: Basic Books.

Fiur, M. (1984). Public relations faces the 21st century. In B. Cantor & C. Burger (Eds.), *Experts in action: Inside public relations* (pp. 381–400). New York: Longman.

Fleckenstein, W. (with Sheehan, F.). (2008). *Greenspan's bubbles: The age of ignorance at the Federal Reserve.* New York: McGraw-Hill.

Fox, J. (2009, August). Is the world ready for Feakonomics again? *Time.* Retrieved November 11, 2009, from www.time.com/time/magazine/article/0,9171,1930520,00.html

Freitag, A. R., & Stokes, A. Q. (2009). *Global public relations: Spanning borders, spanning cultures.* New York: Routledge.

Gilpin, D. R., & Murphy, P. J. (2008). *Crisis management in a complex world.* New York: Oxford University Press.

Glenn, J. C., & Gordon, T. J. (2009). *Futures research methodology version 3.0.* New York: American Council for the United Nations University.

Gordon, A. (2009). *Future savvy: Identifying trends to make better decisions, manage uncertainty, and profit from change.* New York: AMACOM.

Greenspan, A. (2008). *The age of turbulence: Adventures in a new world.* New York: Penguin Books.

Heath, R. L. (Ed.). (2001). *Handbook of public relations.* Thousand Oaks, CA: Sage.

Heath, R. L. (2006). Onward into more fog: Thoughts on public relations' research directions. *Journal of Public Relations Research, 18*(2), 93–114.

Heath, R. L., & O'Hair, H. D. (Eds.). (2009). *Handbook of risk and crisis communication.* New York: Routledge.

Johansen, B. (2007). *Get there early: Sensing the future to compete in the present.* San Francisco: Berrett-Koehler.

Kelly, E. (2005). *Powerful times: Rising to the challenge of our uncertain world.* Upper Saddle River, NJ: Wharton School.

Klein, N. (2007). *The shock doctrine: The rise of disaster capitalism.* New York: Metropolitan Books.

Kotler, P., & Caslione, J. A. (2009). *Chaotics: The business of managing and marketing in the age of turbulence.* New York: AMACOM.

Lattimore, D., Baskin, O., Heiman, S., & Toth, E. (2007). *Public relations: The profession and the practice* (2nd ed.). New York: McGraw-Hill.

Layard, R. (2005). *Happiness.* London: Penguin Books.

Levitt, S. D., & Dubner, S. J. (2005). *Freakonomics: A rogue economist explores the hidden side of everything.* New York: HarperCollins.

Levitt, S. D., & Dubner, S. J. (2009). *SuperFreakonomics: Global cooling, patriotic prostitutes and why suicide bombers should buy life insurance.* New York: HarperCollins.

Lewis, M. (1999, January). How the eggheads cracked. *New York Times.* Retrieved November 21, 2009, from www.nytimes.com/1999/01/24/magazine/how-the-eggheads-cracked.html?pagewanted=1

McKie, D. (2001). Updating public relations: "New science," research paradigms, and uneven developments. In R. Heath (Ed.), *Handbook of public relations* (pp. 75–91). Thousand Oaks, CA: Sage.

Penn, M. J. (with Zalesne, E. K.). (2007). *Microtrends: The small forces behind tomorrow's big changes.* New York: Twelve.

Penn, M. J. (with Zalesne, E. K.). (2009, April). America's newest profession: Bloggers for hire. *Wall Street Journal, 25.* Retrieved October 25, 2009, from http://online.wsj.com/article/SB124026415808636575.html

Phillips, D., & Young, P. (2009). *Online public relations: A practical guide to developing an online strategy in the world of social media.* London: Kegan Paul.

Posner, R. A. (2004). *Catastrophe: Risk and response.* New York: Oxford University Press.

Seitel, F. (2004). *The practice of public relations* (9th ed.). Upper Saddle River, NJ: Prentice Hall.

Solis, B., & Breakenridge, D. (2009). *Putting the public back in public relations: How social media is reinventing the aging business of PR.* Upper Saddle River, NJ: Pearson FT Press.

Sriramesh, K., & Verčič, D. (Eds.). (2003). *The global public relations handbook: Theory, research and practice.* Mahwah, NJ: Lawrence Erlbaum.

Sriramesh, K., & Verčič, D. (Eds.). (2009). *The global public relations handbook: Theory, research, and practice* (Rev. ed.). New York: Routledge.

Stacks, D. W. (2002). *Primer of public relations research.* New York: Guilford Press.

Stigler, J. E. (2007, September). Bleakonomics. *New York Times.* Retrieved November 1, 2009, from www.nytimes.com/2007/09/30/books/review/Stiglitz-t.html?_r=1

Toth, E. (Ed.). (2006). *The future of excellence in public relations and communication management: Challenges for the next generation.* Mahwah, NJ: Lawrence Erlbaum.

Walter, D. (Ed.). (1992). *Today then: America's best minds look 100 years into the future on the occasion of the 1893 World's Columbian Exposition.* Helena, MT: American World Geographic.

Wessel, D. (2009). *In Fed we trust: Ben Bernanke's war on the great panic: How the Federal Reserve became the fourth branch of government.* New York: Random House.

Wessel, D., & Taylor, T. (2009). *Inside the economic crisis.* Retrieved October 30, 2009, from www.haverford.edu/news/stories/31311/51

Wilcox, D., & Cameron, G. (2010). *Public relations: Strategies and tactics* (9th ed.). Boston: Allyn & Bacon.

Wilkinson, R., & Pickett, K. (2009). *The spirit level: Why more equal societies almost always do better.* London: Penguin Books.

CHAPTER 7

Publics and Public Relations

Effecting Change

Shirley Leitch and Judy Motion

This chapter summarizes and extends the work of Leitch and Neilson (2001) published in the 2001 version of the *Handbook of Public Relations.* The chapter begins with a reflective overview of that earlier piece and its critique of the application of the core public relations concepts of "publics," "organizations," and "relations" within dominant public relations theoretical approaches. We then extend the work of Leitch and Neilson by adding the additional core concept of "change." Our discussion is grounded in discourse theory, which, we contend, is both highly relevant and salient for the theory and practice of public relations. We conclude the chapter by considering three significant contemporary challenges for theory development—"multiplicity," "resistance," and "engagement"—that are raised within this new discourse perspective on public relations.

Publics

One of the major contributions offered by Leitch and Neilson (2001) lay in their critique of the way in which the major concept of publics had been theorized and applied within the public relations literature. They began their critique by demonstrating that public relations theory had, for the most part, treated publics and organizations as interchangeable and equivalent entities. The two were interchangeable because from an organizational perspective, another organization could be categorized as a public. The concepts were equivalent because, in addition to being interchangeable, they were treated as if they were equal participants in any public relations process. This odd conceptualization only made sense because of the absence of the concept of power from most public relations theory (Coombs, 1993). The primary outcome of excluding power was to mask the existence and nature of differences and inequalities between organizations and publics, as well as within society more generally.

Leitch and Neilson (2001), therefore, set out to more clearly distinguish the concepts of publics and organizations and to consider how power might figure in the theory and practice of public relations. They argued that ignoring the underlying asymmetries in power relations between organizations and publics had led to a dominant framework of public relations ethics that focused on symmetry in the form of communication (Grunig & Hunt, 1984). Within this highly simplistic model, ethical public relations emerged exclusively from the symmetrical framing of organizational engagement with publics. Thus, organizations or publics that set out to change another's viewpoint would be labeled as unethical simply by virtue of the asymmetrical form of their communication practices. Public rallies, petitions, and street theater—the typical tools of citizens' actions—would all be labeled asymmetrical and, therefore, unethical. Leitch and Neilson (2001) argued that "form" was a relatively superficial indicator of ethics and, therefore, an inadequate basis for ethical public relations practice. A much broader analysis, which considered the context in which engagement occurred and the history, purpose, and resource base of the parties involved, was required (Leitch & Palmer, in press).

A related absence from public relations theory noted by Leitch and Neilson (2001) was, then, a developed concept of the "context" in which organizations might engage with publics. Again, this absence arose as a direct consequence of the neglect of any consideration of power relations. In a decontextualized theory of engagement with publics, the associated complexities—including the social, political, economic, ideological, virtual, and physical components of engagement—had been rendered largely invisible. However, what is "counted in" and what is "counted out" of any analysis makes a considerable difference to the strength of that analysis. A public relations theory that counted out the broader context of the analytical frame was inevitably myopic and, therefore, fundamentally flawed. In this chapter, we outline the ways in which a robust theory of context, drawn from discourse theory, may strengthen public relations research and practice.

Habermas's (1962/1991) distinction between the "system" and the "lifeworld" provided Leitch and Neilson (2001) with a starting point for the development of an adequate theory of the context for public relations engagement (see Figure 7.1). The lifeworld is divided into the "public sphere" and the "private sphere." The public sphere comprises all the public spaces in which citizens may exchange ideas and debate issues. In this respect, in Western democracies at least, the town hall has probably given way to the Internet as the most prominent and accessible dimension of the public sphere. Distinct from the public sphere was the lifeworld, which was the private "habitus" of individuals (Habermas, 1987, 1962/1991). The other half of Habermas's concept of social was the "system," which was divided into the political subsystems of the state and the economic subsystems of the economy (Cohen & Arato, 1992). It is through the public sphere that citizens are able to interact with the state, and it is within the public sphere that public opinion can form and become manifest (Calhoun, 1988, 1992, 1996). Without the concept of the public sphere, public relations literature is unable to deal adequately with the relationship between organizations and publics, particularly in the context of Western democracies.

Figure 7.1 Integrating Social Concepts

	Public	Private
System	Political subsystem or "state"	Economic subsystem
Lifeworld	Public sphere	Private sphere

Source: Cohen and Arato (1992, p. 431).

Another significant issue for Leitch and Neilson (2001) related to the segmentation of publics, a well-established tenet of public relations (see, e.g., Cutlip, Center, & Broom, 1994). They argued that the turn to multiple publics has had some unintended consequences, the most startling of which has been the abandonment of the central democratic concept of "the public," comprising all the citizens of a nation who may engage within the public sphere. There is evidence that this neglect continues. For example, Rawlins and Bowen (2005) opened their *Encyclopedia of Public Relations* entry on "Publics" by confidently stating that "in modern public relations, there is no such thing as a 'general public'" (p. 718). A macrolevel focus on the public and its associated power dynamics has thus been discarded in favor of an exclusively microlevel focus on segmented organizational relationships. However, Leitch and Neilson (2001) argued that the general public should be seen as one of multiple, possible publics with which organizations may engage.

Organizations

Habermas's (1962/1991) distinction between the "system" and the "lifeworld" provided Leitch and Neilson (2001) with a means of reframing the relationships between "organizations" and "publics." The purpose of this reframing was to counter the existing conflation of these two terms. Organizations have generally been theorized as "system"-based entities. However, Cohen and Arato (1992) identified significant changes in the character of the public sphere in terms of its increasing propensity to organize into social movements and thereby to develop its own organizations. One might argue that social movements become part of the system once they develop an organizational structure. However, Leitch and Neilson (2001) contended that the organizations of the lifeworld have a distinctive identity because they emerge from communicative exchanges that occur within the public sphere, while system organizations embody the strategic goals and rationality of the state and economy. They offered the following typology:

1. System organizations of state and economy
2. Lifeworld organizations of the public sphere
3. Boundary organizations, which have some characteristics of both the system and the lifeworld and operate across the system/lifeworld boundary

Within this typology, lifeworld organizations are understood as a subset of lifeworld publics, albeit a high-profile group. Leitch and Neilson (2001) then identified three categories of organization-public relationships:

1. Intersystem organization relations comprising relations between the organizations of the state and the corporate sector
2. Intraorganizational relations comprising relations within an organization
3. Organization-public relations comprising relations between an organization and an external public that is not a system-based organization

Thus, system organizations were differentiated both from "unorganized" publics and from publics that had developed their own organizational structures.

Relations

The final core public relations concept considered by Leitch and Neilson (2001) was "relations." They sought to move the focus of analysis on the relations between organizations and publics to a concern with

> power, strategy, objectives, and the manifold ways each articulates and overdetermines, constructs and deconstructs, organizes and

> disorganizes, the other. Public relations is about the many ways in which different types of publics interact with different types of organizations, and vice versa, on a strategic terrain of competing discourses and unequal access to power and resources. (p. 134)

Rejecting the dominant and demonstrably superficial focus on the form of communicative exchanges of communication, they argued that relations should instead be analyzed in terms of strategy, objectives, and any differences in access to power and resources.

In conceptualizing "relations," Leitch and Neilson (2001) drew on Heath's (1994, p. 364) three-dimensional concept of dialogue, comprising the following:

1. "Values," which are the evaluative frameworks applied by publics to make sense of actions and interactions and thereby create meaning
2. "Meaning," which is formed, reformed, and challenged through the actions of and the interactions between people
3. "Zones of meaning," which are the shared realities of members of particular publics and which combine to form "the fabric of public opinion" (R. Heath, personal communication, June 30, 1998)

Relations are thus viewed as comprising sets of communicative actions that are evaluated by members of publics through value-based frameworks to "make sense" of these interactions and thereby create meanings. These meanings may then come together through further interactions to form the shared realities of publics and, potentially, the shared zones of meaning between organizations and publics. This conceptualization directly challenges the organization-centered representations of engagement with publics that still dominate much public relations theory and research.

From Heath's (1994) perspective, public relations practice may be understood as the intentional fostering of favorable zones of meaning between organizations and publics. An organization's objectives may be negotiated with its publics who then actively participate in the cocreation of meaning. Thus, favorable zones of meaning are outcomes of successful interactions between publics and organizations. Both an organization's and a public's capability and willingness to engage in such interactions will be resource and context dependent. In this respect, Leitch and Neilson (2001) distinguished between unorganized and organized publics. Unorganized publics were defined as those without "an institutional structure, legitimated spokespeople, a clearly articulated agenda, and/or significant discourse resources" and which therefore had limited power (Leitch & Neilson, 2001, p. 136). They noted that it was difficult to engage with such publics or to forge new zones of meaning (Heath, 1994). Unorganized publics are, in effect, merely artifacts of the organizations themselves, which have no existence outside particular public relations strategies.

Some publics do, however, exist independently of system-based organizations and, as discussed above, may have developed into "lifeworld organizations." Such publics offer a fundamental challenge to organization-centered public relations in that they may possess goals of their own. As Leitch and Neilson (2001) argued, the Grunig and Hunt (1984) models assumed that the form taken by public relations interactions would be determined by the organization. However, organized publics may seek to determine their own destinies and may develop resource and power bases that challenge those of system organizations. Heath (1997, p. 156) noted that "activism has become institutionalized" within lifeworld organizations where it is neither readily controlled nor easily manipulated.

Within the next section, we augment the work of Leitch and Neilson (2001) by outlining a discourse approach to public relations. We seek to redirect the attention of both researchers and practitioners to rhetorical understandings of "publics" and "relations" and offer a distinctly poststructuralist focus on understanding these core public relations concepts in particular discourse contexts.

Changing a Discourse

Heath's (2001, p. 31) reference to public relations as "suasive discourse" serves as a reminder that we are not dealing with a symmetrical communicative practice. Rather, a key aim of public relations is to achieve or resist change by persuasively advancing and potentially privileging particular meanings and actions. Although the objectives may be negotiated or consensus sought through engagement with publics, it may also be achieved through persuasion. Public relations, therefore, constitutes a rhetorical practice (Heath, 1992) that establishes a discursive contest between organizations and publics, which, moreover, is neither inherently good nor bad. Indeed, the introduction of such ethical or moral evaluations necessitates the incorporation of the previously neglected contextual dimensions discussed earlier within public relations theory (Leitch & Palmer, in press). Discourse theory—with its emphasis on the understanding of texts within the contexts in which they are produced, distributed, and interpreted—therefore offers a highly relevant and useful body of theory to guide the development of ethical public relations practice. Discourse theory also refocuses our attention away from the form of communication and onto power relationships and the ongoing work by public relations practitioners to legitimate truth claims within discourse contexts (Motion & Leitch, 2009b).

Although a variety of approaches to discourse theory and analysis exist, the poststructuralist works of Michele Foucault and Norman Fairclough are particularly salient to public relations because of the emphasis on language, meaning, and change (Motion & Leitch, 1996, 2009a, 2009b). Fairclough is well established as the most influential discourse theorist within the related field of organization studies (Leitch & Palmer, in press), and work within this field that adopts a discourse perspective is highly relevant to public relations (Alvesson & Kärreman, 2000a, 2000b; Anderson, 2005; Hardy, 2001; Hardy, Palmer, & Phillips, 2000; Heracleous, 2006; Leitch & Davenport, 2005; Maguire & Hardy, 2006; Motion & Leitch, 2009b; Vaara & Tienari, 2008; Vaara, Tienari, & Laurila, 2006).

Fairclough (1992, 1995) offered a three-dimensional model of discourse comprising texts; the discourse practices associated with the production, distribution, and interpretation of texts; and the broader sociocultural context of these texts and practices, including ideological and institutional dimensions. Initially, Fairclough adopted a relatively conservative definition of texts as written language but later expanded this definition to include—as texts—visual images and sound (Fairclough, 2003, p. 2). Fairclough viewed texts as discursive objects that are intended by those who produce them to have causal effects (Leitch & Palmer, in press). These effects are, in turn, mediated by the act of sensemaking on the part of those who interpret them and, thereby, give them meaning. However, as Phillips and Hardy (2002) argued, "It is not individual texts that produce social reality, but structured *bodies* of texts" (p. 82). This focus on understanding the intertextual relationships between bodies of texts is particularly appropriate for public relations practice, which involves the production of sets of texts for organizations and for campaigns to advance organizational objectives.

Fairclough (1992) referred to those who actively engage in seeking to effect change within discourse as "professional technologists who research, redesign and provide training in discourse practices" (p. 8). Public relations practitioners may be seen as an obvious and major subset of Fairclough's profession of discourse technologists (Motion & Leitch, 1996). Discourse technologists seek to achieve change by transforming discourses, which involves changing established ways of thinking about particular objects, concepts, subjects, and strategies (Foucault, 1969/1972) or introducing new language and, therefore, new ways of thinking.

The meanings circulating within a discourse are therefore always potentially in flux as they are produced, reproduced, actively resisted, contested, or transformed by publics and organizations (Hardy et al., 2000).

Foucault (1991, pp. 56–57) explained that a successful discourse transformation may be identified by

1. new boundaries that define and map out what is included,
2. new subject positions and roles for those acting within the discourse,
3. new modes of language, and/or
4. new forms and ways of circulating the discourse within society.

The boundaries of a discourse may have their roots in deep social structures that are imbued with particular ideologies or systems of thought, in which case effecting change is a complex task. For example, a health discourse may have been founded on the social democratic principle of the right of all citizens to receive good quality health care. This discourse may be challenged by a neoliberal government that espouses individual rather than social responsibility for health and, by privileging economic considerations, seeks to introduce a "user-pays" approach into health policy. The ideological shift will be accompanied by the creation of new subject positions and roles for the publics and organizations who act within the health discourse. The subject position of "patient" may be replaced by that of "customer," and of hospital by "service provider," which in turn fundamentally alters the power relationships between publics and organizations within the health discourse context. Leitch and Neilson (2001) argued that organizations deploy public relations strategies to create and then persuade members of publics to accept subject positions that articulate most advantageously with the interests of the organization (Hall, 1986; Moffitt, 1994; Motion & Leitch, 1996; Slack, 1996). The rules that operate within discourse contexts constrain the identity possibilities that are available to individuals and set the framework of power relations between various subject positions. To fundamentally challenge these subject positions is a revolutionary act because it involves a challenge to the rules of the discourse itself.

The third dimension of discourse transformation is the new modes of language that are introduced. The design of language was identified by Fairclough (1992) as one of the key components of the work of discourse technologists as they seek to engineer change because language is the primary vehicle for the meanings that circulate within discourse. To continue the health discourse example, a neoliberal change initiative may introduce and privilege new language drawn from a managerial discourse, such as "key performance indicators," "cost-benefit analysis," and "efficiencies." Power and control within the health discourse then shifts from doctors and other health-related publics to professional managers. These professional managers may have limited understanding of the health context in which they act and, in this sense, apply decontextualized "knowledge." Fairclough used the concept of "marketization" to describe the spread of decontextualized knowledge that privileges the economic over all other considerations and that has been a hallmark of the neoliberalist era that has prevailed within most Western democracies for the past three decades.

The fourth dimension of discourse transformation involves the appearance of new forms and ways of circulating the discourse within society. This dimension takes us from the intradiscursive to focus on the interdiscursive and extradiscursive. As Foucault (1991, p. 58) suggested, it is important to consider

1. how a discourse is transformed internally—the intradiscursive focus,
2. how relations between discourses shift as a result of internal transformation—the interdiscursive focus, and

3. how elements that lie outside discourse are brought into discourse to affect both the intradiscursive and the interdiscursive—the extradiscursive focus.

Taken together, these three foci constitute a powerful analytical tool for understanding the underlying mechanisms and dynamics of discourse change. This tool may be used to design or map

1. the rules within a discourse governing what may be said and what is no longer legitimate;
2. the production, reproduction, transformation, and circulation of meaning;
3. the subject positions available to individuals, publics, or organizations that have access to a discourse;
4. the power relations between organizations that seek to transform discourse and other discourse subjects both within and between discourses;
5. how any resulting power struggles are played out;
6. the "domain" or institutional origin of the discourse (Foucault, 1991); and
7. how externalities affect discourses and how their effects are played out within and between discourses.

This analytical tool, we contend, is central to the work of public relations practitioners when they undertake the design and redesign of discourses (Fairclough, 1992).

Design work may be applied to the creation of identities, relationships, and the language associated with particular ideas (Fairclough, 1992). However, from a public relations perspective, the formation or transformation of a discourse only occurs when established ways of thinking are changed within a particular public. Here we draw on the work of Stuart Hall (1986) to introduce the concepts of "disarticulation" and "articulation" to explain how this change process occurs in practice. Disarticulation is defined as a process whereby undesired meanings are disestablished, whereas articulation is defined as the process of linking existing meanings with the meanings of a new discourse (Motion, Leitch, & Brodie, 2003). One way in which new ideas are brought into discourse is by articulating them with a "legacy" or established discourse (Maguire & Hardy, 2006), so that the change may seem less extensive or alien to publics and to increase the likelihood that the change will be accepted. For example, the introduction of a user-pays approach into health may be argued on the basis that "efficiency" means "providing better health care for more people"—a traditional concern within the health discourse—rather than "cutting costs"—the primary concern within an economic discourse.

Another application of the concepts of articulation and disarticulation within discourse transformations centers on subject positions. Subject positions that are familiar and acceptable to members of a public may be lifted from one discourse and articulated into another as a way of adding legitimacy to new ideas or of changing what existing ideas mean. Members of publics occupy subject positions within multiple discourses, each of which has its own rules of engagement and power relations (Moffitt, 1994). Concepts that are new within a particular discourse context may become familiar (and therefore more acceptable) if they are understood from the perspective of a different subject position. For example, the introduction of the subject position of "taxpayer" into a health discourse may help persuade members of the general public to look at health issues from an economic perspective. The articulation and disarticulation of both ideas and identities may then be seen as part of the "training" of publics by public relations practitioners in their role as discourse technologists (Fairclough, 1992).

The goal of training is always to establish new ways of thinking and acting as legitimate. Vaara et al. (2006) argued that "legitimacy means a discursively created sense of acceptance in specific discourses" (p. 793). The legitimacy of texts, discourse practices, and associated identities; relationships; and ideas must, therefore, always be considered in terms of the specific discourse contexts in which they are situated (Leitch & Palmer, in press). If a discourse succeeds in achieving legitimacy, it also achieves a certain status as "truth." Clegg, Courpasson, and Phillips (2006, pp. 196–197) argued that legitimacy grounds truth somewhat more than truth grounds legitimacy. This statement captures Clegg's view of Foucault's (1980) concept of power/knowledge (Foucault, 1980; Motion & Leitch, 2009a), which is defined in terms of the inseparability of power and knowledge. Foucault (1980) wrote that "the exercise of power perpetually creates knowledge and, conversely, knowledge constantly induces effects of power" (p. 52). Occupying positions of power within a discourse enables some discourse subjects to determine what is to count as knowledge in that discourse context. A parliament may determine the law, while a judge may determine the truth of guilt or innocence under that law. Conversely, the body of knowledge that makes up the law is itself the source of legitimacy for the subject positions of lawmaker and judge. An understanding of power/knowledge and how it operates within and between discourse contexts is central to the task of transforming discourse (Fairclough, 1992) and, therefore, to the theory and practice of public relations. The discursive understanding that power/knowledge is contextual provides a more sophisticated view of how truth functions within discourse—a topic largely neglected by public relations scholars (Motion & Weaver, 2005).

We now turn to the concept of positioning, which is central to advancing our understanding of the process whereby changes are effected in the relations within organizations, between organizations, between organizations and publics, and within publics. The concept of subject positions has been discussed earlier in terms of the positions available for "subjects to take up" (Harré & Van Langenhove, 1991, p. 395) within a discourse. Positioning is a more active concept that explains the processes whereby subject positions are created for publics and transformed relative to other subject positions. This active use of "positioning" may be traced to the field of marketing, where it refers to the communication strategies that allow one to "place" a certain product among its competitor products (Ries & Trout, 1981, as referred to in Harré & Van Langenhove, 1991). The work of positioning publics and organizations involves attempting to determine, for example, what roles they may play and what power and resources they may draw on relative to one another. The concept of discursive positioning is therefore of central importance to public relations work.

The work of Moffitt (1994, which has been drawn on above in our discussion of subject positions) offered the important insight that members of publics do not hold one subject position, viewpoint, or what she termed *image*, but may instead hold multiple, even contradictory positions, viewpoints, or images at the same time. This insight is important for our understanding of positioning because it reminds us that positioning people within discourse is far more complex than positioning products. Marketing theory, therefore, provides a stimulus for thinking about positioning, but it is only a starting point. A theory of positioning that is sufficiently robust for the purposes of public relations means understanding the multiple subject positions and multiple discourse contexts in play. The notion that individuals may hold multiple positions with a discourse also validates the notion that discourse subjects have "agency": They are able to actively engage in constructing their own subject positions and in attempting to reposition others. Some subject positions within a discourse context may offer strategic options to express personal and social identities, or to adopt a moral stance, while others may confer power and legitimacy (Harré & Van Langenhove, 1991). However, some subject positions that confer neither may be forced or involuntary.

In such situations, publics may react negatively to the organization's public relations strategy by choosing to adopt their own strategies of resistance as a way of regaining power within the discourse (Leitch & Motion, 2008).

Concluding Challenges

In this chapter, we have sought to both reflexively revisit and extend the earlier work of Leitch and Neilson (2001) on core public relations concepts. In addition to considering the original concepts of "publics," "organizations," and "relations," we have directed attention at the concept of "change"—the objective that lies at the heart of much public relations work. Change has been theorized here from a critical discourse perspective, which offers a more contextually nuanced approach than has typically been the case within mainstream public relations theory. A discourse approach to public relations directs our attention to a number of key challenges, including how to navigate the multiplicity of discourses and subject positions within these discourses. Resistance to change by publics—particularly organized publics—and the role of engagement are other significant issues for public relations practice. In our concluding statements, we would like to sketch out some specific challenges for theory development raised within this new discourse framework for public relations in the hope that it will stimulate both debate and further research.

The Challenge of Multiplicity

Multiplicity was a major focus for Leitch and Neilson (2001), and—a decade on—it remains a concept with which we are still grappling in both our practice and our theory development. The multiplicity of subject positions, publics, and discourses along with the inherent polysemy of language itself must be considered during the production of even basic public relations texts, such as news releases. A glance at the popular public relations texts suggests that we are not yet equipping our graduates to deal with such complexities. In addition, the neglect of the power relations between organizations, between organizations and publics, and between publics continues to impoverish our theorizing. The concepts of "publics," "relations," and "change" cannot, however, be understood without a concomitant consideration of both multiplicity and power (see Heath, Motion, & Leitch, Chapter 13, this volume). In practice, organizational attempts to discursively position publics and control meaning may be subverted or resisted, particularly as publics develop organizational structures and power bases and become more sophisticated in the ways in which they engage with system organizations. Resistance is, we contend, growing in significance as a major challenge for public relations practice. We now briefly outline what we see as the key dimensions of this challenge.

The Challenge of Resistance

Clegg et al. (2006, p. 319) argued that resistance is "largely done discursively," which means that to understand the phenomenon of resistance to change, we also need to understand discourse and discourse practices. The act of resistance is defined here as a challenging act in relation to the exercise or intended exercise of power within a particular discourse context (Clegg et al., 2006). As discussed by Thomas and Davies (2005), within the organizational literature, there has been an increasing problematization of the concept of resistance centered on two questions: (1) "What counts as resistance?" and (2) "When does resistance count?" They argued for a broad view of resistance that encompasses a wide range of challenging acts and that operates both at the level of meaning and at the level of identity. They concluded,

> Challenging one subject position involves drawing on an alternative or subverting the original, in a process of reinterpreting dominant discourses. Resistance is therefore not only oppositional and negative kicking back against the subjectivity offered but also a critical and ultimately generative reflexive process. (p. 727)

This view of resistance—as both oppositional and generative or creative—is in stark contrast to the view that resistance is generally deviant or aberrant behavior. Foucault (1980) stated that "there are no relations of power without resistance" (p. 142). Similarly, Clegg et al. (2006) asserted,

> Resistance is normal. Only an inability to see that the nature of social reality is socially constructed and thus appears differently to people who have different interests in its co-construction, negotiation and de-construction, would lead one to see resistance as in some way deviant. (p. 131)

The origins of resistance to change may, then, be traced to different sets of interests or, at least, to perceptions that interests differ. In addition, we would argue that change may impact on identities as well as on interests (Leitch & Davenport, 2005; Rowley & Moldoveanu, 2003). Foucault (1991) contended that actors derive power from the discourse context(s) in which they act. Identities that clash with contentious discourses become oppositional and, therefore, positioned as resistant. Thus, organizations seeking to introduce change should anticipate resistance as a normal response from publics with identity positions or interests potentially affected by the desired change. One common response to resistance or civil unrest is engagement. Traditionally, resistance and engagement have been treated as two separate literatures. Yet engagement often results from acts of resistance and power contestation. Resistance may be thought of as a component of engagement—resistance is an attempt to create a conversation or communicate.

The Challenge of Engagement

When an organization initiates change, it has to, in some way, communicate or engage with publics. And it is through this communication process that organizations construct publics and draw the boundaries that the engagement is going to cross. As Leitch and Neilson (2001) argued, the opinions and ideas attributed to such publics are more likely to be both constructed and interpreted through an organizational lens than to actually reflect the positions chosen by publics. The way in which an organization or individual engages across discourse boundaries will, then, to a large extent be determined by the way in which the publics and discourse boundaries have been constructed. Boundaries are artifacts of the people who draw them and mark out differences between discourses, people, and possible subject positions. What happens to the exercise of engaging across boundaries if we move away from this organization-centered approach to a public-centered approach? Is it really possible to think differently about engagement, and where would that thinking lead us? The first place it would lead, we argue, is to see publics as groups of people who can position their own identities and interests and who perhaps also form some kind of shared understanding of their collective interests and elements of shared identity (Leitch & Neilson, 2001). Second, a more collaborative mode of discourse technologization may emerge. Digital and social media offer numerous possibilities for facilitating conversations about change and collaborative engagement.

Increasingly, protests and resistance are being staged through *YouTube*, which is one of the most popular entertainment sites on the Internet. According to its *Wikipedia* (October 2009) entry, a billion video clips are viewed daily on *YouTube*. In 2006, *YouTube* was purchased by that other giant of the Internet, *Google*, for US$1.65 billion in stock. The eclectic content of *YouTube* defies classification; however, people go to *YouTube* for many reasons, including to share their ideas, thoughts, and imaginings about change initiatives and to discuss them with other people.

YouTube has become a significant global site for what we term *unorganized* engagement between people and organizations but which may have been more typically categorized as resistance. However, we still have very little understanding of how to undertake unorganized community engagement. Creative utilization of digital technologies is required to enable public relations professionals to seek out and understand the ways in which publics are choosing to engage.

At first glance, the advent of social media may be viewed as calling into question a discourse technologization model of public relations and change. However, the fundamental understanding of publics as a series of positions, and of relations as a series of power plays, remains unchanged. Instead, what emerges is a convergence of democratization and more traditional discourse technologization approaches in which attempts to influence are acknowledged as complex, multifaceted processes.

References

Alvesson, M., & Kärreman, D. (2000a). Taking the linguistic turn. *Journal of Applied Behavioral Science, 36*(2), 136–158.

Alvesson, M., & Kärreman, D. (2000b). Varieties of discourse: On the study of organizations through discourse analysis. *Human Relations, 53*(9), 1125–1149.

Anderson, D. L. (2005). "What you'll say is . . ." Represented voice in organizational change discourse. *Journal of Organizational Change Management, 18*(1), 63–77.

Calhoun, C. (1988). Populist politics, communications media and large scale societal integration. *Sociological Theory, 6,* 219–241.

Calhoun, C. (1992). Introduction. In C. Calhoun (Ed.), *Habermas and the public sphere* (pp. 1–48). Cambridge: MIT Press.

Calhoun, C. (1996). *Critical social theory: Culture, history, and the challenge of difference.* Oxford, UK: Blackwell.

Clegg, S. R., Courpasson, D., & Phillips, N. (2006). *Power and organizations.* London: Sage.

Cohen, J., & Arato, A. (1992). *Civil society and political society.* Cambridge: MIT Press.

Coombs, W. T. (1993). Philosophical underpinnings: Ramifications of a pluralist paradigm. *Public Relations Review, 19*(2), 111–119.

Cutlip, S., Center, A., & Broom, G. (1994). *Effective public relations.* Englewood Cliffs, NJ: Prentice Hall.

Fairclough, N. (1992). *Discourse and social change.* Cambridge, MA: Polity Press.

Fairclough, N. (1995). *Critical discourse analysis.* New York: Longman.

Fairclough, N. (2003). *Analysing discourse: Textual analysis for social research.* London: Routledge.

Foucault, M. (1972). *The archaeology of knowledge* (A. Sheridan Smith, Trans.). London: Tavistock. (Original work published 1969)

Foucault, M. (1980). *Power/knowledge: Selected interviews and other writings 1972–1977.* New York: Pantheon Books.

Foucault, M. (1991). Politics and the study of discourse. In G. Burchell, C. Gordon, & P. Miller (Eds.), *The Foucault effect: Studies in governmentality, with two lectures by and an interview with Michel Foucault* (pp. 53–72). Chicago: University of Chicago.

Grunig, J., & Hunt, T. (1984). *Managing public relations.* New York: Holt, Rhinehart & Winston.

Habermas, J. (1987). *The theory of communicative action: The critique of functionalist reason.* Cambridge, MA: Polity Press.

Habermas, J. (1991). *The structural transformation of the public sphere* (T. Burger & F. Lawrence, Trans.). Cambridge: MIT Press. (Original work published 1962)

Hall, S. (1986). On postmodernism and articulation. *Journal of Communication Inquiry, 10*(2), 45–60.

Hardy, C. (2001). Researching organizational discourse. *International Studies of Management & Organization, 31*(3), 25–47.

Hardy, C., Palmer, I., & Phillips, N. (2000). Discourse as a strategic resource. *Human Relations, 53*(9), 1227–1248.

Harré, R., & Van Langenhove, L. (1991). Varieties of positioning. *Journal for the Theory of Social Behaviour, 21*(4), 393–407.

Heath, R. L. (1992). The wrangle in the marketplace: A rhetorical perspective of public relations. In E. L. Toth & R. L. Heath (Eds.), *Rhetorical and critical approaches to public relations* (pp. 37–61). Hillsdale, NJ: Lawrence Erlbaum.

Heath, R. L. (1994). *Management of corporate communication.* Hillsdale, NJ: Lawrence Erlbaum.

Heath, R. L. (1997). *Strategic issues management: Organizations and public policy challenges.* Thousand Oaks, CA: Sage.

Heath, R. L. (2001). A rhetorical enactment rationale for public relations: The good organization communicating well. In R. L. Heath (Ed.), *Handbook of public relations* (pp. 31–50). Thousand Oaks, CA: Sage.

Heracleous, L. (2006). A tale of three discourses: The dominant, the strategic and the marginalized. *Journal of Management Studies, 43*(5), 1059–1087.

Leitch, S., & Davenport, S. (2005). The politics of discourse: Marketization of the New Zealand science and innovation system. *Human Relations, 58*(7), 891–912.

Leitch, S., & Motion, J. (2008, July). *The discourse strategies of resistance.* Paper presented at the European Group of Organization Studies (EGOS) Conference, Amsterdam.

Leitch, S., & Neilson, D. (2001). Bringing publics into public relations: New theoretical frameworks for practice. In R. Heath (Ed.), *Handbook of public relations* (pp. 127–138). Thousand Oaks, CA: Sage.

Leitch, S., & Palmer, I. (in press). Analyzing texts in context: Current practices and new protocols for critical discourse analysis in organization studies. *Journal of Management Studies.*

Maguire, S., & Hardy, C. (2006). The emergence of new global institutions: A discursive perspective. *Organization Studies, 27*(1), 7–29.

Moffitt, M. (1994). Collapsing and integrating concepts of "public" and "image" into a new theory. *Public Relations Review, 20*(2), 159–170.

Motion, J., & Leitch, S. (1996). A discursive perspective from New Zealand: Another world view. *Public Relations Review, 22*(3), 297–309.

Motion, J., & Leitch, S. (2009a). On Foucault: A toolbox for public relations. In O. Ihlen, B. van Ruler, & M. Fredriksson (Eds.), *Public relations and social theory* (pp. 83–102). New York: Routledge.

Motion, J., & Leitch, S. (2009b). The transformational potential of public policy discourse. *Organization Studies, 30*(10), 1045–1061.

Motion, J., Leitch, S., & Brodie, R. (2003). Equity in co-branded identity: The case of Adidas and the All Blacks. *European Journal of Marketing, 37*(7/8), 1080–1094.

Motion, J., & Weaver, C. K. (2005). A discourse perspective for critical public relations research: Life sciences and the battle for truth. *Journal of Public Relations Research, 17*(10), 49–67.

Phillips, N., & Hardy, C. (2002). *Discourse analysis: Investigating processes of social construction.* Thousand Oaks, CA: Sage.

Rawlins, B. L., & Bowen, S. A. (2005). Publics. In R. L. Heath (Ed.), *Encyclopedia of public relations* (pp. 718–721). Thousand Oaks, CA: Sage.

Rowley, T., & Moldoveanu, M. (2003). When will stakeholders act? An interest and identity-based model of stakeholder group mobilization. *Academy of Management Review, 28*(2), 204–220.

Slack, J. (1996). The theory and method of articulation in cultural studies. In D. Morley & K.-H. Chen (Eds.), *Stuart Hall: Critical dialogues in cultural studies* (pp. 112–130). New York: Routledge.

Thomas, R., & Davies, A. (2005). What have the feminists done for us? Feminist theory and organizational resistance. *Organization, 12*(5), 711–740.

Vaara, E., & Tienari, J. (2008). A discursive perspective on legitimation strategies in multinational corporations. *Academy of Management Review, 33*(4), 985–993.

Vaara, E., Tienari, J., & Laurila, J. (2006). Pulp and paper fiction: On the discursive legitimation of global industrial restructuring. *Organization Studies, 27*(6), 789–810.

CHAPTER 8

Correspondence(s) to Reality

A Reconstructive Approach to Public Relations

Günter Bentele

A reconstructive approach to public relations was initially developed—as a frame of reference—in the context of analyzing *communication norms for public communication*, for instance, by focusing on journalistic norms of truth and objectivity (Bentele, 1982, 1988c). By reflecting on such key reporting standards within an epistemological, historical, and theory of science framework, the analysis put forward in my "Habilitation" thesis (Bentele, 1988b, 2008) was epistemologically grounded to take account of a central aspect of media reception—the perceived *credibility* of the media. Subsequently, this also incorporated a reflection of *ethical norms in public relations* (Bentele, 1992a), of *references to reality* made by television (Bentele, 1992b) and public relations (Bentele, 1994b), as well as the development of a *theory of public trust* (Bentele, 1994a). In this regard, since the 1980s, theoretical considerations were based on biologically founded evolutionary epistemology (EE), which can be described only briefly within the limited confines of this analysis.

The term *reconstructive approach* refers to a concept of reconstruction, which defines a process of *cognitive (and communicative) model building*, in other words, the process whereby a structural-isomorphic model is created by the observing system, a model that "fits" to the focus of observation. The concept and process of reconstruction therefore refers—in relation to the perceptive and cognitive process—to the relations existing between *the observer and observed*, or (in traditional terms) between *the subject and object*. In terms of the communication process, the concept refers to relations between *the characterization and the signified, the description and what is described*, as well as *the media reality and reality as such*. This process is *cognitively* reconstructed in the *observation* of reality. In the process of the communicative *description* of reality (by signs, words, texts, and topics), natural and social reality is *communicatively reconstructed*. Other observers do this in exactly the same way. Moreover, if they also reconstruct observed reality in communicative forms (texts), this reconstructive character of texts ensures that different communication partners have the impression that they are communicatively referring to *the same* reality.

Communication that is to facilitate understanding requires the same referential realities.

This approach is epistemologically founded and was developed in the critical discussion of constructivist approaches (Bentele, 1993). Moreover, it can be linked with *system theories* that are "recoupled" with the theories of society based on action such as those represented by, for example, Giddens's (1984) theory of structuration or Schimank's (2000) actor theoretical approach to sociology. Although this connection cannot be shown here, a basic assumption features the existence of a functionally structured society (Luhmann, 1995) and, therefore, the existence of functional subsystems, such as the economy, law, politics, education, and science. However, these aspects include *social systems with a capacity for action* as, for instance, companies, political parties, ministries, associations, research communities, social movements, religious sects, or political protest movements. Their actions generally occur within preexisting structures that are set by the systems, while simultaneously producing the action of organizations and the structure of the defining system. In this sense, it is possible to speak of a duality of action and structure (Giddens, 1984, pp. 25–28). The social systems with the capacity to act—generally collective actors (Willke, 1996, 178ff.)—are structural elements of the functioning systems and mutually define each other as strategically calculating. *Specific actor constellations* and *dynamic (action-based) developments* emerge from mutual observation, the collection of information about each other, and interpretation of such information. Social dynamics result from the interplay between these levels.

Based on this outline, it seems reasonable to differentiate between the *three levels of analysis*[1] for the purposes of public relations theory, which meanwhile have largely become commonly accepted in a social science discourse. At the *first level of microanalysis*, observation and analysis are focused on the action taken by individual actors, their motives and objectives, the *rules* that they use and the effects of their actions, and so on. On the *second—organizational—level*, the description focuses on the communication process within the organization and between organizations and their social environments ("publics," "stakeholders"). Organization is understood as the level that mediates between social functional systems, society as a social system in its entirety, and the individual actor. In this case, the analysis centers particularly on the tasks, functions, actions, or—to adopt the terms of systems theory—*decision and action programs* of the public relations organization in connection with the suprastatus of the "parent organization" or client. The *third level* of analysis refers to the *macro-analytical level*, on which questions are posed as to the relations to society, for instance, the question as to whether or to what extent public relations itself can reasonably be outlined as a social functional system or part of a social functional system (e.g., "publicistic system," part of the "public sphere"), or what kind of social system it otherwise portrays. This chapter focuses attention on the first two aforementioned levels.

Structures and Processes of Public Relations or Communication Management

On the first two levels of analysis, public relations is initially viewed as a *structured, communicative action* on the part of individual actors in *organizational contexts*, that is, either *within* social organizations or in systemic relations *with* organizations. *The organizational forms*, within which public relations occurs, as action by actors, are first, *communication departments* within organizations (companies, political organizations, associations, NGOs, etc.) and second, specialized *service organizations* such as public relations firms or advertising agencies, consultancy firms, and so on. In addition, *individual actors* who contribute consultancy and communications services to their clients never exclusively work *in isolation* (e.g., writing press releases and compiling information brochures, organizing a press conference, and advising on redesigning the company logo). They cooperate with individual actors (e.g., with freelancers). At least their service always represents an *interaction* between the client and the commissioned party. Therefore, the *organizational context* is a constituent element of delivery of the communications service, even if individual actors accomplish this service. Within organizational contexts, the actors perform in specific *positions* and *roles*—that is, *a package of behavioral expectations.* Vertically, management positions, *operational* and *support*-related positions (e.g., secretaries), can be distinguished. The first two positions are referred to within empirical public relations role research, for instance, as "communication manager" and "communication technician" (cf. the summary in Grunig, Grunig, & Dozier, 2002, 196ff.). Positions or roles are organized within different *organizational forms* (Kieser & Kubicek, 1992) such as lines, divisional structure, or matrix organization. *Horizontally,* a structure is differentiated according to the object or communication areas: subdepartments or parallel communication departments such as press and media relations, sponsoring, public affairs, investor relations, and location communication, to mention a few examples. They are organized according to the respective *publics* or *instrumental orientation.*

As with all social systems, organizations only exist *by means of* communication (Luhmann, 2000, p. 62). Communication occurs within organizations, and organizations communicate—as collective actors—with their external world (Theis, 1994). *Internal* communication processes can be distinguished as follows:

1. Those that proceed relatively *uncontrolled* (informal communication such as conversations at the lunch table, at the coffee machine, creating rumors) and those that are consciously *controlled* by the organization, that is, internal communication processes.
2. In one sense, this includes the processes that are accomplished by means of (internal) media and communication instruments (e.g., notice board, employee magazines, intranet). However, it also includes procedures that occur in preparation of the actual (internal and external) communication processes, particularly in communication departments themselves. These are oriented toward planning, implementation, and production of communication and organization-specific media. Communicative *products* are generated as *results* (texts, images, topics, public relations media, and events).

Depending on how structured, differentiated, and specialized the process is represented as being, we can refer to the three types of public relations as *unordered, routine,* or *strategically planned.* Insofar as the process approaches the ideal model of strategically planned and implemented public relations, the concepts of communication management or strategic communication are appropriate. Here, the division of work and hierarchically organized *process of control* are to be described as *communication management* (CM), which incorporates the complex processes of (environment) observation, analysis, strategy development, organization, implementation, and evaluation of organization-related communication processes. In the extreme case, this process occurs as an unstructured or only slightly structured chain of action of an individual (within the organization management).[2] In a large company, in terms of the division of labor, this process is organized vertically and horizontally and all the departments are responsible for the individual phases and areas. In this process, *communication instruments* (e.g., press releases, employee magazines), *methods* (e.g., media resonance analysis), and *communication technologies* are implemented, which can involve complex procedures (e.g., issues management or campaigns). The input of these kinds of instruments, media, and procedures ideally relies on strategies.

Strategies are plans of chains of action, which involve conditions and show *objective* and *temporal* dimensions. These are—within a system-theoretical context—also known as *programs* (Luhmann, 1995, p. 317). All internal and external communication programs depend on the available personal and financial *resources.* The chief executive levels within the organization generally take the decision about the magnitude and orientation of organizations' internal communication resources, although the resource allocation also depends on the *external* conditions of the organization (e.g., the level of economic activity).

References to Reality and Reality Reconstruction

Basic Theories: Evolutionary Epistemology (EE) and Hypothetic Realism

Underlying theories basic to the reconstructive approach are *EE* and *hypothetic realism.* EE[3] is an important and—at least in the German-speaking countries—a widely accepted epistemological approach, which shows biologically based solutions for very old epistemological questions and problems. Vollmer (1975, 28ff.) formulated 10 basic postulates of this approach, including the following: (1) the *reality postulate*—a real world is existing independent of perception and consciousness; (2) the *structure postulate*—the real world is structured; (3) the *continuity postulate*—between all areas of reality, there exists a continuous (historical and causal) nexus; (4) the *postulate of the consciousness of the other*—other individuals (human and animalistic individuals) also have sensations and consciousness; (5) *the mutual reaction postulate*—our sense organs are affected by the real world; (6) the *brain function postulate*—thinking and consciousness are functions of the brain; and (7) the *objectivity postulate*—scientific statements should be objective.

Based on these postulates, Vollmer developed a "hypothetic realism," which was mentioned and introduced earlier by Campbell (1974) and Lorenz (1975). *Hypothetic realism* means, basically, that *all propositions about reality are hypothetical.* Realisms, hypothetical realism including are incapable of proof. But many arguments can be taken into discussion that make this realistic position plausible. Arguments, to mention a few, include psychological evidence, the realism of language, the simple structure of this hypothesis, the heuristic value and the success of this hypothesis, the functional convergence of different "knowledge/cognition apparatuses" (a "cognitive apparatus" consists of perception organs [e.g., eye, ear] plus brain), the constancy and stability of perception, the invariance of science, and some others.

The process of knowledge is differentiated on several levels (perception, experience, and thinking/cognition). At all three levels, three basic "mechanisms" are working: *selectivity, perspectivity,* and *constructivity.* These mechanisms work together and are inevitable. They build the "subjective character" (traditionally formulated) of the knowledge process. At least in the level of perception, selectivity, perspectivity, and constructivity can be shown empirically. Examples can be given regarding the perception of colors ("color circle"), the perception of light, the perception of space, and so on.

Moreover, many arguments can be mentioned to support the notion that the *structures of the knowledge process* and the *structures of reality* are similar, that both these entities stand in a relationship of *structural isomorphism.* This structural isomorphism can be called by another name: It is a kind of "fit" between the structures of reality and the structures of perception and maybe also the structures of the knowledge process. At the level of perception, it can be clearly shown that there must be a fit between reality structures and perception structures. Why? From a physical point of view, visible light (what we are able to see) is only a very small sector in the electromagnetic spectrum, which is much broader. We cannot see X-radiation, nor can we see infrared or radio waves. Our eyes are capable of processing information from only a very small sector in the entire electromagnetic spectrum. Similarly, our ears, which are our biological instruments to perceive audible frequencies, are capable of hearing only within a very small range in the whole spectrum of audible frequencies. We cannot hear very low or very high frequencies. But in the evolution of certain species, other perception instruments have evolved. For instance, bats have evolved a mechanism of echolocation to orient themselves in their natural environment. So the evolution of the eye of terrestrial animals (which live on earth) and humans can be seen as an adaptation (fit) of these organisms to their natural environment, in which these organisms have evolved. Vollmer (1975, 1985, 1986, 2002) and others call the natural environment of human beings the "mesocosmos," which means a cosmos with medial dimensions, medial distances, medial velocity, and so on. We are not able to perceive the structures of the macrocosmos and microsomos with our natural biological perception organs. And our brain (at least we know this) has certain difficulties imagining processes in the microcosmos and macrocosmos. Because we cannot observe these dimensions directly, we have to build (mesocosmic) models to improve our capacity to imagine and understand these dimensions. But we are quite well endowed biologically to survive in the mesocosmos.

There are certainly similarities between EE, which was sketched out here very briefly, and the biologically argued concepts of "radical constructivism," as it was developed by philosophers such as Heinz von Foerster (1995, 1999) and Ernst von Glasersfeld (1987, 1992), or biologists such as Humberto Maturana and Francesco J. Varela (1987). One of the common features between the two approaches is that *construction* is a basic mechanism of the knowledge process. But whereas radical constructivism argues against the possibility of objective knowledge, the possibility of truth (knowledge can only be viable from this point of view), EE argues for the possibility and probability of objective knowledge, scientific truth, and also tries to explain this possibility by the "fit mechanism."

Some representatives of *radical constructivism* set the reference to reality to one side by way of the *construction* metaphor (media reality is *not* reproduction *but* construction). However, this does not solve the theoretical problem. Von Glasersfeld (1987, 1992) attempted to approach the problem by the *viability concept.* Viability, that is, cognitive representations' fitness for survival, is correctly introduced as a concept in contradistinction to a naive concept of copy. However, it is no solution to the basic problem of the production of *correct* or *true* statements, because it cannot be explained by this concept, *why* some ideas are viable while others are not. In addition, the constructivist von Glasersfeld (1987) argued—contradictory to his own position—*realistically:* "In order to survive, the organism only has to 'cope with' the restricting conditions in his environment. Expressed metaphorically: it has to force itself through the bars of the cage of these conditions" (p. 137). This is (involuntarily) a key argument for realistic epistemological theory: For the observing system, the point is to recognize these "cage bars" as something that exists and to have the capacity to distinguish the situation from a state in which the bars are not present. This is possible in a much more convincing way with a suitability (fitting) concept of EE (Vollmer, 2002).

The crucial difference between radical constructivism and EE, therefore, lies in the epistemological position: EE advocates and argues for a realistic position, that is, the aforementioned *hypothetical-realistic* position (Lorenz, 1975; Vollmer, 1975). Such a position can also be compatible with the approaches of systems theory, as made clear by the assertion put forward by the systems theorist Helmut Willke, a former colleague of Niklas Luhmann at the University of Bielefeld, Germany, who regards the position of a "reflective reconstructivism" as more appropriate than "radical constructivism":

> Note that this does not mean adopting "radical constructivism" . . . as epistemology. Rather, a *reflected reconstructivism* [italics added] seems

> appropriate, thus a process of gaining recognition, whereby the cognitive system may be exclusively linked to one's *own* means of observation and understanding and can therefore find grounds for the object of its recognition, not as "objective" or "real," nor in fact as "reality." However, on the other hand, this does not mean that the cognitive system simply invents some arbitrary products of fantasy and can define these as the correct recognition. Evidently, a plausible relation is required between explanation and the explained, an alignment, "a goodness of the fit" . . . , a kind of key-lock relationship. (Willke, 1996, 167ff.)[4]

Construction or Reconstruction?

In the same way as it is possible to criticize a lack of reference to the actor in some versions of systems theory (Schimank, 1985), I note a *missing reference to reality* in many approaches adopted by systems theory and constructivism with respect to the theory of communication and public relations. Merten and Westerbarkey (1994), for example, defined public relations—taking a (radical) constructivistic position—as the "process of intentional and contingent construction of desirable realities by production and anchoring images in public" (p. 219). Setting aside the fact that in this definition the idea of "desirable reality" remains unclear, as Merten (2000, p. 251) himself acknowledged, this definition leaves open whether and, as applicable, which *constraints* exist to define what is meant by "desirable" and how these desirable realities behave in relation to the empirically determined organizational realities. Press releases or business reports, as constructed "desirable" public relations realities by the media, are not Christmas wish lists—neither are journalistic news or reports. On the contrary, they have to be "constructed" according to the guidelines and within the context of observed reality. To that extent, therefore, they represent "reconstructed entities." The reasons for discussing this reference to the reality of communication processes and products (cf. texts) as a whole and, in particular, to the public relations process in a theoretical sense lie, first, in the fact that the references to reality occur and are reflected in concepts such as truth, objectivity, precision, accuracy, credibility, and trust. These qualities are just as important in professional practice as in scientific reflection. Second, if an attempt is made to avoid the discussion, significant theoretical problems emerge, and questions remain unanswered.

The Reconstructive Model of Observation and Communication

Perception, Observation, and Reconstruction

In my *reconstructive* model (see Bentele, 1988b, 1994a, 2008), I argue on the basis of the position of "hypothetical realism." Every *construction* of *cognitive* and *communicative reality* can only be adequately described and understood if its *reference to reality* is appreciated, in other words, if these processes are regarded as *reconstructive processes*. In this sense, *reconstruction* can be defined as the information, perception, and observation process, whereby at different levels they process (perception, cognition, and communication) they process reality that exists independently of living beings by virtue of their faculties of perception and cognition. This occurs in such a way that isomorphic (structurally similar) constructs or, more precisely, *reconstructs* emerge. *Cognitive* reconstruction occurs in human perceptual and cognitive processes; *communicative* reconstruction occurs within human communication processes. This is to say that they also occur during the production and comprehension of *communicative realities*. Thus, reconstruction processes also take place in processes of *public communication* that emerge through public relations activities, advertising, and journalistic activities. Of course, reconstruction processes are not the only possible processes to describe reality.

There are many forms of fictitious descriptions (or constructions) of reality (e.g., in entertainment programs, movies, or literature) with the help of different media. But if we look at forms of reality descriptions such as news reporting (in journalism) or press releases or annual reports (in public relations), we expect references to reality that guarantee a kind of structural isomorphism.

Reality as such, which can be understood as everything that ever did, does, or will exist, is defined in terms of information theory. In this case, the assumption is that reality *potentially* "contains" an endless array of many different pieces of information. Reality cannot be grasped in *its entirety* or as *a whole entity* by human perception or cognitive activity, at a specific point in time or within the duration of an individual's lifetime, or within the existence of humankind. From the limitless and abundant *potential information* that fulfills the function of *information offers* for an individual's brain, a specific part of reality is *actualized* within the human perception, cognitive process, and communicative process (Bentele & Bystrina, 1978, 96ff.).[5] While observation of a (biological, physiological, or social) system is always an operation *internal to the system* and based on the generation of distinctions, these are not made *arbitrarily* or even by pure *chance*. Rather, they are made in accordance with the existing *rules*, in accordance with the previously existing objective and subjective information, that is, *also* in accordance with the *observed pattern or structure*. For this reason, the process of actualization is not only a process of *construction* but indeed a process of *reconstruction*.

The production of communicative realities occurs as the production of signs, texts, images, sounds, noises, television programs, advertising spots, or scientific theories. The analysis of communicative realities relies on at least three *main levels: signs, texts*, and *topics/themes or issues*. Production and reception on these levels occur according to specific (human-specific) *rules* that develop historically and change accordingly. Moreover, the rules themselves do not emerge *arbitrarily*, or purely by chance, but in accordance with *constraints* that are to be discovered in social reality and the necessities of human coexistence. The actualization of potential information means to select from a specific perspective (*perspectivity*) and a wide variety (*selection*), thereby generating new information (*construction*). This initially occurs as a reflective process and, in a second stage, with the aid of material media. The material use of information in the mode of communicative and technical media (speech, language, writing, images, texts, books, brochures, films) also initiates the process of communication for others and—as soon as the public realm is involved—the process of public *communication* that many people observe.

Basic Principles of Knowledge and Communication: Perspectivity, Selectivity, and Constructivity

Within the reconstruction process, three essential *basic principles* (also on different levels) play a key role: *perspectivity, selectivity*, and *constructivity*. Every observation and every description of anything takes place from a *specific perspective*. This is necessitated by every observer's and each communication's reference to time and place. The inclusion of specific spatial and temporal perspectives is *constituent* for each actor who observes his or her environment or initiates communicative contact with it. Furthermore, in a social context, there is the necessity to act from within *social perspectives. Perspectives of age* and *gender* may be tied to biological facts, but they also have important social dimensions. Income, education, lifestyle, political interest, and links to political parties are factors that constitute *social perspectives* and thus influence the observation and communication process. *Spatial, temporal*, and *social perspectives* are to that extent constituent for every observation and communication. *Changing perspective* is possible and frequently occurs. However, it is not possible to include all or even only 100 perspectives *simultaneously*. Observing any one subject and communication with any one individual, we can achieve a change of perspective—this may be less or more so, depending on the individual; and it is a skill that must be learned. In public communication conveyed by the media, an important basic principle must be accepted.[6]

In the process of perception and recognition as well as in communication, *selectivity* is an equally fundamental principle and constituent necessity. Selection occurs in every communication process, including public communication (journalism, public relations), in the production, the dissemination/broadcasting, and, equally, the process of comprehension.[7]

In language and speech communication, communication partners select from a particular vocabulary; and they choose specific sound patterns, style and grammatical forms, and semantic and pragmatic forms. This to a great extent is learned in social groups in the human socialization process. In public communication within the relevant responsible organizations, that is, the media, specific *selection patterns* and selection procedures emerge as, for instance, the procedure of selecting information (news) according to *news factors*. One rule of self-presentation of organizations, which is in fact a function of public relations, forbids characterizing one's own organization in a consistently negative or too negative light. Selection occurs not only in the process of surveillance/monitoring the environment but also in generic public relations communication on the three levels of signs, texts, and topics/issues.

The aspect of *construction* of communicative (and media) realities is essential to the understanding of cognition and communication as a whole. During the process of perception and observation, our brain constructs cognitive realities. As actors in the communication process, we construct *communicative realities*, which can be clearly distinguished from other forms of realities (natural, material realities, social realities). However, if the reference to reality of the construction process is not implicitly included in the scientific description, this represents an inadmissible *reduction* of the entire process, which leaves out essential aspects, thus preventing an adequate description.

Yet if the constraints that are inherent to the process of monitoring and communication ("reality constraints") are included in the reflection, the concept of "reconstruction" is quickly arrived at. What establishes the constraints and controls the *perspectives* for the media's construction of reality is not only the observing and monitoring system but also the *structures of reality* themselves. These control the *selection process* within the different phases of communication management and, thus, the *constructivity potential*. What might that imply? In observation and the communication process, yet also in the persuasive dimension of organizational communication, there is a kind of coercion, a necessity to orient according to *reality structures*. This insight has nothing to do with an outright copy of reality, a pure mirroring, but has to be understood as "structural isomorphism," that is, structural similarities between description and the described and between text and social reality. For the public relations process, this means, for instance, that a press release or information released in a press conference with respect to the issue at hand must represent this "correctly." Another example is the requirement for the annual report to reflect the economic situation "adequately," or that a so-called ad hoc announcement of a public limited company contains correct and relevant information. In the sphere of investor relations, where everything is about investors' money, it is essential that the reference to reality of the information produced by the company be *legally* approved.[8]

Types of Events and Rules of the Correspondence to Reality. For professional public relations communicators—individual or corporate actors—"external" reality is primarily represented as a complex of *facts* (*actual situation*) and *events*. These events (cf. Figure 8.1 with regard to the following comments) occur on a natural basis (*natural* events), are socially initiated or

Figure 8.1 Model of Social Information and Communication Relationships in the Reconstructive Approach

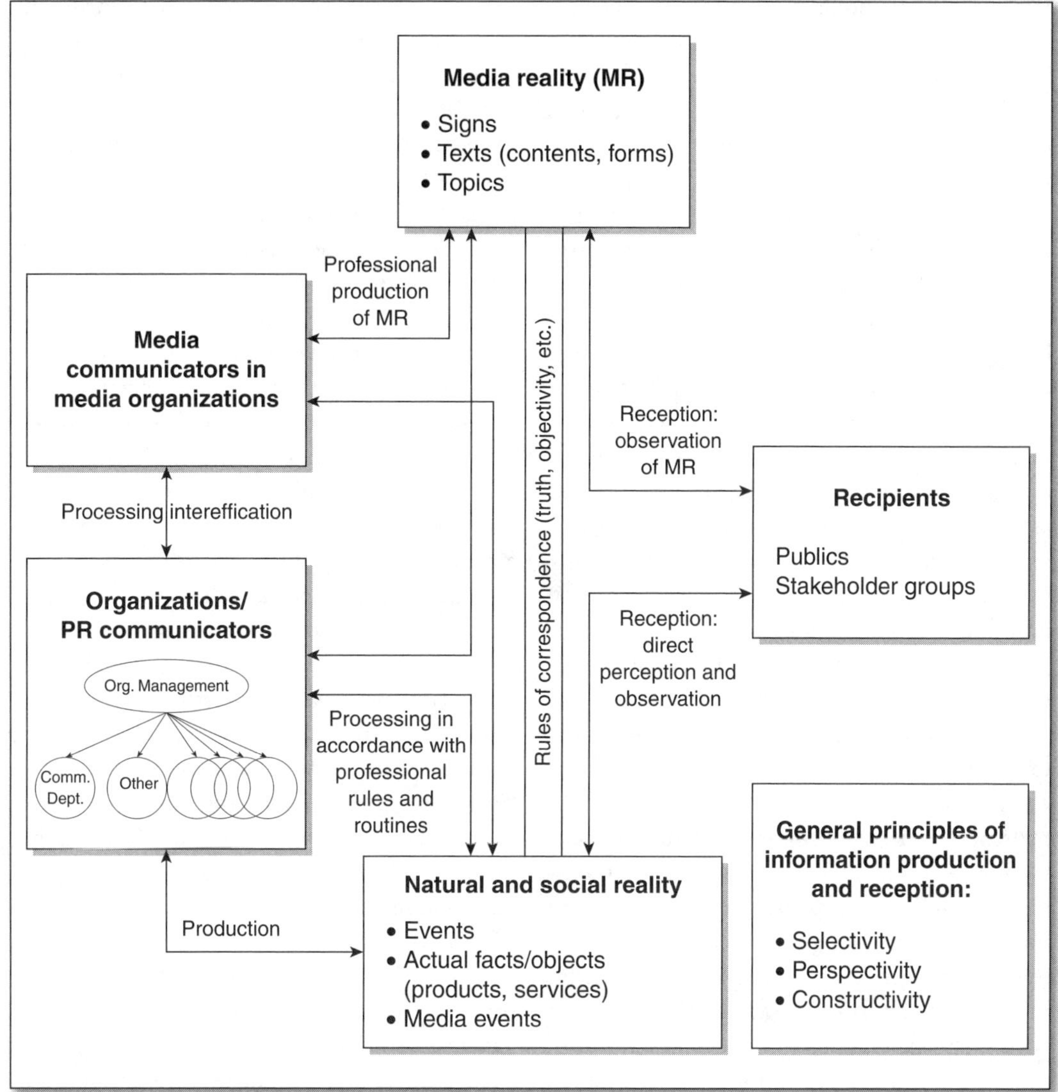

constructed (*social* events), or else are specifically defined for public communication (*media* events such as press conferences, public relations events). Events are perceived in accordance with occupation-related, media-related, and genre-related *rules* and *routines*; they are reconstructed and, in a second phase, translated into *texts* and *topics*, in accordance with media-specific rules and codes.[9] In the case of *media events*, not only the texts but also the events themselves are actually *constructed* in accordance with such or similar rules and professional routines within a social process (social construction) and are linked with texts and mostly with topics.

In the practice of public relations, the existing *rules of the correspondence to reality* are those that set out how the *facts in public relations texts* (e.g., press releases, company reports) are to be accurate and undistorted, how word and deed are to be consistent, and how the generated external company *images* should correspond with the perception the company affiliates and employees have of that company.

The assumption may be that communications activities of actors in social organizations and the media essentially generate the public sphere—understood as a communication system that is comparable with a public arena (Neidhardt, 1994). In this case, it may be observed that communication processes also occur, on the one hand, between public relations actors, public relations organizations, and the professional public relations system and, on the other hand, between journalistic actors and the media as journalistic organizations. These processes can be described as perspective-related selection, construction, and reconstruction processes and subjected to empirical investigation in terms of their reciprocal induction and adaptation action.[10]

The communicative "products" resulting from both communicator subsystems (journalism and public relations) emerge as journalistic texts (in the extended sense) and thus as parts of *media reality*. Texts are combined with other texts, descriptions are commented on, and comments are commented on, again and are building (public) topics/issues. (Public) topics are understood here as sign or meaning complexes that emerge in a complex communication process in an interplay of (a) observed facts and events, (b) expressions of actors (descriptions, interpretations, and evaluations of facts/events), and (c) statements about the statements. Different types of communicators (journalists, public relations professionals, "functional communicators" such as CEOs, politicians, etc.) generate the topics in the context of a historically created reservoir of themes. The topics' career, duration, acceptance, and relevance with the publics depend on how the publics perceive the relationship between the underlying facts/events and the topics themselves (Bentele, Liebert, & Seeling, 1997).

The *thematic function*, that is, the generation, production, and availability of relevant topics for the public, can—at the social macrolevel—be viewed as a key function not only of media but also of public relations.

Media reality can be differentiated for the purposes of analysis into (a) communicative realities of the media as a whole, (b) media reality of specific media, and (c) topics and texts on different levels as a *communicatively constructed* reality. This construction happens in a complex process with different actors. However, in its informative components (news, reports, etc.), it is essentially *reconstructed* media reality, in accordance with existing patterns of reference to reality. Information generated in this way is, in manifold ways, *in relation* to the original potential or currently available information and information structures. The degree of structural *correspondence or isomorphism* between already existing (natural and social) realities on the one hand and media realities that were constructed by the communicators on the other is controlled by professional *norms of adequacy*, such as *truthful reporting* or *objectivity*, and can be examined in this regard. The degree of *adequacy* of media realities is simultaneously a quality criterion for professional communication.

But there is a necessary and indispensable, principal *difference* between social realities on one hand and media realities on the other. This difference between actual facts and events on the one side and their (media) representations on the other also holds true in the case of "media events." Wherever an element of social and communicative reality is built, is organized by public relations professionals (e.g., a press conference, an anniversary event) to generate public awareness and reporting, the description of such an event in the media is also subject to the same *rules of adequacy* for this event type (truth, objectivity) as the reconstruction of other event types. The most *adequate reconstruction* of events that is possible can be characterized as a basic form of the—necessary—*correspondence to reality* (see Figure 8.1).

The *recipients* or the *audience* who are involved in the game as *publics* or *stakeholder groups* observe media realities and, therefore, perceive the facts, events, and media events for the most part only *indirectly* via the mass-communicative construction and reconstruction process. However, this is true only for the most part. This is because, on the one hand, *segments of the audience* participate directly in the events as *participants* or *concerned parties* in relation to reported events. These individuals (similar to journalists reporting on location) can *compare* directly and subjectively experience reality with media reality within the context of a *reality comparison* (Kepplinger, 1992). Every person who participated personally in a certain event (a football game or another sporting event, a political event, a war, etc.), on the other hand, and will later be part of the audience reading or looking at the part of media reality that refers directly to the event, can make a comparison with the social reality of which he or she was part. However, by far the greater part of the audience does not participate in events. These persons will, for instance, have at least a partially independent perception of reality than that reflected in media reports by gaining information through other media sources. In this case, this part of the audience can compare *different information sources* produced by different media.

The audience can evaluate the adequacy of information contained within media reality through both the *reality comparison* and also the *media comparison*. This results in indicators for the perceived *credibility* of reporting of the media as a whole and the professional communicators that are involved in the media (Bentele, 1988a, 1988b). The audience's possibility of undertaking such evaluations of credibility of media reality should be a key cause, historically and functionally, in the emergence of *adequacy rules* (truth, objectivity) on the part of the communicator. If the communicators within communicator systems do not observe these rules, media reality contains perceptible *distortions* or *discrepancies* for the recipients. The audience can perceive *discrepancies* between directly observed parts of reality and media realities (reality comparison) or among the different media realities (media comparison).

Examples of discrepancies are untruths, lies, but also taboos, perceptible glossing over, the omission of negative information, and so on. Perceived discrepancies lead to a decline in credibility and trust values in communication. This trust mechanism (Bentele, 1994a) not only exists between audience and communicator systems but also *between* each of the communicator systems. Journalists also estimate their public relations information sources as more or less credible due to their professional experiences with public relations representatives. This is also a reason for the *rules of adequacy and appropriateness* that exist in public relations professional practice, at least since the times of Ivy L. Lee. *Corporate* (or generally organizational) *transparency* is an important control mechanism, by which statements of media reality can be verified. The more real transparency in politics, business, and other parts of society occurs, the more possibilities there are to verify statements given in public discourse. But this is not a matter of importance to organizations only. There is a kind of transparency game, in which media play a decisive role. Media organizations can force politicians, companies, and the like to show a greater degree of transparency.

Concluding Remarks

Communicators and recipients expect that *media reality*—at least if it does not concern entertainment, but types of informative texts (news reports, etc.)—is in an *adequate* or "*fitting*" *relation* to these events. In this case, similar *rules of the correspondence to reality* are valid for public relations instruments, public relations media, and mass media texts. Of course, due to different perspectives, different *topic constructions* are possible with regard to these social realities. However, if such texts and media representations go beyond a certain "corridor" of reality, the *discrepancies* between immediately experienced reality and the media's version of reality, which is to reflect the former, becomes so vast that this creates problems of credibility and trust. It is very difficult to define precisely the limits and boundaries of these "reality corridors," because the limits are flexible to a certain degree. But it is quite obvious that the corridors are limited. Normally, we can evaluate in our everyday life whether a part of media reality is within the reality corridor or not. Especially in centrally controlled, totalitarian societies, observable discrepancies can be identified between social reality and the state's desired images, insofar as these emerge as negative propaganda effects.

An adequate reconstruction of reality in perception and thought is—for human individuals—a biologically explicable achievement. Adequate reconstruction of reality by public relations and media organizations is a socially justified necessity. If the correspondence rules are hurt, this leads to sanction of losses of credibility and trust. This communicative mechanism seems to be a very crucial feature within the public communication process. This mechanism not only ensures central functions and necessities of human life, such as orientation and correct and accurate information, but also helps those who think that values such as truth (Frankfurt, 2006) and objectivity are not at all out of fashion.

Notes

1. See also Ronneberger and Rühl (1992, 249ff.) for a slightly different definition of the three dimensions.

2. The new sole trader company observes the organizational environment, decides after brief reflection (analysis) to provide the press with information (strategy development), also acts on this decision (implementation), and 2 days later reads the newspaper article (evaluation) that published its information.

3. Cf. instead of many other contributions Campbell (1974), Irrgang (2001), Lorenz (1975), Vollmer (1975, 1985, 1986, 2002), and also Popper (1984). In Bentele (1988b, 1992b, 2008), EE is introduced as a basic theory for communication science.

4. Willke (1996) represented a "functionally genetic" approach in systems theory. This also appears to be ideally compatible with the author's central thoughts, for example, on genetic semiotics (Bentele, 1984) or the functionally integrative strata approach (Bentele, 1997).

5. This idea is entirely compatible with the notion of a basic operation of *observation*, understood as the *determination of a distinction*, as widely acknowledged in systems theory; cf., for example, Willke (1999, 12ff.), Luhmann (1995), and Kneer and Nassehi (1994, 95ff.).

6. When viewing a landscape, with and without a telescope, it is possible to switch quickly from a near to a far perspective. A wall with 40 television monitors can simultaneously show a hotel detective the different rooms and corridors in the hotel; and in television news, the change of perspective is a very important means to facilitate an insight into wider areas of reality.

7. Cf., in this regard, Luhmann's (1995, 139ff.) communication concept that understands communication as "processing of selection" and as a "synthesis" of three selections: information, utterance, and understanding.

8. Cf., for instance, the contributions of Zitzmann, Taubert, and Leis in Kirchhoff and Piwinger (2001).

9. Cf. for the analysis of media-specific codes, for instance, Bentele (1985). On the media-specific routine concept, see also Saxer, Gantenbein, Gollmer, Hättenschwiler, and Schanne (1986).

10. Cf. in this context the intereffication model developed by Bentele, Liebert, and Seeling (1997).

References

Bentele, G. (1982). Objektivität in den Massenmedien: Versuch einer historischen und systematischen Begriffsklärung [Objectivity and mass media: An essay concerning a historical and systematic disambiguation]. In G. Bentele & R. Ruoff (Eds.), *Wie objektiv sind unsere Medien?* [How objective are our media?] (pp. 111–155). Frankfurt am Main, Germany: Fischer.

Bentele, G. (1984). *Zeichen und Entwicklung: Vorüberlegungen zu einer genetischen Semiotik* [Signs and evolution: Considerations toward a genetic theory of semiotics]. Tübingen, Germany: Narr.

Bentele, G. (1985). Die Analyse von Mediensprachen am Beispiel von Fernsehnachrichten [The analysis of media languages: TV news as an example]. In G. Bentele & E. W. B. Hess-Lüttich (Eds.),

Zeichengebrauch in Massenmedien: Zum Verhältnis von sprachlicher und nichtsprachlicher Information in Hörfunk, Film und Fernsehen [The use of signs in mass media: Discussing the relationships of verbal and nonverbal information in radio, film, and TV] (pp. 95–127). Tübingen, Germany: Niemeyer.

Bentele, G. (1988a). Der Faktor Glaubwürdigkeit: Forschungsergebnisse und Fragen für die Sozialisationsperspektive [The factor credibility: Research results and questions for the socialization perspective]. *Publizistik, 33*(2/3), 406–426.

Bentele, G. (1988b). *Objektivität und Glaubwürdigkeit von Medien: Eine theoretische und empirische Studie zum Verhältnis von Realität und Medienrealität* [Objectivity and credibility of mass media: A theoretical and empirical study concerning the relationships between reality and media reality]. Habilitation thesis. Berlin, Germany: Freie Universität Berlin.

Bentele, G. (1988c). Wie objektiv können Journalisten sein? [How objective can media be?]. In L. Erbring, S. Ruß-Mohl, B. Seewald, & B. Sösemann (Eds.), *Medien ohne Moral? Variationen über Journalismus und Ethik* [Media without morality? Variations concerning journalism and ethics] (pp. 196–225). Berlin, Germany: Argon.

Bentele, G. (1992a). Ethik der Public Relations als wissenschaftliche Herausforderung [Ethics of public relations as a challenge for PR research]. In H. Avenarius & W. Armbrecht (Eds.), *Ist Public Relations eine Wissenschaft? Eine Einführung* [Can public relations be scholarly? An introduction] (pp. 151–170). Opladen, Germany: Westdeutscher Verlag.

Bentele, G. (1992b). Fernsehen und Realität: Ansätze zu einer rekonstruktiven Medientheorie [TV and reality: A reconstructive approach to media theory]. In K. Hickethier & I. Schneider (Eds.), *Fernsehtheorien* [TV theories]. Berlin, Germany: Edition Sigma.

Bentele, G. (1993). Wie wirklich ist die Medienwirklichkeit? Einige Anmerkungen zum Konstruktivismus und Realismus in der Kommunikationswissenschaft [How real is media reality? Some notes on constructivism and realism in communication and media research]. In G. Bentele & M. Rühl (Eds.), *Problemfelder, Positionen, Perspektiven* [Problem fields, positions, perspectives] (pp. 152–171). Munich, Germany: Ölschläger.

Bentele, G. (1994a). Öffentliches Vertrauen: Normative und soziale Grundlage für Public Relations [Public trust: Normative and social foundations for public relations]. In W. Armbrecht & U. Zabel (Eds.), *Normative Aspekte der Public Relations. Grundlagen und Perspektiven. Eine Einführung* [Normative aspects of public relations. Foundations and perspectives. An introduction] (pp. 131–158). Opladen, Germany: Westdeutscher Verlag.

Bentele, G. (1994b). Public Relations und Wirklichkeit: Anmerkungen zu einer PR-Theorie [Public relations and reality: A contribution to PR theory]. In G. Bentele & K. R. Hesse (Eds.), *Publizistik in der Gesellschaft* [Public communication in society] (pp. 237–267). Constance, Germany: UVK.

Bentele, G. (1997). PR-Historiographie und funktional-integrative Schichtung: Ein neuer Ansatz zur PR-Geschichtsschreibung [PR historiography and a functional-integrative strata model: A new approach for writing the history of PR]. In P. Szyszka (Ed.), *Auf der Suche nach einer Identität: PR-Geschichte als Theoriebaustein* [In search of identity: PR history as an element of PR theory] (pp. 137–169). Berlin, Germany: Vistas.

Bentele, G. (2008). *Objektivität und Glaubwürdigkeit: Medienrealität rekonstruiert* [Objectivity and credibility: Media reality reconstructed] (S. Wehmeier, H. Nothhaft, & R. Seidenglanz, Eds. & Trans.). Wiesbaden, Germany: VS.

Bentele, G., & Bystrina, I. (1978). *Semiotik: Grundlagen und Probleme* [Semiotics: Foundations and problems]. Stuttgart, Germany: Kohlhammer.

Bentele, G., Liebert, T., & Seeling, S. (1997). Von der Determination zur Intereffikation: Ein integriertes Modell zum Verhältnis von Public Relations und Journalismus [From determination to intereffication: An integrative model concerning the relationships between PR and journalism]. In G. Bentele & M. Haller (Eds.), *Aktuelle Entstehung von Öffentlichkeit: Akteure, Strukturen, Veränderungen* [Actual formation of the public sphere: Actors, structures, and changes] (pp. 225–250). Constance, Germany: UVK.

Campbell, D. T. (1974). Evolutionary epistemology. In P. A. Schilpp (Ed.), *The philosophy of Karl R. Popper* (pp. 413–463). La Salle, IL: Open Court.

Frankfurt, H. G. (2006). *On truth.* New York: Random House.

Giddens, A. (1984). *The constitution of society: Outline of the theory of structuration.* Cambridge, UK: Polity Press.

Grunig, L. A., Grunig, J. E., & Dozier, D. M. (2002). *Excellent public relations and effective organizations: A study of communication management in three countries.* Mahwah, NJ: Lawrence Erlbaum.

Irrgang, B. (2001). *Lehrbuch der Evolutionären Erkenntnistheorie: Thesen, Konzeptionen und Kritik* [Evolutionary epistemology—a textbook: Theses, conceptions, and critique]. Munich, Germany: Reinhardt.

Kepplinger, H. M. (1992). *Ereignismanagement: Wirklichkeit und Massenmedien* [Managing the formation of events: Reality and mass media]. Zurich, Switzerland: Edition Interfromm.

Kieser, A., & Kubicek, H. (1992). *Organisationstheorien II* [Theories of Organizations II]. Stuttgart, Germany: Kohlhammer.

Kirchhoff, K. R., & Piwinger, M. (2001). *Die Praxis der Investor Relations: Effiziente Kommunikation zwischen Unternehmen und Kapitalmarkt* [The practice of investor relations: Communication between companies and the capital market]. Neuwied, Germany: Luchterhand.

Kneer, G., & Nassehi, A. (1994). *Niklas Luhmanns Theorie sozialer Systeme: Eine Einführung* [Niklas Luhmann's theory of social systems: An introduction]. Munich, Germany: Wilhelm Fink Verlag.

Lorenz, K. (1975). *Die Rückseite des Spiegels: Versuch einer Naturgeschichte des Erkennens* [Behind the mirror: Toward a natural history of recognition]. Munich, Germany: Piper.

Luhmann, N. (1995). *Social systems.* Stanford, CA: Stanford University Press. (Original work published 1984 as *Soziale Systeme: Grundriss einer allgemeinen Theorie*)

Luhmann, N. (2000). *Organisation und Entscheidung* [Organization and decision]. Opladen, Germany: Westdeutscher Verlag.

Maturana, H. R., & Varela, F. J. (1987). *Der Baum der Erkenntnis: Die biologischen Wurzeln des menschlichen Erkennens* [Tree of knowledge: Biological roots of human understanding]. Bern, Germany: Scherz.

Merten, K. (2000). *Das Handwörterbuch der PR* [The lexicon of public relations] (Vols. 1 & 2). Frankfurt am Main, Germany: F.A.Z.-Institut.

Merten, K., & Westerbarkey, J. (1994). Public opinion und public relations [Public opinion and public relations]. In K. Merten, S. J. Schmidt, & S. Weischenberg (Eds.), *Die Wirklichkeit der Medien: Eine Einführung in die Kommunikationswissenschaft* [The reality of the media: An introduction into communication science] (pp. 188–211). Opladen, Germany: Westdeutscher Verlag.

Neidhardt, F. (1994). *Öffentlichkeit, öffentliche Meinung, soziale Bewegungen* [Public sphere, public opinion, and social movements]. In F. Neidhardt (Ed.), *Kölner Zeitschrift für Soziologie und Sozialpsychologie* (pp. 7–41). Opladen, Germany: Westdeutscher Verlag.

Popper, K. (1984). *Objektive Erkenntnis: Ein evolutionärer Entwurf* [Objective knowledge: An evolutionary approach]. Hamburg, Germany: Hoffmann und Campe.

Ronneberger, F., & Rühl, M. (1992). *Theorie der Public Relations: Ein Entwurf* [Theory of public relations: An outline]. Opladen, Germany: Westdeutscher Verlag.

Saxer, U., Gantenbein, H., Gollmer, M., Hättenschwiler, W., & Schanne, M. (1986). *Massenmedien und Kernenergie: Journalistische Berichterstattung über ein komplexes, zur Entscheidung anstehendes, polarisiertes Thema* [Mass media and nuclear power: Reporting about complex and polarized topics at issue]. Bern, Germany: Haupt.

Schimank, U. (1985). Der mangelnde Akteursbezug systemtheoretischer Erklärungen gesellschaftlicher Differenzierung: Ein Diskussionsvorschlag [The lack of reference to actors in system theoretical explanations of social differentiation: A proposal for discussion]. *Zeitschrift für Soziologie, 14*(6), 421–434.

Schimank, U. (2000). *Handeln und Strukturen: Einführung in die akteurtheoretische Soziologie* [Acting and structures: Introduction to an action theoretical sociology]. Munich, Germany: Juventa.

Theis, A. M. (1994). *Organisationskommunikation: Theoretische Grundlagen und empirische Forschungen* [Organizational communication: Theoretical foundations and empirical research]. Opladen, Germany: Westdeutscher Verlag.

Vollmer, G. (1975). *Evolutionäre Erkenntnistheorie: Angeborene Strukturen im Kontext von Biologie, Psychologie, Linguistik, Philosophie und Wissenschaftstheorie* [Evolutionary epistemology: Inherent structures in contexts of biology, psychology, linguistics, and philosophy of science]. Stuttgart, Germany: Hirzel.

Vollmer, G. (1985). *Was können wir wissen? Die Natur der Erkenntnis: Beiträge zur Evolutionären Erkenntnistheorie* [What can we know? The nature of knowledge: Contributions to an evolutionary epistemology] (Vol. 1). Stuttgart, Germany: Hirzel.

Vollmer, G. (1986). *Was können wir wissen? Die Erkenntnis der Natur: Beiträge zur modernen Naturphilosophie* [What can we know? The knowledge of nature: Contributions to a modern philosophy of nature] (Vol. 2). Stuttgart, Germany: Hirzel.

Vollmer, G. (2002). *Wieso können wir die Welt erkennen?* [Why can we recognize the world?]. Stuttgart, Germany: Hirzel.

von Foerster, H. (1995). *Einführung in den Konstruktivismus* [Introduction to constructivism]. Munich, Germany: Piper.

von Foerster, H. (1999). *Sicht und Einsicht: Versuche zu einer operativen Erkenntnistheorie* [Sight and understanding: Essays concerning an operative epistemology]. Heidelberg, Germany: Carl Auer.

von Glasersfeld, E. (1987). Die Begriffe der Anpassung und Viabilität in einer radikal konstruktivistischen Erkenntnistheorie [The concepts of adaptation and viability in an epistemology of radical constructivism]. In E. von Glasersfeld (Ed.), *Wissen, Sprache und Wirklichkeit: Arbeiten zum radikalen Konstruktivismus* [Knowledge, language, and reality: Works in radical constructivism] (pp. 137–143). Braunschweig, Germany: Vieweg & Sohn.

von Glasersfeld, E. (1992). Konstruktion der Wirklichkeit und des Begriffs der Objektivität [Construction of reality and the concept of objectivity]. In E. von Glasersfeld (Ed.), *Einführung in den Konstruktivismus* [Introduction to constructivism] (pp. 9–39). Munich, Germany: Piper.

Willke, H. (1996). *Systemtheorie 1: Grundlagen. Eine Einführung in die Grundprobleme der Theorie sozialer Systeme* [System theory 1: An introduction to the basic problem of a theory of social systems]. Stuttgart, Germany: Lucius & Lucius.

Willke, H. (1999). *Systemtheorie 2: Interventionstheorie. Grundzüge einer Theorie der Intervention in komplexe Systeme* [System theory 2: A theory of intervention. Main features of a theory of intervention in complex systems]. Stuttgart, Germany: Lucius & Lucius.

CHAPTER 9

Dialogue as a Basis for Stakeholder Engagement

Defining and Measuring the Core Competencies

Nigel M. de Bussy

Public relations is the profession most often charged with the critical task of engaging with an organization's stakeholders. Yet theoretical advances in the field of stakeholder research have largely occurred within the management discipline, which rarely, if ever, acknowledges the roles and responsibilities of public relations in this regard. In the interests of both advancing our discipline and, more important, building better relationships between organizations and their stakeholders, this chapter aims to contribute to the theory and practice of stakeholder management. Engaging with stakeholders should be one of the most important core competencies of public relations. But fundamental issues remain largely unexplored. What does it mean to be a "stakeholder-oriented" organization, and how can the stakeholder concept be implemented in practice? How can stakeholder orientation be measured, and what is its impact on organizational performance? What is the relationship between stakeholder management and corporate social performance (CSP)?

Despite more than two decades of theorizing in the management discipline, the stakeholder concept remains shrouded in definitional ambiguity and handicapped by poorly conceptualized measurement techniques. This chapter describes the development of STAKOR—a scale to measure stakeholder orientation based on dialogue. STAKOR has been rigorously tested using the data collected in two rounds from 616 Australian companies with more than 80 employees. It offers the opportunity for researchers to answer the fundamental questions posed in the previous paragraph. Above all, STAKOR is a practical tool that public relations managers can use to build the stakeholder engagement capabilities of their organizations and to measure the impact of their activities on firm performance. Rather than equate stakeholder orientation with CSP, which has been the most common approach in the management literature, STAKOR is built on a theory of central importance to many in the field of public relations—the notion of dialogue.

Stakeholders: Problems of Definition and Measurement

It is now more than two decades since the concept of stakeholder management was first popularized by R. Edward Freeman (1984). By 2007, 179 articles directly addressing Freeman's work had appeared in the 11 leading academic journals in the fields of management and business ethics (Laplume, Sonpar, & Litz, 2008). Yet despite this considerable scholarly attention, indeed perhaps partly because of it, the stakeholder concept remains contentious and poorly defined (Stoney & Winstanley, 2001). In particular, as yet there have been only limited attempts at scale development to measure the extent of an organization's stakeholder orientation. This is problematic for both instrumental stakeholder theory, which endeavors to relate the practice of stakeholder management to desired organizational outcomes such as financial performance (Donaldson & Preston, 1995; Freeman, 1999), and the descriptive strand of the theory, which is concerned with how organizations actually behave in practice (Donaldson & Preston, 1995; Jawahar & McLaughlin, 2001).

To measure stakeholder orientation, previous research has generally relied on three types of evidence. One approach is based on data produced by KLD Research & Analytics, an independent CSP ratings agency (e.g., Agle, Mitchell, & Sonnefeld, 1999; Berman, Wicks, Kotha, & Jones, 1999; Berrone, Surroca, & Tribó, 2007; Bird, Hall, Momentè, & Reggiani, 2007; Coombs & Gilley, 2005; Hillman & Keim, 2001; Ruf, Muralidhar, Brown, Janney, & Paul, 2001; Waddock & Graves, 1997). The second method involves content analysis of mission statements and other corporate publications (Bartkus & Glassman, 2008; Moneva, Rivera-Lirio, & Munoz-Torres, 2007; Moore, 2001; Omran, Atrill, & Pointon, 2002). Third, a number of case studies have been published (Driscoll & Crombie, 2001; Harvey & Schaefer, 2001; Heugens, van den Bosch, & van Riel, 2002; Heugens & van Oosterhout, 2002; Ogden & Watson, 1999). A notable aspect of this prior research is the tendency to conflate the constructs of CSP and stakeholder orientation. This chapter describes an alternative approach to measuring stakeholder orientation—STAKOR—a scale designed to evaluate dialogical communication between organizations and their key stakeholders.

The first step in developing a new scale is to specify the construct domain (Churchill, 1979). This proved particularly challenging in the case of STAKOR because of the ambiguities surrounding stakeholder theory and its multifaceted nature. Freeman and Phillips (2002) have argued that stakeholder theory is better understood not as a monolithic theory but rather as a genre of stakeholder theories. STAKOR is conceptualized in terms of dialogue (Bohm, 1990; Buber, 1961; Isaacs, 1999), which has attracted particular attention in recent years in the field of organizational learning (Senge, 2006). The theologian and philosopher Martin Buber is acknowledged as the earliest modern exponent of the theory of dialogue (Matson & Montagu, 1967). For Buber, genuine dialogue involves turning to the other as a partner, although he stressed this does not necessarily imply approval. Rather, "by accepting him as my partner in genuine dialogue I have affirmed him as a person" (Buber, 2002c, p. 214). Buber's philosophical stance provided theoretical grounding for the development of the STAKOR instrument.

Although the role of dialogue in stakeholder engagement has received increased attention in recent years (e.g., Burchell & Cook, 2008; Payne & Calton, 2002; van Huijstee & Glasbergen, 2008), it has not previously been used as a basis for measuring stakeholder orientation. This new approach provides a more direct insight into firms' stakeholder-related behavior than reliance on KLD ratings of CSP. It has the potential to facilitate future stakeholder theory research, particularly its instrumental and descriptive strands, by enabling direct comparisons to be made between firms that adopt a stakeholder management approach versus those adhering to a shareholder value strategy.

Prior Approaches to Measuring Stakeholder Orientation

The Conflation of Stakeholder Orientation and CSP

In 1991, Wood, building on the work of Carroll (1979) and Wartick and Cochran (1985), defined CSP as a business organization's configuration of principles of social responsibility, processes of social responsiveness, and policies, programs, and observable outcomes as they relate to the firm's societal relationships (Wood, 1991, p. 693). However, in 1995, Wood and Jones proposed a significant repositioning of that definition drawing on the by then burgeoning influence of the stakeholder concept. They argued that stakeholder theory is the key to understanding the structure and dimensions of the firm's societal relationships. They redefined "policies, programs, and outcomes" as "internal stakeholder effects, external stakeholder effects and external institutional effects" and argued that stakeholders set norms for corporate behavior, experience that behavior, and also evaluate it (Wood & Jones, 1995). Thus, the stage was set for future researchers to treat CSP and stakeholder management as virtually synonymous (e.g., Bendheim, Waddock, & Graves, 1998; Moore, 2001; Ruf et al., 2001; Waddock & Graves, 1997).

This approach is problematic on conceptual grounds. The model of CSP developed by Wood (1991) and refined by Wood and Jones (1995) is multidimensional. Wood and Jones (1995, p. 253) argued that there is a stronger theoretical relationship between financial performance and the CSP dimension pertaining to corporate social responsiveness than the dimension concerned with corporate social responsibility. They proposed this as one reason for the mixed results obtained by researchers investigating the relationship between corporate social and financial performance (Wood & Jones, 1995). Equally, it is apparent that stakeholder management practices have a more direct conceptual relationship with a firm's processes of social responsiveness than with its principles of social responsibility. Stakeholder management and corporate social responsibility may be related constructs but they are far from synonymous. Indeed, as Walsh (2005, p. 431) has argued, there may be a "calculating" side to stakeholder management. It costs money to build goodwill. Walsh (2005) pointed out that buying a license to operate (the implicit purpose of stakeholder management) is akin to buying insurance.

The KLD Ratings

Related to the conceptual difficulties discussed above are the methodological problems resulting from the nature of the KLD ratings commonly used to measure both CSP and stakeholder management. The KLD ratings include data on five variables (community relations, workplace diversity, employee relations, environmental impact, and product quality), which are assumed in much of the instrumental stakeholder theory literature to equate to orientation toward particular stakeholder groups (Hillman & Keim, 2001; Ruf et al., 2001; Waddock & Graves, 1997). There are also "exclusionary screens" relating to social issues (Hillman & Keim, 2001). In earlier years, these screens resulted in three additional variables used by stakeholder researchers—involvement with either nuclear power, the military, or apartheid-era South Africa (Ruf et al., 2001; Waddock & Graves, 1997). In more recent years, involvement with tobacco, alcohol, and gambling have been added to the list. South Africa has been replaced by other nations with contemporary pariah status, notably Myanmar (Burma). Even corporate operations in Mexico are considered controversial by KLD (Hillman & Keim, 2001).

There are three significant weaknesses in relying on KLD data as a proxy measure for stakeholder orientation. First, in calculating the rankings, equal weight is given to each variable, giving rise to the criticism that they may not be equally valid indicators of the latent variable, stakeholder management (Laplume et al., 2008). Some researchers have attempted to weight the variables post hoc in order to address this problem (Ruf et al., 2001; Waddock & Graves, 1997). However, others have opted to retain the equal weightings (Hillman & Keim, 2001). Second, the relevance to stakeholder management of variables relating to social issues, such as involvement with the military and nuclear power, appears tenuous at best. Indeed using KLD data, Hillman and Keim (2001) separately investigated the impact of stakeholder management and social issue participation on financial performance. They found that while stakeholder management is positively associated with creating shareholder value, the opposite is true for social issue participation (Hillman & Keim, 2001).

Finally, even the five variables assumed to be most closely related to stakeholder orientation may not be valid indicators of the constructs they are purported to represent. For example, doubt can be cast on whether the environment should be considered a stakeholder in its own right. Some scholars have argued in the affirmative (Starik, 1995), while others have taken the opposite position (Phillips & Reichart, 2000). Similarly, does corporate philanthropy (a key measure of community relations) truly capture the nature of a company's relationships with the local community within which it operates? A Machiavellian corporation could use a seemingly generous donation to a worthy cause to mask other less desirable practices, such as exploiting workers or harming the environment. Equally, is a third party assessment of product quality really an adequate measure of customer relationships? Assessments are made by KLD on the basis of a wide range of data—much of it qualitative, such as evaluations of corporate advertising and philanthropy, in addition to public records (Berman et al., 1999). There is inevitably an element of subjectivity in this process, calling into question the reliability as well as the validity of using such ratings to measure the state of a company's stakeholder relations. At a minimum, it is apparent that the empirical evidence based on KLD data needs to be corroborated by studies using different methodological approaches.

Content Analyses and Case Studies

Two alternative methodologies reported in the literature are content analyses of corporate publications such as mission statements (Bartkus & Glassman, 2008; Bartkus, Glassman, & McAfee, 2006; Moneva et al., 2007; Moore, 2001; Omran et al., 2002) and case studies (e.g., Heugens et al., 2002; Ogden & Watson, 1999). Neither Moneva et al. (2007) nor Omran et al. (2002) found any significant relationship between degree of stakeholder orientation (as expressed in mission statements) and financial performance. Taken at face value, these findings seem to disconfirm instrumental stakeholder theory. However, it seems likely that the methodology is confounding the results. Previous research has suggested at best a weak overall relationship between corporate mission statements in general and firm performance (Bart & Baetz, 1998). More recently, Bartkus and Glassman (2008) have seriously undermined the appropriateness of continued reliance on mission statement content analysis as a measure of stakeholder orientation. They found no relationship between firms with mission statements that mention specific stakeholder groups and behaviors regarding these stakeholders, even though the reverse was the case for social issues such as the environment and diversity. KLD rankings were used to measure the dependent variable in this instance (Bartkus & Glassman, 2008). As Ullmann (1985) cautioned more than two decades ago, social disclosure cannot be substituted for social performance without prior empirical verification. Nor do case studies (e.g., Heugens et al., 2002; Ogden & Watson, 1999) offer a convincing alternative. Although the use of case study research in business has increased in recent years, questions remain regarding generalizability—especially when the research objectives involve theory testing (Hillebrand, Kok, & Biemans, 2001).

Prior Scale Development

In an early attempt at stakeholder scale development, Greenley and Foxall (1996, 1997, 1998) surveyed U.K. CEOs and published aspects of their findings in three separate papers. Their approach was to develop a series of scales aimed at measuring orientation toward particular stakeholders, namely, competitors, consumers, shareholders, employees, and unions (Greenley & Foxall, 1996). Unfortunately, the community was excluded from the instrument—a significant limitation given the importance attached to broader social responsibilities in the stakeholder and CSP literatures. Each scale comprised four single-item measures based on the then available literature. In relation to each stakeholder, CEOs were asked to assess (a) the extent of the development of plans for addressing stakeholder needs, (b) the importance of formal research in understanding stakeholder needs, (c) the importance of corporate culture for understanding stakeholder needs, and (d) the relative importance of the stakeholder group in question to the corporate mission (Greenley & Foxall, 1996). A reading of Greenley and Foxall's 1996 and 1997 articles begs the question as to why the researchers did not consider creating "cross-stakeholder" scales, encompassing the four dimensions of planning, research, corporate culture, and corporate mission. The answer appears to lie in the authors' 1998 paper, which reported the coefficient alphas (Cronbach, 1951) for these scales as .50, .62, .31, and .59, respectively, well below the widely accepted standard of .70 (Nunnally, 1978). Thus, the work of Greenley and Foxall (1996, 1997, 1998) was built on the suspect foundations of a series of single-item scales.

More recently, Greenley, Hooley, Broderick, and Rudd (2004; Greenley, Hooley, & Rudd, 2005) and Yau et al. (2007) have both used a scale designed to measure orientation toward customers, employees, shareholders, and competitors in empirical studies of "multiple stakeholder orientation profiles" and firm performance, respectively. The scale items used by the two sets of researchers were almost identical. Both studies have a marketing focus and draw on Narver and Slater's (1990) market orientation scale for the customer and competitor orientation items. Yau et al. (2007) took their shareholder and employee orientation items directly from Greenley et al. (2004). These studies have two significant limitations. First, the inclusion of shareholders and competitors as primary stakeholders in this context is highly problematic. The case against including shareholders in a scale of stakeholder orientation is developed in more detail later. However, the key consideration is that stakeholder management is an *alternative*, not a complement, to the more traditional shareholder value-driven approach. The position of competitors has long presented difficulties for stakeholder theorists (Heath, 2006). The competitor "orientation" measured by Greenley et al. (2004) and Yau et al. (2007) is explicitly based on concepts from the marketing discipline, such as analysis of competitor strengths and weaknesses (Narver & Slater, 1990) and the notion of "competitive aggressiveness" (Lumpkin & Dess, 1996). It is hard to reconcile such postures with a dialogic approach to stakeholding. Hence, competitors cannot be considered as potential partners in dialogue. As Buchholz and Rosenthal (2004, p. 147) colorfully argued, allowing trade associations and the like to police their own industries in the interests of competitor cooperation is akin to "sending the fox to guard the chicken coop."

The second major limitation of the scales developed by Greenley et al. (2004) and Yau et al. (2007) is that even with respect to the two stakeholder groups appropriately included—employees and customers—the items used are focused largely on functional considerations relating to human resource management and marketing. For example, the employee orientation scale refers to employee appraisals, and there are customer orientation items referring to "competitive strategies" and "integrated business functions to serve market needs."

A Dialogical Approach to Stakeholder Orientation

Theoretical Background

As an alternative to equating stakeholder orientation with CSP, STAKOR is conceptualized using the notion of dialogue. Interest in dialogue has been growing in disciplines across the behavioral sciences (Cissna & Anderson, 1998). The word *dialogue* is derived from the Greek *logos*—translated as "word" or "meaning"—and *dia* meaning in this context "through" or "across." Dialogue refers to both a quality of relationship that may arise between two or more people and a way of thinking about human affairs that highlights their dialogic qualities (Cissna & Anderson, 1998).

In *I and Thou*, first published in 1922, Martin Buber introduced the idea of two fundamental human attitudes or modes of existence associated with two basic word pairs—"I-You" and "I-It" (or He or She). Buber claimed that it is not possible to say "I" without meaning either "I-You" or "I-It." Equally, when someone says "You" or "It," the "I" of one or the other basic word pairs is also present (Buber, 2002b, p. 181). Buber drew a distinction between the world as experience and the world of relation. In Buber's philosophy, the former belongs to the basic word "I-It" and the latter to the basic word "I-You" (Buber, 2002b, p. 183). Buber claimed that one does not experience the human being to whom one says "You"; rather, one stands in relation to that person. However, "as soon as the relationship has run its course or is permeated by *means*, the You becomes an Object" (Buber, 2002b, p. 184). Using the metaphor of a chrysalis and a butterfly, Buber wrote that every You is doomed by its nature to enter "thinghood" again and again. The I-It is the chrysalis, the I-You the butterfly. Only the two states do not take turns neatly but are "intricately entangled" (Buber, 2002b, p. 185). In Buber's (2002b) words,

> Even as a melody is not composed of tones, nor a verse of words, nor a statue of lines—one must pull and tear to turn a unity into a multiplicity—so it is with the human being to whom I say You. I can abstract from him the color of his hair, or the color of his speech, or the color of his graciousness; I have to do this again and again; but immediately he is no longer You. (p. 183)

This subtle and far-reaching idea is at the heart of Buber's exposition of dialogue, which came later in his career.

Conceptualizing Dialogue

Buber contrasted dialogue with what he called the "curious sport" of discussion (Buber, 2002a, p. 189)—a distinction also emphasized by more recent authors (Bohm, 1990; Senge, 2006). In a discussion, different views are presented and defended, whereas in dialogue, different views are presented as a means toward discovering a new view (Senge, 2006). In Buber's philosophy, there are three kinds of dialogues (Buber, 2002a, p. 196). *Genuine* dialogue involves each participant really having the others in mind and turning to them with the intention of establishing a living, mutual relation. *Technical* dialogue is prompted solely by the need for objective understanding. Finally, there is what Buber described as *monologue* disguised as dialogue. This can occur in a variety of situations, including debates where thoughts are expressed not as they existed in the mind but only to score points and without those being addressed regarded as in any way present as persons (Buber, 2002a, p. 196).

Writing in 1932, Buber explicitly claimed that it is possible for business leaders to "practice the responsibility of dialogue" (Buber, 2002a, p. 204). For Buber, dialogue occurs in this context when the "leader of a great technical undertaking" experiences the business not as a mechanical structure with its associated "organic servants" (whose identity is merely functional), but "as an association of persons with faces and names and biographies" (Buber, 2002a, p. 204). This is precisely the language used more than seven decades later by McVea and Freeman (2005), who argued for a rethinking of the stakeholder concept emphasizing relationships between stakeholders as real people with names and faces. For Buber, the key to dialogue in business leadership is to comprehend and handle "persons as persons"—albeit for the most part indirectly (Buber, 2002a, p. 204).

Operationalizing Dialogue

In recent years, a number of key requirements for the practice of dialogue have been proposed (Bohm, 1990; Isaacs, 1999; Senge, 2006). These ideas draw, in turn, on principles developed by earlier exponents of dialogue (Buber, 1961; Rogers, 1967). Building on this work, STAKOR operationalizes dialogue in terms of three key attributes: *listening, positive regard,* and *willingness to change.*

Listening. For Isaacs (1999, p. 83), "The heart of dialogue is a simple but profound capacity to listen." In the words of Evered and Tannenbaum (1992, p. 46), one element of dialogue is "the intention to be a better listener." Both Martin Buber and the psychotherapist Carl Rogers, with whom Buber held a famous public conversation on dialogue in 1957, emphasized the importance of listening (Cissna & Anderson, 1998). Indeed, according to Cissna and Anderson (1998, p. 87), both men "stressed listening to an extent unheard of before in either philosophy or psychology." Buber understood listening primarily in terms of "turning towards" the other (Cissna & Anderson, 1998), a notion which, as pointed out above, was central to his philosophy of dialogue. Rogers's (1967) concept of listening was closely linked to the idea of empathy, the ability to suspend one's own frame of reference—at least for a while—and get inside someone else's (Evered & Tannenbaum, 1992). Rogers (1967, p. 250) identified "accurate empathic understanding" as one of the essential attitudinal traits therapists must possess to use dialogue in order to bring about constructive personality change in their clients. The importance to dialogue of suspending one's own assumptions and opinions is stressed in more recent work by both Senge (2006) and Isaacs (1999), with the latter defining "suspension" in terms of the capacity to "see things with new eyes" (Isaacs, 1999, p. 135). Hence, the concepts of listening, suspension of judgment, and empathy are closely interlinked.

Positive Regard. Arguably the most important requirement for dialogue encapsulates Buber's emphasis on treating "persons as persons," in other words valuing and affirming the humanity of others. This aspect of dialogue was summed up by Rogers (1967, p. 249) as "unconditional positive regard." Isaacs (1999) chose the term *respecting.* Senge (2006) stressed the importance of organizational members seeing one another as colleagues. Related themes have already been the focus of some attention in the stakeholder literature. Kant's second formulation of the categorical imperative is, "One ought to treat others as having intrinsic value in themselves, and *not* merely as means to achieve one's end" (Donaldson & Werhane, 1988, p. 13). This is typically interpreted to mean that one should respect every person as a rational and free being (Donaldson & Werhane, 1988). In their article on stakeholder theory and "Kantian capitalism," Evan and Freeman (1988) argued that no stakeholder may be used as a means to the ends of another without having the right to participate fully in the relevant decision. Hence, the manager practicing dialogue should get to know stakeholders as individuals with names and faces (Buber, 2002a; McVea & Freeman, 2005). She should value them as people and not solely because of their roles as employees, customers, suppliers, or members of the community.

Willingness to Change. Dialogue is far more than a mere exchange of ideas. Participants must enter into dialogue with the intent to reach an understanding. The outcome of dialogue is a synthesis (Evered & Tannenbaum, 1992). The key to achieving this is a preparedness to change one's own position in response to the other. As Evered and Tannenbaum (1992, p. 45) put it, in dialogue the participants' egos must be transcended. Drawing on the insights of Carl Rogers in the therapeutic setting, Evered and Tannenbaum

(1992, p. 45) spoke of the need to be willing to risk changing what one thinks one knows. The aim in dialogue is to transcend the understanding of any one person—to gain insights that could not be achieved individually (Senge, 2006). Hence, the practicing dialogic manager will be responsive to the needs of stakeholders. She will be prepared to change the way her organization operates as a result of stakeholder dialogue. Having identified the attributes used to operationalize the concept of dialogue, we now turn our attention to dimensions of the stakeholder orientation construct itself.

The Dimensions of Stakeholder Orientation

As discussed, to evaluate stakeholder orientation, STAKOR draws on the concept of dialogue. There remains, however, the thorny issue of who exactly is a stakeholder—a cause of considerable dissension in the literature (Mitchell, Agle, & Wood, 1997). While there is no universally accepted definition of "stakeholder," there is a reasonable degree of consensus on the identity of the *primary* or *key* stakeholders for most organizations. In proposing his Stakeholder Enabling Principle, which would have had the effect of making stakeholder management obligatory, Freeman (1997) made clear that he was narrowing the definition of stakeholders for this purpose to customers, financiers, employees, suppliers, and communities. Clarkson (1995, p. 106) specified primary stakeholders as shareholders, employees, customers, suppliers, and "the public stakeholder group," by which he meant governments and communities.

STAKOR adopts Clarkson's (1995) classification of primary stakeholder groups—although the term *community* is used in preference to the phrase "the public stakeholder group." In the stakeholder literature, the word *community* is a much more common term than *public stakeholder* (Dunham, Freeman, & Liedtka, 2006; Freeman, 1984, 1997; Lerner & Fryxell, 1994). Therefore, potentially salient dimensions of stakeholder orientation include the posture of the organization toward five key stakeholder groups: employees, customers, shareholders, suppliers, and the community.

However, it is apparent that shareholders are in a different position to other stakeholders. Indeed the term *stakeholder* was coined in the first place as a deliberate counterpoint to *stockholder* or *shareholder*, with the implication that investors are far from the only group to possess a legitimate stake of one form or another in the firm (Freeman, 1984). Much of the theoretical literature over the past two decades has centered on the apparent shareholder value *versus* stakeholder orientation dichotomy, often referred to in terms of the (Milton) Friedman versus Freeman debate (Freeman, 2008; Laplume et al., 2008). STAKOR has the potential to contribute to future instrumental stakeholder theory research, by facilitating performance comparisons between firms taking a stakeholder management approach versus those adopting a shareholder value strategy. Hence, it would be theoretically and methodologically inappropriate to include shareholder orientation as a dimension of overall stakeholder orientation. The implication of stakeholder theory is that the two concepts are in opposition rather than being complementary. From a methodological perspective, the inclusion of shareholders in an instrument to evaluate overall stakeholder management practices could confound future efforts to use that measure in a comparison of the stakeholder versus shareholder approaches. Thus, the STAKOR scale endeavors to measure orientation toward four primary stakeholder groups—customers, employees, suppliers, and the community—in terms of the extent to which firms engage in dialogic communication with members of those groups. Henceforward, when reference is made to stakeholder orientation, it means orientation toward employees, customers, the community, and suppliers but not shareholders. STAKOR is based on the proposition that stakeholder orientation is a second order factor (Garver & Mentzer, 1999; Steenkamp & van Trijp, 1991), that is, it comprises a number of distinct dimensions but the covariation in the scale may also be explained by a single, overall stakeholder orientation factor (see Figure 9.1).

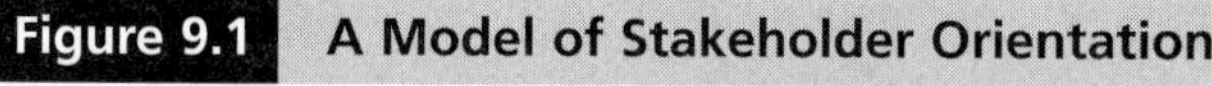

Figure 9.1 A Model of Stakeholder Orientation

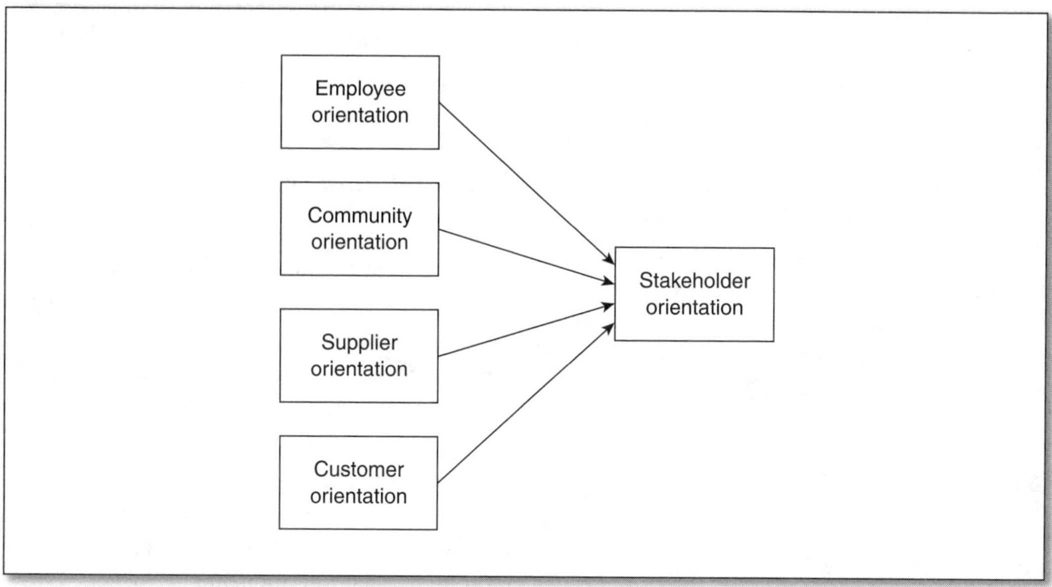

Methods

Scale Development

Drawing on the recommendations of Churchill (1979) and Hinkin (1995), the following steps were followed in the scale development process: The construct domain of stakeholder orientation was specified in terms of dialogic communication, a sample of items was generated, the item pool was reviewed by experts, a first round of data collection was undertaken, the measures were further purified, a second round of data collection took place, and finally the psychometric properties of the new scale were evaluated. The initial sample item pool was derived largely deductively (Hinkin, 1995), based on the literature review. However, nine depth interviews were conducted with senior Australian managers holding stakeholder management responsibilities. Insights from these interviews added an inductive element into the item generation process (Hinkin, 1995). To assess content validity, the initial 60 items relating to dialogic communication with stakeholders were independently reviewed by four academics with relevant expertise. Following this assessment, the number of items was cut to 23 for the first round of data collection. The measurement format comprised 7-point Likert-type scales anchored by *strongly disagree* (1) and *strongly agree* (7).

Sample and Data Collection

The sample frame was a comprehensive, commercially available database of Australian businesses produced by Dun and Bradstreet. In the first round, the survey was administered by mail to 1,806 Australian companies with more than 80 employees. By the cutoff date, a total of 326 usable responses had been received—a response rate of 18.05%. After further purification of the instrument, questionnaires were mailed to a different sample of 1,672 managers resulting in 290 responses—a response rate of 17.34%. Over the course of the two rounds, a survey was sent to every company in the database with more than 80 employees. The survey was targeted at senior financial managers because in general, they are not personally responsible for the management of stakeholder relationships and so are likely to be more objective in their judgments. At the same time, chief financial officers and the like usually have a broad understanding of the status and activities of their companies. To assess the extent of nonresponse bias, data from early and late respondents in both rounds of data collection were compared using *t* tests (Armstrong & Overton, 1977). No significant differences were found. In addition, a comparison was made of the industries represented in the two samples using Australian and New Zealand Standard Industry Codes. A chi-square test revealed no significant difference between the two samples in terms of the proportion of respondents from each of the 17 industry groupings.

Analysis and Results

First Round Data

The first round data were analyzed using principal components factor analysis with varimax rotation and scale reliability analysis (Cronbach, 1951), since at that point the factor structure of the stakeholder orientation construct had not been established. The factor analysis of the proposed stakeholder orientation items resulted in a five-factor solution accounting for 67.48% of the total variance. The rotated component matrix was straightforward to interpret, with Factors 1 to 4 clearly representing orientation toward employees, the community, suppliers, and customers, respectively. Items loading onto the fifth factor were worded more generally in terms of "groups and individuals" rather than specific stakeholder groups. These items were dropped from subsequent analysis as were two additional items relating to nonspecific stakeholder groups, which loaded onto other factors. Factorial validity is said to be demonstrated when the factor structure obtained matches the groupings anticipated prior to analysis (Comrey, 1988). The factor structure obtained from the first round of data analysis suggests that managers perceive stakeholder orientation in terms of specific groups. The alpha coefficients for the four purified scales were as follows. Employee orientation (five items): .89; community orientation (four items): .88; supplier orientation (four items): .82; customer orientation (four items): .80. In all cases, these values exceed the generally accepted minimum of .70 (Nunnally, 1978).

Second Round Data

In the second round, confirmatory factor analysis was used to examine the unidimensionality of the stakeholder orientation construct (Gerbing & Anderson, 1988). Before proceeding with the analysis, 56 cases were deleted because they did not identify themselves as operating in the "for-profit" sector. This left a sample of 234 commercially oriented enterprises, which was used in subsequent analysis. It has been suggested that 200 is in general an acceptable sample size for structural equation modeling (Hoelter, 1983). Given that STAKOR is primarily intended to evaluate the way for-profit organizations interact with their nonfinancial stakeholders, it was important to validate the instrument using a sample comprising fully commercial firms rather than NGOs or government enterprises.

Each of the four STAKOR subscales identified from the first round data was subject to confirmatory factor analysis using the AMOS 6 program. The maximum likelihood estimation procedure was used. A statistically significant factor regression coefficient is a weak condition for convergent validity. A stronger condition is that the coefficient should be substantial, that is, the correlation between the construct and its indicator should exceed .50 (Steenkamp & van Trijp, 1991). Other authors take a more conservative view suggesting that only measurement loadings of .70 and above are considered acceptable, on the grounds that at this level the error variance is lower than the variance in the measure explained by the construct (Hulland, Chow, & Shunyin, 1996). The standardized regression weights (lambdas) and squared multiple correlations (R^2) for each indicator of the four stakeholder orientation dimensions are reported in Table 9.1. The

Table 9.1 Stakeholder Orientation Dimensions: Standardized Regression Weights and Squared Multiple Correlations

Construct	Indicator	Standardized Regression Weight (λ)	Squared Multiple Correlation (R^2)
Employee orientation	Employees valued	.79***	.62
Employee orientation	Managers listen to employees	.83***	.69
Employee orientation	Managers take personal interest in employees	.76***	.58
Employee orientation	Efforts made to ensure employee satisfaction	.82***	.68
Employee orientation	Employee suggestions lead to changes	.79***	.62
Community orientation	Community support believed vital	.89***	.79
Community orientation	Community opinion listened to	.91***	.84
Community orientation	Tailoring operations to meet community expectations	.78***	.61
Community orientation	Changes in response to community wishes	.75***	.56
Supplier orientation	Major suppliers regarded as partners	.67***	.45
Supplier orientation	Important for suppliers to be happy to do business with us	.73***	.53
Supplier orientation	Management listens to ideas from suppliers	.91***	.83
Supplier orientation	Supplier suggestions lead to changes	.77***	.59
Customer orientation	Customer is king or queen	.71***	.51
Customer orientation	Organization listens to customers	.80***	.64
Customer orientation	Do everything possible to give customers what they want	.81***	.65
Customer orientation	Managers get to know customers personally	.52***	.27

***$p < .001$.

R^2 coefficients represent the strengths of the joint linear relationships in the models (Medsker, Williams, & Holahan, 1994). Relatively high squared multiple correlations suggest that the model in question offers an adequate representation of the data that generated it, although R^2 is not a measure of model fit as such (Medsker et al., 1994). It can be concluded from the data that each of the four scales possesses an adequate level of convergent validity.

Unidimensionality is defined as the existence of one construct underlying a set of items and is a critical assumption of measurement theory (Steenkamp & van Trijp, 1991). Overall model fit is a necessary and sufficient determinant of unidimensionality (Kumar & Dillon, 1987); however, there are a variety of model fit measures available. The measures selected for inclusion in Table 9.2 appear to be among the most commonly used and recommended in the business research literature (Hulland et al., 1996). On the basis of the data, all four models appear to exhibit unidimensionality.

The next stage in establishing construct validity was to test for discriminant validity. This involves comparing the correlations between the constructs of a model to a hypothetical model in which all the correlations are set to one (Dunn, Seaker, & Waller, 1994; Joreskog, 1971). A chi-square difference score is then calculated. Significant chi-square difference values indicate that the constructs are distinct and the existence of discriminant validity is supported. The chi-square difference score obtained from a test of the four proposed dimensions of stakeholder orientation was 742.26 with 6 degrees of freedom. Since the relevant critical value of the chi-square statistic with alpha set at .005 is 18.55, the null hypothesis may be rejected, that is, there is evidence in support of the existence of discriminant validity.

Multidimensional constructs must be measured with individual scales—one for each dimension—each of which must demonstrate unidimensionality (Dunn et al., 1994). If there is a sufficient level of correlation between each of the scales, then the overall construct may be treated as a second order factor model (Joreskog & Sorban, 1989). Confirmatory factor analysis was used to test the proposition that overall stakeholder orientation may be regarded as a second order factor. First, the factor scores were obtained for each of the four stakeholder orientation dimensions, that is, employee, community, supplier, and customer orientation. Factor scores are the regression weights for the regression of the unobserved variables on the observed variables (Arbuckle, 1997). These scores were then used to create new, weighted composite scales for each construct to be used in subsequent analysis. The resultant composite variables take into account the individual and joint measurement error of the indicators of each construct and are proportionately weighted by the actual contribution made by each indicator. The formula used to calculate the composite scores was as follows, where w_i is the factor weight for the ith item.

$$\frac{\Sigma(w_1{*}\text{item}_1,\ w_2{*}\text{item}_2, \ldots,\ w_i{*}\text{item}_i)}{\Sigma(w_i)}$$

The results of the confirmatory factor analysis are provided in Table 9.3, while Table 9.4 shows selected model fit statistics. The model appears to offer a good fit with the data, and therefore, the proposition that overall stakeholder orientation may be considered a second order factor model is supported.

Table 9.2 Stakeholder Orientation Dimensions: Selected Model Fit Statistics

Construct	p	CMIN/DF	RMR	GFI	AGFI	NFI	TLI
Employee orientation	.76	0.39	.01	.99	.99	.99	1.00
Community orientation	.28	1.26	.03	.99	.97	.99	0.99
Supplier Orientation	.10	2.67	.02	.99	.94	.99	0.98
Customer orientation	.16	1.86	.03	.99	.96	.99	0.98

Table 9.3 Overall Stakeholder Orientation: Standardized Regression Weights and Squared Multiple Correlations

Indicator	Standardized Regression Weight (λ)	Squared Multiple Correlation (R^2)
Employee orientation	.80***	.64
Community orientation	.64***	.41
Supplier orientation	.69***	.48
Customer orientation	.69***	.47

***$p < .001$.

Table 9.4 Overall Stakeholder Orientation: Selected Model Fit Statistics

p	CMIN/DF	RMR	GFI	AGFI	NFI	TLI
.56	0.34	.01	.99	.99	.99	1.02

Since the traditional measure of reliability, coefficient alpha (Cronbach, 1951), weights all items equally, it is necessary in causal modeling to use measures of reliability that take into account individual item loadings (Fornell & Larker, 1981; Hulland et al., 1996). Variance extracted refers to the overall amount of variance in the indicators accounted for by the latent construct, whereas composite reliability is a measure of the internal consistency of the construct indicators (Hair, Anderson, Tatham, & Black, 1995). The variance extracted should exceed .50 for a construct (Hair et al., 1995). Table 9.5 provides the construct reliability and variance extracted scores for each construct under investigation, in addition to descriptive statistics for each variable. It can be seen that all constructs exceed the accepted .70 standard for reliability (Nunnally, 1978). In addition, all four dimensions of stakeholder orientation, as well as the overall stakeholder orientation construct itself, meet the .50 standard for variance extracted (Hair et al., 1995).

Table 9.5 Construct Descriptive Statistics, Composite Reliabilities, and Variance Extracted

Construct	Mean	SD	CR	VE
Employee orientation	5.26	1.02	.898	.638
Community orientation	4.44	1.33	.903	.701
Supplier orientation	5.04	1.04	.855	.599
Customer orientation	5.42	0.93	.807	.518
Overall stakeholder orientation	5.12	0.83	.800	.501

Discussion and Conclusions

This chapter described the development and validation of a new scale to measure stakeholder orientation based on the concept of dialogue. It was proposed that managers perceive stakeholder orientation in terms of specific groups such as employees, suppliers, customers, and the community. The results from the two rounds of data analysis support the conclusion that STAKOR is a valid and reliable instrument for measuring stakeholder orientation. Moreover, all stakeholders are not equal in this regard. Table 9.3 indicates that dialogical communication with employees makes the strongest contribution to overall stakeholder orientation, with orientation toward the other three primary groups—suppliers, the community, and customers—in approximately equal second place. This is not altogether surprising. Managers are in constant communication with employees, whereas they may have only irregular contact with customers, suppliers, and the community. Hence, the way in which employees are treated is the touchstone for stakeholder engagement in general.

Prior research in the field of instrumental stakeholder theory has produced mixed results (e.g., Berman et al., 1999; Berrone et al., 2007; Meznar, Nigh, & Kwok, 1994). Arguably, there are two major reasons for this. First, there has been a lack of clarity hitherto in conceptualizing stakeholder orientation. Specifically, the construct has become conflated with CSP. While the two constructs may be related, they are far from synonymous. Second, there are methodological issues inherent in the measures generally used in previous studies, such as KLD ratings and content analyses of corporate publications. STAKOR offers a viable alternative for future research. In particular, the use of STAKOR would facilitate structural equation modeling, enabling the relative impact on financial performance of adopting a stakeholder versus shareholder approach to be directly compared. STAKOR also has the potential to contribute to the field of descriptive stakeholder theory (Donaldson & Preston, 1995; Jawahar & McLaughlin, 2001), which deals with how firms actually behave.

Freeman's (1999) formulation of the central proposition of instrumental stakeholder theory states, "To maximise shareholder value over an uncertain time frame, managers ought to pay attention to key stakeholder relationships" (p. 235). This provides a potential answer as to *why* firms should pay attention to their stakeholders but begs the question *how?* STAKOR can contribute to answering both questions. Future research using the scale to examine the relationship between adopting a stakeholder orientation and subsequent financial performance may help confirm or disconfirm the claims of instrumental stakeholder theory. Engaging stakeholders through participating in genuine dialogue seems a promising and ethically sound way for motivated managers to implement the stakeholder concept in practice.

Appendix: Items in the Final STAKOR Scale

Employee Orientation

1. Employees doing a good job are valued in this organization.
2. Managers in this organization are prepared to listen to ideas from employees.
3. Managers in this organization take a personal interest in the well-being of employees.
4. Management in this organization makes every effort to ensure that employees are satisfied with their working conditions.
5. This organization sometimes changes its business processes as a result of employees' suggestions.

Community Orientation

1. Management in this organization believes the support of the community is vital to its operations.

2. This organization listens carefully to community opinion.

3. Management in this organization believes that tailoring our operations to meet community expectations is essential to our survival.

4. This organization sometimes changes its practices in response to community wishes.

Supplier Orientation

1. Management in this organization regards major suppliers as partners.

2. Managers in this organization are prepared to listen to ideas from major suppliers.

3. Management in this organization believes that it's important that major suppliers remain happy to do business with us.

4. This organization sometimes changes its business processes as a result of suggestions from key suppliers.

Customer Orientation

1. Managers in this organization believe that the customer is king or queen.

2. This organization always listens to its customers.

3. Managers in this organization take the trouble to get to know their customers personally.

4. This organization does everything possible to give their customers what they want.

References

Agle, B. R., Mitchell, R. K., & Sonnefeld, J. A. (1999). Who matters to CEOs? An investigation of stakeholder attributes and salience, corporate performance, and CEO values. *Academy of Management Journal, 42*(5), 507–525.

Arbuckle, J. L. (1997). *Amos users' guide version 3.6.* Chicago: SmallWaters.

Armstrong, J. S., & Overton, T. S. (1977). Estimating nonresponse bias in mail surveys. *Journal of Marketing Research, 14*(3), 396–402.

Bart, C. K., & Baetz, M. C. (1998). The relationship between mission statements and firm performance: An exploratory study. *Journal of Management Studies, 35*(6), 823–853.

Bartkus, B. R., & Glassman, M. (2008). Do firms practice what they preach? The relationship between mission statements and stakeholder management. *Journal of Business Ethics, 83,* 207–216.

Bartkus, B. R., Glassman, M., & McAfee, B. (2006). Mission statement quality and financial performance. *European Management Journal, 24*(1), 86–94.

Bendheim, C. L., Waddock, S. A., & Graves, S. B. (1998). Determining best practice in corporate-stakeholder relations using data envelopment analysis: An industry-level study. *Business and Society, 37*(3), 306–338.

Berman, S. L., Wicks, A. C., Kotha, S., & Jones, T. M. (1999). Does stakeholder orientation matter? The relationship between stakeholder management models and firm financial performance. *Academy of Management Journal, 42*(5), 488–506.

Berrone, P., Surroca, J., & Tribó, J. A. (2007). Corporate ethical identity as a determinant of firm performance: A test of the mediating role of stakeholder satisfaction. *Journal of Business Ethics, 76,* 35–53.

Bird, R., Hall, A. D., Momentè, F., & Reggiani, F. (2007). What corporate social responsibility activities are valued by the market? *Journal of Business Ethics, 76,* 189–206.

Bohm, D. (1990). *On dialogue.* Ojal, CA: David Bohm Seminars.

Buber, M. (1961). *Between man and man* (R. G. Smith, Trans.). London: Collins.

Buber, M. (2002a). From "Dialogue" (1932). In A. D. Biemann (Ed.), *The Martin Buber reader* (pp. 189–205). New York: Palgrave Macmillan.

Buber, M. (2002b). From "I and Thou." In A. D. Biemann (Ed.), *The Martin Buber reader* (pp. 181–188). New York: Palgrave Macmillan.

Buber, M. (2002c). Genuine dialogue (1954). In A. D. Biemann (Ed.), *The Martin Buber reader* (pp. 214–215). New York: Palgrave Macmillan.

Buchholz, R. A., & Rosenthal, S. B. (2004). Stakeholder theory and public policy: How governments matter. *Journal of Business Ethics, 51,* 143–153.

Burchell, J., & Cook, J. (2008). Stakeholder dialogue and organisational learning: Changing relationships between companies and NGOs. *Business Ethics: A European Review, 17*(1), 35–46.

Carroll, A. B. (1979). A three-dimensional conceptual model of corporate social performance. *Academy of Management Review, 4*(4), 497–505.

Churchill, G. A., Jr. (1979). A paradigm for developing better measures of marketing constructs. *Journal of Marketing Research, 16*(1), 64–73.

Cissna, K. N., & Anderson, R. (1998). Theorizing about dialogic moments: The Buber-Rogers position and postmodern themes. *Communication Theory, 8*(1), 63–104.

Clarkson, M. B. E. (1995). A stakeholder framework for analyzing and evaluating corporate social performance. *Academy of Management Review, 20*(1), 92–117.

Comrey, A. (1988). Factor analytic methods of scale development in personality and clinical psychology. *Journal of Consulting and Clinical Psychology, 56*, 754–761.

Coombs, J. E., & Gilley, K. M. (2005). Stakeholder management as a predictor of CEO compensation: Main effects and interactions with financial performance. *Strategic Management Journal, 26*(9), 827–840.

Cronbach, L. (1951). Coefficient alpha and the internal structure of tests. *Psychometrika, 16*(3), 297–334.

Donaldson, T., & Preston, L. E. (1995). The stakeholder theory of the corporation: Concepts, evidence, and implications. *Academy of Management Review, 20*(1), 65–91.

Donaldson, T., & Werhane, P. H. (Eds.). (1988). *Ethical issues in business: A philosophical approach* (4th ed.). Englewood Cliffs, NJ: Prentice Hall.

Driscoll, C., & Crombie, A. (2001). Stakeholder legitimacy management and the qualified good neighbor: The case of Nova Nada and JDI. *Business & Society, 40*(4), 442–471.

Dunham, L., Freeman, R. E., & Liedtka, J. (2006). Enhancing stakeholder practice: A particularized exploration of community. *Business Ethics Quarterly, 16*(1), 23–42.

Dunn, S. C., Seaker, R. F., & Waller, M. A. (1994). Latent variables in business logistics research: Scale development and validation. *Journal of Business Logistics, 15*(2), 145–172.

Evan, W. M., & Freeman, R. E. (1988). A stakeholder theory of the modern corporation: Kantian capitalism. In T. L. Beauchamp & N. E. Bowie (Eds.), *Ethical theory and business* (3rd ed.). Englewood Cliffs, NJ: Prentice Hall.

Evered, R., & Tannenbaum, B. (1992). A dialog on dialog: A conversation between Roger Evered and Bob Tannenbaum. *Journal of Management Inquiry, 1*(1), 43–55.

Fornell, C., & Larker, D. (1981). Evaluating structural equation models with unobservable variables and measurement error. *Journal of Marketing Research, 18*(1), 39–50.

Freeman, R. E. (1984). *Strategic management: A stakeholder approach.* Boston: Pitman.

Freeman, R. E. (1997). A stakeholder theory of the modern corporation. In T. L. Beauchamp & N. E. Bowie (Eds.), *Ethical theory and business* (5th ed., pp. 66–76). Upper Saddle River, NJ: Prentice Hall.

Freeman, R. E. (1999). Divergent stakeholder theory. *Academy of Management Review, 24*(2), 233–236.

Freeman, R. E. (2008). Ending the so-called "Friedman-Freeman" debate. *Business Ethics Quarterly, 18*(2), 162–166.

Freeman, R. E., & Phillips, R. A. (2002). Stakeholder theory: A libertarian defense. *Business Ethics Quarterly, 12*(3), 331–349.

Garver, M. S., & Mentzer, J. T. (1999). Logistics research methods: Employing structural equation modeling to test for construct validity. *Journal of Business Logistics, 20*(1), 33–57.

Gerbing, D. W., & Anderson, J. C. (1988). An updated paradigm for scale development incorporating unidimensionality and its assessment. *Journal of Marketing Research, 25*(2), 186–192.

Greenley, G. E., & Foxall, G. R. (1996). Consumer and nonconsumer stakeholder orientation in UK companies. *Journal of Business Research, 35*(2), 105–116.

Greenley, G. E., & Foxall, G. R. (1997). Multiple stakeholder orientation in UK companies and the implications for company performance. *Journal of Management Studies, 34*(2), 259–284.

Greenley, G. E., & Foxall, G. R. (1998). External moderation of associations among stakeholder orientations and company performance. *International Journal of Research in Marketing, 15*(1), 51–69.

Greenley, G. E., Hooley, G. J., Broderick, A. J., & Rudd, J. M. (2004). Strategic planning differences among different multiple stakeholder orientation profiles. *Journal of Strategic Marketing, 12*, 163–182.

Greenley, G. E., Hooley, G. J., & Rudd, J. M. (2005). Market orientation in a multiple stakeholder orientation context: Implicatio ns for marketing capabilities and assets. *Journal of Business Research, 58,* 1483–1494.

Hair, J. F., Anderson, R. E., Tatham, R. L., & Black, W. C. (1995). *Multivariate data analysis* (4th ed.). Upper Saddle River, NJ: Prentice Hall.

Harvey, B., & Schaefer, A. (2001). Managing relationships with environmental stakeholders: A study of U.K. water and electricity utilities. *Journal of Business Ethics, 30,* 243–260.

Heath, J. (2006). Business ethics without stakeholders. *Business Ethics Quarterly, 16*(4), 533–557.

Heugens, P., van den Bosch, F. A. J., & van Riel, C. B. M. (2002). Stakeholder integration. *Business and Society, 41*(1), 36–60.

Heugens, P., & van Oosterhout, H. (2002). The confines of stakeholder management: Evidence from the Dutch manufacturing sector. *Journal of Business Ethics, 40,* 387–403.

Hillebrand, B., Kok, R. A., & Biemans, W. G. (2001). Theory-testing using case studies: A comment on Johnston, Leach, and Liu. *Industrial Marketing Management, 30,* 651–657.

Hillman, A. J., & Keim, G. D. (2001). Shareholder value, stakeholder management, and social issues: What's the bottom line? *Strategic Management Journal, 22*(2), 125–139.

Hinkin, T. R. (1995). A review of scale development practices in the study of organizations. *Journal of Management, 21*(5), 967–988.

Hoelter, J. (1983). The analysis of covariance structures: Goodness-of-fit indices. *Sociological Methods and Research, 11*(3), 325–344.

Hulland, J., Chow, Y. H., & Shunyin, L. (1996). Use of causal models in marketing research: A review. *International Journal of Research in Marketing, 13*(2), 181–197.

Isaacs, W. (1999). *Dialogue and the art of thinking together.* New York: Doubleday.

Jawahar, I. M., & McLaughlin, G. L. (2001). Toward a descriptive stakeholder theory: An organizational life cycle approach. *Academy of Management Review, 26*(3), 397–414.

Joreskog, K. (1971). Statistical analysis of congeneric tests. *Psychometrika, 36*(2), 109–133.

Joreskog, K., & Sorban, P. (1989). *LISREL 7: A guide to the program and application* (2nd ed.). Chicago: SPSS.

Kumar, A., & Dillon, W. (1987). Some further remarks on measurement-structure interaction and the unidimensionality of constructs. *Journal of Marketing Research, 24*(4), 438–444.

Laplume, A. O., Sonpar, K., & Litz, R. A. (2008). Stakeholder theory: Reviewing a theory that moves us. *Journal of Management, 34*(6), 1152–1189.

Lerner, L. D., & Fryxell, G. E. (1994). CEO stakeholder attitudes and corporate social activity in the Fortune 500. *Business and Society, 33*(1), 58–81.

Lumpkin, G., & Dess, G. (1996). Clarifying the entrepreneurial orientation construct and linking it to performance. *Academy of Management Review, 21*(1), 135–172.

Matson, F. W., & Montagu, A. (1967). The unfinished revolution. In F. W. Matson & A. Montagu (Eds.), *The human dialogue: Perspectives on communication* (pp. 1–11). New York: Free Press.

McVea, J. F., & Freeman, R. E. (2005). A names-and-faces approach to stakeholder management. *Journal of Management Inquiry, 14*(1), 57–69.

Medsker, G. J., Williams, L. J., & Holahan, P. J. (1994). A review of current practices for evaluating causal models in organizational behavior and human resources management research. *Journal of Management, 20*(2), 439–464.

Meznar, M. B., Nigh, D., & Kwok, C. C. (1994). Effects of announcements of withdrawal from South Africa on stockholder wealth. *Academy of Management Journal, 37*(6), 1633–1648.

Mitchell, R. K., Agle, B. R., & Wood, D. J. (1997). Toward a theory of stakeholder identification and salience: Defining the principle of who and what really counts. *Academy of Management Review, 22*(4), 853–886.

Moneva, J. M., Rivera-Lirio, J. M., & Munoz-Torres, M. J. (2007). The corporate stakeholder commitment and social and financial performance. *Industrial Management & Data Systems, 107*(1), 84–102.

Moore, G. (2001). Corporate social and financial performance: An investigation in the U.K. supermarket industry. *Journal of Business Ethics, 34,* 299–315.

Narver, J. C., & Slater, S. F. (1990). The effect of a market orientation on business profitability. *Journal of Marketing, 54*(4), 20–35.

Nunnally, J. (1978). *Psychometric theory* (2nd ed.). New York: McGraw-Hill.

Ogden, S., & Watson, R. (1999). Corporate performance and stakeholder management: Balancing shareholder and customer interests in the UK privatized water industry. *Academy of Management Journal, 42*(5), 526–538.

Omran, M., Atrill, P., & Pointon, J. (2002). Shareholders versus stakeholders: Corporate mission statements and investor returns. *Business Ethics: A European Review, 11*(4), 318–326.

Payne, S. L., & Calton, J. M. (2002). Towards a managerial practice of stakeholder engagement: Developing multi-stakeholder learning dialogues. In J. Andriöf, S. A. Waddock, B. Husted, & S. Sutherland Rahman (Eds.), *Unfolding stakeholder thinking* (pp. 121–135). Sheffield, UK: Greenleaf.

Phillips, R. A., & Reichart, J. (2000). The environment as a stakeholder? A fairness-based approach. *Journal of Business Ethics, 23*(2), 185–197.

Rogers, C. R. (1967). The therapeutic relationship: Recent theory and research. In F. W. Matson & A. Montagu (Eds.), *The human dialogue: Perspectives on communication* (pp. 246–259). New York: Free Press.

Ruf, B. M., Muralidhar, K., Brown, R. M., Janney, J. J., & Paul, K. (2001). An empirical investigation of the relationship between change in corporate social performance and financial performance: A stakeholder theory perspective. *Journal of Business Ethics, 32,* 143–156.

Senge, P. M. (2006). *The fifth discipline* (2nd ed.). London: Random House.

Starik, M. (1995). Should trees have managerial standing? Toward stakeholder status for non-human nature. *Journal of Business Ethics, 14*(3), 207–217.

Steenkamp, J.-B. E., & van Trijp, H. C. (1991). The use of LISREL in validating marketing constructs. *International Journal of Research in Marketing, 8,* 283–299.

Stoney, C., & Winstanley, D. (2001). Stakeholding: Confusion or utopia? Mapping the conceptual terrain. *Journal of Management Studies, 38*(5), 603–626.

Ullmann, A. A. (1985). Data in search of a theory: A critical examination of the relationships among social performance, social disclosure, and economic performance of U.S. firms. *Academy of Management Review, 10*(3), 540–557.

van Huijstee, M., & Glasbergen, P. (2008). The practice of stakeholder dialogue between multinationals and NGOs. *Corporate Social Responsibility and Environmental Management, 15,* 298–310.

Waddock, S. A., & Graves, S. B. (1997). The corporate social performance-financial performance link. *Strategic Management Journal, 18*(4), 303–319.

Walsh, J. P. (2005). Book review essay: Taking stock of stakeholder management. *Academy of Management Review, 30*(2), 426–452.

Wartick, S. L., & Cochran, P. L. (1985). The evolution of the corporate social performance model. *Academy of Management Review, 10*(4), 758–769.

Wood, D. J. (1991). Corporate social performance revisited. *Academy of Management Review, 16*(4), 691–718.

Wood, D. J., & Jones, R. E. (1995). Stakeholder mismatching: A theoretical problem in empirical research on corporate social performance. *International Journal of Organizational Analysis, 3*(3), 229–267.

Yau, O. H., Chow, R. P., Sin, L. Y., Tse, A. C., Luk, C., & Lee, J. S. (2007). Developing a scale for stakeholder orientation. *European Journal of Marketing, 41*(11/12), 1306–1327.

CHAPTER 10

"Making It Real"

Anthropological Reflections on Public Relations, Diplomacy, and Rhetoric

Jacquie L'Etang

This chapter features three specifically human activities that share overlapping communicative characteristics and the functions of agency, representing interests through advocacy. There is a comparative element in this discussion, but I have tried to situate this in the context of debates within the respective fields, while endeavoring to position my analysis in an anthropological context. I argue that anthropology offers insights and research tools (ethnography) that can enhance the ability to theorize (including grounded theory) in public relations. Anthropology can help us understand public relations and related occupations (at various points in the human story) as a unique feature of human culture, even though they may have had different manifestations at various points in human history or have emerged in specialized cultures (political, economic, literary, philosophical) and performed a variety of functions (entertainment, persuasion, advocacy, manipulation).

I begin with a more detailed rationale for tackling this analysis and review literature that has explored connections between public relations, diplomacy, and rhetoric. I explain why anthropology is a useful source for public relations and briefly consider literature on culture and public relations. Finally, I suggest that the application of anthropology, its concepts, and research tools offer a much broader understanding of public relations, diplomacy, and rhetoric, as well as the prospect of alternate research agendas.

Rationale

I have long been enthusiastic about the topics of diplomacy and rhetoric and, by nature, am intellectually promiscuous, so this chapter reflects my divergent inclinations. I have also argued, along with others (Daymon & Hodges, 2009; Hodges, 2005, 2006; L'Etang & Pieczka, 1996, 2006; McKie & Munshi, 2007; Pieczka, 1997, 2002, 2006b; Vujnovic & Kruckeberg, Chapter 47, this volume), that anthropological and ethnographic research is long overdue and much underrated in the field of public relations. In this chapter, I have combined these interests and arguments in a way that I hope makes a useful contribution to the field.

Although I first noted the overlaps between diplomacy and rhetoric in 1996, I did not then find any specific literature addressing these in combination with public relations. I focused on detailed comparison and critical comment on public relations and diplomacy (L'Etang, 1994, 1996a, 1996b, 2006b, 2009a) and public relations and rhetoric (L'Etang, 1996a, 1996b, 1997, 2006a). These explorations were different in nature, since in the contemporary world, both public relations and diplomacy constitute a practice and a field of academic study, whereas rhetoric has come to be seen as a communicative discourse or a technique not restricted to a particular class of practitioners, as was the case in ancient Greece. Contemporary considerations of rhetoric have become important to those in linguistics and cultural studies, influenced by debates about relationships between thought, language, epistemology, and society, and have become increasingly interdisciplinary. However, in this chapter, I give emphasis to diplomacy as a comparable practice to public relations, and limit my remarks on rhetoric to a sketch of key problematics that are relevant to consideration of public relations and diplomacy.

In one sense, my interest in the subject has been historical, and, to an extent, genealogical: I wanted to understand the connections between cultural practices of public relations, diplomacy, and rhetoric; the nature of those connections; similarities and differences; and the implications of these for our understanding of human communication, international communication, and intercultural communication. My interest was inspired by the philosophical classics of Plato's *Gorgias*, Aristotle's *Art of Rhetoric*, and Aristophanes's *The Wasps*—hence the themes I focused on from the outset were both ethical and epistemic and influenced by "the new rhetorics" that engaged with postmodern critiques (L'Etang, 1996a, 1996b, 1997, 2006a). My work in diplomacy (partly inspired by a decade of working at the British Council) was more obviously comparative but drew on conceptual frameworks from international relations, especially those that addressed policy and communicative intentions and relational strategies.

My concern is not to justify public relations but to contribute to the generation of multiple insights that elaborate deeper and richer meanings about public relations. As such, this work is differently motivated to idealistic and normative perspectives in the field that seek to legitimize public relations practice. Legitimizing strategies include (a) efforts to prove that public relations is, essentially (and I choose this word both for its literal and its philosophical sense), ethical in facilitating public conversations about issues; (b) efforts to prove legitimacy through alleged contributions to democracy and debate via its role in the economics of information; (c) efforts to prove legitimacy through its effectiveness to organizations/social institutions; and (d) efforts to educate practitioners so that they can gain access to, and participate in, the managerial class. Finally, legitimacy may be sought through conceptual frameworks and historical work that seek to both justify and provide an overall explanation. All these efforts seek to promote rationality and to a degree a consensual view. Much of the work done in public relations scholarship is focused on gaining academic and occupational respectability, and building theoretical and scientific edifices supported by legitimizing discourses. Some have had genuine fears of the consequences of alternative, critical perspectives. For example,

> if I take a rhetorical view of public relations, have I created a rationale for hollow flackery, that is, asymmetrical manipulation? That was my worry. I feared doing more damage to a wounded profession, at least for those of us who believe it has rhetorical roots, could unfortunately end up with a worse name and reputation. . . . My goal was to justify a process of communication and its message content as the foundation of public relations. . . . I thought I could do some good. (Heath, 1997, p. 56)

Historical perspectives can offer insights into the practice, its ideals and ideologies, and its self-identity—so long as it is borne in mind that history writing is partial and depends on sources that are subject to archaeological sedimentation and erosion (L'Etang, 2004, 2008c). However, the motivation behind such work also needs to be laid bare, as it may be ideologically driven as Pearson (2009) pointed out. And, as Der Derian (1987) argued in his exploration of the origins and nature of diplomacy in international relations,

> [there is] a suspicion, supported by historical research, that given the origins of diplomacy have been defined more by diplomacy's present status and need, than by its past principles and practices . . . a genealogy of diplomacy, in the sense of an interpretive history, may produce errors as well as insights. It most surely will not produce the certitude of traditional diplomatic historians who studied diplomacy as an unfolding story of the past neatly creating the present. . . . [T]his genealogy attempts to disabuse the history of diplomacy: it openly looks backward to discover whether there are symptoms of diplomacy's crisis inherent yet hidden in the present definitions of its essential beginning and nearly seamless history. (p. 3)

This quotation highlights the way in which an academic specialist field, closely akin to public relations, has generated a politicized and value-laden historical canon. Precisely the same point may be made of public relations and the way in which its supposed evolutionary path and cultural sites are portrayed in textbooks and academic collections. The predominant story is of U.S. prehistory aligned to the emergence of national identity and the end of the colonial period (the American Revolution) followed by corporate industrial public relations and government propaganda, and successful export of the concept overseas. For example, Van Dyke and Verčič (2009) cited Grunig and Hunt's (1984) description of the American Revolution as "one of the most important products of public relations-like activities in history" and Cutlip's claim that the American Revolution "shaped today's patterns of public relations practice" (Van Dyke & Verčič, 2009, p. 831). Nearly all histories connect U.S. public relations history to events and practices in the ancient world but do not engage with earlier developments in other cultures—a rhetorical effort that bestows a kind of intellectual and historical credibility and legitimacy while writing out intervening developments in other cultures.

Yet despite the historical connections to elites, empirical and conceptual analyses of public relations and power remain rare (but see British scholar Edwards, 2006). In my view, some public relations literature that has pursued themes in diplomacy and rhetoric has idealistic or ideological features. In this chapter, I endeavor to explore underlying elements and identify scope for alternative interpretations. Such an interrogation can demarcate new terrain for empirical studies (Der Derian, 1987, p. 3). Since it has sometimes been suggested that critical scholars are destructive rather than constructive, I have sought approaches that would facilitate the provision of alternative empirical data and theorization. It is my belief that anthropology and ethnographic research offer considerable potential.

My focus on rhetoric and diplomacy was chosen here because of their conceptual and practical overlaps with each other and with public relations, although rhetoric has received greater attention within the public relations discipline. My reading of the literature, which follows, highlights the way in which rhetorical and diplomatic concepts have been used partially and politically. For the moment, it suffices to say that public relations and diplomacy bear comparison, since both occupations act as agents on behalf of principals (governments, clients, organizations, or vested interests) who engage in a range of overt and covert activities, including representation (rhetoric, oratory, advocacy); dialogue (negotiation, compromise, peacemaking); advice (counseling clients); intelligence gathering, surveillance, secrecy, and spying for political or managerial bosses (Dinan & Miller, 2007; Miller & Dinan, 2008); intercultural communication; and psychological operations and propaganda (L'Etang, 1994, 1996a, 1996b, 2006a, 2006b, 2008, 2009a).

Public relations is embedded in diplomacy as strategic communications and media relations within international communications (political and corporate) and plays a key role in political communications of governments and international organizations (multinational corporations, international organizations, nongovernmental organizations [NGOs]). The language of diplomacy has infiltrated public relations practitioner culture evidenced in the terminology of the International Public Relations Association—"The Hermans Memorandum," "The Code of Athens" (based on the UN charter); the existence of a post of "secretary general"; and individual practitioners who have described themselves as "corporate diplomats" (L'Etang, 1996b, p. 18; 2004, pp. 75–80). Of particular interest to those with an interest in public relations are the specialisms of public diplomacy and cultural diplomacy, which primarily focus on nonstate publics outside the host nation (intermestic publics—international domestic publics; Hill & Beshoff, 1994, cited in L'Etang, 1996b) and are intended to develop and foster long-term relationships. Of these types of diplomacy more will shortly be said.

The connections between public relations, diplomacy, and rhetoric operate at various levels. Although both public relations and diplomacy use rhetorical strategies in discourse management, rhetoric historically engages with epistemological issues of truth, knowledge, and ethics in a foundational way. Not only is rhetoric interesting because its earliest professional practitioners and speech consultants—the Sophists—are a source of its first analytical handbook, Aristotle's *The Art of Rhetoric* (L'Etang, 1996a, 1996b), but also because the classical debates foregrounded the dilemma of questionable legitimacy of those who argued for a living but were not subject experts and not specifically concerned with truth. There was criticism of advocates whose focus was on techniques to win arguments rather than on truth-seeking and the acquisition of knowledge.

Defining "truth" in international/intercultural relations contexts is questionable for those who believe that knowledge is socially and culturally constructed. The fracture between those holding relativist and universal epistemological positions is reflected in fault lines within the public relations discipline. This becomes especially noticeable in discussions of the role of public relations in relation to "truth," notably within the rhetorical paradigm. There are also internal tensions in sources that are ostensibly focused on particular cultural perspectives, but which engage with them through the imposition of universalized frameworks. More will be said about this later. Furthermore, the choice of rhetoric and diplomacy in relation to public relations permits reflection on the cultural and intercultural nature of public relations work, a topic that has come to the fore in recent years (Sriramesh & Verčič, 2003, 2009b; Tilson & Alozie, 2004; van Ruler & Verčič, 2004). Since, as I shall argue, public relations is not just about discourse management, rhetoric, and dialectic but also about cultural relations and intercultural communication, it is appropriate to turn to the discipline of anthropology for inspiration and guidance.

Why Anthropology? "Making It Real"

Public relations has had little engagement with anthropology, or with its defining research method—ethnography (L'Etang, 2009b, in press-a). One exception has been a bibliography compiled for use by practitioners (Watson, 2005); another has been Pieczka (1997), who argued that "ethnomethodology and ethnographic approaches to public relations research, might help public relations theory deal with the ethically complex area of strategic action" (p. 66).

The absence of anthropological and ethnographic work is strange, because public relations is a profoundly cultural activity at a number of levels. Public relations work is situated within different national and ethnic cultures, and practitioners participate in international and intercultural communication in a globalized context. Public relations practitioners are members of organizational cultures and engage in intra- and interorganizational cultural communication. Their liaison with those who specialize in marketing, advertising, and design locates the public relations occupational culture within a broader "promotional culture" (Wernick, 1991). Public relations practitioners seek to communicate with stakeholders and publics (who may, of course, perform their own public relations, especially if they metamorphose into social movements or "activists"), which arise within specialized microcultures (financial cultures, political cultures, activist cultures, sporting cultures, digital cultures). Our understanding of these multiple cultural engagements by public relations practitioners is somewhat limited, hence the need for an ethnographic turn.

The purpose of anthropology is to study humankind in specific contexts, from a holistic perspective. Although anthropology combines science, humanities, and archaeology, its main focus is on the creation and practice of culture, and its operation in relation to people's lives, beliefs, values, and knowledge, including spiritual and material elements (Smajs, 2006, p. 636). Anthropology has contributed instrumentally and interpretively to business, organization, and management and marketing studies, specifically ethnographies of work and professions; studies of industrialization; ethnographic design of products and services; and studies of consumer behavior and organizational cultures (Arnould & Wallendorf, 1994; Ashkanasy, Wilderom, & Peterson, 2000; Baba, 2006; Mariampolski, 2006); and it has also generated new concepts within media studies, such as media events and media rituals (Bird, 2009; Rothenbuhler & Coman, 2005). The contribution of anthropology to public relations acquired through its distinctive method, ethnography, lives in its potential to reveal the role and practice of public relations "in everyday life," including its specifically intra- and intercultural manifestations (organizational, regional, national, international). To date, few in public relations have invested the necessary time and patience to do such work, two exceptions being the British-based scholars Hodges (2005, 2006) and Pieczka (1997, 2002, 2006a, 2006b).

Existing literature on public relations and culture is dominated by cross-cultural comparisons, often imposing a particular framework on evidence. The effort is often systematic but has not tended to yield "rich description." For example, Sriramesh and Verčič (2003, 2009b) applied a framework to an ambitious collection of national data focused on political arrangements, ethnic developments, the extent and type of activism, the legal system, media, and a generalized description of the culture. Culture itself is seen as available and explored through a framework of cultural determinants and dimensions (Kaplan & Manners, 1972) of societal culture (Hofstede, 1984, 1991; Hofstede & Paterson, 2000) to link these to "public relations variables" (Sriramesh & Verčič, 2009a, p. 11). In other words, the approach to culture is instrumental, not interpretive. Although Sriramesh (1996) published an "ethnographic study of the southern Indian organisations," his approach was to study a large number of organizations (18), which meant that he was forced to compromise on the amount of time spent at each location (4–8 days) (p. 182), which does not really meet the requirements of in-depth, long-term cultural immersion required by anthropologists.

Indeed, anthropologists have long regretted the bastardization of the term "ethnographic" and criticized practices that Rist (2001) referred to in 1980 as "blitzkrieg ethnography" and "hit and run forays" (p. 199). However, these examples are perhaps not surprising in a discipline that is weak in qualitative research and dominated by functionalism and normative assumptions. I have reviewed methodological approaches to culture within public relations in more detail elsewhere (Sriramesh & Vercic, in press; L'Etang, under review). Furthermore, the overwhelming urge to interpret public relations practice in various cultures through the lens of largely U.S.-inspired frameworks limits the ability to generate data or models that prioritize the themes, concerns, and experiences of practitioners in those cultures

(L'Etang, 2004, 2008c). Anthropology and ethnography offer the concepts and tools to gain thick description and deep insights into the role of public relations in cultures, as well as public relations as a culture. Exploring public relations in specific cultures or adjacent occupational cultures has the potential to generate rich data that may change our approach to the field. Diplomacy is a useful site for such research, both conceptual and ethnographic.

The Role and Scope of Diplomacy and Diplomatic Studies

Diplomacy manages a country's relationship with other countries to further the principal country's ends via direct relations through its representatives (agents). Formal state diplomacy focuses on political relationships and intercourse with other countries through permanent representatives of other nations located outside their host nation in foreign countries or in institutions such as the United Nations (L'Etang, 2006b, p. 374).

Diplomats (political, public, cultural) are political and institutional agents enacting and articulating official versions of values, mores, cultural characteristics, and ideals emerging from and reflecting historical cultural experiences. Such agents seek to use relationships strategically for the benefit of their paymasters. Those in public and cultural diplomacy seek enhanced understanding, and relationships that will produce political and business benefits, and, in corporate communications (instrumental) terms, "strong" identity on the international stage that may reap benefit from other opportunities and strategic alliances. Nevertheless, individuals who work in such roles may well have a deep personal commitment to intercultural cooperation. Those whose careers entail a range of 3- to 6-year overseas postings and the acquisition of multiple languages are necessarily living an anthropologist's life. Such careers entail exposure to cultural dislocation, subjection to inevitable culture shock, homesickness, and regular language training to communicate and empathize with a range of other cultures and their histories in order to facilitate exchange of ideas and lifestyles through a range of techniques.

Jonsson and Langhorne (2004), eminent professors of political science at the Universities of Lund and Rutgers, respectively, recently edited a collection of writing on diplomacy. In their introduction they explained that

> diplomacy can be seen as an institution, understood broadly as a relatively stable collusion of easily recognised *roles* coupled with underlying *norms* and a set of *rules* or *conventions*, prescribing appropriate behaviour, constraining activities, and shaping expectations. . . . Exchange—be it of goods, people, information or services—seems to be central to the origins of diplomacy. Whenever and wherever representatives of distinct identities see the need to establish exchange relations of some kind and realise their interdependence, diplomatic rules and roles are likely to emerge. Today we associate diplomacy with sovereign states, but other entities, such as tribes, clans, cities or churches, have developed diplomatic relations in earlier history. The study of diplomacy is not limited to the modern state system. (p. xiv)

In short, Jonsson and Langhorne (2004) perceived diplomacy as a distinct occupational culture that is involved in relational exchanges and activities, features that provide an excellent rationale for conceiving public relations as a form of diplomacy in multiple contexts, as well as interpreting diplomacy as a form of public relations. Another significant feature of Jonsson and Langhorne's insights is the emphasis given to a variety of cultures that have (and continue) to practice diplomacy. Such insights in relation to identity groupings indicate the anthropological potential of these linked occupations.

Public diplomacy is aimed at foreign publics and aims to advance the nation's interests by achieving understanding of "its ideas and ideals, its institutions and culture, as well as its national goals and policies" (Melissen, 2007a, pp. 11–12). There has been renewed interest in the importance of the concept since 9/11, reflected in the literature on public diplomacy, particularly in its communicative and relational aspects (Cowan, 2008; Jonsson & Hall, 2003; Kelley, 2009; Ronfeldt & Arquilla, 2009; Snow & Taylor, 2009; Zaharna, 2009), for example,

> public diplomacy is part of a newly emerging paradigm of collaborative diplomacy, which requires an approach that is fundamentally dialogue-based.... [N]ation-building and the struggle against international terrorism are two prime examples where such an approach has the potential to contribute to international stability.... [N]ew public diplomacy is increasingly about ideas and values, and involving non-governmental agents is seen as one of the most effective ways of promoting and developing it. (Melissen, 2007b, p. xxi)

Cultural diplomacy is an overlapping concept but describes programs that employ cultural aims and means to achieve medium- and longer-term policy goals by marketing the nation's cultural capital. Cultural access to the language, literature, music, art, history, film and media, science and technology, and medical sciences are all ways of engaging with the nation's values. Scholarships and exchange-of-persons programs facilitate long-term relationships and identification—and identification is an important feature in some rhetorical frameworks (Burke, cited in Heath, 2001a), opening the way to seeing cultural and public diplomacy as a form of rhetoric. Organizations such as the British Council are central to such efforts, but public and cultural diplomacy are not the sole preserve or interest of governments but also engaged in by multinational organizations—"many countries envy the professionalism and public diplomacy muscle of some coal corporations" (Melissen, 2007a, p. 13).

The scope of diplomacy is broad, encompassing relationships in political, cultural, and public dimensions, and also includes nation-building and nation-branding (marketing) activities. While diplomacy has been seen as an adjunct of the field of international relations and is enacted through career diplomats who enjoy a peripatetic lifestyle, the diplomatic activities employed by states, corporations, and multinational organizations and NGOs have expanded. For example, the industries of sport and tourism (Chehabi, 2004; L'Etang, 2006a, 2006b; L'Etang, Falkheimer, & Lugo, 2007), and the cultural industries and education, are all deployed to this end. The concept of "citizen diplomacy" (issue publics, economic representatives, lobbyists, activists, powerful independent agents) has also received attention (Sharp, 2004a, 2004b), a concept that has resonance and relevance for public relations. In a way, these activities may be used to replace or at least supplement formal negotiation. Governments will seek to use key cultural assets to develop and enhance relationships, including those that are also financed by the private sector, such as tourism or sport. Multiple assets imply multiple potential relationships since each distinctive feature may attract support from those external to the country. Hence the fact that Manchester United has supporters in Mauritius adds to the United Kingdom's cultural diplomacy effort. Thus, public diplomacy and cultural diplomacy are not solely the domain of government institutions. They are a vehicle to facilitate many interpersonal exchanges and relationships and to forge direct and indirect connections, often over a long-term generational basis. Industries such as sport and tourism may leverage their diplomatic potential overseas for political and financial enhancements from government in the home country.

The field of diplomacy is largely drawn from international relations, and much has been practitioner-based or historical. However, there has not been a great deal of theorization on the topic of diplomacy, which has tended to become submerged within analyses of power struggles and the threat of force (Jonsson & Langhorne, 2004, p. xv). One framework proposed three categories of assumption: first, the Realist or Machiavellian approach, which assumed a world driven by power, competition, and conflict, and where diplomacy offered inducements or applied pressure; second, the Rationalist approach, which built relationships through promise keeping and truthfulness, trusteeship, and reciprocity; and finally, the Revolutionist model, which focused on the balance of power between nation-states and international society and argued for the international public interest to be guarded by international society (Wight, 1955, cited in L'Etang, 1996b, 2006a, 2006b).

Those in diplomatic studies have tackled communication as a topic in a way that is relevant for public relations studies. For example, Cohen (2004) discussed verbal and nonverbal communication in his essay "Diplomacy as Theatre," which focused on issues of impression management (a field given oddly little attention within public relations) via the media. Jonsson and Hall (2003, 2004) identified key aspects of verbal and nonverbal communication: intelligence, signaling, "necessary ambiguity" (for multiple audiences), formulation and interpretation of messages, semiotics, body language, gift giving, respect, private and public communication, ritualization (protocol, ceremony), and technological communication. Their discussion lays out research themes, which could be usefully explored in public relations, particularly from an anthropological perspective, that would facilitate analysis of rituals, myths, and the lived experience of these forms of human communication in the diplomatic and public relations cultural contexts.

Public and cultural diplomacy also have the complex task of addressing multiethnic populations increasingly from a multiethnic base. The relationship between nation branding and public and cultural diplomacy presents challenges in terms of rhetorical strategies, not least because of the potential danger of mixed or conflicting discourses, for example, the tension between national unity/identity and multiculturalism that acknowledges the diasporic transformative processes of globalization, another theme to which anthropology can contribute.

Public Relations and Diplomacy: A Critical Review

Despite the claim made by Van Dyke and Verčič (2009) that "for decades, scholars and practitioners have debated the issue of separation or convergence between public relations and public diplomacy" (p. 832), the number of sources specifically addressing this topic is relatively small (Grunig, 1993; L'Etang, 1994, 1996a, 1996b, 2006a, 2006b, 2009; Signitzer, 2008; Signitzer & Coombs, 1992; Signitzer & Wamser, 2006; Szondi, 2009; Traverse-Healy, 1988). Much of this work is taken up with role comparisons, including contrasts between theoretical models of public relations and diplomatic practice and theories taken from international relations.

Comparisons are useful beyond the descriptive, in highlighting the importance of intention of the focus of these contributions and the significance of assumptions on which diplomacy/public relations is conducted and how these affect the communicative process. The issue of communication style has been a focus for some discussion; for example, Signitzer and Coombs (1992) took a largely instrumental/behavioral approach drawing on Piesert's (cited in Signitzer & Wamser, 2006) framework and applying it within the public relations dominant paradigm, classifying activities according to "the four models" framework, and the concept of symmetry/asymmetry/public information/publicity. They also drew on sources to distinguish between "tough-minded" and "tender-minded" approaches to public diplomacy (Signitzer, 2008; Signitzer & Coombs, 1992; Signitzer & Wamser, 2006, p. 438), whereas Van Dyke and Verčič (2009) and Xifra (2008, 2009) used the concepts of "hard power" and "soft power" (Nye, 2008). While authors are careful to distinguish between the different forms of diplomacy (political, public, cultural), they have not yet taken sufficient account of technological changes in communication and often seem reluctant to acknowledge that the connection between diplomacy and power has implications for idealistic and normative accounts of public relations. In particular, the acknowledgment of the role of power apparent in diplomacy negates the idealistic features of the dominant paradigm, and the combination of strategic communication and diplomatic motivation leads to an implicitly realistic or Machiavellian approach to diplomacy/public relations based on self-interest (L'Etang, 1994, 1996a, 1996b, 2006, 2009; Wight, 1955).

In particular, the diplomatic analogy and similarity of concept implies rather profound connections between public relations, propaganda, and psychological operations (L'Etang, 1994, 1996a, 1996b, 2006, 2009). Psychological operations are military communications targeted at foreign publics, and according to the U.S. military are "planned operations to convey selected information . . . to foreign audiences to influence the emotions, motives, objective reasoning, and ultimately behaviour of foreign governments, organizations, groups and individuals" (Kilbane, 2009, p. 187).

This definition overlaps with the goals of public diplomacy, propaganda, and public relations and demonstrates strategic intention and operational instrumentalism apparently embedded in these practices. As Melissen (2007a) pointed out,

> Three concepts that deserve brief attention in a discussion on public diplomacy are propaganda, nation-branding and foreign cultural relations. Similar to public diplomacy, propaganda and nation-branding are about the communication of information and ideas to foreign publics with a view to changing attitudes towards the originating country or reinforcing existing beliefs. . . . [T]he practice of cultural relations has traditionally been closed to diplomacy, although it is clearly distinct from it, but recent developments in both fields now reveal considerable overlap between the two concepts. (p. 16)

Although Van Dyke and Verčič (2009) cited Grupp (2008) suggesting that the notion of corporate diplomacy is recent, that concept has been around for at least a couple of decades in public relations (L'Etang, 1994, 1996a, 1996b, 2004; Traverse-Healy, 1988) and is implicit in international relations and international business as evidenced by Strange's (2004) 1988 discussion of "states, firms and diplomacy." The development of organizational, and particularly corporate, diplomacy may not have been much recognized in the literature but may well be a necessary condition of strategic communications practice, and as such, worthy of empirical ethnographic investigation. The civilianization of many military and political concepts and practices, including strategic planning models now taken for granted by senior management (including issues management), has not been subjected to much critical analysis within public relations (although L'Etang, 2006a, 2006b, 2009, and Van Dyke & Verčič, 2009, do touch on this). Interrelationships between the military-industrial complex and other parts of the managerial classes are suggestive of relational strategies and assumptions that will shape communication. Understanding the role of public relations in such "circuits of power" (Pieczka, 2006b, p. 320) can provide a more rounded picture of the occupation and its role in contemporary culture. Anthropological research is one strategy to gather the necessary empirical data and understand practitioner culture in political and international contexts.

The Role and Scope of Rhetoric and Rhetorical Studies: Implications for Public Relations and Diplomacy

Contemporary debates concerning rhetoric vary in scope from the technical to the societal. Discussions include behavioral change and societal impacts as well as the distinctions and relationships between rhetoric, persuasion, dialectic, discourse, argumentation, orality, public discourse, and social movements. Thus, the relevance of this field for the public relations discipline is high, conceptually, critically, and methodologically. Of particular relevance for public relations scholars are the areas of social movement rhetoric (Cox & Foust, 2009) and public discourse studies (Wilson & Eberly, 2009; Zarefsky, 2009). As Zarefsky (2009) explained,

> A growing body of scholarship is devoted to the connections between public discourse and public policy. Sometimes the approach has been to examine discourse devoted to a specific issue or policy; sometimes, it has been to explain choices of policies or their outcomes by reference to considerations of public discourse. In these studies, the unit of analysis is the controversy rather than either the rhetor or the text. Studies of public affairs typically encompass a variety of rhetors and media over time and attempt to account for the resolution of a public issue. (p. 445)

There are multiple paradigms within rhetorical studies and consequently various definitions of the term, some of which are limited to the notion of persuasion; others encompass the scope of social movements. Neoclassical approaches to rhetoric, such as those of Perelmen and Toulmin, "postulate that argumentation is always designed to achieve a particular effect on those for whom it is intended" (van Eemeren,, 2009, p. 16). For some, rhetoric is limited to the political sphere alone; for others, it is liberated as a global concept, "Unfettered by any particular subject matter, rhetoric becomes a power that ranges across the entire domain of human discourse, containing whatever matter it encounters" (Leff, 1987, cited in Lyne & Miller, 2009, p. 168).

The dialectical approach to rhetoric emerged in the late 20th century from the Erlangen School in the form of a formal-dialectical procedure involving a regimented dialogue between the proponent of a thesis and an opponent (van Eenerem, 2009, p. 118). In contrast, pragma-dialectics developed by van Eemeren and Grootendorst viewed argumentation "as a communicative and interactional discourse to be studied from a normative as well as a descriptive perspective" inspired by "critical rationalism . . . speech act theory, Gricean language philosophy, and discourse analysis'"(van Eemeren, 2009, p. 118). In this model, the focus is on analytical stages that are specified as requirements to achieve resolution.

The debating tradition in the United States is a practice-based approach, though there have been departures, such as those who viewed debate as a cooperative rather than a competitive venture (van Eemeren, 2009, pp. 120–121). An influential theorist within public relations has been Kenneth Burke, who saw rhetoric as a form of persuasion or courtship (Heath, 2009, p. 38) in which the competitive exchange of ideas through dialectic offered the potential for shared meanings and transcendent solutions (Heath, 2001b, p. 40). Burke's ideas and their implications for public relations have been analyzed extensively by Heath (2001a, 2001b, 2007, 2009), in particular, drawing out the potential for a rhetorical approach for facilitating choices and collaboration, thus contributing to a consensual approach to public relations.

Western classical concepts of rhetoric have had a useful airing in public relations, not least because classical critiques highlight fundamental problems of legitimacy centered on morality: Is rhetoric a neutral skill that could be applied to any body of knowledge to secure influence? Did rhetoric produce knowledge or truth or simply persuasive effects (attitudinal/behavioral change) through argumentation technique? Such questions have remained important for public relations. Classical philosophers placed rhetoric and philosophy in a dichotomous relationship, as Lunsford, Wilson, and Eberly (2009) explained: "In the Western tradition, the argument between philosophy and sophistry perfectly captures competing conceptions of rhetorical knowledge, with philosophy linking Truth to dialectic and logic and the Sophists linking contingent truth to rhetoric" (p. xx).

Classical philosophers took an essentialist and universalist approach to the notion of truth. The intervening decades of exploration, colonialism, decolonization, and globalization have altered perspectives so that relativist notions of truth and knowledge have become influential. These ideas have reshaped the field of rhetoric and are consistent with approaches taken in anthropology. However, relativism does not appear to be a popular position within public relations. Within public relations, the concept of truth is often used as a way of distinguishing public relations from propaganda, even though there are methodological problems with such a strategy (L'Etang, 2006a, 2006b, 2008). Thus, traditional philosophical ethics are used to underpin the discipline's legitimizing discourses. As Skerlap (2001) pointed out,

> The naïve belief in truth, objectivity and impartiality as the normative criteria of validity of public relations discourse that is professed by public relations textbooks does not elucidate on the discursive dimension of polemical confrontations. Not only has the positivistic concept of truth become controversial with the ascent of postmodern relativism in the last few decades, but the concept of "truth" has been conceptualised altogether differently in rhetorical tradition from ancient times onwards. (p. 183)

Within public relations, there is a dominant U.S. approach to the topic of rhetoric (Heath, 1980, 1992, 1997, 2000, 2001a, 2001b, 2009; Heath & Frandsen, 2008; Heath & Nelson, 1986; Heath, Toth, & Waymer, 2009; Toth & Heath, 1992); but there have also been alternate perspectives (Cheney & Christensen, 2001), including those of some from Europe whose views have not received as much attention as they have deserved, most notably Ihlen (2002, 2005, 2007), who has drawn on social theory to link rhetoric to power processes and sociology of the media and who criticized "the dominant rhetorical approach in public relations and issues management for not integrating symbolic and material dimensions" (2002, p. 259). Similarly, the critical Slovenian scholar Skerlap (2001) criticized the dominant paradigm and "the narrow conception of rhetoric as persuasive and argumentative discourse . . . [and] positivistic understanding of 'truth' and 'objectivity' as normative criteria of public relations discourse" (p. 176).

Within the dominant paradigm, the term *rhetoric* is presented as "dialogue" rather than advocacy yet at the same time to be formulated strategically, as the following quotes illustrate:

> A rationale for effective discourse . . . a well-established body of critical principles . . . regarding how messages need to be proved, structured, framed and worded. (Heath, 2009, p. 22)

> The rhetoric of issue management is best conceived of as dialogue. Both sides have views that they express and preferences they advocate. This dialogue is the product of statement and counter statement, voiced expressions of what organizations do and what they should do, what they prefer as ideology and policy principles. (Heath, 2006, p. 67)

The difficulty with this perspective is that it employs the term *rhetoric* in the traditional classical sense as being concerned with truth and knowledge. However, this does not really describe the public relations function in practice, which is required constantly to frame issues in relation to the organizational mission and function. It is a position that assumes that the public relations function does have influence on policy but does not seem to take account of the public relations role that tries to smooth the way for organizational survival. Many organizations are not explicitly concerned with reaching societal goals (however, these are determined—and whether they are in fact determined openly or simply a consequence of multiple different intentions and drives) but in achieving their own goals and maximizing profit. In other words, many organizations do not operate on the basis of public service as their prime function, even though they may justify what they do in utilitarian terms arguing that the free market benefits the greatest number. In fact, it's an interesting question where the topic of "societal goals" is in fact debated, and the role that public relations does or does not play in that.

Understanding rhetorical practice in public relations and diplomacy requires analysis and understanding of the cultural history and conventions, not just in relation to the practice, but in terms of social context and intellectual tradition and political debate at all levels, including attention to dialectics, argumentation, and argumentative realities. Discussion of rhetoric in public relations needs to be more closely situated within this multiparadigmatic field as there are various interpretations/traditions of rhetoric and many analytic frameworks. Within public relations, rhetoric may be used to solve problems of public relations' legitimacy. Yet, perhaps, there have not been sufficient engagements with more recent rhetorical literature. It is also important for public relations scholars to specify which rhetorical framework they are operating within, and why, and to acknowledge alternative paradigms.

Within public relations, the approach to rhetoric appears to fall within the rhetorical agency paradigm that sees rhetoric as having agency, "especially civic engagement to create public spaces for deliberation and debate" (Leff & Lunsford, 2004, p. 63). Some scholars assume positive agency to public relations and suggest that it has a particular role to play in promoting democracy and civil society (as a part of public diplomacy) around the globe (Taylor & Kent, 2006, p. 398) and argue that "civil society [can be explained] as a rhetorical public relations activity" (Taylor, 2009, p. 83). However, the term *agency* is "polysemic and ambiguous, a term that can refer to invention, strategies, authorship, institutions, power, identity, subjectivity, and subject positions, among others" (Campbell, cited in Lunsford et al., 2009, p. xxii). This challenge points to the necessity for more public relations scholars to engage with social theory and its concepts (Ihlen, van Ruler, & Frederiksson, 2009).

Diplomacy and Rhetoric

Diplomats use rhetoric to position their countries, or, in the case of stateless nations, to make legitimacy claims. Public and cultural diplomacy may be used to support rhetorical strategy and advocacy. The linkage between the two concepts in practice has led to "the nexus between rhetoric and foreign policy studies . . . becoming fertile ground for intellectual exchange, with a growing number of international relations scholars drawing on the concept of argumentation to explain global events" (Mitchell, 2009, p. 248).

Communication has a crucial role in the noosphere (Arquilla & Ronfeldt, cited in Mitchell, 2009, p. 248; and introduced to public relations by the Spanish scholar Xifra, 2008). The "noosphere" is a consequence of

> the rise of a networked global society, characterized by asymmetrical conflicts and heightened efficacy of transnational, non-governmental actors . . . a global "realm of the mind" [that] links actors together in ways that complicate the exercise of traditional modes of state power, hence a new form of political action, "noopolitick." (Mitchell, 2009, p. 248)

In this more complex environment, new cultures of diplomacy arise:

> By noopolitik we mean an approach to statecraft, to be undertaken as much by non-state as by state actors, that emphasizes the role of informational soft power in expressing ideas, values, norms and ethics through all manner of media. This makes it distinct from realpolitik, which stresses the hard, material dimensions of power and treats states as the determinants of the world order. Noopolitick makes sense because knowledge is fast becoming an ever stronger sources of power and strategy, in ways that classic realpolitik and internationalism cannot absorb. (Arquilla & Ronfeldt, cited in Mitchell, 2009, p. 248)

Corporate diplomacy engages in the same processes. Discursive formations combine storylines, values, and morals around fictive organizational personalities and human agents. Public stories may be wallpaper or entertainment, random stream of consciousness, or a focus for debate or a source for contestation, although that may be in digital spaces beyond the ken of corporate issues managers. Rhetorical activities may be engaged in, but they are not all of equal influence or treated as such by powerful actors.

Diplomacy, both political and corporate, is necessarily rhetorical, since it is concerned with local, regional, national, and international positioning, brand, and reputation linked to policy and ambition. Morality is a central discourse mobilized to engender trust, a key component for functional relationships. The problem for those involved in rhetorical and communicative activities on behalf of diplomats, politicians, chief executives, senior public servants, or those heading up hospitals, charities, educational institutions, or activist groups is that their impact on policy may be variable or even minimal—thus leaving them open to criticism that their work is state/organizational advocacy in which relationships are used as a means to the state/organizational end.

Heath suggested that practitioners demonstrate transparency and reflexivity to gain respect and legitimacy for an occupation that he redefined in a way to avoid the classic Platonic criticisms thus:

> The rhetoric of issues management . . . must begin with a consideration of the quality of facts, values/evaluations, and policy positions that are advocated and eventually enacted. As difficult as it is to achieve certain knowledge and truth, those outcomes need to be the constant goal of issues management rhetoric. Without a commitment to better facts, evaluations, and policies, the discipline devolves into the worst of "spin." The public will not tolerate a callous commitment to relativity. Relativity carried to its ultimate extreme suggests that because no truth or knowledge is superior, people are legitimately justified in taking a cynical commitment to abandon the pursuit of truth and knowledge. Nihilism or the power grab thus become alternative strategies. The preferred option is a good-faith effort to use the dialogue of rhetoric to produce and refine facts, evaluations, and policies in the public view through the processes of advocacy and counter advocacy. (Heath, 2006, p. 85)

This rationalist ideal presents one solution to the problems of legitimacy faced by public relations practitioners. However, it is perhaps less helpful in a postmodern and relativist global context, in which the social construction of reality frames the worldview of many. This is particularly true in relation to ideological debates and conflicts, such as those connected to religion and cultural practices, or to those in which truth and knowledge are not easily accessible or resolvable through debate alone, for example, debate over climate change. In other words, although rhetoric in some contexts may produce agreement founded in scientific evidence, much of the time, it is employed interpretively, persuasively, and ideologically, acknowledging multiple perspectives. Thus, cultural diplomacy of Western nations would need to acknowledge, and be responsive to, postcolonial perspectives and alternative readings of their policies.

Relativistic rhetoric may also acknowledge that policy is not necessarily monolithic but has evolved through internal debate. This approach highlights that rhetorical intercultural engagements are multilinear and complex, entered into for multiple reasons and not necessarily to determine a central truth. Discussion of rhetoric within public relations has tended to focus more strongly on classical tradition than on the postmodern "new rhetorics" characterized by diversity, transformation, and dialogue (Enos & Brown, 1993). However, in seeking to understand diplomacy and public relations practice in many different cultures, it is important to understand the necessity for anthropological research, which can gain access to the doubtless multiple understandings and interpretations of rhetorical-type practices that have evolved within a range of historical conditions and microcultures. The use of rationalist definitions and practices drawn from the Western Enlightenment is political and ideological, and it has implications for public relations, diplomacy, and communicative action in cultural contexts that have had alternative histories.

Anthropological Futures in Public Relations, Diplomacy, and Rhetoric

Anthropology could offer holistic, yet empirically grounded, analyses of public relations and diplomacy and their rhetorical aspects. In particular, it would offer comparative insights into the national/cultural/organizational disciplines of public relations and diplomacy (political, public, and corporate) and explore the rhetoric of these practices, occupational rites and rituals, conflict resolution, culture shock, culture change, ethnocentrism, multiculturalism, transnationalism, cultural convergence, and globalization.

Ethnographic studies could uncover the particular experiences of cultural, public, and political diplomats and their communication practices. Likewise, ethnography of public relations practitioners and their professional bodies could uncover the extent of diplomatic concepts and practice in everyday life. Understanding the rhetoric of practitioners is one type of study; the rhetoric of stakeholders and social movements is another. Both could usefully draw on existing work in the anthropologies of communication, media, and business, and greatly enrich the discipline of public relations.

References

Arnould, E., & Wallendorf, M. (1994). Market-orientated ethnography: Interpretation building and marketing strategy formulation. *Journal of Marketing Research, 31*(4), 484–504.

Arquilla, J., & Ronfeldt, D. (1999). *Noopolitik: Toward an American information strategy.* Santa Monica, CA: RAND.

Ashkanasy, N., Wilderom, C., & Peterson, M. (Eds.). (2000). *Handbook of organizational culture and climate.* London: Sage.

Baba, M. (2006). Anthropology and business. In H. Birz (Ed.), *Encyclopedia of anthropology* (pp. 83–125). London: Sage.

Bird, S. (Ed.). (2009). *The anthropology of news and journalism.* Bloomington: Indiana University Press.

Chehabi, H. (2004). Sport diplomacy between the US and Iran. In C. Jonsson & R. Langhorne (Eds.), *Diplomacy* (Vol. 3, pp. 238–252). London: Sage Library of International Relations.

Cheney, G., & Christensen, L. (2001). Public relations as contested terrain: Critical response. In R. Heath (Ed.), *Handbook of public relations* (pp. 167–182). Thousand Oaks, CA: Sage.

Cohen, R. (2004). Diplomacy as theatre. In C. Jonsson & R. Langhorne (Eds.), *Diplomacy* (Vol. 1, pp. 264–278). London: Sage Library of International Relations.

Cowan, G. (2008). Moving from monologue to dialogue to collaboration: The three layers of public diplomacy. *Annals of the American Academy of Political and Social Science, 616*(1), 10–30.

Cox, R., & Foust, C. (2009). Social movement rhetoric. In A. A. Lunsford, K. H. Wilson, & R. A. Eberly (Eds.), *The Sage handbook of rhetorical studies* (pp. 605–628). London: Sage.

Culbertson, C., & Chen, N. (Eds.). (1996). *International public relations: A comparative analysis.* Mahwah, NJ: Lawrence Erlbaum.

Daymon, C., & Hodges, C. (2009). Researching the occupational culture of public relations in Mexico. *Public Relations Review, 35,* 429–433.

Der Derian, J. (1987). *On diplomacy: A genealogy of Western estrangement.* Oxford, UK: Basil Blackwell.

Dinan, W., & Miller, D. (Eds.). (2007). *Thinker, faker, spinner, spy: Corporate PR and the assault on democracy.* London: Pluto Press.

Edwards, L. (2006). Rethinking power in public relations. *Public Relations Review, 32*(3), 229–231.

Edwards, L., & Hodges, C. (in press). *Society, culture and public relations.* London: Routledge.

Enos, T., & Brown, S. C. (Eds.). (1993). *Defining the new rhetorics.* London: Sage.

Grunig, J. E. (1993). Public relations and international affairs: Effects, ethics and responsibility. *Journal of International Affairs, 47*(1), 137–162.

Heath, R. L. (1980). Corporate advocacy: An application of speech communication perspectives and skills—and more. *Communication Education, 29,* 370–377.

Heath, R. L. (1992). The wrangle in the marketplace: A rhetorical perspective of public relations. In E. L. Toth & R. L. Heath (Eds.), *Rhetorical and critical perspectives of public relations* (pp. 17–36). Hillsdale, NJ: Lawrence Erlbaum.

Heath, R. L. (1997). Legitimate "perspectives" in public relations practice: A rhetorical solution. *Australian Journal of Communication, 24*(2), 55–64.

Heath, R. L. (Ed.). (2001a). *Handbook of public relations.* London: Sage.

Heath, R. L. (2001b). A rhetorical enactment rationale for public relations: The good organization communicating well. In R. L. Heath (Ed.), *Handbook of public relations* (pp. 31–50). London: Sage.

Heath, R. L. (2006). A rhetorical theory approach to issues management. In C. Botan & V. Hazleton (Eds.), *Public relations theory II* (pp. 63–100). New York: Routledge.

Heath, R. L. (2007). Management through advocacy. In E. L. Toth (Ed.), *The future of excellence in public relations and communication management: Challenges for the next generation* (pp. 2–19). Mahwah, NJ: Lawrence Erlbaum.

Heath, R. L. (2009). The rhetorical tradition: Wrangle in the marketplace. In R. L. Heath, E. Toth, & D. Waymer (Eds.), *Rhetorical and critical approaches to public relations II* (pp. 17–47). New York: Routledge.

Heath, R. L., & Frandsen, F. (2008). Rhetorical perspective and public relations: Meaning matters. In A. Zerfass, B. van Ruler, & K. Sriramesh (Eds.), *Public relations research: European and international perspectives and innovations* (pp. 349–364). Wiesbaden, Germany: VS Verlag.

Heath, R. L., & Nelson, R. A. (1986). *Issues management.* Beverly Hills, CA: Sage.

Hill, C., & Beshoff, P. (Eds.). (1994). *Two worlds of international relations.* London: Routledge.

Hodges, C. (2005). PRP culture: A framework for exploring public relations practitioners as cultural intermediaries. *Journal of Communication Management, 10*(1), 80–93.

Hodges, C. (2006). *Relaciones humanas: The potential for public relations practitioners as cultural intermediaries.* Unpublished thesis, University of Bournemouth, UK.

Hofstede, G. (1984). *Culture's consequences.* Beverly Hills, CA: Sage.

Hofstede, G. (1991). *Culture and organization: Software of the mind.* London: McGraw-Hill.

Hofstede, G., & Paterson, M. (2000). Culture: National values and organizational practices. In N. Ashkanasy, C. Wilderom, & M. Peterson (Eds.), *Handbook of organizational culture and climate* (pp. 401–416). London: Sage.

Ihlen, O. (2002). Rhetoric and resources: Notes for a new approach to public relations and issues management. *Journal of Public Affairs, 2*(4), 259–269.

Ihlen, O. (2005). The power of social capital: Adapting Pierre Bourdieu to the study of public relations. *Public Relations Review, 31*(4), 492–496.

Ihlen, O. (2007). Building on Bourdieu: A sociological grasp of public relations. *Public Relations Review, 33*(3), 269–274.

Ihlen, O., van Ruler, B., & Frederiksson, M. (2009). *Public relations and social theory: Key figures and concepts.* London: Routledge.

Jonsson, C., & Hall, M. (2003). Communications: An essential aspect of diplomacy. *International Studies Perspectives, 4*(2), 195–210.

Jonsson, C., & Langhorne, R. (Eds.). (2004). *Diplomacy* (Vols. 1–3). London: Sage Library of International Relations.

Kaplan, D., & Manners, K. (1972). *Culture theories.* Englewood Cliffs, NJ: Prentice Hall.

Kelley, J. (2009). Between "take-offs" and "crash landings": Situational aspects of public diplomacy. In N. Snow & P. Taylor (Eds.), *Routledge handbook of public diplomacy* (pp. 72–85). London: Routledge.

Kilbane, M. (2009). Military psychological operations as public diplomacy. In N. Snow & P. Taylor (Eds.), *Public diplomacy* (pp. 187–194). London: Routledge.

Leff, M., & Lunsford, A. (2004). Afterward: A dialogue. *Rhetoric Society Quarterly, 34,* 55–69.

L'Etang, J. (1994, July). *Public relations as diplomacy.* Paper presented at the 1st International Public Relations Research Symposium, Bledcom, Slovenia, Lake Bled.

L'Etang, J. (1996a). Public relations and rhetoric. In J. L'Etang & M. Pieczka (Eds.), *Critical perspectives in public relations* (pp. 106–123). London: ITBP.

L'Etang, J. (1996b). Public relations as diplomacy. In J. L'Etang & M. Pieczka (Eds.), *Critical perspectives in public relations* (pp. 14–34). London: ITBP.

L'Etang, J. (1997). Public relations and the rhetorical dilemma: Legitimate "perspectives," persuasion, or pandering? *Australian Journal of Communication, 24*(2), 33–54.

L'Etang, J. (2004). *Public relations in Britain: A history of professional practice in the 20th century.* Mahwah, NJ: Lawrence Erlbaum.

L'Etang, J. (2006a). Public relations and rhetoric (Revised). In J. L'Etang & M. Pieczka (Eds.),

Public relations: Critical debates and contemporary practice (pp. 359–372). Mahwah, NJ: Lawrence Erlbaum.

L'Etang, J. (2006b). Public relations as diplomacy (Revised). In J. L'Etang & M. Pieczka (Eds.), *Public relations: Critical debates and contemporary practice* (pp. 373–388). Mahwah, NJ: Lawrence Erlbaum.

L'Etang, J. (2008a). *Public relations: Concepts, practice and critique.* London: Sage.

L'Etang, J. (2008b). Public relations, persuasion and propaganda: Truth, knowledge, spirituality and mystique. In A. Zerfass, B. van Ruler, & K. Sriramesh (Eds.), *Public relations research: European and international perspectives* (pp. 251–270). Wiesbaden, Germany: VS Verlag.

L'Etang, J. (2008c). Writing PR history: Issues, methods and politics. *Journal of Communication Management, 12*(4), 319–335.

L'Etang, J. (2009a). Public relations and diplomacy in a globalized world: An issue of public communication. *American Behavioral Scientist, 53*(4), 607–626.

L'Etang, J. (2009b, September). *Public relations anthropology.* Paper presented at Stirling 21, the UK National Conference for public relations scholars, Stirling, Scotland.

L'Etang, J. (in press-a). Thinking about public relations and culture: Anthropological insights and ethnographic futures. In K. Sriramesh & D. Verčič (Eds.), *Culture and public relations.* London: Routledge.

L'Etang, J. (in press-b). Imagining public relations anthropology. In L. Edwards & C. Hodges (Eds.), *Society, culture and public relations.* London: Routledge.

L'Etang, J., Falkheimer, J., & Lugo, J. (2007). Public relations and tourism: Critical reflections and a research agenda. *Public Relations Review, 33*(1), 68–76.

L'Etang, J., & Pieczka, M. (Eds.). (1996). *Critical perspectives in public relations.* London: ITBP.

L'Etang, J., & Pieczka, M. (Eds.). (2006). *Public relations: Critical debates and contemporary practice.* Mahwah, NJ: Lawrence Erlbaum.

Lunsford, A. A., Wilson, K. H., & Eberly, R. A. (2009). Introduction: Rhetorics and roadmaps. In A. A. Lunsford, K. H. Wilson, & R. A. Eberly (Eds.), *The Sage handbook of rhetorical studies* (pp. xi–1). London: Sage.

Lyne, J., & Miller, C. (2009). Introduction: Rhetoric, disciplinarity and fields of knowledge. In A. A. Lunsford, K. H. Wilson, & R. A. Eberly (Eds.), *The Sage handbook of rhetorical studies* (pp. 167–174). London: Sage.

Mariampolski, H. (2006). *Ethnography for marketers: A guide to consumer immersion.* London: Sage.

McKie, D., & Munshi, D. (2007). *Reconfiguring public relations: Ecology, equity and enterprise.* London: Routledge.

Melissen, J. (2007a). The new public diplomacy: Between theory and practice. In J. Melissen (Ed.), *The new public diplomacy: Soft power in international relations* (pp. 3–27). Basingstoke, UK: Palgrave Macmillan.

Melissen, J. (Ed.). (2007b). *The new public diplomacy: Soft power in international relations.* Basingstoke, UK: Palgrave Macmillan.

Miller, D., & Dinan, W. (2008). *A century of spin: How public rations became the cutting edge of corporate power.* London: Pluto Press.

Mitchell, G. (2009). Rhetoric and international relations: More than "cheap talk." In A. A. Lunsford, K. H. Wilson, & R. A. Eberly (Eds.), *The Sage handbook of rhetorical studies* (pp. 247–264). London: Sage.

Nye, J. (2008). Public diplomacy and soft power. *Annals of the American Academy of Political and Social Science, 616*(1), 94–109.

Pearson, R. (2009). Perspectives in public relations history. In R. L. Heath, E. L. Toth, & D. Waymer (Eds.), *Rhetorical and critical perspectives in public relations II* (pp. 92–109). New York: Routledge.

Pieczka, M. (1997). Understanding in public relations. *Australian Journal of Communication, 24*(2), 65–80.

Pieczka, M. (2002). Public relations expertise deconstructed. *Media, Culture & Society, 24,* 301–323.

Pieczka, M. (2006a). "Chemistry" and the public relations industry: An exploration of the concept of jurisdiction and issues arising. In J. L'Etang & M. Pieczka (Eds.), *Public relations: Critical debates and contemporary practice* (pp. 303–330). Mahwah, NJ: Lawrence Erlbaum.

Pieczka, M. (2006b). Public relations expertise in practice. In J. L'Etang & M. Pieczka (Eds.), *Public relations: Critical debates and contemporary practice* (pp. 279–302). Mahwah, NJ: Lawrence Erlbaum.

Rist, R. (2001). Blitzkrieg ethnography: On the transformation of a method into a movement.

In A. Bryman (Ed.), *Ethnography* (Vol. 3, pp. 187–201). London: Sage.

Ronfeldt, D., & Arquilla, J. (2009). Noopolitik: A new paradigm for public diplomacy. In N. Snow & P. Yaylor (Eds.), *Public diplomacy* (pp. 252–366). London: Routledge.

Rothenbuhler, E., & Coman, M. (Eds.). (2005). *Media anthropology.* London: Sage.

Sharp, P. (2004a). Making sense of citizen diplomats. In C. Jonsson & R. Langhorne (Eds.), *Diplomacy* (Vol. 3, pp. 343–361). London: Sage Library of International Relations.

Sharp, P. (2004b). Who needs diplomats? The problem of diplomatic representation. In C. Jonsson & R. Langhorne (Eds.), *Diplomacy* (Vol. 3, pp. 58–78). London: Sage Library of International Relations.

Signitzer, B. (2008). Public relations and public diplomacy: Some conceptual explorations. In A. Zerfass, B. van Ruler, & K. Sriramesh (Eds.), *Public relations research: European and international perspectives and innovations* (pp. 219–232). Wiesbaden, Germany: VS Verlag.

Signitzer, B., & Coombs, W. T. (1992). Public relations and public diplomacy: Conceptual convergences. *Public Relations Review, 18*(2), 137–147.

Signitzer, B., & Wamser, C. (2006). Public diplomacy: A specific governmental public relations function. In C. Botan & V. Hazleton (Eds.), *Public relations theory II* (pp. 435–464). Mahwah, NJ: Lawrence Erlbaum.

Skerlap, A. (2001). Re-evaluating the role of rhetoric in public relations theory and in strategies of corporate discourse. *Journal of Communication Management, 6*(2), 176–187.

Smajs, J. (2006). Culture. In H. Birz (Ed.), *Encyclopedia of anthropology* (pp. 636–640). London: Sage.

Snow, N., & Taylor, P. (Eds.). (2009). *Public diplomacy.* London: Routledge.

Sriramesh, K. (1996). Power distance and public relations: An ethnographic study of Southern Indian organizations. In C. Culbertson & N. Chen (Eds.), *International public relations: A comparative analysis* (pp. 171–190). Mahwah, NJ: Lawrence Erlbaum.

Sriramesh, K., & Verčič, D. (Eds.). (2003). *The global public relations handbook: Theory, research and practice.* London: Routledge.

Sriramesh, K., & Verčič, D. (Eds.). (2009a). *The global public relations handbook: Theory, research and practice.* London: Routledge.

Sriramesh, K., & Verčič, D. (2009b). The relationship between culture and public relations. In K. Sriramesh & D. Verčič (Eds.), *The global public relations handbook: Theory, research and practice* (pp. 47–51). London: Routledge.

Sriramesh, K., & White, J. (1992). Societal culture and public relations. In J. Grunig (Ed.), *Excellence in public relations and communication management* (pp. 597–614). Hillsdale, NJ: Lawrence Erlbaum.

Strange, S. (2004). States, firms and diplomacy. In C. Jonsson & R. Langhorne (Eds.), *Diplomacy* (Vol. 1, pp. 352–366). London: Sage Library of International Relations.

Szondi, G. (2009). Central and East European public diplomacy: A transitional perspective on national reputation management. In N. Snow & P. Taylor (Eds.), *Public diplomacy* (pp. 292–313). London: Routledge.

Taylor, M. (2009). Civil society as a rhetorical public relations process. In R. L. Heath, E. L. Toth, & D. Waymer (Eds.), *Rhetorical and critical approaches to public relations II* (pp. 76–91). London: Routledge.

Taylor, M., & Kent, M. (2006). Public relations theory and practice in nation-building. In C. Botan & V. Hazleton (Eds.), *Public relations theory II* (pp. 341–359). Mahwah, NJ: Lawrence Erlbaum.

Tilson, D. J., & Alozie, E. C. (Eds.). (2004). *Towards the common good: Perspectives on international public relations.* Boston: Pearson.

Toth, E., & Heath, R. (Eds.). (1992). *Rhetorical and critical approaches to public relations.* Mahwah, NJ: Lawrence Erlbaum.

Traverse-Healy, T. (1988). *The credibility factor and diplomacy: A public relations perspective on public affairs* (Koeppler Memorial Lecture). Waco, TX: Baylor University.

Van Dyke, M. A., & Verčič, D. (2009). Public relations, public diplomacy and strategic communication. In K. Sriramesh & D. Verčič (Eds.), *The global public relations handbook: Theory, research and practice* (pp. 822–842). Mahwah, NJ: Lawrence Erlbaum.

van Eemeren, F. (2009). The study of argumentation. In A. A. Lunsford, K. H. Wilson, & R. A. Eberly (Eds.), *The Sage handbook of rhetorical studies* (pp. 109–138). London: Sage.

van Ruler, B., & Verčič, D. (Eds.). (2004). *Public relations and communication management in Europe:*

A nation-by-nation introduction to public relations theory and practice. Berlin, Germany: Walter de Gruyter.

Watson, M. (2005). *Anthropology and public relations: Annotated bibliography of recent and significant research of import to practitioners.* Gainesville, FL: Institute for Public Relations.

Wernick, A. (1991). *Promotional culture: Advertising, ideology and symbolic expression.* London: Sage.

Wilson, K., & Eberly, R. (2009). The common goods of public discourse. In A. A. Lunsford, K. H. Wilson, & R. A. Eberly (Eds.), *The Sage handbook of rhetorical studies* (pp. 423–433). London: Sage.

Xifra, J. (2008, June/July). *Public relations and noopolitik.* Paper presented at the conference Radical PR: Alternative Visions and Future Directions: An International Roundtable, Stirling Media Research Institute, Stirling, Scotland.

Zaharna, R. (2009). Mapping out a spectrum of public diplomacy initiatives: Information and relational communication frameworks. In N. Snow & P. Taylor (Eds.), *Public diplomacy* (pp. 86–100). London: Routledge.

Zarefsky, D. (2009). History of public discourse studies. In A. A. Lunsford, K. H. Wilson, & R. A. Eberly (Eds.), *The Sage handbook of rhetorical studies* (pp. 433–460). London: Sage.

CHAPTER 11

Social Construction and Public Relations

Katerina Tsetsura

This chapter revisits the social construction of reality, taken from sociology (P. L. Berger & Luckmann, 1966), as applied to public relations. Social construction can establish a theoretical basis for understanding public relations as an activity and as a field, and for understanding the identity of the working professionals, the institutions they represent, and people affected by that construction process. A social constructionist perspective helps ensure comprehensive analysis of public relations' role in the coconstruction of meanings among and by individuals who engage in its practices. Social construction offers illuminating ways to understand communication practices in a professional setting.

In-depth research of multiple identity construction uses traditional understandings of multiple identity construction as an integral part of the social construction of reality. This analysis supports comparative cross-disciplinary cross-cultural investigations and identity construction in such professional communication fields. It aims to revive our knowledge of the social construction approach to studying an array of multiple meaning constructions and identities in and through professional communication based on social, professional, cultural, gender, interactional, and contextual expectations. All this analysis explains and applies the theory of social construction and demonstrates its relevance to the study and practice of public relations.

Over the past 40 years, research on the social construction of reality gave rise to numerous theoretical concepts, theory-developing exercises, and a massive number of studies in different fields that focus on social, nonobjective, and interactional constructs of reality (Wilmer, 2002). Some version of the social construction of reality, as Leeds-Hurwitz (1992) pointed out, is generally common to all social approaches, as social approaches concentrate on events that occur in the process of individuals' interactions. P. L. Berger and Luckmann's (1966) original study, unfortunately, is often ignored (Leeds-Hurwitz, 1995). Researchers who choose not to start from a reexamination of P. L. Berger and Luckmann's (1966) social construction of reality miss a great opportunity to ground their basic assumptions in comprehensive analysis of the nature and origins of social construction.

Certainly, one major reason that this sociological project has long been neglected particularly by communication scholars is that interpretive social approaches were not accepted in mainstream research for many years (Craig, 1995). At the same time, researchers reflected a strong desire to part from theories of social psychology and sociology in order to develop independent theories of communication for communication research (Craig, 1995; Leeds-Hurwitz, 1995). Much has been lost as a result of such distancing from the original work on social construction.

Communication researchers have analyzed social construction as a broad, overarching framework to study the influence of social interactions on individuals (Ehrlich & King, 1992; Gergen, 1985; Mumby, 1989; Postmes, Spears, & Lea, 2000; Shotter & Gergen, 1994). This chapter argues that social construction and meaning negotiation provide a basis for complex analysis of the professional field of public relations, especially how it is understood and practiced in society.

Shotter and Gergen (1994) defined social construction as a process of creation, expression, and reinforcement of understanding through continuous and iterative social interaction by social agents situated in contextual environments and identified politically, socioeconomically, and culturally. Miller (2002) specified the problems of studying social construction because of constantly changing social interaction. Because the process of social construction is difficult to pinpoint, its study should focus not only on one interactional event (e.g., single conversation) but also on the variety of such events.

The chapter begins by explaining major assumptions within the social construction of reality and discusses the concept of social institution as well as themes of meaning construction and multiple identity construction. Next, it demonstrates the relationship between social construction and postmodernism. Then, it outlines gaps in previous research, which used social construction in communication and public relations, and poses questions for future research. Finally, it stresses the importance of viewing public relations as a socially constructed field.

The Social Construction of Reality

Social construction, constructionism, and constructivism are sometimes used interchangeably (e.g., Neimeyer, 1993), but often scholars distinguish among the concepts (Chen & Pearce, 1995; Lannamann, 1992; Pearce & Cronin, 1980; Sigman, 1992). All views share the idea that knowledge is not absolute and cannot be separated from the knower (Yerby, 1995). For this reason, constructivism has been advocated in studies of interpersonal communication (Burleson, 1989; Pearce, 1995; Sigman, 1992).

The major difference is that while constructivism emphasizes personal subjectivity (Burleson, 1989), social constructionism focuses on social, interactive, and complex performative relations between individuals' identities (Shotter, 1992). Instead of separating cognitions from communication and predicting behavior based on patterns, social constructionists, such as Lincoln and Guba (1985) and Shotter (1984), proposed that individuals *construct meanings as they interact* with one another. Gergen and Gergen (1991) claimed that social construction stimulates "the fuller realm of shared languages" (p. 79). In social construction, knowledge is a product of language functions in communities of knowledge (Gergen & Gergen, 1991; Pearce, 1995). The process of socially constructed meaning is accomplished through historical and social reflections on how knowledge is understood in communicative interaction (Lannamann, 1992; Pearce, 1995; Yerby, 1995).

The roots of social construction are found in sociology (Craig, 1995; Shotter & Gergen, 1994). P. L. Berger and Luckmann (1966) were the first to define and comprehensively examine the social construction of reality. Practically every social construction project, grounded in sociology, social psychology, or communication, appeared after publication of this benchmark work. P. L. Berger and Luckmann's project was largely a sociological way to approach a new kind of knowledge, an attempt that was taken on by others in more comprehensive ways (Bloor, 1976; Hekman, 1986).

At the time the study was published, the nature of dialogue (Buber, 1970), phenomenology (Merleau-Ponty, 1962), and symbolic interaction (Burke, 1966, 1978) had emerged as central concerns in philosophy (Rorty, 1979). Shortly after publication of P. L. Berger and Luckmann's (1966) work, hermeneutics (Gadamer, 1976; Palmer, 1969) and deconstruction (Derrida, 1976) were on the rise, and Goffman (1974), Heidegger (1971), and Hymes (1972) focused on examination of language and its interpretations.

The concept of the social construction of reality (P. L. Berger & Luckmann, 1966), derived from the French school of sociology, was instrumental in giving rise to a new way of thinking about reality, interactions, and construction of meaning. P. L. Berger and Luckmann (1966) stated that they "modified the Durkheimian theory of society by the introduction of a dialectical perspective derived from Marx and an emphasis on the constitution of social reality through subjective meanings derived from Weber" (p. 15). Looking for systematic theoretical reasoning, they referenced theories of Durkheim (1950) in *The Rules of Sociological Method* and Weber (1947) in *Wirtschaft und Gesellschaft*, "two of the most famous and most influential 'marching orders' for sociology":

> Durkheim tells us, "The first and most fundamental rule is: Consider social facts as things." And Weber observes, "Both for sociology in the present sense, and for history, the object of cognition is the subjective meaning-complex of action." These two statements are not contradictory. Society does indeed possess objective facticity, and society is indeed built up by activity that expresses subjective meaning. And, incidentally, Durkheim knew the latter, just as Weber knew the former. It is precisely the dual character of society in terms of objective facticity *and* subjective meaning that makes its "reality *sui generis*," to use another key term of Durkheim's. The central question for sociological theory can then be put as follows: How is it possible that subjective meanings *become* objective facticities? (P. L. Berger & Luckmann, 1966, p. 16)

Conscious of the multiple realities of everyday life, P. L. Berger and Luckmann (1966) wrote, "The language used in everyday life continuously provides me with the necessary objectifications and posits the order within which these make sense and within which everyday life has meaning for me" (p. 21). Language, in this sense, coordinates one's life in society and fills it with meaningful objects. Language makes subjectivity "more real" (p. 36) not only for conversational partners but also for oneself. The capacity of language to identify and preserve one's subjectivity, albeit with modification, is conserved even after face-to-face interaction is over: "This very important characteristic of language is well caught in the saying that men must talk about themselves until they know themselves" (p. 36). Language, therefore, becomes one's primary reference to everyday life.

P. L. Berger and Luckmann (1966) continued that all human activity is subject to habitualization. If action is repeated frequently, it casts into a pattern and can be reproduced later in a form apprehended by a performer in the beginning. Habitualization implies that even undesirable actions may be performed again in the future "in the same manner and with the same economic effort" (p. 50). This is true for social and nonsocial activities. Since habitualization precedes institutionalization, "institutionalization occurs whenever there is a reciprocal typification of habitualized actions by types of actors"; in other words, "any such typification is an institution" (p. 51).

Construction of a Social Institution

Historically, institutions imply control (Foucault, 1979; Gramsci, 1929–1935/1971). By the very fact of their existence, they strive to control human conduct by setting preferred patterns of conduct, which are iteratively distributed through as many channels as possible (P. L. Berger & Luckmann, 1966). For individuals, institutions are a reality of everyday life; social formations are transmitted to each new generation and thereby become an objective reality. A social institution can be defined as a complex that includes, on the one hand, many normative value-dependent roles and statuses that aim to satisfy certain social necessities; on the other hand, social education that uses resources of society in the form of interaction to satisfy such necessity (Shishkina, 1999). This definition is drawn from Russian sociological perspectives of institutions offered by Gavra (1995) and Komarov, Ionin, and Osipov (1979), who, in their turn, based their knowledge of social institutions on studies of social examination of realities by Durkheim (1950) and Weber (1947). All formal societal order is established by continuous practice and education, which presupposes normative roles, statuses, and practices to satisfy interests of society. Order that is accepted to serve such interests has a potential to become a social institution (Gavra, 1995).

Ultimately, the process of accepting norms and rules of governance of institutions belongs to society at large (Shishkina, 1999). Juridical systems, media (Chong, 2006), and health care (Loe, 2004; Yanovitzky & Bennet, 1999) are examples of such social institutions: Their roles are clearly defined and norms and rules are established and followed by both professionals, who act in the field, and the society, which has a general knowledge about the field and legitimates the profession.

Public Relations as a Social Institution

Public relations can be examined as a social institution (E. Tsetsura, 1997). For instance, in the United States, public relations is often approached as an established social institution. In countries with developing economies and transitional democracies, it is an emerging field and an emerging social institution (Shishkina, 1999). Of course, the process of social institutionalization of public relations is not complete without a general understanding of public relations' goals, norms, and practices by society and across societies.

Such analysis, however, needs caution because all social institutions, regardless of their stability, are in flux. If a society is not stable, how can institutional systems be complete and thus fully developed? If continuous construction of meaning influences the social construction of reality, to what extent can the socially constructed reality be considered as complete at any point in time? In other words, as long as interaction among individuals takes place, as long as discursive practices exist, the completion of any social institution and socially constructed reality cannot be accomplished. At the same time, constructions of meaning and identities of individuals in interaction are necessarily influenced by constructions created and posed by the social institutions and by socially constructed reality (P. L. Berger & Luckmann, 1966). Thus, any study of socially constructed reality and socially constructed meanings requires recognition of a social institution and a comprehensive analysis of multiple identity construction within the institution that frames such construction.

Public relations is a perpetually emerging field not only in countries with a relatively short history of modern public relations, such as Bahrain (AlSaqer, 2008), Colombia and Mexico (Molleda & Moreno, 2008), United Arab Emirates (Kirat, 2006), Russia (K. Tsetsura, in press), and Ukraine (K. Tsetsura & Grynko, 2009), but also in countries where public relations is traditionally considered "emerged," such as Germany (Fröhlich & Peters, 2007) and the United States (Boynton, 2002). Studies in these countries showed that the profession of public relations is still redefining itself as a field within a tradition, changing and adapting meanings of what it represents and what practitioners do and are expected to do and, as a result, refining what it means to do public relations. An emerging social institution with changing social norms, rules, and practices is still in flux. This opens up possibilities for constructing what public relations is and how it should be defined.

Continuous social institutionalization brings opportunities and challenges to the field of public relations. On the one hand, a newly emerging social institution of public relations implies certain historicity and control, which are evident from the onset of institution formation (P. L. Berger & Luckmann, 1966). Previous research on the rise and the development of public relations can help identify historicity and control within the institution that specifically includes the process of creating and sharing common knowledge about itself, recording history of practices, and later, as more practices come into play, establishing norms, rules, and orders that govern this institution in the United States (Cutlip, 1995; Tye, 1998) and other countries, such as Ukraine (K. Tsetsura & Grynko, 2009). Historicity is necessary for successful and timely creation of any social institution, but structure brings control and formation of hierarchy that resists change (Foucault, 1979; Mumby, 1989). On the other hand, because this new social institution is unstable, it is prone to social influences and to more frequent changes than a completely formed institution.

Finally, this commonly shared knowledge penetrates a social institution and forms those normative value-dependent roles of the field and, correspondently, offers social education about the roles for individuals who perform those institutional roles.

Socially Constructed Identities

As social institutions progress through history, move through time, and develop sets of norms, rules, and orders (e.g., stabilize their social structures), they become stronger and gain more control. Soon, they are perceived by society as given (P. L. Berger & Luckmann, 1966).

Even though historicity and control, along with other factors that define public relations or any other field for this matter, seem to be dominant, "it is important to keep in mind that the objectivity of the institutional world, however massive it may appear to the individual, is a humanly produced, constructed objectivity" (P. L. Berger & Luckmann, 1966, p. 57). Such dialectical relationships between an individual and the social world put the product of social construction in a position to act "back upon [the] producer" (p. 57).

Because individuals construct meanings, it is essential to understand what influences identities of individuals. The concept of identity comes directly from the social construction of reality. P. L. Berger and Luckmann (1966) argued, "Identity is, of course, a key element of subjective reality, and like all subjective reality, stands in a dialectical relationship with society" (p. 159). Multiple identities exist because identities can be formed, modified, maintained, and reshaped by multiple social relations. Identities emerge from the dialectic between individual and society and thus are social products. P. L. Berger and Luckmann reasoned that any theorizing about identities has to occur within the framework of theoretical interpretations of socially constructed realities in which identities are located.

During the process of social construction, a social institution is influenced by individuals' identity constructions on the one hand and by negotiations of individuals' identities, the products of socially constructed reality, on the other. Therefore, to study the social construction of any field, one needs to study the essential components of socially constructed realities—socially constructed identities.

The nature of collective identity is grounded in classic sociological constructs such as Durkheim's "collective conscience," Marx's "class consciousness," and Weber's Verstehen (Cerulo, 1997). It is the notion of "we" in a group that lately has been argued as a more viable basis for the collective self. Much of the social construction work in sociology has been done on gender identity (Connell, 1995; Margolis, 1985; West & Zimmerman, 1987) and examination of gender and sex roles (Stacey & Thorne, 1985). The concept of social construction is also actively used in the literature on national identity (Cerulo, 1997; see also works of Bloom, 1990; Bruner, 2002; Gillis, 1994; Spillman, 1997). Fewer studies, however, have examined professional identities from a social constructionist perspective (Lingard, Reznick, DeVito, & Espin, 2002; Marks, Scholarios, & Lockyer, 2002).

The Role of Identity in the Social Construction of Knowledge

Implications of studying one's identities in relation to the social construction of knowledge are clear: Identification of oneself with the objective sense of social action emphasizes both self-experience and a social self. Social identity is formed as a result of coming to terms with social reality. Institutionalization of roles individuals play in each society calls for routine performances of such roles: "One must also be initiated into the various cognitive and even affective layers of the body of knowledge that is directly and indirectly appropriate to this role" (P. L. Berger & Luckmann, 1966, p. 72). Knowledge is socially distributed. Through a dialectical relationship between knowledge and its social base, knowledge becomes a social product and a factor in social change. Social distribution of knowledge has implications for the social construction of identity and repetitious practices of execution of different social identities, depending on which identity is appropriate or desired at a specific point in time. As a result, "whatever the experts do, the pluralistic situation changes not only the social position of the traditional definitions of reality, but also the way in which these are held in the consciousness of individuals" (P. L. Berger & Luckmann, 1966, p. 115).

If socially constructed knowledge changes, so do definitions of reality and constructions of this reality in the minds of individuals. Thus, socially constructed knowledge can explain how specific ideas, including actions and knowledge about certain professional practices, can spread throughout society. If professionals themselves, specifically public relations practitioners, can construct this knowledge about the institution of public relations, it can potentially be adopted by individuals in the society as their knowledge about that institution as well.

Social distribution of knowledge also happens as a result of secondary socialization through means of division of labor and actions of carriers. The role-specific vocabulary is learned by carriers of social institutions through the acquisition of role-specific knowledge when roles are "directly and indirectly rooted in the division of labor" (P. L. Berger & Luckmann, 1966, p. 127). Such distribution of knowledge can face persistence from already formed reality because primary socialization (formation of social structure) takes place first, and secondary socialization has to present knowledge newly constructed through labor, so to speak. P. L. Berger and Luckmann stated, "The reality of everyday life maintains itself by being embodied in routines, which is the essence of institutionalization. Beyond this, however, the reality of everyday life is ongoingly reaffirmed in the individual's interaction with others" (p. 137). Thus, social reality has originated by a social process and is maintained by social processes.

Of course, reality can be transformed through what P. L. Berger and Luckmann (1966) call "alterations" (p. 144). Modifications of reality happen over time. However, recipes for successful alteration of meanings have to include social and conceptual conditions in which society is first willing to construct such a change and then implement it in reality. If one expands P. L. Berger and Luckmann's idea of construction to formulation of social conditions, one can include the social construction of knowledge through individuals' interactions into what constitutes a certain condition and explain how this condition can be changed.

What this means is that the reality of the social institution has an ability to change itself and, if certain conditions exist, can be changed through socially constructed and reconstructed knowledge. Knowledge is reflexive; interacting individuals are involved in constructing reality processes. Reality of institution therefore is subjective; there is no one right reality—only those that are enacted are real. Openness for continuous change becomes feasible, and only openness can be the obvious permanent condition of reality. Institutions thus always have the ability to change and, perhaps, simply cannot resist change since they are socially constructed.

Social Construction and Agency-Structure Tensions

One can easily note a close connection between the concept of social construction and postmodernism. In fact, social construction is a main feature of a postmodern worldview (A. A. Berger, 1998, 2003; Derrida, 1982, 2001). Even though it is tempting to discuss postmodern views in relation to social construction, to keep a theoretical discussion of this overview manageable, the author leaves that exploration to others.

Another close connection is established between social construction and dialectical tensions between agency and structure. Generally, three main theoretical frameworks that aim to integrate agency and structure are structuration, identification, and critical theory (Conrad & Hayes, 2001). Such tensions have been studied to a great extent in organizational communication (Buzzanell, 2000; Cheney, 1991, 1999; Mumby, 1989, 2001; Papa, Singhal, Ghanekar, & Papa, 2000; Putnam & Fairhurst, 2001; Scott, Corman, & Cheney, 1998; Trethewey, 2000; Witmer, 1997). Each of these approaches is different. For instance, under the umbrella of structuration, one can find a variety of works largely based on Giddens's (1984) structuration theory, which examines various angles of the agency-structure relationship at large. Analysis of and using identification deals specifically with issues of unobtrusive control identity formation in organizations (Cheney, 1991, 1999; Scott et al., 1998). Issues of power, empowerment/disempowerment, interests, participation, and democracy are examined by critical theory scholars like Mumby (1989, 2001) and Trethewey (2000). One major thread that unites these studies is examination of agency-structure relations in specific organizational settings.

Identity of individual is examined in studies by Cheney (1991), for example, as tensions between agency of individual and structure of organization implicit in discursive practices. Cheney's focus is on rhetorical examination and classification of identity in relation to organization and on the process of identification. He draws heavily on writings by Kenneth Burke to establish rhetorical connections between the individual and the social. Cheney concentrates on identification with organizations and identity processes resulting in such identification as relevant to organizational communication.

Social construction can help examine public relations not only in relation to a single organization, as is the case with identification, but also in relation to a professional field and in relation to a process of meaning construction. Thus, social construction implies more than just studying public relations processes from a perspective of cocreating meanings (Botan & Taylor, 2004). For this reason, social construction is a more useful approach to understanding all aspects of public relations processes and products than is a cocreational approach.

Social Construction and Poststructuralist Feminist Tradition

Analyses of the social construction of identity are often drawn from a poststructuralist feminist tradition (Weedon, 1987, 1999). As Buzzanell (2001) argued, a poststructuralist perspective presents multiple visions of socially constructed identities of individuals. In poststructuralism, there are no fixed understandings of identity, and the knowledge and perceptions are constructed socially, for example, through cultural, social, and historical factors. One of the major poststructuralist premises formulated by Weedon (1987) emphasized the importance of language through which identities of individuals are socially constructed. Language executes the ways in which organizing, power, meanings, and individual consciousness are presented. According to P. L. Berger and Luckmann (1966), society, identity, and reality all together are subjectively crystallized in this process through the utilization of language, which "constitutes both the most important content and the most important instrument of socialization" (p. 123). Language takes on the vital function of translating objective reality into the subjective and back. Discourse becomes a focus process in studies of socially constructed identities.

Because meanings can be transformed through language, there are no fixed meanings to any phenomenon (Weedon, 1999). Subjectivity, therefore, comes at the center of a poststructuralist perspective. Studying subjectivity (i.e., one's personal views and experiences expressed through language) can help reveal the complexity of multiple identities (more than one identity that an individual has) and negotiation in the process of the social construction of meaning through discourse.

The following section examines social construction in the field of public relations to illustrate how a fragmented, incomplete view of identities undermines the importance and heuristic value of a comprehensive approach to the social construction of reality. The following examples present major trends in the ways social construction is used by public relations scholars.

Unanswered Questions in Public Relations

One common shortcoming of many studies is their inability to recognize the classical concept of the social construction of reality (P. L. Berger & Luckmann, 1966) as a useful overarching framework that can help explain production and reproduction of multiple identities and contexts in which individuals present and negotiate their identities (see, e.g., studies by Aldoory, 2001; Chong, 2006; Harter & Krone, 2001). Many communication studies fail to address the continuity of identity negotiation, a constant identity flux that reflects and is reflected in a broader realm of health communication situations, or contexts, for instance. Thus, identity formation and negotiation tensions among representatives of so-called risk or perceived risk groups, specifically those interactional identities of belonging to a group, are often left unrecognized. Although several studies aimed to address these issues (Fitzpatrick, 2002; Loe, 2004; Myrik, 1995), the limited exposure and use of such studies have kept them on the outskirts of mainstream communication research.

Understanding and exploring the social construction of multiple identities among those who belong to at-risk populations with master identity of risk carriers (individuals with a history of cancer, heart diseases, etc.) as well as individuals with an interactional identity as risk carriers (those who may be at risk due to their professional obligations, lifestyles, personal and social choices, etc.) can greatly benefit public relations scholars. To what extent does one recognize her or his risk? How does an individual communicate with others, such as family members, friends, and health professionals, about the risk? Does one have a sense of belonging, of owning the risk? At which point does the risk become a part of one's identity? With which identities do certain risks become associated? What are the implications of such social construction of meaning of risk for individuals, societal groups, and the community as a whole? Most important, how are such socially constructed meanings produced and reproduced to form a socially constructed reality of an illness or a disease and a socially constructed reality of a social group that has the disease? These important questions can and should be answered by going back to the classic understanding of the social construction of meaning and identity as a basis for the social construction of reality.

Organizational communication research has been actively concentrated on gendered practices and analyses of female identity in the workplace within one organization (Ashcraft & Pacanowsky, 1996; Trethewey, 1997), as well as across professional fields (Ashcraft, 2005; Buzzanell & Liu, 2005; Hochschild, 1983). However, those studies come up short for examining holistic representations of multiple identity negotiation beyond gendered or professional identities. Studies should focus on demonstrating how other cultural and socially defined identities (identities of an organizational employee, a colleague, or a citizen, in addition to identities of a mother, a wife, or an ethnic group member as we are all members of multiple publics) could influence discursive practices of meaning construction within certain societal contexts and interactions and contribute to the social construction of reality through public relations efforts.

The growth of public relations makes it a particularly interesting one in which to examine how professionals talk about their jobs, their profession, and their identities. Most previous studies have concentrated on only one or two social identities of public relations practitioners, such as gender (Aldoory & Toth, 2002; Pompper, 2005a, 2005b), but did not analyze multiple identities in connection with one another.

Some late studies of identity construction at work address professional and social identities (e.g., Girardelli, 2004; Holmes, 2005), yet these studies struggle to define an overarching framework for understanding the implications of such multiple identity negotiation. Performative construction of identity has also become a focus of poststructuralist and deconstructivist narratology as a way to forward a narrative approach to contemporary identity theory (Hofer, 2006; Kraus, 2006). Kraus (2006) articulated a complexity of modern social identity construction, where there is no one given hierarchy of traditionally defined identities, such as gender, class, or nation. Now, "it is composed of others: persons, groups, communities, whether experienced (in personal contact) or 'imagined'" (p. 108). Kraus's approach to understanding the social construction of identity comes closest to the one argued here. His idea that "telling" is "doing" is essential for social construction. Yet he emphasized narrativity as the rationale for construction of belonging, downplaying a social construction of reality as a factor that influences identity construction and is capable of reproducing constructed identities through a synergetic communication effect.

This is a clear gap in understanding the theoretical roots of social construction, which undermines the importance of the social construction of reality as a major implication for studying socially constructed meanings through public relations efforts and a social institution of the field and profession of public relations. To place social construction on the map within a broader realm of communication, communication researchers need to recognize that an outcome of multiple identity construction stretches into the realm of reality and, as such, is capable of defining and influencing communication processes beyond specific instances or communications among certain individuals. In other words, the challenge is to understand how meanings are socially constructed in public relations and through public relations activities. This effort requires recognizing how multiple identities of diverse stakeholders can influence their participation in and understanding of the social institution of public relations as an integral part of creating a social construction of reality. Such understanding can help communication scholars enlighten multiple stakeholders as they deal with health, organizational, intercultural, and societal professional communication challenges in the 21st century.

The Social Construction of Public Relations

Studying the multilayered nature of socially constructed meanings is central to understanding public relations. It can provide a basis for the development of two distinct interests in social construction: meanings as products of social construction and identity negotiations as processes of social construction, in which individuals interact with one another within a social institution. Since the process of social construction presumes a change, identity negotiation can be problematic. The problem could come from dialectic tensions between a newly emerging social structure and a previously socially constructed reality as well as from negotiation of multiple identities.

A change in any social structure of a social institution comes at the price of a previously constructed reality of what was understood as a field (i.e., public relations, organizational or health communication). For instance, those who started to practice public relations 30 years ago have constructed their own reality of what public relations is, sensitive to the dynamics of that era, as those who studied health communication 10 years ago have their own understanding of the reality that informs the field. Either earlier view of reality would be incommensurable with today's more sophisticated and developed view of the field. The central question remains: Can these reflections of changes that a socially constructed institution goes through be found in discourses of professionals, or are they merely theoretical speculations of researchers examining those professionals? More important, can social construction research help understand which identity transformations individuals undergo as they experience, practice, study, or research different areas in communication? Specifically, can a study demonstrate what it means to be a specialist, client, or employee in a certain field?

The argument is that it is possible to answer these questions if one uses social construction as an overarching framework. Many studies of communication failed to answer these questions because communication research as a whole provided no conceptual framework for approaching them comprehensively, addressing all possible identity formations and negotiations. These studies needed to recognize multiple layers of identities and their interconnection with the social construction of meaning, which were developed as a result of the fluctuation of the social institutions and multiple identity crises in a postmodern society.

A lack of research, which exhaustively theorizes about meaning construction in the field of public relations, should motivate scholars to reevaluate and revisit a classical approach to studying socially constructed meanings and identities. Following P. L. Berger and Luckmann (1966), social construction followers will "seek to take cognizance of the transformations of identity that have actually occurred" (p. 165). Theorizing itself may also be transformed in the process. As a result of such theoretical development, one can seek to *problematize* meaning and identity at the level of theory itself (P. L. Berger & Luckmann, 1966).

Social construction opens up possibilities for future analyses to provide unique insight into the construction of meaning by as well as processes of public relations through understanding identities of individuals who engage in public relations practices and thereby negotiate the construction of their identities and the realities of social institutions that they represent.

References

Aldoory, L. (2001). Making health communications meaningful for women: Factors that influence involvement. *Journal of Public Relations Research, 13,* 163–185.

Aldoory, L., & Toth, E. (2002). Gender discrepancies in a gendered profession: A developing theory for public relations. *Journal of Public Relations Research, 14,* 103–126.

AlSaqer, L. (2008). Experience of female public relations practitioners in Bahrain. *Public Relations Review, 34,* 77–79.

Ashcraft, K. L. (2005, May). *Resisting gendered threats in the meeting of occupation and organization: The case of airline pilots.* Paper presented at the International Communication Association Annual Conference, New York.

Ashcraft, K. L., & Pacanowsky, M. E. (1996). "A woman's worst enemy": Reflections on a narrative of organizational life and female identity. *Journal of Applied Communication Research, 24,* 217–239.

Berger, A. A. (Ed.). (1998). *The postmodern presence: Readings on postmodernism in American culture and society.* Walnut Creek, CA: AltaMira Press.

Berger, A. A. (2003). *The portable postmodernist.* Walnut Creek, CA: AltaMira Press.

Berger, P. L., & Luckmann, T. (1966). *The social construction of reality: A treatise in the sociology of knowledge.* New York: Doubleday.

Bloom, W. (1990). *Personal identity, national identity and international relations.* Cambridge, UK: Cambridge University Press.

Bloor, D. (1976). *Knowledge and social imagery.* London: Routledge & Kegan Paul.

Botan, C. H., & Taylor, M. (2004). Public relations: State of the field. *Journal of Communication, 54,* 645–661.

Boynton, L. (2002). Professionalism and social responsibility: Foundations of public relations ethics. *Communication Yearbook, 26,* 230–265.

Bruner, M. L. (2002). *Strategies of remembrance: The rhetorical dimensions of national identity construction.* Columbia: University of South Carolina Press.

Buber, M. (1970). *I and thou* (W. Kaufmann, Trans.). New York: Scribner.

Burke, K. (1966). *Language as symbolic action: Essays on life, literature, and method.* Berkeley: University of California Press.

Burke, K. (1978). (Nonsymbolic) motion/(symbolic) action. *Critical Inquiry, 4,* 809–838.

Burleson, B. R. (1989). The constructivist approach to person-centered communication: A research exemplar. In B. A. Dervin, L. Grossberg, B. J. O'Keefe, & E. Wartella (Eds.), *Rethinking communication: Paradigm exemplars* (Vol. 2, pp. 29–46). Newbury Park, CA: Sage.

Buzzanell, P. M. (Ed.). (2000). *Rethinking organizational and managerial communication from feminist perspectives.* Thousand Oaks, CA: Sage.

Buzzanell, P. M. (2001). *Revising sexual harassment in academe: Using feminist ethical and sense making approaches for analyzing macrodiscourses and micropractices of sexual harassment.* Unpublished manuscript.

Buzzanell, P. M., & Liu, M. (2005). Struggling with maternity leave policies and practices: A poststructuralist feminist analysis of gendered organizing. *Journal of Applied Communication Research, 33,* 1–25.

Cerulo, K. A. (1997). Identity construction: New issues, new directions. *Annual Review of Sociology, 23,* 385–409.

Chen, V., & Pearce, W. B. (1995). Even if a thing of beauty, can a case study be a joy forever? A social constructionist approach to theory and research. In W. Leeds-Hurwitz (Ed.), *Social approaches to communication* (pp. 135–154). New York: Guilford Press.

Cheney, G. (1991). *Rhetoric in an organizational society: Managing multiple identities.* Columbia: University of South Carolina.

Cheney, G. (1999). *Values at work: Employee participation meets market pressure at Mondragón.* Ithaca, NY: ILR Press/Cornell.

Chong, M. (2006). A crisis of epidemic proportions: What communication lessons can practitioners learn from the Singapore SARS crisis? *Public Relations Quarterly, 51,* 6–11.

Connell, R. W. (1995). *Masculinities.* Berkeley: University of California Press.

Conrad, C., & Hayes, J. (2001). Development of key constructs. In F. M. Jablin & L. L. Putnam (Eds.), *The new handbook of organizational communication: Advances in theory, research, and methods* (pp. 47–77). Thousand Oaks, CA: Sage.

Craig, R. T. (1995). Foreword. In W. Leeds-Hurwitz (Ed.), *Social approaches to communication* (pp. v–ix). New York: Guilford Press.

Cutlip, S. M. (1995). *Public relations history: From the 17th to the 20th century.* Hillsdale, NJ: Lawrence Erlbaum.

Derrida, J. (1976). *Of grammatology* (G. C. Spival, Trans.). Baltimore: Johns Hopkins Press.

Derrida, J. (1982). *Margins of philosophy.* Chicago: University of Chicago Press.

Derrida, J. (2001). *Acts of religion.* New York: Routledge.

Durkheim, E. (1950). *The rules of sociological method.* Chicago: Free Press.

Ehrlich, S., & King, R. (1992). Gender-based language reform and the social construction of meaning. *Discourse and Society, 3,* 151–166.

Fitzpatrick, M. A. (2002). Some reflections on meaning and identity in illness. *Journal of Language & Social Psychology, 21,* 68–71.

Foucault, M. (1979). *Discipline and punish: The birth of prison.* New York: Vintage Books.

Fröhlich, R., & Peters, S. B. (2007). PR bunnies caught in the agency ghetto? Gender stereotypes, organizational factors, and women's careers in PR agencies. *Journal of Public Relations Research, 19,* 229–254.

Gadamer, H.-G. (1976). *Philosophical hermeneutics* (D. Linge, Ed. & Trans.). Berkeley: University of California Press.

Gavra, D. P. (1995). *Formirovanie obschestvennogo mneniya: Tsennostnyi aspect. Reprint nauchnogo doklada* [Forming public opinion: Value aspect. Published scholarly presentation]. St. Petersburg, Russia: Rossiiskaia akademiia nauk.

Gergen, K. (1985). The social constructionist movement in modern psychology. *American Psychologist, 40,* 266–275.

Gergen, K., & Gergen, M. (1991). Toward reflexive methodologies. In F. Steier (Ed.), *Research and reflexivity* (pp. 76–95). Newbury Park, CA: Sage.

Giddens, A. (1984). *The construction of society: Outline of the theory of structuration.* Berkeley: University of California Press.

Gillis, J. (1994). *Commemorations: The politics of national identity.* Princeton, NJ: Princeton University Press.

Girardelli, D. (2004). Commodified identities: The myth of Italian food in the United States. *Journal of Communication Inquiry, 28,* 307–324.

Goffman, E. (1974). *Frame analysis.* New York: Harper.

Gramsci, A. (1971). *Selections from the prison notebooks of Antonio Gramsci* (Q. Hoare & G. N. Smith, Eds. & Trans.). New York: International Publishers. (Original work published 1929–1935)

Harter, L. M., & Krone, K. J. (2001). Exploring the emergent identities of future physicians: Toward an understanding of the ideological socialization of osteopathic medical students. *Southern Communication Journal, 67,* 66–83.

Heidegger, M. (1971). *On the way to language* (P. D. Hertz, Trans.). San Francisco: Harper & Row.

Hekman, S. J. (1986). *Hermeneutics and the sociology of knowledge.* Notre Dame, IN: University of Notre Dame Press.

Hochschild, A. R. (1983). *The managed heart: Commercialization of human feeling.* Berkeley: University of California Press.

Hofer, S. (2006). I am they: Technological mediation, shifting conceptions of identity and techno music. *Convergence: The Journal of Research Into New Media Technologies, 12,* 307–324.

Holmes, J. (2005). Story-telling at work: A complex discursive resource for integrating personal, professional and social identities. *Discourse Studies, 7,* 671–700.

Hymes, D. (1972). Models of the interaction of language and social life. In J. Gumperz & D. Hymes (Eds.), *Directions in sociolinguistics: The ethnography of communication* (pp. 35–71). New York: Holt, Rinehart & Winston.

Kirat, M. (2006). Public relations in the United Arab Emirates: The emergence of a profession. *Public Relations Review, 32,* 254–260.

Komarov, M. S., Ionin, L. G., & Osipov, G. V. (1979). *Istoriia burzhuaznoi sotsiologii pervoi poloviny XX veka* [History of bourgeois sociology in the first half of the 20th century]. Moscow: Nauka.

Kraus, W. (2006). The narrative negotiation of identity and belonging. *Narrative Inquiry, 16,* 103–111.

Lannamann, J. W. (1992). Deconstructing the person and changing the subject of interpersonal studies. *Communication Theory, 1,* 179–203.

Leeds-Hurwitz, W. (1992). Forum introduction: Social approaches to interpersonal communication. *Communication Theory, 2,* 131–139.

Leeds-Hurwitz, W. (1995). Introduction to social approaches. In W. Leeds-Hurwitz (Ed.), *Social approaches to communication* (pp. 3–20). New York: Guilford Press.

Lincoln, Y., & Guba, E. G. (1985). *Naturalistic inquiry.* Newbury Park, CA: Sage.

Lingard, L., Reznick, R., DeVito, I., & Espin, S. (2002). Forming professional identities on the health care team: Discursive constructions of the "other" in the operating room. *Medical Education, 36,* 728–734.

Loe, M. (2004). Sex and the senior woman: Pleasure and danger in the Viagraera. *Sexualities, 7,* 303–326.

Margolis, D. R. (1985). Re-defining the situation: Negotiations on the meaning of "woman." *Social Problems, 32,* 332–334.

Marks, A., Scholarios, D., & Lockyer, C. (2002, July). *Identifying a profession: The creation of professional identities within software work.* Paper presented at the 18th Egos Colloquium, Barcelona, Spain.

Merleau-Ponty, M. (1962). *Phenomenology of perception.* New York: Humanities Press.

Miller, K. (2002). *Communication theories: Perspectives, processes, and contexts.* Boston: McGraw-Hill.

Molleda, J.-C., & Moreno, Á. (2008). Balancing public relations with socioeconomic and political environments in transition: Comparative, contextualized research in Colombia, Mexico, and Venezuela. *Journalism & Communication Monographs, 10,* 115–174.

Mumby, D. K. (1989). Ideology and the social construction of meaning: A communication perspective. *Communication Quarterly, 37,* 291–304.

Mumby, D. (2001). Power and politics. In F. M. Jablin & L. L. Putnam (Eds.), *The new handbook of organizational communication: Advances in theory, research, and methods* (pp. 585–623). Thousand Oaks, CA: Sage.

Myrik, R. K. (1995). Communicating about empowerment: The cultural construction of gay identity in public health messages about AIDS. *Political Communication, 12,* 349–350.

Neimeyer, G. J. (Ed.). (1993). *Constructivist assessment: A casebook.* Newbury Park, CA: Sage.

Palmer, R. T. (1969). *Hermeneutics.* Evanston, IL: Northwestern University Press.

Papa, M. J., Singhal, A., Ghanekar, D. V., & Papa, W. H. (2000). Organizing for social change through cooperative action: The [dis]empowering dimensions of women's communication. *Communication Theory, 10,* 90–123.

Pearce, W. B. (1995). A sailing guide for social constructionists. In W. Leeds-Hurwitz (Ed.), *Social approaches to communication* (pp. 88–113). New York: Guilford Press.

Pearce, W. B., & Cronin, V. E. (1980). *Communicating action and meaning: The creation of social realities.* New York: Praeger.

Pompper, D. (2005a). "Difference" in public relations research: A case for introducing critical race theory. *Journal of Public Relations Research, 17,* 139–169.

Pompper, D. (2005b). Multiculturalism in the public relations curriculum: Female African American practitioners' perceptions of effects. *Howard Journal of Communication, 16,* 295–316.

Postmes, T., Spears, R., & Lea, M. (2000). The formation of group norms in computer-mediated communication. *Human Communication Research, 26,* 341–371.

Putnam, L. L., & Fairhurst, G. T. (2001). Discourse analysis in organizations: Issues and concerns. In F. M. Jablin & L. L. Putnam (Eds.), *The new handbook of organizational communication: Advances in theory, research, and methods* (pp. 78–136). Thousand Oaks, CA: Sage.

Rorty, R. (1979). *Philosophy and the mirror of nature.* Princeton, NJ: Princeton University Press.

Scott, C. R., Corman, S. R., & Cheney, G. (1998). Development of a structurational model of identification in the organization. *Communication Theory, 8,* 298–336.

Shishkina, M. (1999). *Public relations v sisteme soctsialnogo upravleniya* [Public relations in the system of social management]. St. Petersburg, Russia: St. Petersburg State University Press.

Shotter, J. (1984). *Social accountability and selfhood.* Oxford, UK: Basil Blackwell.

Shotter, J. (1992). "Getting in touch": The metamethodology of a postmodern science of mental life. In S. Kvale (Ed.), *Psychology and postmodernism* (pp. 58–73). Newbury Park, CA: Sage.

Shotter, J., & Gergen, K. J. (1994). Social construction: Knowledge, self, and continuing the conversation. In S. Deetz (Ed.), *Communication yearbook 17* (pp. 3–33). Thousand Oaks, CA: Sage.

Sigman, S. J. (1992). Do social approaches to interpersonal communication constitute a contribution to communication theory? *Communication Theory, 2,* 347–356.

Spillman, L. (1997). *Nation and commemoration: Creating national identities in the United States and Australia.* New York: Cambridge University Press.

Stacey, J., & Thorne, B. (1985). The missing feminist revolution in sociology. *Sociology Problems, 32,* 301–316.

Trethewey, A. (1997). Resistance, identity, and empowerment: A postmodern feminist analysis of clients in a human service organization. *Communication Monographs, 64,* 281–301.

Trethewey, A. (2000). Revisioning control: A feminist critique of disciplined bodies. In P. Buzzanell (Ed.), *Rethinking organizational and managerial communication from feminist perspectives* (pp. 107–127). Thousand Oaks, CA: Sage.

Tsetsura, E. (1997). *Public relations kak sotsialnyj institut v Rossii* [Public relations as a social institute in Russia]. Unpublished master's thesis, Voronezh State University, Voronezh, Russia.

Tsetsura, K. (in press). Is public relations a real job? How female practitioners construct the profession. *Journal of Public Relations Research.*

Tsetsura, K., & Grynko, A. (2009). An exploratory study of the media transparency in Ukraine. *Public Relations Journal, 3*(2). Retrieved December 20, 2009, from www.prsa.org/prjournal/V013N02/6D-030205.pdf

Tye, L. (1998). *The father of spin: Edward L. Bernays and the birth of public relations.* New York: Crown.

Weber, M. (1947). *The theory of social and economic organization.* New York: Oxford University Press.

Weedon, C. (1987). *Feminist practice and poststructuralist theory.* New York: Basil Blackwell.

Weedon, C. (1999). *Feminism, theory, and the politics of difference.* Malden, MA: Blackwell.

West, C., & Zimmerman, D. (1987). Doing gender. *Gender and Sociology, 1,* 125–151.

Wilmer, F. (2002). *The social construction of man, the state, and war: Identity, conflict, and violence in the former Yugoslavia.* New York: Routledge.

Witmer, D. E. (1997). Communication and recovery: Structuration as an ontological approach to organizational culture. *Communication Monographs, 64,* 324–349.

Yanovitzky, I., & Bennet, C. (1999). Media attention, institutional response, and health behavior change. *Communication Research, 26,* 429–453.

Yerby, J. (1995). Family systems theory reconsidered: Integrating social construction theory and dialectical process. *Communication Theory, 5,* 339–365.

CHAPTER 12

Public Relations and Power

Peter M. Smudde and Jeffrey L. Courtright

"More power!" comedian Tim Allen would exclaim on the mock handyman show, *Tool Time*, on the sitcom *Home Improvement*. Viewers knew that he meant bigger and better machines for home repair, often resulting in destruction and personal injury instead. Would that we recognized as readily what is meant when anyone associated with public relations invokes the word "power." It carries with it semantic baggage—largely negative—that leads many people to believe that they understand the concept. An "armchair" view of power often brings to mind typical ideas of control, domination, and influence. A quick scan of trade publications further reveals notions of public relations' power as capability (Saffir, 1999; Weiner, 2006), as something to be harnessed (Scott, 2007), or as a source of cultural transformation (Cottle, 2003; Miller & Dinan, 2008). For this chapter's purposes, we define power not as something public relations possesses so much as something it exercises through relationships.

Specifically, we believe power is a community-based phenomenon that people confer on each other through their relationships with one another based on hierarchical positions they hold, the rhetorical manifestation and recognition of relationships and positions through communicative acts, and the social implications these dimensions have on individual and, especially, communal views of the system of relationships that exist and evolve among people. In this chapter, we outline three dimensions of power—hierarchical, rhetorical, and social—which represent three distinct lines of research regarding power and public relations. We also present three issues of increasing importance to power and its role in the field's future: technology, activism, and globalization. Ultimately, all these areas fold into the concept of community, which naturally nurtures power through relationships among people and organizations.

Three Dimensions of Power

In the field of public relations, the problem of power is problematic. Yet the problem is solvable through strategic thinking about its three dimensions: hierarchical, rhetorical, and social. In the end, power and public relations are compatible because of people's sensibilities about these three dimensions and abilities to inspire cooperation internally and externally with the groups for which they work.

Hierarchical Dimension

First, the hierarchical dimension of power concerns how it is conferred on people in organizations. The hierarchical nature of organizations is a natural place for power based on individuals' rank and position. In this way, power's hierarchical dimension is captured in such god terms as *control* and *authority.* In contrast, devil terms power include *domination* and *oppression.* In the case of rank and position, power is much more neutral to positive in this sense because it merely refers to one's bailiwick. The problem comes in when power as control or authority is framed in negative terms congruent with those associated with the selfish aims of domination and oppression. In this way, power is associated with the political dynamics that ensue among people organizing with one another at micro- and macrolevels.

In public relations, the hierarchical dimension of power is seen through the ways in which it works within an organizational structure (e.g., Lauzen & Dozier, 1992; Plowman, 1998). Of special importance in the hierarchical dimension of public relations, power is the matter of "getting a seat at the table"—or as J. E. Grunig (1993) called it, inclusion in the "dominant coalition"—which subsumes arguments about why public relations must be included within an organization's formal management team (see Berger, 2005, 2007; D'Aprix, 1997, 2001; Garten, 2001; Hipple, 2007; Lukaszewski, 2001a, 2001b, 2001c, 2008; Oates, 2006; Ries & Ries, 2009; Smudde, 2010). For public relations to be viewed as valuable and valued, as a recent report from the Arthur W. Page Society (2007) argues, public relations people must understand, embrace, and apply business/management concepts and methods more effectively, systematically, and, most of all, strategically. This point is precisely what is behind Lukaszewski's (2008) important treatise about professional communicators becoming and being seen as strategic counselors to management. His key is for public relations officials to sympathize and empathize much more with the needs, pressures, and requirements of organizational leaders by excelling at the seven disciplines of trustworthiness, verbal skillfulness, management acuity, strategic competency, pattern recognition for future application, advising constructively, and advice application.

In other practical terms, the hierarchical dimension of power concerns understanding, navigating, and thriving on the day-to-day dynamics of working with people within an organization. As L. A. Grunig (1992b) argued,

> Power comes to public relations practitioners from different sources. The value the dominant coalition attaches to the public relations function is one key way. . . . The expertise of practitioners, leading to increased professionalism, is another. . . . A third important contingency, according to J. Grunig (1976), is the relationship between placement in the hierarchy and the organization's degree of centralization. (p. 485)

In other words, to borrow a phrase from Shakespeare, some are born with power, some achieve power, and some have power thrust upon 'em. The power-control theory (L. A. Grunig, 1992b) amounts to a situational view of power dependent on management of the resources of power. Important matters about the effective management of public relations personnel and projects are covered in Argenti and Forman (2002), Beard (2001), Croft (2006), and Lordan (2003). Although these volumes are focused on the pragmatic needs for running a public relations function (either a corporate department or an independent agency), issues of power can be teased out of or seen in them and then applied.

Instrumental research related to the hierarchical dimensions of power for public relations people in organizations include Reber and Berger's (2006) study, which shows how practitioners view the limitations of their influence on decision making, and Edwards's (2009) work that focuses on professionals' power-pursuit and power-maintaining behaviors vis-à-vis the work of Pierre Bourdieu. Also, Oksiutycz (2006) advanced a view based on cybernetics that organizational communication's role is one that should both (1) release the productive *power* of employees and (2) introduce recursive organizational structures that result in more effective organizations. Behind these kinds of studies is effective leadership within the public relations function, and Werder and Holtzhausen's (2009) study shows well how two basic leadership styles (i.e., transformational and inclusive) affect the results achieved by staff members. Transformational leaders are more positively associated with "power strategies" (i.e., sound administrative control) and problem-solving approaches that feature effective persuasion, while inclusive leaders are more positively associated with problem-solving approaches that are highly cooperative and informative.

Rhetorical Dimension

The second dimension of power is rhetorical and concerns the effects and effectiveness of one's ability to create, use, and misuse language and symbols, which is a uniquely human capability (Burke, 1970, 1989). This dimension is most associated with manipulative motives behind communication of authoritarian regimes. The key for such negative associations is the selfish side to power as deception, lying, or even spin. On positive or neutral grounds, the rhetorical dimension of power is best associated with persuasion, results, and influence. The presumption here is that someone's or some organization's message making is done on ethical grounds in the first place. The broad, social value of public relations rests on rhetoric, which, as Heath (2000) argued, "is ethical because it empowers participants to engage in dialogue, private or public" (p. 75), and at the same time public relations professionals must "acknowledge the power of rhetoric and be mindful that it can do good and harm" (p. 79).

In public relations, the rhetorical dimension of power is evident in the ways in which practitioners use language, symbols, knowledge, and discourse. Perhaps the most prominent area of note here is the management of messages also pejoratively referred to under terms akin to spin control. In general, this area has been amply addressed in both academic and trade publications, as it is the most visible part of public relations—actual communication acts (referred to in the profession as "tactics") between organizations and their publics. However, in terms of investigations about how public relations specifically exercises its rhetorical power, the research is less plentiful but highly potent.

Courtright and Smudde's (2007) collection of essays specifically investigate power and public relations. The volume features 10 chapters of case studies that survey the breadth of perspectives about power and how it applies to all aspects of the practice and management of public relations. At the heart of this work is the idea that critical perspectives can and must be used to provide deeper understanding and better practice of public relations, especially the symbolic action it features. Research calling for and applying critical theory in investigations of public relations' rhetorical power have grown in recent years (e.g., Courtright, 2007; Elwood, 1995; German, 1995; Heath, 1992; Heath, Motion, & Leitch, 2009; Ihlen, 2005, 2007; Jerome, Moffitt, & Knudsen, 2007; Leitch & Neilson, 2001; Motion & Leitch, 2007; Motion & Weaver, 2005; Smudde, 2004, 2007; Waymer & Ni, 2009). These and other sources, especially Ihlen, van Ruler, and Fredriksson (2009), apply critical theories such as those of Bourdieu, Foucault, Giddens, Goffman, Habermas, and others to focus on the deeper dynamics of rhetoric that public relations professionals enacted and, most important, reveal new insights about how language, symbols, and discourse demonstrate public relations' power. At the intersection of rhetoric and power is choice, so "because it intersects other choices, power calls for stewardship in mutual benefit of those who have an interest in resolving differences and making important choices" (Heath, 2000, p. 77).

Social Dimension

Third and last, the social dimension of power concerns relationships among people. This final dimension is one that most binds together the other two: Organizations and societies are made up of people who act with each other principally through communication. People gather together and invite others to join (or cast others away) because of the common ground they share (e.g., values, goals, worldview). Inherent in this dimension is ethics: People accept and abide by rules of individual and collective good thinking and behavior. The social dimension of power relies on people conferring on other people certain "powerful" attributes. In this way, then, the social dimension intersects with power's hierarchical dimension as it acknowledges micropolitical (i.e., individual to individual) and macropolitical (i.e., individual to group to organization and back) factors. The social dimension also intersects with power's rhetorical dimension because of the natural human capability to use language and symbols to appeal to one's intellect, emotions, and behaviors—to inspire cooperation.

In public relations, the social dimension of power is demonstrable through the interactions of its practitioners with others within and outside their immediate organizations. As Heath (2000) observed, "Rhetorical enactment empowers the practitioner as well as other members of society to decide on their value perspectives and to vet the information they use in making market and public policy decisions" (p. 85). Of special importance in power's social dimension is the concept of professionalism. Much research has been published over the years, and one category that is prominent includes investigations of public relations professionals' practice on a nation-by-nation basis. However, the principal focus for professionalism and public relations power concerns how public relations practitioners' work, attitudes, behaviors, and the like affect and reflect views of the field.

Pieczka and L'Etang (2001) provided a thorough overview of professionalism in public relations. In particular, they point out that the key dimensions of defining professionalism in any field are the presence of a body of knowledge, ethical principles (especially codes of ethics), and certification. Particular topics of occupational interest for public relations have included gender, roles and responsibilities, sociology of the workplace, and engagement with government and society in general. Other research presents the results of studies about public relations professionalism. For example, David (2004) applied the professional values, practice, and pragmatics (3Ps) model to explore the values underlying public relations practices, revealing that the pragmatics component is more symmetrical than originally conceived. Edwards (2006) explores public relations' role in democratic societies, which is primarily based on relationships between organizations and society and the social structures they share. Hoffmann, Rottger, and Jarren (2007) used public relations as practiced in Switzerland to explore and debunk the viability of two models of occupational fields (i.e., trait and power), finding that the two models actually are limited, and a reorientation in their use is needed. Kim and Reber (2009) showed the degrees to which public relations practitioners' attitudes about themselves and their length of service as public relations professionals have a greater appreciation for corporate social responsibility.

Initially, then, research on power in public relations concentrated on the role of public relations professionals in the workplace. A subset of this literature particularly has focused on women in the profession. For example, L. A. Grunig, Toth, and Hon (2001) presented the results of a 10-year study of nearly 2,000 public relations practitioners (women and men) on the role and influence of gender in the public relations field. The authors describe the state of the public relations industry for women (and men) in public and private arenas. Indeed, L. A. Grunig et al. gave us much evidence about how the dynamics of gender, organizational culture, economic factors, personal needs, professional perceptions, pay and promotion, race and ethnicity, and other dimensions intertwine within the profession. As the authors say, "Success in public relations, as in other careers discussed here, comes with an inordinately high price tag for most women. And the positive changes for many women in management we have described here seem to come excruciatingly slowly" (p. 118).

Studies of women in public relations thus hold an important niche in the research literature, and issues of power figure prominently within it (e.g., Aldoory, 2003; Aldoory, Reber, Berger, & Toth, 2008; Choi & Hon, 2002; O'Neil, 2003, 2004; Serini, Toth, Wright, & Emig, 1998). Along with this, more generally, concerns for public relations' ability to influence organizations at managerial and other levels characterize the functionalist view of power: "power over" relations, which Berger (2005) defined as "the traditional dominance model where decision making is characterized by control, instrumentalism, and self-interest" (p. 6). At best, this view should be seen as the amount of *influence* (i.e., "power with"; Berger, 2005, p. 6) public relations people have within the organization, for power qua control is an illusion.

Power Dimensions Taken Together

When taken together, all three dimensions of power actually occur simultaneously, which is why power is problematic. People tend to focus on one of the dimensions more than the others as perhaps a matter of convenience or importance. Clouding one's view of power, too, can be the frame in which one sees power—as a negative (selfish) phenomenon or as a neutral to positive (selfless) means for correction to the status quo. Power's multidimensionality makes it naturally difficult to apprehend but at the same time makes it curiously attractive to apply. The most effective application of power, however, comes from an understanding of these three dimensions. Corporate contexts, whether social, political, economic, technological, or cultural, add further factors to be considered.

A key, then, to power and public relations is looking at power's strategic implications. Strategy means applying an understanding of power's multidimensionality for what it has been in the past (i.e., to learn from it) and, most important, formulating future ways (i.e., to anticipate applications) to inspire cooperation between an organization and its publics through public relations efforts. Such strategizing is possible through five categories of practice (see Smudde & Courtright, in press).

1. *Coalition building:* At an external level, coalition building involves public relations practitioners working on behalf of one's organization to establish common ground with another person or group on which they can collaborate and achieve mutually beneficial ends. At an internal level, coalition building involves public relations professionals working well with others within their own organizations so that the public relations function is valued and valuable. Central here is recognizing the upward and downward flow plus the micro- and macrolevels of power that are at play.

2. *Strategy development:* Public relations professionals must participate in the process and provide counsel for the organization to manage its plans for success in its business and operations. It is the province of public relations to act as a seer of future opportunities and threats to an organization's image, business, and legacy and to address them proactively whenever possible. Strategy development, together with the ancillary practices of message design and genre choices, is the unseen element to public relations that publics and stakeholders do not readily recognize.

3. *Message design:* Taking publics' knowledge, attitudes, and actions into account is the essence of effective message design. Through message design, public relations professionals focus on the relationships among their organizations and the publics/stakeholders that they depend on.

4. *Genre choices:* The actual outputs of public relations professionals' work (i.e., the tactics) must also balance an organization's needs and wants for communication with the publics' needs and wants in communication. In this way, the discourse genres chosen to present any messages must fulfill expectations on multiple levels.

5. *Program execution and evaluation:* The final production and dissemination of public relations work to target publics are what most people recognize as public relations but are, in reality, only the result of much hard planning and preparation. Public relations practitioners must also evaluate how well the program worked for both the target publics and the organization through systematic and appropriate measurement methods (see Daymon & Holloway, 2002; Paine, 2007; Stacks, 2002; van Ruler, Verčič, & Verčič, 2008; Watson & Noble, 2005). With attention to ethics in this and the previous points, public relations may serve as the management of power relations between organizations and publics on whom their success depends.

Future Directions for the Concept of Power in Public Relations

Clearly, the three dimensions of power we have reviewed will continue to be of interest in public relations research. Within these we see at least three subtopics that will generate lines of research of value to the academic field and the practice of public relations: issues of power associated with technology, activism, and globalization.

Technology

It is no secret how utterly fast technology evolves, and it is useless to quote the rate at which technology advances because the quote would be outdated by the time it is published. Nevertheless, new technology, as Coombs (1998) observed, has an enormous potential to equalize things among people and, especially, between people and organizations. Moreover, the Internet has enabled the "haves" and the "have-nots" to engage more equitably in communication about matters important to them both, while fostering constructive engagement between stakeholders and organizations who can better achieve common ground (Jaques, 2006). Indeed, advances in technology have had an extensive impact beyond merely facilitating communication among people—the Internet now hosts communities of people who gather "virtually" to socialize and obtain relationships, help, products, services, resources, support, and so on. Li and Bernoff (2008) referred to this phenomenon as a "groundswell," which they define as "a social trend in which people use technologies to get the things they need from each other, rather than from traditional institutions like corporations" (p. 9).

The power of public relations directly affects and is affected by the groundswell: Information democratization has effectively leveled the playing field on which individuals and organizations can address issues and confront each other (see Bernoff & Li, 2008). This democratization is both good and bad because anyone can obtain and post ("publish") information for everyone to access, which raises issues about source credibility, motives, ethics, law, and so on (see Dahlberg, 2005; Dahlgren, 2000). A raft of books has appeared in the last decade to assist for-profits, nonprofits, and everyday citizens to harness the power of the Internet (e.g., Breakenridge, 2008; Holtz, 2002; Kelleher, 2007; Levine, 2002; Middleberg, 2001; Scott, 2007; Solis & Breakenridge, 2009; Witmer, 2000). Additionally, "the practitioner literature is filled with stories about the need to be Internet savvy and the growing use of intranets for internal communication" (Heath & Coombs, 2006, p. 482). Indeed, Diga and Kelleher's (2009) study shows how frequent social media use is a prized indicator of one's own technology savvy and, most important, a key basis for exercising power as a public relations professional.

For public relations practice, insightful research has addressed key matters in technology, especially the Internet. For example, Kent and Taylor (1998) overviewed what it takes for organizations to inspire dialogue over the Internet. A decade later, Pavlik (2008) deftly showed details about how broadly technology—primarily social media—has made various impacts on public relations practice. Perhaps the best known example of technology's impact on public relations is the role Internet chat groups played in fomenting a crisis for Intel's "flawed" Pentium 2 chip (Hearit, 1999), which, because of the company's inattention to Web rumblings, news organizations framed the chip as flawed in general in spite of the fact that the problem was only possible in rare situations dealing with complex computations. Other examples of technology's role in public relations power include those that address specific aspects or channels of the Internet. First, Kent, Taylor, and White (2003) explored the relationship between Web site design and how well organizations respond to stakeholders. Fernando (2009) examined how Internet social media such as YouTube, YouChoose, and Citizen Tube play a role in perpetuating the power of messages conveyed in video formats. Next, Wright and Hinson's (2008) 3-year study of social media and blog use by public relations professionals showed that the technologies have enabled organizations to respond more quickly to criticism and thereby enhance relationship building with publics. Finally, Porter, Sweetser-Trammell, Chung, and Kim's (2007) study showed how blog use differs among users and the power public relations practitioners hold in their organizations.

Technology has played a major role in bringing our next subject, the power of activism in public relations practice, to the fore.

Activism

At first blush, the topic of activism may seem to be a prominent one within the study of power in public relations, but the fact is that research on activism's role in public relations power has been limited (for reviews, see Smith, 2005; Smith & Ferguson, 2001). Even so, it is important to recognize the role of activism, because

> in today's society, little influence is exerted by individual communicators, unless we acknowledge the power of interpersonal communication—conversation. In matters of public policy, society has grown to a size so large that the key rhetors are organizations—corporations, governmental agencies, and nongovernmental organizations—activist voices, and pressure politics. Each side looks for advantage. Lines are drawn and battles are waged within companies, industries, activist groups, and governmental agencies. Those battles occur between activist groups, governmental bodies, companies, and industries. This process allows, at least in principle, for sides to examine each others' points of view. (Heath, 2000, p. 75)

Indeed, Berger and Reber (2006) recommended an activist role for professionals within organizations. As well, activists as publics "push organizations toward excellence" (L. A. Grunig, Grunig, & Dozier, 2002, p. 442; see also L. A. Grunig, 1992a).

Social movement research on activism (e.g., Jensen, 2001; Simons, 1970; Stevens, 2006) therefore can be extended into analysis about power and public relations. Of particular interest to scholars and practitioners is some insightful research that reveals how organizations have quashed or been adversely affected by activists (e.g., Courtright, 2007; Henderson, 2005; Hon, 2006; Hung, 2003; Lester, 2006; O'Callaghan, 2007; Zoch, Collins, Sisco, & Supa, 2008) and how an application and management of typical activist methodologies are similar to and can enhance public relations practice (e.g., J. E. Grunig, 2000; Holtzhausen & Voto, 2002; Jaques, 2006; Pompper, 2005; Smith & Ferguson, 2001; Thompson, 2008). We believe, however, that future investigations of activism can and should more specifically explore the power dimensions using relevant theoretical orientations and research methodologies similar or in addition to those we covered above (e.g., Berger, 2005, 2007; Berger & Reber, 2006; L. A. Grunig et al., 2002).

One special opportunity for future research is to tie activism and public relations' power through ethics. For example, if we take the Public Relations Society of America's (PRSA) Member Code of Ethics as the springboard to this line of research, a more-focused, profession-specific view of activism becomes apparent. That is, activism predominantly relies on the professional value of advocacy—public relations officials (1) "serve the public interest by acting as responsible advocates for those we represent" and (2) "provide a voice in the marketplace of ideas, facts, and viewpoints to aid informed public debate" (PRSA, 2000, p. 3). This value, then, is the foundation of public relations efforts that uphold all the ethical principles of PRSA's ethics code—ultimately to ensure that the system of power relationships is intact and enables voices to be heard. This view, then, promotes and largely relies on dialogic communication among parties, which, as Johannesen (1990) has shown, is naturally a highly ethical approach and can be easily integrated into more philosophical positions like that drawn out so well by Curtin and Boynton (2001). After all, as Heath (2000) said, "Public relations follows, if it does not help lead, efforts to give voice to the competing advocates and interests that constitute the rhetorical dialogue of society" (p. 85).

Globalization

The previous subjects of technology and activism lead naturally to a third subject of concern, the effects of globalization in international public relations. Multinational corporations (MNCs) enter foreign markets and have great potential to create economic and social side effects for which they may be brought to account (Bomann-Larsen & Wiggen, 2004; Chen, 2004). Bringing them to the court of world public opinion are nongovernmental organizations (NGOs) and activist publics. Exercise of power therefore figures greatly in the future of public relations because of an array of issues: human rights, labor practices, health and environment, and governmental and corporate corruption (United Nations Global Compact Office, n.d.).

The effect that MNCs (and, for that matter, NGOs and activists) can have on the world cannot be overstated. Curtin and Gaither (2005, 2007) argued that all international public relations practice is imbued with power. Seen through articulation theory, public relations research and practice must focus on interactions among five "moments" in Curtin and Gaither's (2005) Circuit of Culture Model: (1) regulation (laws, rules, and norms), (2) production (the encoding of messages), (3) representation (media channels and symbolic forms), (4) consumption (decoding of messages), and (5) identity (of organizations, publics, and other players). Each interaction, or "articulation," between any two moments is where power arises. Thus, Sriramesh and Verčič's (2009) theoretical framework for understanding international public relations provides good direction for attention to power dynamics in the creation and analysis of international public relations campaigns: knowledge of the political system, economic system and level of development, legal constraints, and level of activism in any country in which MNCs, NGOs, and other international actors (e.g., celebrity activists) operate. Power therefore arises in practices as diverse as brand development (Gregory, 2002) and corporate reputation (Morley, 2002), corporate social responsibility (Corbin, 2002; Dayal-Gulati & Finn, 2007; Hirschland, 2006), nation building (Botan & Taylor, 2005), and public diplomacy (Kunczik, 1997; Signitzer & Wamser, 2006).

Conclusion

All together, power is not something public relations possesses so much as it is something it exercises through relationships. Therefore, we believe that power is a community-based phenomenon that people confer on each other through their relationships with one another. This conferring of power is based on the hierarchical positions they hold, the rhetorical manifestation and recognition of relationships and positions through communicative acts, and the social implications these dimensions have on individual and, especially, communal views of the system of relationships that exist and evolve among people.

Public relations therefore has a "powerful" future on the world stage. Practitioners will continue to seek and gain further access to and participation in the circle of key management decision makers and their advisers within organizations. Women will continue to make strides in achieving parity within the profession. New technologies have given organizations and individuals alike a global platform from which to improve the world we live in. In short, public relations has the capability, opportunity, and, indeed, responsibility to exercise power for the betterment of all members of society. Public relations must couple power with ethics due to its potential impact on communities in size ranging from the local to the global (Goddard, 2005). Public relations must nurture power based on relationships among people and organizations.

References

Aldoory, L. (2003). The empowerment of feminist scholarship in public relations and the building of a feminist paradigm. In P. J. Kalbfleisch (Ed.), *Communication yearbook 27* (pp. 221–255). Mahwah, NJ: Lawrence Erlbaum.

Aldoory, L., Reber, B. H., Berger, B. K., & Toth, E. L. (2008). Provocations in public relations: A study of gendered ideologies of power-influence in practice. *Journalism & Mass Communication Quarterly, 85,* 735–750.

Argenti, P. A., & Forman, J. (2002). *The power of corporate communication: Crafting the voice and image of your business.* New York: McGraw-Hill.

Arthur W. Page Society. (2007). *The authentic enterprise: Relationships, values and the evolution of corporate communications.* New York: Author. Retrieved November, 19, 2008, from www.awpagesociety.com/images/uploads/2007AuthenticEnterprise.pdf

Beard, M. (2001). *Running a public relations department* (2nd ed.). London: Kogan Page.

Berger, B. K. (2005). Power over, power with, and power to relations: Critical reflections of public relations, the dominant coalition, and activism. *Journal of Public Relations Research, 17,* 5–28.

Berger, B. K. (2007). Public relations and organizational power. In E. L. Toth (Ed.), *The future of excellence in public relations and communication management: Challenges for the next generation* (pp. 221–234). Mahwah, NJ: Lawrence Erlbaum.

Berger, B. K., & Reber, B. H. (2006). *Gaining influence in public relations: The role of resistance in practice.* Mahwah, NJ: Lawrence Erlbaum.

Bernoff, J., & Li, C. (2008). Harnessing the power of the oh-so-social Web. *MIT Sloan Management Review, 49*(3), 36–42.

Bomann-Larsen, L., & Wiggen, O. (Eds.). (2004). *Responsibility in world business: Managing harmful side-effects of corporate activity.* New York: United Nations University Press.

Botan, C. H., & Taylor, M. (2005). The role of trust in channels of strategic communication for building civil society. *Journal of Communication, 55,* 685–702.

Breakenridge, D. (2008). *PR 2.0: New media, new tools, new audiences.* Upper Saddle River, NJ: Pearson Education/FT Press.

Burke, K. (1970). *The rhetoric of religion: Studies in logology.* Berkeley: University of California Press.

Burke, K. (1989). Poem. In H. W. Simons & T. Melia (Eds.), *The legacy of Kenneth Burke* (p. 263). Madison: University of Wisconsin Press.

Chen, Y.-R. R. (2004). Effective public affairs in China: MNC—government bargaining power and corporate strategies for influencing foreign business policy formulation. *Journal of Communication Management, 8,* 395–413.

Choi, Y., & Hon, L. C. (2002). The influence of gender composition in powerful positions on public relations practitioners' gender-related perceptions. *Journal of Public Relations Research, 14,* 229–263.

Coombs, W. T. (1998). The Internet as potential equalizer: New leverage for confronting social irresponsibility. *Public Relations Review, 24,* 289–304.

Corbin, C. (2002). Silences and lies: How the industrial fishery constrained voices of ecological conservation. *Canadian Journal of Communication, 27,* 7–32.

Cottle, S. (2003). *News, public relations and power.* Thousand Oaks, CA: Sage.

Courtright, J. L. (2007). Internet activism and institutional image management. In J. L. Courtright & P. M. Smudde (Eds.), *Power and public relations* (pp. 151–178). Cresskill, NJ: Hampton Press.

Courtright, J. L., & Smudde, P. M. (Eds.). (2007). *Power and public relations.* Cresskill, NJ: Hampton Press.

Croft, A. C. (2006). *Managing a public relations firm for growth and profit* (2nd ed.). Binghamton, NY: Best Business Books.

Curtin, P. A., & Boynton, L. A. (2001). Ethics in public relations: Theory and practice. In R. L. Heath (Ed.), *Handbook of public relations* (pp. 411–422). Thousand Oaks, CA: Sage.

Curtin, P. A., & Gaither, T. K. (2005). Privileging identity, difference, and power: The circuit of culture as a basis for public relations theory. *Journal of Public Relations Research, 17,* 91–115.

Curtin, P. A., & Gaither, T. K. (2007). *International public relations: Negotiating culture, identity, and power.* Thousand Oaks, CA: Sage.

Dahlberg, L. (2005). The corporate colonization of online attention and the marginalization of critical communication. *Journal of Communication Inquiry, 29,* 160–180.

Dahlgren, P. (2000). The Internet and the democratization of civic culture. *Political Communication, 17,* 335–340.

D'Aprix, R. (1997). Partner or perish: A new vision for staff professionals. *Strategic Communication Management, 1*(3), 12–15.

D'Aprix, R. (2001). Reinventing the strategic communicator. *Strategic Communication Management, 5*(5), 32–35.

David, P. (2004). Extending symmetry: Toward a convergence of professionalism, practice, and pragmatics in public relations. *Journal of Public Relations Research, 16,* 185–211.

Dayal-Gulati, A., & Finn, M. W. (Eds.). (2007). *Global corporate citizenship.* Evanston, IL: Northwestern University Press.

Daymon, C., & Holloway, I. (2002). *Qualitative research methods in public relations and marketing communications.* New York: Routledge.

Diga, M., & Kelleher, T. (2009). Social media use, perceptions of decision-making power, and public relations roles. *Public Relations Review, 35,* 440–442.

Edwards, L. (2006). Rethinking power in public relations. *Public Relations Review, 32,* 229–231.

Edwards, L. (2009). Symbolic power and public relations practice: Locating individual practitioners in their social context. *Journal of Public Relations Research, 35,* 251–272.

Elwood, W. N. (1995). Public relations and the ethics of the moment: The anatomy of a local ballot issue campaign. In W. N. Elwood (Ed.), *Public relations inquiry as rhetorical criticism: Case studies of corporate discourse and social influence* (pp. 255–275). Westport, CT: Praeger.

Fernando, A. (2009). The revolution will be mashed up (and uploaded to YouTube). *Communication World, 26*(1), 10–12.

Garten, J. E. (2001). *The mind of the CEO.* New York: Basic Books/Perseus.

German, K. M. (1995). Critical theory in public relations inquiry: Future directions for analysis in a public relations context. In W. N. Elwood (Ed.), *Public relations inquiry as rhetorical criticism: Case studies of corporate discourse and social influence* (pp. 279–294). Westport, CT: Praeger.

Goddard, T. (2005). Corporate citizenship and community relations: Contributing to the challenges of aid discourse. *Business and Society Review, 110,* 269–296.

Gregory, J. R. (2002). *Branding across borders: A guide to global brand marketing.* New York: McGraw-Hill.

Grunig, J. E. (1976). Organizations and public relations: Testing a communication theory. *Journalism Monographs, 46,* 1–59.

Grunig, J. E. (1993). Image and substance: From symbolic to behavioral relationships. *Public Relations Review, 19,* 121–139.

Grunig, J. E. (2000). Collectivism, collaboration, and societal corporatism as core professional values in public relations. *Journal of Public Relations Research, 12,* 23–48.

Grunig, L. A. (1992a). Activism: How it limits the effectiveness of organizations and how excellent public relations departments respond. In J. E. Grunig (Ed.), *Excellence in public relations and communication management* (pp. 503–530). Mahwah, NJ: Lawrence Erlbaum.

Grunig, L. A. (1992b). Power in the public relations department. In J. E. Grunig (Ed.), *Excellence in public relations and communication management* (pp. 483–501). Hillsdale, NJ: Lawrence Erlbaum.

Grunig, L. A., Grunig, J. E., & Dozier, D. M. (2002). *Excellent public relations and effective organizations:*

A study of communication management in three countries. Mahwah, NJ: Lawrence Erlbaum.

Grunig, L. A., Toth, E. L., & Hon, L. C. (2001). *Women in public relations: How gender influences practice.* New York: Guilford Press.

Hearit, K. M. (1999). Newsgroups, activist publics, and corporate apologia: The case of Intel and its Pentium chip. *Public Relations Review, 25,* 291–308.

Heath, R. L. (1992). The wrangle in the marketplace: A rhetorical perspective of public relations. In E. L. Toth & R. L. Heath (Eds.), *Rhetorical and critical approaches to public relations* (pp. 17–36). Hillsdale, NJ: Lawrence Erlbaum.

Heath, R. L. (2000). A rhetorical perspective on the values of public relations: Crossroads and pathways toward concurrence. *Journal of Public Relations Research, 12,* 69–91.

Heath, R. L., & Coombs, W. T. (2006). *Today's public relations: An introduction.* Thousand Oaks, CA: Sage.

Heath, R. L., Motion, J., & Leitch, S. (2009). *Power and public relations: Paradoxes and programmatic thoughts.* Retrieved December 15, 2009, from www.instituteforpr.org/files/uploads/Power_Public Relations.pdf

Henderson, A. (2005). Activism in "paradise": Identity management in a public relations campaign against genetic engineering. *Journal of Public Relations Research, 17,* 117–137.

Hipple, J. R. (2007, August). Public relations: The critical link to successful business strategy. *Public Relations Tactics,* p. 17.

Hirschland, M. J. (2006). *Corporate social responsibility and the shaping of global public policy.* New York: Palgrave Macmillan.

Hoffmann, J., Rottger, U., & Jarren, O. (2007). Structural segregation and openness: Balanced professionalism for public relations. *Studies in Communication Sciences, 7*(1), 125–146.

Holtz, S. (2002). *Public relations on the net: Winning strategies to inform and influence the media, the investment community, the government, the public, and more* (2nd ed.). New York: AMACOM.

Holtzhausen, D. R., & Voto, R. (2002). Resistance from the margins: The postmodern public relations practitioner as organizational activist. *Journal of Public Relations Research, 14,* 57–84.

Hon, L. (2006). Negotiating relationships with activist publics. In K. Fitzpatrick & C. Bronstein (Eds.), *Ethics in public relations: Responsible advocacy* (pp. 53–69). Thousand Oaks, CA: Sage.

Hung, C.-J. F. (2003). Relationship building, activism, and conflict resolution. *Asian Journal of Communication, 13,* 21–49.

Ihlen, Ø. (2005). The power of social capital: Adapting Bourdieu to the study of public relations. *Public Relations Review, 31,* 492–496.

Ihlen, Ø. (2007). Building on Bourdieu: A sociological grasp of public relations. *Public Relations Review, 33,* 269–274.

Ihlen, Ø., van Ruler, B., & Fredriksson, M. (Eds.). (2009). *Public relations and social theory: Key figures and concepts.* New York: Routledge.

Jaques, T. (2006). Activist "rules" and the convergence with issue management. *Journal of Communication Management, 10,* 407–420.

Jensen, R. J. (2001). Evolving protest rhetoric: From the 1960s to the 1990s. *Rhetoric Review, 20,* 28–32.

Jerome, A. M., Moffitt, M. A., & Knudsen, J. A. (2007). Understanding how Martha Stewart harmed her image restoration through a "micropolitics" of power. In J. L. Courtright & P. M. Smudde (Eds.), *Power and public relations* (pp. 85–106). Cresskill, NJ: Hampton Press.

Johannesen, R. L. (1990). *Ethics in human communication* (3rd ed.). Prospect Heights, IL: Waveland.

Kelleher, T. (2007). *Public relations online: Lasting concepts for changing media.* Thousand Oaks, CA: Sage.

Kent, M. L. (2008). Critical analysis of blogging in public relations. *Public Relations Review, 34,* 32–40.

Kent, M. L., & Taylor, M. (1998). Building dialogic relationships through the World Wide Web. *Public Relations Review, 24,* 321–334.

Kent, M. L., Taylor, M., & White, W. J. (2003). The relationship between Web site design and organizational responsiveness to stakeholders. *Public Relations Review, 29,* 63–77.

Kim, S.-Y., & Reber, B. H. (2009). How public relations professionalism influences corporate social responsibility: A survey of practitioners. *Journalism & Mass Communication Quarterly, 86,* 157–174.

Kunczik, M. (1997). *Images of nations and international public relations.* Mahwah, NJ: Lawrence Erlbaum.

Lauzen, M. M., & Dozier, D. M. (1992). The missing link: The public relations manager role as mediator of organizational environments and power consequences for the function. *Journal of Public Relations Research, 4,* 205–220.

Leitch, S., & Neilson, D. (2001). Bringing publics into public relations: New theoretical frameworks for practice. In R. L. Heath (Ed.), *Handbook of public relations* (pp. 127–139). Thousand Oaks, CA: Sage.

Lester, L. (2006). We too are green: Public relations, symbolic power and the Tasmanian wilderness conflict. *Media International Australia (Incorporating Culture & Policy), 121,* 52–64.

Levine, M. (2002). *Guerilla P.R.Wired: Waging a successful publicity campaign online, offline, and everywhere in between.* New York: McGraw-Hill.

Li, C., & Bernoff, J. (2008). *Groundswell: Winning in a world transformed by social technologies.* Boston: Harvard Business Press.

Lordan, E. J. (2003). *Essentials of public relations management.* Chicago: Burnham.

Lukaszewski, J. E. (2001a). Demystifying strategy: How to develop the mind of a strategist: Part 1 of 3. *Communication World, 17*(4), 13–15.

Lukaszewski, J. E. (2001b). Having strategic impact: How to develop the mind of a strategist: Part 2 of 3. *Communication World, 17*(5), 26–28.

Lukaszewski, J. E. (2001c). See you at the table: How to develop the mind of a strategist: Part 3 of 3. *Communication World, 17*(6), 9–11.

Lukaszewski, J. E. (2008). *Why should the boss listen to you? The seven disciplines of the trusted strategic advisor.* San Francisco: Jossey-Bass.

Middleberg, D. (2001). *Winning PR in the wired world: Powerful communication strategies for the noisy digital space.* New York: McGraw-Hill.

Miller, D., & Dinan, W. (2008). *A century of spin: How public relations became the cutting edge of corporate power.* Ann Arbor, MI: Pluto Press.

Morley, M. (2002). *How to manage your global reputation: A guide to the dynamics of international public relations* (Rev. & updated ed.). Washington Square: New York University Press.

Motion, J., & Leitch, S. (2007). A toolbox for public relations: The oeuvre of Michel Foucault. *Public Relations Review, 33,* 263–268.

Motion, J., & Weaver, C. K. (2005). A discourse perspective for critical public relations research: Life Sciences Network and the battle for "truth." *Journal of Public Relations Research, 17,* 49–67.

Oates, D. B. (2006, October). Measuring the value of public relations: Tying efforts to business goals. *Public Relations Tactics,* p. 12.

O'Callaghan, T. (2007). Disciplining multinational enterprises: The regulatory power of reputation risk. *Global Society: Journal of Interdisciplinary International Relations, 21,* 95–117.

Oksiutycz, A. (2006). Power, empowerment and organisational communication. *Communicare, 25*(2), 25–41.

O'Neil, J. (2003). An analysis of the relationships among structure, influence, and gender: Helping to build a feminist theory of public relations. *Journal of Public Relations Research, 15,* 151–179.

O'Neil, J. (2004). Effects of gender and power on PR managers' upward influence. *Journal of Managerial Issues, 16,* 127–144.

Paine, K. D. (2007). *Measuring public relationships: The data-driven communicator's guide to success.* Berlin, NH: KDPaine.

Pavlik, J. V. (2008, June 4). *Mapping the consequences of technology on public relations.* New York: Institute for Public Relations. Retrieved December 17, 2008, from www.instituteforpr.org/research_single/mapping_the_consequences_of_technology_on_public_relations

Pieczka, M., & L'Etang, J. (2001). Public relations and the question of professionalism. In R. L. Heath (Ed.), *Handbook of public relations* (pp. 223–235). Thousand Oaks, CA: Sage.

Plowman, K. D. (1998). Power in conflict for public relations. *Journal of Public Relations Research, 10,* 237–261.

Pompper, D. (2005). "Difference" in public relations research: A case for introducing critical race theory. *Journal of Public Relations Research, 17,* 139–169.

Porter, L. V., Sweetser-Trammell, K. D., Chung, D., & Kim, E. (2007). Blog power: Examining the effects of practitioner blog use on power in public relations. *Public Relations Review, 33,* 92–95.

Public Relations Society of America. (2000). *Member code of ethics.* New York: Author.

Reber, B. H., & Berger, B. K. (2006). Finding influence: Examining the role of influence in public relations practice. *Journal of Communication Management, 10,* 235–249.

Ries, A., & Ries, L. (2009). *War in the boardroom: Why left-brained management and right-brained marketing don't see eye-to-eye—and what to do about it.* New York: Collins Business.

Saffir, L. (1999). *Power public relations: How to master the new PR* (2nd ed.). New York: McGraw-Hill.

Scott, D. M. (2007). *The new rules of marketing & PR: How to use news releases, blogs, podcasting, viral marketing & online media to reach buyers directly.* Hoboken, NJ: Wiley.

Serini, S. A., Toth, E. L., Wright, D. K., & Emig, A. (1998). Power, gender, and public relations: Sexual harassment as a threat to the practice. *Journal of Public Relations Research, 10,* 193–218.

Signitzer, B., & Wamser, C. (2006). Public diplomacy: A specific governmental public relations function. In C. H. Botan & V. Hazleton (Eds.), *Public relations theory II* (pp. 435–464). Mahwah, NJ: Lawrence Erlbaum.

Simons, H. W. (1970). Requirements, problems, and strategies: A theory of persuasion for social movements. *Quarterly Journal of Speech, 56,* 1–11.

Smith, M. F. (2005). Activism. In R. L. Heath (Ed.), *Encyclopedia of public relations* (Vol. 1, pp. 5–9). Thousand Oaks, CA: Sage.

Smith, M. F., & Ferguson, D. P. (2001). Activism. In R. L. Heath (Ed.), *Handbook of public relations* (pp. 291–300). Thousand Oaks, CA: Sage.

Smudde, P. M. (2004). Implications on the practice and study of Kenneth Burke's "public relations counsel with a heart." *Communication Quarterly, 52,* 420–432.

Smudde, P. M. (2007). Public relations' power as based on knowledge, discourse, and ethics. In J. L. Courtright & P. M. Smudde (Eds.), *Power and public relations* (pp. 207–238). Cresskill, NJ: Hampton Press.

Smudde, P. M. (2010). *Public relations as dramatistic organizing: A case study bridging theory and practice.* Cresskill, NJ: Hampton Press.

Smudde, P. M., & Courtright, J. L. (in press). *Inspiring cooperation & celebrating organizations: Genres, message design & strategy in public relations.* Cresskill, NJ: Hampton Press.

Solis, B., & Breakenridge, D. (2009). *Putting the public back in public relations: How social media is reinventing the aging business of PR.* Upper Saddle River, NJ: Pearson Education/FT Press.

Sriramesh, K., & Verčič, D. (2009). A theoretical framework for global public relations research and practice. In K. Sriramesh & D. Verčič (Eds.), *The global public relations handbook* (Expanded & rev. ed., pp. 3–21). New York: Routledge.

Stacks, D. W. (2002). *Primer of public relations research.* New York: Guilford Press.

Stevens, S. M. (2006). Activist rhetorics and the struggle for meaning: The case of "sustainability" in the reticulate public sphere. *Rhetoric Review, 25,* 297–315.

Thompson, N. (2008). When radicalism pays off. *Third Text, 22,* 599–603.

United Nations Global Compact Office. (n.d.). *The ten principles of the UN Global Compact.* Retrieved April 5, 2009, from www.unglobalcompact.org/AbouttheGC/TheTENPrinciples/index.html

van Ruler, B., Verčič, A. T., & Verčič, D. (Eds.). (2008). *Public relations metrics: Research and evaluation.* New York: Routledge.

Watson, T., & Noble, P. (2005). *Evaluating public relations: A best practice guide to public relations planning, research and evaluation.* Sterling, VA: Kogan Page.

Waymer, D., & Ni, L. (2009). Connecting organizations and their employee publics: The rhetorical analysis of employee-organization relationships (EOR). In R. L. Heath, E. L. Toth, & D. Waymer (Eds.), *Rhetorical and critical approaches to public relations II* (pp. 216–232). New York: Routledge.

Weiner, M. (2006). *Unleashing the power of PR: A contrarian's guide to marketing and communication.* San Francisco: Jossey-Bass.

Werder, K. P., & Holtzhausen, D. (2009). An analysis of the influence of public relations department leadership style on public relations strategy use and effectiveness. *Journal of Public Relations Research, 21,* 404–427.

Witmer, D. F. (2000). *Spinning the Web: A handbook for public relations on the Internet.* New York: Addison Wesley Longman.

Wright, D. K., & Hinson, M. D. (2008). How blogs and social media are changing the way public relations is practiced. *Public Relations Journal, 2*(2). Retrieved May 15, 2008, from www.prsa.org/Intelligence/PRJournal/Spring_08/index.html

Zoch, L. M., Collins, E. L., Sisco, H. F., & Supa, D. H. (2008). Empowering the activist: Using framing devices on activist organizations' Web sites. *Public Relations Review, 34,* 351–358.

CHAPTER 13

Power and Public Relations

Paradoxes and Programmatic Thoughts

Robert L. Heath, Judy Motion, and Shirley Leitch

> *From Plato forward, philosophers have struggled to define power, which is at heart the capacity to bend reality to your will.*
>
> —Meacham (2008, p. 34)

Power is a problematic of public relations: sociopolitical influence that evolves from interests expressed in competing vocabularies. "Meaning structures are filled with privileged interests" (Deetz, 1982, p. 139).

Recognizing this problematic, critics worry that practitioners exert too much, and unethical, power over publics' opinions. In *Unseen Power*, Scott Cutlip (1994) bracketed the good, bad, and ugly sides of this challenge: "Only through the expertise of public relations can causes, industries, individuals, and institutions make their voice heard in the public forum where thousands of shrill, competing voices daily re-create the Tower of Babel" (p. ix). "The social justification for public relations in a free society is to ethically and effectively plead the cause of a client or organization in the free-wheeling forum of public debate" (p. xii). Critics ask to what end and in whose interest meaning is created. Meaning matters; it socially constructs the ideology by which each society shapes its power resources to organize and give individuals and institutions their contextual and enactment integrity.

One pathway to explore this theme features systems (structural/functionalism, networks, structuration); as such, power resources arise from information flow and access to systems that foster or impede harmony/disharmony as goodwill challenges. The other pathway features cocreated meaning that shapes how people think collectively, identify themselves, and collectively enact social order. This second pathway stresses the rich impact language (idioms and vocabulary) has on power resources, as viewed through a rhetorical, discourse analysis, social construction, constitutive, or critical studies lens. Thoughts about reality (social and physical), identities, and identifications, as well as institutional/individual interest alignments, are shaped by words: They define those matters whereby enactable beliefs arise. Discourse has both constitutive (Fairclough, 1992; Foucault, 1972; Stokes, 2005) and social constructionist impact, as words in context privilege certain views of reality bent to various interests, motives, actions, institutions, and relationships (Shotter, 1993; Shotter & Gergen, 1994). Through language, society enacts itself whether meaning is fully cocreated through the discourse of many voices or is the product of one (or a few) voice self-interestedly constructing social reality that the many enact.

The purpose of this chapter is to discuss power as a collective, relational resource codefined and enacted through discourse-generated vocabularies. Resources of power are fostered by terministically bending reality to fit cognitive/ideation, identity/self, and societal/relation interests. The rationale for power arises from meaning by which individuals, organizations, and societies variously and collectively manage relationships and risks. At its best, public relations creates community power resources that empower individual and organizational efficiency, not frustrate it. Before amplifying this theme, the discussion briefly examines power from a systems/structure and functions perspective.

Systems/Structures and Functions Overview

Structuralism/functionalism addresses how public relations helps connect individuals and organizations through power networks. Practitioners bring information and ethical decision making into senior management and work with external systems to foster the kinds and qualities of relationships needed by organizations to achieve goodwill from key publics (J. E. Grunig & Grunig, 2008; L. A. Grunig, 1992; see Berger, 2005, 2007; Berger & Reber, 2006). Stacks (2004) applied part of this logic to crisis response. Interested in leadership and rightfulness, Berger (2007) acknowledged that

> whether researchers seek to advance our understanding of these concepts within a relational and symmetrical perspective, or approach them or other power issues from alternative perspectives, the concepts themselves continue to be crucial terms in our vocabulary of public relations power. (p. 227; see also Berger & Reber, 2006)

Exploring networks of power, Monge and Contractor (2000; Shumate, Fulk, & Monge, 2005) argued that social capital is created through the systemic quality of organizations and relationships as well as the kind of communication they facilitate. Similar analysis of global regimes, including nongovernmental organizations (NGOs; Stohl & Stohl, 2005), helps Taylor (2009) explain the structural/functional *and* rhetorical resources needed for civil society. Systems generate power resources by the structuration of functions defined by transitivity, access (openness/closedness), uncertainty, control, symmetry/asymmetry, complexity, turbulence (stability, randomness, even chaos), linkage, interdependence, adaptiveness, and hierarchy.

Structurally critiquing the formation of the information age, Gandy (1992) explained how public policy systems are manipulated to subsidize some and disadvantage other interests. Baker, Conrad, Cudahy, and Willyard (2009) observed how companies such as Merck gain approval of pharmaceuticals, such as Vioxx, from the Federal Drug Administration through systems and rhetorical positioning developed by the drug industry to protect and promote its interests.

Exploring processes of empowerment, Clegg, Courpasson, and Phillips (2006) observed, "Power and discourses are equally intermingled in so far as they constitute the political structure of organizations through diverse circuits of power" (p. 17). Yet systems, relationships, and attributions make no sense as enactable processes independent of meaning cocreated to collectively manage risks (Heath & Frandsen, 2008; Leitch & Motion, 2009).

Meaning Overview

Power resources are socially constructed interpretations of fact, evaluation, policy, and systems/relationships; as ultimate terms, they form the basis of identification and define the nature and quality of relationships (Courtright & Smudde, 2007). The nexus of power and meaning is not merely the influence—as often explained—that one or more entities exerts on other entities, but the battle by various entities over the rationale of power to determine who are legitimate power resources brokers.

Stressing this grounding principle of power, Barnes (1988) concluded, "Every society possesses a shared body of technical, manipulation-related knowledge, knowledge of nature, and a shared body of social knowledge, knowledge of a normative order" (p. 55). Power resources are enacted normative expectations captured in cocreated views of reality, selves, social relationships, privileges, and obligations. As interest groups and private sector organizations contest assumptions and norms, they define and redefine power, "the structure of discretion" (p. 62). Power, in this sense, is the "capacity for action and the possession of power [is] the possession of discretion in the use of capacity for action" (p. 67). Practitioners engage in the ebb and flow of social meaning (as preferred expectations) and its application to obtain and distribute stakes as manageable power resources.

The traditional definition of power features the ability of X to affect how Y achieves its goals (see, e.g., L. A. Grunig, 1992). As Barnes (1988) argued, this definition does not define power but merely indicates when it is present and "legitimate." This logic forces us to separate the legitimacy that various players enjoy to influence outcomes and the actual, and related, influence those players exert over decisions collectively made. The telling question asks, "What defined and contextually relevant characteristics of X in situation Z give X the ability to affect Y?" Meaning matters, Barnes reasoned, as he directed our attention to this focal point:

> Whether we talk of rights and obligations, or of roles and institutions, or of patterned social relationships, the import is much the same: We are talking of a presumed structure and orderliness in social activity, and a need to understand the nature and the basis of such structure and orderliness is implied. (p. 20)

Power results from definitions of entities as well as situations and value premises and social norms—expected and accepted patterns of thinking and acting.

As understood through discourse analysis and social constructionism, meaning defines power resources and structures/functions that result from and enact them. Clegg et al. (2006) forced attention to this meaning-centric approach: "Organizations and individuals use discourses purposefully to shape the political situation in and through which they can act and perform" (p. 17). Framed from a discourse perspective, power occurs within organizations and among institutions when discussants socially construct the meaning individuals enact in various contexts and to collaborate or compete. Power results when discourse enactors engage via statement and counterstatement (Heath, 2001) as interests compete to become or stay powerful; power can be unequally distributed rather than collectively used to make society more fully functioning (Heath, 2006).

Understanding the discourse nature of power can help organizational leaderships be more reflective and thereby committed and able to sponsor mutually beneficial public relations. This rationale grounds the understanding and criticism of the role public relations can and should play collaboratively in cocreated meaning that results from and guides product/service promotion and reputation building, repair, and management, as well as issue conflict resolution, crisis communication, and risk management.

Perspectives That Frame the Matter: Mead, Foucault, and Others

Power results when private/personal and sociopolitical/marketplace interests are framed so that they motivate choice (including reinforcement). Bernays (1955) captured one polar option in *Engineering Consent*; his philosophy rationalized engineering women's belief that "green," a power word in that context, was fashionable—Lucky Strike green. Bernays's peer, John Hill (1963), warned clients that power resides with key publics' right and ability to decide each matter based on arguments competing voices offer to enlighten choice.

Shared meaning as intersecting zones of meaning is a necessary organizing power resource for collective thought, identity, and relationships, as Clegg et al. (2006) reasoned: "Power is to organization as oxygen is to breathing. Politics are at the core of public life and their expression is invariably dependent on organization, be it in government, business, administration, religion, education, or whatever" (p. 3). This is so because interests are never achieved without connection to other interests (Pfeffer, 1981, 1992).

However well or badly aligned, interests are shaped and deployed collectively through language. As Clegg et al. (2006) observed,

> Power concerns the ways that social relations shape capabilities, decisions, change; these social relations can do things and they can block things unfolding. Power is ultimately about the choices that we make, the actions we take, the evils we tolerate, the good we define, the privileges we bestow, the rights we claim, and the wrongs we do. Power means finding the most effective leverage for particular relations. (p. 3)

This decidedly discourse oriented sense of power focuses on fundamentals of understanding and enactment. The crux of discourse rests on this essential theme: "The ultimate arbiter of what such interests are is not some external agency but the selves whose interests are at issue" (Clegg et al., 2006, p. 4).

At the heart of this problematic is not only willingness to collectively and collaboratively solve problems but also challenges to doing so given the discourse resources that can be and are brought to bear in ways that depend on shared meaning making, the cornerstone of issues management. As Ewing (1987) concluded, "Issues management is about power" (p. 1). Heath (2008; Heath & Palenchar, 2009) featured voices—activist/NGO, governmental, intra-industry, and interindustry—in the battle to increase or narrow the legitimacy gap as the fundamental problematic of each political economy.

Viewed as a discourse challenge, shared definitions, idioms, interests, values, and preferences are brought to life through the meaning that words strategically and idiosyncratically generate. As Roper (2005) argued, mere accommodation to external critics to make the organization less vulnerable, at least for the short term, can reduce the likelihood that issues that need discussion actually receive appropriate attention. Accommodation can preempt the fuller discussion needed for concurrence and collaboration.

Framing Power: Mind/Ideation, Self/Identity, and Society/Relational

Discussion to this point has underscored three foundational concepts. Power and shared meaning are interdependent, coproduced constitutive perspectives that are the foundation for (a) cognition, (b) self-identity, and (c) societal legitimacy as conceptualized by George Herbert Mead (1934). As similarly explained by Motion and Leitch (2007; see also Bentele, 2008), public relations is "a meaning creation process with ideational, relational and identity functions" (p. 264). Drawing on Fairclough (1992) and Foucault (1980, 1982, 1988, 1997), they elaborated:

> The ideational function of public relations would be to influence the concepts and systems of thought that shape how we think about things. The relationship function of public relations would refer to the construction of power relationships between discourse actors or "stakeholders." The identity function of public relations would refer to the creation and transformation of the subject positions available to actors within discourse. (Motion & Leitch, 2007, p. 264)

Discourse is "the vehicle through which power/knowledge circulates and discourse strategies are the means by which the relations of power/knowledge are created, maintained, resisted and transformed" (p. 265). Such meaning can become hegemonic "in that it becomes so pervasive that it is perceived as common sense" (p. 266).

This analysis parallels Castor's (2005) observation: "Social constructionism is an ontological perspective that views knowledge, identity, and social reality as human construction" (p. 482). As van Ruler and Verčič (2005) reasoned, public relations exerts "soft power" because it is "engaged in constructing society by making sense of situations, creating appropriate meanings out of them, and looking for acceptable frameworks and enactments" as the substrata of coproduced societal legitimacy (p. 266). Agents define themselves, give themselves identity, and lay the foundations for higher or lower quality relationships (Leitch & Neilson, 2001; see also, Bentele, 2008).

Power, Barnes (1988) reasoned, is driven by the rationale that makes its enactment legitimate. As interests and concerns are expressed, the vocabulary that matures defines legitimacy, obligation, and compliance as socially constructed power stakeholding/seeking. As Ihlen (2005) reasoned, "social capital can also be seen as one of the several resources used to obtain or maintain positions of power" (p. 492). Such capital arises from connections and memberships: network-framed obligations—or obligations framed as networks.

Public relations, Courtright and Smudde (2007) reasoned, engages "the measured and ethical use of language and symbols to inspire cooperation between an organization and its publics." Rhetorical inquiry "concerns the means by which power constructs, regulates, and perpetuates itself through symbols and the individuals that use them" (p. 4). Such meaning-based logics can be used to examine the "power relations inherent in a corporation's image restoration struggle" (Jerome, Moffitt, & Knudsen, 2007, p. 87; see Foucault, 1972, 1980). Power is exerted and granted by individuals and organizations in deference to standards defined by the dominant hegemony, which attributes responsibility in matters of crisis, consumer marketing decisions, logics of public policy issue debate, and collective management of risk. A central logic of this analysis, according to Smudde (2007), rests on the premise that "people get used to how they think and do things" and, therefore,

> see those systems of thinking and doing as the ways that structure everything humans do, rather than as mere templates for thinking, speaking, and acting. This perspective means that human discourse creates and recreates human reality, including that for organizations, not the other way around. (p. 207)

Advancing this rubric, we are keenly interested in how networks as defined lead members to perceive and think about reality, their identities, and relationships.

Meaning, the fundamental power resource that members of networks use, bends reality to their wills. As such, Clegg et al. (2006) reasoned, "Power is not necessarily constraining, negative or antagonistic. Power can be creative, empowering, and positive" (p. 2; originally Foucault's [1980] insight). As a resource, the strategic use of power and the ends to which it is used determine whether it is positive or negative. "The organizational media that form, condense, and distribute social relations shape power and they can shape it *either way*" (p. 2).

Mind/Ideation

How individuals think about reality serves as a power resource. This proposition addresses the power that results from the language (terminology/idioms) individuals collaboratively and competitively use to bend reality to various interests. Power results from the definitional and generative impact of language, whether informed by positivism, chaos, complexity, or other theoretical underpinnings, that grants or gains power because how people perceive reality conditions their reaction to it and to one another. Power flows from the pressure to achieve collective truth that enables society to make decisions. Institutions, such as science and church, arise to define reality that otherwise is intolerably chaotic and complex. As such, mind/ideation depends on a shared and, therefore, enactable sense of truth.

According to Motion and Leitch (2007), ideational discourse focuses on "the concepts and systems of thought that shape how we think about things" (p. 264). Definitional meaning underpins empowering or marginalizing power resources. "From a Foucauldian perspective, one would argue that the attachment to truth is central to the power/knowledge relationship. Particular knowledges gain the status of truths by virtue of their relationship to power" (p. 266). Attached to interests and strategic skills (as well as professional ethics), we observe,

> Conceptualized from a power/knowledge perspective, public relations shifts from the discourse domain of business, where it is understood as a commercial practice, to the discourse domain of politics, where it is understood as a power effective that produces and circulates certain kinds of truths. (p. 268)

The fundamental connecting tension between discourse and reality is that between word and thing (thoughts about reality and reality as perceived). One explanation of this relationship, referentialism, posits that experience with reality defines words, the meaning that results from experiencing reality (Ogden & Richards, 1923). In contrast, linguistic relativity sees words as defining reality. As Burke (1966) reasoned, "Things are the signs of words" (p. 363). Because words define and attitudinize reality, Burke argued, "there will be as many different worldviews in history as there are people" (p. 52). Our instruments for knowing are nothing but structures of terms and therefore manifest the nature of each terminology (Burke, 1969). Each vocabulary is a reflection, selection, and deflection of how people see and act toward the world they name and, thus, experience. Language is not a microscope for fully understanding reality but a set of terministic screens that enact reality as named (Burke, 1966). Burke (1934) warned, "If language is the fundamental instrument of human cooperation, and if there is an 'organic flaw' in the nature of language, we may well expect to find this organic flaw revealing itself through the texture of society" (p. 330).

As defined by discourse, power as asserted, refuted, and accepted is shaped by dialectical responses encountered through statement/counterstatement; the limits of any one propositional thought are set by counterresponse. Burke (1951, 1969, especially pp. 39–40, 306, 1973, 1983) wrote of the dialect of the act, react, and lesson learned. Shared meaning facilitates, and even frustrates, shared understanding and enactment. "In any process of institutionalization, meaningfulness is never 'given' but has to be struggled for, has to be secured, even against the resistance of others" (Clegg et al., 2006, p. 8). "Thus, power has no essential qualities because *power is not a thing but a relation between things and people as they struggle to secure 'truthfully' embedded meanings*" (p. 10). This discourse-centered approach to power fits neatly with Entman's (2007) views on framing; entities that frame news and issues achieve power because each frame predicts how salient perceived facts will be as they are debated and resolved into shared enactment.

Power and Bending Reality. Humans lack the power to make the sun rise. Even the most powerful ruler cannot extend his or her life beyond what is allotted by forces of nature, but rulers can foster development (or yield to others' influence on that matter) of a religion that leads to the creation of massive tombs in which they will spend the afterlife in stately luxury—even with humans sacrificed for their eternal needs. Faced with an unyielding reality, humans seek empowerment by conceptualizing the afterlife, the creation, and the power of prayer, whereby careful and appropriate invocation of God's will bends reality, such as the parting of a sea or the building of temples and pyramids, or explaining global warming. They even can be implored to provide safe travel, in this world and others. Doctrinal struggles are power battles, as occur between activists and members of industry (or government) who fight over definitions of reality.

Gordon and Pellegrin (2008) featured interaction as the means for social construction of shared reality:

> From the constructionist orientation, *knowledge* is itself a human product as well as an ongoing human production. Social constructionism, in short, contends that reality is a social construction that is created, maintained, altered, and destroyed through the process of human interaction. (p. 105)

Addressing the foundations of ideation, identity, and societal relationships, they observed, "Social constructionism does acknowledge a physical world independent of human interpretation" (p. 105). Operating vocabularies both increase/constrain and define limits of power in regard to reality as interpreted and enacted. Words define and thereby create power resources, such as leadership roles (king, priest, scientist, president, worker, teacher), and ascribe to each, variously constructed, the power and power limits that are societally operable at any time. These linguistic resources define how decisions are made in the face of complexity—by whom and by what process.

Power Discourse and Precaution. Policy struggles create power resources and engage them. The challenge of human ideation is to forge the definition of the character of reality needed for sufficient uncertainty reduction and expedient collective management of risk. Here, we encounter the power of science and with it the mental models approach to risk communication that compares what scientists conclude with what lay audiences believe.

Definitional and propositional battles over controversial interpretations and societal uses of reality necessarily produce power tensions. Attempts at collective definitions and decisions struggle with risk challenges such as biotechnology, global warming, and genetically modified organisms (GMOs); scientists, activists, policymakers, and business leaders yearn for a decision heuristic that would facilitate systematic, responsible, and ethical decision making that may further their interests. Proponents of the precautionary principle reason, in cautionary logics, that changes in biotechnology such as GMOs, for instance, should be conservative.

Intended to empower societal risk decision making, the precautionary principle paradoxically struggles to do that by asking "What is caution?" and wondering when a cautious move toward decision is actually harmful or beneficial (Maguire & Ellis, 2009; Proutheau & Heath, 2009). Ironies of social construction define relationships, ideas, and society in terms of quality of life and effective risk management (McComas, 2003).

Attributional and constitutive aspects of language give insights into how multiple voices define an enactable reality and shape the decision heuristics needed for shared perceptions, enlightened decisions, and collective actions. Balancing what we know and what we want to know, power derives from the ability to name and claim a sense of reality that is adopted and enacted by others. Contests arise because one perspective so instantiated can, and likely does, create hegemonic alienation that fosters friction and disharmony all the while in pursuit of agreement and harmony.

Self/Identity

What individuals think about themselves and others fosters empowering/marginalizing power resources. Language allows people to have rich, enactable, and externalizable definitions of themselves and others. How roles and identities are defined and attitudinized enacts network relationships. The question relevant to social character is "What is identity?" and thus "What is its attributional power?" With and from which organizations or institutions does the individual derive identity, and what power resources do these attachments grant or deny, based on meaning generated identity and forms of alienation so derived? (Burke, 1973). Ever attentive to the role of language, rhetoric, and community, Burke (1965) cautioned, "Let the system of cooperation become impaired, and the communicative equipment is correspondingly impaired, while this impairment of the communicative medium in turn threatens the structure of rationality itself" (p. 163). This analysis builds on Mead's (1934) view: "Our society is built up out of our social interests. Our social relations go to constitute the self" (p. 388), a theme shared by Motion and Leitch (2007).

As humans adopt idioms of their society, they acquire enactable power resources through terms of image, identity, and roles—with attendant empowerment and marginalization. Thus, in a monarchy, the sovereign's sense of self/identity overlays that of the subjects and defines the power and allegiance dynamics, often voiced as expectations. However, no sovereign can be such, even in a totemic manner, unless the assertion of monarchy is reciprocated by submission, compliance, or concurrence of subjects driven by symbols. Persons take their identities from the conventionalized symbol systems into which they are born and which they enact through shared meaning.

Discussions of image (whether individual, organizational, or societal) address processes of identity development, adoption, and enactment. Attributions, privileges, obligations, expectations, and other accoutrements of sociality derive from language that informs power and power limits people have because of their identity. Individuals (as well as organizations) create relationships to foster (or deny), maintain, and repair their identities and those of others. Matters of identification and association are embedded in the idiomatic implications of self/identity.

Society/Relational

What individuals think about societal relationships fosters empowerment/marginalization as power resources. Themes addressed in this chapter are foundational to public relations' role in relationship development, maintenance, and repair as the basis of legitimate stakeholder power resource management (Mitchell, Agle, & Wood, 1997). Terministic screens create and empower/disempower network relationships as power resources. For instance, the U.S. government empowers three branches: (1) the administrative, or executive (president, vice president, cabinet, and departments), (2) legislative (House and Senate), and (3) judicial. By law and tradition, the relationships and responsibilities of each are defined and prescribed—sensitive to debate and structural power resource management. The same is true in other organizations and between them, including relationships between businesses and customers enacted through goods and services. As Motion and Leitch (2007) reasoned, the relational function of public relations features construction of power relationships between discourse actors, or stakeholders, as the rationale for legitimacy and power resource management.

Symbolism and Power-Constituted Relationships

Viewed constitutively, vocabulary guides human activities as undirected plays (Pearce & Cronin, 1980). This conception features logics of discourse—rhetoric, social constructivism, and narrativism—and discourse analysis (see Edwards, 2006, who drew on Bourdieu, 1991). For this reason, a huge and dynamic vocabulary defines the nature, obligation, relationship quality, and expectations of relational entities. Some are political; others are commercial/financial. Many are social.

Privilege may be legitimately enacted and reciprocated terministically. Edwards (2006) voiced concern that "public relations wields unjustified social influence on behalf of already privileged organizational interests" (p. 229) in ways that violate the tenets of democratic society. Discussion, when it occurs, of power and public relations can be biased to "reflect largely agentic or structural perspectives" (p. 229) that hegemonically define the quality of relationships. Edwards recommended practicing and studying public relations "as a socially embedded profession" (p. 229). Such discussions can, and should, define and employ discourse resources to achieve mutually beneficial relationships.

Other agents exist in each field of discourse but tend to be defined in terms that privilege established ways of thinking and power distribution. As several organizations arise to individually and collectively voice concerns and assert propositions, their efforts, however unified or diverse, comprise a social movement (Smith, 2005; Smith & Ferguson, 2001). Cocreated, shared substance, viewed as conjoined and divergent zones of meaning, results in ideology, perspective, and identity/identification. "A social movement becomes a social actor at the point where such an organization takes form" (Leitch & Neilson, 2001, p. 133).

Organizations and the Problematic of Reflectiveness

To right the agentic bias, the challenge is to call on agents to be reflective, considering the dialogic nature of power as discourse and socially constructed meaning. Power develops through many voices, contesting vocabulary that defines and reflects mind, self, and society as a unified concept with scripts, privileges, enactments, attributions, evaluations, and obligations. A fundamental concern is whether assertion privileges one entity, failing to be reflective, in ways that marginalize others. Or we may press for the fully functioning sense of discourse that advances the terministic rationale needed for mutually beneficial relationships.

Agency-centered management theory focuses on principles of *efficiency* and the sociology of organization as *power* "as the central terms of two opposing and antithetical discourses" (Clegg et al., 2006, p. 7). Efficiency is defined as productivity—the ratio of inputs to outputs: "Efficiency may be defined as achieving some predetermined end at the highest output in terms of the least input of resources" (p. 7). As Clegg et al. (2006) reasoned,

> Power and efficiency are not two opposite sides of a continuum constituting the core problematic in organization studies. On the contrary, we claim power and efficiency should be simultaneously analyzed as fundamentally tangled up in the social fabric of power as both a concept and a set of practices. (p. 17)

Organizations that enjoy reflective management seem more capable of working for a fully functioning alignment of shared interests and constructive power resource management (van Ruler & Verčič, 2005). Comparing reflexivity and reflectivity, Holmström (2004) reasoned that reflexivity is monocontextual, whereas reflection (reflectiveness) is polycontextual. At heart, reflectiveness is how well individuals and organizations as a collectivity stay aware of and in harmony with processes that "continuously differentiate, change and reproduce perceptions of legitimacy" (p. 121). Relational success rests on this assumption: "Reflection becomes the production of self-understanding in relation to the environment" (Holmström, 2004, p. 123). The key polarities that define the conditions of reflection offer substantial implications for power resources: integration/domination, interdependence/independence, not sharing/distributing, collaboration/unilateral decision making, and cocreation of social reality/manipulation through propaganda. More indicative than definitive, this list suggests polarities that define the degree to which each organization embraces societal interests as part of its ability to be reflective in its efforts to achieve efficiency.

Power and the Paradox of Legitimacy

Public relations engages in battles for power through hegemonic definitions of legitimacy: The difference between what specific organizations are thought to be doing (what they are actually doing) and how publics expect and prefer them to operate. Involved publics approve or disapprove of any organization according as it is responsive to community interests (Kruckeberg & Starck, 1988), a fundamental principle of strategic corporate responsibility (Crouch, 2006).

Strategies of social construction, as Vaara, Tienari, and Laurila (2006) observed, define legitimacy as a power resource that can be defined taxonomically: normalization, authorization, rationalization, moralization, and narrativization. "From this perspective, *legitimacy means a discursively created sense of acceptance in specific discourses or orders of discourse*" (p. 793). For instance, legitimacy by normalization "seeks to render something legitimate by exemplarity" (p. 798).

Control and the Paradox of Power

Relationships are negotiated and codefined enactments of control, trust, and liking/attachment. Millar and Rogers (1976, 1987) featured control as the right and ability each participant in a relationship has to define, direct, and delimit interaction. Looking for the proactive center of power relationships, Clegg et al. (2006) asked, "What is organization but the collective bending of individual wills to a common purpose?" (p. 2). Is it reasonable by this logic to define society as the collective bending of individual wills to the collective management of risk? (Douglas, 1992).

The question goes to the next layer of analysis. What rationale grants to any entity the right of holding and using power resources as defined symbolically (ideation, identity, and relational)? Power is a combination of rationale (including battles over legitimacy) and resource influence (the ability justified by rationale to shape outcomes). Operating vocabularies define the power sources, resources, and dimensions of relationships.

Power and the Paradox of Risk Management/ Communication

Whether for commercial or issues management purposes, organizations and individuals organize to collectively manage risk (Douglas, 1992; Heath & O'Hair, 2009), a rationale for public relations (Jones, 2002). Cooperation and competition are at heart power resources for observing, managing, and contesting collectively experienced risks.

Power and the Paradox of Empowerment

Power can be positive or negative, constructive or destructive. Within this fluidity, social construction of power gives public relations the rationale, incentive, strategies, and tools to be a force for collaboration and cocreated meaning that shapes and enacts power in ways that bring societal empowerment.

Such problematics force the question of whether power is a zero sum outcome or something that can be magnified through collective engagement. Some conceptualize empowerment as requiring key individuals (such as management) or corporate entities (such as "powerful corporations") to share power with others. In contrast, empowerment (relevant to the mix of ideation, identity, and relationship) can best be viewed as a post hoc sense of what individuals and other entities accomplish collaboratively through collectively asserted power resources (Albrecht, 1988).

Power and the Paradox of the Dialogue as Shared Power

To cocreate meaning as a mix of relevant voices, public relations can work for individual advantage (engineering of consent) or seek a fully functioning society whereby individuals collaborate. Is the emergence and enactment of any vocabulary-driven rationale of mind, self, and society best conceptualized as the empowering pursuit of one interest or the collective need for mutual benefit? Here is the rationale for a dialogic approach to public relations (Kent & Taylor, 2002; Motion, 2005; Pearson, 1989).

Societal power results from meaning that prevails; meaning is the rationale that advances one interest or leads to mutual empowerment through cocreated meaning. Edwards (2006) reflected the influence of Stewart (2001) to conclude, "Even if a norm has been reached, it is always open to future challenges based on the preconditions associated with a particular validity claim. These challenges are evaluated on the basis of Habermas' criteria of truth, legitimacy and sincerity" (p. 230). In keeping with the enriching rhetorical heritage of statement and counterstatement, Edwards (2006) discussed validity claims as efforts to win a case, achieve conclusions, and define reality through engineered consent, or realize "when other evidence introduced into the communicative action process fails to support the argument being presented by practitioners and instead reveals the genuine and arbitrary interests underpinning those arguments" (pp. 230–231).

Giving insight into enriching dialogue, Gordon and Pellegrin (2008) drew on social construction theory to extract three tenets especially relevant to public relations:

> One tenet is that conceptions of reality (including of ourselves) are created through social interaction. A second tenet is that human institutions are created through social interactions and cannot exist independently of human agreement. Finally, a third tenet is that the constructed world of everyday life is itself an important element in the maintenance and reconstruction of social reality, human institutions, and ourselves. (p. 105)

However foundational the first two principles are, the last fundamentally informs public relations theory and practice because of the importance of ideation, identity, and relations.

Conclusion

However fully functioning, power is disposed in public arenas, public spheres, and political economies. Discourse-based courtship and advocacy define mind (perception, attribution, and construction), self (identity/identification), and society (enacted relational narratives) (Heath, 2007). Words construct and attribute power, power distribution, and legitimacy, the battleground for corporate and personal efficiency. Organizations seek through public relations (and other disciplines) to define and attitudinize physical and social reality by seeking to align their interests with those of their stakeholders/stakeseekers.

Mind, self, and society exhibit tensions of the paradox of efficiency and power as problematics of organization. The power of one organization, or entity, to define and achieve its sense of efficiency is constrained and privileged by others. Meaning, as implemented, rationalizes society; a wrangle of views collectively seeks order from chaos. Influence exerted in the marketplace (consumerism) and public policy arena results from power resources acquired and used, however efficiently. Power is the product of resources, their strategic mobilization, and efficiency of that mobilization (Blalock, 1989). Voices of all types work to define, acquire, and use stakes/resources as means for encouraging, reinforcing, opposing, or forcing best practices and change.

Do voices join in some constructive ideal or compete discordantly for visibility, adherents, and influence that deny other voices? "Organizations, above all, are means of constituting relations between people, ideas, and things, that would not otherwise occur. Organizations are performances of various kinds, and power relations constitute the essence of these performances" (Clegg et al., 2006, p. 17). Aligning interests and bending reality to collective wills becomes the rationale and substance of conversation guided by themes of ideation, identity, and relationship. As Gordon and Pellegrin (2008) reasoned, "The making of meaning through human interaction offers routes to redefine, refine, reformulate, and restructure ourselves and our methods relating to both the practice and study of public relations" (p. 104).

Terms and the meaning they bring to sociality count. As our individual and collective minds, terms such as science, sound science, biased science, self-interested science, religion, miracle, chaos, order, and such count. We have raging battles over God's will as order, environmental harm, risk, crisis, and global warming, as starts. For our sense of self, we note the importance of gender, race, age, and profession, as a start—and their isms. Chapters 14, 15, 16, and 17 of this volume address these logics, and their social implications, as well as their impact on identity. At the societal levels (joining the logics of mind and self), we have terms for relationships that bend reality to power outcomes. One is marriage (as in same sex); others include the fundamental principles of pursuit of happiness, freedom, liberty, and life. Of related interest, we have work, production, consumption, profit, conservation, and exploitation. We have the divine right of kings/queens, consent of the governed, and political economy. Meaning matters.

References

Albrecht, T. L. (1988). Communication and personal control in empowering organizations. In J. A. Anderson (Ed.), *Communication yearbook 11* (pp. 380–390). Newbury Park, CA: Sage.

Baker, J. S., Conrad, C., Cudahy, C., & Willyard, J. (2009). The devil in disguise: Vioxx, drug safety and the FDA. In R. L. Heath, E. L. Toth, & D. Waymer (Eds.), *Rhetorical and critical approaches to public relations II* (pp. 170–194). New York: Routledge.

Barnes, B. (1988). *The nature of power.* Urbana: University of Illinois Press.

Bentele, G. (2008). Public relations theory: The reconstructive approach. In A. Zerfass, B. van Ruler, & K. Sriramesh (Eds.), *Public relations research: European and international perspectives and innovations* (pp. 19–31). Wiesbaden, Germany: VS Verlag.

Berger, B. K. (2005). Power over, power with, and power to relations: Critical reflections on public relations, the dominant coalition, and activism. *Journal of Public Relations Research, 17,* 5–28.

Berger, B. K. (2007). Public relations and organizational power. In E. L. Toth (Ed.), *The future of excellence in public relations and communication management: Challenges for the next generation* (pp. 221–234). Mahwah, NJ: Lawrence Erlbaum.

Berger, B. K., & Reber, B. H. (2006). *Gaining influence in public relations: The role of resistance in practice.* Mahwah, NJ: Lawrence Erlbaum.

Bernays, E. L. (1955). *The engineering of consent.* Norman: University of Oklahoma Press.

Blalock, H. M., Jr. (1989). *Power and conflict: Toward a general theory.* Newbury Park, CA: Sage.

Bourdieu, P. (1991). *Language and symbolic power* (G. Raymond & M. Adamson, Trans.). Cambridge, UK: Polity Press.

Burke, K. (1934, May 2). The meaning of C. K. Ogden. *New Republic, 78,* 328–331.

Burke, K. (1951). Rhetoric: Old and new. *Journal of General Education, 5,* 202–209.

Burke, K. (1965). *Permanence and change* (2nd ed.). Indianapolis, IN: Bobbs-Merrill.

Burke, K. (1966). *Language as symbolic action.* Berkeley: University of California Press.

Burke, K. (1969). *A grammar of motives.* Berkeley: University of California Press.

Burke, K. (1973). *The philosophy of literary form* (3rd ed.). Berkeley: University of California Press.

Burke, K. (1983). Counter-gridlock: An interview with Kenneth Burke. *All Area, 2,* 4–35.

Castor, T. R. (2005). Constructing social reality in organizational decision making: Account vocabularies in a diversity discussion. *Management Communication Quarterly, 18,* 479–508.

Clegg, S. R., Courpasson, D., & Phillips, N. (2006). *Power and organizations.* Thousand Oaks, CA: Sage.

Courtright, J. L., & Smudde, P. M. (Eds.). (2007). *Power and public relations.* Cresskill, NJ: Hampton Press.

Crouch, C. (2006). Modeling the firm in its market and organizational environment: Methodologies for studying corporate social responsibility. *Organizational Studies, 27*(10), 1533–1551.

Cutlip, S. M. (1994). *The unseen power: Public relations, a history.* Hillsdale, NJ: Lawrence Erlbaum.

Deetz, S. A. (1982). Critical interpretive research in organizational communication. *Western Journal of Speech Communication, 46,* 131–149.

Douglas, M. (1992). *Risk and blame.* London: Routledge.

Edwards, L. (2006). Rethinking power in public relations. *Public Relations Review, 32*(3), 229–231.

Entman, R. J. (2007). Framing bias: Media in the distribution of power. *Journal of Communication, 57,* 163–173.

Ewing, R. P. (1987). *Managing the new bottom line: Issues management for senior executives.* Homewood, IL: Dow Jones-Irwin.

Fairclough, M. (1992). *Discourse and social change.* Cambridge, UK: Polity Press.

Foucault, N. (1972). *The archaeology of knowledge* (A. M. Sheridan Smith, Trans.). London: Routledge.

Foucault, M. (1978). *The history of sexuality: Vol. 1. An introduction.* London: Penguin Books.

Foucault, M. (1980). *Power/knowledge: Selected interviews and other writings 1972–1977.* New York: Pantheon Books.

Foucault, M. (1982). The subject and power. In H. Dreyfus & P. Rabinow (Eds.), *Michel Foucault: Beyond structuralism and hermeneutics* (pp. 208–226). Brighton, UK: Harvester.

Foucault, M. (1984). *The history of sexuality: Vol. 2. The use of pleasure* (R. Hurley, Trans.). London: Penguin Books.

Foucault, M. (1988). Technologies of the self. In L. Martin, H. Gutman, & P. Hutton (Eds.), *Technologies of the self: A seminar with Michel Foucault* (pp. 16–48). Amherst: University of Massachusetts.

Foucault, M. (1997). On the genealogy of ethics: An overview of work in progress. In P. Rabinow (Ed.) & R. Hurley and others (Trans.), *Michel Foucault: Ethics, subjectivity and truth. The essential works of Michel Foucault 1954–1984* (pp. 340–372). New York: New Press.

Gandy, O. H. (1992). Public relations and public policy: The structuration of dominance in the information age. In E. L. Toth & R. L. Heath (Eds.), *Rhetorical and critical approaches to public relations* (pp. 131–163). Hillsdale, NJ: Lawrence Erlbaum.

Gordon, J., & Pellegrin, P. (2008). Social constructionism and public relations. In T. L. Hansen-Horn & B. D. Neff (Eds.), *Public relations: From theory to practice* (pp. 104–121). Boston: Pearson.

Grunig, J. E., & Grunig, L. A. (2008). Excellence theory in public relations: Past, present, and future. In A. Zerfass, B. van Ruler, & K. Sriramesh (Eds.), *Public relations research: European and international perspectives and innovations* (pp. 327–347). Wiesbaden, Germany: VS Verlag.

Grunig, L. A. (1992). Activism: How it limits the effectiveness of organizations and how excellent public relations departments respond. In J. E. Grunig (Ed.), *Excellence in public relations and communication management* (pp. 503–530). Hillsdale, NJ: Lawrence Erlbaum.

Heath, R. L. (2001). A rhetorical enactment rationale for public relations: The good organization communicating well. In R. L. Heath (Ed.), *Handbook of public relations* (pp. 31–50). Thousand Oaks, CA: Sage.

Heath, R. L. (2006). Onward into more fog: Thoughts on public relations research directions. *Journal of Public Relations Research, 18,* 93–114.

Heath, R. L. (2007). Management through advocacy. In E. L. Toth (Ed.), *The future of excellence in public relations and communication management: Challenges for the next generation* (pp. 41–65). Mahwah, NJ: Lawrence Erlbaum.

Heath, R. L. (2008). Power resource management: Pushing buttons and building cases. In T. L. Hansen-Horn & B. D. Neff (Eds.), *Public relations: From theory to practice* (pp. 2–19). Boston: Pearson.

Heath, R. L., & Frandsen, F. (2008). Rhetorical perspective and public relations: Meaning matters. In A. Zerfass, B. van Ruler, & K. Sriramesh (Eds.), *Public relations research: European and international perspectives and innovations* (pp. 349–364). Wiesbaden, Germany: VS Verlag.

Heath, R. L., & O'Hair, H. D. (Eds.). (2009). *Handbook of risk and crisis communication.* New York: Routledge.

Heath, R. L., & Palenchar, M. J. (2009). *Strategic issues management* (2nd ed.). Thousand Oaks, CA: Sage.

Hill, J. W. (1963). *The making of a public relations man.* New York: David McKay.

Holmström, S. (2004). The reflective paradigm of public relations. In B. van Ruler & D. Verčič (Eds.), *Public relations and communication management in Europe* (pp. 121–133). Berlin, Germany: Mouton de Gruyter.

Ihlen, O. (2005). The power of social capital: Adapting Bourdieu to the study of public relations. *Public Relations Review, 31,* 492–496.

Jerome, A. M., Moffitt, M. A., & Knudsen, J. W. (2007). Understanding how Martha Stewart harmed her image restoration through a "micropolitics" of power. In J. L. Courtright & P. M. Smudde (Eds.), *Power and public relations* (pp. 85–105). Cresskill, NJ: Hampton Press.

Jones, R. (2002). Challenges to the notion of publics in public relations: Implications of the risk society for the discipline. *Public Relations Review, 28*(1), 49–62.

Kent, M. L., & Taylor, M. (2002). Toward a dialogic theory of public relations. *Public Relations Review, 28*(1), 21–37.

Kruckeberg, D., & Starck, K. (1988). *Public relations and community: A reconstructed theory.* New York: Praeger.

Leitch, S., & Motion, J. (2009). Risk communication and biotechnology: A discourse perspective. In R. L. Heath & H. D. O'Hair (Eds.), *Handbook of risk and crisis communication* (pp. 560–575). New York: Routledge.

Leitch, S., & Neilson, D. (2001). Bringing publics into public relations: New theoretical frameworks for practice. In R. L. Heath (Ed.), *Handbook of public relations* (pp. 127–138). Thousand Oaks, CA: Sage.

Maguire, S., & Ellis, J. (2009). The precautionary principle and risk communication. In R. L. Heath &

H. D. O'Hair (Eds.), *Handbook of risk and crisis communication* (pp. 119–137). New York: Routledge.

McComas, K. A. (2003). Citizen satisfaction with public meetings used for risk communication. *Journal of Applied Communication Research, 31,* 164–184.

Meacham, J. (2008, December 29). *The story of power.* Newsweek, pp. 32–35.

Mead, G. H. (1934). *Mind, self, and society.* Chicago: University of Chicago Press.

Millar, F. E., & Rogers, L. E. (1976). A relational approach. In G. R. Miller (Ed.), *Explorations in interpersonal communication* (pp. 87–103). Newbury Park, CA: Sage.

Millar, F. E., & Rogers, L. E. (1987). Relational dimensions in interpersonal dynamics. In M. E. Roloff & G. R. Miller (Eds.), *Interpersonal processes: New directions in communication research* (pp. 117–139). Newbury Park, CA: Sage.

Mitchell, R. K., Agle, B. R., & Wood, D. J. (1997). Toward a theory of stakeholder identification and salience: Defining the principle of who and what really counts. *Academy of Management Review, 22,* 853–886.

Monge, P. R., & Contractor, N. S. (2000). Emergence of communication networks. In F. M. Jablin & L. L. Putnam (Eds.), *The new handbook of organizational communication* (pp. 440–502). Thousand Oaks, CA: Sage.

Motion, J. (2005). Participative public relations: Power to the people or legitimacy for government discourse? *Public Relations Review, 31*(4), 505–512.

Motion, J., & Leitch, S. (2007). A toolbox for public relations: The *oeuvre* of Michel Foucault. *Public Relations Review, 33*(3), 263–268.

Meacham, J. (2008, December 29). The story of power. *Newsweek,* 32–35.

Ogden, C. K., & Richards, I. A. (1923). *The meaning of meaning.* New York: Harcourt, Brace, & Jovanovich.

Pearce, W. B., & Cronin, V. E. (1980). *Communication, action, and meaning.* New York: Praeger.

Pearson, R. (1989). Business ethics and communication ethics: Public relations practice and the idea of dialogue. In C. H. Botan & V. Hazleton Jr. (Eds.), *Public relations theory* (pp. 111–131). Hillsdale, NJ: Lawrence Erlbaum.

Pfeffer, J. (1981). *Power in organizations.* Boston: Pitman.

Pfeffer, J. (1992). *Managing with power: Politics and influence in organizations.* Boston: Harvard Business School Press.

Proutheau, S., & Heath, R. L. (2009). Precautionary principle and biotechnology: Regulators are from Mars and activists are from Venus. In R. L. Heath & H. D. O'Hair (Eds.), *Handbook of risk and crisis communication* (pp. 576–590). New York: Routledge.

Roper, J. (2005). Symmetrical communication: Excellent public relations or a strategy for hegemony? *Journal of Public Relations Research, 17,* 69–86.

Shotter, J. (1993). *Conversational realities: Constructing life through language.* London: Sage.

Shotter, J., & Gergen, K. J. (1994). Social construction: Knowledge, self, others, and continuing the conversation. *Communication yearbook 17* (pp. 3–13). Mahwah, NJ: Lawrence Erlbaum.

Shumate, M., Fulk, J., & Monge, P. R. (2005). Predictors of the international HIV/AIDS NOG network over time. *Human Communication Research, 31,* 482–510.

Smith, M. E. (2005). Activism. In R. L. Heath (Ed.), *Encyclopedia of public relations* (pp. 5–9). Thousand Oaks, CA: Sage.

Smith, M. E., & Ferguson, D. P. (2001). Activism. In R. L. Heath (Ed.), *Handbook of public relations* (pp. 291–300). Thousand Oaks, CA: Sage.

Smudde, P. M. (2007). Public relations' power as based on knowledge, discourse, and ethics. In J. L. Courtright & P. M. Smudde (Eds.), *Power and public relations* (pp. 207–237). Cresskill, NJ: Hampton Press.

Stacks, D. W. (2004). Crisis management: Toward a multidimensional model of public relations. In D. P. Millar & R. L. Heath (Eds.), *Responding to crisis: A rhetorical approach to crisis communication* (pp. 37–61). Mahwah, NJ: Lawrence Erlbaum.

Stewart, A. (2001). *Theories of power and domination.* London: Sage.

Stohl, M., & Stohl, C. (2005). Human rights, nation states, and NGOs: Structural holes and the emergence of global regimes. *Communication Monographs, 72,* 442–467.

Stokes, A. Q. (2005). Metabolife's meaning: A call for the constitutive study of public relations. *Public Relations Review, 31*(4), 556–565.

Taylor, M. (2009). Civil society as a rhetorical public relations process. In R. L. Heath, E. L. Toth, & D. Waymer (Eds.), *Rhetorical and critical approaches to public relations II* (pp. 76–91). New York: Routledge.

Vaara, E., Tienari, J., & Laurila, J. (2006). Pulp and paper fiction: On the discursive legitimation of global industrial restructuring. *Organization Studies, 27*(6), 789–810.

van Ruler, B., & Verčič, D. (2005). Reflective communication management: Future ways for public relations research. In P. J. Kalbfleisch (Ed.), *Communication yearbook 29* (pp. 239–273). Mahwah, NJ: Lawrence Erlbaum.

CHAPTER 14

"Race" in Public Relations

Lee Edwards

Wherever it is practiced, the profession of public relations emerges from a specific social hierarchy, or field of power (Bourdieu, 1984; Koller, 2007), that profoundly marks the nature and identity of public relations through the interests the profession supports and the share of voice it generates for those on whose behalf it is employed (Edwards, 2009; Hackett & Uzelmann, 2003; Hargreaves, 2003; Moloney, 2006). Social hierarchies can be examined along a number of axes, including class, gender, ethnicity, and sexual orientation. While gender has received some attention in public relations scholarship (Aldoory, 2005, 2007; Grunig, Toth, & Hon, 2001; Hon, 1995; Hon, Grunig, & Dozier, 1992), other axes have been largely neglected (L'Etang, 2005; Moloney, 2006). With few exceptions, ethnicity and "race,"[1] in particular, have been overlooked (Pompper, 2005a), despite the fact that "race" is a significant factor in determining social status (Anthias, 2001), social status in turn is reflected in the structure of the public relations profession, and discrimination plays a demonstrable role in the experiences of minoritized practitioners (Ford & Appelbaum, 2009; Pompper, 2004, 2005b; Zerbinos & Clanton, 1993).

This chapter attempts to redress this imbalance by "reading" the profession, its history, and its activities using a *critical race theoretical* lens that foregrounds "race" as an element of the professional habitus. Critical race theory's (CRT) starting point is that, while "race" is socially constructed (Anthias, 1990), racism is the material consequence of that social construction and frequently forms the daily experience of people from minoritized groups. Material conditions are fundamental to the form and evolution of racism, while language and discourse define how "race" and racism may be discussed (Delgado & Stefancic, 2001; Murji & Solomos, 2005; Pompper, 2005a; Valdes, McCristal Culp, & Harris, 2002).

Based on empirical studies in the United Kingdom and the United States, this chapter explores the construction of "race" and the reality of racism in the public relations profession through the experiences of minoritized practitioners. These two countries deserve particular attention because most modern public relations theory and practice comes from them and their influence is widespread (McKie & Munshi, 2007). Furthermore, both cultures have a history marked by the dominance of whiteness in their respective fields of power, and this has shaped the environment in which public relations has developed.

I begin by considering the nature of a professional habitus, which underpins professional cultures and helps shape their identities, and consider how whiteness may be understood as part of a habitus. Habitus is embedded in history, and the importance of the history of public relations in shaping its present is considered as I review briefly the patterns of development that characterize public relations in the United Kingdom and the United States. Finally, the empirical findings from the two countries are considered.

Professional Habitus and Whiteness

Public relations practitioners, like all professionals, are engaged in a struggle over jurisdiction, justifying their existence, protecting their interests, defending their territory, and thereby ensuring their survival. The goal is the control of knowledge, because knowledge permits a specific jurisdiction and thereby generates power (Abbott, 1988).

The processes of generating professional jurisdiction include defining competencies, articulating rules of professional conduct, defining terms of recruitment and promotion, clarifying functional roles, and quantifying return on investment. All these things are shaped by the environment in which they take place. As Abbott (1988) pointed out, "Larger social forces have their impact on individual professions through the structure within which the professions exist, rather than directly" (p. 33). The changing political, social, and economic circumstances that mark a profession over time are therefore important to any understanding of how and why professions such as public relations have taken a particular form.

Jurisdiction is not only about professional function—*what* might be practiced—but also about professional identity—*who* may practice. Professional identity is marked by the possession of appropriate symbolic capital (a particular education, a particular knowledge of art, music, or other cultural forms, a particular family background) and also by the literal embodiment of professionals, who understand that their whole bodies, and not just their minds, must be managed in light of the requirements of the professional field (Sommerlad, 2008). The formation of professional identity occurs in part through the professional habitus, the set of durable dispositions developed and inculcated over time that determine the way we comprehend our social environment and our role within it (Bourdieu, 1990b; Swartz, 1997). As Bourdieu (2000) argued in relation to the professional "game,"

> In reality, what the new entrant must bring to the game is not the habitus that is tacitly and explicitly demanded there, but a habitus that is practically compatible, or sufficiently close, and above all, malleable and capable of being converted into the required habitus, in short, congruent and docile, amenable to restructuring. That is why operations of co-option . . . are so attentive not only to the signs of competence, but also to the barely perceptible indices, generally corporeal ones—dress, bearing, manners—of dispositions to be, and above all, to become, one of us. (p. 100)

The professional habitus plays a significant role in defining what it is to be "a professional" and, like the other processes that define professional jurisdiction, its character is linked to the political, social, and economic circumstances from which the profession has emerged. Consequently, the individuals that the profession attracts tend to be from similar backgrounds and already share common normative assumptions that become absorbed into the professional habitus. As new entrants come into the profession, they adopt this identity because "to fall into line with the rule . . . is to try to put the group on one's side by declaring one's recognition of the rule of the group and therefore of the group itself" (Bourdieu, 2000, p. 125).

Whiteness

Habitus can be shaped by any number of social attributes: gender, class, sexuality, or, of course, ethnicity. In professional contexts where diversity has been limited, whiteness may play a role in shaping the habitus and making it more difficult for those who are "different" to make their way in the professional world.

Whiteness is more than a physical attribute. It is a system that shapes the life experiences of those who are white and those who are not (McIntyre, 1997). Importantly, whiteness cannot exist without the "Other," the groups or categories that act as the foil for whiteness and define what whiteness is. Like "race," whiteness is therefore socially constructed and fluid, responsive to the situations in which it is enacted (McIntyre, 1997; McKinney, 2005).

Whiteness is both physical and associative, symbolic and structural. It encompasses both embodied whiteness and the categorizations normatively associated with white and other ethnic groups. These categorizations construct positions in society for ethnic groups in terms of, for example, class, criminality, intelligence, and occupation. As Ladson-Billings (1999) argued, "In a society where whiteness is positioned as normative everyone is ranked and categorized in relation to these points of opposition. These categories fundamentally sculpt the extant terrain of possibilities even when other possibilities exist" (p. 9). Thus, whiteness functions as a master narrative (Solorzano & Yosso, 2002) that silences multiple voices and perspectives, legitimizes dominant groups, and allocates social status to others in relation to these groups. It permeates social institutions, systems, and spaces such that white interests and norms are central and the interests of other groups remain peripheral (Gillborn, 2008).

Whiteness, like other aspects of habitus, is invisible to those who inhabit it (Dyer, 1997; McKinney, 2005; Perry, 2001). "Seeing whiteness is about living its effects, as effects that allow white bodies to extend into spaces that have already taken their shape, spaces in which black bodies stand out, stand apart, unless they pass, which means passing through space by passing as white" (Ahmed, 2004). Those who live whiteness have been inculcated through family and education systems into this habitus, which validates rather than discriminates against their ethnicity.

Over time, habitus becomes so deeply embedded at all levels of existence that it becomes invisible; to step outside it requires a fundamental questioning of the taken-for-granted world we live in. Whiteness, for example, is transparent until it comes into contact with difference (Flagg, 1997; Frankenberg, 1993; Helms, 1990). This contact represents an opportunity to adopt a new perspective and explore fundamental assumptions: Recognizing whiteness means recognizing its effects and the unearned advantage it represents. Once these are acknowledged, the way is open for a different understanding of what it is to be "othered" in a white context, an understanding that does not desire the "other" to be more like "us" (McIntosh, 1997).

Developing this understanding requires a different view of history, present and future, through the eyes of those who are "othered" by whiteness. In the following discussions of the history and present of public relations, this view is made explicit and a new perspective of the effects of public relations on practitioners and their audiences emerges.

Public Relations History and "Race"

The origins of the modern public relations profession lie in the commercial and political environment in the United States and the United Kingdom in the 19th and 20th centuries. In North America, the 19th century was characterized by a massive expansion of heavy industry and a gradual increase in the use of public relations to promote their interests (Russell & Bishop, 2009; Windle, 1971). The wealth this generated led to the growth of an American middle class able to participate in the production and consumption of economic and social benefits. In contrast, the urban poor and immigrant populations had limited opportunity to consume relative to their wealthier, middle-class neighbors, while nonwhite groups, and particularly black Americans still carrying the legacy of slavery, were legally, economically, and socially defined as subordinate to whites (Harris, 1993; Ross, 1997, 2002). The emergence of new understandings of "mass" publics, easily manipulated and vulnerable to influence by radical movements that might destabilize the status quo, generated a real concern that these working-class poor and "savages" would break out of their allocated spaces and cause chaos (Bernays, 1928/2005; Cutlip, 1994; Ewen, 1996).

The rapid expansion of corporate and government public relations occurred in this context, to manage public opinion and control the "masses." In addition, the new "science" of persuasion articulated by early practitioners was used by commercial organizations to expand their territory, market their products, and encourage consumption. The profession's early practitioners were employed by most of the major corporations and in government, and as the 20th century progressed, public relations became increasingly focused on preserving these interests under the guise of generating prosperity for all Americans (Cutlip, 1994; Ewen, 1996; Martinelli & Mucciarone, 2007; Russell & Bishop, 2009).

Reading this history through a CRT lens offers an alternative view, defined by the perspective of the "Other." In this history, the economic, political, and social structures of the United States promoted by public relations professionals were predicated on the systematic privileging of white interests. This was facilitated by the legal recognition of the material and symbolic benefits of whiteness as a property that could be claimed and enjoyed by those to whom it was accorded (Harris, 1993). These included whiteness as a set of legal rights; as a locator in social systems and structures through employment rights, education entitlements, and other forms of state validation; as the basis for reputation and status; and as a set of expectations about personal and group entitlement to enjoy the benefits of these legal and social rights. Insofar as whiteness was protected and privileged, other groups were not.

Harris (1993) demonstrated the degree to which whiteness shaped every aspect of mainstream life in North America, permeating the discursive positions taken by commercial organizations, educational institutions, and other government departments. Public relations was one of the main mechanisms through which such assumptions were justified and perpetuated, not least because of the invisibility of black Americans in the discourses they produced (Ewen, 1996). Apart from the significant role played by public relations in establishing the Ku Klux Klan in the early 20th century, described by Cutlip (1994) as "unquestionably the saddest chapter in public relations history" (p. 372), the increasing use of public relations to encourage consumption during the 20th century valued audiences in terms of their ability to buy—or, alternatively put, their ability to enjoy the economic and social benefits of whiteness. As consumption increasingly defined the American way of life, it became a central part of the American narrative of belonging, adding another dimension to the process of "othering" that characterized the status of people of color. The growing, consuming, and voting white middle class was increasingly the main audience of interest to corporations and government alike. Progress toward economic well-being became a color-blind story of individual effort generating individual benefits; the social context of that individual effort was, and is, obscured (Carrasco, 2002; Hill-Collins, 2006).

Thus, historically, the structural position of nonwhite groups in North America combined with their legal subordination and discursive exclusion to "other" them culturally, politically, and economically in the discourses of American identity and belonging that most public relations practitioners spent their time communicating.[2] Today, whiteness, as a property that affords access to that identity and belonging, is still protected. Apart from the formal legal environment that provides the structures for this (Harris, 1993), such protection is enacted discursively through public relations activities. The audiences that public relations practitioners address are defined in terms of their material value—their propensity to vote, to buy, to use a particular service. This definition is not "race" neutral; on the contrary, the fact that nonwhite groups are overrepresented in socially marginalized populations means that, by definition, speaking only to those who can claim material value simultaneously "others" those who cannot, by virtue of their place in the country's racial, economic, and political hierarchy (Carrasco, 2002; Hill-Collins, 2006; Said, 1994).

In the United Kingdom, the needs of the political and trading structures of the British Empire were the initial drivers of professional communications activity; consequently, whiteness permeated the early development of the public relations industry here, too. During the 19th and early 20th centuries, the British Empire was at its zenith, with white officials taking up residence and exercising their power in British colonies across the world. Their presence, and the natural superiority of whiteness that it implied, was often taken for granted by those who grew up in this colonized environment (Phillips & Phillips, 1998). The slave trade was the backbone of the British Empire and had required the discursive dehumanization of African peoples in particular, turning them into chattels through texts, material practices, and social structures. A legacy of subordination continued after slavery was abolished, and the primacy of white interests in the Empire's political and economic structures perpetuated arguments in favor of occupying countries for economic and political gain. The notion of empire could not survive without the implicitly and explicitly articulated superiority of the "mother country"—monarchical, white Britain—over the "Other" (Said, 1995).

During the first half of the 20th century, increasing evidence of the Empire's decline prompted the Empire Marketing Board to use film to promote British interests abroad and prolong the appearance of power. These efforts represented a kind of cultural propaganda, which the Foreign Office in 1939 described as "a long term policy that, by promoting an atmosphere of international understanding and cooperation, would ultimately benefit both the political and economic climate in which British interests could flourish" (L'Etang, 2004, p. 38). Naturally, "British" interests were defined in terms of the superiority of white British interests over other nations in the Empire.

As decolonization began and the Empire gradually disintegrated, public relations was used extensively to manage the process, so that transitions were peaceful, and newly independent countries could learn how to govern themselves and manage their societies in a disciplined fashion. Commercial organizations with interests in the former colonies also used public relations to protect their interests during a potentially volatile time. Throughout this process, the superiority of whiteness explicitly and implicitly underpinned communications strategies (L'Etang, 2004).

Public relations also grew in the domestic market. New local government authorities set up after the First World War used public relations to persuade citizens to use new council services available to them. During the Second World War, the Ministry of Information used film, media, and government publications to disseminate propaganda and recruit people from across the Empire for the war effort. Its effectiveness resulted in the proliferation of public relations across a wide range of organizations, and after the war, many military information strategists joined the private and public sectors in senior positions (L'Etang, 2004).

These links with government continued throughout the rest of the century (Miller & Dinan, 2000, 2007), and the development of public relations has been closely connected to the survival of the commercial and political establishment in the United Kingdom (L'Etang, 2004). Underpinned by normative assumptions of the superiority of whiteness over other ethnic groups, the "British culture" disseminated by practitioners through cultural propaganda, and the "British way of life" that was communicated within Britain as a focus of solidarity, were white

British, and not simply "British." Simultaneously, these discourses implicitly marginalized and subordinated nonwhite interests, both at home and overseas (Munshi & Kurian, 2005; Phillips & Phillips, 1998; Shome & Hedge, 2002).

Being "Different" in Public Relations Today

Recognizing the impact of public relations practice on historical racial inequities is an important step toward being able to address its legacy today. Bourdieu (1990a) argued that habitus evolves over time and changes only slowly; history is therefore as relevant to the present as the immediate sociocultural and economic circumstances that define current public relations activity. The following section explores the reality of whiteness today, as a property that one can lay claim to and benefit from, in the words of practitioners who are defined as "other" by this aspect of the professional habitus. The results reveal that whiteness still underpins the assumptions about the relative status of different ethnic groups that mark current public relations habitus, identity, and jurisdiction—in other words, what it is to "be" a public relations practitioner and to "do" public relations. This combines with powerful discourses of merit to make it extremely difficult for minoritized public relations practitioners to voice their concerns or articulate their difference in a way that is perceived as productive rather than destructive.

Whiteness and Merit

Bourdieu (1991) argued that habitus is not only about ways of thinking but also about the physicality of being; the embodiment of habitus is as important an expression of normative assumptions as discourse.

> The modalities of practices, the ways of looking, sitting, standing, keeping silent, or even of speaking . . . are full of injunctions that are powerful and hard to resist precisely because they are silent and insidious, insistent and insinuating. (p. 51)

As practitioners explain, the embodied norms in public relations are embodiments of whiteness.

> *I think one of the stereotypes of PR is a pretty blond girl who's very pretty, a bit of an airhead but is nice to look at and she'll go off and sweet talk the journalist and she'll get lots of nice coverage and she'll find a nice bar or restaurant for us to go to and it is a very old, very stereotyped idea of what PR is but even today it still holds true.* (Interview 18, U.K. practitioner)

> *I'm glad I don't want to be in Public Affairs, 'cause I don't think I would stand much of a chance really. I mean I remember researching agencies and you go on their website and you look at the team and after being knocked back so many times I did start to do that . . . and I started to go on their website, look at the team, look at the type of people, and sometimes they had profiles . . . and I'd read the type of people that were hired and . . . it was those type of people . . . really, you know, good degree, the traditional degree, um, you know, very white background.* (Interview 4, U.K. practitioner)

As Pompper (2004) explained, minoritized individuals are judged on the bases of their distance from whiteness:

> Describing racism as "institutionalized" and "covert," discussants explained that a female African American senior-level manager represents a threat to the status quo because she does not fit the stereotypical mold: "We *can* put a sentence together and we *look* very nice and we *can* present a position," an Atlanta senior level corporate manager declared. (p. 286)

As this quote illustrates, whiteness incorporates not only embodied attributes but also associated assumptions, including the relative skills, intelligence, or professional capability of the practitioner. U.K. practitioners commented on instances when their physical presence, role, and skills had caused some surprise among other practitioners.

> *I've had people think that obviously because I'm from the Caribbean I don't know very much. I think I don't necessarily talk probably like a black British person, I sound different from other people. I think that has caused people to be surprised. I've spoken to people on the phone and then gone to meet them and they're like, "Ha!" Surprised. (laughing) I've had a few of those.* (Interview 12, U.K. practitioner)

> *It does change when you get more senior because people are then completely stunned and shocked and really, you know, they don't know how to deal with it at all. They can't quite believe that you are the boss. There were lots of times I turned up for meetings with other members of staff and people would find it really difficult. They would keep talking to my member of staff or whatever, and they found it really hard to accept that actually I was the decision-maker and I was going to be, you know, giving them the money or whatever it is. They just couldn't cope.* (Interview 14, U.K. practitioner)

Whiteness is also evident in the structures of the profession; practitioners from white backgrounds dominate the industry in both the United States and the United Kingdom, and practitioners from minority ethnic groups are underrepresented (Centre for Economics and Business Research, 2005; PRWeek, 2008). Because of this structural dominance, efforts to highlight the issues facing minoritized practitioners often fall on deaf ears.

> *It was always about "Well, we need to be careful that we're not seen to be positively discriminating." And I thought you couldn't positive discriminate in a million years because you've got so many people who are resistant. It's just, you couldn't over-positively discriminate because there are enough people in the organization with their views who will still not toe the party line about let's be more diverse, let's make sure that we assess people fairly on merit.* (Interview 15, U.K. practitioner)

Whiteness in public relations is complemented by discourses of merit. Merit treats socially contingent outcomes such as educational achievement, political knowledge, cultural capital, or indeed recruitment and promotion, as objective outcomes of individual efforts. Responsibility for becoming the "ideal" professional lies solely with the individual rather than the processes, structures, and managerial judgments through which this is formally achieved. Merit is underpinned by the clearly incorrect assumption that "objective" social systems treat everyone in the same way (Bourdieu, 1999; Carbado & Gulati, 2003). This assumption, and the centrality of merit to professional identity and progress, means that there is very limited discursive scope to address issues of "race" or ethnicity in the profession.

This leaves minoritized professionals in a difficult position. Because merit is focused on individual effort and ignores the social and cultural context in which judgments about that effort are made (Sommerlad, 2002), it does not recognize, for example, that minoritized professionals' identities are continually complicated by historical and current social norms of their ethnicity as the (subordinate) "other." These norms are deeply embedded in habitus and rarely articulated, and yet they have concrete consequences in terms of the spaces and roles that "other" practitioners may legitimately occupy.

> *The awareness of me being the only Asian person in the room is slightly . . . is just an observation, but then I think sometimes it can be a bit more than that. So that I kind of feel I have to . . . kind of outwardly, justify my worth, my reason for being there. And myself a little bit more on certain occasions.* (Interview 9, U.K. practitioner)

> *Later on when we had to recruit more people we did make a very conscious decision to recruit more white faces here for the simple fact that we believed that two Indians going in would meet*

with resistance in both being recommended for pitches, recommended to put our ideas forward, to win business, or not winning once we got to the table and so we would actually, you know, I think in the early days Edward and I went and pitched for every piece of business but over the past two and a half years we didn't, you know, we made a conscious decision to split ourselves up. (Interview 11, U.K. practitioner)

The whiteness of the public relations habitus combined with the subjectivity of "merit in practice" means that, even if minoritized public relations practitioners do achieve a merit-based milestone, they are at risk of being judged, additionally, on the basis of criteria related to their "race" or ethnicity, for example, skin color, dress, adherence to a particular religious diet, or linguistic differences. Whether or not practitioners meet performance criteria, they may be refused promotion or appointment because they do not fit in other ways. Rationales for refusal are usually vague, because they cannot be articulated in terms of merit-based criteria, and there is no alternative discourse available to articulate the other reasons for the rejection.

You feel it. It's not something . . . you feel it. Like when I just finished [my master's degree] I did my internship, it wasn't part of the program, but I wanted to get more experience. I applied for some agencies to work as an intern and my mates that were also interns were all freshers from the university without work experience. I was coming with work experience. I have worked at a very senior level, I've put pitches together, winning pitches, I have worked in London . . . at a senior level as well, but in that agency I realised that they were very reluctant in putting me forward. I think that was where I first of all got the hint. They just saw me like, even though it was clear in my C.V. that my capabilities were much broader than the things they were giving me, they were reluctant at giving me bigger challenges to do. (Interview 27, U.K. practitioner)

This leads inevitably to the uncertainty that characterizes many minoritized professionals' lives.

We had a person come in and give us a case study on her life in PR . . . she works for the Conservative party. And I thought, "Gosh I would have loved to work in, you know, pure PR." I didn't get a chance to do that because that was quite difficult to get into. But there, there are always those kind of thoughts and you do at the back of your mind think, "Oh was it because I am black," or was it just because I didn't push hard enough or whatever. You know it's always that kind of, why did that happen? (Interview 12, U.K. practitioner)

I don't know if I've been sort of treated differently or anything that has made a huge impact. It's really difficult to tell but then I do sometimes think, "Well hang on a minute every time . . ." I mean I have . . . When I joined [company] I was initially just a PR manager and then it's head of media relations a year later and so that happened quite quickly and then now director which is brilliant . . . but I felt as if some of the promotions could have happened earlier in other places. (Interview 16, U.K. practitioner)

While practitioners are not always sure that they are put on a slower track as a result of their ethnicity, they are reluctant to even raise the possibility of it happening with their employer. One professional said,

If there's no one else who looks like you, how can you recognize if you've been put on a slow moving track (compared to a white practitioner)? Unless you live it, it's hard to recognize that this is a problem. (Ford & Appelbaum, 2009)

Uncertainty around the importance of "race" as a basis for others' judgments can also affect the practitioners' confidence in their own skills.

When I do things I always do sometimes think, "Am I, you know, getting this position, getting this job, am I being put forward for this because of my background?" The fact that I'm an ethnic minority. Does it . . . you know, sometimes . . . you know, it's just that little voice sometimes that says . . . but I think I've . . . I don't pay much attention to that. (Interview 9, U.K. practitioner)

Discursive Limitations

The exclusion of "race" or discrimination from professional discourses, and the dominance of merit as an objectively defined assessment of professional competence, means that "race" is not discussed because there is no need to discuss it, given that it should not affect practitioners' progress. And yet, when the occasion arises, stereotypes about minoritized practitioners' "race" are quickly applied, revealing the manner in which "race" or ethnicity always remains relevant in the context of whiteness. Sommerlad (2008) illustrated a similar dynamic in the case of women:

> Identity is socially contingent, but it is structured by actors' understandings of merit and valuations of cultural and symbolic capital which are historical, and which are themselves the product of cultural lag that is derived from antique status understandings of, for instance, gender, ethnicity and class. As a result, whilst the greater autonomy that "women" now enjoy, together with our intersectional understandings of womanhood, may be producing a new and more nuanced politics of equality, at the same time, within that conjecture women can have the abjections of their embodiment re-imposed on them in certain interactions—and at the whim of the dominant actors in the field. (p. 176)

In the same way, the stereotypical assumptions about ethnic groups inherent in whiteness can appear as soon as aspects of difference become visible.

So off we went to the local prison and we're walking around and . . . we were chatting away and then one of the inmates shouts out, "Oy, Angelica, hello!" And I thought, "Oh God, it's my worst nightmare! I'm trying to impress (laughs). Don't tell me, you know, it's some old school friend. Oh what a nightmare (laughs)." So I ignored it. I ignored it . . . but how many people are called Angelica, you know? And anyway he didn't stop, he shouted again. And so James, the Director said, "Oh Angelica, it looks like . . ." and he was black, this guy, so he said, "Oh look, it's one of your relatives." It was awful, an absolutely awful moment, and then the prison governor started teasing me and saying, "Oh, is it someone you know then . . ." you know, "Is it someone from your family?" and this bloke wouldn't stop shouting. Anyway eventually I sort of went "Hmmm," and walked on. And it turned out that I had done some voluntary work . . . where they get people to come in and you go out with the young people and you take them out and talk about their problems, and it was one of those people that we'd obviously not managed to rescue. (Interview 14, U.K. practitioner)

I think women always have an issue but I think the societal view of black women also has an impact on how black women are perceived in the office, so you've got to be quite aware of that when you're working with people. . . . The stereotypical view will be oh, they're sexy, they're exotic, they have tons of kids by different men so they're quite sexual. . . . I think the thing is there aren't enough senior visible black women around to counter the kind of street view of black women. (Interview 15, U.K. practitioner)

Part of the problem for practitioners on the receiving end of this subtle but continuous "othering" is that both whiteness and merit form part of the taken-for-granted worldview held by dominant groups, that disguises the reality of their own privilege. For the majority of white people in any situation, discrimination on the basis of "race" has not been part of their experience and is largely invisible; therefore, the notion of "othering" is simply not in their consciousness

(McIntosh, 1997; Perry, 2001). Consequently, discrimination is defined in very concrete terms, usually with reference to legal obligations. It may be raised in contexts where there is a clear and demonstrable breach of equality principles. But the daily, ongoing, subtle, and multiple processes of "othering" cannot be described or categorized in these terms.

The dominance of merit-based discourses compounds this problem by prioritizing individual effort and responsibility, invalidating group affiliations and ignoring social context. The discursive invisibility of "race" in their professional environment means practitioners' racial or ethnic identity, and issues arising from it, are rarely discussed with white colleagues, since it may generate problems for practitioners who bring up their "othered" status. As Carbado and Gulati (2003) have argued, employers seek employees who represent diversity but in a way that will "fit" with an organization—they have the right cultural capital, the right approach, the right personality:

> In the context of workplaces that are structured around cooperative work, Whites do not have to, in terms of race, think about being the same. They have a limited need to strategize about how and when to signal an integrational capacity to work within teams without causing grit. Whiteness is presumptively grease. Racial minorities, even if they are allowed into the workplace, still have to perform their race in ways that negate the presumptions that their race will engender discomfort and cause disruptions. (p. 1778)

To mention "race" or ethnicity, then, is to point out that in fact, the work done by minoritized practitioners to blend in is a necessary construction of the employer and the employee. It problematizes the "happy diversity" that organizations like to promote (Ahmed, 2009) and introduces grit that creates friction between the practitioner and the dominant group, making him or her less desirable as an employee (Carbado & Gulati, 2003). This is amply illustrated by respondents' comments in the most recent U.S. *Multicultural Survey of PR Practitioners* (Ford & Appelbaum, 2009):

> *This is the quintessential "Catch 22." How do you address your concerns about racism in the workplace without appearing too sensitive. You can't show your real feelings.*
>
> *You can't look down on menial tasks. Do them efficiently and quickly, whether it's compiling media lists or client binders. And if you have to complain, don't complain to a colleague or a supervisor in the workplace, even if you feel comfortable with them. Save it for home.*
>
> *People of color can't be too aggressive, or you'll be shown the door.*

In the United Kingdom, research reveals the same patterns:

> *I try and bring the good stuff into the office so when there's ever . . . like at Jewish festivals I bring in the relevant food, so it might be cheesecake or it might be kind of biscuits or whatever, so I try and make it fun and interesting for them. I don't however, for example when I'm out on a Friday say, "I'm out of office because it's the Jewish Sabbath and here's a link to Wikipedia on Shabbat."* (Interview 8, U.K. practitioner)
>
> *There were people who were [at] more junior levels who went "If this is how it is, I'm not happy." But I think the way that they dealt with it was often in the stereotypical way that people thought, well you're being aggressive, you've got a chip on your shoulder, but actually what they were trying to do is say "I'm not putting up with this and I want you to sort it out now." So I became a harassment adviser, we had a Black minority group that went to talk to management on various issues about what was going around. [It was] very hard, the organization found it very hard to deal with it. Again, you're*

talking to white males, saying that this is an issue. They didn't see it because they were all right, Jack, thank you very much. (Interview 15, U.K. practitioner)

Strategies of Resistance: Managing Identity

Identity work is crucial for practitioners in this position, who have to manage the way people perceive them to be accepted on professional terms (Carbado & Gulati, 2003). Identity is fluid (Hall, 1992), and practitioners regularly contest others' judgments about their skills, roles, and capability to minimize the centrality of "race" and highlight other attributes as part of their ongoing struggle to be recognized.

> *Absolutely, it's a marker, it's a differential and also people sometimes just don't hear you, you know, they don't want to hear your ideas because of who you are rather than listening to the ideas and then considering it. There are people out there and, you know, the way I've dealt with it is that you go and talk to somebody who will end up listening to you, . . . you get knocks and you get up and you then dust yourself down and go forward.* (Interview 11, U.K. practitioner)

> *You have to sort of flag "I'm not happy with where I am, I know I should be doing more." Whereas I think in contrast I saw quite a few people sort of scooped up and "Yes, you're doing really well, let's move you on." And I think that's the real contrast, you have to sort of say "Me!" . . . , you have to make it quite clear that that's where you're heading.* (Interview 15, U.K. practitioner)

> *I think there is still an assumption about Asian women being a bit meek, maybe a bit mild, and not being extrovert and not being assertive, so I think that's still there but, to be honest, I just use that to my advantage. I think, "Well, that's your expectations; that's not what you're going to get."* (Interview 19, U.K. practitioner)

Indeed, for practitioners who enjoy extensive cultural capital in common with their white colleagues (e.g., attendance at a prestigious university, political connections, or access to elite networks), their "race" can be the least pertinent element of their identity during their professional lives. As one focus group participant in the U.K. research argued,

> *The more policies Government puts in place the more obvious it becomes that I'm an ethnic woman. Whereas I don't feel that right now and I'd hate to come into work and think that that's my label.* (FG2)

Minoritized practitioners are, of course, professionals as well as "raced," gendered, and classed individuals, with a stake in the game of professional communications as it is currently constituted. This double (or multiple) consciousness (DuBois, 1903/2008) means that they understand the value of merit for enhancing their position in the profession. Despite the disadvantage it imposes on them, they still have a vested interest in reinforcing its centrality so that they can progress by drawing on it themselves. The longer they practice and the more successful they are, the greater their stake in the status quo. However, they are also aware that merit is itself a complex issue for them. The "liminal space" (Ladson-Billings, 2000, p. 263) they occupy positions them beyond the normative dichotomy of self/other, a place that affords them a unique perspective of the multiple identities and different habitus that inform their position (Ladson-Billings, 2000). This allows them to see clearly when merit alone is insufficient for recognition because it is not objectively assessed. Consequently, they endeavor to accumulate and demonstrate other types of capital to enhance their professional identity, mitigate others' judgments, and enhance their professional opportunities.

> *Getting into PR itself, I think yeah, they saw that extra mile that I would go because by then I was so like downtrodden I guess, that I was . . . now*

> *I know I've got to do that extra bit more than the next person. So, when I did go to that interview, I actually already prepared a press release . . . Yeah, I prepared a press release that was based around the company and from the information that I'd got through my research, and I made up a kind of . . . I just made up something, a new initiative and I wrote around that.* (Interview 4, U.K. practitioner)

U.S. practitioners undertake similar strategies, according to Pompper (2004):

> To compensate for employers' stereotypes, practitioners said they "set the bar very high," "work harder," "arrive early and leave late," "offer something more," and "perform tasks no one else wants to do." Many said they go above and beyond during the job interview process to demonstrate that they can perform the job. (pp. 287–288)

As Sommerlad (2008) suggested in the case of women in the legal profession, the intersectional identity of more privileged minoritized practitioners means that they are able to use gender, class, or other aspects of their identity in their performance of self as strategies to differentiate themselves from stereotypes of their racial groups. This deployment of intersectionality as an "individual stereotype negation strategy" (Carbado & Gulati, 2003, p. 1812) produces a kind of grease that enables them to move more smoothly in and around the professional field. It allows them to understand when to abide by the rules of the professional communications game, when these rules prompt a masking of "otherness," and when interest convergence (Bell, 1980) means that performing the "Other" may be desirable, for example, when an ethnic audience is being targeted and a minoritized practitioner is seen as useful. Thus, in the face of being constructed as the "face that doesn't fit" with the professional habitus, practitioners construct and manage their identity in ways that demonstrate they do.

> *I do think there's this whole . . . juggling thing that you have to juggle, you have to show something that will let them maybe not look at it [ethnicity] so much.* (Interview 4, U.K. practitioner)

> *It's also an advantage because when you have such . . . when they have such low expectations and then they see me and maybe they see my output they go, "Wow this is really good. This report is really good. This proposal is really good." So, I mean, whenever I'm given the opportunity it makes me feel good that, okay yes I'm beginning to prove myself and that has happened over and over again.* (Interview 27, U.K. practitioner)

The multiple consciousness that practitioners exhibit also offers other advantages. Apart from the professional narrative they enact each day, many carry with them narratives from family and community that shape their perceptions of the possibilities available to them. These are aspects of the cultural wealth that Yosso (2005) argued must be accounted for in the lives of minoritized individuals. In the context of professional fields, and of professional communications in particular, this cultural wealth means that the "blank canvas" of the new practitioner is not so blank after all. As Bourdieu (1991) pointed out,

> The power of suggestion which is exerted through things and persons, and which, instead of telling the child what he must do, tells him what he is, and thus leads him to become durably what he has to be, is the condition of effectiveness of all kinds of symbolic power that will subsequently be able to operate on a habitus predisposed to respond to them. (p. 52)

Attempts to define practitioners' professional identity in terms that contradict these family and community narratives may therefore fail, because their primary habitus has furnished them with the strength and resources to fight for their own identity and reject others' claims about what or who they should be. Where practitioners do assert their professional rights, skills, and identity, they can meet with success.

> *I really had to push my way of thinking and my beliefs and how I can do my job as well as practice being a Muslim, and not let it affect my job. So I think everyone hates change and I think that was it. I think there was somebody quite low in the business coming in and they were threatened by it I think in a way. But now I have to admit I have got respect from a lot of my colleagues and so forth. And even people within the PR industry.* (Interview 26, U.K. practitioner)

> *The only way to kind of solve all those problems is for us to all mix and talk more, so you just need to bring more people in, you know, into the room. I just think, by me being with [consultancy], [I've] been working with them for a few months, and it's changed the dynamics. When I walk in now people are not scared anymore, and I could bring another black person and they wouldn't be scared (laughs) you know, it's changed. It's much more relaxed and you can only do that by bringing people in and taking a chance. And, yeah, it might not work out, you know, with that particular person, but give it a try.* (Interview 14, U.K. practitioner)

Professional Structures of Public Relations

The day-to-day "othering" of practitioners through habitus and discourse is reinforced through the structures of the profession. The norms of the wider fields of economic and political power position consultancies, professionals, and their specialist expertise in the overall field of professional practice. Public relations consultancies included in the Top 150 in the United Kingdom are assessed primarily in terms of their financial turnover; those that earn more are higher up in the list. Similarly, the most prestigious specialties are reflected by the focus of these "top" consultancies: public affairs, lobbying, financial public relations, corporate public relations, and a global footprint (Council of Public Relations, 2002; PRWeek, 2009).

Because the client base for public relations is dominated by corporate and government bodies, their interests drive the majority of public relations work. Segmentation within consultancies, for example, tends to operate along the lines of business-defined or government-defined interests (e.g., public affairs, corporate public relations, digital media, consumer, technology, or business-to-business divisions). This has several consequences. First, it means that the professional hierarchy is reflected in the relative importance attached to different types of audience and reinforces historical patterns of privilege. By prioritizing voters and consumers, public relations perpetuates the stigmatization of socially, politically, and economically excluded populations, where minoritized groups are overrepresented.

Second, when minoritized groups do become a focus for public relations activity, perhaps under the rubric of "diversity" or "multicultural communications," they are of interest because of their income, their voting habits, the need to "manage" the problem they present to policymakers, or their spectacle as the exotic "Other." In other words, they are framed in terms of their relevance to whiteness and its (business or political) interests. In the United Kingdom, only one of the top 20 agencies has a multicultural division and justifies its focus purely in terms of the need for organizations to recognize the spending power of different ethnic groups (Weber Shandwick, 2007). In the United States, awareness of the need to improve diversity is greater, and efforts to reach more diverse populations are more developed, but results are patchy and practitioners argue that diversity will only improve if there is a clear "business case" for it (PRWeek, 2008). This limits opportunities for practitioners who may have strengths in this area.

> *I suppose a lot of companies do bring in practitioners who are from a BME background or specialize in those audiences and you see a lot of that with the Asian market in particular because there*

is this perception that Asians have money, there's a higher disposable income that is up for grabs by mainstream companies who do the right thing by them and so there's one or two individuals . . . who kind of get those contracts, but then when you look at what they're actually asked to do, . . . there's no planning from the absolute launch of a product to say, "Okay, we've got a great product, this is our marketing plan and within that marketing plan how do we market this differently for different audiences?" (Interview 22, U.K. practitioner)

In this context, the opportunities for minoritized practitioners to use their cultural wealth (Yosso, 2005) as a valuable professional asset are limited—there is no interest convergence when the dominant group is not interested. While there are agencies that specialize in diversity communications, a role just in this area—or other stereotypical areas such as communicating to "hard to reach groups"—may compromise practitioners who want to avoid being pigeonholed into a single area of expertise. Moreover, the assignment of this particular "place" in the profession is made according to criteria set by the dominant group, which defines the context in which diversity communications are of interest and places them on the periphery rather than at the center of communications exercises.

Practitioners in this position may benefit from having a role, but they simultaneously enact a professional habitus that does not always work to their advantage, and they perpetuate the structure of the professional field such that it sustains others' superiority. Minoritized practitioners therefore have a choice between taking advantage of interest convergence where it exists, and supporting the professional norm, or challenging it, but risking their personal comfort and, potentially, their career progression.

Conclusion

Symbolic efficacy, Bourdieu (1991) argued, is determined by "the relationship between the properties of discourses, the properties of the person who pronounces them and the properties of the institution which authorizes him to pronounce them" (p. 111). In this chapter, I have shown how assumptions of whiteness permeate public relations history in the U.K. and U.S. environments and continue in the present through the professional habitus, merit-based discourses, and professional structures. This produces symbolic power that focuses on minoritized professionals' "race" as a point of difference with the potential to affect their professional lives on the most fundamental level.

Flintoff, Fitzgerald, and Scraton (2008) defined difference as "fundamentally about hierarchy and value—about relations between different groups, rather than simple characteristics held by different groups" (p. 77), while McIntosh (1997) argued that discrimination is not about episodic violence as much as about the ongoing balance between the interests of different groups. From this perspective, if the public relations profession wants to genuinely improve diversity and address the discrimination that minoritized practitioners face, it must recognize the pervasiveness of whiteness and give up some of that privilege to make room for something new. Once the past and present are recognized for what they are, strategies to change the future can evolve.

Notes

1. I use quotation marks around the word "race" throughout this chapter to underline the fact that it is a social construction rather than an objective reality (Delgado & Stefancic, 2001).

2. This is not to dismiss the major efforts made by practitioners during the civil rights movement and on behalf of organizations advancing black interests, such as the NAACP (Hon, 1997; Straughan, 2004). These efforts were a crucial part of the struggle for greater equality in the United States. However, the majority of public relations work was done on behalf of white interests.

References

Abbott, A. (1988). *The system of professions: An essay on the division of expert labour.* Chicago: University of Chicago Press.

Ahmed, S. (2004). Declarations of whiteness: The non-performativity of antiracism [Electronic version]. *borderlands, 3*(2).

Ahmed, S. (2009). Embodying diversity: Problems and paradoxes for black feminists. *Race, Ethnicity and Education, 12*(1), 41–52.

Aldoory, L. (2005, December). A (re)conceived feminist paradigm for public relations: A case for substantial improvement. *Journal of Communication,* 668–684.

Aldoory, L. (2007). Reconceiving gender for an "excellent" future in public relations scholarship. In E. Toth (Ed.), *The future of excellence in public relations and communication management: Challenges for the next generation* (pp. 399–412). Mahwah, NJ: Lawrence Erlbaum.

Anthias, F. (1990). "Race" and class revisited: Conceptualising "race" and racisms. *Sociological Review, 38*(1), 19–42.

Anthias, F. (2001). The concept of "social division" and theorising social stratification: Looking at ethnicity and class. *Sociology, 35*(4), 835–854.

Bell, D. (1980). *Brown v Board of Education* and the interest covergence dilemma. *Harvard Law Review, 93,* 518–533.

Bernays, E. (2005). *Propaganda.* New York: Ig. (Original work published 1928)

Bourdieu, P. (1984). *Distinction: A social critique of the judgment of taste.* London: Routledge & Kegan Paul.

Bourdieu, P. (1990a). *In other words: Essays towards a reflexive sociology.* Oxford, UK: Polity Press.

Bourdieu, P. (1990b). *The logic of practice.* Cambridge, UK: Polity Press.

Bourdieu, P. (1991). *Language and symbolic power* (G. Raymond & M. Adamson, Trans.). Cambridge, UK: Polity Press.

Bourdieu, P. (1999). *The weight of the world: Social suffering in contemporary society.* Cambridge, UK: Polity Press.

Bourdieu, P. (2000). *Pascalian meditations.* Stanford, CA: Stanford University Press.

Carbado, D., & Gulati, M. (2003). The law and economics of critical race theory. *Yale Law Journal, 112,* 1757–1828.

Carrasco, E. R. (2002). Critical race theory and post-colonial development: Radically monitoring the World Bank and the IMF. In F. Valdes, J. McCristal Culp, & A. P. Harris (Eds.), *Crossroads, directions and a new critical race theory* (pp. 366–375). Philadelphia: Temple University Press.

Centre for Economics and Business Research. (2005). *PR Today: 48,000 professionals; £6.5 billion turnover.* London: Author.

Council of Public Relations. (2002). *2002 Industry documentation and rankings.* Retrieved October, 1, 2009, from www.prfirms.org/_data/n_0001/resources/live/cons_rank.xls

Cutlip, S. M. (1994). *The unseen power: Public relations, history.* Hillsdale, NJ: Lawrence Erlbaum.

Delgado, R., & Stefancic, J. (2001). *Critical race theory: An introduction.* New York: New York University Press.

DuBois, W. E. B. (2008). *The souls of black folk.* Oxford, UK: Oxford University Press. (Original work published 1903)

Dyer, R. (1997). *White.* New York: Routledge.

Edwards, L. (2009). Symbolic power and public relations practice: Locating individual practitioners in their social context. *Journal of Public Relations Research, 21*(3), 251–272.

Ewen, S. (1996). *PR! A social history of spin.* New York: Basic Books.

Flagg, B. (1997). Transparently white subjective decision making: Fashioning a legal remedy. In R. Delgado & J. Stefancic (Eds.), *Critical white studies: Looking behind the mirror* (pp. 85–88). Philadelphia: Temple University Press.

Flintoff, A., Fitzgerald, H., & Scraton, S. (2008). The challenges of intersectionality: Researching difference in physical education. *International Studies in the Sociology of Education, 18*(2), 73–85.

Ford, R., & Appelbaum, L. (2009). *Multicultural survey of PR practitioners.* Retrieved September 22, 2009, from www.ccny.cuny.edu/prsurvey

Frankenberg, R. (1993). *White women, race matters: The social construction of whiteness.* Minneapolis: University of Minnesota Press.

Gillborn, D. (2008). *Racism and education: Coincidence or conspiracy?* Abingdon, UK: Routledge.

Grunig, L. A., Toth, E. L., & Hon, L. C. (2001). *Women in public relations.* New York: Guilford Press.

Hackett, R. A., & Uzelmann, S. (2003). Tracing corporate influences on press content: A summary of recent Newswatch Canada research. *Journalism Studies, 4*(3), 331–346.

Hall, S. (1992). New ethnicities. In J. Donald & A. Rattansi (Eds.), *"Race," culture and difference.* London: Open University/Sage.

Hargreaves, I. (2003). Spinning out of control. *History Today, 53*(3), 38–39.

Harris, C. (1993). Whiteness as property. *Harvard Law Review, 106*(8), 1707–1791.

Helms, J. (1990). *Black and white racial identity development.* Westport, CT: Praeger.

Hill-Collins, P. (2006). *From black power to hip hop.* Philadelphia: Temple University Press.

Hon, L. C. (1995). Toward a feminist theory of public relations. *Journal of Public Relations Research, 7*(1), 27–88.

Hon, L. C. (1997). To redeem the soul of America: Public relations and the civil rights movement. *Journal of Public Relations Research, 9*(3), 163–212.

Hon, L. C., Grunig, L. A., & Dozier, D. M. (1992). Women in public relations: Problems and opportunities. In J. E. Grunig & L. A. Grunig (Eds.), *Excellence in public relations and communication management* (pp. 419–438). Hillsdale, NJ: Lawrence Erlbaum.

Koller, A. (2007, May). *The public sphere, the field of power and comparative historical research.* Paper presented at the International Communication Association: Communication, Control, Critique, San Francisco.

Ladson-Billings, G. (1999). Just what is critical race theory and what's it doing in a *nice* field like education? In L. Parker, D. Deyhle, & S. Villenas (Eds.), *Race is . . . race isn't: Critical race theory and qualitative studies in education* (pp. 7–30). Boulder, CO: Westview Press.

Ladson-Billings, G. (2000). Racialized discourses and ethnic epistemologies. In N. K. Denzin & Y. S. Lincoln (Eds.), *Handbook of qualitative research* (pp. 257–277). Thousand Oaks, CA: Sage.

L'Etang, J. (2004). *Public relations in Britain: A history of professional practice in the 20th century.* Mahwah, NJ: Lawrence Erlbaum.

L'Etang, J. (2005). Critical public relations: Some reflections. *Public Relations Review, 31,* 521–526.

Martinelli, D. K., & Mucciarone, J. (2007). New deal public relations: A glimpse into FDR press secretary Stephen Early's work. *Public Relations Review, 33,* 49–57.

McIntosh, P. (1997). White privilege and male privilege: A personal account of coming to see correspondences through work in women's studies. In R. Delgado & J. Stefancic (Eds.), *Critical white studies: Looking behind the mirror* (pp. 291–299). Philadelphia: Temple University Press.

McIntyre, A. (1997). *Making meaning of whiteness: Exploring racial identity with white teachers.* New York: State University of New York Press.

McKie, D., & Munshi, D. (2007). *Reconfiguring public relations: Ecology, equity and enterprise.* Abingdon, UK: Routledge.

McKinney, K. D. (2005). *Being white: Stories of race and racism.* New York: Routledge.

Miller, D., & Dinan, W. (2000). The rise of the PR industry in Britain 1979–98. *European Journal of Communication, 15*(1), 5–35.

Miller, D., & Dinan, W. (2007). *Thinker, faker, spinner, spy: Corporate PR and the assault on democracy.* London: Pluto Press.

Moloney, K. (2006). *Rethinking public relations: PR propaganda and democracy* (2nd ed.). Abingdon, UK: Routledge.

Munshi, D., & Kurian, P. (2005). Imperializing spin cycles: A postcolonial look at public relations, greenwashing, and the separation of publics. *Public Relations Review, 31,* 513–520.

Murji, K., & Solomos, J. (Eds.). (2005). *Racialization: Studies in theory and practice.* Oxford, UK: Oxford University Press.

Perry, P. (2001). White means never having to say you're ethnic: White youth and the construction of "cultureless" identities. *Journal of Contemporary Ethnography, 30*(1), 56–91.

Phillips, M., & Phillips, T. (1998). *Windrush: The irresistable rise of multiracial Britain.* London: HarperCollins.

Pompper, D. (2004). Linking ethnic diversity and two-way symmetry: Modeling female African-American practitioners' roles. *Journal of Public Relations Research, 16*(3), 269–299.

Pompper, D. (2005a). "Difference" in public relations research: A case for introducing critical race theory. *Journal of Public Relations Research, 17*(2), 139–169.

Pompper, D. (2005b). Multiculturalism in the public relations curriculum: Female African-American practitioners' perceptions of effects. *Howard Journal of Communications, 16*(4), 295–316.

PRWeek. (2008, December 15). *PR Week diversity survey 2008.* London: Author.

PRWeek. (2009, April 24). *PR Week top 150 consultancies 2009.* London: Author.

Ross, T. (1997). The rhetorical tapestry of race. In R. Delgado & J. Stefancic (Eds.), *Critical white studies: Looking behind the mirror* (pp. 89–97). Philadelphia: Temple University Press.

Ross, T. (2002). The unbearable whiteness of being. In F. Valdes, J. McCristal Culp, & A. P. Harris (Eds.), *Crossroads, directions and a new critical race theory.* Philadelphia: Temple University Press.

Russell, K. M., & Bishop, C. O. (2009). Understanding Ivy Lee's declaration of principles: U.S. newspaper and magazine coverage of publicity and press agentry, 1865–1904. *Public Relations Review, 35,* 91–101.

Said, E. (1994). *Culture and imperialism.* London: Vintage Books.

Said, E. (1995). *Orientalism* (2nd ed.). Harmondsworth, UK: Penguin Books.

Shome, R., & Hedge, R. (2002). Postcolonial approaches to communication: Charting the terrain, engaging the inheritance. *Communication Theory, 12*(3), 249–270.

Solorzano, D. G., & Yosso, T. J. (2002). Critical race methodology: Storytelling as an analytical framework for education research. *Qualitative Inquiry, 8*(1), 23–44.

Sommerlad, H. (2002). Women solicitors in a fractured profession: Intersections of gender and professionalism in England and Wales. *International Journal of the Legal Profession, 9*(3), 213–234.

Sommerlad, H. (2008). That obscure object of desire: Sex equality and the legal profession. In R. Hunter & M. Drakopoulou (Eds.), *Rethinking equality projects in law: Feminist challenges* (pp. 171–194). Oxford, UK: Hart.

Sommerlad, H., & Sanderson, P. (2008, July). *Professions, intersectionality and cultural capital: Understanding choice and constraint in occupational fields.* Paper presented at the Third International Legal Ethics Conference, Gold Coast, Australia.

Straughan, D. M. (2004). "Lift every voice and sing": The public relations efforts of the NAACP, 1960–1965. *Public Relations Review, 30,* 49–60.

Swartz, D. (1997). *Culture and power: The sociology of Pierre Bourdieu.* Chicago: University of Chicago Press.

Valdes, F., McCristal Culp, J., & Harris, A. P. (Eds.). (2002). *Crossroads, directions, and a new critical race theory.* Philadelphia: Temple University Press.

Weber Shandwick. (2007). *The multi-cultural insight study: Understanding the multicultural market.* London: Author.

Windle, R. (1971). *British and American economic history, 1850–1950.* London: Macdonald & Evans.

Yosso, T. J. (2005). Whose culture has capital? A critical race theory discussion of community cultural wealth. *Race, Ethnicity and Education, 8*(1), 69–91.

Zerbinos, E., & Clanton, G. A. (1993). Minority practitioners: Career influences, job satisfaction, and discrimination. *Public Relations Review, 19*(1), 75–91.

CHAPTER 15

Toward an Intersectionality Theory of Public Relations

Jennifer Vardeman-Winter and Natalie T. J. Tindall

Identities like race, gender, class, and sexuality/sexual orientation can act together, simultaneously, to place groups in distinct situations of power. How power is distributed unequally based on multiple, overlapping identities is called of intersectionality (Collins, 2000; Dill, McLaughlin, & Nieves, 2007; McCall, 2005; Weber, 2001). Within the logic of intersectionality, these concepts become salient characteristics that shadow individuals in everyday interactions (e.g., Brewer, 1995; Collins, 1993, 2000; King, 1988; Weber, 2001; Zinn & Dill, 1996). As Collins (1993) noted, these identity markers are systems of power that influence and filter through all social interactions, relations, and organizations.

As the field of public relations is interested in how relationships are managed between organizations and communities, an exploration of how intersectionality exists at multiple levels of public relations is worth examination. There is a need to analyze and understand how practitioner identities impact the creation and implementation of strategic messages. Analyzing barriers to change and researching communication strategies for *others* outside dominant social groups is incomplete if it is viewed consistently through a single lens, with a myopic gaze that omits multiple realities and identities, or if the research relies on myths that construct groups as monolithic entities (Fletcher & Ely, 2003).

To link intersectionality and public relations, we first outline the origins, characteristics, examples, and debates within research on intersectionality theory. We then propose an intersectionality theory of public relations by presenting cases for how identities can be seen on nine levels of public relations praxis, scholarship, and pedagogy. We encourage researchers, educators, and practitioners to adopt a refined lens when considering publics, students, the discipline, and policy making to uncover systemic power differentials and illuminate solutions to equalize access to opportunities for all participants in public relations and in all contexts where public relations operates.

Theory of Intersectionality

Intersectionality examines how some individuals and communities exist at the convergence where oppressions take on a cascading, multiplying effect. In other words, to some individuals and communities, race, gender, class, sexuality, or disability are not the only identities on which people are oppressed by systemic power, nor do any of these identities exist within a vacuum. Instead, systemic oppressions can happen simultaneously, in an interlocking way, thereby creating a web of inequality (Zinn & Dill, 1996).

Simply put, intersectionality is "the study of multiple, complex social relations" (Dill et al., 2007, p. 629). Legal academics (Bell, 1990; Bell & Nkomo, 2001; K. Crenshaw, 1991; Matsuda, 1996; Williams, 1997), sociology scholars (e.g., Collins, 2000), feminist scholars (Zinn & Dill, 1996), and education researchers (hooks, 1984; Ladson-Billings, 2005, 2006; Ladson-Billings & Tate, 1995; Pillow, 2003) have discussed and highlighted intersectionality as a way to understand the structural, political, and representational connections that exist and limit access to some groups and have offered an alternative lens through which to view diversity, power, culture, and identity in public relations scholarship, praxis, and pedagogy (K. Crenshaw, 1991). This concept emerged from discourse about women of color's unique knowledges gained from the work and the social relations they experienced in living and working in vastly different cultures (Dill et al., 2007). Understanding the relevance of race, gender, and class and how they affect an individual's life cannot be understood unless a researcher acknowledges and understands the context in which they are achieved (West & Fenstermaker, 1995).

Intersectionality originated from feminist standpoint epistemology (Dill et al., 2007), which involves research conducted by women, for women (Olesen, 2003). The advocacy of research conducted by women reflects long-term, structural, and methodical negligence by political, economic, social, legal, academic, and biomedical systems of women's particular knowledge (Harding, 1991). Theoretical assumptions include the following:

1. Women's standpoint in society and knowledge are different from men's.
2. Women's knowledge has not been considered equal in most official, legitimized social systems.
3. Women's knowledge has been relegated to a very few sites within society, such as the home and around children, rather than in public sites (Acker, Barry, & Esseveld, 1983; Reinharz, 1992).

Because of this fractional presence in public spaces, censorship of women's voice, and historic blockades to access to certain informational sites, such as politics, legal privilege, education, and even within the home, women have come to know the world from a partial, situated standpoint (Haraway, 1988).

Furthermore, women—and in particular, women from historically oppressed groups such as African American women and Chicanas—learn subaltern and multiple layers of partial knowledge because of the intersections and coexistence of oppression based on gender, race, ethnicity, class, nationality, embodiment, and sexual orientation (Moraga & Anzaldúa, 1983; Zinn & Dill, 1996). Intersectionality rests on the basis that race or gender tell only part of the story of an individual's and a group's everyday, lived experiences and their access to opportunities (Weber, 2001). These intersections represent not only the realities of overlapping oppression but also the possibility that subjugation and privilege can coexist. Furthermore, intersectionality analysis largely emerged from the limitations of investigations conducted around individual identities (e.g., only race, only gender).

Intersectionality is also based on a rejection of essentialism of gender or race because these social constructions do not stand alone but, instead, exist because of one another. To this point, Collins (2000) argued that intersectionality is produced through a "matrix of domination," which is the "overall social organization within which intersecting oppressions originate, develop, and are contained" (pp. 227–228). The matrix of oppression suggests that depending on one's social location, people can experience their identities in different manners. Zinn and Dill (1996) offered this example:

> People of the same race will experience race differently depending upon their location in the class structure as working class, professional managerial class, or unemployed; in the gender structure as female or male; and in structures of sexuality as heterosexual, homosexual, or bisexual. (pp. 326–327)

Scholars have categorized intersectionality in several ways. For example, Weber (2001) reasoned that intersectionality exists across five themes, which explain how race, class, gender, and sexuality (a) are historically and geographically/globally contextual, (b) are socially constructed, (c) are a result of power relationships, (d) exist along macro social structural and micro social psychological levels, and (e) are always simultaneously expressed. Similarly, some scholars believe intersectionality to exist primarily within the social sphere (e.g., McCall, 2005), whereas others argue that intersectionality is more of a product of structural, political, and cultural/representational oppressions (K. Crenshaw, 1991).

In one of the most in-depth studies of intersectionality to date, Kimberlé Crenshaw (1991), a legal scholar, provided evidence of distinct levels of intersectionality. For example, the oppressions faced by battered women, including immigrants, serve as structural examples of intersectionality in that the institutions established to aid battered women do not have the financial, personnel, or political capacity to address all the "multilayered and routinized forms of domination" (p. 1245) many women face. To exemplify this point, she cited an event when a "Latina in crisis was repeatedly denied accommodation at a shelter because she could not prove that she was English-proficient" (p. 1262). K. Crenshaw described structural intersectionality from a system perspective:

> Many women of color, for example, are burdened by poverty, child care responsibilities, and the lack of job skills. These burdens, largely the consequence of gender and class oppressions, are then compounded by the racially discriminatory employment and housing practices women of color face, as well as by the disproportionately high unemployment by women of color that makes battered women of color less able to depend on the support of friends and relatives for temporary shelter. (pp. 1245–1246)

At the political level of intersectionality, K. Crenshaw (1991) pointed to domestic abuse statistics where black women are mutually oppressed because of political ramifications of reporting these statistics according to both their race and gender identities. Her analysis revealed that "most crime statistics are classified by sex or race but none are classified by sex *and* race. Because we know that most rape victims are women, the racial breakdown reveals, at best, rape rates for Black women" (p. 1252). She reasoned that domestic abuse activists fear that releasing such statistics will indicate to authorities and other publics to "dismiss domestic violence as a minority problem and, therefore, not deserving of aggressive action" (p. 1253).

In summary, intersectionality offers an analysis of "intersecting forms of domination [that] produce *both* oppression *and* opportunity" (Zinn & Dill, 1996, p. 327). Therefore, an intersectionality framework offers analytic points into power relationships across many hierarchical relationships such as those between organizations and publics, producers and consumers, and policymakers and affected communities.

Why Should Intersectionality Be Pursued in Public Relations

Public relations has been and continues to be defined as an ethical advocacy function that serves the publics' interests. It is in the best interest of the practice to know the structural, political, and representational conditions of the publics with whom we communicate.

Reason 1: Lack of Theoretical Explanation of Complexities Publics Face

Excellence theory (L. A. Grunig, Grunig, & Dozier, 2002) worked to explain difference and diversity through the concept of requisite variety. Yet, as scholars have argued, the concept of requisite variety is flawed and reductionist. Sha and Ford (2007) concluded that the concepts of identity and difference explicated in excellence theory and subsequent research is limited to additive categorizations and the homogenization of groups to the simplest factor.

Plus, Sha and Ford's (2007) work echoes the concerns of K. Crenshaw (1991), that while categorizations are natural, intersectionality is distinct in its efforts to analyze "the particular values attached to [categories] and the way those values foster and create social hierarchies" (p. 1297). Identities are reconceptualized within frameworks of race and gender, and K. Crenshaw claimed that "recognizing that identity politics takes place at the site where categories intersect thus seems more fruitful than challenging the possibility of talking about categories at all" (p. 1299). Following K. Crenshaw, Sha and Ford (2007) wrote that previous researchers had not "problematize[d] extant theoretical constructs and ask whether they are appropriate for a public relations discipline that incorporates multiple diversities" (p. 390), but that more comprehensive analyses were required in this complex discipline.

Reason 2: Our Role as Advocates

Public relations serves the public interest; the role of the public relations practitioner is one of responsible advocacy for clients (Fitzpatrick & Bronstein, 2006). Advocacy is grounded in the First Amendment legal concepts of "the marketplace of ideas" and "the free trade in ideas" (Heath, 1992). Fitzpatrick and Bronstein (2006) contextualized the communication strategies of public relations within its advocacy role to society:

> The concept of a marketplace of ideas in democratic societies governed by the people reflects a deep and sustained belief that self-government is made possible by properly informed citizens who engage in informed decision making. The public interest is best served when the voices of diverse special interests are heard. (p. 4)

Four principles guide the marketplace advocacy principle—access, process, truth, and disclosure. The need to understand difference and intersectionality is important for the first two principles. With access, the speaker must have access to the marketplace, and the listener must have access to the information. The process requires that "truthful information flows to and from marketplace participants" (Fitzpatrick & Bronstein, 2006, p. 10). Simply reducing the marketplace participants—the publics for our messages—to demographics and psychographics negates the nuances of lived experiences and personal identities that impact how individuals will select, receive, react to, and process the messages that are spread, debated, and refined in the marketplace.

A Model of Intersectionality in Public Relations

If public relations practitioners and scholars further explore how intersectionality operates within and external to the discipline, the discipline can contribute better to achieving a "fully functioning society" in which publics have the full information they need to make important decisions, and organizations aid this information freedom through challenging discourse, corporate social responsibility, and equitable policy making (Heath & Palenchar, 2009, p. 234). As a consideration of how publics experience power relationships in their everyday, lived experiences (Smith, 1987), this section outlines major areas where intersectionality should be analyzed in public relations research.

A theory of intersectionality in public relations consists of the need for analysis on multiple levels: (a) the intraindustrial level, (b) the interorganizational level, (c) the organization-publics relational level, (d) the publics and community level, (e) the representational level, (f) the media level, (g) the multinational/global level, (h) the theoretical level, and (i) the pedagogical level.

Intraindustrial Level

Public relations research shows a persistent subjugation of women of color and gay, lesbian, and bisexual practitioners (Tindall, 2007b). In particular, women of color receive the lowest pay, the slowest promotion rates, and fewer opportunities for professional development, and they tend to work in technician roles more than managerial roles when compared with white women and especially white men (L. A. Grunig, Toth, & Hon, 2001). Although few studies have examined sexuality, research shows that public relations is a field within which gay, lesbian, bisexual, and transgender people cannot readily reveal their true sexual identities for fear of damaged relationships and professional restrictions (Tindall, 2007a; Waters & Tindall, 2007).

Furthermore, research about the status of the public relations discipline within an organization has revealed that because of the identities of public relations practitioners, the public relations function is often relegated to marketing, legal, human resources, or advertising departments/teams (L. A. Grunig, et al., 2002; L. A. Grunig, et al., 2001). The excellence project explained this trend by arguing that the public relations function is not empowered unless it is part of the dominant coalition, and to be part of the dominant coalition, members of the public relations function should be invited to meetings with upper management (L. A. Grunig, et al., 2002). Tindall (2007b) suggested that this phenomenon in public relations reflects Kanter's (1977) theory of homosocial reproduction, which proposes that corporate executives tended to socialize with and promote men more, thus resulting in a glass ceiling for women in corporations.

Interorganizational Level

Intersectionality in public relations operates across organizations according to how power is distributed among types of organizations. This is a factor of intersectionality that is observed primarily in power tensions between large corporations and smaller activist groups. Heath and Palenchar (2009) suggested that power resource dependency theory explains how groups gain power through accumulations of tangible wealth (e.g., money, materials, employees) and intangible wealth (e.g., relationships with policymakers, access to media personnel, public goodwill), and that this wealth is limited within a society; thus, groups must compete to garner these types of wealth. To better understand how the individual and collective identities of activist members and groups impact their access to power, an intersectionality analysis should be used to further understand the nature of activist groups and the unique barriers they face as organizations in the accomplishment of their public relations goals because of the complex ways their multiple identities may interact within more mainstream political and representational social structures.

Organization-Publics Relational Level

A vast amount of public relations research, practice, and pedagogy is based on the strategic management of public relations and issues (Heath & Palenchar, 2009). This often requires the segmentation and prioritization of publics according to (a) their potential impact on the organization's bottom line as well as (b) the extent to which they are likely to communicate with or about the organization (J. E. Grunig, 1992; L. A. Grunig et al., 2002). Some publics-based, intersectionality research has suggested that the essence of strategic management and ethical principles of public relations may contradict one another (Aldoory, 2001, 2009; Tindall, 2007a, 2007b; Tindall & Vardeman, 2008; Vardeman, 2008; Vardeman & Tindall, 2008). Specifically, some research has focused on how the segmentation and prioritization of publics in communication campaigns have contradicted the proposed missions of organizations sponsoring the campaigns.

For example, in their study of how women of color make meaning of a heart disease communication campaign, the *Heart Truth*, sponsored by the U.S. National Heart, Lung, & Blood Institute with the mission to educate women "that heart disease is the #1 killer of American women" (National Heart, Lung, and Blood Institute [NHLBI], n.d.), Vardeman and Tindall (2008) questioned why, if women of color are at higher risk for complications from cardiovascular disease, was a specialized effort within the campaign for women of color initiated 3 years after the general campaign? Furthermore, they found that the women participating in their study felt that their identities were compromised in certain behavioral suggestions made by the campaign. The materials suggested that women eat fresh fruits and vegetables and exercise regularly. However, some Latinas perceived the cost of fresh produce to be higher than the foods they buy, and they did not know how to adapt their traditional ethnic and cultural foods to the American versions, particularly in ways that their families would eat. Thus, problems with neglecting intersectionality arose when assumptions were made by campaign designers about the ease with which cultural members could change their lifestyles, and the designers did not consider how class and ethnicity differences might significantly determine whether women of color were empowered to make healthy changes.

Risk communication is an important area of study for intersectionality (Aldoory, 2009). Organizations make suggestions to publics based on organizations' perspectives of how publics should live and behave around public health threats; then campaign designers communicate with publics using organization-approved, "culturally competent" symbols (Rakow, 1989; Salmon, 1990). An example of this is the red dress used as the "national symbol for women and heart disease awareness" used in the Heart Truth campaign (NHLBI, n.d.). This symbolization essentializes women's gender as preferential of the color red and as exemplified by a dress. However, some interview participants critiqued the campaign for its use of the symbol, questioning whether lesbians or women who do not wear dresses of any color, shape, or pattern would feel comfortable with that representation (Tindall & Vardeman, 2008).

Furthermore, the communication events surrounding Hurricane Katrina provide a keen example of the need to look at public relations, including crisis communication, from an intersectional lens. Those severely affected by the disaster were poor, mostly black, and older, whereas those who escaped safely were primarily middle and upper class, white, and younger (Rowan, Botan, Kreps, Samoilenko, & Farnsworth, 2009; Waymer & Heath, 2007). The negligence of recognizing multiple identities by authorities in Hurricane Katrina highlights other dimensions of oppression, including disability and the elderly and, in particular, how people with disabilities and older, sick people are able to cope and escape disasters.

Risk communication scholars have noted the dynamic and historically cultivated nature of health disparities based on identity (e.g., Aldoory, 2009; Dutta, 2007; Heath & O'Hair, 2009), yet the impact of identity and the intersection of culture, race, gender, age, sexuality, and socioeconomic factors have not been addressed fully in most risk communication campaigns. For some, structuring health/risk campaigns around racial categories alone have not been successful strategies (see also Campbell & Jovchelovitch, 2000; Carpiano, 2006; Dinham, 2005; Guareschi & Jovchelovitch, 2004). Perhaps campaigns see smaller effect sizes because designers fail to recognize that social identities are not fixed or rooted; rather, identity is negotiated, and it is this negotiated identity—achieved and constructed through everyday social interactions and relations—that must be considered when creating campaigns (Stephens, 2007).

Publics and Community Level

Individual communities and cultures experience intersectionality that can be examined from a public relations perspective. Based on stereotypes and perceptions of those within group versus the *other*, or those outside the group (Hall, 1997), intersectionality exists across groups, or cultures, and perpetuates real or perceived differential access to opportunities based on how identities overlap. As an example of intersectionality within intergroup politics, Vardeman (2008) studied how intersectionality affected teen girls' perceptions of the Gardasil media campaign, and how racial, ethnic, and sexual activity/motherhood statuses may affect perceptions differently. For example, when asked how she thinks that teen girls from different races or ethnicities may perceive the media differently than she does, one white, 17-year-old, middle-upper-class teen girl expressed differences based on race and motherhood status. White teen girls interviewed about their perceptions of the Gardasil HPV/cervical cancer vaccine campaign discussed that nonwhite girls whom they perceived to be promiscuous (because they either were already sexually active or were pregnant) do not care about their sexual health and, therefore, need different communication because of their skin color, sexual activities, and gender.

Intersectionality also exists for communities on a structural level. For example, those with easy access to resources are able to alleviate social and structural problems for themselves, whereas resource-poor communities may be less able to fix the problem from within. In research on environmental racism, racially and ethnically diverse populations and low-income neighborhoods show higher concentrations of lead, have larger groups that work with pesticides, and are located where agricultural runoff and wastewater contribute to the degradation of nearby rivers and streams (U.S. Environmental Protection Agency, 2009). In connecting issues management—a business discipline related to public relations through the importance of research, strategic management, and corporate social responsibility—to risk communication, Heath and Palenchar (2009) illuminated this problem of environmental racism:

> Key publics feel deeply that companies and governmental organizations (and even nonprofits, including activists) create or allow risks to occur that will affect the health, safety, environmental quality, and economic well-being of community residents and users of products. Of related importance is the emerging concern that the placement of manufacturing companies, waste disposal facilities, and hazardous occupations does not equitably expose rich persons to risks as often or as severely as poor persons and those of color. (p. 314)

The trend to counter environmental racism—dubbed environmental justice—is one that uses communication, research, media advocacy, and policy making to reduce the persistent health risks that people of color and of low-income backgrounds are subjected to by the locating of undesirable facilities and contaminants (Wallack, Dorfman, Jernigan, & Themba, 1993).

Another compelling argument for intersectionality at the community and cultural level is the persistence of public health disparities in the United States as well as internationally. In the United States, people of color and people from low-income, resource-poor communities experience higher morbidity and mortality rates in major diseases that plague the U.S. population as well as the public health care budget, such as infant mortality, cancer, heart disease and stroke, diabetes, mental health, and HIV and AIDS (National Center on Minority Health and Health Disparities, 2002). Furthermore, in some cases, gender also contributes to persistent, intersectional public health disparities. For example, although cervical cancer is a highly preventable disease (Dignan, Michielutte, Wells, & Bahnson, 1994; Williams, 1997)—particularly in the United States due to the availability and wide use of the Pap smear detection method (American Cancer Society, 2005)—women of color from low-income communities are overrepresented among those who constitute the roughly 10,000 women who get cervical cancer annually and 4,000 women who die annually of the disease. These morbidity and mortality rates are concentrated among poor Latinas and black women because of their lack of knowledge about the Pap smear method (National Cancer Institute, 2004) and their inability to pay for the procedure or lack of insurance to cover the costs (American Cancer Society, 2005), as well as a lack of follow-up when abnormal Pap test results are revealed (Dignan et al., 1994).

Representational Level

Within a culture, representation occurs when meanings are inscribed through symbols and language into texts, such as media (Acosta-Alzuru, 2003; du Gay, Hall, Janes, Mackay, & Negus, 1997). As public relations practitioners use media in almost every communication effort, and as the words, symbols, and images we build into campaigns represent the attitudes we hope to convey in messaging, how groups are differentially represented in campaign materials, events, and media is of importance. Some media studies have shown that some groups are disproportionately portrayed in media and in campaign work negatively because of their overlapping, multiple identities (C. Crenshaw, 1997; Ehlers, 2004; Holland, 2009; Meyers, 2004).

Media Level

Some communities have little access to media resources, and this reduces some groups' ability to get important risk and crisis information as well as the extent to which some groups can illuminate the problems within their communities themselves by conducting media advocacy (Wallack et al., 1993). Studies show that communities of color and low-income communities have less access to communication technologies such as the Internet, newspapers, and magazines as well as more barriers (such as a lack of transportation) to interpersonally reaching information sources such as health clinics, emergency disaster groups, and public health and safety offices (National Center on Minority Health and Health Disparities, 2002). Thus, some researchers have hypothesized a knowledge gap in which knowledge is disseminated faster among information-rich communities than in information-poor communities (see Tichenor, Donohue, & Olien, 1970; Viswanath & Finnegan, 1996). Furthermore, while media advocacy is one way that communities with less resource-wealthy advocates can attract media attention to issues, Wallack et al. (1993) advised that ethics issues and difficulties exist in doing advocacy work in communities of color and low-income communities, particularly in how communities are represented. As public relations practitioners hoping to break through persistent disparities, the authors recommended that advocates think through the stereotypes they have of the experts and the communities they are trying to help to recognize how *othering* and stereotypes could be limiting the effectiveness of their work because of damaging effects of representation, particularly in mass media.

Multinational/Global Level

Intersectionality in public relations exists in multinational, particularly international, communication campaigns. Campaigns sponsored by Western organizations that strive to reach international publics using mass media—particularly those in less economically, politically, and structurally developed countries—have been dubbed *development communication* by communication scholars. Early development communication was characterized from a modern, diffusion perspective (Servaes, 1999; Vargas, 1998) and was considered a paternalistic approach (Moemeka, 2000).

A current, more participatory model of development communication is termed *another development* because the practice now implies using the media to influence changes at not only the economic level but also the social justice level to enable disenfranchised peoples to share in their own communal improvements (Servaes, 1999). Rather than using media in a top-down relationship and only talking to audiences (Moemeka, 2000), "another" development communication attempts to facilitate the participation and talking with audiences in local, horizontal communication relationships within grassroots contexts via emphasizing the accessibility—physically and intellectually—of media (Vargas, 1998).

The connection between intersectionality and global public relations is evidenced by the practice of development communication, which uses mass media messages and technologies to change a group's perceptions, attitudes, and behaviors for the betterment of the quality of their lives. Despite the variable goodwill motivation for the campaign, development communication has often been rooted in patriarchal processes that neglect the participation of the publics. These theoretical connections are important for review for public relations to reinvigorate the necessity of intersectionality analysis within global, humanitarian communication efforts.

Theoretical Level

Intersectionality is evident in the scholarship of public relations in the area of global, multinational, international, and transnational theory building since Western, modern public relations theories and concepts have largely served as the primary framework on which all research, practice, and pedagogy have been compared (Sriramesh, 2003). The trend toward Westernization in international public relations research has garnered criticism from scholars who believe that these frameworks represent only one out of many types of public relations management models and theories (Bardhan, 2003; Holtzhausen, 2000; Holtzhausen, Petersen, & Tindall, 2003; Sriramesh, 2006; van Heerden & Ströh, 2005). These scholars believe that the Western, modern perspective is ethnocentric in assuming the West's approach to public relations to be the norm, with countries outside the West practicing *other* or deviant types of public relations. These scholars believe that Western public relations metanarratives constitute top-down, asymmetrical principles and emphasize the unequal power that organizations ultimately and inherently hold over publics.

In reaction to the extent of international public relations research being conducted from a Western perspective—or using basic Western theories—some scholars (Bardhan, 2003; Holtzhausen, 2000; Holtzhausen et al., 2003; van Heerden & Ströh, 2005) have attempted to "build endogenous models, micronarratives, and literature as local alternatives to the dominant metanarratives of public relations" (Bardhan, 2003, p. 246). For example, Holtzhausen et al. (2003) and van Heerden & Ströh (2005) connected a traditional *Ubuntu* African ethic concerned with the treatment of other human beings, which involves participation, sharing, harmony, reciprocation, empathy, understanding, and cooperation, to the Western, modern perspective of global public relations. Van Heerden and Ströh offered this postmodern perspective of public relations in South Africa "to enlighten Western public relations practitioners to the positive postmodern values that African public relations practitioners can contribute to the field" (p. 18).

The postmodern, micronarrative, "alternative" perspective to global public relations management presented here is only one perspective different from the dominant paradigm, and there are many topical areas of global public relations that remain to be explored. For example, feminist, rhetorical, and intersectional paradigms have yet to be explored in global public relations management.

Pedagogical Level

Closely related to the realities of intersectionality within public relations theory is the intersectionality that exists for non-American students in public relations graduate education. Because the United States is the irrefutable global leader in public relations knowledge production and education, many students from abroad travel there to attend academic institutions and receive their education (Sriramesh, 2003). Although these opportunities exist for international students, the curriculum of education and theoretical and practical application of public relations endures as a U.S.-centric body of knowledge (Sriramesh, 2002, 2003).

Furthermore, as organizations grow increasingly transnational and publics also grow exponentially more diverse, there exists a "dire need for making public relations education and practice multicultural" (Sriramesh, 2003, p. 519) so that practitioners are better educated and trained to manage multicultural communication relationships. Furthermore, multicultural education is vital for public relations as a function to continue to provide holistic strategic management counsel for how groups can communicate with each other mutually, ethically, and symmetrically (Sriramesh, 2003; Vardeman, 2005).

In summary, intersectionality operates on multiple *individual* levels within the field of public relations creating problems of systemic, consistent subjugation of certain groups for the privilege of other groups. *Taken together*, identities often operate at multiple levels concomitantly. In other words, some public relations participants experience marginalized status in the field at multiple levels. For example, research suggests that a lesbian of color working in public relations may be relegated to communicating only with publics from her same race, may not receive the same salary as her heterosexual, white female or male counterparts, and, as a public of certain campaigns, may not be communicated with about diseases for which she is at higher risk than are white, female, heterosexual publics.

Conclusion

Public relations exists not only within organizations but also as a social, political, rhetorical, and economic function. Practitioners have a stake in understanding the complexity within which they, their publics, their organization's missions, and policy reforms exist. The purpose of this chapter was to introduce the theory of intersectionality into public relations research, praxis, and pedagogy so that practitioners and researchers can better know the "mutually constitutive relations among social identities" (Shields, 2008, p. 301). As a discipline, we can begin to strengthen an intersectional theory of public relations through reflexivity about, understanding, and negotiating our differences.

References

Acker, J., Barry, K., & Esseveld, J. (1983). Objectivity and truth: Problems in doing feminist research. *Women's Studies International Forum, 6*, 423–435.

Acosta-Alzuru, C. (2003). "I'm not a feminist . . . I only defend women as human beings": The production, representation, and consumption of feminism in a *telenovela*. *Critical Studies in Media Communication, 20*, 269–294.

Aldoory, L. (2001). Making health messages meaningful for women: Factors that influence involvement. *Journal of Public Relations Research, 13*, 163–185.

Aldoory, L. (2009). The ecological perspective and other ways to (re)consider cultural factors in risk communication. In R. L. Heath & H. D. O'Hair (Eds.), *Handbook of risk and crisis communication* (pp. 227–246). New York: Routledge.

American Cancer Society. (2005, January 1). *Overview: Cervical cancer. What causes cancer of the cervix? Can it be prevented?* Retrieved May 15, 2005, from www.cancer.org/docroot/CRI/content/CRI_2_2_2X_What_causes_cancer_of_the_cervix_Can_it_be_prevented_8.asp?sitearea=

Bardhan, N. (2003). Rupturing public relations metanarratives: The example of India. *Journal of Public Relations Research, 15*, 225–248.

Bell, E. L. (1990). The bicultural life experience of career-oriented black women. *Journal of Organizational Behavior, 11*, 459–477.

Bell, E. L., & Nkomo, S. M. (2001). *Our separate ways: Black and white women and the struggle for professional identity.* Boston: Harvard Business School Press.

Brewer, M. B. (1995). Managing diversity: The role of social identities. In S. E. Jackson and M. N. Ruderman (Eds.), *Diversity in work teams: Research paradigms for a changing workplace* (pp. 47–68). Washington, DC: American Psychological Association.

Campbell, C., & Jovchelovitch, S. (2000). Health, community and development: Towards a social psychology of participation. *Journal of Community & Applied Social Psychology, 10*, 255–270.

Carpiano, R. M. (2006). Toward a neighbourhood resource-based theory of social capital for health: Can Bourdieu and sociology help? *Social Science & Medicine, 62*, 165–175.

Collins, P. H. (1993). Toward a new vision: Race, class, and gender as categories of analysis and connection. *Race, Sex, and Class, 1,* 557–571.

Collins, P. H. (2000). *Black feminist thought: Knowledge, consciousness, and the politics of empowerment.* London: HarperCollins Academic.

Crenshaw, C. (1997). Women in the Gulf War: Toward an intersectional feminist rhetorical criticism. *Howard Journal of Communications, 8,* 219–235.

Crenshaw, K. (1991). Mapping the margins: Intersectionality, identity politics, and violence against women of color. *Stanford Law Review, 43,* 1241–1299.

Dignan, M., Michielutte, R., Wells, H. B., & Bahnson, J. (1994). The Forsyth County Cervical Cancer Prevention Project—I. Cervical cancer screening for black women. *Health Education Research, 9,* 411–420.

Dill, B. T., McLaughlin, A. E., & Nieves, A. D. (2007). Future directions of feminist research: Intersectionality. In S. N. Hesse-Biber (Ed.), *Handbook of feminist research: Theory and praxis* (pp. 629–637). Thousand Oaks, CA: Sage.

Dinham, A. (2005). Empowered or over-powered? The real experiences of local participation in the UK's New Deal for Communities. *Community Development Journal, 40,* 301–312.

du Gay, P., Hall, S., Janes, L., Mackay, H., & Negus, K. (1997). *Doing cultural studies: The story of the Sony Walkman.* London: Sage.

Dutta, M. J. (2007). Communicating about culture and health: Theorizing culture-centered and cultural sensitivity approaches. *Communication Theory, 17,* 304–328.

Ehlers, N. (2004). Hidden in plain sight: Defying juridical racialization in *Rhinelander v. Rhinelander. Communication & Critical/Cultural Studies, 1,* 313–334.

Fitzpatrick, K., & Bronstein, C. (Eds.). (2006). *Ethics in public relations: Responsible advocacy.* Thousand Oaks, CA: Sage.

Fletcher, J. K., & Ely, R. J. (2003). Introducing gender: Overview. In R. J. Ely, E. G. Foldy, M. A. Scully, & the Center for Gender in Organizations (Eds.), *Reader in gender, work, and organization* (pp. 3–9). Malden, MA: Blackwell.

Grunig, J. E. (1992). *Excellence in public relations and communication management.* Hillsdale, NJ: Lawrence Erlbaum.

Grunig, L. A., Grunig, J. E., & Dozier, D. M. (2002). *Excellent public relations and effective organizations: A study of communication management in three countries.* Mahwah, NJ: Lawrence Erlbaum.

Grunig, L. A., Toth, E. L., & Hon, L. C. (2001). *Women in public relations: How gender influences practice.* New York: Guilford Press.

Guareschi, P., & Jovchelovitch, S. (2004). Participation, health and the development of community resources in southern Brazil. *Journal of Health Psychology, 9*(2), 311–322.

Hall, S. (Ed.). (1997). *Representation: Cultural representations and signifying practices.* London: Sage (in association with the Open University).

Haraway, D. (1988). Situated knowledges: The science question in feminism and the privilege of partial perspective. *Feminist Studies, 14,* 575–599.

Harding, S. (1991). *Whose science? Whose knowledge?* Ithaca, NY: Cornell University Press.

Heath, R. L. (1992). The wrangle in the marketplace: A rhetorical perspective of public relations. In R. Heath & E. L. Toth (Eds.), *Rhetorical and critical approaches to public relations* (pp. 17–36). Hillsdale, NJ: Lawrence Erlbaum.

Heath, R. L., & O'Hair, H. D. (2009). The significance of crisis and risk communication. In R. L. Heath & H. D. O'Hair (Eds.), *Handbook of risk and crisis communication* (pp. 5–30). New York: Routledge.

Heath, R. L., & Palenchar, M. J. (2009). *Strategic issues management: Organizations and public policy challenges* (2nd ed.). Thousand Oaks, CA: Sage.

Holland, S. L. (2009). The "offending" breast of Janet Jackson: Public discourse surrounding the Jackson/Timberlake performance at Super Bowl XXXVIII. *Women's Studies in Communication, 32,* 129–150.

Holtzhausen, D. R. (2000). Postmodern values in public relations. *Journal of Public Relations Research, 12,* 93–114.

Holtzhausen, D. R., Petersen, B. K., & Tindall, N. T. J. (2003). Exploding the myth of the symmetrical/asymmetrical dichotomy: Public relations models in the new South Africa. *Journal of Public Relations Research, 15,* 305–341.

hooks, b. (1984). *Feminist theory: From margin to center.* Boston: South End Press.

Kanter, R. M. (1977). *Men and women of the corporation.* New York: Basic Books.

King, D. K. (1988). Multiple jeopardy, multiple consciousness: The context of black feminist ideology. *Signs: Journal of Women in Culture and Society, 14,* 42–72.

Ladson-Billings, G. J. (2005). New directions in multicultural education: Complexities, boundaries, and critical race theory. In J. A. Banks and C. M. Banks (Eds.), *Handbook of research on multicultural education* (pp. 50–65). San Francisco: Jossey-Bass.

Ladson-Billings, G. J. (2006). They're trying to wash us away: The adolescence of critical race theory in education. In A. D. Dixson and C. K. Rousseau (Eds.), *Critical race theory in education: All God's children got a song* (pp. v–xiii). New York: Routledge.

Ladson-Billings, G. J., & Tate, W. (1995). Toward A critical race theory of education. *Teachers College Record, 97,* 47–68.

Matsuda, M. (1996). *Where is your body? Essays on race, gender and the law.* Boston: Beacon Press.

McCall, L. (2005). The complexity of intersectionality. *Signs: Journal of Women in Culture and Society, 30,* 1771–1800.

Meyers, M. (2004). African American women and violence: Gender, race, and class in the news. *Critical Studies in Media Communication, 21,* 95–118.

Moemeka, A. A. (2000). *Development communication in action: Building understanding and creating participation.* Lanham, MD: University Press of America.

Moraga, C., & Anzaldúa, G. (Eds.). (1983). *This bridge called my back: Writings by radical women of color.* Berkeley, CA: Third Woman Press.

National Cancer Institute. (2004, February). *A snapshot of cervical cancer.* Retrieved May 8, 2004, from http://prg.nci.nih.gov/snapshots/Cervical-Snapshot.pdf

National Center on Minority Health and Health Disparities. (2002). *Strategic research plan and budget to reduce and ultimately eliminate health disparities: Vol. 1.* Retrieved October 13, 2009, from www.ncmhd.nih.gov/our_programs/strategic/pubs/VolumeI_031003EDrev.pdf

National Heart, Lung, and Blood Institute. (n.d.). *The Heart Truth: A national awareness campaign for women about heart disease.* Retrieved April 25, 2006, from www.nhlbi.nih.gov/health/hearttruth/index.htm

Olesen, V. L. (2003). Feminisms and qualitative research at and into the millennium. In N. K. Denzin & Y. S. Lincoln (Eds.), *The landscape of qualitative research: Theories and issues* (2nd ed., pp. 332–397). Thousand Oaks, CA: Sage.

Pillow, W. S. (2003). Race-based methodologies: Multicultural methods or epistemological shifts? In G. Lopez & L. Parker (Eds.), *Interrogating racism in qualitative research methodology* (pp. 181–202). New York: Peter Lang.

Rakow, L. F. (1989). Information and power: Toward a critical theory of information campaigns. In C. T. Salmon (Ed.), *Information campaigns: Balancing social values and social change* (pp. 164–184). Newbury Park, CA: Sage.

Reinharz, S. (1992). *Feminist methods in social research.* New York: Oxford University Press.

Rowan, K. E., Botan, C. H., Kreps, G. L., Samoilenko, S., & Farnsworth, K. (2009). Risk communication education for local emergency managers: Using the CAUSE model for research, education, and outreach. In R. L. Heath & H. D. O'Hair (Eds.), *Handbook of risk and crisis communication* (pp. 168–191). New York: Routledge.

Salmon, C. T. (1990). God understands when the cause is noble. *Gannett Center Journal, 4*(2), 23–34.

Servaes, J. (1999). *Communication for development: One world, multiple cultures.* Cresskill, NJ: Hampton Press.

Sha, B.-L., & Ford, R. (2007). Redefining "requisite variety": The challenge of multiple diversities for the future of public relations. In E. Toth (Ed.), *The future of excellence in public relations and communication management: Challenges for the next generation* (pp. 381–398). Mahwah, NJ: Lawrence Erlbaum.

Shields, S. A. (2008). Gender: An intersectionality perspective. *Sex Roles, 59,* 301–311.

Smith, D. E. (1987). *The everyday world as problematic: A feminist sociology.* Boston: Northeastern University Press.

Sriramesh, K. (2002). The dire need for multiculturalism in public relations education: An Asian perspective. *Journal of Communication Management, 7,* 54–70.

Sriramesh, K. (2003). The missing link: Multiculturalism and public relations education. In K. Sriramesh & D. Verčič (Eds.), *The global public relations handbook: Theory, research, and practice* (pp. 505–522). Mahwah, NJ: Lawrence Erlbaum.

Sriramesh, K. (2006). The relationship between culture and public relations. In E. L. Toth (Ed.), *The future of excellence in public relations and communication management: Challenges for the next generation* (pp. 507–526). Mahwah, NJ: Lawrence Erlbaum.

Stephens, C. (2007). Participation in different fields of practice: Using social theory to understand participants in community health promotion. *Journal of Health Psychology, 12,* 949–960.

Tichenor, P. J., Donohue, G. A., & Olien, C. N. (1970). Mass media flow and differential growth in knowledge. *Public Opinion Quarterly, 34,* 159–170.

Tindall, N. (2007a). *Identity, power, and difference: The management of roles and self among public relations practitioners.* Unpublished doctoral dissertation, University of Maryland, College Park.

Tindall, N. (2007b, August). *Invisible in a visible profession: Lesbian public relations professionals and their roles, responsibilities, and functions in organizations and public relations.* Paper presented at the Association for Education in Journalism and Mass Communication, Washington, DC.

Tindall, N., & Vardeman, J. E. (2008, November). *Complications in segmenting campaign publics: Women of color explain their problems, involvement, and constraints in reading heart disease communication.* Paper presented to the Public Relations Division, National Communication Association, San Diego.

U.S. Environmental Protection Agency. (2009, February 12). *Environmental justice: Frequently asked questions.* Retrieved September 29, 2009, from www.epa.gov/oecaerth/resources/faqs/ej/index.html

van Heerden, G., & Ströh, U. (2005, July). *Exploring postmodern public relations in "Dark Africa."* Paper presented at the 12th International Public Relations Research Symposium, Lake Bled, Slovenia.

Vardeman, J. E. (2005). *How Chinese graduate students make meaning of U.S. public relations education.* Unpublished manuscript.

Vardeman, J. E. (2008). *How teen girls and parents make meaning of a cervical cancer vaccine campaign: Toward a feminist, multicultural critique of health communication.* Unpublished doctoral dissertation, University of Maryland, College Park.

Vardeman, J. E., & Tindall, N. T. J. (2008, August). *"If it's a woman's issue, I pay attention to it": Identity in the Heart Truth campaign.* Top faculty paper presented to the Commission on the Status of Woman, Association for Education in Journalism and Mass Communication, Chicago.

Vargas, L. (1998). Development communication. In M. A. Blanchard (Ed.), *History of the mass media in the United States: An encyclopedia* (pp. 182–184). Chicago: Fitzroy Dearborn.

Viswanath, K., & Finnegan, J. R. (1996). The knowledge gap hypothesis: Twenty-five years later. In B. R. Burleson (Ed.), *Communication yearbook 19* (pp. 187–227). Thousand Oaks, CA: Sage.

Wallack, L., Dorfman, L., Jernigan, D., & Themba, M. (1993). *Media advocacy and public health: Power for prevention.* Newbury Park, CA: Sage.

Waters, R., & Tindall, N. (2007). *Coming out to tell our stories: The career experiences of gay men in public relations.* Paper presented at the annual meeting of the Association for Education in Journalism and Mass Communication, Washington, DC.

Waymer, D., & Heath, R. L. (2007). Emergent agents: The forgotten publics in crisis communication and issues management research. *Journal of Applied Communication Research, 35*(1), 88–108.

Weber, L. (2001). *Understanding race, class, gender, and sexuality: A conceptual framework.* Boston: McGraw-Hill.

West, C., & Fenstermaker, S. (1995). Doing difference. *Gender and Society, 9,* 8–37.

Williams, P. J. (1997). *Seeing a color-blind future: The paradox of race.* New York: Noonday Press.

Zinn, M. B., & Dill, B. T. (1996). Theorizing difference from multiracial feminism. *Feminist Studies, 22,* 321–331.

CHAPTER 16

Does Public Relations Scholarship Have a Place in Race?

Damion Waymer

As I sat down to write this chapter, I struggled to come up with a title for it. "What's in a name?" one might ask. "Everything!" I would reply. An earlier title for this chapter was, "Does Race Have a Place in Public Relations Scholarship?" My response was an emphatic, "Yes!" Isn't it obvious? Globalization and the continuous expansion of transnational corporations present myriad employee and community management issues (often stemming from racial and cultural difference) for public relations professionals (Waymer & Ni, 2009). Moreover, the U.S. population is more diverse than ever before due to the continual influx of ethnically and racially diverse persons. Many organizations provide services to, employ, and have relationships with publics who are members of racial minorities (Stewart & Perlow, 2001). Although it appears that race should have a place in public relations practice and scholarship, it seems to date that few scholars are writing about and studying this diversity, and many of these organizations have not found ways to strategically manage it. As a result, issues and crises involving race and racial discrimination cases are omnipresent in the contemporary United States. And public relations scholars have yet to fully pursue this charge of addressing this important area of research. But if race has a place in public relations, how broad is its scope? Will race be reduced to a variable in a strategic communication campaign effort? Will race only be thought of as dimensions of likeness and similarity so that organizations can craft better "audience-friendly" messages to achieve their own ends?

A more provocative question, however (and the eventual title of this chapter), is whether public relations scholarship has a place in race. Race has a rich literature, and studies that problematize race have a long history. If public relations scholarship has a place in race, what will that look like? I provide two contemporary U.S. examples for consideration.

First, during the summer of 2009, the Creative Steps camp arranged for 65 children—most of whom were black and Hispanic—to swim each Monday afternoon at a private suburban Philadelphia swim club. The director of Creative Steps camp communicated that shortly after she and the group arrived to the swim club, some of the children in her group reported hearing racial comments. A few days later, Creative Steps' money was refunded and the group was no longer allowed to swim at the club. John Duesler, president of the Valley Club, voiced concern that so many children would "change the complexion" or atmosphere of the club. In his and the club's defense, Duesler said that he used a terrible choice of words and that the decision to not allow the Creative Steps camp access to the pool was not motivated by race. The decision was motivated by safety concerns for the large number of children in the pool at one time. Due to public outcry, the Pennsylvania Human Relations Committee launched a formal investigation into the matter.

Some might question whether this is a public relations matter; however, by taking a "does race have a place in public relations scholarship" approach, the question is rather easily addressed. Consider these implications: How does the Valley Club restore its tarnished image? What can the club do to restore lost goodwill? Consider the speed at which this isolated incident in a small Philadelphia suburb became a much larger issue and a crisis situation for the Valley Club. Consider the speed at which seemingly unrelated persons from across the United States mobilized and placed pressure on a regulatory body (the Pennsylvania Human Relations Committee) to "do something" about this perceived injustice. Public relations, however, has far greater, untapped potential. Public relations can do more than just repair images tarnished by racial misunderstandings, address disgruntled publics who are not happy about some racial concern, or contribute to some organization's bottom line by "managing" race responsibly or by demonstrating its corporate social responsibility (CSR)—though these functions are very important. Public relations scholarship can be transformative, enabling scholars to use these theories to contribute more broadly to society and spark a more fruitful societal discussion about race.

Second, in May 2009, former Speaker of the House Newt Gingrich and fellow conservatives such as Rush Limbaugh branded the then Supreme Court justice nominee Sonia Sotomayor a "reverse racist" for her comments that she hoped that a "wise Latina woman with the richness of her experiences would more often than not reach a better conclusion than a white male who hasn't lived that." Some might ask what makes this situation a public relations challenge. In response, I argue that contestable questions of value and fact (components of "issues" in the issue management literature) are at the heart of this issue. The contestable question of value deals with empathy as a valuable emotional trait for a judge. The contestable questions of fact build from the value of empathy. Do different lived experiences correlate with a judge's ability to be more empathetic? Does empathy correlate with the ability to make better judgments as a judge? The reason that Justice Sotomayor's comments were scrutinized so heavily and were subject to criticism, in part, was because various publics arrived at different answers to the aforementioned questions. Although Latino represents a culture and not a race of people, it is important to note that various subsets of the Latino culture (e.g., Mexican Americans) are subject to racism and racially based discrimination in the United States based on perceived biological differences and physical characteristics. As such, critics of Sotomayor (who represents a nonwhite race) suggested that her comments served as a form of reverse racism directed toward white men. These discussions, of what counts as racism, how racism is communicated, and ultimately what role political entities and/or organizations can play in advancing discussions of race, demonstrate the power of public relations in race—if the field will embrace the challenge.

For public relations scholarship to have a place in race, scholars must continue to find ways for public relations scholarship to showcase and to expose the roots of power, the notions of privilege, and the injustice that are by-products of race and racial prejudice. So if public relations scholarship is to have a place in race, then one must explore ways that public relations scholarship might be best fit to problematize race and address societal problems caused in part by matters of race. This chapter is a product of that lofty goal.

Based on these highlighted incidences from the year 2009, it is evident that race still matters in the United States; it matters in people's communities whether they have access to services for which they have paid; it matters in people's schools whether a Latino judge can speak openly about Supreme Court justices, those justices' ages and race, and how those demographic variables might be a factor in how those justices reach their decisions. Race also matters in people's workplaces. The classic case study in many public relations textbooks is Texaco and the "black jelly bean" incident. In short, race continues to be a hot-button issue in the United States, and as such, this chapter provides more discussion about this topic as it relates to public relations scholarship.

This chapter is important because of the financial, business, and societal implications of race. I first demonstrate the financial and business implications of race and public relations. Next, using public relations normative theory such as the fully functioning society theory as a foundation, I argue that public relations managers who deal with crisis, risk, and issues management would be wise to plan for, welcome, and take into account this diversity. Moreover, I argue that the field might be better served if scholars actively pursued the question of whether public relations has a place in race.

Race and CSR: It Makes Good Business Dollars and (Cents) Sense

CSR is the notion that organizations are responsible for addressing matters—whether they be employee, consumer, community, or economic related—that are important to the communities in which they operate (Carroll, 1991, 1999; Ihlen, 2009; May, Cheney, & Roper, 2007). Jacoby (1974), more than three decades ago, argued that the public "has endowed it [corporate social responsibility] with a very broad meaning":

> Thus, when consumers raise their voices in protest against unsafe, faulty or misrepresented products; when employees complain about routinized jobs, bureaucratic paralysis, or inhumane working environments; . . . when protests emanate from university campuses over the failure of corporations to eliminate poverty, hard-core unemployment, racial discrimination, crime and urban decay; when stockholders demand that their companies leave South Africa, boycott Angola, or appoint women, blacks, and youths to their board of directors—all are complaining in one way or another that business is not discharging its social responsibilities. (p. 224)

Today, the breadth of the meaning and society's expectations of what is deemed socially responsible still rings true. Simply put, "social responsibility is an important value among American consumers . . . [and] an essential element for organizations seeking long-term success" (Sellnow & Brand, 2001, p. 293). Thus, for organizations to retain their privileges of operation, they need to assess, audit, and address the social pressures applied by multiple stakeholders (Davenport, 2000; Dawson, 1998). One common pressure applied to many organizations today, from universities to corporations, relates to issues of race.

Corporate social performance (CSP) was introduced as a method for evaluating how well organizations were meeting their corporate social responsibilities (Albinger & Freeman, 2000). Diversity issues/treatment of women and minorities is one of the five most commonly used dimensions of CSP (Luce, Barber, & Hillman, 2001; Sharfman, 1996). Scholars in the field of business have begun assessing what social responsibility activities (including diversity) are valued by the market (Bird, Hall, Momentè, &

Reggiani, 2007) and the potential of financial success for firms that cultivate relationships with diverse stakeholders (Weigand, 2007).

The business management literature has plenty of examples of why understanding matters of diversity in general and race specifically is beneficial for corporations. Similar discussions can be applied to government agencies, and nonprofits, nongovernment organizations, and activists often deal directly on behalf of diverse publics, or exploit bias, dislike, and even hatred for them. In short, understanding diversity is proven to affect organizations' bottom lines. Financial gains, as they relate to business practices and even nonprofit fundraising, should not be the sole reason that public relations scholarship should venture down the path of exploring race. As such, although joining race and public relations makes good dollars and cents, race, especially as it relates to risk, issues, and crisis management, has far broader practical, theoretical, and societal implications.

Race and Communication

Race merits theoretical and practical study because it is an enduring, contested phenomenon with important communicative implications (Allen, 2007). Many communication scholars (Allen, 1995, 2004, 2007; Ashcraft & Allen, 2003; Buzzanell, Waymer, Tagle, & Liu, 2007; Jackson, 2002; Orbe, 1998; Waymer, 2008) argue that race matters. In fact, scholars such as Giroux (2003) have considered race as "one of the most powerful ideological and institutional factors for how identities are categorized and power, material privileges, and resources distributed" (Giroux, 2003, p. 200).

With this said, contemporary organizations are actively seeking to value diversity, usually with race as a high priority, due to population projections about increasing numbers of racial minorities; in fact, visit most major companies' Web sites, and one will find statements about diversity. Simply put, organizations are and can be considered sites where organizational members can develop and implement policies, programs, and training to embrace racial differences and to counteract racism (Allen, 2007). Yet, despite these compelling conditions, communication and public relations scholars in general seldom investigate race.

Normative public relations theory suggests that public relations can be defined as the establishment and management of symmetrical, mutually beneficial relationships between an organization and its myriad publics (Grunig, 2001). Embedded deep in this definition is a suggestion that "diverse publics," as well as their interests and needs, should be addressed. Hon and Brunner (2000) argued that diversity in public relations adds value to society's discourse because it increases the likelihood that concerns will be heard and given regard. As Heath, Lee, and Ni (2009) noted, "A growing assumption is that multiple voices add value to dialogue" (p. 128). And that dialogue must continue and must be meaningful.

Heath (2006) suggested that "the fully functioning theory of public relations argues that it is a force (through reflective research and best practices) to foster community as blended relationships, resource distribution, and shared meanings that advance and yield to enlightened choice" (p. 110). Thus, if scholars use theory to guide the practice and profession, should not theory and practice plan for, prepare for, and include racially diverse citizens and their perspectives—as they can be considered a major component of moving society toward becoming more fully functioning? If we take this perspective, it moves us beyond seeing race as something to be managed by or through public relations to a point where we see public relations as being a theoretically rich vehicle to address an enduring construct that can advance or impede the vision of what Heath (2006) called community. Should not theory be used to address race at its core?

"Race Matters" as Crisis Communication Situations

Crises are studied in great detail in public relations literature (Benoit, 1997; Brinson & Benoit, 1996;

Coombs, 1995, 1999; Hearit, 1994; Seeger, Sellnow, & Ulmer, 1998; Seeger & Ulmer, 2002); however, Waymer and Heath (2007) and Kim and Dutta (2009) asserted that almost overwhelmingly crisis communication research and literature is void of discussions about race, and even when business and communication scholars have explored crises in terms of such issues as race (see Chin et al., 1998; Williams & Olaniran, 2002; Brinson & Benoit, 1999), their focus has been to suggest strategies that may enable organizations to respond to such crises more effectively. Moreover, Baker (2001), in her discussion of race and reputation, warned that fallout from racial discrimination can be severe because companies find themselves responding to crises instead of preventing them; yet, she only offered image restoration strategies and did not use other strategies that would seek to anticipate and minimize racial crises from the outset. There was no mention of strategic issues management or relationship building from the outset. In such analyses, there is little or no attention paid to those communicative efforts designed to avoid such crises or to be socially responsible in such efforts of inclusion and diversity.

According to Millar (2004), "The perception that organizational crises are most frequently fires, explosions, workplace violence, and chemical spills is wrong; it is a misperception of organizations in crisis" (p. 28). Moreover, Millar (2004) found that

> most crises are neither accidental nor sudden. Rather they reveal questionable, illegal, or unethical activity by someone within the organization frequently involving other members of the organization or people who routinely interact with organizational personnel. Not only does the problem exist, someone in the organization knows, or has neglected to learn, of its existence. The problem is not lack of knowledge, but rather an unwillingness to report the problem or resolve it. (pp. 28–29)

In fact, Millar (2004) found that there had been a 26.4% increase in class action lawsuits that organizations faced between the years 1990 and 2000. This shift, in part, might be attributed to what Lerbinger (1997) called a crisis of skewed management values. Moreover, issues of race and racial discrimination likely would fall under this domain.

Lerbinger (1997) stated that crises of skewed management values are often caused when managers "favor short-term economic gain and neglect broader social values and stakeholders other than investors" (p. 186). Moreover, this situation of unbalanced values stems from "the classical business creed that focuses on the interests of stockholders and tends to view the interests of its other stakeholders—such as customers, employees, and the community—not only as subsidiary but as relatively unimportant" (pp. 186–187). There are noncorporate organizations such as governmental entities that can both suffer from crisis and practice public relations. These types of organizations, however, suffer the sharpest wrath from concerned publics, when their actions seem to be discriminatory on the basis of race or class—for the government is held to the standard of being "of the people, by the people, and for the people" (Waymer, 2009). So how can a government that is for the people discriminate against the people or allow questionable, unethical, and illegal conditions to linger? Herein lies the role (or in the case of the following example, the failing to fulfill the role) of risk management.

Effective Risk Management: Building "True Community" With Racial Minorities

Some scholars have argued that society might exist essentially for the collective management of risk (Douglas, 1992). If organized society is not managing to fulfill its duty, it is challenged vehemently by critics. Kim and Dutta (2009) argued that Hurricane Katrina victims were subject to conditions of vulnerability long before the hurricane made landfall; the distressed communities of New Orleans owed "their circumstances to decades of politics and policies that perpetuated racism and exclusionary political and economic practices" (p. 152). They argued for a rethinking of crisis communication; the authors articulated a viewpoint that challenges practitioners and scholars alike to hear and appreciate the voices of the subaltern. These are the individuals whose voices are largely absent in public discourse, and their structural environment is often characterized by extreme lack of resources (Beverly, 1999; Dutta-Bergman, 2004, 2005). These voices should and must be heard—especially in an age where many voices for members of these populations and voices that have been muted traditionally for a host of reasons are emerging with frequency (see Waymer, 2007; Waymer & Heath, 2007, for a discussion of emergent agents)—as these voices allow for a more thorough and effective management of risk. Moreover, Waymer and Heath (2007) noted that organizations should be reflective, inclusive, and proactive when dealing with marginalized (and oftentimes racialized) publics because "engaging in reflection, inclusion, and being proactive also might spare the responsible organization from moments of embarrassment should these voices come to emerge with a vengeance" (p. 106).

Vengeance is related to Sandman's (1993) work that categorizes risk as outrage (cultural, personal view) and to a lesser degree hazard (technical assessment). Moreover, Heath and Palenchar (2009) argued that few strategic issues management challenges "loom as ominously as those that arise from risks people suffer or fear they suffer" (p. 310). As such, from a cultural theory perspective (Douglas, 1992), it is paramount for organizations to engage in meaningful dialogue with minority publics to gain a better understanding of what risks they deem important and how organizations can work together with them to collectively manage these risks. Race must be thought of as more than a variable. Because it is such a divisive construct, by exploring matters of race, public relations has the potential to be an applied contributor to the problematizing of race. One current community challenge that highlights this discussion of race, risk, issues, and risk/crisis management and demonstrates the potential role of public relations in race is the omnipresent debates surrounding environmental racism.

"Race Matters" as Issues Management

An issue can be defined as a contestable question of fact, value, or policy (Heath & Palenchar, 2009). What contestable questions of fact, value, or policy are most pertinent to racial minorities? The answer is most likely issues of limited access and issues of systemic exclusion.

Environmental racism is often defined as the intentional or unintentional location of hazardous waste sites, landfills, incinerators, and polluting industries in communities inhabited mainly by minorities, including, but not limited to, African Americans, Hispanics, Native Americans, Asians, migrant farm workers, and the working poor. These groups are particularly vulnerable because they are perceived as passive publics who will not fight back against the poisoning of their neighborhoods in fear that it may jeopardize jobs and economic survival. They do not tend to organize or fight back (likely due to a lack of resources) as do their white counterparts (for a related discussion, see "not in my backyard," or NIMBY, discussed in Chapters 31 and 32, this volume).

As such, in an attempt to address contemporary issues and challenges, public relations scholars have begun to seek the input from diverse publics so that there can be a better collective management of risk. For example, Heath et al. (2009) surveyed more than 600 white, black, Asian, and Hispanic Americans in Houston, Texas. What they found was that about half of the people surveyed did not feel adequately prepared to respond during times of crises—be it a chemical plant explosion or natural disaster, to name a few. Moreover, of those who did feel adequately prepared to respond, minority publics voiced that diverse voices (source similarity and message sensitivity) increased residents' sense of self-, expert, and community preparedness—meaning that if citizens have access to risk and crisis information that is from sources similar to them and stated in messages that are sensitive to them, they feel more prepared to deal with crisis emergency response. This line of research is not focused on an organization's bottom line; rather, the focus is on being more inclusive to welcome perspectives from minority perspectives so that there can be further efforts to realize a more fully functioning society.

Conclusion

To date, the scholarly literature provides tactics for organizations to use to deal with race in general, and it is usually as a result of some crisis that has manifested. These strategies are often reactive, and many of them involve the use of rhetorical strategies, such as shifting the blame, scapegoating, or evading responsibility through claims of defeasibility, to repair a tarnished image once such crises occur. There is very little work that highlights the import of diversity and diverse perspectives as it relates to effective issues, crisis, and risk management.

Race is a serious matter, and it must be taken seriously by public relations and crisis communication scholars. Due to the volatile nature of race matters, organizations cannot afford "not" to pay earlier attention to such diversity concerns. Moreover, society cannot afford or be allowed to continue to marginalize the voices of key societal members. Anderson (1996) argued that as communication scholars, the choice is ours; we can "either participate in the meanings that produce the deepening violence, the racial injustice, the sexual harassment, the conditions of the homelessness, the inequalities of our society or we actively resist and oppose them at the sites of their production" (p. 197). Calling for a discussion of whether public relations has a place in race is one way to engage in such resistance. Scholars engaging in and supporting activism is another.

Activist pressures often come into play as these groups attempt to influence the public policy process. For an example of activist pressures stemming from matters of race, one need look no further than the creation and continuation of the National Association for the Advancement of Colored People (NAACP) and its (along with other organizations') involvement during and its influence in effecting the outcome of the Civil Rights Movement. The public relations efforts of the NAACP, including its publication called *The Crisis*, help the organization continue protecting and enhancing the civil rights of African Americans and other minorities. From a public relations scholarly perspective, Heath and Waymer (2009) showed how Frederick Douglass in his Fourth of July address spoke against slavery and addressed the perplexing paradox (in the eyes of freed slaves and slaves) in the United States called Independence Day. Douglass emerged as a leading voice against slavery, but he was not alone in his efforts. There is no doubt that Douglass's articulate argument won the hearts of some. It is that open discussion, especially as it pertains to matters of race, that is paramount for the advancement of public relations and the society. But a more important observation with public relations implications is that it appears that for these coordinated activist efforts to have broad-reaching societal implications, there must be a professional voice in terms of balancing the needs of a diverse population and the desires of the other (organization, government, society at large).

Public relations scholars have recently observed that this discipline and this profession can help organizations be reflective, which, in turn, enhances their managerial abilities and perspectives (van Ruler & Verčič, 2005). Embracing racial differences—making diversity a key component of organizations and changing antiquated organizational cultures—is probably the best way to foster mutually beneficial relationships and to help society become more fully functioning.

Implications for Future Research

While this chapter focused on the area of race and public relations in society, it did not address such matters in the profession itself—with the exception of highlighting in the Heath et al. (2009) study how diverse publics wanted and valued a similar voice and a sensitive voice to communicate with them during times of risk and crisis. This seems to support the call for hiring and training diverse persons in public relations—not as a tool but as a means of enabling voices to be heard that are often forgotten. This will hopefully better serve society and the organizations where these persons are employed. But to be sure that these racially diverse persons are not seen as mere tools, further steps should be taken to problematize race. First, how do these diverse persons feel about "diversity" in their own organizations where they are employed? Do they feel like tokens? While corporate Web sites provide a wealth of information about an organization's diversity initiatives and are the easiest and probably the most widely recognized way to find information about an organization, accounts from the individuals who create diversity plans and critical dialogue about those plans from the employees they are made to benefit and the publics they are designed to reach would create a much more complete representation of diversity and public relations management. As such, a possible study might ask members of minority public relations organizations, such as the National Black Public Relations Society (NBPRS) and the Hispanic Public Relations Association (HPRA), whether the organizations they work for have diversity initiatives, whether they perceive such initiatives (if present) to be more than mere window dressing, whether they perceive the organizations that they work for to be committed to diversity, and if those organizations are prepared for or have the means to mitigate and deal with potential crises of race that might arise. Finally, the study proposes asking these diverse members what thoughts they have that might help their companies make diversity a meaningful and integral part of their organizational culture. This is important because most crises of race emerge from some issue that is left unaddressed in an organization's culture. Simply put, it is better to gather input from diverse publics prior to a crisis and embrace those perspectives as opposed to feeling their wrath and scorn, and experiencing public scrutiny after a crisis manifests itself. Image restoration strategies that instruct organizations about how to deal with crises of race are valuable, but they should be the organization's last resort—being socially responsible and caring about what matters to diverse publics should always be the higher ranking option. Does public relations scholarship have a place in race? Yes! And it's time that scholarly efforts reflect that position.

References

Albinger, H. S., & Freeman, S. J. (2000). Corporate social performance and attractiveness as an employer to different job seeking populations. *Journal of Business Ethics, 28,* 243–253.

Allen, B. (1995). "Diversity" and organizational communication. *Journal of Applied Communication Research, 23,* 143–155.

Allen, B. J. (2004). *Difference matters: Communicating social identity.* Long Grove, IL: Waveland.

Allen, B. J. (2007). Theorizing communication and race. *Communication Monographs, 74,* 259–264.

Anderson, J. A. (1996). *Communication theory: Epistemological foundations.* New York: Guilford Press.

Ashcraft, K. L., & Allen, B. J. (2003). The racial foundations of organizational communication. *Communication Theory, 13,* 3–38.

Baker, G. F. (2001). Race and reputation: Restoring image beyond the crisis. In R. L. Heath (Ed.), *Handbook of public relations* (pp. 513–520). Thousand Oaks, CA: Sage.

Benoit, W. L. (1997). Image restoration discourse and crisis communication. *Public Relations Review, 23,* 177–186.

Beverly, J. (1999). *Subalternity and representation: Arguments in cultural theory.* Durham, NC: Duke University Press.

Bird, R., Hall, A. D., Momentè, F., & Reggiani, F. (2007). What corporate social responsibility activities are valued by the market? *Journal of Business Ethics, 76,* 189–206.

Brinson, S. L., & Benoit, W. L. (1996). Attempting to restore a public image: Dow Corning and the breast implant crisis. *Communication Quarterly, 44,* 29–41.

Brinson, S. L., & Benoit, W. L. (1999). The tarnished star: Restoring Texaco's damaged public image. *Management Communication Quarterly, 12,* 483–510.

Buzzanell, P., Waymer, D., Tagle, M., & Liu, M. (2007). Different transitions into working motherhood: Discourses of Asian, Hispanic, and African American women. *Journal of Family Communication, 7,* 195–220.

Carroll, A. B. (1991). The pyramid of corporate social responsibility: Toward the moral management of organizational stakeholders. *Business Horizons, 34*(4), 39–48.

Carroll, A. B. (1999). Corporate social responsibility: Evolution of a definitional construct. *Business & Society, 38,* 268–295.

Chin, T., Naidu, S., Ringel, J., Snipes, W., Bienvenu, S. K., & Desilva, J. (1998). Denny's: Communicating amidst a crisis. *Business Communication Quarterly, 61*(1), 180–196.

Coombs, W. T. (1995). Choosing the right words: The development of guidelines for the selection of the "appropriate" crisis-response strategies. *Management Communication Quarterly, 8,* 447–476.

Coombs, W. T. (1999). *Ongoing crisis communication: Planning, managing, and responding.* Thousand Oaks, CA: Sage.

Davenport, K. (2000). Corporate citizenship: A stakeholder approach for defining corporate social performance and identifying measures for assessing it. *Business and Society, 39,* 210–219.

Dawson, E. (1998). The relevance of social audit for Oxfam GB. *Journal of Business Ethics, 17,* 1457–1469.

Douglas, M. (1992). *Risk and blame.* London: Routledge.

Dutta-Bergman, M. J. (2004). The unheard voices of Santalis: Communicating about health from the margins of India. *Communication Theory, 14,* 237–263.

Dutta-Bergman, M. J. (2005). Civil society and communication: Not so civil after all. *Journal of Public Relations Research, 17,* 267–289.

Giroux, H. A. (2003). Spectacles of race and pedagogies of denial: Anti-black racist pedagogy under the reign of neoliberalism. *Communication Education, 52,* 191–211.

Grunig, J. E. (2001). Two-way symmetrical public relations: Past, present, and future. In R. L. Heath (Ed.), *Handbook of public relations* (pp. 11–30). Thousand Oaks, CA: Sage.

Hearit, K. M. (1994). Apologies and public relations crises at Chrysler, Toshiba, and Volvo. *Public Relations Review, 20,* 113–126.

Heath, R. L. (2006). Onward into more fog: Thoughts on public relations' research directions. *Journal of Public Relations Research, 18*(2), 93–114.

Heath, R. L., Lee, J., & Ni, L. (2009). Crisis and risk approaches to emergency management planning and communication: The role of similarity and sensitivity. *Journal of Public Relations Research, 21,* 123–141.

Heath, R. L., & Palenchar, M. J. (2009). *Strategic issues management: Organizations and public policy challenges* (2nd ed.). Thousand Oaks, CA: Sage.

Heath, R. L., & Waymer, D. (2009). Activist public relations: A case study of Frederick Douglass' "Fourth of July Address." In R. L. Heath, E. L. Toth, & D. Waymer (Eds.), *Rhetorical and critical approaches to public relations II* (pp. 195–215). New York: Routledge.

Hon, L. C., & Brunner, B. (2000). Diversity issues and public relations. *Journal of Public Relations Research, 12,* 309–340.

Ihlen, O. (2009). Good environmental citizens? The green rhetoric of corporate social responsibility. In R. L. Heath, E. L. Toth, & D. Waymer (Eds.), *Rhetorical and critical approaches to public relations II* (pp. 360–374). New York: Routledge.

Jackson, R. L. (2002). Exploring African American identity negotiation in the academy: Toward a transformative vision of African American communication scholarship. *Howard Journal of Communication, 13,* 43–57.

Jacoby, N. H. (1974). The corporation as social activist. In S. P. Sethi (Ed.), *The unstable ground: Corporate social policy in a dynamic society* (pp. 224–244). Los Angeles: Melville.

Kim, I., & Dutta, M. J. (2009). Studying crisis communication from the subaltern studies framework: Grassroots activism in the wake of Hurricane Katrina. *Journal of Public Relations Research, 21,* 143–164.

Lerbinger, O. (1997). *The crisis manager: Facing risk and responsibility.* Mahwah, NJ: Lawrence Erlbaum.

Luce, R. A., Barber, A. E., & Hillman, A. J. (2001). Good deeds and misdeeds: A mediated model of the effect of corporate social performance on organizational attractiveness. *Business and Society, 40,* 397–415.

May, S. K., Cheney, G., & Roper, J. (Eds.). (2007). *The debate over corporate social responsibility.* New York: Oxford University Press.

Millar, D. P. (2004). Exposing the errors: An examination of the nature of organizational crises. In D. P. Millar & R. L. Heath (Eds.), *Responding to crisis: A rhetorical approach to crisis communication* (pp. 19–31). Mahwah, NJ: Lawrence Erlbaum.

Orbe, M. P. (1998). From the standpoint(s) of traditionally muted groups: Explicating a co-cultural communication theoretical model. *Communication Theory, 8,* 1–26.

Sandman, P. M. (1993). *Responding to community outrage: Strategies for effective risk communication.* Fairfax, VA: American Industrial Hygiene Association.

Seeger, M. W., Sellnow, T. L., & Ulmer, R. R. (1998). Communication, organization, and crisis. In M. E. Roloff (Ed.), *Communication yearbook 21* (pp. 231–275). Thousand Oaks, CA: Sage.

Seeger, M. W., & Ulmer, R. R. (2002). A post-crisis discourse of renewal: The case of Malden Mills and Cole Hardwoods. *Journal of Applied Communication Research, 30,* 126–142.

Sellnow, T. L., & Brand, J. D. (2001). Establishing the structure of reality for an industry: Model and anti-model arguments as advocacy in Nike's crisis communication. *Journal of Applied Communication Research, 29,* 278–295.

Sharfman, M. (1996). The construct validity of the Kinder, Lydenberg, and Domini social performance ratings data. *Journal of Business Ethics, 15,* 287–296.

Stewart, L. D., & Perlow, R. (2001). Applicant race, job status, and racial attitude as predictors of employment discrimination. *Journal of Business and Psychology, 16,* 259–279.

van Ruler, B., & Verčič, D. (2005). Reflective communication management, future ways for public relations research. In P. J. Kalbfleisch (Ed.), *Communication yearbook 29* (pp. 239–273). Mahwah, NJ: Lawrence Erlbaum.

Waymer, D. (2007). Minority opinions go public: Implications for online issues management and the spiral of silence hypothesis. In S. C. Duhé (Ed.), *New media and public relations* (pp. 77–87). New York: Peter Lang.

Waymer, D. (2008). A man: An autoethnographic analysis of black male identity negotiation. *Qualitative Inquiry, 14,* 968–989.

Waymer, D. (2009). Liberty and justice for all? The paradox of governmental rhetoric. *Communication Quarterly, 57,* 334–351.

Waymer, D., & Heath, R. L. (2007). Emergent agents: The forgotten publics in crisis communication and issues management research. *Journal of Applied Communication Research, 35,* 88–108.

Waymer, D., & Ni, L. (2009). Connecting organizations and their employee publics: The rhetorical analysis of employee-organization relationships (EOR). In R. L. Heath, E. L. Toth, & D. Waymer (Eds.), *Rhetorical and critical approaches to public relations II* (pp. 216–232). New York: Routledge.

Weigand, R. A. (2007). Organization diversity, profits and returns in U.S. firms. *Problems and Perspectives in Management, 5,* 69–83.

Williams, D. E., & Olaniran, B. A. (2002). Crisis communication in racial issues. *Journal of Applied Communication Research, 30,* 293–313.

CHAPTER 17

Feminist Scholarship and Its Contributions to Public Relations

Brenda J. Wrigley

Feminist scholarship is sometimes viewed with skepticism and misunderstanding about its methodology, purpose, and conclusions. Since the 1980s, feminist scholarship has contributed to the understanding of the public relations profession and the challenges faced by both men and women working in this field. Understanding the origins of this research and the evolution of feminist scholarship in public relations provides a context for future researchers who seek to explain the challenges and opportunities posed by the increasing feminization—majority female composition—of the field.

Emergence of Feminist Scholars

In the past 25 years, feminist theory and methodology, the focus of feminist scholarship by listening to women's voices and experience, make up the framework for this research. Issues affecting women in the workplace are considered in the context in which they take place. Treichler and Wartella (1986) outlined a number of concerns addressed by feminist theory and methodology:

> (1) a more sophisticated and pointed analysis of power relations, (2) a social theory which attempts to account for the social and cultural construction of sexual difference, (3) a commitment to lived experience which links communication to the contexts in which it occurs, (4) a theoretical analysis which links differences of gender to those of class, age, race, and ethnicity, and (5) an explicit agenda for social change. (p. 1)

Feminist researchers have adopted strategies for shifting the debate and recapturing the conversations about women's lives to transform them into works more reflective of women's experience and standpoint.

> The phrase "standpoint epistemology" has become a central notion in feminist work in these fields, because it refers to both the

> importance of perspective and experience to conceptions of truth and to the existence of differing concepts of knowledge for people of differing experiences. (Cirksena & Cuklanz, 1992, p. 40)

Even among feminist scholars, there is a continuing debate about the merits of standpoint epistemology. Mathison (1997) suggested that although it is important to acknowledge some of the biases that have influenced earlier research, there are inherent problems with looking at issues strictly from a women's standpoint. She cautioned that what may result is not a representation of women's real experience but rather a distortion based on feminist beliefs.

> What seems important is a clear acknowledgement of the frame of reference of the researcher and a statement of honesty about using research to bring about social change. These are basic tenets of feminist scholarship. This approach acknowledges the patriarchal nature of traditional academic research approaches and eschews them for an approach designed to allow women to express their own experiences for themselves. (Punch, 1994)

A growing group of feminist communication scholars emerged during the 1980s. Among them, Lana F. Rakow (1986), whose contributions have been important and numerous, insisted that gender be better defined, and that we look to feminist theory as a framework for gender research in communication. Rakow (1992) felt that it is important to draw on many different disciplines, including sociology, history, and philosophy, to develop communication gender research frameworks:

> We feminist scholars in communication are, in turn, making a substantial contribution to feminist theory, even while we undertake two major challenges. One is to insist that scholars in our own field not only recognize the existence of feminist work but that they also be held accountable for it, preventing feminist scholarship from being marginalized into simply another approach to studying communication. A second challenge is to complete our own internal revolution, accounting for and theorizing our own political, epistemological, and cultural differences as women and as feminists. (p. 3)

Rakow (1989) viewed the progress in feminist scholarship as remarkable, given the relatively short period of time since its beginnings. She believes that for feminist scholarship in media studies to move forward, women must become more aware of other feminist scholars in the field, must participate in the discourse, must collaborate with other feminists, and must create new visions for the changes they wish to see take place. Cirksena and Cuklanz (1992) concurred with Rakow:

> Feminist theories have much to offer the study of communication. . . . Feminists have proposed alternatives: . . . integration; valorizing the female; and rejecting binarisms for more multifaceted ways of thinking about the world. (pp. 18–37)

Steeves's (1987) work outlined four bodies of feminist theory: radical feminism, liberal feminism, Marxist feminism, and socialist feminism. Radical feminism states that biological differences between men and women are assumed. Some of this type of feminist work promotes so-called radical alternatives, such as separatism and lesbian communities where women create their own language, have children by benefit of science rather than traditional intercourse, and develop and employ separate feminist media channels. Radical feminism's more subjective methodologies include depth interviews, participant observation, consciousness-raising, and a variety of other qualitative methods. Some radical feminists argue that only women should do research about women. Steeves noted that radical feminism lacks a body of systematic research.

Steeves (1987) traced liberal feminism's roots to liberal philosophy and economic considerations. The most widely represented of the feminist theories, liberal feminism has often championed causes such as the right to vote, to own property, and to attain equal pay and fair employment policies. Liberal feminists, Steeves noted, want to work within the structure (not throw out the structure, as radical feminists wish to do); they believe that sound arguments will create the changes needed in society. Liberal feminists use quantitative methodology, including content analysis, often examining the number of women represented, the stereotypes, and the depictions that devalue women (p. 101).

Theories used by liberal feminists include agenda setting, cultivation, social learning, and modeling theory. The liberal feminist literature contains historical studies from a chiefly *compensatory feminist* perspective, where the stories of isolated, successful, and championing women are noted.

Marxist feminism examines class oppression and the capitalist system's oppression of women. Marxist feminism advocates for wholesale social change, which would include radical economic change as well. The capitalist system and ideologies, which support and reinforce it, play off one another in mass media, creating a dominant reading of texts (i.e., one that reinforces the dominant ideology of capitalism) (Steeves, 1987, p. 113).

Socialist feminism embraces a similar philosophy but adds that the patriarchy contributes to oppression. Socialist feminism urges alliances between feminists and other oppressed groups to achieve equality. Methodologies commonly employed include critical scholarship and qualitative methods. Socialist feminism was strongly influenced by British critical cultural studies. Textual analysis, which features hegemonic, negotiated, and oppositional readings of texts, is a cornerstone of socialist feminist research. Semiotics is often used in socialist feminist research, particularly using psychological theories like those of Lacan, who characterized the displaying of body parts as objectifying the female body, a theory known as the *male gaze* (Steeves, 1987, p. 112).

Steeves (1987) contended that no one feminist theory will suffice. She was, however, encouraged by the number of young scholars examining the feminist theoretical literature and approaching communication studies using feminist theories. More theory building, she added, is clearly needed. Mere counting of representations is not enough; we must examine the theoretical foundations for those representations. Only then can we take them apart and put them back together in a way that works to change women's traditional devaluation.

Pioneering Public Relations Gender Research

In 1986, a landmark research report by Cline et al. brought our attention to the increasing numbers of women in public relations. The study, *The Velvet Ghetto: The Impact of the Increasing Percentage of Women in Public Relations and Business Communication*, is a classic examination of the public relations and communications workforces and how women were faring in those fields. The study examined the impact of having greater percentages of women in the communications profession and what this feminization of the field means for salary and status of those women:

> The most serious impact is an economic one. While some economists contend that the depressed salaries in women's fields are a result of the overcrowding of women into a profession, thus raising supply over the demand, there appears to be a direct relationship between a job's sex typing and its wage-status ranking. In fact, one researcher argues that it is sex segregation, not sex discrimination (unequal pay for equal work) that accounts for the bulk of the male-female earnings differential. (pp. 1–3)

One finding of the *Velvet Ghetto* study was that women take the first step in their own discrimination by self-selecting technician roles (supporting roles, as opposed to managerial roles). The study rested on three premises:

1. Women are more likely to perceive themselves as filling a technical rather than a managerial role.
2. Women are paid substantially less than men, even when other variables are controlled for.
3. When other professions have gone from male-dominated to female dominated, those professions have all diminished in salary and status. (Cline et al., 1986, p. II-1)

The study's results were most disheartening for women. They were entering technician roles in increasing numbers and were paid less than men, and their gender was the strongest predictor of low salary, even when controlling for other factors such as education and experience. Salaries were $6,000 to $30,000 per year lower, on average, for women. Over a lifetime, salary differentials could amount to a more than million-dollar price tag for being a woman (Cline et al., 1986, V-2).

But the news got worse. The study also found that the route to top management was *not* through the communications or public relations department. Furthermore, because of increasing feminization in the field, and socialization about gender stereotypes, women were being excluded from management jobs (Cline et al., 1986, V-3–V-4).

The *Velvet Ghetto* researchers found other factors at work, including confusion about the role and function of the communications department; hiring bias; the exclusion of women from the so-called good ol' boy network; and perceptions of women as being inferior managers but better nurturers, being emotional rather than rational, being sidetracked by childbearing, and being unwilling or unfamiliar with learning how to be a team player (Cline et al., 1986, V-4–V-8).

The authors concluded that a number of factors are causing depressed salaries and status for women in communications. The two most important are undervaluing of the communications role (and feminization of the field, which results in salary depression and status diminution) and the socialization process, which steers women to self-select a technical role, avoiding management as a career option and aspiration.

The *Velvet Ghetto* study explored several major themes with regard to women in communications management and the barriers to their advancement. From the 1986 study's report, key feminization themes included "adverse impact of women on the field of public relations; the overt bias favoring men over women; the socialization problems of women who want careers; and themes concerning women's personalities" (Toth, 1989, p. 71).

In 1989, the International Association of Business Communicators (IABC) published the follow-up study, *Beyond the Velvet Ghetto*. Wilma Mathews, Chair of the IABC Research Foundation, led off the report with a review of how the first *Velvet Ghetto* study had been received:

> People who read about or listened to the Velvet Ghetto results reacted vehemently, angrily or passively to the word that the public relations/communication profession is in serious danger of losing status, prestige and power. Since the team and Foundation members have continued for four years to spread the word of concern, we'd had an opportunity to look at these reactions over time and discern if any patterns exist . . . [M]uch of the problem of inequality is rooted in perceptions that there is no problem. If there is a pattern, that is it: a flat, almost frightening denial that a problem exists. If perception is reality, then the perception of the lack of a problem becomes the reality. (Mathews, 1989, p. 1)

Survey results from the 1989 study included these conclusions:

- Having a higher percentage of women in public relations and business communication was depressing salaries and reducing the influence of the field.

- For women, their gender worked against them: they faced double standards, unequal opportunities for advancement, and lower salaries than those paid to men, and suffered from sex discrimination problems unique to women.
- Bias was pervasive with regard to issues of gender and levels of motivation, commitment, and sacrifice for those in management and those aspiring to management.
- A major salary gap still existed between men and women in these fields, with men making at least $15,000 to $30,000 per year more than women. (Toth & Cline, 1989)

In writing about the study's findings, Mathews (1988) highlighted suggestions for women in public relations, including being more proactive about networking and mentoring, working to combat lethargy, and striving to work with other women to address glass ceiling issues (p. 28).

Fagenson's (1992) subsequent research found that gender was not a factor in protégés' need for power and achievement. Tam, Dozier, Lauzen, and Real (1995) examined how mentoring relationships can affect career advancement. Their 1995 study suggested that same-sex mentoring pairings result in a more intensive mentoring process, but superior mentoring by women in management resulted in less advancement for their subordinates than did mentoring by male superiors (p. 259).

In a follow-up article to the *Beyond the Velvet Ghetto* study, Toth and Cline (1991) examined the issues addressed in the 1989 study. They concluded that there was certainly a salary disparity between men and women in public relations and business communication and that a double standard existed for men and women in terms of opportunities for advancement. Their study ended on an ambivalent note:

> Despite career inequities, the field of public relations seems welcoming to women where other occupations do not. In public relations, women seem to have found options for such life choices as work, marriage, and family. Women do perceive that salary, advancement, and treatment inequities exist in this field and that they must make more and different sacrifices than men to achieve senior-level positions. However, they are still choosing to work in public relations. Further research should focus on why women make this career choice. (p. 174)

Recognizing public relations was not the only profession to suffer from salary and promotion inequities for women, the Public Relations Society of America (PRSA) nonetheless realized the leadership role the profession could play in building an understanding of the issue; public relations sees itself as a leading advocate for mutual understanding and conflict resolution. In 1991, the Women in Public Relations Task Force released its report on gender issues in American public relations, *Under the Glass Ceiling: An Analysis of Gender Issues in American Public Relations.* This study combined a nationwide survey of more than 1,000 public relations professionals with focus groups of both men and women (Wright, Grunig, Springston, & Toth, 1991).

Not surprisingly, this PRSA task force study also concluded that gender discrimination was a very real problem in public relations in the United States. The salary gap was particularly noticeable after the first 4 years in the field. While finding that the wage gap between men and women might be narrowing a bit, the researchers remained generally pessimistic about women's prospects in the field. Women were generally less positive about their current jobs and less optimistic for their future in their current jobs. Women, overall, reported a higher incidence of sex discrimination than did men (Wright et al., 1991):

> Women are professionally oppressed and are entrenched in a secondary status when compared with men. Women strongly believe sexual harassment exists in public relations. In most cases women perceived the gender inadequacies to be greater throughout the field of public relations than they are within their current organization. (pp. 16–17)

Men in the PRSA survey commented on their resentment of affirmative action policies, which they believed sometimes allowed women to be hired unfairly. Women expressed their frustration about women's limited advancement opportunities. Roles for practitioners took two main forms: technician and manager. Women were often relegated to a technician's role, resulting in lower salaries and greatly increased frustrations for women (Wright et al., 1991).

Focus group research conducted with separate groups of men and women bore out the earlier skepticism men had expressed over just how bad things really are for women in public relations. Distrust of the survey results was a common male response; women, however, reinforced the survey results and suggested reasons why they were as they were. Among the factors contributing to the glass ceiling, institutional factors within organizations were noted. A kind of "blame the victim" syndrome, expressed by both men and women, indicated that women would continue to receive lower salaries as long as they didn't insist that they be treated better in salary negotiations. Women said that family and home responsibilities were different for them and believed that a choice between work and family was essential for success in the workplace. Some expressed having paid the price of giving up a personal life to maintain success in the workplace. The study concluded with the importance of addressing these issues for both men and women in the profession, indicating that they will suffer and the profession as a whole will be diminished by unfair treatment (Wright et al., 1991). This notion of work-life balance will come up in later studies as feminist scholarship in public relations progresses.

In 1995, Linda Childers Hon examined discrimination against female public relations practitioners and urged academic researchers to look beyond dichotomies, much as Creedon (1991) has done to explain what's going on for women in public relations. Women frustrated by an inability to be treated fairly in the corporate world are urged to strike out on their own and start their own businesses (Hon, 1995).

Hon's 1995 research also suggested that women should recognize the socialization process at work that devalues women and their contributions. Scholarship about women will serve to enlighten and inspire public relations students about the future of women in the profession. Educators should prepare women honestly and openly for what lies ahead.

Summary of Early Studies

As this review has indicated, several major early studies looked at gender issues in public relations. The glass ceiling is a recurring theme. Gender discrimination and salary disparities are a recurring theme in studies conducted between the mid-1980s and the late 1990s. Underlying these themes is feminization of the field (the increasing number of women in public relations resulting in women making up a majority in the field). This feminization theme is often characterized by those in the field as a self-fulfilling prophecy, in that women self-select technician roles and, therefore, participate unwittingly in their own discrimination.

The link between gender and salaries is clear and has been shown in all the studies reviewed here. Yet another pattern emerging is the clear denial by males participating in these studies that gender inequities are as great as women have claimed (Toth & Cline, 1991). Even faced with hard numbers, both men and women deny that inequities are as pronounced as the research indicates. This interesting phenomenon is highlighted in Wrigley's (2002) study of the glass ceiling in public relations.

One factor that may create cracks in the glass ceiling is turbulent economic times, which may force organizations to rely on public relations more than ever, thus giving women an opportunity to advance. Yet, despite this hopeful prediction, research indicates this has not happened. Women are still kept out of managerial roles in disproportionate numbers (J. E. Grunig, 1992; L. A. Grunig, Toth, & Hon, 2001).

Playing by male rules is another strategy some researchers have suggested. If men made the rules and women understand the rules, then women can use the rules to their advantage. Creedon (1991, 1993b) and Hon (1995) have asked whether women really want to play by the male rules (i.e., is the "prize" of advancing to management really such a great thing after all?).

Playing by male rules includes networking, finding a mentor, and redoubling efforts to have more energy to tackle the problems created by gender inequities. These strategies have worked for men, so why won't they work for women? One reason why these strategies may not be working is that they do not address the larger issues of socialization and the resulting institutional barriers in place to prevent women from being promoted. When women improve their salary positions, they sometimes experience backlash in the form of hostility from men; some studies indicate men cry "reverse discrimination" when affirmative action policies benefit women.

What Creedon (1991, 1993a, 1993b, 1993c) and Hon (1995) have suggested is that we need to rid ourselves of just thinking in terms of dichotomies (technician vs. manager) and instead begin thinking about job satisfaction and the nature of roles in public relations work.

Public Relations Roles Research

Broom's (1982) early work in roles research in public relations demonstrated that women were outnumbered by men in managerial roles; women were more often technicians. Salaries for men and women were significantly different, and gender was a strong predictor of role. Subsequent studies tried controlling for several variables, such as education, years of experience, and type of organization, but these variables were not the predictor of salary; gender was (Dozier, Chapo, & Sullivan, 1983; Theus, 1985; Turk, 1986). Similar findings resulted when women in the Canadian public relations industry were studied (Scrimger, 1985).

Broom's (1982) manager/technician dichotomy has persisted in public relations roles research. Roles for practitioners surveyed by PRSA in 1991 took two main forms: technician and manager. Women were found to be often relegated to a technician's role, resulting in lower salaries and greatly increased frustrations (Wright et al., 1991, p. 25).

Understanding of roles enactment and the relationship of gender to roles, salary, and status is a major contribution to the research in public relations. However, just as the *Excellence Study* has helped frame our thinking in public relations, so has roles research set up a dichotomy that limits our thinking. To the extent that roles research helps us explore gender issues, it has value; when it limits our ability to create other models—to examine the concept of role as more of a continuous variable—it tends to restrict our thinking. This limits the possibilities practitioners may envision in shaping new working roles that fit their definitions of job satisfaction and their talents and abilities (Dozier, Grunig, & Grunig, 1995).

The literature review for the 1991 *Excellence Study* addressed a number of explanations for how roles are developed, acknowledging that they probably are the result of a complex societal process. The study noted that biological determinism and its influence on popular notions of male aggression are contributors. Organizational reinforcement of male attributes, socialization for women and men, contextual rewards such as interpersonal relationships and working conditions, risk-taking versus risk-averse behaviors, and gender stereotypes all contribute to roles enactment (Hon, Grunig, & Dozier, 1992, pp. 424–425).

Broom and Dozier (1986) have found that women have a harder time moving up from a technician role to a managerial role than do men. Structural mechanisms in place within organizations help perpetuate gender discrimination. Men in charge of organizations, who make promotion decisions, may not believe that they practice overt discrimination; rather, they tend to promote people who are most like themselves (i.e., white males) because these are the people with whom they are most comfortable.

Lauzen's (1991, 1992, 1994) studies have examined the likelihood of women advancing into management positions in public relations. She concluded that with the acquisition of more skills and years of experience, women can assume a managerial role, but those women who start out as technicians in the organization are often passed over for promotion by men, who enter the ranks of top management through a process called *encroachment*, where those from fields such as finance or the law assume top public relations positions. This supports the notion that the route to top management is *not* through the public relations department.

Dozier and Broom (1995) later discussed the way in which the manager's role has evolved in public relations, suggesting that gender no longer predicted salary, but experience did. They concluded that the feminist movement had had some impact in reducing overt salary discrimination and gender role segregation. However, they cautioned that their findings should not be used to justify further sex discrimination.

Toth and Grunig tackled the issue of roles for women in public relations in 1993 in a feminist analysis of the "under the glass ceiling" research. They found that women who are public relations managers blur the dichotomy of technician/manager and end up "doing it all" by assuming both a technical role and a managerial role, at times, and for less money.

In suggesting strategies for change, Toth and Grunig (1993) said that urging women to be more like men—to assume male characteristics—not only misses the point but also causes undue stress for women. They recommended a reevaluation of society's expectations of women and their gender roles. Indeed, they found inherent problems in the structure, which an application of feminine values could remedy. As Rakow (1987, 1989) and many others have suggested, the structure needs dismantling before real change for women in public relations can ever come about.

These studies prompted research in the area of gender differences; women may bring unique attributes and approaches to the business world. In a study examining gender differences, conducted in 1996 by Lariscy, Sallot, and Cameron, the perception of the concepts of justice and equity by men and women were studied. The researchers concluded that men and women have different perceptions of justice and equity as public relations practitioners. In a separate study, Weaver-Lariscy, Cameron, and Sweep (1994) found that female public relations practitioners take on a role of "conscience of the organization," while men are more likely to assume a "dominant insider" role (p. 137).

These studies posit that there are fundamental differences between men and women in terms of their approaches to their roles in the workplace. Based on a review of the literature in the area of gender role differences, Marshall (1993) characterized male values or principles as "self-assertion, separation, independence, control, competition, focused perception, rationality, analysis, clarity, discrimination, and activity," while women are described by "interdependence, cooperation, receptivity, merging, acceptance, awareness of patterns, wholes and contexts, emotional tone, personalistic perception, being, intuition, and synthesizing" (pp. 122–123). While Marshall believed that both men and women can be ascribed certain characteristics traditionally reserved for the other gender, she also believed that biological and physical characteristics, socialization, and social roles play a part in determining gender values and perceptions that are different for men than women.

Role enactment and the link to gender-attributed characteristics also has been a theme in the management literature. Weider-Hatfield (1987) found that "self-reported differences in communicative behavior in a leadership context are better explained by psychological gender" than by biological sex (p. 11). Male managers prefer "punishment-based strategies" and female managers use "altruism—and rationale-based strategies," according to findings by Harper and Hirokawa (1988, p. 157). They believed, however, that such approaches are situational in nature and that as more women become managers, the popular view that women somehow manage differently will dissipate. How that will happen, however, is not made clear.

What about within-gender perceptions? Heald, Contractor, Koehly, and Wasserman (1998) conducted a study of workers' perceptions of organizational social structure. They found that coworkers from the same department held similar views of the organization's social structure, and employees of the same gender held similar views of organizational structure. This poses the question "Do women share similar views about organizational barriers to their advancement?"

While promotions to a managerial role and increased financial compensation may be related to job satisfaction for women entering public relations, there may be other factors that relate to job satisfaction in equal or greater amounts. Some studies have explored number of hours per week worked, seniority, and commitment to organizations as important measures (Bell, Roloff, Van Camp, & Karol, 1990).

Because of the way in which they approach their roles in public relations work, women may well have job satisfaction definitions different from those of men. In addition, Creedon (1991) suggested that male models, who assume role satisfaction will be greater for women if they become managers, may overlook the inherent job satisfaction found in technician roles.

This overview of roles research in public relations makes an important underlying assumption: Roles as studied in the public relations literature are defined based on male models. Moving up to a managerial position is seen to be desirable and important to achieving status, increased salary, and greater job satisfaction. But how do women perceive these roles? What constitutes job satisfaction for them? If women remain technicians, are they really in a "lesser" role from their point of view? Creedon (1991) made a strong case for deconstructing male models of public relations roles. She advocated discarding the male models and creating new ones that better relate to women's experience.

Thus, it is less desirable to be a technician, and women are chiefly technicians. Gender is a strong predictor of role, and gender is the strongest predictor of salary. Where roles are blurred, as in the case of Toth and Grunig's (1993) follow-up to the 1991 PRSA study, women are doing a combination of both roles and still being paid less than their male counterparts. But Toth and Grunig argued that asking women to become more like men to advance misses the point; it's the structure that needs fixing.

Doing "better" is always relative, and improvements for women in the public relations and communications industries must be tempered with the fact that there is still substantial underrepresentation of women in management in these fields. In fields where women are the majority—70% or more in public relations—one might assume that they have a better chance to achieve equity (Sha & Toth, 2005, p. 93). It appears that they do not.

Even with the prospects for increases in the numbers of women in the communications industry, the larger problem of underrepresentation in management remains:

> Despite some favorable overall trends . . . women's gains are, if not illusory, certainly compromised, falling far short of meeting policy goals of true integration and parity. Women are doing better, but too often they are not doing well enough when compared to men. Traditional gender/status hierarchies are maintained by strongly gendered processes, which appear to operate as effectively in the newly emerging postindustrial as the industrial economy. (Stone, 1995, p. 421)

Society's clear delineation between the genders starts early—at birth. Gender-appropriate behavior is established from the beginning. Gender-appropriate roles soon follow. Gender-appropriate jobs provide the last step in gelling the gender role. Well before men and women enter the workforce, they have become conventionally gender typed (Bem, 1993). Breaking free of these gender stereotypes is nearly impossible, given the structure in place to support and reinforce them. Penalties for attempting to deviate from gender stereotypes can be great; at their worst in the workplace, they can shut women out of management.

Summary of Roles Research

In examining roles research for women in public relations and communications management, we have seen a number of explanations for women's roles. These include self-selection by women into lower-paying, lower-status positions; sex discrimination because of organizational scale (size), market factors, and institutional arrangements, which make discrimination and segregation more endemic; promotion bars and barriers; gender role socialization; labor market discrimination and institutional mechanisms; cultural beliefs, norms, and practices; attributed biological differences between the sexes; legislative restrictions; and, finally, gender stereotyping.

This results in lower salaries for women; lower representation of women in top management groups, as CEOs and on boards of directors; fewer opportunities for advancement; different (i.e., double) standards of evaluation; noninclusion in the so-called inner circle; isolation; exaggerated visibility; criticism for management style; lower status; undervaluing of the communication role; and sex discrimination problems unique to women.

Suggested solutions have included mentoring, education, learning about networks and the way male colleagues work together, an evaluation of career paths and planning strategies for advancement, and a willingness to play by the rules established by men in the organization.

Bees, Bitches, and Other Public Relations Characters

Prior research highlighted the fact that women sometimes blame other women for their inability to achieve promotions and other opportunities. Participants in Wrigley's (2002) research on the causes of the glass ceiling for women in public relations and communications management discussed the "corporate bitch," a woman who advances into management and then works to prevent other women from advancing. These women have also been characterized as "Queen Bees," since they appear to be the sole female in an all-male environment who systematically works to "eliminate" female competition for top positions in the organization (pp. 39–40). The larger question is "Who are the beekeepers?"

Women facing workplace discrimination in these public relations and communications environments dealt with the cognitive dissonance they felt about not being able to achieve promotions, pay equity, or equal treatment by practicing what Wrigley (2002) termed *negotiated resignation.*

> A conceptual definition of negotiated resignation was developed by analyzing how women described glass ceiling contributing factors as well as the strategies they mentioned as useful in overcoming the glass ceiling . . . getting along and fitting in, attempting to please by working harder and building consensus, or being a peacemaker in resolving conflicts between coworkers. These conciliatory strategies do not address the larger question of whether or not the structure is at fault; they smooth the workplace waters sufficiently to allow individuals to adapt to their workplace environment and continue to function without disruption to the status quo. . . . Indeed, participants resisted the feminist label altogether. (p. 49)

This approach to discrimination results in a denial that such inequities exist, because acknowledging them would mean doing something about them. Pushing away a feminist label is one form of such denial.

Moving Beyond Dichotomies: Work-Life Balance

Larissa Grunig (1995, 2000) has contributed much to feminist scholarship in public relations. Her earlier Feminist Phase Analysis research examined the five phases to studying women in public relations: male scholarship and compensatory, bifocal, feminist, and multifocal approaches. In 2006, she proposed a sixth phase in Feminist Phase Analysis, termed the *integrative phase*, which recommends examining communications professionals as people trying to balance work-life issues (L. A. Grunig, 2006, p. 115).

Her premise is that while earlier research emphases were important for their time, pushing feminist scholarship in public relations forward will require a more contextual approach to the lives of men and women in public relations. She acknowledged the importance of all the earlier phases of feminist scholarship in public relations and challenged future feminist scholars to move beyond them.

In 2008, Aldoory, Jiang, Toth, and Sha conducted a study funded by the PRSA Foundation that sought to fill what they perceived as a gap in the literature—and one that answers L. A. Grunig's call to conduct more integrative studies. The study they conducted on work-life balance used eight focus groups of men and women to determine the challenges practitioners face and to uncover strategies for both men and women to achieve work-life balance.

The researchers propose a work-personal continuum, where the personal aspects of one's life go beyond family to include personal time to maintain health and pursue personal interests:

> The factors that help professionals measure their place on the continuum include societal pressure; contradictions between organizational policies and culture; the unpredictable nature of public relations work; use of technology; perceived professional identity; parenthood; and a timeshifting process that favors work. (Aldoory et al., 2008, p. 14)

A Book of Their Own: Women in Public Relations

In 2001, three of the best known and most prolific feminist scholars in public relations released the first book to examine the influence of gender on the practice. *Women in Public Relations* reports the results of a study of 2,000 public relations practitioners funded by the PRSA and chronicles the gender research conducted in public relations.

The book is an ambitious look at the evolution of gender research in public relations and reminds readers that many of the issues uncovered in previous decades of research continue to exist today. In their "Last Word," L. A. Grunig et al. (2001) spelled out the implications of ignoring gender inequities in the public relations profession:

> Most feminist treatises end with the notion that the solution to sex discrimination hinges on political, institutional, and organizational policies. Women alone, even women aligning themselves with like-minded men, cannot overcome either the blatant or the subtle sexism we have described here. We agree. We also acknowledge, as have most writers before us, that societal transformation is not so easy as it might seem on paper. Change takes longer than anyone expects. Without moving toward equity for women in public relations, however, the field risks losing the talents of well more than half of what we have established as its most effective practitioners. (p. 360)

Conclusions

What can we learn from the decades of feminist scholarship in public relations? First, it has been the life's work of several key scholars since the mid-1980s. Larissa Grunig, Elizabeth Toth, Linda Hon, and Lana Rakow have made immeasurable contributions to our understanding of the impact of gender on the profession. Second, many of the challenges highlighted in earlier decades continue to plague the profession today. And despite the belief by younger practitioners and students in public relations programs at colleges and universities today that such discrimination has disappeared, current research shows that issues of salary inequity, lack of women in upper management, and struggles with work-life balance continue (Aldoory & Toth, 2002) today.

Widening the lens to see these issues as challenges for both men and women has been suggested as a way to solve the gender challenge to public relations. But the larger issues of workplace and societal structure and values—and their inherent oppression—cannot be ignored if we are to unpack the inequities and create a field that is truly as equitable for women as it has been welcoming (Choi & Hon, 2002).

Many avenues remain open for feminist scholarship in public relations for those who come after us. Gender represents just one type of diversity. Ethnicity, sexual orientation, socioeconomic factors, and other diversities offer many opportunities for further exploration. International research, while conducted relative to more mainstream topics, has yet to truly examine the challenges of gender in worldwide practice. Articles by Fröhlich and Peters (2007) and AlSaqer (2008) are recent exceptions.

Earlier feminist scholars made this their life's work; we must do the same.

References

Aldoory, L., Jiang, H., Toth, E. L., & Sha, B. L. (2008). Is it still just a women's issue? A study of work-life balance among men and women in public relations. *Public Relations Journal, 2*(4), 1–20.

Aldoory, L., & Toth, E. L. (2002). Gender discrepancies in a gendered profession: A developing theory for public relations. *Journal of Public Relations Research, 14*(2), 103–126.

AlSaqer, L. (2008). Experience of female public relations practitioners in Bahrain. *Public Relations Review, 34,* 77–79.

Bell, R. A., Roloff, M. E., Van Camp, K., & Karol, S. H. (1990). Is it lonely at the top? Career success and personal relationships. *Journal of Communication, 40*(1), 9–23.

Bem, S. L. (1993). *The lenses of gender: Transforming the debate on sexual inequality.* New Haven, CT: Yale University Press.

Broom, G. M. (1982). A comparison of sex roles in public relations. *Public Relations Review, 8*(3), 17–22.

Broom, G. M., & Dozier, D. M. (1986). Advancement for public relations role models. *Public Relations Review, 12,* 37–56.

Choi, Y., & Hon, L. C. (2002). The influence of gender composition in powerful positions on public relations practitioners' gender-related perceptions. *Journal of Public Relations Research, 14,* 229–263.

Cirksena, K., & Cuklanz, L. (1992). Male is to female as ____ is to ____: A guided tour of five feminist frameworks for communication studies. In L. F. Rakow (Ed.), *Women making meaning* (pp. 18–44). New York: Routledge.

Cline, C. G., Toth, E. L., Turk, J. V., Walters, L. M., Johnson, N., & Smith, H. (1986). *The velvet ghetto: The impact of the increasing percentage of women in public relations and business communication.* San Francisco: IABC Foundation.

Creedon, P. J. (1991). Public relations and "women's work": Toward a feminist analysis of public relations roles. *Public Relations Research Annual, 3,* 67–84.

Creedon, P. J. (1993a). Acknowledging the infrasystem: A critical feminist analysis of systems theory. *Public Relations Review, 19,* 157–166.

Creedon, P. J. (1993b). The challenge of re-visioning gender values. In *Women in mass communication* (2nd ed., pp. 3–23). Newbury Park, CA: Sage.

Creedon, P. J. (Ed.). (1993c). *Women in mass communication* (2nd ed.). Newbury Park, CA: Sage.

Dozier, D. M., & Broom, G. M. (1995). Evolution of the manager role in public relations. *Journal of Public Relations Research, 7*(1), 3–26.

Dozier, D. M., Chapo, S., & Sullivan, B. (1983, August). *Sex and the bottom line: Income differences among women and men in public relations.* Paper presented at the meeting of the Public Relations Division, Association for Education in Journalism and Mass Communication, Corvallis, OR.

Dozier, D. M., Grunig, L. A., & Grunig, J. E. (1995). *Manager's guide to excellence in public relations and communication management.* Mahwah, NJ: Lawrence Erlbaum.

Fagenson, E. A. (1992). Mentoring: Who needs it? A comparison of proteges' and nonproteges' needs for power, achievement, affiliation, and autonomy. *Journal of Vocational Behavior, 41*(1), 48–60.

Fröhlich, R., & Peters, S. B. (2007). PR bunnies caught in the agency ghetto? Gender stereotypes, organizational factors, and women's careers in PR agencies. *Journal of Public Relations Research, 19*(3), 229–254.

Grunig, J. E. (Ed.). (1992). *Excellence in public relations and communication management.* Hillsdale, NJ: Lawrence Erlbaum.

Grunig, L. A. (1995, July). *A feminist phase analysis of research on women in postmodern public relations.* Paper presented at the Second International Public Relations Research Symposium, Bled, Slovenia.

Grunig, L. A. (2000). A feminist phase analysis of research on women in postmodern public relations. In D. Moss, D. Verčič, & G. Warnaby (Eds.), *Perspectives on public relations research* (pp. 89–120). London: Routledge.

Grunig, L. A. (2006). Feminist phase analysis in public relations: Where have we been? Where do we need to be? *Journal of Public Relations Research, 18*(2), 115–140.

Grunig, L. A., Toth, E. L., & Hon, L. C. (2001). *Women in public relations: How gender influences practice.* New York: Guilford Press.

Harper, N. L., & Hirokawa, R. Y. (1988). A comparison of persuasive strategies used by female and male managers: An examination of downward influence. *Communication Quarterly, 36,* 157–168.

Heald, M. R., Contractor, N. S., Koehly, L. M., & Wasserman, S. (1998). Formal and emergent predictors of coworkers' perceptual congruence on an organization's social structure. *Human Communication Research, 24*(4), 536–563.

Hon, L. C. (1995). Toward a feminist theory of public relations. *Journal of Public Relations Research, 7*(1), 27–88.

Hon, L. C., Grunig, L. A., & Dozier, D. M. (1992). Women in public relations: Problems and opportunities. In J. E. Grunig (Ed.), *Excellence in public relations and communication management.* Hillsdale, NJ: Lawrence Erlbaum.

Lariscy, R. A. W., Sallot, L., & Cameron, G. T. (1996). Justice and gender: An instrumental and symbolic explication. *Journal of Public Relations Research, 8*(2), 107–121.

Lauzen, M. (1991). Imperialism and encroachments in public relations. *Public Relations Review, 17*(3), 245–255.

Lauzen, M. (1992). Effects of gender on professional encroachment in public relations. *Journalism Quarterly, 69,* 173–180.

Lauzen, M. (1994). Public relations practitioner role enactment in issues management. *Journalism Quarterly, 71*(2), 356–369.

Marshall, J. (1993). Viewing organizational communication from a feminist perspective: A critique and some offerings. In S. A. Deetz (Ed.), *Communication yearbook 16* (pp. 122–141). Newbury Park, CA: Sage.

Mathews, W. (1988). Women in PR: Progression or retrogression? *Public Relations Review, 14*(3), 24–28.

Mathews, W. (1989). Killing the messenger. In E. Toth & C. Cline (Eds.), *Beyond the velvet ghetto.* San Francisco: IABC Research Foundation.

Mathison, M. A. (1997). Complicity as epistemology: Reinscribing the historical categories of "woman" through standpoint feminism. *Communication Theory, 7*(2), 149–161.

Punch, M. (1994). Politics and ethics in qualitative research. In N. K. Denzin & Y. S. Lincoln (Eds.), *Handbook of qualitative research* (pp. 83–97). Thousand Oaks, CA: Sage.

Rakow, L. F. (1986). Rethinking gender research in communication. *Journal of Communication, 36*(4), 11–26.

Rakow, L. F. (1987). Looking to the future: Five questions for gender research. *Women's Studies in Communication, 10,* 79–86.

Rakow, L. F. (1989). Feminist studies: The next stage. *Critical Studies in Mass Communication, 6*(2), 209–215.

Rakow, L. F. (Ed.). (1992). *Women making meaning: New feminist directions in communication.* New York: Routledge.

Scrimger, J. (1985). Profile: Women in Canadian public relations. *Public Relations Review, 11*(3), 40–46.

Sha, B. L., & Toth, E. L. (2005). Future professionals' perceptions of work, life, and gender issues in public relations. *Public Relations Review, 31,* 93–99.

Steeves, H. L. (1987). Feminist theories and media studies. *Critical Studies in Mass Communication, 4*(2), 95–135.

Stone, P. (1995). Assessing gender at work: Evidence and issues. In J. A. Jacobs (Ed.), *Gender inequality at work* (pp. 409–423). Thousand Oaks, CA: Sage.

Tam, S. Y., Dozier, D. M., Lauzen, M. M., & Real, M. R. (1995). The impact of superior-subordinate gender on the career advancement of public relations practitioners. *Journal of Public Relations Research, 7*(4), 259–272.

Theus, K. T. (1985). Gender shifts in journalism and public relations. *Public Relations Review, 9*(1), 42–50.

Toth, E. L. (1989). Whose freedom and equity in public relations? The gender balance argument. *Mass Comm Review, 16*(1/2), 70–76.

Toth, E. L., & Cline, C. G. (1989). *Beyond the velvet ghetto.* San Francisco: IABC Research Foundation.

Toth, E. L., & Cline, C. G. (1991). Public relations practitioners' attitudes toward gender issues: A benchmark study. *Public Relations Review, 17,* 161–174.

Toth, E. L., & Grunig, L. A. (1993). The missing story of women in public relations. *Journal of Public Relations Research, 5*(3), 153–175.

Treichler, P. A., & Wartella, E. (1986). Interventions: Feminist theory and communication studies. *Communication, 9,* 1–18.

Turk, J. V. (1986, June). The shifting salary scene. *Currents, 12*(6), 20.

Weaver-Lariscy, R. A., Cameron, G. T., & Sweep, D. D. (1994). Women in higher education public relations: An inkling of change? *Journal of Public Relations Research, 6*(2), 125–140.

Weider-Hatfield, D. (1987). Differences in self-reported leadership behavior as a function of biological sex and psychological gender. *Women's Studies in Communication, 10,* 1–14.

Wright, D. K., Grunig, L. A., Springston, J. K., & Toth, E. L. (1991). *Under the glass ceiling: An analysis of gender issues in American public relations.* New York: PRSA Foundation.

Wrigley, B. J. (2002). Glass ceiling? What glass ceiling? A qualitative study of how women view the glass ceiling in public relations and communications management. *Journal of Public Relations Research, 14*(1), 27–55.

CHAPTER 18

Reflective Management

Seeing the Organization as if From Outside

Susanne Holmström

The Importance of Public Relations in Managing Organizations Reflectively

Society's turbulence strikes organizations. As society evolves and faces new challenges, the legitimating notions mediating the interrelations between an organization and its social environment change in attempts to meet these challenges.[1] Since the latter half of the 20th century, new legitimating paradigms and practices have evolved to cope with modernization's increasing strains on life and nature, with society's accelerating complexity and diversity, and with the growing global interdependence.

This evolution has changed the premises of organizational decision making and puts new demands on the managing of organizations. Conventional narcissist perspectives no longer suffice for an organization to be seen as a responsible and legitimate part of society. Decision making of most organizations of Western orientation has to relate to *the public* (understood as a specific way of reasoning on matters of common interest from the perspective of a societal horizon) as well as to *publics* (understood as different stakeholders, each with their particular interest in and perspective on the world and on the organization).[2]

These transformations are part of the evolution of modernity. Although the structures and processes analyzed below constitute a strong global trend, they relate closely to the degree of societal complexity found in particular in well-developed regions where society has grown highly complex and is characterized by fluid modernity. Full, or *solid*, modernity was characterized by inclinations to reflexive, petrified structures and norms that were seen as natural and necessary and by passive confidence, stable patterns of expectation, and taken-for-granted institutions. In contrast, late, or *fluid*, modernity is characterized by the acknowledgment of social norms and institutions as contingent (Luhmann, 1998) and consequently by fluid patterns of expectation, continuous reflective and discursive legitimization processes, hyperirritation, and an active generation of trust. From decision premises being given by following society's solid, common norms, monocontextual market considerations, and the law, we now see decision premises being generated along with decision making as social constructions that are products of continual choice. Decision making can no longer relate to solid, common norms only but must also relate to what is "reasonable" and "responsible" in continuously changing contexts—without the possibility of reaching any general consensus or ultimate reason, without a given, unambiguous environment, but in an interplay with different and even conflicting perspectives and positions.

From being relatively simple and a question of legal relations and unambiguous functional relations mainly, the interrelations between an organization and its social environment have grown significantly more complex, dynamic, and ambiguous, complicating the managing of organizations by requiring sensitivity to an increasingly diverse and dynamic environment integrated into its decision making. We can identify two basic requirements. First, where public relations in a previous paradigm worked disconnected from the central decision processes of most organizations, public relations competences and processes are becoming a central part of navigating organizations in fluid modernity to install the necessary optics for decision making to consider a wide variety of society's rationales as well as to partake in public communication processes. Second, along with the new sensitivity required for an organization's decision processes to be more than a narcissistic mirroring of the organization, a reflective, second-order perspective is required, seeing the organization as if from outside, in the condition of sociodiversity.

New Demands on Management

Second-Order Reflection

Reflection can be analytically identified as the social mechanism fundamentally characterizing contemporary ideals of legitimacy. The rise from the first-order, narrow, unambiguous, monocontextual perspective of reflexivity to the second-order broad, open, polycontextual perspective of reflection has huge implications for the relationship between an organization and its social environment and for the premises of decision making (Holmström, 1997, 1996/1998, 2002, 2004, 2005b).

Reflexivity implies a narcissistic perspective from within, a perspective from where decision premises are taken for granted and are applied blindly, and from where what is seen with this perspective is taken to be the one reality, the only truth. The perspective consequently conflicts blindly with different worldviews, different sets of decision premises. The reflexive, first-order perspective implies a view in which the organization reflects itself only in the environment, as in a mirror. For business companies, it implies a reconstruction of the public as a market and of publics as mainly consumers and shareholders. Reflexive decision making is inattentive to the broader context and to the unintended, however often far-reaching, side effects involved in its consequences.

In *reflection*, the organization sees itself as if from outside, in the condition of sociodiversity. Reflective decision making views the organization within a larger interdependent societal context and leads to the approach that the environment is to be respected instead of managed.

Triple Synthesis: The Public Relations Part in Decision Processes

The evolution of a reflective paradigm in the legitimating notions mediating the interrelation between organizations and their social environment involves the integration of previously disconnected practices and perspectives in central management's decision processes. From a *sociological* aspect, the evolution makes decision making's sensitivity to more and to different social categories imperative, involving a broad range of rationales designated "publics" or "stakeholders," and to the representation of society within society, whether denoted the *public sphere, public opinion, society*, or the *population*.

From a *communication* aspect, the communicative processes with the *public* and *publics* today go far beyond enabling only the results of decision making; they are constitutive of decision processes and are so in several contexts and in two dimensions. First, as will be unfolded below, six fundamental trends—each in its way—demand involvement in continuous reflective and discursive processes. Second, interaction with the new environments requires communicative competences and strategies beyond the conventional exchange processes of the market and beyond the reference to the legal regulation of the state.

Reflective decision making consequently integrates three interrelated functions: *Self-understanding*, *sensitivity*, and *self-presentation* functions, which each in its way takes a very different form in the reflexive first-order and the reflective second-order mode, respectively (see Figure 18.1).

Figure 18.1 Whether Management Practice Is Characterized by First-Order Reflexivity or by Second-Order Reflection Can Be Identified on Three Interrelated Organizational Functions

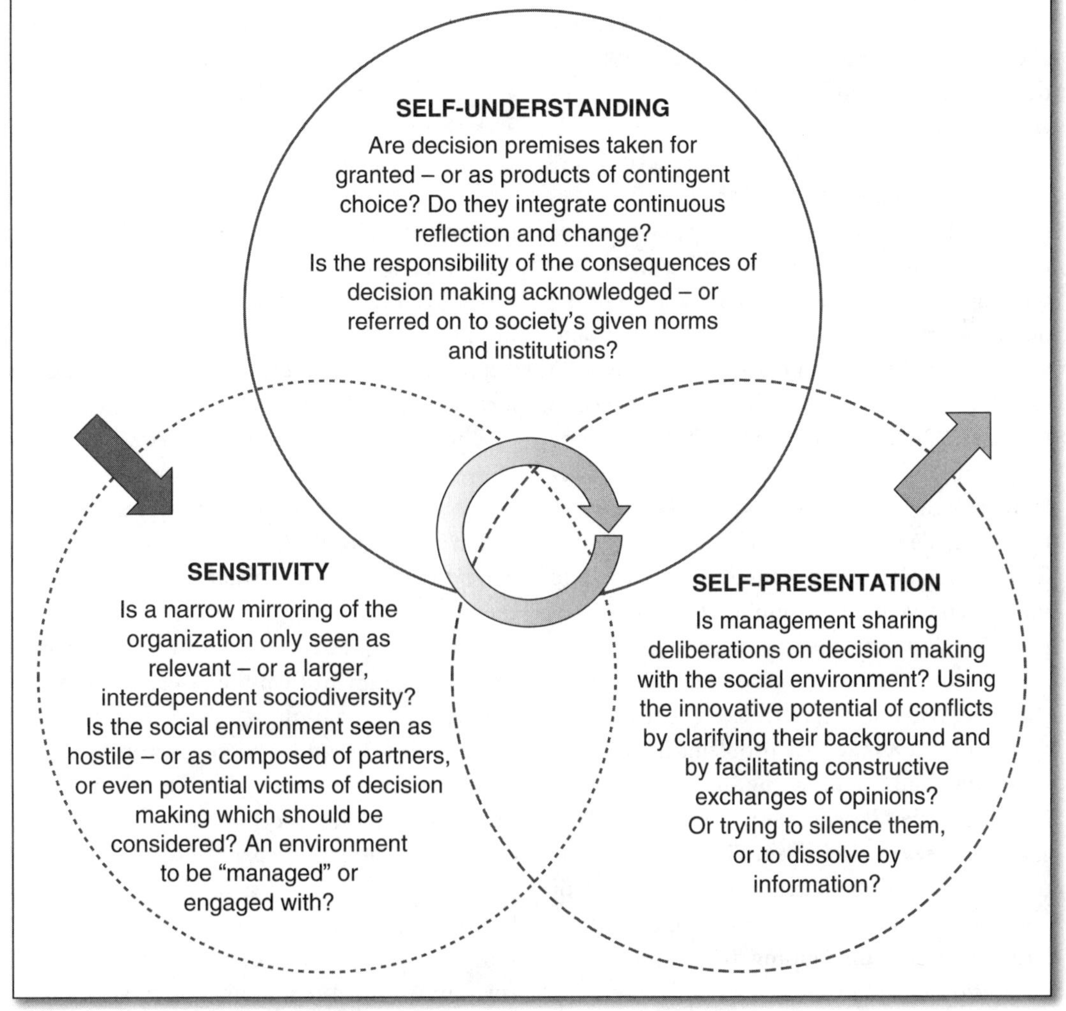

Reflective Self-Understanding. The organization's self-understanding is a key determinant of reflective management. Self-understanding is about the integrity, role, and responsibility of the organization in society; about identity and values; and, consequently, about how the organization interprets and processes the input from its environment. The fluidity and diversity of contemporary society prompt an increasing focus on self-understanding. An organization's decision premises are no longer given; they are continuously regenerated in engagement with a turbulent social environment of different and diverse rationales. Fundamentally, however, any organization can synchronize its decision premises with itself only, since the environment is observed and interpreted from the self-understanding and social optics of the organization (Bakken & Hernes, 2003; Luhmann, 1996/2000). It can consequently do so in ways that are more or less sensitive to its environment.

To minimize self-oscillation, a reflective second-order perspective in the organization's view of itself in relation to its social environment is decisive for the organization's continuous balancing of its self-understanding. On the one hand, the organization must be open and sensitive to a broad range of perspectives to ensure a continuous updating of its decision premises. On the other hand, this sensitivity puts self-understanding and identity under increasing pressure. It takes a reflective perspective to enable the organization to clearly define itself in relation to the environment even in intense engagement in public communication processes and with diverse stakeholder publics and to remain the same although continuously changing. Without a reflective self-understanding, an organization may have problems in defining, renewing, and maintaining its identity; the intense stakeholder engagement will make decision processes overcomplex. The risk is that the organization will be paralyzed into inaction or will surrender to the social environment, which basically means disclaiming the responsibility of decision making.

Reflective Sensitivity. Reflective second-order *sensitivity* is needed to take decision making to a new level that mirrors decisions in a diversity of specific rationales as well as on the larger societal horizon. In a reflexive first-order position, sensitivity to more than market[3] and state is basically disconnected from corporate core decisions, whereas from a reflective position, sensitivity is closely interrelated with core decision processes and overall corporate policies.

Sensitivity refers to the way the organization observes its environment. The environment is not a given thing: It is reconstructed by the organization, and the organization will always reconstruct the world in its own image. Stakeholder salience will vary distinctively from a reflexive versus a reflective perspective. Any organization's stakeholders remain the product of subjective judgment, depending on the worldview, complexity, and, consequently, sensitivity of the organization. The issues of public communication processes and the stakeholder publics to which decision processes pay attention depend on the organization's often tacit criteria of relevance. And what is seen and heard is interpreted from the organization's perspective and self-understanding. For instance, a reflexive business perspective sees the public as a market, not as a horizon mirroring the idea of a common interest.

Blind spots are inherent in any observation. However, by raising the observation to the reflective second-order perspective, the organization acknowledges its blind spots, and that its perspective determines what it can see. When the organization sees itself as if from outside, in the societal context, a larger and more complex social environment than the given environment of market and state emerges. Sensitivity to stakeholders goes beyond a mere mirroring of the organization. In contrast, the reflective perspective makes decision processes sensitive to different, even conflicting, perspectives, including their rationales, interests, and expectations—to those potentially influenced by decisions. From a basic approach of respect for the social environment, the organization endeavors to see the world as through the eyes of stakeholders and attempts to understand their perspectives on the organization.

Reflective Self-Presentation. A reflective second-order perspective is decisive for the organization's *self-presentation* to be relevant and meaningful to the social environment. Self-presentation is about output from the organization, about building expectations and trust, about attempting transparency by sharing deliberations on and results of decision processes with the social environment; about justifying decisions and decision premises; and about contributing to society's constitutive communication. This takes self-presentation far beyond merely enabling results of decision processes and makes it a focal matter of managing organizations in contemporary society's fluidity and diversity.

When expectations are no longer more or less fixed and determined by common, stable norms seen as natural and inevitable (as in the solid society of yesterday), a consistent but sensitive and consequently constantly changing self-presentation is required to build and sustain trust. When decision processes relate to a diversity of different stakeholder publics, the self-presentation must consider their individual perspective on and interest in the organization as a basic precondition of meeting with their criteria of relevance and of meaning. And when addressing *the public*, it must be from an appreciation of the specific rationality of this societal horizon, from an understanding of the notion of common interest. These challenges are highlighted in Table 18.1.

Table 18.1 Perspectives and Implications of Reflexive Versus Reflective Management

	Reflexivity	Reflection
Self-understanding		
Approach	Solid identity: Decision premises taken for granted, natural, necessary	Fluid identity: Decision premises seen as contingent; continuously questioned, updated
Self-observation	Monophone functional logic unquestioned trump of decision making; blind self-interest	Polyphone sensitivity; enlightened self-interest (profit in regard of people, planet)
Responsibility	Refers responsibility on to society's well-established norms; does not acknowledge the risk inherent in any decision (rather sees itself as victim)	Sees that risky decisions are inevitable; acknowledges responsibility as decision maker
View on social environment	Relies on (blind) confidence from the social environment when conforming with society's given, stable patterns of expectation and shared norms	Sees that a precondition of society's confidence is to relate reflectively and consistently to the expectations of the social environment
Relation	Autonomous, arbitrary decision making	Social environment involved in deliberations on decision making

(Continued)

Table 18.1 (Continued)

	Reflexivity	Reflection
Sensitivity		
Approach	Sees only the inherent environment (to business: stakeholders, monocontextual markets) and state	Sees a larger and more complex environment as relevant (stakeholders, polycontextual markets, public)
Self-observation	Monocontextual, self-centered, narcissist view from within; narrow, unambiguous perspective	Polycontextual view as if from outside, sees itself in the larger context; tries to see the world through the perspectives of the social environment
Responsibility	Does not see the consequences of decision making in the larger perspective	Extensive sensitivity to the consequences of decision making and to the position of potential victims
View on social environment	Turbulent environment seen as hostile: society split in black/white positions; prejudice prevails	Understands conflicts as inherent in society's construction
Relation	Managing the social environment (socio-uniformity)	Engagement with the social environment (sociodiversity)
Self-presentation		
Approach	Closed, blind counteraction, "asymmetrical communication"	Sharing deliberations on decision premises with the social environment
Self-observation	Blind self-presentation from within from an idea of universality: "Objective" information and transparency produces dissent instead of consensus	Self-presentation sensitive to sociodiversity, takes into consideration different worldviews (consensus on dissent)
Responsibility	Believes that information will dissolve conflicts; does not see the inherent conflict between decision maker and potential victim	Openly acknowledges responsibility as decision maker; commits the organization in relation to society
View on social environment	Does not see the environment's need for more than market information	Precise, continuous, consistent signals to the environment about expectations to be met by the organization
Relation	Does not see conflicts or tries to silence them	Sees the potential of conflicts, exposes their background, and facilitates exchange of views

Synthesis. Where self-understanding, sensitivity, and self-presentation in a reflexive first-order paradigm tend to lead their own lives separated from core decision processes, in a reflective second-order paradigm, they are closely interrelated and integrated. Sensitivity is constitutive to decision-making processes, and self-presentation not only enables results of decision making but is part of the organization's fundamental interaction with its social environment.

For self-understanding to live up to contemporary legitimating norms requires sensitivity to the social environment. Sensitivity, however, is determined by self-understanding: An organization's reconstruction of the organization's environment mirrors the organization's self-understanding. Too much sensitivity will get decision making out of balance, out of step with the organization's own values, role, and responsibility in society. Too little sensitivity will get decision making out of step with the environment. Consequently, reflective second-order sensitivity is decisive to ensure management's attention to material issues and stakeholders instead of drowning in noise and irrelevant complexity by relating to the most visible matters only and to vociferous stakeseekers. The self-presentation must rely on sensitivity to stakeholder expectations as well as to the organization's self-understanding, values, and way of operating to be trustworthy.

Relating to Six Issues

As will be evident from the above exposition of the differences between first-order reflexivity and second-order reflection, reflection requires considerable resources in the managing of organizations. It is not a question of leadership by heart, of doing good, or of personal moral inclinations—a reduction of complexity that comes easy to most of us as human beings but that does not suffice in managing organizations sustainably in the hypercomplexity of contemporary society (Qvortrup, 2003; Willke & Willke, 2008). Rather, it is a question of leadership by brain, of understanding not only the immediate self-referential environment but also the complex social and societal contexts within which the organization is embedded.

From this also follows that reflection does not come easily. It is no panacea, nor is it automatically activated, and when activated, the nature of social processes will work against reflection within the organization. Empirically, we most often see reflection activated by shocks and legitimacy crises and often following a period of turbulence in the social environment, of misunderstandings and of failing support (Holmström, 2002, 2005b), as was the case with Shell and Brent Spar in 1995 (Mirvis, 2000).[4] Also, reflective ideals are spread by isomorphism—that is, by professional best practices and by role models. However, the most sustainable vehicle in making management reflective is insight into the interrelation between society and organizations, into the transformations of these interrelations, and consequently of the premises of the organization's prosperity for the longer term and in the larger perspective.

Trends That Change the Interrelation Between Organization and Society

The social complexity involved in the legitimating notions evolved during recent decades can be unfolded on six structural dimensions that each in its own specific way contributes to provoking the need for reflection and each in its way provokes public relations processes (Table 18.2). They are interrelated and tend to intensify each other, and they all originate from the specific stage of modern society's full functional differentiation. However, each category constitutes specific dynamics and requires specific

Table 18.2 Six Interrelated Social Dimensions

Feature	Dimension	Problem	Impact on Management
Insensitive society	The relation between society's meaning structures on the one hand, life and nature on the other	The insensitivity of society's meaning systems to life and nature	To integrate considerations for life and nature in decision premises and processes
Trust society	Character of norms and institutions, of social security strategies	Dissolution of stable, shared patterns of expectation threatens social cohesion	To establish stable expectations and make the organization live up to them
Polycontextual society	The condition of sociodiversity	Balancing the interdependence of the increasingly specialized societal spheres with their increasing mutual interdependence	To balance independence and interdependence; to reflect several rationales in decision processes
Politicized society	Political regulation of society	The coordination of society's increasing complexity, diversity, and dynamism together with the lack of global governing structures	To politicize and make decisions from a societal perspective (e.g., corporate social responsibility, public affairs)
Decision society	Organizations as the primary decision makers of society	The asymmetrical relation between a decision maker and those influenced by the decision	To demonstrate responsibility, sustainability, transparency
Global society	The interrelation between different societal, political, and cultural forms	The mutual interdependence between previously independent cultures and societal forms activates latent conflicts of legitimacy	To adopt a metareflective approach that sees the company's local context as if from outside, within global diversity

responses and considerations within the core decision processes of an organization.

Managing the Balancing of People, Planet, and Profit

The first structural dimension relates to society's strains on life and nature caused by the side effects of modernization and full functional differentiation. For organic, chemical, biological, psychical, and physiological processes to be observed, interpreted, and communicated in society, they must be reconstructed into social processes according to society's meaning structures. The following is perhaps a counterintuitive observation, but a fundamental problem as society develops is that it grows increasingly insensitive to nonsocial processes (Luhmann, 1986/1989). Since the 1600s, society's communication processes have gradually clustered around various specialized rationales in functional meaning systems (Luhmann, 1968/1982, 1984/1995, 1997a).

In modern society, meaning is structured according to functional filters such as economy, politics, law, family, science, education, and mass media. Society automatically tends to reconstruct anything, including the well-being of nature and human beings, from its social filters with their criteria of relevance and success. This applies to anything from taking action on climate change to the obesity pandemic. The economic filter will activate questions such as "Does it pay? Does it improve our competitiveness?" The economic rationale cannot see its strains on nature and life until economic criteria are influenced. And what is seen is then automatically reconstructed from economic premises. A corresponding (in)sensitivity goes for all social dynamics. Politics: Will we gain votes, power? Science: Does it generate new knowledge? News media: Is it new information? Law: Can we regulate the matter legally? And so on. This isolation serves as a protective shield to build up specific complexity (Luhmann, 1997b).

Consequently, functional differentiation has decisively increased society's knowledge. However, gradually, the monofunctional specialization has evolved to an extent where the self-centered functional systems' strain on life and nature has reached a critical mass (Beck, 1994). Increasing strains such as pollution, global warming, deforestation, lifestyle disease, and stress have activated the demand for decision making to balance considerations of these functional rationales with life and nature—most prominently expressed in regard to business and the economic filter in the phrases, "people, planet, profit" and "the triple bottom line" (Elkington, 1997)—that is, the balancing of social, environmental, and economic considerations.

During recent decades, we have seen the relation to life and nature progress from exploitation to socioeconomic (Porter & Kramer, 2006) and holistic paradigms. In a holistic business paradigm, the challenge is for decision making to balance as mutual preconditions what was previously seen as opposites: maximizing profitability by contributing to sustainable development and balanced growth; demonstrating financial responsibility by acknowledging social and environmental responsibility; or exploring business opportunities by initiatives that address social needs or help reduce environmental impact. For this delicate balancing to succeed requires a complete rethinking of basic self-understandings and decision premises, and consequently of the approach to the environment: from the reflexive short-term perspective based in a blind, particular self-interest to a reflective long-term perspective based in enlightened self-interest (Annan, 1999); from relating to the market horizon from an unambiguous economic exchange rationality to continuous negotiations in public communication processes and in interplays with NGOs representing the interests of life and nature.

Managing Trust

The second dimension relates to the character of society's norms and of safety strategies for social interaction. Society is growing increasingly diverse, complex, fluid, uncertain, and unpredictable, relying less on knowledge, control, and confidence and more on trust. Trust facilitates interaction even in complex and uncertain social contexts and is the glue of contemporary society (Bentele & Seidenglanz, 2008; Jalava, 2003; Luhmann, 1968/1982). However, distrust is constantly lurking and threatening social interaction. A fundamental task of management is to continuously prove the organization worthy of trust.

All social interaction requires some kind of safety mechanism for anyone to risk engagement in interaction. Society's form of coordination has changed during recent decades. The solid society of yesterday was relatively familiar and uniform. You more or less knew what to expect. Social interaction was framed by common, stable norms determined by tradition or convention, by law and institutional control. A general confidence prevailed. Organizations used to rely on a certain degree of confidence based on expectations from their social environment that shared, well-established, evident norms framed their decision processes. An organization's stakeholders were mainly passive. Relations rested in a well-ordered view of the world.

Today, society is fluid, hypercomplex, diverse, dynamic, and chaotic. Often, you cannot be completely certain what to expect outside small circles of family, colleagues, and friends. Trust is required—a need that is intensified by the five other fundamental features of society today identified by the research presented in this chapter. For instance, to relieve the pressure on conventional law as a basic social safety strategy, new forms of political governance rely on mutual trust as a coordinating mechanism.

Trust is based on extrapolation from information and experience that are insufficient for certain knowledge and secure anticipations but that establish some expectations about the future behavior of an organization. Based on these expectations, stakeholders choose whether they dare trust the organization. Often, this is a long process—depending also on the relation between the risk and benefit perceived by the individual stakeholder in trusting the organization. In addition, management has to be always prepared to justify decisions and their premises in public. Solid modernity's conventional control mechanisms are replaced by the public searchlight on single cases that are generalized. The random test samples of mass media are *trust* checks—as opposed to solid modernity's *truth* checks.

The challenges in managing trust consequently require a reflective position. From a reflexive first-order perspective, management will take its decision premises for granted. Social norms and institutions are seen as necessary, natural, inevitable, and self-evident, and by conforming to these norms and institutions, reflexive management takes the social environment's confidence for granted. In contrast, in the reflective second-order perspective, decision premises are acknowledged as contingent, that is, as social constructions that are products of continual choice and that consequently need to be continuously updated and justified in relation to the dynamic social environment. Precise and continuous self-presentation on what is to be expected from the organization based on a consistent and at the same time continuously changing self-understanding that relates to external expectations is a focal part of reflective management to continuously earn, build, and sustain trust.

Managing Sociodiversity

The third dimension relates to the growing differentiation of society, which increasingly requires that the organization collaborate with multiple and diverse stakeholders and consequently that decision making reflectively consider a wide range of rationales and perspectives. Conflict and diversity energize society today. Sociodiversity ensures high levels of diversified knowledge, competence, and resources, but also demands collaboration based on mutual respect and flexible and tolerant relations between the diverse societal positions to turn conflicts and diversity into prospects of innovation, inspiration, dynamism, and cross-fertilization.

To ensure collaboration between the diverse societal positions requires that decision making understand and respect individual independence as well as mutual interdependence. This position implies a reflective self-understanding in relation to the sociodiverse context, that is, an understanding of the dynamics within the social environment as well as of the organization's own boundaries and integrity. A reflective position reveals the inevitability of conflicts and makes it possible to use innovative potential by clarifying their background and by facilitating constructive exchanges of opinions, taking into account different worldviews. In contrast, a reflexive first-order position does not see that conflicts are inherent in society's construction and tries to silence them or to dissolve them by information—in this way enhancing dissent from the reflexive perspective of universality.

Consequently, reflection on this dimension implies that decision making intensify sensitivity to diverse stakeholders out of respect for sociodiversity and the integrity of different perspectives. Decision processes reflect how decisions made from their own basic perspective, whether, for instance, economy, science, or health, are seen from different rationales such as education, family, care, politics, or mass media. The basic driver of most organizations remains monofunctional: A business company's primary rationale continues to be economy, a research institution's science. However, what is new is that the fundamental functional rationale of the reflective organization is not always the indisputably taken-for-granted trump in the decision process.

Managing Governance

On the fourth dimension, new forms of societal regulation evolve, characterized by encouraging society's actors to self- or coregulation. Society is increasingly regulated everywhere—and nowhere. Government structures and conventional law on the one hand and competitive market coordination on the other are complemented or substituted by societal governance structures and increasing communicative complexity (Sand, 2004; Sørensen & Torfing, 2005). Societal governance involves a large number of interdependent but independent actors who, from enlightened self-interest, partake in governance networks, based on *negotiation* rationality. Stakeholder engagement and public relations processes function as coregulators of the relationship between society and organization, and the need for generating trust becomes an important motive for self-constraint and taking on societal responsibility.

From the *state* perspective, a double pressure drives the governance trend. First, to cope with society's accelerating degree of complexity, knowledge, and dynamism, and with the consequences that are analyzed on the five other social dimensions presented in this chapter, and to do so in inclusive and flexible ways, political initiatives not only intervene from outside by conventional law. They increasingly subtly influence organizations' internal reflections on their own role and responsibility (Teubner, 2005) by incentives to environmental and social considerations and reporting and to voluntary compliance with ethical standards. Second, the growing global interdependence activates global governance structures to cope with the lack of global governing structures. For instance, global standards such as the UN Global Compact impose self-regulation on the global business community. From the *market* perspective, competitive market regulation no longer seems capable of considering contemporary society's complex interrelatedness. Instead, for the business community to generate trust increasingly means integrating societal considerations. The organization is *politicized* to the extent that this notion implies taking into account the societal horizon and the common interest in decision premises and processes. The organization *politicizes* by contributing to the production of public purpose in the broad sense of societal visions, ideas, plans, and regulations. Politicization involves partaking in the public debate and qualifying political decisions by supplying knowledge and assessments on issues of relevance to the organization.

From unicentric state control and multicentric competitive market regulation; from compliance via legal sanctions and fear of economic loss, then, the new societal governance forms are characterized by polycontextual networks. Together, private companies, public institutions, and NGOs endeavor to solve societal issues by producing tools for reflective self-restriction. The need for trust and the co-ownership of decisions stimulate compliance. Governance coordination relies on the regulating force of polycontextual interplays between the public perspective, news media, various NGOs, and an increasing number of stakeholder publics. Correspondingly, control mechanisms and sanctions take new, polycontextual forms such as mass mediated legitimacy crises, distrust, and failing support from a diversity of stakeholders.

Whenever you interfere with the production of public purpose, whenever you enter the political arena, your decision premises, processes, and actions become matters of public interest. The inherent legitimating reference of the political system, public opinion, grows relevant to organizations outside the political sector and causes a pronounced increase of public relations structures. Procedural qualities such as transparency and publicly available information are key elements of polycontextual governance. The cohesion of the governance society depends on society's actors being trustworthy. Instead of focusing primarily on conformance to conventional law, organizations today also have to be prepared for random sample tests by the mass media in their controlling function as trust checkers.

Where polycontextual governance offers high flexibility, dynamism, and social energy while maintaining the basic structure of society, it also makes high demands on a company's decision making. More than any of the trends and issues of contemporary society, societal governance regulation requires for the management of organizations to be capable of adopting a reflective perspective: first and foremost, because it requires a clear recognition of its own role in society for the organization to involve itself in political processes without taking on illegitimate political power on the one hand, and on the other hand, to do so without confusing its own decision processes by turning into a semipolitical institution. Furthermore, the governance form requires management's sensitivity to the societal horizon, to the public sphere, and to public opinion, in respect of the notion of common interest, without decision processes growing negligent to market rationales that to a business company would mean disclaiming responsibility as part of society's economic foundation. Finally, it takes a reflective self-presentation on the societal horizon to legitimize the company's decision premises and processes and to influence public purpose by partaking in society's constitutive communication processes and in governance networks in an accountable and transparent way without undermining democracy's basic principles and institutions.

Managing Anxiety

The fifth dimension focuses on the fundamentally asymmetrical relation between decision makers and those affected by a decision and contributes to explaining the demand for responsible, accountable, and transparent decision making (Holmström, 2005a).

When decisions are seen as contingent choices, decision makers are made responsible for their consequences (Luhmann, 1991/1993). Everything from climate change to obesity is attributed to decisions that could have been made differently. Organizations are made *responsible* for the consequences of their decisions. Correspondingly, *sustainability*—which involves taking responsibility for the future—has become a prominent issue. And with the increasingly pronounced conflict between decision makers and those who are potentially influenced by decisions without having the final say or even being involved in the decision making, *accountability* is wanted and *transparency* required, that is, access to or even participation in decision-making processes, often in the form of stakeholder engagement and NGO partnerships. With the increasing recognition that even seemingly trivial decisions by organizations can affect—for good or bad—individual well-being on a global scale, the victim's perspective explodes and finds immediate resonance with the selection criteria of news media (Luhmann, 2000); fear, worry, and distrust spread. The legitimacy of decisions is constantly questioned by the perspective representing potential victims—increasingly organized in NGOs to build decision-making power and influence.

From reflexive positions, the decision maker/victim dichotomy leads to a social climate characterized by black-and-white prejudices and futile, deadlocked conflicts. Reflexive management passes responsibility on to society's well-established norms, does not acknowledge the risk involved in any decision, but tends to feel as the victim in the frequent legitimacy crises fed by this conflict that is inherent in society's construction. In contrast, reflective management takes on the responsibility of decision making, endeavors to consider the consequences from the potential victim's perspective, accounts for decision premises and processes, sees the potential of conflicts, exposes their background, and facilitates exchange of views.

Managing Globalization

The sixth structural dimension relates to the conflicts between legitimating notions as globalization increases the interdependence and sensitivity between societal and cultural forms that were previously separated. Globalization's activation of formerly latent conflicts leads to the local/global dichotomy that causes diverging cultural interpretations of an issue and leads to even remote events having a major influence on the organization—a growing trend as social media entail global connectivity. It becomes a pivotal management problem to navigate an organization legitimately in still more cultural and societal contexts where its decisions may have consequences, that is, all the way back to peripheral subsuppliers and all the way forward to side effects of a product in a distant country.

Generic patterns in the multitudinous diversity of legitimacy conflicts can be identified by relating them to society's constitution and to its form of social coordination: between contemporary variations of modernity's functionally differentiated society, and between two different societal forms, with function and stratification respectively as their primary differentiation. Where modernity's functional differentiation has its roots in European ideas and has replaced the stratified type of society in particular in Western-oriented regions, hierarchical stratification still dominates society in some other regions. Modernity's values of individualism, plurality, fluidity, and horizontal diversity confront values of collectivism, uniformity, tradition, and vertical diversity (Baraldi, 2006; Luhmann, 1998). These different types of societal constitution breed different legitimating corporate settings (Holmström, 2008; Kostova & Zaheer, 1999).

To navigate legitimately within a multitudinous diversity of societal and cultural forms requires for decision making to take on a metareflective position. The principle of metareflection implies that by seeing the diversity of societal, political, and cultural forms as if from outside, management acknowledges that self-understanding and decision premises are basically rooted in a specific culture and in specific ideals of legitimacy—and at the same time is able to take into consideration different cultural and societal contexts within which the organization operates. Where a first-order reflexive perspective leads to blind ethnocentric positions, metareflective decision making is based on a self-understanding that relates one's own role and cultural roots to global diversity based on a metareflective sensitivity to a broad range of diverse cultures and societal forms, and a self-presentation that relates the deliberations of decision premises and the results of decision processes to this diversity (Holmström, Falkheimer, & Gade Nielsen, 2010).

Public Relations as Part of Reflective Management

In today's complex societies characterized by fluid modernity, managing major organizations involves complex decision-making processes, relating reflectively to the public horizon and to stakeholder publics. Society's turbulence strikes in organizations. As society faces new challenges, the legitimating notions mediating the interrelation between an organization and its social environment change and transform the premises of decision making. Where legitimacy in solid modernity was more or less given by common, solid norms, by central state regulation, and by unambiguous competitive market coordination, in today's fluid modernity, distinguished by liquid, ambiguous norms, organizations have to continuously justify their decisions and the underlying rationales without the possibility of relating to any ultimate reason—but in interplays with different and even conflicting perspectives and positions. Because this justification basically determines the organization's license to operate in society and is a basic precondition of support and resources from stakeholders, it becomes a concern of central management to continuously regenerate, renew, test, and adjust decision premises by mirroring them in a diversity of rationales and to continuously earn, build, and sustain trust in ongoing interrelations with stakeholder publics and in public communication processes.

While this social environment is often dealt with diffusely, relating it to different structural problems activated by society's evolution toward the full functional differentiation of modernity identifies six specific social trends, issues, and contexts for decision making to consider. Each has its particular dynamics and requires its particular response and considerations within management decision processes, but all activate paradigms and practices with a common denominator that can be analytically identified as the ideal of the second-order perspective of reflection.

First, with the increasing attention to the strains on life and nature by the side effects of modernization, growth, efficiency, profit, and market success no longer suffice to gain legitimacy and trust. Business companies must balance profit with considerations of people and planet in ongoing negotiations with stakeholders and in public relations processes. A reflective position helps management understand the complex interplay between issues, interests, and institutions and consequently helps balance considerations of life and nature with economic concerns.

Second, with society growing increasingly diverse, complex, fluid, uncertain, and unpredictable, social relations rely less on knowledge, control, and confidence and more on trust. A fundamental task of management is to continuously prove the organization worthy of trust. A reflective perspective is a precondition for decision processes to earn, build, and sustain trust by continuously relating to expectations from the environment, in attempts to see the world through the eyes of the social environment.

Third, the growing diversity of knowledge, competency, and capability in today's increasingly functionally differentiated society requires the organization's collaboration with multiple and diverse stakeholders and requires for decision making to respect sociodiversity and a growing range of different perspectives. A reflective perspective is a precondition of collaboration based on mutual respect and flexible and tolerant relations in between diverse societal positions.

Fourth, to cope with society's increasing complexity and dynamism, new political forms of societal governance call for corporate coregulation and coresponsibility and continuous discursive legitimization, based on participation in public debate and on sensitivity to the representation of society-within-society—whether this is denoted the *population*, the *public sphere*, or *public opinion*. A reflective position enables an understanding of the organization in a larger interdependent societal context and stimulates self-restrictive measures, ultimately as a basic precondition of securing the organization's own independence and self-referential development for the long term.

Fifth, with fluid modernity's increasing acknowledgment of the far-reaching consequences of contingent decisions, the perspective of being a potential victim explodes and continuously challenges the responsibility, accountability, sustainability, and transparency of corporate decision making. A reflective perspective makes decision premises and processes sensitive to those influenced by decisions in the larger perspective.

Sixth, globalization activates latent legitimacy conflicts between previously independent cultures and societal forms. A metareflective view on the diversity of cultural, societal, and political forms is a precondition for management to meet the challenges of globalization.

On all dimensions, public relations in a previous paradigm worked disconnected from the core decision processes of most organizations. Today, public relations is central to navigating organizations in fluid modernity. Furthermore, the second-order perspective of reflection is required, seeing the organization as if from outside, in the condition of sociodiversity, for an organization to navigate in the complexity and diversity of contemporary society from an understanding of the delicate balancing of people, planet, and profit; of consistency and change; of interdependence and independence; of market and society; of decision maker and victim; and of global and local values.

The legitimating paradigms and practices of reflection are bred by a specific stage of modernity and may be neither relevant nor possible in other types of society. For instance, the need for trust is a specific product of fluid modernity. A mainly stratified society as found in particular in some Asian countries is characterized by stable norms, tradition, convention, and collectivism. Instead of trust, social security strategies range from top-down control and confidence in conventional relations and collective norms to social security found in direct experience and personal family or friend relations. As to the governance trend, even though ideals of CSR increasingly permeate corporate semantics, the governance trend will be met with very different interpretations—depending in particular on whether the political culture is based in a strong tradition of central state control, as, for instance, the former USSR, in a basic culture of competitive market regulation, as, for instance, the United States, or on the mixed regulation of the welfare state, as in, for instance, Scandinavia. In addition, cultures based in the stratified society's hierarchical regulation, often with a strong religious reference, are not consistent with the basic values and the ideas and ideals of reflection that mediate the governance trend.

To conclude, to take contentions of reflective management beyond normative statements that reduce complexity from moral or political stances or from a specific professional niche, and to fully understand the challenges to management and the increasing importance of attention to an organization's public relations, requires an understanding of the social dynamics driving the evolution that activates reflective paradigms and practices.

Notes

1. The research presented in this chapter is based on Niklas Luhmann's theories on the nature and dynamics of social processes and on the constitution of society and of organizations (Holmström, 2007, 2009; Luhmann, 1984/1995, 1997b).

2. See Jensen (2001), for example, for a discussion of the differences between the notions of the public in American and European research and practice.

3. This goes for business companies. Other types of organizations with other primary rationales—for instance, science, for a nonprofit research institution, politics, for a political party or an NGO, news, for public news media, or religion, for a church—will relate each to their specific social environment.

4. For a case based on the theory of the reflective paradigm, see Holmström et al. (2010).

References

Annan, K. (1999). *Introduction to global compact.* Retrieved March 8, 2010, from http://www.un.org/News/Press/docs/1999/19990201.sgsm6881.html

Bakken, T., & Hernes, T. (Eds.). (2003). *Auopoietic organization theory.* Copenhagen, Denmark: Copenhagen Business School Press.

Baraldi, C. (2006). New forms of intercultural communication in a globalized world. *International Communication Gazette, 68*(1), 53–69.

Beck, U. (1994). The reinvention of politics: Towards a theory of reflexive modernization. In U. Beck, A. Giddens, & S. Lash (Eds.), *Reflexive modernization* (pp. 1–55). Cambridge, UK: Polity Press.

Bentele, G., & Seidenglanz, R. (2008). Trust and credibility. In A. Zerfass, B. van Ruler, & K. Sriramesh (Eds.), *Public relations research: European and international perspectives and innovations* (pp. 49–62). Wiesbaden, Germany: Westdeutscher Verlag.

Elkington, J. (1997). *Cannibals with forks: The triple bottom line of 21st century business.* Oxford, UK: Capstone.

Holmström, S. (1997). An intersubjective and a social systemic public relations paradigm. *Journal of Communications Management, 2*(1), 24–39.

Holmström, S. (1998). *An intersubjective and a social systemic public relations paradigm.* Roskilde, Denmark: Roskilde University. Retrieved January 15, 2010, from www.susanne-holmstrom.dk/SH1996UK.pdf (Original work published 1996)

Holmström, S. (2002). Public relations reconstructed as part of society's evolutionary learning processes. In D. Verčič, B. van Ruler, I. Jensen, D. Moss, & J. White (Eds.), *The status of public relations knowledge* (pp. 76–91). Ljubljana, Slovenia: Pristop Communications.

Holmström, S. (2004). The reflective paradigm. In B. van Ruler & D. Verčič (Eds.), *Public relations in Europe* (pp. 121–134). Berlin, Germany: de Gruyter.

Holmström, S. (2005a). Fear, risk, and reflection. *Contatti (Udine University: FORUM), 1*(1), 21–45.

Holmström, S. (2005b). Reframing public relations: The evolution of a reflective paradigm for organizational legitimization. *Public Relations Review, 31*(4), 497–504.

Holmström, S. (2007). Niklas Luhmann: Contingency, risk, trust and reflection. *Public Relations Review, 33*(2), 255–262.

Holmström, S. (2008). Reflection: Legitimising late modernity. In A. Zerfass, B. van Ruler, & K. Sriramesh (Eds.), *Public relations research: European and international perspectives and innovations* (pp. 235–250). Wiesbaden, Germany: Westdeutscher Verlag.

Holmström, S. (2009). On Niklas Luhmann: Contingency, risk, trust and reflection. In Ø. Ihlen, M. Fredriksson, & B. van Ruler (Eds.), *Public relations and social theory* (pp. 187–211). New York: Routledge.

Holmström, S., Falkheimer, J., & Gade Nielsen, A. (2010). Legitimacy and strategic communication in globalization: The Cartoon Crisis and other legitimacy conflicts. *International Journal of Strategic Communication, 4,* 1–18.

Jalava, J. (2003). From norms to trust: The Luhmannian connections between trust and system. *European Journal of Social Theory, 6*(2), 173–190.

Jensen, I. (2001). Public relations and emerging functions of the public sphere. *Journal of Communication Management, 6*(2), 133–147.

Kostova, T., & Zaheer, S. (1999). Organizational legitimacy under conditions of complexity: The case of the multinational enterprise. *Academy of Management Review, 24*(1), 64–81.

Luhmann, N. (1982). *Trust and power.* Hoboken, NJ: Wiley. (Original work published 1968)

Luhmann, N. (1989). *Ecological communication.* Cambridge, UK: Polity Press. (Original work published 1986)

Luhmann, N. (1993). *Risk: A sociological theory.* New York: de Gruyter. (Original work published 1991)

Luhmann, N. (1995). *Social systems.* Palo Alto, CA: Stanford University Press. (Original work published 1984)

Luhmann, N. (1997a). *Die Gesellschaft der Gesellschaft* [Society's society]. Frankfurt, Germany: Suhrkamp.

Luhmann, N. (1997b). Limits of steering. *Theory, Culture & Society, 14*(1), 41–57.

Luhmann, N. (1998). *Observations on modernity* (W. Whobrey, Trans.). Palo Alto, CA: Stanford University Press.

Luhmann, N. (2000). *Organisation und Entscheidung* [Organization and decision]. Opladen, Germany: Westdeutscher Verlag.

Luhmann, N. (2000). *The reality of the mass media.* Cambridge, UK: Polity Press. (Original work published 1996)

Mirvis, P. H. (2000). Transformation at Shell: Commerce and citizenship. *Business and Society Review, 105*(1), 63–84.

Porter, M. E., & Kramer, M. R. (2006). Strategy and society: The link between competitive advantage and corporate social responsibility. *Harvard Business Review, 84*(12), 78–92.

Qvortrup, L. (2003). *The hypercomplex society.* New York: Peter Lang.

Sand, I.-J. (2004). Polycontextuality as an alternative to constitutionalism. In C. Joerges, I.-J. Sand, & G. Teubner (Eds.), *Transnational governance and constitutionalism.* Oxford, UK: Hart.

Sørensen, E., & Torfing, J. (2005). The democratic anchorage of governance networks. *Scandinavian Political Studies, 28*(3), 195–218.

Teubner, G. (2005). Substantive and reflexive elements in modern law. In C. Seron (Ed.), *The law and society canon* (pp. 75–122). Aldershot, UK: Ashgate.

Willke, H., & Willke, G. (2008). Corporate moral legitimacy and the legitimacy of morals. *Journal of Business Ethics, 81,* 1–12.

CHAPTER 19

Symmetry and Its Critics

Antecedents, Prospects, and Implications for Symmetry in a Postsymmetry Era

Robert E. Brown

Almost from its rollout in J. E. Grunig and Hunt's (1984) *Managing Public Relations*, the concept of symmetry established itself as the dominant paradigm of public relations, generating considerable attention, research, and publication. But parallel to its ascendancy and for nearly as long as the theory's career, a growing chorus of critics has arisen to challenge it. After a quarter century of querulous criticism, the scholarship of public relations may be said to have entered a postsymmetrical age.

A multifaceted, complex theory in its original form, symmetry has been dramatically downsized and reshaped. Symmetry proved a watershed not only for public relations scholarship but also for the way in which the public relations industry was encouraged to view the practice. Symmetry theory sought to reframe public relations from an influential and creative management practice to an ethical and professional practice based on a communication system amenable to rigorous, quantitative evaluation and capable of producing equitable outcomes not only for organizational management but also for their publics. That view signaled a shift from what had been the dominant perspective of public relations during much of the 20th century: persuasive communication.

A social scientist by training and sensibility, J. E. Grunig (2001) wrote that with the first of a series of publications in 1976, he "began to look at public relations as a dependent variable to be explained, rather than as an independent variable whose effects are to be described" (p. 11). J. E. Grunig's initial conceptualization of symmetry, in the 1984 textbook he coauthored with Hunt, proposed four models: (1) press-agentry/publicity, (2) public information, (3) two-way asymmetric, and (4) two-way symmetric. The models were characterized as follows: press-agentry/publicity as a one-way, source-to-receiver, unethical model whose exemplary practitioner was P. T. Barnum, the circus promoter and flimflam man plying his trade in mid-19th-century America; public information as a one-way, ethically problematic, source-to-receiver model intended to convey information;

and two-way asymmetry (the Bernays model), which that orchestrated communication back and forth between the source and the receiver, with the intention of using research techniques to evaluate attitudes in order to persuade publics and win victories for management.

The fourth model contained the essence of J. E. Grunig's major contribution to public relations theory: two-way symmetry. He proposed it as the most "evolved" of the theoretical models in that it proposed a normative concept of public relations practice that reconceived what the practice could and should be: not the persuasive, pro-management model named by Bernays (1952), but rather a whole new state of affairs described by the balance of fairness for both an organization and its publics. Less than a decade after positing symmetry as the most evolved model of public relations; J. E. Grunig proposed an enhanced form of symmetry as the only excellent way of practicing public relations.

Not surprisingly, the ambitious claims for symmetry have come under considerable criticism, particularly from rhetoricians, critical thinkers, historians, and proponents of cultural diversity. These scholars challenged symmetry's assumptions and presumptions. The intellectual foundations of symmetry theory sought to brand public relations as a science, rooted in systems theory, with the effects of public relations to be rendered measurable primarily by reliance on quantitative methodologies. Other key elements of symmetry were its "evolutionary" or progressive historiography that viewed the practice as developing from deception and impulse to an emphasis on reason and ethics, its American-centric cultural focus, its intellectual allegiance to the precision and objectivity associated with modernity, and the assumption that human nature and its social expression are benign and rational, enabling productive negotiation.

Almost since symmetry theory's introduction, its critics have challenged its assumptions. Under the impress of these challenges, J. E. Grunig and symmetry's adherents have modified the theory, so that two decades after its introduction, symmetry has been largely truncated from its four original models to the enhanced fourth model, symmetry, and the concept of symmetry itself has come to be understood far more simply as the willingness to change.

Still, after a generation as the dominant paradigm of public relations research and publication, and after almost as many years under attack by symmetry's critics, J. E. Grunig's normative conceptualization continues to enjoy widespread influence on the way public relations is taught, discussed, researched, published, and, perhaps to a lesser extent, practiced worldwide. Symmetry continues to be a frequently cited theoretical foundation for public relations research, as well as an ethically aspirational corrective to the persistence of popular, cynical, dismissive, and uninformed notions of public relations.

Periodic History of Public Relations

Like Bernays, Cutlip, and other scholars with a serious interest in the history of public relations, Heath (2005) traced the antecedents of public relations to antiquity and even to the dawn of civilization. Despite the obvious risks of speculating in the absence of much evidence, scholars have attempted to explore the apparent but elusive associations of public relations with other historical forms of influence. As historical sociology insists, all social theory needs to be grounded in history; and because public relations theory is social theory, it, too, needs to be historically grounded because "sociological explanation is necessarily historical" (Borgatta & Borgatta, 1992, p. 838). Public relations scholarship, however, has not generated a particularly large or impressive body of historical or historiographical literature.

Despite the historical efforts of a few public relations scholars, including Cutlip and Hiebert, the field lacks a definitive scholarly history. What does exist in public relations textbooks and scholarly publications is a consensus narrative of the development of public relations. Generally, public relations scholars have described public relations as the institutional child of the 19th-century and early 20th-century industrialism and communication technology. Three decades after his publication of *Crystallizing Public Opinion* (Bernays, 1923), one of the field's seminal texts, Edward L. Bernays (1952) sketched just such a narrative of public relations. Bernays's historical narrative established the periodicity and the progressivist history of the field that became the template for J. E. Grunig's four models. But J. E. Grunig rejected the persuasive core of the Bernays model as insufficiently evolved.

Bernays's Periodicity

After citing examples of public relations–like activities in antiquity, Bernays identified several paradigmatic periods of American history, beginning with the end of the American Civil War. The first of these periods was 1865–1900, seen as an era of rapid growth, expansion, and industrialization marked by the prominence of the railroad and oil empire builders and their ethically free, "public be damned" attitude, the imperious phrase of the American railroad tycoon, Cornelius Vanderbilt (Bernays, 1952, p. 51). Bernays identifies the next period of public relations as 1900–1919, characterized by the U.S. government's regulatory reaction against the abuses of empire builders, spawning what Bernays calls public relations' early modern development whose motto was "the public be informed" (p. 63). The information model was a step forward from Barnum and Vanderbilt.

What follows is the period from 1919 to 1929, which Bernays identified as the rise of public relations as a new profession, when increasing attention was paid to the close analysis of the power of public opinion, most famously by Walter Lippmann (1922) with the publication of *Public Opinion*. This bracing period saw the benefits of public relations' association with social science in the rise of the perception of public relations' power and influence. But there was a dark side, too, as public relations came to be associated with the period's totalitarian propaganda, a perceptual stain that continues to haunt the reputation of public relations. In Bernays's historical account of public relations, it was during this period of professionalization that the public relations industry began to place considerable emphasis on social responsibility, in part to offset public relations' invidious association with the rising tide of fascism and communism. It was also during this period that Bernays changed the name of his agency, and by extension the industry's identity as well, from "propaganda bureau" to "public relations counsel," and introduced the "two-way" concept (Bernays, 1952) that continues to be a definitive attribute of public relations.

Bernays's final period, 1929–1941, traced the rise of public relations in world affairs, taking the practice through the Great Depression and up to the start of World War II in Europe. J. E. Grunig's original four models of public relations replicate Bernays's historiographical narrative of the field.

Two-Way Street

Eric Goldman (1948, p. 3) credited N. S. B. Gras (1945) with tracing the origins of public relations to the medieval guild. Goldman credited Bernays with being the essential theoretician of public relations, advancing the notion of two-way communication. Bernays's framing of public relations found its way into Scott Cutlip and Allen Center's (1952) early and influential textbook with its emphasis on defining public relations as "adequate two-way communication and interpretation" (p. 5), and its promulgation of the conventional historical idea of public relations as a practice that had progressed substantially from the press-agentry of P. T. Barnum to the rise of professionalism.

Systems Theory Foundation

While Bernays's progressivist history influenced the concept of public relations, and later played a key role in J. E. Grunig's theory of symmetry, an equally important influence was systems theory. The GST (general systems theory) paradigm is credited to the biologist Karl Ludwig von Bertalanffy (1976). For decades to come, systems theory spawned applications of greater and lesser rigor across a broad range of disciplines, including psychology, sociology, anthropology, political science, economics, and information systems. The influence of systems theory was evident in the development of the symmetrical concept of public relations.

J. E. Grunig regarded the persuasive head of Bernays's approach to have overwhelmed its ethical heart. If J. E. Grunig found in Bernays's emphasis on science and engineering a like-minded appreciation of science's prestige, he also found Bernays's approach to science to be impressionistic and inferior to the scientific and quantitative rigor of systems theory. In his doctoral research and early publications, J. E. Grunig (1969) applied systems theory, economic decision-making theory, and quantitative and qualitative methodologies. As a doctoral candidate in mass communication, J. E. Grunig focused attention on economic theory as applied to the analysis of decision-making processes—including those of farmers in Colombia, South America. He concluded, in part, that communication behavior played a major role in the strategies, successes, and failures of peasant farmers (J. E. Grunig, 1966, 1969).

In applying systems thinking to public relations theory, J. E. Grunig sought to transcend Bernays methodologically and ethically by making symmetry scientifically testable and replacing the problematic and wishful ethics of manipulative persuasion with an ethics based on the systems concept of balance. As he sought to develop a theory that would explain the behavior of organizations, J. E. Grunig appears to have been influenced by Lee Thayer (1968), a communication theorist who demonstrated how systems theory could be used to explain social, economic, interpersonal, and organizational behavior. Making use of cybernetics—an application of systems theory to the analysis of information flows—Thayer proposed that organizational communication could be categorized as "diachronic" and "synchronic" (p. 129), terms that roughly corresponded, he said, to the difference between "monologue" and "dialogue" (p. 129). Conversation had trumped persuasion.

Thayer's distinction played a role in J. E. Grunig's early development of symmetry theory. Where the objective of synchronic communication is to bring about a change in the actions or behavior of another person to be consistent with the approach of the communicator, diachronic communication brings about a whole new state of affairs between communicators rather than moving one party in the direction or under the influence of another. In other words, synchronic communication is persuasive, whereas diachronic communication is negotiated. In his introduction of symmetry theory in 1984, J. E. Grunig drew distinctions between what he posited as a two-way asymmetric model (sometimes called the Bernays model) and a single two-way symmetric model. In doing so, J. E. Grunig and Hunt (1984) used Thayer's terms of "dialogue" and "monologue" (p. 23) to contrast the symmetric and asymmetric models. With Thayer's distinction, J. E. Grunig sought to open an entirely new space for public relations. Whether he did has been a matter for long and serious debate in the scholarly community.

It was this crucial, systems theory–based distinction between asymmetry and symmetry that took center stage in J. E. Grunig's development of symmetry theory. The distinction amounted to the rejection of Bernays as an inadequate role model for public relations, despite Bernays's lifelong campaign to establish ethical standards and an academic curriculum for the nascent profession. In J. E. Grunig's original conception of symmetry, Bernays was credited with developing the two-way communication approach that emphasized organizational research of publics. But J. E. Grunig saw Bernays as failing to base public relations on the premise of ethical balance, or equilibrium, between organization and publics, the systems theory concept that J. E. Grunig adapted from Thayer. Before symmetry, persuasion had been fundamental to public relations; but symmetry rejected persuasion as ethically and effectively inferior to what could and should be achieved through the properly balanced management of systems.

Excellence Theory

Another major influence on symmetry theory came from the enormous popularity of Peters and Waterman's (1982) publication on excellence in the management of companies. Their book, *In Search of Excellence*, sold several million copies during the 1980s. A short time after the introduction of symmetry theory in 1984, J. E. Grunig and Hunt began to engage in research that sought to meld symmetry theory with the concepts of organizational excellence that were far more widely known. J. E. Grunig's (1992) *Excellence in Public Relations and Communication Management* sought to join the theories of excellence and symmetry. L. A. Grunig, Grunig, and Ehling (1992) claimed that the nexus of symmetry and excellence had moved beyond all other conceptualizations of public relations, including the "values perspective" associated with Cutlip's idea of effectiveness (J. E. Grunig, 1992, pp. 68–75). In his elaboration of symmetry theory, J. E. Grunig sought to position symmetry-excellence theory as the dominant paradigm of public relations. To accomplish this, he broadened symmetry-excellence's intellectual reach by acknowledging the contributions of Jurgen Habermas's theory of the "ideal communication situation" (J. E. Grunig, 1992, p. 54) and favorably citing a number of rhetorical scholars, including Kenneth Burke, as well as feminist theorists and quantitative methodologists (p. 54). As early as 1992, J. E. Grunig appears to have begun to open symmetry to incorporate a rhetorical perspective.

Symmetry's Phases

Theories have a way of changing over time. It is not possible to understand the criticism of symmetry or its place in a postsymmetrical world without reviewing its alterations over time. Symmetry's critics weigh in with different perspectives and new research. Like many other theorists with a big idea, J. E. Grunig began tinkering with symmetry almost as soon as he introduced it in 1984 (J. E. Grunig & Hunt, 1984). The complex relationship of advocacy to symmetry is attributable to these revisions. So are the revisions and simplifications crafted by J. E. Grunig's scholarly disciples.

Phase 1

The overture to the curtain rising on symmetry theory came in the 1960s with J. E. Grunig's research into the communication variables and other variables associated with the economic decision making of Colombian farmers (J. E. Grunig, 1966, 1969). The phases of symmetry can be said to begin with J. E. Grunig and Hunt's (1984) introduction of four models culminating in "two-way symmetrical" public relations, which contained the essence of what would come to be known simply as symmetry. Unlike existing, and for J. E. Grunig relatively impressionistic perspectives on public relations, he reversed the conception of public relations to view it as a "dependent variable to be explained rather than as an independent variable whose effects were to be described" (J. E. Grunig, 2001, p. 11).

Phase 2

The first phase was followed by a second, characterized by J. E. Grunig's project to weld symmetry theory to the management theory of excellence with the publication of *Excellence in Public Relations* in 1992. With its emphasis on the management of large and powerful corporations, excellence theory came under attack with special vehemence from critical thinkers such as L'Etang and Pieczka (2006), who questioned what they regarded as the narrowness of excellence theory's ethical claims and its insensitivity to the power differentials between powerful organizations and their publics.

Phase 3

The beginning of the third phase saw J. E. Grunig defending symmetry-excellence throughout the 1990s and into the following decade. By the turn of the 21st century, J. E. Grunig (2001) began to deemphasize, if not openly retreat from, the systems theory perspective that had been symmetry's foundation. At the same time, J. E. Grunig defended symmetry against the objection that the theory is "utopian" (J. E. Grunig, 2001, p. 17). In this phase, J. E. Grunig appeared to move symmetry into closer alignment with the rhetorical perspective that "would envision public relations as a force that allows competing groups in a pluralist society equal access to decision makers, maintains functional equilibrium in a society, and produces goodwill and harmony" (J. E. Grunig, 2001, p. 17). Toth (2009) finds "some complementary understandings" among the symmetrical, rhetorical, and critical perspectives (p. 56).

J. E. Grunig's third phase of theoretical development consisted not simply in rebutting his critics but also in repositioning the symmetry-excellence concept. He took pains to admit to a semantic confusion: For in choosing the terms "symmetry" and "balance," J. E. Grunig admitted that he had "failed to convey" his sense that symmetry refers "more to a process than to an outcome" (J. E. Grunig, 2001, p. 28). On further reading and reflection, J. E. Grunig repositioned his concept with reference to Spicer (1997) and asserted that Spicer's thinking has "moved me beyond the relative notion of consensus as an end-product to the more process-oriented experience of collaboration" (J. E. Grunig, 2001, p. 28).

Continuing his efforts to defend symmetry theory from what he regarded as misconceptions about the role and meaning of measurement in public relations research, J. E. Grunig (2008) asserted that "the greatest problem in public relations is not the lack of measurement but the lack of conceptualization" (p. 89). In 1976, J. E. Grunig framed public relations broadly as the dependent variable to be explained rather than as an independent variable that produced effects to be described. Two decades later, he offered "reputation" (p. 93) as an example of a dependent variable that can be measured. In contrast, the public relations pioneer Bernays (1952) framed public relations descriptively in language that would mark it, in J. E. Grunig's terms, as independent variables that Bernays identified as "information given to the public" and "persuasion directed at the public to modify attitudes and actions" and "efforts to integrate attitudes and actions of an institution with its publics and of publics with that institution" (p. 3). As someone not working in what J. E. Grunig called the "research tradition" (p. 114), the public relations pioneer Bernays did not express his ideas of public relations as "variables." But all three of the definitive attributes of public relations Bernays cited are independent variables (Bernays, 1952, p. 3).

Phase 4

It is the fate of theories to move beyond their creators, sometimes unrecognizably. Freud might not be a Freudian or Marx a Marxist. In what appears to be the fourth and latest phase of symmetry's development, J. E. Grunig's theory has been appropriated by its adherents, who have interpreted it variously, including quite simply as the willingness to change.

Symmetry's Critics

Notwithstanding J. E. Grunig's attempts to broaden the concept of symmetry, and explain and defend it against its critics, objections to symmetry theory began soon after its introduction and have multiplied ever since. At the same time, the influence of symmetry theory persists in the United States and internationally.

Symmetry theory has come under increasing attack from five principal directions: (1) rhetoric, (2) critical thinking, (3) postmodernism, (4) qualitative methodology, and (5) a mixture of globalism, internationalism, and multiculturalism. What unites the critics of symmetry is their emphasis on the values of pluralism, interdisciplinarity, and cultural and methodological diversity, and their rejection of symmetry—or any other approach—to be the single, dominant, legitimate paradigm.

Rhetorical Problems

While there is no consensus on symmetry among rhetorical theorists, some rhetorical scholars, notably Heath, regard symmetry theory as problematic. Heath's (2001) approach to public relations stresses the value of the cocreation of meaning, along with advocacy, argument, and dialogue—attributes not emphasized, if not absent, in symmetry theory. For Heath, public relations is primarily about meaning rather than the result of systems-driven, cybernetic processes. Public relations is regarded as the outcome of vigorous disputes between advocates who may interpret facts differently but in a democratic society can manage to find common ground. Public relations ethics derive from the ethical discourse of rhetoric itself. For Heath, as for Aristotle, advocacy is a crucial part of rhetoric's ethical nature. Heath has objected to symmetry founding its ethics on a systems explanation, regarding systems-based symmetry not as unethical but aethical as it fails to rise to the rhetorically derived standards for ethics that Heath insists are "basic to the full functioning of a community" (Heath, 2001, p. 49). Unlike Heath's rhetorical perspective, symmetry is not primarily about meaning, or shared or cocreated meaning, but rather misplaced in the physical equations of systems theory and cybernetics. Systems-based symmetry may be sufficient for physics but not for citizenship.

In a key passage, Heath (2001) challenges symmetry theory's implication that rhetoric somehow falls short of symmetrical excellence by insisting that rhetoric

> is symmetrical because each idea placed in the marketplace and public policy arena stands on its own merit. No idea is privileged even if it has an advocate with deep pockets. Rhetoric empowers policy discussants to seek adherents and to have their say in circumstances that affect them even if they only privately reject the points made by corporate or other organizational rhetors. (p. 49)

He added to this the concept of a "fully functioning society" (p. 49) in which "policy and preference are forged through assertion and counter-assertion" (p. 49). Such a conception of excellence is what Heath calls "organic" (p. 49), in contrast to symmetry's predominantly mechanistic conceptualization of excellence as a balance of systemic forces and counterforces.

Role of Advocacy

J. E. Grunig doesn't reject advocacy, claiming instead that it is accounted for in a symmetrical communication system as a "countervailing power" typically wielded by activist groups (J. E. Grunig, 2001, p. 18). It is possible to interpret J. E. Grunig's position as a way of reconciling the symmetrical and rhetorical endorsement of advocacy, although for J. E. Grunig, advocacy is an incidental rather than a central feature of an ethical communication system. For Heath, rhetoric establishes a more robust, reliable, and inclusive standard for public relations ethics than symmetry because Aristotelian rhetoric "blended advocacy and symmetry" (Heath, 2009, p. 29).

From Heath's perspective, symmetry's "equilibrium" amounts to nothing more than a mechanical perception of feedback from a mechanical source. The symmetrical theory of public relations ethics and excellence is seen as distant from any socially grounded basis of fairness for organizational relationships with stakeholders. It is not symmetry's mechanical balancing act that's central to the ideals or the conceptualization of public relations; rather, it is meaning that is cocreated (Heath & Coombs, 2006, p. 20) in the dialogue that comprises advocacy and argument. Historically, the rhetorical tradition follows the intellectual path from *Ars Rhetorica* through the medieval university of Aquinas, the philosophers of the Enlightenment, and the framers of American democracy.

Not all rhetoricians agree with Heath's assessment of symmetry. Toth (2009) saw in symmetry's emphasis on improving organizations and strengthening their relationships values consistent with the ethical roots of rhetoric. Toth sees sufficient common ground in the rhetorical and symmetrical approaches to public relations. In particular, it is excellence theory that Toth finds to be particularly compelling as a "paradigm or world view of public relations" (Toth, 2009, p. 56). Toth quoted J. E. Grunig approvingly in describing symmetry as "a process-oriented experience of collaboration, of mixed motives, collaborative advocacy, and cooperative antagonism" (J. E. Grunig, 2001, p. 28). In seeking to marry symmetrical theory with excellence theory, J. E. Grunig argued that "asymmetry and symmetry (or advocacy and collaboration) work in tandem in excellent public relations" (p. 30), adding that "we now seem to have a much better developed theory of symmetrical (dialogic, collaborative advocacy)" (p. 30).

But for Heath that marriage cannot be intellectually consummated. For one thing, J. E. Grunig and Heath regard very differently the failure of parties to collaborate. For J. E. Grunig (2001), symmetry theory offers the guidance that the failure of parties to reach accommodation constitutes ethical grounds for either side pursuing the "advocacy of its interests of withdrawal from the dialogue" (p. 16). But for Heath this guidance belies a misunderstanding of the organic nature of the give-and-take of dialogue and advocacy and creates an unsatisfying and ethically problematic context for communication.

Like Toth, Bowen (2005) has sought to find common ground between the symmetrical and rhetorical concepts of public relations. Bowen described symmetrical public relations in the rhetorical terms of "debate," "discussion," "negotiation," and "collaboration" (p. 839). For Bowen, symmetry is a way of doing public relations so that it "performs an idealistic social role" acting to "grease the wheels of society" and moving organizations and publics toward engagement in "informed debate" (p. 839).

But none of the three authors—Bowen, Toth, or J. E. Grunig—has been able to bridge the intellectual gap between symmetry and its critics. From the perspective of intellectual history, contrasting sensibilities may also play a role in the long, complex, contentious, and sometimes arcane and even mystifying battles engendered by symmetry. Historically, the intellectual heritage of rhetoric—from Aristotle in antiquity to Burke in modernity—occupies a very different space from that of Bertalanffy and Thayer, which is roughly the gulf between the humanities and the sciences. That contrast in sensibilities echoes intellectual history, including the schism that led the poet and critic T. S. Eliot to speculate on a "dissociation of sensibilities" that occurred in the late 16th and early 17th centuries, when it became no longer possible for even highly educated individuals to understand the world as a whole, owing to the rise of empirical science with its dazzling but mystifyingly quantifiable methodologies (Eliot, 1964). Plato's repudiation and Aristotle's defense of rhetoric cast a long shadow that fell on public relations.

Critical Thinking Critiques

Another source of objections to symmetry theory's claim to dominance and legitimacy comes from the camp of critical thinkers. According to L'Etang (2008), critical thinking challenges existing assumptions, policies, and practices, an also opens analysis to new, interdisciplinary, and creative ways of approaching a subject (p. 4). For L'Etang, the nexus of symmetry and excellence represents the failure of self-criticism and creative imagination. From the perspective of critical thinking, symmetry's legacy has been the unfortunate narrowing of the conception, practice, and ethical character of public relations.

For critical thinkers, symmetry's insensitivity to power differentials sets public relations' ethical bar too low. Fundamental to critical thinking is its deeply skeptical attitude toward power. For critical thinkers, symmetry theory's assumptions about organizations and stakeholders mask the realities of the vastly unequal power differential between organizational management and its stakeholders. Critical thinkers reject symmetry's assertion of a public relations ideal of "excellence" as a standard of fairness and balance. On the contrary, critical thinkers see the world asymmetrically, as a field of unequally equipped competitors, where powerful and well-resourced organizations dominate not only through overt force but also by covert, invisible, unacknowledged, symbolic strategies and unexamined assumptions. From a critical thinking perspective, symmetry not only fails to remediate this asymmetry, as it claims to do, but may also actually harden, institutionalize, and defend it with the illegitimately borrowed prestige and quantified rigor of science. Critical thinking challenges what it perceives to be the hegemonic power that lies underneath symmetrical-excellent programs such as corporate social responsibility, benefiting management at the expense of its constituencies.

Critical thinking places public relations—and, in particular, symmetry theory—squarely in its crosshairs. From the critical vantage point, the confluence of excellence theory and symmetry theory is based on the uncritical acceptance of the assumption that public relations practitioners should "align themselves with management" (L'Etang, 2008, p. 163). This pro-organizational assumption is seen as irreconcilable with symmetry theory's claims to ethical normativeness.

In a similar vein, critical thinking challenges the assumptions of excellence theory that endorse the values of the world's most powerful corporations. Critical thinking challenges symmetry theory's conception of excellence on the ground that the management idea of excellence reflects the management bias of the popular "excellence" books of the 1980s. As a pluralistic approach to ideas and institutions, critical thinking rejects symmetry's assumption that there is a single, dominant, unitary, or universal concept of excellence when it comes to the highly complex, interpersonal, political, economic, and symbolic interactions that constitute public relations.

Another criticism leveled against symmetry is its adoption of excellence, which is regarded by critical thinkers as one of the management fads of the 1980s and 1990s, along with total quality management and statistical quality control, part of the rise in prestige of the organizationally fashionable management "guru" (L'Etang, 2008, pp. 162–163).

Europe has been a source of critical-thinking objections to symmetry theory. Pieczka (2006), a leading critical thinker, challenged symmetry's functionalist and systems foundational assumptions, which led to symmetry's dictum that the function of public relations is to manage subsystems to produce outcomes of equilibrium. Another assumption about public relations that has come under fire is that its goal must be adaptation, harmony, and negotiation, as elaborated in J. E. Grunig's book on excellence.

Critical thinkers like L'Etang and Pieczka (2006) have not failed to recognize the intention of symmetry-excellence theory to set ethical standards. Pieczka regarded the excellence project as a "deductive process" (p. 355), which offered a limited idea of excellence, an approach that "puts answers before questions," in the sense of limiting the possibilities of what the answers might be (p. 355). Put simply, the excellence project produced a concept of excellence that lacked sufficient depth and breadth.

Notwithstanding its critics, symmetry theory has its European adherents in the scholarly and practitioner communities. Among the most productive European scholars influenced by symmetry are Günter Bentele and Stefan Wehmeir (2003), whose perspective on public relations is rooted in systems theory. Bentele has endorsed symmetry's affirmation of scientific objectivity. In the wake of fascism and communism, European scholars have been acutely sensitive to the dark association of public relations with propaganda and sought to expunge every trace of propaganda from public relations.

But other European scholars have objected to symmetry as a narrowly American creation. That public relations came to be regarded as American is not particularly surprising, even apart from the popular influence of Bernays, Ivy Lee, and other American pioneers of public relations. Especially after World War I, the growing perception of the power of public relations in the affairs of business, politics, and other arenas came to be associated with the rapidly increasing power and influence of the United States in world affairs, particularly in business, entertainment, and communication. America's identification with public relations became the basis for a chorus of European objections to the damaging influence of America's exporting its consumer and entertainment industries, lowering standards, and promoting cultural mediocrity.

Long before J. E. Grunig's introduction of symmetry, both the institution and the idea of public relations were lumped together with advertising and branded as peculiarly American. Whether intentionally or not, the introduction of symmetry has served its adherents as a rigorous, intellectually complex, quantitatively supported, sometimes passionately defended reaction against the plainly notorious reputation of public relations—a bad name that has been faithfully, if ruefully, documented for decades by public relations scholars themselves. If public relations professionals and scholars have occasionally acknowledged the industry's reputation for dishonesty, critics of public relations outside the public relations practice have not hesitated to heap abuse and ridicule on public relations and its practitioners. Daniel Boorstin's (1992) *The Image* and Edward S. Herman and Noam Chomsky's (2002) *Manufacturing Consent* attacked public relations as powerful and illegitimate, pointing to its regrettable orchestration of what Boorstin derided as "pseudoevents." In the spirit of Marxist critiques, Chomsky enlarged that criticism by associating public relations with propaganda used to advance U.S. capitalism and imperialism.

Postmodernism Versus Modernism

Among the most severe critics of symmetry are thinkers whose work is associated with the tenets of postmodernism, defined broadly speaking as a collection of worldviews that have in common the rejection of "claims of absolute certainty, objective truth, ... and intrinsic meaning" (Agnes, 2000, p. 1125). This worldview is associated most famously with the ironic and subversive antiphilosophy of Nietzsche in the 19th century, and in the 20th with Foucault and many others. Postmodernists—queer theorists, feminists, culture theorists, popular culture theorists—have elaborated the contrast between the Enlightenment veracities held sacred by conventional wisdom and hegemonic power, and the material critique of the flawed foundation of those veracities. In the visual and literary arts, where modernism is said to value representationalism and depth, postmodernism offers abstraction and surfaces. Jameson (1993) regarded postmodernism as a "revolt" (p. 315) against the "frantic economic urgency of producing fresh waves of ever more novel-seeming goods (from clothing to airplanes) at ever greater rates of turnover" (p. 316).

Pomo Economics

The role of economics can hardly be underestimated in the origins and development of symmetry, in its marriage to excellence theory, and in the postmodernist critique of its assumptions. Symmetry-excellence theory reflects a modernist, progressivist, and fundamentally procapitalist worldview that postmodernism regards as neoliberalism. Postmodernist critiques attack symmetry not only on the cultural front but also by challenging the fairness, legitimacy, and material reality of neoliberalism's belief in the legitimacy of free market economics, itself a part of the intellectual legacy of modernism associated with Adam Smith's *Wealth of Nations* published in 1776.

In the spirit of antimaterialism and empty novelty, postmodernism stands in direct opposition to the symmetrical concept of public relations that fails to account for the hegemony of powerful industrial and corporate organizations versus their publics. In recent decades, among the most prominent postmodernists was Guy Debord (1983), who argued that the rise of American advertising and public relations had created "false choice in spectacular abundance" (p. 56), a degrading spectacle that was addicting the world to material and fatuous products and services.

For postmodern theorists, the 21st-century world can in no way be adequately described in terms of symmetry, a concept whose scientificism, rationalism, mechanism, insularity, and claims to objectivity, truth, ethics, and excellence appear arrogant, parochial, and naive. From a postmodern perspective, any good and useful theory of public relations would have to move beyond the culturally reductive narrowness of symmetry and instead embrace multiple perspectives and methodologies, cultural diversity, and interdisciplinarity and display more sensitivity to power differentials between management and its publics than is admitted by the symmetry theory.

Postmodernism itself is, in no small measure, a question of economics. Its cultural critique can claim an intellectual pedigree that includes Hegel and Marx, the deconstructive sociology of Simmel, and more recently poststructuralists and cultural theorists who have sought to unpack what Jameson (1993) called "the logic of late capitalism" (p. 312).

Postmodernity is also the source of much criticism of public relations—and indirectly of symmetry. The fashion for public relations bashing has fueled the reception of facetious attacks, including Henry Frankfort's (2005) *On Bullshit*, Laura Penny's (2005) *Your Call Is Important to Us*, and Larry Tye's (2002) *The Father of Spin: Edward L. Bernays and the Birth of Public Relations.* What these views of public relations have in common is the equation of public relations with the perception of organizational mendacity, manipulation, soullessness, and buffoonery. Taken together, these popular, middlebrow books, together with the works of highbrow scholars, have helped perpetuate the negative reputation of public relations.

It should not be surprising, then, to see how symmetry could have been embraced by the public relations industry—teachers, scholars, and textbook writers.

Qualitative Imperatives

The fox knows many things, but the hedgehog knows one big thing. Isaiah Berlin made his famous observation in an essay on Leo Tolstoy. Much the same distinction might be said to characterize the basic objection of qualitative scholars to the methodological approach fostered and favored by symmetrists. From the perspective of ethnographers, rhetoricians, critical thinkers, feminists, phenomenologists, focus group researchers, historiographers, unstructured interviewers, communitarians, and other qualitative researchers, they're the fox seeking their share of attention in a discipline that has been dominated by the hedgehog symmetrists who know only quantitative methodology. Qualitative research sensibility tends toward pluralism, endorsing intersubjectivity; quantitative methodology is regarded by its critics as monistic, unrealistic, and naive. Symmetry theory's positivistic identification with science has led researchers to think probabilistically and editors to favor the publication of the hedgehogs over the foxes. Postpositive researchers find the quantitative approach to be problematic. Champions of qualitative approaches to knowledge believe it to "provide multiple truths, alternative visions and critical perspectives" (L'Etang, 2008, p. 249).

Broadly speaking, European scholars have demonstrated a wider range of methodological approaches to public relations than U.S. scholars. Much of the qualitative scholarship has been produced by scholars outside the United States, while public relations scholarship in the United States has been strongly represented by quantitative approaches based on the theory developed by J. E. Grunig. Intellectual skirmishes have resulted. Citing the Polish scholar Magda Pieczka, L'Etang (2008) argued that symmetry is a "self-referential" product of U.S. scholarship (p. 251). Noting that opposition to the legitimacy of symmetry theory arose in the mid-1990s, L'Etang cited Pieczka's characterization of a "paradigm struggle" (p. 253). Symmetry's adherents replied that a critical theory could never qualify as a good theory. L'Etang identified that argument as one between the positivists who favor symmetry and the postpositivists who value "thick description" generally associated with cultural anthropology, ethnography, and other "richly patterned and detailed analysis of research participants" (p. 253). Among these postpositivist, nonsymmetrist approaches, L'Etang included feminism, relationalism, communitarianism, rhetoric, and the critical historiography that challenged the flawed conventional, symmetrist historical account of public relations as originating in the United States during the middle of the 19th century (Brown, 2006).

Historiographical Critiques

While the scholarship of public relations has been concerned with the problem of ethics, it remains largely unconcerned with history or historiography, including its own. Apart from a small number of public relations scholars with a serious interest in history—notably, Cutlip, Hiebert, and Pearson—Brown (2003) asserted that public scholarship has been fundamentally ahistorical (Brown, 2003; Cutlip, 1995; Hiebert, 1966; Pearson, 2009). This relative lack of attention to history may account for what Pearson (2009) asserted to be the scholarly consensus that public relations began in "the last decades of the nineteenth century and first two decades of the twentieth century" (p. 105). Recognizing that the ahistorical nature of public relations scholarship was at odds with symmetry theory's historiographical assertions of public relations embedded in the upward progression of the symmetrical models, Brown (2003) criticized the conventionally accepted origins of public relations as flawed. Brown (2003, 2004) sought to apply symmetry theory to the influential practices of St. Paul (2003) and the patronage strategies of the Catholic Reformation popes (2004). In the postmodern spirit of turning an argument upside down, Brown constructed a challenge to symmetry's historiography. Applying symmetry theory's four original models to the communication strategies of the rhetorically educated missionary St. Paul, Brown concluded that while symmetry's models would mark Paul as a sophisticated public relations practitioner, it would not qualify him as an excellent or ethical one because of the saint's missionary predilection for persuasion, thus elevating the ethics of J. E. Grunig's models above the canonization of a saint.

Cultural and Internationalist Approaches

Notwithstanding the conventional wisdom that public relations arose amid the febrile technological and geographical expansion of the United States in the 19th century, few would doubt that today public relations is a phenomenon of global proportions. Among the early 21st century's most powerful trends—along with the explosion of digital communication—has been globalization. For Sriramesh (2003), "in the new millennium, *every* public relations professional must have a global perspective in order to be effective, and such an outlook should not be considered the domain of *international public relations specialists his* anymore" (p. xxv). From this perspective, the rise of globalization and international public relations has revealed a weakness of symmetry's more narrowly, if ambitiously, monocultural focus. While preserving what they perceive to be symmetry's emphasis on two-way and ethical communication, Sriramesh and Verčič's (2003) approach to international public relations differs from J. E. Grunig's in its breadth, scope, and cultural diversity. From an internationalist perspective, public relations must be understood by first accounting for its "three infrastructural ingredients" at the national level: (1) the political system, (2) the level of economic development, and (3) the level of activism (Sriramesh & Verčič, 2003, p. 2). From those rubrics flow numerous subcategories, including a nation's legal system. But even more attention is paid to the influence of culture, its "determinants" and "dimensions," including its social stratification, social mobility, collectivism, masculinity-femininity, tolerance for uncertainty, orientation to short-term or long-term time, and quality of interpersonal trust, in addition to considerations of the nature of the media environment (pp. 8–10).

An Emerging Pluralism: Implications for the Postsymmetrical World

It is no longer surprising to make the case that we are living in an asymmetrical world. For some observers, this asymmetry has been framed by events such as the attacks of September 11 and the uprisings of insurgencies and nonstatist organizations against traditional world powers.

Nevertheless, the emerging internationally authored scholarship on public relations has not been so much an objection to symmetry—both Sriramesh and Verčič (2003) have been strongly influenced by J. E. Grunig—as the opening of public relations scholarship to a broader, more culturally and politically complex and diverse array of ideas and assumptions.

Above and beyond the heated skirmishes of the symmetry wars, public relations itself appears to be changing. McKie and Munshi (2009) regard the role of public relations as a major influence on the way students "see both society and the role of the profession in society" (p. 61). Without failing to recognize the valuable role played by rhetorical and critical theorists in framing the vigorous debate about the legitimacy and limitations of symmetry, readers are asked to "open themselves to other disciplines to overcome public relations' lack of awareness of other fields and a lack of engagement with other major academic currents over the past 40 years" (p. 61). Listing these "gaps" alphabetically to avoid the trap of prioritizing them, the authors include anthropologists, cultural theorists, ecofeminists, philosophers, poets, novelists, scientists, and sociologists (p. 61).

The implications of this intellectual pluralism suggest that public relations appears to have entered a new era in which the battles over symmetry are giving way to a broader and deeper theoretical, intellectual, and cultural pluralism. A newly minted conversation is taking place, which is opening public relations to the bracing voices of the anthropologist Arjun Appadurai's ethnographies (McKie & Munshi, 2009, p. 62), the cultural theorist Julia Kristeva's Eurofeminism (p. 66), and the worldviews of the Maori and Native Americans (p. 67). In the globalized, intensified, and anxious zeitgeist of the 21st century, public relations can no longer risk marginalizing such voices as "merely" radical or exotic or poetic.

Among symmetry's postmodernist critics, McKie (2001) found the prevailing symmetrical conceptualization of public relations to be out of touch with new currents of thought, particularly chaos theory and postmodernism. Echoing Hiebert's (1996, p. 188) observation of a sharp "divide" in the conception of public relations by scholars compared with practitioners, McKie found that it is scholars, not corporations, who are out of touch with postmodern sensibility. Global companies have learned to operate successfully in the environment of postcolonial, multicultural, pluralistic inclusivity that is required of postmodern business operations no longer characterized by the "scientific managerialism associated with modernity" (McKie, 2001, p. 78).

The Crisis Perspective

Throughout history, the advent of a new millennium has produced radical and even apocalyptic visions of change. The 21st century is no exception. Events such as the spectacular attacks of 9/11, anxieties about nuclear proliferation, controversies about global climate change, the putative clash of civilizations, economic "meltdowns," and warnings of disease pandemics are common to our century's discourse. If anything, this mounting and panicky conversation has cast radical doubt on symmetry theory's fundamentally progressive, benign, and optimistic assumptions. The character of our era would appear to be anything but symmetric or objectively quantifiable.

In the postsymmetrical era, the world has been characterized in scholarly terms as chaotic, complex, and even frightening. For public relations in the past two decades, it is therefore unsurprising to note that there has emerged a rapidly growing body of literature on crisis management. Crisis has increasingly been used to frame many sorts of events, trends, and predictions. In the age of postsymmetry, public relations has taken on the coloration of crisis.

Digital Revolution

The explosion of digital technologies has magnified the perception of crisis, adding to a general sense of time-starved urgency, and heightening anxiety about loss of personal privacy and organizational reputation. The digital Web, with its real and persistently potential threat to organizations, has become a priority for the theory and practice of public relations. Amid the rapid, exotic, technical, and global atmosphere of crisis, symmetry theory can appear to be outmoded and out of touch. The nexus of digitization and crisis, with its video, audio, and social media transmission of images of terrorism, ethnic warfare, economic collapse, and climatic apocalypse projects a potentially uncontrollable world consistent with chaos and complexity theory (McKie, 2001, p. 78). As McKie contended, such a world is better served by a theoretical approach that favors the many over the one, the intersubjective over the naively, if idealistically, objective, the international and global over the predominantly American. From a similarly critical perspective sensitive to cultural diversity, Cheney and Christensen (2001) ask what would a "non-Western, nonmanagerial, and nonrationalist form of public relations look like?" (p. 182).

The recognition of the postsymmetrical world emerged several decades before the turn of the new millennium. Its seminal texts can be found in the changing paradigms of anthropology, linguistics, philosophy, theology, education, and the arts. Contrary to symmetry's vision of managerial competence and human rationality, scholars outside the field of public relations have offered a very different vision of a world marked by crisis, chaos, violence, and complexity. As the 21st-century world moves beyond the reassuring paradigm of symmetry, a generation of scholars have moved away from the mathematics of probability, opting instead to look for answers in the chaos and complexity known to ethnographers and phenomenologists.

In the last two decades of the 20th century, these new paradigms of social science were pioneered by a generation of qualitative thinkers, including the anthropologists Geertz, Douglas, and Turner, the sociologist Goffman, and the performance studies scholar Schechner. They immersed themselves in the quotidian drama of social life and discerned the complex structure and rhythm of theatrical rituals and choreographed dramas that led to either social integration or communal dissolution. Building on the microsociology of Goffman (1959), Schechner (1977) found meaning in exquisitely repetitive choreographed scenes and movements. The anthropologist Turner (1987) discovered a deep structure that resolved crises in the staged rituals of African villages and the narratives of popular culture. Douglas (1992) considered crisis through the lens of the primal importance of risk and the assignment of blame, which parallels the communication theory of attribution cited by Coombs (2007). Geertz (1977) reframed cultural anthropology as an act of ethnographic and literary creation.

These and other innovators from outside the discipline of public relations have created the foundation for the epistemological paradigm shift that has moved public relations beyond the biases of modernism and the limitations of symmetry. The preference for new, exploratory, self-reflexive, intersubjective, dialogic, realistic, and relativistic methodologies does not preclude the acceptance of rigorous quantitative approaches. But it can be fairly said that public relations is no longer under the sway of any single dominant paradigm.

References

Agnes, M. (2000). *Webster's new world college dictionary* (4th ed.). Foster City, CA: IDG Group.

Bentele, G., & Wehmeier, S. (2003). From literary bureaus to a modern profession: The development and current structure of public relations in German. In K. Sriramesh & D. Verčič (Eds.), *The global public relations handbook: Theory, research, and practice* (pp. 192–221). Mahwah, NJ: Lawrence Erlbaum.

Bernays, E. L. (1923). *Crystallizing public opinion.* New York: Boni & Liveright.

Bernays, E. L. (1952). *Public relations.* Norman: University of Oklahoma Press.

Bertalanffy, L. von. (1976). *General systems theory.* New York: George Braziller.

Boorstin, D. J. (1992). *The image: A guide to pseudo events in America.* New York: Vintage Books.

Borgatta, E. F., & Borgatta, M. L. (Eds.). (1992). *Encyclopedia of sociology* (Vol. 2). New York: Macmillan.

Bowen, S. (2005). Symmetry. In R. L. Heath (Ed.), *Encyclopedia of public relations* (Vol. 2, pp. 837–839). Thousand Oaks, CA: Sage.

Brown, R. (2003). St. Paul as a public relations practitioner: A metatheoretical speculation on messianic communication and symmetry. *Public Relations Review, 29,* 229–240.

Brown, R. (2004). The propagation of awe: Public relations, art and belief in Reformation Europe. *Public Relations Review, 30*(3), 381–389.

Brown, R. (2006). The myth of symmetry: Public relations as cultural styles. *Public Relations Review, 32*(3), 206–212.

Cheney, G., & Christensen, L. T. (2001). Public relations as contested terrain: A critical response. In R. L. Heath (Ed.), *Public relations handbook* (pp. 167–182). Thousand Oaks, CA: Sage.

Coombs, W. T. (2007). *Ongoing crisis communication: Planning, managing, and responding* (2nd ed.). Thousand Oaks, CA: Sage.

Cutlip, S. (1995). *Public relations history: From the 17th to the 20th century.* Hillsdale, NJ: Lawrence Erlbaum.

Cutlip, S., & Center, A. (1952). *Effective public relations.* New York: Prentice Hall.

Debord, G. (1983). *Society of the spectacle.* Detroit, MI: Black & Red.

Douglas, M. (1992). *Risk and blame.* New York: Routledge.

Eliot, T. S. (1964). The metaphysical poets. In *Selected essays* (pp. 241–250). New York: Harcourt, Brace & World.

Frankfort, H. G. (2005). *On bullshit.* Princeton, NJ: Princeton University Press.

Geertz, C. (1977). *The interpretation of cultures.* New York: Basic Books.

Goffman, E. (1959). *The presentation of self in everyday life.* New York: Doubleday.

Goldman, E. (1948). *Two-way street: The emergence of the public relations counsel.* Boston: Bellman.

Gras, N. S. B. (1945). Shifts in public relations. *Bulletin of the Business Historical Society, 19,* 107–118.

Grunig, J. E. (1966). The role of information in economic decision making. *Journalism Monographs, 3,* 1–51.

Grunig, J. E. (1969). Economic decision-making and entrepreneurship among Colombian latinfundistas. *Inter-American Economic Affairs, 23*(2), 21–46.

Grunig, J. E. (Ed.). (1992). *Excellence in public relations and communication management.* Hillsdale, NJ: Lawrence Erlbaum.

Grunig, J. E. (2001). Two-way symmetrical public relations: Past, present, and future. In R. L. Heath (Ed.), *Handbook of public relations* (pp. 11–30). Thousand Oaks, CA: Sage.

Grunig, J. E. (2008). Conceptualizing quantitative research in public relations. In B. van Ruler, A. T. Verčič, & D. Verčič (Eds.), *Public relations metrics: Research and evaluation* (pp. 88–119). New York: Routledge.

Grunig, J. E., & Hunt, T. (1984). *Managing public relations.* Fort Worth, TX: Holt, Rinehart & Winston.

Grunig, L. A., Grunig, J. E., & Ehling, W. (1992). What is an effective organization? In J. E. Grunig (Ed.), *Excellence in public relations and communication management* (pp. 65–90). Mahwah, NJ: Lawrence Erlbaum.

Heath, R. L. (2001). A rhetorical enactment rationale for public relations: The good organization communicating well. In R. L. Heath (Ed.), *Handbook of public relations* (pp. 31–59). Thousand Oaks, CA: Sage.

Heath, R. L. (2005). Antecedents of modern public relations. In R. L. Heath (Ed.), *Encyclopedia of public relations* (Vol. 1, pp. 32–37). Thousand Oaks, CA: Sage.

Heath, R. L. (2009). The rhetorical tradition: Wrangle in the marketplace. In R. L. Heath, E. L. Toth, & D. Waymer (Eds.), *Rhetorical and critical approaches to public relations II* (pp. 17–47). New York: Routledge.

Heath, R. L., & Coombs, W. T. (2006). *Today's public relations.* Thousand Oaks, CA: Sage.

Herman, E. S., & Chomsky, N. (2002). *Manufacturing consent: The political economy of the mass media.* New York: Pantheon Books.

Hiebert, R. (1966). *Courtier to the crowd: The story of Ivy Lee and the development of public relations.* Ames: Iowa University Press.

Hiebert, R. (1996). Review of the books *Critical perspectives in public relations,* eds. J. L'Etang & M. Pieczka; and S. Ewen, *PR: A short history of spin. Public Relations Review, 23*(2), 187–196.

Jameson, F. (1993). Excerpts from *Postmodernism, or the cultural logic of late capitalism.* In J. Natoli & L. Hutcheon (Eds.), *A postmodern reader* (pp. 312–332). Albany: State University of New York Press.

L'Etang, J. (2008). *Public relations: Concepts, practice and critique.* London: Sage.

L'Etang, J., & Pieczka, M. (Eds.). (2006). *Public relations: Critical debates and contemporary practice.* Mahwah, NJ: Lawrence Erlbaum.

Lippmann, W. (1922). *Public opinion.* New York: Harcourt, Brace.

McKie, D. (2001). Updating public relations: "New science," research paradigms, and uneven developments. In R. L. Heath (Ed.), *Handbook of public relations* (pp. 75–92). Thousand Oaks, CA: Sage.

McKie, D., & Munshi, D. (2009). Theoretical black holes: A partial A to Z of missing critical thought in public relations. In R. L. Heath, E. L. Toth, & D. Waymer (Eds.), *Rhetorical and critical approaches to public relations II* (pp. 61–75). New York: Routledge.

Pearson, R. (2009). Perspectives on public relations history. In R. L. Heath, E. L. Toth, & D. Waymer (Eds.), *Rhetorical and critical approaches to public relations II* (pp. 92–109). New York: Routledge.

Penny, L. (2005). *Your call is important to us: The truth about bullshit.* New York: Three Rivers Press.

Peters, T. J., & Waterman, R. H. (1982). *In search of excellence.* New York: Harper & Row.

Pieczka, M. (2006). Paradigms, systems theory and public relations. In J. L'Etang & M. Pieczka (Eds.), *Public relations: Critical debates and contemporary practice* (pp. 333–357). Mahwah, NJ: Lawrence Erlbaum.

Schechner, R. (1977). *Performance theory.* London: Routledge.

Spicer, C. (1997). *Organizational public relations: A political perspective.* Mahwah, NJ: Lawrence Erlbaum.

Sriramesh, K. (2003). Introduction. In K. Sriramesh & D. Verčič (Eds.), *The global public relations handbook: Theory, research, and practice* (pp. xxv–xxxvi). Mahwah, NJ: Lawrence Erlbaum.

Thayer, L. (1968). *Communication and communication systems: In organization, management and interpersonal relations.* Homewood, IL: Richard D. Irwin.

Toth, E. (2009). The case for pluralistic studies of public relations. In R. L. Heath, E. L. Toth, & D. Waymer (Eds.), *Rhetorical and critical approaches to public relations II* (pp. 48–60). New York: Routledge.

Turner, V. (1987). *The anthropology of performance.* New York: Performing Arts Journal.

Tye, L. (2002). *The father of spin: Edward L. Bernays and the birth of public relations.* New York: Picador.

CHAPTER 20

Strategy, Management, Leadership, and Public Relations

Finn Frandsen and Winni Johansen

Public relations is a discipline and a profession that cherishes ambitions on its own behalf. As an academic discipline, it has the ambition to develop into an autonomous social scientific discipline, or even better, to become a theory per se. Nowhere is this ambition expressed more clearly than in the two seminal books, *Public Relations Theory* (1989) and *Public Relations Theory II* (2006), edited by Botan and Hazleton, with more than a decade between the two publications. In the first of these books, public relations is presented as "a rapidly emerging social science discipline" (Botan & Hazleton, 1989, p. 13). In the second, this perspective has clearly expanded:

> Although we both still feel that it is useful to understand public relations as a social science, neither of us would argue today that a social, scientific perspective is necessarily the best way to understand public relations. In fact, we argue instead that what are needed today are actual theories of public relations, rather than just a social science approach . . . a theory of public relations per se. (Botan & Hazleton, 2006, p. 4)

As a profession or organizational practice, public relations has the ambition to develop into a strategic management discipline. This ambition is manifested in the definition of public relations as "the management of communication between an organization and its publics" (J. E. Grunig & Hunt, 1984, p. 6) and in the idea that (at least some) public relations practitioners must move away from just being "communication technicians" to become "communication managers," or even better, "communication executives," contributing to or participating in the strategic decision-making processes of the organizations along the lines of their missions, visions, and objectives (cf. the research on the organizational roles of public relations practitioners).

But how are words such as *strategy*, *management*, and *leadership* defined and used within the discipline and the profession of public relations? How do public relations researchers and practitioners in the United States and Europe study and understand these concepts and the phenomena to which they refer? And especially, do the points of development within this discipline correspond to those within disciplines that have strategy, management, and leadership as their primary object of study? Has the first-mentioned type of research reached the same level, and is it in phase with the second type of research? These are some of the questions that we will address in this chapter.

The chapter is divided into four sections. In the first section, central findings from some of the studies of the ongoing institutionalization of public relations, corporate communication, and strategic communication within private and public organizations, conducted in the United States and in Europe after the year 2000, are briefly presented and discussed. The focus is on how public relations practitioners understand and practice strategy, management, and leadership in their organizations. In the second section, a picture is drawn of how the research within the general field of strategic management has developed since the beginning of the 1960s. Then, points of development identified are compared with the corresponding type of research within the field of public relations. To what extent is there accord between the points of development within these two areas? Does the study of public relations defined as a strategic management discipline lag behind the research within the general field, or is it situated at the same level? And if not, what then is the potential of this research for public relations research in the future? The third section discusses the results of an empirical study of how a class of executive MBA students in Corporate Communication understand and work with strategy, management, and leadership. In the last section of the chapter, two scenarios for the future study of strategy, management, and leadership within public relations research are finally presented, serving as a kind of open conclusion.

Institutionalization of Public Relations, Corporate Communication, and Strategic Communication

The annual conference of the European Public Relations Education and Research Association (EUPRERA) in 2008 took place in Milan, Italy, and had the following theme: "Institutionalizing Public Relations and Corporate Communication." The overall goal of the conference was to investigate how and to what extent public relations has been institutionalized as a strategic organizational function and practice over the years and how this has affected not only the profession as such but also the many private and public organizations where this process of institutionalization is taking place. In this section, the EUPRERA conference will serve as an occasion to take a look at some of the most important empirical studies of the institutionalization of public relations, corporate communication, and strategic communication that have been conducted in the United States and in Europe during the past decade or so. We will briefly present four of these studies in chronological order. What can they tell us about strategy, management, and leadership within the discipline and the profession of public relations?

Researchers from the Amsterdam School of Communication Research (ASCoR) at Amsterdam University have conducted a longitudinal study of communication management in Dutch organizations. The first study was conducted in 1995 and repeated in 1999 (cf. van Ruler & de Lange, 2003) and again in 2005 (cf. Elving & van Ruler, 2005). The aim of the study was to look into the communication management processes defined as "how to manage communication, how to improve this, and elements of management" (Elving, van Ruler, & Goodman, 2008). The study deals among other themes with the following topics: size and responsibilities of communication management, background of respondents, glass ceiling (the more or less invisible mechanisms that prevent women from climbing to the top of the organizational ladder), encroachment (assignment of top positions in communication management departments or units to individuals without training or experience in the field), tasks of communication management, and budget. In 2005, the survey was sent to 25% of the 8,776 private companies and to 25% of the 8,588 communication agencies in the Netherlands (response rate 7%, i.e., 355 respondents). However, through the Dutch Professional Communication Association, they got another 87 respondents and a total of 556 organizations and 266 agencies. Compared with the previous studies, the findings of the most recent survey from 2005 show, among other things, that the glass ceiling for female communication managers seems to have disappeared, that encroachment is disappearing, that the tasks of communication departments are increasing, and that communication is considered vital for organizations.

Researchers from the Strategic Public Relations and Communications Center at the University of Southern California Annenberg School for Communication have conducted a series of annual or biannual Generally Accepted Practices (GAP) studies of public relations and communication practices since 2002 (2003, 2004, 2005, 2007, and 2009). The aim is "to advance the study, practice and value of the public relations profession by conducting practical, applied research in partnership with other visionary organizations" (Annenberg School of Communication, 2009, Introduction). In the 2007 GAP study, the researchers involved surveyed 520 communication professionals from public organizations (30%), private companies (23%), government agencies (11%), and not-for-profit organizations (36%) in the United States. The respondents were asked to answer a series of 38 questions concerning their profile and title, organizational data (branches), public relations budget, evaluation, reporting lines, use of outside public relations agencies, methods of public relations evaluation, perception of senior management's views/support, public relations/communications function, and the extent to which communications functions are integrated within the public relations/communication organization and with other departments. The focus is clearly on functions, size, and budget, but there is also an interest in reporting lines and senior management views and support that may reflect their perception of strategy, management, and leadership.

GAP V (GAP Study 2007) shows that the issue of public relations in 2007 is no longer (as in previous GAP studies) whether public relations has gained access to the C-suite (Chairman, CEO, COO) but rather what it does with that access. The study found that 64% were reporting directly to the C-suite, with 23% reporting to marketing and the remainder to human resources, legal, finance, and strategic planning. Those who were reporting to the C-suite indicated that they received a higher level of support and serious consideration within the organization and that public relations was likely to be included in organizational strategic planning and senior level meetings of all types. Furthermore, the study shows that "even among smaller organizations, public relations practitioners are more and more involved in the important strategy meetings at which the key decisions and direction of their organizations are planned and analyzed" (Annenberg School of Communication, 2009, II, p. 7). Finally, there seems to be a strong conviction among public relations practitioners that CEOs value the contributions of public relations.

Swerling and Sen (2009) discussed the institutionalization of the strategic communication function in the United States based on the 2007 GAP study. They concluded that four constructs serve as key indicators of the institutionalization of the communication function, namely, line of reporting, senior management perceptions, evaluation, and integration. The line of reporting construct clearly shows that "communication professionals are involved in strategic meetings, their recommendations are taken seriously and they contribute to strategic decision making" (p. 143), and the perceptions of senior management have clearly improved since earlier GAP studies. However, when it comes to evaluation and integration, there is significant work to be done. Communication professionals are still using traditional evaluation methods measuring media relations and publicity, neglecting more sophisticated metrics such as, for instance, contribution to profitability, influence on corporate culture, and impact on stakeholders' opinions. The communication function still needs to become more integrated with other organizational disciplines such as marketing, finance, and human resources. In fact, according to Swerling and Sen (2009), the communication function "should become the champion of cross functional cooperation" (p. 141).

Researchers from or affiliated with Corporate Communication International (CCI) at Baruch College, City University of New York, have conducted a series of studies of Corporate Communication Practices & Trends in Fortune 1000 companies since 1999 (2001, 2002, 2003, 2005, 2007, and 2009). Benchmark studies were made in China in 2006/2008 (Wang, 2008; Wang & Goodman, 2006), in South Africa in 2007/2008 (De Wet, Meintjes, Niemann-Struweg, & Goodman, 2008), and in two Scandinavian countries in 2008: Denmark and Norway (Brønn, Frandsen, Johansen, & Goodman, 2008; Frandsen & Johansen, 2008). The CCI studies use a triangulated method consisting of a survey (online questionnaire mailed to Fortune 1000 companies in the United States), additional interviews, and site visits. The 2009 CCI study had a response rate of 7%, including 15 interviews (Goodman, 2009). The survey focuses on the following topics: educational background of the corporate communication executives, salary, reporting lines, functions, budget, use of agencies and consultants, and events influencing the practice of corporate communication. In 2009, when ranking the functions that best describe the role of corporate communication in private companies, 23% of the respondents ranked the role of counsel to the CEO and corporation as the most important, 18% manager of company's reputation, and almost 13% source of public information about the company. Furthermore, a new function appeared in the 2009 study: 3.5% ranked member of the strategic planning leadership team most important.

In 2007, EUPRERA started a series of annual transnational surveys studying trends in communication management and public relations in Europe. The quantitative research project is run in conjunction with academics from 11 universities throughout Europe and the European Association for Communication Directors and *Communication Director* magazine. The online survey, titled the *European Communication Monitor* (ECM), conducted in English, consists of an electronic questionnaire sent to practitioners working with public relations and management of communication in private companies, including communication agencies, and in public organizations and institutions in more than 34 countries (N = 1,863 in 2009) asking them to answer a series of questions and items concerning their activities. In 2009, the research highlights were (a) challenges for communication management in the recession and media crises, (b) strategic issues and development of the discipline and communication instruments, (c) trends in internal communication, measurement/evaluation, and interactive communication, (d) communication executives' roles and influence on management decisions, and (e) salaries and qualification needs (Zerfass, Moreno, Tench, Verčič, & Verhoeven, 2009, p. 5). For a discussion of the findings of the 2008 ECM study and the institutionalization of strategic communication in Europe, see Tench, Verhoeven, and Zerfass (2009).

Concerning strategy, management, and leadership, the ECM study (Zerfass et al., 2009) includes questions about the roles of public relations professionals and their contribution to organizational objectives as well as public relations and management decisions. According to the findings, the survey proves that

> PR professionals can foster business goals basically in two distinct ways: a) by solving problems deriving from business or functional strategies that can (probably) be solved by communication activities, i.e. selling goods by marketing communication, motivating employees through internal communication etc.; b) by helping to define organizational objectives by adding the communicative dimension to strategy formulation, i.e. by reporting results from issues management and stakeholder research, by managing reputation risks, etc. This combines either with dissemination or with listening and reflecting activities. (p. 29)

The answers show that almost 85% of the respondents have a focus on supporting business goals by planning and executing communication, whereas only 61% feel responsible for helping to define business strategies. While 56% declare that they use both means, enacting the "strategic facilitator" role, this seems to be prevalent mostly among heads of communications, in private companies, in NGOs, and in Northern Europe.

Concerning public relations and management decisions ("How seriously are public relations recommendations taken by senior management?" and "To what extent are public relations and reputational considerations factored into strategic decision making and planning in your organization?"), the answers in the 2009 study show that public relations practitioners (73%) are trusted advisers but that only 64% are involved in decision making and planning. And finally, concerning the question of "Strategic issues: issues that might become relevant for public relations and communication management within the next three years," linking business strategy and communication (47%) and coping with the digital evolution and the social web (45%) seem to be the two main issues. Dealing with sustainable development and social responsibility, according to 38%, has lost ground (–3%), whereas building and maintaining trust is a major issue (+4%). Internal communication is seen as a driver of organizational change and restructuring in times of crisis, with a clear link to strategy, and 74% of the respondents indicate that training managers to act as communicators is the most relevant future action in internal communication.

To these four (trans)national studies of the institutionalization of public relations, corporate communication, and strategic communication, one can add an even longer series of purely national studies (see, e.g., Hamrefors, 2009; Invernizzi & Romenti, 2009).

The epistemological motives behind the four studies presented above are often defensive, having grown out of the need for legitimizing public relations as a profession and an organizational practice. The studies are rarely anchored within specific theoretical frameworks accounting for the institutionalizing process as such. Most of the studies are quantitative in nature, primarily surveys or diffusion studies, based on (online) questionnaires. Furthermore, two of the studies concentrate on communication management and public relations practices in one country only; only the CCI studies and the ECM have been conducted as transnational studies.

However, they all aim at describing what characterizes the work of public relations practitioners or professionals, at revealing the kind of issues and topics they are dealing with, and their strategic position inside the organization (dominant coalition, reporting line, reference to CEO, dealing with business strategies, etc.). All the studies seem to indicate that communication managers or communication executives have become more influential within both private and public organizations and that the communication management function has indeed been institutionalized. But how the public relations practitioners or professionals understand and work with strategy, management, and leadership is less obvious from these studies. The ECM studies are the only studies that distinguish between two ways of looking at strategy and leadership. How they perceive strategy, management, and leadership is only revealed in a very indirect way.

Strategy, Management, Leadership, and Public Relations: From Normative Idealism to Critical Realism

The concepts of strategy, management, and leadership are multidimensional concepts applied, with more or less diverging meanings, within a series of different theoretical and practical contexts. Based on a new approach to strategic management, Cummings and Wilson's *Images of Strategy* (2003) highlights some of the many dimensions, or "maps," or "images," contained by or ascribed to the concept of strategy: strategy as *decision making*, as *intention*, as *orientation*, as *organizing*, as *numbers*, as *creativity*, as *process*, *power*, *change*, and so on. However, the overall idea behind the approach is not to point out one single map or image as the best definition of strategy but to combine the various maps or images when mapping the organization's strategic course (pp. 1–5). Also, within the field of public relations, the concept of strategy is often used with diverging meanings: from *corporate strategy* and *business strategy* to *message strategy* (Tench & Yeomans, 2009, p. 188; see also Moss, 2005). Common to all these fundamental dimensions, meanings, or definitions is the idea of *directed* and *planned activities* within the organization as a whole, or within specific areas or at specific levels of the organization, to reach a specific goal or specific objectives. In this section, we will focus on the field of strategic management, consciously neglecting the many other relevant contexts where the concept of strategy plays an important role.

Strategic management forms a large field of study that has developed in many directions since the beginning of the 1960s, when the first books on "business strategy formulation" (cf. Ansoff, 1965; Chandler, 1962) were published in the United States (Pettigrew, Thomas, & Whittington, 2002, p. 5). It is therefore obvious that we will not be able to cover all the issues serving as drivers in this development. On the other hand, the issues selected are all relevant for the study and practice of public relations as a strategic management discipline.

The development within the field of strategic management can be described as a long and complex journey, moving away from a position that can be described as *normative idealism* to a position that can be described as *critical realism*. The following four major points of development can be identified.

One: From a Prescriptive to an Emergent Perspective on Strategic Management

The first major point of development is the movement from a prescriptive to an emergent perspective on strategic management. The prescriptive perspective, or the rational-analytic view of strategy, is the oldest, most widespread, and most conventional approach. This is also the reason why it is the foundational perspective where all further developments within the field find their starting point. Characteristic of a prescriptive strategy is the conviction that the objective of the strategy can be defined in advance and that the main elements of the strategy can be developed before it is implemented (Lynch, 2009, p. 37). A prescriptive strategy is based on a linear-hierarchical view of the strategy process. On the one hand, the process is viewed as a linear sequence of separate stages or steps following one after another (Johnson, Scholes, & Whittington, 2009, pp. 16–17). On the other hand, the strategy process is also viewed as a procedure, which is led and carried out by top management (the strategic level) from where it is "sent down" through the organizational hierarchy to be implemented by middle or lower management and the employees (the tactical and operational levels).

The following stages or steps are normally represented in the strategy process:

1. A situational analysis of the strategic position of the organization that includes an examination of both the external environment (e.g., the expectations of the stakeholders, competition, or developments taking place in society at large) and the internal environment (e.g., the economic and human resources and competences that the organization has at its disposal). The purpose of the situational analysis is to produce an overview of the existing strategic options and the consequences of each of these options. In this context, the objectives of strategy are then identified.
2. The formulation of the strategy where the options and consequences identified in the first stage are weighed up against each other before the strategic choices are made (strategic decision making). Top management is expected to make precisely the strategic choices that are best suited for the achievement of the goal and objectives of the organization.
3. The implementation of the chosen strategy option including the structures, processes, and changes needed to turn the content of the strategy into reality. Thus, implementation is viewed as a separate and distinctive stage or step that only comes after the strategy has been formulated.

According to Lynch (2009), the prescriptive perspective on strategic management is represented by theories such as, for example, the resource-based theories of strategy, the game-based theories of strategy, and the cooperation- and network-based theories of strategy.

The emergent perspective saw the light of day less than a decade later, mainly as a reaction to the oversimplified strategy view represented by the prescriptive approach. Characteristic of an emergent strategy is the claim that the final objective of the strategy will remain unclear and that its elements are developed during the course of its life, as the strategy proceeds (Lynch, 2009, p. 42). Strategies do not always develop as intended or planned but tend to emerge in organizations over time as a result of new opportunities, organizational learning, or even accidental actions (Johnson et al., 2009, p. 17). Therefore, the value of a prescriptive strategy can only be limited.

Where as the prescriptive perspective was based on a linear-hierarchical view defining the strategy process as a rational and analytic process, the emergent perspective views the strategy process as a process where the strategy of the organization is derived as a result of trial, repeated experimentation, and small steps forward. Thus, strategies emerge from a more or less confused background and often in a nonlinear, muddled, and disorganized way, where power and cultural and political forces and processes also have an important role to play (Lynch, 2009, p. 43).

According to Lynch (2009), the emergent perspective on strategic management is represented by theories such as, for example, the uncertainty-based theories of strategy, the human-resource-based theories of strategy, and the innovation and knowledge-based theories of strategy.

Two: From Empirical Studies to Evidence-Based Management

The first point of development starts at the beginning of the 1960s, culminating at the beginning of the 1990s, where representatives of the rational-analytic view and the emergent view, personified by Igor Ansoff and Henry Mintzberg, respectively, were fighting "turf wars" over which perspective most accurately represented the organizational strategy process: the top-down design or planning school or the bottom-up emergence school (cf. the exchange between Mintzberg, 1990, and Ansoff, 1991).

The second point of development was initiated at the end of the 1960s and the beginning of the 1970s, and once again, Henry Mintzberg played a leading part. Until this point, the empirical research in management in general, and in strategic management in particular, had been sparse. Researchers as well as practitioners based their understanding of strategy and management on general views such as Fayol's (1918) description of the manager's job as consisting of a series of basic functions: to plan, to organize, to coordinate, to command, and to control. But in 1973, in his seminal work *The Nature of Managerial Work*, Henry Mintzberg raised an essential question: What do managers really do when they manage? (Mintzberg, 1973). Following the study of the work of five chief executives from different types and hierarchical levels of private and public organizations, Mintzberg concluded that the jobs of managers are very much alike and that their work can be described in terms of 10 basic roles (3 interpersonal roles, 3 informational roles, and 4 decisional roles) and 6 sets of working characteristics (managerial work is taxing, the activities are characterized by brevity, variety, and fragmentation, verbal communication is important, etc.); that the manager is both a generalist and a specialist and that the power of managers derives from their access to many sources of information; that managerial work is highly complex; and that there is no science in this work. "Managers work essentially as they always have—with verbal information and intuitive (nonexplicit processes)" (p. 3).

Mintzberg's study was conducted more than 40 years ago. However, it still serves as an important source of inspiration for new research projects within the field of strategic management, such as the new *Strategy as Practice* community, which has sprung into existence since the year 2000 and to which we will return later. This also applies to the new interest in *evidence-based management*, which has emerged recently and where Mintzberg's original question "What do managers really do when they manage?" has been replaced by a new, yet related, question: "What is really effective when managers manage?" Evidence-based management is inspired and to some extent guided by the evidence-based medicine movement (Pfeffer & Sutton, 2006), departing from the idea that management decision making must always be built on the best available evidence, that is, ideally speaking, unambiguous cause-and-effect connections (Rousseau, 2006). But contrary to evidence-based medicine, evidence-based management still remains at a hypothetical stage of development.

Three: Critical Management Studies

After two decades, the 1970s and especially the 1980s, where the prescriptive perspective on strategic management "struck back" with a new focus on competition and industrial organization economics (cf. Porter, 1980, 1985), a third point of development started at the beginning of the 1990s, with the publication of Mats Alvesson and Hugh Willmott's *Critical Management Studies* (1992).

Up to this point, the majority of studies conducted within strategic management research had been characterized by a lack of critical reflection on the field (Whipp, 1996). With critical management studies (CMS), the dominant management principles of organizing (such as efficiency, rationality, homogeneity, and masculinity) are challenged (Phillips & Dar, 2009). According to the scholars representing this new line of thinking, critical management research includes three tasks: an *insight* task demonstrating a commitment to "the hermeneutic, interpretive and ethnographic goals of local understandings closely connected to and appreciative of the lives of real people in real situations," a *critique* task counteracting the "dominance of taken-for-granted goals, ideas, ideologies and discourses that put their imprints on management and organization ideas," and a *transformative redefinition* task demonstrating a commitment to the pragmatic aspects of a critical approach, "recognizing that insight and critique without support for social action leaves research detached and sterile" (Alvesson & Deetz, 2000, p. 17).

The early version of CMS was inspired by the critical theory of the Frankfurt School, rooted in

Western neo-Marxism (historical materialism), and by poststructuralism and postmodernism, rooted in "French Theory" (Foucault, Derrida, Bourdieu, and others), but has since then developed in many directions, including feminist theory, critical discourse analysis, and so on. Although not always departing from mutually compatible sources of inspiration, the representatives of CMS share the critique of managerialism and the idea of emancipation. The overall research topics are conflict, power, exploitation, and politics and the effects these phenomena have on the management of organizations.

Strategy has become an increasing focus of attention within CMS. So far, strategy has been studied as an *ideology* serving the interest of the top management of organizations and securing the internal balance of power (Shrivastava, 1986), or as a *discourse* creating power effects such as providing a rationalization for success and failure, generating a sense of personal and organizational security, or communicating rationality to outsiders and employees (Knights & Morgan, 1991). Scholars within critical management studies have also studied how the growing tendency to label more and more activities as "strategic" can be interpreted as part of the esteem-enhancing identity work of managers.

Looking at critical management studies from a broader perspective, this point of development may also include the *organizational politics* school, represented by, among others, Andrew Pettigrew, studying the organizational role of power and culture as shapers of decision and strategy outcomes (Pettigrew, 1973, 1977).

Four: Strategy as Practice

The last major point of development is also the most recent. It concerns the academic community that has developed since the beginning of the new millennium, naming itself Strategy as Practice. This new community is inspired by the pragmatist tradition in philosophy (Rorty), the process or work activity tradition within management research (Mintzberg), and the "practice turn" in the social sciences exemplified by Giddens and Bourdieu (Johnson, Langley, Melin, & Whittington, 2007). Thus, the strategy as practice researchers want to study what people actually *do* when working with strategy in organizations:

> Strategy as practice attempts a fundamental inversion of dominant conceptions of strategy. Whereas strategy has traditionally been seen as something an organization has—for example, a diversification strategy or an internationalization strategy—for strategy as practice researchers, strategy is something you do. (Jarzabkowski & Whittington, 2008, p. 101)

According to the traditional approach to strategic management (cf. the prescriptive approach presented above), a strategy is something that an organization *has*; a strategy is the result of one-off decisions; and a strategy is developed in specific places (the boardroom), at specific times (during strategy seminars), and by specific persons at the top of the organizational hierarchy (top management). And a strategy is always formulated before it is implemented. The Strategy as Practice researchers take a somewhat different approach. To them, strategy is first of all *strategizing*, something *people do*, an activity embedded in a specific organizational context. The result is a new focus on the complex microprocesses and micropractices constituting the everyday activities of organizational life and involved in strategy making. Strategy making is not a rational, analytic, disembodied, and asocial activity but an interactive and contextually situated type of behavior.

The theoretical, methodological, and empirical consequences of the microtheory of strategy as practice are important. Strategy formulation and implementation are no longer seen as completely separate phenomena in a linear-hierarchical sequence of stages and steps, and the traditional macro approach to strategy is linked to a micro approach within a new integrative framework.

Old quantitative approaches to research design are supplemented with new qualitative approaches (ethnography, in-depth case studies, etc.). And there is a new focus on strategic practitioners, including more than just the C-suite.

The expected outcomes of this new line of thought within strategic management research are also important: a type of research that reflects the real work of practitioners, particularly in terms of strategic competence, skill, and learning under different situations; a new awareness of the power residing in dominant discourses of strategic action; and a point of reflexivity for researchers, teachers, students, and practitioners in the strategy field.

Above, we have attempted to draw a picture of how research within the general field of strategic management has developed since the beginning of the 1960s from an inside to an outside perspective and from a focus on the economic dimension of organizations to a focus on the social dimension. The picture is far from exhaustive, and it is far from objective, but it presents how strategic management research has developed from normative idealism to critical realism.

How does the study of public relations defined as a strategic management discipline relate to this picture? Previous research on strategy, management, and leadership conducted by public relations researchers has been closely linked to a series of specific topics: the organizational roles of public relations practitioners (Dozier, 1992; Dozier, Grunig, & Grunig, 1995), how the dominant coalition views the public relations function (L. A. Grunig, Grunig, & Dozier, 2002), how the practitioners can gain access to the dominant coalition, and how they can contribute to strategic decision making (Berger & Reber, 2006), leadership in public relations (Bowen, 2009), power (Berger, 2007), and such. Although important exceptions exist, strategy, management, and leadership are still very much viewed from a prescriptive perspective. Therefore, the important question is "How can we make use of the many new insights challenging our traditional strategic understanding?"

Strategic Understanding of Communication Managers

To study the strategic understanding (including both perceptions and behavior) of communication managers or communication executives, a small experimental study was conducted in 2009 with participants from the Executive Master's Program in Corporate Communication at the Aarhus School of Business, Aarhus University.

The study forms part of a larger research project, the aim of which is to contribute to a better, more realistic, and more contextualized understanding of the managerial work of communication managers. The research design is qualitative, consisting of 20 semistructured "double interviews" in 10 different organizations. The research questions are "How do communication managers and CEOs belonging to the same organization perceive and work with strategic management? How do they perceive themselves and each other as managers? And how do they interact with each other as managers?"

The research design for the experimental study was also qualitative, consisting of "written interviews" with 24 interviewees (Executive Master's Students) who all had several years of experience in communication management from both private and public organizations. They were asked to answer 26 open-ended questions about their perception of and work with management and strategy. By means of content analysis, the answers were then categorized in themes, analyzed, and interpreted according to the cognitive mapping model presented in Figure 20.1.

As presented in the model, three types of factors have an influence on the sociocognitive structures and the socioconative patterns of managers in their daily work: (1) organizational factors, such as type of organization and the life cycle of the organization; (2) personal factors, such as

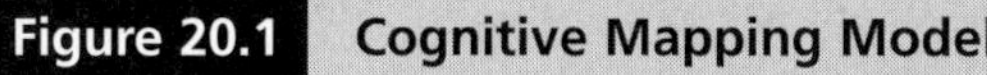

Figure 20.1 Cognitive Mapping Model

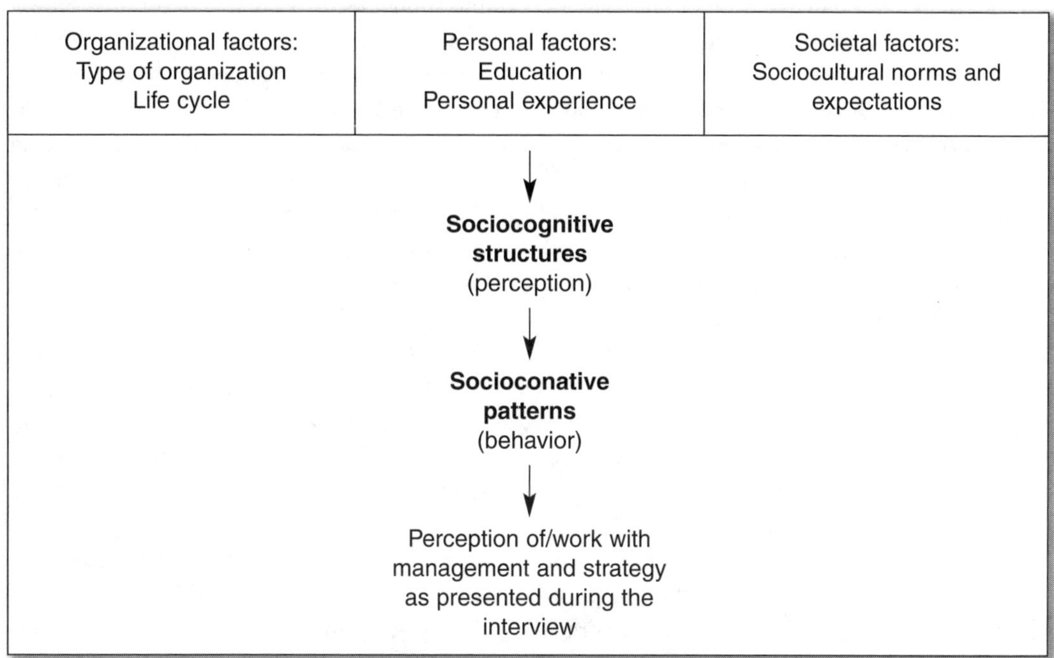

experience and educational background; and (3) societal factors, such as sociocultural norms and expectations that have been institutionalized or are in the process of institutionalization in the organization. The sociocognitive structures and the socioconative patterns are expected to come forward during the "written" interviews, through the use of mental maps, rhetoric, and discourse.

The first set of questions in the "written interview" sheds light on the following topics: How do communication managers or executives and CEOs define strategy, management, and leadership? What kind of strategy perspective do they apply—a prescriptive perspective or an emergent perspective?

The interviewees define *management* in almost 20 different ways, but many of them are closely related. The four most widespread definitions are (1) "to take the lead," "to set a common course or direction," (2) "to inspire and to motivate," (3) "to coach and to counsel," and (4) "to make other people change their behavior." When it comes to the use of management metaphors, the three most popular metaphors are (1) captain or shepherd, (2) lighthouse, and (3) light, guiding star, or direction mark. According to the interviewees, a CEO would define management as "having control," "the right to decide," "he knows better," "having focus on economy and financial results," and "being the conductor of a high-speed train."

The interviewees define *strategy* in three ways: (1) "to set up a long-term goal," (2) "a planned route to go," and (3) "the ability to constantly adjust the direction to follow." And they often make use of terms from the corporate vocabulary such as "mission" and "vision." The most-used strategy metaphors are "a curved road," "military commander," "military precision," "timetable, map, or schema," "chess," "jigsaw puzzle," "bull's-eye," and "a rope that ties things together."

According to the interviewees, a CEO would define strategy as "the road (to the goal) being more direct (less curved)," "business focus," "something the directors or members of the board have decided," "a long-term plan," and "the rationale behind things." Seventeen of the interviewees stated that the CEO of their organization perceived and worked with strategy and management in a different way when compared with communication managers or communication executives, who are more operational and practical, developing strategies to support the overall corporate strategy.

The second set of questions in the "written" interview sheds light on the following topic: "What is the purpose of a strategy, and how are strategies formulated and implemented in your organization?"

The interviewees had almost the same perception of the primary purpose of a strategy, and except for one, all agreed that this would also be the perception of a CEO: "to make the organization work towards the same goal," "alignment of the direction to go," "to set a direction to go in order to fulfill the goals," and "to make the organization move from A to B."

Concerning the question "What will typically happen when a new strategy is to be developed in your organization?" 17 interviewees described the typical process as a top-down process. However, 4 of them indicated that it was often preceded by a brainstorm process, where different groups of people give input to the strategy process. Three persons indicated that there was no typical way and that strategy processes were more a matter of damage control.

And finally, to the question "What will typically happen when a new strategy is going to be implemented in your organization?" followed by two options, (a) "What you have decided to happen happens" and (b) "Something different than what you have decided happens," the answers were distributed in the following way: Five interviewees said (a) "My organization is very goal oriented"; three said (b) "The goal is clear, but not how we get there, and something different always happens"; seven indicated a mix between (a) and (b); and finally, four interviewees indicated that "It fizzles out," "It comes to nothing," and "We always turn back to where we started."

As it appears from the answers presented above, the communication managers and communication executives selected for the experimental study are rather traditional in their way of understanding strategy and management. The prescriptive approach is dominant, although the interviewees also seem to be aware of emergent factors. When it comes to working with strategy and management, many organizations still formulate and implement strategies in the traditional way. A new strategy is typically initiated, formulated, and implemented in a top-down process, although there seems to be a high awareness of the fact that prescriptive strategies often are not being fully achieved or in some cases not achieved at all, due to unclear or incompetent goal setting, unforeseen changes in the market, and the organizational culture being resistant and just ignoring new "ideas." The study also showed that some organizations do not work with strategic planning in a proactive way, but are only reacting and doing damage control.

Future Directions

In the introduction to this chapter, public relations was depicted as an ambitious discipline focusing on the development of a theory of public relations per se and as a likewise ambitious profession wanting to promote its practitioners as communication managers or communication executives. When it comes to the study of strategy, management, and leadership, these ambitions can be administered according to (at least) two different scenarios. On the one hand, public relations scholars and practitioners may keep focusing on themselves and their academic or organizational status, that is, remain a community that can be described as introvert or centripetal. This will allow us to continue refining an important body of theoretical knowledge and practical functions that has been under construction since the end of the 1980s. We can continue contributing to our own academic journals, attending our own conferences, and sharing our own practical experiences. And this will certainly keep public relations alive, but for how long?

On the other hand, public relations scholars and practitioners may choose a somewhat different route, transforming our community into a more open and extrovert environment. This not only implies that we seek inspiration from other disciplines within the social sciences or the humanities (such as social theory, anthropology, rhetoric, or discourse analysis) but also means that we must interact in a more direct way with researchers working within these disciplines and that we must contribute to their journals and their conferences. Strategy, management, and leadership are most certainly among these disciplines.

References

Alvesson, M., & Deetz, S. (2000). *Doing critical management research.* London: Sage.

Alvesson, M., & Willmott, H. C. (Eds.). (1992). *Critical management studies.* London: Sage.

Annenberg School of Communication. (2009). *Fifth annual public relations generally accepted practices (GAP) Study 2007 (GAP V).* Retrieved January 21, 2010, from http://annenberg.usc.edu/CentersandPrograms/ResearchCenters/SPRC.aspx

Ansoff, H. I. (1965). *Corporate strategy.* Homewood, IL: Dow Jones-Irwin.

Ansoff, H. I. (1991). Critique of Henry Mintzberg's "The design school: Reconsidering the basic premises of strategic management." *Strategic Management Journal, 12*(6), 449–461.

Berger, B. K. (2007). Public relations and organizational power. In E. L. Toth (Ed.), *The future of excellence in public relations and communication management: Challenges for the next generation* (pp. 221–234). Mahwah, NJ: Lawrence Erlbaum.

Berger, B. K., & Reber, B. H. (2006). *Gaining influence in public relations: The role of resistance in practice.* Mahwah, NJ: Lawrence Erlbaum.

Botan, C. H., & Hazleton, V. (1989). The role of theory in public relations. In C. H. Botan & V. Hazleton (Eds.), *Public relations theory* (pp. 3–15). Hillsdale, NJ: Lawrence Erlbaum.

Botan, C. H., & Hazleton, V. (2006). Public relations in a new age. In C. H. Botan & V. Hazleton (Eds.), *Public relations theory II* (pp. 1–18). Mahwah, NJ: Lawrence Erlbaum.

Bowen, S. A. (2009). What communication professionals tell us regarding dominant coalition access and gaining membership. *Journal of Applied Communication Research, 37*(4), 418–443.

Brønn, P. S., Frandsen, F., Johansen, W., & Goodman, M. B. (2008). *Corporate communication practices & trends: Norwegian benchmark study 2008.* Oslo, Norway: Norwegian School of Management, Centre for Corporate Communication.

Chandler, A. R. (1962). *Strategy and structure: Chapters in the history of the industrial enterprise.* Cambridge, MA: MIT Press.

Cummings, S., & Wilson, D. (Eds.). (2003). *Images of strategy.* Malden, MA: Blackwell.

De Wet, G., Meintjes, C., Niemann-Struweg, I., & Goodman, M. B. (2008). *Corporate communication practices & trends: South Africa Benchmark Study 2007/08.* New York: CCI. Retrieved December 27, 2009, from www.corporatecomm.org/studies.html

Dozier, D. M. (1992). The organizational roles of communications and public relations practitioners. In J. E. Grunig (Ed.), *Excellence in public relations and communication management* (pp. 327–355). Hillsdale, NJ: Lawrence Erlbaum.

Dozier, D. M., Grunig, L. A., & Grunig, J. E. (1995). *Manager's guide to excellence in public relations and communication management.* Mahwah, NJ: Lawrence Erlbaum.

Elving, W. J. L., & van Ruler, B. (2005). *Trendonderzoek communicatiemanagement* [Trends in communication management]. Amsterdam: Amsterdam School of Communication Research.

Elving, W. J. L., van Ruler, B., & Goodman, M. (2008, October). *Communication management in the Netherlands: Trends, developments, and benchmark with US benchmark study.* Paper presented at the EUPRERA 2008, Milan, Italy.

Fayol, H. (1918). *Administration industrielle et générale* [General and industrial management]. Paris: Dunod.

Frandsen, F., & Johansen, W. (2008, June). *Corporate communication practices & trends: A European benchmark study 2008 (Denmark).* Paper presented at the Conference on Corporate Communication 2008, Wroxton, UK.

Goodman, M. B. (2009). *2009 CCI corporate communication practices & trends.* New York: CCI. Retrieved December 27, 2009, from www.corporatecomm.org/studies.html

Grunig, J. E., & Hunt, T. (1984). *Managing public relations.* Fort Worth, TX: Harcourt Brace.

Grunig, L. A., Grunig, J. E., & Dozier, D. M. (2002). *Excellent public relations and effective organizations: A study of communication management in three countries.* Mahwah, NJ: Lawrence Erlbaum.

Hamrefors, S. (2009). *Kommunikativt ledarskap: Den nya tidens lederskap i värdeskapende nätverk* [Communicative leadership: Today's leadership in value-creating networks]. Falun, Sweden: Norstedts Akademiska Förlag.

Invernizzi, E., & Romenti, S. (2009). Institutionalization and evaluation of corporate communication in Italian companies. *International Journal of Strategic Communication, 3*(2), 116–130.

Jarzabkowski, P., & Whittington, R. (2008). Hard to disagree, mostly. *Strategic Organization, 6*(1), 101–106.

Johnson, G., Langley, A., Melin, L., & Whittington, R. (2007). *Strategy as practice: Research directions and resources.* Oxford, UK: Oxford University Press.

Johnson, G., Scholes, K., & Whittington, R. (2009). *Fundamentals of strategy.* Harlow, UK: Prentice Hall.

Knights, D., & Morgan, G. (1991). Corporate strategy, organisations and subjectivity: A critique. *Organization Studies, 12*(2), 191–215.

Lynch, R. (2009). *Strategic management.* Harlow, UK: Prentice Hall.

Mintzberg, H. (1973). *The nature of managerial work.* New York: Harper & Row.

Mintzberg, H. (1990). The design school: Reconsidering the basic premises of strategic management. *Strategic Management Journal, 11*(3), 171–195.

Moss, D. A. (2005). Strategies. In R. L. Heath (Ed.), *Encyclopedia of public relations* (Vol. 2, pp. 823–826). Thousand Oaks, CA: Sage.

Pettigrew, A. M. (1973). *The politics of organizational decision making.* London: Tavistock.

Pettigrew, A. M. (1977). Strategy formulation as a political process. *International Studies of Management and Organization, 7*(2), 78–87.

Pettigrew, A., Thomas, H., & Whittington, R. (2002). Strategic management: The strengths and limitations of a field. In A. Perrigrew, H. Thomas, & R. Whittington (Eds.), *Handbook of strategy and management* (pp. 3–30). London: Sage.

Pfeffer, J., & Sutton, R. I. (2006). *Hard facts, dangerous half-truths and total nonsense: Profiting from evidence-based management.* Cambridge, MA: Harvard Business School Press.

Phillips, N., & Dar, S. (2009). Strategy. In M. Alvesson, T. Bridgman, & H. Willmott (Eds.), *The Oxford handbook of critical management studies* (pp. 414–432). Oxford, UK: Oxford University Press.

Porter, M. E. (1980). *Competitive strategy.* New York: Free Press.

Porter, M. E. (1985). *Competitive advantage.* New York: Free Press.

Rousseau, D. M. (2006). Is there such a thing as evidence-based management? *Academy of Management Review, 31,* 256–269.

Shrivastava, P. (1986). Is strategic management ideological? *Journal of Management, 12*(3), 363–378.

Swerling, J., & Sen, C. (2009). The institutionalization of the strategic communication function in the United States. *International Journal of Strategic Communication, 3*(2), 131–146.

Tench, R., Verhoeven, P., & Zerfass, A. (2009). Institutionalizing strategic communication in Europe—An ideal home or a mad house? Evidence from a survey in 37 countries. *International Journal of Strategic Communication, 3*(2), 147–164.

Tench, R., & Yeomans, L. (2009). *Exploring public relations.* Harlow, UK: Prentice Hall.

van Ruler, B., & de Lange, R. (2003). Barriers to communication management in the executive suite. *Public Relations Review, 29*(2), 145–158.

Wang, J. (2008). *Corporate communication practices and trends: A China study 2008—Phase II.* New York: CCI. Retrieved December 27, 2009, from www.corporatecomm.org/studies.html

Wang, J., & Goodman, M. B. (2006). *Corporate communication practices and trends: A China study 2006.* New York: CCI. Retrieved December 27, 2009, from www.corporatecomm.org/studies.html

Whipp, R. (1996). Creative deconstruction: Strategy and organizations. In S. R. Clegg, C. Hardy, & W. R. Nord (Eds.), *Handbook of organization studies* (pp. 261–275). Thousand Oaks, CA: Sage.

Zerfass, A., Moreno, A., Tench, R., Verčič, D., & Verhoeven, P. (2009). *European communication monitor. Trends in communication management and public relations: Results of a survey in 34 countries.* Brussels, Belgium: Euprera. Retrieved December 9, 2009, from www.communicationmonitor.eu

CHAPTER 21

Reputation, Communication, and the Corporate Brand

Peggy Simcic Brønn

In public relations, image and reputation management are referred to as impression management, a process whereby organizations attempt to control what people think of them (Coombs, 2001). Forman and Argenti (2005) asserted that the function of corporate communication is to "manage the impressions of a firm's constituencies in order to enhance the organization's reputation" (p. 248). They referred to Rindova and Fombrun (1999), who believe communications should be managed "so as to mold the interpretations and perceptions of constituents" (Forman & Argenti, 2005, p. 248). The use of words such as *manage, control, mold,* and *influence* are unfortunate because they give the impression that organizations can make people believe what they want them to believe. This is in sharp contrast to the variables of transparency, authenticity, and responsiveness—the building blocks of good reputations. These variables invite dialogue—real dialogue based on stakeholder involvement. In this chapter, we look at the concept of reputation, arguing first that it is impossible to understand reputation without first understanding the concepts of identity and image. This is followed by a discussion of the corporate brand and corporate branding, how organizations use their identity to build reputation. Finally, we discuss the communication practices that are correlated with organizations with high reputations.

Organizational and Corporate Identity

The concept of identity is complex and includes organizational identity, organizational identification, and corporate identity. Very simplified definitions of organizational identity and corporate identity are offered here, with less weight on organizational identification. Albert and Whetten (1985) described organizational identity as what is central, distinctive, and enduring about an organization and answers the questions "Who are we?" and "What are we?" Hatch and Schultz (2000) described it as the many different elements that all of an organization's members have an opinion on and how they think of themselves. Organizational identity is *how* an organization's members perceive and understand: "who we are" and "what we stand for." Organizational identity is seen from the perspective of all members of the organization, who are also the recipients of messages. Interpersonal communication is the dominant communication channel. Organizational identification, on the other hand, is "the degree to which a member defines him- or herself by the same attributes that he or she believes define[s] the organization" (Dutton, Dukerich, & Harquail, 1994, p. 39). It is tightly associated with organizational identity in that individuals seek organizations whose characteristics reflect how they see themselves; thus, organizational identity is often described as residing in the values of the organizational members.

Dowling (2001) defined corporate identity as the symbols and nomenclature used by an organization to identify itself to people. Corporate identity as visual identity is probably most recognized and encompasses a variety of media. Gregory (1998) listed seven categories of materials that can carry a firm's name: stationery, literature, transportation, packing, architecture, signs, and marketing/sales. Gregory then listed nearly 100 specific things encompassed by these categories, including letterheads, business cards, news releases, annual reports, sales bulletins, cartons, labels, stamps, logos, trucks, ships, cars, building design, interiors, landscaping, uniforms—the list is endless. Using a global survey by Millward Brown linking branding and sensory awareness, Lindstrom (2005) discussed building brands using touch, taste, smell, sight, and sound. This author attempts to explain how firms can capitalize on the fact that 75% of our emotions are generated by what we smell.

Corporate identity helps people find or recognize an organization (Dowling, 2001). Ind (1997) referred to identity as the outward manifestation of an organization. Some well-known examples are McDonald's, Disney, and Nike, just to name a few. Nike doesn't even need to use its name anymore; the "Swoosh" is sufficient. Hatch and Schultz (2000) viewed corporate identity as the *idea* of the organization and how it is represented to different audiences, in this case primarily external stakeholders. Here, identity is defined by top managers and their advisers, and communication channels are mediated, that is, are delivered, in most cases by the mass media, or nonpersonal channels such as newsletters, annual reports, and so on.

Due to the overlap of internal and external stakeholders, however, there may be no clear lines between the two definitions, and employees' impressions of corporate identity are likely to carry over into their direct experiences with organizational identity. It is easy to see that organizations that don't realize the distinctions between these two concepts by focusing too much on corporate identity, that is, externally, can find themselves with problems. For instance, organizations can alienate employees when they allow their customers to define who they are, forgetting that it is the employees who have to live, so to speak, the identity, and that perhaps they should be included as major actors here. Hatch and Schultz (2000), however, saw a positive trend among decision makers taking internal and external stakeholders' perceptions and reactions into consideration when formulating identity.

Image

One definition of image asks "What do we believe others think of us?" where the organization as actor is directing the question to others and asking for feedback (Brown, Dacin, Pratt, & Whetten, 2006). The authors defined corporate identity as a set of associations that the organization wants to send to various stakeholders. They label these as *intended* associations. Because managers often want to focus on organizational attributes that they view as the most important, this then becomes the *intended image* of the organization, or the associations that the organization *wants* the stakeholder group to have of the organization. Image is defined as the mental associations that organizational members believe others have of them. The researchers label these *construed* or *interpreted* associations and the stronger associations as *construed image*.

Van Riel and Fombrun (2007) defined image as being like a mirror; it reflects the identity of the organization. Van Riel introduced this when he used Birkigt and Stadler's (1986) model in his 1995 book on corporate communication to illustrate the influence of the corporate identity mix (communication, behavior, and symbols) on image. However, van Riel and Fombrun believed that the Birkigt and Stadler model is problematic in that

1. it does not consider that image is affected by other sources;
2. it does not reflect that image should not be an end in itself but a means to achieve organizational success;
3. it does not distinguish between static identity elements such as culture, which changes slowly, and dynamic identity elements, such as communication and symbolism, which can change quickly; and
4. it does not recognize the unequal impact of static and dynamic identity elements on image, where static elements are likely to have far greater impact.

Reputation

Reputation asks the question "What do others actually think about us?" (Brown et al., 2006). It represents the reality of the organization for the stakeholder regardless of what the organization believes about itself, chooses to communicate, or thinks it knows about what stakeholders are thinking. The difference between image and reputation, according to Brown et al., is that image is about asking stakeholders if they concur with what we believe they think, versus reputation asking what you *really* think.

While image and reputation are definitely interrelated, according to Giardini, Gennaro, and Conte (2008), reputation is a distinct phenomenon and, for them, an influential and persistent one. Image is the output of evaluating a "target," but reputation is "both the process and the effect of transmission of that image." Giaridini et al. see reputation as dynamic in that it is subject to change, for example, if there is bad behavior in the form of corruption or deception. Reputation is what people think about organizations and also what organizations are in the eyes of others.

Reputation is an exchange of social evaluations, which "are crucial to partner selection, social control and coalition formation" (Giardini et al., 2008, p. 232). It acts as a compass, steering us away from bad or dangerous affiliations, and helps us to find reliable associates in both small and large social groups. Furthermore, image is often traceable, that is, the "evaluator" is often known, while reputation's source is anonymous. It is something people say about someone or something, but the source is unclear, and it is spread more easily.

Brønn and Ihlen (2009) summarized the work of several researchers in defining reputation. Barnett, Jermier, and Lafferty (2006), for example, reported 49 different definitions. Some authors have also demonstrated the different uses of the term in different academic disciplines (Fombrun, 1996; van Riel & Fombrun, 2007), including psychology, economics, strategy, accounting, marketing, sociology, and communication. In an attempt to find similarities and differences between and within the different disciplines, the different definitions have been grouped into three categories, where weight is on three different characteristics (Barnett et al., 2006):

- Definitions that center on reputation being the attention that a stakeholder gives an organization; reputation is seen as a perception of impression.
- Definitions that point out that the term involves an evaluation; reputation says something about status of an organization; it has to do with meanings.
- Definitions that emphasize reputation as a value for an organization; reputation is tightly associated with its consequences.

It should be emphasized that there are overlaps between categories, but they can also be differentiated.

Reputation as Relationships

It has been suggested that relationships are reputation. Reputation is described as a magnet that attracts people (Fombrun & van Riel, 2004). People want to work for organizations with a good reputation and want to invest in firms with a good reputation. In other words, they want a relationship with the organization: To "acquire a reputation that is positive, enduring, and resilient requires managers to invest heavily in building and maintaining good relationships with their company's constituents" (Fombrun, 1996, p. 57).

J. E. Grunig (1993) proposed that one characteristic of effective organizations is their ability to achieve their goals through the development of relationships with their stakeholders. Based on the results of the Excellence Study, L. A. Grunig, Grunig, and Dozier (2002) suggested that the quality of relationships determines reputation, that quality relationships and reputation result more from the behavior of organizations than from messages disseminated, and that the value of relationships includes the value of reputation. Coombs (2000) conceptualized reputation as an organization's relational history (i.e., a collection of past events in a relationship) with multiple stakeholders.

MacMillan, Money, Downing, and Hillenbrand (2004) contended that at the heart of any business relationship is trust of and commitment to a business by its stakeholders. MacMillan, Money, Downing, and Hillenbrand (2005) concluded that reputation affects organizations through stakeholder relationships. Research by Brønn (2007) showed a clear correlation between relationship building and impact on reputation.

Organizations that communicate effectively with stakeholders develop better relationships because management and stakeholders understand one another and because both are less likely to behave in ways that have negative consequences for the interests of the other (Hon & Grunig, 1999). Relational capital, according to Roberts, Brønn, and Breunig (2003), is what makes human capital succeed; it combines and relates people to each other and allows them to exchange their knowledge, skills, and insights in business situations. Accordingly, it produces reputation and image when parties successfully exchange insights, experience, and information.

Reputation as Trust

It is possible to assert that it is not reputation that is damaged when organizations fail to live up to expectations; it is rather our trust in them. Trust, like reputation, can take years and resources to build up, and while it may be difficult to break, it, again, like reputation, can take considerable time and even more resources to restore. According to Kramer (1999), individuals' perceptions of others' trustworthiness and their willingness to engage in trusting behavior when interacting with them increases or decreases as a function of long-term interaction. Through interaction, parties gain information that allows them to assess each other's disposition, intentions, and motives. Based on this information, each party can then decide whether or not the others are trustworthy and if they can be trusted in the future. Reputation therefore becomes a resource representing the beliefs that contribute to creating a feeling of trust. Someone who has a good reputation is very likely trustworthy.

The Edelman public relations agency publishes an annual survey measuring the state of trust. This Trust Barometer asks college-educated people in the top 25% income level in 20 countries whom they trust. Government was dead last in the United States, North and South America, and Europe in the 2008 Edelman survey, and business was trusted more than government in 12 of the 20 countries surveyed. Europeans and North Americans trust nongovernmental organizations (NGOs) and religious organizations more than the business community. People trust their peers, that is, a "person like themselves." This was true for all geographical regions.

Garry Honey (2007), senior fellow at the Centre for Risk Research at the University of South Hampton, lists five stages of losing trust: (1) *disappointment* with inconsistent behavior where trust is questioned, but it is possible for organizations to recover quickly; (2) *surprise* at the poor judgment or lack of control by an organization where trust is dented, but with time and good relationship building, an organization can recover; (3) *concern* about an accident or safety issue such as a product recall where trust is diminished and recovery comes at considerable cost; (4) *disgust* at the incompetence and poor management decision making of the organization where trust is severely damaged and trust is never fully recovered; and finally, (5) *outrage* that the organization would engage in things such as fraud, embezzlement, or other illegal activity and trust is completely lost and impossible to recover.

As noted by the Edelman Trust Barometer (n.d.), when people no longer trust an organization, their first reaction is that they no longer purchase its products and services. This is true for almost all countries. People also do not want to work for the organization or invest in it. And they tell others what they think about the organization.

Branding the Organization

Sandstrom (2006) made the point that it would be surprising to find an organization with a strong corporate brand that did not have a good reputation. Van Riel and Fombrun (2007) described corporate branding as the activities carried out by organizations to "build favorable associations and positive reputation with both internal external stakeholders" (p. 107). The term *branding* is most closely associated with marketing but in the last several years has become more and more used by people working in public relations or corporate communication.

Corporate branding applies typical branding constructs to the entire organization and is not limited to customers, but rather encompasses all stakeholders (internally and externally). As noted by Hatch and Schultz (2008), the corporate brand targets all stakeholders, "influences organizational activities from top to bottom and it infuses everything an organization is, says and does, now and forever" (p. 10). It is "based on an integrated and interdisciplinary mindset based on the central ideas about who the organization is. It emphasizes developing relationships with all stakeholders and invites stakeholders to participate in defining who the organization is—and wants to be" (Schultz, 2005, p. 24).

The first wave of corporate branding is described as the recognition that the organization itself (and not products) plays an increasingly important role in differentiation and stakeholder relations (Schultz, Antorini, & Csaba, 2005). The problem is that corporate branding has been very tightly associated with marketing and propaganda. The results were short-term expressions from the organization and not long-term relationship building with stakeholders. There are a number of myths associated with the concept of building the organization as a brand. Schultz et al. (2005) tried to clear these themes up. According to them,

- Corporate branding is NOT the same as normal branding. Corporate branding puts weight on the organization as a central and long-lasting power.
- Corporate branding is NOT solely the responsibility of marketing departments. The long-term strategic nature of corporate branding means that it is better placed under corporate communication.
- Corporate branding is NOT about creating a beautiful impression. It is decisive for organizations' believability that there is a correlation between the organizational and corporate identities.
- The goal of corporate branding is NOT just simply communicating. The goal is clear

and concise communication over time and loyalty to basic vision and values, and not empty talk, so-called corporate speak.

- Corporate branding does NOT automatically mobilize the organization's employees. The organization cannot just start activities and take for granted that everyone will follow along.
- Corporate branding is NOT just for commercial enterprises. The concept can be applied to countries, regions, nonprofits, and governmental organizations.

Schultz et al. (2005) suggested that corporate branding is already on its second wave, where it is seen as a strategic strength that is anchored in the organization and that encompasses all stakeholder groups, both internal and external. For example, in organizations with strong brands, there tends to be a stronger connection between the vision, culture, and image (Hatch & Schultz, 2008) that together constitute the organization's identity. Vision is top leaders' desires for the future, culture is what the employees have always known or believed (organization's heritage and values and beliefs), and image is what external interests expect or want from an organization (p. 11).

Bickerton (2000) believed that it is important that organizations understand and find ways to coordinate things to streamline activities tied to corporate branding. When there is a gap between vision, culture, and image, the organization's brand is at risk—in other words, the reputation is either damaged or not useful. It is thus imperative that vision, culture, and image be linked (Hatch & Schultz, 2008). This demands a multifunctional approach where all functions participate, including marketing, strategy, human resources, design, and communication (Table 21.1).

Communication and Reputation

Communication can create attention to, understanding for, and recognition of an organization's strategic goals. This can be a competitive advantage for an organization in the form of a better image and reputation. There are three levels for

Table 21.1 Progressive Approach to Corporate Branding

	Traditional Approach	Progressive Approach
Purpose	Managing; conveying information	Build/strengthen relationships
Role	Produce/distribute information on initiatives, programs, industry awards/recognition	Provide context, interpretation, relevance
Perspective	Reactive	Anticipative, creative
Integration with strategy	Little, sporadic	Extensive, well-planned
Approach	Push	Holistic
Skills	Journalistic	Human behavior; sense what people need to know, feel, do
Information flow	Top down	Two-way, sideways
Measures	Clips/clicks/hits	Organizational success

processing of information that can influence how people perceive an organization (Bromley, 2000, in van Riel & Fombrun, 2007):

1. *Primary Level:* Personal experience
2. *Secondary Level:* What friends and colleagues say about an organization or products
3. *Tertiary Level:* Mass media information such as paid advertising and unpaid publicity

The greatest degree of impact on reputation is at the primary level, but this tends to be the least used. As noted by van Riel and Fombrun (2007), most people get their information from secondary sources and the mass media. Together, they are the biggest sources of information, but also the least influential. There can be an immediate impact on image, but not on reputation.

Kim, Bache, and Clelland (2007) described two communication approaches to reputation building—a symbolic management approach and a behavioral management approach. In the symbolic approach, organizations use communication to generate positive impressions in a particular audience. Emphasis is on media visibility and favorability, and organizations that take this approach put a lot of resources into media relations. In the behavioral management approach, on the other hand, the organization aligns its actions or behavior with the messages being sent through the organization's communications. Behavior can be a code of conduct, a social audit, incentive schemes, compliance schemes, public ratings, philanthropy, value-based statements of intent, and templates such as the Balanced Scorecard (Dowling, 2006).

Organizations that concentrate only on the symbolic approach assume that if they tell a stakeholder what he or she wants to hear, it will enhance their reputation and thus performance (Kim et al., 2007). According to Dowling (2006), such proclamations may be

- to employees: "we are a good, safe place to work";
- to customers: "we stand behind our products and services";
- to society: "we are a good corporate citizen";
- to investors: "our reports and forecasts are reliable";
- to insurers: "we are a sensible risk";
- to government: "because of our economic and social contribution, support us"; and
- to regulators: "trust our interpretation of and compliance with the law."

Analyzing 7 years of data from international research based on the Reputation Quotient and RepTrak, van Riel and Fombrun (2007) identified six principles for communication that are associated with high reputation ranking:

- Visibility
- Distinctiveness
- Authenticity
- Transparency
- Consistency
- Responsiveness

The drivers of *visibility* are public prominence and market prominence. Public prominence occurs when an organization has high street exposure. This may come from a strong national heritage or a strong media presence. Market prominence also comes from being listed on a public stock exchange, which invites scrutiny and media coverage, and highly publicized corporate citizenship. In other words, the more people know you, the more likely they are to like you. Strong reputations tend to come from positive visibility, but negative publicity tends to be the rule. It doesn't take much imagination to list firms with poor reputations based on their high negative profiles.

According to Fombrun and van Riel (2004), without visibility, there can be no reputation. Those who want a good reputation must communicate with all relevant stakeholders as they build relationships with them. It is possible to purchase visibility in the media, but the best is to deserve positive media coverage. The downside is that visible organizations can be more vulnerable to criticism. When a new car model from Mercedes tips over in a test, the reaction is much larger than when a model from Hyundai does the same (Brønn & Ihlen, 2009).

Top-ranked firms distinguish themselves from their rivals by building reputation through a "core reputation platform" based on their *distinctive* characteristics, those attributes that make every organization unique. What the organization stands for is expressed through slogans, trademarks and logos, and corporate stories that speak to all stakeholders.

Authenticity is one of the most important drivers of reputation. It starts with organizational identity, that "beating heart of the organization" (van Riel & Fombrun, 2007, p. 165), that which makes the organization real, genuine, accurate, reliable, and trustworthy. This is where the organization demonstrates that there are no gaps between who they are, what they say they are, and what they do. This is a difficult challenge and the one where organizations often find themselves in difficulty. Organizations would like for us to believe that they are real, genuine, reliable, and trustworthy, but upper management doesn't always deliver on the promises of this rhetoric.

Transparent organizations allow stakeholders access to information that helps them make an accurate assessment of the organization. Organizations are being forced to be more transparent due to pressures from the market, society, politicians, and the law. Stakeholders want information on products and services, financial performance, vision, and leadership and visible leaders, social responsibility, and workplace environment. One trend in this area is product information, where, for example, McDonald's provides nutritional information on the raw materials used in its products. Some of the information in this category is regulated through laws, particularly if a firm is registered on the stock exchange. Voluntary release of information is where some organizations have problems.

Communicating that one is transparent can strengthen a reputation because it builds confidence in the organization. Fombrun and van Riel (2004) pointed out four criteria for openness:

1. Information must be detailed enough that stakeholders can get an accurate picture of the organization.
2. Information that is available must be relevant and provided at the right time.
3. Information must be accurate.
4. It must be possible to use information as comparison.

The best-regarded organizations manage their communication so that they express themselves *consistently* and coherently, that is, they are consistent in both words and deeds. This means that marketing messages must be in harmony with public relations messages, which must be in harmony with messages being sent internally in the organization. It is not enough to create a great vision, with strong ethical guidelines, if it is not shared with the rest of the organization, and if employees are not coached on what it means to enact the guidelines. This is achieved through consistency: consistency through a shared identity that guides consistent behavior and consistent communication.

Key to achieving consistency is aligning the various identities of the organization. The task of aligning identities can be challenging. It is quite possible that an organization's desired identity may conflict with how its identity is conceived, which conflicts with the actual identity, which in turn clashes with the communicated identity (see Balmer & Greyser, 2002). An example from a business school illustrates this point (Brønn & Ihlen, 2009). The school's administration created a branding campaign that suggested that its market position was so strong that it shared characteristics with some of the great brands of our times, including McDonald's. Many faculty members resented the association, as they did not see themselves as delivering a readymade, machine generated, and impersonal educational "product." What seemed a good idea, in that the school has strong brand awareness in the marketplace, backfired because the communicated identity was totally out of harmony with the employees' perception of the values within their organization.

The last communication principle is to be *responsive.* This is a core theme of dialogue, which builds on the premise that the organization will adjust its attitudes and behavior based on feedback from the environment. This is also a key aspect of research on strategic communication, where there is often talk of two-way symmetrical communication (J. E. Grunig, 2001). This means that organizations should try to balance their own interests against those of their operating environment. This is not only viewed as being ethically correct; it is also profitable in the long run. All organizations depend on public acceptance to survive; organizations must demonstrate that they are open to feedback. This is the responsibility of everyone in the organization. A quick test to assess an organization's degree of responsiveness is to send a message to a firm that promises dialogue on its Web page and see how long it takes them to answer.

Corporate Branding/ Communication Activities

Examples of corporate branding activities include corporate advertising, advocacy or issues advertising, and cause-related marketing (Brønn, 2005). Corporate advertising is the term given to paid-for messages placed by the organization telling about the organization. There are very few if any product references. Examples of corporate advertising are general image or positioning ads that announce plant openings, new identities, innovations, and so on. This area also encompasses sponsorships of sports, broadcasts, and music. Rolex sponsors golf tournaments such as the Masters and the British Open and regularly advertises that it does so. Although the product is often pictured, the advertisement is about the company's sponsorship. Recruitment ads for employees also fall into this category. L'Oreal has as a goal to be the company most preferred to work for among graduating female science and business students. It therefore uses considerable resources profiling the company toward this market, including advertising in student newspapers and sponsoring different events. Similarly, advertising aimed at the financial sector is a way to release information on financial results and to generate investment and is often used as a defense against a takeover.

Advocacy advertising is a way for organizations to communicate their position on public issues that are connected with their business activities. This may include taking a position on social or business issues, resolving misunderstandings, or countering a negative editorial. In the 1970s, this was a popular method used by energy companies to try to persuade the American public not to listen to the government, which wanted to institute regulations and environmental controls. Nike and other companies use this type of advertising today to defend themselves against accusations of producing their products in sweatshops. Shell's Profits and Principles campaign was probably one of the largest campaigns of this type. The company would like consumers and other groups to believe that the company does its utmost to protect the environment, work with local populations, and have an open dialogue with its stakeholders. Ford and Rolex take a slightly different tack. Both organizations reward individuals for personal excellence, either for environmental work or for helping humankind. Ford had its Heroes for the Planet award, and Rolex still has an award titled Spirit of Enterprise. The companies then advertise the granting of these awards in the media, featuring the recipient of the award.

Corporate Social Responsibility Communication

Communicating social responsibility is one of the biggest challenges facing firms today. Corporate social responsibility (CSR) communication is defined as communication created and transmitted by the organization about its CSR initiatives (Morsing, 2006). Brønn (2005) defined it as marketing or branding of the firm as socially responsible (the firm's vision that they have something to contribute to society over and above profit maximization) through the firm's communication activities. The range of activities here is large and may include a variety of media such as labeling on packaging, affinity/cobranded credit cards, licensing agreements, and sponsorships, advertising, or sales promotions. Sales promotions may include assistance in raising donations, purchase-triggered donations, and so on. Other activities range from corporate statements regarding value chain decisions, environmental compliance, women and minority issues, investment guidelines, support of local communities, and so on.

A well-known form of CSR communication is cause-related marketing (CRM). The term has been attributed to American Express, which, in 1983, raised money for the Statue of Liberty's restoration project by donating a sum of money based on consumers' use of its credit card. There are a number of definitions of CRM, most of which define the key characteristic of CRM as the firm's donation to a designated cause (not-for-profit organization) that links to customers engaging in revenue-producing transactions (see, e.g., Varadarajan & Menon, 1988). In the United States, CRM is used as a corporate term for "working together in financial concert with a charity . . . to tie a company and its products to a cause" (Ptacek & Salazar, 1997, p. 9). Adkins (1999) defined CRM as using marketing money, techniques, and strategies to support worthwhile causes while at the same time building the business. Furthermore, it is the commercial activity by which businesses and charities or causes form a partnership with each other to market an image, product, or service for mutual benefit.

A related concept is corporate social marketing (CSM). Drumwright and Murphy (2004) defined CSM as "encompass[ing] marketing initiatives that have at least one noneconomic objective related to social welfare and use the resources of the company and/or one of its partners" (p. 164). Hoeffler and Keller (2002) described how CSM can build brand equity for firms through, among other things, building brand awareness, enhancing image, establishing credibility, and eliciting engagement in the brand above and beyond purchasing, for example, by getting involved in a cause-related activity supported by the brand.

Kotler and Lee (2004) defined CSM more narrowly as a strategy that "uses marketing principles and techniques to foster behavior change in a target population, improving society while at the same time *building markets for products or services*" (p. 14). In other words, firms engage in CSM for commercial purposes. Kotler and Lee contended that the emphasis on behavior change differentiates CSM from typical corporate social initiative activities engaged in by business. According to the authors, these activities as used by firms are designed to raise money, create goodwill, and build awareness of a cause or brand but not to change individual behavior. A well-crafted CSM campaign, according to Kotler and Lee, is one where the firm chooses a social problem whose solution *requires* people to change their individual behavior. The full marketing benefit comes when the targeted behaviors relate to one or more of the company's products or services.

There is a long list of companies who are involved in causes or support nonprofit organizations based on their vision of their CSR. These types of associations generally receive a lot of scrutiny, and many consumers are skeptical about them (Mohr, Eroglu, & Ellen, 1998). Therefore, organizations (both NGOs and firms) must be very careful when entering into these alliances. Companies must be extremely careful that they "walk the talk," as a legitimacy gap in this area can be disastrous for the noncommitted firm.

CSR Communication and Public Relations

Black and Härtel (2004) proposed that an organization's ability to be socially responsible is contingent on the skills of public affairs (public relations) professionals within the organization to help their organization engage in balanced two-way communication. Socially responsive organizations also depend on the ability of other managers to take into consideration stakeholders and social factors in their decision making. These authors recommended the same processes employed in reputation risk analysis as key for success in this area: environmental scanning, issues management, and stakeholder management.

A model of social responsibility developed by Black and Härtel is shown in Figure 21.1. The authors believe that all organizations should be stakeholder engaged, that is, recognize that they depend on others to survive, and also that their behavior affects others, who sometimes are in conflict with the organization. This can be measured by their public relations orientation and their CSR orientation. The public relations orientation is demonstrated by what they call (a) value attuned public relations and (b) dialogue. Value attuned public relations is defined as the ability of public relations managers to "detect and transmit information about social values to guide executive decision-making" (p. 130). Dialogue is the "conscious and respectful effort to share power in a discourse" (p. 130), where parties can feel free to cocreate and challenge each other. The authors warn that not engaging in true dialogue means that the organization's claim of stakeholder engagement is in danger of being seen as merely symbolic with little or no substance, thus damaging the organization's reputation.

Harmonizing Communication

The discussion in this chapter perhaps leaves the impression that building reputation through communication strategies is relatively easy—just follow the six principles, align organizational and corporate identity, and there should be no problems. In fact, the principles are quite complicated and difficult to communicate and live up to. If an organization is to succeed, the reputation platform must not

Figure 21.1 Public Relations and Attitude to CSR

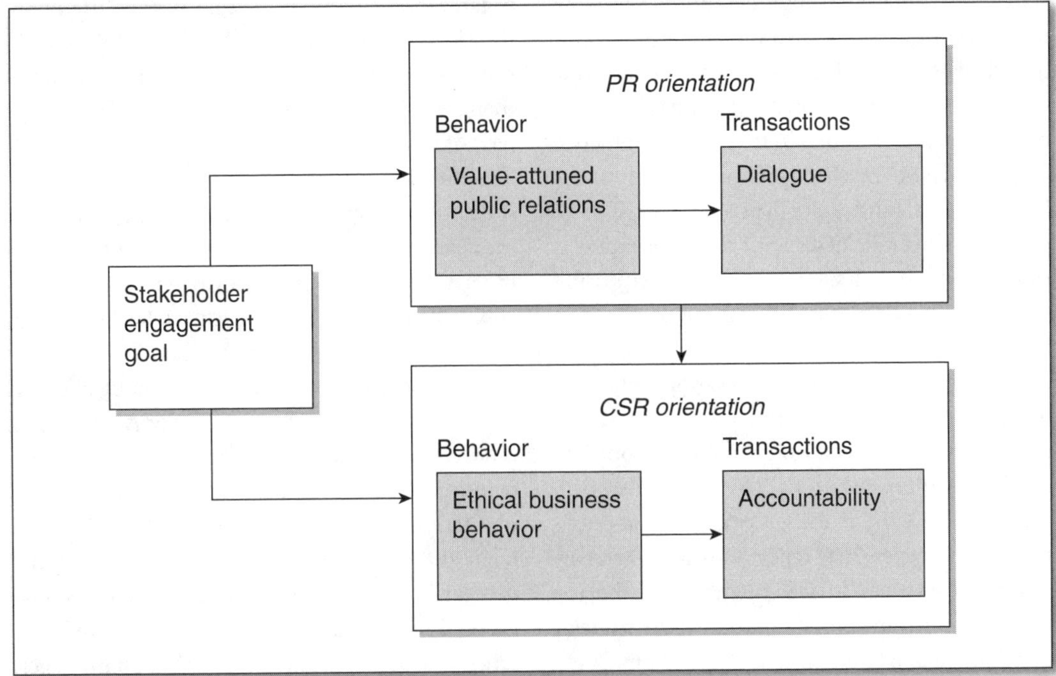

Source: Black and Härtel 2004.

only be strategically positioned; it must also create an emotional appeal and offer a surprise (Fombrun & van Riel, 2004). External communications should express aspects of the organization's mission and vision while at the same time creating emotional appeal and helping differentiate the organization. In addition, all internal and external communication should be harmonized "as effectively and as efficiently as possible, so as to create a favorable basis for relationships within groups upon which the company is dependent" (van Riel, 1995, p. 26).

This means orchestrating the instruments constituting the corporate identity mix: communication, symbols, and behavior. Key is getting all the communication functions to cooperate. This can be done, according to van Riel (1995), through anchoring an organization's communication in what he calls common starting points. These are described as central values that provide the common basis for all communication forms used by organizations in their profiling.

Corporate communication has been offered as a framework that could coordinate communication from a strategic level and oversee both public relations and marketing communication activities (Cornelissen, 2008). Harmonizing communication through a corporate communication department responsible for both marketing communication and traditional PR activities sounds reasonable but is difficult to put into practice. Discussions on marketing communication and PR structural and role differences have been prevalent since the 1970s with the publication of Kotler and Mindak's (1978) article on possible configurations of marketing and public relations. Since the 1990s, the discussion has centered on integrated marketing communication, and then integrated communication, with the argument that organizations need a more strategic approach to their communications (see Cornelissen & Thorpe, 2001). Today, there is evidence that public relations managers may report to the CEO but are still not viewed as formal members of the top management team providing input into strategic decision making (Cornelissen, van Bekkum, & van Ruler, 2006). In such situations, communication can rapidly become a one-way tool to convince stakeholders of the organization's position instead of a strategic instrument in relationship building that can lead to good reputations. Research indicates that marketing and public relations do often work together, but the relationship is often more informal than formal and often depends on the relationship between members of the departments. Cornelissen and Thorpe (2001) suggested that organizations should consider a more flexible and less structural approach to their external communication activities.

Conclusion

Reputation risk is seen as the gap between what organizations communicate to external stakeholders and the behavior they expect from the organization. Put another way, there is a gap between organizational identity, corporate identity, and image. This is perhaps the largest challenge in building reputations. Messages from organizations through, for example, advertising or other communication activities to some degree and for a certain amount of time influence an organization's reputation regardless of the organization's basic activities (Bromley, 2002). It is therefore clear that what organizations say about themselves and how they say it is a very important part of any discussion on reputation.

Attempting to manage the impressions of stakeholders by communicating only positive messages has been shown to have little to no impact on reputation performance (Kim et al., 2007). In fact, such an approach can backfire if, for example, a firm overpromises or builds false expectations. Merely communicating without aligning behavior is not a sustainable strategy. A reputation is not a result of packaging, catchy slogans, or clever communications campaigns. An organization's reputation rests on every single thing it does, from the way it manages its employees to the demeanor of the receptionist. Trust, which reputation is all about, is a result of observed and repeated trustworthy behavior, not good messages. A successful communication strategy makes sure that corporate identity is aligned with organizational identity. In other words, who we say we are is in fact who we are. This approach satisfied Bromley (2002), who wondered if reputation is a by-product of an organization's activities or if it is possible that reputation can be a communication goal. The answer is yes to both questions.

References

Adkins, S. (1999). *Cause related marketing: Who cares wins.* Oxford, UK: Butterworth Heinemann.

Albert, S., & Whetten, D. A. (1985). Organisational identity. In L. C. Cummings & B. M. Staw (Eds.), *Research in organizational behavior* (pp. 263–295). Greenwich, CT: JAI Press.

Balmer, J. M. T., & Greyser, S. A. (2002). Managing the multiple identities of the corporation. *California Management Review, 44*(3), 72–86.

Barnett, M. L., Jermier, J. M., & Lafferty, B. A. (2006). Corporate reputation: The definitional landscape. *Corporate Reputation Review, 9*(1), 26–38.

Bickerton, D. (2000). Corporate reputation versus corporate branding: The realist debate. *Corporate Communications, 5*(1), 42–48.

Birkigt, K., & Stadler, M. M. (1986). *Corporate identity, Grundlagen, Funktionen, Fallspielen* [Corporate identity: The foundation, functions, and case descriptions]. Landsberg am Lech, Germany: Verlag Modern Industrie.

Black, L. D., & Härtel, C. E. (2004). The five capabilities of socially responsible companies. *Journal of Public Affairs, 4*(2), 125–144.

Bromley, D. B. (2002). An examination of issues that complicate the concept of reputation in business studies. *International Studies of Management and Organizations, 32*(3), 65–81.

Brønn, P. (2005). Corporate communication and the corporate brand. In P. Brønn & R. Wiig-Berg (Eds.), *Corporate communication: A strategic approach to building reputation.* Oslo, Norway: Gyldendal.

Brønn, P. S. (2007). Relationship outcomes as determinants of reputation. *Corporate Communications: An International Journal, 12*(4), 376–393.

Brønn, P., & Ihlen, Ø. (2009). *Åpen eller Innadvent, Odømmebygging for Organisasjoner* [Open or closed, reputation building for organizations]. Oslo, Norway: Gyldendal.

Brown, T. J., Dacin, P. A., Pratt, M. G., & Whetten, D. A. (2006). Identity, intended image, construed image, and reputation: An interdisciplinary framework and suggested terminology. *Journal of the Academy of Marketing Science, 34*(2), 99–106.

Coombs, T. (2000). Crisis management: Advantages of a relational perspective. In J. A. Ledingham & S. D. Bruning (Eds.), *Public relations as relationship management: A relational approach to the study and practice of public relations* (pp. 73–93). Mahwah, NJ: Lawrence Erlbaum.

Coombs, T. (2001). Interpersonal communication and public relations. In R. L. Heath (Ed.), *Handbook of public relations* (pp. 105–114). Thousand Oaks, CA: Sage.

Cornelissen, J. P. (2008). *Corporate communication: A guide to theory and practice.* Thousand Oaks, CA: Sage.

Cornelissen, J. P., & Thorpe, R. (2001). The organization of external communication disciplines in UK companies: A conceptual and empirical analysis of dimensions and determinants. *Journal of Business Communication, 38,* 413–438.

Cornelissen, J. P., van Bekkum, T., & van Ruler, B. (2006). Corporate communications: A practice-based theoretical conceptualization. *Corporate Reputation Review, 9*(2), 114–133.

Dowling, G. (2001). *Creating corporate reputations.* New York: Oxford University Press.

Dowling, G. (2006). Reputation risk: It is the board's ultimate responsibility. *Journal of Business Strategy, 27*(1), 59–68.

Drumwright, M. E., & Murphy, P. E. (2004). How advertising practitioners view ethics. *Journal of Advertising, 33*(2), 7–24.

Dutton, J. E., Dukerich, J. M., & Harquail, C. V. (1994). Organizational images and member identification. *Administrative Science Quarterly, 39,* 239–263.

Edelman Trust Barometer. (n.d.). Retrieved March 16, 2010, from www.edelman.com/trust/2008

Fombrun, C. J. (1996). *Reputation: Realizing value from the corporate image.* Boston: Harvard Business School Press.

Fombrun, C., & van Riel, C. B. M. (2004). *Fame and fortune: How successful companies build winning reputations.* Upper Saddle River, NJ: Pearson Education.

Forman, J., & Argenti, P. (2005). How corporate communication influences strategy implementation, reputation and the corporate brand: An exploratory qualitative study. *Corporate Reputation Review, 8*(3), 245–264.

Giardini, F., Gennaro, D. T., & Conte, R. (2008). A model for simulating reputation dynamics in industrial districts. *Simulation Modeling Practice and Theory, 16,* 231–241.

Gregory, J. R. (with Wiechmann, J. G.). (1998). *Marketing corporate image: The company as your #1 product.* Chicago: NTC Business Books.

Grunig, J. E. (1993). Image and substance: From symbolic to behavioral relationships. *Public Relations Review, 19*(2), 121–139.

Grunig, J. E. (2001). Two-way symmetrical public relations: Past, present, and future. In R. L. Heath (Ed.), *Handbook of public relations* (pp. 11–20). Thousand Oaks, CA: Sage.

Grunig, L. A., Grunig, J. E., & Dozier, D. M. (2002). *Excellent public relations and effective organizations: A study of communication management in three countries.* Hillsdale, NJ: Lawrence Erlbaum.

Hatch, M. J., & Schultz, M. (2000). Scaling the Tower of Babel: Relational differences between identity, image and culture in organizations. In M. Schultz, M. J. Hatch, & M. H. Larsen (Eds.), *Expressive organizations* (pp. 11–35). Oxford, UK: Oxford University Press.

Hatch, M. J., & Schultz, M. (2008). *Taking brand initiative: How companies can align strategy, culture, and identity through corporate branding.* San Francisco: Jossey-Bass.

Hoeffler, S., & Keller, K. L. (2002). Building brand equity through corporate societal marketing. *Journal of Public Policy & Marketing, 21*(1), 78–89.

Hon, L. C., & Grunig, J. E. (1999). *Guidelines for measuring relationships in public relations.* Gainesville, FL: Institute for Public Relations.

Honey, G. (2007, November). *Reputation and principal risks.* Paper presented at the TERF conference (The Enterprise and Risk Forum), London.

Ind, N. (1997). *The corporate brand.* New York: New York University Press.

Kim, J.-N., Bache, S. B., & Clelland, I. J. (2007). Symbolic or behavioral management? Corporate reputation in high-emission industries. *Corporate Reputation Review, 10*(2), 77–98.

Kotler, P., & Lee, N. (2004). *Corporate social responsibility: Doing the most good for your company and your cause.* Hoboken, NJ: Wiley.

Kotler, P., & Mindak, W. (1978). Marketing and public relations: Should they be partners or rivals? *Journal of Marketing, 42,* 13–20.

Kramer, R. M. (1999). Trust and distrust in organizations: Emerging perspectives, enduring questions. *Annual Review of Psychology, 50,* 569–598.

Lindstrom, M. (2005). *Brand senses.* London: Kogan Page.

MacMillan, K., Money, K., Downing, S., & Hillenbrand, C. (2004). Giving your organization SPIRIT: An overview and call to action to directors on issues of corporate governance, corporate reputation and corporate responsibility. *Journal of General Management, 3,* 2–42.

MacMillan, K., Money, K., Downing, S., & Hillenbrand, C. (2005). Reputation in relationships: Measuring experiences, emotions and behaviors. *Corporate Reputation Review, 8*(3), 214–232.

Mohr, L. A., Eroglu, D., & Ellen, S. P. (1998). The development and testing of a measure of skepticism toward environment claims in the marketers' communications. *Journal of Consumers Affairs, 32*(1), 30–55.

Morsing, M. (2006). Corporate social responsibility as strategic auto-communication: On the role of external stakeholders for member identification. *Business Ethics: A European Review, 15*(2), 171–182.

Ptacek, J. J., & Salazar, G. (1997). Enlightened self-interest: Selling business on the benefits of cause-related marketing. *Nonprofit World, 15*(4), 9–14.

Rindova, V. P., & Fombrun, C. J. (1999). Constructing competitive advantage: The role of firm-constituent interaction. *Strategic Management Journal, 20*(8), 691–710.

Roberts, H., Brønn, P. S., & Breunig, J. (2003). *Intangible assets and communication* (IABC Research Report). San Francisco: IABC.

Sandstrom, L. (2006). *Corporate branding: Et verktøj til stratgisk kommunikation* [A tool for strategic communication] (2nd ed.). Frederiksberg, Denmark: Forlaget Samfundslitteratur.

Schultz, M. (2005). A cross-disciplinary perspective on corporate branding. In M. Schultz, U. M. Antorini, & F. F. Csaba (Eds.), *Corporate branding: Purpose/people/process* (pp. 23–54). Copenhagen, Denmark: Copenhagen Business School Press.

Schultz, M., Antorini, U. M., & Csaba, F. F. (Eds.). (2005). *Corporate branding: Purpose/people/process.* Copenhagen, Denmark: Copenhagen Business School Press.

van Riel, C. B. M. (1995). *Principles of corporate communication.* Hemel Hempstead, UK: Prentice Hall.

van Riel, C. B. M., & Fombrun, C. J. (2007). *Essentials of corporate communication.* London: Routledge.

Varadarajan, P. R., & Menon, A. (1988). Cause-related marketing: A coalignment of marketing strategy and corporate philanthropy. *Journal of Marketing, 52*(3), 58–74.

PART II

The Practice of Public Relations as Change Management

Robert L. Heath

Part I of this *Handbook* featured major theories and bodies of research as well as discussions relevant to them. Those chapters addressed conditions and challenges facing organizations, the public(s)/stakeholders, and society/community relevant to the rationale for and practice of public relations. That discussion addressed various challenges of change management central to the value public relations can add to society. Its value includes its ability to help create and adjust relationships and assist various personae as they plan, manage, debate, contest, push, and shove—the wrangle of the narrative of society as the blending and collision of interests.

Extending, applying, and adding logics to those explored there, Part II focuses on where the rubber meets the road. Some commentators treat these topics as subfunctions or the work of technicians. One can bet, however, that authors in Part II have at times (perhaps often and even always) viewed what they discuss as a much bigger picture, rather than a subfunction. Such is the problem of the vocabulary of the discipline—how its supporters and others have defined, segmented, and parsed the discipline. Also, no matter how essentially public relations practitioners engage in development and implementation of the organization's missions and vision through a change management philosophy, sooner or later, there is the need for implementation. And in implementation, changes are designed to satisfy one or a set of publics/stakeholders, but one can predict that these may disturb other constituencies. Postchange, communication can continue the process of change in varying degrees of contention and collaboration.

For instance, risk communication can (and is) seen as a subfunction by some. Others, especially in light of the risk management initiative in management theory, see it as central to and even the driver of public relations. For instance, if discussants adopt the perspective of the cultural theory of risk, they will argue that societies thrive or perish (as is true of individuals and organizations) based on the collective ability to manage risks.

Thus, if public relations is engaged in change management, the change managed is very likely to be risk identification, interpretation, assessment, and response to minimize impact and perhaps even occurrence of various risks. Thus, the engagement between organizations and stakeholders discusses acceptable levels of risk and fairness of risk bearing. These discussions may debate the willingness and ability of organizations and individuals to achieve appropriate levels of corporate responsibility to deserve support rather than suffering opposition.

This theme obviously applies to high-risk industries (such as banking/financial, petrochemical, extraction, food production and processing, medical, and nuclear generation), but it can also extend to a marketing model and to governmental agencies and NGOs (nongovernmental organizations). In a marketing model, are not the selling points used to define (most or all?) products and services designed to manage risk—including carefully crafted statements designed to withstand product safety litigation? Dialogue in this narrative might include the following: "As we near allergy season, ask your doctor about the green pill!" Note also the power leverage of the voice of the ad, the physician, and the medication as defined by regulation. Then, we have the FDA (U.S. Food & Drug Administration) prescribed precaution: "This medication can affect the ability to operate machinery." "In rare occasions, users may suffer diarrhea, nausea, and suicidal thoughts. If any of these symptoms occur or if thoughts of suicide occur, stop using the medication and contact your physician," but not a lawyer. "Contact a lawyer" is a different risk management ad.

Are we wise to consider what follows in part and perhaps whole as contexts or domains (rhetorical problems?) calling for public relations? The narrative of the chapters in Part II sets the scene for the contextual enactment of "public relations" (featuring process as structures/functions and cocreation of meaning). The contextual nature of an organization, for instance, one that is high risk, might well do more to define public relations (public affairs, corporate communication, strategic communications, marketing communication, etc.) than any research-based understanding of public relations might define these research areas and practices.

In all the contexts in the following chapters, change is a possibility, and perhaps even the probable solution, but never independent of relevant discourse. Crisis, for instance, presumes that some performance ability or policy might need to be changed. And communication may not solve the crisis as crisis. If a risk is greater, such as emergency storm management, than the current level of management of that risk, then new risk management best practices are needed. Communication may not reduce the risk or mitigate its consequences, but certainly it is not irrelevant—or merely a technician role. If a college suffers the loss of students and faculty—those performing community service—in an earthquake in Haiti, does the college manage the crisis by a lesson learned—change managed—to discontinue the service outreach or only work in "low"-risk communities?

If a company's performance is undervalued by investors, communication may solve the problem. If the performance of the company does not deserve a higher valuation, then communication simply can't solve the problem.

Themes of this sort are implicitly and explicitly central to Part II and link it conceptually with Part I. It is important, however, to realize that topics discussed there are not merely "implementable" as strategic technician functions. Rather, theory in Part II, specific to these contexts, must necessarily challenge and refine discussions in Part I.

Finally, as much as themes of some of the chapters in Part I feature management, contexts in Part II not only do so as well but also have evolved with management wisely and purposefully included in their names. Key contexts require and have developed their specific rationale, process, and meaning development and enactment. Whereas the management cadre of any specific organization might not immediately understand and appreciate the contributing role of public relations, such is not the case for research, issues, risk, crisis, community relations, investor relations, and such. The tension between contexts and the umbrella concept of public relations often occurs not because contexts are trivialized by management but because management does not always see these as what public relations contributes. Thus, for instance, general counsel may play a dominant role in an organization's crisis management and communication, whereas we would like for public relations to do so—in coordination with other disciplines. Optimally, however, crisis management and communication are a team effort—matrixed management.

The contexts discussed here are not exhaustive, but we have a long list: issue management, crisis, risk, community engagement, community relations, ethics management, military media relations, sports relations, marketing communication, and publicity. We also are attentive to the channel alternatives that continue to evolve and change. By exploring contextual exigencies, we advance our understanding of how public relations serves an important management role because of its relevance to the shaping and enacting of missions and visions vital to making society fully functioning.

CHAPTER 22

The Use of Research in Public Relations

Marcia W. DiStaso and Don W. Stacks

The use of research in public relations is a hot topic in both academia and the practice. Its importance has been highlighted due to the increasing demand for accountability and transparency in organizations (Bowen, Rawlins, & Martin, 2010). Public relations research focuses on the entire public relations process and examines the relationships that exist between organizations or persons and their target publics (Lindenmann, 2006).

Public relations research is the "effort aimed at discovering the facts or opinions pertaining to an identified issue, need or question" (Stacks, 2006, p. 18). Public relations research differs slightly from what many other disciplines call research in that in the practice of public relations, it has been primarily used in support of business objectives.

The role of public relations research from the early 20th century to date has shifted from the simple act of counting publicity materials to a more sophisticated evaluation of public relations effectiveness. Using research methods similar to the methods used by scientists in other disciplines is what legitimates the practice and study of public relations. Research in the practice of public relations differs from academic public relations research in that its focus is practical and often for the use of establishing the impact of public relations on return on investment (ROI).

Both the 1998 and the 2006 Commission on Public Relations Education identified research as an integral part of public relations "curricular essentials" for public relations professionals (National Curriculum Commission, 2007).

Because of the growing importance of research in both academia and the practice of public relations, the purpose of this chapter is to explore its use.

Literature Review

Research in Academia

Public relations academic research is informed by both practice and theory. Examples of public relations theory include contingency theory (Cameron, Cropp, & Reber, 2001), excellence theory (Grunig, Grunig, & Dozier, 2002), relationship management theory (Ledingham, 2003), PR^3 (Stacks, 1995), and situational crisis communication theory (Benoit, 1995; Coombs, 1995). For more details on public relations theory, see Botan (2009).

Until the late 1980s, the public relations journals (*Public Relations Quarterly* and *Public Relations Journal*) focused on practical research with most publications consisting of historical case studies, surveys, interviews, or focus groups (Stacks & DiStaso, 2009). In 1975, the journal *Public Relations Review* was founded. From 1989 to 1991, the *Public Relations Annual* (Volumes 1–3, edited by Larrisa and James Grunig), which later became the *Journal of Public Relations Research*, produced the first academically oriented journal in public relations with a theoretical research base.

Research in the Practice

In the practice of public relations, research is conducted for all aspects of a campaign from precampaign activities to implementation and the evaluation of the campaign's effectiveness (Stacks & DiStaso, 2009). Research, then, can be assessed by the methods employed in each of the campaign phases.

In addition to meeting the research goals of the campaign, it is also important to evaluate how well the campaign helped the business (company, client, product) achieve its overall objectives. Ultimately, business objectives should drive research objectives, which, in turn, should contribute to the ROI.

Disconnect Between Academia and Practice

Although there have been many changes in public relations practice and academia over the years, there is still a disconnect between the two groups (Stacks & DiStaso, 2009; Wright & VanSlyke Turk, 2007). There are many possible explanations for this, and neither group is solely to blame.

Part of the problem may be the lower number of senior-level public relations executives and managers who have formally studied public relations, and many entry-level positions are filled by applicants without a degree from a university-based public relations program (Wright & VanSlyke Turk, 2007). As a result, there is a lack of understanding of best practices and research principles in the profession (Michaelson, 2009). Another reason may be the claim by educators that professionals do not understand or appreciate the theoretical aspects of the science beneath the art of the field.

The lack of agreement about a common research agenda is yet another possible reason for the disconnect. Also, only a few professionals subscribe to or read the public relations research journals. Unfortunately, each of these reasons is exacerbated by the lack of communication between the groups. Although there are exceptions, most academics allocate only a small portion of their time to professional service, and with relatively small travel budgets, educators must choose more academic conferences in lieu of other gatherings with professionals. Therefore, educators and professionals don't mix as much as necessary to improve the field.

Given the disconnection, it is helpful to look at the changes in the perceptions of research in the practice of public relations. To do this, we reflect on the 1998 study of 258 public relations educators and professionals (see Stacks, Botan, & VanSlyke Turk, 1999) compared with the 2006 study of 312 public relations educators and professionals (see DiStaso, Stacks, & Botan, 2009).

The 1998 study identified that research skills were desired but not often found in entry-level and advanced-level professionals. In 2006, the gap improved slightly, but research skills were more highly desired than found. Both professionals and educators felt that research skills were more desired and existed more often with the advanced-level professionals than with the entry-level applicants. Furthermore, educators believed that research skills were more important than professionals did, and they were less optimistic about how often the skills were found. Possibly, the educators saw the need for the use of research more than professionals, so they expected to have a higher level of desire in the practice. Plus, it looks like the students are learning and retaining more research skills than the educators thought. No matter who believed research skills were more important, both groups felt strongly that research was important for professionals.

Research Methodology

A variety of research methods are available to the public relations scholars and professionals, but ultimately, the research question or problem dictates which method to use (Hocking, Stacks, & McDermott, 2003; Stacks, in press). It is wrong to believe that one method is better than another; therefore, the best approach to research is to select the method that will appropriately explore what is needed.

Over the years, there has been great debate about epistemological positions with qualitative-quantitative methodologies serving as a proxy for these presuppositions. Again, instead of placing an emphasis on one over the other, we support the idea of a marketplace of ideas with the use of a variety of research methods.

Qualitative. According to the *Dictionary of Public Relations Measurement and Research* (a document prepared by an academic but closely reviewed for accuracy by public relations academics and professionals and earning the Commission on Public Relations' "Gold Standard" designation), qualitative research "usually refers to studies that are somewhat to totally subjective, but nevertheless in-depth, using a probing, open-ended, response format or reflects an ethnomethodological orientation" (Stacks, 2006, p. 17). Qualitative methods are informed by an interpretive worldview.

Lindlof and Taylor (2002) suggested that questions drive qualitative research. This includes inquiries such as the following: What's going on here? What is the communicative action that is being performed? How do they do it? What does this mean? Once a question is selected, choices about the research orientation can be made. Qualitative methods include (but are not limited to) interviews, focus groups, case studies, ethnography, observation, and critical analysis (Denzin & Lincoln, 2003). In public relations, the three most common types of qualitative methods are interviews, focus groups, and case studies.

Interviewing is a method of data collection that is relied on quite extensively by qualitative researchers. In general, there are three main types of interviews: (1) the informal conversational interview, (2) the general interview guide approach, and (3) the standardized open-ended interview (Patton, 1990). Interviews involve personal interaction that allows the participant's perspective on the phenomenon to unfold through conversation.

Focus groups are a "controlled group discussion" (Wimmer & Dominick, 2003, p. 124). Often materials are used to stimulate the discussion as it is guided by a moderator. Advantages of focus groups are the interaction between the participants and the speed with which a large amount of data can be collected.

According to Yin (2003), case studies for the purpose of research are one of the most challenging endeavors in the social sciences. This is because case studies are an "informal research methodology that gathers data on a specific individual, company or product with the analysis focused on understanding its unique qualities" (Stacks, 2006, p. 2). The benefit of case studies is that they allow the researcher to retain the holistic and meaningful elements of real-life events.

Although not used often in public relations, participant-observation should be a sociological method employed by the professionals. Stacks (2010) points out that all public relations professionals regardless of practice area should understand what the "normal" daily activity of a client or staff is. Indeed, he goes on to state that practicing participant-observation methodology may provide insights into potential problems either in the company or with the client.

It is important to note that qualitative research, unlike quantitative research, cannot be truly replicated. This is because the researcher himself or herself sees the world through a unique lens, which can influence the data collection and analysis. Another reason is because each study follows a different path simply because of the nature of qualitative research. Instead of duplicating qualitative studies, it may be helpful to apply some of the findings to different settings or situations.

Quantitative. According to the *Dictionary of Public Relations Measurement and Research*, quantitative research "usually refers to studies that are highly objective and projectable, using closed-ended, forced-choice questionnaires; research that relies heavily on statistics and numerical measures" (Stacks, 2006, p. 17).

Quantitative research is more of an objective analysis that often uses statistical programs. According to Levine (2009), quantitative research is applied to many topics, and the methodology used within those topics is also diverse, ultimately, indicating that quantitative research can be "applied to anything that can be quantified" (p. 59). Quantitative methods include (but are not limited to) survey research, content analysis, and experimental designs.

The most popular quantitative method is the survey, and this is also the most common research method used in public relations (Stacks & Watson, 2006). Survey methodology can be through telephone, face-to-face, or using the Internet and can consist of cross-sectional or longitudinal designs (Hocking et al., 2003; Stacks, in press).

Content analysis is defined as "the systematic, objective, quantitative analysis of message characteristics" (Neuendorf, 2002, p. 1). This does not include rhetorical, narrative, discourse, critical, or other types of analysis. Ultimately, the goal of content analysis is to produce counts of key categories and measurements of other variables (Neuendorf, 2002).

Although experimental or quasi-experimental methodologies are available, they are rarely conducted in public relations (especially in the practice) (Stacks, 2010). The evidence of causality through the use of control gives experimental designs advantages over all other methodologies.

By following specific rules, quantitative methodology allows for the describing of a subset of a population in such a way as to present accurate depictions of how the total population would respond—this is called generalizability.

Multiple Methods. Public relations research often entails employing several research methods to explore a single problem. This allows for the combining of methods to use the individual strengths of each. Combining two or more research methods is called triangulation (Hocking et al., 2003). It is important to note that triangulation is simply the combining of methods and not the combining of qualitative and quantitative methods.

Research Questions

To further explore the use of research in public relations academia and practice, the following research questions were explored:

> RQ1: What categories of methodology (quantitative, qualitative, or a combination of both) were used in public relations academic research from 1999 to 2008?
>
> RQ2: What categories of methodology (quantitative, qualitative, or a combination of both) were used in the practice of public relations from 1999 to 2008?
>
> RQ3: What are the differences between the categories of methodology (quantitative, qualitative, or a combination of both) used in public relations academic and practical research from 1999 to 2008?
>
> RQ4: What types of methodology (i.e., interviews, focus groups, survey) were used in public relations academic research from 1999 to 2008?
>
> RQ5: What types of methodology (i.e., interviews, focus groups, survey) were used in the practice of public relations from 1999 to 2008?
>
> RQ6: What are the differences between the types of methodology (i.e., interviews, focus groups, survey) used in public relations academic and practical research from 1999 to 2008?
>
> RQ7: Were there changes in the categories of methodology (quantitative, qualitative, or a combination of both) used in public relations academic research from 1999 to 2008?
>
> RQ8: Were there changes in the categories of methodology (quantitative, qualitative, or a

combination of both) used in the practice of public relations from 1999 to 2008?

RQ9: Were there changes in the types of methodology (i.e., interviews, focus groups, survey) used in public relations academic research from 1999 to 2008?

RQ10: Were there changes in the types of methodology (i.e., interviews, focus groups, survey) used in the practice of public relations from 1999 to 2008?

Method

A content analysis was conducted to look at the differences between the use of research in academia and in the profession over the past 10 years. The public relations academic research was reviewed by analyzing the *Journal of Public Relations Research* and *Public Relations Review*, and the research used in the practice of public relations was reviewed by analyzing the Public Relations Society of America (PRSA) Silver Anvil Award winners. A census was conducted for 10 years from 1999 to 2008. This resulted in an analysis of 730 items: 148 articles in the *Journal of Public Relations Research*, 415 articles in *Public Relations Review*, and 167 Silver Anvil Award winners.

Each item was manually analyzed for the type(s) of research that was used (editor notes, prefaces, bibliographies, and book reviews were excluded from the review). All types of methodology used were recorded, and they were later collapsed into the following eight categories for the academic research: (1) interviews, (2) focus groups, (3) survey, (4) content analysis, (5) experimental, (6) case study, (7) other qualitative (i.e., rhetorical, historical, critical), and (8) other quantitative (i.e., secondary data analysis). The research in the practice of public relations was collapsed into the following five categories: (1) interviews, (2) focus groups, (3) survey, (4) content analysis, and (5) secondary. According to the PRSA (2009), secondary research includes "searching existing resources for information or data related to a particular need, strategy or goal (e.g., online computer database searches, Web-based research, library searches, industry reports and internal market analyses)" (p. 5). In addition to this, each item was categorized as either quantitative, qualitative, or both when any combination of quantitative and qualitative methodologies were used. The journal, volume, issue, and year were also recorded.

Two coders were used, with each coding roughly half of the items. Intercoder reliability was assessed using Holsti (1969), with each researcher coding the same 20%. It was 93.1 for the methodologies and 90.0 for the characterization of the methodologies. The results of the analysis are as follows.

Results

RQ1: What categories of methodology (quantitative, qualitative, or a combination of both) were used in public relations academic research from 1999 to 2008?

In the public relations academic research, quantitative methodologies were dominant. For all the academic research ($N = 563$), quantitative methods were used 51.5% ($n = 290$) of the time, qualitative 22.0% ($n = 124$), a combination of quantitative and qualitative 7.1% ($n = 40$), and 19.4% did not use any methodology ($n = 109$) (see Figure 22.1).

Each of the journals had a relatively similar breakdown, with *Public Relations Review* having a slightly higher emphasis on quantitative and the *Journal of Public Relations Research* having a higher percentage use of combined methods. Out of the 148 articles in the *Journal of Public Relations Research*, 46.6% used quantitative methods ($n = 69$), 22.3% used qualitative ($n = 33$), 8.1% used a combination of quantitative and qualitative ($n = 12$), and 23.0% did not use any methodology ($n = 34$). Out of the 415 articles in *Public Relations Review*, 53.3% used quantitative methods ($n = 221$), 21.9% used qualitative ($n = 91$), 6.7% used a combination of

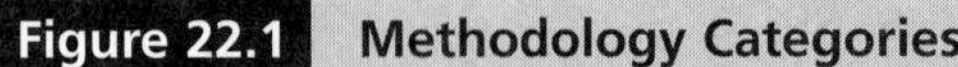

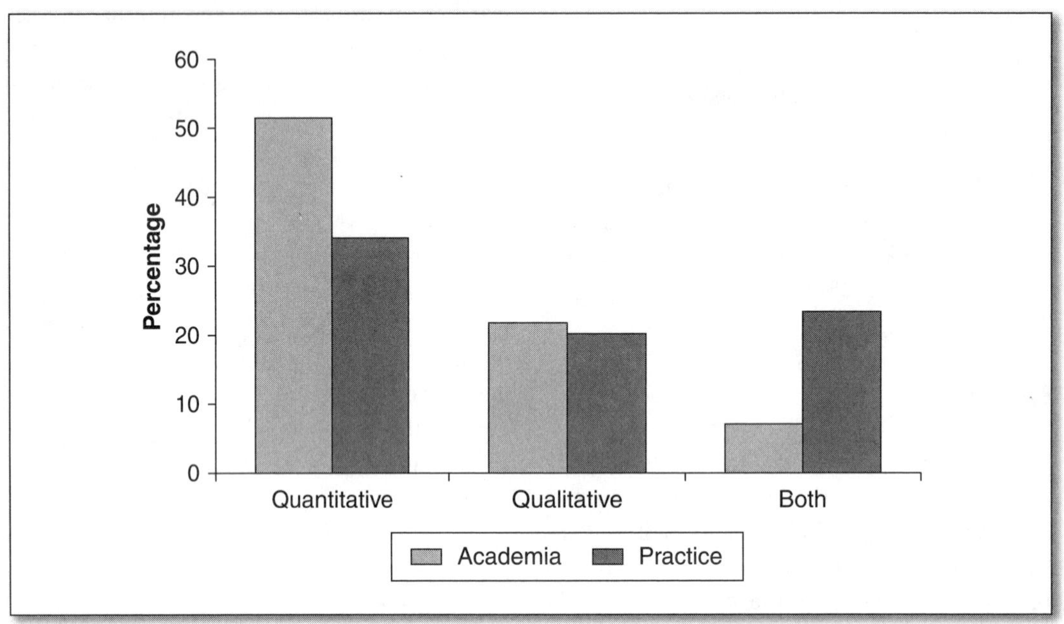

quantitative and qualitative ($n = 28$), and 18.1% did not use any methodology ($n = 75$).

RQ2: What categories of methodology (quantitative, qualitative, or a combination of both) were used in the practice of public relations from1999 to 2008?

In the practice of public relations (as determined through the Silver Anvil Award winners), quantitative methodologies were only slightly more prominent than qualitative, and the combined use of both methodologies was more frequent than in the academic research. Out of the 167 Silver Anvil Award winners, 34.1% used quantitative methods ($n = 57$), 20.4% used qualitative ($n = 34$), 23.4% used a combination of quantitative and qualitative ($n = 39$), and 22.2% did not use any methodology ($n = 37$) (see Figure 22.1).

RQ3: What are the differences between the categories of methodology (quantitative, qualitative, or a combination of both) used in public relations academic and practical research from 1999 to 2008?

The practical research was more spread out between quantitative and qualitative, while the academic research contained a larger percentage of quantitative research (see Figure 22.1). Practical research also contained more than three times the frequency of use of the combination of both methods.

RQ4: What types of methodology (i.e., interviews, focus groups, survey) were used in public relations academic research from 1999 to 2008?

There was a total of 618 methodologies used in the public relations academic research. Of this, 12.9% used interviews ($n = 80$), 2.9% used focus groups ($n = 18$), 23.6% used surveys ($n = 146$), 17.3% used content analysis ($n = 107$), 4.7% used experimental designs ($n = 29$), 8.9% used case studies ($n = 55$), 9.4% used other qualitative methods ($n = 58$), and 2.6% used other quantitative methods ($n = 16$) (see Figure 22.2).

Figure 22.2 Types of Methodology in Academia

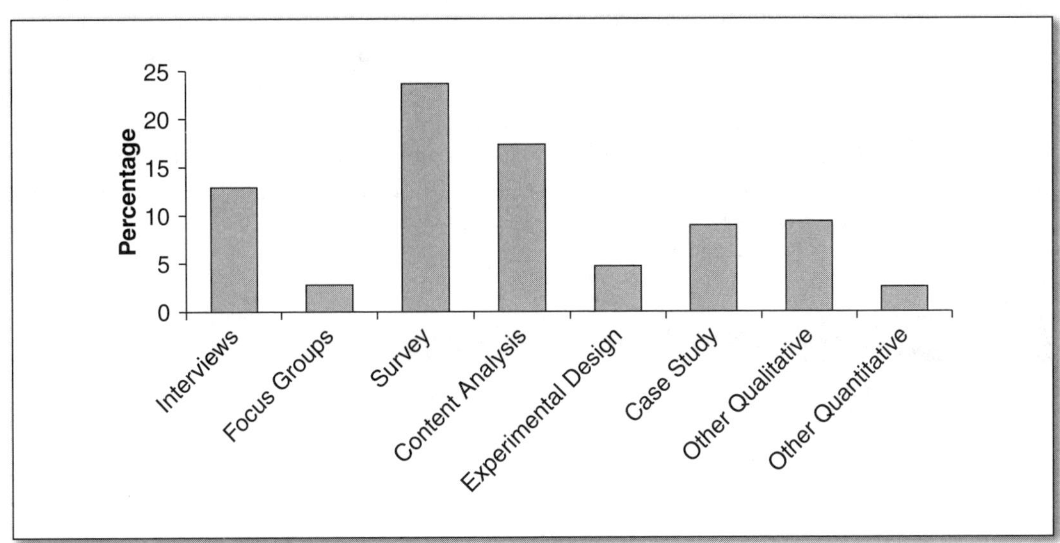

RQ5: What types of methodology (i.e., interviews, focus groups, survey) were used in the practice of public relations from 1999 to 2008?

There were a total of 317 methodologies used in the public relations practical research. Of this, 15.5% Silver Anvil Award winners used interviews (*n* = 49), 14.5% used focus groups (*n* = 46), 29.0% used surveys (*n* = 92), 3.5% used content analysis (*n* = 11), and 37.5% used secondary methods (*n* = 119) (see Figure 22.3).

Figure 22.3 Types of Methodology in the Practice

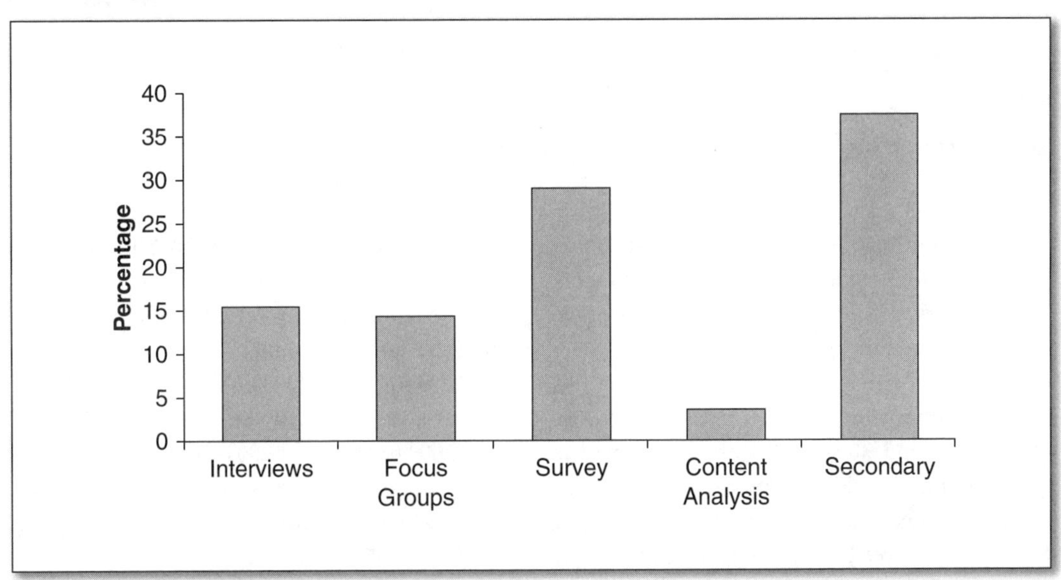

RQ6: What are the differences between the types of methodology (i.e., interviews, focus groups, survey) used in public relations academic and practical research from 1999 to 2008?

A large percentage of the research conducted in the practice was what PRSA calls secondary, and this is not necessarily a separate methodology in academia. For example, this includes literature searches, which are typically included in academic research but as part of the paper leading to the method and not as the method per se. Therefore, this category is included only in the practical research. Another difference is that experimental design is not used at all in the practice, and nor were the other types of quantitative and qualitative methodologies (see Figure 22.4).

Figure 22.4 Types of Methodology

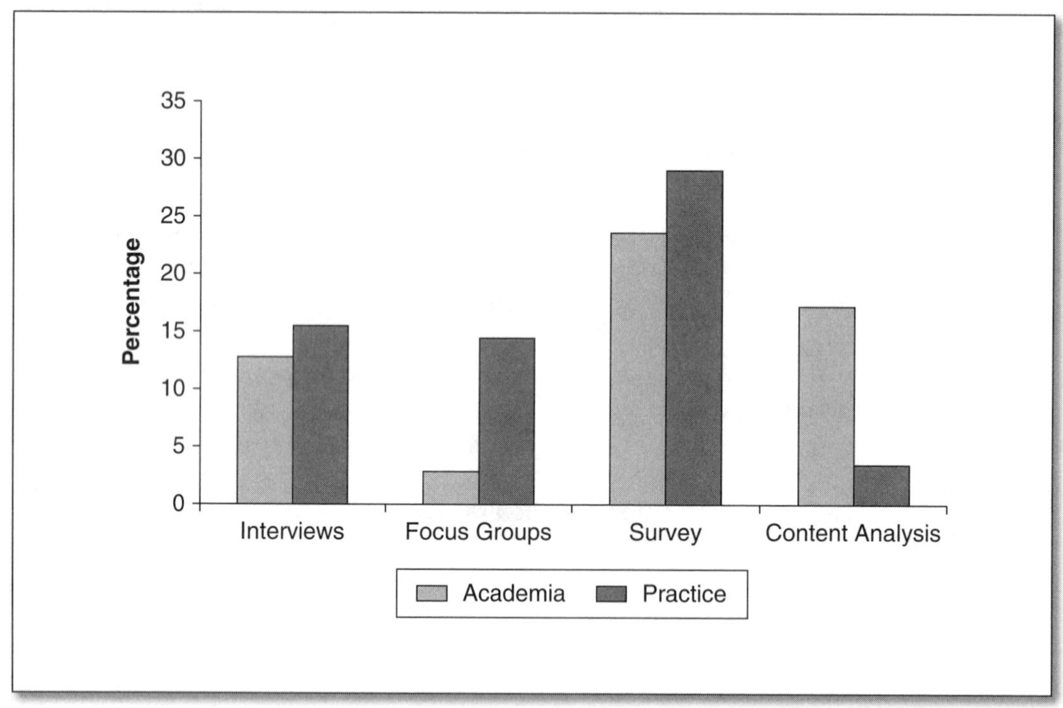

RQ7: Were there changes in the categories of methodology (quantitative, qualitative, or a combination of both) used in public relations academic research from 1999 to 2008?

By breaking the 10 years into two groups (1999–2003 and 2004–2008), the differences in academic public relations research were mainly in the use of qualitative methodologies (see Figure 22.5). Over both groups, the quantitative methodologies were used about half the time (49.8% for 1999–2003 and 52.6% for 2004–2008) and the combination of both methodologies remained fairly constant (7.0% for 1999–2003 and 7.2% for 2004–2008). The articles published without a methodology declined from 23.7% in 1999–2003 to 16.7% for 2004–2008. The other difference found was in the use of qualitative methodologies, which went from 19.5% in 1999–2003 to 23.6% in 2004–2008.

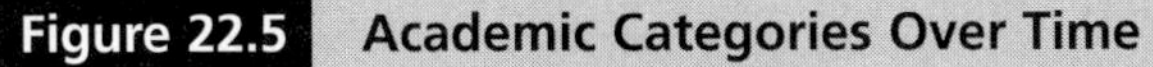

Figure 22.5 Academic Categories Over Time

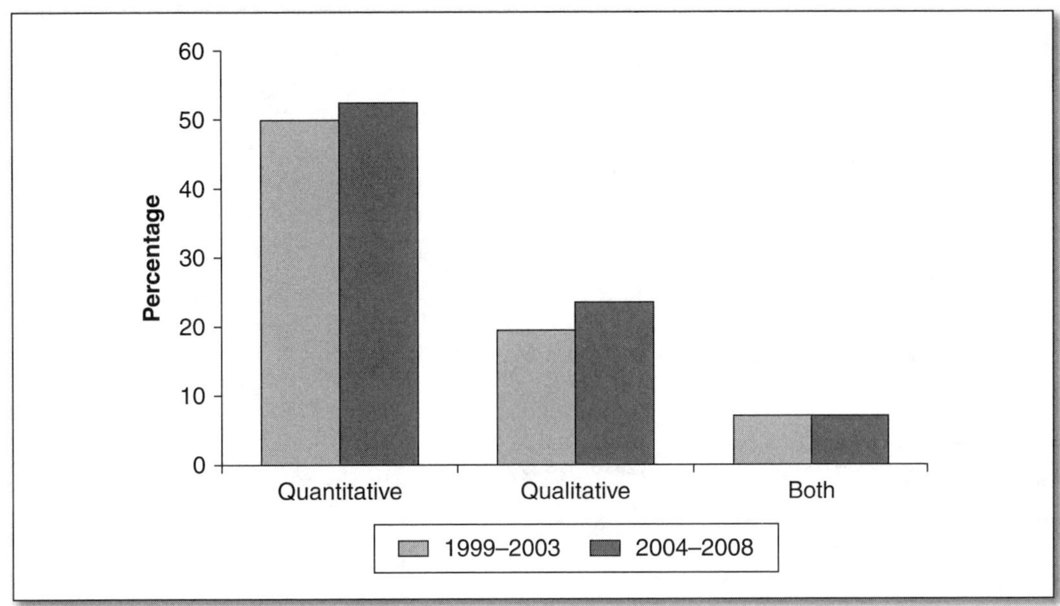

RQ8: Were there changes in the categories of methodology (quantitative, qualitative, or a combination of both) used in the practice of public relations from 1999 to 2008?

For the 5 years from 1999 to 2003, quantitative methodologies were used 41.7% of the time, qualitative were used 16.7% of the time, and both were used 25.0% of the time (see Figure 22.6).

Figure 22.6 Categories Over Time in the Practice

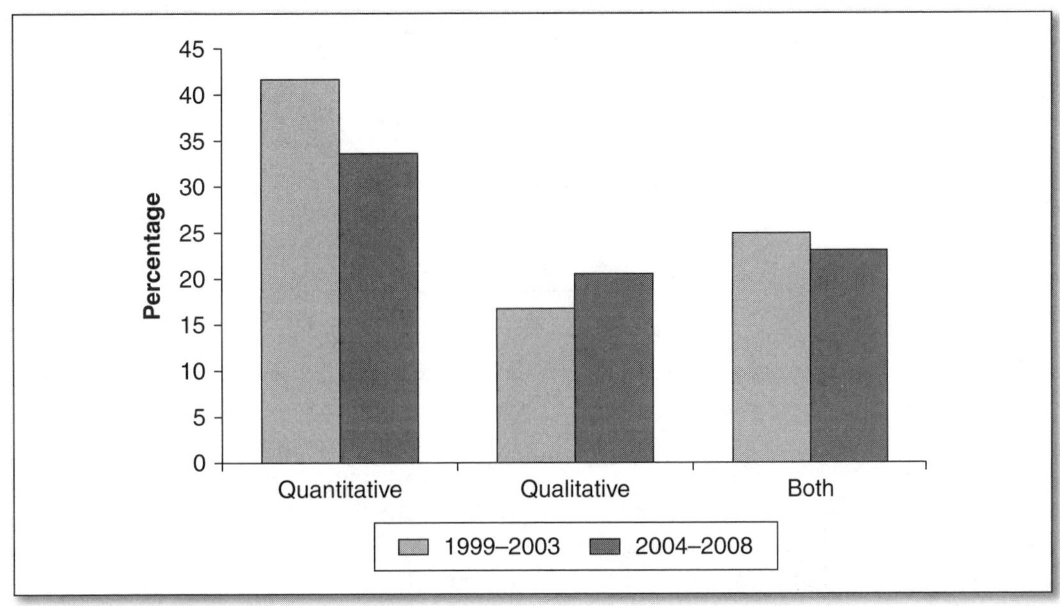

In the following 5 years, quantitative methodologies were used 33.5% of the time, qualitative were used 20.6% of the time, and both were used 23.2% of the time. In addition, Silver Anvil Award winners who did not use a method increased from 16.7% to 22.6%.

RQ9: Were there changes in the types of methodology (i.e., interviews, focus groups, survey) used in public relations academic research from 1999 to 2008?

For public relations academic research from 1999–2003 to 2004–2008, the use of interviews increased from 9.8% to 12.9%, the use of focus groups increased from 1.9% to 2.3%, the use of surveys decreased from 25.1% to 21.0%, the use of content analysis increased from 8.4% to 22.7%, the use of experimental design increased from 4.2% to 5.5%, the use of case studies decreased from 11.6% to 8.6%, the use of other qualitative methodologies decreased from 14.4% to 16.7%, the use of other quantitative methodologies increased from 0.9% to 3.7%, and the use of no methodology decreased from 23.7% to 16.7% (see Figure 22.7).

Figure 22.7 Methodology in Academia Over Time

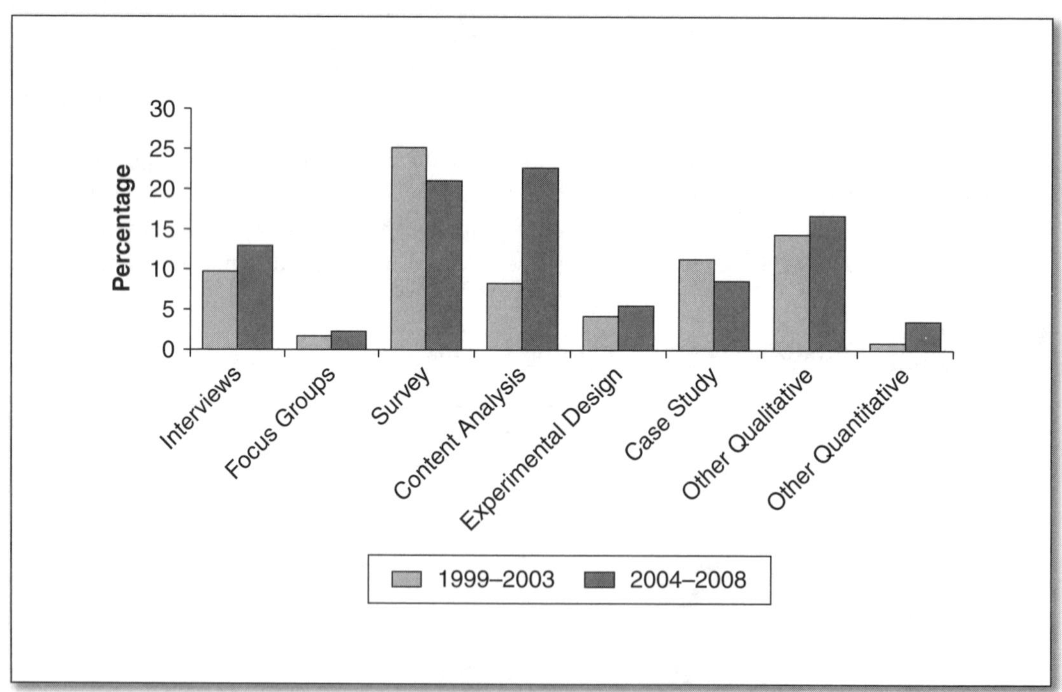

RQ10: Were there changes in the types of methodology (i.e., interviews, focus groups, survey) used in the practice of public relations from 1999 to 2008?

For Silver Anvil Award winners from 1999–2003 to 2004–2008, the use of interviews increased from 8.3% to 28.4%, the use of focus groups decreased from 25.0% to 13.5%, the use of surveys decreased from 50.0% to 32.3%, the use of content analysis increased from 0.0% to 1.9%, and the use of secondary methodologies increased from 16.7% to 23.9% (see Figure 22.8).

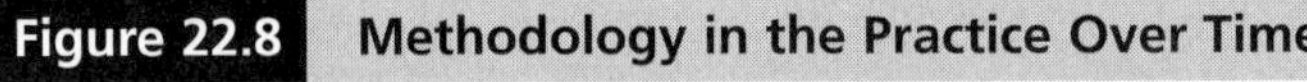

Figure 22.8 Methodology in the Practice Over Time

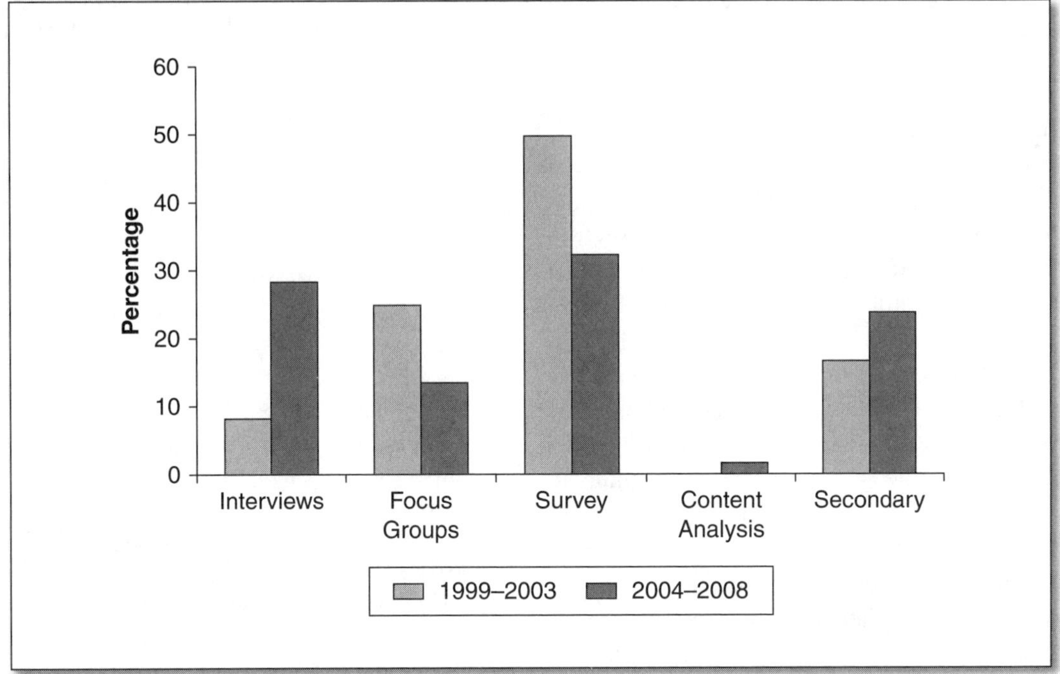

Discussion

The findings from this study indicate that professionals and scholars use a variety of research methods, and both epistemological approaches seem to coexist. In fact, the differences between the two groups are not as large or as significant as what some have speculated.

Academically, we saw a greater use of quantitative methods, especially survey methodology and content analysis. Content analysis was the one method that saw a substantial increase when looking at just the past 5 years. There were some studies with experimental design, but it was used very infrequently over the years. Although qualitative methods were not used as often as quantitative methods, interviews were more common than focus groups, with very few studies using focus groups.

The largest percentage of the research in the practice contained what PRSA calls secondary research. This "research" is typically included in academic research but as part of the study leading to the methodology and not as the method, so this was unique to the practice. It is important to note, however, that secondary research has been covered in public relations research texts for a number of years (e.g., Brody & Stone, 1989; Broom & Dozier, 1990; Stacks, 2002, 2010).

There was a more equal distribution between the use of quantitative, qualitative, and combined methods in the practice of public relations than in academia, although quantitative methods were used slightly more frequently. The quantitative method that was the most common was the survey, but it does appear to have lost some of its popularity over the past 5 years. The qualitative methods were split almost equally between interviews and focus groups, but looking at just the past 5 years, interviews are more common. Experimental design was not used at all in practice.

Overall, quantitative methodology was more frequently used in the academic research, while the practical researchers used a combination of both methods much more often.

Summary

The results of this study further stress the importance of academic and professional research in public relations. Any discipline or profession that does not work diligently to first create and then add to its body of knowledge and, second, test assumptions based on that body of knowledge will neither advance in its understanding of its practice nor survive in the long term. This is especially true as market forces continue to change the role of public relations in daily communication activities.

In this regard, research must continue to demonstrate a relationship between public relations and business outcomes—outcomes that the public relations professional has to prove to show ROI. The days of "good writing" must now be supplemented with "strategic thought" based on research into the nonfinancial indicators that public relations so successfully works with: client, product, institutional credibility, relationship, reputation, trust, and now confidence (Stacks, 2010). Or, as the Institute of Public Relations' tagline states, proving the "science beneath the art."

References

Benoit, W. L. (1995). *Accounts, excuses, and apologies: A theory of image restoration.* Albany: State University of New York Press.

Botan, C. (2009). Theories and effects of public relations. In W. F. Eadie (Ed.), *21st century communication: A reference handbook* (pp. 698–705). Thousand Oaks, CA: Sage.

Bowen, S. A., Rawlins, B., & Martin, T. (2010). *An overview of the public relations function.* New York: Business Expert Press.

Brody, E. W., & Stone, G. C. (1989). *Public relations research.* New York: Praeger.

Broom, G. M., & Dozier, D. M. (1990). *Using research in public relations: Applications to program management.* Englewood Cliffs, NJ: Prentice Hall.

Cameron, G. T., Cropp, F., & Reber, B. H. (2001). Getting past platitudes: Factors limiting accommodation in public relations. *Journal of Communication Management, 5,* 242–261.

Coombs, W. T. (1995). Choosing the right words: The development of guidelines for the selection of the "appropriate" crisis response strategies. *Management Communication Quarterly, 8,* 447–476.

Denzin, N. K., & Lincoln, Y. S. (2003). *The landscape of qualitative research* (2nd ed.). Thousand Oaks, CA: Sage.

DiStaso, M. W., Stacks, D. W., & Botan, C. H. (2009). State of public relations education in the United States: 2006 Report on a national survey of executives and academics. *Public Relations Review, 35*(3), 254–269.

Grunig, L. A., Grunig, J. E., & Dozier, D. M. (2002). *Excellent public relations and effective organizations: A study of communication management in three countries.* Mahwah, NJ: Lawrence Erlbaum.

Hocking, J. E., Stacks, D. W., & McDermott, S. T. (2003). *Communication research* (3rd ed.). Boston: Allyn & Bacon.

Holsti, O. (1969). *Content analysis for social sciences and humanities.* Reading, MA: Addison-Wesley.

Ledingham, J. A. (2003). Relationship management as a general theory of public relations. *Journal of Public Relations Research, 15,* 181–198.

Levine, T. R. (2009). Quantitative approaches to communication research. In W. F. Eadia (Ed.), *21st century communication: A reference handbook* (pp. 57–64). Thousand Oaks, CA: Sage.

Lindenmann, W. K. (2006). *Public relations research for planning and evaluation.* Gainesville, FL: Institute for Public Relations. Retrieved March 10, 2010, from www.instituteforpr.org

Lindlof, T. R., & Taylor, B. C. (2002). *Qualitative communication research methods.* Thousand Oaks, CA: Sage.

Michaelson, D. (2009). *Setting best practices in public relations research.* Gainesville, FL: Institute for Public Relations. Retrieved March 10, 2010, from www.instituteforpr.org

National Curriculum Commission. (2007). *Report of the National Curriculum Commission on Public Relations.* New York: Public Relations Society of America.

Neuendorf, K. A. (2002). *The content analysis guidebook.* Thousand Oaks, CA: Sage.

Patton, M. Q. (1990). *Qualitative research and evaluation methods* (2nd ed.). Newbury Park, CA: Sage.

Public Relations Society of America. (2009). *2009 Silver Anvil call for entries.* Retrieved March 18, 2010, from www.prsa.org/Awards/SilverAnvil/Documents/SA_CFE_10.pdf

Stacks, D. W. (1995). Travel public relations models—public relations and travel: A programmed approach to communication in the 1990s. *Southern Public Relations, 1,* 24–29.

Stacks, D. W. (2002). *Primer of public relations research.* New York: Guilford Press.

Stacks, D. W. (2006). *Dictionary of public relations measurement and research.* Gainesville, FL: Institute for Public Relations. Retrieved March 10, 2010, from www.instituteforpr.org

Stacks, D. W. (2010). *Primer of public relations research.* New York: Guilford Press.

Stacks, D. W., Botan, C., & VanSlyke Turk, J. (1999). Perceptions of public relations education. *Public Relations Review, 25*(1), 9–28.

Stacks, D. W., & DiStaso, M. W. (2009). Public relations research. In W. F. Eadia (Ed.), *21st century communication: A reference handbook* (pp. 706–714). Thousand Oaks, CA: Sage.

Stacks, D. W., & Michaelson, D. (2010). *A practitioner's guide to public relations research, measurement, and evaluation.* New York: Business Expert Press.

Stacks, D. W., & Watson, M. L. (2006). Two-way communication based on quantitative research and measurement. In E. L. Toth (Ed.), *Excellence in public relations and communication management: Challenges for the next generation* (pp. 67–84). Mahwah, NJ: Lawrence Erlbaum.

Wimmer, R. D., & Dominick, J. R. (2003). *Mass media research: An introduction.* Belmont, CA: Thompson Wadsworth.

Wright, D. K., & VanSlyke Turk, J. (2007). Public relations knowledge and professionalism: Challenges to educators and practitioners. In E. L. Toth (Ed.), *The future of excellence in public relations and communication management* (pp. 571–588). Mahwah, NJ: Lawrence Erlbaum.

Yin, R. K. (2003). *Case study research: Design and methods* (3rd ed.). Thousand Oaks, CA: Sage.

CHAPTER 23

Reputation Models, Drivers, and Measurement

Tom Watson

Reputation was, is, and always will be of immense importance to organizations, whether commercial, governmental, or not for profit. To reach their goals, stay competitive, and prosper, good reputation paves the organizational path to acceptance and approval by stakeholders. Even organizations operating in difficult ethical environments—perhaps self-created—need to sustain a positive reputation where possible.

Argenti and Druckenmiller (2004) argued that "organizations increasingly recognize the importance of corporate reputation to achieve business goals and stay competitive" (p. 368). While there are many recent examples of organizations whose leadership and business practice behaviors have destroyed their reputations, such as Enron, Arthur Andersen, Bear Stearns, and Lehman Brothers, the positive case for reputation is that it has fostered continued expansion of old stagers such as Johnson & Johnson and Philips and innovators such as Cisco Systems, who have led rankings of the most respected organizations in the United States and Europe.

What is evident is that reputation *does not occur by chance.* It relates to leadership, management, and organizational operations; the quality of products and services; and—crucially—relationships with stakeholders. It is also connected to communication activities and feedback mechanisms.

This chapter will consider the definitions and nature of reputation and its management, best practice, and evaluation, particularly in relation to organizations in ethically threatened situations.

What Is Reputation?

In the corporate world, reputation is seen as a major element of an organization's provenance alongside and included in financial performance and innovation. It is socially complex and intangible, highly specific to each organization, and part of a process of "social legitimization" of the organization (Martin de Castro, Navas Lopez, & Lopez Suez, 2006). There is also a historical aspect (Hall, 1992; Murray & White, 2005; Yoon, Guffey, & Kijewski, 1993). It is perceptual

(Fombrun, 1996; Wartick, 2002), emotive (Groenland, 2002), and composed of affective and cognitive dimensions (Llewellyn, 2002; Schwaiger, 2004). Dowling (1994) defined corporate reputation as "the evaluation (respect, esteem, estimation) in which an organization's image is held by people" (p. 8). Argenti and Druckenmiller (2004) referred to it as "the collective representation of multiple constituencies' images of a company built up over time and based on a company's identity programs, its performance and how constituencies have perceived its behaviour" (p. 369). This is also reflected in Coombs's scholarship on crisis communication (Situational Crisis Communication Theory), which argues that past crises form a reputational threat to organization at varying levels of intensity (Coombs, 2004). Llewellyn (2002) expanded the definitions to include affective and cognitive elements: "Reputation occurs as stakeholders evaluate their knowledge of or encounters with an organization [cognitive] vis-à-vis their expectations, which are couched within their individual values (personal identities) or collective norms [affective]" (p. 447).

The definitions of Dowling and Argenti and Druckenmiller indicate that reputation is a "collective representation" of images and perceptions, not merely a self-promotional message. It involves relationships with all stakeholders and is gained, maintained, enhanced, or detracted from over time. For greater understanding of reputation, these primarily organizational management approaches can be improved with the inclusion of emotional (affective/cognitive) elements, as proposed by Llewellyn (2002) and Schwaiger (2004), which separate the perception of the stakeholders from their behavior. Two case studies—Ansett Airlines and Rover—discussed later demonstrate the separation of these factors and the outcomes when they occlude negatively.

A factor that has not appeared prominently in public relations and communications literature is "predictability." In political science and political economy, it is the key factor. "The fundamental appeal and importance of this concept [reputation] for economists, and political scientists influenced by their writing, is that reputation lets actors predict others' moves during strategic interaction, according to the 'extrapolation principle'" (Sharman, 2007, p. 20). This principle is

> the phenomenon that people extrapolate the behaviour of others from past observations and this extrapolation is self-stabilising because it provides an incentive to live up to these expectations. . . . By observing others' behaviour in the past, one can fairly confidently predict their behaviour in the future without incurring further costs. (von Weizsacker, 1980, p. 72)

Fombrun and van Riel (2004) touched on predictability by proposing that reputation involves stakeholder judgements "about a company's ability to fulfil their expectations," but most definitions and descriptions consider that reputation is a collection of images and behaviors (see also Argenti & Druckenmiller, 2004; Dowling, 1994). In public relations, the extrapolation principle has not been explored widely, and the case studies in this chapter will consider its impact in the form of predictability. While the historical aspect of reputation and the ability to deliver future results is noted, it is not explicated as predictability. Coombs (2004) referred to crisis history and crisis type as the basis for planning the communication response: "By accounting for the effects of crisis history, crisis managers can craft messages that more effectively protect the organization's reputational assets" (p. 287), but this relevant advice is aimed at communicators and not the responses of stakeholders and so also falls short of predictability.

Bringing this discussion together, a new definition of organizational (or corporate) reputation is proposed as "the sum of predictable behaviors, relationships, and two-way communication undertaken by an organization as judged affectively and cognitively by its stakeholders over a period of time." It will be explored in the case studies and subsequent discussions leading to proposals for new applied theory.

Can Reputation Be Managed?

The validity of the term *reputation management* is also discussed in this chapter. In the new field of reputation management, there is academic research, a body of knowledge, and a specialist academic journal, *Corporate Reputation Review,* as well as many public relations consultancies that have rebranded as "reputation managers" (Hutton, Goodman, Alexander, & Genest, 2001, pp. 247–248). There is also an assumption that all organizations have a reputation, be it good, neutral, or bad. But how well can this be managed, controlled, or directed? Hutton et al. (2001) described the dilemma succinctly:

> [U.S. public relations academics] David Finn, Doug Newsom and others have pointed out that concepts such as "reputation" and "image" are not generally something that can be managed directly, but are omnipresent and the global result of a firm's or individual's behavior. Attempting to manage one's reputation might be likened to trying to manage one's own popularity (a rather awkward, superficial and potentially self-defeating endeavor).
>
> On the other hand, some advocates see reputation management as a new guiding force or paradigm for the entire field, in keeping with Warren Buffet's admonition that losing reputation is a far greater sin for an organization than losing money. (p. 249)

So questions about the validity of reputation management are balanced against the reality of the importance of reputation for businesses.

Fombrun (1996) argued a different case that reputation is built in a planned manner by organizations taking necessary notice of the environment in which they operate.

> Better regarded companies build their reputations by developing practices which integrate social and economic considerations into their competitive strategies. They not only do things right—they do the right things. In doing so, they act like good citizens. They initiate policies that reflect their core values; that consider the joint welfare of investors, customers and employees; that invoke concern for the development of local communities; and that ensure the quality and environmental soundness of their technologies, products and services. (p. 8)

The paradigm of reputation management is that the organization's reputation depends on its behavior as a corporate citizen, as a part of the societies in which it operates and not above or apart from them. Reputational considerations are embedded in policy and actions, not just bolted on when convenient. Hutton et al. (2001) and Fombrun (1996) are approaching reputational management from different perspectives—communications management versus organizational policy. This is a theme that is also part of the continuing debate on the nature of reputation management.

Good and Bad Reputation

Definitions of *reputation* tend to favor the positive, with emphasis placed on "being well thought of," "in public esteem," and "delivering on promises." But reputation has two sides. In this section of the chapter, two views will be taken on the value of reputation. The first uses a survey method to identify the reputations of organizations in North America and Europe. The second studies four case studies of large corporate organizations entering severe crises in which their notional reputational value may or may not lead to their survival.

In 2000, Gardberg and Fombrun (2002) investigated the reputation of companies at both ends of the reputational spectrum. They sought the views of samples of Americans and Europeans in 11 countries on companies with the best and worst corporate reputations (p. 385) (Tables 23.1, 23.2, 23.3, and 23.4). Using a combination of telephone and online polling, they garnered more than 10,000 nominations.

Table 23.1 The Top Five "Best Overall Reputations" in the United States

Rank	Company
1	Cisco Systems
2	Johnson & Johnson
3	Home Depot
4	Ben & Jerry's
5	HP (Hewlett Packard)

Table 23.2 The Worst Reputation Nominees in the United States

Rank	Company
1	Firestone
2	ExxonMobil
3	Philip Morris (now Altria)
4	Nike
5	Kmart

Table 23.3 The Best Corporate Reputation Nominations in Europe

Rank	Company
1	Carrefour
2	Philips
3	Daimler Chrysler
4	Ford
5	Volkswagen

Table 23.4 The Worst Reputation Nominees in Europe

Rank	Company
1	McDonald's
2	TotalFinaElf
3	Shell
4	Deutsche Bank
5	Microsoft

Source: Tables 23.1–23.4 adapted from Gardberg and Fombrun (2002, pp. 387–390) and summarized by the author.

On the positive side, Cisco Systems was one of the strong performers in the (information technology) IT business, while Johnson & Johnson had "made" its reputation nearly 20 years earlier with its prompt and ethical response to the Tylenol extortion situation. Home Depot was more warmly regarded than Wal-Mart, which dominates U.S. retailing. Ben & Jerry's, a niche ice-cream brand owned by Unilever, had captured an immense place in the hearts of corporate America because it wasn't positioned as big and successful but quirky and human. Hewlett-Packard (HP), which was later wracked by criticism for its takeover of Compaq, was then seen as part of the engine room of the U.S. IT sector that was soon to be hit by the early-decade "tech wreck" recession.

On the negative side, Firestone was suffering (as was Ford) from catastrophic tire failures on the Explorer sport utility vehicle (SUV). ExxonMobil had become a long-term target for environmental groups after the Exxon Valdez pollution disaster in Alaska, while Philip Morris (now Altria) was constantly in the spotlight for its production and marketing of cigarettes, which also affected the reputation of its nontobacco brands and subsidiaries. Nike, once the darling of sports brands, was under attack from public interest groups for sourcing production from low-cost economies with abysmal labor practices, while Kmart was suffering from poor financial performance and being seen as an also-ran compared with Wal-Mart and Home Depot.

In Europe, three motor vehicle makers were ranked in the top five in a list headed by a discount retailer, equivalent to Wal-Mart, and a long-established electrical and electronics manufacturer. Ironically, while Ford was being hammered in the United States for the failings of its Explorer SUV, it was simultaneously being lauded in Europe. Since 2000, Daimler Chrysler's star has been falling as the transatlantic motor manufacturing merger has failed to deliver value and was broken up.

The negative picture contains two U.S.-owned corporations (McDonald's and Microsoft) and two European oil groups (TotalFinaElf and Shell), along with Deutsche Bank. Yet all continue to be successful despite this negative reputation.

The conclusions drawn by Gardberg and Fombrun (2002) were as follows:

- Positive nominations are given to companies with strong corporate brands that have identifiable subsidiary brands often of the same name. The gaining of favorable "top-of-mind" visibility speaks to the historical associations created in the minds of the public through strategic communications.
- Negative associations with some equally strong megabrands whose names have become synonymous with crisis speak to the inability these companies have in adjusting public perception (p. 391).

The Value of Reputation in a Crisis

"Good" reputation can, some argue, accumulate like assets in a bank (Alsop, 2004) and help balance out rainy days when the organization runs into problems. Research using case studies from Australia and the United Kingdom (Watson, 2007) found that the reputational equation is loaded with caveats and conditions for this outcome to be predicted. The four case studies were on a national airline, a grain exporter, a building materials manufacturer, and a vehicle manufacturer. They were chosen for the national impact of their behaviors and subsequent plight, for their prominence in media coverage, and for their use of corporate communication strategy and tactics and similar types of unethical behavior or what was perceived by stakeholders to be so. Their analysis has led to new propositions on applied theory on the role of reputation in managing crises.

Ansett Airlines: National Airline

After operating since 1937, the long-established Australian airline Ansett collapsed in 2001 after aircraft maintenance crises eroded public confidence. After the third of these crises, travelers' intentions to travel by Ansett had fallen to 25%. In response, the airline placed its chief executive before the media to apologize to customers and to assure them of improvements in the quality of service. It followed this with a A$20 million advertising campaign, using the chief executive and high-profile sports and entertainment stars (Easdown & Wilms, 2002), but this campaign had a boomerang effect on customers. Facing insolvency, Ansett shut down its operations on September 15, 2001.

McDonald (2006) applied attribution theory to Ansett's problems and found that the dominant customer attitude to the airline had been one of anger and distrust in the senior executive staff to manage effectively and tell the truth. Even using the chief executive officer (CEO) as the chief spokesperson, normally best practice, was a failure because it reinforced the image of an airline that did not care for the safety of its customers and crews but put its effort into image development.

> Additionally, when crisis messages, such as that delivered by the Ansett CEO, were perceived as lies, anger resulted and negative character attributions were made about company management. Such dispositional attributions revealed strong negative attitudes to those companies caught lying and contribute to the public's lack of trust in the integrity of organizations. (McDonald, 2006, p. 10)

AWB International: Grain Exporter

Australia has been a major exporter of agricultural produce since the mid-19th century, and wheat has always ranked highly in importance in volume and value. Australia's (then) sole licensed wheat exporter, AWB International (the privatized Australian Wheat Board), provided sales to the post–Gulf War I Iraqi market of 10 million tons of wheat for more than a decade. This was notionally supplied at market price through a United Nations–approved process, but the Volcker report on the Oil-for-Food program found that there was "a sink of corruption" ("Feeding a Dictator," 2005) and that AWB was one of the traders with Iraq that engaged in practices that inflated the price of imports and provided income to the Sadaam Hussein regime.

This revelation led to the appointment by the federal government of a commission to inquire into the behavior of AWB. It recommended that 11 former AWB executives and an oil businessman face criminal charges for allegedly deceiving the United Nations and the Australian government over the scandal. Subsequently, the government took the sole export right away and handed it to a grower group from 2008 onward, with an important judgment being that AWB's ethical behavior was no longer defendable or predictable. AWB has since produced poor financial performance (a 71% fall in half-year after-tax profits to end of March 2007) (ABC Radio National, 2007) and suffered the loss of its business reputation (a continuing decline in share price). Because it had national commercial interests that were separate from international trading, AWB has survived as a much-reduced business but had lost its international reputation and its freedom of operation.

James Hardie Industries: Building Materials Manufacturer

From the early 20th century onward, asbestos was mined in Australia and processed into building materials, principally for internal and external wallboards. In the latter part of the 20th century, it became apparent that many thousands of miners and building workers were suffering from the lung diseases mesothelioma and asbestosis caused by exposure to asbestos fibers. One of the major producers of these asbestos products (from 1917 to 1987) was James Hardie Industries, which was faced with increasingly large compensation demands.

In a defensive move, the company moved its ownership offshore to Holland in 2001 and created a body called the Medical Research and Compensation Foundation, which took over the rump of its Australian interests and was to handle compensation claims. At this time, Hardie issued a news release stating that adequate funds had been set aside for compensation claims. Actuarial assessments later estimated the liability over the next 40 years as five times higher than the company had allowed for (SMH.com, 2007). Three years later, the state government in New South Wales convened a Special Committee of Enquiry into the Foundation. It found that senior management were deliberately dishonest and were "prepared to be deceitful" about the extent of the asbestos claims. It also reported that the corporate communications activity in 2001 had been deliberately misleading and had been planned as such (Howell, Miller, & Bridges, 2006).

The outcomes of this period of organizational behavior and subsequent investigations were that both criminal and civil court cases against the company and its senior executives took place. The former chief executive has been heavily fined and banned from directing a company. Smaller fines and bans were imposed on two other Hardie executives and seven nonexecutive directors. Hardie has extended its compensation package and reduced its legal restrictions on claimants. The company has not failed, nor has it lost its place in the worldwide market for building products, but it has lost the trust of many as an ethical and responsible business. Many building contractors are reluctant to order Hardie products due to a lingering doubt on its credibility that will take many years to eradicate. The company's share price has remained solid, compared with the benchmark ASX (Australian Securities Exchange) 200.

Hardie's attempt to manage its reputation in 2001 signally failed because of the deceptive behavior of senior executives and the failure of the organization to correct them quickly. Subsequently, its ability to operate freely has been severely limited by vastly increased government oversight, community antipathy, and increased costs for compensation and legal services. It can also be argued that the degraded reputational situation has engendered a loss of predictability in relationships with many key stakeholders, including the government, which has instituted the major inquiry.

Rover: Mass Market Vehicle Manufacturer

The case of Rover (and its antecedents) can be accurately described as a saga because of the longevity of its problems. From the early 1970s, large-scale vehicle production in the United Kingdom was in doubt because of competition from non-U.K. manufacturers and a range of factors that made profitable production problematic (quality, industrial issues, and marketing). By the early 1990s, the Rover group (formerly British Leyland and BL) was again foundering. Its then owner, British Aerospace, sold the business to the German BMW (Bavarian Motor Works) car business. By the late 1990s, BMW, which had invested heavily in Rover, was losing £2,000 on every car that was made and sold (Brady & Lorenz, 2005).

The decline and fall of Rover is well documented, but its reputation was severely damaged by corporate behavior at two crucial points. In 2000, when BMW's exasperation with Rover's performance was reaching a terminal stage, as its market share had slumped from 11.3% to 4.6%, it undertook "what amounted to a disinformation programme throughout the first quarter" (Brady & Lorenz, 2005, p. 165) and told staff and car dealers that it was proceeding with a reorganization and had no intentions of selling Rover. It also made assuring comments to the then industry secretary and sought his support for an EU (European Union) aid package worth £152 million. In the meantime, BMW was secretly seeking to sell Rover to competitors and was in negotiations with a private equity firm to break up the business. When the news of the potential sale broke in March 2000, Rover's reputation among all stakeholders sank to a new low. One newspaper headline, "It's All Over Rover" (Brady & Lorenz, 2005, p. 171), summed up the sentiment. BMW did not complete the deal with the private equity firm and sold it for a notional £10 to a group of former Rover managers. BMW had destroyed what was left of Rover's reputation with British stakeholders by its action in the "disinformation" activity in the first half of 2000.

Phoenix's ownership of Rover was disastrous and the car maker shut down in 2005. The expected benefit of a return to British ownership stimulating national sales did not eventuate. While British buyers were sympathetic to Rover (the affective element), they had known about the problems of the marque and its products for 30 years (the cognitive element), and because of the long-term decline in both product and corporate reputation they chose not to purchase them. During the Phoenix period, the new management was unsuccessful in turning the business around or engaging the support of key stakeholders, especially the government, which had long ceased to be supportive of Rover. Although there was a long history of political and financial support for Rover, one of the factors for its demise was surely its behavior, which was demonstrably no longer predictable or apparently ethical. In 2005, after being misled by BMW and then Phoenix, it decided to not intervene again in the West Midlands motor industry. That was the end of Rover, which had no beneficial reputation left.

Applied Theory Proposals

In all the case studies, poor management, unethical practices, a lack of engagement with customers and other stakeholders, indifferent or aggressive performances by CEOs, misleading corporate communication, and a lack of preparedness for crisis communication severely or terminally affected these companies. They also failed the test of "predictability."

Reputation has affective and cognitive elements in its makeup (Llewellyn, 2002; Schwaiger, 2004). Having one element, such as sympathy (affective), does not—as exemplified by Ansett and Rover—sustain an organization's existence if the cognitive (experience of the organization) is not balanced with it. The loss of predictability in Ansett's and Rover's cases was one of the main reasons that led to the withdrawal of government and political support, because of the erosion or elimination of their reputation. AWB's ethical and operational performance has resulted in the removal of its valued "single-desk status," with predictability also being one of the factors, because government could no longer support its operations on international markets as being ethical and representative of the country's normal business behavior.

James Hardie is a partial exception to the cognitive/affective and predictability analyses. Its reputation and operations have suffered within Australia, as evidenced by union boycotts and government regulations, but it has returned to profit from operations in other countries, where the asbestos disease issue has little impact. So any claim to universality of these factors may be tempered by the physical situation of the crisis/behavior (despite the reach of the Internet).

Two proposals for new applied theory are made:

Proposition 1:

Reputation is an asset in a crisis when it has these characteristics:

- Affective and cognitive elements are in an organizationally beneficial alignment.
- The organization operates in a historically predictable manner with a set of ethical and organizational behaviors that are acceptable to governmental and other key regulatory stakeholders.
- There is ethical leadership by the CEO and management (dominant coalition) that is supported by two-way communication and engagement with stakeholders.
- The ability to manage the immediate crisis is less important if the organization satisfies the characteristics of affective-cognitive alignment, predictability, and ethical leadership. Without these characteristics, crisis management is likely to be unsuccessful in creating strong recovery conditions and can lead to a prolonged struggle for survival.

Proposition 2:

- Failure, rather than survival, is the most likely outcome for organizations with weak cognitive/affective balance and predictability, especially if they depend on goodwill from government and regulators.

The implication of the propositions are that the consideration of reputation as a determinant of postcrisis response and an influence on survival or failure of an organization should include consideration of two aspects of reputation and whether the notion of reputation as a source of defensive "capital" (Alsop, 2004) is a false one. Predictability of organizational behavior offers defensive value that is potentially greater than the immediate crisis response, which is so often the focus of public relations and organizational communication research. It is a factor that deserves greater consideration because of its linkage with a wider range of stakeholders than is offered by current crisis communication theory and best practice.

Best Practice in Reputation Management

In an eight-country study, Kitchen and Laurence (2003) explored corporate reputation management practice, with an emphasis on the role of the CEO and the management of reputation, across cultures and national borders. They also identified the critically important role of clear and ethical leadership by organization CEOs and dominant coalitions. Table 23.5 shows that corporate reputation is of the greatest importance in achieving corporate objectives, with the highest ranking in the anglophone (i.e., the United States, Canada, and the United Kingdom) world.

Table 23.5 The Importance of Company Reputation in Achieving Corporate Objectives

Country	Very Important (%)	Somewhat Important (%)
United States	94	6
Canada	90	8
United Kingdom	89	10
Belgium	86	14
France	86	14
Italy	83	17
Netherlands	76	24
Germany	71	29

As for the measurement of this element, Kitchen and Laurence (2003) commented that "despite the apparent importance devoted to corporate reputation, sustained increase in systematized formal measurement procedure was not in marked evidence in the countries concerned" (p. 108) (Table 23.6). More than half the respondents in the Netherlands and Canada undertook formal measurement, but there was little or no progress in other countries.

Table 23.6 Formal Systems to Measure a Company's Reputation

Country	Yes	No
Netherlands	62	36
Canada	52	48
United States	42	57
France	50	56
Belgium	37	63
United Kingdom	37	63
Germany	33	67
Italy	29	71

Corporate Reputation Measurement

Where evaluation took place, the majority of companies in the eight countries nominated "custom research" as both their main method of monitoring and measuring reputation and the one metric that is "most meaningful" (Table 23.7). Kitchen and Laurence (2003) commented that "custom research" is a category that covers a wide range of quantitative and qualitative research techniques that can be undertaken by in-house facilities and external suppliers (p. 110). The relevant factor that was identified was that "media coverage" was much less important than "custom research" and "informal feedback" in most countries and was lowly ranked as a "most meaningful" metric in only three out of eight countries (in the Netherlands 7%, in the United States and the United Kingdom 5% each). As media relations is the main activity in most corporate communications programs, it is

Table 23.7 Corporate Reputation Influencers (Mean Rank Order)

Rank/Influence	Mean
Customers	4.58
Employees	3.92
CEO reputation	3.70
Print media	3.24
Shareholders	3.05
The Internet	2.90
Industry analysts	2.87
Financial analysts	2.78
Regulators/government	2.64
Broadcast media	2.29
Labor union leaders	2.29
Plaintiff's lawyers	2.03

Note: 5 = extremely influential; 1 = does not influence at all.

revealing that it appears to have so little importance in the measurement of (and thus contribution to) corporate reputation.

Kitchen and Laurence (2003, p. 113) commented that, apart from the third-ranked role of CEO reputation, it was notable that print media has a higher ranking (3.24) than broadcast media (2.29). Internet (2.90) also ranks higher than broadcast media, despite its often unmediated and unchecked content. Another observation was "the very low ranking awarded to labour union leaders," which may indicate that the power and importance of unions is well on the wane, a trend very noticeable throughout Europe.

A theme of this study is the weight given to the CEO's reputation in determining corporate reputation (Table 23.8). Citing van Riel (1999) that there is a close interrelationship between corporate reputation and the reputation of the CEO, Kitchen and Laurence (2003) found that it is "most important in Italy, closely followed by Canada, then the USA." On the reverse, it "is . . . least likely to impact on corporate reputation in Belgium, the UK and France" (p. 113).

Table 23.8 **What Percentage of Your Company's Corporate Reputation Is Based on the CEO's Reputation?**

Country	50% to 100%
Italy	83
Canada	66
United States	54
Netherlands	44
Germany	42
France	36
United Kingdom	33
Belgium	26

"The CEO's reputation becomes more important when choosing a successor to move the company on to new and better heights," with the United States (64%), Germany (55%), and Italy (52%) placing greatest weight and Canada (38%) and France (34%) placing least emphasis on this factor (Kitchen & Laurence, 2003, pp. 113–114).

Summarizing the eight-country study, Kitchen and Laurence (2003) offered six conclusions:

1. Corporate reputation has increased and is increasing in importance.
2. The need to systematize measurement is growing in importance.
3. The key influencers on reputation are—despite some caveats—customers, employees, and then the CEO.
4. A good corporate reputation precedes and helps business grow internationally and helps in preparing the ground in new markets among key constituencies.
5. CEO reputation and corporate reputation are increasingly intertwined. The CEO is inevitably cast in the role of chief communicator.
6. The responsibility for managing reputation is a key management responsibility and—led by the CEO—it must be managed in an integrated manner. (pp. 115–116)

It is clear that if the organization or its CEO cannot communicate its mission, brands, or values, some other organization, stakeholder, or irate public with communication capabilities can or will. "Corporate communication must be mastered by the corporation and those duly appointed to speak on its behalf; or it will master the corporation" (p. 116).

Measuring Reputation

Although Kitchen and Laurence's (2003) eight-country study found that the majority of organizations do not measure reputation well, there is a wide range of literature that proposes reputational measurement. One of the measures most prominently discussed by practitioners is Fombrun's Reputation Quotient model. From a study of data collected by Harris Interactive and analysis of focus groups, Fombrun (2000) proposed a taxonomy for perception of companies. Based on the respondents' comments on the companies they liked and disliked, he has nominated six categories of factors:

1. Emotional appeal	How much the company is liked, admired, and respected
2. Products and services	Perceptions of the quality, innovation, value, and reliability of the company's products and services
3. Financial performance	Perceptions of the company's profitability, prospects, and risk
4. Vision and leadership	How much the company demonstrates a clear vision and strong leadership
5. Workplace environment	Perceptions of how well the company is managed, how good it is to work for, and the quality of its employees
6. Social responsibility	Perceptions of the company as a good citizen in its dealings with communities, employees, and the environment

From these factors, Fombrun has developed a reputation quotient (RQ) to "benchmark the reputations of companies as seen by different stakeholder segments" (2000, p. 2). This, he claimed, was a valid instrument for measuring corporate reputations. Fombrun argued that corporate reputation has economic value, but, "unfortunately, efforts to document this value have run up against the fact that a company's reputation is only one of many intangibles to which investors ascribe value" (p. 2). Three factors—crisis effects, supportive behaviors, and financial analyses—confirm that "reputations have bottom-line financial value" (p. 2).

For *crisis effects*, he pointed to the recovery that corporations such as Johnson & Johnson (Tylenol), ExxonMobil (Exxon Valdez), and Motorola (brain tumors and mobile phones) have had after crises. This has varied in financial and reputational terms, with research by Gardberg and Fombrun (2002) identifying Johnson & Johnson as one of the most respected companies and ExxonMobil as one of the least respected companies.

Supportive behavior is evidenced by the attitude of resource holders (banks, suppliers, regulators, and staff). Most companies are not in a crisis state and thus their reputation remains stable if not improving. That, said Fombrun (1996), creates a value cycle, when perceptions and performance "[demonstrate] approval of the company's strategic initiatives and [are] made possible by more attractive financial valuations" (p. 42).

Financial analyses can also support the value of corporate reputation with measurement of intangible assets such as patents and goodwill (reputational capital). Other technical devices, such as notional licensing of a corporate name, can demonstrate value. Fombrun (1996) pointed to research by Srivastava, McInish, Woods, and Capraro (1997), who compared companies with similar risk and return but different average reputation scores in 1990. This study found that a 60% difference in reputation score was associated with a 7% difference in market value. Since this average capitalization was $3 billion, "a point difference in reputation score from 6 to 7 on a 10-point scale would be worth an additional $52m in market value" (Srivastava et al., 1997, p. 6). Later studies of Fortune 500 corporations between 1983 and 1997 indicated that a 1-point difference on the scale was worth $500 million in market value (Black, Carnes, & Richardson, 2000).

A challenge to Fombrun's (1996) analysis and methodology has been mounted from public relations academics. Hutton et al. (2001) argued that there is a confusion between correlation and causality: "Reputation researchers have claimed significant correlations between reputation and financial performance; unfortunately such studies are largely meaningless and circular in their logic, given that *Fortune* [italics added] and other reputation measures they are studying are largely *defined* [italics added] by financial performance" (p. 258).

The relationship between reputation and spending on corporate communication activities has been studied by Hutton et al. (2001). They did not find a smooth, consistent relationship between corporate communication spending and reputation, with the overall correlation being just .24. They also found that the correlation between company size and reputation was .23. "In other words, there was a modest correlation between reputation and spending on communication activities, but most of that was accounted for by the fact that larger companies—which presumably benefit from greater visibility—tend to have better reputations" (Hutton et al., 2001, p. 249). The significant correlation between corporate activity and reputation was "foundation funding" (charitable donations), which was .69. High levels of expenditure for investor relations, executive outreach, and media relations were other activities that correlated highly with positive reputation. Acidly, they noted that social responsibility, corporate advertising, and industry relations have negative correlations (Hutton et al., 2001, pp. 252–253).

Thus, there is a mixed picture in the academic debate over the valuation of corporate reputation. Simple verities such as good behavior and practices equal good reputation are challenged by the correlation between the sheer size of a company and its expenditure in some areas of communication.

References

ABC Radio National. (2007, May 23, 12:21:00). *The World Today: AWB records massive profit slump.*

Alsop, R. J. (2004). *The 18 immutable laws of corporate reputation: Creating, protecting, and repairing your most valuable asset.* New York: Free Press.

Argenti, P. A., & Druckenmiller, B. (2004). Reputation and the corporate brand. *Corporate Reputation Review, 7*(4), 368–374.

Black, E., Carnes, T., & Richardson, V. (2000). The market value of corporate reputation. *Corporate Reputation Review, 3*(1), 31–42.

Brady, C., & Lorenz, A. (2005). *End of the road: The true story of the downfall of Rover* (2nd ed.). Harlow, UK: Pearson Prentice Hall.

Coombs, W. T. (2004). Impact of past crises on current crisis communication. *Journal of Business Communication, 41*(3), 265–289.

Dowling, G. (1994). *Corporate reputations.* Melbourne, Victoria, Australia: Longman Professional.

Easdown, G., & Wilms, P. (2002, July 27). Crash landing. *Herald-Sun,* p. 19

Feeding a dictator. (2005, October 29). *The Australian,* p. 18.

Fombrun, C. J. (1996). *Reputation: Realizing value from the corporate image.* Cambridge, MA: Harvard Business School Press.

Fombrun, C. J. (2000, December 4). The value to be found in corporate reputation. *Financial Times,* p. 2.

Fombrun, C. J., & van Riel, C. B. M. (2004). *Fame and fortune: How successful companies build winning reputations.* Upper Saddle River, NJ: FT Prentice Hall.

Gardberg, N. A., & Fombrun, C. J. (2002). For better or worse: The most visible American corporate reputations. *Corporate Reputation Review, 4*(4), 385–391.

Groenland, E. (2002). Qualitative research to validate the RQ dimensions. *Corporate Reputation Review, 4*(4), 308–315.

Hall, R. (1992). The strategic analysis of intangible resources. *Strategic Management Journal, 13,* 135–144.

Howell, G., Miller, R., & Bridges, N. (2006). Cardinal rule of the media release: Get your facts right. *Asia Pacific Public Relations Journal, 6*(2). Retrieved from http://www.deakin.edu.au/arts-ed/apprj/vol6no2.php#5

Hutton, J. G., Goodman, M. B., Alexander, J. B., & Genest, C. M. (2001). Reputation management: The new face of corporate public relations. *Public Relations Review, 27,* 247–261.

Kitchen, P. J., & Laurence, A. (2003). Corporate reputation: An eight-country analysis. *Corporate Reputation Review, 6*(2), 103–117.

Llewellyn, P. G. (2002). Corporate reputation: Focusing on the zeitgeist. *Business and Society, 41*(4), 446–455.

Martin de Castro, G., Navas Lopez, J. E., & Lopez Suez, P. (2006). Business and social reputation: Exploring the concept and main dimensions of corporate reputation. *Journal of Business Ethics, 63,* 361–370.

McDonald, L. (2006). Perceiving is believing: How consumers attributions about the cause of Ansett Airlines' safety crisis impacted outcomes. *Asia Pacific Public Relations Journal, 6*(2). Retrieved March 18, 2010, from www.deakin.edu.au/arts-ed/apprj/vol6no2.php#7

Murray, K., & White, J. (2005). CEOs' views on reputation management. *Journal of Communication Management, 9*(4), 348–358.

Schwaiger, M. (2004). Components and parameters of corporate reputation: An empirical study. *Schmalenbach Business Review, 56*(1), 46–71.

Sharman, J. C. (2007). Rationalist and constructivist perspectives on reputation. *Political Studies, 55,* 20–37.

SMH.com. (2007, May 28). *James Hardie profit up, asbestos liability estimate down.* Retrieved May 29, 2007, from www.smh.com.au/news/business/james-hardie-profit-up-asbestos-liability-estimate-down/2007/05/28/1180205161229.html

Srivastava, R. K., McInish, T. K., Woods, R. A., & Capraro, A. J. (1997). The value of corporate reputation: Evidence from equity markets. *Corporate Reputation Review, 1*(1), 1–8.

van Riel, C. B. M. (1999). *Principles of corporate communication.* Upper Saddle River, NJ: Prentice Hall.

von Weizsacker, C. (1980). *Barriers to entry.* New York: Springer-Verlag.

Wartick, S. (2002). Measuring corporate reputation: Definition and data. *Business and Society, 41*(4), 371–392.

Watson, T. (2007). Reputation and ethical behaviour in a crisis: Predicting survival. *Journal of Communication Management, 11*(4), 371–384.

Yoon, E., Guffey, H. J., & Kijewski, V. (1993). The effects of information and company reputation on intentions to buy a service. *Journal of Business Research, 27,* 215–228.

CHAPTER 24

Come Together

Rise and Fall of Public Relations Organizations in the 20th Century

Julie K. Henderson

As the practice of public relations expanded in the United States during the 20th century, so did the desire of those who worked in the discipline to unite, to come together, to define their roles. Rex Harlow (1981), public relations leader, writer, and researcher, reflected on the need at that time for

> the honest, decent members of the new craft to join hands in counteracting the work of quacks and slickers with shoddy whitewashing tactics and unconscionably high fees. The dishonest activities of this unprincipled group, which were bringing public relations into disrepute, had to be stopped. Only through organized efforts could this be done. (p. 39)

Thus, a number of public relations organizations, some successful, some not, formed over the 20th century. Common threads run through many of these attempts: The organizers were driven to set high standards for this new profession, to create a guide for ethical behavior, and to specify who merited the designation of public relations practitioner.

Which Was the First?

At least five public relations organizations have been designated as the first by one measure or another. One is the Public Relations Society of America (PRSA); two others, the National Association of Accredited Publicity Directors, Inc. (NAAPD) and the Institute for Public Relations, were antecedents of PRSA. The remaining two are the Bank Marketing Association (BMA) and the Council for the Advancement and Support of Education (CASE).

Edgar Waite (1947), an early leader of PRSA, wrote that it was "the first truly national and professional organization in the country" for public relations people (p. 1). Others, including PRSA itself, made the claim that NAAPD was the first. A PRSA document, the *PRSA Timeline* (PRSA, n.d.), noted that "organized public relations is born" in 1936 when the National Association of Publicity Directors held its first meeting. However, the term *national* was used loosely; the group was strictly New York based. A 1970 article in *Public Relations Journal* (Smith, 1970, p. 124) also named the National Association of Publicity Directors as the first, although both references omit the "accredited" part of the group's name.

Harlow, who founded the Institute for Public Relations in 1939, seemed to consider it the first, for he was quoted as observing, "Since it was the first and only national organization in the country, it had to provide a high grade of leadership—which I think it did" (Schoch, 1982, p. 16).

Organization or association? In *This is PR*, a public relations textbook, the authors argued that CASE is the oldest public relations *organization* in the world, because its roots date back to the American Association of College News Bureaus begun in 1917 (Guth & Marsh, 2003). They, and Kathleen Schoch (1982), cited BMA as the first *association* of public relations people, even though *public relations* was not in the original (or current) name. The BMA began in 1915 as the Financial Advertising Association, consisting of bankers who were dissatisfied with their membership in the Associated Advertising Clubs of the world. The group changed its name three times: in 1947 to the Financial Public Relations Association, in 1966 to the Bank Public Relations and Marketing Association, and in 1970 to the Bank Marketing Association (Schoch, 1982).

Early Stumbles

Was Edward Bernays, frequently referred to as the father of public relations, responsible for the failure of two early attempts to organize public relations people?

In 1927, 13 members from the Advertising Club in New York City formed a committee to professionalize public relations. Bernays was the chair; Ivy Lee was a member. When Bernays released a story about the effort to *Editor and Publisher*, other members were said to be angry because the article focused on Bernays. The public relations historian Scott Cutlip (1994) wrote that Bernays's "lust for publicity and self-glorification" killed the committee (p. 215).

Another short-lived group, the Council on Public Opinion, was described by *Time* magazine ("Propaganda Battle," 1938) this way: "Around a dinner table in Manhattan frequently gather some 20 of the ace propagandists in the U.S. . . . [The] chairman is the nation's No. 1 publicist, dark Machiavellian Edward L. Bernays." *Time* seemed to dismiss the Council's importance when adding, "This small group might easily be the seat of a sinister super-government were it not that no two members of the Council on Public Opinion completely agree on anything very important" (p. 24).

Again, the other members were offended by the implication that Bernays was the guru and they were his followers. The Council ceased to be, but another group sprang from it—the Wise Men. Bernays was never invited to a Wise Men meeting.

Deep Roots: PRSA and IABC

The two largest public relations/business communications organizations in the United States today, the Public Relations Society of America (PRSA) and the International Association of Business Communicators (IABC), both have roots that date back nearly 100 years.

Public Relations Society of America

PRSA was formed when the National Association of Public Relations Counsel (NAPRC), basically an East Coast organization, merged with the American Council on Public Relations (ACPR), a West Coast group, in 1948.

NAPRC. The NAPRC began as the NAAPD, in 1936 (Baldwin, 1937). Among the people cited as key to this effort are Hamilton Wright II, William Baldwin, and Harry Bruno.[1]

Membership was limited to those with five or more years of publicity or public relations experience who were highly placed either in an agency or on a public relations staff. One stated objective was to "promote and maintain the highest standards of service and conduct by all members of the publicity profession." The group was aimed at "serving the press and the public effectively through the raising of standards and the improvement of methods in the development of public relations for business and industry" (Baldwin, 1937, p. 140). In 1944, the group changed its name to the National Association of Public Relations Counsel, reflecting the maturation of public relations from strictly publicity.

Edward Bernays apparently had a fairly low opinion of NAAPD standards. In 1959, Scott Cutlip interviewed Bernays and quoted him as saying,

> A man announced himself as an individual who promoted trade associations. I saw him and he told me he was promoting a publicity association. And he wanted me to be president of it. I asked him what his profit would be, and he said his Organization acted as secretary of organizations he helped form. I told him that I was not interested in treating the field on such a basis. That did not deter him and he organized the NAPD (no accreditation). I did not want to be a part of any such promotion then, now, or ever, for I do not think that this is the way to develop a professional organization that has criteria of education, skill, know-how and character as a basis for joining. (Cutlip, 1994, p. 216)

ACPR. ACPR began life as the Institute for Public Relations with Rex Harlow as its founder (Guth & Marsh, 2003). Its charter was issued in 1939; after only 2 days, it was renamed the American Institute of Public Relations. Later the name was changed to the American Council on Public Relations.

The Merger. Details of the merger of ACPR and NAPRC to become PRSA were hammered out during a "four-day marathon session in the heat of a Chicago August" in 1947 (Rankin, 1948, p. 11). Chicago was the geographical middle ground for the New York/East Coast NAPRC and the San Francisco/West Coast ACPR. The merger committee included three members from each: Homer Calver, Averell Broughton, and Sam Fuson of NAPRC and Edgar Waite, Rex F. Harlow, and Virgil Rankin of APRC. This meeting had been preceded by about 2 years of study (Waite, 1947). Edgar Waite (1947), ACPR delegation chair, noted that "the public relations fraternity today has a brand new professional organization which for the *first time* [italics added] promises a truly nation-wide program" (p. 1).

About 6 months after the Chicago meeting, PRSA became official. A "Certificate of Incorporation of the Public Relations Society of America, Inc." was submitted on January 17, 1948, signed by six original incorporators, the six men from the Chicago meeting (PRSA, 1948). The corporate charter was granted by the State of New York on February 4, 1948 (PRSA, n.d.).

Officers named to serve until the first annual meeting were Earle Ferris as chairman of the board, Virgil L. Rankin as president, and five vice presidents representing five districts.[2] Standing committees, appointed to focus on crucial issues, included Professional Standards, Educational, and Eligibility (Rankin, 1948). The executive headquarters would be in New York, with the editorial and educational offices in San Francisco. It was agreed that dues should be at least $50 a year (Waite, 1947). The bylaws stated that members had to be "free of affiliation . . . with any subversive organization," have a "reputation for ethical conduct and integrity," and have at least 5 years of professional experience (Waite, 1947, p. 1).

PRSA absorbed the *Public Relations Journal*, published by the ACPR for 4 years, and it was designated the official magazine of PRSA, with Rankin continuing as editor (Rankin, 1948). The Silver Anvil Awards were absorbed in 1961 when the American Public Relations Association eventually merged with PRSA, having declined to do so during the 1947 Chicago meeting (Smith, 1970).

During the 1960s, PRSA continued to evolve. In 1959, the PRSA board approved special interest sections; in 1960, the first of these, the Counselors Section (now Academy), was recognized. Beginning in 1964, PRSA offered its members an accreditation program, with holders earning the designation APR, or Accredited in Public Relations.

PRSA administered the accreditation program until 1998, when the Universal Accreditation Board was formed and assumed that duty. The board includes eight other groups: the Agricultural Relations Council, Puerto Rico Public Relations Association, Florida Public Relations Association, Maine Public Relations Council, National School Public Relations Association, Religion Communicators Council, Southern Public Relations Federation, and Texas Public Relations Association (Universal Accreditation Board, 2009).

Public Relations Student Society of America. By the late 1960s, student public relations clubs were springing up on college campuses around the country, independent and with no professional guidance. Seeing a need, the 1967 PRSA Assembly voted to create the Public Relations Student Society of America (PRSSA). By March 1968, nine chapters were chartered, with total membership of 196. For the first few years, PRSA supported the group financially, but in 1973, the students voted for a national dues structure to make PRSSA self-supporting. Originally run by a PRSA Committee on Student Organizations, in 1974, the students voted to change to a nationally elected student chairperson, plus other student officers and a board of directors.

In 1976, circumstances led to PRSSA establishing its own annual national conference. Because it was the bicentennial year, PRSA decided to cosponsor a World Congress in August instead of the usual October/November date. PRSSA students had attended previous conferences, but few were able to attend in August. In response, students at the University of Dayton organized their own national PRSSA conference. That set a precedent: From that time on, students had their own conference, concurrent with the PRSA conference, and were included in pre-conference PRSA meetings to make sure that their needs would be met (Teahan, 1980).

International Association of Business Communicators

IABC also has a heritage that dates back to the 1930s, grounded mainly in various groups of industrial and internal communicators.

In June 1970, at a joint conference of the International Council of Industrial Editors (ICIE), the American Association of Industrial Editors (AAIE), and the Canadian Industrial Editors Association (CIEA), the first two groups decided to join together to form the IABC. The first president was William G. Irby of Sylacauga, Alabama. In 1974, Corporate Communicators Canada (formerly CIEA) decided to join IABC, making it officially an international association.

ICIE and AAIE. In 1941, Robert B. Newcomb called representatives of national and regional associations of industrial editors together for the purpose of creating a national voice; from this, the National Council of Industrial Editors Association (NCIEA) was formed. The following groups ratified its constitution:

- The Industrial Editors Associations of Chicago, Detroit, St. Louis, and Massachusetts
- Southwestern and Pacific Coast Associations of Industrial Editors
- The House Magazine Institute
- Syndicate of House Magazine Editors
- The American Association of Industrial Editors (AAIE; formally organized at the 1938 National Safety Congress)

The NCIEA later changed its name to the National Council of Industrial Editors, and then in 1946 to the *International* Council of Industrial Editors when the Canadian Industrial Editors Association became an affiliate. The same year, the American Association of Industrial Editors, an original charter member begun in 1938, withdrew (Abshier, 1990).

Like PRSA, IABC sponsors student chapters and offers accreditation for its members who achieve their ABC (Accredited Business Communicator) by completing a written and oral examination and submitting a portfolio of their work for review (IABC, n.d.).

By Invitation Only

Three of the groups of public relations practitioners that sustain an elite membership by keeping a tight rein on who can join include the Wise Men, Public Relations Seminar, and the Arthur W. Page Society (Arthur W. Page Society, n.d.). The first two also maintain a low profile, eschewing publicity and news coverage, and absent even a Web site.

The Wise Men

Accounts of the establishment of the Wise Men are found in the personal files of John W. Hill, a cofounder of the Hill and Knowlton agency. Looking back to the group's first meeting on November 18, 1938, Hill described it this way: "A little group of earnest toilers in the field of public relations assembled one evening in a small flat in midtown Manhattan to dine and discuss the state of the nation and other matters appertaining thereto" (Hill, 1946). Among the 15 or so men present, he recalled Pendleton Dudley, Northrop Clarey, Claude Robinson, Frank Mason, Bronson Batchelor, Jim Selvage, Allan Brown, Herb Smith, and John Long (Hill, 1950).

When issuing an invitation for membership to a new candidate in 1956, Hill said of the Wise Men:

> You will find it the darnest [*sic*] group you every [*sic*] imagined—it has no constitution, no bylaws, no officers, no regular meeting place and, most important of all, no entrance fees or dues! Really, it has no name. Some wag member of the Group dubbed it "The Wise Men" years ago, and this has stuck.
>
> You might say it is a non-existent organization but, actually, it has gone on month after month for 17 years. It just so happens that the first meeting was held in my apartment on November 18, 1938. I asked some 15 or so people in public relations to join me for dinner[3] and they have been having dinner each month since that time. I think that the lack of formalities of any kind has been one of the reasons for the continuance of the Group.
>
> I suppose it could be said that the Group contains the cream of the crop in public relations brains of this country, because such individuals as Paul Garrett, Tommy Ross, Arthur Page, Harold Brayman, Frank Waltman, Pen Dudley and John Long, and others, are members. The membership numbers about 30, and the new ones have been selected very carefully over the years by the Group itself. In fact, the only formality upon which the Group insists is that there be a very thorough screening of each new member. The reason for this is that meetings are purely social and there is no agenda. The host for the evening is self-appointed and he selects the time and place for his meeting—then bills each member for his share of the cost of the dinner. Attendance is usually around 15 to 18 men.
>
> I have found over the years that this is one of the most rewarding groups or associations to which I belong—not only because of the stimulating discussions which usually cover every subject under the sun (but usually within the realm of public relations and public affairs), but also because of the close friendships with other people in our profession that have developed. (Hill, 1956, pp. 1–2)

The only way to become a member was (and is) to get another member to offer a recommendation, and then the entire group had to approve. Although the inside information shared among members was sometimes incorrect, such as James Irwin suggesting in 1945 that the upcoming Roosevelt-Churchill-Stalin conference would be held in Alaska (Irwin, 1945), members held their group in highest regard. "The wise men is one of the most unique and interesting dinner groups I have ever known" (Robinson, 1945). "We are a most remarkable group. . . . Great minds contributing in a major degree to human progress" (Irwin, 1952). "The Wise Men are one of the greatest aggregations of intelligence and good fellowship in the world. . . . [T]he boys are deeply indebted to you [Hill] for having the vision to call the group together in the beginning" (Robinson, 1947).

In his writing about early efforts to organize public relations, Harlow (1981) provided an outsider's view of the Wise Men:

> The joining of efforts (to organize public relations) at first was through small exclusive groups. The Wise Men is an example. It was a group composed of some 15 of the public relations directors or officers of the largest, most prestigious corporations, and the heads of the leading public relations counseling firms in New York. These men ruled the roost as far as public relations in their city was concerned—and, in their opinion, throughout the country as well. (p. 39)

Public Relations Seminar

> The Public Relations Seminar is an annual 3-day gathering of 100 to 120 of the leading business public relations men and women, and the top people of public relations consulting firms which have business accounts. It is restricted to business people in order to encourage frank and uninhibited discussion of the public problems of American business.
>
> Membership is limited to not more than two persons for each industrial company or agency, the members are chosen by a Sponsoring Committee of the leading business public relations people in the country, and invitations are issued only to those persons who can make a substantial contribution to the thinking of the conference, regardless of the size or importance of their companies. (Brayman, 1969, p. 3)

This description was included in the history of the Public Relations Seminar written by Harold Brayman, one of the Seminar founders.

The first Public Relations Seminar was held in 1952. It sprang from a larger, broader, more accessible meeting that had been held from 1944 to 1951 called the National Conference of Business Public Relations Executives.

The National Conference itself grew from a discussion during a dinner meeting of a small group of public relations people that sounds suspiciously like a Wise Men meeting. Those in attendance included John W. Hill, Pendleton Dudley, Thomas J. Ross, Paul Garrett, and others[4] who reportedly had been meeting regularly since 1939 (Brayman, 1969). Garrett, of General Motors, noted that American business finally had a golden opportunity to speak from "strength" due to the heightened production during the War years after repeatedly being on the defensive during the Depression years. But, he maintained, business first had to recognize the importance of public relations and practitioners (Brayman, 1969).

To address this opportunity, the Conference on Public Relations was organized, held on November 30, 1942, with about 150 in attendance. It received financial support from the National Association of Manufacturers, which basically paid costs not covered by registration fees. In stating its purpose, Garrett noted that

> unlike the lawyers, the doctors, and the engineers, we have never come together in any formal way as public relations specialists to exchange views. We have never put down any set of public relations principles. . . . Basically our job is designed to help management understand, and give consideration to, the

> public relations aspects of its moves. (Brayman, 1969, p. 7)

In 1950, this annual conference evolved into 3-day sessions called the Conference of Business Public Relations Executives, still under the auspices of the National Association of Manufacturers (NAM) and held at the same time as the NAM annual meeting. The purpose of the 1950 conference, sponsored by 30 leading public relations executives, was "to consider ways of improving public understanding of business and industry, particularly of their roles in economic progress" ("Business Is," 1950), according to news reports.

During 1950 and 1951, there was some discussion among members about the similarity between this conference and the new PRSA annual conference and about whether the two should be merged. Instead, it was determined that there was a need for an alternative—a smaller, more exclusive group—and thus, the first Public Relations Seminar was held June 6 to 8, 1952, in Pocono Manor, Pennsylvania, with the "whole purpose of the Seminar to review intensively and creatively the problems and questions that are uppermost in the minds of responsible business public relations executives today" (Brayman, 1969, p. 16). The Seminar was invitation only and continues as such today.

Arthur W. Page Society

At the 1951 conference of the Business Public Relations Executives, Arthur Page, often referred to as the Dean of Corporate Public Relations, declared,

> The way to melt all these suspicions [of big business] is to operate the big business in such a manner that there is nothing to hide and then hide nothing. But it goes further than this. It is necessary to actively expose the business to view in so far as the public will take time to look at it. (Page, 1951, p. 1)

Page was vice president of public relations for American Telephone and Telegraph (AT & T) for nearly 20 years and the first public relations executive to serve as an officer and member of the board of directors of a major public corporation. His years with AT & T certainly gave him a perspective on the public's view of big business and public relations' role: "Public Relations in this country is the art of adapting big business to a democracy, so that the people have some confidence that they are being well served and at the same time the business has freedom to serve them well" (Page, 1958, p. 1).

The management concepts Page practiced were condensed into the Page Principles and are regarded as a guideline for ethical corporate public relations behavior. They form the foundation for the Arthur W. Page Society, begun in 1983, a professional association exclusively for senior public relations and corporate communication executives who seek to enrich and strengthen their profession (Arthur W. Page Society, n.d.).

Society members are chosen through strict criteria; the Society seeks to bring together senior executives from a wide spectrum of industries who want to perpetuate the high standards of Page. Its mission is "to strengthen the management policy role of the corporate public relations officer by providing a continuous learning forum and by emphasizing the highest professional standards" (Arthur W. Page Society, n.d.).

This society maintains a much higher profile than the previous two groups. Its administration includes a media relations department, and it sponsors a variety of programs to promote the ethical practice of public relations, including the Page Legacy Scholars, which supports research by professors.

The Institutes

The Institute *for* or *of* Public Relations has been a fairly popular name for public relations groups throughout the decades.

As noted earlier, Rex Harlow founded the Institute for Public Relations in 1939, which later became the ACPR. Bernard Lichtenberg also headed an Institute of Public Relations in the 1930s and often gave speeches using President of that Institute as his title. However, this appears to have been an agency offering services, not a membership organization (Lichtenberg, 1936).

Another Institute of Public Relations was founded in 1948 by public relations officers from commerce, industry, and government in the United Kingdom. It was incorporated in 1964. Among its main objects were "to encourage and foster the observance of high professional standards by its members" (Black & Sharpe, 1983, p. 204).

The contemporary American group associated with the name The Institute for Public Relations—IPR—was originally chartered as the Foundations for Public Relations Research and Education in 1956 as a unit of PRSA. Pendleton Dudley, first president and chair, established the foundation with other senior practitioners to build a professional body of knowledge, a necessary step on the path to making public relations a profession. The original purpose of IPR was "to improve the practice of public relations through research and education" (IPR, 2006, p. 6).

The name was changed to the Institute for Public Relations Research and Education in 1989 when the organization left PRSA to become an independent foundation. Its headquarters are in the College of Journalism at the University of Florida in Gainesville.

IPR's strategic plan focuses on the science beneath the art of public relations. Its well-known annual research conference, the only conference devoted exclusively to public relations research, began in 1998 and now is held every March, cosponsored with the University of Miami. This international (originally interdisciplinary) conference is distinctive because it includes research presentations by both university scholars and practitioners from around the world.

IPR's Commission on Measurement seeks ways to prove the effectiveness of public relations, and its Essential Knowledge Project is building a library of research available without charge to students, educators, and practitioners. In addition, IPR sponsors symposia, lectures, conferences, executive forums, and other training programs in the United States and overseas.

Unlike many other groups, IPR is not membership based. The nonprofit organization is supported through program revenues and contributions from public relations agencies, corporations, research companies, and educators (IPR, 2008).

Beyond American Borders

American public relations practitioners have also been involved in a variety of public relations organizations overseas. The Public Relations Coalition boasts more than 50,000 members worldwide from 17 groups home based in the United States and abroad, such as the Asian American Advertising and Public Relations Alliance, the IABC, and PRSA (Public Relations Coalition, n.d.). The Global Alliance, composed of more than 60 member organizations, was established in 2000 to enhance the public relations profession and its practitioners throughout the world ("Global Alliance," 2005). The North American Association of Independent Public Relations Agencies (NAIPRA) exists only online as a network of public relations agencies that are not owned by another company. Its purpose is to promote the value of independent agencies and to provide a way for these agencies to connect with each other. Despite the name, members extend beyond North America and include agencies in China, New Zealand, and Australia (NAIPRA, n.d.).

Headquartered outside the United States, the Canadian Public Relations Society and the International Public Relations Association have nevertheless attracted significant American involvement.

Canadian Public Relations Society

The Canadian Public Relations Society, Inc., historically has its roots in two primarily local groups, one in Montreal, Quebec, and one in Toronto, Ontario. The Montreal group was called the Canadian Public Relations Society, or La Société canadienne des Relations extérieures, and the Toronto group, the Public Relations Association of Ontario. The two amalgamated in 1953 to form the national Canadian Public Relations Society (CPRS), with chapters identified as CPRS-Toronto and CPRS-Montreal (later becoming CPRS-Quebec). The first national president after amalgamation was J. W. Lawrence, from Toronto (M. Barker, personal communication via e-mail, April 28, 2008).

Mary Barker, APR, FCPRS(H), the national chair of the CPRS 60th Anniversary Committee, notes that the need for a national public relations organization in Canada became evident following World War II. Public relations people were in demand because public relations had been used so effectively by the government and the military during the war, and companies saw the benefits it could provide. Indeed, large industries such as water and power companies, electric companies, food companies, and others were among the leaders who pushed for such a group. Gordon Hulme of Shawinigan Water & Power Co., in Toronto, and Jack Lawrence of Bordon Co., also in Toronto, were two such leaders who foresaw the local groups as forerunners of a national group. Other experienced public relations people also saw "a need for some sort of development of these skills (not just ex-journalists)" (M. Barker, personal communication via e-mail, April 28, 2008). CPRS began with these objectives: to promote discussion of all phases of public relations; to provide a clearinghouse for ideas and experience in public relations activities; and to advance the knowledge, skill, and professional status of individuals engaged in public relations (M. Barker, personal communication via e-mail, April 28, 2008).

National conferences began in 1953 in Montreal. The first Joint CPRS-PRSA International Conference was held in 1972 in Detroit, with popular authors Arthur Hailey and Harold Robbins among the guest speakers. The CPRS Code of Ethics was formally adopted in 1961, although it was under development from the beginning. Qualified members first achieved accreditation in 1969. A College of Fellows was formally established in 1998 (CPRS, 2008). The first two CPRS Fellows who were selected, Charles Tisdall and David Eisenstadt, both of Toronto, were at the time already Fellows of PRSA.

Currently, the Canadian Society has 16 member societies from coast to coast and in every province.

International Public Relations Association

In 1949, two Dutch and three British public relations men meeting in London talked of "organising public relations officers in collective groups with the object of raising the standard of public relations practice, and enhancing the prestige as well as the efficiency of public relations men," according to the published history of the International Public Relations Association (IPRA), stored with the papers of Robert Bliss, IPRA president from 1965 to 1967 (IPRA, n.d., p. 1). A Provisional International Committee worked over the next 5 years, mainly during the weekend conferences of the British Institute of Public Relations. IPRA was intended to "provide a channel for the exchange of ideas and professional experience between those engaged in public relations practice of international significance" and to "foster the highest standards of public relations practice" (IPRA, n.d., p. 1).

The constitution of the IPRA was adopted in London on May 1, 1955 (IPRA, 1955a); its council was to consist of three members from each of the five countries representing the founding bodies: France, Great Britain, the Netherlands, Norway, and the United States. At the first Council meeting in Bath, England, Odd Medboe of Norway was appointed chair and Fife Clark was appointed president (IPRA, 1955b).

Membership was limited to

> persons devoting their full time to and being fully responsible for the planning and execution of a coherent and significant part or the whole of the activities of a corporation, company, union, government, government department or other organization . . . provided that these activities shall possess international significance. (IPRA, n.d., p. 3)

The International Code of Ethics, called the Code of Athens, was based on the United Nations Declaration of Human Rights and adopted by the IPRA General Assembly on May 12, 1965 (Bliss, 1967a). The IPRA began sponsoring a World Congress in 1958, with the first held in Brussels (Bliss, 1967b).

Public Relations Education

Various groups with interests beyond public relations alone have carved out special niches for public relations education. Three are national education groups: the Association for Education in Journalism and Mass Communication (AEJMC), the National Communication Association (NCA), and the International Communication Association. The PRSA, whose membership consists of public relations professionals, sponsors a professional interest section for educators, the Educators Academy.

AEJMC and NCA both had their beginnings early in the 20th century. AEJMC was born in 1912 at a conference of journalism teachers called by W. G. Bleyer of Madison, Wisconsin. The name of the group was the American Conference of Teachers of Journalism, changed by 1915 to the American Association of Teachers of Journalism (AATJ). Membership in this organization was for individuals. Concurrently, Walter Williams was assembling the American Association of Schools of Journalism (formed in 1917), membership in which consisted of schools and departments of journalism. At the first meeting, the name was expanded to reflect the membership to the Association of American Schools and Departments of Journalism (AASDJ).

In 1949, the Association for Education in Journalism (AEJ) was created through the merger of three groups: AATJ, AASDJ, and the American Society of Journalism School Administrators (ASJSA), which was formed in 1944. AEJ was based on individual memberships and provided an umbrella for other organizations, such as AASDJ and ASJSA, plus other media groups.

In 1965, the Public Relations Division became one of the 10 special-interest divisions to qualify under the new constitution, meeting the requirement of at least 30 members who could demonstrate the value of the proposed division in terms of teaching, research, and service. The first division chair was James R. Young of West Virginia University (Emery & McKerns, 1987).

The NCA began life as the National Association of Academic Teachers of Public Speaking in 1914. It went through many name changes: National Association of Teachers of Speech in 1923, Speech Association of America in 1946, Speech Communication Association in 1970, and NCA in 1997.

NCA's Public Relations Division promotes research, teaching, and the ethical practice of public relations (NCA, n.d.).

The International Communication Association, originally called the National Society for the Study of Communication when it was formed in 1950, also has a Public Relations Division (International Communication Association, 2009).

Early Inroads Into Specialization

Association for Women in Communications

The Association for Women in Communications (AWC) began its life as a women's journalism society, Theta Sigma Phi, in 1909. The seven originators, Georgina MacDougall, Helen Ross, Blanche Brace, Rachel Marshall, Olive Mauermann, Helen Graves, and Irene Somerville, were all students of the new journalism program at the University of Washington in Seattle. By 1915, Theta Sigma Phi chapters were established at seven universities. The first national president was Lenore White. The group published *The Matrix*, a magazine for women journalists, and held its first national convention in 1918 (AWC, n.d.).

Theta Sigma Phi changed its name to Women in Communication, Inc. (WICI) in 1972 and at that time allowed men to become active members. In 1996, WICI was dissolved and immediately replaced with the AWC.

Specialization Throughout the Century

A variety of other organizations begun in the early 1900s were based on a specialized area of public relations practice.

The concept of a Religious Publicity Council originated at a meeting in March 1929 of the Conference on Religious Publicity; today it is known as the Regional Communicators Council (Dugan, Nannes, & Stross, 1979). CASE has a long and involved genealogy. Both of its parents, the American Alumni Council (AAC) and the American College Public Relations Association (ACPRA), can trace their origins to the early 1900s; they merged to form CASE in 1974 (CASE, n.d.).

The National School Public Relations Association began life in 1935 as the National Association for Educational Publicity, started by members of the National Education Association. A year later, the name was changed to School Public Relations Association, and in 1950 to the National School Public Relations Association (NSPRA; n.d.).

Midcentury saw the development of the Agricultural Relations Council (1953) and the Library Public Relations Council (1940) (Schoch, 1982). The Investor Relations Association (1966) was one of the originating chapters of the new National Investor Relations Institute (1969) (Morrill, 1995).

New organizations of public relations professionals continue to develop, such as the Council of Public Relations Networks, whose beginnings in 1997 were announced in a *New York Times* article (Stuart, 1997), and the Council of Public Relations Firms (CPRF), begun in 1998 by dozens of America's leading public relations firms to create a national association to represent the interests of public relations firms (CPRF, n.d.). The Plank Center, named for Betsy Ann Plank, was established at the University of Alabama in 2005 to help develop leadership values and skills in public relations education and practice (Plank Center, n.d.).

Conclusion

Various themes are repeated in discussing the formation of public relations organizations during the 20th century. The founders of these groups often expressed common goals. These included the following:

- To promote high standards and ethical conduct, often defined in a member code of ethics
- To limit the practice of public relations to a select group
- To establish clout through numbers
- To encourage continuous improvement, often through continuing education or accreditation
- To promote public relations as a management function
- To meet the growing practice of and need for public relations
- To create a body of knowledge
- To exchange information; to promote discussion

- To distinguish public relations from advertising and expand it beyond strictly publicity
- To provide the practice of public relations with leadership
- To create a national organization

As public relations continues to grow, but continues to fight negative perceptions, the need for such organizations certainly will not decrease. Indeed, they should play a major role in moving public relations to a professional status.

Notes

1. When discussing the formation of the PRSA, Scott Cutlip (1994, p. 88) quoted Hamilton Wright II as saying, "I was one of 12 men who founded this [PRSA] back in the 1920s." Cutlip observed that Wright is probably referring to the NAAPD, even though it was not organized officially until 1936.

2. Averelle Broughton, Eastern; Conger Reynolds, Central; Edgar A. Waite, Western; Maxwell Benson, Southern; and Lee Trenholm, Canada.

3. Following several members' disenchantment with the Council on Public Opinion.

4. John P. Syme, James. W. Irwin, Robert S. Peare, and Ralph C. Champlin.

References

Abshier, A. (1990). Stuck in the eighties. *Communication World.* Retrieved May 5, 2008, from http://findarticles.com/p/articles/mi_m4442/is_n6_v7ai_8457746

Arthur W. Page Society. (n.d.). *About the society.* Retrieved May 9, 2008, from the Arthur Page Society Web site at www.awpagesociety.com/site/about

Association for Women in Communications. (n.d.). *AWC is one of the originals.* Retrieved April 15, 2008, from www.womcom.org/about_us/history.asp

Baldwin, W. H. (1937, October). Association of Publicity Directors. *Public Opinion Quarterly, October,* 139–140.

Black, S., & Sharpe, M. L. (1983). *Practical public relations: Common-sense guidelines for business and professional people.* Englewood Cliffs, NJ: Prentice Hall.

Bliss, R. (1967a, May 17). *Is public relations equal to its international opportunity?* Address presented to the Finnish Public Relations Association, Helsinki, Finland, May 17 (Robert Bliss Papers, Mss. 234, Vol. 1). Madison: Wisconsin Historical Society.

Bliss, R. L. (1967b, October 14). *IV. Public Relations World Congress report* [draft] (Robert Bliss Papers, Mss. 234, Vol. 1). Madison: Wisconsin Historical Society.

Brayman, H. (1969). *Developing a philosophy for business action: A history of the Public Relations Seminar.* Baltimore: Public Relations Seminar Committee.

Business is told it talks to itself. (1950, May 4). *New York Times,* p. 1.

Canadian Public Relations Society. (2008). *Let's celebrate in 2008!* Retrieved May 16, 2008, from www.cprs.ca/AboutCPRS/e_60.htm

Council for the Advancement and Support of Education. (n.d.). *CASE history.* Retrieved May 3, 2008, from the CASE Web site at www.case.org/About_CASE/CASE_History.html

Council of Public Relations Firms. (n.d.). *At-a-glance.* Retrieved April 28, 2008, from www.prfirms.org/index.cfm?fuseaction=Page.viewPage&pageId=471

Cutlip, S. (1994). *The unseen power: Public relations, a history.* Hillsdale, NJ: Lawrence Erlbaum.

Dugan, G., Nannes, C. H., & Stross, R. M. (1979). *RPRC: A 50-year reflection.* Available from the Religious Public Relations Council, Inc. Web site at www.religioncommunicators.org/history_toc.html

Emery, E., & McKerns, J. P. (1987, November). AEJMC: 75 years in the making. *Journalism Monographs.* 1–2, 9–10, 13–16, 26, 35, 44, 73.

Global Alliance launches efforts to sustain rebuilding Asia. (2005, February 8). *Canada Newswire.* Retrieved March 22, 2010, from www.lexisnexis.com.www.remote.uwosh.edu/us/lnacademic/search/newssubmitForm.do

Guth, D., & Marsh, C. (2003). *Public relations: A values-driven approach* (2nd ed.). Boston: Allyn & Bacon.

Harlow, R. (1981, Summer). Rex Harlow: A public relations historian recalls the first days. *Public Relations Review, Summer,* 33–42.

Hill, J. W. (1946, November 27). *Letter to Bronson Batchelor* (John W. Hill Papers, Mss. 62AF, Box 30). Madison: Wisconsin Historical Society.

Hill, J. W. (1950, November 10). *Letter to Pendleton Dudley* (John W. Hill Papers, Mss. 62AF, Box 30). Madison: Wisconsin Historical Society.

Hill, J. W. (1956, January 17). *Letter to Phelps Adams* (John W. Hill Papers, Mss. 62AF, Box 30). Madison: Wisconsin Historical Society.

Institute for Public Relations. (2006). *Dedicated to the science beneath the art.* Retrieved April 30, 2008, from www.instituteforpr.org/about/50_year_report

Institute for Public Relations. (2008). *Year in review.* Retrieved May 3, 2008, from www.instituteforpr.org/about/year_in_review

International Association of Business Communicators. (n.d.). *Accredited Business Communicator* [Brochure]. Retrieved March 22, 2010, from www.iabc.com/abc/

International Communication Association. (n.d.). *Public relations division.* Retrieved March 20, 2010, from www.icahdq.org/sections/secdetinfo.asp?SecCode=DIV12

International Public Relations Association. (1955a, May 1). *Constitution* (London) (Robert Bliss Papers, Mss. 234, Vol. 1). Madison: Wisconsin Historical Society.

International Public Relations Association. (1955b, May 1). *Minutes of the first meeting of the Council of the IPRA* (Bath, England) (Robert Bliss Papers, Mss. 234, Vol. 1). Madison: Wisconsin Historical Society.

International Public Relations Association. (n.d.). *IPRA history: Policy and purpose* [Pamphlet] (Robert Bliss Papers, Mss. 234, Vol. 1). Madison: Wisconsin Historical Society.

Irwin, J. (1945, January 18). *Letter to WM* (John W. Hill Papers, Mss. 62AF, Box 30). Madison: Wisconsin Historical Society.

Irwin, J. (1952, November 28). *Letter to John W. Hill* (John W. Hill Papers, Mss. 62AF, Box 30). Madison: Wisconsin Historical Society.

Lichtenberg, B. (1936). *Speeches and articles* (Bernard Lichtenberg, Mss. 104AF, Book 4, 1936–1937). Madison: Wisconsin Historical Society.

Morrill, D. C. (1995). *Origins of NIRI.* Retrieved April 29, 2008, from the National Investor Relations Institute Web site at www.niri.org/FunctionalMenu/About/Origins.aspx

National Communication Association. (n.d.). *NCA member knowledge communities.* Retrieved September 25, 2009, from www.natcom.org/index.asp?bid=10830

National School Public Relations Association. (n.d.). *What is NSPRA?* Retrieved May 5, 2008, from www.nspra.org

North American Association of Independent Public Relations Agencies. (n.d.). *NAIPRA.* Retrieved October 20, 2009, from www.naipra.org

Page, A. W. (1951, May 17). *Business in a republic.* Speech before the Business Public Relations Conference, New York City (Arthur Page Papers, Mss. 51AF, Box 57). Madison: Wisconsin Historical Society.

Page, A. W. (1958, December 16). *Address to the 4th annual meeting of the Institute of Life Insurance* (Arthur Page Papers, Mss. 51AF, Box 57). Madison: Wisconsin Historical Society.

Plank Center for Leadership in Public Relations. (n.d.). *About us.* Retrieved September 29, 2009, from www.plankcenter.ua.edu/about.html

Propaganda battle. (1938, January 24). *Time,* pp. 24, 26.

Public Relations Coalition. (n.d.). *PR coalition.* Retrieved October 20, 2009, from http://72.32.147.97/pr_coalition/index.html

Public Relations Society of America. (1948). *Certificate of incorporation.* New York: Author.

Public Relations Society of America. (n.d.). *PRSA timeline.* New York: Author.

Rankin, V. (1948). Public Relations Society of America: A report. *Public Relations Journal, March,* 10–13.

Robinson, C. (1945, October 10). *Letter to John W. Hill* (John W. Hill Papers, Mss. 62AF, Box 30). Madison: Wisconsin Historical Society.

Robinson, C. (1947, December 1). *Letter to John W. Hill* (John W. Hill Papers, Mss. 62AF, Box 30). Madison: Wisconsin Historical Society.

Schoch, K. S. (1982, July). *The uniting of a profession: The history of public relations organizations.* Paper presented at the annual meeting of the Association for Education in Journalism, Athens, Ohio.

Smith, R. W. (1970, October). The PR chronicle. *Public Relations Journal, October,* 124–125.

Stuart, E. (1997, February 20). Public relations alliance formed. *New York Times* (Late edition), p. 5.

Teahan, F. (1980, Summer). PRSSA history. *Forum, Summer,* 4–5.

Universal Accreditation Board. (n.d.). *Universal Accreditation Board.* Retrieved September 28, 2009, from www.praccreditation.org

Waite, E. A. (1947, August). PRSA: The Public Relations Society of America. *Public Relations Journal, August,* 1–3, 39.

CHAPTER 25

Public Relations Identity

Evolving From Academic and Practitioner Partnerships

Bonita Dostal Neff

The historical identity of public relations is a contrast of views. Often an invisible entity to publics in the past, current mentions from the media about superficial and failed events are incidents labeled as "public relations." These relentless negative media interpretations hinder the development of appreciative publics supporting public relations. The challenge to reconcile this complex mix of commentary about public relations has traceable roots in the historical development of the discipline.

Academic and practitioner efforts to refine, establish, and justify public relations roles and functions remain largely a varied and multidisciplinary effort. Public relations professionals are more energized than ever to confirm and improve the identity of the discipline, through either action or publication. These varied and strongly held conflicting interpretations occur within a context of globalwide initiatives in public relations practice, policy, research, theory, and pedagogy. Public relations is codified, for example, in curriculums established in community colleges (a system developed in the United States) as well as at the graduate school level worldwide. It is taught through professional seminars and as part of accreditation.

Despite the media's negative depiction of public relations, career job descriptions are plentiful. During the recession, the spending on public relations increased 3% in 2009 to $3.4 billion (which does not include public relations' word-of-mouth activities). But advertising contracted by 3% and marketing decreased by 8% (*The Economist,* 2010). Such a strong showing during a recession is significant for a discipline that is largely invisible to the public while struggling to define itself for a century. However, this does not diminish the importance of acknowledging the serious challenges that remain to define and improve the identity of the profession for both practitioners and academics.

Movement toward reshaping a public relations identity nurtures spurts of publishing energy within the discipline about itself to educate students and working professionals. Consequently, the rapidly expanding job responsibilities are accompanied by multiple publishing outputs producing an extensive body of knowledge refining many levels of public relations insights.

The lack of solidarity regarding its identity presently gives the field many options to keep alive the "wrangle in the marketplace" within full view of professionals, academics, students, and critics, as well as the public, in some instances.

Some of this momentum is clearly away from a "public relations" identity. Alternative terms are offered for public relations, and substitute concepts have been coined and promoted to avoid the negative aura. No doubt some professionals are acting on the belief that public relations has a negative persona, particularly within the public purview. In fact, such a negative identity can give them license to practice in ways that confirm rather than dispel the negative image. The question is: Can the practice counter Brody's (1992) assertion about "public identification with public relations becoming more of a liability"? (p. 44). Will renaming the discipline make a difference ultimately? The response is "perhaps." The renaming process can lead to a continued identity with public relations if the role and functions are primarily similar. However, if renaming the discipline brings in some element of negative connotation (greater than already interpreted) or a greater vagueness toward public relations, the consequences could be less supportive of a "public relations" identity.

Regardless, the emerging effort to improve the reputation along with proliferation of public relations expertise creates a common ground of dialogue for both groups (those working on image for short or long terms) of public relations professionals—academics and practitioners. Voices producing varied input to interpret public relations identity have a number of primary influences. The ability for public relations to be so varied in function partially stems from the variety of academic sources developing the field of study. The blending of these various disciplines into the public relations curriculum, however, often provides a useful mix of approaches for the practice.

By the mid-1980s, a survey of the college and university catalogs, a publication considered a legal contract, documented where public relations is taught (Neff, 1989). Countering the accepted perception of journalism departments as the discipline primarily offering public relations, the data established a mix of disciplines. The findings also documented communication(s) departments offering the *most* courses and *greatest* range of offerings in public relations curriculum. This overall listing of departments established public relations course offerings as the following: communication(s) (41%), journalism (21%), business (17%), interdisciplinary (8%), mass communication (7%), public relations (2%), and miscellaneous (4%). This surprising finding countered the popular notion of where public relations is taught and established guidelines to ensure that future research will require all departments with public relations to be included in relevant studies.

Today young practitioners and academics are philosophically complex and trained in crucial areas of expertise. This might also explain the range of public relations involvement from public diplomacy, risk communication, and crisis communication, to political and/or health campaigns. Some students emerge with a political science interest or double major in public relations and biology, for example. Hence, the second academic degree often creates the "context" for public relations practice. This richness or matrix of possibilities provides an almost limitless number of combinations for public relations students. Students can now emerge with social media expertise or a strong global expertise level with multilingual abilities. So perhaps the ability for public relations to be so malleable really allows the discipline to meet the future challenges of society—wherever these challenges may lead public relations professionals. Furthermore, the academic preparation affects the public relations discipline very early in a professional's career today.

Cropp and Pincus articulated the concern in 2001 that the increasing ambiguity of the central role of public relations with the proliferation of jargon may be countered now by a growing number of forces in the field of public relations. First, the ambiguity of the role of public relations may really reflect more where public relations is studied as well as the historical development of the context in which public relations is practiced. The wide variety of possibilities provides a range of perspectives in most sectors of the economy, including government, social institutions, and cultural entities. Second, the jargon may reflect a more considered view of the functions practiced. Obviously, the discipline continues to explore the possibilities and needs more time and effort to sort out these various professional paths of study and application in public relations.

With this rapidly developing focus on public relations, the potential for improving the public relations profession's reputation is growing. Bringing the discipline's issues into the research arena for review and challenge is perhaps the most rigorous way to address the discussion on the core attributes of a public relations identity. Currently, a solid list of formalized and mature public relations associations are devoting resources and priorities to public relations questions and needs. More extensive research means more opportunities to rigorously review or challenge views. For example, at this time, fully developed divisions or interest groups in public relations associations examine a variety of public relations perspectives: communication, journalism, business, or a more integrated public relations curriculum. Those associations housing public relations academic units (data as of November 2010) include the following:

- Association for Education in Journalism and Mass Communication (AEJMC—journalism context, public relations division [PRD] established in 1965)
- International Communication Association (ICA—global communication(s) context with PRD established in 1984)
- National Communication Association (NCA—communication(s) context with PRD established in 1987)
- Central States Communication Association (CSCA—communication(s) context with PR Interest Group established in 1988)
- International Academy of Business Disciplines (IABD—global business context with association established in 1989 with a track in Public Relations/Corporate Communication)
- Public Relations Society of America (PRSA) founded in 1947 and developed the Educators Academy (PRSA membership is largely practitioner based with an Educators Academy)
- International Public Relations Association (IPRA—global public relations associations based in Switzerland) is a more non-U.S.-based organization
- State associations such as Texas Public Relations Association
- Associations by country such as Public Relations Institute of New Zealand, Public Relations Institute of Australia, and European Public Relations Education and Research Association (EUPRERA)

A stand-alone U.S. organization devoted solely to public relations is the Florida-based Institute for Public Relations (IPR) established in 1987. This nonprofit organization conducts extensive research, partners academics and practitioners in public relations, and sponsors the Miami International Public Relations Research Conference (IPRRC) annually. Having a robust body of knowledge in the public relations discipline, professionals are now poised to "take a stand" publicly on the identity of public relations.

The Tipping Point: The Discipline Responds

In 2009, Coombs and Holladay articulated a new model of response to the media's negative mantra about public relations. Quoting academics and practitioners from the public relations profession, the authors took a stand on the damaging journalistic statements about the public relations discipline. In *This Is Not Just Public Relations: Public Relations in Society* (2007), Coombs and Holladay challenged the popular media tendency to reduce public relations to the frivolous or failed "events" surfacing in the news. The "colloquial usage" of public relations by the media is repudiated with documented academic and practitioner research and experience by defending the usefulness of the public relations discipline to society. In addition, the role of ethics in public relations illustrated the unique boundary-spanning capacity of public relations and the counterbalancing merit that public relations brings to the element of power. Last, the long-term impact and influence of the role of public relations are explored in three areas: (1) public diplomacy, (2) the private volunteer organizations as a form of activism, and (3) the increased corporate global network.

At last, the public relations professionals are responding publicly in print and "taking a stand" to establish the value of a "multibillion-dollar" industry to society. Now, the work begins to disseminate the research to the public at large. The "guiding questions" proposed by Cropp and Pincus in 2001 are, 10 years later, more fully researched by formal bodies of academic and practitioners associations, institutes, colleges and universities, and foundations—to name a few. Now with a more intense mix of practitioner and academic experience, more informed statements are countering and rectifying the demeaning public media statements. Key shifts beyond the earlier Cropp and Pincus concern include the following topics.

The loci of public relations are no longer viewed as just servicing clients or organizations. Increasingly, researchers and practitioners are asking the question, Should public relations assume more of a leadership role in society (activists, representing marginalized populations, organizing volunteers or stakeholders in society, not just the organization's interests)?

Should the central role of public relations focus on servicing organizational managements be part of the dominant coalition or should public relations be independent of this top-level influence? How do various cultures interpret the term *public relations*? How do these metaphors or interpretations provide some guidance for understanding how the public relations profession is practiced globally? How are the forces of technology, culture, religion, issues, environment, politics, arts, and so on challenging the education and training of public relations professionals within a global spectrum?

How should the process of public relations be described to most fully provide authentic, ethical, and socially responsible approaches to the roles and functions of public relations? Most important, the critical review of the literature was largely based on other disciplines: anthropology, psychology, business, political science, history, and the like. Now the literature is increasingly sourced by those from public relations backgrounds—academics that teach public relations and/or directing graduate students in public relations research programs as well as public relations practitioners who provide data-based conclusions. This shift provides more opportunity for a public relations focus to be addressed in research and gives the discipline a deeper commitment to the research process. This also gives rise to a cadre of public relations practitioners who are not just corporate voices serving their single organization but voices outside the corporate setting involved in developing a substantial infrastructure of stand-alone public relations agencies with independent standards and ethics. Such an influence gives rise to a greater potential for ethnicity and professionalism in the public relations discipline, including a stronger identity.

Now to examine the nexus of the issues in the public relations discipline, this more engaged discipline is demonstrated to reflect a perspective having multifaceted versions of the profession. These clashes of views, the directions of identity possibilities, and the ultimate foundational and critical elements of the profession illustrate the contributions that are currently establishing a larger and yet more contextually defined role for public relations on a global stage.

More Independent Thought Toward an Identity

Rather than viewing the "decades-long confusion over the nature and applications of public relations as a deteriorating clarity of its transcending purpose" (Cropp & Pincus, 2001, pp. 190–191), the foci of this larger current discussion integrates more current streams of thought representing disciplinary approaches and/or context framing. For example, the growth of associations in public relations, the establishment of institutes concentrated on public relations research, and more high-level, recognized, refereed, and awarded scholarship (journals, books, research projects) provide a more rigorous basis for examining the foundational ways to explore "streams of independent thought."

Furthermore, the rapid development of public relations in public relations agencies and the roles and functions of public relations in nonprofits, business, and government in the late 1980s represent a large practitioner database of experience. Now, one should ask the following questions: How does research define public relations roles and functions? At what juncture do cultural interpretations affect one's view of public relations? How does the broadened purview of public relations (from client to organization to publics to perhaps a more holistic mission of saving the universe or universes) shape, frame, and define the process of the discipline? How do the pressures of the context define, refine, confuse, exclude, or reinforce the identity of public relations? Most important, does the emerging leadership role of public relations affect the process beyond the context?

In summary of this examination of the historic development of public relations, the focus of the problem centers on the failure of professionals to treat the discipline in a holistic way. A number of early studies reported on only one discipline's findings (only surveying public relations professionals from one association, for example) and then reported the conclusions as if the data reflected the entire field. This disparity in research interpretations occurs through either ignorance or a strongly felt opinion that one discipline has the "right" answer. One observes department chairs, for example, reporting survey results from one association as the gospel for the entire discipline. So the problem continues as to how this information is applied and, consequently, how these distortions affect the discipline of public relations. So perhaps it is not the absence of a universally accepted and functionally accurate understanding of the essential role of public relations but more a matter of false perceptions hindering and interfering with the authentic interpretation of the findings. Yet, on another level, the coordinated work of the more interdisciplinary and global groups is providing the leadership out of this morass of narrow mindlessness—maybe. So in some respect, there is light at the end of the tunnel—but not necessarily full enlightenment.

Another major area of constraint focuses on the contexts of public relations practice. Public relations is often defined narrowly in marketing-dominated departments, relegated to "special events" or media in some organizations, and excluded entirely in other areas. The bias is often reflecting the "business" bottom line emphasis, and public relations is viewed as "soft" when there is no understanding of the full range of public relations functions. When public relations professionals begin to challenge these situations and confront them, there may be opportunities for intervention. The Integrated Marketing Communication (IMC) approach that captured the imagination of many is an example of this denigration of public relations role and functions. Why not just IC—Integrated Communications? Furthermore, the resistance to fully acknowledge the value of public relations is in light of evidence to the contrary.

An examination of the most current association descriptions of public relations focuses on the various approaches established by associations, institutes, and academic and practitioner scholarship/research projects. Reviewing the descriptions of each of these associations provides a framework of study for examining the momentum of public relations activity.

Comparing and contrasting associations with a public relations focus frames the discussion around the various themes in public relations development. On one level, you have the more academic associations fostering a public relations division and/or interest group: examples include AEJMC (division), CSCA (interest group), IABD (track), ICA (division), IPR (100% public relations with academic membership), NCA (division), and PRSA (educators academy). AEJMC's PRD, for example, focuses on public relations research with themes on education, professional freedom and responsibility, and graduate international research. Within a journalism and mass communication context, the emphasis is on diversity and developing liaisons with professionals in the field. IABD's track in public relations/corporate communication is considered one of the "support disciplines of business." As a business academic association supporting a public relations discipline emphasis, the Academy bridges "theory and practice" and seeks "to increase individual awareness of business problems and opportunities in the international marketplace."

ICA's PRD, a global intense association, focuses on "theory and laboratory/practice between publics and organizations; theory advancement for solving pragmatic PR problems; consultant clients or corporate employers." ICA's PRD has a transnational PR research team focusing on cultural issues. NCA, the largest academic communication organization, "seeks to build and maintain mutually beneficial relationships between organizations and their stakeholders." The NCA PRD is also the largest division among all the academic associations and offers the international PRide Award for outstanding publishing in public relations (open to nonmembers). The more practitioner-oriented associations, PRSA, the Association for Women in Communications (AWC), and the International Association of Business Communicators (IABC), focus on "advancing the field of public relations education by collaborating with college and university public relations educators and practitioners." The only association fully devoted to public relations, the IPR, "bridges the academy and the profession, supporting PR research and mainstreaming this knowledge into practice through PR education."

Most important, what you are seeing is the shift from the narrow focus of "defining" public relations to an emerging infrastructure capable of handling intense research into the very nature of public relations—allowing the body of knowledge to bring the necessary clarification to the surface. Indeed the momentum as a research-driven discovery process yields multilayered insights into the functions and basic nature of the role of public relations in society worldwide. No longer is this a "chronic state of confusion." The anecdotal approach to the territorial battle was responded to by the popular book *The Fall of Advertising and the Rise of Public Relations* (Ries & Ries, 2002). Now the research approach verifies and documents the value of public relations in integrated communication. For example, research on the effectiveness of advertising and PR message sequencing in product introductions applied four experimental conditions: (1) public relations alone, (2) public relations followed by advertising, (3) advertising followed by public relations, and (4) advertising alone. The research team established that *only* public relations significantly affected the outcomes (Ivanov, Parker, & Sims, 2009). Such findings are bringing disciplines into better focus and should reorient the IC question to more accurately reflect what really "works." This is the age of research supporting the impact of public relations efforts fundamentally.

Moving Beyond Static Approaches: An Interactive Communication Process

As the public relations process is more securely connected to "communication," the research is now more fluid in reflecting public relations as a process grounded in communication and not an artificial diagram of a continuum. So public relations is seen as the interrelated loop of communication moving beyond the static "categorical approach" or a single-dimensional continuum to a multifaceted, interactive process more reflective of communication per se.

The symmetrical and asymmetrical models of Grunig and Grunig (1992) identified as press-agentry or publicity, public information, two-way asymmetric, and two-way symmetric models (symmetry suggesting "ideal public relations") are better represented by speech act theory where "people create social reality through their language per se or 'speech acts.'" This is also a distinct "shift from the idea that communication is information" (Neff & Hansen-Horn, 1998, p. 356). Akin to this approach is the work of Gordon (2008) on social constructionism and public relations. She examined the historical perspective and intellectual traditions as operable through the process of social construction through language. This theoretical approach helps establish public relations as a meaning-creating discipline. Focus on dialogue brings into question the way public relations as "relationship *management*" is cast. The shift away from information exchange and/or management moves the concept of relationship from a static concept to allow one to peruse the following idea:

> I first began . . . with a seemingly innocent and obvious question: What makes a good relationship? It soon became apparent, at least to me, that this question needed to be reworded to "What makes a good communication process?" Communication is the observable practice of a relationship, and so it was to the actual process of communicating that I had to attend. (Penman, 2000, p. 1)

When one realizes that the very essence of public relations is grounded in communication, the discussion of continuums for studying public relations seems more of an artifice primarily useful for clarifying concepts. A variety of research paradigms have developed to define public relations and improve its reputation such as symmetrical asymmetry (Grunig, 1992), conflict to cooperation (Murphy, 1991), contingency theory (Cameron, Pang, & Jin, 2008), or situational theory (Grunig, 2005). Such analysis should capture the interactivity of the communication process, however. Even in social media the metaphor is compared with neural networks of interactivity. Dialogue as interaction is featured in the rhetorical view of the public relations discipline as interactivity of communication as in the Burkian image of a "wrangle in the marketplace" (Heath, 2008). Thus, the role of rhetoric as a suasory discourse becomes central to the discipline of public relations and connects us to the basic ethical and analytical foundations outlined in early history by Aristotle, Plato, Cicero, Quintilian, and other notables of rhetoric.

Now the depiction of the forces shaping perspectives "across public relations" becomes more integrated and evolutionary. The rapid expansion of public relations associations brings a dynamic dimension to the public relations perspectives. With the interconnections between professions (academics and practitioners), communication history, interdisciplinary relationships, multiple organizational infrastructures, and public relations per se, it is viewed as an interactive process, and the integration potential is evident. Figure 25.1 describes the integration of public relations across key perspectives. The generation of extensive research has allowed a rich body of knowledge to develop, allowing a better understanding of the complex process of public relations. There is now enough evidence to provide a more definitive approach to the execution and application of public relations theories, principles, and practices. It is, as outlined below, largely a merging of public relations perspectives.

Figure 25.1 Merging Perspectives Within Public Relations

Academic and professional partnering on research

History grounding and shaping the mission and vision of public relations (a rhetorical basis)

Public relations training/thinking incorporates multiple disciplines (diplomacy, business, NGOs)

Public relations research incorporating and generating new interdisciplinary terminology

Public relations constituencies viewed from an ombudsman and/or boundary-spanning perspective

Tactical and strategy intertwined in terms of socially responsible, legal, and ethical frameworks

Note: These statements reflect how the discipline of public relations is evolving strongly through the academic and practitioner professional partnerships. Now strongly supported by research, the public relations body of knowledge is defining and refining the complexities of the web of communication relationships.

Defining, Refining, and Analyzing Public Relations

The study of public relations needed to more clearly and effectively establish itself, because a reputable profession can take many twists and turns. One is the reality that since public relations is practiced in a multitude of contexts (health, tourism, government, technology, parks and recreation, education, etc.), the language used to discuss the context may vary to accommodate the situational needs. Often the term *public relations* is ignored or avoided in such discussions. Government bodies, for example, distance themselves from the word *public relations* in deference to the more neutral-sounding titles such as "public affairs" or "public information"; such moves may also be taken to abide by the legal constraints. Today, more and more public relations professionals compete for government funding to run campaigns on health, citizenship, and other national concerns. It is ironic that the term is denied within the government on one hand and funded on the other.

Ultimately, public relations professionals provide the bridge to connect people through their boundary-spanning responsibilities. From organization to organization, from organization to publics, from publics to publics, or to the population as a whole, public relations practice emerges as a leadership function connecting people, ideas, and actions. Perhaps the search is to find inclusive terms describing the value of the public relations communication process. The question then becomes how to reduce this vast infrastructure of activity so clearly that the functions of public relations are identified and the evolving roles are defined. One response to this richly developing body of knowledge in the discipline was to organize the information along the infrastructure lines to codify the concepts.

Major Academic and Professional Initiatives

In 2005, the discipline gained a bit more firm grounding when Heath (2005) edited the two-volume *Encyclopedia of Public Relations.* The encyclopedia organizes concepts and clusters topics in a dual-index approach. The encyclopedia's appendixes list various codes of ethics, include the national commission reports for undergraduate and graduate education, provide a list of PRSA local chapters, list online resources, and include a "Dictionary of Public Relations Measurement."

The range and depth of discussion provide the discipline with guidance and focus.

In addition, there has been significant in-depth publishing in areas where public relations professionals have recognized responsibilities. Heath, for example, has published in crisis management (Heath & Coombs, 2006), strategic issues management (Heath, 1988), corporate issues management (Heath, 1990), communication technologies (Heath, 1998), and theory and rhetoric (Heath, 2008). Such contributions provide a broad and solid foundation for the discipline to build on. Similarly, Coombs contributed to the crisis literature (Coombs, 1999, 2004a, 2004b, 2007a, 2007b) and published with Holladay on various crisis projects (Coombs & Holladay, 1996, 2002, 2004). A series of studies on dialogic communication applied to technology were developed by Taylor, Kent, and White (2001). Such a significant listing of efforts on central topics strengthens the body of knowledge as a vital part of shaping and affirming the identity of public relations.

John Pavlik (1987) contended that "the public relations emphasis on the practice at the expense of the theoretical" produced a serious gap (p. 1). However, it is not clear which discipline he was referring to—journalism perhaps? At that time, journalism offered primarily a practical approach to public relations. When Thomsen (1995) examined the *Public Relations Review (PRR)* from 1985 to 1994, he confirmed that only 19% of the 96 articles coded had basic research. However, during this period, Neff's (1989) research established that communication(s) departments had nearly twice as many public relations programs as journalism ones. Communication academics, a more theoretical academic area, was most likely not included in these studies.

Communication(s) departments offer a more theoretical perspective, and this discipline offers a rich history of rhetorical theory within a wide range of contexts: inter/intrapersonal, organizational, public, community relations, media communication, and multi/intercultural communication, for example. As mentioned, *Public Relations Theory*, by Carl H. Botan and Vincent Hazleton (1989), offered a series of articles on theoretical areas of interest. Their second volume (2006) continued to update theory discussion. Another scholarly book, *Public Relations: From Theory to Practice*, addressed the relationship between theory and practice (Hansen-Horn & Neff, 2008). Thus, the platform for theoretical development is now well received, bringing a larger purview of thinking to the public relations process. Today, publications with theory are abundant throughout the discipline.

During this period, the well-respected academic and trade outlets for public relations publications reflected a deep professional commitment to and articulation of the discipline. For example, *PRR*, the most tenured journal in public relations, is the only journal published five times a year. Established as a scholarly journal, *PRR* is "devoted to articles that examine public relations in depth" (Elsevier, 2009). The publication remains today one of the more central publications in the field of public relations.

In 1989, Grunig and Grunig launched a theory and research-based annual that became *the Journal of Public Relations Research (JPRR)*. This journal is now housed in the PRD of AEJMC. It addresses theory specifically as described in the journal's mission statement: *JPRR* "publishes research that creates, tests, or expands public relations theory" (Malone & Coombs, 2009).

The *International Journal of Strategic Communication*, established and edited by Derina Holtzhausen, is housed in the Routledge Taylor & Francis Group publishing company. Although the editor establishes the publication as independent of public relations, the journal remains of great interest to those in public relations. A review of a special issue features a number of public relations academics on familiar public relations topics—crisis communication, corporate social responsibility, and strategic communication (Zerfass, 2009).

The move toward taking public relations academic research and translating and applying it to the practice is now a well-established approach in the annual conference sponsored by the IPR. This is the only practitioner-academic partnership conference.

The Public Relations Journal is published by the Public Relations Society of America. This quarterly electronic "research" journal is dedicated to "facilitating the transfer of knowledge from the educational community to the professional community." Such partnership between the educators and practitioners is giving intense renewal to the impetus of public relations research (*Public Relations Journal*, PRSA).

Other initiatives continue to develop. The *Journal of Communication* (ICA), the *Applied Journal of Communication* (NCA), *Journalism Quarterly*, the *Business Research Yearbook*, the *Journal of International Business Disciplines*, and other journals in communication, journalism, and business are scholarly outlets for public relations work. The PRD of ICA is currently proposing a division journal. Specialty journals are also being proposed by those who are active in public relations risk communication. For instance, Sellnow, Seeger, and Ulmer are developing a journal focused on risk and crisis, particularly in agriculture and emergency management *(Panel on "Bad Food,"* 2009). Interest in extending the discipline to journals already established on other continents is growing. So the explosion of research outlets serves as another indicator of the rapid growth of public relations in academia with well-established research agendas.

Meanwhile, the trade publications in public relations are equally growing and rapidly becoming central to the profession for both academics and practitioners. These publications include *PRWeek*, *PR News*, the Public Relations Student Society of America's *Tactics* and *The Strategist*, IABC's *The World*, and IPRA's published white papers. So the public relations discipline is rich with dialogue on concepts, experience, case studies, and analysis. Perhaps the area most lacking is multicultural aspects of public relations. Although there have been inroads with various publications, only one major scholarly text has been published on the public relations discipline in this area. Stephen P. Banks's (2000) *Multicultural Public Relations: A Social-Interpretive Approach* set the standard for the discipline and remains the most articulate theoretical published piece addressing multicultural public relations. Banks made a call for the "need for theory" (p. 24) and articulated well the multicultural dimension of such a theory. Banks defined the public relations role as a communication development facilitator (p. x).

In search of an "international identity" globally, Curtin and Gaither (2007) offered the most dedicated conceptual discussion of global public relations. The title speaks well to the central focus of the text: *International Public Relations: Negotiating Culture, Identity, and Power.* With more multicultural and global public relations research, the discipline of public relations will further mature toward a high level of professionalism. This move is defined in Figure 25.2.

The public relations role develops as facilitating and leading a vast web of relationships. With the emergence of a rich body of knowledge through the establishment of associations with public relations divisions/interest groups/academics, the field has extended the discipline into published outlets globally. This has moved the discipline from a corporate-centric model to a web of complex relationships. The integration of the tactical-strategy ethical approach provides a basis for operation on standards. The more multidisciplinary approach adds a richness of context to the operations of public relations. Thus, public relations can be seen as an independent ombudsman, part of an organization, a key role in the dominant coalition, or a separate agency entity facilitating the relationships in the world.

The shortsighted view of public relations, what Coombs and Holladay (2010) called "corporate centric," has not given public relations a particularly good reputation. These authors correctly visualize a web of relationships with corporate as only one element. This approach sets the stage for a very different outcome when reviewing the evolution of public relations. Instead of viewing public relations practitioners as "managers" (an unrealistic concept), they are considered to be

Figure 25.2 Factors Considered When Preparing for a Career in Public Relations

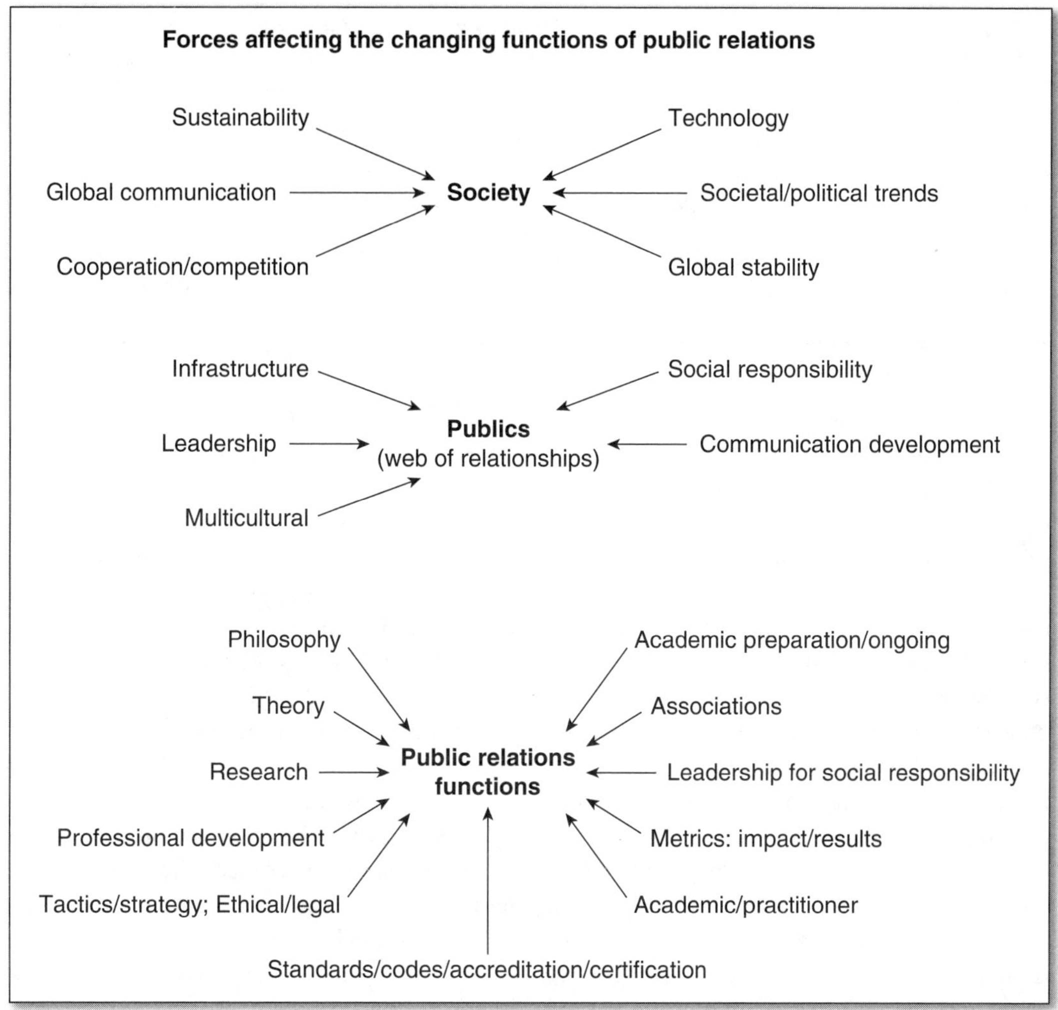

communication facilitators. This means that the cadre of public relations professionals will be required to have a much higher level of training. The public relations process is also viewed as more interactive and not as a simple continuum.

Public Relations: An Integrative Process

The public relations professional is responsible for integrating society's needs within dialogic exchange, the cultural elements, the understanding of the relationships, and the level of process—self/public/organization (Hansen-Horn & Neff, 2008). It is a theory-driven field beyond just simple case study approaches. Most important, the progress of public relations, as viewed from all the disciplines contributing to the profession, looks most fully as developed in the diagram in Figure 25.3.

The influence of the environment on public relations is well documented. As academics and practitioners merge and use and publish research, the impact shapes the preparation and training of public relations professionals.

Figure 25.3 The Communication Process in the Public Relations Discipline

Press-Agentry	Publicity	Promotions	Relationship Management	Organizational Positioning	Communication Development Facilitator
non/media	persuasion		managing	contextual influence	development
1900s	1940/1950s	1960s/1970s	1980s	1990s	21st century
Practitioner-based experience	some academic		academic	interdisciplinary	practitioners/academics

The primary forces shaping the discipline of public relations focused on increased practitioner and academic experience and research. From an understanding of how public relations academic programs developed, to how training programs supported public relations practitioners, the partnerships formed between the two groups reveal how public relations has become needed by society. The challenge is now to continually develop these professionals on levels that meet the communication demands of society.

The 1960s through the 1980s focused more on promotion and relationship development. Contributing to this context today is the development of the World Wide Web. The tactical idea comes from the need to account for outputs. This is the age of "impressions." As persuasion is integrated into the "tactical" approach, the idea of strategy is married to the development of tactics. Unfortunately, the movement toward "strategic" was a direction away from ethics, whereas strategy allowed for more flexibility in representing the larger sense of society.

The shift away from media to a more decentralized communication network facilitated some of this change. The gatekeeping process is now diminished in the social media and digital age. The average citizen is now fully represented in communication interaction. The emergence of new values such as sustainability emphasized the shift away from a corporate-centric view. Now the web of relationships (Coombs & Holladay, 2010) illustrates the interactivity that no longer can be managed but can only be inspired through leadership. Instead of a manager of public relations, professionals now are more leaders in boundary-spanning roles, represent socially responsible roles as ombudsmen, and provide the leadership necessary to help society.

One, again, needs to be reminded that symbolic and behavioral relationships are grounded in communication. Only through communication can one sustain a viable relationship.

Context drives the development of the role of public relations. Obviously, the integration of public relations requires a higher level of communication skills. Thus, the context provides some of the infrastructure possibilities, but the leadership role of public relations professionals often furthers the range of possibilities even more. Public relations professionals can now choose to be independent of the dominant coalition or develop a more flexible role through boundary-spanning activities. There are choices. By realizing that organizations and publics do not live in a corporate-centric situation but really belong to a web of relationships, the context rather than the type of the organization determines the relationship development possibilities. Importantly, it is not just a management approach. Thus, the range of possibilities includes contexts such as diplomacy, government, nonprofits, the Web and electronic viral environs, and obviously business. So whether a boundary spanner or an independent leader, the public relations professional blends tactics and strategy concepts with concepts such as social responsibility.

Future: The Role of Creating the Vision for Society

The academic associations have incorporated the public relations discipline, and the practitioner associations have increased their level of professionalism. *Challenging?* Of course. When you have more complexity, the challenges are greater. With a more global approach, culture and languages become more important. When more expertise is needed, the depth and breadth of education and training must be increased. *Demanding?* The increased professionalism of public relations has led to a greater need for public relations services. The increased challenges and complexities require more standards and monitoring of the profession. But then the career is exciting and certainly rewarding. *Promising?* The growth of public relations as the third fastest growing profession is ample proof of the discipline's need. The growth of public relations during difficult economic times further substantiates the importance of public relations to society. The rating of public relations as the top communication position further highlights the contributions of the profession. There are so many more new ways of experiencing the public relations lifestyle.

Indeed, the communication skills required will become more and more complex when one is practicing as a communication development facilitator. Now, a greater number of organizational matrixes will have to be understood, and so also their mission and purpose. The adaptation to a web of relationships will be far more complex and will challenge the profession. The leadership development needed will take experiential training and a high level of academic preparedness.

Moving away from a narrow "employee communication" approach to social responsibility will truly engage the profession. When public relations cares for the children, the elderly, and those without substantial means or abilities, this will be a society that is not just tied to economics. The less selfish, less greedy, and more authentic approach to public relations will provide a major social emphasis and consequently greater impact.

Ultimately, communication development without a "managing" relationship approach integrates tactics and strategy (not being narrowly strategic) within ethical and legal standards. Because it incorporates knowledge of a number of complex contexts (both global and local), it will enhance the diplomacy, the culture, the businesses, the nonprofits, government, and the future networks that will be developed. Whatever the social and digital world brings to us, the public relations professional must be prepared to "make the world work."

References

Banks, S. (2000). *Multicultural public relations: A social-interpretive approach.* Ames: Iowa State University Press.

Botan, C. H., & Hazleton, V., Jr. (Eds.). (1989). *Public relations theory.* Hillsdale, NJ: Lawrence Erlbaum.

Botan, C. H., & Hazleton, V., Jr. (Eds). (2006). *Public relations theory II.* Mahwah, NJ: Lawrence Erlbaum.

Brody, E. W. (1992). We must act now to redeem PR's reputation. *Public Relations Quarterly, 37*(3), 44.

Cameron, G. T., Pang, A., & Jin, Y. (2008). Contingency theory: Strategic management of conflict in public relations. In T. L. Hansen-Horn & B. D. Neff (Eds.), *Public relations: From theory to practice* (pp. 134–155). Boston: Pearson.

Coombs, W. T. (1999). *Ongoing crisis communication: Planning, managing, and responding.* Thousand Oaks, CA: Sage.

Coombs, W. T. (2004a). Impact of past crises on current crisis communications: Insights from situational crisis communication theory. *Journal of Business Communication, 41,* 265–289.

Coombs, W. T. (2004b). A theoretical frame for post-crisis communication: Situational crisis communication theory. In M. J. Martinko (Ed.), *Attribution theory in the organizational sciences: Theoretical and empirical contributions* (pp. 275–296). Greenwich, CT: Information Age.

Coombs, W. T. (2007a). *Ongoing crisis communication: Planning, managing, and responding* (2nd ed.). Thousand Oaks, CA: Sage.

Coombs, W. T. (2007b). Protecting organization reputations during a crisis: The development and application of situational crisis communication theory. *Corporate Reputation Review, 10*(3), 163–177.

Coombs, W. T., & Holladay, S. J. (1996). Communication and attributions in a crisis: An experimental study of crisis communication. *Journal of Public Relations Research, 8,* 279–295.

Coombs, W. T., & Holladay, S. J. (2002). Helping crisis managers protect reputational assets: Initial tests of the situational crisis communication theory. *Management Communication Quarterly, 16,* 165–186.

Coombs, W. T., & Holladay, S. J. (2004). Reasoned action in crisis communication: An attribution theory-based approach to crisis management. In D. P. Millar & R. L. Heath (Eds.), *Responding to crisis: A rhetorical approach to crisis communication* (pp. 95–115). Mahwah, NJ: Lawrence Erlbaum.

Coombs, W. T., & Holladay, S. J. (2007). *This is not just public relations: Public relations in society.* Malden, MA: Wiley-Blackwell.

Coombs, W. T., & Holladay, S. J. (2010). *PR strategy and application: Managing influence.* West Sussex, UK: Wiley.

Cropp, F., & Pincus, D. J. (2001). The mystery of public relations: Unraveling its past, unmasking its future. In R. L. Heath (Ed.), *Handbook of public relations* (pp. 189–204). Thousand Oaks, CA: Sage.

Curtin, P., & Gaither, T. K. (2007). *International public relations: Negotiating culture, identity, and power.* Thousand Oaks, CA: Sage.

The Economist. (2010, January 14). New York. Retrieved March 20, 2010, from www.economist.com/business-finance/displaystory.cfm?story_id=15276746

Elsevier. (2009). *Public Relations Review.* Retrieved March 31, 2009, from www.elsevier.com/wps/find/journaldescription.cws_home/620188/authorinstructions

Gordon, J. (2008). Social constructionism and public relations. In T. L. Hansen-Horn & B. D. Neff (Eds.), *Public relations: From theory to practice* (pp. 104–121). Boston: Pearson.

Grunig, J. E. (1992). *Excellence in public relations and communication management: Contributions to effective organizations.* Hillsdale, NJ: Lawrence Erlbaum.

Grunig, J. E. (2005). Situational theory of publics. In R. L. Heath (Ed.), *Encyclopedia of public relations* (Vol. 2, pp. 778–780). Thousand Oaks, CA: Sage.

Grunig, J. E., & Grunig, L. A. (1992). Models of public relations and communications. In J. E. Grunig (Ed.), *Excellence in public relations and communication management* (pp. 285–326). Hillsdale, NJ: Lawrence Erlbaum.

Hansen-Horn, T. L., & Neff, B. D. (Eds.). (2008). *Public relations: From theory to practice.* Boston: Pearson.

Heath, R. L. (Ed.). (1988). *Strategic issues management: How organizations influence and respond to public interests and policies.* San Francisco: Jossey-Bass.

Heath, R. L. (1990). Corporate issues management: Theoretical underpinnings and research foundations. In L. A. Grunig & J. E. Grunig (Eds.), *Public relations research annual* (Vol. 2, pp. 29–65). Hillsdale, NJ: Lawrence Erlbaum.

Heath, R. L. (1998). New communication technologies: An issues management point of view. *Public Relations Review, 24,* 273–288.

Heath, R. L. (Ed.). (2005). *Encyclopedia of public relations.* Thousand Oaks, CA: Sage.

Heath, R. L. (2008). Rhetorical theory, public relations, and meaning: Giving voice to ideas. In T. L. Hansen-Horn & B. D. Neff (Eds.), *Public relations: From theory to practice* (pp. 208–225). Boston: Pearson.

Heath, R. L., & Coombs, W. T. (2006). *Today's public relations: An introduction.* Thousand Oaks, CA: Sage.

Ivanov B., Parker, K., & Sims, J. (2009, November). *Effectiveness of advertising and PR message sequencing in product introductions: Corporate credibility and image as moderator of sequencing success.* Top paper presentation, Public Relations Division, at the 2009 National Communication Association Conference, Chicago.

Malone, P. C., & Coombs, W. T. (Guest Eds.). (2009). Crisis communication [Special issue]. *Journal of Public Relations Research, 21*(2).

Murphy, P. (1991). The limits of symmetry: A game theory approach to symmetric and asymmetric public relations. In L. A. Grunig & J. E. Grunig (Eds.), *Public relations research annual* (Vol. 3, pp. 115–131). Hillsdale, NJ: Lawrence Erlbaum.

Neff, B. D. (1989). The emerging theoretical perspective in public relations: An opportunity for communication departments. In C. Botan & V. Hazleton (Eds.), *Public relations theory* (pp. 159–172). Hillsdale, NJ: Lawrence Erlbaum.

Neff, B. D. (1998). Speech act theory: An approach to public relations leadership. In T. L. Hansen-Horn & B. D. Neff (Eds.), *Public relations: From theory to practice* (pp. 208–225). Boston: Pearson.

Neff, B. D., & Hansen-Horn, T. L. (Eds.). (1998). *Public relations: From theory to practice.* Boston: Allyn & Bacon.

Panel on "Bad Food Required Good PR: Crisis Communication and the Food Industry." (2009). Public Relations Division, National Communication Association annual conference, Chicago.

Pavlik, J. (1987). *Public relations: What research tells us.* Beverly Hills, CA: Sage.

Penman, R. (2000). *Reconstructing communicating.* Mahwah, NJ: Lawrence Erlbaum.

Ries, A., & Ries, L. (2002). *The fall of advertising and the rise of public relations.* New York: HarpersBusiness.

Taylor, M., Kent, M. L., & White, W. J. (2001). How activist organizations are using the Internet to build relationships. *Public Relations Review, 27,* 263–284.

Thomsen, S. R. (1995, November). *Emerging agendas and pedagogical applications: What Public Relations Review tells us.* Paper presented at the annual meeting of the Speech Communication Association, San Antonio, TX.

Wright, D. K. (Ed.). *Public Relations Journal.* Retrieved January 17, 2010, from www.prsa.org/prjournal

Zerfass, A. (Ed.). (2009). Institutionalization of strategic communication theoretical analysis and empirical evidence [Special issue]. *International Journal of Strategic Communication, 3*(2).

CHAPTER 26

Relationship Management Projects Public Relations Image

Analysis of Living History *and* Dreams From My Father

Gayle M. Pohl

Living History is about a woman—Hillary Rodham Clinton—the current U.S. Secretary of State. Before assuming that role, she was the junior U.S. Senator from New York. A former candidate for the Democratic nomination in the 2008 presidential election, Hillary Clinton is married to Bill Clinton, the 42nd president of the United States, also making her the First Lady of the United States from 1993 to 2001.

In 2003, Hillary Clinton released a 562-page autobiography, *Living History.* The publisher Simon & Schuster paid Hillary Clinton an advance of $8 million. The book set a first-week sales record for a nonfiction work and went on to sell more than 1 million copies in the first month following publication, and was translated into 12 languages. Hillary Clinton's audio recording of the book earned her a nomination for the Grammy Award for the Best Spoken Word Album.

Although *Living History* is not the only publication about Hillary Clinton, it is her only autobiography. Comparing this book with other publications about Hillary Clinton (Bernstein, 2007; Estrich, 2005; Gerth & Van Natta, 2007) that may contain less than flattering statements, *Living History* is Hillary Clinton's opportunity to set the record straight, as she had control over the materials, both in their selection and in their interpretation. Readers were eager to read about her side of the story. Much like other autobiographies, *Living History* is, thus, a reflexive and contrived public presentation to offer an alternative public discourse of Hillary Clinton.

Dreams From My Father: A Story of Race and Inheritance follows Barack Obama's autobiographical journeys through life. Elected as the first half-white, half-black president of the United States, Obama tells what it was like to be the son of a white mother, who was often absent, and a black father, whom he never knew. Obama was raised by his white grandparents and was raised in Hawaii. He was the first black (self-acknowledged) president of the Harvard Law Review and then went on to become a community organizer and civil rights attorney in Chicago. Obama dismisses terms such as *mulatto* and states that we are all caught in contradictions and disparate communities. He talks about racism, poverty, and corruption.

Much like books written by other politicians such as John Edwards (2006), *Living History* and *Dreams From My Father* are purposeful presentations with an election in mind. Both were published in a timely manner to pave the way for the presidential election that Hillary Clinton and Barack Obama were expected to campaign for hard. However, unlike other politicians who started this purposeful presentation with a clean slate, Hillary Clinton carried the extra baggage to provide a transparent presentation of the scandals she encountered from her time as the First Lady of Arkansas through her tenure as the First Lady of the United States. Obama entered the election as a virtual unknown.

This study is an analysis of *Living History* and *Dreams From My Father* to find out how these books were contrived to achieve the goal of paving the way for the presidential elections as well as clarifying misunderstanding and restoring a favorable image for Hillary Clinton and Barack Obama. In other words, the author seeks to identify elements of relationship management evident in the books. The elements of relationship management identified in the books help Clinton and Obama establish a public relations image of choice and highlight their individual strengths and political message to the American people. It is through the use of relationship management theory that they were placed in the offices they hold today. This study not only highlights the utilization of relationship management but also extends the literature of relationship management, a traditionally interpersonal relationship management study, to include mediated communication.

Book as a Platform for Relationship Building

Using these books as platforms for analysis provides a solid foundation because unlike radio, these books are suitable for announcements. The books also have the space and length needed to explain how the candidates built relationships with their supporters.

Unlike television, the books are suitable for evocative presentations and clear explanations. The books allow for both the discursive and emotive content to be thoroughly explained.

The books, unlike newspaper reports, which generally lack historical contexts and interpretations, offer an ideal arena to provide an overtime evolutionary and in-depth analysis and understanding of events reported. Also unlike news reports, which are written by reporters with unpredictable predispositions, autobiographies provide the author an enhanced control over the content presented.

Literature Review

Ledingham and Bruning (1998) viewed public relations from a relational perspective—that is, a "*management* function that uses communication strategically" (p. 56). Bruning and Ledingham (2000) explained that the relational management perspective moves public relations practice away from "manipulating public opinion through communication messages" to a combination of "symbolic communication messages and organizational behaviors to initiate, nurture, and maintain mutually beneficial organization-public relationships" (p. 87).

Ledingham and Bruning (1998) defined organization-public relationships as "the state that exists between an organization and its key publics that provides economic, social, political, and/or cultural benefits to all parties involved, and is characterized by mutual positive regard" (p. 62). This definition of relationships is quite narrow in that it excludes negative relationships that can develop. Hon and Grunig (1999) explained that an organization-public relationship occurs when a possibility of consequences occurring exists.

Many researchers have put effort into developing relationship constructs. Broom, Casey, and Ritchey (1997) suggested relationship concepts, antecedents of relationships, and consequences of relationships in their three-stage model of relationships. Bruning and Ledingham (1998) surveyed literature in interpersonal communication and social psychology and identified five dimensions of relationships: trust, openness, understanding, involvement, and commitment.

In reviewing relationship management studies, trust appears to be a vital factor. Trust is described by Leichty and Springton (1993) as "a small risk by disclosing personal information.... If the other party reciprocates the self-disclosure, then the first party is likely to self-disclose again ... and mutual trust emerges from a positive feedback spiral" (pp. 180–188). Leichty and Springton (1993) stated that this process is similar for an organization and its various publics.

Grunig (1993) noted that these behavioral concepts referred to by Leichty and Springton (1993) are endemic to interpersonal communication. The measures of trust, openness, understanding, commitment, and involvement can be used to measure the quality of behavioral relationships of organizations. Ledingham and Bruning (1998) said that these measures can also engender loyalty toward an organization among key publics when that involvement is known by key publics.

A theory focused on political communication is called constituent relationship management (CRM). It uses the same premise that Bruning and Ledingham (1999) introduced with the relationship management theory. CRM (Crawley, 2003) is defined as the art of leveraging people (voters), information/data, process, and technology to optimize the way in which an organization (politician/candidate) markets, engages, and services its constituents. This relationship management method is important because it adds value and trust with a candidate's constituents by allowing them to control their preferences—ranging from the format and frequency of e-mail communications to the type of information they receive both online and off-line. The constituents' privacy is guaranteed through databases and the constituent can answer surveys he or she chooses. The ability to interact directly with the candidate's team is also available. Creating opportunities for interaction helps you direct the information received to the right place right away. User self-identification of interests saves costly research into finding out who are the candidates' most important audiences. These values suggest that constituents want to understand the candidate's views, want the candidate to be open to interaction with them, and want the candidate to be involved in the campaign and have a commitment to the voter. Adding a user's engagement history to his or her profile enables surgical targeting of future outreach messages and calls to action. CRM also adds value to the candidate by saving the person time and resources. The candidate is also able to more effectively target the segments of the constituency most wanted.

Ledingham and Bruning (1999) and CRM (Crawley, 2003) supported the notion that a candidate needs to solicit the voters' trust, openness, understanding, involvement, and commitment.

Research Methodology

To determine if Hillary Clinton and Barack Obama connected with their readers on Ledingham and Bruning's (1998) relationship levels of (1) trust, (2) openness, (3) understanding, (4) involvement, and/or (5) commitment, a thematic analysis was used. Thematic analysis is defined by Boyatzis (1998) as an analysis of themes that relies on scientific methods and is not limited to the types of variables that may be measured or the context in which the themes are created or presented (p. 3).

Boyatzis said that thematic analysis is a way of seeing a phenomenon or, in this study, a relationship. It is a process for encoding qualitative information. The encoding requires an explicit "code." A theme is a pattern found in the information that at the minimum describes and organizes the possible observations or at the maximum interprets aspects of the phenomenon. A theme may be interpreted at the manifest level (directly observable in the information) or at the latent level (categorizing issues underlying the phenomenon). A code may be a list of themes; a model with themes, indicators, and qualifications that are causally related; or something in between these two forms. A codebook is the compilation or integration of a number of codes in a study (Boyatzis, 1998, pp. 160–161).

Three methods of developing themes include the following:

1. Generating themes inductively from raw data
2. Generating themes from theory
3. Generating themes from prior research

The method used in this study was the generation of themes from theory. Five of Ledingham and Bruning's (1998) relationship management elements were used as codes.

The relationship elements are operationalized in the following way:

1. Trust: a belief in disclosures—"I believe in what he or she says and/or does."
2. Openness: making an effort to be open about him- or herself to the public
3. Understanding: wanting the public to understand him or her and his or her behaviors
4. Involvement: being aware of the country and its people and wanting to be involved with the problems and problem-solving process for the nation and its people
5. Commitment: being dedicated to the health and welfare of the nation and its people

Every page of each autobiography was examined for quotes that illustrated one or more of the five relationship management elements described above. Many quotes demonstrated more than one theme; however, only one to three quotes were chosen for illustration purposes for the written study. Each of the five elements is represented in each of the autobiographies. The themes are central to each of the autobiographies and clearly represent how a public relations image is formed through the use of relationship management theory.

As a public relationship academic and practitioner myself, I have seen clients develop a trusting, committed, and open relationship with their customers/constituents that has led to some type of professional involvement such as volunteerism or sponsorship and has been enriched with a deep understanding of the organization and its commitment to the community. I truly believe that this is relationship management at its best. This study of Clinton's and Obama's autobiographies reaffirms my ardent belief.

Analysis

Trust. Hillary Clinton (2003) disclosed a great deal of information in her autobiography, *Living History.* As relationship management demands, she opens herself up to the reader and appears to disclose intimate moments of trust. As a child, Hillary said, she was mostly concerned with her family, school, and sports.

> I loved school, and I was lucky enough to have some great teachers. . . . It was an assignment . . . that led me to write my first autobiography. I rediscovered it in a box of old papers after I left the White House. . . . I was still very much a child at that age, and mostly concerned with family, school, and sports. . . . But grade school was ending; and it was time to enter a more complicated world than the one I had known. (Clinton, 2003, pp. 14–15)

As a young woman, Hillary leaves home to go to college and is excited, but as a mother, who leaves her daughter at college, she experiences a different reaction. It is at this point in the book that Clinton seeks the trust of the reader, as she discloses and relates her experiences both as a woman and as a human being.

> I didn't know anyone else going to Wellesley. Most of my friends were attending Midwestern colleges to be close to home. My parents drove me to college . . . My mother has said that she cried the entire thousand-mile drive back from Massachusetts to Illinois. Now that I have had the experience of leaving my daughter at a distance university, I understand exactly how she felt. But back then, I was only looking ahead to my own future. (Clinton, 2003, pp. 25–26)

When Clinton was faced with her husband's infidelity, she reports that he initially lied to her about the details of the situation. At first, Bill told her that a female intern mistook his attention. She says that she believed him. When he later told her he did have a sexual relationship with Monica Lewinsky, Hillary reports feeling angry, betrayed, and hurt. She also felt her relationship with her husband was a private situation. The nation should not have been allowed to be involved. She also felt that her president was serving her country well. Her husband, however, was not in favor with either her or Chelsea.

> I told him (Bill) he had to tell Chelsea. His eyes filled with tears. He betrayed the trust in our marriage, and we both knew it might be an irreparable breach. These were terrible moments for all of us. . . . As the hour for his [public] statement approached, everyone was putting in his or her two cents, and this was not helping Bill. . . . So, I finally said, "Well, Bill, this is your speech. You're the one who got yourself into this mess, and only you can decide what to say about it." Then Chelsea and I left the room. (Clinton, 2003, pp. 466–468)

Clinton trusts her reader to see her as a woman, a human being, and a political leader. That is why she discloses this information. The more her readers trust Clinton, the more they feel they have a relationship with her.

In *Dreams From My Father*, Barack Obama (1995) asks the reader to trust him by disclosing intimacies about his reactions to his race and himself. In the book, he presented himself as a student living in New York, busy with work, seeing others as necessary distractions. Obama found comfort in solitude.

> I was living in New York . . . in an uninviting block, treeless, and barren. . . . I was prone to see other people as unnecessary distractions. It wasn't that I didn't appreciate company exactly. I enjoyed exchanging Spanish pleasantries with my mostly Puerto Rican neighbors, and on my way back from classes I'd usually stop to talk to the boys who hung out on the stoop all summer long about the Knicks or the gunshots they'd heard the night before. (Obama, 1995, pp. 3–4)

Obama openly speaks of race during his college days. He and his roommate made fun of white people walking in the neighborhood.

> When the weather was good, my roommate and I might sit out on the fire escape to smoke cigarettes or . . . watch white people from the better neighborhoods nearby walk their dogs down our block to let the animals shit on our curbs—"Scoop the poop, you bastards!" my roommate would shout with impressive rage, and we'd laugh at the faces of both master and beast, grim and unapologetic as they hunkered down to do the deed. (Obama, 1995, p. 4)

Obama (1995) trusts his reader with his self-disclosures about his less than complementary reactions to white people during his college days and his fraternizations with mixed-race neighbors who used guns.

Openness: Relationship management openness is defined as an individual making an effort to be open about himself or herself to the public. In *Living History,* Hillary Clinton offers many examples of openness. One example is when Clinton cites getting fired from a fishing job in Alaska.

> Sliming fish in Valdez in a temporary salmon factory on a pier. My job required me to wear knee-high boots and stand in bloody boots in bloody water while removing guts from the salmon with a spoon. When I didn't slime fast enough, the superiors yelled at me to speed up. . . . I noticed that some of the fish looked bad. When I told the manager, he fired me and told me to come back the next afternoon to pick up my last check. When I showed up, the entire operation was gone. (Clinton, 2003, p. 43)

Clinton is also open about handling scandals and explaining why she has stayed with her husband after his infidelities.

> I'm often asked why Bill and I stay together. . . . What can I say to explain a love that has persisted for decades and has grown through our shared experiences of parenting a daughter, burying our parents, and tending our extended families, a lifetime's worth of friends, a common faith, and an abiding commitment to our country? All I know is that no one knows me better and no one can make me laugh the way Bill does. . . . Bill Clinton and I started a conversation in the spring of 1971, and more than thirty years later we are still talking. (Clinton, 2003, p. 75)

Obama (1995), as a teen, pictured himself as resentful and desperate to prove himself.

> I remember the days when I would have been sitting in a car like that, full of inarticulate resentments and desperate to prove my place in the world. The feelings of righteous anger as I shout at Gramps for some forgotten reason. The blood rush of a high school bawl. The swagger that carries me into a classroom drunk or high, knowing that my teachers will smell beer or reefer on my breath, just daring them to say something. (Obama, 1995, p. 270)

He also openly discusses what it means to be black.

> Mostly I kept quiet when these subjects [what it's like to be black] were broached, privately measuring my own degree of infection. But I noticed that such conversations rarely took place in large groups, and never in front of whites. Later, I would realize that the position of most black students in predominately white colleges was already too tenuous, our identities too scrambled, to admit to ourselves that our black pride remained incomplete. And to admit our doubt and confusion to whites, to open up our psyches to general examination by those who had caused so much of the damage in the first place, seemed ludicrous, itself an expression of self-hatred—for there seemed no reason to expect that whites would look at our private struggles as a mirror into their own souls rather than yet more evidence of black pathology. (Obama, 1995, p. 193)

Understanding. Crawley (2003) stated that people/readers want to understand candidates' views and want the candidates to clearly articulate their ideas and views. Self-identifying candidate views save the reader/voters costly time and money on research.

Hillary Clinton (2003) traveled from throughout the United States to China, Africa, Eastern Europe, and Latin America in 1997. She reported that this trip gave her a renewed reverence for the United States government and new ideas about how to put it to work for all citizens.

> Harriet Tubman is one of my heroines. A former slave, she escaped to freedom on the Underground Railroad and then courageously

> returned to the South time and again to lead other slaves to freedom.... [She] became a grassroots activist who raised money to school, clothe, and house newly freed black children.... She was a force unto herself and an inspiration to Americans of all races.... [She said] "If you are tired, keep going. If you are scared, keep going. If you are hungry, keep going. If you want a taste of freedom, keep going." (Clinton, 2003, p. 462)

The journey across the continents convinced Hillary Clinton to run for office.

> The emotional capstone of the tour was an event at the Women's Right's National Historical Park in Seneca Park, attended by sixteen thousand people. This marked the 150th anniversary of the campaign for women's suffrage.... I urged women to be guided into the future by the vision and wisdom of those who had gathered in Seneca Falls.... It was fitting that my spring and summer of discovery should end on this historic ground. I had witnessed the fragile bloom of democracy taking root in China, Africa, Eastern Europe, and Latin America. The drive for freedom in those countries was the same drive that made America.... Because so much blood has been shed for the right to vote here and all over the world, I have come to think of it as a secular sacrament. Choosing to run for elected office is a tribute to those who sacrificed for our equal right to vote for our leaders. I returned home with a renewed reverence for our flawed but vigorous system of government and new ideas about how to put it to work for all citizens. (Clinton, 2003, pp. 462–463)

Obama (1995) took a trip to Kenya to try to fill an emptiness he was feeling and comfort an anger he was nurturing.

> Kenyatta International Airport was almost empty.... I completed the form and Miss Omoro gave it the once-over before looking back at me. "You wouldn't be related to Dr. Obama, by any chance?" she asked. "Well, yes—he was my father." Miss Omoro smiled sympathetically. "I'm very sorry about his passing. Your father was a close friend of my family's . . ." For the first time in my life, I felt comfort, the firmness of identity that a name might provide, how it could carry an entire history in other people's memories.... My name belonged and so I belonged, drawn into a web of relationships, alliances, and grudges that I did not yet understand. (Obama, 1995, p. 305)

Obama (1995) reports feeling his father's presence in Kenya and begins to understand his father as a man, his father's way of life, and therefore his own roots.

> I see him [my father] in the school boys who run past us, their lean, black legs moving like piston rods between blue shorts and oversized shoes. I hear him in the laughter of the pair of university students who sip sweet, creamed tea, and eat samosas in a dimly lit teahouse. I smell him in the cigarette smoke of the businessman who covers one ear and shouts into a payphone; in the sweat of the day laborer who loads gravel into a wheelbarrow, his face and bare chest covered with dust. The old man's here, I think, although he doesn't say anything to me. He's here, asking me to understand. (Obama, 1995, p. 32)

Involvement. According to Ledingham and Bruning's (1998) relationship management theory, an involved candidate is one who strategically develops programs that communicate with internal and external publics and provide opportunities for the country and eliminate threats (Rhee, 2004, p. 17).

Hillary Clinton was involved as a First Lady. In fact, she was the first to have offices in the West Wing.

> My staff became known around the White House as "Hillaryland." We were fully immersed in the daily operations of the West Wing, but

> we were also our own little subculture within the White House. (Clinton, 2003, p. 133)

Health care was a special interest of Clinton's, so Bill asked Hillary to lead the health care charge.

> Bill [asked] that I lead the [health care costs] task force and work with Ira [Magaziner] on this signature initiative of his Administration.... The terrible cycle of escalating costs and declining coverage was largely the result of a growing number of uninsured Americans. Patients without insurance seldom could afford to pay for their medical expenses out-of-pocket, so their costs were absorbed by the doctors and hospitals that treated them. Doctors and hospitals, in turn raised their rates to cover the expenses of caring for patients who weren't covered or couldn't pay, which is why $2 aspirin tablets and $2,400 crutches sometimes appear on hospital bills. Insurers, confronted with having to cover higher doctor and hospital rates, began trimming coverage and raising the price of premiums, deductibles and co-payments for people with insurance. As the price of premiums went up, fewer employers were willing or able to provide coverage for their workers, so more people lost their insurance. (Clinton, 2003, pp. 144–145)

Clinton also decided to be involved with the State Department when asked.

> The State Department had asked me to go as an emissary to Bosnia-Herzegovina to reinforce the importance of the Dayton Peace Accords, which had been signed in November. Gains on the ground by the Croat-Muslim coalition that the United States had helped support, coupled with the NATO air strikes that Bill had advocated, finally forced the Serbs to negotiate a settlement. I was also scheduled to make stops at U.S. military bases in Germany and Italy and spend a week in Turkey and Greece, two important U.S. and NATO (North Atlantic Treaty Organization) allies that had a difficult, tense relationship over Cyprus and other unresolved issues. (Clinton, 2003, p. 341)

Obama (1995) decided to become involved by becoming a community organizer. He organized black people through a grassroots movement and began mobilizing the poor.

> In 1983, I decided to become a community organizer.... I'll organize black folks. At the grass roots. For change.... I can show how becoming an organizer was a part of that larger narrative, starting with my father and his father before him, my mother and her parents, my memories of Indonesia with its beggars and farmers. (p. 133)

He started his organizing efforts with the African American community.

> I saw the African American community becoming more than just the place where you'd been born or the house where you'd been raised. Through organizing, through shared sacrifice, membership had been earned. And because membership was earned—because this community I imagined was still in the making, built on the promise that the larger American community, black, white, and brown, could somehow redefine itself—I believed that it might, over time, admit the uniqueness of my own life. (Obama, 1995, pp. 134–135)

Commitment: Huang (1997) described relational management and commitment as the willingness to invest in the health and growth of a relationship. Readers/voters are seeking and expecting candidates to show commitment to the nation and public through their actions and ideas.

Hillary Clinton illustrated commitment through her ideas and her dedication to her country. Throughout her husband's impeachment trial, Hillary Clinton never doubted that she would prevail in the end. She was committed to her husband and that justice would prevail.

> Throughout the trial, I never doubted that we would prevail in the end. I was relying more on my faith every day. It reminded me of an old saying from Sunday school: Faith is like stepping off a cliff and expecting one of two outcomes—you will either land on solid ground or you will be taught to fly. (Clinton, 2003, p. 494)

Imaging a commitment to serving the people of the country, Clinton decided in 1999 to run for a Senate position representing New York. People questioned her as to why she would run for a seat from New York. She responded by saying,

> I think that's a very fair question, and I fully understand people raising it. And I think I have some real work to do to get out and listen and learn from the people of New York and demonstrate that what I'm for is maybe as important, if not more important, than where I'm from.
>
> A few minutes later, Senator Moynihan and I walked back to his farm house for brunch. . . . Soon I was on my way. (Clinton, 2003, p. 507)

Obama worked as a community organizer in Chicago, Illinois, in the Altgeld Gardens Public Housing Projects. In his autobiography, he imaged himself as moving toward the center of people's lives in Chicago as a community organizer.

> A dump—and a place to house poor blacks. Altgeld may have been unique in its physical isolation, but it shared with the city's other projects a common history: the dreams of reformers to build decent housing away from white neighborhoods, and prevented working families from living there; the use of the Chicago Housing Authority—the CHA—as a patronage trough; the subsequent mismanagement and neglect. . . . [E]verything about the Gardens seemed in a perpetual state of disrepair. Ceilings crumbled. Pipes burst. Toilets backed up. . . . [M]ost children in Altgeld grew up without ever having seen a garden. . . . I was there to meet some of our key leaders to talk about the problems in our organizing effort, and how we might get things back on track. (Obama, 1995, pp. 165–166)

The mayor allowed Obama to get things on the right track, but it could not just stop there, so he began spending time with the mothers who were raised by teenage mothers themselves.

> They [mothers] spoke without self-consciousness about pregnancy at fourteen or fifteen, the dropping out of school, the tenuous links to the fathers who slipped in and out of their lives. They told me about working the system, which involved mostly waiting; waiting to see the social worker, waiting to exchange to cash their welfare checks, waiting for the bus, . . . I would find myself fighting off the urge to gather up these girls and their babies in my arms. . . . My plans for the parents were simple . . . to improve the basic services in Altgeld—the toilets fixed, the heaters working, the windows repaired. (Obama, 1995, pp. 233–234)

Investing in constituents and voters is strategy that is remembered as commitment to the people.

Discussion

Bruning and Ledingham (2000) stated that "relationship management is a process of symbolic communication through messages and organizational behaviors to initiate, nurture, and maintain mutually beneficial organization-public relationships" (p. 87). Both Hillary Clinton and Barack Obama initiated, nurtured, and maintained mutually beneficial relationships with their readers (potential voters) by evoking a level of trust, commitment, involvement, openness, and understanding with and among them in each of their autobiographies as illustrated in each of the cited quotes.

The communication styles of the authors are different. Throughout the narratives used in this study, there is an elitist's tone to Clinton's writing. She used a top-down communication style. Due to her experience, she referred to the "White House" and foreign leaders by name. Clinton easily relayed anecdotes of the rich and famous and actually lived experiences that people are curious and envious of in a vicarious way. While Clinton demonstrated in the autobiography that she understood history, the workings of Washington, and the White House, she did not demonstrate an understanding of the voters' need of change (as evidenced by the outcome) during the campaign. When Hillary Clinton ponders her own historic presidential campaign, she will understand that the millennials took a woman's right and ability to be president for granted, not out of lack of appreciation for their elders or history, but because it is just so obvious to them that an alternative does not even exist.

Obama wrote his book in an egalitarian style. He used a bottom-up communication approach. He imaged himself as a grassroots type of advocate and communicator. He was a community organizer who went into a poor neighborhood in Chicago to improve it. He tried to understand the hardship of the rank and file and lived the everyday experience of those who struggle with life's simple necessities. He also visited Kenya to try to learn about his father. He came across as understanding the people and what they wanted.

If Hillary Clinton used this autobiography to help create her image for her presidential campaign, she made some misjudgments. This study revealed that Clinton misjudged the involvement and commitment of her constituents and voters. She relied on her experience, preparedness, and name (as a brand), when her voters were looking to her for change instead of the "old guard." Relationships with voters and constituents are fluid and dynamic. They need to be renewed and refreshed. Involvement of "new" blood is essential in a new campaign if a public relations image is to be effective. The old guard is not effective with the millennial generation. This is also a way to maintain trust in a relationship. Her constituents did not need to hear about the Washington insider, they needed to hear about the way in which she would transform Washington.

Hillary Clinton played the trust, involvement, openness, commitment, and understanding elements well in the sense that those who liked Bill Clinton thought that she would maintain a similar White House, because her initial strategic positioning was one of a Washington insider with insight, knowledge, and know-how.

Barack Obama took on the theme of change and the people went wild. He understood that Americans wanted a different style of government. They wanted new buzzwords, they wanted a new economy, and they wanted a difference. He emphasized the relational aspect of understanding.

Clinton had people on her team because she trusted them. Instead, she needed people who were more techno-savvy, millennia-savvy, and caucus-savvy. Obama had people who understand the proportional allocation of votes, the necessity of winning the caucus states, and the power of Internet fund-raising. CRM (Crawley, 2003) reasoned that leveraging technology optimizes the market and engages voters. Clinton's advisers relied on the old money and did not reach out effectively to the college-age voters for fund-raising. Understanding the current voter calls for understanding current technology and its myriad uses. Millennials disproportionately populate the Internet. Understanding and representing each of your publics images you as a candidate of all the people.

Super Tuesday was Clinton's destination. She believed that if she could beat Obama on that date, she would win. Early on, Clinton was not open to gearing up forces to go beyond Super Tuesday. Even though Clinton did campaign to the end, she was not prepared to do so from the beginning of her campaign. This proved to be a mistake. Obama understood from the beginning that he needed to be prepared to campaign until election day. Again, emphasis is on the relational element "understanding."

Obama imaged himself as the everyday person with everyday experiences. The voter who wanted this type of understanding in a political official voted for him, while the voter who wanted experience, preparedness, connections, trust, involvement, and commitment voted for Hillary Clinton.

This study showed that all five elements helped shape the public relations images of Hillary Clinton and Barack Obama. Most scholars believe that the critical component in relationship management is trust. However, for Obama, in the political sense, for the 2008 presidential campaign, the relational element "understanding" was the key.

References

Bernstein, C. (2007). *A woman in charge: The life of Hillary Clinton.* New York: Alfred Knopf.

Boyatzis, R. (1998). *Transforming qualitative information: Thematic analysis and code development.* Thousand Oaks, CA: Sage.

Broom, G. M., Casey, S., & Ritchey, J. (1997). Toward a concept and theory of organization-public relationships. *Journal of Public Relations Research, 9,* 83–98.

Bruning, S. D., & Ledingham, J. A. (1998). Organizational-public relationships and consumer satisfaction: The role of relationships in the satisfaction mix. *Communication Research Reports, 15*(2), 199–209.

Bruning, S. D., & Ledingham, J. A. (1999). Relationships between organizations and publics: Development of a multi-dimensional organization-public relationship scale. *Public Relations Review, 25*(2), 157–170.

Bruning, S. D., & Ledingham, J. A. (2000). Perceptions of relationships and evaluations of satisfaction: An exploration of interaction. *Public Relations Review, 26,* 85–95.

Clinton, H. R. (2003). *Living history.* New York: Simon & Schuster.

Crawley, P. (2003, March). *Relationship management for political communicators: Best practices for constituent relationship management.* Presented to the Politics Online Conference at George Washington University, Washington, DC.

Edwards, J. (2006). *Home: The blueprints of our lives.* New York: Collins.

Estrich, S. (2005). *The case for Hillary Clinton.* Los Angeles: Regan Books.

Gerth, J., & Van Natta, D. (2007). *Her way: The hopes and ambitions of Hillary Clinton.* New York: Little Brown.

Grunig, J. E. (1993). Image and substance: From symbolic to behavioral relationships. *Public Relations Review, 19*(2), 121–139.

Hon, L. C., & Grunig, J. E. (1999). *Guidelines for measuring relationships in public relations* (pp. 1–40). Gainesville, FL: Institute for Public Relations.

Huang, Y. H. (1997). *Public relations, organization-public relationships, and conflict management.* Unpublished doctoral dissertation, University of Maryland, College Park.

Ledingham, J. A., & Bruning, S. D. (1998). Relationship management in public relations: Dimensions of organization-public relationship. *Public Relations Review, 24,* 55–65.

Leichty, G., & Springton, J. (1993). Reconsidering public relations models. *Public Relations Review, 19*(4), 327–339.

Obama, B. (1995). *Dreams from my father: A story of race and inheritance.* New York: Three Rivers Press.

Rhee, Y. (2004). *The employee-public-organization chain in relationship management: A case study of a government organization.* Unpublished doctoral dissertation, University of Maryland, College Park.

CHAPTER 27

Activism 2.0

Michael F. Smith and Denise P. Ferguson

The price of liberty is eternal publicity.

—Seeger and Schwartz (1972, p. 472)

Between 2003 and 2008, Addyson, Ohio, was the scene of the Ohio Citizen Action Good Neighbor Campaign directed toward the Bayer/Lanxess Chemical Plant (Zoller, 2009). The plant had experienced several malfunctions, which had produced air and water emissions that exceeded the Environmental Protection Agency's standards, and neighbors complained of odors, alleged chemical emissions, and fear of illness. The plant was situated near an elementary school, which heightened parents' fears. An organizer from Ohio Citizen Action helped create a local organization, the Westside Action Group (WAG), to pressure Lanxess to improve its environmental performance. WAG petitioned the company to make changes, attempted to document neighbors' complaints, generated media coverage about the issue, and pressed state and federal environmental protection agencies to make a finding against the chemical manufacturer. The company itself had already established a Public Advisory Group to engage other local stakeholders; however, some Addyson citizens felt as if the company controlled too much of the agenda during the group's meetings. After nearly 5 years of meetings, trading accusations about motives and expertise, and pressure from both citizens and regulators, Lanxess invested more than $2 million in equipment upgrades to reduce emissions and avoid future malfunctions.

The Addyson case demonstrates the process by which an activist organization can elicit change on the part of an organization. However, the case illustrates other dimensions of the interplay between activists and corporations. The corporation had developed a conduit through which it could consult with its community, the Public Advisory Group—a common corporate mechanism for engaging with activists (Heath & Palenchar, 2009). WAG questioned the legitimacy of the advisory group, and the company questioned the ability of WAG to understand the science behind its emissions problem. The contest between the various groups included advocacy through the media but also moved from direct pressure to engagement through meetings to the lobbying of regulators by citizens' groups. This progression represented the interplay between activists' and the corporation's strategies as the issue evolved. As the citizens' group sought to influence the company's actions, it sought to gain power by marshaling expert information and the regulatory power of the Environmental Protection Agency. As Zoller (2009) noted, "Activists seek to build sources of legitimacy, power, and urgency that increase their likelihood of being heard by a corporation" (p. 94).

Despite a decade of activism research, represented by the case above and numerous other examples of activism, the role of activists in public relations scholarship and practice is still unclear and evolving. One line of scholarship suggests that activists are cocreators of the relationships between organizations and their publics, contributing to the development and resolution of issues and, ultimately, to social good. Heath (2006) and Heath and Waymer (2009) argued that "the dialogue of society is best when it helps organizations be more reflective and work for legitimacy; it voices perspectives to help society be more fully functional" (p. 201). Only when society experiences the engagement of activists in dialogue on issues are we likely to realize "the democratic exchange long championed as the essence of public relations" (p. 195). One important social role of activists and their organizations is to elevate a society's value standards, as environmental groups have pushed for higher environmental standards in the United States. A second common role or theme of activist organizations is "stressing the failure to live up to hallowed values" (p. 209).

Scholars continue to claim that activists challenge public relations managers in business and government to be better equipped to engage constructively (L. A. Grunig, 1992; Heath & Waymer, 2009). There also is a recognition that organizations, especially corporations, build alliances with activist groups for the appearance of concern and support for activists' issues and to appear socially responsible; however, these alliances are actually benefiting the corporation's interests and limiting the activist group's interference. In actuality, the corporation is "co-opting" the activist organization and is able to gather information and "know the enemy" (Coombs & Holladay, 2007, p. 11; Stauber & Rampton, 1995).

In this chapter, we review the progress that has been made in activism research since the publication of the previous edition of the *Handbook of Public Relations* in 2001. In some respects, the chapter's title is a little misleading, suggesting that we will focus on the development of the Internet and its impact on activism. While technology's influence has been more widely examined than it was a decade ago, our purpose is to summarize and extend the first version of our treatment of activism, reaffirming the role that public relations plays in activism, as well as exploring some conceptual terrain that has framed activist research and public relations scholarship more broadly.

Activist Public Relations: Two Key Purposes

In our previous work (M. F. Smith & Ferguson, 2001), we explored the theoretical explanations for the origins of activism, highlighted some of the strategies and tactics used by both activists and institutions, and sought to identify directions for future research. In the years since, much of the scholarship in public relations and activism has traced the use of activism in public relations throughout history, continuing in a postmodern, informational era, and explored the public relations goals of activist organizations and the means by which they pursue those goals. In this section, we review the recent understandings of these purposes and means and some of the research that has extended those lines of thought.

The arguments to move away from a corporate-centric view of public relations are stronger and being heard from increasing numbers of scholars (Coombs & Holladay, 2007, 2010; Heath, 2006; Heath & Waymer, 2009; Leitch & Neilson, 2001).

Recent scholars acknowledge that part of the historical evolution of public relations is connected to activism. Coombs and Holladay (2007) claimed that activists were practicing public relations before the existence of large corporations, and their efforts to be heard and press for change "spurred the growth of corporate public relations" (p. 75). Corporations viewed activists

> as barriers to overcome or challenges to meet, and helped create the "need" for modern public relations. If we shift the focus a bit, activism can be seen "as" modern public relations. In the 1960s activists utilized public relations to attract the attention of the corporate elite, developing and utilizing many of the modern tools of public relations. (p. 52)

The abolition and temperance movements, muckrakers, women's movements, and Saul Alinsky and the activists of the 1960s all are examples of activism directed toward corporate, governmental, and societal change. Heath and Waymer (2009) examined the "Fourth of July Address" by Frederick Douglass, whose famous abolitionist rhetoric illustrates "the role of activist organization in the issue dialogue that is a vital part of issues management" and that "force(s) responses by other organizations" (pp. 195–196).

> Anti-slavery groups lobbied; they created alliances to promote and oppose legislation.... They raised money and mobilized forces; they created and sustained speakers bureaus and publications. In short, they strategically created conflict or the conditions for conflict. They defined and pressed issues, created platforms of fact, and advocated enlightened policy. They engaged in media relations and community relations, as well as offering testimonials and providing data for the (re)formation of public opinion. (p. 200)

Coombs and Holladay (2007) described Alinsky's *Rules for Radicals* as "a public relations primer for activists with its focus on communication as a mechanism for influence" (p. 70). They claimed that although there was evidence for nearly 100 years that activists were public relations practitioners, it was "not until the mid-1990s that public relations researchers considered activists to be practicing public relations rather than simply posing an obstacle" (p. 53). Thinking of public relations and promotion only from the perspective of corporations or business interests ignores the reality that activist organizations and groups strategically use promotion to "call attention to, frame, and advocate" their issue(s), positions, and activities (Heath & Waymer, 2009, p. 195; Knight & Greenberg, 2002).

Activist organizations use public relations for two primary, interrelated purposes. The first is to rectify the conditions identified by the activist publics. For example, environmental groups pursue environmental issues; antiwar activists seek an end to an armed conflict. Generally, there are three sorts of goals activist organizations pursue: (1) to either elicit or resist change on the part of a target organization or, more broadly, an industry or field; (2) to seek public policy or regulatory changes that would, in turn, effect change in institutional or public behavior; or, most broadly, (3) to change social norms. Many activist organizations pursue all three outcomes (Coombs & Holladay, 2010). Heath and Waymer (2009) argued that "the typical rhetorical stance of activism challenges the status quo by demonstrating through assertion and proof the weakness or hypocrisy of the ideals on which the status quo operates" (p. 209). Activist organizations operate in the "tensions between what is and what ought to be" (Heath & Waymer, 2009, p. 201) or act in ways that violate what the activists believe would be more legitimate and socially responsible. This legitimacy gap (Sethi, 1977) can create the strain that motivates activists and leads them to execute strategies to get their messages out and push for change.

The second major goal of activist public relations is to maintain the organization(s) established to pursue the activists' purpose(s) or, more broadly, to sustain the movement. The principal purpose here is to secure ongoing support for the organization's goals in the form of followers, volunteers, and monetary donations.

These goals reflect the dual publics for which an activist organization must account. On the one hand, there are the targets of activists' advocacy efforts, or those organizations, legislators, regulators, or other publics that might help achieve their goals and resolve issues. On the other hand, there are the targets of their advocacy efforts and the publics that might follow them (Heath & Palenchar, 2009; Jiang & Ni, 2009). Activist organizations have their own publics with varying levels of awareness and involvement in the group's activities (Heath & Palenchar, 2009).

As is the case with much of the research and practice this past decade, there is a temptation to focus attention on the use of public relations tactics, especially the use of the Internet. We would contend that, from an activist's viewpoint, the Internet is a public relations tactic used to achieve the two primary goals identified earlier. There is no mistaking the impact of the Internet and other inexpensive forms of communication on activism—as well as on organizations of all kinds and the public relations field more broadly. It should be remembered, however, that activists have used a variety of tactics, not just the Internet, to achieve their goals. Since 2001, a great deal of the research on activism and public relations has investigated these two primary goals.

A number of studies have examined how activists use public relations to achieve their goals. These studies have primarily looked at public relations strategies, or the general approach to communicating to achieve a goal, and tactics, or the particular tools used in public relations, such as press releases, Web sites, and other computer-generated, technology-dependent techniques (Knight & Greenberg, 2002). Several of the studies in this area seek to refine the typologies of tactics used by activists and by institutions in responding to activism. Previous studies grouped activist tactics by their function, such as informational activities, meant to educate publics about issues, or legalistic activities, which seek solutions to issues through the courts or legislative/regulatory venues (Jackson, 1982). Zietsma and Winn (2008) categorized activist strategies as issue raising, issue suppressing, positioning, and solution seeking. Generally, scholars indicated that various strategies and tactics would be used depending on the status of an issue or the position in its life cycle (Crable & Vibbert, 1985; Heath & Palenchar, 2009). Thus, early in the life cycle of an issue, activists and institutions seek to frame the issue in terms that influence later discussion and resolution of the issue (Crable & Vibbert, 1985; Heath & Palenchar, 2009).

The typologies developed have been somewhat limited in that they viewed the process from either the activists' or the institutions' viewpoint. In addition, the typologies tend not to recognize the dynamic nature of issue engagement, the natural conflict that results when opposing viewpoints clash. More recent studies have sought to determine how tactics evolve as activists and institutions debate an issue (Murphy & Dee, 1992; Zietsma & Winn, 2008; Zoller, 2009). For example, den Hond, de Bakker, and de Haan (2008) examined the evolution of antisweatshop activism directed toward sports apparel manufacturers from 1998 through 2002. Framing the interaction between activists and the corporations as a chain of action and response, they examined how the conflict was initiated and escalated as the issue of foreign labor in the supply chain moved through its life cycle. Various activist organizations used different strategies, and target companies differed in their responses, yet the overall movement was from confrontation to the establishment of industry-wide certification standards. This study addresses a methodological need we will discuss later in the chapter.

In addition to general typologies of strategies used by activists to pursue action on their issues, recent research has focused on specific tactics activists use, particularly the Internet. As Coombs and Holladay (2007) pointed out, activists were early adopters of low-cost communication technology, long before "corporations realized their relevance and incorporated them into the mix of public relations and marketing communication" (p. 73). This is not too surprising, given the limited resources with which most activists work and their need to communicate their messages to members and issue-oriented stakeholders. Such Internet activism is sustained through a variety of communication tools and distribution outlets, and this ongoing attention shapes public thinking. To traditional public relations devices, such as news releases and public statements, are added public relations tools adapted to the Internet, such as Web pages, discussion groups, Listservs, and blogs (Coombs & Holladay, 2007; Bullert, 2000). Other more nontraditional tactics are made possible (e.g., blogs) and more effective (e.g., boycotts) by the Internet's ability to instantaneously communicate to an activist organization's constituents.

For example, the American Family Association (AFA) capitalized on Internet technology's ability to instantaneously and inexpensively communicate with members and followers of the organization when it mobilized thousands of people to pressure organizations to stop advertising on television programs that promote lifestyles and values that are in opposition to the AFA, and to boycott organizations that offered benefits to same-sex couples and donated money to homosexual organizations and events. The AFA developed the boycottford.com Web site, posting numerous documents "exposing and indicting Ford's pro-homosexual agenda" and links to Web sites that provide Ford's "gay-themed advertisements" (Coombs & Holladay, 2007, p. 72). Word of the boycottford.com Web site spread virally, and more than 700 Web sites had links to the AFA Web site within 3 days. This mobilization blitz was effective: Within 1 week, Ford dealers met with the AFA, and soon after, the AFA suspended its boycott. At the meeting, Ford was given a deadline for making changes related to the organization's concerns, or face another boycott. Other uses of Internet technology by the AFA included Listservs, discussion groups, and Weblogs. A number of activist Web sites feature media relations materials such as press releases, backgrounders, position papers, and multimedia material meant to tell the organization's story, frame its issue, and generate media coverage (Illia, 2003; Reber & Kim, 2006).

The second major function that public relations serves in activism is to maintain their organizations and their functions. As with other organizations, activist movements tend to move through various stages of development (Heath & Palenchar, 2009; Stewart, 1980). At each stage, the organization faces communication and organizational challenges (M. F. Smith, 2004). Heath and Palenchar (2009) identified five stages of activist organization development: strain, mobilization, confrontation, negotiation, and resolution (p. 179). The organizational and communication challenges facing activist groups are many, and these change as they move through the organization's developmental life cycle. Activist groups must recruit members, gather resources, and establish the organization as a legitimate advocate for an issue during the strain and mobilization stages.

As we noted in 2001, the organizational maintenance goal and functions of activism have not received as much research attention as have the efforts activists use to achieve their goals. Taylor, Kent, and White (2001) evaluated the Web sites of 100 environmental organizations for evidence of dialogic public relations variables and serendipitously discovered that activists' Web sites were targeted more to volunteers than to the media, suggesting that the Internet serves an important organizational maintenance function. While the relationship-building features of dialogue were not universally found in the Web sites, there was evidence to suggest that the sites sought to develop ongoing relationships with volunteers, such as encouraging return visits. Jiang and Ni (2009) explicated the strategies activists used to manage the twin goals of advocacy and maintenance. They suggested that funneling relevant, reliable information and clearly defining an organizational identity that embraces core followers are key ways in which activists maintain their organizations.

Implicit in much of this research is the acknowledgement that activism is a legitimate line of inquiry that can contribute to public relations theory building. Interestingly, conceptualizing about activism has been extended to a postmodern view of the public relations practitioner. Postmodern theorists suggest that "we should conceive of PR as being able to perform a broader ethical role within society, working to insure that disparate voices both outside and inside the organization are heard by the organization" (Coombs & Holladay, 2007, pp. 46–47). Such a postmodern approach calls for public relations practitioners not only to fulfill activist roles on behalf of their stakeholders (Berger, 2005) but also to enable those groups to become activists. Holtzhausen (2000) and Holtzhausen and Voto (2002) argued that public relations professionals who take a more activist role in their organizations demonstrate a more ethical public relations practice, acting as the "conscience" of the organization and "giving voice to those stakeholders who lack power in their relationships with the organization" (Coombs & Holladay, 2007, p. 47).

This line of research also responds to the call for approaches to public relations research that include publics and their efforts to communicate with and influence institutions (Karlberg, 1996; Leitch & Neilson, 2001). Research into activism reflects both the functional and cocreational perspectives in public relations research (Botan & Taylor, 2004). The interaction between activists and target organizations helps create and frame issues, while the focus on activist tactics presumes that communication serves an instrumental function in helping organizations achieve their goals and maintain their operations.

Our earlier work sought to describe various theoretical approaches that explained how activist organizations formed, the ways in which activists use public relations to attain their goals and maintain their organizations, and some of the ways in which corporations respond. While those concepts provide a basis for describing the interplay between activists and their target organizations, given the growing research and focus on activism's yet still unclear conclusions, we now explore a trio of concepts that deepen our understanding of activism as well as public relations broadly.

Emerging Key Concepts in Activism Research

The two goals of activism—goal attainment and organizational maintenance—have provided a fertile ground for public relations theory building, particularly around three interrelated concepts: issues, legitimacy, and power. These three concepts not only contribute to our understanding of activism but also contribute to public relations theory development and provide some guidance for understanding public relations' role in shaping civil society.

Issues

At the heart of activism research is the identification, development, and resolution of issues, and an issues management perspective dominates most scholarly work on activism. Botan and Taylor (2004) argued that "at the heart of issues management is a belief that organizations and publics can engage each other in ways that allow for one or both parties to change" (p. 654). The goal attainment function of activism clearly centers on issues, which tend to be either questions ready for decision (Jones & Chase, 1979), organizational decisions that create problematic conditions for publics (J. E. Grunig, 1989; J. E. Grunig & Hunt, 1984), or conditions to which people attach meaning and about which they create arguments (Crable & Vibbert, 1985). Activists "recognize issues earlier and package them to shape the interpretation of others" (Zietsma & Winn, 2008, p. 71). During the "strain" phase in the development of activism, the definition and framing of issues contributes to the interaction between activists and organizations (Heath & Palenchar, 2009; Jaques, 2004). Activists pursue a preferred resolution to an issue, which provides the first goal of activist public relations, the outcome desired by the organization.

However, issue communication is also essential to activist organization maintenance. The attractiveness of an issue, as well as an activist organization's approach to resolving that issue, helps attract followers and other resources and provides a framework for advocacy activities. For example, when an issue has reached a current stage, receiving media attention and generating interaction between an activist group and its target, activist organizations associated with the issue attract supporters and donations. However, once an issue reaches a dormant stage and appears resolved, resources for the activist organization tend to fall. Activist organizations must adjust to changes in their issue's life cycle, using communication strategies that convince members their issue (and the organization) is still salient (M. F. Smith, 1995). They must also adjust issue communication strategies in responses to counterstrategies employed by their target organizations or fields. Zietsma and Winn (2008), in a study that traced a 24-year-long conflict among a number of stakeholders and stakeseekers in British Columbia's forestry industry, claimed that activist organizations "build influence chains by linking issues to other groups that have resource control over important targets" (p. 69).

Legitimacy

The concept of legitimacy appears in a variety of ways in activism scholarship. Activists seeking to pursue their goals face a dual legitimacy challenge. On the one hand, they must establish the legitimacy of their own issues or social values. On the other hand, they must undermine the legitimacy of their target organization and/or the values it represents. One important step in the early stages of an issue's life cycle is establishing the issue's legitimacy, or acceptance of the issue by increasingly broader segments of the public (Crable & Vibbert, 1985). As noted before, issues provide the grounds for activist organizations' goals. Both activists and institutions marshal arguments and premises designed to legitimize their positions on issues and, indeed, the legitimacy of the issue itself.

Activists attempt to convince publics of the legitimacy of their issue by questioning the legitimacy of target organizations or industries. The legitimacy gap (Sethi, 1977) represents the perceived difference between an institution's performance and a society's expectations for right and proper performance. Nonprofit activism "is a crucial factor in the evolutionary history of issues management" as it "creates or builds on the legitimacy gap between the activists and the target organization, whether business, government, or other nonprofit" (Heath, 1997; Heath & Waymer, 2009, p. 196). This legitimacy gap, which requires the exigence of a solution, provides the "motivation" for activism and social movement and the "grounds" for the five stages of activism—strain, or stress, mobilization, confrontation, negotiation, and resolution—which are "the key elements of activism" (Heath & Waymer, 2009, p. 206). "This strain is the motive that attracts followers and sustains nonprofits in their efforts to correct what they target or frame as the evils of society" (p. 213), while "activist organizations employ the strategy of 'incremental erosion'... challeng[ing] the legitimacy of its target by chipping away at premises that are needed by the business to sustain its current means for generating revenue" (p. 197).

Activists and their targets perform a legitimacy dance, each questioning the other's issues, motives, and right to exist. Questioning activists' legitimacy has long been a corporate response strategy. Oliver (1991), for instance, suggested that one corporate response strategy is defiance, which involves ignoring explicit norms and values, challenging new requirements, and attacking the sources of institutional pressure. In post-9/11 America, corporations and other institutions have branded some activists "terrorists," a label that gained some legitimacy itself (Heath, 2008). While some activist groups, such as the Earth Liberation Front, have used violent acts to pursue their issues, the "terrorism" label has been used widely to brand other activist groups whose approaches were more benign. For example, the Maryland State Police department's antiterrorism unit conducted surveillance and used state troopers to infiltrate more than 60 activist groups in the state. The activist organizations that were infiltrated include Amnesty International, People for the Ethical Treatment of Animals, and a group advocating the construction of bicycle lanes in major cities (Rein & White, 2009). Similarly, New York City police attended the meetings of activist organizations across the United States, Canada, and Europe prior to the 2004 Republican National Convention (Dwyer, 2007), and some environmentalists have been labeled "ecoterrorists," despite engaging in acts of civil disobedience, not violence (R. K. Smith, 2008).

Power

Power, like legitimacy and issues, is a concept that helps explain the twin, mirror image roles that public relations plays in activism. Activist organizations and their targets attempt to influence each other through the use of power.

Activists claim that corporations exert a tremendous amount of power, which influences their interactions with activists. Indeed, Coombs and Holladay (2007) cited issues of power and marginalization as primary reasons for the "failure to treat activism as public relations" (p. 53). Corporations are presumed to have greater financial resources, which translates into greater ability to influence what issues are discussed and greater ability to purchase controlled media, such as issue advertising. Greater financial resources also allow corporations to engage in other means of influence, such as lobbying, campaign contributions, and legal fees associated with court challenges to activism.

Despite these resources, corporations have claimed that activists can leverage influence in a variety of ways. Corporate public relations practitioners claim that activists often win coverage from sympathetic media outlets (L. A. Grunig, 1992). Zietsma and Winn (2008) used the term *chains of influence* to describe the ways in which activist organizations link with others to exert influence. They also noted that often, activist efforts are directed not only at a target organization but at other stakeholders on which the target organization depends, such as suppliers or customers. In this way, activists seek to disrupt a resource on which a corporation depends. Spar and LaMure (2003) suggested that activists gain influence when they are able to have an impact on the perception of an organization's brand and its competitive position. They argued that activists "frequently target the otherwise positive image that a firm may have spent decades nurturing. The stronger and cleaner this image, ironically, the more enticing the target" (p. 84). Here, the relationship between power and legitimacy becomes clearer. As Heath (2008) argued, "Reputation is crafted and used to legitimize the person's or organization's ability to have and exert power" (p. 4). The ability to influence an opponent's reputation is a means of exerting influence.

Activists gain power to the extent to which they can mobilize resources, especially people and money. Ten people complaining about a corporation's actions may have little influence; 10,000 people writing to Congress or boycotting the organization's products might have more influence and perhaps effect change. The key challenge for activist groups is "how to move from the margin to claim the attention of organizational leadership" (Coombs & Holladay, 2007, p. 62). To get the attention of organizational decision makers requires activist leaders to manage mutually influential relationships between the activist group and its supporters and to encourage management to recognize that these stakeholders are gaining influence. Activist organizations rely on traditional public relations tactics to attract the attention and support necessary to achieve these goals; "the more people, especially high profile people, who support a cause the greater the perceived power of the activist group" (Coombs & Holladay, 2007, p. 62; Ryan, 1991), which explains why activists spend significant time in training their members in how to use the media and Internet to best reach and mobilize their supporters and get out their messages. Greenpeace is a model for other nongovernmental organizations (NGOs); it is one of the few NGOs "that have power based on their years of activity, strong organizational structure, and communication skills" (Coombs & Holladay, 2007, p. 59).

Clearly, many activist organizations lack the resources and skills necessary to exercise influence and power in their relationships with corporations, legislators, and government agencies. Some argue that activists have power equal to corporations and that they have greater access to public attention than do corporations (Coombs & Holladay, 2007). This claim of activist influence is attributed "to the news media being enamored with activists and having an anti-corporate bias in news reporting" (p. 54). But the majority of "societal structures, such as government policy-making and news sources, still favor organizations over activists. Activists must compete with a wide array of events and issues when trying to capture public attention" (p. 55).

Activist organizations can themselves attempt to recruit a sufficient number of people to their cause; however, more often they attempt to form coalitions with other organizations advocating for the same issue or for issues whose arguments rest on similar value premises. For example, the anti–nuclear weapons organization Sane/Freeze aligned itself with environmental organizations as the disposal of nuclear weapons material became current (M. F. Smith, 1995). Similarly, among the partners in the coalition on Smoking OR Health against R.J. Reynolds Company (Condit & Condit, 1992) were the American Heart Association, American Cancer Society, and medical researchers Alton Ochshner and Ernest Wynder, who "chipped away" at the "foundations of legitimacy that had sustained the industry's position on tobacco and health" (Heath & Waymer, 2009, p. 197).

One recognition of the use of alliances to reach the objective of influencing public policy is the Advocacy Coalition Framework (ACF; Sabatier & Jenkins-Smith, 1993). The premises and strategies the ACF uses to effect change are intriguingly similar to those found in activist literature and practice. The ACF assumes that stakeholders are "primarily motivated to convert their beliefs into actual policy and thereby seek allies to form advocacy coalitions to accomplish this objective" (p. 120). A basic premise of the ACF, as in the understanding of activism, is that individuals exercise their abilities and the right to free expression of their deeply held values by joining groups, or coalitions, made up of like-minded members for the purpose of effecting public policies that are compatible with their core beliefs (Ferguson, 1999).

Advocacy coalitions include actors (individuals and groups) of similar policy core beliefs who are committed to policy change and willing to execute activities directed toward those ends. Coalition actors must seek to convince other actors of "the soundness of their position concerning the problem and the consequences of one or more policy alternatives" (Sabatier & Jenkins-Smith, 1993, p. 45). In the ACF, there are five types of resources that enable advocacy coalitions to carry out their strategies and achieve their goals (Weible, 2007): access to legal authority to make policy, public opinion, information, mobilizable troops, and skillful leadership.

One study has integrated the ACF with communication theory. Paystrup (1993) examined the "not in my backyard" (NIMBY) response from Wyoming, Idaho, and Montana residents to plans to reintroduce the gray wolf into Yellowstone National Park as a rhetoric of risk, driving the selection of certain argumentative tactics. Paystrup used the ACF to inform the application of Burke's dramatistic method to analyze how the NIMBY advocacy coalition's rhetoric culturally constructed a risk assessment of wolves. We shall discuss additional ways in which application of the ACF may inform our understanding of activist organizations' alliances and activities directed toward reaching objectives related to public policy change.

Research Directions and Unmet Needs

In 2001, we argued that two interrelated needs existed in activism research: the need for longitudinal studies that focused on the interaction between activists and other organizations, and the need for greater methodological diversity in studying this interaction.

Since then, several studies have employed a longitudinal perspective in examining the interaction between activists and institutions. As noted earlier, Zietsma and Winn (2008) examined 24 years' worth of public documents and interviewed participants to analyze the evolution of public protests regarding clear-cutting of forests. Zoller's (2009) study of Addyson, Ohio, that began our chapter covered 5 years and used ethnography, media accounts, public documents, and interviews, while Walton (2009) analyzed the decade-long work of the Citizen's Council in Mississippi to resist efforts toward desegregation. While these scholars have not reached consensus on the dynamics that influence activist/organizational interaction, they provide useful models of the longitudinal studies required to make sense of social change.

The ACF is one type of analysis of stakeholder alliances and their activities directed at public policy change. It offers a mechanism to explain policy change over time (study of over at least a decade), and focuses on policy subsystems as the most useful units of analysis (Ellison, 1998; Jenkins-Smith & Sabatier, 1994; Jenkins-Smith, St. Clair, & Woods, 1991; Sabatier & Jenkins-Smith, 1993). According to the ACF, since "policy core beliefs are resistant to change and structure participation in advocacy coalitions, coalition membership is predicted to remain stable for a decade or more, extending its utility for a stakeholder analysis" (Zafonte & Sabatier, 2004, p. 99).

In addition to offering the possibility of answering our original call for longitudinal analysis of activist efforts and impact, and that of their alliances, the ACF extends the methodological diversity activism research requires to build theory and understanding. The longitudinal stakeholder analysis of the ACF combines multiple qualitative and quantitative methods. For example, when Weible (2007) tested the ACF by examining alliances and activities directed toward implementation of the Marine Life Protection Act (MLPA) in California, he used a variety of methods: interviewing stakeholders, which informed the creation of a survey; establishing a stakeholder advisory committee; and taking a snowball sample of additional stakeholders drawn from a list of 310 stakeholders, including environmentalists, professional boating and touring associations, commercial and recreational fishers, and local, state, and federal officials. Employing an ACF stakeholder analysis, or adapting useful elements for shorter-term or non-public-policy change analysis, may offer "a systematic evaluation of the different categorizations of stakeholder policy core beliefs, coalition membership, usable resources, and accessible venues" (Weible, 2007, p. 112).

Finally, we are encouraged to see that the interest in activism research has been integrated into the equally significant trend in international public relations scholarship. Just as traditional views of corporate public relations practice shift when situated in different international contexts, so too has the view of activism (Wakefield, 2008). Guiniven (2002) examined how national culture might shape the interaction between activists and organizations, while Weber, Rao, and Thomas (2009) traced how activism influenced corporate decision making in the German biotechnology industry. Notably, Sriramesh and Verčič's (2003) framework for understanding the development of global public relations, rooted in the excellence model, features activism as an important environmental variable shaping public relations practice. The second edition of the *Global Public Relations Handbook* (Sriramesh & Verčič, 2009) even features a separate chapter on activism; however, the authors take the traditional, narrow approach that views activism as shaping more legitimate corporate public relations practices (Kim & Sriramesh, 2009). Indeed, much of the chapter examines how society might shape activism (and, in turn, corporate public relations), rather than vice versa.

Clearly, the study of activism has animated public relations scholarship over the past decade.

However, the perspective that activism is a legitimate public relations practice, contributing to the marketplace of ideas essential to the development of a fully functioning society, has not been fully embraced by either scholars or practitioners. Even as scholars suggest that activism and socially responsible organizations go hand in hand (Bies, Bartunex, Fort, & Zald, 2007; Holtzhausen, 2007), some activists express skepticism of public relations' role in this interaction: "Show me an institution that doesn't profess abiding commitment to the progress and prosperity of the wretched of the earth and I'll show you an institution that hasn't paid its public relations bill" (Gitlin, 2003, p. 100). As in 2001, we conclude with the hope that "further research and methodological diversity will help researchers and practitioners understand the dynamic nature of activism and its influence on public relations practice and, ultimately, society itself" (M. F. Smith & Ferguson, 2001, p. 300).

References

Berger, B. K. (2005). Power over, power with, and power to relations: Critical reflections on public relations, the dominant coalition, and activism. *Journal of Public Relations Research, 17*(1), 5–28.

Bies, R. J., Bartunex, J. M., Fort, T. L., & Zald, M. N. (2007). Corporations as social change agents: Individual, interpersonal, institutional, and environmental dynamics. *Academy of Management Review, 32*(3), 788–793.

Botan, C. H., & Taylor, M. (2004, December). Public relations: State of the field. *Journal of Communication, December,* 645–661.

Bullert, B. J. (2000). Progressive public relations, sweatshops, and the net. *Political Communication, 17,* 403–407.

Condit, C., & Condit, D. (1991). Smoking OR health: Incremental erosion as a public interest group strategy. In E. L. Toth & R. L. Heath (Eds.), *Rhetorical and critical approaches to public relations* (pp. 241–256). Hillsdale, NJ: Lawrence Erlbaum.

Coombs, W. T., & Holladay, S. J. (2007). *It's not just PR: Public relations in society.* Malden, MA: Blackwell.

Coombs, W. T., & Holladay, S. J. (2010). *PR strategy and application: Managing influence.* Chichester, UK: Wiley-Blackwell.

Crable, R. E., & Vibbert, S. L. (1985). Managing issues and influencing public policy. *Public Relations Review, 11,* 3–16.

den Hond, F., de Bakker, F. G., & de Haan, P. (2008). The sequential patterning of tactics: Institutional activism in the global sports apparel industry, 1988–2002. *Conference on Environmental Governance and Democracy: Institutions, public participation and environmental sustainability.* New Haven, CT: Yale University Press.

Dwyer, J. (2007, March 25). City police spied broadly before GOP convention. *New York Times.* Retrieved December 10, 2009, from www.nytimes.com/2007/03/25/nyregion/25infiltrate.html

Ellison, B. (1998). The advocacy coalition framework and implementation of the Endangered Species Act: A case study in western water politics. *Policy Studies Journal, 26*(1), 11–29.

Ferguson, D. (1999). *Rhetorical public relations and issue management strategies of social movement orgnaizations: The communication of values and policy preferences.* Unpublished dissertation, Purdue University, West Lafayette, IN.

Gitlin, T. (2003). *Letters to a young activist.* New York: Basic Books.

Grunig, J. E. (1989). Sierra Club study shows who become activists. *Public Relations Review, 15*(3), 3–24.

Grunig, J. E., & Hunt, T. (1984). *Managing public relations.* Fort Worth, TX: Harcourt Brace.

Grunig, L. A. (1992). Activism: How it limits the effectiveness of organizations and how excellent public relations departments respond. In J. E. Grunig (Ed.), *Excellence in public relations and communication management* (pp. 503–530). Hillsdale, NJ: Lawrence Erlbaum.

Guiniven, J. E. (2002). Dealing with activism in Canada: An ideal cultural fit for the two-way symmetrical public relations model. *Public Relations Review, 28,* 393–402.

Heath, R. L. (1997). *Strategic issues management: Organizations and pubilc policy challenges.* Thousand Oaks, CA: Sage.

Heath, R. L. (2006). Onward into more fog: Thoughts on public relations' research directions. *Journal of Public Relations Research, 18*(2), 93–114.

Heath, R. L. (2008). Power resource management: Pushing buttons and building cases. In T. L. Hansen-Horn & B. D. Neff (Eds.), *Public relations: From theory to practice* (pp. 2–19). Boston: Pearson.

Heath, R. L., & Palenchar, M. J. (2009). *Strategic issues management: Organizations and public policy challenges* (2nd ed.). Thousand Oaks, CA: Sage.

Heath, R. L., & Waymer, D. (2009). Activist public relations and the paradox of the positive: A case study of Fredick Douglass' "Fourth of July Address." In R. L. Heath, E. L. Toth, & D. Waymer (Eds.), *Rhetorical and critical approaches to public relations* (2nd ed., pp. 195–215). New York: Routledge.

Holtzhausen, D. R. (2000). Postmodern values in public relations. *Journal of Public Relations Research, 12,* 93–114.

Holtzhausen, D. R. (2007). Activism. In E. L. Toth (Ed.), *The future of excellence in public relations and communication management* (pp. 357–380). Mahwah, NJ: Lawrence Erlbaum.

Holtzhausen, D. R., & Voto, R. (2002). Resistance from the margins: The postmodern public relations practitioner as organizational activist. *Journal of Public Relations Research, 14*(1), 57–84.

Illia, L. (2003). Passage to cyberactivism: How dynamics of activism change. *Journal of Public Affairs, 3*(4), 326–337.

Jackson, P. (1982). Tactics of confrontation. In J. S. Nagelschmid (Ed.), *The public affairs handbook* (pp. 211–220). New York: AMACOM.

Jaques, T. (2004). Issue definition: The neglected foundation of effective issue management. *Journal of Public Affairs, 4*(2), 191–200.

Jenkins-Smith, H., & Sabatier, P. (1994). Evaluating the advocacy coalition framework. *Journal of Public Policy, 14,* 175–203.

Jenkins-Smith, H., St. Clair, G., & Woods, B. (1991). Explaining change in policy subsystems: Analysis of coalition stability and defection over time. *American Journal of Political Science, 35*(4), 851–872.

Jiang, H., & Ni, L. (2009). Activists playing a dual role: Identities, organizational goals, and public relations activities. *Journal of Public Affairs, 9,* 288–300.

Jones, B. L., & Chase, H. W. (1979). Managing public policy issues. *Public Relations Review, 7,* 3–23.

Karlberg, M. (1996). Remembering the public in public relations research: From theoretical to operational symmetry. *Journal of Public Relations Research, 8*(4), 263–278.

Kim, J.-N., & Sriramesh, K. (2009). Activism and public relations. In K. Sriramesh & D. Verčič (Eds.), *The global public relations handbook: Theory, research, and practice* (2nd ed., pp. 85–104). New York: Routledge.

Knight, G., & Greenberg, J. (2002). Promotionalism and subpolitics. *Management Communication Quarterly, 15*(4), 541–570.

Leitch, S., & Neilson, D. (2001). Bringing publics into public relations: New theoretical frameworks for practice. In R. L. Heath (Ed.), *Handbook of public relations* (pp. 127–138). Thousand Oaks, CA: Sage.

Murphy, P., & Dee, J. (1992). Du Pont and Greenpeace: The dynamics of conflict between corporations and activist groups. *Journal of Public Relations Research, 4*(1), 3–20.

Oliver, C. (1991). Strategic responses to institutional processes. *Academy of Management Review, 16*(1), 145–179.

Paystrup, P. (1993). *The wolf at Yellowstone's door: Extending and applying the cultural approach to risk communication to an endangered species recovery plan controversy.* Unpublished dissertation, Purdue University, West Lafayette, IN.

Reber, B. H., & Kim, J. K. (2006). How activist groups use websites in media relations: An evaluation of online press rooms. *Journal of Public Relations Research, 18*(4), 313–333.

Rein, L., & White, J. (2009, January 4). More groups than thought monitored in police spying. *Washington Post.* Retrieved November 12, 2009, from www.washingtonpost.com/wp-dyn/content/article/2009/01/03/AR2009010301993.html?sid=ST2009010302013

Ryan, C. (1991). *Prime Time Activism.* Boston: South End Press.

Sabatier, P., & Jenkins-Smith, H. (1993). *Policy change and learning.* Boulder, CO: Westview Press.

Seeger, P., & Schwartz, J. M. (1972). *The incompleat folksinger.* New York: Simon & Schuster.

Sethi, S. J. (1977). *Advocacy advertising and large corporations: Social conflict, big business image, the news media, and public policy.* Lexington, MA: D. C. Heath.

Smith, M. F. (1995). Sane/freeze, issue status, and rhetorical diversification. In W. N. Elwood (Ed.), *Public relations inquiry as rhetorical criticism* (pp. 191–212). Westport, CT: Praeger.

Smith, M. F. (2004). Activism. In R. L. Heath (Ed.), *Encyclopedia of public relations.* Thousand Oaks, CA: Sage.

Smith, M. F., & Ferguson, D. P. (2001). Activism. In R. L. Heath (Ed.), *Handbook of public relations* (pp. 291–300). Thousand Oaks, CA: Sage.

Smith, R. K. (2008). Ecoterrorism: A critical analysis of the villification of radical environmental activists as terrorists. *Environmental Law, 38*(2), 537–576.

Spar, D. L., & LaMure, L. T. (2003). The power of activism: Assessing the power of NGOs on global business. *California Management Review, 45*(3), 78–101.

Sriramesh, K., & Verčič, D. (2009). *The global public relations handbook: Theory, research, and practice* (2nd ed.). New York: Routledge.

Stauber, J., & Rampton, S. (1995). *Toxic sludge is good for you: Lies, damned lies, and the public relations industry.* Monroe, ME: Courage Press.

Stewart, C. J. (1980). A functional approach to the rhetoric of social movements. *Central States Speech Journal, 30,* 298–305.

Taylor, M., Kent, M. L., & White, W. J. (2001). How activist organizations are using the Internet to build relationships. *Public Relations Review, 27,* 263–284.

Wakefield, R. I. (2008). Theory of international public relations, the Internet, and activism: A personal reflection. *Journal of Public Relations Research, 20,* 138–157.

Walton, L. R. (2009). Organizing resistance: The use of public relations by the Citizen's Council in Mississippi, 1954–1964. *Journalism History, 35*(1), 23–33.

Weber, K., Rao, H., & Thomas, L. G. (2009). From streets to suites: How the anti-biotech movement affected German pharmaceutical firms. *American Sociological Review, 74*(1), 106–127.

Weible, C. M. (2007). An advocacy coalition framework approach to stakeholder analysis: Understanding the political context of California Marine Protected Area Policy. *Journal of Public Administration Research and Theory, 17*(1), 95–117.

Zafonte, M., & Sabatier, P. (2004). Shared beliefs and imposed interdependencies as determinants of ally networks in overlapping subsystems. *Journal of Theoretical Politics, 10*(4), 473–505.

Zietsma, C., & Winn, M. I. (2008). Building chains and directing flows: Strategies and tactics of mutual influence in stakeholder conflicts. *Business and Society, 47*(1), 68–101.

Zoller, H. (2009). Narratives of corporate change: Public participation through environmental health activism, stakeholder dialogue, and regulation. In L. M. Harter, M. J. Dutta, & C. E. Cole (Eds.), *Communicating for social impact: Engaging communication theory, research, and pedagogy* (pp. 91–114). Cresskill, NJ: Hampton Press.

CHAPTER 28

Activism in the 20th and 21st Centuries

Pamela G. Bourland-Davis, William Thompson, and F. Erik Brooks

"Utilization of publicity and press agentry to promote causes, tout land ventures, and raise funds is older than the nation itself," wrote Cutlip (1995, p. 1). Introductory public relations textbooks, too, recognize cause-related groups or organizations as using publicity during the 19th century (Wilcox, Cameron, Ault, & Agee, 2003), and as being important in the development of public relations practices.

Historic treatments of public relations often identify early cause-related work under the auspices of precursors to public relations, as is evident in Cutlip's (1995) *Public Relations History: From the 17th to the 20th Century—The Antecedents.* From the American Revolution and ratification of the Constitution to political campaigns and even corporations recognizing a need to carry their messages to the public, Cutlip traced how communication techniques have been used to advocate causes throughout the history of the United States. He recognized that in the latter 19th century, "pressure groups" became more evident, using the example of the Anti-Saloon League. Cutlip noted the Sierra Club and its founder and president, John Muir, who incorporated highly successful communication efforts, which included authoring magazine articles, letters, and telegrams as well as public speaking to fulfill the group's goals in creating legislation to protect natural resources. Cutlip's final chapter in this text highlights the myriad social groups that emerged between 1866 and 1917, groups such as the Salvation Army (1880), the National Association for the Advancement of Colored People (1909), and the National Committee for the Prevention of Blindness (1915). This chapter asserts that the development of social groups, advocacy groups, or activist organizations follows attempts of organized groups of individuals attempting to redress power imbalances or unequal access to resources. The authors, using cases involving activist organizations, begin with the premise that conflict is not inherently bad and is a naturally occurring condition in social life and human communication (Wilmot & Hocker, 2007). Activist leaders, attempting to remedy disparities between groups and power resources, use conflict to their advantage and assume publicity roles in recognition that more equalized access to communication resources then could mobilize support for causes. In fact, Smith and Ferguson (2001) defined activist organizations as relying on public relations. The authors established criteria for activist groups: that activists are organized, that they have goals, and that they use communication to reach those goals.

These power struggles continue today; they may loom larger than a national concern, or can be very localized. The study of activist or cause-based groups will always be important wherever and whenever there is potential for conflict derived from differential access to resources. Thus, this chapter examines two early 20th-century activist groups, the National Association for the Advancement of Colored People (NAACP) and the International Labor Defense (ILD), specifically looking at the public relations methods (or antecedents of public relations work) incorporated for advocacy. Then, a contemporary application of cause-related advocacy will be presented, based on one author's personal counseling experience. These cases allow for introspection based on the use of public relations to provide an opportunity to equalize power resources and emerge, then, as legitimate applications of the profession. As such, the cases also allow us to consider the definitional foundations of public relations.

In using communication successfully, the activist organization has the capacity to change societal discourse. This is much as Heath (2000) and Henderson (2005) asserted, advocating as they do the use of rhetorical strategies in examining activist groups, especially in creating shared meaning between stakeholders (Henderson, 2005) and in emphasizing the need for a multiple stakeholder model (Heath, 2000). Dozier and Lauzen (2000) called attention to critical theory as an analytical framework for activist groups representing social movements.

Contemporary literature typically considers cause-related groups from a corporate point of view, or in terms of what organizations can do when confronted by such groups (Smith & Ferguson, 2001). Berger and Reber (2006), in *Gaining Influence in Public Relations*, also discussed how corporate practitioners can use pressure from activists and advocates to obtain bargaining within their organizations and ensure that their voices are heard by corporate leaders. Berger (2005) and particularly Holtzhausen (2000) and Holtzhausen and Voto (2002) have confronted these troubling questions of power differentials of franchised organizations and disenfranchised publics by arguing for internal activism. Each has argued that public relations practitioners can be a force for good by actively soliciting for ethical practice and less powerful publics. Berger (2005) classified these as sanctioned resistance (gaining more education, becoming more knowledgeable about internal political maneuvering, etc.) and unsanctioned resistance (whistle-blowing, leaks to the press about corporate actions, etc.).

Several cases of public relations and activist organizations have been forwarded that add to the discussion. Straughan (2004) addressed public relations activities of the NAACP during the early 1960s to mid-1960s, such as the sit-ins and marches. Perkins (2005) conducted an analysis of the NAACP's responses to the 2000 presidential election. Walton (2009) examined the use of public relations, between 1954 and 1964, by the Citizens' Council in Mississippi, a group advocating for maintaining segregation in public schools. Among other cases, Henderson (2005) looked at public activism in New Zealand, while McCown (2007) considered internal activism and public relations responses.

This chapter adds to these cases of activist organizations and their incorporation of public relations. To begin, the discussion starts with the NAACP's early years as an organization, specifically looking at the efforts from the lens of a public relations practitioner. That lens is then directed toward an interest group's legal arm, the ILD, and the Scottsboro case. The chapter then moves forward to the 21st century to a localized case of a union.

Social Movements and Activist Organizations

According to Dozier and Lauzen (2000),

> Social movements, such as abolitionism, involve broad shifts in attitudes, agendas, and behaviors of diverse peoples over extended periods of time. Despite emancipatory rhetoric that demands immediate change, social movements often bring about changes only slowly; at the same time, social movements can profoundly affect public policy and fundamentally alter and destroy institutions. (p. 13)

The African American community provides ample evidence of the long-term commitment needed to bring about and sustain change.

While the Boston Tea Party of 1773 is an oft-cited demonstration of U.S. activism, blacks had already held a few protests (Bennett, 1993). In 1644, the first legal protest in America occurred when 11 blacks petitioned for their freedom in New Netherlands, now New York. In 1688, the first formal protest against slavery was organized by Quakers in Germantown, Pennsylvania. In 1775, the first abolitionist society was organized in Philadelphia, Pennsylvania, followed in 1832 by Boston's New England Anti-Slavery Society and the American Anti-Slavery Society in 1833. In 1847, Frederick Douglass undertook what practitioners would recognize as formal communication activities by publishing the abolitionist newspaper *The North Star*. By the 1850s, abolitionists began assuming direct action tactics such as in two 1851 cases, when abolitionists invaded courtrooms to rescue fugitive slaves.

W. E. B. Du Bois, in *The Negro* (2005), chronicling the emergence of the National Association for the Advancement of Colored People in 1909, wrote that the NAACP "with its monthly organ, *The Crisis*, is now waging a nation-wide fight for justice to Negroes" (p. 227). As to its impact, he wrote,

> Instead of being led and defended by others, as in the past, American Negroes are gaining their own leaders, their own voices, their own ideals. Self-realization is thus coming slowly but surely to another of the world's great races, and they are to-day girding themselves to fight in the van of progress, not simply for their own rights as men, but for the ideals of the greater world in which they live; the emancipation of women, universal peace, democratic government, the socialization of wealth, and human brotherhood. (p. 231)

The NAACP was one venue through which African Americans could provide recognized leadership, and as a membership group, it provided a voice to many. At its start, the NAACP was an interracial and Northern-based group of highly educated individuals who believed that more aggressive actions were needed to obtain equal rights. The NAACP grew out of an earlier vanguard, the Niagara Movement, with a platform, formulated by Du Bois (1905), focusing on freedom of speech and criticism, freedom of the press, full manhood suffrage, and abolition of caste distinctions based on race and color. The NAACP adopted these goals and broader goals recognized in the name with the words "advancement" and "colored persons" deliberately chosen so that the organization could help people of color from any country (Lewis, 1993).

The NAACP fairly quickly moved to an organized group, representing a cause, and using communication (e.g., *The Crisis*), thus meeting the criteria established by Smith and Ferguson (2001). Central to the NAACP fitting the criteria for an activist group is W. E. B. Du Bois, whose work and correspondence (Aptheker, 1973) provides the base for examining the NAACP's early work. It would be difficult to talk about the NAACP's inception without including him: Du Bois served on the organization's board of directors, the goals adopted were largely based on his work with the Niagara Movement, and he served as editor of *The Crisis.* Although Du Bois has been accorded distinction primarily as a journalist (Sloan, 2008) rather than as an early public relations practitioner, his official title was Director of Research and Publicity. As such, it appears he is the first African American whose official job title focused on promoting an organization and its cause.

His title appeared to be a work in progress. According to Aptheker (1973),

> Symbolic of the nature and purpose of the projected NAACP was Du Bois's relationship to it. A struggle ensued among the sponsors of the 1909 meeting as to whether or not Du Bois was to be a permanent and full-time officer of the association, especially in the function he demanded—namely, the direction of research and propaganda. (p. 169)

In June of 1910, William English Walling, one of the NAACP cofounders, wrote to Du Bois, "I can reassure you that the whole effort and hope of our Committee is built almost exclusively on obtaining you as director of its investigations" (p. 169). Underscoring the importance of the research, Du Bois noted in a response to Walling, related to the position and its funding, that "no provision is made for research work, unless something is included under postage" (pp. 170–171).

Walling also noted,

> The moment is a critical one for your work and public activities; but such moments come in the lives of all, and there are certain risks which ought to be taken, both from our own personal standpoints and for the sake of the cause. (Aptheker, 1973, p. 169)

As is evident, Du Bois was no stranger to publicity work, referring, in his correspondence, to the concepts of publicity and propaganda. He had done much to raise funds for research support in his academic role at Atlanta University. He had been publisher and editor of two other publications, *The Moon* and *The Horizon*; the latter was affiliated with the Niagara Movement and would become *The Crisis* (Aptheker, 1973). His published research was also highly recognized.

Du Bois described *The Crisis,* an important communication tool, as follows: "It will record important happenings and movements in the world which bear on the great problem of interracial relations, and especially those which affect the Negro-American" (Moon, 1970, p. 2). Named after a popular poem, *The Present Crisis* by James Russell Lowell (Greene, 2002), its goals are described by Du Bois (Moon, 1970): "The object of this publication is to set forth those facts and arguments which show the danger of race prejudice, particularly as manifested today toward colored people" (p. 2). Du Bois's vision for *The Crisis* was that it would be a newspaper, serve as a review of opinion and literature, and stand "for the rights of men, irrespective of color or race, for the highest ideals of American democracy, and for reasonable but earnest and persistent attempts to gain these rights and realize these ideals" (Moon, 1970, p. 2).

Aptheker (1973) reported that the initial November 1910 publication had a circulation of 1,000, growing to 22,500 by April 1912. *The Crisis* itself supported typical goals of activist organizations by addressing the conditions serving as the impetus for the organization and then supporting organizational sustenance (Smith & Ferguson, 2001). A critical issue of the time was the practice of lynching. *The Crisis* included editorials, notes, and pictures or drawings to focus attention on how lynching supported hegemonic concerns. (The NAACP also worked to provide legal support for African Americans to try to eliminate this practice.) Other common themes and commentaries during Du Bois's editorship included women's suffrage, Negro suffrage, and Jim Crow laws (Dyja, 2008).

With many of the NAACP founders being educated in the arts and humanities, they believed that many whites were just uninformed about blacks and black culture, and relied on negative images pervading newspapers and film

(Chong, 1991). Specifically, they wanted to combat the negative race portrayals, which they thought could be accomplished through news, pamphlets, and *The Crisis.* Du Bois wanted to counteract the negative imagery by publishing in *The Crisis* works of black artists and writers. He also conducted studies rooted in sociology and politics and published the results in *The Crisis* in an attempt to show that blacks were not intellectually inferior to whites.

Du Bois's approach as editor is reflected in his 1914 letter to the new NAACP chair, Joel Spingarn, in which he noted that he saw *The Crisis* as very new with significant potential. He wrote,

> It can be a center of enterprise and co-operation such as black folk have not themselves dreamed. . . . What I am working for with the *Crisis* is to make the N.A.A.C.P. *possible.* Today it is *not* possible. . . . The men who will fight in these ranks must be educated and the *Crisis* can train them: not simply in its words, but in its manner, its pictures, its conception of life, its subsidiary enterprises. (Aptheker, 1973, p. 204)

Du Bois's work with *The Crisis* appears to have consumed much of his time in the area of the publicity part of his job title. Clearly, his reputation in social research was central to his invitation to join the NAACP staff. His 1915 publication of *The Negro* was described by Aptheker (1973) as "the first overall examination of the history of African and African-derived peoples" (p. 177). It was part of a series of the Home University Library, resulting from a request from the English editors for his contributions, to which Du Bois replied that a planned summer lecture series could be transformed into essays for the publication. Many of the period's thinkers and writers, including the likes of Upton Sinclair, would correspond with Du Bois concerning their appreciation for his work on this publication.

While Du Bois clearly served as an important voice for the NAACP, his time was not without confrontation with other NAACP members. Aptheker (1973) wrote that Du Bois, serving as the NAACP's public voice, was apparently too often a voice independent of and not in complete accord with "management." "One of the problems arose from the fact that Du Bois was, uniquely, both a member of the board and, in his position as director of research and publications, also its employee" (p. 181). Aptheker attributed the conflict in part to chauvinism of white board members and to possible conflict of interest with Villard, chair of the board, who was also an author and editor.

The confrontations appeared to lead to attempts to alter the organizational structure, putting the work of Du Bois under the organization's secretary. Du Bois wrote in 1914 (Aptheker, 1973), "In the proposed measures . . . the *Crisis* and its editor are put under the 'immediate' charge of the executive committee and absolutely barred from all real initiative. No other executive officer is thus humiliated" (p. 189). He added,

> To these *The Crisis* is a source of acute unrest and they want it changed in to a periodical which will say nothing that any person, or at least many persons can disagree with. They propose, therefore, to stifle all initiative of thought or action on my part and yet to use my name as editor. (p. 191)

Another lens for looking at the communication involved in an activist organization is Jackson's (1982) five tactical categories: (1) informational, (2) organizational, (3) symbolic, (4) legal, and (5) civic disobedience. A review of early NAACP activities finds numerous examples. Informational activities included *The Crisis,* editorials, letters to presidents and presidential candidates, speeches, and Du Bois's research in the form of publications. Symbolic activities were also evident, including the hiring of Du Bois, a graduate of Harvard and a recognized author, researcher, and professor from Atlanta University. Other symbolic activities included publishing in *The Crisis* photos of lynchings as well as of graduates of higher education. Du Bois was involved in event management work such as the 50th anniversary of the Emancipation Proclamation, to which he invited Robert Todd Lincoln as a guest of honor (Lincoln's son declined) (Aptheker, 1973). Organizing activities are also evident ranging from meetings and conferences to establishing local NAACP chapters. Early legal activities focused on providing representation for African Americans in judicial proceedings and organizing the group's National Legal Committee. Finally, civil disobedience included forming a picket line for the New York showing of *Birth of a Nation* (Dyja, 2008).

As is evident, this early 20th-century activist group certainly incorporated many public relations methods in its advocacy work, an advocacy centered on a social movement and significant conflict. The methods were true to the time period, although it is possible that Du Bois's background in research elevated the public relations work to another level. His seat at the management table may have been fraught with interpersonal conflict, but that and his independent advocacy puts his work as a practitioner well ahead of its time. Historically, then, the case of the NAACP and its director of research and publicity has allowed for examination of the public relations practitioner in the activist role, a role that challenged society, politics, business, and indeed the heart of America, and ultimately represented the disenfranchised.

The Communist Party, the ILD, and the Scottsboro Case

Interest groups, whether representing activist causes or corporate causes, attempt to shape policy and public opinion through direct and indirect lobbying (Sidlow & Henschen, 2002). Direct lobbying techniques include making personal contact with key legislators, providing expertise and research results for legislators, offering expert testimony before Congress, and providing legal advice. Indirect techniques include attempting to influence public policy indirectly through third parties or the general public, shaping public opinion, fighting in the courts, and holding demonstrations. While indirect techniques appear spontaneous, they are usually as well planned as direct techniques. They may include media publicity, advertisements, mass mailings, and the use of public relations techniques designed to cultivate the group's image. These direct and indirect methods were central to one of the most famous cases that showcased the power of an interest group to organize, intervene, and strike a blow against racial inequality—the Scottsboro Boys case.

In 1925, the Central Committee of the Communist Party of the United States formed the ILD. The ILD became the party's legal muscle, and the organization's goal was to provide legal and moral aid to people it considered victims of an ongoing class war. The ILD was a driving force in the defense of strikers and workers confronting labor injustices, foreign-born individuals faced with discrimination, and African Americans in the Deep South challenged by Jim Crow laws and discrimination. Around 1927, the organization began to take a more aggressive approach to challenging the system, subscribing to a more militant strategy that included direct action (Anker, 2005). ILD leadership believed that this new philosophy would lead to equality and would empower a working-class movement that could seize the methods of production. Also, the ILD believed that direct action would lead to equality and eliminate politically motivated and racist legal practices against the poor, immigrants, and African Americans. With that in mind, the group launched political protests and campaigns that included legal defense, as well as massive levels of publicity-garnering action. The scope and aggressiveness of ILD protests, however, often contrasted sharply with the less-combative methods of other civil rights groups such as the NAACP.

During the 1930s, the Scottsboro case brought the ILD center stage. The Scottsboro case began in 1931 after two white women on a freight train near Paint Rock, Alabama, accused nine African American men of rape. All were traveling on the freight train as vagrants and a fight occurred between the African American men and some whites also traveling on the train. The men were arrested, held in jail, and eight were sentenced to death at trial. The ILD protested that the men were tried without adequate access to counsel.

The ILD initiated a campaign to gain the men's freedom; however, this led to a turf battle with the NAACP for control of the case. As bitter rivals, the ILD and NAACP would battle for control of the legal defense and the support of African Americans for the duration of the case. The ILD recognized the case's potential to become a lightning rod for a national struggle against racism, as well as a powerful propaganda vehicle and recruitment tool for the Communist Party. As a result, a large number of African Americans began to affiliate with the Communist Party.

The ILD pursued the case through the conventional legal channels of state and federal courts of appeals. However, it did not believe that justice could be secured through the direct action of litigation alone. The ILD also used indirect methods resulting in a relentless media campaign with sponsored rallies and parades, and nationwide speaking tours designed to raise money for the defense and to expose the court of public opinion to the gross inequities in the Alabama justice system. ILD publicity efforts transformed the case from a local matter into an international spectacle. The ILD used publicity to help persuade the Alabama Supreme Court to review the case and block the defendants' immediate execution. The Alabama court received scores of letters from non-Communists, and black and white people from across the country who learned about the case through ILD promotional efforts (Feldman, 2004).

By the mid-1930s, the ILD had lost its appeal and turned to coalition building. In a tenuous alliance, the ILD, NAACP, and ACLU formed the Scottsboro Defense Committee (SDC), which opted for a more reformist, legally oriented campaign in lieu of mass tactics (Feldman, 2004). After failing to win the defendants' release in a 1936 trial, the SDC agreed to a divergent plea bargain in 1937, whereby four defendants were released and the remaining five endured lengthy prison sentences with the last defendant not being freed until 1950.

Although the ILD did not secure unconditional release, its campaign to "Free the Scottsboro Boys" had tremendous legal and political implications. In one of its legal actions, the ILD in 1935 intervened with the U.S. Supreme Court, securing a landmark ruling of constitutional rights being violated because blacks were systematically excluded from jury rolls. The ILD's major contributions challenged traditional liberalism and the politics of racial accommodation and popularized the tactics of "mass pressure," which became a mainstay for civil rights activity.

The roles of Du Bois in the NAACP and the ILD leaders in the Scottsboro Boys case are both revealing and potentially obscuring as to the relationship between public relations and activism. In both cases, activities we now define as public relations played a key role in the rise of public consciousness of formerly disenfranchised groups. But the massive historical importance accorded the gradual overthrow of blatant racial discrimination may obfuscate the central role activism plays in public relations practice today. The insights into public relations theory that we can gain from escaping the automatic acceptance of the corporate-style environment of public relations practice opens a window to the possibility of activism permeating more of public relations practice than is currently considered and reveals more about the potential power of public relations.

Contemporary Conflict and an Arts Union

As is evident, the need for representation, for a voice, applies to all those with causes represented by groups organizing and needing to communicate their positions, and the number of causes has not diminished over time. The reason for many groups, however, is far more localized, although always personalized.

According to the second author of this chapter, William Thompson, vast power differentials exist between the disenfranchised activist groups for which he works and the franchised corporate actors with which his clients vie for resources. The enfranchised groups have little need to actively seek a sharing of views because they feel that they have the capacity to impose their own. In this environment, according to Thompson, there is no relationship because there is no equality.

To illustrate this, Thompson offered a case study for which he served as lead consultant. An orchestra musicians' union with which Thompson had a long relationship was asked to renegotiate its contract during the second year of what had originally been intended as a 4-year agreement. The 67 musicians in the bargaining unit were told that the orchestra's management (whose board comprised 53 of the city's wealthiest and most socially prominent individuals) could not fulfill its payroll commitment in 26 days and would declare bankruptcy when it ran out of cash. In that process, the musicians' former contract would be vacated and a bankruptcy judge would impose a new, supposedly less generous, contract that would cut the musicians' $27,000 annual salary enough to allow the orchestra to emerge from its financial problems. But if the orchestra musicians would submit to a 21% pay cut immediately, the board had donors prepared to infuse the orchestra's accounts to avert its cash-flow problems.

The musicians hired a labor lawyer and Thompson. The lawyer advocated a strike to respond to the management's unwillingness to fulfill a contractual obligation. But after examining the orchestra's truly troubling financial projections, Thompson worried about the message of intransigence that a strike by the musicians would signal to the community.

Similarly, Thompson was concerned over the loss of control over the musicians' financial fate that would accompany a bankruptcy hearing. While the musicians might receive one or possibly two paychecks before the orchestra's management ran out of money, emerging from the bankruptcy process might take months. If they called a strike, the musicians would have to depend on a diminishing and finally disappearing union strike fund to sustain them and their families. If they allowed the orchestra to go into full bankruptcy, the musicians could only depend on unemployment payments.

Thompson suggested an entirely different idea to the musicians' governing committee and the musicians' lawyer. If the orchestra's management retained a positive balance in its bank account, it couldn't declare bankruptcy. And if the management couldn't declare bankruptcy, it would have no justifiable reason, at least in the short term, to escape from the contract that bound it to the musicians.

So Thompson proposed that if the musicians simply continued to play the rest of the season's concerts, but refused any pay until the orchestra's management fixed its finances, the musicians could gain time to find a solution to the problem and garner valuable community attention and respect that could be converted into financial support later.

In Thompson's mind, this proposal would give the musicians the time to assemble a working coalition of community members, assess the orchestra's financial situation more adroitly, and perhaps assemble the critical funding to fulfill the contract. From a public relations standpoint, it would provide a stark contrast between a group of musicians who were willing to work for nothing to keep the orchestra afloat and a group of the city's wealthiest and most influential citizens who were complacent enough about the institution's importance, and callous enough about the sanctity of a contract, to declare the organization bankrupt.

The governing committee for the musicians and then the musicians of the full orchestra agreed to undertake this unconventional strategy. The subsequent announcement of their willingness to continue to play out the season, even if not being paid, provided immediate benefits to the musicians, both strategically and from a public relations standpoint.

Strategically, as Thompson hoped, the maneuver effectively blocked the orchestra's management from declaring bankruptcy. While management could have insisted that its obligations overmatched potential revenues, Thompson perceived that management felt constrained from shutting down a community institution sustained by people working for free.

As Thompson hoped, the community's perception of the crisis swelled and support for the musicians was evident throughout the city. As their public relations counselor, Thompson prompted several front-page newspaper articles and television packages and citizens responded with numerous letters to the editor supporting the musicians.

And, while the overall approach emerged from economic and strategic considerations, Thompson often used press-agentry methods to solicit media coverage. In a most blatant example, Thompson suggested that the musicians apply for unemployment benefits while wearing their formal concert attire.

Similarly, Thompson used press-agentry methods to solve strategic problems and increase the pressure on management. Because Thompson knew that it would be critical to maintain health insurance coverage for all musicians and help sustain younger musicians who could not survive even a single lost paycheck, he had the orchestra's musicians establish a revolving loan fund that would cover such expenses. Soon media outlets were running stories on contributions to the welfare fund made by orchestra supporters, and by fund-raisers organized by teenagers studying classical music and even small children with lemonade stands.

Maneuvers on the media stage were delaying any precipitous action by the management against the musicians, but this was not achieved by any mutual communication between the parties, and battle lines between the sides likely hardened during this time. However, the delay in bankruptcy filing provided an opportunity to undertake a more detailed analysis of the orchestra's funding structure. When Thompson noticed anomalies between ecstatic annual announcements of record fund-raising increases by the city's united arts fund, and the fund's static appropriations to the orchestra (which was supposed to be its primary beneficiary), he examined 15 years of corporate and individual giving to the orchestra and the united arts fund.

During the first 7 of those 15 years, the united fund's appropriations to the orchestra rose at an 8.5% annual rate, almost the precise level of the fund's own additional revenue increases. But during the last 8 years of the period, while the united fund had an average 9.0% annual fund-raising increase, the fund's appropriation to the orchestra increased only 0.4% annually. Over those 8 years, the diminished allied arts fund's percentage distribution to the orchestra had transformed what would have been a $126,000 accumulated surplus into a $1.1 million accumulated deficit.

Armed with that information, the musicians were able to forge a tighter partnership with their formerly antagonistic management, who accompanied them for a presentation of their findings to the city's mayor. Simultaneously, a former orchestra united arts fund and orchestra board member who had resigned under testy circumstances had commissioned his own accountant to verify the musicians' financial analysis. He used his own standing as the former publisher of the metropolitan newspaper to highlight the disbursement disparity to the public in two articles he solicited from his former newspaper.

The final part of the puzzle came into place when the musicians extended their list of powerful partners to include unions representing the local public school teachers, auto workers, teamsters, and union workers at a major local appliance factory. Each of the unions vowed to place their members' payroll checkoffs for the united arts fund into an escrow account until the arts fund resolved the funding difficulties that prevented the orchestra musicians from being paid.

Within 24 hours, two major local corporations made a joint media announcement with the united arts fund in which they pledged themselves to a plan to liquidate the accumulated deficits of all the major local performing arts organizations. The orchestra musicians received all their back pay retroactively, and labor peace reigned again for a while.

Conclusion

This chapter has highlighted the need to examine some of the intellectual constrictions under which the public relations field operates when it predominantly envisions its practitioners as plying their trade in corporate environments. In particular, these cases emphasize areas for future research based on public relations as practiced in activism and on how public relations is taught.

First, if public relations practitioners truly believe that excellent public relations can be practiced only when public relations practitioners sit within the dominant coalition, these cases highlight instances in which central decision-making figures within activist groups may be individuals who, regardless of their titles, were still intimately involved in the organization's communication strategies. In fact, in many cases, the very "product" of an activist organization could be considered to be its messages, and the leaders of such organizations, from W. E. B. Du Bois to Margaret Sanger or Martin Luther King Jr., then become public relations practitioners in providing voices for their organizations and causes. The advocacy of a cause (or causes) appears to be so endemic to the organization that it becomes difficult to separate the work of the organization from the leaders and from public relations practices, thus reaffirming the need to analyze the rhetoric and symbols of the group.

A second issue is raised because each case, from different time periods and subsequently different media options, also highlights the dramatic relevance of information, of thoughtful analysis. Du Bois's title of Director of Research and Publicity and Thompson's economic analysis are intriguing examples of how a spot within the dominant coalition flows from a strategic vision and organizational knowledge, not just communication competency.

Third, the cases point to weaknesses in applying traditional public relations models to activist organizations. The examples shown here demonstrate that activist organizations are often more successful in graphically highlighting differences with the organizations with which they are competing for power resources. By developing situations in which perceptions of conflict are heightened (often through press-agentry tactics), activist organizations may gain more attention than if they had tried to collaborate in the face of evident power disparities. Consequently, the need for public action and resolve will be more firmly established. So while press-agentry tactics may be employed, they are employed with critical data secured through research. Interestingly, Du Bois's work at the NAACP was described by W. Burghart Turner with Joyce Moore Turner in the reprint of *The Negro* (Du Bois, 2005): "He was no longer just the scholar; he became the gladiator" (p. xii).

Finally, the activist cases cited illustrate the foreshortened view that we in the field, by our own allegiance to particular practice models, may be imposing on our students' education, their career choices, their leadership and promotion opportunities, and their ultimate role in participating in a democratic society. The oft-lamented failure of public relations practitioners to be admitted into the dominant coalitions of corporations appears counterbalanced by the refreshing instances in which activist groups are guided by individuals trained in or exhibiting high-level public relations skills. By restricting public relations roles and training our students within the narrow spectra of strategic orientations that we define as "normative" within the corporate environment, we not only limit their effectiveness to see other career possibilities in nonprofit or activist contexts but also unconsciously contribute to the continuance of the status quo by suggesting that the default position of excellent public relations entails abandoning many of the tactics that equalize power differentials between established powers within our society and disenfranchised groups. While an amoral framework of power does not certainly privilege an outcome favorable to disenfranchised groups, few would disagree that the working of a marginally democratic society depends on the perception that all society's groups have access to public debate.

Cutlip (1995) concluded his history of the antecedents of public relations, saying,

> Propagandist, press agent, public information officer, public relations or public affairs officer, political campaign specialists, trade association lobbyists—all are protected in our democratic system by the same First Amendment rights that journalists enjoy, enabling them to play a far more important opinion-making role than the public perceives, or than journalists . . . are willing to admit. (p. 283)

Ultimately, the precept that we as public relations practitioners will strive for consensus may be damaging to our most defensible and applaudable role in a democratic society. We cannot, through our educational methods or our philosophical foundations, institutionally tip the balance as honest brokers of information from which the polity can make a decision it perceives as in its best interest at the time.

References

Anker, D. (2005). Scottsboro: An American tragedy [DVD]. On *American experience series.* Alexandria, VA: PBS Home Video.

Aptheker, H. (1973). *The correspondence of W.E.B. Du Bois: Vol. 1. Selections, 1877–1934.* Amherst: University of Massachusetts Press. Retrieved August 19, 2009, from www.netlibrary.com

Bennett, L. (1993). *Before the Mayflower: A history of Black America.* Chicago: Penguin Books.

Berger, B. K. (2005). Power over, power with, and power to relations: Critical reflections on public relations, the dominant coalition, and activism. *Journal of Public Relations Research, 17*(1), 5–28.

Berger, B., & Reber, B. (2006). *Gaining influence in public relations.* Mahwah, NJ: Lawrence Erlbaum.

Chong, D. (1991). *Collective action and the civil rights movement.* Chicago: University of Chicago Press.

Cutlip, S. M. (1995). *Public relations history: From the 17th to the 20th century—The antecedents.* Hillsdale, NJ: Lawrence Erlbaum.

Dozier, D. M., & Lauzen, M. M. (2000). Liberating the intellectual domain from the practice: Public relations, activism, and the role of the scholar. *Journal of Public Relations Research, 12*(1), 3–22.

Du Bois, W. E. B. (1905, July). *A proposed platform for the conference at Buffalo for the Niagara Movement,* Buffalo, NY. Retrieved March 12, 2010, from www.library.umass.edu/spcoll/dubois/?page_id=896

Du Bois, W. E. B. (2005). *The Negro.* Baltimore: Black Classic Press.

Dyja, T. (2008). *Walter White: The dilemma of black identity in America.* Chicago: Ivan R. Dee.

Feldman, G. (2004). *Before Brown: Civil rights and white backlash in the Modern South.* Tuscaloosa: University of Alabama Press.

Greene, M. (2002). *Crisis born: NAACP. A history.* Peterborough, NH: Cobblestone.

Heath, R. L. (2000). A rhetorical perspective on the values of public relations: Crossroads and pathways toward concurrence. *Journal of Public Relations Research, 12*(1), 49–68.

Henderson, A. (2005). Activism in "paradise": Identity management in a public relations campaign against genetic engineering. *Journal of Public Relations Research, 17*(2), 117–137.

Holtzhausen, D. R. (2000). Postmodern values in public relations. *Journal of Public Relations Research, 12*(1), 93–114.

Holtzhausen, D. R., & Voto, R. (2002). Resistance from the margins: The postmodern public relations practitioner as organizational activist. *Journal of Public Relations Research, 14*(1), 57–84.

Jackson, P. (1982). Tactics of confrontation. In L. S. Nagelschmidt (Ed.), *The public affairs handbook* (pp. 211–220). New York: American Management Association.

Lewis, D. L. (1993). *W.E.B. Du Bois: Biography of a race, 1868–1919.* New York: Henry Holt.

McCown, N. (2007). The role of public relations with internal activists. *Journal of Public Relations Research, 19*(1), 47–68.

Moon, H. L. (1970). *History of The Crisis.* Retrieved March 23, 2010, from www.thecrisismagazine.com/TheCrisisHistory.html

Perkins, S. C. (2005). Un-presidented: A qualitative framing analysis of the NAACP's public relations response to the 2000 presidential election. *Public Relations Review, 31,* 63–71.

Sidlow, E., & Henschen, B. (2002). *America at odds.* Belmont, CA: Wadsworth/Thomson Learning.

Sloan, W. D. (2008). *The media in America.* Northport, AL: Vision Press.

Smith, M., & Ferguson, D. P. (2001). Activism. In R. Heath (Ed.), *Handbook of public relations* (pp. 291–300). Thousand Oaks, CA: Sage.

Straughan, D. M. (2004). "Lift every voice and sing": The public relations efforts of the NAACP, 1960–1965. *Public Relations Review, 30*(1), 49–60.

Walton, L. (2009). Organizing resistance: The use of public relations by the Citizens' Council in Mississippi, 1954–64. *Journalism History, 35*(1), 23–33.

Wilcox, D. L., Cameron, G. T., Ault, P. H., & Agee, W. K. (2003). *Public relations strategies and tactics.* Boston: Allyn & Bacon.

Wilmot, W. W., & Hocker, J. L. (2007). *Interpersonal conflict.* Boston: McGraw-Hill.

CHAPTER 29

Public Relations Practitioners and the Leadership Challenge

Bruce K. Berger and Juan Meng

Leaders are crucial to the success, image, and future of nations, organizations, and professions. Our own experiences instruct us that leaders touch our work and social lives in many ways. Leaders make important strategic decisions. They affect employee attitudes, beliefs, and performance. They shape organizational culture and communication climate and influence stakeholders' perceptions. Given the importance of leaders, it's not surprising that leadership research is pervasive. Two decades ago, Yukl (1989) claimed that research articles about leadership numbered in the thousands, and the pace of scholarship has continued. A recent search of Amazon.com yielded more than 28,000 book titles about leaders and leadership.

Broadly, this vast body of research suggests that leadership takes many forms, its definitions are myriad, its dynamics are complicated, and context counts. Leaders speak and act in specific situations, within distinct organizational cultures, and are embedded in networks of relationships with followers and stakeholders. They also bring varying sets of skills, traits, styles, beliefs, and experiences to the task.

Leaders in public relations also are vital to the profession's success, image, and future (Berger & Reber, 2006). Communication is growing in strategic importance for organizations due to increasing global competition and the rapid diffusion of new information and communication technologies (Meng, 2009). Public relations practice also is now considered by many to be a valuable management function that helps organizations achieve their goals in a dynamic environment.

Few research studies, however, have directly explored leadership in the field. The purpose of this chapter is to do that and to begin what we hope will be a national dialogue about leadership in public relations or what we refer to as the "leadership challenge." We believe that many issues in the profession today are leadership issues, for example, ethical dilemmas, employee trust and engagement challenges, and increasing demands from stakeholders for greater transparency and social responsibility. Yet we face a knowledge gap in understanding the dimensions and dynamics of what we call "excellent leadership" in practice. To address this challenge, we do the following:

- Briefly review the landscape of leadership research and summarize a handful of indirect studies of leadership in the public relations literature.
- Present a meta-analysis of 16 recent leadership studies initiated or supported by the Plank Center for Leadership in Public Relations. We use these and the indirect studies to (a) make four broad observations about leadership in the field, (b) define the construct of "excellent leadership" in public relations, and (c) propose a normative theory of public relations leadership based on nine principles of excellent leaders.
- Suggest ideas for converting our emerging knowledge of leadership into actions in professional practice and educational exercises in the classroom.

The Large and Shifting Field of Leadership Studies

The study of leadership rivals in age the emergence of civilization (Bass, 1997), and over the centuries, the effort was focused on identifying what leaders did and why they did it. Only in the past century have theories of leadership emerged that are more narrowly focused on specific dimensions of leadership. These different perspectives have contributed to a growing body of knowledge, though one marked by widespread disagreements about the definition of leadership. As Bass (1997) noted,

> Leadership has been conceived as the focus of group processes, as a matter of personality, as a matter of inducing compliance, as the exercise of influence, as particular behaviors, as a form of persuasion, as a power relation, as an instrument to achieve goals, as an effect of interaction, as differentiated role, as initiation of structure, and as many combinations of these definitions. (p. 17)

Researchers do agree, however, that leadership is a "complex multifaceted phenomenon" (Yukl, 1989, p. 253). This is reflected in the broad range of leadership studies in the past century (Northouse, 2007), which have viewed leadership primarily as a set of traits and characteristics (1920s); particular styles and behaviors (1940s); a mix of technical, human, and conceptual skills (1950s); effective teamwork and direction (1960s); contingent and situational (1970s); transactional or transformational (1970–1980s); and authentic in nature (1990s).

Each of these areas of study still attracts research attention, but given the vast size of the corresponding literature, we do not review them here. We do, however, briefly examine transformational leadership theories, which are the most widespread and influential theories today, given their dynamic qualities and the combination of rational and affective dimensions (Northouse, 2007).

Transformational and Charismatic Leadership

Research of the late 1970s and early 1980s signaled a shift toward charismatic and transformational theories (Northouse, 2007). Unlike traditional leadership theories, which emphasized rational processes, the new approaches focused more on affective dimensions, for example, emotions, values, ethics, and long-term relationships, as well as followers' motives, needs, and satisfaction (e.g., Bass, 1985; Conger, 1999; Conger & Kanungo, 1987; House, 1977). These theories also combine leadership traits, power, behaviors, and situational variables in a dynamic model, as opposed to earlier linear models. In addition, charismatic and transformational leaders articulate a vision of the future that can be shared by subordinates. In these and other ways, transformational leaders elevate the interests of followers, generate awareness and acceptance among the followers of the organization's mission, and motivate followers to go beyond self-interests for the good of the organization (e.g., Bass, 1985; Beyer, 1999; Conger, 1999; House, 1977).

Conger and Kanungo (1987) suggested that charisma is an attributional phenomenon: Followers ascribe charismatic qualities to a leader based on their observations of the leader's behavior. Leaders who make self-sacrifices, take personal risks, and are willing to incur high costs to achieve a shared vision will more likely be perceived as charismatic by their subordinates. Bass (1985) suggested that transformational leaders focus on developing followers to their full potential—that is, they transform followers by making them more aware of the importance and values of task outcomes and by activating their higher-order needs.

Transformational leaders, then, help create an environment of trust and serve as role models (Bass, 1985, 1990). They influence the beliefs, values, behaviors, and success of organizational members (Sosik, Godshalk, & Yammarino, 2004). Indeed, they bear a responsibility to model desired behaviors for the benefit of the organization and those they supervise: "Leaders model the standards, the climate and the expectations of the organization" (Scarnati, 2002, p. 181).

Perspectives on Leadership in the Public Relations Literature

Though few studies in public relations have directly explored leaders and the practice of leadership (Aldoory & Toth, 2004), the concept of leadership is implicit in several theoretical perspectives in the field. Some scholars also have recognized the importance of applying leadership skills to enhance practice, develop practitioners, and help them participate successfully in strategic decision-making arenas (e.g., Berger & Reber, 2006; Berger, Reber, & Heyman, 2007; L. A. Grunig, Grunig, & Dozier, 2002; Werder & Holtzhausen, 2009).

Excellence and Role Theories

One of the most comprehensive research projects in the field, the International Association of Business Communicators (IABC) Excellence Study, identified the key characteristics of excellence in public relations as general principles (J. E. Grunig, 1992; L. A. Grunig et al., 2002; S. Lee & Evatt, 2005). The well-known principles reflect characteristics and values that a public relations unit could (and should) have at the program, departmental, organizational, and economic levels. We can also view the principles as a conceptual framework for leadership. Applying some of the generic principles to leadership, for example, we might conclude that (a) public relations leaders should be involved in strategic management of the organization, (b) senior public relations executives should be empowered as members of the dominant coalition, (c) public relations leaders should possess a managerial worldview and professional knowledge and experience, and (d) public relations leaders should use and model two-way communication (Broom & Dozier, 1986; Dozier & Broom, 1995; J. E. Grunig, 1992).

Excellence theorists also concluded that an organization's structure and culture influence the role and effectiveness of public relations. They advocated for a "culture for communication," which is characterized by a participative work environment, a symmetrical system of internal communication, and equal opportunities (L. A. Grunig et al., 2002).

Contingency Theory

Cameron and colleagues (e.g., Cameron, Cropp, & Reber, 2001; Reber & Cameron, 2003; Shin, Cameron, & Cropp, 2006) developed contingency theory, which focuses on strategic and conflicted relationships between an organization and its publics. Public relations leaders help strategically manage their organizations by making choices based on issues and actors in the external environment. These choices fall within an organization-public relationship continuum that ranges from pure advocacy to pure accommodation. Public relations may be accommodative in one situation but adversarial in another. This view suggests that public relations leaders must be able to assess external threats and opportunities, choose the right position on the continuum, and advocate effectively for their choices with organizational leaders. Presumably, such approaches might reflect a situational theory of leadership (Waller, Smith, & Warnock, 1989), where leaders also change and adapt their style, depending on the environment and circumstances.

Power Relations Theory

Berger and Reber (2006) explored how power can make public relations units more active, effective, and ethical in organizational decision making. They claimed that public relations is inherently political and argued that "individual professionals can increase their influence if they become more politically astute, employ more diverse influence resources and tactics, and exert greater political will in organizational arenas where decisions are shaped through power relations" (p. 2). Berger et al. (2007) further explored factors that help public relations leaders achieve professional success and maintain their leadership positions. They found a complex set of factors and patterns linked to success, including communication and rhetorical skills; diverse experiences and assignments; a proactive nature; and strong relationship building, networking, and interpersonal skills.

Leadership Styles and Gender

Aldoory (1998) interviewed female leaders in public relations to examine their language and leadership style. She found that they exhibited transformational and interactive styles of leadership, grounded in a situational context. Aldoory and Toth (2004) conducted one of the few studies that focused directly on leadership in the field. They examined which leadership styles are the most effective for public relations and how leadership perceptions vary by gender. They found that practitioners strongly favored the transformational leadership style over the transactional style. Overall, the survey revealed few differences between female and male participants and their preference for style. Focus group participants in the research project, however, expressed preference for the situational leadership style in addition to the transformational style. They also generally agreed that women had fewer opportunities for leadership positions in public relations, though they believed that women made better leaders due to their perceived empathy and collaborative efforts.

In short, previous research in public relations suggests, often indirectly, that leaders are crucial to (a) increasing the value of public relations, (b) achieving effectiveness in and for organizations, and (c) helping organizations make good strategic choices and do the right thing. In addition, principles of excellence in public relations practice appear linked with some qualities of excellent leaders, for example, participation in dominant coalitions, possession of a managerial worldview, and use of transformational leadership style and two-way communication.

The Plank Center Studies

These perspectives have been supplemented in the past few years by a number of research projects initiated or supported by the Plank Center for Leadership in Public Relations at the University of Alabama. The Center seeks to recognize and help develop outstanding leaders and role models in public relations practice and education, and it does so through awards, scholarships, speaker programs, research grants, publications, video interviews with leaders, and other approaches. In one important initiative, the Center has set out to help build a research-based foundation of knowledge regarding leadership in the field. To date, 16 leadership studies have been carried out, and they are beginning to shed light on public relations leadership in a number of areas, such as the following:

- The construct of "excellent leadership" in public relations and its corresponding qualities and dimensions of excellent leaders (Berger, 2008; Berger et al., 2007; Choi & Choi, 2008; Jin, 2009; Meng, 2009; Meng, Berger, Gower, & Heyman, 2009; Meng & Heyman, 2009)
- Leadership styles and practitioner preferences (Jin, 2009; Werder & Holtzhausen, 2009) and the influence of role models and mentors on leadership beliefs and values (Berger, Meng, & Heyman, 2009)
- Leadership education in university public relations programs (Erzikova & Berger, 2009a) and students' perceptions of leadership in the field (Erzikova & Berger, 2009b)
- The pivotal role of ethics in leadership (Kang, 2009; Kang & Berger, 2009a; S.-T. Lee & Cheng, 2008)
- The influences of organizational conditions (Kang & Berger, 2009a) and the type of organization (Liu & Horsley, 2009) on leadership styles and practices

For this chapter, we completed a meta-analysis of the 16 studies to locate recurring themes or patterns. The studies employed surveys, interviews, and focus groups with public relations practitioners, educators, and students largely in the United States, though some research was conducted in Europe and in Singapore too. We also drew from previous studies in the public relations literature, described above. Glass (1976) first used the term *meta-analysis* to refer to statistical analysis of the findings from a large body of research studies to integrate those findings. We didn't conduct statistical analysis of the 16 studies; rather, we examined findings in the studies to determine if there were recurring themes and patterns that might reflect principles of excellent leaders.

Our analysis yielded four broad observations about leadership in public relations and suggested nine qualities of excellent leaders. We first describe the four observations, which provide a framework for thinking about leadership in the field. We then define the construct of "excellent leadership" in public relations and outline a normative theory of such leadership. We express the nine qualities of leadership as principles of excellence for leaders. We acknowledge that this is a preliminary and incomplete theoretical framework, but we propose it nevertheless to stimulate greater discussion and research about this important topic.

Four Observations About Leadership in the Field

1. Comprehensive research by Meng and colleagues suggests that excellent leadership in public relations is a complex mix of at least six interrelated dimensions: self-dynamics, team collaboration, ethical orientation, relationship-building skills, strategic decision-making capability, and communication knowledge and expertise (Meng, 2009; Meng et al., 2009; Meng & Heyman, 2009). The key factor structure and patterns of the research indicate that all six dimensions are largely complementary and related in a meaningful way: None of the six dimensions alone was of significantly greater weight than the others (see Figure 29.1 for the conceptual measurement model of public relations leadership). This research suggests that public relations leadership should not be seen as an isolated perspective, but rather, it should be seen and developed in a comprehensive and balanced manner.

Testing and validating the six dimensions provides a foundation to develop a theoretical framework for excellent leadership in public relations. As Yukl (1989) suggested, leadership, and its content, use, and role within organizations, is complex, and these six dimensions may represent the core of leadership in the field. Through integration of the dimensions, public relations leaders may be able to embed organizational knowledge through the development of specific and strategic routines designed to manage knowledge and leverage perceptions of public relations values in the organization.

Figure 29.1 A Multilevel Measurement Model of Excellent Leadership in Public Relations (Theoretical Model)

2. Survey research suggests that leadership in public relations may be different from other professions in two primary ways: (1) Public relations leaders must possess a compelling vision for what public relations can be and how it connects organizations with publics and the larger social system, and (2) public relations leaders must possess a complex communication skill set and knowledge of media and new technologies and information systems. However, diverse practitioners in three survey samples were nearly perfectly divided on whether leadership is different in public relations versus other professions (Erzikova & Berger, 2009b; Meng, 2009; Meng et al., 2009). Younger practitioners and students appear to believe in this difference to a greater extent than do older professionals (Erzikova & Berger, 2009b; Meng, 2009).

3. Female and male professionals and practitioners at diverse organizations, large and small, in the United States share more or less similar perceptions about excellence in public relations leadership (Berger et al., 2007; Meng, 2009; Meng et al., 2009). One exception is that women and professionals working in agencies and large public relations units rate the vision dimension of leadership significantly higher than do men and those professionals working in private corporations and small units. A more limited international survey sample (n = 101) and in-depth interviews with 19 professionals in London and Singapore provided results similar to those in the United States.

These results are largely consistent with the findings of Aldoory and Toth (2004), who found that professional women and men both strongly preferred a transformational leadership style. However, in related focus group research, professional women were seen to have fewer opportunities than men for leadership positions due to various social, structural, and environmental factors.

4. Organizational culture and structure exert great influence on the extent to which public relations leadership can be excellent and effective (J. E. Grunig, 1992; L. A. Grunig et al., 2002; Kang & Berger, 2009b; Liu & Horsley, 2009; Meng, 2009). This influence is greatest in two ways: the extent to which (1) top management supports ethics and models ethical behaviors and (2) an open and participative communication system is present (Kang, 2009; Kang & Berger, 2009b). Interviews with international practitioners suggested that, in a rapidly changing environment, deeply rooted cultural values and practices may be even more powerful at the organizational level than at the societal level (Meng, 2009).

At the same time, public relations leaders can push back on culture and structure: They can be agents for changing how things get done, who participates, and how people feel about their organizations (Berger & Reber, 2006; Choi & Choi, 2008). Leaders directly affect organizational climate through their styles, values, attributes, and actions. Climate refers to the "feel of an organization," or the current attitudes, perceptions, and beliefs about the organization shared by its members (Clark, 1997).

Excellent Leadership in Public Relations: Construct and Theoretical Framework

Based on the analysis of the public relations leadership studies, we propose that *excellent leadership in public relations is a dynamic process that encompasses a complex mix of individual skills and personal attributes, values, and behaviors that consistently produce ethical and effective communication practice. Such practice fuels and guides successful communication teams, helps organizations achieve their goals, and legitimizes organizations in society.*

This definition of leadership, unlike those in most previous work, integrates skills, attributes, styles, and behaviors. As Northouse (2007) and others have suggested, many traditional approaches are more limited in scope. Using the conceptual measurement model (Figure 29.1) developed by Meng (2009), we argue that excellent leadership is a complex and dynamic process. It combines and draws on the six crucial dimensions mentioned earlier (Meng, 2009).

These six dimensions, interrelated and complementary, represent the core of excellent leadership in public relations, which produces positive outcomes at the team, organizational, and societal levels. The extent to which public relations leaders can be excellent and effective is also influenced by other factors, notably organizational culture, structure, and external environment. To date, this model has been tested and validated through three surveys (n = 562) of diverse practitioner samples in the United States, one survey (n = 101) with practitioners in Europe and Singapore, and depth interviews with 19 practitioners in London and Singapore.

In pursuing the construct of excellent leadership in public relations—what people evaluate as excellence—we are seeking to learn what excellent leaders do, or what they ought to be like. This represents a normative theoretical framework, which we believe is an appropriate approach to leadership theory development, because the most important evaluations of leaders' qualities and values occur in the minds of followers. They determine the relative strengths, weaknesses, and success of leaders based on behaviors they observe and what they believe to be the best or most appropriate values and behaviors (Clark, 1997).

Nine Principles of Excellent Leadership in Public Relations

Based on this construct and our meta-analysis of the studies, we propose nine principles for excellence in leadership in the field. Each principle is supported by 3 to 6 case studies. These principles more fully describe our theoretical framework, and each may be tested in future research projects. We contend that excellent public relations leaders should have the following qualities:

1. *Lead by example: They should model the way through two-way communication and exemplary behaviors.* Role models and mentors exert the greatest influence on practitioner beliefs about what constitutes excellent leadership qualities and values (Berger, 2008; Berger et al., 2009; Erzikova & Berger, 2009a; S.-T. Lee & Cheng, 2008; Meng et al., 2009).

In-depth interviews with 20 young public relations leaders suggested that "leading by example" is one of the most important qualities of excellent leaders (Berger, 2008). Twenty high-level public relations executives and pioneers in the field said in interviews that ethical role modeling is far more influential than formal ethics approaches (such as ethics codes, training programs) in transferring ethics knowledge and appropriate behaviors in organizations (S.-T. Lee & Cheng, 2008). Educators indicated that greater access to role models would help students learn appropriate values and behaviors (Erzikova & Berger, 2009a).

2. *Participate effectively and credibly in strategic decision-making arenas in organizations.* Strategic decision-making capability is the most crucial dimension of leadership, according to senior practitioners (Kang, 2009; Meng, 2009; Meng et al., 2009). The ultimate public relations leader is a strategic counselor who's engaged in important decision-making moments in the dominant coalition in the organization (J. E. Grunig, 1992; L. A. Grunig et al., 2002). This capability involves interpersonal communication and rhetorical skills, as well as credibility and rapport with senior organizational leaders (Berger et al., 2007). It also requires an understanding of organizational culture, political intelligence, knowledge of power relations, and professional courage—the ability and willingness to speak truth to power (Berger & Reber, 2006).

3. *Exemplify a strong ethical orientation and set of values for doing the right thing and practicing professional standards at all times.* Ethical orientation touches every aspect of leadership practice and is crucial to individual reputation, organizational success, and the profession's image and future (Erzikova & Berger, 2009a; Kang, 2009; Kang & Berger, 2009b; Meng, 2009). Values define how organizations conduct business and how and to what extent they are concerned with employees, communities, and so forth (Clark, 1997).

Many surveyed educators said that a strong ethical orientation was among the most important values for public relations students to possess, and American public relations students defined leadership in public relations primarily through an ethics prism, emphasizing trustworthiness and strong values (Erzikova & Berger, 2009b). In interviews, 20 longtime leaders in the field argued that ethics are grounded more in personal than in professional values. Personal ethics, along with interpersonal behaviors and the active advocacy of ethical standards, are the most important characteristics of public relations leaders who help spread ethical behavior throughout the organization (S.-T. Lee & Cheng, 2008).

4. *Possess complex communication and rhetorical skills.* We take this knowledge requirement for granted in the profession: Leaders should be technically proficient and familiar with the tasks of employees. However, research begins to reveal the multilayered nature and complexity of this capability and suggests four levels of knowledge and skill (Berger et al., 2007; Meng, 2009; Meng et al., 2009).

1. Level 1 involves strong writing and technical skills and knowledge of a range of communication channels and media.
2. At Level 2, practitioners use their knowledge and skills to select and implement appropriate communication strategies and tactics. Knowledge and expertise in new social media are involved at both Levels 1 and 2.
3. At Level 3, practitioners use interpersonal skills to build relationships, collaborate, negotiate, and work effectively in teams.
4. At Level 4, practitioners possess and employ excellent rhetorical and persuasive communication skills and strategies that make them effective participants in senior decision-making circles.

5. *Possess clear self-knowledge that guides successful interactions, formation of relationships, and self-development.* Self-knowledge—knowing the strengths and limitations of one's character, skills, and knowledge—helps guide successful decisions. Many individual traits contribute to successful leadership, but self-dynamics may be the core set: self-insights, sense of vision, and team collaboration. Self-insights help locate and deal effectively with blind spots that can produce unintended consequences. They also help practitioners interact more effectively with others (S.-T. Lee & Cheng, 2008; Meng, 2009; Meng & Heyman, 2009). Self-improvement is closely linked to self-insights, and excellent leaders may continually seek to strengthen their attributes through reflection, formal development, and experiences.

6. *Possess a strong desire to lead.* Individual initiative and desire to lead appear to be fundamental to excellent leadership over the long term. This principle may be at the center of transformational leadership (Clark, 1997). Practitioners can improve their professional skills, process ethics codes, study role models, and participate in management development programs. But the fundamental desire to lead is a rich, continuing source of energy, power, learning, and determination (Berger et al., 2009; Meng, 2009; Meng et al., 2009).

7. *Employ transformational and inclusive styles of leadership that are sensitive to context and environment, as well as individual needs and differences.* Transformational and inclusive leadership styles are consistently preferred by public relations professionals (Aldoory, 1998; Aldoory & Toth, 2004; Choi & Choi, 2008; Jin, 2009; Werder & Holtzhausen, 2009). Transformational leaders have a vision for the future, motivate change, inspire others through communication, and are innovative risk takers. Inclusive leaders are collaborative, share decision making, and engage in participative processes. These styles are more effective in gaining trust with employees and teams, managing employee hopes and frustrations, and resolving conflicts and solving problems (Jin, 2009; Werder & Holtzhausen, 2009). A study by the Hay Group found that trust and confidence in top leaders was the most reliable predictor of employee or member satisfaction (Lamb & McKee, 2004).

8. *Demonstrate passion for the work and the profession that encourages and inspires others.* Passion for work and the profession may be the lifeblood of leadership. Exhibiting passion and positive energy on the job brings projects to life and spurs hope. Passion for work also is a positive contagion that may facilitate shared vision, build esprit de corps, and enrich organizational

climate. Excellent leaders in public relations fully engage in the challenges of leadership on the job and often in the community and profession (Berger, 2008; Berger et al., 2007; S.-T. Lee & Cheng, 2008).

9. *Serve as agents for change and for helping create a culture for communication.* The extent to which public relations leaders can be effective and excellent is affected by organizational culture, structure, and environment (J. E. Grunig, 1992; L. A. Grunig et al., 2002; Kang & Berger, 2009b; Liu & Horsley, 2009; Meng, 2009). Public relations leaders may be most effective and excellent in open communication environments and when organizational leaders support and model ethical behaviors (Kang, 2009; Kang & Berger, 2009b). Thus, excellent public relations leaders push back on restrictive or closed communication environments and inappropriate behaviors for the benefit of employees, the overall organization, and the practice and profession.

The Leadership Challenge

If excellent leadership is crucial to the public relations profession and its future, it seems important to examine these principles more closely and to use the knowledge we gain to better prepare students and practitioners to meet future challenges. As noted above, each of the theoretical principles may be tested in new research projects. In this section, we move beyond research to discuss the current state of leadership development in practice and in the classroom, both important sites for engaging the leadership challenge.

The Leadership Challenge in Practice

The landscape of leader development and cultivation in public relations practice is populated with diverse and somewhat disconnected structures and approaches (Berger et al., 2009). Some companies, agencies, and nonprofits, for example, have established internal development programs, where individual or team-mentoring programs are formalized, and leadership development programs help prepare individuals for broader responsibilities (e.g., Whirlpool's Worldwide Leadership Academy). These programs may use internal experts or specialist providers, for example, the Center for Creative Leadership, to develop and deliver training. Participants volunteer or are more often selected for such programs based on future promise, past performance, or favorable relationships.

Professional associations such as the Public Relations Society of America (PRSA), the Arthur W. Page Society (AWP), and the Institute for Public Relations (IPR), among others, play key roles in leader development too. First, they carry out a mentorship role by providing professionals with challenging association assignments, recognition for their work, social networks, and professional and career development opportunities (Eby, 1997). Second, associations deliver leadership development programs for some members or member organizations. Typically, such programs consist of 2- or 3-day sessions, where professional experts deliver knowledge or skills training and where participants are provided social opportunities to build networks and share experiences firsthand.

All these are valuable learning opportunities, but there are some associated limitations and issues. First, only 10% to 20% of public relations professionals belong to associations, so relatively few of the more than 250,000 practitioners in the United States today actually benefit from the direct association experiences and opportunities. Second, the costs of development programs for some practitioners are prohibitive. Third, not all professional education and development programs are created equally, and the quality of content and instruction vary. Fourth, such programs are but moments in a long professional chain; once participants reenter the workplace, they confront ongoing issues and responsibilities that may constrain their efforts or desires to enact what they've learned. Fifth, the job marketplace today is dynamic, and professionals may or may not transport and use their learning in their new positions or organizations.

Sixth, participants in professional development programs often evaluate the perceived quality of their workshops and training, but there appear to be few if any metrics to assess the long-term outcomes of development and educational programs. We know little about the extent to which those who participate in leadership development programs actually model or enact desired behaviors or values on the job, or go on to become outstanding leaders in the field.

In short, though a number of leadership development programs are available today, their capacity is limited, their quality is inconsistent, and the extent to which their effects are evaluated in the short term or long term is unknown, which makes it difficult to improve such efforts systemically in the profession. Believing that leadership growth and development are important in public relations, we suggest three steps to enhance and advance leadership development:

1. *Designate the leadership challenge as a national priority.* This seems especially crucial at a time when public trust in organizations and the profession is very low, and new technologies, globalization, and the rise of new and empowered stakeholders are reshaping traditional communication practices and placing a premium on ethical and transparent practice and leadership.

2. *Create a national forum through which we can begin to develop consensus regarding the key dimensions or qualities of excellent leadership in the field.* We know that there are many definitions of leadership and approaches to leadership preparation. Some agreement in the field about what leadership is and how we address it seem to be important prerequisites to improving education and development programs.

3. *Catalog and analyze existing leadership development programs—in associations, organizations, and universities—to identify content, delivery approaches, metrics, best practices, and so forth.* This initiative might provide the basis for meaningful systemic change in the preparation of leaders, and it would afford an opportunity for educators, researchers, and practitioners to work together.

We believe that there's already a strong foundation for such actions. AWP, for example, is populated by 300 high-level corporate and agency executives and leading academics. This is an ongoing forum for information sharing and problem solving by current leaders in the field. IPR has long supported and led efforts to create and make visible research and measurement approaches to enhance ethical and effective practice. PRSA possesses expertise in the delivery of skill and career development programs and in the distribution of information and knowledge to thousands of practitioners. The Page Center for Integrity in Public Communication and the Plank Center for Leadership in Public Relations, among others, provide expertise and resources at the university level.

Imagining the possibility of these and other groups and associations working together to address the leadership challenge in public relations is a crucial first step to actualization. Moreover, it's an opportunity for current leaders in the field to perform an important role-modeling function for the entire profession.

The Educational Challenge

We know that public relations students learn about leadership through role models and mentors (e.g., Pompper & Adams, 2006). They also learn through experiences in campaign courses, through shadowing exercises with professionals, teams, or club project assignments and involvement in the Public Relations Student Society of America (PRSSA). However, we know little about how and to what extent leadership concepts are incorporated into university education programs, which are widespread and growing.

A recent survey of 159 educators and two focus groups (10 educators) by Erzikova and Berger (2009a) captured some baseline information in this regard. They found that teachers are advocates for leadership education, and they believe that they help develop leaders in the field. Though few universities or colleges offer specific courses in leadership, the educators said that leadership elements are integrated throughout the public relations curricula. They also indicated that the most important leadership skills and values for public relations students to gain are a strong ethical orientation, problem-solving ability, and communication knowledge and skills.

The surveyed educators said that the most effective approaches to teaching leadership are case studies, group discussions, and student-led projects. Overall, the educators favored a more holistic approach to teaching leadership, which would include a primary course, more leadership development opportunities outside the classroom, and greater access to public relations leaders.

If we consider the issue of access to leaders and role models, we believe that educators and students today have greater access through the Page Center and the Plank Center, among other resources. The Page Center supports research in ethical practice and has produced a video series of oral histories of longtime leaders in the field. The Plank Center has compiled a series of 20-minute video interviews with 15 recognized public relations leaders, who speak of their own experiences and leadership qualities. The Plank Center Web site also includes the book *Legacies From Legends in Public Relations*, a collection of brief messages written to public relations students by 34 leaders.

Drawing from these two Centers, then, and in the absence of public relations speakers to talk in the classroom about leadership, how might educators do more to incorporate role models and leaders in their public relations classes? Here are five suggestions:

1. Assign, or let students select, one or several oral histories or video interviews to review as the basis for writing a brief reflection paper on the topic. Use the reflection papers to guide class discussion about leaders, their experiences, and students' perceptions of them.
2. Assign, or let students select, 5 to 7 brief messages from the *Legends* book as the basis for writing refection papers. Use the papers as the basis for a class session in which the students compare and contrast key themes in the *Legends* messages.
3. Arrange a 30-minute conference call to your classroom with one of the profiled leaders, who could share personal experiences and lessons and respond to student questions. Consider a series of calls tied to key subjects or topics in a management or writing class.
4. Give students a project assignment that requires them to gather information about, and conduct an online or telephone interview with, a profiled leader of their choosing.
5. Assign a class a collective research project to content analyze the oral histories, leader video interviews, or leaders in the *Legends* book. This approach combines learning how to plan and conduct content analysis research with learning about leadership themes and patterns. The final products of the exercise could include a class conference paper, or preparation and delivery of a presentation to other students, faculty, or local PRSA or PRSSA chapters.

All these assignments focus on leaders as role models, one important principle of excellent leaders. However, we suggest that each principle highlighted in this chapter offers similar opportunities for creatively translating leadership into the classroom to inform and even inspire students.

In closing, we reaffirm our belief that leadership in public relations is too important an issue to be overlooked, or taken for granted in research, education, and practice. We outlined a tentative theory of excellent leadership and offered some practical suggestions to begin to address the challenge. Our intention is not to claim that our theory is THE theory about public relations leadership, or that our list of suggestions is complete, but rather to provoke discussion and more research about this crucial issue. We believe the future of our profession depends on it.

References

Aldoory, L. (1998). The language of leadership for female public relations professionals. *Journal of Public Relations Research, 10,* 73–101.

Aldoory, L., & Toth, E. (2004). Leadership and gender in public relations: Perceived effectiveness of transformational and transactional leadership styles. *Journal of Public Relations Research, 16*(2), 157–183.

Bass, B. M. (1985). *Leadership and performance beyond expectations.* New York: Free Press.

Bass, B. M. (1990). *Bass and Stogdill's handbook of leadership: Theory, research, and managerial applications* (3rd ed.). New York: Free Press.

Bass, B. M. (1997). Does the transactional-transformational leadership paradigm transcend organizational and national boundaries? *American Psychologist, 52*(2), 130–139.

Berger, B. (Ed.). (2008). *Profiles of success: Stories of emerging leaders in public relations.* Tuscaloosa: University of Alabama. Retrieved February 11, 2010, from http://viewer.zmags.com/showmag.php?mid=gspqr#/page0/

Berger, B., Meng, J., & Heyman, W. (2009, March). *Role modeling in public relations: The influence of role models and mentors on leadership beliefs and qualities.* Paper presented at the 12th International Public Relations Research Conference, Miami, FL.

Berger, B. K., & Reber, B. H. (2006). *Gaining influence in public relations: The role of resistance in practice.* Mahwah, NJ: Lawrence Erlbaum.

Berger, B. K., Reber, B. H., & Heyman, W. C. (2007). You can't homogenize success in communication management: PR leaders take diverse paths to top. *International Journal of Strategic Communication, 1*(1), 53–71.

Beyer, J. M. (1999). Taming and promoting charisma to change organizations. *Leadership Quarterly, 10,* 307–330.

Broom, G. M., & Dozier, D. M. (1986). Advancement for public relations role models. *Public Relations Review, 12*(1), 37–56.

Cameron, G. T., Cropp, F., & Reber, B. (2001). Getting past platitudes: Factors limiting accommodation in public relations. *Journal of Communication Management, 5*(3), 242–261.

Choi, Y., & Choi, J. (2008, May). *Dimensions of leadership in public relations: Exploring an organization-wide perspective.* Paper presented at the annual meeting of the International Communication Association, Montreal, Quebec, Canada.

Clark, D. (1997). *Concepts of leadership.* Retrieved March 27, 2010, from www.skagit.com/~donclark/leader/leadercon.html

Conger, J. A. (1999). Charismatic and transformational leadership in organizations: An insider's perspective on these developing streams of research. *Leadership Quarterly, 10*(2), 145–179.

Conger, J. A., & Kanungo, R. N. (1987). Toward a behavioral theory of charismatic leadership in organizational settings. *Academy of Management Review, 12,* 637–647.

Dozier, D. M., & Broom, G. M. (1995). Evolution of the manager role in public relations practice. *Journal of Public Relations Research, 7*(1), 3–26.

Eby, L. T. (1997). Alternative forms of mentoring in changing organizational environments: A conceptual extension of the mentoring literature. *Journal of Vocational Behavior, 51,* 125–144.

Erzikova, E., & Berger, B. (2009a). *Leadership education in the PR curriculum: Reality, opportunities, and benefits.* Manuscript submitted for publication.

Erzikova, E., & Berger, B. (2009b). *Russian and US public relations students' perceptions of professional leadership and leaders.* Paper presented at the 12th International Public Relations Research Conference, Miami, FL.

Glass, G. V. (1976). Primary, secondary, and meta-analysis of research. *Educational Research, 5,* 3–8.

Grunig, J. E. (Ed.). (1992). *Excellence in public relations and communication management: Contributions to effective organizations.* Hillsdale, NJ: Lawrence Erlbaum.

Grunig, L. A., Grunig, J. E., & Dozier, D. M. (2002). *Excellent public relations and effective organizations:*

A study of communication management in three countries. Mahwah, NJ: Lawrence Erlbaum.

House, R. J. (1977). A theory of charismatic leadership. In J. G. Hunt & L. L. Larson (Eds.), *Leadership: The cutting edge* (pp. 189–207). Carbondale: Southern Illinois University Press.

Jin, Y. (2009, May). *Emotional leadership as a key dimension of public relations leadership: A national survey of public relations leaders.* Paper presented at the annual conference of the International Communication Association, Chicago.

Kang, J. (2009). *Antecedents and consequences of ethical leadership of public relations practitioners.* Unpublished doctoral dissertation, University of Alabama, Tuscaloosa.

Kang, J., & Berger, B. (2009a). *The influence of organizational conditions on public relations practitioners' dissent.* Paper presented at the annual conference of the Association for Education in Journalism and Mass Communication, Boston.

Kang, J., & Berger, B. (2009b). *Organizational environment, autonomy, and the ethics counsel role of public relations.* Paper presented at the annual conference of the International Communication Association, Chicago.

Lamb, L. F., & McKee, K. B. (2004). *Applied public relations: Cases in stakeholder management.* Mahwah, NJ: Lawrence Erlbaum.

Lee, S., & Evatt, D. S. (2005). An empirical comparison of the predictors of excellence in public relations. *Corporate Reputation Review, 8*(1), 31–43.

Lee, S.-T., & Cheng, I.-H. (2008, August). *Ethical leadership in public relations: Roles, dimensions and knowledge transfer.* Paper presented at the annual conference of the Association of Education in Journalism and Mass Communication, Chicago.

Liu, B. F., & Horsley, S. (2009, May). *Public relations leaders in the public and private sector: Peas in a pod or polar opposites?* Paper presented at the annual conference of the International Communication Association, Chicago.

Meng, J. (2009). *Excellent leadership in public relations: An application of multiple-group confirmatory factor analysis models in assessing cross-national measurement in variance.* Unpublished doctoral dissertation, University of Alabama, Tuscaloosa.

Meng, J., Berger, B., Gower, K., & Heyman, W. (2009, May). *A test of excellent leadership in public relations: Key qualities, valuable sources, and distinctive leadership perceptions.* Paper presented at the annual conference of the International Communication Association, Chicago.

Meng, J., & Heyman, W. (2009, March). *Measuring excellent leadership in public relations: A second-order factor model in the dimension of self-dynamics.* Paper presented at the 12th International Public Relations Research Conference, Miami, FL.

Northouse, P. G. (2007). *Leadership: Theory and practice.* Thousand Oaks, CA: Sage.

Pompper, D., & Adams, J. (2006). Under the microscope: Gender and mentor-protégé relationships. *Public Relations Review, 32*(3), 309–315.

Reber, B., & Cameron, G. T. (2003). Measuring contingencies: Using scales to measure public relations' practitioner limits to accommodation. *Journal of Mass Communication Quarterly, 80*(2), 431–446.

Scarnati, J. T. (2002). Leaders as role models: 12 rules. *Career Development International, 7*(3), 181–189.

Shin, J., Cameron, G. T., & Cropp, F. (2006). Occam's razor in the contingency theory: A national survey of 86 contingent variables. *Public Relations Review, 32,* 282–286.

Sosik, J. J., Godshalk, V. M., & Yammarino, F. J. (2004). Transformational leadership, learning goal orientation, and expectations for career success in mentor-protégé relationships: A multiple levels of analysis perspective. *Leadership Quarterly, 15,* 241–261.

Waller, D. J., Smith, S. R., & Warnock, J. T. (1989). Situational theory of leadership. *American Journal of Hospital Pharmacology, 46,* 2335–2341.

Werder, K. P., & Holtzhausen, D. R. (2009). An analysis of the influence of public relations department leadership style on public relations strategy use and effectiveness. *Journal of Public Relations Research, 21*(4), 404–427.

Yukl, G. W. (1989). *Leadership in organizations* (2nd ed.). Englewood Cliffs, NJ: Prentice Hall.

CHAPTER 30

Embedding Issue Management

From Process to Policy

Tony Jaques

Issue management is not about how to manage an issue, but how to manage because of an issue.

When issue management[1] was becoming established in the late 1970s and early 1980s, its founders explicitly envisaged a discipline that would enable corporations and business associations to proactively deal with issues that affect them, rather than merely reacting to such issues.

Over the subsequent decades, issue management evolved beyond the corporate sector and attracted a great deal of attention from practitioners and academics, some of whom introduced complex work processes and mathematical modeling intended to promote a structural framework for the discipline and to help carve out a unique role, language, and identity.

But the past few years have seen renewed focus on issue management both as a core suite of proven tools and processes and also as a critical element embedded within the broader continuum of management practice. Reviewing this evolution helps reinforce the important contribution of issue management and its emerging positioning as part of an integrated response to organizational and societal risks, threats, and challenges.

The Beginning of Issue Management

Of all the disciplines in public relations, issue management is the only one whose formal birth can be traced to an exact time and place. The occasion was April 15, 1976, when public relations pioneer Howard Chase (1910–2003) released the inaugural issue of his new publication *Corporate*

Public Issues and Their Management, which formally introduced for the first time the term *issue management* (Chase, 1976).

During the 1970s, Chase and a number of colleagues became increasingly concerned about the lack of corporate capacity to respond to the growing influence of activist and other nongovernmental organizations (NGOs) in the development of public policy. Accordingly, they promoted issue management as a business discipline explicitly designed to enable corporations to participate in, and not simply respond to, public policy issues that have the potential to affect the organization. Chase (1980) himself described it as "a methodology by which the private sector can get out of the unenviable position of being at the end of the crack-the-whip political line" (p. 5).

More specifically, Chase (1982) described issue management as "the capacity to understand, mobilize, coordinate and direct all strategic and policy planning functions, and all public affairs/public relations skills, toward achievement of one objective; meaningful participation in creation of public policy that affects personal and organizational destiny" (p. 1).

There have been many attempts to refine and restate the definition of issue management (including Crable & Vibbert, 1986; Heath & Cousino, 1990; Heugens, 2005; Wartick & Mahon, 1994). Indeed, Heath (1997) observed that no definition of issue management had yet achieved consensus, and nothing since has altered that judgment.

A key reason for this continuing absence of consensus is the evolution of issue management itself and its application. Instead of still being just a mechanism to allow the corporate sector to participate in the formation of public policy, issue management is now also used by government agencies themselves to promote and implement new policy, and by NGOs, activists, and community groups to facilitate public participation in the process. As a result of this migration, the nature and application of issue management has changed substantially (for discussion of this evolution, see Jaques, 2009b).

Meanwhile, the fundamental definition of issue management evolved from a focus mainly on public policy toward an increasing focus on internal processes, with a strong emphasis on the basic nature of issue management itself—that is, a formal process to identify and prioritize issues early, to mobilize resources across the organization, and to develop and implement practical plans in order to achieve planned, positive outcomes. In addition to a focus on tools and processes, issue management also began to resume its original strategic intent, with a growing emphasis on the essential links between issue management and strategic planning (see Jaques, 2009a).

What Is an Issue?

In his groundbreaking book *Issue Management: Origins of the Future*, Chase (1984) defined an issue as "an unsettled matter which is ready for decision" (p. 38). But it is clear that this definition was neither sufficiently specific nor sufficiently distinguished from everyday organizational problems. Since then, three distinct approaches emerged to define the nature of an issue, and each of these approaches is still in use.

As long ago as 1994, Wartick and Mahon reviewed the literature and identified three distinct definitional issue constructs: (1) the controversy theme, (2) the expectational gaps theme, and (3) the impact theme. For the discussion that follows, the author prefers to substitute the description disputation theme for the controversy theme, because the word *controversy* can itself be perceived as a loaded term (Jaques, 2009b).

The Disputation Theme

Following the lead provided by the 1984 Chase definition, a number of scholars and commentators introduced other descriptions developing the disputation theme. A typical early example of this approach is Crable and Vibbert (1986): "An issue occurs when a problem becomes focused in a particular question that calls for dispute and some sort of resolution" (p. 62). Other scholars substituted alternative qualifiers such as "a public dispute in which the public interest is unclear" (Stanley, 1985, p. 18) or a dispute that "leads to confrontations and political battles" (Lerbinger, 1997, p. 318).

Unfortunately, the disputation approach can become very general and rather passive. This limitation is exemplified in a more recent presentation of the disputation theme from Heath and Coombs (2006): "An issue is a contestable difference of opinion, a matter of fact, evaluation or policy that is important to the parties concerned" (p. 262).

Yet the disputation theme is useful because it emphasizes that an issue requires, by definition, a dispute between two or more parties. If the matter under discussion is so self-evident that there are no contending opinions, then no issue exists. The principal limitation of this theme is that many disputes or "unsettled matters" exist in society which would not be classified as issues in the sense of requiring the full application of formal issue management. In other words, although every legitimate issue involves matters of dispute, not every dispute constitutes an issue.

The Expectation Gap Theme

The concept of an issue being a gap in expectation was also developed very early and came to be defined as a gap between the actions of the organization concerned and the expectations of its stakeholders (Issue Management Council, n.d.; Regester & Larkin, 2002).

This theme has the merit of simplicity, and it also has strong support among the activist/NGO community, particularly in the field of corporate social responsibility (CSR), where there is a clear focus on corporate performance versus stakeholder expectation. However, the gap theme is losing favor among scholars because the concept of an expectation gap is too general, lacks sufficient specificity, and is very subjective. And like the disputation theme, it too can be a very passive concept. A gap in stakeholder expectation can certainly *lead* to an issue, especially if the gap and/or the stakeholder is of sufficient importance. Furthermore, analysis of the gap can help *characterize* an issue. But it is difficult to argue that the gap itself constitutes an issue as such.

The Impact Theme

The third approach, the impact theme, was typified very early in work by the Conference Board, a not-for-profit international business research organization based in New York, which introduced what it called "impact taxonomy." The Board's adopted definition was as follows: "An issue is a condition or pressure, either internal or external to an organization that, if it continues, will have a significant effect on the functioning of the organization or its future interests" (Brown, 1979, p. 1).

The impact theme has subsequently been much adapted and modified in a variety of forms. One of the most recent and effective restatements is by Regester and Larkin (2002): "An issue is a condition or event, either internal or external to the organization which, if it continues, will have a significant effect on the functioning or performance of the organization or on its future interests" (p. 42).

It can be argued that this impact approach is less applicable to community/NGO groups, which sometimes elect to participate in an issue that they feel affects society as a whole rather than affecting their particular organization. However, it has some very strong merits that make it a leading working definition.

The first of these merits is that the impact theme emphasizes the dynamic nature of an issue. Unlike the passivity of the other two approaches, which focus on an existing dispute or gap, the impact theme highlights the continuous nature of the issue as a moving and developing risk. Moreover, its future focus on potential effect rather than just a present problem emphasizes the importance of intervention, which is very much aligned with a generally more proactive modern response.

Perhaps most important is that the impact definition also provides a very clear statement that the focus is, and must be, on what is *significant.* While organizations face problems every day, of varying nature and importance, the great strength of the impact theme in issue definition is its emphasis that issue management is not a general-purpose problem-solving tool, applied to every dispute or gap in expectation, but is most appropriately employed when the impact is, or is likely to be, significant.

Beyond this focus on definitions, there is real value in a better understanding of the nature of issues, or more precisely the quality of issues, as this helps distinguish between different types of problems and issues and helps counter the careless use of the word *issue.*

Some managers describe every challenge they face as an "issue," be it market share, staff retention, competitive pricing, timing a product launch, or getting a new publication out on schedule. However, Jaques (2007b) said that situations properly defined as issues, and which warrant mobilization of formal issue management processes, are normally those

- which involve external parties,
- for which there is no black-and-white answer,
- which may involve public policy or regulation,
- where emotions rather than data often prevail,
- which happen in public or in the news media, and
- where the risks of failure are greatest and, if left unmanaged, have the potential to become crises and threaten the entire organization.

The Development of Process Models

From the earliest days of issue management, there was a strong emphasis on charts and diagrams to illustrate the process. Shortly after first launching the "new science" of issue management, Chase and his colleague Barrie Jones published the first formal issue management process diagram (Chase & Jones, 1977), which reinforced the foundation on which the structure was built.

The Chase-Jones model comprised five basic steps—issue identification, issue analysis, issue change strategy options, issue action program, and evaluation of results—and is still regarded as "the most influential issue management model" (Coombs & Holladay, 2007, p. 81).

At the same time Chase and Jones also published a "wall chart" that expanded on their five-stage model and depicted 88 distinct steps presented as a series of concentric circles within each stage.[2] While the wall chart has fallen out of use, mainly because it was too complicated, the simple five-step Chase-Jones model provided the blueprint for most other graphic representations of key processes. In fact, Ewing (1997) asserted that "all issue management models published by others since 1997 are variations on this model" (p. 174). Yet the effective demise of the multielement Chase-Jones "wall chart" provides another important lesson for today, at a time when modern computer graphic programs make it all too easy to produce highly complex models and flow charts. Process models are important in both the operation and communication of issue management and are now accepted as essential to issue management best practice (Jaques, 2005). But the models need to be simple, logical, and intuitive.

One such simplified model is the Do-It Plan© (Jaques, 2000a, 2000b) (Figure 30.1). The four steps of this model, which spell out its name, are (1) definition (defining the issue in a single, structured sentence), (2) objective (agreeing on a single, overarching objective), (3) intended outcomes (manageable subobjectives), and (4) tactics (specific name-bound, time-bound actions to deliver each outcome).

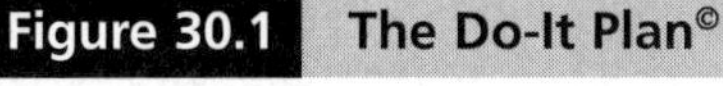

Figure 30.1 The Do-It Plan©

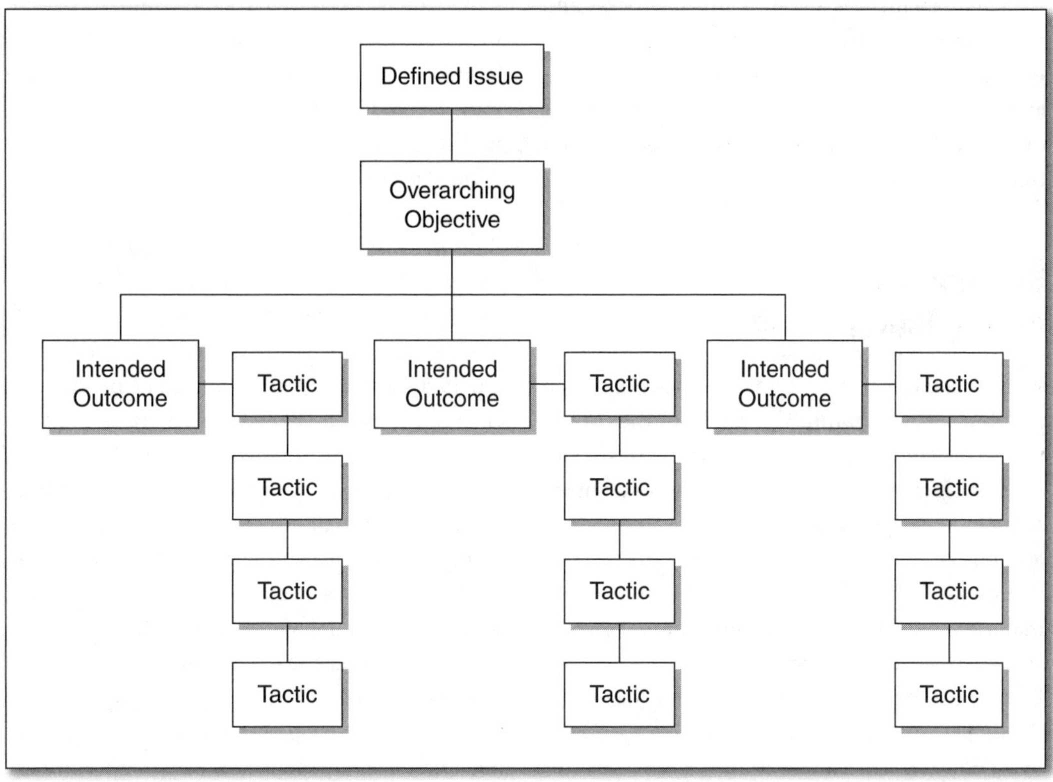

Source: Jaques (2000a, p. 129).

The Issue Life Cycle

The other key area where models have been widely used in issue management relates to graphic presentations of the issue life cycle, sometimes known as the issue attention cycle. An early example of such a model is seen in the work of Meng (1992), who characterized issues moving over time through five phases of a life cycle—potential, emerging, current, crisis, and dormant—and moving at the same time through parallel phases of ability to influence or affectability—origin, mediation/amplification, organization, and resolution.

There are other models using alternative descriptions for the progressive stages, such as societal expectation, political developments, legislation, and regulation/litigation. Or yet again emerging issues, politicization, legislation/mandated requirements, and litigation (for detailed discussion of issue life cycles, see Bigelow, Fahey, & Mahon, 1993; González-Herrero & Pratt, 1996; Jaques, 2000a, 2000b; Mahon & Waddock, 1992; Zyglidopoulos, 2003).

The different terminology in various models is less important than the two common concepts that run through them all: first, that issues unattended generally deteriorate toward greater risk and second, that the longer an issue survives and the later intervention occurs, the fewer choices remain open, the greater the cost, and the less the chances of achieving positive outcomes.

Such models can be effective in illustrating the importance of early intervention to maximize the opportunities and minimize the potential bottom line impact. However, these models do have a fundamental weakness in that they suggest issue management is a logical, linear process and that issues lend themselves to "resolution." In reality, issues are inherently unpredictable and evolutionary, and the issue management process does not take place in isolation but as part of a total management environment.

Embedding Issue Management

While issue management has developed a strong tradition of proven models and tools, the proper focus of issue management is not on issues but on management. Or put another way, issue management is not about how to manage an issue but about how to manage *because* of an issue. And it is this embedding of issue management as a core management discipline that underpins the transition from process to policy.

A great deal of academic effort has been expended on analyzing—and occasionally overanalyzing—complex management systems for recognizing, categorizing, and prioritizing issues. In fact, Coombs (2002) suggested that there are more than 150 different forecasting techniques to project the potential effects an issue might have on an organization. Academics and practitioners have also introduced novel taxonomy in an attempt to distinguish different management approaches, including anticipatory management (Ashley, 1995), risk issue management (Leiss, 2001), reputation risk management (Larkin, 2003), environmental issue management (Heugens, 2006), strategic issue management (Ansoff, 1980; Schwarz, 2005), and crisis issue management (Kovoor-Misra, 2002).

But in recent years, there has also been an increasing focus on the role of core issue management itself within the broader continuum of management practice, leading to its emergent positioning as part of an integrated response to organizational and societal risks, threats, and challenges.

The two key disciplines within this continuum—issue management and crisis management—saw remarkably similar patterns of development. While issue management as a defined activity began in the late 1970s, the first book devoted solely to issue management was not published until 1984 (*Issue Management: Origins of the Future* by Howard Chase). Significantly, one of the seminal works on the emerging discipline of crisis management was published just two years later (*Crisis Management: Planning for the Inevitable* by Steve Fink, 1986).

Although crisis study developed in the 1960s and 1970s, especially in the fields of psychology, sociology, and disaster response (Booth, 1993), the era of formal organizational crisis management as a business discipline reportedly began in the United States after the notorious Tylenol poisoning scandal of 1982 (e.g., Heath & Palenchar, 2009). And it has been claimed that it was not established as an independent research area in Europe until after the Chernobyl disaster in 1986 (e.g., Falkheimer & Heide, 2006).

The parallel progress of issue management and crisis management has in fact been a very important factor in embedding both disciplines within a more integrated response. Defining crisis and crisis management is outside the scope of this chapter (for detailed definitional analysis, see Jaques, 2009b), but more recent developments within crisis management have been critical to the evolution of issue management.

Unlike issue management, where both strategic and tactical elements are well recognized, crisis management as originally conceived was very much a reactive discipline focusing on the situation *after* a crisis has occurred, which perpetuates superficial distinctions and impedes progress. While a crisis is by definition a situation out of control (Benedict, 1994), the concept of crisis management as a purely reactive tactical discipline is now being superseded by a much more comprehensive approach.

Within this more strategic context, crisis management should be seen not just as a tactical reactive response when a crisis hits but as a proactive discipline embracing interrelated processes ranging from crisis prevention and crisis preparedness through crisis response and on to crisis recovery.

From an early period, crisis management was recognized both as constituting the response to a triggering event and as part of an ongoing process. And while the two approaches are naturally complementary, it has been acknowledged that most practitioners appear to agree on the fact that crises are processes, yet nevertheless often treat them as events. Indeed, Roux-Dufort (2007) concluded that the crisis management literature still mostly develops the event approach, while the process-oriented approach has been less used and developed, both theoretically and in practice.

Similarly, Pauchant and Mitroff (1992) claimed that 90% of the literature focuses on what to do when everything falls apart, for which they coined the neat expression "crash management." Their key distinction was that total crisis management focuses not only on what to do in the heat of a crisis but also on why crises happen and what can be done to prevent them.

A key disadvantage of the event approach is that it has the potential to inhibit examination of the trends and incidents that lead to triggering a crisis. In contrast, the conceptualization of crisis management as a process continuum promotes analysis of the activity extending back before the triggering event and deeper into the preceding phases to identify what Roux-Dufort calls "accumulation of organizational imperfections" (see, e.g., Forgues & Roux-Dufort, 1998; Roux-Dufort, 2007, 2009; Smith, 2005).

In addition to improved characterization of the period leading up to a crisis, the process approach also permits better analysis of the postcrisis situation. Specifically, it explores the management options not just for recovery and business resumption after the event but also for learning from crises (Elliott, Smith, & McGuinness, 2000; Stern, 1997) and addressing longer-term issues that can arise in the wake of a crisis (Heath & Millar, 2004; Jaques, 2009c; Ulmer, Seeger, & Sellnow, 2007).

Although there is obvious complementarity between the event approach and the process approach to crisis management, the process approach is gaining increasing attention, with important implications for the wider areas of management practice. Understanding crisis management in this holistic way helps turn the focus to process rather than definitions and also helps emphasize that the various processes are interrelated clusters of activities rather than being steps within a linear model. In this way, the process approach provides a basis for properly understanding the integral relationship between issue management and crisis management and the other management disciplines that surround them.

Issue and Crisis Management: An Integrated, Relational Model

The model presented here (Jaques, 2007a) is predicated on the holistic view of crisis management, that crisis prevention and crisis preparedness are just as much parts of the overall process as the tactical steps to take once a crisis strikes (Figure 30.2). Furthermore, the postcrisis cluster of activities has a critical function looping back to preparing for and managing future crises.

The model's nonlinear structure emphasizes that the elements should be seen as clusters of related and integrated disciplines, not as steps to be undertaken in a sequential fashion. While the precrisis and crisis management hemispheres of the model naturally follow each other, some individual elements may occur either overlapping or simultaneously. Indeed, crisis prevention and crisis preparedness, for example, most often *should* happen simultaneously.

It has been said that the best way to manage crises is to understand and manage issues, and in the context of this relational model the full scope of issue management is positioned in both crisis prevention and postcrisis management. In contrast, Heath (1997, p. 289) believes that crisis management is a *part* of issue management, and not vice

Figure 30.2 Issue and Crisis Management Relational Model©

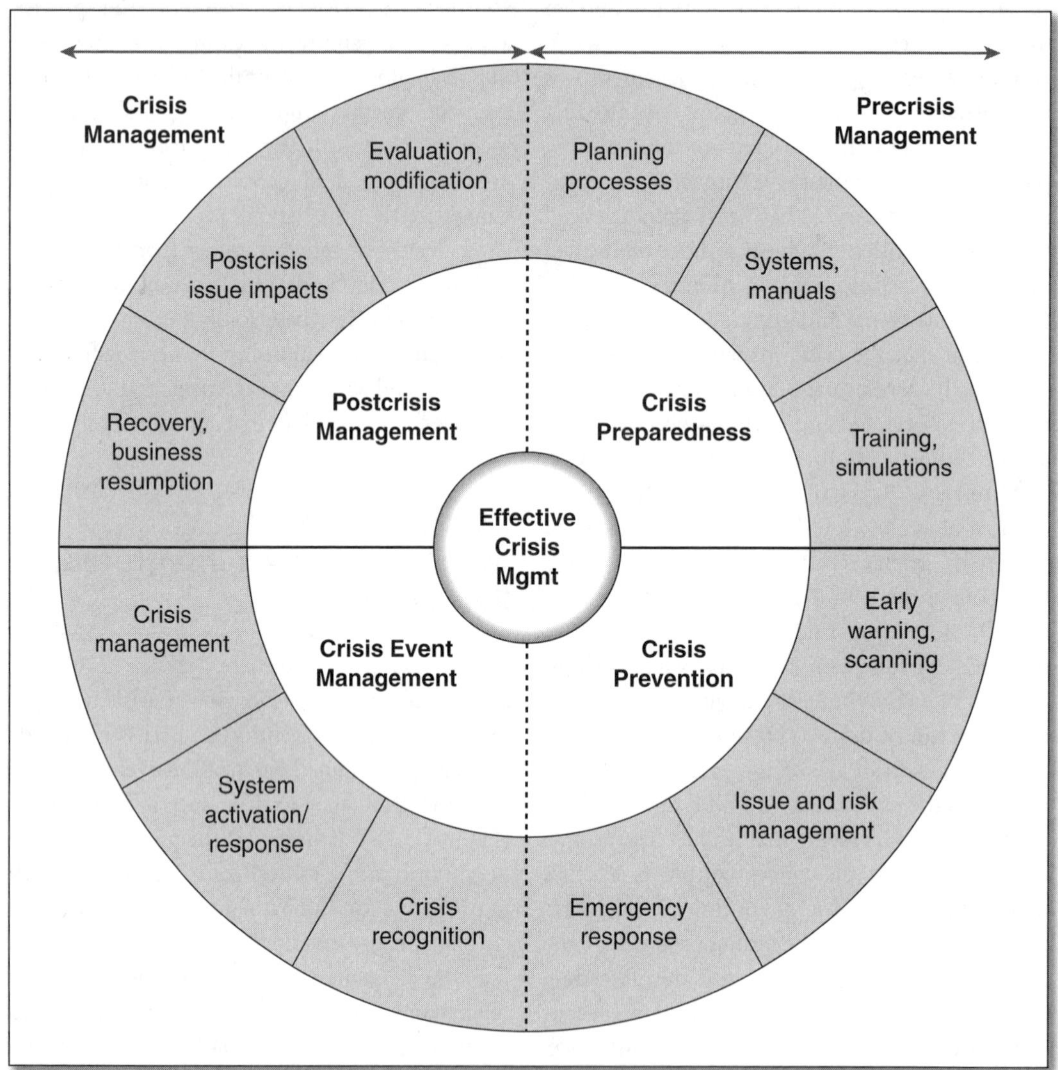

Source: Jaques (2007a), p. 150.

versa. Indeed, he goes further and asserts that crisis management is actually a *function* of issue management. Heath also argued persuasively for going beyond the traditional problem-issue-crisis-resolution linear sequence, emphasizing that not only can crises arise from issues; issues can arise from crises, too.

Although this relational model illustrates the interdependence between issue management, crisis management, and the related activities, there is at present no generally agreed taxonomy to define the different elements of management response to potential problems. In this case, the attempt is to distinguish between precrisis management and crisis management and, more important, to introduce and characterize a critical distinction between crisis preparedness and crisis prevention.

Crisis preparedness focuses primarily on systems planning, manuals, documentation, infrastructure, war rooms, functional checklists, resources, and training, all of which are very important. Indeed, they are the foundation of effective crisis response. But they make no direct contribution to preventing a crisis happening in the first place. This is the role for the interrelated cluster of activities identified as part of crisis prevention—including audits, risk assessment, social forecasting, environmental scanning, anticipatory management, future studies, and, most critically, issue management.

However, for issue management to be embedded in broader management, it is essential that the process provide effective mechanisms for information to be translated into action. As Stocker (1997) commented,

> Getting information about a potential crisis can be as sophisticated as a formal issues management program or as simple as interviewing your own employees about what could go wrong, or what may be going wrong. . . . In most internally generated crises, the knowledge and potential for a problem was well known in advance of the onset of the public crisis, and top management found out about it as it was going public. (p. 192)

Clearly, early warning and scanning are important in helping prevent a crisis—either chronic or acute—but they are of no value whatever if management ignores, denies, or tries to suppress the warnings.

There has been extensive research into the reasons and rationalizations as to why organizations fail to become crisis prepared, and why issue and crisis warning signs are ignored (e.g., Elliott et al., 2000; Lagadec, 1997; Mitroff & Pauchant, 1990; Smith & Elliott, 2007). But for the present discussion, the important point is that formal issue management provides tools and processes to reduce that risk.

Issue Management After a Crisis

The other key conclusion to be drawn from this model is the importance of issue management as a postcrisis discipline. There is a broad modern recognition that the greatest risk from a crisis, especially legal and reputational, can arise from how the organization responds after the triggering event. Phelps (1986) warned that "when the dust begins to settle, the aftershocks are often more devastating and costly to the organization over the long term than the original crisis" (p. 5), and 't Hart and Boin (2001) later coined the phrase "the crisis after the crisis."

Much of the literature on the postcrisis phase focuses on business recovery, continuity, and renewal, and, from a communication perspective, on postcrisis discourse (e.g., Coombs & Holladay, 2007; Ulmer et al., 2007). But a holistic management approach recognizes the risk from a range of longer-term postcrisis events, such as coroners' inquests, judicial or political inquiries, prosecution, prolonged litigation, and hostile media scrutiny. Such issues can persist for years or even decades and may affect a whole industry, not just the organization initially involved. A good example of this is the notorious *Exxon Valdez* incident, which was first an environmental crisis (a major oil spill), then a management crisis (slow and inadequate response), then a management/litigation issue (sustained legal and public review of management response), and finally an industry safety issue.

In the immediate aftermath of the incident, there was an industry review of bulk tanker construction and navigation in enclosed waters, which led to important changes. But for Exxon-Mobil another long-term effect was a prolonged and costly reputational issue. Although the oil spill happened in March 1989, the legal compensation argument dragged on for 19 years through acrimonious and damaging appeals and counterappeals, until it was finally settled in the U.S. Supreme Court in June 2008.

In the same way, the Challenger disaster of 1986 led to a prolonged and extremely damaging reputational issue for NASA, and in 2005 Hurricane Katrina triggered a maelstrom of reputational issues for the Federal Emergency Management Agency, long after the natural storm and its aftermath had subsided.

All three high-profile examples serve to reinforce, from an organizational perspective, that the longer-term issues resulting from a crisis can cause longer-lasting damage than the crisis itself and require effective and very well focused management response. By embedding issue management into the continuum of management response, organizations are able to proactively manage issues to reduce the risk of crises developing, to identify and manage the issues that arise in the wake of crises, and to learn from their own experience and the experience of others to adapt and improve the process to address future issues.

Notes

1. The terms *issue management* and *issues management* are both commonly used. Howa rd Chase, the "father" of the discipline, reportedly quipped it should be issue management, not issues management, in the same way that it is *brain* surgery, not *brains* surgery.

2. The wall chart was later published as a fold-out in *Issue Management: Origins of the Future* (Chase, 1984).

References

Ansoff, H. I. (1980). Strategic issue management. *Strategic Management Journal, 1*(2), 131–148.

Ashley, W. C. (1995). *Anticipatory management: 10 power tools for achieving excellence in the 21st century.* Stamford, CT: Issue Action.

Benedict, A. C. (1994). After a crisis: Restoring community relations. *Communication World, 11*(8), 20–23.

Bigelow, B., Fahey, L., & Mahon, J. F. (1993). A typology of issue evolution. *Business and Society, 32*(1), 18–29.

Booth, S. A. (1993). *Crisis management strategy: Competition and change in modern enterprises.* London: Routledge.

Brown, J. K. (1979). *This business of issues: Coping with the company's environments.* New York: Conference Board.

Chase, W. H. (1976). Objectives of CPI. *Corporate Public Issues and Their Management, 1*(1), 1.

Chase, W. H. (1980). Issues and policy. *Public Relations Quarterly, 25*(1), 5–6.

Chase, W. H. (1982). Issue management conference: A special report. *Corporate Public Issues and Their Management, 7*(3), 1–2.

Chase, W. H. (1984). *Issue management: Origins of the future.* Stamford, CT: Issue Action.

Chase, W. H., & Jones, B. L. (1977). CPI presents. *Corporate Public Issues and Their Management, 2*(14), 1–4.

Coombs, W. T. (2002). Assessing online issue threats: Issue contagions and their effect on issue prioritisation. *Journal of Public Affairs, 2*(4), 215–229.

Coombs, W. T., & Holladay, S. J. (2007). *It's not just PR: Public relations in society.* Malden, MA: Blackwell.

Crable, R. E., & Vibbert, S. L. (1986). *Public relations as communication management.* Edina, MN: Bellwether Press.

Elliott, D., Smith, D., & McGuinness, M. (2000). Exploring the failure to learn: Crises and the barriers to learning. *Review of Business, 21*(3/4), 17–24.

Ewing, R. P. (1997). Issues management: Managing trends through the issue life cycle. In C. L. Caywood (Ed.), *The handbook of strategic public relations and integrated communications* (pp. 173–187). New York: McGraw-Hill.

Falkheimer, J., & Heide, M. (2006). Multicultural crisis communication: Towards a social constructionist perspective. *Journal of Contingencies and Crisis Management, 14*(4), 180–189.

Fink, S. (1986). *Crisis management: Planning for the inevitable.* New York: American Management Association.

Forgues, B., & Roux-Dufort, C. (1998, May). *Crises: Events or processes? Paper presented at the* Hazards and Sustainability Conference, Durham, UK.

González-Herrero, A., & Pratt, C. B. (1996). An integrated symmetrical model for crisis-communication management. *Journal of Public Relations Research, 8*(2), 79–105.

Heath, R. L. (1997). *Strategic issues management: Organisations and public policy challenges.* Thousand Oaks, CA: Sage.

Heath, R. L., & Coombs, W. T. (2006). *Today's public relations: An introduction.* Thousand Oaks, CA: Sage.

Heath, R. L., & Cousino, K. R. (1990). Issues management: End of first decade progress report. *Public Relations Review, 16*(1), 6–18.

Heath, R. L., & Millar, D. P. (2004). A rhetorical approach to crisis management: Management, communication processes and strategic responses. In R. L. Heath & D. P. Millar (Eds.), *Responding to crisis: A rhetorical approach to crisis management* (pp. 1–17). Mahwah, NJ: Lawrence Erlbaum.

Heath, R. L., & Palenchar, M. J. (2009). *Strategic issues management: Organizations and public policy challenges* (2nd ed.). Thousand Oaks, CA: Sage.

Heugens, P. P. M. A. R. (2005). Issues management: Core understandings and scholarly development. In P. Harris & C. S. Fleischer (Eds.), *The handbook of public affairs* (pp. 481–500). Thousand Oaks, CA: Sage.

Heugens, P. P. M. A. R. (2006). Environmental issue management: Towards multi-level theory of environmental management competence. *Business Strategy and the Environment, 15*(6), 363–376.

Issue Management Council. (n.d.). Retrieved March 30, 2010, from www.issuemanagement.org

Jaques, T. (2000a). Developments in the use of process models for effective issue management. *Asia Pacific Public Relations Journal, 2*(2), 125–132.

Jaques, T. (2000b). *Don't just stand there: The do-it plan for effective issue management.* Melbourne, Victoria, Australia: Issue Outcomes.

Jaques, T. (2005). Using best practice indicators to benchmark issue management. *Public Relations Quarterly, 50*(2), 8–11.

Jaques, T. (2007a). Issue management and crisis management: An integrated, non-linear, relational construct. *Public Relations Review, 33*(2), 147–157.

Jaques, T. (2007b). Issue or problem? Managing the difference and averting crises. *Journal of Business Strategy, 28*(6), 25–28.

Jaques, T. (2009a). Integrating issue management and strategic planning: Unfulfilled promise or future opportunity? *International Journal of Strategic Communication, 3*(1), 19–33.

Jaques, T. (2009b). Issue and crisis management: Quicksand in the definitional landscape. *Public Relations Review, 35*(3), 280–286.

Jaques, T. (2009c). Issue management as a post-crisis discipline: Identifying and responding to issue impacts beyond the crisis. *Journal of Public Affairs, 9*(1), 35–44.

Kovoor-Misra, S. (2002). Boxed in: Top managers' propensities during crisis issue diagnosis. *Technological Forecasting and Social Change, 69*(8), 803–817.

Lagadec, P. (1997). Learning processes for crisis management in complex organizations. *Journal of Contingencies and Crisis Management, 5*(1), 24–31.

Larkin, J. (2003). *Strategic reputation risk management.* Basingstoke, UK: Palgrave Macmillan.

Leiss, W. (2001). *In the chamber of risks: Understanding risk controversies.* Montreal, Quebec, Canada: McGill-Queens University Press.

Lerbinger, O. (1997). *The crisis manager: Facing risk and responsibility.* Mahwah, NJ: Lawrence Erlbaum.

Mahon, J. F., & Waddock, S. A. (1992). Strategic issues management: An integration of issue life cycle perspectives. *Business and Society, 31*(1), 19–32.

Meng, M. (1992). Early identification aids issue management. *Public Relations Journal, 48*(3), 22–24.

Mitroff, I. I., & Pauchant, T. C. (1990). *We're so big and powerful nothing bad can happen to us: An investigation of America's crisis-prone corporations.* New York: Birch Lane.

Pauchant, T. C., & Mitroff, I. I. (1992). *Transforming the crisis prone organization.* San Francisco: Jossey-Bass.

Phelps, N. L. (1986). Setting up a crisis recovery plan. *Journal of Business Strategy, 6*(4), 5–8.

Regester, M., & Larkin, J. (2002). *Risk issues and crisis management: A casebook of best practice* (2nd ed.). London: Kogan Page.

Roux-Dufort, C. (2007). A passion for imperfections: Revisiting crisis management. In C. M. Pearson, C. Roux-Dufort, & J. A. Clair (Eds.), *International handbook of organizational crisis management* (pp. 221–252). Thousand Oaks, CA: Sage.

Roux-Dufort, C. (2009). The devil lies in details! How crises build up within organizations. *Journal of Contingencies and Crisis Management, 17*(1), 4–11.

Schwarz, J. O. (2005). Linking strategic issue management to futures studies. *Futures Research Quarterly, 21*(3), 39–55.

Smith, D. (2005). Business (not) as usual: Crisis management, service recovery and the vulnerability of organizations. *Journal of Services Marketing, 19*(5), 309–320.

Smith, D., & Elliott, D. (2007). Exploring the barriers to learning from crisis: Organizational learning and crisis. *Management Learning, 38*(5), 519–531.

Stanley, G. D. D. (1985). *Managing external issues: Theory and practice.* Greenwich, CT: JAI Press.

Stern, E. (1997). Crisis and learning: A conceptual balance sheet. *Journal of Contingencies and Crisis Management, 5*(2), 69–86.

Stocker, K. (1997). A strategic approach to crisis management. In C. L. Caywood (Ed.), *The handbook of strategic public relations and integrated communications* (pp. 189–203). New York: McGraw-Hill.

't Hart, P., & Boin, R. A. (2001). Between crisis and normalcy: The long shadow of post-crisis politics. In U. Rosenthal, R. A. Boin, & L. K. Comfort (Eds.), *Managing crises: Threats, dilemmas and opportunities* (pp. 28–46). Springfield, IL: Charles C Thomas.

Ulmer, R. R., Seeger, M. W., & Sellnow, T. L. (2007). Post crisis communication and renewal: Expanding the parameters of post-crisis discourse. *Public Relations Review, 33*(2), 130–134.

Wartick, S. L., & Mahon, J. F. (1994). Toward a substantive definition of the corporate issue construct: A review and synthesis of the literature. *Business and Society, 33*(3), 293–311.

Zyglidopoulos, S. C. (2003). The issue life cycle: Implications for reputation for social performance and organizational legitimacy. *Corporate Reputation Review, 6*(1), 70–81.

CHAPTER 31

Risk Communication

Michael J. Palenchar

Risk concerns suffuse every level of society, from policymakers to field-level enforcement, from risk generators to risk bearers, from affluent societies with not in my backyard (NIMBY) neighborhoods to communities near industrial complexes inundated with environmental risks and associated environmental justice concerns. Following the lead of Mary Douglas (1992) that every society since humans became social animals is a risk society, the rationale for the industrialized and the evolving technological society is the collective management of risk. As Douglas has noted, our current version of society may be more aware of risk, and while it is always different for each society, it is not necessarily unique. Some of these differences relate to Beck's (1992) notion that humans live in a risk society with its unwanted side effects that result from incredible economic growth, technological advancement, and welfare and society wealth unrivaled in the history of humankind. Goffman (1959, 1967) had it right when he penned his discussions on chance that risk is where the action is.

Concepts of risk have one common element, according to Renn (1992): the distinction between possible and chosen action (contingency). "Thinking about risks helps people to select the option that promises at least a marginal benefit compared to all other available options" (Renn, 2008, p. 1). Humans have the option of choice, to identify different options, "to design different futures" (p. 1); risk is inherent in being human. Risk communication can be part of and influence these choices, these futures that people choose. Beyond that, humans, as risk bearers, learn to live in varying degrees of comfort with ambiguity, contradiction, and imperfection. The challenge when addressing risk is uncertainty; that change has no constituency. There is always a constituency for staying the same, but change is a risk. So change (risk) needs a voice, an advocate in favor or disfavor, and that advocacy is often through risk communication.

Some key concerns related to risk and risk communication were addressed in 2006 at the Society for Risk Analysis and the National Science Foundation Symposium on Strategic

Acknowledgment: The author would like to thank the following graduate students for their research assistance with this chapter: Karen Freberg, Tatjana M. Hocke, and Nicole Merrifield.

Risk Communication. What kinds of risk information can humans readily process and appreciate? What kinds are likely to be misunderstood? Are some risk communication efforts bound to result in failure and increased controversy? Do risk analyses misrepresent or even underestimate risks if they do not account for perception issues? What features improve a risk communication effort's likelihood of success? These questions and more are the foci of risk communication researchers and practitioners. Many of these questions fit under issues of blame and mortality, which are central to Douglas's understanding of risk. Whose fault is it, what action is being taken, with what damages and what compensation? According to Douglas (1992) and based on her observations, people respond to risk in a way that is often directed at organizations, often including government, that either generate risk or fail to protect, which explains why risk communication is or should be of fundamental interest to public relations students, researchers, and practitioners.

Approximately two decades ago, Pearson (1990) asked a question about functionalism and public relations that pertains directly to risk communication. Is the management function of public relations "on a model that sees system imperatives as best served when publics are shielded from some of the complexities of policy decisions? Or can public relations be a communication process that facilitates genuine discussion and critique of policy questions?" (p. 227). Pearson's questions go right to the heart of the role of risk communication.

Modern risks, crises, and disasters challenge humans with a new species of trouble (Erikson, 1994) that public relations and risk communication practitioners must communicatively manage. The industrial and information ages have created a whole new range of risks and crises, while advances in communication and information technologies have increased people's awareness of these risks as well as increasing the opportunities for dialogue and shared decision making based on risk assessment and associated political and social discussions. As Palenchar (2009) noted, "Risk, crisis and ultimately disaster are the definitive challenge to communication and public relations scholars and practitioners" (p. 31) whose business, political, or social missions involve managing health, safety, and environmental risks.

Risk quandaries are the study of science, social science, and humanities, while risk communication is both a social and behavioral science field of study and an applied field that works to manage and communicate about risk with stakeholders, gaining from perspectives advanced by communication, psychology, sociology, anthropology, political science, and economics. Communication based on trust built through meaningful and effective public dialogue, according to Renn (2004), is more likely to produce legitimate decisions supported by risk bearers, even regarding controversial matters. This move reflects the general trend of risk communication from the power of information within education to one of consensus building through dialogue. However, according to Renn and Kastenholz (2000),

> The popularity associated with the concepts of two-way communication, trust-building, and stakeholder participation, however, obscures the challenge of how risk communicators can and should put these noble goals into practice and ensure that risk management reflects competence, efficiency, and fair burden sharing. (p. 8)

With the formation of society about managing risk, new species of trouble, and consensus building through dialogue as primary concepts, the purpose of this chapter is to better appreciate the challenges in understanding what is risk and risk communication, risk communications' rapid growth, evolvement of the field, the multidisciplinary nature of some key areas of risk communication research, and best practices. This chapter argues that the evolvement and advancement of risk communication is one of the stronger contributions to the public relations body of knowledge.

A Risk by Any Other Name

The study of risk features probabilities and causal modeling leading to predictions and recommendations related to managing uncertainty. The flip-side study of risk features a social and cultural theory approach to risk (Renn, 1992); those theories examine the crossroads among people, culture, society, risk, and crisis (Heath & O'Hair, 2009c).

Reviewing three decades of risk research, Renn (1998) noted the lack of a commonly accepted definition of risk in science and the public understanding of risk. His review also identified four images of risk in public perception that provides a basic overview of the meaning of risk: (1) *pending danger* from an artificial risk source with large catastrophic potential, inequitable risk distribution and perception of chance; (2) *slow killers* that have delayed and noncatastrophic effects, contingent on information rather than experience with a strong incentive for blame; (3) *cost-benefit ratio*, which is confined to monetary gains and losses, asymmetry between risks and gains; and (4) *avocational thrill*, which is personal control over degree of risk, voluntary activity with noncatastrophic consequences.

From an epistemological status of risk, Althaus (2005) provided an excellent review of disciplinary perspectives. For example, the disciplines of logic and mathematics view risk as a calculable phenomenon, and science and medicine view risk as an objective reality. Within the social sciences, anthropology typically views risk as a cultural phenomenon, sociology as a societal phenomenon, and economics as a decisional phenomenon. History views risk as a narrative, the arts as an emotional phenomenon, and philosophy as a problematic phenomenon. Law views risk as a fault of conduct and a judicable phenomenon, while psychology views risk as a behavioral or cognitive phenomenon. With this basic understanding of risk, the next section discusses the renaissance in risk communication.

Renaissance in Risk Communication

Risk communication grew organically out of a variety of perspectives and initiatives, whether they are community-based activism, government response, or industry initiated (Palenchar, 2009). Modern-era interest in risk communication can be traced back to the 1950s and the "Atoms for Peace" campaign and to the 1970s antinuclear movement (Kasperson & Stallen, 1991), while interest in risk communication was considered "quite recent" as of the late 1980s (Krimsky & Plough, 1988).

While risk communication research is not considered an independent scholarly discipline, according to Heath and O'Hair (2009b), the study of risk "has lingered on the fringe of academics for years, but only in the past three decades has its broad application and examination become adopted" (p. xi). Along with the founding of the Society for Risk Analysis in 1980 and the National Research Council's (NRC) 1989 publication *Improving Risk Communication*, the role of governmental and nongovernmental research centers, including university affiliated centers, cannot be underestimated in the rapid development of risk communication (see Palenchar, 2009, for more details on this history).

More and more governmental agencies are acknowledging this vital role for risk communication as it relates to regulation based on risk and crisis management. For example, risk and crisis communication are core elements of the U.S. National Incident Management System, which in coordination with the National Response Framework, ideally provides a national systematic, proactive approach to managing risk and crisis events (Federal Emergency Management Agency, n.d.). In 2009, the U.S. Department of Health and Human Services' Food and Drug Administration announced an ambitious long-term strategic plan for risk communication, supported by the assertion from the FDA's Commissioner and Deputy Commissioner that "one of the greatest challenges facing any public health agency is that of risk communication" (Hamburg & Sharfstein, 2009, p. 2493). Overall, according to Krimsky and Golding (1992), the field of risk studies developed from the practical needs of industrialized societies to regulate technology and to protect its citizens from human-made and natural hazards.

Also, with the tremendous rise of citizen environmental groups, a major institutional shift in society has moved from trust in public institutions to trust in citizens groups (Heath & O'Hair, 2009c; Laird, 1989). The long-term decline in public confidence and trust in traditional social institutions has paralleled the growth in risk communication. Fischhoff (1990) has long argued that stakeholders have insisted on a role in deciding how health, safety, and environmental risks will be managed, while Renn and Kastenholz (2000) claimed that numerous risk communication projects were launched during the 1980s and 1990s as a response to both the environmental regulation requiring open information and the public's increasing demands to be informed about potential hazards. Perhaps what is different today, according to Macauley (2006), "is the widespread attention throughout all echelons of modern society—the public at large; governments at the federal, state and local levels; industry; and universities and other nongovernmental organizations—to questioning the limits and applications of risk analyses" (p. 1).

What Is Risk Communication?

Much of the early work in risk communication focused on discussions of risk associated with personal health and safety practices involved in living and working in close proximity to harmful activities and toxic substances (NRC, 1989). This view of risk communication typically involves large organizations whose activities can pose a risk to members of a community, as opposed to risk communication scholarship from an interpersonal or health communication perspective based on persuasive health messages to do or not do something related to personal health practices.

Risk communication has always had a functional intent based on the differences between experts and risk bearers' threat assessments. The NRC (1989) described risk communication as "an interactive process of exchange of information and opinion among individuals, groups, and institutions" (p. 2), while Covello (1992) concisely defined risk communication as "the exchange of information among interested parties about the nature, magnitude, significance, or control of a risk" (p. 359). His famous definition does not, however, tell us how the information exchanged is analyzed, debated, and reconciled into public policy and acceptance of risks.

According to the NRC (1989), the U.S. Environmental Protection Agency helped establish risk communication as a means to open, responsible, informed, and reasonable scientific and value-laden discussion of risks. From this perspective, risk communication is successful to the extent that risk bearers can become more knowledgeable about and confident that sufficient control is imposed by the risk generator and by government or other external organizations that are responsible for monitoring the risk. When looked at in hindsight, however, these definitions are more likely not intentionally linear and information-push oriented but rather accidental in their writing composition (based on initial research in risk and risk meaning) and not based in a theoretically grounded construction.

A more recent general definition of risk communication by McComas (2006) says that "risk communication can be broadly understood as an iterative exchange of information among individuals, groups, and institutions related to the assessment, characterization, and management of risk" (p. 76). According to Palenchar (2005),

> Risk communication provides the opportunity to understand and appreciate stakeholders' concerns related to risks generated by organizations, engage in dialogue to address differences and concerns, carry out appropriate actions

> that can reduce perceived risks, and create a climate of participatory and effective discourse. (pp. 752–753)

This definition includes the notion that the purpose of risk communication campaigns is not necessarily to reduce risk awareness but to engage and encourage vigilant community stakeholders regarding the discussion and management of risk.

The Organization for Economic Co-Operation and Development (2002) in Europe developed the *Guidance Document on Risk Communication for Chemical Risk Management* and identified the major risk communication issues as the need to provide information to the public about the risk, provide information to the public about the process for conducting risk assessment, organize effective two-way communication, enhance trust and credibility, and involve stakeholders in the process to resolve conflicts. From these perspectives, risk communicators work toward shared dialogue rather than only an information push of rational risk assessments by experts in industry and government.

Recently, under the leadership of the Centers for Disease Control and Prevention and several leading risk and crisis communication scholars, traditional concepts of risk communication and crisis communication have been combined under one comprehensive model—*crisis and emergency risk communication* (CERC). Comprising five stages (precrisis, initial event, maintenance, reassurance, and evaluation), the CERC model differs from traditional risk communication because oftentimes a decision must be made within a narrow window of time and without all the necessary information.

> Crisis and emergency risk communication is the effort by experts to provide information to allow an individual, stakeholder, or an entire community to make the best possible decisions about their well-being within nearly impossible time constraints and help people ultimately to accept the imperfect nature of choices during the crisis. (Reynolds, 2002, p. 6)

This combined perspective toward risk and crisis communication is intensely explored in Heath and O'Hair's (2009a) *Handbook of Risk and Crisis Communication.*

Evolvement of Risk Communication

An appreciation for the evolvement of risk communication has been demonstrated by several noted scholars, including Covello, Fischhoff, Heath, Krimsky, Leiss, McComas, Otway, Renn, Rowan, and Sandman. In one of the more recent reviews, Krimsky (2007) suggested three stages to the evolution of risk communication, which started with a linear communication process of delivering messages to most likely unrealistic and irrational stakeholders. The next stage was founded on the acknowledgment of scientific uncertainty, and the subjective and cultural aspects of risk, while the last and current stage is tied to postmodernist and social constructionist views of risk.

Morgan, Fischhoff, Bostrom, and Atman (2002) discussed seven stages in the evolution of risk communication, moving from the original concept of the legal requirements of risk communication, which is based on the notion of getting the numbers (facts) right, to the current stage of multidirectional flow of communication among stakeholders, which is based on the notion of partnerships in managing risk. Fischhoff (1995) summarized well and in simple terms the first 20 years of risk communication research into the developmental stages in risk management, moving through the various developmental stages characterized by the primary communication strategy:

> All we have to do is get the numbers right, all we have to do is tell them the numbers, all we have to do is explain what we mean by the numbers, all we have to do is show them they've accepted similar risks before, all we have to do is show them that it's a good deal for them, all we have to do is treat them nice, all we have to do is make them partners, and finally, all we have to do is all of the above. (p. 139)

Risk communication is a global area of study, and risk communication in Europe has undergone profound changes over the past 20-plus years (Lofstedt, 2004). Similar to Leiss's (1996) and McComas's (2006) reviews of risk communication, Lofstedt (2004) traced European regulation and risk communication from a model of consensual regulation and communication based on decisions made among industry and policymakers with those decisions passed down to the community as "participatory-transparent" (p. 1). According to Lofstedt, the modern approach calls for more inclusive public and stakeholder participation, regulatory strategies to be open and transparent, taking into consideration social values and the use of the precautionary principle, a distinct separation of risk assessment from risk management (policy making), and the view that scientists are another stakeholder group, no more or less important.

In essence, the scientific approach, or as Leiss (1996) termed the technical risk assessment period, deals directly with the cold, hard facts of a risk—focusing specifically on the probability of an adverse occurrence, the most likely victims of such an event, and what might be the perfect conditions for turning the risk into a crisis (Heath & O'Hair, 2009c). The typical scientific approach was to "let experts determine the probabilities of risks, hold a public meeting, share this expertise with those who attended, and move on with the project" (p. 5).

The objective science approach to risk communication rarely took into account the lay audience and its interpretation of the risk. Instead, it relied on scientists—who for much of the 20th century had been secluded in universities and research centers—to engage with and meet the needs of the general public (Calsamiglia & Ferrero, 2003). Krimsky (2007) commented that early risk communication "was largely a euphemism for translating technical risks into a publicly accessible and digestible form, which eventually would be acceptable to the audience" (p. 159).

While the first phase centered on the *risk component* of risk communication, the next phase—the mid-1980s until the early 1990s—emphasized the *communication element*; in other words, risk communication was regarded as "messages intended to persuade a listener of the correctness of a point of view" (Leiss, 1996, p. 89). Strategies were based on refined marketing efforts to interpret an audience's perceived reality through source credibility, message clarity, and effective use of communication channels. Despite a seemingly more audience-centered approach, as well as a movement away from peddling the superiority of technical expertise, persuasion was still fraught with credibility issues. Attempts to construct a dialogue were often perceived as manipulation techniques that were eerily similar to propaganda (Leiss, 1996).

The third phase features *social relations* that work to achieve a level of discourse that can treat the content issues of the risk—technical assessment—and the quality of the relationships along with the political dynamics of the participants. Different from both its predecessors, the social context phase—starting around the mid-1990s—is based on social and cultural theories, which postulated that risk and crisis communication can only be effective when response strategies extend beyond scientific models and examine the nature and societal norms of the people affected by the crises (Heath & O'Hair, 2009c). When compared with objective science, the social context phase rejects the transfer of information model, assumes the existence of multiple, eclectic, and active audiences, and is sensitive to creating fluid relationships among people and their societies (Tansey & Rayner, 2009). It recognizes that regardless of the inherent merits of any scientific line of inquiry, the benefits have to be seen and judged by many different persons and cultures (Hasian & Plec, 2002).

Providing more data on the evolution of risk communication, Gurabardhi, Gutteling, and Kuttschreuter (2005) reviewed 349 peer-reviewed articles related to risk communication published from 1988 to 2000, and their results indicated an increase in publishing articles on risk communication, a decrease in articles referring to one-way flow of information, and an increase in concern for two-way risk communication, with a gradual increase in reference to stakeholder participation in risk decisions. In summary of the overviews of the development of risk communication, risk communicators first started with the notion that they wanted to obtain and share the correct numbers. According to Stern and Fineberg (1996), this approach obviously failed, and so risk communication practices evolved until the professional risk community came to the conclusion that ideally risk communication entails working with publics as partners in the mutual attempt to manage risks.

Research Agendas

This section includes very brief overviews of some of the significant research agendas related to risk communication, including risk perception/expressed preference, mental models, precaution advocacy/outrage management, and community infrastructural, sociocultural, and critical theoretical. By no means an exhaustive typology or explanation, and quite arguable, this section provides a starting point for understanding and appreciating the complex and multidisciplinary approach to risk communication. Within these and other research orientations are an eclectic and expansive range of key constructs and contexts of risk communication, including rhetoric, influence and persuasion, interpersonal and organizational communication, the affect heuristic, the precautionary principle, social dramaturgy, the ecological perspective, science literacy, renewal, restorative enrichment, ethics, decision making, disaster sociology, mass media studies, and communication and information technology.

Risk Perception/ Expressed Preference

From years of risk analysis and perception research, it is becoming more evident that observed discrepancy is a fundamental challenge of risk communication researchers—the discrepancy between potential and actual risk bearers' perceptions of environmental and technological risks, and those of the science and policy experts. Better understanding this divide, and related communication questions, remains a core challenge to the field.

Identified as risk perception research specifically including expressed preference research, psychological studies were at the forefront of risk communication research, addressing cognitive and attitudinal processes through which risks are interpreted. Early research conducted by Starr (1969) focused on whether risk exposure was voluntary or involuntary and the value of benefits to the risk. Researchers such as Fischhoff, Slovic, Lichtenstein, Read, and Combs (1978) and Slovic, Fischhoff, and Lichtenstein (1979) extended this research based on expressed views of risk rather than behavioral research.

They found that experts based their risk perspectives on probability of fatality, while lay people's evaluations are based more on subjective characteristics of the hazard. Their landmark research focused on concepts such as dread and unknown as key psychometric variables within risk communication. Other variables included involuntary, unfamiliar, uncontrollable, unfair, memorable, acute, focused in time and space, fatal, delayed, artificial, and undetectable, as well as the question of whether individual mitigation is impossible. Three of the strongest psychometric variables within this line of research, which have also been advanced in other research orientations, are control, trust, and uncertainty.

Some work has been conducted that is bridging psychological and sociocultural research. For example, Finucane, Slovic, Mertz, Flynn, and Satterfield (2000) conducted traditional psychological metrics research while also including a range of social factors such as values, gender, race, emotions, trust, and stigma in shaping risk perceptions.

Mental Models

Obtaining a strong understanding of mental modeling theory is another area of study that helps practitioners when developing risk communication message strategies. Through the integration of decision theory and behavioral research, the mental models approach of risk communication is built on the research of Fischhoff, Morgan, Bostrom, and associates (e.g., Morgan et al., 2002). The mental models approach is based on the concept of how people understand and view various phenomena grounded in cognitive psychology and artificial intelligence research (Geuter & Stevens, 1983). Mental modeling suggests that those affected by a risk will create their own interpretation of the event based on the construction and interpretation of the information within their own cognitive processes. Successful integration of information with existing beliefs, according to the mental models approach, "requires creating coherent *mental models*, allowing people to make sense of what they hear and make consistent inferences regarding the situations they face" (Downs, de Bruin, Fischhoff, Hesse, & Maibach, 2009, p. 508).

What is also significant is the potential barrier due to the sheer number and complexity of evaluations and choices related to risk decisions (e.g., Fischhoff, 2005); quite possibly the more information an individual has to sift through to develop a solution to the problem, the slower and less accurate the reasoning becomes (Vandierendonck, Dierckx, & De Vooght, 2004). Depending on the type of risk or crisis, information overload is all too common, especially when practitioners resort to a data dump of incident specifics.

Precaution Advocacy/ Outrage Management

Precautionary communication is used to alert people to hazards that people are insufficiently concerned about, while outrage management is used to calm people who are overconcerned about less hazardous situations. Sandman's (1993) work on risk as a function of hazard (technical assessment) and outrage (cultural, personal view) has provided a framework and reference for much of this work in risk communication and health communication.

Originally examined by Fischhoff, Sandman, and Slovic, among others, hazard and outrage have been extended and advanced by numerous other researchers. From this research perspective, the risk bearers' view of the risk reflects the danger (hazard) and also, just as importantly, how they feel about the risk and their related emotions about the action (outrage). Sandman's (1986) classic argument is that the ultimate goal of risk communication is rational alertness, and the task of risk communication is to alert people when they need to be alerted and reassure them when they need to be reassured because the public often ignores serious risks and overreacts to less serious risks.

Community Infrastructural

Decades of risk management and communication research argue for an infrastructural, community-based approach (Palenchar & Heath, 2007). While a general definition of risk communication from this perspective was provided earlier in the chapter, "an infrastructural approach to crisis and risk reasons that individual, expert, and community efficacy are focal points for determining whether a community is properly organized to plan and communicate about various risks" (Heath, Lee, & Ni, 2009, p. 124). A fully functioning society is aware of risk, or at least does its best to be aware of, assess, and discuss, and develops plans tailored to particular risk-bearing communities and their individual and group unique risk decision heuristics. "These messages need to survive experiences and conversations of people in the community" (p. 128).

Risk democracy is a central theme within community infrastructures, and in association with various experts, individual voices of risk bearers must be brought together to create systems and shared perspectives that appropriately assess, mitigate, and respond to risks that may be unevenly borne throughout any community or larger society. "Opinions are formed, held, shared, and reinforced by social units, what can be called community units of like-minded people" (Heath, Palenchar, & O'Hair, 2009, p. 472).

This approach builds on key psychometric variables such as trust, control, and uncertainty, combined with a community construction of the meaning and the communication and management of risk through the lens of rhetorical heritage. Uncertainty governs the risk communication process. "In turbulent times, uncertainty and distrust soar. Highly involved people struggle to control sources of risks that affect their self-interests. Information and knowledge become less relevant to the need to exert control because they are only loosely related to risk tolerance" (Heath, 1995, p. 273).

A general view of risk communication from a community infrastructural perspective assumes multiple voices in the community. Heath and Lee (2009) demonstrated the need to attune to multiple voices in risk discussions in the high risk community study, and emergency management experts need to understand potential risks and crises, plan appropriate response protocols to mitigate damages, exert appropriate control measures, and "communicate in ways that provide expert advice (mental modes approach to risk communication) sensitive to cultural concerns. Done properly, recommendations are more likely to be sustained, rather than contradicted or dismissed by various publics" (p. 137).

Sociocultural

A sociocultural perspective toward risk communication is based on the experiences of everyday life. A social theory or sociological-oriented view of public relations is not necessarily about management problems but about "the relationship public relations has with respect to the societies in which it is produced and to the social systems it co-produces" (Ihlen & van Ruler, 2007, p. 244). A sociological orientation in this ongoing struggle of meaning in the creation of social reality and risk has advanced understanding of risk concerning ontological status and testable models that connect sociological variables with individual attitudes, perceptions, and meanings of risk.

Heath and O'Hair (2009c) argued that to understand fully the impact of a risk on a given population, communication theorists must search for insight into the cultural and societal practices employed by those individuals. Their argument was founded on the rationale that risk and crisis communication demand more than just a transfer of information and that "we can only understand crisis and risk communication by first examining the nature of people and the society they build" (p. 5).

Kasperson and Kasperson's (1996) social amplification of risk framework is a social theory approach that seeks to explain why some incidents that were determined to have very little potential of harm to the lay audience would end up becoming the focus of an unreasonable amount of attention. Their framework as they described it is "capable of illuminating risk in its full complexity, is sensitive to the social settings in which risk occurs, and also recognizes that social interactions may either amplify or attenuate the signals to society about the risk" (p. 96). Lay publics will form judgments based on any number of perceived factors such as controllability, catastrophic potential, scientific understanding, effects on future generations, and dread. In addition to the threat against the public, the social amplification of the risk may also lead to increased potential for liability, financial burdens, and reputational damage (Kasperson & Kasperson, 1996). It is also widely accepted that while intense media coverage could result in a social amplification of risk, messages of self-efficacy may help counteract this trend (McComas, 2006).

Alaszewski (2005) reviewed risk communication pieces in recent issues of *Health, Risk and Society* and argued for the importance of social contexts in the study of risk communication—that humans' response to information is shaped by social contexts, such as the need for personal security and trust for information sources.

The arguments stand against a rational actor decision-making model in risk communication: "There is little evidence that risk communication based on the rational actor model shapes an understanding or behavior in ways in which health-policy makers and public health experts want" (p. 101). Bickerstaff (2004) argued that over the past decade, there has been a significant shift in convergence between the social and cultural risk perception research to the psychological risk perception research.

Critical Theoretical

Critical theoretical scholarship has only recently become a focus of public relations (L'Etang, 2005) and risk communication scholarship. While applied scholarship has been critical of policy and practice within the field, as well as challenging early assumptions of risk communication, it routinely, either intentionally or unintentionally, disregarded issues such as socioeconomic status and power, especially historically constructed power relations. Like public relations, risk communication scholarship is global with insightful research coming out of most parts of the world, though many have argued that risk communication research remains too Western or American orientated. Oftentimes, risk communication studies are still fundamentally dominated by rational, logical, and predictable approaches.

If risk communication, however, is moving to a user-created information sharing and discourse-centered communication approach, legitimacy is even more important. Legitimization is provided by civil society for political institutions when policies and actions are considered to be rational because it aligns with present social norms (Habermas, 1976); thus, risk decisions in this sense should be collaboratively negotiated.

Risk communication that operates within and accepts dissymmetry and dissensus might be more effective in risk assessment and risk communication. According to Holtzhausen (2000),

> The understanding of consensus and symmetry in public relations is seriously challenged by the postmodern concepts of dissensus and dissymmetry. Seeking consensus implies seeking an unjust settlement in which the most powerful, usually organizations, get their way.... Consensus sacrifices the recognition of differences for superficial treatment. (pp. 106–107)

The discussion of and acceptance of different viewpoints is important, even those considered on the fringes or the edges.

Wardman's (2008) extensive literature review on the constitution of risk communication in advanced liberal societies brings some additional clarity to the increasingly large field of risk communication research and related policy and management issues. Wardman listed three imperatives typically employed in the utilization of risk communication. First, a normative imperative for risk communication based on a process that suggests risk communication is the right thing to do, without regard for outcomes. Second, the instrumental imperative identifies risk communication as a purposeful resource that can be used by individuals or organizations to meet established objectives. The third, substantive, imperative is that risk communication should be used to improve risk dialogue and the quality of knowledge available for risk decisions; better outcomes are possible with insights from multiple stakeholders with different points of view.

Best Practices of Risk Communication

After reviewing what are risk and risk communication, as well as the evolution and numerous research orientations to the field, this chapter turns to three best practical typologies of risk communication. For example, the World Health Organization (2004) developed risk and crisis communication guidelines in response to the communication problems faced in dealing with the severe acute respiratory syndrome (SARS) epidemic of 2003. The guidelines include five fundamental risk communication principles: (1) building trust, (2) announcing early, (3) being transparent, (4) respecting public concerns, and (5) preparatory planning.

Second, risk communication researchers with the National Center for Food Protection and Defense (NCFPD) developed and refined over several years 10 best practices for effective risk communication (NCFPD, n.d.; see also Seeger, 2006). These are as follows: (1) risk and crisis communication is an ongoing process; (2) conduct pre-event planning and preparedness activities; (3) foster partnerships with publics; (4) collaborate and coordinate with credible sources; (5) meet the needs of media and remain accessible; (6) listen to publics' concerns and understand audience; (7) communicate with compassion, concern, and empathy; (8) demonstrate honesty, candor, and openness; (9) accept uncertainty and ambiguity; and (10) give people meaningful actions to do (self-efficacy).

Last, Palenchar and Heath (2006) provided responsible advocacy guidelines within the context of strategic risk communication to guide ethical choices and strategic actions by public relations and risk communication practitioners. These included advice to (1) work with community residents to develop and use emergency response measures that can mitigate severe outcomes in the event of a risk event; (2) acknowledge, research, and appreciate the depths of desire on the part of stakeholders to exert control over factors they perceive to have a negative effect; (3) acknowledge uncertainty in risk assessments, and do not trivialize this uncertainty but use it as an incentive for constantly seeking better answers to the questions raised by members of the community; (4) work with community members to effectively participate in decision-making systems so that they become a constructive part of the risk assessment and risk management process; (5) build trust over time through community outreach and collaborative decision making; (6) feature legitimate benefits while acknowledging harms in communications, but do not assume that all persons' decision heuristics or values lead them to the same weightings of risk harms and benefits; (7) participate in the risk assessment and communication process through dialogue, and understand concerns in terms of the experiences and values of community members; and (8) recognize the value-laden, personalized decision process community residents apply, and frame the risk assessment accordingly (p. 140).

Conclusion

Leiss (1996) correctly suggested that with the transition of a new phase in the evolution of risk communication, newer approaches would build on the strengths and weaknesses of the ones that had come before. The variety of perspectives in risk communication has made it a truly universal field of study (Gurabardhi et al., 2005), while the past 30-plus years have seen a continued maturation of the field of risk communication as indicated by not just the evidence but the explosion of research. Renn (2008) suggested, however, that there is still a major debate about how society views risk. Veil, Reynolds, Sellnow, and Seeger (2008) argued that "although much is known about the role of communication, a comprehensive picture of the process in risks and crises has yet to emerge" (p. S31), while Pidgeon, Kasperson, and Slovic (2003) similarly argued that research concerning risk communication, despite tremendous advances, remains "seriously fragmented: between the psychometric paradigm and cultural theories of risk perception; between post-modernist and discourse-centered approaches and behavioral studies of risk; between economic/utility-maximization and economic-justice approaches; and between communications and empowerment strategies for risk communication" (p. 2).

Rowan's (1994) suggestion that there are three types of risk communication research that could provide a foundation for future risk communication is especially applicable today. These include (1) a technical perspective that tends to privilege persuasive scientific data versus a more democratic perspective that is concerned more with matters of justice and fairness, (2) phenomenological analyses of people's everyday experience and notions of environmental risk, and (3) a research perspective that builds on broad philosophical principles for what constitutes excellent risk communication.

As the field continues to evolve in concept and expand in concerns of stakeholders and related private, governmental, and nongovernmental organizations, there remains a tremendous opportunity for additional research and applications. One example is the area of risk communication and children. The rise in significant risk events over the past several decades has highlighted the need to improve the gaps in preparedness, response, and recovery policies that specifically address the needs of children. According to the U.S. National Commission on Children and Disasters (2009),

> Public health departments and hospitals will need to improve their ability to handle a surge of pediatric patients due to influenza, provide appropriate risk communication and community mitigation guidance to schools, child care providers and other child congregate care facilities and potentially execute mass vaccinations and mass prophylaxis, with special considerations to safely and effectively administer medications and interventions to children. (p. 5)

Another emerging research area is the role of new information technology, especially new media and social media, in relation to the distribution of risk information and the dialogue among risk stakeholders.

Ultimately, is risk communication about objective phenomena or social construction? Following Renn's (2008) advice, risk communicators should try to "avoid the naïve realism of risk as a purely objective category, as well as the relativistic perspective of making all judgments subjective reflections of power and interests" (p. 3). When Leiss's article on the three phases of the evolution of risk communication was published in 1996, he considered this third, social phase to be the stage the communications industry was experiencing at that time; however, it is evident that the field is expanding into a new era of dialogue that builds on the strengths of the diversity of research being conducted while focusing on real-time application of the theory to better manage resources and better manage health, safety, and environmental risks.

References

Alaszewski, A. (2005). Risk communication: Identifying the importance of social context. *Health, Risk and Society, 7*(2), 101–105.

Althaus, C. E. (2005). A disciplinary perspective on the epistemological status of risk. *Risk Analysis, 25*(3), 567–588.

Beck, U. (1992). *Risk society: Towards a new modernity.* London: Sage.

Bickerstaff, K. (2004). Risk perception research: Socio-cultural perspectives on the public experience of air pollution. *Environment International, 30,* 827–840.

Calsamiglia, H., & Ferrero, C. L. (2003). Role and position of scientific voices: Reported speech in the media. *Discourse Studies, 5*(2), 147–173.

Covello, V. T. (1992). Risk communication: An emerging area of health communication research. In S. A. Deetz (Ed.), *Communication yearbook 15* (pp. 359–373). Newbury Park, CA: Sage.

Douglas, M. (1992). *Risk and blame: Essays in cultural theory.* London: Routledge.

Downs, J. S., de Bruin, W. B., Fischhoff, B., Hesse, B., & Maibach, E. (2009). How people think about cancer: A mental models approach. In R. L. Heath & H. D. O'Hair (Eds.), *Handbook of risk and crisis communication* (pp. 507–524). New York: Routledge.

Erikson, K. (1994). *A new species of trouble: The human experience of modern disasters.* New York: W. W. Norton.

Federal Emergency Management Agency. (n.d.). *About the national incident management system.* Retrieved www.fema.gov/emergency/nims/AboutNIMS.shtm

Finucane, M. L., Slovic, P., Mertz, C. K., Flynn, J., & Satterfield, T. A. (2000). Gender, race, and perceived risk: The "white male" effect. *Health, Risk and Society, 2*(1), 59–72.

Fischhoff, B. (1990). *Risk issues in the news: Why experts and laymen disagree.* Washington, DC:

News Backgrounders, Foundation for American Communities.

Fischhoff, B. (1995). Risk perception and communication unplugged: Twenty years of process. *Risk Analysis, 15*(2), 137–145.

Fischhoff, B. (2005). Decision research strategies. *Health Psychology, 21,* S1–S8.

Fischhoff, B., Slovic, P., Lichtenstein, S., Read, S., & Combs, B. (1978). How safe is safe enough? A psychometric study of attitudes toward technological risks and benefits. *Policy Sciences, 9*(3), 127–152.

Geuter, D., & Stevens, A. L. (1983). *Mental models.* Hillsdale, NJ: Lawrence Erlbaum.

Goffman, E. (1959). *The presentation of self in everyday life.* New York: Anchor Books.

Goffman, E. (1967). *Interaction ritual: Essays in face-to-face behaviour.* Garden City, NJ: Anchor Books.

Gurabardhi, Z., Gutteling, J. M., & Kuttschreuter, M. (2005). An empirical analysis of communication flow, strategy and stakeholders' participation in the risk communication literature 1988–2000. *Journal of Risk Research, 8*(6), 499–511.

Habermas, J. (1976). *Legitimation crisis* (T. McCarthy, Trans.). London: Heinemann.

Hamburg, M. A., & Sharfstein, J. M. (2009). The FDA as a public health agency. *New England Journal of Medicine, 360*(24), 2493–2495.

Hasian, M., Jr., & Plec, E. (2002). The cultural, legal and scientific arguments in the human genome diversity debate. *Howard Journal of Communications, 13,* 301–319.

Heath, R. L. (1995). Corporate environment risk communication: Cases and practices along the Texas Gulf Coast. In B. R. Burleson (Ed.), *Communication yearbook 18* (pp. 255–277). Thousand Oaks, CA: Sage.

Heath, R. L., Lee, J., & Ni, L. (2009). Crisis and risk approaches to emergency management planning and communication: The role of similarity and sensitivity. *Journal of Public Relations Research, 21*(2), 123–141.

Heath, R. L., & O'Hair, H. D. (Eds.). (2009a). *Handbook of risk and crisis communication.* New York: Routledge.

Heath, R. L., & O'Hair, H. D. (2009b). Introduction. In R. L. Heath & H. D. O'Hair (Eds.), *Handbook of risk and crisis communication* (pp. xi–xii). New York: Routledge.

Heath, R. L., & O'Hair, H. D. (2009c). The significance of crisis and risk communication. In R. L. Heath & H. D. O'Hair (Eds.), *Handbook of risk and crisis communication* (pp. 5–30). New York: Routledge.

Heath, R. L., Palenchar, M. J., & O'Hair, H. D. (2009). Community building through risk communication infrastructure. In R. L. Heath & H. D. O'Hair (Eds.), *Handbook of risk and crisis communication* (pp. 471–487). New York: Routledge.

Holtzhausen, D. R. (2000). Postmodern values in public relations. *Journal of Public Relations Research, 12*(1), 93–114.

Ihlen, O., & van Ruler, B. (2007). How public relations works: Theoretical roots and public relations perspectives. *Public Relations Review, 33,* 243–248.

Kasperson, R. E., & Kasperson, J. X. (1996). The social amplification and attenuation of risk. *Annals of the American Academy of Political and Social Science, 545,* 95–105.

Kasperson, R. E., & Stallen, P. J. M. (1991). Risk communication: The evolution of attempts. In R. E. Kasperson & P. J. M. Stallen (Eds.), *Communicating risks to the public* (pp. 1–14). Boston: Kluwer.

Krimsky, S. (2007). Risk communication in the Internet age: The rise of disorganized skepticism. *Environmental Hazards, 7,* 157–164.

Krimsky, S., & Golding, D. (1992). Preface. In S. Krimsky & D. Golding (Eds.), *Social theories of risk* (pp. xiii–xvii). Westport, CT: Praeger.

Krimsky, S., & Plough, A. (1988). *Environmental hazards: Communicating risks as a social process.* Dover, MA: Auburn House.

Laird, F. N. (1989). The decline of deference: The political context of risk communication. *Risk Analysis, 9*(2), 543–550.

Leiss, W. (1996). Three phases in the evolution of risk communication practice. *Annals of the American Academy of Political and Social Science, 545,* 85–94.

L'Etang, J. L. (2005). Critical public relations: Some reflections. *Public Relations Review, 31,* 521–526.

Lofstedt, R. (2004). *Risk communication and management in the 21st century* (Working paper). London: AEI-Brookings Joint Center for Regulatory Studies.

Macauley, M. K. (2006, January). *Issues at the forefront of public policy for environmental risk.* Paper presented at the American Meteorological Society's Annual Policy Colloquium, Washington, DC.

McComas, K. A. (2006). Defining moments in risk communication research: 1996–2005. *Journal of Health Communication, 11,* 75–91.

Morgan, M. G., Fischhoff, B., Bostrom, A., & Atman, C. J. (2002). *Risk communication: A mental modes approach.* New York: Cambridge University Press.

National Center for Food Protection and Defense. (n.d.). *10 risk communication best practices.* Retrieved March 23, 2010, from www.ncfpd.umn.edu/research/risk.cfm

National Research Council. (1989). *Improving risk communication.* Washington, DC: National Academy Press.

Organization for Economic Co-Operation and Development. (2002). *OECD guidance document on risk communication for chemical risk management* (Series on risk management, No. 16, Environment, Health and Safety Publications). Paris: Author.

Palenchar, M. J. (2005). Risk communication. In R. L. Heath (Ed.), *Encyclopedia of public relations* (pp. 752–755). Thousand Oaks, CA: Sage.

Palenchar, M. J. (2009). Historical trends of risk and crisis communication. In R. L. Heath & H. D. O'Hair (Eds.), *Handbook of risk and crisis communication* (pp. 31–52). New York: Routledge.

Palenchar, M. J., & Heath, R. L. (2006). Responsible advocacy through strategic risk communication. In K. Fitzpatrick & C. Bronstein (Eds.), *Ethics in public relations: Responsible advocacy* (pp. 131–153). Thousand Oaks, CA: Sage.

Palenchar, M. J., & Heath, R. L. (2007). Strategic risk communication: Adding value to society. *Public Relations Review, 33,* 120–129.

Pearson, R. (1990). Ethical values or strategic values? The two faces of systems theory in public relations. *Journal of Public Relations Research, 1*(1/4), 219–234.

Pidgeon, N., Kasperson, R. E., & Slovic, P. (2003). Introduction. In N. Pidgeon, R. E. Kasperson, & P. Slovic (Eds.), *The social amplification of risk* (pp. 1–11). Cambridge, UK: Cambridge University Press.

Renn, O. (1992). Concepts of risk: A classification. In S. Krimsky & D. Golding (Eds.), *Social theories of risk* (pp. 53–89). Westport, CT: Praeger.

Renn, O. (1998). Three decades of risk research: Accomplishments and new challenges. *Journal of Risk Research, 1*(1), 49–71.

Renn, O. (2004). Participatory processes for designing environmental policies. *Land Use Policy, 23,* 34–43.

Renn, O. (2008). *Risk governance: Coping with uncertainty in a complex world.* London: Earthscan.

Renn, O., & Kastenholz, H. (2000). *Risk communication for chemical risk management: An OECD background paper.* Berlin, Germany: OECD Workshop.

Reynolds, B. (2002). *Crisis and emergency risk communication.* Atlanta, GA: Centers for Disease Control and Prevention.

Rowan, K. E. (1994). What risk communicators need to know: An agenda for research. In B. R. Burleson (Ed.), *Communication yearbook 18* (pp. 300–319). Thousand Oaks, CA: Sage.

Sandman, P. M. (1986). *Explaining environmental risk: Some notes on environmental risk communication* [Brochure]. Washington, DC: U.S. Environmental Protection Agency.

Sandman, P. M. (1993). *Responding to community outrage: Strategies for effective risk communication.* Fairfax, VA: American Industrial Hygiene Association.

Seeger, M. W. (2006). Best practices in crisis communication: An expert panel process. *Journal of Applied Communication, 34*(3), 232–234.

Slovic, P., Fischhoff, B., & Lichtenstein, S. (1979). Facts and fears: Understanding perceived risk. *Policy and Practice in Health and Safety, 2,* S65–S102.

Starr, C. (1969). Social benefit versus technological risk. *Science, 165,* 1232–1238.

Stern, P. C., & Fineberg, H. V. (Eds.). (1996). *Understanding risk: Informing decisions in a democratic society.* Washington, DC: National Academy Press.

Tansey, J., & Rayner, S. (2009). Cultural theory and risk. In R. L. Heath & H. D. O'Hair (Eds.), *Handbook of risk and crisis communication* (pp. 53–79). New York: Routledge.

U.S. National Commission on Children and Disasters. (2009, October). *Interim report.* Washington, DC: Author.

Vandierendonck, A., Dierckx, V., & De Vooght, G. (2004). Mental model construction in linear reasoning: Evidence for the construction of initial annotated models. *Quarterly Journal of Experimental Psychology, 57A*(8), 1369–1391.

Veil, S., Reynolds, B., Sellnow, T. L., & Seeger, M. W. (2008). CERC as a theoretical framework for research and practice. *Health Promotion Practice, 9*(4, Suppl.), S26–S34.

Wardman, J. K. (2008). The constitution of risk communication in advanced liberal societies. *Risk Analysis, 29*(2), 1619–1637.

World Health Organization. (2004). *Outbreak communication: Best practices for communicating with the public during an outbreak.* Geneva, Switzerland: Author.

CHAPTER 32

Community Engagement and Risk Management

Katherine A. McComas

Since the publication of the 2001 version of the *Handbook of Public Relations* (Heath, 2001) nearly a decade ago, our society has arguably become more aware of the daily risks it faces at the local, national, and global levels. From the terror attacks of September 11, 2001, to the devastation of Hurricane Katrina in 2005, to the more mundane yet ever-present nationwide recalls of food products, plastic water bottles, pharmaceuticals, and children's toys, we are inundated with information about hazards in our lives. One has only to turn on the evening news or listen to a local radio newscast to learn about local controversies related to risk management, ranging from concerns about water quality, secondhand smoke, deer overpopulation, and wildfire-related hazards. For the more active information seeker, the Internet provides countless resources for people to access databases about toxic chemicals in their neighborhoods, lead levels in their backyards, and registered sex offenders in their local areas.

People's concern about risk, coupled with their need to "do something," has underscored the need to find appropriate and meaningful ways to engage citizens in risk management. In addition to long-standing efforts, such as restoration advisory boards, watershed protection groups, and local emergency planning committees, the last decade has also witnessed a growing number of voluntary organizations sponsored by the U.S. Department of Homeland Security and the U.S. Department of Justice geared toward capitalizing on people's patriotic desire to protect themselves and their communities from risk. These include programs such as Citizen Corps, which seeks to augment the capacity of first responders through the use of volunteers; the Community Emergency Response Team, which trains volunteers in disaster preparedness skills; the USAonWatch, which is an expanded neighborhood watch program that goes beyond local crime to include terrorism awareness; and the Volunteers in Police Service, which seeks to enhance the ability of local police forces to use volunteers (Drabczyk, 2007; National Office of Citizen Corps, 2009).

This chapter examines community engagement in risk management. Its intent is to offer a conceptual foundation that might be useful for someone seeking to understand or explore what the distinct or cumulative impact might be for society's preoccupation with risk and safety and the public and private sectors' organized efforts to engage community members in risk management. With the intent of informing theory and practice in public relations, it explores ways to structure and benefit from people's growing demand for a sense of agency or control over their exposure to risk, while also examining the challenges associated with community engagement. It operates from a perspective that appropriate and ethical community engagement is not only something for which we should strive from a normative sense but also something essential to the management of risk as well as the health and welfare of society.

Risk Management and Risk Communication

Risk management pertains to the regulatory and procedural measures we employ to minimize unnecessary or unwanted exposure to risk, which can include everything from traffic laws, to airport security measures, to warning labels on consumer products. In its most basic sense, risk can be understood as the "things, forces, or circumstances that pose danger to people or to what they value" (National Research Council, 1996, p. 215). The challenge for risk management is that while some people seek zero risk in their daily lives, others are willing to accept some level of risk to obtain some type of benefit. People still drive on highways, for example, despite the risk of being in a traffic accident; they still live in cities, despite the higher likelihood of being a victim of crime; some even still smoke cigarettes, despite the risk of dying from lung cancer. Understanding how people evaluate costs versus benefits, also known as risk trade-offs, and then incorporating this information into management choices is a key aspect of risk management and an important area of risk research (Heath, Liao, & Douglas, 1995; Johnson, 2004; Nathan, Heath, & Douglas, 1992; Zaksek & Arvai, 2004).

Exposure to some risks occurs at a level of personal choice, such as the choices of where to drive or live, or decisions about whether to purchase organic produce to avoid the risks of pesticide residues. As such, they never rise to the level of a public health issue requiring an organized, risk management response. Other risks affect groups of individuals, such as decisions about building new power plants or allowing for more natural gas drilling, and require legal, political, or societal action. Even seemingly personal choices, like whether to smoke cigarettes or talk on a cell phone while driving, can require societal action, when by partaking in an activity individuals expose someone else to a risk, such as the risk of cancer from secondhand smoke or a car accident due to inattentive driving. This chapter focuses on the management of public and environmental health risks that pose risks beyond the individual level and, as such, require legal, political, or societal response.

Effective risk management includes risk communication with affected publics, not only to inform them of risks but also, ideally, to involve them in deciding the boundaries for risk acceptability (National Research Council, 1996, 2008). Risk communication, narrowly defined, can be understood as a purposeful, iterative exchange of information among individuals, groups, and institutions related to the assessment, characterization, and management of risk. It is important to recognize, however, that any organized risk communication effort also takes place within a broader, social context that includes intentional and unintentional messages conveyed by individuals, groups, and institutions about the origins and nature of risk (Boholm, 2008; Plough & Krimsky, 1987; Wardman, 2008). Given the likelihood of competing risk messages, effective risk communication may hinge less on the accurate interpretation of any one message and more on the extent to which health officials are considered trustworthy and legitimate providers of risk information (Fischhoff, 1995).

Some prefer to distinguish public health-risk communication from environmental risk communication (Gurabardhi, Gutteling, & Kuttschreuter, 2004), arguing that public health risk communication more often entails voluntary than involuntary risks, such as cigarette smoking, and may require different approaches. Persuasive approaches, for example, may be more justifiable in public health risk communication efforts, where significant medical or scientific opinion concurs on both the relative risk and the need to convince individuals to take preventative actions to avoid harm. Environmental risks, in comparison, often pertain to risks that are involuntary or that a minority is asked to accept, such as the siting of a landfill. In such cases, the use of persuasive approaches to encourage people to accept involuntary or disproportionate risk is arguably unethical and can lead to considerable backlash or outrage on behalf of those being asked to bear the brunt of the risk. In this regard, research addresses how to assist individuals as they evaluate risk trade-offs associated with risk management decisions (see, e.g., Arvai & Gregory, 2003; Arvai, Gregory, & McDaniels, 2001; McComas, Arvai, & Besley, 2009; McDaniels, Gregory, & Fields, 1999; Renn, 1999; Zaksek & Arvai, 2004).

The emphasis on deliberation and integration of public input into risk management decisions is a relatively modern development. Historically, risk communication followed a much more one-sided approach, and decisions about risk acceptability were largely based on scientific risk assessments with little public input (Leiss, 1995; Lynn, 1990). Lynn (1990) described these early approaches as "a right-to-hear-what-has-already-been-decided approach" (p. 96). After it became apparent that the public was not always willing to accept such decisions, the next phase of risk communication emphasized persuasive approaches (Leiss, 1996), which might be described as a "decide-announce-defend" approach. The current phase reflects the importance that psychological and social factors have on risk acceptability (Bostrom & Lofstedt, 2003; Fischhoff, 1995; Leiss, 1995, 1996).

Psychological research on risk perceptions examines why, for example, people are more willing to accept some risks over others, even when science suggests the risks of dying from either are relatively equal. Namely, research on the psychometric paradigm has determined that people base their perceptions on subjective qualities of risk, including its voluntariness, controllability, fairness, benefits, catastrophic potential, scientific understanding, scientific uncertainty, delayed effects, effects on future generations, dread, personal stake, and human versus natural origin (Slovic, 1999, 2000). Furthermore, risk perceptions tend to map onto two factors related to the extent to which a risk is perceived as "dreaded" and its effects "known" or observable. In turn, research has found that people often want more risk reduction and greater regulation for risks that they perceive are less known and more dreaded, such as radioactive waste, pesticides, and electromagnetic fields; risks associated with bicycles, lawn mowers, trampolines, fireworks, and even smoking, in comparison, are perceived as less dreaded and more observable or known (Slovic, 1987). Field research has extended the measures of risk perception into community settings and found that they worked well to predict people's orientation toward local hazards (Heath, Seshadri, & Lee, 1998; Trumbo, 1996; Trumbo, McComas, & Besley, 2008).

Along with psychological factors, social factors, such as trust in risk managers, also play a major role in people's orientation to and acceptance of risk (Leiss, 1995, 1996). Indeed, the past two decades have witnessed a substantial increase in research examining trust in risk communication (Cvetkovich & Lofstedt, 1999; Fessenden-Raden, Fitchen, & Heath, 1987; Johnson & Chess, 2003; Poortinga & Pidgeon, 2003; Slovic, 1993; Trumbo & McComas, 2003), including the role of trust in community engagement activities (Boeckmann & Tyler, 2002; Heath et al., 1998; Lofstedt, 2005; McComas & Trumbo, 2001; Palenchar & Heath, 2007; Siegrist, Cvetkovich, & Gutscher, 2001). In particular, research has consistently found that the less trustworthy people perceive risk managers, the more concerned they are about the risks (Freudenburg, 1993; McComas & Trumbo, 2001; Poortinga & Pidgeon, 2003). Research has also found that people tend to trust risk managers with whom they believe they share similar values (Siegrist, Cvetkovich, & Roth, 2000; Siegrist et al., 2001). The extent to which community engagement can amplify concern about risk and decrease trust in risk managers is one of the questions examined in the next section.

Methods of Community Engagement

From the neighborhood crime watch team that meets in someone's living room, to the terror alerts posted along highways, to the local emergency planning committee that meets during regularly scheduled sessions at a municipal building, methods of community engagement in risk management vary widely. Given that much of the research that applies to theory and practice in public relations focuses on the more formalized processes of community engagement, which are often mandated and sponsored by the public or private sector, this chapter focuses on the latter, more formal approaches.

One means of organizing the methods is by their objectives. Some methods, such as workshops or meetings, seek primarily to engage community members in specific decisions and are relatively short term. Others involve longer-term, capacity building, partnership roles for community members, such as local emergency planning committees or restoration advisory boards. Table 32.1 lists of some of the most common methods used to inform risk management activities as well as frequent objectives.

Table 32.1 Selected Methods of Community Engagement

Method	Description	Studies
Community survey	• Random sample or targeted population used to assess the attitudes and desires of community residents	Ballard and Kuhn (1996), Burger (2004), Charnley and Engelbert (2005), Heath and Palenchar (2000), Jardine (2003), McComas and Scherer (1999), and Pellizzoni and Ungaro (2000)
Focus groups or other controlled discussion group	• Participants recruited by sponsors to respond to key questions	Charnley and Engelbert (2005), Dietrich and Schibeci (2003), Dürrenberger, Kastenholz, and Behringer (1999), Jardine (2003), Pellizzoni and Ungaro (2000), Rowe, Horlick-Jones, Walls, and Pidgeon (2005), and Smith and McDonough (2001)
Written comments on draft material/ interactive Web site	• Open call for comments on an issue of concern and/or proposed policies or actions, which may be provided in hard copy or through an electronic forum	Drew, Nyerges, and Leschine (2004), Lidskog and Soneryd (2000), O'Riordan (1976), Pidgeon et al. (2005), Roth, Dunsby, and Bero (2003), Rowe, Horlick-Jones, Walls, and Pidgeon (2005), and Schotland and Bero (2002)

Method	Description	Studies
Availability session/open house	• Representatives from sponsors or other experts answer one-on-one questions; often held in concert with a more traditional public meeting	McComas (2003b)
"Traditional" public meeting/public hearing	• Open to all community members but agenda set by officials (Such meetings often include an official presentation followed by questions or comments from the audience.)	Adams (2004), Baker, Addams, and Davis (2005), Boholm (2008), Gundry and Heberlein (1984), Hamilton (2003), Kuhn and Ballard (1998), Lidskog and Soneryd (2000), McComas (2001, 2003a), McComas, Besley, and Trumbo (2006), and O'Riordan (1976)
Advisory board/committee	• Select group of stakeholders who play an advisory role to the risk management authority	Aronoff and Gunter (1994), Burger (2002), Burroughs (1999), Heath, Bradshaw, and Lee (2002), Kinney and Leschine (2002), McDaniels, Gregory, and Fields (1999), Murdock, Wiessner, and Sexton (2005), O'Riordan (1976), Rothstein (2004), Santos and Chess (2003), and Wolfe and Bjornstad (2003)
Discussion events/community dinner/workshops/ priority setting	• Public events designed to facilitate and encourage discussion among community members	Abelson et al. (2003), Halvorsen (2001, 2003), and Webler, Rakel, Renn, and Johnson (1995)
Consensus conference/deliberative forum/deliberative workshops	• Public events wherein sponsors create a public forum for substantive and substantial debate and learning by participants (Experts are generally made available to lay persons and participants often play a role in shaping discussion agenda.)	Abelson et al. (2003), Arvai, Gregory, and McDaniels (2001), Einsiedel (2002), Einsiedel and Eastlick (2000), Einsiedel, Jelsoe, and Breck (2001), Goven (2003), Joss and Durant (1995a, 1995b), Mayer, de Vries, and Geurts (1995), Renn, Webler, and Johnson (1991), and Rowe, Marsh, and Frewer (2004)

Source: Adapted from McComas, Arvai, and Besley (2009).

In terms of effectiveness, each method has its strengths and limitations (Chess & Purcell, 1999). For example, well-done community surveys can provide a representative "snapshot" of residents' views on a matter of broad interest (Blendon, Benson, Desroches, & Weldon, 2003; McComas & Scherer, 1999; Pidgeon et al., 2005). Such views could change, however, if residents do not hold strong opinions or are exposed to new information. Surveys also do not allow for direct interaction with decision makers. On the other hand, public meetings can provide direct, face-to-face opportunities for interaction and build community cohesion (McComas, Trumbo, & Besley, 2007), but they can lead to decreased trust in risk managers and increased risk when managed poorly or disingenuously (Boholm, 2008; McComas, 2003b, 2003c).

Part of the limitation of the methods may be based in the historical underpinnings of community engagement, which was geared more to allow the public an opportunity to comment but not necessarily to have a meaningful voice in policy making. Much like early approaches to risk communication, early methods of community engagement emphasized the superiority of scientific assessments or expert knowledge. Thus, rather than seeking information from citizens, participation more often entailed one-way transfers of information from scientists or technical experts to citizens or nonexperts in the audience (Beierle & Cayford, 2002; Lynn, 1990). Beierle and Cayford (2002), for example, described how traditional approaches to public participation reflected managerial models that gave decision-making power to authorities that were expected to make choices in the public's behalf. In many ways, these approaches reflected the dominant view that gave scientific authority priority over public input. The legislation that followed, however, carried a much more pluralistic appeal, reflecting the aims of making decision making more democratic. The most recent approach, referred to as participatory democracy, maintains that the act of participation itself can have substantive benefits beyond the immediate issue, including creating social capital, political efficacy, and community capacity (Beierle & Cayford, 2002).

This evolution in thinking about community engagement can be seen within the context of the common justifications for community engagement, which can be grouped as normative, substantive, and instrumental (Fiorino, 1990). Normative arguments reflect a fundamental belief that, in a democracy, people have a right to have a voice in decisions that affect their interests. For instance, either through direct participation or representation, people should have a say in how communal resources are managed. Substantive arguments argue that citizen input can improve the substantive quality of risk management decisions (National Research Council, 2008). This rationale lies in contrast with an approach that prioritizes scientific assessments and instead recognizes that community members, who are often acutely tuned in to the risk in the context of their everyday lives, can bring unique wisdom to risk assessments (Jasanoff, 1997; Wynne, 1992). Instrumental arguments emphasize the instrumental benefits of community engagement, which include the belief that having community members engage in the decision making can lead to greater acceptance of decisions and build trusting relationships between community members and authorities. As the National Research Council stated (2008),

> Participation ideally should improve the *quality* of assessments and decisions and their *legitimacy* among those involved and potentially affected. It should lead to increased understanding and decision-making *capacity* among agency officials, scientists, and the interested and affected parties involved and the interests they represent. And it should enhance the ability to implement decisions once they are made both by producing better decisions and by producing legitimate, credible, and well-understood decisions. (p. 225)

One could argue, however, that the evolution in practice has not kept up with evolution in theory about community engagement. In particular, some efforts tend to emphasize the normative or instrumental role of community engagement over the substantive role. For instance, many have criticized public meetings for being used by public agencies as means to minimize public input or co-opt meeting attendees, who by their mere attendance can no longer argue that they did not have a chance to voice their opinions on the decision (Berry, Portney, Bablitch, &

Mahoney, 1997; Checkoway, 1981; Heberlein, 1976). Early on, Arnstein (1969) provided a scathing critique of public participation programs designed to manipulate citizens and minimize their impact on agency decisions. Arnstein's (1969) "ladder of citizen participation" categorized various methods according to the extent to which they ceded control to citizens in agency decision making. Indeed, the question of control remains central 40 years later.

Granted, some of the delay in practice may be due to legal constraints, economic constraints, or organizational culture. On the other hand, it may reflect a concern about how best to engage citizens and use their input. Specifically, to what extent should risk assessments and management decisions incorporate lay or nonexpert opinions? To avoid "capture" by political interests, risk assessment has traditionally been separated from risk management (National Research Council, 1996). In light of the evolution in thought, how should values, ethics, and perceptions of risk be incorporated into risk characterizations? Is shared decision making possible, or even desirable in all cases? Rather than a "one-size-fits-all" or best practice approach, the National Research Council (2008) recommended taking more of a best process approach based on its findings that (a) little evidence suggests that one technique is better than the others, (b) research and practical experience suggest that "best" is situation dependent, (c) change can occur and techniques may need to change accordingly, and (d) "best practice" techniques can lead to formulaic applications that can hinder change and innovation.

In terms of process, however, research on procedural justice suggests that fairness is among the most important factors (Thibaut & Walker, 1975). Early research on procedural justice in legal settings suggested that people's fairness evaluations were strongly related to their control over the process (Thibaut & Walker, 1975). Subsequent research found that people valued other factors related to the enactment of the procedures, including the perceived trustworthiness and neutrality of authorities, and the degree to which they were treated with respect (Tyler, 1989, 1994, 2000; Tyler & Lind, 1992).

In the context of risk management, research has demonstrated that shared control over the decision-making procedures is also important to perceptions of fairness (Heath, Bradshaw, & Lee, 2002). Furthermore, perceived fairness of the process can influence a host of outcome variables, including satisfaction with the process (Arvai, 2003; McComas, 2003a; Webler & Tuler, 2000), satisfaction with the risk managers (Lauber & Knuth, 1997), risk perceptions (Boholm, 2008; McComas et al., 2007), and willingness to accept the outcomes of decisions (Wolsink & Devilee, 2009). Attention to procedural fairness, as well as outcome fairness, is also considered important to efforts seeking to maintain or rebuild trust in risk management institutions (Heath & Abel, 1996a; Lofstedt, 2005; McComas, Besley, & Yang, 2008).

Even so, some fears may linger that any consultation with community members relating to risk may lead to an all-out refusal or a "not-in-my-backyard" (NIMBY) response. Indeed, fear of such kneejerk reactions has even led some countries to propose legislation to limit local input on planning activities (Wolsink, 1994). Research has suggested, however, that local opposition is often much more nuanced than a simple claim of NIMBYism might suggest (Hunter & Leyden, 1995; Kraft & Clary, 1991; Lober, 1996). Furthermore, dismissing local concerns as NIMBYist might exacerbate conflict and prove counterproductive (Wolsink, 1994), whereas a focus on fairness in decision making might prove more useful (Wolsink & Devilee, 2009).

Indeed, in its 2008 report, the National Research Council offered several recommendations to enhance public participation in environmental assessment and decision making, including an admonition to design processes that are inclusive, collaborative, transparent, and honest. Furthermore, it recommended that organizations that undertake public participation do so with a commitment to allow public input to inform their decisions, as well as to learn from the process. Finally, they suggested greater investment in social science research to inform the practice of public participation.

Incentives and Barriers to Community Engagement

If we accept that community engagement can improve risk assessment and risk management, the next step is to examine the reasons that motivate community members to participate. Recognizing the multiple meanings associated with the term *community*, this chapter uses the term in its geographical sense to denote the place where people live, work, raise their children, and conduct most of their daily activities (Poplin, 1972), while noting that one person's geographical boundaries of his or her community may not align exactly with another person's, even if they live next door. In this sense, a person's community has a subjective quality, which might be seen as reflecting that person's unique values and priorities. Accordingly, individuals' commitment to their community will likely differ according to the "boundaries" that they place on their community, which may influence their orientation toward risk (Devine-Wright, 2009). Furthermore, for some people, these boundaries may not extend past their neighborhood, whereas for others, they may include the town, city, or county. Thus, for any particular risk management issue, there will be varying degrees of interest in engagement.

In some sense, much of the discussion surrounding community engagement has focused more on organizational incentives and barriers to engage community members than on incentives and barriers for community members to engage. The underlying assumption appears to be, "If organizations offer community members the opportunity to engage, those who care enough will engage." Unfortunately, such assumptions fail to consider the institutional, social, and psychological factors that might pose barriers to community members. In addition to low levels of voter turnout, Putnam (2000) chronicled a diminishing desire among Americans to engage in local, civic activities despite an increase in opportunities to participate, which he related to diminishing social capital, or the "social glue" that connects people to one another. This decrease in social capital is particularly problematic for risk management, where greater involvement can lead to better outcomes on multiple levels (Portney & Berry, 1997).

Depending on their perceived stakes in the decision's outcome, some members of the community will be interested in participating in the decision-making process and others will not. Perhaps the most extensively studied approach in public relations to predicting individuals' level of activity with regard to a given issue is the situational theory of publics (Grunig, 1983; Grunig & Hunt, 1984; Grunig & Repper, 1992), which offers a means of predicting communication behaviors depending on problem recognition, constraint recognition, and level of involvement. Briefly summarized, problem recognition explores the extent to which an individual recognizes something amiss in a situation and stops to think about it. Constraint recognition relates to the extent to which an individual perceives limitations to carrying out a type of behavior related to the situation. Finally, level of involvement refers to the degree to which an individual feels some connection to the situation. The theory predicts that high problem recognition, low constraint recognition, and high level of involvement encourage active communication, or information seeking behavior, as opposed to passive communication, or information processing behavior.

In the context of community engagement in risk management, research suggests multiple barriers to active communication, such as attending a community meeting or workshop, or searching out information on a Web site. In terms of problem recognition, research has found that people may be unaware of or uninformed about risks or community engagement opportunities (Heath & Abel, 1996b; Heath et al., 2002; McComas, Besley, & Trumbo, 2006; Pirie, de Loe, & Kreutzwiser, 2004). In turn, research has examined strategies for increasing awareness (Jardine, 2003; Neuwirth, Dunwoody, & Griffin, 2000; Rich & Conn, 1995).

Furthermore, structural or institutional constraints may bar individuals from having access to information or opportunities to participate, ranging from scheduling conflicts or transportation difficulties (Bryan, 2004; McComas et al., 2006) to difficulties understanding the risk information (Atlas, 2007). Environmental justice research has examined how the placement of industrial facilities in economically disadvantaged communities has placed unfair burdens on certain groups that too often host a disproportionate share of the risk while also having less of a voice in the process (Chess, Burger, & McDermott, 2005; Pollock, 1995; Satterfield, Mertz, & Slovic, 2004). In turn, efforts to improve community engagement have commented on the importance of reaching people who may not have the economic means to participate (Quigley, Handy, Goble, Sanchez, & George, 2000; Vaughan, 1995). Furthermore, research has found that the extent to which a community's diversity is represented in risk management infrastructures may enhance community members' confidence in the management's ability to respond to crises (Heath, Lee, & Ni, 2009). Similarly, the extent to which community members trust agency members in charge of the risk management activities may influence their intentions to engage (McComas et al., 2006).

More generally, communication research examines the mobilizing influence of interpersonal and mass communication on individual civic engagement (McLeod, Scheufele, Moy, Horowitz et al., 1999; McLeod, Scheufele, & Moy, 1999; Scheufele, 2000). Most of this research has focused more on traditional acts of political engagement surrounding political campaigns (e.g., voting) than on activities more associated with public participation (e.g., attending a meeting, participating on a citizen advisory committee). Even so, relevant studies have shown that the size and heterogeneity of discussion networks influence civic participation. That is, when individuals had larger and more diverse networks, they were more likely to engage in civic activities (McLeod, Scheufele, Moy, Horowitz et al., 1999). Higher levels of civic engagement are also found to be associated with readership of certain media, primarily news or public affairs (Shah, McLeod, & Yoon, 2001). Research on risk information in the media has also found that it can influence individuals' intention to seek information, particularly when media included information about a risk's severity (Neuwirth et al., 2000). Although some research has examined the use of the Internet, including social networking and blogging, related to risk communication (Capriotti, 2007; Macias, Hilyard, & Freimuth, 2009), much room remains for additional inquiry.

In sum, understanding incentives and barriers to communication can help risk managers address the challenge of representativeness, which can be defined as the degree to which people who engage represent, or share similar characteristics (e.g., demographics, attitudes, values, opinions) with, people who do not yet have some type of stake in the issue (e.g., live in the affected area). Although risk managers may not be legally required to ensure the representativeness of community members, several compelling reasons suggest why they should strive for it. From a normative sense, representation can help ensure that community members have a voice in decisions that affect them (Fiorino, 1990). From a substantive sense, having a representative sample of community input can increase the accuracy of risk characterizations (National Research Council, 1996). From an instrumental sense, it can assist risk communication efforts by helping relay information back to stakeholders not able to attend. Finally, representativeness is a key criterion for evaluating fairness in decision making (Leventhal, Karuza, & Fry, 1980; Renn, Webler, & Kastenholz, 1996; Renn, Webler, & Wiedemann, 1995), which has been noted above as an important component in risk management activities.

Conclusions

As we look to the future, the need to engage communities in risk management and, indeed, build their capacity for risk-based decision making is likely to increase. These needs will be borne out of a demand to solve today's most pressing resource issues, such as issues related to climate change, renewable energy, water quality, and waste management, as well as respond to any number of unforeseen hazards. This chapter has sought to provide an overview of some of the major research themes that inform the theory and practice of community engagement in risk management. These included the role of risk acceptability and risk perceptions, as well as the importance of risk communication that reflects an iterative and dialogical process. The chapter examined the justifications for engaging community members, as well as some of the psychological, social, and institutional barriers community members might face. It also explored some of the persisting challenges and concerns about community engagement, such as how much power to cede to community members and concerns about NIMBYism.

Meeting the challenges of risk management will not come easily, but the evidence in support of community engagement has grown annually and offered additional justifications for the effort. This evidence is perhaps most extensively reviewed and succinctly summarized in the National Research Council (2008) report, which found that, when done well, community engagement can improve the quality and legitimacy of decisions while also building trust among community members, organizational representatives, scientific experts, and public officials (National Research Council, 2008). Done poorly, the bad memories may not be soon forgotten. A truism, which research supports, is that trust is more easily lost than regained (Cvetkovich, Siegrist, Murray, & Tragesser, 2002; Poortinga & Pidgeon, 2004; Slovic, 1993). Slovic (1993) argued that this was due to individuals' likelihood to give more weight to "trust-destroying" than "trust-building" events. In turn, one means of rebuilding trust is to share control over the process of risk management—a significant challenge likely to define the next decade of risk management research.

References

Abelson, J., Eyles, J., McLeod, C. B., Collins, P., McMullan, C., & Forest, P. G. (2003). Does deliberation make a difference? Results from a citizens panel study of health goals priority setting. *Health Policy, 66*(1), 95–106.

Adams, B. (2004). Public meetings and the democratic process. *Public Administration Review, 64*(1), 43–54.

Arnstein, S. (1969). A ladder of citizen participation. *Journal of the American Institute of Planners, 35,* 216–224.

Aronoff, M., & Gunter, V. (1994). A pound of cure: Facilitating participatory processes in technological hazard disputes. *Society & Natural Resources, 7*(3), 235–252.

Arvai, J. L. (2003). Using risk communication to disclose the outcome of a participatory decision making process: Effects on the perceived acceptability of risk-policy decisions. *Risk Analysis, 23,* 281–289.

Arvai, J. L., & Gregory, R. (2003). A decision focused approach for identifying cleanup priorities at contaminated sites. *Environmental Science & Technology, 37,* 1469–1476.

Arvai, J. L., Gregory, R., & McDaniels, T. L. (2001). Testing a structured decision approach: Value-focused thinking for deliberative risk communication. *Risk Analysis, 21*(6), 1065–1076.

Atlas, M. (2007). TRI to communicate: Public knowledge and the federal Toxics Release Inventory. *Social Science Quarterly, 88*(2), 555–572.

Baker, W. H., Addams, H. L., & Davis, B. (2005). Critical factors for enhancing municipal public hearings. *Public Administration Review, 65*(4), 490–499.

Ballard, K. R., & Kuhn, R. G. (1996). Developing and testing a facility location model for Canadian nuclear fuel waste. *Risk Analysis, 16*(6), 821–832.

Beierle, T. C., & Cayford, J. (2002). *Democracy in practice: Public participation in environmental decisions.* Washington, DC: Resources for the Future.

Berry, J. M., Portney, K. E., Bablitch, M. B., & Mahoney, R. (1997). Public involvement in administration:

The structural determinants of effective citizen participation. *Journal of Voluntary Action Research, 13*, 7–23.

Blendon, R. J., Benson, J. M., Desroches, C. M., & Weldon, K. J. (2003). Using opinion surveys to track the public's response to a bioterrorist attack. *Journal of Health Communication, 8*, 83–92.

Boeckmann, R. J., & Tyler, T. R. (2002). Trust, respect, and the psychology of political engagement. *Journal of Applied Social Psychology, 32*(10), 2067–2088.

Boholm, A. (2008). The public meeting as a theatre of dissent: Risk and hazard in land use and environmental planning. *Journal of Risk Research, 11*(1/2), 119–140.

Bostrom, A., & Lofstedt, R. E. (2003). Communicating risk: Wireless and hardwired. *Risk Analysis, 23*(2), 241–248.

Bryan, F. M. (2004). *Real democracy: The New England town meeting and how it works.* Chicago: University of Chicago Press.

Burger, J. (2002). Restoration, stewardship, environmental health, and policy: Understanding stakeholders' perceptions. *Environmental Management, 30*(5), 631–640.

Burger, J. (2004). Fish consumption advisories: Knowledge, compliance and why people fish in an urban estuary. *Journal of Risk Research, 7*(5), 463–479.

Burroughs, R. (1999). When stakeholders choose: Process, knowledge, and motivation in water quality decisions. *Society & Natural Resources, 12*(8), 797–809.

Capriotti, P. (2007). Chemical risk communication through the Internet in Spain. *Public Relations Review, 33*(3), 326–329.

Charnley, S., & Engelbert, B. (2005). Evaluating public participation in environmental decision-making: EPA's superfund community involvement program. *Journal of Environmental Management, 77*(3), 165–182.

Checkoway, B. (1981). The politics of public hearings. *Journal of Applied Behavioral Science, 17*(4), 566–582.

Chess, C., Burger, J., & McDermott, M. H. (2005). Speaking like a state: Environmental justice and fish consumption advisories. *Society & Natural Resources, 18*(3), 267–278.

Chess, C., & Purcell, K. (1999). Public participation and the environment: Do we know what works? *Environmental Science & Technology, 33*, 2685–2692.

Cvetkovich, G., & Lofstedt, R. E. (Eds.). (1999). *Social trust and the management of risk.* London: Earthscan.

Cvetkovich, G., Siegrist, M., Murray, R., & Tragesser, S. (2002). New information and social trust: Asymmetry and perseverance of attributions about hazard managers. *Risk Analysis, 22*(2), 359–367.

Devine-Wright, P. (2009). Rethinking NIMBYism: The role of place attachment and place identity in explaining place-protective action. *Journal of Community & Applied Social Psychology, 19*(6), 426–441.

Dietrich, H., & Schibeci, R. (2003). Beyond public perceptions of gene technology: Community participation in public policy in Australia. *Public Understanding of Science, 12*(4), 381–401.

Drabczyk, A. L. (2007). Ready, set, go: Recruitment, training, coordination, and retention values for all-hazard partnerships. *Journal of Homeland Security and Emergency Management, 4*(3). Retrieved March 16, 2010, from www.bepress.com/jhsem/vol4/iss3/12

Drew, C. H., Nyerges, T. L., & Leschine, T. M. (2004). Promoting transparency of long-term environmental decisions: The Hanford decision mapping system pilot project. *Risk Analysis, 24*(6), 1641–1664.

Dürrenberger, G., Kastenholz, H., & Behringer, J. (1999). Integrated assessment focus groups: Bridging the gap between science and policy? *Science and Public Policy, 26*(5), 341–349.

Einsiedel, E. F. (2002). Assessing a controversial medical technology: Canadian public consultations on xenotransplantation. *Public Understanding of Science, 11*(4), 315–331.

Einsiedel, E. F., & Eastlick, D. L. (2000). Consensus conferences as deliberative democracy: A communications perspective. *Science Communication, 21*(4), 323–343.

Einsiedel, E. F., Jelsoe, E., & Breck, T. (2001). Publics at the technology table: The consensus conference in Denmark, Canada, and Australia. *Public Understanding of Science, 10*(1), 83–98.

Fessenden-Raden, J., Fitchen, J. M., & Heath, J. S. (1987). Providing risk information in communities: Factors influencing what is heard and accepted. *Science, Technology, & Human Values, 12*(3/4), 94–101.

Fiorino, D. J. (1990). Citizen participation and environmental risk: A survey of institutional mechanisms. *Science, Technology, & Human Values, 15*(2), 226–243.

Fischhoff, B. (1995). Risk perception and communication unplugged: Twenty years of process. *Risk Analysis, 15*, 137–145.

Freudenburg, W. R. (1993). Risk and recreancy: Weber, the division of labor, and the rationality of risk perceptions. *Social Forces, 71*(4), 909–932.

Goven, J. (2003). Deploying the consensus conference in New Zealand: Democracy and de-problematization. *Public Understanding of Science, 12*(4), 423–440.

Grunig, J. (1983). Communication behaviors and attitudes of environmental publics: Two studies. *Journalism Monographs, 81*, 1–47.

Grunig, J., & Hunt, T. (1984). *Managing public relations.* New York: Holt, Rinehart & Winston.

Grunig, J., & Repper, F. (1992). Strategic management, publics, and issues. In J. Grunig (Ed.), *Excellence in public relations and communication management* (pp. 117–158). Hillsdale, NJ: Lawrence Erlbaum.

Gundry, K. G., & Heberlein, T. A. (1984). Do public meetings represent the public? *Journal of the American Planning Association, 50*, 175–182.

Gurabardhi, Z., Gutteling, J. M., & Kuttschreuter, M. (2004). The development of risk communication. *Science Communication, 25*(4), 323–349.

Halvorsen, K. E. (2001). Assessing public participation techniques for comfort, convenience, satisfaction, and deliberation. *Environmental Management, 28*(2), 179–186.

Halvorsen, K. E. (2003). Assessing the effects of public participation. *Public Administration Review, 63*(5), 535–543.

Hamilton, J. D. (2003). Exploring technical and cultural appeals in strategic risk communication: The Fernald radium case. *Risk Analysis, 23*(2), 291–302.

Heath, R. L. (Ed.). (2001). *Handbook of public relations.* Thousand Oaks, CA: Sage.

Heath, R. L., & Abel, D. D. (1996a). Proactive responses to citizen risk concerns: Increasing citizens' knowledge of emergency response practices. *Journal of Public Relations Research, 8*(3), 151–171.

Heath, R. L., & Abel, D. D. (1996b). Types of knowledge as predictors of company support: The role of information in risk communication. *Journal of Public Relations Research, 8*(1), 35–55.

Heath, R. L., Bradshaw, J., & Lee, J. (2002). Community relationship building: Local leadership in the risk communication infrastructure. *Journal of Public Relations Research, 14*(4), 317–353.

Heath, R. L., Lee, J., & Ni, L. (2009). Crisis and risk approaches to emergency management planning and communication: The role of similarity and sensitivity. *Journal of Public Relations Research, 21*(2), 123–141.

Heath, R. L., Liao, S.-H., & Douglas, W. (1995). Effects of perceived economic harms and benefits on issue involvement, use of information sources, and actions: A study in risk communication. *Journal of Public Relations Research, 7*(2), 89–109.

Heath, R. L., & Palenchar, M. (2000). Community relations and risk communication: A longitudinal study of the impact of emergency response messages. *Journal of Public Relations Research, 12*(2), 131–161.

Heath, R. L., Seshadri, S., & Lee, J. (1998). Risk communication: A two-community analysis of proximity, dread, trust, involvement, uncertainty, openness/accessibility, and knowledge on support/opposition toward chemical companies. *Journal of Public Relations Research, 10*(4), 35–56.

Heberlein, T. A. (1976). Some observations on alternative mechanisms for public involvement: The hearing, the public opinion poll, the workshop and the quasi-experiment. *Natural Resources Journal, 16*, 197–212.

Hunter, S., & Leyden, K. M. (1995). Beyond NIMBY: Explaining opposition to hazardous waste facilities. *Policy Studies Journal, 23*(4), 601–619.

Jardine, C. G. (2003). Development of a public participation and communication protocol for establishing fish consumption advisories. *Risk Analysis, 23*(3), 461–471.

Jasanoff, S. (1997). Civilization and madness: The great BSE scare of 1996. *Public Understanding of Science, 6*(3), 221–232.

Johnson, B. B. (2004). Risk comparisons, conflict, and risk acceptability claims. *Risk Analysis, 24*(1), 131–145.

Johnson, B. B., & Chess, C. (2003). Communicating worst-case scenarios: Neighbors' views of industrial accident management. *Risk Analysis, 23*(4), 829–840.

Joss, S., & Durant, J. (Eds.). (1995a). *Public participation in science: The role of consensus conferences in Europe*. London: British Science Museum & European Commission Directorate General XII.

Joss, S., & Durant, J. (1995b). The UK national consensus conference on plant biotechnology. *Public Understanding of Science, 4,* 195–204.

Kinney, A. G., & Leschine, T. M. (2002). A procedural evaluation of an analytic-deliberative process: The Columbia River Comprehensive Impact Assessment. *Risk Analysis, 22*(1), 83–100.

Kraft, M. E., & Clary, B. B. (1991). Citizen participation and the NIMBY syndrome: Public response to radioactive-waste disposal. *Western Political Quarterly, 44*(2), 299–328.

Kuhn, R. G., & Ballard, K. R. (1998). Canadian innovations in siting hazardous waste management facilities. *Environmental Management, 22*(4), 533–545.

Lauber, T. B., & Knuth, B. A. (1997). Fairness in moose management decision-making: The citizens' perspective. *Wildlife Society Bulletin, 25*(4), 776–787.

Leiss, W. (1995). Down and dirty: The use and abuse of public trust in risk communication. *Risk Analysis, 15*(6), 685–692.

Leiss, W. (1996). Three phases in the evolution of risk communication practice. *Annals of the American Academy of Political and Social Science, 545,* 85–94.

Leventhal, G. S., Karuza, J., & Fry, W. R. (1980). Beyond fairness: A theory of allocation preferences. In G. Mikula (Ed.), *Justice and social interaction* (pp. 167–218). New York: Springer-Verlag.

Lidskog, R., & Soneryd, L. (2000). Transport infrastructure investment and environmental impact assessment in Sweden: Public involvement or exclusion? *Environment and Planning A, 32*(8), 1465–1479.

Lober, D. J. (1996). Why not here? The importance of context, process, and outcome on public attitudes toward siting of waste facilities. *Society & Natural Resources, 9*(4), 375–394.

Lofstedt, R. E. (2005). *Risk management in post-trust societies.* London: Palgrave Macmillan.

Lynn, F. M. (1990). Public participation in risk management decisions: The right to define, the right to know, and the right to act. *Risk: Health, Safety and Environment, 1,* 95–102.

Macias, W., Hilyard, K., & Freimuth, V. (2009). Blog functions as risk and crisis communication during Hurricane Katrina. *Journal of Computer-Mediated Communication, 15*(1), 1–31.

Mayer, I., de Vries, J., & Geurts, J. (1995). An evaluation of the effects of participation in a consensus conference. In S. Joss & J. Durant (Eds.), *Public participation in science: The role of consensus conferences in Europe* (pp. 109–124). London, UK: British Science Museum & European Commission Directorate General XII.

McComas, K. A. (2001). Public meetings about local waste management problems: Comparing participants to nonparticipants. *Environmental Management, 27*(1), 135–147.

McComas, K. A. (2003a). Citizen satisfaction with public meetings used for risk communication. *Journal of Applied Communication Research, 31*(2), 164–184.

McComas, K. A. (2003b). Public meetings and risk amplification: A longitudinal study. *Risk Analysis, 23*(6), 1257–1270.

McComas, K. A. (2003c). Trivial pursuits: Participant views of public meetings. *Journal of Public Relations Research, 15,* 91–115.

McComas, K. A., Arvai, J. L., & Besley, J. C. (2009). Linking public participation and decision making through risk communication. In R. L. Heath & D. H. O'Hair (Eds.), *Handbook of risk and crisis communication* (pp. 364–385). New York: Routledge.

McComas, K. A., Besley, J. C., & Trumbo, C. W. (2006). Why citizens do and do not attend public meetings about local cancer cluster investigations. *Policy Studies Journal, 34*(4), 671–698.

McComas, K. A., Besley, J. C., & Yang, Z. (2008). Risky business perceived behavior of local scientists and community support for their research. *Risk Analysis, 28*(6), 1539–1552.

McComas, K. A., & Scherer, C. W. (1999). Providing balanced risk information in surveys used as citizen participation mechanisms. *Society & Natural Resources, 12*(2), 107–119.

McComas, K. A., & Trumbo, C. W. (2001). Source credibility in environmental health-risk controversies: Application of Meyer's credibility index. *Risk Analysis, 21*(3), 467–480.

McComas, K. A., Trumbo, C. W., & Besley, J. C. (2007). Public meetings about suspected cancer clusters: The impact of voice, interactional justice, and risk perception on attendees' attitudes in six communities. *Journal of Health Communication, 12*(6), 527–549.

McDaniels, T., Gregory, R., & Fields, D. (1999). Democratizing risk management: Successful public involvement in local water management decisions. *Risk Analysis, 19,* 497–510.

McLeod, J. M., Scheufele, D. A., & Moy, P. (1999). Community, communication, and participation: The role of mass media and interpersonal discussion in local political participation. *Political Communication, 16*(3), 315–336.

McLeod, J. M., Scheufele, D. A., Moy, P., Horowitz, E. M., Holbert, R. L., Zhang, W. W., et al. (1999). Understanding deliberation: The effects of discussion networks on participation in a public forum. *Communication Research, 26*(6), 743–774.

Murdock, B. S., Wiessner, C., & Sexton, K. (2005). Stakeholder participation in voluntary environmental agreements: Analysis of 10 Project XL case studies. *Science, Technology, & Human Values, 30*(2), 223–250.

Nathan, K., Heath, R. L., & Douglas, W. (1992). Tolerance for potential environmental health risks: The influence of knowledge, benefits, control, involvement, and uncertainty. *Journal of Public Relations Research, 4*(4), 235.

National Office of Citizen Corps. (2009). *Citizen Corps: Programs and partners.* Retrieved December 1, 2009, from www.citizencorps.gov/programs

National Research Council. (1996). *Understanding risk: Informing decisions in a democratic society.* Washington, DC: National Academies Press.

National Research Council. (2008). *Public participation in environmental assessment and decision making.* Washington, DC: National Academies Press.

Neuwirth, K., Dunwoody, S., & Griffin, R. J. (2000). Protection motivation and risk communication. *Risk Analysis, 20*(5), 721–734.

O'Riordan, J. (1976). The public involvement program in the Okanagan Basin study. *Natural Resources, 76,* 177–196.

Palenchar, M. J., & Heath, R. L. (2007). Strategic risk communication: Adding value to society. *Public Relations Review, 33*(2), 120–129.

Pellizzoni, L., & Ungaro, D. (2000). Technological risk, participation and deliberation. Some results from three Italian case studies. *Journal of Hazardous Materials, 78*(1), 261–280.

Pidgeon, N. F., Poortinga, W., Rowe, G., Jones, T. H., Walls, J., & O'Riordan, T. (2005). Using surveys in public participation processes for risk decision making: The case of the 2003 British GM nation? Public debate. *Risk Analysis, 25*(2), 467–479.

Pirie, R. L., de Loe, R. C., & Kreutzwiser, R. (2004). Drought planning and water allocation: An assessment of local capacity in Minnesota. *Journal of Environmental Management, 73*(1), 25–38.

Plough, A., & Krimsky, S. (1987). The emergence of risk communication studies: Social and political context. *Science, Technology, & Human Values, 12*(3/4), 4–10.

Pollock, P. H. (1995). Who bears the burdens of environmental-pollution? Race, ethnicity, and environmental equity in Florida. *Social Science Quarterly, 76*(2), 294–310.

Poortinga, W., & Pidgeon, N. F. (2003). Exploring the dimensionality of trust in risk regulation. *Risk Analysis, 23*(5), 961–972.

Poortinga, W., & Pidgeon, N. F. (2004). Trust, the asymmetry principle, and the role of prior beliefs. *Risk Analysis, 24*(6), 1475–1486.

Poplin, D. E. (1972). *Communities: A survey of theories and methods of research.* New York: Macmillan.

Portney, K. E., & Berry, J. M. (1997). Mobilizing minority communities: Social capital and participation in urban neighborhoods. *American Behavioral Scientist, 40*(5), 632–644.

Putnam, R. D. (2000). *Bowling alone: The collapse and revival of American community.* New York: Simon & Schuster.

Quigley, D., Handy, D., Goble, R., Sanchez, V., & George, P. (2000). Participatory research strategies in nuclear risk management for native communities. *Journal of Health Communication, 5*(4), 305–331.

Renn, O. (1999). A model for an analytic-deliberative process in risk management. *Environmental Science & Technology, 33*(18), 3049–3055.

Renn, O., Webler, T., & Johnson, B. B. (1991). Public participation in hazard management: The use of citizen panels in the U.S. *Risk: Health, Safety and Environment, 2,* 197–226.

Renn, O., Webler, T., & Kastenholz, H. (1996). Procedural and substantive fairness in landfill siting: A Swiss case study. *Risk: Health, Safety and Environment, 7,* 145–168.

Renn, O., Webler, T., & Wiedemann, P. M. (1995). *Fairness and competence in citizen participation: Evaluating models for environmental discourse.* Dordrecht, The Netherlands: Kluwer Academic.

Rich, R. C., & Conn, W. D. (1995). Using automated emergency notification systems to inform the public: A field experiment. *Risk Analysis, 15*(1), 23–28.

Roth, A. L., Dunsby, J., & Bero, L. A. (2003). Framing processes in public commentary on US federal tobacco control regulation. *Social Studies of Science, 33*(1), 7–44.

Rothstein, H. F. (2004). Precautionary bans or sacrificial lambs? Participative risk regulation and the reform of the UK food safety regime. *Public Administration, 82*(4), 857–881.

Rowe, G., Horlick-Jones, T., Walls, J., & Pidgeon, N. (2005). Difficulties in evaluating public engagement initiatives: Reflections on an evaluation of the UK GM Nation? Public debate about transgenic crops. *Public Understanding of Science, 14*(4), 331–352.

Rowe, G., Marsh, R., & Frewer, L. J. (2004). Evaluation of a deliberative conference. *Science, Technology, & Human Values, 29*(1), 88–121.

Santos, S. L., & Chess, C. (2003). Evaluating citizen advisory boards: The importance of theory and participant-based criteria and practical implications. *Risk Analysis, 23*(2), 269–279.

Satterfield, T. A., Mertz, C. K., & Slovic, P. (2004). Discrimination, vulnerability, and justice in the face of risk. *Risk Analysis, 24*(1), 115–129.

Scheufele, D. A. (2000). Talk or conversation? Dimensions of interpersonal discussion and their implications for participatory democracy. *Journalism & Mass Communication Quarterly, 77*(4), 727–743.

Schotland, M. S., & Bero, L. A. (2002). Evaluating public commentary and scientific evidence submitted in the development of a risk assessment. *Risk Analysis, 22*(1), 131–140.

Shah, D. V., McLeod, J. M., & Yoon, S. H. (2001). Communication, context, and community: An exploration of print, broadcast, and Internet influences. *Communication Research, 28*(4), 464–506.

Siegrist, M., Cvetkovich, G. T., & Gutscher, H. (2001). Shared values, social trust, and the perception of geographic cancer clusters. *Risk Analysis, 21*(6), 1047–1053.

Siegrist, M., Cvetkovich, G., & Roth, C. (2000). Salient value similarity, social trust, and risk/benefit perception. *Risk Analysis, 20*(3), 353–362.

Slovic, P. (1987). Perception of risk. *Science, 236,* 280–285.

Slovic, P. (1993). Perceived risk, trust, and democracy. *Risk Analysis, 13*(6), 675–682.

Slovic, P. (1999). Trust, emotion, sex, politics, and science: Surveying the risk-assessment battlefield. *Risk Analysis, 19*(4), 689–701. (Reprinted from *Environment, Ethics, and Behavior,* 277–313, 1997)

Slovic, P. (Ed.). (2000). *Perception of risk.* London: Earthscan.

Smith, P. D., & McDonough, M. H. (2001). Beyond public participation: Fairness in natural resource decision making. *Society & Natural Resources, 14*(3), 239–249.

Thibaut, J. W., & Walker, L. (1975). *Procedural justice: A psychological analysis.* Mahwah, NJ: Lawrence Erlbaum.

Trumbo, C. W. (1996). Examining psychometrics and polarization in a single-risk case study. *Risk Analysis, 16*(3), 429–438.

Trumbo, C. W., & McComas, K. A. (2003). The function of credibility in information processing for risk perception. *Risk Analysis, 23*(2), 343–353.

Trumbo, C. W., McComas, K. A., & Besley, J. C. (2008). Individual- and community-level effects on risk perception in cancer cluster investigations. *Risk Analysis, 28*(1), 161–178.

Tyler, T. R. (1989). The psychology of procedural justice: A test of the group-value model. *Journal of Personality and Social Psychology, 57*(5), 830–838.

Tyler, T. R. (1994). Psychological models of the justice motive: Antecedents of distributive and procedural justice. *Journal of Personality and Social Psychology, 67,* 850–863.

Tyler, T. R. (2000). Social justice: Outcome and procedure. *International Journal of Psychology, 35*(2), 117–125.

Tyler, T. R., & Lind, E. A. (1992). A relational model of authority in groups. *Advances in Experimental Social Psychology, 25,* 115–191.

Vaughan, E. (1995). The significance of socioeconomic and ethnic diversity for the risk communication process. *Risk Analysis, 15*(2), 169–180.

Wardman, J. K. (2008). The constitution of risk communication in advanced liberal societies. *Risk Analysis, 28*(6), 1619–1637.

Webler, T., Rakel, H., Renn, O., & Johnson, B. (1995). Eliciting and classifying concerns: A methodological critique. *Risk Analysis, 15*(3), 421–436.

Webler, T., & Tuler, S. (2000). Fairness and competence in citizen participation: Theoretical reflections from a case study. *Administration & Society, 32,* 566–595.

Wolfe, A. K., & Bjornstad, D. J. (2003). Making decisions about hazardous waste remediation when even considering a remediation technology is controversial. *Environmental Science & Technology, 37*(8), 1485–1492.

Wolsink, M. (1994). Entanglement of interests and motives: Assumptions behind the NIMBY-theory on facility siting. *Urban Studies, 31*(6), 851–866.

Wolsink, M., & Devilee, J. (2009). The motives for accepting or rejecting waste infrastructure facilities: Shifting the focus from the planners' perspective to fairness and community commitment. *Journal of Environmental Planning and Management, 52,* 217–236.

Wynne, B. (1992). Sheep farming after Chernobyl: A case study in communicating scientific information. In B. Lewenstein (Ed.), *When science meets the public* (pp. 43–67). Washington, DC: American Association for the Advancement of Science.

Zaksek, M., & Arvai, J. L. (2004). Toward improved communication about wildland fire: Mental models research to identify information needs for natural resource management. *Risk Analysis, 24*(6), 1503–1514.

CHAPTER 33

Crisis Communication

A Developing Field

W. Timothy Coombs

Crisis communication is a dynamic and rapidly expanding field of study. Look through a few issues of any public relations or communication journal or the program for any communication-oriented conference and crisis communication will be featured prominently. The challenge in this chapter is to cover the topic in a meaningful fashion without being redundant, with respect to other reviews and commentaries on crisis communication. This chapter will explore crisis communication through its conceptualization, history, and focal tensions. There will be a short review of where we have been to help us understand where crisis communication research still needs to go.

Conceptualizing Crisis Communication: Foundational Definitions

Any discussion of crisis communication requires consideration of what constitutes a crisis. This chapter defines crisis as "the perception of an unpredictable event that threatens important expectations of stakeholders and can seriously impact an organization's performance and generate negative outcomes" (Coombs, 2007b, pp. 2–3). Crises are perceptual. If stakeholders believe there is a crisis stemming from expectation violations, a crisis exists and negative outcomes will occur if the situation is neglected. We should not call any event a crisis. Crisis should be reserved for only those events that have the potential to or do seriously affect the organization. The event must warrant assembling the crisis team. Many events we call crises really may not be. In part, organizations have developed routines for handling common crises such as product harm leading to a product recall. As crisis managers develop routines for handling crises, what would once have been a crisis requiring the crisis team is now a negative event that can be handled without the entire team. The negative event will require only the reputation repair aspect of crisis.

While crisis communication is emerging as a distinct field of study, it is important to contextualize it within the broader discipline of public relations. Crisis communication is closely linked to the allied fields of risk communication, issues management, and reputation management. Risk communication involves the exchange or dialogue between risk bearers and the organizations creating the risk. Risk bearers learn about the risks presented by an organization and the actions being taken to control the risks. Organizations listen to risk bearers to appreciate their concerns and perceptions of the risks (Palenchar, 2005). Risk communication can be a critical component in prevention and preparation. Risk communication can be used to avert a risk and to prepare people for it, if and when a risk escalates into a crisis. Part of crisis communication can involve elements of risk communication. Failures at risk communication can precipitate a crisis, while a crisis may create the need for risk communication.

We find a similar pattern with issues management. Issues management involves the systematic application of procedures designed to influence an issue's resolution. Failed efforts to manage an issue can create a crisis, while a crisis may generate issues in need of management (González-Herrero & Pratt, 1996; Heath, 1994). Failure to effectively manage the crisis can invite government scrutiny and even new regulations.

Reputation management is gaining attention in public relations because of its connection to a number of important outcomes such as valuation of stock, recruitment and retention of employees, and sales (Fombrun & van Riel, 2004). Crises have long been viewed as a threat to reputations—that is, how stakeholders perceive the organization. Thus, crisis management is closely linked to reputation management. Moreover, some believe that a strong reputation prior to a crisis is an asset to organizations during the crisis. Some argue for a halo effect that protects the organizations (Dowling, 2002), while others argue any crisis costs reputational capital, so having a strong reputational account prior to a crisis helps ensure a healthy reserve after the crisis hits (Coombs & Holladay, 2006). Crisis communication does act in concert with other elements of public relations.

Communication is ubiquitous throughout the entire crisis management process. The various applications of crisis communication can be divided into two categories: (1) managing information and (2) managing meaning. Managing information includes the collection and analysis of information and the dissemination of knowledge. Decision making by crisis teams and informing stakeholders are both driven by managing information. This would include the critical warnings provided to stakeholders about safety and how to protect themselves from the crisis (instructing information) as well as follow-up information after a crisis.

Managing meaning is accomplished through efforts to shape how people perceive the crisis situation. The targets for crisis meaning management are all stakeholders, including those inside the organization. Convincing others in the organization that a crisis does exist, providing adjusting information (helping people cope psychologically with the crisis), and managing reputations are examples of managing meaning. Managing meaning encompasses the growing interest in crises and affect. Researchers have been examining the emotions generated by crises and the effects of those emotions on stakeholder behavioral intentions (e.g., Coombs & Holladay, 2005; Jin & Pang, 2010).

We can cross the two categories of crisis communication with the three phases of crisis management to construct a 2 × 3 crisis communication array for organizing crisis communication research. Crisis communication can span multiple cells. The crisis communication array in Table 33.1 is designed as a guide for discussion, not as a rigid set of boxes for arranging research. The crisis communication array consists of six cells: (1) precrisis managing information, (2) precrisis managing meaning, (3) crisis response managing information, (4) crisis response managing meaning, (5) postcrisis managing information, and (6) postcrisis managing meaning. Currently, the bulk of the extant crisis communication

Table 33.1 Crisis Communication Array

Crisis Phase	Managing Information	Managing Meaning
Precrisis/prevention and preparation		
Crisis response		
Postcrisis/learning		

literature focuses on managing meaning. Below are some possible topics to pursue along with citations for research relevant to the various cells.

1. *Precrisis managing information:* educating stakeholders about emergency communication and response systems, scanning for crisis-related risks, and monitoring crisis-related risks (González-Herrero & Pratt, 1996; Heath & Abel, 1996; Heath, Lee, & Ni, 2009).
2. *Precrisis managing meaning:* selling crises to management, inoculation, vigilance, plan efficacy, and self-efficacy of stakeholders for a crisis response (Wan & Pfau, 2004; Williams & Olaniran, 1998).
3. *Crisis response managing information:* decision making by crisis management teams, effectiveness of instructing information, and effectiveness of warning/notification systems (Kolfschoten & Appelman, 2006; Sellnow & Sellnow, in press).
4. *Crisis response managing meaning:* reputation repair, effectiveness of adjusting information, and ability to present the organization's side of the story and effectively communicate the risks created by the crisis (Benoit, 1995; Coombs & Holladay, 1996; Holladay, 2009).
5. *Postcrisis managing information:* organizational learning and postmortems of crisis responses (Roux-Dufort, 2000).
6. *Postcrisis managing meaning:* healing and memorials, renewal, managing issues arising from a crisis, and managing risks made salient by crises (Ulmer, Seeger, & Sellnow, 2007).

The precrisis cells have some promising research but are underdeveloped. The best way to manage a crisis is to avoid one. Risk management and issues management are a natural fit with precrisis. Reducing risks or effectively managing an issue can eliminate the trigger event for a crisis. Moreover, we have only just begun to scratch the surface in our understanding of how crisis communication shapes the preparation of stakeholders for a crisis and the effects of crisis response messages during a crisis. The recent engagement between crisis and risk communication holds great promise for precrisis communication and postcrisis communication. We shall see similar gains as crisis communication and issues management converge.

Crisis response has dominated the crisis communication research with a heavy emphasis on managing meaning. There are other questions to pursue in crisis response meaning management such as the ability of crisis managers to place their messages into traditional and online media outlets—telling their side of the story (Holladay, 2009). We see some interesting research emerging on managing information that examines the work of crisis teams (e.g., Kolfschoten & Appelman, 2006). Also, researchers have been exploring instructing information in greater depth (Sellnow & Sellnow, in press). However, managing information remains a small slice of the crisis response research.

Postcrisis/learning depends on a careful examination of the crisis management effort to determine what was done well, what was done poorly, and what can be done to improve before the next crisis. Postcrisis makes crisis management cyclical, as the learning feeds back into the other aspects of the crisis management process. Managers are encouraged to learn from crises. However, researchers find little evidence of learning from crises (Roux-Dufort, 2000). In part, crisis learning is managing information, as data about the crisis management effort must be collected and analyzed. However, there is no learning if that information is not incorporated into the organization. Taking lessons from a crisis and infusing them into organizational practices is, to a large extent, managing meaning. Although there are rough guides for points to consider when evaluating a crisis management effort, there is little discussion of the limitations and problems associated with the process.

We can layer two additional factors onto the crisis communication array: (1) international crises and (2) online communication. Crises are becoming more international as they span multiple countries and cultures (Coombs, 2008). We need a greater understanding of how culture and other variables introduced by international crises affect crisis communication across the six cells. There is limited research on international crisis communication (e.g., Frandsen & Johansen, 2010; Huang, Lin, & Su, 2005; Lee, 2005; Taylor, 2000). Similarly, we have just begun to understand the effect of online communication across the six cells. Clearly, there are implications for precrisis (scanning) and crisis response. Yet researchers have just begun to scratch the surface of the online world (e.g., Choi & Lin, 2009; Taylor & Perry, 2005). The potential research topics increase exponentially as we introduce international crises and online communication to the mix.

Historical Development

The earliest crisis communication writings were practical in nature. The focus was on "how-to advice" for a crisis. The emphasis was on the form and format of crisis responses such as be quick and avoid "no comment" (Coombs, 2007b). This section will focus on the strategic use of crisis communication. How has communication been used to address concerns and to pursue desired outcomes during a crisis? The history of strategic crisis communication can be traced through two dominant research approaches: rhetorical and social science. The rhetorical approach is the older of the two and will be considered first.

Rhetorical Approaches to Crisis Communication

Crises are situations that create a need for management to respond—crises trigger the need for communication. Crisis communication tends to be public communication, so it is natural that rhetoric would be applied as crisis communication can be viewed as a type of public address. The rhetorical approach thus focuses on crisis communication as a type of public address. There are four notable lines of rhetorical crisis communication research: (1) corporate apologia, (2) image restoration, (3) focusing event, and (4) renewal. This section reviews the major approaches in a cursory manner because detailed discussions about the research lines are available elsewhere (e.g., Coombs, 2009).

Corporate apologia was the earliest rhetorical application to crisis communication. Apologia is a genre within rhetoric devoted to the study of self-defense. When rhetors are faced with a challenge to their character, they use communication to defend their character. Apologia was designed for individuals, not corporations. Dionisopoulos and Vibbert (1988) were the first to argue that organizations could face the same character (reputation) threats as individuals and had the same need to protect their characters in public.

Hearit's (2001, 2006) work came to define corporate apologia. His research was not just a series of loosely connected case studies applying corporate apologia. Rather, Hearit (1995) refined and expanded our understanding of corporate apologia, transforming it into a distinct perspective for examining corporate rhetoric.

Image restoration theory, now called image repair theory, can be treated as a derivation of corporate apologia (Benoit & Pang, 2008). Benoit (1995) shares the view that public reputations can be threatened, are valuable, and warrant protection. Benoit fuses apologia with ideas from account giving to create a set of crisis response strategies—communicative options for crisis managers. Benoit's list of crisis response strategies is exhaustive and a significant development for crisis communication.

Fishman (1999) introduced the idea of the focusing event to crisis communication. A focusing event is "sudden and unpredictable" but becomes widely known in a short period of time. Type 1 focusing events are "normal" and include natural disasters. Type 2 focusing events are new, violation expectations, and create uncertainty that demands public attention. Fishman argues that some crises qualify as Type 2 focusing events because not all crises become widely known in a short period of time. The power of the focusing event is that it helps set the public agenda, thereby potentially influencing policy decisions. Crisis communication can be used to influence the ensuing policy discussion, essentially merging it with issues management. Fishman's work builds a critical bridge to issues management but is often overlooked because it generated limited research.

The rhetoric of renewal, now called the discourse of renewal (DR), shifts the focus of crisis communication in two ways. First, the emphasis becomes the positives that can be taken away from the crisis. Crisis becomes an opportunity for organizational change and development. DR is consistent with writings that consistently posit that crises are an opportunity for organizational learning. Second, the emphasis is on the future, not on the crisis itself and not on addressing issues of blame or responsibility for the crisis. Crisis managers should focus on the "prospective vision of the future in their crisis communication rather than focusing retrospectively on responsibility for the event" (Ulmer, Sellnow, & Seeger, 2010, p. 692). However, DR has limits. Not all organizations are in a position to execute DR because there are certain conditions that must exist for DR to be effective. Moreover, some crises demand attention to issues of responsibility, and an organization would be viewed as unethical for avoiding them (Coombs, 2009).

What unites these four approaches are their object of study and method. The object of study is the crisis response strategy—that is, what crisis managers say and do after a crisis. The method is the case study approach. The conclusions based on these qualitative/interpretative methods must be taken as tentative because they illustrate rather than prove the aspects of a theory.

Multivocal Approach

The multivocal approach is consistent with the rhetorical tradition and evolves from what Frandsen and Johansen (2010) call the rhetorical arena that emerges around a crisis. While linked to rhetoric and a text-oriented focus, the multivocal approach is more complex as it draws on a grounded theory approach and on the work of Luhmann (1996). A crisis event helps form a rhetorical arena. The rhetorical arena can begin to form before the crisis event (precrisis) and last into the postcrisis phase; thus, it is not restricted only to the crisis response phase. The approach is multivocal because the voices of many actors within the rhetorical arena are considered; it is not just a dominant sender and receiver. There are multiple actors serving as senders and receivers and these various communicative processes interact in the rhetorical arena. The rhetorical arena is constituted by these various voices. The analysis reflects a macro level when these various voices are examined as the rhetorical arena as a whole.

The multivocal approach includes a micro level that is sociorhetorical. Here, the individual communicative process between specific senders and receivers is examined. The focus is on the crisis communication, the sender, the receiver, and the four parameters (context, media, genre, and text). The analysis must seek to understand both the macro and micro levels and uses a case study approach. Multiple voices must be considered when analyzing and evaluating the crisis communication that transpires within the rhetorical arena. The emphasis on the multivocality is a significant development in crisis communication thinking. As Frandsen and Johansen (2010) note, "Actors very often accelerate the course of events and spin a crisis in new directions, contributing to its dynamics" (p. 430). It is not just the organization engaging in crisis communication; it can be politicians, the news media, and/or customers as well. The multivocal approach complicates our thinking and is especially well suited for international crisis communication, where multiple voices are the norm. For a more detailed discussion of the multivocal approach and its application in the international crisis communication setting, see Frandsen and Johansen (2010).

Social Science Approaches to Crisis Communication

The social science tradition is rooted primarily in the attribution theory (AT). The core of AT is people's need to make sense of events they encounter, especially those that are sudden and unexpected. Causes for events are attributed to either the individual(s) involved in the event or the circumstances surrounding an event (Kelley, 1971; Weiner, 1986). AT research uses experimental designs. The subject pool is broad since AT is a general theory about human behaviors—it should be common to all humans, though culture can have some effect on attributions (e.g., Huang et al., 2005).

Marketing researchers were the first to link AT and crises with the works of Mowen (1980) and Jolly (Jolly & Mowen, 1985). Crisis communication was a consideration but not the dominant factor in the early AT marketing crisis communication research. Later researchers like Jorgensen (1996) and Bradford and Garrett (1995) explored the effect of crisis response strategies on people's reactions to crises, including behavioral intentions. The research was restricted to a limited range of crisis, including product harm and ethical misconduct. It did not generate a more macro theoretical framework for addressing a range of crisis types and for the application of crisis response strategies.

Situational crisis communication theory (SCCT) was developed to more fully articulate the connection between crisis types and crisis response strategies. The central assumption is that the situation shapes what will be seen as an effective response. Hence, the crisis situation guides the selection of appropriate crisis responses. So what makes a response effective? To answer this question, we must appreciate the influence of Sturges (1994) on SCCT. Sturges (1994) argued that crisis communication has three functions: (1) instructing information, (2) adjusting information, and (3) managing reputation.

Instructing information tells stakeholders how to protect themselves physically from a crisis. Adjusting information helps people cope psychologically with a crisis. Finally, crisis response strategies can be used to repair the reputation damage inflicted by a crisis. These three functions should be pursued in the order just presented. However, it is common to present instructing and adjusting information simultaneously (Holladay, 2009). SCCT follows this advice with the belief that public safety is the top priority in a crisis. The initial or base response in a crisis consists of instructing and adjusting information. Initial effectiveness is the ability to protect people physically and to comfort those in psychological distress. Situational factors are then used to guide reputation repair. The marker of effectiveness then shifts to reputation repair/protection.

Reputation is a complex concept, because it can affect stakeholder behavioral intentions and affect. AT was used to understand the connection between a crisis and organizational reputation. The key to selecting crisis response strategies became how stakeholders attribute organizational responsibility for a crisis. The greater the stakeholder attributions of organizational responsibility for the crisis, the greater the threat posed by the crisis. Attributions of crisis responsibility are linked to organizational reputation, behaviors toward the organization, and affect toward the organization. Assessing the crisis situation is a two-step process. First, crisis managers determine the crisis type. A crisis type is the frame used by stakeholders to interpret the crisis event. Crisis types vary in the strength of attributions of organizational crisis responsibility they generate. SCCT research clusters crises into three types based on the attributions of organization crisis responsibility each generates: (1) victim (low attributions of organizational crisis responsibility), (2) accidental (modest attributions of organizational crisis responsibility), and (3) preventable (strong attributions of organizational crisis responsibility) (Coombs & Holladay, 2002).

The second step is to consider intensifiers of the crisis threat. So far, research has identified crisis history and prior relationship reputation as intensifiers. Crisis history includes similar crises, if any, that occurred in the past. Prior relationship reputation is how well or poorly the organization has treated stakeholders in the past (Schwarz, 2008). For both intensifiers, the threat is intensified if the variable is negative. This means people attribute greater organizational crisis responsibility when there is either a history of past crises or the prior relationship reputation is unfavorable. The effect of the intensifiers has been called the Velcro effect (Coombs, 2004; Coombs & Holladay, 2006).

SCCT proposes four groups of crisis response strategies. (1) Denial strategies seek to prevent any connection between the organization and some crisis event and include denial, attacking the accuser, and scapegoating. (2) Diminish strategies try to reduce the perceived responsibility for the crisis and include justification and excuse. (3) Rebuild strategies attempt to improve the reputation and include compensation and apology. (4) Bolstering strategies try to draw on existing goodwill and should be used as a secondary strategy in support of other strategies. Bolstering strategies include reminding, ingratiation, and victimage (Coombs, 2006). SCCT holds that as attributions of organizational crisis responsibility become stronger, crisis managers must use more accommodative crisis response strategies. Victim and accidental crises with no intensifiers require just instructing and adjusting information. Once intensifiers appear, crisis managers should consider moving to more accommodative strategies such as compensation and apology. Refer to Coombs (2007c) for a more detailed discussion of the various strategies and specific recommendations.

SCCT research has begun to explore the role of affect in the crisis situation and response. Following Weiner (1986, 2006), SCCT focuses on the emotions of anger, sympathy, and Schadenfreude (taking joy from the pain of others). SCCT research supports the contention that stronger attributions of crisis responsibility lead to greater anger and even to Schadenfreude in extreme cases. Moreover, anger has proven to be an energizer for behavior. Greater anger increases the likelihood of people engaging in negative word of mouth (saying bad things about an organization or product). When posted online, these negative messages can linger well past the negative affect created by the crisis. Put another way, people's anger can dissipate, but their words can remain in cyberspace for others to see. The motivation from anger has been called the negative communication dynamic (Coombs & Holladay, 2007). Future research needs to explore how crisis response strategies can reduce anger and thereby reduce the likelihood of negative word of mouth.

Contingency theory is a grand theory of public relations and attempts to explain how public relations operates as a whole. Contingency theory researchers seek to understand what guides policy-level decisions. Key elements of contingency theory include conflict, stance, and the factors that can shape a stance. Conflict is considered natural in contingency theory. Stakeholders can experience conflict with an organization or with other stakeholders. Stance is the general way in which management in an organization approaches conflict. Stances range from accommodative, a willingness to make concessions, to advocacy, a willingness to persuade others to your position. Managers will have a preferred stance that can be anticipated by examining past reactions to conflict. However, 87 variables have been identified that can change a stance. Contingency theory seeks to understand how the variables come to change an organization's typical stance. The variables shaping a stance can be grouped as internal or external (Cameron, Pang, & Jin, 2008; Shin, Cameron, & Cropp, 2006).

When contingency theory is applied to crisis communication, the crisis is the conflict and the stances become the crisis response strategies. Threat appraisal is used to assess the crisis situation. The threat appraisal comprises an assessment of the threat type (internal or external to the organization) and threat duration (long term or short term). The threat is used to guide the stance (crisis response). The greatest threat is believed to be internal and long term, and a more accommodative response is favored when the threat is greater (Hwang & Cameron, 2008; Jin & Cameron, 2007).

Emotion has emerged as an important topic from the contingency theory approach to crisis communication. Pang, Jin, and Cameron (2010) have integrated the appraisal model of emotion with contingency theory to form the integrated crisis mapping (ICM) model. ICM centers on four emotions: (1) anger, when an offense has occurred; (2) fright, when facing uncertainty and threat; (3), anxiety, when facing immediate danger; and (4) sadness, when a sense of loss develops. ICM proposes two dimensions that are crossed to form four quadrants. The first dimension is the public coping strategy ranging from problem-focused (taking action) to cognitive-focused coping (changing interpretation of relationship). The second dimension is the level of organizational engagement and indicates the amount of resources devoted to the crisis.

The quadrants are used to anticipate the emotion created by the crisis. Quadrants 1 (high engagement and conative coping) involves reputational damage leading to anger and then anxiety. Quadrant 2 (high engagement and cognitive coping) includes natural disasters and leads to sadness and then fright. Quadrant 3 (low engagement and cognitive coping) involves terrorism and leads to fright and sadness. Quadrant 4 (low engagement and conative coping) involves security issues and leads to anxiety and then anger. Thus far, research has shown Quadrant 1 to be tied to anger, while Quadrants 2 to 4 are dominated by anxiety (Jin, 2009; Jin & Pang, 2010).

Synthesizing SCCT and Contingency Theory

Researchers have noted the similarities between SCCT and contingency theory, leading to speculation that they could be integrated (Holtzhausen & Roberts, 2009). Integration of the two theories is a viable idea. A potential synthesis should retain the AT aspect of SCCT, because the common usage of AT allows for comparison with studies in marketing and management (Laufer & Coombs, 2006). Contingency theory's value is in identifying other intensifying or even mitigating factors in the crisis situation derived from its stable of internal and external variables. Contingency theory would extend the search for intensifiers and possible moderators well beyond the current set of variables derived from AT. While the integration has yet to be accomplished, there is potentially a rich yield from a more robust theory of crisis communication created by fusing SCCT and contingency theory.

Tensions in the Crisis Communication Research

Capturing the major themes evident in the rapidly growing crisis communication research would take a book, not a book chapter. However, two driving themes emerge: (1) sender-receiver and (2) concern for organization and concern for stakeholders. These themes can be viewed as tensions that exist within the crisis communication research.

Sender Versus Receiver

An early sender bias appears in the crisis communication research as a result of its links to rhetoric. The focus was on identifying what strategies were used and inferring how people should react to the strategies. Moreover, the research assumed that the crisis managers were the ones defining the crisis event. This perspective leads to the creation of various lists of crisis response strategies that are available for crisis managers to use and some discussion of crisis types. It was assumed that stakeholders would react in prescribed ways to the definition of the crisis and the crisis response strategy. Receivers would share the same interpretation of the crisis and the strategies as the senders. This crisis communication research reflects the focus on the rhetor/sender of the message. Lee (2004) was among the first to question this bias overtly. However, social scientific research had begun examining the receiver prior to Lee's critique.

A receiver orientation seeks to understand the crisis and the crisis response strategies from the stakeholder's perspective. The definition of crisis used in this chapter reflects a focus on the receiver as crises are in large part based on perceptions of stakeholders. The social science approaches to crisis communication reflect much greater attention to the receiver. From the beginning, SCCT was rooted in a receiver orientation. SCCT sought to understand how stakeholders (1) perceived the crisis and (2) reacted to the crisis response strategies. SCCT holds that the crisis type (how stakeholders define the crisis situation) is a critical element in crisis communication. Early SCCT research sought to categorize various crises according to the way in which they were perceived by the stakeholders. We witness a similar interest in stakeholders' crisis perceptions in contingency theory. The research generated by SCCT and contingency theory examines how stakeholders perceive the crisis.

SCCT and contingency theory also seek to understand how stakeholders react to crisis response strategies. The research in SCCT and contingency theory explores stakeholder reactions to the crisis response strategies, including the effects on affect and behaviors (e.g., Coombs & Holladay, 2007; Jin & Cameron, 2007). It is the understanding of how stakeholders will respond to crises and crisis response strategies that allows the social science crisis communication research to produce evidence for evidence-based crisis communication (Coombs, 2007a, 2010). Of course, understanding the receiver is used to help crisis managers to be more effective. This raises the second tension: "More effective for whom?"

Concern for Organization Versus Concern for Stakeholders

An accurate critique of crisis communication is that the research is corporate centric (Kent, 2010; Tyler, 2005). The research centers on organizations and seeks to find ways to protect reputational resources, purchase intention, and prevent negative word of mouth. Researchers are privileging the organization over the stakeholders in terms of outcomes for the crisis communication endeavor. This privileging is found in both the rhetorical and the social science crisis communication research. The corporate-centric bias reflects the origins of crisis communication in practitioner interests of how to improve their efforts. Effectiveness tends to be defined as what helps the organization maintain a reputation, sales, or favorable comments from stakeholders.

A case can be made that stakeholder interests are a part of crisis communication. Both instructing and adjusting information are stakeholder centric because they are designed to help stakeholders in some way. Of course, we should be mindful that helping stakeholders helps the organization as well, but that connection is unavoidable. The first concern in a crisis should be stakeholder safety, not organizational assets. A crisis response that violates this principle is doomed to hurt rather than to help the organization. I would argue that instructing and adjusting information serve as the base response for most crisis communication. In fact, most crises would be resolved effectively (favorable to the organization) by simply using instructing and adjusting information (Coombs, 2007b).

However, we have little research into the use of instructing and adjusting information. How might we improve instructing and adjusting information? For which stakeholders ? What makes for effective (beneficial to the stakeholder) instructing and adjusting information? The connection between risk communication and crisis communication is relevant here. Risk communication can provide insights into improving/creating effective adjusting and instructing information. An example of that research is Heath, Lee, and Ni's (2009) examination of the role of similarity and sensitivity in creating more effective community emergency management and communication. We need to understand what can be done prior to a crisis to ensure that people follow instructing information, how best to communicate instructing and adjusting information during a crisis, and the ways in which instructing and adjusting information remain relevant and useful after a crisis is considered to be over. More research is needed to understand instructing and adjusting information in the precrisis, crisis, and postcrisis phases.

Conclusion

Crisis communication, while growing rapidly, is a nascent field with ample room for expansion. The quick review of crisis communication's development helped us understand its current trajectory and future opportunities. In referring back to the crisis communication array, we see that research has concentrated in one of six cells. In general, we know little about information management, precrisis communication, and postcrisis communication. Moreover, we need to understand the unique demands of international crisis communication and the effects online channels have on the full spectrum of crisis communication. However, with the expansion of crisis communication will come the challenge of integration. How do we make sense of all the research? What are the real lessons evolving from this maelstrom of research activity? Those will be issues for later reviewers to address. For now, crisis communication stands as a dominant presence in public relations that will only grow stronger in the future.

References

Benoit, W. L. (1995). *Accounts, excuses, and apologies: A theory of image restoration.* Albany: State University of New York Press.

Benoit, W. L., & Pang, A. (2008). Crisis communication and image repair discourse. In T. L. Hansen-Horn & B. D. Neff (Eds.), *Public relations: From theory to practice* (pp. 243–261). New York: Pearson.

Bradford, J. L., & Garrett, D. E. (1995). The effectiveness of corporate communicative responses to accusations of unethical behavior. *Journal of Business Ethics, 14,* 875–892.

Cameron, G. T., Pang, A., & Jin, Y. (2008). Contingency theory. In T. L. Hansen-Horn & B. D. Neff (Eds.), *Public relations: From theory to practice* (pp. 134–157). New York: Pearson.

Choi, Y., & Lin, Y. H. (2009). Consumer responses to Mattel product recalls posted on online bulletin boards: Exploring two types of emotion. *Journal of Public Relations Research, 21*(2), 198–207.

Coombs, W. T. (2004). Impact of past crises on current crisis communications: Insights from situational crisis communication theory. *Journal of Business Communication, 41,* 265–289.

Coombs, W. T. (2006). The protective powers of crisis response strategies: Managing reputational assets during a crisis. *Journal of Promotion Management, 12,* 241–260.

Coombs, W. T. (2007a). Attribution theory as a guide for post-crisis communication research. *Public Relations Review, 33,* 135–139.

Coombs, W. T. (2007b). *Ongoing crisis communication: Planning, managing, and responding* (2nd ed.). Thousand Oaks, CA: Sage.

Coombs, W. T. (2007c). Protecting organization reputations during a crisis: The development and application of situational crisis communication theory. *Corporate Reputation Review, 10*(3), 163–177.

Coombs, W. T. (2008). The future of crisis communication from an international perspective. In T. Nolting & A. Thiessen (Eds.), *Krisenmanagement in der Mediengesellschaft: Potenziale und Perspektiven in der Krisenkommunikation* (pp. 275–287). Wiesbaden, Germany: VS-Verlag.

Coombs, W. T. (2009). Conceptualizing crisis communication. In R. L. Heath & H. D. O'Hair (Eds.), *Handbook of risk and crisis communication* (pp. 100–119). New York: Routledge.

Coombs, W. T. (2010). Pursuing evidence-based crisis communication. In W. T. Coombs & S. J. Holladay (Eds.), *Handbook of crisis communication* (pp. 719–725). Malden, MA: Blackwell.

Coombs, W. T., & Holladay, S. J. (1996). Communication and attributions in a crisis: An experimental study of crisis communication. *Journal of Public Relations Research, 8*(4), 279–295.

Coombs, W. T., & Holladay, S. J. (2002). Helping crisis managers protect reputational assets: Initial tests of the situational crisis communication theory. *Management Communication Quarterly, 16,* 165–186.

Coombs, W. T., & Holladay, S. J. (2005). Exploratory study of stakeholder emotions: Affect and crisis. In N. M. Ashkanasy, W. J. Zerbe, & C. E. J. Hartel (Eds.), *Research on emotion in organizations: Vol. 1. The effect of affect in organizational settings* (pp. 271–288). New York: Elsevier.

Coombs, W. T., & Holladay, S. J. (2006). Unpacking the halo effect: Reputation and crisis management. *Journal of Communication Management, 10*(2), 123–137.

Coombs, W. T., & Holladay, S. J. (2007). The negative communication dynamic: Exploring the impact of stakeholder affect on behavioral intentions. *Journal of Communication Management, 11,* 300–312.

Dionisopoulos, G. N., & Vibbert, S. L. (1988). CBS vs Mobil Oil: Charges of creative bookkeeping. In H. R. Ryan (Ed.), *Oratorical encounters: Selected studies and sources of 20th century political accusation and apologies* (pp. 214–252). Westport, CT: Greenwood Press.

Dowling, G. (2002). *Creating corporate reputations: Identity, image, and performance.* New York: Oxford University Press.

Fishman, D. A. (1999). ValuJet flight 592: Crisis communication theory blended and extended. *Communication Quarterly, 47*(4), 345–375.

Fombrun, C. J., & van Riel, C. B. M. (2004). *Fame & fortune: How successful companies build winning reputations.* New York: FT Prentice Hall.

Frandsen, F., & Johansen, W. (2010). Crisis communication, complexity, and the cartoon affair: A case study. In W. T. Coombs & S. J. Holladay (Eds.), *Handbook of crisis communication* (pp. 425–448). Malden, MA: Blackwell.

González-Herrero, A., & Pratt, C. B. (1996). An integrated symmetrical model for crisis communications management. *Journal of Public Relations Research, 8*(2), 79–105.

Hearit, K. M. (1995). "Mistakes were made": Organizations, apologia, and crises of social legitimacy. *Communication Studies, 46,* 1–17.

Hearit, K. M. (2001). Corporate apologia: When an organization speaks in defense of itself. In R. L. Heath (Ed.), *Handbook of public relations* (pp. 501–511). Thousand Oaks, CA: Sage.

Hearit, K. M. (2006). *Crisis management by apology: Corporate response to allegations of wrongdoing.* Mahwah, NJ: Lawrence Erlbaum.

Heath, R. L. (1994). *Management of corporate communication: From interpersonal contacts to external affairs.* Hillsdale, NJ: Lawrence Erlbaum.

Heath, R. L., & Abel, D. D. (1996). Proactive response to citizen risk concerns: Increasing citizens' knowledge of emergency response practices. *Journal of Public Relations Research, 8,* 151–171.

Heath, R. L., Lee, J., & Ni, L. (2009). Crisis and risk approaches to emergency management planning and communication: The role of similarity and sensitivity. *Journal of Public Relations Research, 21*(2), 123–141.

Holladay, S. J. (2009). Crisis communication strategies in the media coverage of chemical accidents. *Journal of Public Relations Research, 21*(2), 208–217.

Holtzhausen, D. R., & Roberts, G. F. (2009). An investigation into the role of image repair theory in strategic conflict management. *Journal of Public Relations Research, 21,* 165–186.

Huang, Y. H., Lin, Y. H., & Su, S. H. (2005). Crisis communicative strategies in Taiwan: Category, continuum, and cultural implication. *Public Relations Review, 31,* 229–238.

Hwang, S., & Cameron, G. T. (2008). Public's expectation about an organization's stance in crisis communication based on perceived leadership and perceived severity of threats. *Public Relations Review, 34,* 70–73.

Jin, Y. (2009). The effects of public's cognitive appraisal of emotions in crises on crisis coping and strategy assessment. *Public Relations Review, 35*(3), 310–313.

Jin, Y., & Cameron, G. T. (2007). The effects of threat type and duration on public relations practitioner's cognitive, affective, and conative responses to crisis situations. *Journal of Public Relations Research, 19,* 255–281.

Jin, Y., & Pang, A. (2010). Future directions of crisis communication research: Emotions in crisis—the next frontier. In W. T. Coombs, & S. J. Holladay (Eds.), *Handbook of crisis communication* (pp. 677–682). Malden, MA: Blackwell.

Jolly, D. W., & Mowen, J. C. (1985). Product recall communications: The effects of source, media, and social responsibility information. *Advances in Consumer Research, 12,* 471–475.

Jorgensen, B. K. (1996). Components of consumer reaction to company-related mishaps: A structural equation model approach. *Advances in Consumer Research, 23,* 346–351.

Kelley, H. H. (1971). *Attribution in social interaction.* New York: General Learning Press.

Kent, M. L. (2010). What is a public relations "crisis"? Refocusing crisis research. In W. T. Coombs & S. J. Holladay (Eds.), *Handbook of crisis communication* (pp. 705–712). Malden, MA: Blackwell.

Kolfschoten, G. L., & Appelman, J. H. (2006, June). *Collaborative engineering in crisis situations.* Paper presented at ISCRAM-TIEMS 2006 Summer School, Tilburg, The Netherlands.

Laufer, D., & Coombs, W. T. (2006). How should a company respond to a product harm crisis? The role of corporate reputation and consumer-based cues. *Business Horizon, 10*(2), 123–137.

Lee, B. K. (2004). Audience-oriented approach to crisis communication: A study of Hong Kong consumers' evaluations of an organizational crisis. *Communication Research, 31,* 600–618.

Lee, B. K. (2005). Crisis, culture, and communication. In P. J. Kalbfleisch (Ed.), *Communication yearbook 29* (pp. 275–308). Mahwah, NJ: Lawrence Erlbaum.

Luhmann, N. (1996). *Social systems.* Stanford, CA: Stanford University Press.

Mowen, J. C. (1980). Further information on consumer perceptions of product recalls. *Advances in Consumer Research, 8,* 519–523.

Palenchar, M. J. (2005). Risk communication. In R. L. Heath (Ed.), *Encyclopedia of public relations* (Vol. 2, pp. 752–755). Thousand Oaks, CA: Sage.

Pang, A., Jin, Y., & Cameron, G. T. (2010). Contingency theory conflict management: Directions for the practice of crisis communication from a decade of theory development, discovery, and dialogue. In W. T. Coombs & S. J. Holladay (Eds.), *Handbook of crisis communication* (pp. 527–549). Malden, MA: Blackwell.

Roux-Dufort, C. (2000). Why organizations don't learn from crises: The perverse power of normalization. *Review of Business, 21,* 25–30.

Schwarz, A. (2008). Covariation-based causal attributions during organizational crises: Suggestions for extending situational crisis communication theory. *International Journal of Strategic Communication, 2,* 31–53.

Sellnow, T. L., & Sellnow, D. D. (in press). The instructional dynamic of risk and crisis communication: Distinguishing instructional messages from dialogue. *Review of Communication.*

Shin, J. H., Cameron, G. T., & Cropp, F. (2006). Occam's razor in the contingency theory: A national survey of 86 contingent variables. *Public Relations Review, 32,* 282–286.

Sturges, D. L. (1994). Communicating through crisis: A strategy for organizational survival. *Management Communication Quarterly, 7*(3), 297–316.

Taylor, M. (2000). Cultural variance as a challenge in global public relations: A case study of the Coca-Cola scare in Europe. *Public Relations Review, 28,* 277–293.

Taylor, M., & Perry, D. C. (2005). The diffusion of traditional and new media tactics in crisis communication. *Public Relations Review, 31,* 209–217.

Tyler, L. (2005). Towards a postmodern understanding of crisis communication. *Public Relations Review, 31*(4), 566–571.

Ulmer, R. R., Sellnow, T. L., & Seeger, M. W. (2007). Post-crisis communication and renewal: Expanding the parameters of post-crisis discourse. *Public Relations Review, 33*(2), 130–134.

Ulmer, R. R., Sellnow, T. L., & Seeger, M. W. (2010). Considering the future of crisis communication research: Understanding the opportunities inherent to crisis events through the discourse of renewal. In W. T. Coombs & S. J. Holladay (Eds.), *Handbook of crisis communication* (pp. 691–697). Malden, MA: Blackwell.

Wan, H. H., & Pfau, M. (2004). The relative effectiveness of inoculation, bolstering, and combined approaches in crisis communication. *Journal of Public Relations Research, 16*(3), 301–328.

Weiner, B. (1986). *An attributional theory of motivation and emotion.* New York: Springer-Verlag.

Weiner, B. (2006). *Social motivation, justice, and the moral emotions: An attributional approach.* Mahwah, NJ: Lawrence Erlbaum.

Williams, D. E., & Olaniran, B. A. (1998). Expanding the crisis planning function: Introducing elements of risk communication to crisis communication practice. *Public Relations Review, 24*(3), 387–400.

CHAPTER 34

Expanding the Parameters of Crisis Communication

From Chaos to Renewal

Matthew W. Seeger, Timothy L. Sellnow, and Robert R. Ulmer

Both research into and practice of the communication dimensions of crises and disasters have exploded in the past decade. What was once a relatively narrow specialization within the larger public relations field has morphed into an interdisciplinary and integrative field employing multiple methods guided by diverse and broad-based theoretical frameworks from several fields and informed and facilitated by a steady stream of dramatic crisis events. In fact, in some ways, it has eclipsed public relations theory, redefined it, and reimagined it.

Research includes the wide-ranging postcrisis communication body of knowledge known as image restoration and apologetic discourse (Benoit, 1995; Coombs, 1999; Hearit, 2005) and significant research programs into evacuations, recalls, and warnings (Mileti & Fitzpatrick, 1992; Mileti & Peek, 2000; Mileti & Sorensen, 1990; Perry & Lindell, 2006; Seeger & Novak, in press). Scholars have also responded to practical crisis communication questions by exploring best practices, specific strategies associated with specific stages, and strategies for communicating during natural disasters (see Reynolds & Seeger, 2005; Seeger, 2006; Vanderford, Nastoff, Telfer, & Bonzo, 2007). Moreover, links are being forged between the large interdisciplinary body of inquiry into risk communication and work in crisis communication (see Morgan, Fischhoff, Bostram, & Altman, 2002; Slovic, 2000). Recently, some efforts have positioned risk and crisis communication as part of a larger integrated study field (see Heath & O'Hair, 2009; Reynolds & Seeger, 2005).

The crisis communication field is clearly undergoing a fundamental and dynamic expansion and reshaping, so much so that the parameters are no longer distinct. Some observers have described this rapid expansion as a "blessing and a curse" in that a plethora of insights are being generated but in a kind of fragmented and dispersed manner that makes integration and synthesis challenging (Coombs, 2010, p. 24). The field's dynamic nature, however, also signals a certain urgency to understand the communication dimensions of these transformative events.

In this chapter, we discuss factors and cases that have contributed to a crisis communication repositioning and describe the integration of research and the development of new interdisciplinary work in this dynamic research and practice field. We also identify factors and trends in crisis communication, including the emergence of new threats, and the mainstreaming and development of routine crisis communication through models such as ongoing crisis communication and crisis and emergency risk communication (CERC). In addition, we describe the emerging theoretical frameworks driving crisis communication and argue that they occupy a central position in this work. Finally, we describe some implications for crisis communication research based on this new framework for understanding crisis communication.

A Case-Driven Field

Dramatic events have repositioned crisis communication, as both a public practice challenge and a topic of diverse interdisciplinary research. Arguably, crisis communication has been driven by a public agenda formed by an ongoing stream of what Thomas Birkland (1997) described as "focusing events." These events demonstrate the deficiencies of current crisis communication and management practice; illustrate the range of failures that may result in crises; offer learning opportunities for scholars, crisis managers, and members of the public; and focus attention and resources toward research, planning, mitigation, and response. The list of crises that have driven the public and research agenda is quite long and extends back to public relations' development as a profession in response to industrial accidents and labor actions. Four events, however, are particularly important in modern crisis communication research development: the Tylenol poisonings, the *Exxon Valdez* oil spill, the 9/11 terrorist attacks, and Hurricane Katrina. We describe these below.

Heath and O'Hair (2009) suggested that the 1986 Tylenol poisoning episode and the *Exxon Valdez* oil spill mark the modern resurgence of crisis communication scholarship. The Tylenol poisonings involved the intentional adulteration of a popular over-the-counter pain medication. The crisis was centered on Chicago suburbs in the fall of 1982 and resulted in seven deaths from two separate cyanide poisoning incidents. The Johnson & Johnson company was forced to recall its best-selling product and mount an aggressive public relations campaign to reassure the public about the product's safety and save the brand (Pinsdorf, 1999, pp. 87–88). This included an appearance by the CEO, James Burke, with talk show host Phil Donahue. Burke helped rebuild public trust by providing an open and candid description of the company's response. He also announced new product and packaging designs that reduced tampering possibilities. The Tylenol episode illustrates consumer products' vulnerability and the impact proactive public relations can have in the face of a crisis. While some scholars note that Johnson & Johnson had the advantage of being a crisis victim and, thus, was able to credibly deny responsibility (Benoit, 1995), others note that this effective public relations response was a function of a core set of beliefs and a corporate culture that emphasized responsibility to customers, employees, communities, and stockholders (Marra, 1998).

While the Tylenol episode is generally considered a successful public relations case, the March 24, 1989, Exxon Valdez oil spill is often cited as an environmental disaster compounded by ineffective public relations. The episode involved a spill of 10.8 million gallons of crude oil, which eventually covered some 11,000 square miles. The pristine environment of Prince William Sound, Alaska, was devastated. Vivid images of dying birds and oil-soaked otters dominated media coverage.

Small (1991) poignantly concluded that although Exxon spent more than a billion dollars in an attempt to repair its image, the company failed to muster a favorable public portrayal of its efforts. Williams and Treadaway (1992) noted that the company initially chose a reactive stance, sought to scapegoat, and only late in the crisis accepted responsibility. The company initially tried to deny that the spill was significant, then sought to shift blame to the *Valdez* captain and the state of Alaska, creating the impression the company was avoiding responsibility. Denial; a slow, indecisive response; failure to take responsibility; and scapegoating compounded the harm to the company's already tarnished image (Williams & Treadaway, 1992).

In contrast to the Tylenol and Exxon cases, the 9/11 events involved a dramatic terrorist attack and highlighted government agencies' and the community's responses. Moreover, the event radically shifted security, terrorism, and communication public policy agendas. Not only did it involve the largest ever terrorism attack on U.S. soil; it also illustrated mass communication's power to create a common understanding of the event and leverage significant resources to address a common threat (Carey, 2003; Cohen, Ball-Rokeach, Jung, & Kim, 2003; Wakshlag, 2002). The World Trade Center collapse was a worldwide media event, allowing a remote global audience to participate in the crisis in real time. The crisis was also accompanied by the failure of first responder communication systems, which led to additional deaths of emergency workers who did not receive the order to evacuate the burning towers. The events directly affected a number of organizations in and around ground zero, created sharp declines in several industries, and had ripple impacts throughout the economy. Communication was instrumental in rebuilding these industries and, in some cases, renewing specific organizations (Seeger, Ulmer, Novak, & Sellnow, 2005).

Hurricane Katrina was similar to 9/11 in the sense that it was most directly associated with governmental agencies rather than private firms. While 9/11 created unity opportunities and consensus, Katrina illustrated government response deficiencies and some populations' vulnerability (Eisenman, Cordasco, Asch, Gordan, & Gliuck, 2007; Spence, Lachlan, & Griffin, 2007). These included existing warning systems' inadequacies and challenges faced in delivering information, including "rapid dissemination of health messages; adaptation of messages for diverse audiences, locations, and circumstances; and phasing of key risk messages" (Vanderford et al., 2007, p. 12). Among the dramatic failures was federal officials' disconnect from the situation on the ground and preoccupation with image rather than with providing substantive aid to those affected (Waymer & Heath, 2007).

One of the most politically important aspects of Hurricane Katrina was President George W. Bush's failure to acknowledge response deficiencies while asserting that the Federal Emergency Management Administration (FEMA) was managing the event successfully (Kellner, 2007; Liu, 2007). Media portrayals of victims on rooftops or wading through flooded streets highlighted both the deficiencies and the residents' plight. Like 9/11, Katrina was a media event, allowing the remote public to experience the disaster. Mishra (2006) found that many firms not affected by the disaster featured messages on their Web pages about the hurricane and made donations to relief agencies. She described these activities as corporate social responsibility strategies designed to bolster these firms' images.

These and many other cases have driven the research agenda for public relations and crisis communication. They have also illustrated the ways in which the research agenda has expanded from image restoration to broader issues of evacuations, warnings, and consensual meaning creation and communication during a crisis. Crisis communication has also expanded beyond those events associated with specific firms to broader crises and disasters affecting entire communities, regions, or the nation. Interdisciplinary approaches have similarly expanded the crisis communication research domain and provided opportunities to integrate new perspectives and approaches.

The Integration of Interdisciplinary Research

These and other cases influenced the crisis communication research agenda in two additional ways. First, they indicated to both scholars and practitioners the need to adopt a broader interdisciplinary perspective in approaching these complex events. Second, they prompted communication scholars to reach beyond traditional disciplinary boundaries for new constructs and theories. Crisis has become an important study domain in a number of fields, including political science (Birkland, 1997), emergency management (Auf Der Heide, 1989), anthropology (Douglas, 1992; Erickson, 1976), and sociology (Kreps, 1984; Tierney, 2003).

Early efforts to describe disasters were grounded in political science (Hermann, 1972) and drew heavily from notions of political disasters such as war, governmental collapse or loss of legitimacy, or sudden economic declines. As Cuny (1983) noted, disasters are inherently political events and "often highlight the social struggles in a society and underscore the inherent inequities within a political system" (p. 54). Natural disasters are generally seen as creating political and social unrest (Albala-Bertrand, 1993), although political and social instability may also be described generally as crises. Political scientists have also examined the role of crises and disasters in setting the public policy agenda. Birkland (1997), for example, characterized sudden, rare, and harmful or potentially harmful occurrences as focusing events. Because these events are known to both the public and policymakers, they often garner widespread attention and set the subsequent public policy agenda (Birkland, 1997).

Emergency management, as a field, has focused primarily on information communication between first responder agencies for coordination purposes and for public information officers training. The emphasis is usually on supporting technologies such as 800 megahertz radios and geographic information systems (GIS) that allow for more timely situational awareness through real-time information exchange. This ability to share information between agencies is called interoperability (Auf der Heide, 1989; Liebenau, 2003) and is generally seen as a prerequisite to an interorganizational coordination. Liebenau (2003) examined emergency communication during the World Trade Center disaster and concluded that firefighters' radios were not synchronized with the radios of the police, other groups of firefighters, or other emergency service providers. Coordination across agencies was thus limited (p. 48). Post 9/11, interoperability has been a major goal of first responder agencies and of research (see "Interoperability," n.d.). In addition, the public information spokesperson has been described as a specialized emergency management and criminal justice officer who serves as gatekeeper for information disseminated to the media and the public (Motschall & Cao, 2002; Surrette & Alfrado, 2001).

Applied anthropology has also made important contributions to crisis and disaster understanding, in part through the application of ethnographic methodologies at the scene but also through an interest in these events' cultural dimensions and their impact on societies. In his comprehensive literature review, Oliver-Smith (1996) noted that disasters "signal a failure of a society to adapt successfully to certain features of its natural and socially-constructed environment in a sustainable way" (p. 303).

Although anthropologists are interested in a variety of factors related to crises, such as culturally constructed notions of risk and responses to risk (Douglas, 1992), the meaning of a crisis has been an important study focus. This includes rituals of loss and grieving for persons, places, and institutions (Bode, 1989; Maida, 1996). Erickson's (1976) investigation of the 1972 *Buffalo Creek Dam failure* in Logan County, West Virginia, for example, explored the impact on a community dislocated and dispersed by a disaster. In addition, anthropologists have examined the contested meaning of the crisis and the role the media plays in this process (Benthall, 1993; Button, 1995).

The most robust body of work with the most direct interest in communication is disaster sociology (Comfort, 2005; Drabek & McEntire, 2003; Kreps, 1984). Broadly constructed, disaster sociology focuses on the mutual influence of disasters and social systems, including communities, institutions, organizations, and networks (Quarantelli, 1978; Turner, 1976). Thus, disaster sociology includes examination of social factors associated with disasters' onset and sociological factors influenced by disasters. As such, disaster sociology intersects with many other fields, including anthropology and communication.

Much of disaster sociology research has explored the development of myths of disasters (Tierney, 2003), the role of the media (Quarantelli, 1981; Quarantelli & Dynes, 1977), and process and variables in evacuations (Mileti & Peek, 2000; Mileti & Sorensen, 1990; Lindell, Prater, & Peacock, 2007). This includes robust efforts to understand variables such as gender, income, and race and their impact on natural disaster evacuations. Wenger and Friedman (1986) explored the role of the media in propagating disaster myths.

Interdisciplinary approaches to crisis communication have significantly enriched and broadened the understanding of roles, functions, processes, and outcomes. Because crises are such complex events, these approaches are necessary in any effort to build a comprehensive understanding.

Emergence of New and Expanded Theoretical Frameworks

Crisis communication developed as a practice-driven field. In public relations and emergency management areas, the practical need to communicate about crises and disasters drove the development of a field based in experiences and basic principles. One of the earliest crisis public relations practitioners was Ivy Lee, who is also described as a public relations founding father. Some of Lee's most important early successes as a public relations practitioner involved managing the communication association with accidents and union strikes in the rail and mining industries (Hallahan, 2002; Hiebert, 1966). Among other things, Lee advocated for comparative openness when organizations face a crisis—a principle that still frames much of public relations practice. The 1986 Tylenol poisoning episode and the 1989 *Exxon Valdez* oil spill mark the modern resurgence of crisis communication scholarship (Heath & O'Hair, 2009). While the former was an open proactive communication success marker, the latter epitomized stonewalling and a reactive stance. While models such as press-agentry and two-way symmetrical approaches inform public relations efforts during crisis, specific crisis communication theories did not emerge as an important factor in the field until apologia was expanded into a general image restoration theory (see Benoit, 1995). Image restoration theory and its recent variants, such as situated crisis communication theory and the discourse of renewal, remain the primary theoretical framework for crisis communication. This perspective has been joined, however, by the application of chaos and complexity theory, cultural theory, the development of elaborate integrated developmental models such as CERC, and the application of organizational learning theory to crisis communication study.

Chaos theory, complexity theory, and organizational learning theory examine crisis communication from the perspective of recovery or resilience. Chaos theory is applied as a metaphor for comprehending crisis communication's complexity (Tsoukas, 2005). As such, chaos theory contrasts sharply with traditional linear views of communication. Chaos theory has been applied to risk and crisis communication as a means of understanding both the disruption and restoration of order in organizations. In studies focusing on crisis communication, chaos theory is typically dissected into four interacting elements: bifurcation, fractals, strange attractors, and self-organization (Freimuth, 2006; Murphy, 1996; Seeger, Sellnow, & Ulmer, 2003; Sellnow, Ulmer, Seeger, & Littlefield, 2009). Bifurcation occurs at the onset of the crisis's most acute and unanticipated point. Weick (1993) described bifurcation as a cosmology episode where existing forms of sense making fail to account for the unforeseen experiences. Fractals are pieces of information that must be interpreted, sorted, and prioritized to gain an understanding of the cause and consequences of the bifurcation. The process of identifying patterns from fractal data, Murphy (1996) explained, is difficult because "concentration on individual units can yield insignificant or misleading information" (p. 99). Strange attractors, from the crisis communication perspective, are those values, principles, and social assumptions that draw people together in pursuit of common goals (Wheatley, 1999). The collapse of order produced by bifurcation demands that existing biases, tensions, and conflict be replaced by unprecedented collaboration. Seeger et al. (2003) explained that "bifurcation creates a moment in which the status quo is suspended and established relationships are amenable to a fundamental reordering" (p. 34). Ultimately, organizations recover from bifurcation through the self-organization process. Self-organization is an essential and naturally occurring process through which systems realign in bifurcation's wake (Sellnow, Seeger, & Ulmer, 2002). Wheatley (2007) explained that, within the organizational setting, "only leaders can commit their organization to this path" (p. 43). Although crises constrain all organizational leaders with some degree of uncertainty, leaders who embrace self-organization are better able to consider inconsistent or conflicting information and to encourage employees to do likewise. In this manner, organizations and communities develop lasting and meaningful changes that actually enhance resilience and renew organizations after a crisis event.

Complexity theory and chaos theory apply many of the same principles. In fact, the terms are often used in conjunction with one another. Both theories share components such as "attractors, bifurcation, unpredictability, and nonlinearity" (Gilpin & Murphy, 2008, p. 38). While chaos theory focuses on nonlinear systems that move from simple to highly complex situations, complexity theory concentrates on movement in the opposite direction. Thus, complexity theory seeks to understand the alignment of the many small or subtle interactions that create networks or patterns that function at a higher level. From the perspective of complexity theory, crisis is not seen as a blunder on the part of the organization. Rather, crises are caused by an "incidental interaction between variables whose result the organization could not have anticipated" (Murphy, 2000, p. 452). Gilpin and Murphy (2008) characterized chaos theory's primary objective as identifying "the manifestation of order from the confusion of myriad local interactions" (p. 39).

Complexity theory application to crisis communication has focused on the concept of attractor basins. Attractor basins are "discrete areas of behavior, attitudes, or values that capture a system for a while" (Gilpin & Murphy, 2008, p. 39). Crises such as reputational harm cause a "sudden leap from one 'attractor basin' or organizational image held by the public to another" (p. 39). Various stakeholders of an organization may have distinct attractor basins that "exert pull on the organization" (p. 40). From the complexity theory perspective, crisis planning involves identifying an organization's attractor basin boundaries and avoiding these boundaries. Violating these boundaries can result in an inevitable leap to another attractor basin.

Ultimately, both chaos theory and complexity theory seek to elucidate the self-organization process. Chaos theory sees self-organization as postcrisis renewal. In contrast, complexity theory views self-organization as unpredictable patterns' emergence through the process of co-evaluation by an organization's internal and external agents. In both cases, the patterns emerging through self-organizations are neither linear nor predictable.

The self-organization process identified by chaos and complexity theories is depicted as a learning process in organizational learning theory. Organizational learning occurs retrospectively as organizations observe errors, share these observations, derive lessons from the error, and share that knowledge throughout the organization. In this manner, organizational learning can change an organization's behavior range (Huber, 1996). Sitkin (1996) saw failures as "an essential prerequisite for learning" (p. 541). These failures alert organizations to their inadequacies and inspire change. Crisis, then, is seen as an urgent need for learning and change. Veil (2007) argued that in crisis situations "organizational learning can expedite image restoration, rebuild legitimacy, and better prepare organizations for future crises" (p. 337).

Whereas chaos, complexity, and organizational learning theories make sense of crises retrospectively, cultural theory, situational crisis communication theory (SCCT), and the CERC model expand the crisis communication focus to include a proactive or predictive dimension. Cultural theory provides a distinct view of risk perception and risk communication at the organizational or institutional level. Cultural theory views "institutional structure" as the "ultimate cause of risk perception" (Tansey & Rayner, 2009, p. 60). Institutions serve to represent and publicly communicate a collective view of risk issues from the perspectives of the distinct groups competing. Thus, institutions, rather than individuals, debate one another in the politicized context of risk issues. Controversies over risk issues are, at best, resolved through compromise rather than consensus. For example, housing ordinances developed in response to San Diego's wildfires represent a compromise among local government, resident organizations, and environmental groups. None of the three parties are completely satisfied, but the compromise provides a "clumsy solution" to the current problem (Tansey & Rayner, 2009, p. 75).

The CERC model provides a comprehensive and integrated approach to risk communication, emergency response, and crisis communication (Reynolds & Seeger, 2005). The model includes five stages: (1) precrisis, (2) initial event, (3) maintenance, (4) resolution, and (5) evaluation. Precrisis focuses on risk messages that provide warnings and preparation advice. Communication during the initial event concentrates on reducing uncertainty, providing the public with self-efficacy strategies, and offering the public reassurances. The maintenance stage provides ongoing uncertainty reduction and reassurance as well as continuing to provide self-efficacy strategies. Communication in the resolution stage focuses on updating the public regarding resolution and discussion about the cause of the crisis. The resolution stage typically provides a new risk understanding and produces future resilience strategies. The model concludes with an evaluation stage, during which the response's adequacy is debated and lessons learned are discussed. This model has been used to plan for and assess organizational response to natural disasters, epidemics, pandemics, and food-borne illness outbreaks (Seeger, Reynolds, & Sellnow, 2009; Veil, Reynolds, Sellnow, & Seeger, 2008). As such, the model serves as an effective tool for risk communicators to manage and respond to risk issues that can and do evolve into full-blown crises.

Benoit's (1995) work with image repair offers a pragmatic taxonomy of crisis response strategies for organizations. This work, however, is limited to case study analysis relying predominantly on external messages from the organization and media coverage of the event. SCCT moves beyond descriptive case studies to provide experimental and quasi-experimental designs for organizational crisis communication study (Coombs, 2009). Specifically, SCCT tests the correlational relationship between an organization's responsibility for a crisis and the organization's reputation (Coombs & Holladay, 2002). Organizations may seek to alter either perceptions of the crisis at hand or the organization's reputation. To do so, organizations may deny responsibility for the crisis, diminish perceptions of responsibility, rebuild the organization's reputation, or bolster the organization's reputation through goodwill acts. SCCT makes a valuable contribution to crisis communication study by providing a data-driven and verifiable model that, at minimum, provides a means of empirically testing response strategies in the context of varying constraints. At best, the theory enables crisis communicators to predict various response strategies' outcomes.

An additional image restoration expansion known as renewal discourse seeks to understand growth and development opportunities inherent in a system's collapse (Seeger et al., 2005).

Renewal argues that communication processes are central to framing a prospective vision for how organizations may be reconstituted following a crisis. In several cases, organizations have experienced renewal following devastative crises. This renewal is accompanied by positive relations with stakeholders, visible and active leadership, a prospective vision of the organization, and a strong value orientation.

New Areas of Practice

In addition to the development of interdisciplinary research and more focused theoretical frameworks, crisis communication has seen the development of much broader practice areas in both public and government arenas. While once seen as an activity practiced only rarely and for short periods of time, crisis communication increasingly is part of ongoing crisis planning and risk management efforts. Coombs (1999), for example, has suggested that the ongoing crisis communication model should be adopted as a public relations practice standard. Seeger et al. (2003) have suggested that crisis management and communication is developing into a key managerial competency necessary for organizational success in increasingly risky business environments.

Crisis communication's expanded role has become standard practice in the domains of health, public safety and security, and emergency management with industry groups as well as with specific organizations. The creation of the Department of Homeland Security (DHS) in 2002 centralized many federal activities formerly dispersed throughout several agencies. Primarily through its Web site, *Ready.Gov*, DHS has promoted crisis communication efforts in a number of arenas, including business and industry, community groups and organizations, and families. DHS also promotes interoperability through unified standards and the National Emergency Communications Plan. DHS created the Homeland Security Alert System in 2002. This color-coded system was designed to alert the public and institutions to heightened risks of terrorist events. The system generated so much controversy that DHS acknowledged that it is no longer effective and that the public is largely indifferent to alerts. Plans are currently in place for revising the system. The Centers for Disease Control and Prevention (CDC) have similarly embraced a greatly expanded crisis communication role in the public health area. In response to events such as the 2001 anthrax attacks, the emergence of Sudden Acute Respiratory Syndrome (SARS), and the pandemic influenza threat, the CDC developed the CERC framework and associated training. CERC is based on an integrated and developmental crisis and risk communication framework. CERC training has been widely disseminated as part of efforts to create crisis communication capacities within the general public health community.

In addition to governmental agencies, specific industries have expanded their issue management and public relations efforts. Associations such as the International Food Industry Council (IFIC) and the Independent Petroleum Association of America (IPAA) have expanded efforts to provide members with resources for managing issues and threats and responding to crises. Among other things, professional associations seek to promote awareness and preparedness, in part because crises centered on particular organizations also impact the entire industry's reputation.

Broad-based crisis communication activities at the governmental and industry levels will become increasingly important as new threats emerge and their consequences become manifest. Climate change, the threat of widespread technological failure, the emergence or reemergence of new infectious diseases, global terrorism, and the interaction of these and other threats creates a greatly expanded need for effective crisis communication.

Conclusion

Crisis communication boundaries are expanding because of the increasing frequency of crisis events. The frequency of crises can be attributed to the complex, efficient, technologically intense, dynamic, and tightly coupled systems that characterize our society. In this context, organizations, governments, federal and state agencies, and ultimately the public are experiencing more "normal accidents" of greater severity and broader impact (Perrow, 1999, p. 356). Many of these normal accidents exemplify technological failures and communication failures. In some cases, technological failures are often masked or influenced by communication problems. Current crisis research and practice suggests that effective communication is crucial to managing and ultimately recovery from the crisis event. At its roots, much interdisciplinary crisis management research emphasizes communication's central role. Whether the research emphasizes psychological risk perception, anthropological studies of how individuals cope with disasters, or sociological examinations of evacuation procedures, communication plays a key role in each of these research programs. As the theory and practice of managing crises continues to develop, it is unlikely that communication's role will diminish. That being the case, communication and public relations researchers should be well positioned to contribute to this expanding interdisciplinary study field.

References

Albala-Bertrand, J. M. (1993). *Political economy of large natural disasters.* Oxford, UK: Clarendon Press.

Auf Der Heide, E. (1989). *Disaster response: Principles of preparation and coordination.* Toronto, Ontario, Canada: C.V. Mosby.

Benoit, W. L. (1995). *Accounts, excuses and apologies.* Albany: State University of New York Press.

Benthall, J. (1993). *Disaster relief and the media.* London: Tauris.

Birkland, T. A. (1997). *After disaster: Agenda setting, public policy and focusing events.* Washington, DC: Georgetown University Press.

Bode, B. V. (1989). *No bells to toll: Destruction and creation in the Andes.* New York: Scribner.

Button, G. V. (1995). "What you don't know can't hurt you": The right to know and the Shetland Island oil spill. *Human Ecology, 23*(2), 241–257.

Carey, J. (2003). The functions and uses of media during the September 11 crisis and its aftermath. In A. M. Noll (Ed.), *Crisis communications: Lessons from September 11* (pp. 1–17). New York: Rowman & Littlefield.

Cohen, E. L., Ball-Rokeach, S. J., Jung, J., & Kim, Y. (2003). Civic actions after September 11: A communication infrastructure perspective. In A. M. Noll (Ed.), *Crisis communications: Lessons from September 11* (pp. 31–34). New York: Rowman & Littlefield.

Comfort, L. (2005). Risk, security, and disaster management. *Annual Review of Political Science, 8,* 335–356.

Coombs, W. T. (1999). *Ongoing crisis communication: Planning, managing, and responding.* Thousand Oaks, CA: Sage.

Coombs, W. T. (2009). Conceptualizing crisis communication. In R. L. Heath & D. H. O'Hair (Eds.), *Handbook of risk and crisis communication* (pp. 99–118). New York: Routledge Taylor & Francis.

Coombs, W. T. (2010). Parameters of crisis communication. In W. T. Coombs & S. J. Holladay (Eds.), *Handbook of crisis communication* (pp. 17–54). Malden, MA: Wiley-Blackwell.

Coombs, W. T., & Holladay, S. J. (2002). Helping crisis managers protect reputational assets: Initial tests of situational crisis communication theory. *Management Communication Quarterly, 16,* 165–186.

Cuny, F. C. (1983). *Disasters and development.* Oxford, UK: Oxford University Press.

Douglas, M. (1992). *Risk and blame: Essays in cultural theory.* London: Routledge & Chapman Hall.

Drabek, T. E., & McEntire, D. A. (2003). Emergent phenomena and the sociology of disaster: Lessons, trends and opportunities from the research literature. *Disaster Prevention and Management, 12*(2), 97–112.

Eisenman, D. P., Cordasco, K. M., Asch, S., Golden, J. F., & Gliuck, D. (2007). Disaster planning risk communication with vulnerable communities: Lessons from Hurricane Katrina. *American Journal of Public Health, 97,* S1.

Erickson, K. (1976). *Everything in its path: The destruction of a community in the Buffalo Creek mining disaster.* New York: Simon & Schuster.

Freimuth, V. S. (2006). Order out of chaos: The self-organization of communication following the anthrax attacks. *Health Communication, 20*(2), 141–148.

Gilpin, D. R., & Murphy, P. J. (2008). *Crisis management in a complex world.* New York: Oxford University Press.

Hallahan, K. (2002). Ivy Lee and the Rockefellers' response to the 1913–1914 Colorado Coal Strike. *Journal of Public Relations Research, 14*(4), 265–315.

Hearit, H. M. (2005). *Crisis management by apology: Corporate response to allegations of wrongdoing.* Mahwah, NJ: Lawrence Erlbaum.

Heath, R. L., & O'Hair, D. H. (Eds.). (2009). *Handbook of risk and crisis communication.* New York: Routledge Taylor & Francis.

Hermann, C. F. (1972). Threat, time and surprise: A simulation in international crisis. In C. F. Hermann (Ed.), *International crises: Insights from behavioral research* (pp. 187–214). New York: Free Press.

Hiebert, R. E. (1966). *Courtier to the crowd: The story of Ivy Lee and the development of public relations.* Ames: Iowa State University Press.

Huber, G. P. (1996). Organizational learning: The contributing processes and the literatures. In M. D. Cohen & L. S. Sproull (Eds.), *Organizational learning* (pp. 124–162). Thousand Oaks, CA: Sage.

Interoperability as a function of disaster response. (n.d.). *Annotated bibliographies.* Retrieved September 22, 2009, from www.colorado.edu/hazards/resources/bibliographies.html

Kellner, D. (2007). The Katrina Hurricane spectacle and crisis of the Bush presidency. *Cultural Studies ↔ Critical Methodologies, 7*(2), 222–234.

Kreps, G. A. (1984). Sociological inquiry and disaster research. *Annual Review of Sociology, 10,* 309–330.

Liebenau, J. (2003). Communication during the World Trade Center disaster: Causes of failure, lessons, and recommendations. In A. M. Noll (Ed.), *Crisis communications: Lessons from September 11* (pp. 45–54). New York: Rowman & Littlefield.

Lindell, M. K., Prater, C. S., & Peacock, W. G. (2007). Organizational communication and decision making for hurricane emergencies. *Natural Hazards Review, 8,* 50–60.

Liu, B. F. (2007). President Bush's major post-Katrina speeches: Enhancing image repair discourse theory applied to the public sector. *Public Relations Review, 33*(1), 40–48.

Maida, C. A. (1996). *Crisis and compassion in a world of strangers.* New Brunswick, NJ: Rutgers University Press.

Marra, F. J. (1998). Crisis communication plans: Poor predictors of excellent crisis public relations. *Public Relations Review, 24,* 461–474.

Mileti, D. S., & Fitzpatrick, C. (1992). The causal sequence of risk communication in the Parkfield Earthquake Prediction Experiment. *Risk Analysis, 12,* 393–400.

Mileti, D. S., & Peek, L. (2000). The social psychology of public response to warnings of a nuclear power plant accident. *Journal of Hazardous Materials, 75,* 181–194.

Mileti, D. S., & Sorensen, J. H. (1990). *Communication of emergency public warnings* (ORNL-6609). Washington, DC: Federal Emergency Management Administration.

Mishra, K. E. (2006). Help or hype: Symbolic or behavioral communication during Hurricane Katrina. *Public Relations Review, 32,* 358–366.

Morgan, M. G., Fischhoff, B., Bostram, A., & Altman, C. J. (2002). *Risk communication: A mental models approach.* Cambridge, UK: Cambridge University Press.

Motschall, M., & Cao, L. (2002). An analysis of the public relations role of the police public information officer. *Police Quarterly, 5*(2), 152–180.

Murphy, P. (1996). Chaos theory as a model for managing issues and crises. *Public Relations Review, 22,* 95–113.

Murphy, P. (2000). Symmetry, contingency, complexity: Accommodating uncertainty in public relations theory. *Public Relations Review, 26,* 447–462.

Oliver-Smith, A. (1996). Anthropological research on hazards and disasters. *Annual Review of Anthropology, 25,* 303–328.

Perrow, C. (1999). *Normal accidents* (2nd ed.). New York: Basic Books.

Perry, R. W., & Lindell, M. K. (2006). *Emergency planning.* Hoboken, NJ: Wiley.

Pinsdorf, M. K. (1999). *Communicating when your organization is under siege: Surviving public crisis.* Bronx, NY: Fordham University Press.

Quarantelli, E. L. (Ed.). (1978). *Disasters: Theory and research.* London: Sage.

Quarantelli, E. L. (1981). *The command post point of view in the local mass communication system* (Preliminary Paper No. 22). Newark: University of Delaware Disaster Research Center.

Quarantelli, E. L., & Dynes, R. R. (1977). Response to social crisis and disaster. *Annual Review of Sociology, 3,* 23–49.

Reynolds, B., & Seeger, M. W. (2005). Crisis and emergency risk communication as an integrative model. *Journal of Health Communication Research, 10,* 43–55.

Seeger, M. W. (2006). Best practices in crisis and emergency risk communication. *Journal of Applied Communication Research, 34*(3), 232–244.

Seeger, M. W., & Novak, J. M. (in press). Modeling the recall and warning process in the foodborne contamination event: Perspectives from disaster warnings and crisis communication. *International Journal of Mass Emergencies and Disasters.*

Seeger, M. W., Reynolds, B., & Sellnow, T. L. (2009). Crisis and emergency risk communication in health contexts: Applying the CDC Model to pandemic influenza. In R. L. Heath & D. H. O'Hair (Eds.), *Handbook of risk and crisis communication* (pp. 302–322). New York: Routledge Taylor & Francis.

Seeger, M.W., Sellnow, T. L., & Ulmer, R. R. (2003). *Communication and organizational crisis.* Westport, CT: Praeger.

Seeger, M., Ulmer, R. R., Novak, J., & Sellnow, T. L. (2005). Post crisis discourse and organizational change: Failure and renewal. *Journal of Change Management, 18*(1), 78–95.

Sellnow, T. L., Seeger, M. W., & Ulmer, R. R. (2002). Chaos theory, informational needs, and natural disasters. *Journal of Applied Communication Research, 30,* 269–292.

Sellnow, T. L., Ulmer, R. R., Seeger, M. W., & Littlefield, R. S. (2009). *Effective risk communication: A message-centered approach.* New York: Springer.

Sitkin, S. B. (1996). Learning through failure: The strategy of small losses. In M. D. Cohen & L. S. Sproull (Eds.), *Organizational learning* (pp. 541–578). Thousand Oaks, CA: Sage.

Slovic, P. (2000). *The perception of risk.* London: Earthscan.

Small, W. J. (1991). *Exxon Valdez:* How to spend billions and still get a black eye. *Public Relations Review, 17*(1), 9–25.

Spence, P., Lachlan, K. A., & Griffin, D. R. (2007). Crisis communication, race, and natural disasters. *Journal of Black Studies, 37,* 539–554.

Surrette, R., & Alfrado, R. (2001). Public information officers: The civilianization of a criminal justice profession. *Journal of Criminal Justice, 23*(4), 107–117.

Tansey, J., & Rayner, S. (2009). Cultural theory and risk. In R. L. Heath & D. H. O'Hair (Eds.), *Handbook of risk and crisis communication* (pp. 53–79). New York: Routledge Taylor & Francis.

Tierney, K. (2003). Disaster beliefs and institutional interests: Recycling disaster myths in the aftermath of 9-11. *Research in Social Problems and Public Policy, 11,* 33–51.

Tsoukas, H. (2005). *Complex knowledge: Studies in organizational epistemology.* Oxford, UK: Oxford University Press.

Turner, B. (1976). The organizational and interorganizational development of disasters. *Administrative Science Quarterly, 21,* 378–397.

Vanderford, M., Nastoff, T., Telfer, J., & Bonzo, S. (2007). Emergency communication challenges in response to Hurricane Katrina: Lessons from the Centers for Disease Control and Prevention. *Journal of Applied Communication Research, 35*(1), 9–25.

Veil, S. (2007). Mayhem in the Magic City: Rebuilding legitimacy in a communication train wreck. *Public Relations Review, 33*(3), 337–339.

Veil, S., Reynolds, B., Sellnow, T. L., & Seeger, M. W. (2008). CERC as a theoretical framework for research and practice. *Health Promotion Practice, 9*(4), 26S–34S.

Wakshlag, J. (2002). Introduction: Reflections on media in times of crisis. In B. Greenberg (Ed.), *Communication and terrorism* (pp. xiii–xv). Cresskill, NJ: Hampton Press.

Waymer, D., & Heath, R. L. (2007). Emergent agents: The forgotten publics in crisis communication and issues management research. *Journal of Applied Communication Research, 35,* 88–108.

Weick, K. E. (1993). The collapse of sensemaking in organizations: The Mann Gulch disaster. *Administrative Science Quarterly, 38,* 628–652.

Wenger, D., & Friedman, B. (1986). *Local and national media coverage of disaster: A content analysis of the print media's treatment of disaster myths.* Newark: University of Delaware Disaster Research Center.

Wheatley, M. J. (1999). *Leadership and the new science: Discovering order in a chaotic world* (2nd ed.). San Francisco: Berrett-Koehler.

Wheatley, M. (2007). *Finding our way: Leadership for an uncertain time.* San Francisco: Berret-Koehler.

Williams, D. E., & Treadaway, G. (1992). Exxon and the Valdez accident: A failure in crisis communication. *Communication Studies, 43,* 56–64.

CHAPTER 35

Red Cross Crisis Communication in the Wake of September 11, 2001

Kimberly A. Schwartz

Due to an act of terrorism, not just one, but four passenger planes crashed on September 11, 2001. In addition to the hundreds who died on board, thousands more died at the locations where the planes crashed—the Pentagon and both the World Trade Center's Twin Towers, which gave way due to damage sustained by the crashes. At the same time the emergency responders rushed to rescue the few victims who had survived in the wake of the four plane crashes, the news media simultaneously rushed to keep the Americans current about the events as they unfolded.

In addition to the unknown number that died following the collapse, thousands more became homeless or jobless within New York City. Nationwide, business as usual in the United States ground to a halt, as the U.S. Federal Aviation Administration grounded all flights across the nation, and Wall Street also suspended trading. In all, this catastrophe directly affected at least 25,000 families, with unofficial estimates gauging that about one in five people in the United States economically or emotionally felt the impact left by this tragedy.

In the wake of this turmoil, people turned to television and radio broadcasts, which were not only all-encompassing but also around the clock. However, America's attention to this tragedy did not wane as the hours folded into days, and days into weeks, leaving the mass media to search for more news content to fulfill their audience's increased hunger for news about the September 11 tragedies. To satisfy this desire for information, the mass media devoted intensive coverage to survivors and human service agencies, presenting these organizations with a rare forum to deliver their message. Consequently, charitable giving soared to unknown heights, but with these donations came an increased expectation for accountability. This public expectation for transparency far exceeded the previous experience of these nonprofits, leaving some charitable organizations unprepared, and in some cases, revealing internal strife.

Media Influence and Donor Contributions

Among the charitable organizations responding to the needs of the September 11, 2001, victims was the American Red Cross, a nonprofit, humanitarian service organization, well recognized chiefly for its blood services program and disaster relief services. The latter service—that is, disaster relief—has been part of the organization since its founding 120 years ago. At that time, founder Clara Barton agreed to provide disaster relief and relief services to members of the military and their families in exchange for receiving a federal charter to operate a society of the International Red Cross. Although this made Red Cross the only federally recognized agency to deliver disaster relief, it did not include financial support from the government. Therefore, the funds needed to deliver disaster relief had to come from private sources (Schwartz, 2002).

Over time, Red Cross learned that disaster donations, in-kind contributions, or volunteering not only are spontaneous acts but also involve little or no previous contact by the donor with the charity. Moreover, speculation has long been that larger disasters provoke a whole host of emotions ranging from disbelief to ultimately shock and finally an urge to help (Schwartz, 2002). With the onset of broadcasting, the American Red Cross and International Red Cross have found that news coverage, especially television coverage of large-scale disasters, has been a very strong motivator that results in a tremendous outpouring of unsolicited financial support. An example includes the Loma Prieta earthquake, which occurred during one of the 1989 World Series games in San Francisco, resulting in media coverage that obtained more than $90 million for earthquake relief efforts (Schwartz, 2002). The assumption in this and other instances is that the news media influenced the resulting donations, but until recently, this has been difficult to prove. Nevertheless, Adam Simon (1997) established a link between media coverage and an individual making a charitable contribution. His findings indicate that media exposure of an international earthquake was a contributing cause in inducing private individuals to make a charitable contribution. Greater earthquake severity resulted in more media coverage, and this media coverage increased private contributions. Thus, in the wake of such a devastating catastrophe, it could be expected that either an internal or an external motivational factor would generate more than half a billion dollars in financial donations, thousands of pints of donated blood, and thousands of new disaster volunteers for the American Red Cross.

Message Formulation

Despite donor desire and media coverage, Red Cross is aware that a humanitarian service organization must communicate its need to the potential charitable donor. A review of both news and feature releases publicized by the American Red Cross from September 11 to November 20, 2001, reveals that the organization publicized three messages: (1) the need to donate blood, (2) the need for financial donations, and (3) the availability of crisis counseling. These messages, delivered through a combination of communication methods (e.g., formal and informal), helped Red Cross detail the assistance provided in the wake of the tragedy, explained how the public could help the organization provide disaster relief to those in need, and explained how the public could obtain the assistance they needed.

The phrase "To help the victims of disaster . . . " was included in every news release, even if it was only at the bottom. One release spelled out this directive in a bit more detailed manner: "To help provide support for people in need following this disaster as well as emerging human needs resulting from this tragedy . . . " was included in the release (American Red Cross, 2001a). The next most prominent message was the availability of crisis counseling. This began with the publication on September 12 of the Red Cross writer Cynthia Long's article (Long, 2001). In this, Red Cross emphasized the availability of this service, due to the extremely traumatic nature of the event, for the families of victims who lost their lives, for those who lost their home or job in the collapse of the Twin Towers, or for those who felt traumatized by this catastrophe.

The Messengers

As expected, continual response to media inquiry and the resulting wave of public demand and response presented an overwhelming administrative prospect as well as challenges for all Red Cross direct service workers and media respondents for many weeks. Within the disaster public affairs function, a diverse communication method emerged as a direct result of the national headquarters lacking overall coordination. This occurred as four separate groups were working with the news media: (1) local chapter public relations staff, (2) rapid response team members (e.g., trained to respond to air traffic tragedies), (3) trained national disaster public affairs personnel, and (4) the national headquarters public relations function in Washington, D.C. While this was a problem in itself, only the rapid response and disaster public affairs personnel had been trained to deal with the news media in the wake of disaster. A fourth source of news distributed countrywide came from national headquarters. They publicized not only the fact sheets received from the disaster relief operation but also news and feature stories.

Two additional studies with Red Cross disaster public affairs personnel, following this disaster, by Terry (2003) and Reed (2004), identified a similar progression of growing discourse failure in the wake of this disaster relief effort. Reed additionally maintained that an organization needs to learn from a crisis, noting that it is imperative for an organization to evaluate each stage of the crisis for applicable lessons. However, the willingness of the organization to learn from the crisis also may make a difference in the outcome of the crisis.

External Communication Amid Internal Strife

Despite the availability of formal communications issued by American Red Cross National Headquarters or its onsite disaster public affairs personnel, the majority of news media relied on personal interviews and their own research. For example, a release on Red Cross's immediate and continuing response (American Red Cross, 2001b) resulted in CNN interviewing Red Cross spokesman Phil Zepeda (Brown & O'Brien, 2001). In addition, interviews occurred where assistance was being given, resulting in Red Cross personnel with no disaster public affairs training being interviewed, resulting in mixed outcomes for the organization. On September 20, 2001, CNN correspondent Bill Hemmer, during CNN's *Live at Daybreak* program, interviewed Ann Carol, a Red Cross registered nurse (King & Hemmer, 2001). Although Hemmer reported that the Red Cross had told CNN that in-kind donations should no longer be requested, Carol said, "What we really need is foot insoles for people's feet. . . . We are taping them up and treating the blisters, but we have a need for this, not food, not money" (p. 2).

In addition to mixed media messages, internal issues began to attract media interest. An October 4 story by Paul Farhi (2001) in the *Washington Post* partially placed blame for what was happening on Red Cross president Dr. Bernadine Healy. This piece speculated that Healy's assertive reputation was the reason behind the organization conducting excessive fund-raising, having a lack of donor communication, refusing to support a shared victim database with other organizations, and asking for more blood donations when independent blood banks were already full. Also, during this period, media reports focused on a similar fund-raising crisis that Red Cross faced during the 1989 San Francisco earthquake relief efforts. This issue was the subject of the October 11 FOX News Network *O'Reilly Factor* television program (O'Reilly, 2001b). Host Bill O'Reilly's guest on that program, the former San Francisco mayor Art Agnos, reflected on the Loma Prieta earthquake relief, stating that the Red Cross was "spending approximately $10 million for their standardized formula of service, which really didn't fit the needs of the people of San Francisco at that time" (p. 2).

Media Critique Continues

As time went on, news media coverage emphasized what Red Cross was not doing rather than the disaster relief services it provided (Farhi, 2001). In the *Chronicle of Philanthropy*, a cross section of media editorials censured Red Cross for the organization's response to the attacks (Newspaper Editorials, 2001). In its editorial, the *Chicago Tribune* recognized that "credibility is everything" (p. 11) when it comes to a charitable organization's reputation. In their view, the crisis erupted because the disaster relief organization's message was deceptive (p. 11). To regain its good name, the newspaper recommended that Red Cross must make a concerted effort to repair its standing in the eyes of the American public (p. 11). The *Los Angeles Times* paralleled the *Chicago Tribune* by agreeing that Red Cross must "rectify what could be a tremendous loss of faith with its donors everywhere" (p. 11).

However, *USA Today* believed that Red Cross had not disguised its intended uses, but instead, it had neglected to mention that some funds would provide existing programs assistance and some would go for educating the public (Newspaper Editorials, 2001, p. 11). In the end, this publication felt that aiding those in need would be the determining measure for success (p. 11). Meanwhile, another editorial in the *Washington Post* somewhat agreed with the commentary made by *USA Today*. Even though the newspaper felt that Red Cross may have had excellent grounds to keep on asking for blood and setting aside funds for the September 11 relief efforts, the publication felt these measures "sent strong messages and the organization was mostly deaf to their implications" ("The Perils of Success," 2001, p. 1). Their suggestion to solving the problem required that Red Cross be thoroughly honest and candid in the future (p. 2).

Organizational and Individual Critique

Susan Moeller (1999), director of the Journalism Program at Brandeis University and author of *Compassion Fatigue: How the Media Sell Disease, Famine, War and Death*, previously established the importance of knowledge to humanitarian organizations, stating that information had become "a more powerful—and more volatile tool for humanitarian organizations than a sack of rice or flour ever was" (p. 44). In her *Chronicle of Philanthropy* commentary, she stated that charities desiring to remain a credible news source need not only to supply reliable facts but also to be above reproach when it comes to representing their clientele. Moeller added that nonprofit organizations distributing news either to benefit themselves or for reasons that are biased will find it rebounds unfavorably on them (p. 44).

Within less than 2 weeks after September 11, 2001, organizations joined the media in questioning how the American Red Cross planned to use the funds given to the organization. An example of this was the *St. Louis Post Dispatch* story on September 21 (Schneider, Jonsson, & Holland, 2001). This article featured Kathleen McCarthy, director of City University of New York's Center for the Study of Philanthropy, and Bennett Weiner of the Better Business Bureau's Wise Giving Alliance, who both stated that they felt troubled about the spending and distribution of collected funds (pp. 1–2).

Joining the public dialogue were communication professionals, including Anthony De Cristofaro (De Cristofaro et al., 2001), director of communications for the United Way of Washington.

Formerly the United Way of America spokesman, in 1992, when the agency experienced a management crisis, he felt that this crisis occurred due to two factors: first, the American public did not understand that it takes time to deliver disaster relief, and second, donors expected a disaster relief response similar to the instant gratification they could obtain on the Internet. De Cristofaro added that this crisis would affect the Red Cross in the future, as the organization would have to explicitly explain how it delivers disaster relief. Crisis communications consultant James E. Lukaszewski held a similar view about how the crisis affected the Red Cross. It was his belief that nonprofit organizations do their work while not realizing that people have no idea what they do every day. To correct the current situation, Lukaszewski believed that the Red Cross had to be open and honest, describe how its procedures led to the current crisis, admit it made a mistake, be sincere about it, and admit that public trust is very important to the organization (p. 12).

Two other communication professionals had opinions that differed from the others. Larry L. Smith, president of the Institute for Crisis Management and a local Red Cross volunteer, believed that communicating with internal publics is most important. His recommendation is that financial supporters should be reassured that funds are being properly used by going to those who need them (De Cristofaro et al., p. 15). Meanwhile, Andy Burness, president of Burness Communications, felt that an organization can avoid a crisis altogether by anticipating what the public wishes to understand and educating them before they ask (p. 13).

Crisis Communication Emerges

Even though questions arose about Red Cross handling of this disaster less than 1 week after September 11, it did not fully reach crisis proportions until October 26, 2001. All the pending issues and questions came to a head that day with the resignation of Dr. Bernadine Healy as president and chief executive officer of the American Red Cross. According to a report filed by Ahan Kim (2001) for Cox News Service, Dr. Healy bluntly informed reporters that the board demanded her resignation (p. 1).

In the wake of Dr. Healy's resignation, entertainment news began full-scale exposés on what the Red Cross was doing. Bill O'Reilly (2001a), during the *O'Reilly Factor* on FOX News Network, confronted Red Cross vice president of communications Bill Blaul, on November 1, asking him to reply to "charges that it is not donating enough money to the families of the terror victims" (p. 1). In the interview, Blaul confronted one of the primary concerns raised by the media—how would Red Cross spend the monies placed into the Liberty Fund that had been created by the then Red Cross president, Healy? (p. 2). Blaul reported that Red Cross would direct all its funds to go toward assisting the victims, with another Red Cross budget source to fund other support programs and indirect costs (pp. 2–3). Officially, the Red Cross took this stance on November 14 during a news conference (Orfinger, 2001).

Mainstream media followed shortly not only with reports of current Red Cross disaster relief efforts but also with in-depth investigative reporting. On November 19, the *Washington Post* published an article written by staff reporters Pat Flaherty and Gilbert M. Gaul (2001). In their article, the reporters outlined previous disasters where Red Cross was accused of being unclear about how it used charitable contributions: the 1995 Oklahoma City bombing, the Red River flooding in Minnesota and North Dakota in 1997, and a January 2001 wildfire near San Diego.

Recommendations

To begin with, Red Cross should have foreseen that the following issues could pose future problems, or else it should have handled these issues better:

- There was a lack of response to media questions and reports about the Liberty Fund or the handling of disaster donations until 1 month after the disaster. A full explanation of this issue did not occur until 2 months after the disaster.

- News releases were too general in nature with few specific details given (e.g., the first publication of relief statistics occurred 6 days after the disaster). The usual key Red Cross fund-raising phrase used in disasters on news releases, "to help the victims of this and other disasters," was not included in Red Cross news or feature releases, which would have been helpful in educating donors.
- Red Cross ignored its own previous disaster fund-raising crises issues, which could have provided lessons for communicating in the wake of this disaster, such as confronting or correcting misconceptions before a crisis arose.

Second, even though communication experts provided differing views on how the fund-raising crisis affected the organization, all agreed that a good reputation is the most important item the Red Cross could possess. Their recommendations included reassuring internal donors that their funds were properly used, informing the public that the organization had made a mistake, establishing that public trust is everything to the Red Cross, and explaining how the organization delivers disaster relief.

Thus, this author felt that, in addition to the suggested recommendations, the Red Cross needs to do the following to avoid future communication crises in the wake of a catastrophic disaster:

1. Use the lessons learned from previous Red Cross disaster crises to avoid future issues.
2. Make education about Red Cross disaster relief a priority at the local, regional, and national levels to educate the news media, external publics, and internal Red Cross supporters.
3. Crisis communications training, including media training, should be required for national headquarters communications personnel and at least one person at every chapter.
4. Only trained disaster public affairs personnel should handle media inquiries in the wake of a disaster, even if this excludes the local chapter from this function.
5. Have only one disaster public affairs resource not separate teams, to avoid message diffusion.
6. During a disaster, respond immediately to confront or correct misconceptions before a crisis arises.
7. In the wake of disaster, the organization must immediately be truthful and honest about the usage of donor funds (including direct costs).

Conclusion

A prediction that September 11, 2001, could be another disaster fund-raising crisis for Red Cross was the subject of Jane Eisner's (2001) story in the October 28 issue of the *Philadelphia Inquirer*. In the article, the author questioned whether too much money had been raised for the disaster relief. Adding that very little information existed about the spending of these funds, she advised that charities should be forthcoming with details because "the controversies are only beginning to surface" (p. 2). At that time, her comments seemed prophetic, pointing out something that Red Cross should never have lost sight of—that Red Cross donor communication must be accurate and detailed. Both the news media and communications experts concurred with this viewpoint when it came to the Red Cross handling of donor funds after September 11. They concluded that the organization must frankly and honestly admit that they made a mistake, establish that public trust meant everything to the Red Cross, and make an extra effort to reclaim its reputation.

In addition, the American Red Cross could have prevented some issues from becoming topics for discussion, primarily by their lack of response to media questions about the Liberty Fund or the handling of disaster donations. Second, Red Cross ignored the growing crisis, not confronting or correcting misconceptions until they became a crisis, which had occurred in a previous disaster. However, Red Cross could not control media interest in researching and publicizing internal issues such as the then Red Cross president, Bernadine Healy, confessing her reason for leaving the organization during her resignation announcement and unauthorized volunteers talking to the news media.

However, it is always easy to judge an organization after the fact. To its credit, the American Red Cross responded to the best of its ability to an unprecedented disaster, the scope of which far exceeded previous relief efforts. In addition, the organization also had to deal with audiences that possessed very little understanding of the way in which the organization operated. This included donors who had never given blood, donated money, or volunteered for Red Cross, as well as recipients who had never before received assistance from the organization. However, as a portion of the Red Cross mandate from the U.S. Congress includes disaster preparedness, education, and mitigation, therein lies the opportunity to prevent future donor and news media misunderstanding.

References

American Red Cross. (2001a, September 12). *American public joins the Red Cross in unprecedented relief efforts around the country* [Press release]. Washington, DC: Author. Retrieved March 20, 2010, from www2.redcross.org/press/disaster/ds_pr/010912relief.html

American Red Cross. (2001b, September 11). *Red Cross responds to World Trade Center, Pentagon and Pittsburgh plane crashes* [Press release]. Washington, DC: Author. Retrieved March 20, 2010, from http://old.911digitalarchive.org/crr/documents/1272.pdf

Brown, A., & O'Brien, M. (2001, September 11). America under attack: Terrorist launch successful attacks against targets in New York and Washington. *CNN Breaking News*. Retrieved from LexisNexis database.

De Cristofaro, A., Lukaszewski, J., O'Reilly, B., Burness, A., Huffington, A., Smith, L., et al. (2001, November 15). Recovering from controversy: Experts offer advice to the Red Cross. *Chronicle of Philanthropy*, pp. 12+.

Eisner, J. (2001, October 28). Perhaps it's time to refocus our charitable contributions. *Philadelphia Inquirer*. Retrieved from LexisNexis database.

Farhi, P. (2001, October 8). In the face of disaster: Red Cross president Bernadine Healy activated her troops—and riled her critics. *Washington Post*. Retrieved from LexisNexis database.

Flaherty, M., & Gaul, G. (2001, November 19). Red Cross has pattern of diverting donations. *Washington Post Online*.

Kim, A. (2001, October 26). Healy had "no choice" but to leave Red Cross, she says. *Cox News Service*. Retrieved from LexisNexis database.

King, J., & Hemmer, B. (2001, September 20). America's new war: New York site cleanup continues. *CNN Live at Daybreak*. Retrieved from LexisNexis database.

Long, C. (2001, September 12). *Horror of attack takes emotional toll on nation* [Press release]. Washington, DC: American Red Cross. Retrieved March 20, 2010, from http://old.911digitalarchive.org/crr/documents/1271.pdf

Moeller, S. (1999, March). Relief groups and the press: A delicate balance. *Chronicle of Philanthropy*, pp. 44–45.

Newspaper editorials rebuke Red Cross for response to attacks. (2001, November 15). *Chronicle of Philanthropy*, p. 11.

O'Reilly, B. (2001a, November 1). Follow-up: Interview with Bill Blaul. *FOX News Network The O'Reilly Factor*. Retrieved from LexisNexis database.

O'Reilly, B. (2001b, October 11). Unresolved problem: Getting relief money to families. *FOX News Network The O'Reilly Factor*. Retrieved from LexisNexis database.

Orfinger, B. (2001, November 14). *Red Cross announces major changes in Liberty Fund* [Press release].

Washington, DC: American Red Cross. Retrieved March 20, 2010, from www.redcrosslv.org/news/2001/libertyfund.html

The perils of success. (2001, November 20). *Washington Post Online.*

Reed, K. E. (2004). A public affairs case study of the American Red Cross after September 11. *Master's Abstracts International, 43*(3), 649.

Schneider, A., Jonsson, G., & Holland, E. (2001, September 21). Unprecedented cash flow floods charities: Watchdog urges donors to be wary when giving. *St. Louis Post Dispatch.* Retrieved from LexisNexis database.

Schwartz, K. (2002). *Disaster public affairs and crisis communication in the wake of catastrophe: An analytical examination of the American Red Cross after September 11, 2001.* Master's thesis. Retrieved March 16, 2010, from www.dbq.edu/library/collectionsPDF/schwartz.pdf

Simon, A. (1997). Television news and international earthquake relief. *Journal of Communication, 47*(3), 82–93.

Terry, H. L. (2003, May). Public relations and the American Red Cross: Surviving the attack on America, September 11, 2001. *Masters Abstracts International, 41*(5), 1237.

CHAPTER 36

Defining the Relationship Between Public Relations and Marketing

Public Relations' Most Important Challenge

James G. Hutton

Confusion, misunderstandings, and occasional skirmishes among marketing, advertising, and public relations became the norm in the late 1980s and early 1990s as advocates of "integrated marketing communications" (IMC) sought to combine a variety of marketing, advertising, and public relations functions. Some public relations educators and practitioners cried foul, claiming that IMC represented a form of marketing imperialism that sought to subordinate public relations to marketing (Duncan, Caywood, & Newsom, 1993; Lauzen, 1991; Rose & Miller, 1994). From the beginning, however, IMC was mostly a false issue, driven primarily by the advertising industry, that has long served to obscure a more basic concern that is much more important to the future of public relations—the fundamental nature of the relationship between marketing and public relations.

Historically, the debate was generally about whether marketing and public relations should be partners or rivals in competing for organizational attention and resources. Today, the issue is quite different: Under a variety of monikers, the marketing field is reinventing itself to include or subsume much or all of public relations.

The public relations field has been very slow to respond to the challenge. In fact, from both practical and intellectual perspectives, the public relations field may well have created the vacuum that marketing is now filling. There remains a critical need for public relations to define its intellectual and practical domain, especially vis-à-vis marketing, to regain control of its own destiny.

Marketing and Public Relations: Independent Functions?

A logical place to begin the discussion of the relationship between marketing and public relations is an analysis of the similarities and differences between the two fields.

Few would disagree that marketing and public relations share much in common. Within organizations, they are the two functions most focused on external constituencies. Both deal with communication, persuasion, and relationships. Both deal with messages and media, increasingly focusing on new technologies that include social media and mobile marketing. Both deal with public opinion and segmentation of audiences. Ideally, both are strategic management functions that are anchored in research.

On the other hand, the differences are substantial. In terms of their scope of operation, marketing also is concerned with product development, physical distribution, location analysis, retailing, pricing, and customer service, while public relations is more concerned with the news media, various government entities, community relations, investor relations, and employee relations.

Marketing practitioners need to be better versed in break-even analysis, competitive analysis, package design, and queuing theory, whereas public relations practitioners must know the ins and outs of journalism, the legal and policy requirements of the Securities and Exchange Commission and stock markets, how best to manage the organization's charitable-contributions process, how to write speeches, and how to develop and implement an issues management program.

Regarding attitude, as well, there appear to be substantial differences. Marketing tends to demand a more aggressive, competitive, hyperbolic, "selling" mind-set, whereas public relations often demands a more conciliatory, peacemaking approach. So, while their research, processes, and objectives are often similar, the knowledge base, audiences, and mind-sets of marketing and public relations frequently are quite different.

Throughout most of their histories, the differences between marketing and public relations outweighed the similarities, causing them to tread generally divergent paths. For the most part, marketing focused on market research, product development, pricing, distribution, selling, advertising, and sales promotion functions, while public relations devoted most of its attention to media relations, public opinion, publicity, internal communications, government relations, and investor relations.

Over time, however, the differences between marketing and public relations diminished somewhat, to the point where they began bumping into one another with greater regularity and competing more directly for organizational resources. Clearly, the two fields could not act entirely independently any longer, at least without compromising organizational effectiveness and efficiency.

Marketing and Public Relations: Partners or Rivals?

Kotler and Mindak (1978) were among the first to directly address the increasingly important issue of the marketing/public relations interface, by asking whether marketing and public relations should be partners or rivals. The authors laid out five possible relationships: (1) marketing and public relations as independent functions, (2) marketing and public relations as overlapping functions, (3) marketing as a subset of public relations, (4) public relations as a subset of marketing, and (5) marketing and public relations as the same function.

Unfortunately, they did not really provide any criteria for choosing from among the five relationships. A simple but generally effective scheme is outlined in Figure 36.1 (Hutton, 1996a). The scheme is based on two simple questions: "What proportion of the marketing tasks confronting the organization are communication related?" and, conversely, "What proportion of the organization's communication tasks are marketing related?"

Figure 36.1 **Heuristic for Helping to Determine the Appropriate Relationship Between Public Relations and Marketing**

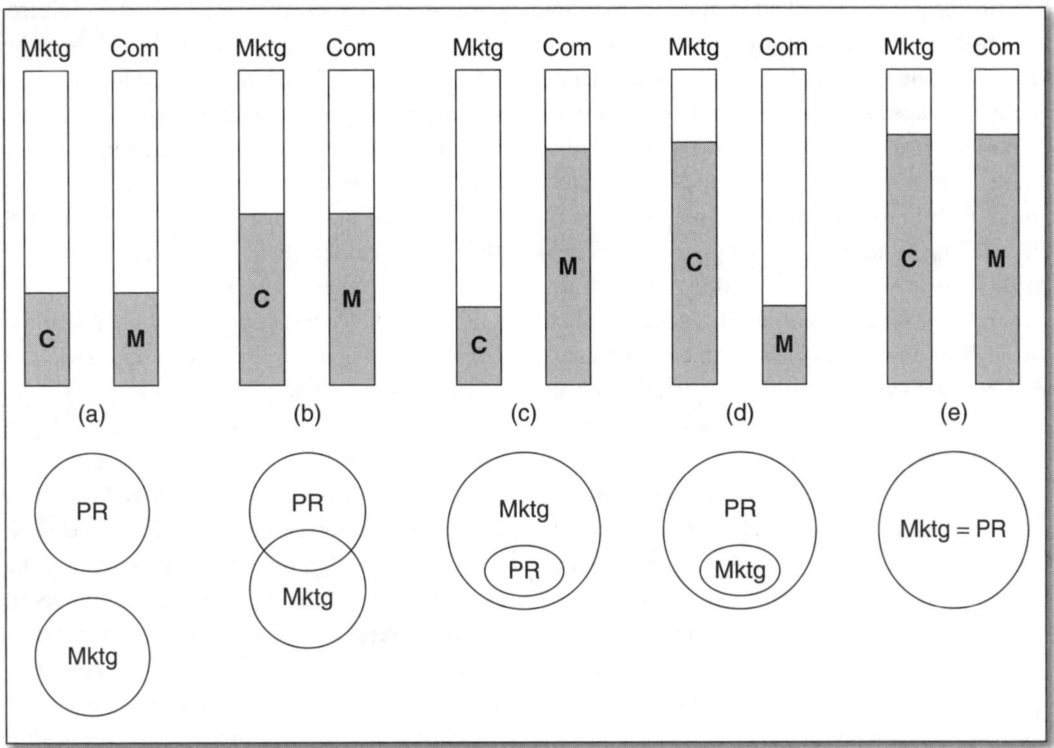

Source: Hutton (1996a). Reprinted with permission.

Note: Mktg or M = marketing; Com or C = communication; PR = public relations.

For example, if communication issues are a relatively small part of marketing and vice versa, an organization might wish to opt for the "separate but equal" model ("a" in Figure 36.1). Public utilities would generally be well suited to this model, given the importance they place on community, government, and media relations and the fact that media representatives, community-interest groups, and government agencies are generally more comfortable dealing with a separate "corporate communications," "public relations," or "public affairs" department, rather than a "marketing" department or a public relations department that reports to a marketing executive. Conversely, the noncommunication marketing functions of a public utility—especially physical distribution, capacity utilization, and product development issues—constitute a high percentage of the utility's marketing efforts.

If a moderate proportion of the marketing issues confronting an organization are communication related, and vice versa, then the "overlapping" model ("b" in Figure 36.1) is probably appropriate. Most large corporations likely fall into this category, given the size, complexity, and frequent independence of the marketing and public relations issues confronting such organizations. Typically, day-to-day marketing activities such as product publicity, promotion, and sales-force communications would be handled by the various line operations of the company. A corporate public relations or communications department, meanwhile, would handle financial communications, employee communications, the corporate identity program, the corporate advertising program, and other global communications because each of those functions touches many audiences ("publics" or "stakeholders") besides prospects, customers, and other members of the marketing channel. A company with a limited number of strong, independent brands might wish to develop a strong "marketing public relations" function, as suggested by Harris (1991). In any case, cooperation between the functions still is essential but accomplished through staff meetings between the departments and at the highest level of the organization as well as through personal relationships and other informal means.

Of course, in many large, complex organizations, there are multiple levels of some communication functions. For example, it is common to have corporate advertising, and organization-wide employee communications emanate from the corporate level, while product advertising and local employee communications emanate from the division level.

The "marketing dominant" model ("c" in Figure 36.1) is probably appropriate for a multi-brand consumer products company whose brands are more visible to the public than is its corporate persona. In such cases, care must be taken not to slight other key audiences, but it may be appropriate to operate with a skeleton corporate communications staff and to let marketing supervise almost all public relations activities as a line function because of the importance of product publicity, crisis communication (e.g., product recalls), sponsorships, special events, and other marketing-related public relations activities to developing and maintaining brand loyalty.

The "public relations dominant" model ("d" in Figure 36.1) probably would be appropriate for most professional services organizations, associations, hospitals, universities, and assorted nonprofit organizations, which typically have fewer pricing and distribution channel issues than do consumer or industrial product manufacturers. The public-relations-dominant mode would be more appropriate for such organizations because, at least conceptually, it focuses on longer-term issues of organizational culture, identity, and community outreach, befitting the nature of those institutions. In addition, this model generally is more appropriate and effective for such organizations to engage in a subtler form of marketing, making greater use of softer-sell tactics such as sponsorships and institutional advertising, rather than harder-sell techniques such as price-related advertising.

Finally, the "marketing = public relations" model ("e" in Figure 36.1) would be appropriate to most situations where a high percentage of marketing issues are communication related and vice versa, typical of a small business where there is great overlap between the two areas and neither is likely to be very sophisticated or highly developed.

In practice, of course, the choice among the five options will often be complicated by special circumstances, not to mention political and personnel considerations. Still, the scheme just described provides a general rationale and simple guidelines for the appropriate relationship between marketing and public relations in a given context. In both theoretical and practical terms, the choices first laid out by Kotler and Mindak (1978) suggested that no one model is best in all circumstances and that marketing and public relations should align themselves in whatever fashion is most conducive to accomplishing the organization's objectives. That commonsense approach to defining the marketing/public relations interface probably remains good advice but has been ignored by those who insist that there is one correct model (e.g., Grunig, 1992) and who tend to dismiss or ignore a constructive partnership between marketing and public relations.

IMC: Public Relations as Subordinate to Advertising?

Beginning in the late 1980s, a wild card that greatly complicated the marketing/public relations relationship was advertising, most notably in the form of IMC.

Critics of IMC suggested that it was simply the latest in a long line of attempts made by the advertising industry to expand its revenue base at the expense of other communication disciplines without a legitimate conceptual foundation. Ad industry veterans recall aborted variations on a similar theme, such as the "Whole Egg," "orchestration," and the "New Advertising" (Kalish, 1990), which sought to make advertising and related communications more consistent and coherent. The failure of such schemes (Levine, 1993) was largely the result of the mainstream advertising businesses' unwillingness to let go of a system that, while antiquated, had been very lucrative to agency owners (Schultz, 1993).

That self-contained system was (and occasionally still is) characterized by a media-commission compensation structure that defied economic logic (Ogilvy, 1963); ego- and award-driven creativity; a "who stole whose client this week" trade press mentality; and a "let's put on a show" style of business in which agencies routinely subjected themselves to wasteful and often demeaning business pitches and competitive account reviews (M. Martin, 1994).

In pushing the IMC concept, the consensus among advertising executives (Duncan, 1993) seemed to be that this time, IMC would take hold because it was not simply about finding new sources of revenue and growth but about survival of the advertising agency business. Fragmentation of the media, new communication technologies, new segmentation techniques, and the rise of databases were conspiring to threaten major advertising agencies' dependence on traditional mass media advertising and traditional ways of viewing advertising.

Unfortunately, although many of the major advertising agencies embraced IMC and trumpeted their role in integrating clients' marketing communications, there were serious questions about their sincerity. For example, major agencies generally were reducing or even eliminating their research functions (Ziff, 1992, p. RC2) at precisely the time one would presume that research would be emphasized as the foundation of a truly integrated marketing communications program. Wolter (1993) reported that IMC practice suffered from "superficiality," "ambiguity," and "blurred focus." The binge of major advertising agency takeovers of the major public relations firms in the 1970s and 1980s resulted in little real integration of those functions and often a great deal of turmoil.

So, while *IMC* may be a necessary transitional term between *advertising* and *marketing communication*, an astute observer will recognize that the word *integrated* is superfluous, at best, and is little more than a confession that *non*integrated or *dis*integrated communications have been the norm in the past.

As suggested schematically in Figure 36.2, few would disagree, from either a conceptual or practical perspective, that all elements of marketing communications should work in unison and that organizations should use all appropriate means of marketing communication at their disposal. Clearly, there seldom would be a circumstance when marketing communications should *not* be integrated. In practice, the lack of integration is generally a function of poor communication or lack of cooperation rather than any philosophical or theoretical disagreement about whether marketing communications should or should not be integrated.

The more meaningful debate is about the relationship between what might be termed *integrated marketing* (i.e., an organizational structure or authority in which all elements within the "marketing" circle in Figure 36.2 are united) and *integrated communications* (i.e., an organizational structure or authority in which all elements within the "public relations" circle are united). Theoretically, of course, it is highly desirable to have all functions of the firm integrated. Realistically, however, in most situations, marketing-communications functions must be placed under the organizational authority of either marketing or communications.

Figure 36.2 Relationships Among Marketing, Advertising, Marketing Communication, and Public Relations

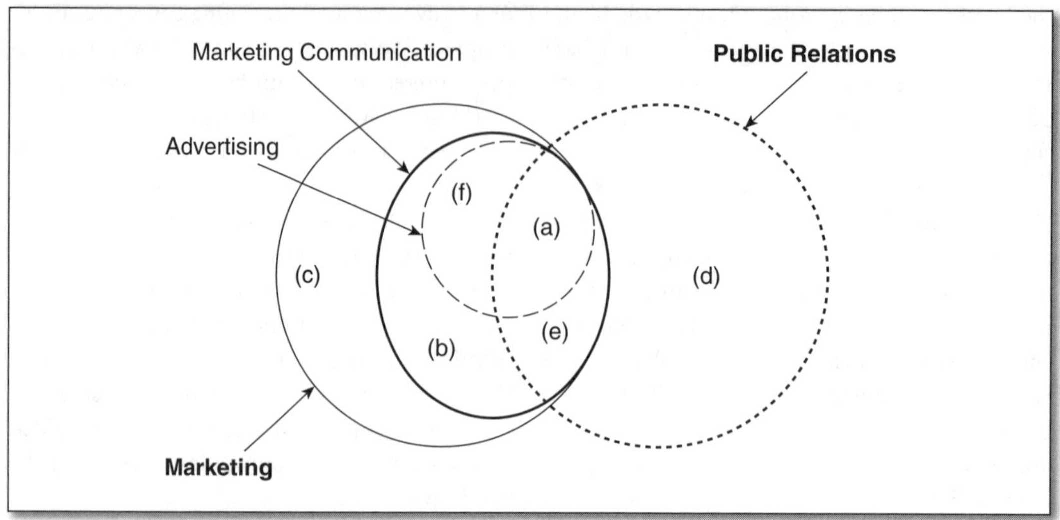

Source: Hutton (1996a). Reprinted with permission.

Note: (a) = corporate advertising; (b) = sales force and marketing channel communications, trade shows, packaging, direct marketing, sales promotion, and the like; (c) = distribution, logistics, location analysis, pricing, new product development, and the like; (d) = investor relations, community relations, employee communications, public affairs/government relations, media relations, crisis communications, corporate identity, executive communications, charitable donations, and the like; (e) = product publicity, brochures, and other collateral materials, part of media relations, part of crisis communications, part of corporate identity, sponsorships, and the like; (f) = traditional mass media advertising.

Organizations' frequent inability to resolve questions of how to organize and implement marketing, advertising, and public relations functions in an efficient, coherent manner continues to be a major issue. Despite persistent criticisms of IMC and absent any consistent definition of IMC, a study of senior marketing executives by the Association of National Advertisers (the most recent available) found that IMC was the marketing executives' highest priority, surpassing even "accountability" and "brand building" (Association of National Advertisers, 2008). A major reason for the ongoing concern about IMC appears to be marketers' inability and/or unwillingness to integrate digital marketing media with traditional advertising media (Association of National Advertisers, 2009).

Marketing and Public Relations: The Same Function?

While the IMC debate rages on in many quarters, it often obscures a trend that is even more important to the future of public relations: Marketing (not just advertising) scholars and practitioners have been methodically redefining the field of marketing as public relations. "Employee communications" has become "internal marketing" (Gronroos, 1981), "crisis communications" has become "crisis marketing" (Marconi, 1992), and virtually the whole of "public relations" is now "relationship marketing."

In a *Journal of Marketing* article, Duncan and Moriarty (1998) graphically depicted "marketing" as the replacement for "public relations" at the corporate staff level, relegating "public relations," even as a line function, to a role as one of seven marketing-communication "message sources" (along with personal sales, advertising, sales promotion, direct marketing, packaging, and events).

Many public relations practitioners and scholars are not even aware of the trend. Others see it as little more than a grab for power and turf by marketers.

From another perspective, however, it appears that marketing's interest in public relations is a natural stage of marketing's evolution. To understand why, it is necessary to look a little deeper into the history of modern marketing thought (beginning roughly with the Industrial Revolution) from a marketing channels perspective (Hutton, 1996a).

From their origins in economics, marketing thinkers were initially concerned primarily with issues of economic efficiency, focusing on the production end of the producer-to-consumer channel and on questions surrounding economies of scale, pricing, and the relationship among mass production, mass distribution, and mass consumption. Within a few decades, the leading edge of marketing theory and practice had moved down the channel to distribution issues, including extended discussions of the role of middlemen, ownership of goods in the channel, and power relationships in the channel.

As marketing theory and practice continued to progress down the marketing channel, the "selling concept" came to the fore, with its focus on sales management and selling techniques, followed by the rise of the "marketing concept," with its focus on (a) product branding and positioning and (b) customer wants and needs as the engine of the marketing process and the basis of the entire organization's philosophy.

Having reached the end of the channel (the consumer), the natural progression for the most forward-thinking marketers was to explore two new frontiers: (1) the application of the so-called marketing concept to nonbusiness organizations and activities and (2) a focus on the *context* of the entire marketing channel, which most marketing texts (e.g., McCarthy, 1975) had previously regarded as fixed or uncontrollable.

Explorations of the first frontier are documented in the debates about "Broadening the Concept of Marketing" (Kotler & Levy, 1969), while exploration of the second frontier is perhaps best illustrated by Kotler's (1986) concept of "megamarketing," which added two more "Ps," politics and public relations, to marketing's traditional "4 Ps" (product, place, price, and promotion). Interestingly, in both cases, the focus of marketing thought shifted from the channel itself to a range of external issues dealing with societal issues and relationships with noncustomer publics or stakeholders such as governments, activist groups, employees, and investors—the traditional domain of public relations.

The critical point is that marketing thought is evolving toward a public relations perspective, to such an extent that marketing is essentially redefining itself as public relations. Duncan (1993), for example, defined IMC as "the process of strategically developing and controlling or influencing all messages used to build and nourish *relationships* [italics added] with customers and other *stakeholders* [italics added]." Plummer (1993) described advertising's job as "controlling the message," public relations' job as "managing the dialogue" (including crisis management and what Plummer called "positive communications"), and relationship marketing's job as "interacting with publics."

Kotler, perhaps marketing's most visionary thinker over the past 35 years, has been writing about public relations extensively during this period but under a variety of different names: "total" marketing" (Kotler, 1992), "megamarketing" (Kotler, 1986), and "generic" marketing (Kotler, 1972). In his article on generic marketing, Kotler (1972) outlined three levels of marketing "consciousness." In Consciousness 1, he defined marketing as a business subject concerned with buyers, sellers, and economic products, in which the core concept was market transactions. In Consciousness 2, marketing was distinguished by organization-client transactions, not necessarily requiring payment, as practiced by museums, universities, churches, and the like, as well as by businesses. Finally, in Consciousness 3, marketing applied to an organization's attempts to relate to all of its publics, not just its consuming public.

Thus, Kotler's definition of generic marketing, Plummer's definition of relationship marketing, and Duncan's definition of IMC are nearly identical—and all are definitions of public relations as it has been practiced by more enlightened organizations for decades.

The Continuing Identity Crisis of Public Relations

Marketing's lack of acknowledgment or even recognition of its own reinvention of public relations is due largely to the general lack of understanding of what public relations is and does. Marketing and advertising textbooks and "how-to" business books (e.g., Hotchkiss, 1940; McCarthy, 1975; Wasson, 1983) traditionally have mistaken publicity or marketing-related public relations as the whole of public relations, often portraying public relations as an afterthought to an advertising campaign, designed to garner whatever "free advertising" can be generated to complement the basic ad campaign. Top executives, typically trained in business schools, tend to perpetuate such misconceptions in practice.

Before public relations practitioners and scholars accuse marketing of imperialism, however, it would be prudent to examine a number of factors that have actually encouraged marketers to fill a large void created by public relations practitioners and scholars. Among the most important issues are the following:

1. *The ineffectiveness of public relations in educating businesspeople and business schools about public relations.* Pincus and others have looked at this issue extensively (e.g., Pincus, Ohl, & Rayfield, 1994). Ironically, many of the topics that have come to the forefront of business school research—things such as reputation management (G. Martin, 2008), corporate culture (Hutton, 1996c), and "humanistic" approaches to relationships (Hutton, 1996b) are topics about which public relations practitioners have a wealth of knowledge and experience.

2. *Public relations' frequent lack of understanding of marketing and business, in general.* Despite incessantly describing itself as a management function, public relations continues to suffer from a general lack of respect for and frequent lack of success in meeting organizational goals because so few of its practitioners and scholars exhibit a clear understanding of business subjects. Ehling, White, and Grunig (1992), for example, in describing the relationship between marketing and public relations, made a number of claims that would be considered nonsense by sophisticated marketing practitioners:

- "In contrast to public relations, marketing communication is characterized by unilateral design, unidirectional message flow, and one-stage operation" (p. 389). (The entire industry of database marketing is *based* on the notion of two-way message flow and continuous feedback.)
- "Marketing rationale and techniques are not . . . even useful to nonbusiness organizations such as educational institutions, not-for-profit hospitals, and public welfare agencies" (p. 359). (It would be difficult to find a major nonprofit organization that does not effectively use marketing techniques, at least to some degree. Many such organizations are more sophisticated marketers than the average for-profit organization.)
- "The resolution of conflict and the mediation of disputes is essentially a public relations function and not a concern of marketing" (p. 369). (During the late 1950s and early 1960s, one of the most important areas of marketing research concerned conflict management and conflict resolution, in the context of marketing channels. It remains an important and active research topic.)

3. *The failure of public relations to define itself and to develop sophisticated and progressive theory.* In not developing a widely accepted definition and a central organizing principle or paradigm, the field of public relations has left itself vulnerable (a) to marketing and other fields that are making inroads into public relations' traditional domain and (b) to critics who are filling in their own (typically very derogatory) definitions of public relations (Hutton, 1998).

Olasky (1984) described the problem as the "aborted debate within public relations" about what should be the fundamental purpose or nature of public relations. According to Olasky, the public relations profession chose not to challenge Edward Bernays's paradigm, developed during the 1920s (including advocacy of the client's position and concurrent lack of concern for objectivity), because it was too lucrative for its practitioners:

> The public relations occupation was too profitable for its beneficiaries to accept the reformation and reconstruction that paradigm changes require.... The trade was made: acceptance of a low status for public relations in return for acceptance of fat paychecks. (p. 94)

Others (e.g., Dover, 1995; Hutton, 1994; Ragan, 1994) have suggested that the problem is more related to factors such as closed-mindedness, arrogance, inbreeding, and the fear of new theories and new theorists than to financial gain. In any case, Olasky's basic observation about the lack of theory development in public relations appears to be correct and still applicable more than two dozen years later.

Another dimension of the "definition" problem in public relations is the field's unfortunate but frequent forays into misguided definitions. Over the years, public relations has been terribly distracted by a mind-numbing variety of definitions. The current distraction for the field is "reputation management." Some major public relations agencies have enjoyed financial success with the approach, and certainly it makes sense for some organizations in some situations. But it is an ill-advised strategy for defining the whole of public relations. Besides its lack of a generally accepted definition, "reputation management" represents an extremely risky path for public relations. A reputation is not something that can be managed, in any real sense, given that it results from the actions of all members of an organization, as interpreted by a host of outside observers. Even more important, evidence (Therkelsen et al., 2008) strongly suggests that chief executive officers (CEOs) do not perceive public relations as being in charge of their organizations' reputations. To stake the future of the public relations field on something that is inherently unmanageable and that CEOs do not believe is—or can be—managed by public relations people, in particular, seems to be seriously misguided.

4. *The inflexibility of public relations theorists.* As suggested earlier, the idea that there is one "best" structural relationship between marketing and public relations, regardless of context, probably is false and not in keeping with a true management orientation, which would argue that form should vary according to situation and objectives.

Theorists must be very sensitive to practical considerations, as well. For example, in developing countries or in countries where public relations is a developing field, the typical organization may not have the luxury of devoting resources to a public relations department that downplays marketing-support responsibilities (Kent, Taylor, & Turcilo, 2006).

5. *The failure of public relations to develop its central tenet or core concept.* Pavlik (1987, p. 122) and Broom, Casey, and Ritchey (1997) reported that while relationships are often discussed in public relations as a central theme or *the* central theme in the field, (a) the term *relationship* is seldom even defined and (b) there has been little substantive research in the field of public relations regarding the measurement of relationships, the theoretical constructs of relationships,

or relationships as the unit of analysis. Broom et al. "found the same paucity of useful definitions in the literature of other fields in which the concept of relationships is central" (p. 83), including interpersonal communication, psychotherapy, interorganizational relationships, and systems theory.

Surprisingly, however, Broom et al. (1997) overlooked a wealth of information from marketing. The omission of marketing as a domain of relationship theory is particularly puzzling given that some of the relationship-marketing theory deals with precisely the issues they were attempting to explain, such as the antecedents and consequences of relationships.

More specifically, one of the marketing theories directly relevant to public relations was titled the "commitment/trust" theory of relationship marketing (R. Morgan & Hunt, 1994). In their model, R. Morgan and Hunt (1994) posited trust and commitment as the core of relationships in a marketing context. The antecedents included shared values ("corporate culture," in public relations parlance), communication, and the costs of exiting the relationship. The desired outcomes or consequences of trust and commitment included acquiescence, (reduction in) uncertainty, cooperation, and functional (as opposed to dysfunctional) conflict. The authors made a compelling case for their theory, including an empirical pilot test of their trust/commitment model with a competing model, using higher-order statistical techniques.

Only later, in the late 1990s and early 2000s, did the public relations field begin to develop substantive theory regarding relationships, and much of it was based (often without giving proper credit) on the R. Morgan and Hunt model and other research outside of the public relations field.

6. *Implicit overreliance on "communications" or "communication" as the central tenet of public relations.* While public relations has not formally identified or developed its core concept, there is little doubt that a large majority of both public relations scholars and public relations practitioners were trained in communication(s) of one sort or another and tend to operate with that bias. To whatever extent R. Morgan and Hunt (1994) are correct in their hypothesis that trust and commitment are the foundation of strong relationships, and that communication is just one antecedent (and probably not the most important one), public relations might need to go back to the drawing board and reassess its dominant focus on communication as the field's implicit foundation.

7. *The continuing disintegration of public relations.* A major consequence of the semantic confusion surrounding public relations is that—contrary to much talk about "integrated" communications—the public relations field is generally *dis*integrating. Particularly the higher-end functions (i.e., those that are best paid, most influential, and closest to top management), such as investor relations and government relations, are being lost to other functional areas within organizations. For example, the National Investor Relations Institute (NIRI) reported that the percentage of investor relations managers reporting to chief financial officers (CFOs) or treasurers rose from 44% to 56% in just the 4-year span from 1988 to 1992 (Sweeney, 1994). As of 2008, a study by NIRI and Korn Ferry International (J. D. Morgan, 2008) found that only 3% of investor relations officers reported to chief public relations officers, despite the fact that about one in five investor relations officers came from public relations or communications backgrounds. An even more recent global study of investor relations (Bank of New York Mellon, 2009) found that about 60% of investor relations heads reported to the CFO, about 30% reported to the CEO, and so few reported to public relations that it was not even on the radar.

Similarly, many corporate public relations departments have lost responsibility for crisis communications to management consulting firms and marketing departments; some have lost responsibility for corporate identity programs to marketing; some have lost government relations to the legal department; and some have lost internal/employee communications to the human resources department. The extreme of this phenomenon was illustrated by Burger King about 10 years ago when it "integrated" its communications function into the organization by disbanding the public relations department. Its media relations (the only communications function that could not halfway logically be assigned to another functional area with the organization) was given to the "diversity" department.

Perhaps the key point, relative to the relationship between marketing and PR, is that as public relations loses its nonmarketing-related functions, marketing becomes a greater percentage of the overall public relations function, and thus it becomes more likely and more logical that marketing will annex or subsume public relations.

8. *Public relations' failure to stake out its most logical core domain.* For reasons that are not entirely clear, public relations has never staked a solid claim to territory that it logically should dominate, both in practice and in theory development. For example, Rotfeld (2001) and other marketing scholars have argued that marketing has overstepped its bounds and been guilty of "misplaced marketing" when it comes to the marketing of education, health care, and other social institutions. Along the same lines, Hutton, Leung, Mak Ka Ying, Varey, and Watjatrakul (2010) found moderate to very strong public resistance to the idea of treating students, patients, members of religious organizations, and similar audiences as "customers." Clearly, the application of marketing concepts to social institutions (e.g., hospitals and other health care organizations, religious organizations, and government entities of all kinds) makes many people uncomfortable, leaving a huge opportunity for public relations. Yet public relations does not have the kind of presence one would expect, relative to marketing, in most such organizations.

Similarly, public relations has not done a particularly good job of staking its claim to emerging fields of relationship management such as social networking. Marketing has staked at least an equal claim, and in large measure, the distinction between marketing and public relations is being blurred even further in the minds of businesspeople and the general public because "marketing" and "public relations" are so often used interchangeably in the digital world. One of the most popular books about the use of blogs, viral marketing, podcasting, and the other new media was titled *The New Rules of Marketing and PR* (Scott, 2007) and talked about the two fields almost as though they were one. At the same time, the term *marketing public relations* seems to have taken hold in the world of social media (Giannini, 2010).

Conclusion

The relationship between public relations and marketing is increasingly being defined by the marketing side. The reasons, however, have less to do with marketing imperialism than with (a) marketing's natural progression toward relationships and noncustomer publics and (b) the void that public relations has created, inviting marketing and other fields to assume responsibility for traditional public relations functions.

The result, one might argue, will probably not be good for either field. Marketing has more than enough to worry about, in tending to customer demands, product development, pricing, advertising, sales promotion, sales management, market research, and other core marketing issues, and it might well be spreading itself too thin in attempting to manage relationships with a host of noncustomer publics. Public relations, on the other hand, will almost certainly suffer as both a practice and an intellectual discipline if it is subordinated or assimilated by marketing.

To stem the tide, public relations needs to systematically address the issues that have led to its frequent marginalization in the marketing/public relations relationship. If public relations fails to meet the challenge, its future will be uncertain and largely in the hands of others. If it succeeds, public relations' future will be in its own hands and very bright, indeed.

References

Association of National Advertisers. (2008). *Senior marketing executives weigh in on top issues* (news release, April 8). Retrieved March 30, 2010, from www.ana.net/news

Association of National Advertisers. (2009). *ANA and 4A's study shows marketers face internal and external challenges integrating traditional and digital media* (news release, April 24). Retrieved March 30, 2010, from www.ana.net/news

Bank of New York Mellon. (2009). *Global trends in investor relations: A survey analysis of IR practices worldwide* (5th ed.). Retrieved March 30, 2010, from www.vcall.com/CustomEvent/conferences/bankofny/confpage.asp?ID=140213

Broom, G. M., Casey, S., & Ritchey, J. (1997). Toward a concept and theory of organization-public relationships. *Journal of Public Relations Research, 9*(1), 83–98.

Dover, C. J. (1995). The shearing of the lambs: An irreverent look at excellence. *Journal of Management Advocacy Communication, 1*(1), 38–44.

Duncan, T. (1993, September). *Perspectives on integrated marketing communication.* Paper presented at the seminar sponsored by District IV of the International Association of Business Communicators, Des Moines, IA.

Duncan, T., Caywood, C., & Newsom, D. (1993). *Preparing advertising and public relations students for the communications industry in the 21st century.* Boulder: University of Colorado.

Duncan, T., & Moriarty, S. (1998). A communications-based marketing model for managing relationships. *Journal of Marketing, 62*(2), 1–13.

Ehling, W. P., White, J., & Grunig, J. E. (1992). Public relations and marketing practices. In J. E. Grunig (Ed.), *Excellence in public relations and communication management* (pp. 357–393). Hillsdale, NJ: Lawrence Erlbaum.

Giannini, G. T. (2010). *Marketing public relations: A marketer's approach to public relations and social media.* Upper Saddle River, NJ: Prentice Hall.

Gronroos, C. (1981). Internal marketing: An integral part of marketing theory. In J. H. Donnelly Jr. & W. R. George (Eds.), *Marketing of services* (pp. 236–238). Chicago: American Marketing Association.

Grunig, J. E. (Ed.). (1992). *Excellence in public relations and communication management.* Hillsdale, NJ: Lawrence Erlbaum.

Harris, T. L. (1991). *The marketer's guide to public relations.* New York: Wiley.

Hotchkiss, G. B. (1940). *An outline of advertising: Its philosophy, science, art and strategy.* New York: Macmillan.

Hutton, J. G. (1994, November 7). Excellence study: Political and narrow. *The Ragan Report, 25*(19), 1.

Hutton, J. G. (1996a). Integrated marketing communications and the evolution of marketing thought. *Journal of Business Research, 37,* 155–162.

Hutton, J. G. (1996b). Integrated relationship-marketing communications: A key opportunity for IMC. *Journal of Marketing Communications, 2,* 191–199.

Hutton, J. G. (1996c). Making the connection between public relations and marketing: Building relationships, corporate equity and a "culture-to-customer" business philosophy. *Journal of Communication Management, 1*(1), 37–48.

Hutton, J. G. (1998, May). *The nature and scope of public relations.* Paper presented at the 11th annual conference on Corporate Communications, Madison, NJ.

Hutton, J. G., Leung, V., Mak Ka Ying, A., Varey, R., & Watjatrakul, B. (2010). *Students, patients, citizens and believers as "customers": A cross-national exploratory study* (Working paper).

Kalish, D. (1990). The new advertising. *Agency,* Fall, 28–33.

Kent, M. L., Taylor, M., & Turcilo, L. (2006). Public relations by newly privatized businesses in Bosnia-Herzegovina. *Public Relations Review, 32,* 10–17.

Kotler, P. (1972). A generic concept of marketing. *Journal of Marketing, 36*(2), 46–50.

Kotler, P. (1986). Megamarketing. *Harvard Business Review, 64*(2), 117–124.

Kotler, P. (1992, September). Total marketing. *Business Week's Advance Briefs.* (Mailed to selected subscribers of *Business Week* in September)

Kotler, P., & Levy, S. (1969). Broadening the concept of marketing. *Journal of Marketing, 33*(1), 10–15.

Kotler, P., & Mindak, W. (1978). Marketing and public relations: Should they be partners or rivals? *Journal of Marketing, 42*(3), 13–20.

Lauzen, M. (1991). Imperialism and encroachment in public relations. *Public Relations Review, 17,* 245–256.

Levine, J. (1993, March 15). Teaching elephants to dance. *Forbes,* 100–101.

Marconi, J. (1992). *Crisis marketing: When bad things happen to good companies.* Chicago: American Marketing Association.

Martin, G. (2008). Employer branding and reputation management. In C. Cooper & R. Burke (Eds.), *High performing organizations* (pp. 252–274). London: Routledge.

Martin, M. (1994, November 4). HHCl rethinks to reclaim the integrated initiative. *Campaign London,* p. 11.

McCarthy, J. (1975). *Basic marketing: A managerial approach.* Homewood, IL: Richard D. Erwin.

Morgan, J. D. (2008). *NIRI releases summary results of inaugural NIRI–Korn/Ferry International IRO compensation study.* (Executive Alert news release from the National Investor Relations Institute, April 7, Vienna, VA)

Morgan, R., & Hunt, S. (1994). The commitment-trust theory of relationship marketing. *Journal of Marketing, 58*(3), 20–38.

Ogilvy, D. (1963). *Confessions of an advertising man.* New York: Atheneum.

Olasky, M. N. (1984, August). *The aborted debate within public relations: An approach through Kuhn's paradigm.* Paper presented to the Qualitative Studies Division of the Association for Education in Journalism & Mass Communication, Gainesville, FL.

Pavlik, J. V. (1987). *Public relations: What research tells us.* Newbury Park, CA: Sage.

Pincus, D., Ohl, C. M., & Rayfield, B. (1994). Public relations education in MBA programs: Challenges and opportunities. *Public Relations Review, 20,* 55–71.

Plummer, J. (1993, August). Presentation to the American Marketing Association's annual educators conference, Boston.

Ragan, L. (1994, September 13). It's time to look more closely at IABC's $400,000 *Excellence* report. *The Ragan Report, 25*(13), 2.

Rose, P. B., & Miller, D. A. (1994). Merging advertising and PR: Integrated marketing communications. *Journalism Educator, 49*(2), 52–63.

Rotfeld, H. J. (2001). *Adventures in misplaced marketing.* Westport, CT: Quorum Books.

Schultz, D. E. (1993, April 26). Why ad agencies are having so much trouble with IMC. *Marketing News,* p. 12.

Scott, D. M. (2007). *The new rules of marketing and PR.* Hoboken, NJ: Wiley.

Sweeney, P. (1994, April 3). Polishing the tarnished image of investor relations executives. *New York Times,* p. F-5.

Therkelsen, D., Fiebich, C., Groehler, K., Freeman, B., Piltingsrud, B., Hutton, J. G., et al. (2008). *Reputation management: Conflicting expectations between public relations practitioners and top management* (Working paper).

Wasson, C. R. (1983). *Marketing management: The strategy, tactics and art of competition.* Charlotte, NC: ECR Associates.

Wolter, L. (1993, September 13). Superficiality, ambiguity threaten IMC's implementation and future. *Marketing News, 12,* 21.

Ziff, W. B. (1992). The crisis of confidence in advertising. *Journal of Advertising Research, 32*(4), RC2–RC5.

CHAPTER 37

Being Public

Publicity as Public Relations

Kirk Hallahan

Publicity involves the use of communication to make an entity publicly known. One dictionary defines publicity as "the state or quality of being public"—and suggests that publicity is an "act or device to attract public interest" and support (*Merriam-Webster's Dictionary*, 2009). *Being public* thus implies visibility, attention, prominence, identification, understanding, and openness—and is the opposite of being private or secretive.

Modern public relations (PR) originated with publicity, although the term has generally fallen out of favor except in segments of the public relations practice devoted to promotion of creative works such as movies, plays, and books. Yet publicity—in the broad sense of an entity acting in public view—is a necessary condition for effective public relations. Indeed, "PR = performance + recognition."

For the past half century, publicity has been narrowly defined within public relations to mean obtaining media coverage in the news and entertainment portions of newspapers, magazines, television, and radio. However, publicity can be defined more generically as the "dissemination of information and materials." In this sense, advertising and publicity are equivalent, and the paid use of the former can even be viewed as a tool for obtaining the latter.

The distinction between the broad and narrow senses of *publicity* is important in today's rapidly changing communication environment where practitioners use a combination of public media and direct communication vehicles to reach publics. Moreover, when critics refer to questionable public relations practices, they are usually referring to the *publicity* aspects of public relations—not its assessment, planning, or counseling functions.

As this chapter suggests, publicity is a metaconstruct that can be examined from professional, historical, managerial, economic, interpersonal, behavioral, cultural, critical, philosophical, ethical, legal, and technological perspectives. Moreover, publicity provides an alternative and potentially valuable paradigm for understanding how entities of all types promote themselves—including individuals and institutions.

Professional Perspectives

Reaching the public is a primary reason why clients retain public relations consultants, recruit public relations volunteers, and establish public relations departments. Publicity skills also represent the principal focus of tactical training in public relations programs offered by educational institutions in the United States. Publicity can be deployed for various purposes in all four of the basic kinds of public relations programs.

1. Promotional programs
   - Create awareness; promote trial; and encourage repeat use of products and services.
2. Relational programs
   - Maintain mutually beneficial patterns of interaction and exchanges by key stakeholders.
3. Issues management programs
   - Create awareness and understanding, marshal support, and prompt action related to a social problem, public policy matter, or dispute.
4. Crisis communication programs
   - Provide information, give directions, explain organizational actions, or assume (or deny) responsibility during periods of uncertainty following an extraordinary event.

Publicity about an entity can be initiated either internally or externally and can be either favorable or unfavorable. This suggests the four-part typology illustrated in Figure 37.1.

Controlled publicity involves favorable messages generated by an entity that helps advance its mission or cause and appears before audiences essentially as desired. *Compromised publicity* entails messages modified substantially by a third party when being distributed (such as by the news media) and might harm achievement of the entity's goal. Problems include errors, favorable information about competitors, alternative solutions to a problem or situation, or negative comments. *Corroborative publicity* is generated by a third party that supports an entity's purpose or position on an issue. Examples include, but are not limited to, reports issued by outside organizations, endorsements by prominent people, and favorable media news reports, editorials, or reviews. *Countervailing publicity* is generated by critics or competitors and can work against the interests of the entity by mentioning contradictory information, criticisms, or attacks.

Importantly, controlled or corroborative publicity does not always need to be positively valenced. Indeed, a neutral tone, the avoidance of hype, and inclusion of some negative information can lend credence to the arguments presented and accrue credibility to the source. This phenomenon has been observed in terms of *language expectancy theory* (Burgoon, Denning, & Roberts, 2002; Hallahan, 1999a), the *paradox of the positive* (Heath & Waymer, 2009), *inoculation theory* (Szabo & Pfau, 2002), and *stealing thunder*

Figure 37.1 A Typology of Publicity

	Source	
Valence	**Internal**	**External**
Favorable	Controlled	Corroborative
Unfavorable	Compromised	Countervailing

or the purposeful release of negative information in a crisis (Arpan & Pompper, 2003). Similarly, compromised and countervailing publicity can help advance a cause by encouraging public consideration or discussion of the arguments.

Historical Perspectives

The antecedents to modern publicity date to the use of drums among tribal peoples and the dissemination of papyrus leaflets promoting farming practices in ancient Iraq. For-profit and not-for-profit organizations have used publicity to promote their activities since the 16th century (Cutlip, 1995).

The emergence of modern publicity in the early 20th century reflected the increased complexity of society, the emergence of large and complex institutions, the heightened pluralism and diversity in society, and people's dependence on organizations. The trend also reflected Progressive Era ideals about the rational nature of people, the emerging power of large newspapers and magazines, and the attacks on corporations and government by muckraking journalists (Cutlip, 1994; Ewen, 1996; Thompson, 2003).

Publicity was the term most often used to describe public relations activities in the early 20th century. Although he occasionally described his role as being an "advisor on public relations" as early as 1916 (Raucher, 1968, p. 122), public relations pioneer Ivy L. Lee (1925) almost always called his craft *publicity*. Definitions of publicity at the time were strikingly similar to modern descriptions of public relations (I. L. Lee, 1925, p. 8; Wilder & Buell, 1923, p. 6). Publicity eventually subsumed *press-agentry*—the practice of obtaining notices in newspapers about plays, books, lectures, and movies—and was used interchangeably with press-agentry and public relations in the 1930s (Washburn, 1937).

Publicity's impact raised considerable public concern by the early 1900s (Hallahan, 2002; Lucarelli, 1993; Russell & Bishop, 2009). Despite the success of wartime government information programs (Creel, 1972a, 1972b; Lasswell, 1927), *propaganda* was considered a scourge by the end of World War I. Not surprisingly, savvy practitioners like Edward L. Bernays started using "counsel on public relations" as an innocuous and more dignified term to describe publicity work (Bernays, 1923, 1965; Curtis, 2005). At the same time, a spate of books appeared on the topic (Cutlip, 1994; Raucher, 1968; Wilder & Buell, 1923). In 1922, journalist Walter Lippmann (1922) observed, "The development of the publicity man is a clear sign that the facts of modern life do not spontaneously take a shape in which they can be known. They must be given shape by somebody" (p. 218).

Managerial Perspectives

Publicity is a form of *management communication* used to lead organizations.

Organization of the Function

The first publicity department for a corporation was established by Westinghouse in 1889. Traditionally, the publicity function focused on external media relations. Managers of the early 20th century, who often focused on efficiency and control, centralized publicity in public relations departments where the function could be controlled (L. A. Grunig, Grunig, & Dozier, 2002). But postmodern management approaches suggest that publicity can and ought to be decentralized (Hallahan, 2007). Today, publicity is an important function both *outside* and *within* organizations and can be pursued by units such as marketing communications, investor relations, employee communications, and even corporate journalism (Kounalakis, Banks, & Daus, 1999).

The focus on publicity as a management tool—not merely a promotional vehicle—began in the early 20th century when practitioners like I. L. Lee convinced corporate executives to look at situations from the public's perspective and to provide factual and accurate news to the press. Meanwhile, public relations pioneers like Arthur W. Page stressed the importance of supplying information directly to employees and other stakeholders. Publicity played an important tactical role as businesses embraced public relations during the early half of the 20th century (Ewen, 1996; Olasky, 1987; Raucher, 1968; Safire, 1963; Tedlow, 1979). Yet, today, most large complex organizations pay little strategic attention to publicity at the executive level. Publicity suffers from any kind of strategic or long-term planning (Doorley & Garcia, 2007; Holstein, 2008).

Publicity Seeking and Avoidance

Most entities seek controlled publicity that helps advance their mission and strive to avoid compromised or countervailing publicity. Organizations not only release information routinely in the form of news and feature stories but also stage *pseudo events* (Boorstin, 1960), *spectacles* (Debord, 1995; Spencer, 2000), and *stunts* (Fuhrman, 1989) that have no other purpose than to generate attention. Entities obsessed with gaining exposure are referred to as *publicity hounds.*

Some organizations purposely shun publicity. The 11th Tradition of Alcoholics Anonymous (2009), for example, emphasizes attraction rather than promotion and stresses maintaining the anonymity of members in the media. Legitimate reasons for publicity avoidance include (a) the unintended or premature disclosure of business plans, (b) the disclosure of proprietary information (such as a trade secret), and (c) security concerns about crimes against senior and other personnel. Other reasons include (d) executive shyness or fear, (e) distrust or disdain for the media, (f) concerns about misrepresentation, (g) lack of personnel with publicity skills, and (h) worries about repercussions resulting from publicity gone awry (see Doorley & Garcia, 2007; Grant, 1995).

Strategic Uses

Publicity serves as a strategic management tool in at least five ways:

First, publicity can be used to *signal an entity's planned activities* to the marketplace. Preannouncements about future activities provide implicit clues (and often explicit instructions) for how vendors, business partners, distributors, suppliers, customers, competitors, investors, public officials, or employees should anticipate an entity's forthcoming actions (e.g., gear up production or defer purchases).

Second, publicity allows entities to articulate their values and goals publicly. Thus, publicity serves an educational function for employees and other stakeholders and can explain the entity's aims and activities. Publicity thus also sets a standard against which performance can be later judged. Importantly, stakeholders assess the verisimilitude of publicity by comparing an entity's words with their personal experience.

Third, publicity helps an entity fulfill its mission by stimulating stakeholder behaviors that contribute to revenue or other performance goals. Stakeholder actions can include buying, investing, donating, working, voting, adopting spiritual beliefs, engaging in prosocial activities, and avoiding risk. In marketing, publicity often *supplements* or serves an *alternative* (in the absence of adequate budget) for advertising, direct selling, or sales promotion (Hallahan, 1996). While initially resisted by advertising professionals (Tedlow, 1979), publicity today plays a critical role in *integrated marketing communication* (Hallahan, 2007).

Fourth, publicity is a tool that can be used for *impression management* or to enhance an entity's *reputation.* People prefer to identify with and be affiliated with entities with good reputations (Doorley & Garcia, 2007; van Riel & Fombrun, 2007). Positive reputation alternatively can be measured in terms of perceived goodwill and brand equity. Reputation operates as a heuristic that enables people to make judgments about an entity without having in-depth knowledge of or a relationship with the entity (Hallahan, 2000b).

Fifth, publicity represents a publicly accessible historical record of an entity's activities. Newspaper clippings, digital archives, employee publications, and other publicity records serve as artifacts that chronicle an entity's evolution.

Assessment

Demonstrating publicity's effectiveness remains a managerial challenge. Although the metrics for media publicity measurement are well known, most publicists and their clients rely on subjective assessments or readily available circulation figures or readership/viewership/access data. Actual impact is often imputed because the costs of more rigorous assessments (such as surveys to measure awareness, attitudes, or behavioral intent) can easily equal or exceed the expenditures for the activity being measured. When measurement is applied to larger, multifaceted campaigns, the challenge becomes distinguishing between the effect of publicity and that of all other campaign components. In the same vein, calculating publicity's *return on investment* is conceptually straightforward (Merims, 1972; McElreath, 1997), but requires identifying fully the amount spent and agreeing on the percentage that publicity (vs. all other efforts) contributed to the results obtained. Alternatively, clients have a penchant to assess publicity's costs and benefits in terms of space or time equivalency to advertising—a dubious exercise because the two content classes are not directly comparable.

Economic Perspectives

For economists, publicity is a tool of *social coordination* that enables entities to signal the availability of resources and to communicate incentives in order to match consumption to production (Wills, 1997). Publicity information is a *public good* that can be reproduced and reused without depleting its value.

Publicity and Economic Behavior

Classical economics assumes that people are rational beings. Publicity facilitates decision making and exchanges in a free market economy to the extent that the information is material and complete. However, available information is rarely perfect (*symmetrical*). Thus, publicity can bias decision making, resulting in irrational choices. Examples of this phenomenon include reliance on price or quality ratings found in magazines such as *Consumer Reports* (Archibald, Haulman, & Moody, 1983).

Publicity hype has contributed to frenzied economic activity dating back to the Dutch Tulip Bubble of 1624, and today primes confidence in the economy during periods of both recession and recovery. Brennan and Pettit (2004) argued that publicity can affect performance through what they term the *economy of esteem:* Publicity increases the size of an entity's audience and thus an entity's reputation or prestige, which in turn provides incentives for the entity to perform. Behavioral economists have demonstrated the effects of news and publicity on economic transactions and movements in a variety of contexts. Among these are trading and investments, financial planning, public procurement, real estate and construction, international trade, and demand for consumer products considered hazardous.

Publicity and Economic Structures

Neoclassical economists challenge the premise of the rational consumer and the effectiveness of free markets. Transaction cost analysis, for example, suggests that organizations will abandon market mechanisms and enter into hierarchical relationships whenever costs are lower (Podnar, Lah, & Golob, 2009; Williamson, 1996). Resource dependency theory similarly posits that organizations will establish relationships with others to obtain needed resources and will maximize the dependence of others on them (Pfeffer & Salancik, 1978). In such cases, publicity facilitates relationship formation and maintenance by supplying vital information that promotes or reinforces the benefits of such arrangements. In systems theory, publicity similarly represents the outputs and inputs used by boundary-spanning units.

Publicity and Media Economics

Publicists are a key component in a society's extended *public information system* (Cutlip, 1994). Estimates suggest that 40% or more of news content originates with or involves publicity sources (Cutlip, 1989). Extensive research has examined the media's reliance on public relations–generated materials and the role of publicists in the production of news (for a review, see Cameron, Sallot, & Curtin, 1997; Sallot, Steinfatt, & Salwen, 1998).

As *sources* of news, publicists and their clients operate as *information sponsors* that subsidize news media operations. Gandy (1982) explained that an *information subsidy* involves a party interested in influencing government, media, or other organizations and who bears the cost of generating information favorable to the party's position (see also Curtin, 1999; McManus, 1994, 1995; Turk, 1986). Publicists and their clients reduce the cost of media news gathering by facilitating efficient *work routines* for media workers (Tuchman, 1978) and by providing *official sources* (Fishman, 1980; Gans, 2003). These institutionalized arrangements bias the news production process. This phenomenon is best illustrated by the membership press clubs (*kisha kurabu*) through which much media publicity is distributed in Japan (Schudson, 2003).

Information subsidies take three basic forms—and these represent the three core strategies used in all publicity. First, publicists supply *materials* that can be used as is or require only modest editing. Prepackaged information saves media time and money by eliminating the need to create content from scratch. Second, publicists arrange for *spokespersons* to deliver information in readily accessible forms such as speeches, testimony, or media interviews. Third, publicists organize provocative *events* that journalists and others are invited to attend. Events are easy and compelling ways for media personnel to experience an idea, individual, or institution.

Interpersonal Perspectives

Beyond institutional exchanges, publicity depends heavily on interpersonal communication or exchanges. These include *publicist-gatekeeper negotiations, spokesperson exchanges,* and *audience information sharing.*

Publicist-Gatekeeper Negotiations

To gain access to major speech platforms, governmental bodies, or media, publicists often propose ("pitch" or "sell") an idea and then negotiate arrangements with a designated organizational representative or *gatekeeper.* Examples of gatekeepers include program chairs for major speech forums, staff members for legislative bodies conducting hearings, and media editors or producers (Shoemaker & Vos, 2008). Gatekeeping involves subprocesses of screening and selection, and the accompanying negotiation is a dyadic process in which each party pursues a distinct role and goal (Belz, Talbott, & Starck, 1989; Charron, 1989). The publicist seeks exposure for a client, while the gatekeeper wants to advance the organization's mission or agenda. Such negotiations are *transactional exchanges* (McManus, 1994, 1995) and can be analyzed in terms of *game theory* (Murphy, 1989) where the parties seek a mutually beneficial ("win-win") outcome. Both negotiators can grant *rewards* or impose *punishments* by allowing or blocking access to the party they represent. Negotiators use the authority, stature, or knowledge of the party they represent as leverage. French and Raven (1959) referred to these as *legitimate, referent,* and *expert* power, respectively.

Much publicity work involves *relational exchanges* wherein the parties strive for an ongoing pattern of mutually beneficial exchanges, not just a single transaction. Social exchange theory suggests that people will maintain such relationships until the point when perceived costs exceed perceived benefits (Prior-Miller, 1989). Lobbyists, agents representing artists, and media relations specialists all generally recognize the potential value of future access. So all of them try to establish and maintain positive relationships with gatekeepers by using their professional training and experience to anticipate and accommodate the needs, production processes, and protocols followed by gatekeepers (Taylor, 2009).

Spokesperson Exchanges

Interpersonal communication plays a critical role whenever a spokesperson shares information with others. A publicist who negotiates access might also serve as a spokesperson. However, clients often assume the separate spokesperson role by giving a speech, testifying before a government body, or being interviewed. These interactions usually involve another key person who talks with or questions the spokesperson—the emcee at a speech, the chairman of a legislative panel, or a media interviewer. As with publicist-gatekeeper negotiations, the parties in spokesperson interactions have distinct roles and goals. The spokesperson is the expert source of information whose goal is to persuasively communicate key messages (*talking points*) in a compelling and persuasive way. The role of the host is to facilitate the presentation and thus advance the mission or agenda of the sponsoring organization—whether through cordial hospitality or tough interrogation. The host can also serve as an audience's representative to ask the questions that audiences would ask if they could do so.

Importantly, spokespersons engage in a *dialogue* (not monologue) when presenting information and often can pose questions and obtain valuable feedback. Serving as a spokesperson, regardless of the venue, requires careful training and preparation and knowledge of the dynamics of successful interpersonal communication (Knapp & Daly, 2002). Spokespersons must "stay on message" while following learned routines, customs, and communication rules (Berger, 2002; Len-Rios, 2008; Pearson, 1989). Complaints about spokesperson interactions or interviews usually can be explained by the fact that one of the parties either (a) impeded the other party from achieving a desired goal or (b) violated the other party's expectations based on explicit or implicit rules of conduct.

Audience Information Sharing

Many publicity campaigns focus on *word-of-mouth* advertising or *buzz marketing*, where the aim is to prompt audiences to share information with others (Hughes, 2005; Thorne, 2008). As part of the resulting conversations, audience members thus become as *advocates* or *evangelists*. Publicity and social marketing campaigns commonly employ multitier approaches, where a portion or all of the effort is intentionally targeted to information *intermediaries* because of their roles or stature in a community or organization and their abilities to reach the ultimate target audiences. Examples include distributors and retailers who share product information with consumers, financial analysts who make recommendations to individual investors, and health care providers who advise at-risk populations and their families or friends. Individuals with strong knowledge or involvement in a topic can play critical roles in a publicity program as sources of *interpersonal influence* and *social support*—consistent with the theories of the *two-step flow of mass communication* and *opinion leadership* (Katz & Lazarsfeld, 1955).

Behavioral Perspectives

Publicity as Persuasion

Publicity attempts to influence people's knowledge, attitudes, or actions. These represent the *cognitive, affective,* and *conative* dimensions of human behavior recognized by psychologists (Christen & Hallahan, 2005). As a form of *persuasion*, publicity uses communication (vs. physical force, patronage, or purchase) to influence others (Miller & Levene, 2008), including the formation and maintenance of mutually beneficial organizational-public relationships.

Contrary to early theorizing that suggested persuasion effects were uniform and driven by human instincts, behavioral research suggests a wide variety of factors influence the persuasion process. Among these, audiences engage in *selective perceptions, attention*, and *retention* of publicity messages based on their interests. Publicity can also have a differential effect based on the degree to which groups are information advantaged or information disadvantaged and are in a position to use new information (Gaziano & Gaziano, 2008). Publicists and other persuaders thus must enhance the *motivation, ability*, and *opportunity* to process publicity (Hallahan, 2000a).

Persuasion process models suggest that people respond to persuasive messages in two ways—that is, there are two routes to persuasion (Chaiken, Wood, & Eagly, 1996; Petty, Briñol, & Priester, 2009). Individuals with high involvement in a topic will systematically or effortfully consider the quality of arguments presented—while individuals for whom a topic has low relevance or consequence are less attentive and engaged in processing messages. Instead, low-involvement individuals are cognitive misers who rely on simple peripheral or heuristic cues to make judgments. In the context of publicity, such cues might include the association of an entity with a respected organization or cause, or involvement by prominent public figures or celebrity endorsers. Other examples include the appearance of a news story in a particularly prestigious medium, or merely whether a topic is covered in the news at all. Hallahan (1999a, 1999b) argued that the much-touted *third-party endorsement* effect attributed to media news can be explained as a form of heuristic processing.

Publicity, Awareness, and Learning

Behavioral effects from publicity are rooted in learning the content of publicity messages. *Diffusion of innovation theory* suggests that the adoption of new ideas involves a sequence of steps or *hierarchy of effects* that involves knowledge, persuasion, trial, decision, and reinforcement (Rogers, 2003). Alternative approaches suggest that emotion can be critical: People can become aroused or involved, which then prompts them to learn (Christen & Hallahan, 2005; Hallahan, 2001). Learning can involve thoughtful consideration of arguments, the use of heuristic cues, or simple observation and emulation as posited in *social learning theory* (Bandura, 2009). Anecdotal evidence about the effectiveness of observed publicity can be evidenced in *fads* and *crazes*, the perpetuation of *myths* and *legends*, and risky *copycat behaviors* (pranks, crimes, and suicides) patterned after media portrayals.

Publicity, like all communications messages, stimulates thinking through a process of *priming*, where particular memory nodes (also referred to as schemas or associative networks) are stimulated so that new information is categorized and understood in the context of particular preexisting memory traces or knowledge (Kosicki, 2002; Roskos-Ewoldsen, Roskos-Ewoldsen, & Carpentier, 2009). Publicity thus strives to make particular knowledge more readily available and accessible in memory. Publicity's effect on awareness is evident in media *agenda-setting* research, which demonstrates a strong correspondence between media coverage and the topics that people report as being on their minds or that they talk about with others. Similarly, people think about the *attributes* of a topic in the same way those attributes are covered in the media (McCombs & Reynolds, 2009; Valenzuela & McCombs, 2008).

Publicity and Intent

Beyond awareness, publicity is used to help crystallize positive attitudes and prompt desired actions. In the absence of the ability to control actual future behavior, much publicity is directed at fostering *behavioral intent*, which can serve as a proxy measure of probable behavior based on the psychological theories of *reasoned action* and *planned behavior* (Christen & Hallahan, 2005; Fishbein & Ajzen, 2010). Creating behavioral intent is the goal of information campaigns that seek commitments to support prosocial causes (Rice & Atkin, 2009) as well as promises from people to pursue healthy behaviors (Atkin & Silk, 2008). Political polls are essentially measures of behavioral intent that assess plans to vote for particular candidates or ballot measures or to support public policy initiatives based on electioneering or exposure in public forums (Kaid, 2008).

Negative Publicity

Extensive research on decision making has demonstrated the overwhelming effects of negative information. People react more strongly to negative information suggesting the prospect of hazard or loss than to positively valenced messages that promise gains (Hallahan, 1999c). This phenomenon reflects people's autonomic responses and automatic vigilance that guards them against danger (Pratto & John, 1991). Negative psychological reactions require organizations to respond to *crises*, *risky situations*, and *controversies or disputes* involving clients. Cognitive dissonance theory suggests that people suffer discomfort when presented contradictory information and seek cognitive balance (Cooper, 2007). Importantly, audiences with direct personal experiences with a situation are more likely to dismiss negative publicity inconsistent with their experience. Or more negative publicity might prompt others to reevaluate their knowledge based on new information. For individuals with negative personal experiences, negative publicity resonates with and reinforces negative perceptions. Negative publicity can result in unfavorable purchase intent related to products and brands or the avoidance of entities accused of malfeasance or corporate irresponsibility based on a person's knowledge or values.

Credibility and Contextual Effects

More than a half-century of research suggests that publicity is more effective when the source, spokesperson, vehicle, or channel presenting a persuasive message demonstrates a higher level of *credibility*—as measured in *trustworthiness*, *expertise*, *independence*, or *attractiveness*. However, even information from a low credibility source can be effective if people later dissociate message content and sources in memory—the so-called sleeper effect (Self, 2008).

The format or *content class* in which publicity appears also biases assessments of the publicity messages. People consistently report that they prefer to obtain information and recommendations about products, services, and public affairs from friends or family. When asked to choose, people say that they think news is more credible than advertising and *prefer* to obtain information about products from news reports rather than advertising (Hallahan, 1999b). Experiments analyzing the comparative effectiveness of media publicity versus media advertising have provided mixed results but draw into question the contention that media publicity is uniformly more effective than advertising. But most experiments presumably force participants to actually process the message (e.g., see Hallahan, 1999a). Because people react negatively to persuasion attempts (Burgoon, Alvaro, Grandpre, & Voulodakis, 2002), evidence suggests that people are more likely to avoid, resist, or discount advertising compared with publicity messages. Whereas people think that *advertising sells*, publicity's advantage might be that people think *publicity tells*. Hallahan (1999a) argued that more attentiveness or openness to publicity results from people deploying different format-related schemas or cognitive rules for processing persuasive messages. This phenomenon is particularly relevant to the new emerging content classes found on the Internet (Wang, 2009) where the promotional intent of message formats (such as blogs or social networking profiles) are not always clear to users. Similarly, audiences can become confused about *hybrid messages* (advertorials, video news releases, product placements, edutainment, etc.) where the message's persuasive purpose is often obfuscated (Balasubramanian, 1994; Goodman, 2006).

Publicity Uses and Knowledge

People *depend* on the information provided to them through publicity in living their daily lives (Ball-Rokeach & DeFleur, 1976) and are motivated to use publicity to various purposes. Cognitive needs include surveillance of the environment, solving problems, and the desire for intellectual stimulation known as *need for cognition* (Hallahan, 2008). Other uses of publicity can be examined from a *uses-and-gratifications perspective* and include the formation of *personal identities*, *social utility* (the usefulness of the information for social vs. problem-solving purposes), and *diversion/entertainment* (Papacharissi, 2008; Rubin, 2009).

Interestingly, people's responses to publicity and other persuasion attempts vary based on their knowledge of persuasion processes (Friestad & Wright, 1994). In general, people are ignorant about publicity processes—such as how news makes its way into the media. They are also generally unaware of how publicity might affect them: People tend to underestimate the effect of mediated publicity on them but overstate its effects on others—a phenomenon known as *third-person effect* (Perloff, 2009). They are also unaware of *cultivation effects* or how consumption of heavy concentrations of unbalanced publicity fare might distort their views of social reality (Shrum, 2009; Signorelli & Morgan, 2008). Finally, people generally don't recognize how their group memberships (*social identification*) can bias their media choices and their interpretation of information that contradicts their worldviews. This effect is commonly evidenced in complaints about *media bias* and observed as the *hostile media phenomenon* (Eveland, 2002).

Cultural Perspectives

Publicity and the Social Construction of Culture and Social Reality

As a major source of ideas in people's lives, publicity is integrally involved in the creation of culture—the systems of beliefs, values, ideals, traditions, customs, and mores that characterize a society and the subcultures or communities within it. Publicity serves essentially the same functions in society as the mass media: surveillance, correlation, transmission, entertainment, and mobilization (Lasswell, 1948; Wright, 1975).

Publicists help construct the social reality or worldviews shared among individuals and groups through recommendations about actions that clients should undertake and through *rhetoric*, or the use of culturally significant mediating symbols: words, images, and sounds. As with all rhetoric, publicity involves a process of signification whereby message producers ascribe and recipients derive meaning (Heath, Toth, & Waymer, 2009). Publicity can contribute to introspective processes such as *sense making* (Dervin, 1992; Weick, 1995) and can be examined using *symbolic interactionism*, which argues that people derive meaning through interactions with others (Blumer, 1969). *Structuration theory* suggests that publicity serves as a structural property that can be drawn on by social actors as they create or transform an institutional relationship or other social relationships and structures in their own discourse.

Publicity as Narrative

As rhetors, publicists help create a *persona* (personality) for an entity by creating an image and giving the entity a "voice." Group, organizational, and corporate *narratives* (Gilpin, 2008) can be delivered in the form of *lectures*, where a source speaks directly to the audience, or *dramas*, where players in a scene act out a situation and audiences draw their own conclusions (Wells, 1989). Both lectures and dramas can be analyzed using rhetorical tools such as Aristotle's *persuasion triad* (logos, pathos, ethos), Burke's (1969) *dramatic pentad* (act, scene, agent, agency, purpose), Toulmin's (1958) *argument analysis* (grounds, warrants, backing, rebuttal, qualifiers, claims), *frame analysis* (Goffman, 1974), or *sociodrama* (Mickey, 2003).

Publicity employs argumentation, evidence, emotion, and figurative language (see reviews in Dillard & Pfau, 2002; Walton, 2007). Much of how publicity works also can be explained through *framing theory*—how message producers prime audiences by focusing attention on only particular aspects of a situation while excluding others (Hallahan, 1999c; Tewksbury & Scheufele, 2009). Framing devices include *catchphrases*, *depictions*, *metaphors*, *exemplars*, and *visual imagery* (Gamson, Croteau, Hoynes, & Sasson, 1992). Publicity involving issues or disputes can also entail *claims making*, where social problems are identified through a process of *typification*, where situations are characterized as of a particular category familiar to the audience. Claims makers not only use argumentation and framing techniques but also employ *celebrities*, *large and official numbers*, and *symbols* (Best, 1987; Salmon, 1990). Many of the rhetorical devices used in publicity are variations on propaganda devices identified in the 1930s—*name-calling*, *glittering generalities*, *transfer*, *testimonial*, *plain folks*, *card stacking*, and *bandwagon* (A. M. Lee & Lee, 1972). Importantly, effective publicity and rhetoric draw on the core values in a society, the enduring values of gatekeepers (Gans, 2003), and the inherent *news values* of information (Brighton & Foy, 2007).

Publicity, Identification, and Community

As an alternative model to persuasion, Burke (1969) argued that the fundamental process that people use to connect to others in a culture is *identification*—an intrapersonal process wherein people look for associations and seek affinities and affiliations based on common interests (stakes), attitudes, values, experiences, perceptions, or material properties. Recognizing such *consubstantiality* involves a semiconscious or subconscious process of *self-persuasion.* Heath et al. (2009) observed that public relations practitioners use publicity to create identification and to inform, evaluate, and recommend actions.

Although publicity is commonly dismissed as a self-serving, one-way form of rhetoric, publicity plays a vital role in the *free marketplace of ideas* (Milton, 1927) and adds value to a society by prompting people to engage in dialogue, to identify or align with common interests, and to seek cooperation (Heath et al., 2009). Philosopher John Dewey (1927) argued that the role of media and publicity was to facilitate the "great conversation" vital to a democracy, not merely to transmit objective information to the public (cf. Lippmann, 1922, 1925). In a similar vein, Burke (1969) described rhetoric as a way in which people with competing interests participate in the "wrangle in the marketplace" (Heath, 1992; Heath et al., 2009). Publicity thus helps build social capital by encouraging *civic engagement* (Shah, Rojas, & Cho, 2009), by fostering a *civil society*, and by promoting a sense of *community* (Hallahan, 2004).

Publicity and Cultural Expression

Publicity is integrally involved in preserving and encouraging public interest in the fine arts and other forms of serious creative expression—painting, sculpture, dance, symphonic and chamber music, theater, serious fiction, and so on. Publicity is also crucial to the commercial viability of popular culture by creating popular demand for books, plays, movies, music recordings, TV shows, electronic games, and other entertainment fare. Publicity exposure serves as an *extension* or an *alternative* to actually experiencing cultural works themselves. Exposure occurs through previews and reviews by critics and consumers; news, feature stories, and documentaries; and discussions about culture trends. Publicity also has contributed to the rise of today's *celebrity culture* where personalities seek and audiences grant *fame* to people for their accomplishments in the arts, entertainment, professions, commerce, sports, and politics (Herwitz, 2008; James, 2007; Rein, Kotler, & Stoller, 1997). Publicity also serves as an arbiter of public tastes related to products and services such as food, fashion, travel and tourism, and sports. In much the same way, publicity itself has become a fixture in popular culture—celebrated through fictional portrayals of publicists in movies and books and the memoirs of famous (and infamous) publicists.

Critical Perspectives

Manipulating symbols and driving topics onto the public, government, and media agendas of discussion (Mannheim, 1987) are sources of considerable power to those who possess the financial and creative resources to generate publicity. Public exposure in media and other public forums provides *legitimization* and confers *status* on particular ideas (Lazarsfeld & Merton, 1948).

Publicity and Social Change

Publicity is a primary tool used by social activists and social advocates to effect social change. Social change typically begins on the periphery (not at the center) of society and involves a sometimes long and arduous process of *agenda building* to create public awareness of a social problem and then mobilize support (Cobb & Elder, 1983; Hallahan, 2001; Perloff, 1998). Resource mobilization theory (McCarthy & Zald, 2001) and power resource management theory (Heath, 2008) suggest that publicity is one of the advantages that can be exploited by activists and otherwise disadvantaged social movements. Various tactics are available to capture public attention and jolt mainstream society out of complacency. Among these are *hate speech* (Cortese, 2006), *counterpublicity* (Downey & Fenton, 2003; Ryan, 1991), *outlaw discourse* (Boyd & VanSlette, 2009), and publicity-driven terrorism (Clark & Newman, 2006; Nacos, 2007; Wilkinson, 1990).

Publicity and Social Control

Critics argue that media and other institutions too often ridicule, marginalize, and trivialize dissent. By reflecting the values of mainstream society, publicity produced by mainstream organizations often enforces social norms and the status quo (Carey, 1989/2009). Marxist theorists argue that publicity is one of the principal tools by which the dominant ideologies in society are preserved and extended. Karl Marx (1845/1998) defined *ideology* as a false consciousness that upper classes impose on the working class to perpetuate their power. Neo-Marxists further suggest that social control operates through a process of *hegemony*, whereby citizens unquestioningly accept and tacitly consent to the actions of the dominant class—and their own actions reinforce dominance over them (Gramsci, 1971). Thus, by reinforcing predominant social values, publicity can be seen as an unobtrusive form of capitalistic control.

Social control involving publicity can also be examined from political economy perspectives that center on *conspiratorial* and *constraint* explanations for how communications systems operate (e.g., see Herman & Chomsky, 2002). Examples of collusion include the unchecked ability of media organizations to self-promote their own activities and those of other powerful interests while often ignoring negative news involving themselves or their business partners. Media are also subject to direct influence attempts by government, special interest groups, and advertisers. Even governments in democratic societies occasionally pressure publishers to squelch controversial stories and employ threats ranging from prosecution to curtailing access to future information. Media advocacy groups pressure media to portray society in ways consistent with their worldviews and values—and threaten reprisals ranging from boycotts to legislative reform (Fortunato, 2005; Gallagher, 2001; Suman & Rossman, 2000; Toplin, 2006). Advertisers similarly complain about adverse coverage and threaten to withdraw business (An & Bergen, 2007; Koc, 2006; Price, 2003). Fears of reprisals and other negative consequences hold media in check, discourage controversial or countervailing publicity, and encourage *puff pieces* and other publicity coverage favorable to powerful interests.

Philosophical Perspectives

Publicity is integrally involved in questions related to privacy versus secrecy—or what Hannah Arendt (1998) differentiated as our *public lives* versus our *private lives.* Indeed, communicating publicly alters the constitutive forms and functions of communication and has been shown to affect the behaviors of people and entities in arenas ranging from literature, politics, and commerce to interpersonal communication and human relationships (e.g., see Goffman, 1959).

In most democratic societies, people are guaranteed the right to publicize ideas as part of the protection of free expression and free press (Splichal, 2002) but are protected from disclosing private matters against their will. That same protection does not apply to government and other institutions, and philosophers have debated for more than two centuries about the importance of transparency.

Publicity and Governance

In libertarian societies, access to information about government activities is a vital right of citizens. Utilitarian philosopher Jeremy Bentham (1791/1994) observed, "Without publicity, no good is permanent; under the auspices of publicity, no evil can continue" (p. 589). In a similar vein, the philosopher Immanuel Kant (1795/1991) argued that laws to which people were required to adhere are invalid unless publicly known. He argued, "All actions related to the right of other human beings are wrong if their maxim is incompatible with publicity" (translated in Luban,

1996, p. 155). Publicity is similarly an essential ingredient in Kant's concept of the public use of reason (Gosseries, 2005).

Much of the credit for the dissolution of the former USSR in 1991 was attributed to *glasnost*, which is often defined as "openness" but also can be translated as "publicity." Openness is the foundation of laws found in democracies that require citizen access to government processes—open meetings, open records, media access to crime scenes, and so on. Yet even staunch advocates of public disclosures recognize the value of confidentiality in certain matters. For example, in providing for the national defense, a government must balance the needs for publicity and secrecy (Cunningham, 2003; Shils, 1956).

Publicity and Deliberation

Kant argued for publicity as an abstract principle, but others contend that the dissemination of information (*actual publicity*) is essential for the public discussion of issues. Kant defended the importance of the secret ballot for citizens, but called for the public disclosure of legislators' voting records. Drawing on the example of Ancient Greece, John Stuart Mill argued that the psychological constraint of being in the eye of the public promotes honesty and has an important place in republican theory. But Mill (1861/1962) observed, "Publicity . . . is no impediment to evil, nor stimulus to good, if the public will not look at what is done; but without publicity, how could they either check or encourage what they were not permitted to see?" (chap. 2). Numerous writers from Karl Marx to publisher Joseph Pulitzer have expressed similar sentiments. Lippmann (1915, p. 199) observed, "A special interest openly avowed is no terror to democracy; it is neutralized by publicity." Importantly, this notion of openly competing perspectives and the ready identification of sources differentiates publicity from one-sided or surreptitious *propaganda*.

Contemporary theorists argue that publicity does not always facilitate discussion. Elisabeth Noelle-Neumann (1994) contended that media coverage and polls reporting that a majority in society hold a particular view actually creates a *spiral of silence* wherein those in the minority will become reticent to speak (Salmon & Glynn, 2008). Jürgen Habermas (1962/1989) similarly chided one-sided media publicity (and advertising) for the demise of the robust *public sphere* of public discussion that he argued characterized 18th-century Europe (see Mayhew, 1997).

Publicity and Fairness

Kant argued that people are important because they are human beings and deserve to be treated with respect and dignity—and not merely exploited as the means toward an end (Kant, 1785/2002). According to Kant, enabling people to exercise their free will and their capability to reason promotes their freedom. Thus, being forthright and transparent, and avoiding deception, are essential for entities to behave ethically (Plaisance, 2009).

In a similar vein, the 20th-century philosopher John Rawls (1971) contended that an ethical society is one that is grounded in fairness and justice. According to Rawls, publicity enables people to know the bases of their social and political relationships and the underlying principles and enforceable rules that govern them and society. Publicity thus operates as one of the five formal constraints on rights (Rawls, 1993, 2001). Publicity also permits an entity's actions to stand up to public scrutiny. Thus, entities have an obligation to be transparent in and accountable for their actions. According to Rawls, those with power should not monopolize public communications. Instead, they must balance self-interest with the public interest—especially to ensure that the concerns of the most vulnerable members of society are addressed.

Publicity and Justice

Publicity plays a critical role in the formal and informal systems of justice in society. Throughout the centuries, governments have routinely made examples of criminals and political dissidents by publicly exposing them and their misdeeds through actions ranging from humiliation to public executions (Foucault, 1995). Today, publicized court trials ostensibly serve as deterrents to crime in a similar way. However, *fear of publicity* often discourages victims from coming forward, thus impeding justice by preventing prosecutions. Publicity similarly can play a negative role in justice through *prejudicial pretrial publicity* and *prejudicial media coverage.* Both can jeopardize the right of a defendant to a fair trial (Kovera & Greathouse, 2008). Meanwhile, attorneys increasingly push the limits on professional guidelines related to *litigation* of *trial publicity* to seek public sympathy for their clients or causes (American Bar Association, 2007; Roschwalb & Stack, 1995). In the contemporary restorative justice movement that seeks out-of-court resolution of crimes, publicity can serve as *reparation* and play a crucial role in involving and reassuring a community affected by a crime (Schiff, 2007). Publicity has been used as a tool to discourage corporate offenses (Fisse & Braithwaite, 1983), while *corrective publicity* and corrective advertising have been ordered as remedies in administrative law actions (Bernhardt, Kinnear, Mazis, & Reece, 1981; Liu, 1998; Tyebjee, 1998).

Ethical Perspectives

As an activity that attempts to influence the behavior of others, publicity has been a topic of suspicion and scrutiny since its inception. Ethics represent guidelines for decision making or socially agreed-on standards of conduct based on actions deemed right or wrong, fair or unfair. Ethical standards stem from previous transgressions and can be established at the societal, professional, organizational, employer, and personal levels. Ethics involve *expectations* for performance that generally exceed the *minimum* standards required by law.

Media publicists have been criticized for manufacturing news, for cluttering media channels with trivia, for blocking access to newsmakers by journalists, and for holding their duty to clients above their responsibility to the public. Publicists confront a variety of ethical dilemmas related to the release of information. A partial inventory of publicity practices deemed unethical include *lying, stonewalling, sandbagging, selective (vs. full) disclosure of available information, failure to seek out information that a publicist should know, puffery, leaking, rumormongering, gossiping, false fronting, unfair dealing/favoritism, failure to correct errors, blackmailing,* and *spin-doctoring.*

Outright *bribery* (paying gatekeepers to obtain exposure) is prohibited in most Western nations. But bribing government officials or paying journalists for coverage is a customary practice in nations around the world such as Mexico and Russia and in Asia and Africa. In many nations, journalists *moonlight* (also work for corporations or government) or receive payments whether or not they perform legitimate work. More subtle forms of bribery include free meals, event tickets, product samples (*freebies*), gifts, and paid trips (*junkets*).

The struggle to establish ethical standards for publicity, including proper levels and forms of disclosure by organizations, has led about a dozen professional associations to establish codes of conduct. The Public Relations Society of America's (2000) Code of Ethics, for example, stresses six professional values: (1) responsible advocacy, (2) honesty, (3) professional expertise, (4) independence, (5) loyalty, and (6) fairness. These self-regulation attempts are informal, voluntary, and aspirational (prescriptive rather than restrictive). Most codes lack effective enforcement powers and provide for only weak penalties, such as expulsion from the sponsoring organization. Ironically, fears of libel suits and adverse publicity precludes organizations from using publicity to name offenders.

Legal and Regulatory Perspectives

Although publicity involves the free expression of ideas, publicity activities can be highly regulated.

In totalitarian states, publicity activities by entities other than the government are simply prohibited. In partially free nations, publicity materials can be scrutinized prior to dissemination. In most Western nations, publicity content is free from such prior restraint but the *manner* in which publicity activities are undertaken is subject to oversight.

Publicists generally must comply with tort laws, including prohibitions against defamation or misuse of others' intellectual property (copyrights, trademarks, etc.). In the United States, celebrities and others enjoy a specific property right known as the *right of publicity*, which requires obtaining permission and providing compensation whenever using another person's words or images for financial gain (Bunker, 2008; McEvoy & Windom, 2003).

In the United States, political speech and publicity are protected by the First Amendment's guarantees of "free speech, and of the press." Promotional publicity for profit-making entities is considered *commercial speech*, which has enjoyed increased protection but can be regulated as part of the oversight of activities in which the government has a "compelling state interest." Commercial speech regulation (a) cannot interfere with political speech and (b) cannot be used to preclude entities from engaging in otherwise legal activities. Under the regulations of the Federal Trade Commission, a news release is considered *advertising*. Meanwhile, the Food and Drug Administration considers publicity a form of *labeling*. Publicly traded companies must conform to the prompt and full disclosure requirements of the Securities and Exchange Commission's Regulation FD (Fair Disclosure) and to publicity restrictions governing public offerings of securities. Publicists for foreign organizations or governments must register with the Department of Justice under the Foreign Agents Registration Act of 1938. Specific rules apply to publicity during bargaining governed by the National Labor Relations Act. Various government agencies are responsible for enforcing antidiscrimination rules that call for organizations to affirmatively promote equal opportunity in promotional communications related to employment, education, real estate, banking, and lending.

Technological Perspectives

The forms, story genres, conventions, and channels used in publicity have changed over time and are inevitably shaped by technology. Whereas publicity in the 20th century was predominated by reliance on public media, major changes took place at the dawn of the 21st century—most notably, the rise of interactive media employing the Internet and mobile devices (Hallahan, 2010).

Publicists have always relied on direct communications to reach audiences. Examples range from drums and carrier pigeons to lectures and speeches. Printed ephemera have included trade cards, bulletins, and brochures. During the 19th and 20th centuries, publicists seized the opportunity to distribute information quickly, broadly, and at low cost using third-party newspapers and magazines as well as radio and television. (The resulting saving in distribution costs almost always offset the labor costs represented in providing information subsidies to the media.) But today many of the cost, speed, and distribution advantages of mass media have been negated by electronic networks that allow the publicists to circumvent the press (Hallahan, 1994).

Digitization of text, images, and sounds has altered how publicity is produced and packaged. More important, however, the ways in which publicity is distributed, archived, and used have been transformed. In addition to "pushing" out information, modern publicity involves "pulling" in audiences seeking information using Web sites. Search engines such as Google and Yahoo! have become master publicity aggregators and directories for organizational information. Optimizing the lowly news release has become a prerequisite to enable search engine users to find information. Online communication has transformed the structure and language used in publicity stories and, in particular, has elevated the importance of *keywords.* In the past, publicity was a fleeting commodity and often lost to audiences, except for clipping an occasional article or recording a TV air check.

Today, Web and mobile phone users can reread and retain publicity messages. Moreover, users can look up publicity information or seek additional facts using these same devices. Audiences have become content producers who can forward publicity to friends or family, create new e-mail or text messages, or post information or opinions on personal blogs, microblogs, or social networking pages.

Academic Perspectives

The *Gannett Center Journal* observed, "We live in an age of publicity" and described publicity as "the oxygen of recognition." The editors added, "As such it's bound to be on the mind of anyone who wants to gain the notice of the public" (Publicity, 1990, p. vi).

This review suggests that publicity is an important, multifaceted construct that can be examined from multiple perspectives. Publicity—as both the general concept of *being public* and the narrower concept of gaining media visibility—has made an impact on world events and plays a critical role in economics and the management of organizations. Understanding publicity processes requires knowledge of basic psychological and communication processes and how people then use publicity in a social context. Because of publicity's power, the proper use of publicity has been debated, and publicity practices continue to be scrutinized and regulated. Publicity is also evolving with the advent of new media.

Within public relations research, publicity has languished as a concept. Theorizing about publicity over the past 25 years was biased, in part, by J. E. Grunig and Hunt's (1984) advocacy of symmetrical two-way communication as a normative standard for practicing public relations. In their four-part model of public relations, the authors lumped press-agentry and publicity together with propaganda in a single form of public relations practice where "practitioners spread the faith of the organization involved, often through incomplete, distorted or half-truth information" (p. 21). Yet if publicity is conceptualized as an entity *being public,* or more narrowly as gaining exposure through media, it should be readily evident that characteristics of messages are not defining characteristics of publicity as a process. Indeed, the full spectrum of message accuracy, completeness, and candor can be represented in publicity messages. Moreover, publicity plays a vital role in all four models of public relations practice.

Heath (2001, pp. 1–2) observed that all the introductory chapters of the 2001 version of this *Handbook* defined public relations in terms of reducing conflict. He noted that while most academics focused on advancing harmony, most practitioners spent the bulk of their time on "other dynamics of the marketplace" such as attracting buyers, protecting or promoting an image, promoting donations, or attracting taxpayer support of government initiatives. These inevitably involve publicity. Ferguson (1984) had suggested that the *relationships* might serve as the construct to provide coherence to the field—an idea that blossomed a decade later. However, as a generic concept, publicity stands on equal footing with relationships as a potential framework for examining the field. Publicity subsumes a variety of constructs and approaches for examining an entity's public activities; the promotion and measurement of organizational-public relationships might be only one (albeit desirable) outcome of *being public.*

Some evidence suggests a glimmer of recognition for publicity's importance today. Heath and Coombs's (2006, p. 7) textbook, for example, includes "publicity" and "promotion" in their definition of public relations. Zoch and Molleda (2006, p. 295) proposed an integrated model of media relations that combines framing, information subsidies, and agenda building. Most recently, Heath et al. (2009, p. 40) acknowledged the role of publicity in adding value to public discourse.

Importantly, publicity is a pursuit not limited to public relations. Various social actors seek or shun public attention—with no pretext of engaging in public relations. Instead of relegating publicity to a tool used in public relations, public relations can be seen as only one of the varied contexts or reasons why entities pursue public attention and understanding. Future research needs to examine in more depth and breadth the many dimensions of publicity, its alternative relationships to public relations, and its importance in public communication.

References

Alcoholics Anonymous. (2009). *11th tradition.* Retrieved September 1, 2009, from www.aa.org/bigbookonline/en_appendicei.cfm

American Bar Association. (2007, February). *Model rules of professional conduct. Advocate: Rule 3.6 Trial Publicity.* Retrieved September 1, 2009, from www.abanet.org/cpr/mrpc/rule_3_6.html

An, S., & Bergen, L. (2007). Advertiser pressure on daily newspapers. *Journal of Advertising, 36*(2), 111–121.

Archibald, R. B., Haulman, C. A., & Moody, C. E., Jr. (1983). Quality, price, advertising and published quality ratings. *Journal of Consumer Research, 9*(4), 347–356.

Arendt, H. (1998). *The human condition* (2nd ed.). Chicago: University of Chicago Press.

Arpan, L. M., & Pompper, D. (2003). Stormy weather: Testing "stealing thunder" as a crisis communication strategy to improve communication flow between organizations and journalists. *Public Relations Review, 29*(3), 291–308.

Atkin, C., & Silk, K. (2008). Health communication. In D. W. Stacks & M. B. Salwen (Eds.), *An integrated approach to communication theory and research* (2nd ed., pp. 489–503). New York: Routledge.

Balasubramanian, S. K. (1994). Beyond advertising and publicity: Hybrid messages and public policy issues. *Journal of Advertising, 23*(4), 29–46.

Ball-Rokeach, S. J., & DeFleur, M. L. (1976). A dependency model of mass media effects. *Communication Research, 3,* 3–21.

Bandura, A. (2009). Social cognitive theory of mass communication. In J. Bryant & M. B. Oliver (Eds.), *Media effects: Advances in theory and research* (pp. 94–124). New York: Routledge.

Belz, A., Talbott, A. D., & Starck, K. (1989). Using role theory to study cross perceptions of journalists and public relations practitioners. *Public Relations Research Annual, 1,* 125–140.

Bentham, J. (1994). Of publicity. *Public Culture, 6*(3), 581–595. (Original work published 1791 in *An Essay on Political Tactics, or Inquiries Concerning the Discipline and Modes of Proceeding Proper to be Observed in Political Assemblies: Principally Applied to the Practice of the British Parliament, and to The Constitution and Situation of the National Assembly of France,* chap. 2)

Berger, C. R. (2002). Goals and knowledge structures in social interaction. In M. L. Knapp & J. A. Daly (Eds.), *Handbook of interpersonal communication* (3rd ed., pp. 181–212). Thousand Oaks, CA: Sage.

Bernays, E. L. (1923). *Crystallizing public opinion.* New York: Boni & Liverright.

Bernays, E. L. (1965). *Biography of an idea: Memoirs of public relations counsel Edward L. Bernays.* New York: Simon & Schuster.

Bernhardt, K., Kinnear, T., Mazis, M., & Reece, B. (1981, January). The impact of publicity on corrective advertising effect. *Advances in Consumer Research, 8,* 414–415.

Best, J. (Ed.). (1987). *Images of issues: Typifying contemporary social problems.* New York: Aldine de Gruyter.

Blumer, H. (1969). *Symbolic interactionism: Perspective and method.* Englewood Cliffs, NJ: Prentice Hall.

Boorstin, D. (1962). *The image: Or what happened to the American dream?* New York: Atheneum.

Boyd, J., & VanSlette, S. H. (2009). Outlaw discourse as postmodern public relations. In R. L. Heath, E. L. Toth, & D. Waymer (Eds.), *Rhetorical and critical approaches to public relations II* (pp. 328–342). New York: Routledge.

Brennan, G., & Pettit, P. (2004). *The economy of esteem: An essay on civil and political society.* New York: Oxford University Press.

Brighton, P., & Foy, D. (2007). *News values.* Thousand Oaks, CA: Sage.

Bunker, M. (2008, Summer). Free speech meets the publicity tort: Transformative use analysis in right of publicity law. *Communication Law & Policy, 13*(3), 301–320.

Burgoon, M., Alvaro, E., Grandpre, J., & Voulodakis, M. (2002). Revising the theory of psychological reactance. In J. P. Dillard & M. Pfau (Eds.), *The persuasion handbook: Developments in theory and practice* (pp. 213–232). Thousand Oaks, CA: Sage.

Burgoon, M., Denning, V. P., & Roberts, L. (2002). Lanaguage expectancy theory. In J. P. Dillard & M. Pfau (Eds.), *The persuasion handbook: Developments in theory and practice* (pp. 117–136). Thousand Oaks, CA: Sage.

Burke, K. (1969). *A rhetoric of motives* (2nd ed.). Berkeley: University of California Press.

Cameron, G. T., Sallot, L. M., & Curtin, P. A. (1997). Public relations and the production of news: A critical review and a theoretical framework. In B. R. Berelson (Ed.), *Communication yearbook 20* (pp. 111–115). Thousand Oaks, CA: Sage.

Carey, J. W. (2009). *Communication as culture.* Boston: Unwin Hyman. (Original work published 1989)

Chaiken, S., Wood, W., & Eagly, A. H. (1996). Principles of persuasion. In E. T. Higgins & A. Kruglanski (Eds.), *Social psychology: Handbook of basic principles* (pp. 702–744). New York: Guilford Press.

Charron, J. (1989). Relations between journalists and public relations practitioners: Cooperation, conflict and negotiation. *Canadian Journal of Communication, 14*(2), 41–54.

Christen, C. T., & Hallahan, K. (2005). Psychological processing. In R. L. Heath (Ed.), *Encyclopedia of public relations* (Vol. 2, pp. 660–665). Thousand Oaks, CA: Sage.

Clark, R. V. G., & Newman, G. R. (2006). Situational techniques and publicity. In *Outsmarting the terrorists* (pp. 209–217). Westport, CT: Praeger Security.

Cobb, R. W., & Elder, C. D. (1983). *Participation in American politics: The dynamics of agenda-building* (2nd ed.). Baltimore: Johns Hopkins University Press.

Cooper, J. (2007). *Cognitive dissonance: Fifty years of a classic theory.* Thousand Oaks, CA: Sage.

Cortese, A. J. P. (2006). *Opposing hate speech.* Westport, CT: Praeger.

Creel, G. (1972a). *The Creel report: Complete report of the Chairman of the Committee on Public Information.* New York: Da Capo Press. (Original work published 1917–1919)

Creel, G. (1972b). *How we advertised America.* New York: Arno Press. (Original work published 1920)

Cunningham, B. (2003). Pluralist democracy: Balancing publicity, privacy and secrecy. *Administrative Theory and Praxis, 25*(2), 299–308.

Curtin, P. A. (1999). Reevaluating public relations information subsidies: Market driven journalism and agenda-building theory and practice. *Journal of Public Relations Research, 11*(1), 53–90.

Curtis, A. [Writer, Producer]. (2005). *Century of the self* [DVD]. bnpublishing.com. Retrieved June 30, 2009, from www.archive.org/details/AdamCurtisCenturyoftheSelfPart2of4

Cutlip, S. M. (1989). The manufacture of news. *Gannett Center Journal, 3*(2), 105–115.

Cutlip, S. M. (1994). *The unseen power: Public relations, a history.* Hillsboro, NJ: Lawrence Erlbaum.

Cutlip, S. M. (1995). *Public relations from the 17th to 20th century: The antecedents.* Hillsboro, NJ: Lawrence Erlbaum.

Debord, G. (1995). *The society of the spectacle.* New York: Zone Books. (Original work published as *Société du spectacle*).

Dervin, B. (1992). From the mind's eye of the user: The sense-making qualitative-quantitative methodology. In J. D. Glazier & R. R. Powell (Eds.), *Qualitative research in information management* (pp. 61–84). Englewood, CO: Libraries Unlimited.

Dewey, J. (1927). *The public and its problems.* Chicago: Swallow Press.

Dillard, J. P., & Pfau, M. (Eds.). (2002). *The persuasion handbook: Developments in theory and practice.* Thousand Oaks, CA: Sage.

Doorley, J., & Garcia, H. F. (2007). *Reputation management: The key to successful public relations and corporate communication.* New York: Routledge.

Downey, J. W., & Fenton, N. (2003). New media, counter publicity and the public sphere. *New Media & Society, 5*(2), 185–202.

Eveland, W. P., Jr. (2002). The impact of news and entertainment on perceptions of social reality. In J. P. Dillard & M. Pfau (Eds.), *The persuasion handbook: Developments in theory and practice* (pp. 691–727). Thousand Oaks, CA: Sage.

Ewen, S. (1996). *PR! A social history of spin.* New York: Basic Books.

Ferguson, M.A. (1984, August). Building theory in public relations. Interorganizational relationships as a public relations paradigm. Paper presented to Association for Education in Journalism and Mass Communication, Gainesville, FL.

Fishbein, M., & Ajzen, I. (2010). *Predicting and changing behavior: The reasoned action approach.* New York: Psychology Press.

Fishman, M. (1980). *Manufacturing the news.* Austin: University of Texas Press.

Fisse, B., & Braithwaite, J. (1983). *The impact of publicity on corporate offenders.* Albany: State University of New York Press.

Fortunato, J. A. (2005). *Making media content: The influence of constituency groups on mass media.* Mahwah, NJ: Lawrence Erlbaum.

Foucault, M. (1995). *Discipline and punish: The birth of the prison.* New York: Vintage Books.

French, J. R. P., & Raven, B. (1959). The bases of social power. In D. Cartwright (Ed.), *Studies in social power* (pp. 150–167). Ann Arbor: University of Michigan Press.

Friestad, M., & Wright, P. (1994). The persuasion knowledge model. How people cope with persuasion attempts. *Journal of Consumer Research, 21*(1), 1–31.

Fuhrman, C. (1989). *Publicity stunt! Great staged events that made the news.* San Francisco: Chronicle Books.

Gallagher, M. (2001). *Gender setting: New agendas for media monitoring and advocacy.* New York: Zed Books.

Gamson, W. A., Croteau, D., Hoynes, W., & Sasson, T. (1992). Media images and the social construction of reality. *American Review of Sociology, 18,* 373–393.

Gandy, O. (1982). *Beyond agenda setting: Information subsidies and public policy.* Norwood, NJ: Ablex.

Gans, H. (2003). *Democracy and the news.* New York: Oxford University Press.

Gaziano, C., & Gaziano, E. (2008). Theories and methods in knowledge gap research. In D. W. Stacks & M. B. Salwen (Eds.), *An integrated approach to communication theory and research* (2nd ed., pp. 122–136). New York: Routledge.

Gilpin, D. R. (2008). Narrating the organizational self: Reframing the role of the news release. *Public Relations Review, 34*(1), 9–18.

Goffman, E. (1959). *The presentation of self in everyday life.* Garden City, NY: Doubleday.

Goffman, E. (1974). *Frame analysis: An essay on the organization of experience.* Cambridge, MA: Harvard University Press.

Goodman, E. (2006). Stealth marketing and editorial integrity. *Texas Law Review, 85*(1), 83–152.

Gosseries, A. (2005). Publicity. In *Stanford encyclopedia of philosophy.* Retrieved June 30, 2009, from http://plato.stanford.edu/entries/publicity

Gramsci, A. (1971). *Prison notebooks* (J. A. Buttigieg & A. Callari, Trans.). New York: Columbia University Press.

Grant, D. M. (1995, August). Why publicity may not be right for your client. *Public Relations Tactics, 2*(8), 15.

Grunig, J. E., & Hunt, T. (1984). *Managing public relations.* New York: Holt, Rinehart & Winston.

Grunig, L. A., Grunig, J. E., & Dozier, D. M. (2002). *Excellent public relations and effective organizations: A study of communication management in three countries.* Mahwah, NJ: Lawrence Erlbaum.

Habermas, J. (1989). *The structural transformation of the public sphere: An inquiry into a category of bourgeois society* (T. Burger with F. Lawrence, Trans.). Cambridge: MIT Press. (Original work published 1962)

Hallahan, K. (1994, Summer). Public relations and circumvention of the press. *Public Relations Quarterly, 38*(2), 17–19.

Hallahan, K. (1996). Product publicity: An orphan of marketing research. In E. Thorson & J. Moore (Eds.), *Integrated communication: Synergy of persuasive voices* (pp. 305–330). Mahwah, NJ: Lawrence Erlbaum.

Hallahan, K. (1999a). Content class as a heuristic cue in the processing of news versus advertising. *Journal of Public Relations Research, 11*(4), 293–320.

Hallahan, K. (1999b). No, Virginia, it's not true what they say about publicity's third-party endorsement effect. *Public Relations Review, 25*(4), 331–350.

Hallahan, K. (1999c). Seven models of framing: Implications for public relations. *Journal of Public Relations Research, 11*(3), 205–242.

Hallahan, K. (2000a). Enhancing motivation, ability and opportunity to process public relations messages. *Public Relations Review, 26*(4), 463–480.

Hallahan, K. (2000b). Inactive publics: The forgotten publics in public relations. *Public Relations Review, 26*(4), 499–515.

Hallahan, K. (2001). The dynamics of issue activation and response: An issues processes model. *Journal of Public Relations Research, 13*(1), 27–59.

Hallahan, K. (2002). Ivy Lee and the Rockefellers' response to the 1913–1914 Colorado coal strike. *Journal of Public Relations Research, 14*(4), 265–315.

Hallahan, K. (2004). "Community" as the framework for public relations theory and research. In P. J. Kalbfleisch (Ed.), *Communication yearbook 28* (pp. 233–279). Thousand Oaks, CA: Sage.

Hallahan, K. (2007). Integrated communication: Implications for and beyond public relations excellence. In E. L. Toth (Ed.), *The future of excellence in public relations and communication management: Challenges to the next generation* (pp. 299–337). Mahwah, NJ: Lawrence Erlbaum.

Hallahan, K. (2008). Need for cognition as a motivation to process publicity and advertising. *Journal of Promotion Management, 14,* 169–194.

Hallahan, K. (2010). Online public relations. In H. Bidgoli (Ed.), *Handbook of technology management* (Vol. 2., chap. 36, pp. 497–517). Hoboken, NJ: Wiley.

Heath, R. L. (1992). The wrangle in the marketplace: A rhetorical perspective of public relations. In E. L. Toth & R. L. Heath (Eds.), *Rhetorical and critical approaches to public relations* (pp. 17–36). Hillsdale, NJ: Lawrence Erlbaum.

Heath, R. L. (2001). Shifting foundations: Public relations as relationship building. In R. L. Heath (Ed.), *Handbook of public relations* (pp. 1–9). Thousand Oaks, CA: Sage.

Heath, R. L. (2008). Power resource management: Pushing buttons and building cases. In T. L. Hansen-Horn & B. D. Neff (Eds.), *Public relations: From theory to practice* (pp. 2–19). Boston: Allyn & Bacon.

Heath, R. L., & Coombs, W. T. (2006). *Today's public relations: An introduction.* Thousand Oaks, CA: Sage.

Heath, R. L., Toth, E. L., & Waymer, D. (Eds.). (2009). *Rhetorical and critical approaches to public relations II.* New York: Routledge.

Heath, R. L., & Waymer, D. (2009). Activist public relations and the paradox of the positive. In R. L. Heath, E. L. Toth, & D. Waymer (Eds.), *Rhetorical and critical approaches to public relations II* (pp. 194–215). New York: Routledge.

Herman, E. S., & Chomsky, N. (2002). *Manufacturing consent: The political economy of the mass media* (2nd ed.). New York: Pantheon Books.

Herwitz, D. A. (2008). *The star as icon: Celebrity in the age of mass consumption.* New York: Columbia University Press.

Holstein, W. J. (2008). *Manage the media (Don't let the media manage you).* Boston: Harvard University Press.

Hughes, M. (2005). *Buzzmarketing: Get people to talk about your stuff.* New York: Portfolio.

James, C. (2007, May 19). Right time, wrong publicity. *New York Times.* Retrieved April 8, 2010, from www.nytimes.com/2007/05/19/arts/television/19hass.html

Kaid, L. L. (2008). Political communication. In D. W. Stacks & M. B. Salwen (Eds.), *An integrated approach to communication theory and research* (2nd ed., pp. 457–472). New York: Routledge.

Kant, I. (1991). Perpetual peace, Appendix II (H. B. Nisbet, Trans.). In H. Reiss (Ed.), *Kant: Political writings* (2nd ed., pp. 93–130). Cambridge, UK: Cambridge University Press. Retrieved March 17, 2009, from www.mtholyoke.edu/acad/intrel/kant/kant6.htm (Original work published 1795)

Kant, I. (2002). *Groundwork for the metaphysics of morals* (A. W. Wood, Ed. & Trans.). New Haven, CT: Yale University Press. (Original work published 1785)

Katz, E., & Lazarsfeld, P. F. (1955). *Personal influence: The part played by people in the flow of mass communications.* Glencoe, IL: Free Press.

Knapp, M. L., & Daly, J. A. (Eds.). (2002). *Handbook of interpersonal communication* (3rd ed.). Thousand Oaks, CA: Sage.

Koc, E. (2006). Order three advertisements and get one news story free: Public relations ethics practices of Turkish and international companies in Turkey. *Public Relations Review, 32*(4), 331–340.

Kosicki, G. M. (2002). The media priming effect: News media and considerations affecting political judgments. In J. P. Dillard & M. Pfau (Eds.), *The persuasion handbook: Developments in theory and practice* (pp. 63–81). Thousand Oaks, CA: Sage.

Kounalakis, M., Banks, D., & Daus, K. (1999). *Beyond spin: The power of strategic corporate journalism.* San Francisco: Jossey-Bass.

Kovera, M. B., & Greathouse, S. M. (2008). Pretrial publicity: Effects, remedies and judicial knowledge. In E. Borgida & S. T. Fiske (Eds.), *Beyond common sense: Psychological science in the courtroom* (pp. 261–280). Malden, MA: Blackwell.

Lasswell, H. (1927). *Propaganda technique in the world war.* New York: A. A. Knopf.

Lasswell, H. (1948). The structure and function of communication in society. In L. Bryson (Ed.), *The communication of ideas* (pp. 203–243). New York: Institute for Religious and Social Studies.

Lazarsfeld, P., & Merton, R. (1948). Mass communication, popular taste, and organized social action. In L. Bryson (Ed.), *The communication of ideas* (pp. 95–118). New York: Institute for Religious and Social Studies.

Lee, A. M., & Lee, E. B. (1972). *The fine art of propaganda.* New York: Octagon Books.

Lee, I. L. (1925). *Publicity: Some of the things it is and is not.* New York: Industries Publishing.

Len-Rios, M. E. (2008). Following communication rules: A communication-centered theory for public relations. In T. L. Hansen-Horn & B. D. Neff (Eds.), *Public relations: From theory to practice* (pp. 181–194). Boston: Allyn & Bacon.

Lippmann, W. (1915). *The stakes of diplomacy.* New York: H. Holt.

Lippmann, W. (1922). *Public opinion.* New York: Macmillan.

Lippmann, W. (1925). *The phantom public.* New York: Macmillan.

Liu, L. (1998, February 2). *The FDA's use of adverse publicity.* Cambridge, MA: Harvard Law School. Retrieved April 8, 2010, from http://leda.law.harvard.edu/leda/data/204/leoliu.html

Luban, D. (1996). The principle of publicity. In R. E. Goodin (Ed.), *The theory of institutional design* (pp. 154–198). New York: Cambridge University Press.

Lucarelli, S. (1993). The newspaper industry's campaign against spacegrabbers, 1917–1921. *Journalism Quarterly, 70*(4), 883–892.

Mannheim, J. B. (1987). A model of agenda dynamics. In M. L. McLaughlin (Ed.), *Communication yearbook 10* (pp. 499–516). Thousand Oaks, CA: Sage.

Marx, K. (with Engels, F.). (1998). *The German ideology* (R. M. Baird & S. E. Rosebaum, Eds.). Amherst, NY: Prometheus Books. (Original work published 1845 as *Deutsche ideologie*)

Mayhew, L. H. (1997). *The new public: Professional communication and the means of social influence.* New York: Cambridge University Press.

McCarthy, J. D., & Zald, M. N. (2001). The enduring vitality of resource mobilization theory of social movements. In J. H. Turner (Ed.), *Handbook of sociological theory* (pp. 535–565). New York: Kluwer Academic.

McCombs, M., & Reynolds, A. (2009). How news shapes our civic agenda. In J. Bryant & M. B. Oliver (Eds.), *Media effects: Advances in theory and research* (pp. 1–16). New York: Routledge.

McElreath, M. (1997). *Managing systematic and ethical public relations campaigns.* Boston: McGraw-Hill.

McEvoy, S., & Windom, W. (2003). A tale of two cases: Right of publicity versus the First Amendment. *Communications and the Law, 25*(2), 31–46.

McManus, J. (1994). *Market-driven journalism: Let the citizen beware?* Thousand Oaks, CA: Sage.

McManus, J. (1995). A market-driven model of news production. *Communication Theory, 5,* 301–338.

Merims, A. M. (1972). Marketing's stepchild: Product publicity. *Harvard Business Review, 50,* 107–113.

Merriam-Webster's dictionary. (2009). Publicity. Retrieved June 30, 2009, from http://m-w.com

Mickey, T. J. (2003). *Deconstructing public relations: Public relations criticism.* Mahwah, NJ: Lawrence Erlbaum.

Mill, J. S. (1962). *Considerations on representative government.* Chicago: Regnery Press. (Original work published 1861)

Miller, M. D., & Levene, T. R. (2008). Persuasion. In D. W. Stacks & M. B. Salwen (Eds.), *An integrated approach to communication theory and research* (2nd ed., pp. 245–260). New York: Routledge.

Milton, J. (1927). *Areopagitica and other prose works.* New York: Dutton.

Murphy, P. (1989). Game theory as a paradigm for the public relations process. In C. H. Botan & V. Hazleton Jr. (Eds.), *Public relations theory* (pp. 173–192). Hillsdale, NJ: Lawrence Erlbaum.

Nacos, B. L. (2007). *Mass-mediated terrorism: The central role of the media in terrorism and counterterrorism* (2nd ed.). Lanham, MD: Rowman & Littlefield.

Noelle-Neumann, E. (1994). *The spiral of silence.* Chicago: University of Chicago Press.

Olasky, M. N. (1987). *Corporate public relations: A new historical perspective.* Hillsdale, NJ: Lawrence Erlbaum.

Papacharissi, Z. (2008). Uses and gratifications. In D. W. Stacks & M. B. Salwen (Eds.), *An integrated approach to communication theory and research* (2nd ed., pp. 137–152). New York: Routledge.

Pearson, R. (1989). Beyond ethical relativism in public relations: Coorientation, rules and the idea of communication symmetry. *Public Relations Research Annual, 1,* 67–68.

Perloff, R. M. (1998). Agenda building. In *Political communication: Politics, press, and public in America* (pp. 221–242). Mahwah, NJ: Lawrence Erlbaum.

Perloff, R. M. (2009). Mass media, social perception and the third-person effect. In J. Bryant & M. B. Oliver (Eds.), *Media effects: Advances in theory and research* (pp. 252–268). New York: Routledge.

Petty, R. E., Briñol, P., & Priester, J. R. (2009). Mass media attitude change: Implications of the elaboration likelihood model of persuasion. In J. Bryant & M. B. Oliver (Eds.), *Media effects:*

Advances in theory and research (pp. 125–164). New York: Routledge.

Pfeffer, J., & Salancik, G. R. (1978). *The external control of organizations: A resource dependence perspective.* New York: Harper & Row.

Plaisance, P. L. (2009). *Media ethics: Key principles for responsible practice.* Thousand Oaks, CA: Sage.

Podnar, K., Lah, M., & Golob, U. (2009). Economic perspectives on public relations. *Public Relations Review, 35*(4), 340–345.

Pratto, F., & John, O. P. (1991). Automatic vigilance: The attention-grabbing power of negative social information. *Journal of Personality and Social Psychology, 61,* 380–391.

Price, C. J. (2003). Interfering owners or meddling advertisers: How network television news correspondents feel about ownership and advertiser influence on news stories. *Journal of Media Economics, 16*(3), 175–188.

Prior-Miller, M. (1989). Four major social scientific theories and their value to the public relations researcher. In C. H. Botan & V. Hazleton Jr. (Eds.), *Public relations theory* (pp. 67–81). Hillsdale, NJ: Lawrence Erlbaum.

Publicity [Introduction to special issue]. (1990). *Gannett Center Journal, 4*(2), vi–xi.

Public Relations Society of America. (2000). *Code of ethics.* Retrieved June 30, 2009, from www.prsa.org/aboutUs/ethics/preamble_en.html

Raucher, A. R. (1968). *Public relations and business, 1900–1929.* Baltimore: Johns Hopkins Press.

Rawls, J. (1971). *A theory of justice.* Cambridge, MA: Harvard University Press.

Rawls, J. (1993). *Political liberalism.* New York: Columbia University Press.

Rawls, J. (2001). Grounds falling under publicity. In E. Kelly (Ed.), *Justice as fairness, a restatement* (pp. 120–222). Cambridge, MA: Harvard University Press.

Rein, I., Kotler, P., & Stoller, M. (1997). The voice of visibility. In *High visibility: The making and marketing of professionals into celebrities* (pp. 271–298). Lincolnwood, IL: NTC Business Books.

Rice, R. E., & Atkin, C. K. (2009). Public communication campaigns: Theoretical principles and practical applications. In J. Bryant & M. B. Oliver (Eds.), *Media effects: Advances in theory and research* (pp. 436–468). New York: Routledge.

Rogers, E. (2003). *The diffusion of innovations* (5th ed.). New York: Free Press.

Roschwalb, S. A., & Stack, R. A. (Eds.). (1995). *Litigation public relations: Courting public opinion.* Littleton, CO: F. B. Rothman.

Roskos-Ewoldsen, D. R., Roskos-Ewoldsen, B., & Carpentier, F. D. (2009). Media priming: An updated synthesis. In J. Bryant & M. B. Oliver (Eds.), *Media effects: Advances in theory and research* (pp. 74–93). New York: Routledge.

Rubin, A. R. (2009). Uses-and-gratifications perspectives on media effects. In J. Bryant & M. B. Oliver (Eds.), *Media effects: Advances in theory and research* (pp. 165–184). New York: Routledge.

Russell, K., & Bishop, C. (2009, June). Understanding Ivy Lee's declaration of principles: U.S. newspaper and magazine coverage of publicity and press agentry, 1865–1904. *Public Relations Review, 35*(2), 91–101.

Ryan, C. (1991). *Prime time activism: Media strategies for grassroots organizing.* Boston: South End Press.

Safire, W. (1963). *The relations explosion: A diagram of the coming boom and shakeout in corporate relations.* New York: Macmillan.

Sallot, L. M., Steinfatt, T. M., & Salwen, M. B. (1998). Journalists' and public relations practitioners' news values: Perceptions and cross-perceptions. *Journalism and Mass Communication Quarterly, 75*(2), 366–377.

Salmon, C. T. (1990). God understands when the cause is noble. *Gannett Center Journal, 4*(2), 23–34.

Salmon, C. T., & Glynn, C. J. (2008). Spiral of silence: Communication and public opinion as control. In D. W. Stacks & M. B. Salwen (Eds.), *An integrated approach to communication theory and research* (2nd ed., pp. 153–168). New York: Routledge.

Schiff, M. (2007). Satisfying the needs and interests of stakeholders. In G. Johnstone & D. W. Van Ness (Eds.), *Handbook of restorative justice* (pp. 228–246). Portland, OR: Willan.

Schudson, M. (2003). News sources. In *The sociology of news* (pp. 134–153). New York: W. W. Norton.

Self, C. C. (2008). Credibility. In D. W. Stacks & M. B. Salwen (Eds.), *An integrated approach to communication theory and research* (2nd ed., pp. 435–456). Mahwah, NJ: Lawrence Erlbaum.

Shah, D., Rojas, H., & Cho, J. (2009). Media and civic participation: On understanding and misunderstanding communication effects. In J. Bryant & M. B. Oliver (Eds.), *Media effects: Advances in theory and research* (pp. 207–227). New York: Routledge.

Shils, E. (1956). *The torment of secrecy.* Carbondale: Southern Illinois University Press.

Shoemaker, P. J., & Vos, T. P. (2008). Media gatekeeping. In D. W.Stacks & M. B. Salwen (Eds.), *An integrated approach to communication theory and research* (2nd ed., pp. 75–89). New York: Routledge.

Shrum, L. J. (2009). Media consumption and perceptions of social reality: Effects and underlying processes. In J. Bryant & M. B. Oliver (Eds.), *Media effects: Advances in theory and research* (pp. 50–73). New York: Routledge.

Signorelli, N., & Morgan, M. (2008). Cultivation analysis: Research and practice. In D. W. Stacks & M. B. Salwen (Eds.), *An integrated approach to communication theory and research* (2nd ed., pp. 106–121). New York: Routledge.

Spencer, V. (2000). Publicity in the political arena: Metaphor of spectacle, combat and display. In P. Corcoran & V. Spencer (Eds.), *Disclosures* (pp. 15–43). Brookfield, MA: Ashgate.

Splichal, S. (2002). *Principles of publicity and press freedom.* Lanham, MD: Rowman & Littlefield.

Suman, M., & Rossman, G. (Eds.). (2000). *Advocacy groups and the entertainment industry.* Westport, CT: Praeger.

Szabo, E. A., & Pfau, M. (2002). Nuances in inoculation: Theory and applications. In J. P. Dillard & M. Pfau (Eds.), *The persuasion handbook: Developments in theory and practice* (pp. 233–258). Thousand Oaks, CA: Sage.

Taylor, M. (2009). Protocol journalism as a framework for understanding public relations-media relationships in Kosovo. *Public Relations Review, 35*(1), 23–30.

Tedlow, R. S. (1979). *Keeping the corporate image: Public relations and business 1900–1950.* Greenwich, CT: JAI Press.

Tewksbury, D., & Scheufele, D. A. (2009). New framing theory and research. In J. Bryant & M. B. Oliver (Eds.), *Media effects: Advances in theory and research* (pp. 17–33). New York: Routledge.

Thompson, J. A. (2003). *American progressive publicists and the First World War.* New York: Cambridge University Press.

Thorne, L. (2008). *Word-of-mouth advertising, online and off: How to spark buzz, excitement, and free publicity for your business or organization with little or no money.* Ocala, FL: Atlantic.

Toplin, R. B. (2006). Media wars. In *Radical conservatism: The right's political religion* (pp. 237–264). Lawrence: University Press of Kansas.

Toulmin, S. (1958). *The uses of argument.* Cambridge, UK: Cambridge University Press.

Tuchman, G. (1978). *Making news: A study in the construction of social reality.* New York: Free Press.

Turk, J. (1986). Information subsidies and media content. *Journalism Monographs,* No. 100.

Tyebjee, T. T. (1982). Role of publicity in FTC corrective advertising remedies. *Journal of Marketing & Public Policy, 1,* 111–121.

Valenzuela, S., & McCombs, M. (2008). The agenda-setting function of the news media. In D. W. Stacks & M. B. Salwen (Eds.), *An integrated approach to communication theory and research* (2nd ed., pp. 90–105). New York: Routledge.

van Riel, C. B. M., & Fombrun, C. J. (2007). *Essentials of corporate communication.* London: Routledge.

Walton, D. N. (2007). *Media argumentation: Dialectic, persuasion, and rhetoric.* New York: Cambridge University Press.

Wang, A. (2009). *Content class effects on consumer online information processing: In integrated marketing communication context.* New York: VDM Verlag.

Washburn, C. (1937). *Press agentry.* New York: National Library Press.

Weick, K. E. (1995). *Sense-making in organizations.* Thousand Oaks, CA: Sage.

Wells, W. D. (1989). Lectures and dramas. In P. Cafferata & A. M. Tybout (Eds.), *Cognitive and affective responses to advertising* (pp. 13–20). Lexington, MA: Lexington Books.

Wilder, R. H., & Buell K. L. (1923). *Publicity: A manual for the use of business, civic or social organizations.* New York: Ronald Press.

Wilkinson, P. (1990). Terrorism and propaganda. In Y. Alexander & R. Latter (Eds.), *Terrorism and the media: Dilemmas for government, journalists and the public.* Washington, DC: Brassey's.

Williamson, O. E. (1996). *The mechanisms of governance.* New York: Oxford University Press.

Wills, I. (1997). *Economics and the environment: A signalling and incentives approach.* St. Leonards, New South Wales, Australia: Allen & Unwin.

Wright, C. R. (1975). Functional analysis and mass communication revisited. In J. Blumer & E. Katz (Eds.), *The uses of mass communications* (pp. 197–212). Beverly Hills, CA: Sage.

Zoch, L. M., & Molleda, J. (2006). Building a theoretical model of media relations using framing, information subsidies and agenda-building. In C. H. Botan & V. Hazleton (Eds.), *Public relations theory II* (pp. 279–310). Mahwah, NJ: Lawrence Erlbaum.

CHAPTER 38

The Role of Public Relations in Promoting Healthy Communities

Jeffrey K. Springston and Ruthann Weaver Lariscy

Remarkable progress has been documented in the past few decades in both understanding and treating human health. One major change is the shift in emphasis in health care from treatment to prevention (Clymer, 2009). Whether a message is attempting to persuade individuals to not smoke, to exercise more, or to daily consume a half aspirin, we are surrounded by pro–healthy lifestyle messages, most of which are designed to prevent serious disease, illness, or premature death. It is also true that these prohealthy messages must compete in an environment where people are regularly exposed to messages encouraging the consumption of highly processed foods and where people's environment, lifestyles, and work often make it difficult to exercise and eat healthy foods.

Perhaps not surprisingly, given limited health communication resources, the overall health of communities has received less attention than most individual health behaviors and activities. *Healthy communities* were defined and some strategies were introduced in the *Healthy People 2010* initiative (Department of Health and Human Services, 2000). There are also a variety of nonprofit organizations, such as CityNet, Association for Community Health and Improvement, an initiative from the National Civic League, plus some individual state programs (Municipal Research and Services Center [MRSC], 2008), whose goals share some overlap with the federal program. There are excellent examples of individual communities achieving milestones in community health, but such efforts remain largely fragmented.

While a community effort to improve health is not a solution for all problems, a community-level approach has the potential of achieving goals that are beyond the reach of individuals and has some important advantages over efforts by state or national agencies/organizations that often lack the local knowledge and support that a community-level coalition can achieve. As Ratzan (2009) urged, as communication scholars we need to focus our attention on helping people "make appropriate health decisions by building healthy, participatory communities and effective health care delivery systems, supported by enlightened health policy. Health is not just the imperative for the individual or the government, but everyone's responsibility" (p. 99).

In this chapter, we seek to place public relations as a central element in the development of community collaborations to promote health. We will provide a common definition of what is meant by healthy communities, and, in an effort to provide a contextual framework, we will highlight a couple of the major health threats facing most communities. We will then discuss how a public relations approach can be used to promote community health by facilitating the creation of community collaboration, promote compromise between community stakeholders, and assist in the development of realistic and achievable goals that include providing credible information to policymakers to help shape local systems and the environment to be more conducive for a healthy population. Finally, we will provide a case example of a community development effort.

What Is a Healthy Community?

The concept of health is something that has changed throughout history, and even in contemporary times, many definitions of a healthy community exist. To medical professionals, a healthy community may be defined as one in which free or affordable health care is available to all citizens (American Medical Association, 2009). The Centers for Disease Control and Prevention (CDC) define a healthy community as

> a community that is continuously creating and improving those physical and social environments and expanding those community resources that enable people to mutually support each other in performing all the functions of life and in developing to their maximum potential. (CDC, 2000)

The *Healthy People 2010* initiative defined a healthy community more broadly as "one which includes those elements that enable people to maintain a high quality of life and productivity" (Department of Health and Human Services, 2000).

While the definitions themselves obviously vary somewhat from one another, the explication of specific programs, environmental features, and a healthy environment is similar across organizations. Common components in most discussions of healthy communities include available, affordable health care for all citizens; emphasis on prevention as well as treatment of both illnesses and accidents; safety; presence of roads, playgrounds, schools, and other facilities needed for the community to function safely; and a healthy environment (i.e., air and water quality).

Additionally, some attention is being given to the role of community design as an important contributor to healthy communities (Robert Wood Johnson Foundation, 2000). Bike paths, walkways, safe playgrounds, swimming pools, and athletic fields and venues are all cited as examples of planning community design to include numerous types of physical activities. Citing information provided by the CDC, the Foundation White Paper emphasized that "despite the clear health benefits of physical activity, two-thirds of American adults do not meet the CDC recommendations, which suggest that adults engage in physical activity at least five days a week, for 30 minutes or more" (Robert Wood Johnson Foundation, 2000, p. 3).

Poor Diet and Lack of Exercise: Two Major Threats to Healthy Communities

Technology and innovative practices in recent decades have yielded some dramatic improvements in health, and we have seen some important improvements in the prevalence of some healthy behaviors, such as cancer screening. As a result, the overall mortality and morbidity rates for cancer have dropped significantly since the 1950s (Kort, Paneth, & Vande Woude, 2009). Unfortunately, the same cannot be said for other health indicators such as obesity and type 2 diabetes. According to the CDC, there has been a dramatic increase in the level of obesity, with only one state (Colorado) that had a prevalence of obesity less than 20%. CDC data indicate that the southeastern United States is particularly hard hit by prevalence of both obesity and type 2 diabetes (CDC, 2009). While the causes of these diseases are complex, there is little doubt that they are strongly associated with Western diets and a lack of exercise (Cordain et al., 2005). Unlike periodic cancer screening, eating healthy diets and getting enough exercise are behaviors that need to be engaged in daily.

Communication campaigns to educate and persuade individuals to promote healthier eating and exercise are critically important, but such efforts are dwarfed by the industries that promote unhealthy products and behaviors. Recent studies have shown evidence that food advertising and marketing have an important influence on the population's consumption of less healthy foods (e.g., Aktas, 2006; Batada, Seitz, Wootan, & Story, 2008; Royne & Levy, 2008). However, David Kessler, former director of the U.S. Food and Drug Administration, argues that it is not marketing alone that has changed the average American's diet so markedly from the typical pre-1980 American diet. He made a compelling argument that through rigorous research and development testing, the food industry has created processed foods that cause many people to become addicted in much the same manner that people become addicted to controlled substances (Kessler, 2009). While Kessler did not specifically accuse the food industry of purposefully creating addicting foods, he argued that it is the result of their work. We are beginning to see physiological studies that bear this out. For example, a study using magnetic resonance imaging revealed that the brain activity stimulated by the thought of certain foods is very similar to the activity drug addicts exhibit when thinking about their drug (Rolls, 2005). Kessler posited that this is achieved by carefully modulating the amount of a food's sugar, fat, and salt content to create hyperpalatable taste. Essentially, eating sugar, fat, and salt compels many people to want to eat more sugar, fat, and salt.

It is very difficult to avoid exposure to food industry promotions. Food-related advertising and marketing are common fixtures in many aspects of our society, ranging from our public schools to our media. The impact of food industry practices is beginning to gain attention among elected officials. In an attempt to avoid regulatory restrictions, the food industry often argues that advertising and promotion don't influence people to eat such foods if they aren't otherwise inclined. Rather, advertising affects only brand selection. Some theorists would agree that promotional efforts do not have the power to initiate the adoption of new behaviors. Since the mid-1970s, Ehrenberg and colleagues have argued for a "weak" theory of advertising, namely, that the effect of advertising is primarily one of reinforcing existing behaviors (e.g., Ehrenberg, 1974). While at first blush that seems to support the food industry's claim, it does not minimize the negative impact of such promotions because they may serve to reinforce already existing unhealthy behavior patterns. The combination of what is essentially a processed food addiction and the omnipresence of food advertisements and marketing is likely having a very significant influence on people's eating behaviors.

In addition to the forces at work to promote poor dietary habits, there are also a number of influential factors at play that explain the decreasing level of physical activity of many Americans. Brownson, Boehmer, and Luke (2005) analyzed current conditions and long-term trends in physical activity, employment and occupation, travel behavior, land use, and related behaviors such as television watching and video game playing. They noted that all these factors contributed to a sedentary lifestyle. Many jobs are becoming less physical, the average commute time is increasing, there has been a precipitous rise in strip malls and other types of development that discourage walking, and people are increasingly spending more time in front of a computer or a television.

There are many dimensions of living a healthy lifestyle, and each community faces unique challenges and opportunities to facilitate community health. Two factors that would maintain and improve everyone's lives are eating healthier and getting an adequate amount of physical exercise. There is little doubt that communication is essential to promoting these healthier behaviors. However, informing people about healthy behaviors and persuading them that such behaviors are a good idea are often insufficient to promote sustained behavior changes. Some researchers make the argument that we also need to put a strong focus on shaping environmental stimuli that trigger and reinforce people's behavior patterns (e.g., Foxall & Greenley, 2000; Hoek & Gendall, 2006).

The Role of Public Relations

While individuals have some ability to shape their environment to make it more conducive for exhibiting healthy behaviors, community groups can often have more power to facilitate changes and to influence local, state, and federal governments to do so. Fraser (1982) pointed to two key reasons for forming coalitions. Such groups can pool resources and save money, and collectively, people can have more influence with policymakers than individuals typically can. The adoption of an issues management perspective can provide a critical component to the success of community collaboration efforts. Issues managers can help by helping to define problems and select ones on which to focus. They can also help identify allies and opponents and decide how participants will be attracted to coalitions.

Public relations can serve a critical role in the success of building community coalitions and of promoting a coalition's goals. R. L. Heath and Palenchar (2009) stated that

> the wise issues manager realizes that in a multiple stakeholder environment, the concerns that must be addressed are not likely to be narrowed to the relationship between one company and one group of activists. Bridging differences and achieving mutual interests can be challenging, requiring the marshaling of a variety of resources through a business plan, a public policy plan, and a communication plan. (p. 165)

Issues management entails balancing relationships with multiple stakeholders.

This is no simple task, given that every community has competing interests and that often, some of those interests conflict with healthy behavior. For example, restaurants often upsize their meal portions to compete for patrons. Developers often create residential and commercial space that discourages walking. City and county governments often loathe implementing plans for mass transit, bikeways, and other infrastructure improvements because of the expense to riders and taxpayers, particularly in an economic downturn such as the one we are currently experiencing. However, times of scarcity often result in creativity, and the politically impossible may become possible.

The impetus for forming a community coalition to improve health could come from a variety of sources, but Wolff (2001) argued that the effort is much more likely to succeed when it originates from the community. He offered some cautions that issues managers should heed. First, prior history with community coalition building will be an important factor in the potential success of any effort. All communities are likely to have had at least some history of collaborative efforts, and communities that have fewer successful attempts will find it more difficult to succeed. He also cautioned about the dangers of communities that are "overcoalitioned." It is common for government or private agencies to mandate that a coalition be formed as a condition for receiving funds to combat a particular health problem. As a result, there may be an overlapping focus between groups, creating communication and coordination difficulties between groups, for example, a sustainable environment coalition, a tobacco coalition, and an asthma coalition. Such an environment underscores the need for experienced professional communicators who can facilitate communication and keep the community informed.

Wise (2009) pointed out that public relations experts are bridge builders. While his point was made with regard to international efforts, the same principles apply to building bridges between different classes or other demographic subdivisions in a community.

Formation of Community Collaboration/Coalitions to Promote Health

A community is defined as an informally organized set of loose associations among residents (McKnight, 1994). In a thorough review of current studies about community organizing, Dearing (2003) assessed that most research falls into one of two camps: (1) individual attitude and behavior change campaigns and (2) community empowerment through grassroots activities and initiatives (p. 208). He advanced that if a problem is with individuals, the solution is self-help (individual level) or behavior change campaigns (institution level). If a problem is within an institution, the solution for individuals is grassroots activism, and for institutions it is social ecology interventions (supporting the coalitions and organizations that in turn promote health in their communities) (p. 209). Rothschild (1999) indicated that health campaigns may occur at the individual, community, or societal level.

For years, the emphasis in health campaigns has been at the individual level. These campaigns often have an institution behind them, but targeting individuals can be a systematic approach to obtain specific outcomes within a large population of individuals (Salmon & Atkin, 2003). Behavior changes are seen as the responsibility of individuals with guidance from experts in institutions that sponsor the campaigns (Dearing, 2003). Rothman (1970) labeled this type of community effort *social planning* and advanced that it is often not the best approach.

There has also been study of grassroots community organizing, labeled *community building* (Dearing, 2003; Walter, 1997); while they can be quite successful, Dearing (2003) said "such efforts often languish for years" (p. 210). One alternative to individual efforts, whether as health information campaigns or grassroots organizing, is when an external organization (e.g., a foundation or institute) enters a community to initiate change (Dearing, 2003). Such organizations typically bring funding and other resources to the community but are not always embraced by local citizens, as these efforts can be viewed as "outsiders' influence."

Thus, the preferred approach to community organizing for change is *resident centric*, according to scholars (Dearing, 2003; Guttman, 2000; LaBonte, 1997) and is increasingly termed *community building*. It is from this perspective that we believe public relations health practitioners can most effectively contribute to changing the health environment of communities.

Such successful community building requires that key stakeholders in a community organize with the overarching goal of improving community quality of life, with health being a critical element. These stakeholders could include elected and unelected government officials (including environmental, transportation and city planning, law enforcement, and parks and recreation), health experts and providers, community foundations, community leaders (business, church, civic groups, etc.), and leaders from area schools and universities. Such efforts should also include stakeholders from underserved segments of the community, as it is often these individuals who face the most challenges to living a healthy lifestyle. Many factors exist in communities that negatively influence healthy behaviors. To address these factors in a holistic way, broad-based coalitions are necessary to contribute the needed expertise to identify problems and proffer solutions. Coalitions that represent the spectrum of interests in the community stand the best chance of gaining wider support from the community.

Facilitate Negotiation and Compromise Between Stakeholders

R. L. Heath and Coombs (2006) advised to look for concurrence and shared control as well as distribution of resources in a win-win style. Public relations can play a useful role in negotiation as well as in its more standard role of media relations. Depending on how a coalition is formed, it could be viewed by local government and/or businesses as an activist group opposed to status quo business or government operations. If a coalition forms as an outgrowth of government or business recognition of an important problem, it may be seen in a more positive, collaborative light. In either event, R. L. Heath and Coombs recommended that it may be much more productive to see coalition activists as allies than as foes.

Renee Guarriello Heath (2007) argued that the best model in which to conceive of community collaboration should be informed by an approach in which stakeholders are chosen for their ability to think differently, and the most innovative solutions will be when potential positions are contested and examined and disagreements with other stakeholders on particular subject matters are allowed to occur. Stakeholders with diverse perspectives should be sought after. R. G. Heath and Frey (2004) pointed out that true community collaboration consists of autonomous stakeholders who cooperate in a relatively nonhierarchical relationship that is negotiated through dialogue. Community offers a context and boundary for these types of collaborations.

R. G. Heath (2007) cautioned about several forces that are often at play to work against stakeholder diversity. One is a history of volunteerism-facilitated homogeneity. Often, such groups have a history where individuals volunteered for a particular cause, and this evolved into a more formal coalition. This history can often develop into a group culture that excludes dissimilar thinking about a problem. A second force can be related to mandated partnerships. Grants or other funding often stipulate that specific groups be included on an advisory board. While this can be positive in placing people with established connections, it can also lend itself to inertia in perspective taking. A third force that can promote homogeneity over diversity is an orientation toward resources. Selection of stakeholder membership can be strongly influenced by what finances or other resources the stakeholder brings to the table, not necessarily whether that person has a different perspective on the problem. Finally, group procedures and logistics can greatly influence who can actively participate. For example, meeting times might exclude people if their work flexibility doesn't allow them to take time from work. Location can be another major obstacle. Meeting places that are not convenient can be problematic, particularly if individuals lack transportation.

A person skilled in public relations and issues management can help the coalition build trust, anticipate challenges that come with homogeneity, and help the group understand that airing disagreement and challenging perspectives can be a good thing. Potapchuk, Crocker, and Schechter (1998) cautioned against neglecting this phase of coalition formation. Without building trust with key stakeholders, the risks of damaging or delaying efforts are great. The public relations specialist can also help the group implement procedures and structures that lend themselves to greater participation. This might include the careful rotation of meeting places and times and the creation of events that work to build trust between potential opponents, for example, sharing meals together.

Development of Realistic and Achievable Goals

Merzel and D'Affitti (2003) analyzed 25 community-based health intervention projects that targeted problems such as cardiovascular disease, smoking prevention, cancer screening and prevention, HIV prevention, and substance abuse. The authors indicated that differences in the goals and between community stakeholders and health researchers and health officials often limited the success of the interventions. As Wolff (2001) pointed out, early development of a common shared vision and mission is vital to the success of community coalitions. If the coalition provides a good representation of the community and all voices are encouraged to contribute, any resulting vision and mission stand a much better chance of success. A skilled issues manager can help facilitate this. The resulting vision and mission must be clear to participating stakeholders and relate to the group's goals, objectives, and activities on a day-to-day basis. The goals and objectives must be concrete, attainable, and, ultimately, measurable. Wolff notes that community coalitions often find this requirement to be challenging. If a coalition sets out a broad agenda, it can become easily distracted by side issues and unexpected events. In a discussion of activist groups, R. L. Heath and Palenchar (2009) argued that it is vitally important that groups pick battles they know they can win. Such success will motivate members and demonstrate to all community stakeholders that the coalition has a degree of power and influence. Kreuter, Lezin, and Young (2000) indicated that realistic expectations for collaborative efforts include the exchange of information among coalition members, the promotion of collaboration among coalition members, and the legitimization of the issue or focus of a coalition within a community. The authors also argued that it can be realistic that coalitions can achieve meaningful program planning to attack or address an issue, influence policy, and influence resource allocation for a given problem or issue. They indicate that it is not realistic to expect full program implementation, major direct changes in organizational systems, or large changes in specific individual health outcomes.

Harris and McGrath (2008) pointed out that coalition partners very often decide to work together on a policy issue as a way of leveraging the assets each partner possesses. This includes resources such as information, membership, funding, and access to legislators. Even though partners may otherwise be competitors, it is often to their advantage to set aside those differences to maximize their joint impact on public policy. A coalition can make an argument more effective by more clearly demonstrating that a particular position is in the public interest, and a coalition can reduce and simplify the overall amount of information policymakers are subject to receiving by reducing multiple messages they would have otherwise received.

Additionally, a public relations expert could help facilitate media attention on the coalition's efforts, and this can have an important influence on public policy. Yanovitsky (2002) examined two decades of data regarding the role of media attention to public policy attention and action. He found that public policy attention is most intense early in the life cycle of an issue. Attention does not equal action, however. The more one-sided the coverage, the more likely action will take place. The more public debate and disagreement over positions, the less likely quick or sweeping action will take place. This supports the argument that a diverse coalition needs to be formed at the outset, and for as many compromises to be worked out as possible so that a broader consensus for action is endorsed by the coalition.

Case Example

An Existing Underused Community Opportunity. Within the boundaries of Macon/Bibb County in Georgia lies an 1,800-acre publicly owned and maintained lake surrounded by large outdoor recreation areas divided into three separate parks, each containing unique activities (e.g., camping, hiking, disk golfing). In spring, 2009, recreation and other facilities were in need of repair or replacement—much damage from a tornado the previous year accelerated the need for city planners to renovate facilities and activity venues. The

Board of Commissioners, representing every district in the unified city-county government, knew something had to be done, but they were reluctant in the existing economic climate to ask taxpayers to assume another tax increase. Some federal funds would come to the site as a direct result of the tornado damage. The opportunity seemed "right" to begin rebuilding a "hidden treasure" within the county. Such a situation is perfectly suited to launch a healthy community initiative.

The first step the Commission took was to open the bid process for public opinion research firms. They wanted to know what citizens in their own and surrounding counties wanted Lake Tobesofkee and its recreational facilities to provide. They retained a research and public relations firm that proceeded to conduct interviews with key stakeholders and town hall meetings with various interest groups (e.g., citizens living around the lake; biking and walking special interest groups) in addition to both a scientific random direct dial telephone survey and a nonscientific Internet survey advertised through local media (television ads and talk shows, radio announcements, and newspaper stories and advertisements).

Findings from the multipronged research initiatives revealed strong preferences among various constituencies; additionally, and, initially, of surprise to both the public relations team and the commissioners, strong voluntary participation from several interest groups emerged. One example: a representative from Southern Off-Road Bicycle Association, a regional advocacy and interest group for mountain bikers, attended each town meeting. Indicating that he represented 150 members who wanted more bike trails, he committed the organization to help build them. The Macon Running Club was equally interested in providing volunteers to help build paths and routes for runners and hikers.

One strength public relations brings to the process of building healthy communities is providing means through which various coalitions, like these mountain bikers, runners, and hikers, are brought together and organized for the greater good of the community. Without the critically important public opinion research that was conducted, these coalitions may very well never have coalesced.

This case illustrates the role public relations occupies in developing healthy communities in several ways. First, a firm public opinion research foundation established priorities of citizens' interests, thus providing a blueprint for the commissioners to guide spending. One such interest that emerged from the research, which had not previously existed at the lake or any of its recreational areas, was for a children's swimming/play area, isolated from boating and fishing areas on the lake. This relatively inexpensive addition would not have been considered had the opinion research not been initiated.

Second, public relations brought previously isolated interests together in meaningful coalitions. It became apparent, through the town hall meetings, focus groups, interviews, and call-ins to radio and television talk shows, that a number of specific interest groups were willing to volunteer their personal labor as well as work reciprocally with other special interests. Equestrian supporters, for example, provided data on the importance of having separate paths for horses, cycles, and hiking. All three groups concurred and agreed to work jointly on the formation of separate venues for each.

Third, public relations performs public education functions through numerous strategies and tactics. In this case study, stakeholder education was accomplished in numerous ways: Highly interested, self-motivated parties could attend events and learn about the lake and parks renovations and express their preferences. For motivated individuals who were unable to physically attend a meeting, an online survey was provided. This was promoted in media advertisements as well as in television and radio talk shows and a utility bill insert sent to all residents. Finally, traditional tactics such as brochures and announcements in newsletters, as well as nontraditional ones such as online social media, were used to educate a breadth of stakeholders and stimulate interest in development of healthy recreational activities and facilities.

Finally, and of great importance, public relations provided credible information to policymakers on which they could base decisions regarding taxpayers' monies in challenging economic times. With the public opinion evidence in hand, coalitions formed (and producing armies of volunteers to supplement professional designers and construction agents), and massive (yet relatively inexpensive) public education programs in place, policymakers could have confidence in the decisions they made.

Conclusion

In this chapter, we have discussed the important role that public relations can play in promoting healthier communities through an issues management approach. This includes helping the community leaders work with experts in health to better understand and anticipate health challenges and opportunities and facilitating the formation of community coalitions that can collaboratively address these issues. While such efforts have often not demonstrated dramatic statistical improvements in specific health indicators, Kreuter et al. (2000) suggested that this may not be the best measure. Instead, it may be more useful to view the benefits of increased community awareness, participation, and empowerment as important first steps to health status and systems changes. As public relations scholars and practitioners our focus should be placed on how knowledge and practices in our field can be applied to community health. The facilitation of collaboration between community stakeholders is a good place to invest our energies.

References

Aktas, A. Y. (2006). The effects of television food advertisement on children's food purchasing requests. *Pediatrics International, 48,* 138–145.

American Medical Association. (2009). *Public health: Healthy communities/Health America.* Retrieved March 20, 2010, from www.ama-assn.org/ama/pub/aboutAMA/amafoundation/publichealth

Batada, A., Seitz, M. D., Wootan, M. G., & Story, M. (2008). Nine out of 10 food advertisements shown during Saturday morning children's television programming are for foods high in fat, sodium, or added sugars, or low in nutrients. *Journal of the American Dietetic Association, 108,* 673–678.

Brownson, R. C., Boehmer, T. K., & Luke, D. A. (2005). Declining rates of physical activity in the United States: What are the contributors? *Annual Review of Public Health, 26,* 421–443.

Centers for Disease Control and Prevention. (2000). *Designing and building healthy places.* Retrieved March 20, 2010, from www.cdc.gov/healthyplaces

Centers for Disease Control and Prevention. (2009). *U.S. trends in obesity.* Retrieved March 20, 2010, from www.cdc.gov/obesity/data/trends.html#State

Clymer, J. (2009). *National health care reform: Moving from treatment to prevention* (Partnership for Prevention). Retrieved March 20, 2010, from www.prevent.org/content/view/182

Cordain, L., Eaton, S. B., Sebastian, A., Mann, N., Lindebert, S., Watkins, B. A., et al. (2005). Origins and evolution of the Western diet: Health implications for the 21st century. *American Journal of Clinical Nutrition, 81,* 341–354.

Dearing, J. W. (2003). The state of the art and the state of the science of community organizing. In T. Thompson, A. Dorsey, K. Miller, & R. Parrott (Eds.), *Handbook of health communication* (pp. 207–220). Mahwah, NJ: Lawrence Erlbaum.

Department of Health and Human Services. (2000). *Healthy people 2010.* Retrieved March 20, 2010, from www.healthypeople.gov

Ehrenberg, A. S. (1974). Repetitive adertising and the consumer. *Journal of Advertising Research, 14,* 25–34.

Foxall, G. R., & Greenley, G. E. (2000). Predicting and explaining responses to consumer environments: An empirical test and theoretical extension of the behavioural perspective model. *Service Industries Journal, 20,* 39–63.

Fraser, E. A. (1982). Coalitions. In J. S. Nagelschmidt (Ed.), *The public affairs handbook* (pp. 192–199). New York: AMACOM.

Guttman, N. (2000). *Public health communication interventions.* Thousand Oaks, CA: Sage.

Harris, P., & McGrath, C. (2008, March). *Lobbying and political marketing: A neglected perspective and research agenda.* Paper presented at the 5th International Political Marketing Conference, Manchester, UK.

Heath, R. G. (2007). Rethinking community collaboration through a dialogic lens: Creativity, democracy, and diversity in community organizing. *Management Communication Quarterly, 21,* 145–171.

Heath, R. G., & Frey, L. (2004). Ideal collaboration: A conceptual framework for community collaboration. In P. Kalbfleisch (Ed.), *Communication yearbook 28* (pp. 189–232). Mahwah, NJ: Lawrence Erlbaum.

Heath, R. L., & Coombs, W. T. (2006). *Today's public relations.* Thousand Oaks, CA: Sage.

Heath, R. L., & Palenchar, M. J. (2009). *Strategic issues management: Organizations and public policy challenges.* Thousand Oaks, CA: Sage.

Hoek, J., & Gendall, P. (2006). Advertising and obesity: A behavioral perspective. *Journal of Health Communication, 11,* 409–423.

Kessler, D. (2009). *The end of overeating: Taking control of the insatiable American appetite.* New York: Macmillan.

Kort, E. J., Paneth, N., & Vande Woude, G. F. (2009). The decline in U.S. cancer mortality in people born since 1925. *Cancer Research, 69,* 6500–6505.

Kreuter, M. W., Lezin, N. A., & Young, L. A. (2000). Evaluating community-based collaborative mechanisms: Implications for practitioners. *Health Promotion Practices, 1,* 49–63.

LaBonte, R. (1997). Community, community development, and the forming of authentic partnerships. In M. Minkler (Ed.), *Community organizing and community building for health* (pp. 880–1002). New Brunswick, NJ: Rutgers University Press.

McKnight, J. L. (1994). Two tools for well-being: Health systems and communities. *American Journal of Preventive Medicine, 10,* 23–25.

Merzel, C., & D'Affitti, J. (2003). Reconsidering community-based health promotion: Promise, performance, and potential. *American Journal of Public Health, 93,* 557–574.

Municipal Research and Services Center. (2008). What is a healthy community? Retrieved March 20, 2010, from www.mrsc.org/Subjects/HumanServices/healthyWhat.aspx

Potapchuk, W. R., Crocker, J., & Schechter, W. H. (1998). *Systems reform and local government: Improving outcomes for children, families, and neighborhoods.* Retrieved from ERIC database (ED427102).

Ratzan, S. C. (2009). Health competent societies: Our challenge and future. *Journal of Health Communication, 14,* 99–101.

Robert Wood Johnson Foundation. (2000). *Active living through community* [White paper]. Retrieved March 20, 2010, from www.rwjf.org/pr/product.jsp?id=34038

Rolls, E. T. (2005). Taste, olfactory, and food texture processing in the brain, and the control of food intake. *Physiology and Behavior, 85,* 45–56.

Rothman, J. (1970). Three models of community organization practice. In F. M. Cox, J. L. Erlich, J. Rothman, & J. E. Tropman (Eds.), *Strategies of community organization* (pp. 20–36). Itasca, IL: Peacock.

Rothschild, M. L. (1999). Carrot sticks, and promises: A conceptual framework for the management of public health and social issues behavior. *Journal of Marketing, 63,* 24–37.

Royne, M. A., & Levy, M. (2008). Does marketing undermine public health? *Journal of Consumer Marketing, 25,* 473–475.

Salmon, C., & Atkin, C. (2003). Using media campaigns for health promotion. In T. Thompson, A. Dorsey, K. Miller, & R. Parrott (Eds.), *Handbook of health communication* (pp. 449–472). Mahwah, NJ: Lawrence Erlbaum.

Walter, C. L. (1997). Community building practice: A conceptual framework. In M. Minkler (Ed.), *Community organizing and community building for health* (pp. 68–83). New Brunswick, NJ: Rutgers University Press.

Wise, K. (2009). Public relations and health diplomacy. *Public Relations Review, 35,* 127–129.

Wolff, T. (2001). A practitioner's guide to successful coalitions. *American Journal of Community Psychology, 29,* 173–192.

Yanovitsky, I. (2002). Effects of news coverage on policy attention and actions: A closer look into the media-policy connection. *Communication Research, 29,* 422–451.

CHAPTER 39

Community Relations and Corporate Social Responsibility

Robert L. Heath and Lan Ni

Over the years, the focus of public relations practice and scholarship has changed in dramatic as well as subtle ways. One of these changes has been to de-emphasize the functions and structures of public relations as practiced. Starting in the 1950s, agencies began to feature specialties. They not only provided public relations, public affairs, or corporate communication consulting, but also touted various specialties. One can find a huge list of specialties by looking at old business cards as well as agency flyers and advertisements. The announced specialties might feature government relations, community relations (CR), investor relations, financial relations, graphics, fund-raising, publicity, promotion, and such. Later, some added issues management and marketing communications. They might even include advertising and special event planning. Lists of agency specialization constantly change in ways that seek to connect to client needs.

Similar trends exist for public relations units in businesses (as well as in nonprofits and governmental agencies). Especially, the departments for big companies (and therefore big departments) often divide responsibilities by structure and function. These functions may also result from the strategic need to decentralize. Such decentralization might occur because companies have operating locations that pose special needs for public relations engagement. CR, therefore, might be a centralized function in the major department with specialists assigned to operating locations such as operations and plant facilities. These points of engagement can also consist of national operating facility locations owned or contracted by multinational companies.

It's common to find CR efforts, if not departments by that name, associated with, for instance, police departments. Community outreach can not only reduce friction between officers and citizens but also increase partnership relationships, where citizens work with police to fight community crime. Similar initiatives can lead to community engagement for city beautification and community cleanup.

As will be explored more in the remainder of this chapter, CR can be directly and explicitly, or by implications, associated with the continuing interest by scholars who seek to understand the requirements of relationship, community, and communitarianism. In addition, CR is a companion topic to corporate social responsibility (CSR), a term that can include a range of public relations initiatives from strategic philanthropy to risk management and communication.

Community Relations: Definition and Variations on a Theme

In this section, we define the uniqueness (as specific challenges and objectives) to the enactment of corporate/organizational public relations. CR is one of the many structures/functions that allows us to discuss the specifics of engagement in practical terms as well as being theoretically grounded.

Writing for the *Encyclopedia of Public Relations*, Neff (2005) defined CR as "largely a public relations responsibility focusing on the management of potential and existing communication interactive networks of organizations and publics for the benefit of both groups" (p. 174). This definition is foundational and functional because it blends two key themes salient in the public relations literature. It featured networks and infrastructures that can imply one-way and two-way communication. Another theme is the mutual benefit (MBR, mutually beneficial relationships; hence the logic of connecting CR and CSR) that the organization receives by having good "community relations" and operations that mutually benefit the community where operations occur.

The term *community* is used in two major ways: as a "locality—people grouped by geographic location" and as a "nongeographic community of interest—people with a common interest" (Grunig & Hunt, 1984, p. 266). These authors believe that the second definition of community actually refers to a public that arises spontaneously on a common problem or interest, regardless of geographic location. They pointed out that nearly all CR programs are designed for the first type of community. Therefore, they defined CR as "specialized public relations programs to facilitate communication between an organization and publics in its geographic locality" (p. 267).

Idioms unique or important to each era often are used to define and discuss CR, such as peacemaker, dealing with community tensions, or accommodating to diversity. Answers.com's (n.d.) definition emphasized MBR and CSR themes:

> Community relations refers to the various methods companies use to establish and maintain a mutually beneficial relationship with the communities in which they operate. The underlying principal of community relations is that when a company accepts its civic responsibility and takes an active interest in the well-being of its community, then it gains a number of long-term benefits in terms of community support, loyalty, and good will.

Boston College created a Center for Corporate Citizenship (www.bcccc.net) to conduct research and use those findings (including organizational testimony) to establish a white paper rationale for the mutual benefits of community citizenship, positive engagement that brings reciprocated endorsement. This program sees community citizenship as a management tool that connects with other related tools such as employee volunteer programs. It champions businesses that are locally owned and/or operated, hire locally, and perform community service that demonstrates a desire to build community as a foundation for relationships. Worth noting, this Center is located in the Carroll School of Management.

In this sense, CR is strategic implementation of objectives to create, maintain, enhance, and repair relationships with stakeholders and stakeseekers whose interests can be aligned with those of the organization. Apart from structure and function, CR entails the creation of socially constructed reality—the meaning-building aspect of public relations. If this only implements the organization's view of the work, the situation is likely to be less enduring than if it is mutual and cocreated. Thus, the quality of the infrastructures and the dialogue that occurs can produce a shared view, aligned interests, or a fractured relationship and divergent views and interests. These options as outcomes and challenges seem to get us to the heart of effective and ethical CR. In this sense, one standard theme of CR is to plan and act on the assumption that each day what the organization does and says should be designed to justify its being welcomed as a neighbor: Act and communicate in ways that don't take the relationship for granted but seek to understand this requirement, renew it continually, and enhance it through all that is said and done. Seek to have stakeholders and stakeseekers in the community willing to embrace and wish the organization well as a member of the community.

A brief review of public relations texts on the topic can help us understand the relevance of the concept and how it is viewed in practice—and research. In this glimpsing, we are like tourists taking snapshots of the scenes as they pass to recall our tradition on this topic rather than trying to capture the entire landscape.

In *The Practice of Public Relations*, Seitel (2001) featured the topic in his chapter on community diversity and connected it to "social responsibility." He reasoned that tangible and intangible outcomes are important, as he listed the latter: appearance, participation, stability, and pride. Cutlip, Center, and Broom (2006) touched lightly on the concept through the comments of Kern-Foxworth:

> **Community relations** must reach out to communities that include multiracial audiences and participants when planning events and selecting sponsorship partners. . . . This can include sponsoring social action programs that demonstrate understanding of the heritages of various community groups, seeking constituents' input on issues that affect their communities. (p. 46)

The description of tactics by Guth and Marsh (2009) pointed out that senior practitioners maintain "contact with local special-interest groups such as environmental organizations" whereas "new practitioners also often help coordinate special events such as tours of their organizations' facilities" (p. 36). They noted CR's connections to company charitable contributions and special events.

The theme of mutual benefit runs throughout the discussion. Baskin, Aronoff, and Lattimore (1997) featured that theme in their definition and devoted a chapter to CR, which emphasized employee volunteerism, corporate philanthropy, and special events. There was similar emphasis in Wilcox, Cameron, Ault, and Agee (2003; see also Wilcox & Cameron, 2009), who defined it as "planned activity with a community to maintain an environment that benefits both the organization and the community" (p. 10). They addressed it as a means for listening and responding to key audiences.

While acknowledging traditional themes relevant to community relationships, Heath and Coombs (2006) not only featured relational quality and mutual benefit (and thus philanthropy, including corporate sponsorship) but also emphasized the goals that

> center on doing what is necessary to improve and strengthen the community. Risk communication, for instance, is one aspect of community relationships. People who live and work in proximity to sources of danger, such as chemical companies or nuclear generation plants, want to know how safe they are and what to do in the event of an emergency. (p. 29)

Here explicitly is the confluence of CR, community risk, relationship development, aligned interests, and CSR. It is a centerpiece to solving the puzzle of crisis management, prevention, mitigation, and response. Demonstrating this point with the Texas Eastern Transmission Company Edison, New Jersey, pipeline crisis, Heath and Coombs (2006) noted that CR was the central theme to its crisis response plan: helping to restore the community, even though the company was not culpable for the explosion. And, in their response to one community's concern, the company enlisted credible commentary about the company's character from the head of the Gulf Coast United Way in Houston. Being known as a good citizen benefits marketing, hiring, and expeditious operations, as well as crisis response.

One of the few textbooks that discussed CR explicitly is Grunig and Hunt (1984). In their chapter on CR, they emphasized the interdependence of organizations and community and differentiated "expressive" (i.e., promoting organizations and showing goodwill) and "instrumental" (i.e., truly improving the community) CR activities. They stressed the value of instrumental rather than merely expressive community participation.

This brief reflection on the discussion of CR, especially in textbooks, suggests that authors see it in various ways and as serving different purposes. The centering theme, however, is that CR is a key part of the engagement of organizations (business, nonprofit—including activists, and government) with local citizens, residents, organizations, and consumers.

The troika of crisis, risk, and issues offers substantial rationale for effective CR programs, which include building community infrastructures by which citizens and officials can productively address key issues and concerns. Heath (1995) noted, for instance, the virtue of community advisory committees (CACs) and other communication opportunities in communities where substantial, but manageable, risks exist.

Where the Rubber Meets the Road

In her discussion of CR, Neff (2005) advanced the notion that it can be a strategic opportunity to benefit both parties:

> This assumes that public relations utilizes communication functions to interact with intent and commitment to create dialogue. The framework guiding this process is grounded in the concepts of the participants' rights and responsibilities and is "trim-tabbed" by the power of public opinion. (p. 174)

As such, CR has a grassroots quality, although sometimes the "astroturfing" strategy of public relations professionals can distort public dialogue and foster division rather than unity of purpose and cause. Neff (2005) reasoned that CR is not merely cosmetic but essential to "public input," issues, crisis, and network—infrastructures vital to each local environment.

In addition to communication, effective CR calls for management engagement, budgeting, and the development and implementation of standards of CSR. As such, although CR is a way for organizations to demonstrate that they play a positive role in the lives of communities, it also is a way for them to understand the expectations local residents have of what actions, policies, and commitment—aligned interests—the organization must be willing and able to implement to demonstrate its citizenship.

In general, CR exists as a structure and function, job position, or job assignment (or variations of all three), when operations call for individuals to be in close proximity to key publics/stakeholders, especially where concerns might exist on the part of community residents as well as local officials and employees about the safety of the facility operations. In such cases, CR can and probably does blend with strategic skills in crisis communication, issues management, and risk communication. This arrangement is designed so that the corporate communication and management cadre can have strategic dialogue with individuals who have interests in and special needs because of the nature of local operations. This configuration is very typical of heavy manufacturing and extraction industries, for example.

With the comments in mind that we have offered to this point, the remainder of this section explores in more detail the variations of CR to better understand in practice and through theory how CR can help create mutual benefit rather than simply be a means—basically one-way—that can use kindness to actually colonize local communities to the interest of the larger organization in its efforts to achieve its mission and vision. To this end, we feature subsections of kinds of neighbors, leading from the least challenging to the most—and probably the most mutually beneficial. We conceptualize types of CR as three kinds of neighbors. Before launching into this discussion, however, we caution against assuming that all three types might be required of a fully functioning CR program and note that even the least engaged may suffice depending on conditions, what we might call the nature of the rhetorical problem (Bitzer, 1968, 1987).

Nice Neighbor

One CR type exists that even operates with slightly different job titles on behalf of government agencies with local offices and activist/nongovernmental organization (NGO)/nonprofits. For instance, we find Federal Emergency Management officials engaged in preventive and emergency response at the local level. And NGOs often have local operatives. By this paradigm, national organizations—including businesses—have specific CR rollouts in communities where the organization operates. These kinds of units/structures/functions often are more one-way than two-way. In this situation, you might have CR programs that can even be implemented by local managers who are supplied with the communication tools to accomplish the efforts. In this configuration, we find companies, such as retail specialists, who help sponsor community activities such as fund-raisers and even community awareness efforts such as hurricane preparedness.

These sorts of CR are often used to build marketing communication relationships through reputation and goodwill strategies. Thus, we have discount stores providing school supplies to schools and school districts for needy children. Such organizations participate in events as well as sponsor them. A company, for instance, may have employees volunteer to help with a livestock show (fairs, fund-raiser walks, and other similar events—including cleanups). They might buy teenagers' livestock. They might sponsor a larger goodwill campaign, as Wrangler Western wear (www.toughenoughtowearpink.com/) sponsored a Tough Enough to Wear Pink campaign through local rodeos and livestock shows. This was a goodwill fund-raiser where local participants were acknowledged for raising funds to fight breast cancer.

The point of being a nice neighbor is to work to demonstrate that you add value to the community by participation and contribution. You put a face on the organization. For instance, a state agency might put out a sign at new road construction that announces: "Your tax dollars at work. $4,000,000 for road improvements." A manufacturing and distribution plant facility might announce the number of hours worked safely, post the phone number of the local emergency planning committee, remind the public to drive safely since schools are opening for the fall semester, or announce a fund-raiser (or similar event). Signage and notices in the local paper might remind people that the Lion's Club meets on Tuesday at noon (and periodically raises money and gathers eyeglasses for the "less fortunate"). And the list goes on.

This kind of CR relies heavily on identification (Burke, 1969) and can easily be seen as one-way. This characterization is not inherently unethical or dysfunctional since the purpose is to be a sort of town crier bringing good news and goodwill engagement to the community. Such CR programs often tout the taxes the company pays to the community, the volunteer hours and other service strategies the company employees engage in to generate goodwill, and the number of employees it employs. It may provide the company facilities for community activities (such as playgrounds, golf courses, fishing and camping facilities, or meeting rooms). Utility companies, for instance, may have large cooling ponds of which a portion is set aside for recreation. (By the way, that kind of facility can also reduce the likelihood that children and even adults will trespass and use the facility without authorization and supervision.) Such violations are best prevented or reduced by proaction that truly leads to "CR." Large companies, and even government agencies, sponsor activities such as fund-raisers. Either might sponsor with others a "walk for health." A cosponsor would likely be a nonprofit, such as the the Humane Society, one of the several major breast cancer nonprofits, and such. Large retail outlets might discount and raise funds to fight hunger (a typical activity for food chains and even mom- and- pop operations) or recover from a disaster (such as hardware stores/chains helping raise money and elicit volunteers to help recover, or participate in Habitat for Humanity). County and state highway departments are willing to foot the bill for a sign announcing that a section of road has been adopted by some group willing to pick up litter. Groups of local merchants, the local school district, a regional university, and a state agency might cosponsor a clean the beaches, or rivers, or parks, or something, day.

This nice neighbor works to be helpful and rarely engages in controversy. The outcome can be community benefit; also, the organization can benefit by having higher employee satisfaction/productivity because it is a good place to work. Since we so often see public relations as only engaged in disputes and working with angry stakeholder publics, we can forget the value of being a nice neighbor simply for the benefits that accrue to both the organization and the members of the community touched by the "kindness." However, we must also realize that the responsibility of CR can (and often does) go beyond sponsoring a Little League team, and only the most ignorant company (unreflective management) believes that Little League sponsorship is sufficient payment for unethical employment practices or toxic emissions into the air.

Good (Generous) Neighbor

This kind of neighbor is nice, but with a fuller checkbook. Strategic philanthropy is a typical corporate option. And it is not without controversy, as will be noted below in the discussion of CSR. For instance, Milton Friedman (1970) reasoned that money spent on philanthropy and unnecessarily on any "feel good" project was economically unethical. The purpose of companies is to make a profit and reward shareholders. It is not intended to be a generous citizen who spends shareholder dollars, for instance, to fight poverty, to help special needs citizens, or offer scholarships (unless the latter bring the alumni back to be productive employees).

In contrast is the kind of company or other organization that spends money on philanthropy either merely for reputation or to create the sort of community lifestyle that attracts the best and brightest employees. Generations of businesses sponsored an array of cultural events (museums, opera, symphony, concert series, theater) with a variety of motives in mind and often with little more than executive ego gratification as an outcome. Such generosity is likely to benefit some citizens, such as symphony patrons, and anger others, such as lower income people who still can't afford or don't appreciate the symphony (thus suggesting that the sponsorship might best be devoted to helping the symphony reach out to needy and talented children and members of the community who are not traditional symphony goers). Aha! So strategic philanthropy is not easy and can be counterproductive and dysfunctional.

Hall (2006) addressed the connection between strategic philanthropy and relationship building. She discovered that community members who know about company philanthropy exhibit a stronger positive relationship with the company than those who do not know about the giving. Of additional importance, those who know about the philanthropy exhibit more of a communal relationship than an exchange relationship with the sponsoring organization. But we emphasize that what community members know about the philanthropy is evaluated by their expectations: how they think it helps the community, not merely by the act of giving itself.

Good neighbors quickly learn that CR works best when the organization embraces many sponsorships and does not seem to be self-serving. Sponsorships may need to be linked with the larger effort to be reflective and responsive. Thus, members of the petrochemical industry, operating along a body of water harmed by their and other organizations, may sponsor a "bay day." It is likely to be best when it allows for issues discussion on environmental quality rather than being limited to hot dogs and softball in a park near the body of water.

Strategic philanthropy may be the price of operation, not, as Friedman (1970) argued, its destruction. As multinational companies operate abroad, and this is not a new phenomenon or merely international, they are often expected to provide community services. For instance, oil and gas companies have always been the engine in the garden, raising environmental questions with their operations and creating profits that may not be reasonably shared. The same is true for manufacturing, extraction in general, railroads, shipping, air transport, and all kinds of businesses that materially reshape communities where they operate. Reshape can be a code word for enhance or destroy. United Fruit Company became notorious for bringing roads to parts of South and Central America, but they only seemed to go where the company needed them to haul produce to market. Sponsorship and corporation colonialism are often coconspirators for damaged relationships.

A case in point is the peril of what is known as the "oil curse." As oil/gas exploration occurs in countries, companies may build roads, which are abandoned once not needed for industrial operations. Jobs and living conditions are likely to be good, until the company (or industry) moves operations. Such companies operating in countries with struggling economies and dysfunctional governments are necessarily entering waters full of piranhas. In a country such as Angola, operating companies are licensed to operate by paying various amounts of their generated revenue to the state and local governments. These can be fortunes. Corruption keeps the money from benefiting the people. NGOs and local persons, such as doctors, request expenditures from the companies for "a medical facility." Once that commitment is made, endless requests follow: nurses, more doctors, better facilities, better medical materials and equipment, and such. One day the company(ies) leave, and all that was good becomes a wreck. See a case study of Exxon's efforts (Ball, 2006).

Reflective/Responsive Neighbor

Many clues suggest that beyond the sort of feel-good aspect of CR (despite the perils of strategic philanthropy), the real significance of CR began and has continued in tandem with the corporate interest in issues management, crisis management and communication, and risk management and communication. Explicit interest in issues began in the 1960s and 1970s. Even though not explicitly using the word *issues,* Grunig and Hunt (1984) highlighted the importance of engaging in instrumental rather than expressive community participation as well as the criticality of engaging rather than avoiding controversial topics in CR (p. 278). Crisis as a practitioner cottage industry and academic topic began with Johnson & Johnson's Tylenol case. Risk management and communication became intensely studied and practiced in the late 1980s. In all, the question that drove CR became ever more clearly stated as how safe is safe and how fair is safe?

Noting changes in perception of role, practice, and outcome, Wilson (2001) saw constructive changes in how organizations, especially businesses, understood and undertook CR to the end of developing communitarian relationships. As she noted,

> Public relations counselors' role will be to ensure that the organization recognizes and accepts its responsibility to its employees, customers, and neighbors to engage in cooperative action for the growth, benefit, and improvement of the community. Corporate participation in the community will be driven by the strategic pursuit of an improved quality

> of life for all community participants, not because it is financially profitable but rather because it is the morally responsible course. (pp. 524–525)

However much she overemphasized by implication the ability of practitioners to achieve this outcome, she nevertheless rightly placed the burden of responsibility and reflection on management, including public relations. She underscored the need for proaction, planning, and execution. Both the processes and outcomes are guided by the morality of mutual interest.

In 1997, Heath connected issues, crisis, and risk drawing on a decade of research and observation of CR in the petrochemical industry, nuclear waste remediation, and use of nuclear fuel to generate electricity (see also Heath, 1995, for a discussion of how industry responds to shifting grounds of CR and CSR—an important nexus for strategic issues management). Heath featured issues management as more of a management function than more narrowly a communication function and, therefore, suggests that public relations/public affairs personnel engage with other members of senior management to shape, define, guide, and budget the organization to manage itself in troubled waters, including engagement with key stakeholders and stakeseekers.

In 2006, Lerbinger produced *Corporate Public Affairs*, which addressed, as did Heath (2006), the sociopolitical conditions that surround organizations, especially businesses, that can affect their operations. (Note that similar positioning is used to define public relations, which also can be seen as coupling with marketing communication.) Lerbinger viewed public affairs as an extension of public relations. (Note that public affairs at the corporate level often is a common departmental—structure and function—title, one that often serves as an umbrella for public relations and even marketing communication.) Lerbinger reasoned that public affairs is expected "to attain sufficient power to engage an organization to achieve preferred outcomes in the political arena and to forge and maintain a sociopolitical environment favorable to it" (p. 1).

The upshot of such overarching definitions is not trivial or academic. The point of this discussion is to give rationale for the guidance, definition, and engagement aspects of management and communication. In all this, a trend has developed that argues that management needs to be responsive and reflective, considering not only its interests but how others' interests are important to organizational and societal success.

Lerbinger (2006) did not include CR in his index but does suggest this important point of engagement through topics such as community advisory councils (CACs) and community involvement programs. Thus, one finds the following:

> The private sector has applied the principles of public participation to community relations, often using the term *community involvement.* This approach is fostered because of the proximity of local interest groups to a specific organization. Business has learned that it can gain greater freedom in finding ways to cut pollution by engaging in dialogue with government officials and environmental groups. (p. 54)

In this discussion, he noted the creation of community advisory panels through the initiative of the Chemical Manufacturers Association (now the American Chemistry Council) in the 1990s. For an in-depth history of these infrastructural risk communication and community organization trends (see Palenchar, 2009).

The discussion of CR as part of the excellence tradition also features key aspects of infrastructure. Rhee's (2007) case study investigated Brookhaven National Laboratory's (BNL's) release of strontium 90 and tritium into the environment, particularly water sources. After fighting complaints and lawsuits and battling scandal, the lab capitulated and engaged in environmental cleanup; those activities were reported and monitored through CACs. Rhee observed that "BNL developed [a] CAC as a forum for it to interact with the community on a regular basis. During and after the crisis, the CAC meetings served to create relationships between the lab and the different community groups" (p. 105). This case features a reactionary use of CACs rather than something more proactive to engage with the community before risks become crises and manifest themselves into issues (Heath, 1995; Heath & Palenchar, 2009).

For this sort of CR to work, and mature into something that is mutually beneficial, the organization's management must first of all be committed to be reflective and responsive. Success may, and often does, require continual definition, redefinition, deployment, and redeployment of standards of CSR. This then becomes an excellent means for monitoring issues as they are discussed by participants. And these infrastructures provide the basis for discussions of fact, value, and policy as a step toward collaborative decision making and alignment of interests (Heath & Palenchar, 2009). If operated properly, they can foster mutual interests instead of breeding or exacerbating antagonism. The goal is to create and maintain processes of dialogue that achieve concurrence, shared knowledge, and meaning, if not consensus.

Insights into ways to create useful CR (sensitive to crises, issues, and risks) have increased over the years and continue to be refined. Rowan, Botan, Kreps, Samoilenko, and Farnsworth (2009) noted the number of contexts in which community outreach was either required or engaged in voluntarily: Community Right to Know, guidelines for and from Centers for Disease Control, and state or federal licensing, such as that to design, build, and operate a nuclear generating facility or petrochemical facility; waste (including nuclear waste) remediation, which often requires community input; Superfund Recovery guidelines for specific community engagement; and the list goes on and on.

A generic occupational category has grown because of legislation, regulation, and company initiatives: emergency management. Such individuals are part of a troika of CR efforts: senior management (at least at the site, such as plant or facility manager), emergency manager (with various discipline backgrounds such as environmental expert or plant/operations safety officer), and the communication specialist or team. In such settings, Rowan et al. (2009) offered guidelines for the education of logical emergency managers based on the CAUSE model for research, education, and outreach: Confidence, Awareness, Understanding, Satisfaction (with proposed solutions), and Enactment, or moving from agreement to action. Work such as that by Rowan and her team is often accomplished through collaboration between companies, activist/NGOs, and government officials such as the Environmental Protection Agency or the Nuclear Regulatory Commission.

McComas, Arvai, and Besley (2009) centered their examination of risk communication on the public sphere to understand why public engagement on risk succeeds or fails. One of the difficulties with this sort of discourse is its dependence on technical, even highly technical, data and sophisticated analysis. Understanding, therefore, is one substantial challenge. Another is motivating stakeholders to participate. They can see such CR events as marginalizing rather than engaging primarily because it is technical and sponsored by the organizations who have an interest in achieving support for their operations. Thus, CR requires understandable analysis, often requiring independent third parties' opinions and various motivations: rational, socioeconomic, and relational. If the community is to be engaged, alternatives considering ends and means need to be discussed. This dialogic approach seems best as opposed to one where the sponsoring company "sells" its preferred alternative.

In these ways, CR at the highest level of responsiveness and with reflection needs a communitarian to drive the discourse. As have others, Heath and Palenchar (2009) recommend that the character of the organization engaging in CR is important; mutual empowerment is imperative. Thus, based on decades of research, they offer 14 guidelines, including the following:

> Accept the desire on the part of key publics to exert control over factors they worry affect them and other entities for which they have concern.

> Collaborate with them to engage in information gathering, risk assessment, and risk control.
>
> Recognize the value-laden personalized decision process they apply and frame the risk assessment accordingly. (pp. 342–343)

The process of being a responsive/reflective neighbor requires engagement, patience, and empowerment. The goal is a stronger community, not just a more profitable company. Part of this commitment requires constant refinement of health, safety, and environmental (HSE) policy, as well as transparent reporting of the objectives, standards, measures, and success in this regard.

Connecting CR and CSR

This brief overview, which features metaphorically types of neighbors enacted through CR, sets the stage for the remainder of this chapter. It is intended to help the reader appreciate the strategic logic of organizations that designate units and personnel with the specific mission of making contact, for various outcomes, with key local publics. With that in mind, the next section delves into the strategic logic of CR with marketing communication, reputation building/maintenance, crisis management/communication, risk management/communication, and issues management purposes/objectives. This matrix of specialties fits within the organization's mission and vision and its larger philosophy of public relations (public affairs or corporate communication).

That said, why connect this topic with a discussion of CSR? The simplest answer is that CSR strategically and ethically has a very local connection if, for instance, the company commits to a high standard of environmental responsibility that requires budgeting and management policy from the executive level—from the headquarters. But such commitment and policy, however management or community centered, always rolls out at the local levels. This is true for petrochemical and refinery operations, for instance. In that industry, public health and safety are real challenges, and continual engagement is crucial. Local connections are vital to bring the organization, similar organizations, community residents, local government, and NGOs into meaningful dialogue. Events, often central to reputation management, occur at the local level. Community standards, public norms, local customs, and community dynamics are essential to successful CSR programs, which invariably link to savvy CR programs. For an extensive discussion of CSR and public relations, see the Institute for Public Relations (www.instituteforpr.org/essential_knowledge/list/category/Corporate%20Social%20Responsibility/)

Lerbinger (2006) is one of many academics and practitioners who see CSR as an essential rather than peripheral aspect of community engagement. He offered the Pyramid of CSR as a set of guidelines for public affairs engagement:

> 1. Perform basic economic function of producing goods and services for society, and, thereby, also provide jobs.
> 2. Minimize the social costs imposed on society [by the organization's operations].
> 3. Help solve social problems.
> 4. Make social investments to strengthen society's infrastructure.
> 5. Support public policies that are in the public interest. (p. 408)

In this discussion, he cautioned that Friedman's and others' admonition against CSR is narrow, dysfunctional, and counterproductive to profit optimization.

Even the briefest review of CSR literature suggests that it goes in many directions and makes different assumptions. Some discussants feature CSR as having marketing value; companies profit from CSR reputations (see, e.g., Gildea, 1994–1995; Kotler & Lee, 2005). At minimum, this approach to CSR and CR would feature the company as being a nice neighbor.

Other discussants feature more of an ethical than pragmatic, profit-orientated approach. They argue, for instance, that the organization needs to apply revenue to build a better community and even to solve local problems. Here we have that range of strategic philanthropy from supporting cultural events to solving collective problems, which might extend to financial support (beyond taxes) for public schools and even for scholarships (see, e.g., Ihlen, 2005; Sen, Bhattacharya, & Korschun, 2006).

Finally, we have the CSR challenge of the responsive/reflective neighbor (Mahon & McGowan, 1991; Rochlin, Witter, Monaghan, & Murray, 2005). Battles over the past 40 years in corporate America have revealed that activism, and even government policy (regulation, legislation, and litigation), result when the operating standards of companies fall short of community expectations. The standards of HSE, as noted above, result from concerns that business operations harm health, safety, and environmental quality. Organizations can attempt to disprove such concerns or prove that the organization meets the expected standards. So goes CR, but it may require changing policy (budgeting and management policy) to operate at a higher level, so that the community standards are not offended and their expectations are met.

Conclusion

Among the richest theoretical foundations and research agendas for CR are those that connect it to the rich bodies of literature in crisis communication, risk management and communication, and issues management. It draws on the enormous discussion of CSR.

The purpose of this chapter is to expand the examination and appreciation of CR and to foster additional theorizing, research, and best practices. At minimum, this chapter is useful to organizations seeking to know local opinions and expectations of what the company or other organization needs to think and do to be a nice neighbor. But it also presumes that more can be expected to build, maintain, and repair relationships between the organization and the community where it operates. The organization needs to consider what is expected for it to be good, as well as responsive and reflective. Thus, CR is not merely a communication activity but begins with management policy and decision making with the desire to be a constructive member of each community where it operates: local, regional, national, and global. For these reasons, public relations, through CR and CSR efforts, has an excellent opportunity, but a daunting challenge, to make society more fully functioning (Heath, 2006). Heath's (2006) article includes the following premise:

> To help society to become more fully functioning, managements of organizations (for profit, nonprofit, and governmental) must demonstrate the characteristics that foster legitimacy, such as being reflective; being willing to consider and instrumentally advance others' interests; being collaborative in decision making; being proactive and responsive to others' communication and opinion needs; and working to meet or exceed the requirements of relationship management, including being a good corporate citizen. (p. 100)

References

Answers.com. (n.d.). Retrieved August 17, 2009, from www.answers.com/topic/community-relations

Ball, J. (2006, January 10). As Exxon pursues African oil, charity becomes a political issue. *Wall Street Journal,* pp. A1, A10.

Baskin, O., Aronoff, C., & Lattimore, D. (1997). *Public relations: The profession and the practice.* Madison, WI: Brown & Benchmark.

Bitzer, L. (1968). The rhetorical situation. *Philosophy and Rhetoric, 1,* 1–15.

Bitzer, L. (1987). Rhetorical public communication. *Critical Studies in Mass Communication, 4,* 425–428.

Burke, K. (1969). *A rhetoric of motives.* Berkeley: University of California Press.

Cutlip, S. M., Center, A. H., & Broom, G. M. (2006). *Effective public relations* (9th ed.). Upper Saddle River, NJ: Prentice Hall.

Friedman, M. (1970, September 13). The social responsibility of business is to increase its profits. *New York Times,* pp. 122–126.

Gildea, R. L. (1994–1995). Consumer survey confirms corporate social action affects buying decisions. *Public Relations Quarterly, 39*(4), 20–21.

Grunig, J. E., & Hunt, T. (1984). *Managing public relations.* New York: Holt, Rinehart, & Winston.

Guth, D. W., & Marsh, C. (2009). *Public relations: A values-driven approach* (4th ed.). Boston: Pearson.

Hall, M. R. (2006). Corporate philanthropy and corporate community relations: Measuring relationship-building results. *Journal of Public Relations Research, 18,* 1–21.

Heath, R. L. (1995). Corporate environmental risk communication: Cases and practices along the Texas Gulf Coast. In B. R. Burleson (Ed.), *Communication yearbook 18* (pp. 255–277). Thousand Oaks, CA: Sage.

Heath, R. L. (1997). *Strategic issues management: Organizations and public policy challenges.* Thousand Oaks, CA: Sage.

Heath, R. L. (2006). Onward into more fog: Thoughts on public relations' research directions. *Journal of Public Relations Research, 18,* 93–114.

Heath, R. L., & Coombs, W. T. (2006). *Today's public relations: An introduction.* Thousand Oaks, CA: Sage.

Heath, R. L., & Palenchar, M. J. (2009). *Strategic issues management: Organizations and public policy challenges* (2nd ed.). Thousand Oaks, CA: Sage.

Ihlen, O. (2005). The power of social capital: Adapting Bourdieu to the study of public relations. *Public Relations Review, 31,* 492–496.

Kotler, R., & Lee, N. (2005). *Corporate social responsibility.* Hoboken, NJ: Wiley.

Lerbinger, O. (2006). *Corporate public affairs: Interacting with interest groups, media, and government.* Mahwah, NJ: Lawrence Erlbaum.

Mahon, J. F., & McGowan, R. A. (1991). Searching for the common good: A process-oriented approach. *Business Horizons, 34*(4), 79–86.

McComas, K. A., Arvai, J., & Besley, J. C. (2009). Linking public participation and decision making through risk communication. In R. L. Heath & H. D. O'Hair (Eds.), *Handbook of risk and crisis communication* (pp. 364–385). New York: Routledge.

Neff, B. D. (2005). Community relations. In R. L. Heath (Ed.), *Encyclopedia of public relations* (pp. 174–177). Thousand Oaks, CA: Sage.

Palenchar, M. J. (2009). Historical trends of risk and crisis communication. In R. L. Heath & H. D. O'Hair (Eds.), *Handbook of risk and crisis communication* (pp. 31–52). New York: Routledge.

Rhee, Y. (2007). Interpersonal communication as an element of symmetrical public relations: A case study. In E. L. Toth (Ed.), *The future of excellence in public relations and communication management: Challenges for the next generation* (pp. 103–117). Mahwah, NJ: Lawrence Erlbaum.

Rochlin, S., Witter, K., Monaghan, P., & Murray, V. (2005). Putting the corporate into corporate responsibility. In P. Raymond (Ed.), *Accountability forum: Corporate responsibility and core business* (pp. 5–13). London: Greenleaf.

Rowan, K. E., Botan, C. H., Kreps, G. L., Samoilenko, S., & Farnsworth, K. (2009). Risk communication education for local emergency managers: Using the CAUSE Model for research, education, and outreach. In R. L. Heath & H. D. O'Hair (Eds.), *Handbook of risk and crisis communication* (pp. 168–191). New York: Routledge.

Seitel, F. P. (2001). *The practice of public relations* (8th ed.). Upper Saddle River, NJ: Prentice Hall.

Sen, S., Bhattacharya, C. B., & Korschun, D. (2006). The role of corporate social responsibility in strengthening multiple stakeholder relationships: A field experiment. *Journal of the Academy of Marketing Science, 34,* 158–166.

Wilcox, D. L., & Cameron, G. T. (2009). *Public relations: Strategies and tactics* (9th ed.). Boston: Pearson.

Wilcox, D. L., Cameron, G. T., Ault, P. H., & Agee, W. K. (2003). *Public relations: Strategies and tactics* (7th ed.). Boston: Pearson.

Wilson, L. J. (2001). Relationships within communities: Public relations for the new century. In R. L. Heath (Ed.), *Handbook of public relations* (pp. 521–526). Thousand Oaks, CA: Sage.

CHAPTER 40

The Nature of Good in Public Relations

What Should Be Its Normative Ethic?

Shannon A. Bowen

> *The discovery of what is true and the practice of that which is good, are the two most important aims of philosophy.*
>
> —Voltaire (Goodman, 1997)

Consider, for a moment, the ontological nature of good. How do you know that something is good? What makes an action worthy of being termed *good*? What do we really *mean* when we say the word *good*? Do we define good through its own intrinsic qualities or as outcomes that it creates? When the nature of public relations is assessed, is it intrinsically good or evil? From that nature, can a normative ethics for the field be derived?

Communication is among that class we can call good or morally worthy in the eyes of philosophers who closely examine the question. It creates bonds between humankind, it allows us to organize, share, and record knowledge; communication makes it possible to thrive and produce rather than to simply exist. One can say that communication is then good, although it does not foster thriving alone in a vacuum, as other factors that one might also consider good must be present. But focusing on communication allows scholars to see the worthy nature of the enterprise, the exchange and order it creates, as the backbone of society.

Communication creates a thriving, industrious society, and one can therefore say that that is a good. Does the outcome of thriving mean that a concept is good? Consider the weeds thriving in your garden, and you will quickly see the problem

Author's Note: Acknowledgment is due to the profound work of the philosopher W. David Ross on the moral nature of good and right actions. His book *The Right and the Good* (1930/2002) inspired this chapter.

with this argument. There must be something more to communication than thriving industriousness to make it one among the good. Is it because it is a tool of building relationships? And cannot communication also be used for evil purposes, such as lying, malicious gossip, perjury, and many forms of deceit? Despite these and other drawbacks, communication can still be considered among the good.

Without communication, we could not examine matters in depth. We could not analyze, explain, justify, contemplate, and dissect ideas until we discover the truth based on the rational analysis of a situation, phenomenon, specimen, or cause. Communication can be said to be an inherent good because in its purest form—that is, of good intent as opposed to deceit or malice—it leads to the shared creation of knowledge and truth.

What is the good in public relations? Is it good because it is a form of communication, or is it a weed among the roses? Can it *both* build trust and persuade? These questions haunt the public relations industry and its practitioners, those who hire public relations agencies, and the scholars who study ethics in public relations. By exploring the nature of good in public relations, I seek to help clarify what we really mean when we say "public relations ethics."

Defining the Field

Examining some leading definitions allows the critical scholar to understand if authors assume that public relations is ethical or unethical, if they use words implying duty or obligation versus public good to tell us what form of ethics they might prefer, or if an asymmetrical or symmetrical worldview underlies these definitions.

Among the hundreds of definitions of public relations, Heath and Coombs (2006) defined it in this manner:

> Public relations is the management function that entails planning, research, publicity, promotion, and collaborative decision-making to help any organization's ability to listen to, appreciate, and respond appropriately to those persons and groups whose mutually beneficial relationships the organization needs to foster as it strives to achieve its mission and vision. (p. 7)

Their definition is accurate and comprehensive and includes an ethical vision for the role of public relations in building collaborative decisions and appreciating publics, akin to the duty of respect to which many ethicists obligate communicators. Heath and Coombs's (2006) definition is normative in that it relies on relationships being mutually beneficial—an ideal state for relationships but one not always possible to achieve. Class action lawsuits, boycotts, and other problems, with mutually beneficial relationships, are common in the relationships between organizations and publics. Still, the value of the definition offered by Heath and Coombs is that it includes the ethical concept of collaboration, meaning that publics have participative control over the decisions that affect them. Also, the ethical concepts of listening and appreciating are highly valued by modern philosophers in both rationalist and deontological traditions.

In offering an ethically rounded discussion of how to define public relations, Heath and Coombs (2006) emphasized a "smart" approach to public relations. Smart is an acronym the authors designed to remind public relations practitioners to think of these considerations:

- Societal value and meaning—focusing on the consequences an action can have on society
- Mutually beneficial relationships—fostering the interests of all involved parties
- Advantages through objectives—achieving certain goals based on motivating action and shared interests
- Rhetorical strategies—strategic planning using certain messages and tactics to achieve desired objectives

- Tactics—strategy should drive which tools, such as news releases or publicity events, practitioners use (2006, p. 3).

Three of the five guidelines Heath and Coombs (2006) included in their smart acronym can be said to have originated with moral philosophy: (1) societal value and meaning, a utilitarian construct for measuring the impact that certain decisions have on members of society; (2) mutually beneficial relationships fostering the interests of involved parties, which is said to be ethical because it is based on dialogue and understanding rather than only on self-interest; and (3) rhetorical strategies that are based on ancient rhetoric in which the person of character speaks on behalf of an idea in pursuit of truth.

Offering another definition, Cameron, Wilcox, Reber, and Shin (2008) wrote that public relations is "the management of competition and conflict on behalf of one's organization, and when possible, also in the interests of the publics that impact the organization" (p. xv). This definition addresses the problem common in other definitions that relationships cannot always be mutually beneficial but should seek to foster the interests of all parties when possible. However, this definition also takes a decidedly competitive approach that leaves much of how to manage the competition and conflict up to the ethics of the individual, which is at times a risky proposition.

A text by Newsom, Turk, and Kruckeberg (2004) defined public relations thus: "As a management function, public relations involves responsibility and responsiveness in policy and information to the best interests of the organization and its publics" (p. 2). This definition focuses on responsibility and responsiveness in public relations, therefore encouraging ethical behavior. The definition is normative because it obligates one to act in the best interest of both the organization and its publics, which could be impossible if those interests are diametrically opposed. The definition does not say to whom the practitioners are to be responsible, leaving in question whether that responsibility is first to the organization and second to publics or vice versa. However, this definition does hold that responsibility is to be considered an intrinsic good of public relations. It also specifies that responsiveness is a good, building on the rhetorical paradigm of enhancing dialogue.

A classic definition of public relations from J. E. Grunig and Hunt (1984) offered that public relations is "the management of communication between an organization and its publics" (p. 4). They do not obligate public relations to be practiced in the interest of any particular party, nor to be mutually beneficial. By placing the field squarely in a management discipline, they allow the autonomy necessary for ethical decision making, but they do not specify a normative ethic to be ascribed.

This brief review of definitions suggests that a normative or aspirational ethic for public relations can be achieved. These scholars hold that public relations can contribute to the good of society by building discussion. Reviewing the ethical constructs within each definition, we can say that the ethical nature of the good (Ross, 1930/2002) in public relations exists within the following concepts:

- Collaborative decision making
- Listening and appreciating
- Social value and meaning
- Dialogue and responsiveness
- Managing competition and conflict
- Responsibility
- Autonomy

These concepts define the nature of "good" in public relations, as seen in the definitions offered by leaders in the field. These definitions aspire to explain how public relations functions should ideally be conducted. They abhor dishonesty, vociferous advocacy, spin, or manipulation among "the good" and valuable aspects of public relations within society; however, we know that these activities happen every day. Researchers

(Bowen et al., 2006; Parsons, 2004) found little ethics training in public relations except among managers at the higher levels of their organizations, who act as ethics counselors as part of their role in issues management. Furthermore, a higher level of moral reasoning is reported among public relations practitioners with more years of experience in the field (Baker & Martinson, 2002; Wright, 1985).

Determining the Nature of Good in Public Relations

By examining the concepts bulleted in the list above as being inherently good in public relations and discussing them in the sense of what they mean in moral philosophy or ethics, this section offers understanding of the nature of good as a normative ethic for public relations. Three concepts from the literature of moral philosophy will be added to those already discussed, and a model illustrating their integration and use in an organization as reflective management will be offered later in this chapter (Figure 40.1). Reflective management builds on the work of van Ruler and Verčič (2005). This model of management can be used by scholars to discuss and research topics related to ethics and as a guide to enhance the ability of practitioners to conduct ethical public relations.

Figure 40.1 The Reflective Model of Ethical Public Relations Management in an Organization

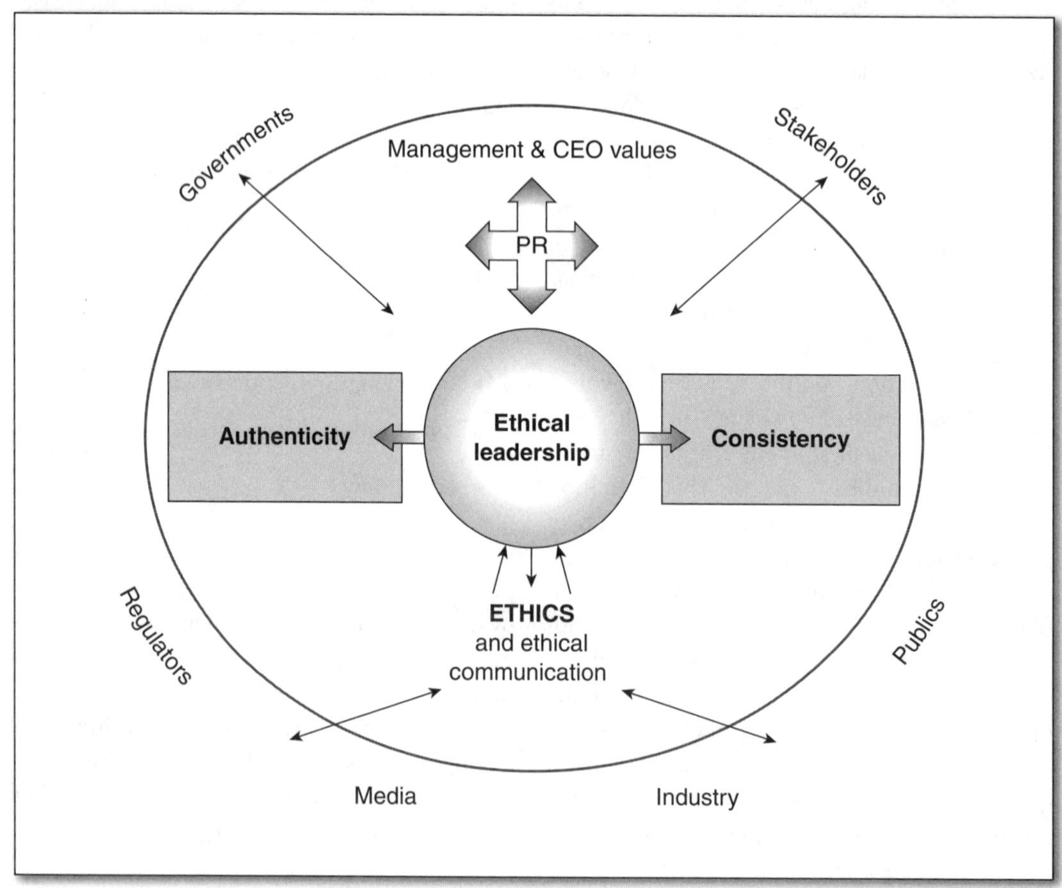

Collaborative or Integrative Decision Making

Collaborative decision making is thought to be inherently ethical because it allows people to share in creating their own destiny rather than having that outcome decided arbitrarily by others. Creating integrative decisions, or agreements, which integrate the interests of others, is a method of problem solving that has been shown over time to create more enduring and satisfying decisions than those made from a one-sided perspective (Lewicki, Litterer, Saunders, & Minton, 1993). From a moral philosophy perspective, collaborative decision making is often defined as good because it respects the interests of other parties rather than basing a decision in one entity's self-interest alone. Collaborative or integrative decisions are arrived at through using dialogue to discuss and align interests, creating ethics "in and through communication" (Jovanovic & Wood, 2006, p. 389). Although more will be said about dialogue in a few sections, collaborative decision making constitutes an ethical good according to philosophers: Bakhtin (1993) saw it as communicative action in creating a world of life and Buber (1970) saw it as an equalizing force between parties, demanding equal consideration and respect from each.

The collaborative decision-making process is often termed *symmetrical public relations.* Symmetrical public relations should be interactive and built to maintain the interests of both parties. L. A. Grunig, Grunig, and Dozier (2002) explained that symmetrical relationships "balance the interests of the organizations with the interests of publics on which the organization has consequences and that have consequences on the organization" (p. 11). Kent and Taylor (2002) stressed the collaborative aspect of dialogue, noting that it is a conversation in which both sides have a viewpoint but remain interested and open to the view of others.

Listening and Appreciating

Listening is inadequately studied in public relations scholarship. The listening scholar Andy Wolvin pointed out the inherently ethical nature of listening when he said that it respects the value of the view from another perspective (A. Wolvin, personal communication, April 17, 2005). Wolvin and Coakley (1996) reviewed several studies and found that "we spend more time listening than we spend in any other form of verbal communication" (p. 14), concluding that "listening plays a vital role in our lives" (p. 15) and even "influences personal development" (p. 19). The inherently good nature of true, active listening is rooted in the moral philosophy of respect and value for the rational analysis, views, or being of "the other" (Levinas, 1990). The ethics of care discussed by the philosopher Seyla Benhabib (1992) and the developmental psychologist Carol Gilligan (1982) builds on the concept of listening as an ethical act, as does the concept of empathetic dialogue (Kent & Taylor, 2002). Listening is a foundational part of the public relations process for idea formation, environmental scanning, understanding the values of publics, and cocreating meaning on which to move forward in strategic management.

Appreciating is also a value that is rooted in the moral-philosophical conception of respect (Acton, 1970; Sullivan, 1989) for publics, both internal and external to the organization and to the decision maker. Appreciating requires ascribing inherent value to publics simply because they exist, thus upholding the value of equality. It implies appreciating the value of the relationship even though it might not be one of financial significance to the organization. Appreciating the divergence of ideas, of thought, and of values and solutions to common problems can form the basis of a collaborative relationship between an organization and publics. Appreciating publics for the humanity they bring to an organization values the internal publics whose human capital contributes to its output and efficacy, drives its mission, and contributes to its success or failure. Appreciation is deeply related to the Kantian conceptualization of respect; appreciation implies an outward manifestation of that respect, through an appreciative attitude, action, stance, or response.

Social Value and Meaning

Understanding the social value and meaning of public relations holds the inherent notion that the function does have a positive and useful role in society. Scholars (Heath, 2006; van Ruler & Verčič, 2005) would prefer that role to be a prosocial one, meaning that the function encompasses an important social function that allows publics to know, understand, and interact effectively with organizations. The consequences on society of any organization's (big or small, governmental, for profit, or nonprofit) mission can therefore be communicated with publics, because it is these consequences that create issues for publics (J. E. Grunig & Repper, 1992). As a social value of public relations, those publics can have some governing hand in the way in which organizations operate—the moral good of collaborative decision making.

A deeper moral analysis reveals that the public relations function does perform the role of information provider, news provider, and liaison and also fosters an open exchange of information between organizations, governments, and publics in society (Spicer, 2000). Truthful and accurate information must flow in society for democracy to operate (Day, 1997). The implications of public relations functioning in this manner are greater personal involvement in the governing, prioritizing, value formation, norm setting, and operations of organizations within society. That involvement of individuals supports the ideal of an informed and fair democratic process (Heath, 2006), which we can say is a moral good. Removing the understanding necessary for involvement in informed decision making or the power of liberty that such a system entails can be said to be unethical because it does not respect the rationality or dignity of the individual. In this sense, public relations can be defined as good because it enhances individual moral autonomy, informed rational decision making, and the liberty of choice that is the backbone of a democratic society. Public relations itself does not guarantee moral autonomy and informed rational decision making, but it must exist within each complex society as a necessary condition for the survival and thriving of those democratic ideals. In a system with one voice or with government-controlled public relations, the diversity of ideas needed for an informed, rational decision are withheld from the public. Such denial of moral agency is unethical because it offers neither respect and dignity nor recognition of the rational autonomy necessary in making an informed choice. Given that restriction, this analysis can conclude that public relations is both a necessary and inherently good social process when it respects autonomy, rationality, and the liberty of informed decision making and governance.

Dialogue and Responsiveness

Philosophers have long considered the concept of "dialogue" imbued with inherent goodness or moral worth. The repeated appearance of the term *dialogue* in both the definitions of public relations and within the body of knowledge shows that communication scholars value its inherent good. Definitions of public relations mention the term *responsiveness* as a core value of the function, and the mutuality of dialogue necessitates a responsive communication function as an inherent good. Responsiveness can also be thought of in the co-orientational sense of dialogue studied by Ron Pearson (1989a, 1989b), who described dialogue as an ethic to guide public relations.

Responsiveness can also be thought of as engagement (Heath, 2001). Richard Edelman (2009) defined public engagement as the "reassessment of corporate policy and continuous communication" (p. 3). Engagement can take place with an idea, an issue of concern, or a public. The ethical aspect of engagement affords value and importance within management to publics and their causes; it recognizes the initiative to seek information and the moral autonomy of publics. Conducting public relations in a manner of authentic engagement means that publics are respected for their moral autonomy rather than being viewed as simply uninformed people to be persuaded to the organization's point of view or as critics to be assuaged by accommodation. Therefore, responsiveness or engagement is an inherently ethical concept because respect and moral autonomy are maintained.

Deontological philosophers like Immanuel Kant (1793/1974) viewed the term *dialogue* as good because it maintains dignity and respect for others. Following Kant, Habermas (1987) argued that dialogue is good because it fulfills our moral obligation under deontology, because all people are obligated equally by rationality and thus equally worthy of dialogue. Buber (1970) argued that dialogue creates all real living as seen through what he called the I-Thou connection. Buber's I-Thou dialogue is characterized by "mutuality, directness, intensity, and ineffability" (Friedman, 2002, p. 65). According to Friedman (2002), the culmination of Buber's (1970) philosophy was to explain the "sphere of between" as a basic reality of the interdependence of human existence. Buber argued that "the participation of both partners is in principle indispensable to this sphere" that he called "the dialogical" (p. 98). For Buber, the ultimate good is created when dialogue is genuine and creates "authentic existence" (p. 100). Authentic existence is discussed in the public relations literature as authenticity and as an inherent good in moral philosophy. For its creation of genuine dialogue, and thus authenticity, public relations can be said to be inherently good.

Managing Competition and Conflict

Public relations as the management of competition and conflict can be supported through the moral philosophy of justice, again with the caveat that the communicator must be honest. Philosophers since Plato have maintained that justice is a core component of a healthy society. Plato named justice as the most important cardinal virtue in *The Republic*, along with the other cardinal virtues of wisdom, courage, and temperance (Plaisance, 2009). Justice implies fairness, responsibility, and the participation of organizations and publics. Ross (1930/2002) argued that a basic moral obligation of all humans is to bring about justice. Rawls's (1971) well-known theory of justice requires the ethical decision maker to use what he called the "veil of ignorance" so that he or she would be stripped of social position, rank, and identity, blind to the consequences of a decision, yet potentially affected by the decision. His theory of justice seeks to include the concepts of objectivity, impartiality, and reversibility in a less abstract and more useful, real-world model than found in prior philosophy. Benhabib (1992) and Gilligan (1982) each, separately, added perspectives of care for a generalized other to the concept of justice.

The real question in this analysis is "Do public relations practitioners consider justice when they manage competition and conflict or do they consider only creating an advantage and achieving a self-interested win?" Normatively, public relations practitioners would place themselves behind a veil of ignorance when considering their activities. The evidence (Bowen et al., 2006) suggests that only the highest level decision makers within the public relations profession actively consider concepts of justice in their decision making and that those at lower levels of responsibility most often consider creating advantage through persuasive advocacy.

A large part of the practice of public relations engages in managing conflict and leading change (Rawlins & Stoker, 2003). Normatively, public relations professionals would consider their role in creating justice through the management of competition and conflict. In failing to create fairness or justice, practitioners do not meet the standard of inherent good. Those at higher levels of responsibility, approximately 29.8% of practitioners worldwide (Bowen et al., 2006), who report directly to CEOs (chief executive officers), are in a position to enhance justice or level the playing field of competition and conflict. Normatively, public relations can and should embrace that role as part of the inherent value creation and worth of the field.

Responsibility

Responsibility is a foundational principle within a moral philosophy, as developed by Kant (1781/1997) and numerous other scholars. Responsibility, in moral philosophy, is often discussed in conjunction with the term *duty*, and the two concepts are often used interchangeably (Sullivan, 1989). Kant (1785/1993) explained that moral law obligates each rational decision maker equally to do his or her duty to uphold moral principle. Kantian scholars (Baron, 1995; Bennett, 1966; Paton, 1927; Sullivan, 1989) discuss responsibility, accountability, attribution, and judgment as central concepts in understanding duty. Responsibility or duty is a commitment to taking the action that is right. Baron explained, "One governs one's conduct by a commitment to doing what is right and be(ing) prepared so to act even in the face of strong opposing desires" (p. 132). Duty provides the motive to act on that which is encouraged by moral considerations. Acting from a basis of responsibility does not need to be the only consideration in a decision-making process for public relations practitioners, but it does need to be one of them. Baron elucidated that point: "We can value the motive of duty without placing special value on acting from duty as a primary motive" (p. 133). In public relations, it is a complex interplay between the duties required to employers, clients, publics, the media, and regulatory agencies or other governmental officials. Acting from responsibility or duty means that the public relations practitioner must consider the duties that exist on an equal footing, without preferential treatment or bias for selfish desires, motives of greed, or fear of retribution.

A duty to do that which is morally right means that each practitioner must rationally consider all the viewpoints as equal and decide the correct course of action based on ethical duties that go beyond capriciousness, selfishness, or other biased concerns. In this sense, public relations has inherent goodness when practitioners consider the divided loyalties that come with the field and regard their responsibility as doing that which is morally right. Preliminary research (Lieber, 2008) has "yielded tangible data that a duty to society rationale is, in fact, a part of everyday public relations" (p. 249), although we do not know how that reasoning occurs.

The nature of public relations is good only if and when practitioners ask, "Does my action have moral worth?" (Baron, 1995). That consideration does not mean that an action must be done against one's will, without regard for the self and without regard for inclination. Self and inclination must be regarded equally along with other considerations. Baron (1995) argued that the "presence of inclination is consistent with the actions being done from duty, and thus having moral worth" (p. 152). If those in public relations consider it a duty or responsibility to do what is right in upholding moral law, not just what is right for a client or employer, then the field has moral worth. This weighty responsibility brings with it the obligation of veracity, or honesty and truthfulness, in public relations.

Autonomy

Bivins (2006) noted the link between responsibility and autonomy and argued that the role of an autonomous professional presumes objectivity "to use reason to determine action" (p. 27). Autonomy can be seen in J. E. Grunig and Hunt's (1984) definition of public relations as a management function. In that definition, management has the autonomy to determine what constitutes a morally good action, considering the interests of publics in addition to those of the organization, including profit margin. Philosophers argue that autonomy is necessary to base impartial judgment on principle alone rather than on selfish concerns.

The idea of autonomy stems from Immanuel Kant, who argued that moral agency rests with autonomy's basis in the ability for rational analysis, which separates man from beast (Kant,

1785/1964). In explaining Kant's (1783/1977) moral theory, Sullivan (1994) argued that each person "has the power of autonomy and therefore the right and the responsibility to be self-governing, in control of his or her own destiny in so far as that is possible" (pp. 22–23). By freeing ourselves from the constraints of only satisfying organizational goals, only creating mutually beneficial goals, or only accommodating the needs of publics, being an autonomous and rational manager implies that public relations can do what is best based on a moral analysis alone.

Autonomy requires access to truthful and accurate information and an honesty on behalf of the communicator. Public relations practitioners must be honest and truthful not only because deception damages an organization's reputation and diminishes relationships with publics and stakeholders but also because honest communication is the only morally worthy way of communicating. Day (1997) wrote,

> The notion of individual autonomy is based, in part, on freedom of choice.... First, a lack of integrity in human communications undermines the autonomy of the individual. As rational beings, we depend on truthful and accurate information to make informed judgments about a whole host of activities; ... a lack of veracity among advertising and public relations practitioners would understandably create a climate of public distrust of the business community. (pp. 74–75)

Public relations is uniquely suited to conduct an autonomous moral analysis within an organization because it maintains relationships with internal publics (employees) and external publics (people outside its boundary). Those relationships allow it to know and understand the values of many varied publics around the organization, not just those limited to one organizational function such as marketing understanding consumers or legal understanding regulatory requirements. Therefore, it can include those interests in organizational decision making on an equal basis with the interests of management and finance in a rational, responsible, and thoroughly considered deliberation about what constitutes the morally worthy action—or what is the right thing to do. Only a communication manager with the autonomy to stand up to the CEO or others in management and who can voice disagreement with a decision that may be unethical is truly contributing to the responsible and effective management of the organization.

New Factors of Ethical Public Relations

As a normative pursuit, the field brings value and meaning to society by fostering collaborative decision making, listening, and appreciating while respecting others; offering information within a democratic society; creating dialogue and responsiveness; managing competition, conflict, and divided loyalties through duty and responsibility; and maintaining an independent or autonomous perspective to use in the analysis of organizational decisions. Each of those factors interacts within the "sphere" of an organization in its environment, with communication flowing symmetrically to create ethically responsible organizations.

Before an ethic of reflective management can be firmly established as a normative guide for the field based on the inherent good it pursues, we must include concepts from moral philosophy that are thought to be inherently good in and of themselves. Thus, three considerations remain to be added to create a thorough understanding of the normative ethic of public relations practice: ethical leadership, authenticity, and consistency. Each is discussed below, and Figure 40.1 conceptualizes how these factors interact within an organization to create ethical public relations.

Ethical Leadership

A defining factor of an organization is its leadership, especially "the power holders of the organization" (J. E. Grunig, 1992, p. 24). A corporation is socially defined by all its constituencies (Spicer, 1997), but top executives have a unique responsibility in directing the ethical decision making of the organization (Bowen, 2002; Sriramesh, Grunig, & Buffington, 1992; Waters, 1988) because the firm exists as an entity with the legal rights of an individual, but by permission of society. Many scholars (Berger & Reber, 2006; Bowen, 2009; Goodpaster, 2007; Seeger, 1997; Sims, 1991, 1994) argued that an ethical organizational culture must begin with the leaders at the top. A stream of scholarship on ethical leadership (Cavanaugh & Moberg, 1999; Paine, 1999; Parks, 1993) has identified one key component of a successful leader to be *moral courage.* Cavanaugh and Moberg (1999) wrote, "Courage is demanded within every organization in order to achieve honesty and integrity" (p. 3). As the Enron debacle illustrated, the courage, attitudes, intelligence, integrity, ethics, and moral character of executives have a critical impact on the goals and mission of an organization, its values, and communication about those standards (Bowen & Heath, 2005; Goodpaster, 2007; Sims & Brinkman, 2003) with stakeholders and publics.

The leaders of an organization envision and set the tone of the organization's ethical values system (Morgan, 2006; Seeger, 1997). Yeager and Kram (1995) termed this concept the organization's *ethical climate* (p. 46), although there is some dispute over whether that term encompasses all the necessary variables, such as the moral values of leaders and founders (Dickson, Smith, Grojean, & Ehrhart, 2001). Based on its ethical climate and the values of its leadership, a corporation develops its own code of ethics specifying the moral norms of the organization. A code of ethics is potentially a powerful tool of organizational leadership and strategic decision making (Murphy, 1998).

A useful code of ethics becomes a part of organizational culture, and the organizational culture reinforces the values specified in the code of ethics. For Morgan (1986), organizational culture is "a process of reality construction that allows people to see and understand particular events, actions, objects, utterances, or situations in distinctive ways" (p. 128). Using Morgan's definition, organizational culture would have a tremendous impact on leadership values, ethical decision making, and communicating those decisions, as well as what is codified in a code of ethics. Research on corporate leaders is diverse and considers many factors that link leadership with ethical decision making. Some of these are the personal characteristics of leaders (Howell & Avolio, 1992; Howell & Frost, 1989; Levine, 1949), the communicative dimensions of leader-subordinate relationships (Lee, 2001; Lee & Jablin, 1995), the organizational structure variables (Katz & Kahn, 1966; Seeger, 1997; Shockley-Zalabak & Morley, 1994), the transformational leadership (Bass, 1985; T. Burns & Stalker, 1961; Lee & Jablin, 1995), the management styles (J. M. Burns, 1978; McGregor, 1960), the moral courage (Cavanaugh & Moberg, 1999; Kidder, 2005), and the individual values versus group values (Ciulla, 1998; Smircich & Calas, 1987).

Moral courage and the leadership variables mentioned above point to the fact that resolving ethical dilemmas in a morally worthy way is important to the survival of an organization. Buchholz, Evans, and Wagley (1994) argued that the survival of an organization depends on how successfully it makes decisions in the complex arena of public issues. An organization's ethics statement gives its leaders valuable guidelines regarding how issues are to be approached and what core values are central in the decision.

Many executives might not be cognizant of the role ethics plays in decision making. Ethical values are often obscured by the phrase "It feels right" or "I know this is the right thing to do." However, only decisions based on a rational analysis of communication options through the perspective of a philosophical paradigm achieve the necessary rigor to be deemed ethical. Decision making in ethics should go beyond an intuitive analysis (Baker & Martinson, 2002; Bivins, 1992, 2006; Gower, 2003; Parsons, 2004).

Authenticity

Authenticity means being the same on the inside as one appears to be outside an organization, or even personally. Before one can be authentic, a manager of an organization must reflectively examine his or her own beliefs, values, and ethical decision-making paradigms, so that they can be represented authentically in discussions with others. Rawlins and Stoker (2006) agreed: "Being authentic requires a strong sense of self" (p. 426). The complex concept of authenticity comprises these three general concerns: transparency, truthfulness (veracity, honesty, or credibility), and genuineness—an intention or a morally good will.

Transparency refers to being open with how business is conducted, meaning that operations are visible and understandable from outside the organization. Rawlins (2009) defined transparency as the opposite of secrecy. Transparency goes beyond the requirements of disclosure because it allows the organization not only to disclose but also to be knowable in its inner workings, its policies, its decision-making processes, its priorities, and its relations with stakeholders and publics. Rawlins (2007) cited an industry study that found that the number one response among publics to the question "How can organizations rebuild trust?" was "Be open and honest in business practices" (agreement = 94%).

Honesty or truthfulness in public relations is vital to goodness. As the obverse of deception, truthfulness is morally worthy because it allows the freedom to make an individual choice, respecting moral autonomy, rationality, and dignity. To lie is morally unworthy because it erodes the fabric of society; if everyone lied, no one would expect truth. Only truthful communications can be generalized with equal respect for all people, making honesty morally worthy. Therefore, the principle of veracity holds that the truth must be told, even when ugly or not advantageous to an organization's own desires.

Genuineness speaks to the heart of moral intention in that an organization is genuinely pursuing an ethical course of action rather than just using ethics as "window dressing" to keep itself out of trouble by appearing ethical. The organization wants to be ethical and demonstrates that through its actions rather than simply wanting to appear or seem good. L'Etang and Pieczka (1996) posed serious challenges to the genuineness of an organization by questioning how respectful and symmetrical communication can coexist between an organization and publics given the power differential that exists between the two. The only answer to that challenge is to question the motivation of the organization in its communication and decision making with regard to publics. If the moral intention is less than simply "to do the right thing," philosophers like Kant would deem the action unethical (Kant, 1785/1993). He held that a morally good will is the only thing that can exist as an incorruptible good, in and of itself (Kant, 1783/1977). A good intention or a morally good will is the highest standard of ethics in moral philosophy.

Authenticity comprises transparency, honesty, and genuineness or a morally good will. Philosophers regard these concepts as *prima facie* good, or morally worthy in and of themselves, placing authenticity as a core concern of any ethical organization. Authenticity is to "be" rather than "to seem." Rawlins and Stoker (2006) included the concept of authenticity as vital in public relations, along with sincerity and autonomy. They explained, "An authentic person is not as concerned with how well the message is received as much as how well it represents his or her true thoughts" (p. 426).

The Arthur W. Page Society issued a study in 2007, named *The Authentic Enterprise.* In that report, CCOs (chief communications officers) averred, "In a word, authenticity will be the coin of the realm for successful corporations and for those who lead them" (p. 6). The Authentic Enterprise advised that "values, principles, beliefs, mission, purpose or value proposition—must dictate consistent behavior and actions" (pp. 5–6).

Consistency

Consistency is a deceptively simple concept. It is tempting to think of a definition of consistency that implies a rigid or even routine decision-making paradigm and little else. However, understanding consistency, in terms of the moral-philosophical meaning of the word, signifies relying on a rationally devised and thorough means of analysis before any decision is possible. The analytic approach to decision making renders snap judgments useless and decisions based on feeling or instinct not worthy of being termed *ethical* in the philosophical sense. A reliance on enlightenment, modern, and rationalist moral philosophy means that decisions can be made from an understandable and consistently applied framework. A rational-economic model of decision making requires an enormous amount of research and information to arrive at an optimal decision; a bounded rationality model requires decision makers to operate in an imperfect information environment in which all information or risks are not known (Sims, 1994). A bounded rationality approach, employed by morally autonomous decision makers, results in the most enduring decisions being made in an imperfect information environment. By eliminating bias, capriciousness, selfishness, and other preinfluencing concerns from the decision-making process, publics can understand the decisions of management as both logical and defensible, even if they do not agree with the values or conclusions inherent in the decision.

In public relations, consistency raises the question of loyalty to an organization as an advocate versus loyalty to professional ideals as an adviser to the organization. Each perspective on the ideal, ethical role of public relations practitioners has merit, and each perspective has pros and cons. By maintaining a consistent decision-making process, moral philosophy engages public relations practitioners with the normative ideal of being autonomous, objective, and rational decision makers rather than simply advocating organizational positions. As difficult as the prospect to implement rational objectivity and autonomy in the real workplace may be, the mental exercise alone of attempting to remove bias, pressures, and other personal desires from the decision may allow practitioners to have a better view of the organization through the eyes of publics. Research of Baker and Martinson (2002) supported the argument for consistency in applying ethical paradigms. "There is a very real danger that public relations practitioners will too often play a dysfunctional societal role as professional persuasive communicators if they have not established ethical principles to guide their communication practices" (p. 18).

Establishing standards of ethical decision making in public relations and implementing that same standard consistently across issues and with varying publics produces a consistency that disavows capriciousness. Though complete objectivity is not possible in a human state, the philosophers who advocate this mental exercise realize that more thoroughly considered, respectful, and reversible decisions should ensue through the mental exercise of rational autonomy. When decisions consistently reflect thought on behalf of publics, in addition to the normal thought on behalf of an organization, they are consistently more respectful and inherently ethical than nonobjective decisions.

Consistency allows organizations to build trusting relationships with publics. If a public knows what to expect of an organization because it has been consistently rational in the past, it tends to trust the organization to continue being rational and fair in the relationship.

Reflective Management

Combining all these concerns of moral decision making, as evidenced in the inherent good seen in the definitions of public relations, as well as in a philosophical analysis of the field, helps define a normative ethic for the field. We can term all these concepts as *reflective management* and operationalize them in the model as seen in Figure 40.1. Reflective management builds on the positive social role established by van Ruler and Verčič (2005) while significantly expanding on the ethical role of public relations. This role is based in moral philosophy, the analytical means through which it achieves a normative ethical status, and it describes the normative role that public relations should play both within organizations and in society.

References

Acton, H. B. (1970). *Kant's moral philosophy.* London: Macmillan.

The Arthur W. Page Society. (2007). *The authentic enterprise.* New York: Author.

Baker, S., & Martinson, D. L. (2002). Out of the red-light district: Five principles for ethically provocative public relations. *Public Relations Quarterly, 47*(3), 15–19.

Bakhtin, M. M. (1993). *Toward a philosophy of the act* (V. Liapunov, Trans.). Austin: University of Texas Press.

Baron, M. W. (1995). *Kantian ethics almost without apology.* Ithaca, NY: Cornell University Press.

Bass, B. M. (1985). *Leadership and performance: Beyond expectations.* New York: Free Press.

Benhabib, S. (1992). *Situating to self: Gender, community and postmodernism in contemporary ethics.* London: Routledge.

Bennett, J. (1966). *Kant's analytic.* Cambridge, UK: Cambridge University Press.

Berger, B. K., & Reber, B. H. (2006). *Gaining influence in public relations: The role of resistance in practice.* Mahwah, NJ: Lawrence Erlbaum.

Bivins, T. H. (1992). A systems model for ethical decision making in public relations. *Public Relations Review, 18*(4), 365–383.

Bivins, T. H. (2006). Responsibility and accountability. In K. Fitzpatrick & C. Bronstein (Eds.), *Ethics in public relations: Responsible advocacy* (pp. 19–38). Thousand Oaks, CA: Sage.

Bowen, S. A. (2002). Elite executives in issues management: The role of ethical paradigms in decision making. *Journal of Public Affairs, 2*(4), 270–283.

Bowen, S. A. (2009). What communication professionals tell us regarding dominant coalition access and gaining membership. *Journal of Applied Communication Research, 37*(4), 427–452.

Bowen, S. A., & Heath, R. L. (2005). Issues management, systems, and rhetoric: Exploring the distinction between ethical and legal guidelines at Enron. *Journal of Public Affairs, 5,* 84–98.

Bowen, S. A., Heath, R. L., Lee, J., Painter, G., Agraz, F. J., McKie, D., et al. (2006). *The business of truth: A guide to ethical communication.* San Francisco: International Association of Business Communicators.

Buber, M. (1970). *I and thou* (W. Kaufmann, Trans.). New York: Scribner.

Buchholz, R. A., Evans, W. D., & Wagley, R. A. (1994). *Management responses to public issues: Concepts and cases in strategy formulation* (3rd ed.). Upper Saddle River, NJ: Prentice Hall.

Burns, J. M. (1978). *Leadership.* New York: Harper & Row.

Burns, T., & Stalker, G. M. (1961). *The management of innovation.* London: Tavistock.

Cameron, G. T., Wilcox, D. L., Reber, B. H., & Shin, J. H. (2008). *Public relations today: Managing competition and conflict.* Boston: Pearson Education.

Cavanaugh, G. F., & Moberg, D. J. (1999). The virtue of courage within the organization. In M. L. Pava & P. Primeaux (Eds.), *Research in ethical issues in organizations* (pp. 1–26). Stamford, CT: JAI Press.

Ciulla, J. (1998). Leadership ethics: Mapping the territory. In J. Ciulla (Ed.), *Ethics, the heart of leadership* (pp. 3–25). Westport, CT: Praeger.

Day, L. A. (1997). *Ethics in media communications: Cases and controversies* (2nd ed.). Belmont, CA: Wadsworth.

Dickson, M. W., Smith, D. B., Grojean, M. W., & Ehrhart, M. (2001). An organizational climate regarding ethics: The outcome of leader values and the practices that reflect them. *Leadership Quarterly, 12*(2), 197–217.

Edelman, R. (2009). *Edelman Trust Barometer: The tenth global opinion leaders study.* Retrieved November 11, 2009, from www.edelman.com/trust/2009/docs/Trust_Book_Final_2.pdf

Friedman, M. S. (2002). *Martin Buber: The life of dialogue.* New York: Routledge.

Gilligan, C. (1982). *In a different voice: Psychological theory and women's development.* Cambridge, MA: Harvard University Press.

Goodman, E. C. (Ed.). (1997). *The Forbes book of business quotations.* New York: Black Dog & Leventhal.

Goodpaster, K. E. (2007). *Conscience and corporate culture.* Malden, MA: Blackwell.

Gower, K. K. (2003). *Legal and ethical restraints on public relations.* Prospect Heights, IL: Waveland Press.

Grunig, J. E. (1992). Communication, public relations, and effective organizations: An overview of the book. In J. E. Grunig (Ed.), *Excellence in public relations and communication management* (pp. 1–30). Hillsdale, NJ: Lawrence Erlbaum.

Grunig, J. E., & Hunt, T. (1984). *Managing public relations.* New York: Holt McDougal.

Grunig, J. E., & Repper, F. C. (1992). Strategic management, publics, and issues. In J. E. Grunig (Ed.), *Excellence in public relations and communication management* (pp. 117–157). Hillsdale, NJ: Lawrence Erlbaum.

Grunig, L. A., Grunig, J. E., & Dozier, D. M. (2002). *Excellent public relations and effective organizations: A study of communication management in three countries.* Mahwah, NJ: Lawrence Erlbaum.

Habermas, J. (1987). *The theory of communicative action: Reason and the rationalization of society* (T. McCarthy, Trans.; Vol. 2). Boston: Beacon Press.

Heath, R. L. (2001). A rhetorical enactment rationale for public relations: The good organization communicating well. In R. L. Heath (Ed.), *Handbook of public relations* (pp. 31–50). Thousand Oaks, CA: Sage.

Heath, R. L. (2006). A rhetorical theory approach to issues management. In C. Botan & V. Hazleton (Eds.), *Public relations theory II* (pp. 63–99). Mahwah, NJ: Lawrence Erlbaum.

Heath, R. L., & Coombs, W. T. (Eds.). (2006). *Today's public relations: An introduction.* Thousand Oaks, CA: Sage.

Howell, J. M., & Avolio, B. J. (1992). The ethics of charismatic leadership: Submission or liberation? *Academy of Management Executive, 6*(2), 43–54.

Howell, J. M., & Frost, P. J. (1989). A laboratory study of charismatic leadership. *Organizational Behavior and Human Decision Processes, 43,* 243–269.

Jovanovic, S., & Wood, R. V. (2006). Communication ethics and ethical culture: A study of the ethics initiative in Denver city government. *Journal of Applied Communication Research, 34*(4), 386–405.

Kant, I. (1964). *Groundwork of the metaphysic of morals* (H. J. Paton, Trans.). New York: Harper & Row. (Original work published 1785)

Kant, I. (1974). *On the old saw: That may be right in theory but it won't work in practice* (E. B. Ashton, Trans.). Philadelphia: University of Pennsylvania Press. (Original work published 1793)

Kant, I. (1977). *Prolegomena to any future metaphysics that will be able to come forward as science* (J. W. Ellington & P. Carus, Trans.). Indianapolis, IN: Hackett. (Original work published 1783)

Kant, I. (1993). Metaphysical foundations of morals (C. J. Friedrich, Trans.). In C. J. Friedrich (Ed.), *The philosophy of Kant: Immanuel Kant's moral and political writings* (pp. 154–229). New York: Modern Library. (Original work published 1785)

Kant, I. (1997). *Critique of pure reason* (P. Guyer & A. W. Wood, Trans.). Cambridge, UK: Cambridge University Press. (Original work published 1781)

Katz, D., & Kahn, R. L. (1966). *The social psychology of organizations* (2nd ed.). New York: Wiley.

Kent, M. L., & Taylor, M. (2002). Toward a dialogic theory of public relations. *Public Relations Review, 28*(1), 21–37.

Kidder, R. M. (2005). *Moral courage: Taking action when your values are put to the test.* New York: HarperCollins.

Lee, J. (2001). Leader-member exchange, perceived organizational justice, and cooperative communication. *Management Communication Quarterly, 14*(4), 574–589.

Lee, J., & Jablin, F. M. (1995). Maintenance communication in superior-subordinate work relationships. *Human Communication Research, 22,* 220–257.

L'Etang, J., & Pieczka, M. (Eds.). (1996). *Critical perspectives in public relations.* London: International Thomson Business Press.

Levinas, E. (1990). *Nine Talmudic readings* (A. Aronowicz, Trans.). Bloomington: Indiana University Press.

Levine, S. (1949). An approach of constructive leadership. *Journal of Social Issues, 5,* 46–53.

Lewicki, R. J., Litterer, J. A., Saunders, D. M., & Minton, J. W. (1993). *Negotiation: Readings, exercises, and cases* (2nd ed.). Boston: Irwin.

Lieber, P. (2008). Moral development public relations: Measuring duty to society in strategic communication. *Public Relations Review, 34,* 244–251.

McGregor, D. (1960). *The human side of enterprise.* New York: McGraw-Hill.

Morgan, G. (1986). *Images of organization.* Beverly Hills, CA: Sage.

Morgan, G. (2006). *Images of organization: Updated edition of the international bestseller.* Thousand Oaks, CA: Sage.

Murphy, P. E. (1998). *Eighty exemplary ethics statements.* Notre Dame, IN: University of Notre Dame Press.

Newsom, D., Turk, J. V., & Kruckeberg, D. (2004). *This is PR: The realities of public relations* (8th ed.). Belmont, CA: Thomson Wadsworth.

Paine, L. S. (1999). Managing for organizational integrity. In T. Donaldson & P. H. Werhane (Eds.),

Ethical issues in business: A philosophical approach (6th ed., pp. 526–538). Upper Saddle River, NJ: Prentice Hall.

Parks, S. D. (1993). Professional ethics, moral courage, and the limits of personal virtue. In B. Darling-Smith (Ed.), *Can virtue be taught?* (pp. 181–183). Notre Dame, IN: University of Notre Dame Press.

Parsons, P. J. (2004). *Ethics in public relations: A guide to best practice.* London: Kogan Page.

Paton, H. J. (1927). *The good will: A study in the coherence theory of goodness.* New York: Macmillan.

Pearson, R. (1989a). Beyond ethical relativism in public relations: Coorientation, rules, and the idea of communication symmetry. In J. E. Grunig & L. A. Grunig (Eds.), *Public relations research annual* (Vol. 1, pp. 67–86). Hillsdale, NJ: Lawrence Erlbaum.

Pearson, R. (1989b). *A theory of public relations ethics.* Unpublished doctoral dissertation, Ohio University, Athens.

Plaisance, P. L. (2009). *Media ethics: Key principles for responsible practice.* Los Angeles: Sage.

Rawlins, B. (2007). Trust and PR practice [Electronic version]. *Institute for Public Relations.* Retrieved November 28, 2009, from www.instituteforpr.org/essential_knowledge/detail/trust_and_pr_practice/

Rawlins, B. (2009). Give the emperor a mirror: Toward developing a stakeholder measurement of organizational transparency. *Journal of Public Relations Research, 21*(1), 71–99.

Rawlins, B., & Stoker, K. (2003). Dropping a loaded gun: Using topical transformation to explain how Smith & Wesson failed to influence the influential. *Journal of Communication Management, 6*(3), 269–279.

Rawlins, B., & Stoker, K. (2006, March). *Taking the B.S. out of P.R.: Creating genuine messages by emphasizing character and authenticity.* Paper presented at the International Public Relations Research Conference, Miami, FL.

Rawls, J. (1971). *A theory of justice.* Cambridge, MA: Harvard University Press.

Ross, W. D. (2002). *The right and the good.* Oxford, UK: Clarendon Press. (Original work published 1930)

Seeger, M. W. (1997). *Ethics and organizational communication.* Cresskill, NJ: Hampton Press.

Shockley-Zalabak, P., & Morley, D. D. (1994). Creating a culture: A longitudinal examination of the influence of management and employee values on communication rule stability and emergence. *Human Communication Research, 20,* 334–355.

Sims, R. R. (1991). The institutionalization of organizational ethics. *Journal of Business Ethics, 10*(7), 493–506.

Sims, R. R. (1994). *Ethics and organizational decision making: A call for renewal.* Westport, CT: Quorum Books.

Sims, R. R., & Brinkman, J. (2003). Enron ethics (or, culture matters more than codes). *Journal of Business Ethics, 45*(3), 243–256.

Smircich, L., & Calas, M. B. (1987). Organizational culture: A critical assessment. In F. M. Jablin, L. L. Putnam, K. H. Roberts, & L. W. Porter (Eds.), *Handbook of organizational communication: An interdisciplinary perspective* (pp. 228–263). Newbury Park, CA: Sage.

Spicer, C. (1997). *Organizational public relations: A political perspective.* Mahwah, NJ: Lawrence Erlbaum.

Spicer, C. (2000). Public relations in a democratic society: Value and values. *Journal of Public Relations Research, 12*(1), 115–130.

Sriramesh, K., Grunig, J. E., & Buffington, J. (1992). Corporate culture and public relations. In J. E. Grunig (Ed.), *Excellence in public relations and communication management* (pp. 577–595). Hillsdale, NJ: Lawrence Erlbaum.

Sullivan, R. J. (1989). *Immanuel Kant's moral theory.* New York: Cambridge University Press.

Sullivan, R. J. (1994). *An introduction to Kant's ethics.* New York: Cambridge University Press.

van Ruler, B., & Verčič, D. (2005). Reflective communication management, future ways for public relations research. In P. J. Kalbfleisch (Ed.), *Communication yearbook 29* (pp. 239–273). Mahwah, NJ: Lawrence Erlbaum.

Waters, J. (1988). Integrity management: Learning and implementing ethical principles in the workplace. In S. Srivastva (Ed.), *Executive integrity: The search for human value in organizational life* (pp. 172–196). San Francisco: Jossey-Bass.

Wolvin, A., & Coakley, C. G. (1996). *Listening* (5th ed.). Boston: McGraw-Hill.

Wright, D. K. (1985). Can age predict the moral values of public relations practitioners? *Public Relations Review, 11*(1), 51–60.

Yeager, P. C., & Kram, K. E. (1995). Fielding hot topics in cool settings: The study of corporate ethics. In R. Hertz & J. B. Imber (Eds.), *Studying elites using qualitative methods* (pp. 40–64). Thousand Oaks, CA: Sage.

CHAPTER 41

Military Spokespeople and Democracy

Perspectives From Two Israeli Wars

Margalit Toledano

L'Etang (2006) called for a discussion "to understand the perspective of practitioners as they too struggle to come to terms with the nature and social role of their practice, its ethical implications, and connections with propaganda and the associated historical and ideological baggage" (p. 40). In response, this chapter addresses the underresearched area of military spokespeople in times of war. In looking at the way two Israeli military spokespeople functioned on the battlefield of public opinion, the chapter identifies influences from the sociopolitical environment, public opinion, and the media and analyzes the implications for democracy.

Origins

In the public relations literature, the emergence of the profession is linked to wartime propaganda. Histories (Cutlip, 1994; Ewen, 1996) and textbooks (Broom, 2009; Lattimore, Baskin, Heiman, & Toth, 2007) connect the emergence of the profession with war. Cutlip's (1995) *Public Relations History: From the 17th to the 20th Century: The Antecedents* identified early public relations efforts on behalf of army units and generals during the American Revolution as the "American antecedents" to public relations.

Most U.S. public relations textbooks credit their government's World War I propaganda as an inspiring experience for many of the founders of modern public relations, who used it for developing their careers. Edward Bernays and Carl Byoir, for example, both served on the U.S. "Committee on Public Information." L'Etang's (2004) research on the origins of the British profession features a list of prominent British practitioners who were involved in British propaganda and intelligence in World War II (p. 49). Both American and British practitioners later applied lessons from war propaganda in civil society so that "the overlap between the apparently distinct occupations of public relations and propaganda" (p. 48) is evident.

Traces can still be found in contemporary public relations. The overlap has had an impact on the profession's self-image, concepts, and role in society and is still visible in the continuing use of military terms such as *campaigns, strategy, tactics*, and *target publics*. Outside of wartime, such language still connotes an aggressive and partisan attack, if now directed at publics on behalf of organizations. Grunig (1989) presented war as a metaphor for asymmetrical models of public relations used by organizations that believe they know best, that the public just needs to understand them, and to cooperate. In this context, he mentioned the title of a speech at the 1986 annual meeting of the Public Relations Society of America: "Waging and Winning the War of Ideas" (Grunig, 1989, p. 32). Yet the public relations literature rarely deals with the specific role played by the public relations practitioner in a military organization, and especially not during the very challenging circumstances of war.

There are relatively few published examples of academic research into propaganda and public relations during wartime (Hiebert, 1991, 1993, 2003; Smith, 2005). This research contributed to the body of knowledge in a number of ways, including overviews of different military approaches to communication in different wars and the results of these different strategies. It also had a useful focus on evaluating the propaganda/public relations effort and discussing important issues such as the role of public relations in a democratic society, the value of "freedom of expression" and the "right to know," in situations where survival is at stake. It did not, however, contain evidence from actual military practitioners.

This chapter seeks to redress that absence and to add material from other wars to the research. It analyzes the two recent wars that Israel launched: against Hezbollah in Lebanon in 2006 and against Hamas in Gaza in 2008/2009. These wars provided a rare opportunity to see behind the scenes and to examine some of the complex challenges faced by military spokespeople. The two spokespeople examined are different and exercised different communications strategies in different political and military contexts. What makes the study possible is that much of their work was subsequently brought into the public eye through postwar investigation committees, academic debates, media interviews, and books.

What's So Special About the Military Spokesperson Role?

The military spokesperson is positioned at the intersection between a citizen's rights to national security and to freedom of information. The security of the state is actually a precondition to a citizen's ability to realize all his or her other rights—even the "right to know" that is fundamental to a democratic system. In addition, the military spokesperson actually represents a public organization, funded by the government, which has the right to keep information about its activities secret. Often, it cannot be transparent for state security reasons.

Public criticism of the military via media, especially during wartime, might be seen as weakening its ability to defend the state and is, therefore, open to censorship. Military institutions do not usually consider the possibility that criticism might also serve as a positive wakeup call, for example, to end the war in a way that may eventually strengthen the military and the democratic society that is being defended. Dor, Iram, and Voldavsky (2007) noted, "Courageous ethical journalism is meaningless when offered in retrospect. Truly difficult questions must be posed during wartime because that is when there is still a chance to effect change" (p. 12).

In fact, histories of the relationships between the media and the military show very little criticism by national media during wartime. Journalists are also citizens and, in times of emergency, such as war, they tend to choose unity and solidarity and to "protect the national interest, strengthen the consensus and limit criticism. This is what happened to the British media during the Blitz, and to the American media during the Gulf War, and after the September 11th terror attack" (Weiman, 2002, p. 13; Author's translation from Hebrew [ATH]).

The military spokesperson, just like the journalist, is a citizen and influenced by the sociopolitical environment. Accordingly, when the political culture holds the army above public scrutiny, and the public gives up its right to know for the sake of security, the military spokesperson will be likely to close the system and use the army's power of censorship to stop criticism from being published.

Over the past two decades, this traditional communication strategy has been challenged. New technology, which has increased citizens' access to information in real time, and cultural and legal liberalization, has enforced a policy of relative openness to the public and transparency about military institutions (Lebel, 2005, p. 20). In these circumstances, the military is expected, like any other public institution, to communicate with, and be responsible to, external stakeholders as well as being open and truthful. The transparency, however, needs to be accepted by the highest level of military authority because the professional military spokesperson is a soldier lower in the chain of command and so needs to obey orders, even when they do not observe professional standards of ethics.

To motivate, and achieve legitimacy for, the military institution, the spokesperson has to communicate effectively with major stakeholders such as serving officers and soldiers, young future soldiers, those on the home front, decision makers, and international opinion. Spokespeople need to aim at persuading all stakeholders that the military is fighting for a just and legitimate cause. Military spokespeople need to present their nation as behaving legitimately, conducting a defensive operation, acting as the underdog and more the victim of enemy activities than an aggressor, and as justified in taking the actions it takes. At the same time, they have to present their military as being strong, motivated, highly ethical, and able to win.

In a democratic system, military intelligence, not the spokesperson/public relations, is supposed to take charge of conducting psychological warfare against the enemy. Propaganda efforts to mislead and manipulate the enemy are accepted as legitimate military functions, but the Spokesperson Unit should not be involved. Otherwise, they might lose their effectiveness as a credible source of information.

Context 1: The Israeli Defense Force

Israel is the fourth strongest military power in the world today. Since its inception, it has been involved in military operations against neighboring Arab countries and engaged in long-term and violent conflict with the Palestinians, who claim indigenous rights to the land on which the State of Israel was built. The military, called the Israeli Defense Force (IDF), is a major social institution, reflecting Israeli society and considered "the army of the people." Military service is mandatory for all non-Arab Israelis, and reserve service of up to one month a year lasts until the age of 43. Thus, almost all Israelis, apart from groups exempted on the grounds of religion or disability, know the army from within. According to public opinion polls, Israeli Jews' level of trust in the IDF, and in its spokespeople, is higher than in any other public institution (Lebel, 2005, p. 19). Consequently, criticism about IDF deficiencies, or claims that it has acted illegally, or inhumanely, are very hard for Israelis to accept.

The IDF spokesperson is the highest authority responsible for IDF communications and relationships with stakeholders. The mission statement of the IDF Spokesperson Unit is

> to report on the accomplishments and activities of the IDF to the Israeli and International public, to nurture public confidence in the IDF, and to serve as the IDF's primary professional authority on matters of public relations and distribution of information to the public. (IDF, n.d.)

The spokesperson participates in general staff meetings to consult and recommend communication strategy.

The unit employs about 400 soldiers, of whom 300 are very young soldiers in regular service and 100 are professional communicators. About 800 professionals serve in the unit on their reserve duty (Yaron, personal communication with the author in Modyin, October 19, 2009). Psychological warfare aimed at the enemy is conducted by the Intelligence Unit, which operates separately from the Spokesperson Unit. There are ongoing efforts to coordinate and make sure one does not contradict the other, but each unit is trying to achieve different objectives (Yaron, personal communication with the author in Modyin, October 19, 2009).

According to Yaron (personal communication with the author in Modyin, October 19, 2009), the first woman to serve as military spokesperson (2002–2005), it was 2003 before the IDF consulted with the spokesperson in the planning stages of operations. At that point, the then chief of staff, Bugi Yaalon, decided in principle to include representatives of the Spokesperson Unit in planning meetings at all levels of command and, when possible, to open activities to embedded journalists. Yaron set the values of relevance, credibility, and legitimacy as guidelines for the unit work.

Context 2: Lebanon 2006

In the Second Lebanon War, which started on July 12, 2006, and lasted 34 days, Israel attacked Hezbollah targets in Lebanon by massive air bombardment and then by a ground operation, while Hezbollah launched about 5,000 rockets on the northern towns of Israel. On the Israeli side, there were 4,000 casualties, most of them suffering from anxiety attacks, 42 dead, and 32 severely injured. On the Lebanese side, according to various reports, the air strikes killed more than 11,000 people, with a third of them children. More than 4,000 people were injured, and the vast majority of casualties were not related to Hezbollah (Dor et al., 2007, p. 9).

The explicit government goals for this 2006 campaign—it was not called a war—were to bring two soldiers, abducted by Hezbollah on July 12, back to Israel and to disarm Hezbollah, which had a missile arsenal hidden in southern Lebanon. Those goals were approved and supported by Western countries, especially the United States, which identified Hezbollah as a terrorist organization and regarded the operation as part of the war against international terror. The goals were to be achieved by a military operation. The government did not aim for any political or diplomatic effort to pressure the Lebanese government to limit Hezbollah from within, nor did it seek to empower the Lebanese central government to do so (Brom, 2007, p. 21). As the war continued, and the destruction in Lebanon increased, many Europeans became outraged and accused Israel of committing war crimes. World calls for a halt to the fighting ended it with an agreement involving the UN forces.

The campaign was declared by a newly elected Israeli government 2 months after a general election. It was conducted by inexperienced leaders. Nevertheless, the prime minister, Ehud Ulmert, and the minister of defence, Amir Peretz (who had no military background), were eager to show themselves as popular war heroes. The chief of staff, Lt. General Dan Halutz, was a controversial political appointment with a reputation as an arrogant, insensitive, and self-centered officer (Shelah & Limore, 2007, p. 170).

On the first night of the war, the IDF destroyed strategic Hezbollah targets (including 59 missile launchers), in 34 minutes of a massive airstrike (Ben, 2006, p. 7). In a euphoric mood, Halutz, Ulmert, and Peretz decided to continue the war. They ignored messages from Lebanese ministers calling for a ceasefire and kept going in spite of lacking clear military and political targets. "To stop now," asked General Halutz in a discussion with Ulmert, "when we are winning?" (cited in Shelah & Limore, 2007, p. 83). The barrage of rockets aimed at Israeli civilians continued, and the IDF did not provide any effective response. Around the middle of the war, the army entered Lebanon with ground units, which were not actually prepared to take part in this kind of operation.

At the end of the war, neither goal was achieved. The abducted Israeli soldiers were not returned to their families, and, although Hezbollah received significant blows, and lost hundreds of militants, it was not disarmed. The IDF was exposed as unprepared for war, and its reputation was badly damaged. This decreased the IDF's deterrent power, long regarded as essential for Israel's survival among hostile Arab countries. Most Israelis found the results of the war disappointing, and the war was considered a failure. The disappointment led to several official postwar investigation committees, which also examined the role of the media and the way the IDF Spokesperson Unit functioned during the war.

The Media and Public Opinion in the 2006 War

Many Israelis, frustrated by the outcome, blamed the media for the failure. Public opinion surveys found the public accused the media of reporting irresponsibly, revealing too much information to the enemy, being too critical, not supporting the IDF, and having a demoralizing effect (Weiman, 2007, pp. 17–22). Complaints to broadcasting authorities increased dramatically. A survey conducted by the Second TV & Radio Authority found that 91.7% of the Israelis thought that the media had to boost the national morale, and 85.4% thought that the media needed to report in a patriotic way (Rozen, 2006, p. 22). Israelis also expressed dissatisfaction with the publicity given to casualties and funerals. Only a few dissident peace activists complained that the Israeli media ignored, or justified, the destruction and human suffering caused by indiscriminate IDF bombing. Most Israelis did not expect the IDF spokespeople and the media to question the war goals or the conduct of the IDF.

The reality was different. Research conducted by Keshev, the Center for the Protection of Democracy in Israel, analyzed 9,000 news items in the Israeli print and electronic media during the war and found that the Israeli media "created a general atmosphere of full and unqualified support for the war and its justness, systematically suppressing questions that arose from day one of the war" (Dor et al., 2007, p. 3). Some criticism about tactical issues did become louder toward the end of the war but "ultimately conveyed the following message: The war is both right and just, but the decision makers are not conducting it properly, so we are losing. None of them said: something is fundamentally wrong with this war" (Dor et al., 2007, p. 7). Peri's (2006) independent analysis confirmed that "the Israeli media did not present any political option to solve the conflict. Instead, it kept repeating the official Israeli narrative and ignoring both Arab and international narratives." The author herself also observed how two leading evening newspapers sponsored patriotic public relations campaigns with billboards and advertisements using slogans such as "Israel is strong," "We shall win," and other messages supportive of the war.

Neither the fact that the 2006 war was covered online nor that the Internet served as major source of information changed the tone of the patriotic coverage: "The speed that is enabled by the medium was the only message of the Internet . . . [which] provided mainly flash headlines for immediate updating . . . and it enabled users to release pressure by responding online" (Tausig, 2006, p. 27; ATH). While the Internet did spread lots of rumors and misinformation, it did not appear to have much influence on events, although both sides used it for propaganda: "There were online campaigns with petitions and surveys. The IDF spokesperson placed videos on the net and the Ministry of Foreign Affairs used its cadets to write responses to blogs and articles" (Tausig, 2006, p. 28).

In the postwar mood of dissatisfaction, the Israel Press Council set up a special committee to create a media code of ethics for wartime. This committee commented that "if the media had been more critical at the first week of the war, it might have ended earlier. The media has given in to briefings of officers who presented a fake image of IDF accomplishments" ("The Media Is Not Guilty," 2007, p. 9; ATH).

Brigadier General Miri Regev: Publicizing the IDF

Brigadier General Regev headed the Spokesperson Unit during the 2006 war. She was appointed in 2005 by the then chief of staff (COS), General Dan Halutz. Regev had attained the post with "on-the-job training" in various positions within the IDF Spokesperson Unit and the Prime Minister Office, and a role in charge of the IDF Censor's office in 2004.

In Regev's first year as IDF spokesperson, Israel withdrew unilaterally from the Gaza strip, and the IDF enforced the controversial evacuation of Israeli settlements there. Backed by the COS, Regev conducted the "Disengagement" operation as a media event, in which military activities were planned or postponed according to the media's timetable and needs (Shoen, 2005). This was the first time a massive group of Israeli and international reporters and photographers participated in an IDF operation, and many were embedded within army and police units. The goals included presenting the IDF as acting effectively, while being sensitive to human rights, and showing the world the high costs Israel's government was ready to pay for its decision to evacuate Israeli citizens from their homes in occupied territories.

Regev won praise for her success in changing the IDF communication culture and building a positive reputation for the IDF by opening its units to the media. As she explained in an interview, "We need to learn to work in an environment in which every citizen has a cellular phone, can take a picture and broadcast it in real time on the Internet" (Regev, cited in Kaspit, 2007, p. 22; ATH). Her rationale for openness was rooted in her belief that censorship would not work when soldiers were able to report live from the battlefield and information is easily accessible in a very competitive media environment. She also believed that embedding journalists within army units would result in favorable reports supporting the army line (Regev, 2006).

Regev stayed with the strategy of openness following the disengagement operation in Gaza for the War in Lebanon. In a media interview, she claimed to "recommend embedding journalists with the army from day one" (Kaspit, 2007, p. 24; ATH). However, on this occasion, the COS and general staff refused although, according to Regev, 29 Israeli and 14 international correspondents eventually entered Lebanon with Israeli units (Ganon, 2006, p. 6; ATH). She claimed that officers objected to embedding journalists for a number of reasons: disturbing soldiers in the battlefield, not being prepared for war, not having appropriate equipment, and for their editors refusing to pay the high cost of insurance for journalists entering a war zone (Regev, 2006). In another interview, she admitted that "officers feared that 'unflattering' information about internal debates, contradicting commands, shortcomings in the preparedness and the fitness of the armed forces for an extensive ground operation would be exposed" (Kanti, 2006, p. 12; ATH). This information was eventually published anyway: "Reporters walked up to soldiers sitting around on the Lebanon border, interviewed them, and broadcast complaints" (Goldman, 2009).

As a matter of fact, there was not much pressure from the media to get permission to enter Lebanon. In her testimony to the Israel Press Council committee, Regev's (2006) only complaints about the Israeli media were that it did not give enough publicity to IDF "accomplishments" and did not show the damage done to Hezbollah; otherwise, "the media was cooperative and very patriotic."

Her predecessor in the role of IDF spokesperson, Brigadier General Ruth Yaron (personal communication with the author in Modyin,

October 19, 2009), criticized Regev for being too keen on publicity, for her strategy of "coloring the media in green [the IDF uniform is green] to increase the love of the people to the army by providing human stories to weekend magazines." From a professional perspective, Yaron (personal communication with the author in Modyin, October 19, 2009) thought Regev was wrong in defining "her major clients as the journalists" and should have seen that "the spokesperson's client is not the media but rather the Israeli public, who owns the army."

The Israeli public were angry with Regev's policy of openness because they saw it as irresponsible. People saw no need to publish information that helped Hezbollah target Israeli towns and no need to publicize internal arguments. Openness was considered out of place when the enemy was a terrorist organization. Marvin Kalb (2007) commented that "an open society becomes the victim of its own openness. During the war, no Hezbollah secrets were disclosed, but in Israel secrets leaked, rumors spread like wildfire" (p. 44). Hezbollah controlled its communication in a very centralized system, with no permission for journalists to move in the region or to embed with its militants.

Staging the "Image of Victory" and Political Ambitions

The first night's airstrike, which was a significant accomplishment for the IDF, was planned secretly. Regev learned about it only when it was over and too late for her to optimize its use in the media. After the war, she claimed that if she had been included in the planning discussions, she would have been able to leverage the media coverage so that the successful airstrike would have been fixed in the public mind as the "image of victory" and that there would have been no pressure for the continuation of the war (Shelah & Limore, 2007, p. 83; ATH). The quest for a "victory photo," motivated partly by the political ambitions of the COS (and other high commanders, including Regev), became an obsession that dictated military operations. Shelah and Limore (2007) described an "obsession" about raising awareness in Halutz's time as COS to the extent that even "the instructions for military operations read almost like propaganda. . . . Halutz was determined to shape the consciousness of leaders, soldiers, and the public in relation to the success of the war" (pp. 84–85; ATH).

Eventually, the COS was accused of initiating purposeless operations and putting soldiers' lives at risk for the sake of a photo opportunity. Soldiers were equipped with cameras, and the Spokesperson Unit sent its photographers to take pictures of the bodies of Hezbollah militants: "In the last week of the war the COS summoned a meeting about 'creating a consciousness of victory' in which Regev said: 'We need to stage a story of victory'" (Shelah & Limore, 2007, p. 271).

Because the IDF consists of so many civilians on reserve service, high-ranking officers care for their image in the workplace, where they often serve as CEOs or political leaders. During the war, many conducted their own media relations so that military information leaks increased (Commission for the Investigation of the Campaign, 2008, p. 465). Halutz's investigation of officers' telephone use found that 460 of them conducted unauthorized conversations with journalists during one day (Peper, 2009). The IDF spokesperson was accused of using her role for personal exposure, building herself as a "brand" (in her own words) (Shoen, 2005), and she did indeed join the Likud party when she had to retire after the war, and she was elected to the Knesset in the 2009 elections.

One of the results of personal political considerations being involved in military strategy is the focus on local publicity to impress future voters. This can lead to neglect of the international media. There is also an assumption that the army needs to do what needs to be done to secure the state without taking international criticism into account. Certainly, Regev focused solely on the domestic media and delegated the entire international media operation to a reserve officer.

Almost until the end of the war, Regev demonstrated absolute loyalty to the COS who appointed her. In interviews, while still in office, she said she would follow him to politics. She supported his personal publicity efforts and tried to cover up his failures. When the COS was exposed selling private stocks in the first day of the war, Regev tried to convince the editor not to publish the story (he held it back until after the war). When the COS was hospitalized during the war, she succeeded in getting the media to cooperate in playing down the story.

Speaking With "One Voice"

Journalists and filmmakers, who depended on the IDF spokesperson's approval for filming in army-controlled territory, complained about "draconian" contracts, and one producer claimed, "The army assists only those who self-censor" (Pinto, 2007; ATH). Similar evidence was given by documentary producer Nurit Keidar, who during the 2006 war interviewed a high-ranking IDF officer for a film called *War Room*. Keidar had to sign the IDF spokesperson contract, which allowed the spokesperson to withdraw permission, whenever, and for whatever reason. The officer interviewed by Keidar expressed deep frustration with the war and criticized his superiors. Regev demanded, based on the contract Keidar signed, that the documentary be prevented from screening on Israeli television. Keidar said that as long as the interviewee approved the screening, she was not giving the film up even though she was threatened with legal action by Regev. Keidar (personal communication with the author in Tel Aviv, December 1, 2006) said, "I was treated by colleagues in the media as a traitor. . . . [S]oldiers lost their lives for nothing and the spokeswoman was pressuring the TV channel directors to take the evidence off the screen."

One representative of the Spokesperson Unit explained the policy as follows: "When we see that a movie has an educational, social, Zionist objective, which does not harm the IDF's image or the State of Israel, we offer our help" (cited in Pinto, 2007; ATH). Thus, Regev's declared liberal approach to open the army to media, which underpinned the embedding strategy, was actually a tool for controlling and censoring communication about the army and not for letting other voices be heard. It was up to the spokesperson to decide which messages were educational and did not harm the IDF or Zionist values. The Spokesperson Unit could use, and abuse, its power for political control of messages. Regev did not see the IDF as a public entity in a democratic state that was obliged to provide the same service to all, without discrimination based on points of view.

Regev Under Public Scrutiny

Israeli academic research found a high level of public dissatisfaction with the IDF spokesperson. At the end of the war, Professor Gabi Weiman's (2007) survey of 300 Israeli Jews found that Regev's media interviews and appearances provoked criticism and antagonism:

> During emergencies and war the public and the media express a need for "a national interpreter" . . . that combines charisma, credibility, knowledge, and media skills, including an ability to communicate, clarity, and external empathy. During the Lebanon war the IDF spokeswoman Miri Regev was positioned in the communication front but according to many she failed her job, not only because of personal attributes but mainly because she was perceived as "public relations executive for the army and the COS." (Weiman, 2007, p. 26; ATH)

The 2007 state comptroller's report stated that a great deal of classified material was revealed to the media throughout the war. The head of the operations division did not examine Regev on the significance of the COS instruction regarding openness:

> As the war progressed, there was a lack of clarity among the IDF officers concerning how open they could be with the media, their boundaries, and how the commanders and officials supervised this and ensured enforcement.

> This led, inter alia, to the release of classified information. . . . The IDF spokeswoman also failed to provide written instructions dictating how reporters would be embedded with IDF units in the field. (Azoulay, 2007, p. 7)

The government-appointed investigation Commission, headed by former judge Eliyahu Winograd, submitted a report based on inquiries conducted within the army. The report criticized both the COS and the military spokesperson for the openness policy resulting in live reports and loss of control over publication of army secrets. In his testimony, the COS defended the openness policy and put the blame on unauthorized leaks from within the army. He identified a need to integrate the efforts of censorship and the Spokesperson Unit to avoid publicity for information that puts IDF soldiers at risk (Commission for the Investigation of the Campaign, 2008, p. 465).

The Israel Press Council committee considered the way the spokesperson reported about Israeli casualties. It stressed the need to protect the privacy of families, which were harassed by journalists, and concern about the effect bad news on Israeli casualties had on public morale. Regev responded that she was unable to delay the publicity about casualties. Journalists testifying at the Israel Press Council complained about Regev's openness and said that the access she gave them to army secrets shocked them. In response, Regev said that as spokesperson she was not the censor. Her job was to serve the media and she trusted the censor's office would prevent publicity of classified information (Toledano, 2006).

Context 3: Gaza 2008/2009 and the Counteraction to Lebanon

The IDF military operation in Gaza was planned ahead as an opportunity to restore the IDF's deterrence power, which was dangerously damaged in the 2006 war. The Gaza war started on December 27, 2008, with a week of massive airstrikes, followed by 2 weeks of IDF ground incursion. The attack was presented as retaliation for Hamas rockets fired at Israeli civilians in the south, at the end of 6 months of a relatively quiet ceasefire. The 22 days of military operation ended with more than 1,300 Palestinians and 13 Israelis dead and with more than 5,000 Palestinians injured and brought huge destruction to Gaza.

The dead included many Palestinian children and civilians who, because of the blockade imposed by Israel, and the high-density Gaza population, were unable to flee the fighting. The IDF claimed that the large number of Palestinian civilian victims resulted from Hamas using civilians as human shields and operating from residential and public buildings. The distinction between civilians and Hamas militants became one of the central issues in condemnations of IDF actions in the Gaza operation. It led to accusations of war crimes and initiations of legal action abroad against Israeli political leaders and IDF officers. Other condemnations related to the use, forbidden by international law, of white phosphorus bombs in civilian areas; and to the deprivation of medical supplies, electricity, and basic supplies from Palestinian civilians. Accusations about war crimes were published by human rights organizations during and after the war and by Israeli soldiers who participated in the operation and witnessed incidents of inhumane and unethical activities.

Most Israelis perceived the Gaza operation, called "Cast Lead," as a necessary means to stop Hamas rockets, which had been terrorizing Israeli civilians in the south for 8 years. Public opinion surveys showed massive support for the war, with up to 90% thinking it was just (Goldman, 2009). A small minority of hundreds of Israeli peace activists demonstrated against the war from day one but did not get much attention from the media or the public. Journalist Gideon Levi (2009) said, "The media prepared the support for the war before it started and then took its place in the chorus line and cheered. Another opinion? Public debate? Not in our place" (ATH).

Demonstrators against the war, who claimed that the operation was not the way to secure Israelis' safety, and that only peace negotiations would help, were labeled "anti-Israeli Israelis" by one prominent reporter (Shavit, 2009, p. 5; ATH).

The media aligned with the public expectations:

> Israeli reporters . . . understood that the public was not interested in critical reporting about the war or in human interest stories about the Palestinians in Gaza. Israelis wanted stories about the home front, about civilians within rocket range, the soldiers called up for the ground incursion, and the worried or grieving families left behind. (Goldman, 2009)

The international media, especially Al Jazeera, broadcast shocking pictures of the destruction caused by the IDF, but Israelis chose not to expose themselves to these reports. Most Israelis were informed by Israeli media, traditional and online, even though international outlets were available (Caspi, 2009). There was high consensus about the justness of the operation and the need to leave the IDF to do what it needed to do. In Israel, international public opinion is often considered to be biased against Israel anyway, and thus not expected to influence Israel's decisions. As Nachman Shai (2009), a former IDF spokesperson, put it, "At this stage the first priority is to calm down Gaza and stop the rockets even if we pay in terms of our public relations and in terms of our public diplomacy."

Dissident Israeli voices claimed that the real intention of the war leaders was political—to throw down the Hamas government in the Gaza strip and to gain voters' sympathy in Israel (Noi, 2009). Mainstream commentators noted that the chief of staff for the Gaza operation, General Gabi Ashkenazi, was less interested in publicity than his predecessor: "Ashkenazi brought the army back to training and improved fitness, and he used restraint and caution in his actions" (Harel, 2009, p. 1; ATH). There was no quest for "an image of victory" this time, and the IDF spokesperson of the period functioned differently in a very different environment.

The outcomes of the Gaza operation are still happening while this chapter is being written, and the long-term Israeli blockade of Gaza is still in place in spite of international demonstrations condemning it. Complaints about war crimes also surfaced from Israeli soldiers who participated in the war, from Palestinian representatives of victims, and from the international community (e.g., human rights organizations, the United Nations). Legal action against Israeli military and political leaders for war crimes is on the agenda in some countries, and Israel's reputation in the world has deteriorated dramatically. Although the rocket attacks on the south of Israel stopped, Hamas is stronger than ever in Gaza. Nevertheless, public opinion in Israel still supports the Cast Lead operation and sees it as a success.

Brigadier-General Avi Benayahu: IDF Spokesperson and Censor

Benayahu was appointed as IDF spokesperson in 2007, following a career as a military reporter, adviser, and director of the IDF radio station. His communication strategy for the Gaza operation was designed in response to criticism about the 2006 IDF openness policy. The strategy was simple: no permission to media to enter Gaza, no soldier cellular phone communication allowed, no unauthorized interviews permitted, zero tolerance for leaks, the massive use of media—especially the Internet—to deliver the IDF message, and the delegitimization of groups criticizing the IDF. The IDF Spokesperson Unit was the only source of information for media, and reporters depended on Benayahu's briefings and narratives.

In fact, Goldman (2009) claimed that

> Israeli reporters were not permitted to enter the territory [Gaza] until the final days of the operation, when a handful of military

> correspondents were chosen for a limited embed. Even the border area inside Israel was a closed military zone. The ministry of defence also kept Gaza closed to international media, defying a Supreme Court order to let a pool of reporters in.

Most Israeli reporters accepted the limitations and, as they too responded to the criticism of the media in 2006, they followed a patriotic line to satisfy reader and viewer expectations. International correspondents, however, protested. They described Israel as a country that "used to be a democracy." Ethan Broner, head of the New York Times bureau, is quoted as being horrified that "there had not been a single editorial in the Israeli press about the moral dimension of the decision to keep the press out of Gaza" (Goldman, 2009).

The IDF posted their narrative about the Gaza operation rationale on an IDF YouTube channel (www.youtube.com/user/idfnadesk). According to Irit Atsmon (personal communication with the author in Tel Aviv, October 28, 2009), who was responsible for communication with international reporters as a reserve officer in the IDF Spokesperson Unit during the Gaza operation, Benayahu distributed 120 videos in four languages illustrating how Hamas used civilians and children as human shields. A total of 1,300 interviews were organized by the unit within 22 days of operation: "Communication was centralized and worked well," Atsmon said in an interview with the author.

An example of the ability of Benayahu to manipulate the Israeli media is the way he set the agenda regarding "Shovrim Shtika" (Breaking the Silence). This was an organization established by reserve soldiers to share their troubling experiences in the occupied territories with the Israeli public. The organization documented and verified 670 testimonies of IDF soldiers who participated in the war and were involved in, or witnessed, inhumane behavior. The report was released to international media and in Israel was given exclusively to *Haaretz* newspaper. Benayahu responded immediately. He took advantage of the other media outlets' anger at not being included to downplay the story and, eventually, to have it taken off the agenda. Instead of dealing with the soldiers' evidence, the media gave publicity to Benayahu's allegations against the organization's credibility and his claims that Shovrim Shtika was a company, not a nongovernmental organization (NGO), and was not transparent about their funding institutions. The fact that the organization faxed the documents to prove it was indeed an NGO and provided its financial report to all media editors did not make any difference (Grossman & Matan, 2009, p. 42). Thus, Israelis were much less exposed to the soldiers' stories than international audiences.

Israelis did not seem to care. Avinoam Brug (personal communication with the author in Tel Aviv, October 4, 2009), a director of an Israeli public opinion research company said,

> In crisis situations such as war, individuals are looking for a sense of mastery of their lives. The openness of 2006 gave them a feeling of chaos which they resented, whereas Benayahu in 2008/9 gave the feeling that things were under control. The Israeli public liked it.

However, the cost of the closure policy in international public opinion was devastating.

Conclusion

In discussing propaganda and public relations, Weaver, Motion, and Roper (2006) observed that in "a democracy other competing discourses (supposedly) also have avenues for expression and promotion" (p. 21). The military spokesperson's strategy actively restricted the idealistic "multiple discourse," and neither spokesperson attempted dialogue or allowed competing voices to be heard. Both used their privileged power to restrict the public discourse: Regev's openness was severely limited and, as much as Benayahu, she tried to cover up mistakes and malpractice and to silence alternative voices.

In Weaver et al.'s (2006) claim that "the merits of propaganda and public relations practice can only be judged in terms of the contexts and ends to which it was used" (p. 21), there is an assumption that public relations works for the public interest whereas propaganda works against the public interest. But who decides what the public interest is? The analysis of each spokesperson's work stresses the shaping role played by public opinion. When the public prefers messages that boost morale over messages that expose failures and question war goals, which strategy better serves the democratic system? Should the spokesperson follow the public demand or the commitment to truth? The two cases illustrate how public opinion and political pressures mattered more than democratic values. Neither spokesperson was interested in allowing an argument for advancing peace, or allowing criticism of possible human rights abuse, although, over time, these may serve the public interest better. The citizens' right to know is a fundamental value for ethical public relations. However, in certain situations, such as war, the public might not want to know the truth and prefer to surrender freedom of speech for the sake of such emotional needs as fear reduction and national pride.

Heath (2001) raised the following questions: "To what extent are certain practices universal? Are some unique to each context?" (p. 444). Following Heath, this chapter explored how military spokespeople represent public relations practice in war situations. Such practitioners are certainly an important part of the industry, and the Public Relations Society of America is currently preparing a special accreditation for military public relations executives (Accredited Public Relations—Military or APR-M). Questions remain: Are military practitioners able to follow the ethical demand to be truthful? Able to develop a dialogue? And to enable critical voices to be heard? Are they representatives of the public relations industry? In responding to L'Etang's (2006) call for research on "the perspective of practitioners" (p. 40), these two cases illuminated the intersections where the public relations practitioner, the media, and public opinion interact in shaping democracy.

References

Azoulay, Y. (2007, November 20). From the mouth of the IDF—not the government. *Haaretz* [The Land; English edition], p. 7.

Ben, A. (2006, October 24). 59 Iranian missile launchers were destroyed within only 34 minutes. *Haaretz* [The Land], p. 7.

Brom, S. (2007). Military and political goals in a limited war against a guerrilla organization. In M. Elarm & S. Brom (Eds.), *The second Lebanon war: Strategic dimensions* (pp. 15–24). Tel Aviv, Israel: Yediot Aharonot.

Broom, M. (2009). *Cutlip & Center's effective public relations* (10th ed.). Upper Saddle River, NJ: Prentice Hall.

Caspi, D. (2009). *A victory in search of a photo.* Retrieved January 25, 2009, from www.ynet.co.il/Ext/Comp?ArticleLayuout/CdaArticlePrintPreview/1,2506,L-336

Commission for the Investigation of the Campaign in Lebanon 2006, State of Israel. (2008). *The Second Lebanon War: Final report.* Retrieved February 5, 2008, from www.vaadatwino.co.il/reporets.html

Cutlip, S. M. (1994). *The unseen power.* Hillsdale, NJ: Lawrence Erlbaum.

Cutlip, S. M. (1995). *Public relations history: From the 17th to the 20th century: The antecedents.* Hillsdale, NJ: Lawrence Erlbaum.

Dor, D., Iram, S., & Voldavsky, O. (2007). *War till the last moment: Israeli media in the second Lebanon war.* Jerusalem, Israel: Keshev, Center for Protection of Democracy in Israel.

Ewen, S. (1996). *PR! A social history of spin.* New York: Basic Books.

Ganon, T. (2006, September). Militants discourse. *Hayin HaShviit* [The Seventh Eye], *64*, 6–9.

Goldman, L. (2009, May/June). Covering Gaza from Israel: What the Israelis wanted to know about the war. *Columbia Journalism Review.* Retrieved June 15, 2009, from http://www.cjr.org/campaign_desk/covering_gaza_from_israel_1.php?page=all&print=true

Grossman, L., & Matan, O. (2009, July 24). The major censor. *Ha'ir Tel Aviv* [The City], *1503,* 38–42.

Grunig, J. E. (1989). Symmetrical presuppositions as a framework for public relations theory. In C. H. Botan & V. Hazleton Jr. (Eds.), *Public relations theory* (pp. 17–44). Hillsdale, NJ: Lawrence Erlbaum.

Harel, A. (2009, August 14). There is no reason for a party. *Haaretz* [The Land], *Hashavua* [The Week], p. 1.

Heath, R. L. (2001). Learning best practice from experience and research. In R. L. Heath (Ed.), *Handbook of public relations* (pp. 441–444). Thousand Oaks, CA: Sage.

Hiebert, R. E. (1991). Public relations as a weapon of modern warfare. *Public Relations Review, 17*(2), 107–116.

Hiebert, R. E. (1993). Public relations, propaganda, and war: A book review and essay on the literature. *Public Relations Review, 19*(3), 293–302.

Hiebert, R. E. (2003). Public relations and propaganda in framing the Iraq war: A preliminary review. *Public Relations Review, 29*(3), 245–255.

Israel Defense Force. (n.d.). *IDF* spokesperson *unit.* Retrieved December 1, 2009, from http://dover.idf.il/IDF/English/units/branches/amatz/Spokesperson/default.htm

Kalb, M. (2007). The Israeli-Hezbollah war of 2006: The media as a weapon in asymmetrical conflict. *Harvard International Journal of Press/Politics, 12*(3), 43–66.

Kanti, M. (2006, September). IDF spokesperson sums up: Our functioning was excellent. *Hayin HaShviit* [The Seventh Eye], *64,* 12–15.

Kaspit, B. (2007, October 8). In many aspects, the Hasbarah was more successful than the war. *Haaretz* [The Land], *Sof Shavua* [Weekend], p. 21–28.

Lattimore, D., Baskin, D., Heiman, S. T., & Toth, E. (2007). *Public relations: The profession and the practice* (2nd ed.). New York: McGraw-Hill.

Lebel, U. (2005). Confrontation or co-dependency? The relationship between security and communication at war and in routine times: Theoretical framework. In U. Lebel (Ed.), *Security and communication: Dynamics of relationships* (pp. 13–48). Beer Sheva, Israel: Ben Gurion University, Ben Gurion Institute for Israel Research.

L'Etang, J. (2004). *Public relations in Britain: A history of professional practice in the 20th century.* Hillsdale, NJ: Lawrence Erlbaum.

L'Etang, J. (2006). Public relations and propaganda: Conceptual issues, methodological problems, and public relations discourse. In J. L'Etang & M. Pieczka (Eds.), *Public relations: Critical debates and contemporary practice* (pp. 23–40). Mahwah, NJ: Lawrence Erlbaum.

Levi, G. (2009). Galei Zahal. *Haaretz* [The Land]. Retrieved January 3, 2009, from http://elections.walla.co.il/?w=/100/1410086/@@/item/printer

The media is not guilty [Editorial]. (2007, April 20). *Haaretz* [The Land], p. 9.

Noi, O. (2009). *Forget "scorching the consciousness."* Retrieved January 6, 2009, from www.ynet.co.il/Ext/Comp/ArticleLayout/CdaArticlePrintPreview/1,2506,L-3651

Peper, A. (2009, July 29). During "Cast Lead" operation: IDF checked phones of hundreds officers and have not found leaks. *Haaretz* [The Land], p. 3.

Peri, Y. (2006, November). *The media in the Second Lebanon War.* Paper presented at a seminar organized by the communication departments of Sapir Academic College and the Netanya Academic College, Tel Aviv, Israel.

Pinto, G. (2007, March 7). Under the IDF spotlight. *Haaretz* [The Land]. Retrieved August 22, 2007, from www.haaaretz.com/hasen/objects/pages/PrintArticleEn.jhtml?itemNo=834

Regev, M. (2006, October 20). *An oral testimonial to the "Israel Press Council committee to set ethical code for media during war."* Presented at a public meeting attended by the author in Tel Aviv, 2006.

Rozen, G. (2006). *Ombudsman: 11th annual report 2005.* Jerusalem: The Second Television & Radio Authority.

Shai, N. (2009). *Former military PR guru explains thoughts behind the words* [Video recording]. Retrieved December 23, 2009, from www.youtube.com/watch?v=9UyYqUBSbPA

Shavit, A. (2009, January 1). Defensive war. *Haaretz* [The Land], p. 5.

Shelah, O., & Limore, Y. (2007). *Captives of Lebanon.* Tel-Aviv, Israel: Yediot Ahronoth Books and Chemed Books.

Shoen, A. (2005). If you want it or not: Miri Regev is a brand. *Iton Tel Aviv.* Retrieved September 3, 2006, from www.tam.co.il/14_10_2005/magazine1.html

Smith, M. F. (2005). Warfare and public relations. In R. L. Heath (Ed.), *Encyclopedia of public relations*

(Vol. 2, pp. 893–897). Thousand Oaks, CA: Sage.

Tausig, S. (2006, September). A non-virtual war. *Hayin HaShviit* [The Seventh Eye], *64*, 26–28.

Toledano, M. (2006, October 20). *Personal transcripts from a meeting of the "Israel Press Council committee to set ethical code for media during wartime," Tel Aviv.*

Weaver, C. K., Motion, J., & Roper, J. (2006). From propaganda to discourse (and back again): Truth, power, the public interest, and public relations. In J. L'Etang & M. Pieczka (Eds.), *Public relations: Critical debates and contemporary practice* (pp. 7–21). Mahwah, NJ: Lawrence Erlbaum.

Weiman, G. (2002, July). A lot of criticism is published against the media, from right and left, during war time and crisis, and afterwards. *Hayin HaShviit* [The Seventh Eye], *39*, 13–15.

Weiman, G. (2007). *The public criticism of the media in the Lebanon War 2006.* Tel Aviv, Israel: Tel Aviv University.

CHAPTER 42

Sport Public Relations

Thomas E. Isaacson

Sport public relations has myriad opportunities for scholars, educators, and practitioners. The growth in professional and university sports in the United States and around the world has resulted in many live and mediated viewing options for fans. The demand by fans for sport information has resulted in increased media coverage. Burton and Howard (1999) bluntly stated, "Professional sports command constant media and consumer attention" (p. 44).

Consequently, increased media coverage has helped generate additional revenue for sport organizations that supplements ticket and merchandise sales. In 2005, ESPN (Entertainment and Sports Programming Network) signed an 8-year contract with the National Football League (NFL) to televise Monday Night Football at the cost of $1.1 billion per year. The NFL maintains separate contracts with CBS (Columbia Broadcasting System), FOX, and NBC (National Broadcasting Company) for other games and provides game coverage and analysis through its league-owned channel NFL Network.

Television programming, which covers all the major sports in the United States, provides one of a number of media revenue streams for sport organizations. Major League Baseball created an advanced media division to manage the sport's digital assets in 2000. Seven years later it generated close to $400 million in revenue that was shared equally among the league's 30 teams (Torre & Verducci, 2009). Satellite television and radio produced additional revenue.

University sport teams generate significant revenues of their own. In addition to media broadcast contracts, universities have focused on stadium expansions, premium seating options, merchandise sales, and lucrative sponsorship deals. In college football, this resulted in 10 different teams earning at least $45 million in 2005 (Schwartz, 2007). *Forbes*'s 2009 list of the most valuable men's college basketball teams shows that 8 of the top-10 most valuable teams generated more than $10 million in revenue the previous season (Schwartz, 2009).

In these environments, sport public relations practitioners fill roles dealing with media relations, new media, Web management and design, print publication development, community relations, promotion, special event planning, integrated communication, and sport marketing. This chapter will review approaches to university education in sport public relations and discuss research opportunities for scholars in the field before concluding with a discussion on research outlets.

Education in Sport Public Relations

Public relations educators have recognized the student interest in sport public relations and its career options. Recent editions of popular undergraduate public relations textbooks discuss the topic from a variety of perspectives. Wilcox and Cameron (2009) included an entertainment, sport, and travel chapter that briefly discusses sport publicity and sponsorship. Similarly, Newsom, Turk, and Kruckeberg (2007) included sport in their description of specialization areas within public relations. Although Cutlip, Center, and Broom (2006) do not include a specific section on sport public relations, sport examples are provided to illustrate concepts in the textbook (e.g., China's 2008 Olympic bid, the community relations activities by the Chicago Bulls).

Beyond these references in textbooks, however, Neupauer (2001), when discussing needs in the university sports information field, wrote that "educators, scholars, athletic directors, and sports information directors (SIDs) need to make sure that those aspiring to enter the field are prepared to handle the job by providing appropriate coursework and training" (p. 554). The comment applies to the preparation for public relations employment at a professional sport level as well. Universities have taken a variety of approaches in response.

Through curriculum changes, some universities now offer individual courses exclusively focused on sport public relations, sport information, and sport communication. Other universities have taken it a step further by creating entire programs in sport public relations. Northern Michigan University created an entertainment and sport major that is designed to follow the Public Relations Society of America (PRSA) curriculum guidelines. The public relations faculty developed the program and teach the courses. Created in 2003, the major attracts 40 students annually to its introductory courses (K. Rybacki, personal communication, August 26, 2009).

An alternative approach has been taken by universities such as the University of North Carolina (UNC) at Chapel Hill and Bradley University. These universities include sport public relations education as a part of their integrated programs. UNC's Sport Communication Program, started in 2002, offers a variety of courses, including sport communication, ethical issues in sport communication, and sport marketing and advertising. Bradley's Sport Communication Program is designed to familiarize students with sport journalism, promotion and publicity, production and performance, and sport media relations.

While these examples show that some university public relations departments are capitalizing on the demand for specialized sport public relations education, at other universities this need is being fulfilled by other academic departments. For example, the University of Michigan offers a sport management program that is housed in its School of Kinesiology. This program includes courses designed to familiarize students with organizational strategy and behavior, promotion and marketing, media, and research methods. In addition to preparing students for management positions in sport, it also educates them for positions in sport information and communication. Similarly, Indiana University offers a sport marketing and management program through its Department of Kinesiology that offers courses in sport promotion and public relations and sport communication. Additionally, the department partners with the university's business school for integrated course offerings.

The universities and programs described here are not intended to provide a comprehensive list of sport public relations education. Indeed, many more universities in the United States offer similar programs. Instead, the examples simply show the diverse approaches being taken to fill educational needs in this specialized area and are intended to raise awareness of the opportunities.

Within the public relations field, university administrators and educators will have to decide if their institution will develop courses and programs to address the sport public relations needs. If not, these educational opportunities are likely to be met with increasing frequency by kinesiology, marketing, and management departments.

Research in Sport Public Relations

Academic research exploring sport public relations topics is relatively limited but appears to be increasing as scholars in public relations and related disciplines have published a variety of related studies in academic journals (e.g., Desmarais & Bruce, 2008; Fortunato, 2000; Funk & Pritchard, 2006; Hardin & McClung, 2002; L'Etang, 2006; McCleneghan, 1995; Neupauer, 1999; Stoldt, Miller, & Comfort, 2001; Woo, An, & Cho, 2008). This section reviews a number of the pertinent articles that have contributed to our understanding of the work of sport public relations practitioners.

Online survey research by Hardin and McClung (2002) gathered demographic information about college sports information directors (SIDs)—the term often used to describe sport public relations practitioners at a college or university level—and solicited advice from respondents for students interested in the field. Unlike the overall public relations field that is about 70% female (Wilcox & Cameron, 2009), results show that males make up a majority (89%) of the practicing SIDs. Although random sampling was not used in the survey, these numbers are generally consistent with earlier research (McCleneghan, 1995; Neupauer, 1999).

The typical SID has 16.81 years of experience in the sports field, has been at his or her current institution for nearly 12 years, has a bachelor's degree in journalism/public relations or a related field, and is a member of the College Sports Information Directors Association (CoSIDA). More than 60% make at least $45,000 per year, although 18% make less than $35,000.

Responses were solicited to the following open-ended question: "What would you tell a current college student who wants to enter the sports information/media relations profession?" The qualitative responses were coded and revealed the following general themes:

> Get as much writing experience as possible, gain as much experience as possible as an undergraduate, be prepared to work long hours, and plan on a career with little pay and little appreciation, but also plan on it being a lot of fun. (Hardin & McClung, 2002, p. 38)

McCleneghan (1995) used a cluster sampling method to survey SIDs from regional areas around the United States. Demographic information of survey participants was similar to that reported by Hardin and McClung (2002). The top external publics SIDs work with most frequently include members of the media at radio stations, TV stations, and newspapers. Qualitative open-ended questions were used to help describe the overall work environment and job responsibilities. The most common response to the question "What takes up most of the SID's time during the week?" was administrative duties (55%).

Neupauer (1999) surveyed SIDs in the mid-Atlantic region of the United States using a purposive sample to determine if communication trait differences existed among practitioners employed at large and small universities. No significant differences were found among respondents. While the study contributes to the development of an SID profile, Neupauer added that "the next generation of SID research needs to clearly define the Sports Information Director's role within all intercollegiate athletic environments" (p. 169).

Stoldt et al. (2001) surveyed athletic directors at NCAA (National Collegiate Athletic Association) Division I, II, and III institutions to gain an understanding of their perceptions of the work done by SIDs. Results showed that a majority of the SIDs (92.3%) are perceived to primarily fill technical roles. The athletic directors' highest levels of confidence in the sport information staff's ability to perform public relations tasks were on producing sport information materials, working with coaches and athletes, maintaining media contacts, and coordinating special events. Conversely, the lowest levels of confidence were for conducting public relations research, mediating conflicts, setting public relations goals, and identifying emerging issues.

When athletic directors were asked to identify the benefits they received from public relations programs, those cited least frequently included a variety of ways by which to generate increased revenue (e.g., ticket and merchandise sales). In response to items related to strong and weak departmental relationships, the weakest perceived relationships were with students, alumni, and boosters.

Stoldt et al. (2001) summarized the results by stating, "If SIDs are indeed their athletic departments' top public relations officers, and yet serve in limited public relations capacities, then it seems likely that college athletic departments are failing to maximize their public relations effectiveness" (p. 170).

The studies by McCleneghan (1995) and Stoldt et al. (2001) raise troubling questions about the role of SIDs in strategic public relations planning. If the majority of their time is spent on administrative duties and they are perceived to fill only technical roles by athletic directors, who are likely to be part of the dominant coalition in the athletic department, their opportunities to provide strategic public relations advice will be limited. If true, this could have important and negative implications for practitioners. Depending on the types of publicity SIDs are asked to engage in, this perhaps may be the reason that Grunig and Hunt (1984) listed sport as an area where press-agentry/publicity is still practiced. Future research should further explore the topic.

In a study focused on strategies used by practitioners working in professional sport, Fortunato (2000) used a case study approach to determine the effectiveness of the National Basketball Association's (NBA's) media relations strategies and the success the organization had in its efforts to influence media coverage. After conducting in-depth interviews with league executives and public relations staff, Fortunato concluded that "NBA personnel certainly believe they are a very powerful agent in the agenda-setting process and that mass media coverage would be vastly different without the public relations and promotional strategies that are implemented by the NBA" (p. 496).

While also focusing on professional sport, Funk and Pritchard (2006) used an experimental design to explore the effects of positive and negative newspaper coverage on attitudes toward a professional Major League Baseball team. Using a repeated measures prepost design, they found that commitment influences a reader's processing of messages and, as a result, can moderate reader responses. Committed readers had better recall of supportive articles and less committed readers recalled more facts from negative articles.

These results are useful for sport public relations practitioners who may be asked to advise on media relations tactics and develop organizational responses to negative publicity. The study "emphasizes how important media relations are for altering consumer beliefs and feelings about organizations" (Funk & Pritchard, 2006, p. 618). In addition, practitioners should consider different message development strategies depending on the commitment level of the target public and the valence of any recently published news about the organization. The authors' article summary notes that future research would benefit from comparing source characteristics that include both team-sponsored and nonteam-sponsored communication.

The aforementioned articles contribute to a profile of the university sports information profession and begin to explore media relations issues that influence public relations practice in professional sports. Future research should build on topics described here and consider additional research questions that can improve the practical application of results and improve educators' ability to prepare students for careers in sport public relations. A number of research possibilities are discussed in the next section.

Research Opportunities

Given the growth of professional and university sports during the past few decades, an increase in sport public relations research topics is not surprising. However, a number of important issues and topics that can further improve our understanding of sport public relations remain untested. Indeed, despite the research increase, Neupauer's (2001) plea for helping the unknown field of sport public relations through the development of more scholarly articles on related topics remains relevant. This section explores some of the opportunities.

Similar to public relations practice in other areas, media relations activities make up a large portion of the sport public relations practitioner's work. In one of the few textbooks focused specifically on sport public relations, Stoldt, Dittmore, and Branvold (2006) wrote, "The public that perhaps has the greatest potential effect on a sport organization, however, may be the mass media" (p. 64). Their rationale for the statement is supported by describing the extensive attention paid to sport in the media (e.g., all-sport television and radio stations, sport sections of newspapers, and weekly sport magazines). The authors noted the unique partnership that exists between media and sport organizations through their combined efforts to deliver sport content to fans.

Depth interviews that I conducted in 2008 with public relations practitioners working for professional sport organizations and university sports information departments confirm the media relations emphasis in their day-to-day work. Comments from professional sport public relations practitioners working with two different Major League Baseball teams in the Midwest included "The majority of our time is spent on media relations" and "I am continually working on my relationships with the media." University sports information directors working at NCAA Division I and Division II institutions expressed similar sentiments but noted that the sports associated with the media relations work changed frequently during the academic year.

Research opportunities include an in-depth analysis and an improved understanding of the relationships between media members and practitioners and evaluations of the media relations tactics typically used in sport.

Media-Practitioner Relationships

Little is known about media-practitioner relationships in sport public relations. The consumer demand that exists for sport information has the potential to influence the power balance of the relationships. Instead of a situation where the practitioner is actively promoting his or her organization to media members in an effort to increase media coverage, many practitioners in sport are managing requests from the media and making decisions about media access that will be provided to key organizational spokespeople (e.g., players, coaches, owners, and general managers).

The media demand requires organizations to develop credential policies that determine eligibility and provide varied access levels at events (Stoldt et al., 2006). At a professional sport level, a team may issue season credentials to more than 300 media members on an annual basis (B. Britten, personal communication, April 25, 2008).

To accommodate media demands, sport organizations have created press boxes that provide the media with opportunities to work while watching an event (Stoldt et al., 2006). A press box is typically managed by the home team's public relations staff. This creates an environment that encourages the development of interpersonal relationships between practitioners and the media, particularly with those who attend regularly. Additional opportunities for interactions take place when both practitioners and members of the media travel to road sporting events. Not only do relationships develop during the course of a season; they also continue from year to year, as many members of the media will cover the same team for an extended period of time.

Depending on the size of the media market, the number of media members covering a team on a regular basis will vary. For example, the Chicago White Sox have beat writers from four local newspapers who cover the team from spring training through the end of the season (Beghtol, 2008). The newspapers employing the writers also have 13 sports columnists on staff who will cover the team on an irregular basis. Conversely, the Minnesota Twins, located in Minneapolis, are regularly covered by beat writers from two local newspapers, and each of the papers employs three sports columnists (M. Herman, personal communication, April 22, 2008).

Although media-practitioner relationships in sport remain uninvestigated, power in media-practitioner relationships has been extensively covered in the communication and public relations literature. This provides an appropriate theoretical background and approach for investigating the topic in sport.

The importance of power in human communication is illustrated by its inclusion in the development of theories and as a key variable to test research hypotheses across communication disciplines (Giles & Wiemann, 1987; McCombs & Shaw, 1972; McGuire, 2001; Millar & Rogers, 1987). Similarly, in public relations research, power has impacted theory development and academic research.

Definitions of power in public relations research vary slightly. Plowman (1998) defined it as something that "involves interactions among different players and the ability to employ some means to achieve an intended effect" (p. 241). The basis of this definition focuses on relationships between people (Dahl, 1957). Dozier, Grunig, and Grunig (1995) defined power simply as "the capacity to exert influence, a transaction in which you get others to change their behavior as you intended" (p. 75). However, they note that this definition of power is indicative of a one-way view of public relations. To extend the definition to include a two-way perspective, Dozier et al. (1995) explained power as follows:

> Excellent communication programs incorporate another dimension of power: the communicator's ability to influence decisions about an organization's goods and services, its policies, and its behavior. The communication department must have power and influence within the dominant coalition to help organizations practice the two-way symmetrical model. (p. 75)

A 2005 special issue of *Journal of Public Relations Research* was dedicated to the continued influence of power on public relations. Within it, Berger (2005) argued that "any public relations theory is deficient to the extent it fails to account for power relations and structures in organizations" (p. 23). This supports the common perspective on power in public relations that focuses on the need for practitioners to become part of an organization's dominant coalition, defined as "that group of people with the power to set directions and affect structure in organizations" (Dozier et al., 1995, p. 15).

Approaching the issue from a postmodern perspective, Holtzhausen and Voto (2002) agreed that power is important in public relations, but they argue that practitioners can exercise power outside the dominant coalition using personal characteristics, relationship building, and expertise. Consistent across the different approaches is a focus on power and relationships within an organization. Indeed, Holtzhausen and Voto noted that additional research on power relations between counselors and clients would be valuable to the public relations field.

A logical, yet related, approach would be to investigate power differences between public relations practitioners and a critical external public—the media. A lack of attention to the power differences between these two groups exists despite the dominant role of media relations as a method of communicating messages with targeted publics in modern public relations.

Cho (2006) investigated the impact of types of power and contingent factors that may limit or facilitate power related to health public relations practitioners and their media relationships. Previous research results "suggest that journalists perceive themselves as more powerful and valuable than public relations practitioners" (p. 564).

However, in health reporting, when public relations practitioners play a mediating role between journalists and experts in the industry and the subject matter is often complex, the power in the relationship is expected to be different. Results of a Web survey conducted with PRSA members shows expert power to have the highest mean value, and the respondents both perceived themselves to be experts and were used by reporters covering health news. In addition, expert power was significantly correlated with frequency of media contact and years of experience in health care.

Cho's (2006) research provides a good starting point for studies exploring the relationship between the media and practitioners in sport. While sport's subject matter is not typically complex, practitioners do play a key mediating role between journalists and the "experts" they want to interview. Particularly in professional sport organizations and prominent university sport programs, demand from consumers for sport information creates a situation where media members are relying on practitioners for story ideas, supporting content for story ideas, and, most important, providing access to sources needed to complete stories.

Consumer demand also creates a situation where the media members are asked to repeatedly report on sport organizations. For example, print journalists, television broadcasters, and radio broadcasters not only cover all the games of a particular athletic team; they are also asked to produce content on nongame days and, increasingly, during the team's off-season as well.

Few public relations practitioners working for corporations or representing clients in an agency setting have the luxury of consumer demand for media coverage of their employer or client on a daily basis. The impact that this has in a sport environment on public relations practices and the key media-practitioner relationship should be explored.

Media Relations Tactics

Media relations in public relations practice has been defined as "working with mass media in seeking publicity or responding to their interests in the organization" (Wilcox & Cameron, 2009, p. 10). The value of engaging in media relations is to capitalize on the third-party credibility associated with a message published or broadcast by a member of the independent media (Sweetser, Porter, Chung, & Kim, 2008). Its use as a tactic by public relations practitioners has been widespread and prevalent, but in sport public relations, it may be even more popular.

Stoldt et al. (2006) call media relations the most commonly used tactic by sport public relations practitioners. Practical application of the tactic often involves tasks intended to facilitate media coverage of sporting events. These tasks include managing press credentials, organizing and managing a press area (e.g., press box, postgame interview room), designing and writing extensive media guides, writing news releases, and researching and writing game notes. The primary result of this attention to the media is consistent coverage of sporting events and the development of game stories summarizing the outcome.

The impact of game stories on fan behavior, however, is unknown, and it provides an opportunity for research that has practical implications. Scholars should consider measuring the effectiveness of game stories and other tactics at producing behavioral changes among target publics.

It is logical to expect that most of the readers and viewers of media-produced games stories are already fans of one of the participating teams. In many instances, the fans may have even watched or listened to the event prior to exposing themselves to the subsequent media coverage. If true, this means that game stories may have a limited impact on fan behavior. Instead, it is people who are already fans who consume the coverage and reinforce their already positive attitudes. This would do little to attract new fans or generate additional revenue.

Sport public relations practitioners, like their colleagues in other parts of the field, are challenged by owners at a professional level and athletic directors at a university level to show how their work affects the organization's bottom line (e.g., in generating revenue, protecting against lost revenue). Alternative approaches to media relations should be considered that could potentially attract new fans or increase the financial commitment of casual fans.

Another media relations approach involves the promotion and development of human interest stories. These stories use the human element, often in the form of an individual story, to inform an audience of a topic. The emphasis of the story tends to be either unusual (i.e., unexpected behaviors or events) or based on emotional appeals (Ryan & Tankard, 2005). These stories, which are used less frequently by sport public relations practitioners, only receive a brief mention by Stoldt et al. (2006) in their sport public relations textbook.

Reasons for the limited emphasis on human interest stories by sport public relations practitioners are unknown. They may simply be overwhelmed with a high number of tactical responsibilities, an issue identified in previous research (McCleneghan, 1995; Stoldt et al., 2001), and the result may be a lack of time for story identification and promotion. Other possibilities include a lack of recognition of newsworthy human interest stories within the organization or a low perceived value of the placement of such stories. Regardless of the reasons, the lack of emphasis on human interest story promotion by sport public relations practitioners could be a missed opportunity.

Practitioners may be able to use human interest stories to influence key target publics. Intuitively, it seems possible that human interest stories will generate more word-of-mouth discussion and, in the new media environment, are more likely to be forwarded to other people or posted on a social networking site such as Facebook. When athletic directors, often the immediate supervisors of sports information directors, were asked to rate the strength of their programs' relationships with various stakeholders, the weakest relationship was with students (Stoldt et al., 2001). This could help improve weak relationships and enhance SIDs' credibility with athletic directors.

However, empirical research is needed to substantiate these claims. One approach to rigorously testing these ideas is to develop experimental research designs. This would allow researchers to manipulate message sources and isolate the effects of different story types. It would also improve the generalizability of the findings and generate results that would be immediately useful to practitioners. Experimental research has been advocated by public relations scholars as a way to help determine causality and to evaluate communication message effectiveness (Boynton & Dougall, 2006; Stacks, 2002), and such an approach would also be beneficial in sport public relations research.

An exhaustive list of research possibilities is not within the scope of this chapter. Certainly, a number of relevant topics important to sport public relations deserve further examination by scholars. Future chapters and articles should address the following topics:

- Public relations strategies and tactics that can be used to generate additional revenue and increase fan support (e.g., new media possibilities, evaluating media guide influence on media coverage and the university recruiting process, and an improved understanding of fan motivational factors)
- Sport sponsorship and its impact on consumer behavior
- Product placement in sport and its value as competition for consumer attention increases
- Community relations activities and their impact on consumer perceptions of corporate social responsibility

- Crisis public relations issues stemming from the behavior of sponsors (e.g., Enron as a sponsor of the Houston Astros' home ballpark), fans (e.g., college basketball fans rioting after team success or failure), and athletes (e.g., illegal use of performance-enhancing substances)

In some instances, scholars will be able to draw from existing public relations material and related research areas. This can help expose them to a variety of theoretical perspectives that can, when appropriate, be applied to sport public relations. For example, sport sponsorship has been covered extensively in sport marketing journals (e.g., Alexandris, Tsaousi, & James, 2007; Dees, Bennett, & Villegas, 2008; Jensen & Butler, 2007; Kuzma, Veltri, Kuzma, & Miller, 2003).

Research Outlets

Outlets for sport public relations research exist at multiple academic association and professional organization national conferences. In the academic area, the Association for Education in Journalism and Mass Communication (AEJMC) and National Communication Association (NCA) provide two options.

While each association's public relations division is a possible outlet, scholars should consider other divisions and interest groups as well. For example, AEJMC's Entertainment Studies Interest Group includes sport studies as a part of its specialization along with video games and entertainment media.

Smaller specialized conferences focusing exclusively on sport issues to consider include the Scholarly Conference on College Sport and Summit on Communication and Sport.

A variety of options exist through professional associations. PRSA has an entertainment and sport specialization area that meets at its annual international conference. CoSIDA holds an annual summer meeting designed to improve SIDs' job proficiency through technical panels dealing with communications, publications, and promotions.

Journals that practitioners typically consider as outlets for public relations research—such as *Public Relations Review* and the *Journal of Public Relations Research*—are also appropriate for sport public relations work. A 2008 special issue of *Public Relations Review* was dedicated to sport topics and attempted to "draw attention to the considerable scope that sport has for public relations practice in the field and for applied and critical scholarship" (L'Etang & Hopwood, 2008, p. 87). Other journals that have published sport public relations articles include *Sport Marketing Quarterly*, *International Journal of Sport Marketing and Sponsorship*, *Journal of Business Research*, and *The Social Science Journal*. Traditional communication and media journals may also be considered when the topic is an appropriate fit.

Conclusion

The ability of sport to capture consumers' attention and money appears to be increasing. This means that there will be additional job opportunities in sport public relations and related areas as the magnitude of public relations successes and failures are enhanced. A likely consequence of having significant financial rewards at stake is a demand for evidence-based decisions by owners and athletic directors.

In this environment, a variety of academic departments at universities—public relations, communication, marketing, management, and kinesiology—are positioning themselves to be the educational providers for students interested in the field. Decisions need to be made by public relations educators about the role they will play in sport public relations education. This chapter is intended to increase awareness in the following areas:

- The different approaches to sport public relations education

- Research topics that will improve our understanding of sport public relations
- Research outlets that exist for sport public relations scholars

Educators, scholars, and practitioners can expand the topics covered here, and doing so will benefit public relations in sport. Many of the proposed research ideas will benefit from practitioner-scholar collaboration, perhaps improving the practical application of research results. In fact, some topics are impossible to effectively research without practitioner support.

In an area where most practitioners do not maintain membership or involvement in traditional public relations professional organizations (e.g., PRSA) or academic associations (e.g., AEJMC), collaborative work could increase the links between this group of practitioners and the rest of the public relations field. More interaction between the groups would strengthen sport public relations education and, based on research results, potentially change some of the normative media relations tactics used in the field.

References

Alexandris, K., Tsaousi, E., & James, J. (2007). Predicting sponsorship outcomes from attitudinal constructs: The case of a professional basketball event. *Sport Marketing Quarterly, 16*(3), 130–139.

Beghtol, B. (Ed.). (2008). *Chicago White Sox media guide* [Brochure]. Chicago, IL: Graphic Arts Studio.

Berger, B. K. (2005). Power over, power with, and power to relations: Critical reflections on public relations, the dominant coalition, and activism. *Journal of Public Relations Research, 17*(1), 5–28.

Boynton, L., & Dougall, E. (2006). The methodical avoidance of experiments in public relations research. *PRism, 4*(1). Retrieved February 18, 2010, from http://praxis.massey.ac.nz/prism_online_journ.html

Burton, R., & Howard, D. (1999). Professional sports leagues: Marketing mix mayhem. *Marketing Management, 8*(1), 37–46.

Cho, S. (2006). The power of public relations in media relations: A national survey of health PR practitioners. *Journalism & Mass Communication Quarterly, 83*(3), 563–580.

Cutlip, S. M., Center, A. H., & Broom, G. M. (2006). *Effective public relations* (8th ed.). Upper Saddle River, NJ: Prentice Hall.

Dahl, R. (1957). The concept of power. *Behavioral Science, 2*, 201–215.

Dees, W., Bennett, G., & Villegas, J. (2008). Measuring the effectiveness of sponsorship of an elite intercollegiate football program. *Sport Marketing Quarterly, 17*(2), 79–89.

Desmarais, F., & Bruce, T. (2008). Blurring the boundaries of sports public relations: National stereotypes as sport announcers' public relations tools. *Public Relations Review, 34*(2), 183–191.

Dozier, D. M., Grunig, J. E., & Grunig, L. A. (1995). *Manager's guide to excellence in public relations and communications management.* Mahwah, NJ: Lawrence Erlbaum.

Fortunato, J. (2000). Public relations strategies for creating mass media content: A case study of the National Basketball Association. *Public Relations Review, 26*(4), 481–497.

Funk, D., & Pritchard, M. (2006). Sport publicity: Commitment's moderation of message effects. *Journal of Business Research, 59*(5), 613–621.

Giles, H., & Wiemann, J. M. (1987). Language, social comparison, and power. In C. R. Berger & S. H. Chaffee (Eds.), *The handbook of communication science* (pp. 350–384). Newbury Park, CA: Sage.

Grunig, J. E., & Hunt, T. (1984). *Managing public relations.* New York: Holt McDougal.

Hardin, R., & McClung, S. (2002). Collegiate sports information: A profile of the profession. *Public Relations Quarterly, 47*(2), 35–39.

Holtzhausen, D. R., & Voto, R. (2002). Resistance from the margins: The postmodern public relations practitioner as organizational activist. *Journal of Public Relations Research, 14*(1), 57–84.

Jensen, R., & Butler, B. (2007, October). Is sport becoming too commercialized? The Houston Astros' public relations crisis. International Journal of Sport Marketing & Sponsorship, 23–32.

Kuzma, J. R.,Veltri, F. R., Kuzma, A. T., & Miller, J. J. (2003). Negative corporate sponsor information: The impact on consumer attitudes and purchase intentions. *International Sports Journal, 7*(2), 140–147.

L'Etang, J. (2006). Public relations and sport in promotional culture. *Public Relations Review, 32,* 386–394.

L'Etang, J., & Hopwood, M. (2008). Sports public relations. *Public Relations Review, 34,* 87–89.

McCleneghan, J. S. (1995). The sports information director: No attention, no respect, and a PR practitioner in trouble. *Public Relations Quarterly, 40*(2), 28–32.

McCombs, M., & Shaw, D. L. (1972). The agenda setting function of mass media. *Public Opinion Quarterly, 36,* 176–187.

McGuire, W. J. (2001). Input and output variables currently promising for constructing persuasive communications. In R. E. Rice & C. K. Atkin (Eds.), *Public communication campaigns* (pp. 22–48). Thousand Oaks, CA: Sage.

Millar, F. E., & Rogers, L. E. (1987). Relational dimensions of interpersonal dynamics. In M. E. Roloff & G. R. Miller (Eds.), *Interpersonal processes: New directions in communication research* (pp. 117–139). Newbury Park, CA: Sage.

Neupauer, N. C. (1999). A personality traits study of sports information directors at "big" vs. "small" programs in the East. *The Social Science Journal, 36*(1), 163–172.

Neupauer, N. C. (2001). Sports information directing: A plea for helping an unknown field. In R. L. Heath (Ed.), *Handbook of public relations* (pp. 551–555). Thousand Oaks, CA: Sage.

Newsom, D., Turk, J., & Kruckeberg, D. (2007). *This is PR: The realities of public relations.* Belmont, CA: Thompson Advantage Books.

Plowman, K. D. (1998). Power in conflict for public relations. *Journal of Public Relations Research, 10*(4), 237–261.

Ryan, M., & Tankard, J., Jr. (2005). *Writing for print and digital media.* New York: McGraw-Hill.

Schwartz, P. J. (2007, November 20). The most valuable college football teams. *Forbes.* Retrieved September 2, 2009, from www.forbes.com/2007/11/20/notre-dame-fooball-biz-sports-cx_ps_1120collegeball.html

Schwartz, P. J. (2009, March 16). The most valuable college basketball teams. *Forbes.* Retrieved September 2, 2009, from www.forbes.com/2009/03/16/most-valuable-college-basketball-teams-business-sports-final-four.html

Stacks, D. W. (2002). *Primer of public relations research.* New York: Guilford Press.

Stoldt, G. C., Dittmore, S. W., & Branvold, S. E. (2006). *Sport public relations: Managing organizational communication.* Champaign, IL: Human Kinetics.

Stoldt, G., Miller, L., & Comfort, P. (2001, September). Through the eyes of athletics directors: Perceptions of sports information directors, and other public relations issues. *Sport Marketing Quarterly, 10*(3), 164–172.

Sweetser, K., Porter, L., Chung, D., & Kim, E. (2008). Credibility and the use of blogs among professionals in the communication industry. *Journalism and Mass Communication Quarterly, 85*(1), 169–185.

Torre, J., & Verducci, T. (2009). *The Yankee years.* New York: Doubleday.

Wilcox, D., & Cameron, G. (2009). *Public relations: Strategies and tactics* (9th ed.). New York: Pearson.

Woo, C. W., An, S. K., & Cho, S. H. (2008). Sports PR in message boards on Major League Baseball websites. *Public Relations Review, 34*(2), 169–175.

CHAPTER 43

Investor Relations

Alexander V. Laskin

In October 2008, shares of Apple Inc. plunged 10% over the course of just 10 minutes. What caused such a rapid decline: poor sales of iPods, technological problems with iPhones, or virus threats to Apple computers? It was actually none of the above. The decline was attributed to the report that Apple's chief executive officer (CEO), Steve Jobs, was rushed to a hospital emergency room. Later, it was discovered that the information was nothing but a rumor that originated on a site with user-generated content, where essentially anybody can post anything without identifying themselves. Yet such gossips present a real challenge to the investor relations professionals whose job is to ensure people have complete and accurate understanding of the company and its value.

This chapter provides a brief overview of investor relations—a specialization of public relations. First, the definition of investor relations is provided, followed by the discussion of the role of the investor relations profession in the corporate world. This chapter also draws attention to the history of investor relations and talks about some of the future trends likely to make an impact on the profession.

Investor Relations: Definition

The professional association of investor relations practitioners, National Investor Relations Institute (NIRI), defined investor relations as "a strategic management responsibility that integrates finance, communication, marketing and securities law compliance to enable the most effective two-way communication between a company, the financial community, and other constituencies, which ultimately contributes to a company's securities achieving fair valuation" (NIRI, 2003). This definition was adopted by the Board of Directors of NIRI in 2003 and reflects the current view on the profession as it evolved over the years.

Investor relations is a strategic activity. Investor relations officers do not wait for shareholders to contact them with questions and then simply respond to investors' queries. Instead, they have a plan of action sometimes designed weeks, months, or even years in advance. This plan has a certain goal in mind to support larger organizational needs and is based on a comprehensive research program.

Investor relations is a management function. Investor relations officers must have a seat at the table when the key organizational decisions are being made. Investor relations cannot be successful as a purely communicative function—that is, just explaining corporate decisions to investors. Rather, investor relations practitioners are involved in developing business strategies and tactics. Investor relations professionals contribute an important perspective to the process—that is, knowledge of how shareholders and investors will react to corporate decisions.

Investor relations is at the border of several academic disciplines. Successful investor relations professionals should be more than great public relations practitioners. They must also be proficient in accounting and finance. Often, investor relations officers deal with financial issues and discuss them internally and externally with very specialized audiences, such as the chief financial officer (CFO) or financial analysts. Without a deep understanding of the financial position of a company and the effect of business decisions on corporate finances, investor relations officers won't be able to contribute much to the success of their organizations. Investor relations is a highly regulated area. Thus, investor relations officers should also be knowledgeable of the many laws governing the issuance and trading of securities, the disclosure of corporate information, and corporate governance.

Investor relations is based on two-way communication. It is important to establish the flow of information from the company's management to investors, shareholders, financial analysts, media, and other interested parties. Timely and accurate disclosure of information is an essential part of the investor relations work. At the same time, it is equally important to establish the opposite flow of information: from outsiders to the company's management. Investor relations officers should carefully listen to the financial publics and relay their concerns to the organization's senior management.

Finally, the ultimate goal of investor relations is a fair valuation of the company's securities. The share price should not be as high as possible—the higher is not necessarily the better. Rather, the share price should reflect the actual honest value of the company. Overvaluation can be as harmful as undervaluation and may even lead to a company's demise. As a result, investor relations officers should not be trying to inflate or deflate the company's achievements, hide its failures or successes, or withhold information vital for the proper understanding of its corporate value.

Investor Relations: Significance

Investor relations has always been an important function for corporations. In fact, investor relations is the highest paid specialization among all other public relations subfunctions. According to a 2006 salary survey sponsored by *PRWeek*, the median salary for practitioners specializing in "financial/investor relations" was $165,620, followed by "crisis management" ($150,000) and "reputation management" ($143,000). Salaries for the remaining specializations ranged from $98,500 for "public affairs" to $59,910 for "community relations."

Today, the importance of investor relations is increasing even more. One of the reasons for the increased significance of investor relations is the chain of corporate scandals caused by senior management's manipulation of information disclosed to investors, and, as a result, the inability of investors, both private and corporate, to properly understand the company's business and its value. In the chain of corporate scandals, the companies once believed to be among the leaders in their respective fields, such as Adelphia, Global Crossing, WorldCom, Tyco International, Kmart, and Waste Management, experienced significant drops in their share prices and some even faced bankruptcies. Of course, the largest scandal of all was Enron: "The collapse of energy giant Enron is the largest bankruptcy and one of the most shocking failures in U.S. corporate history" (Allen, 2002, p. 206). Some call Enron "the Watergate of business" and suggest that companies now have to rely on their investor relations to inspire confidence in their investors.

In fact, investor relations today probably has to restore the investors' confidence in the whole model of corporate America. Investor relations professionals must communicate faster, provide more information, make information more relevant to understanding the company's business and its value, and use the appropriate communicative channels. After the corporate scandals caused shockwaves throughout the U.S. economy, the legislature could not leave the changes up to corporations. Enron served as a catalyst for legal reform. The new law, the Public Company Accounting Reform and Investor Protection Act of 2002, is often referred to by the names of its sponsors, Senator Paul Sarbanes (D-MD) and Representative Michael G. Oxley (R-OH), as the Sarbanes-Oxley Act, or simply SOX. While signing the bill on July 30, 2002, President Bush declared that this legislation represents "the most far-reaching reforms of American business practices since the time of Franklin D. Roosevelt." SOX became another important reason for the increased importance of investor relations.

Investor relations, previously guided by the Securities Act of 1933 and the Securities Exchange Act of 1934, received long-needed reform in a variety of areas, including disclosure procedures. SOX demanded enhanced disclosure of information to investors and introduced personal responsibility of senior management for accuracy of the information disclosed to investors. Some call SOX the most welcome gift to shareholders; others call it a regulatory backlash. For better or worse, however, SOX is the new reality of investor relations.

The significance of investor relations is also underscored by the changing nature of a corporate value chain. Today, much of the corporate value is in intangibles. In fact, Baruch Lev (2004) explained that in the modern economy, intangible assets generate most of shareholder value and account for more than half the market capitalization of public companies. This requires investor relations practitioners to adapt by expanding the disclosure from obligatory financial information to a variety of nonfinancial indicators. Various techniques of measuring and reporting nonfinancial information emerged. Investor relations practitioners must be able to relate this information to the investment community and explain the influence of these factors on the company. Seely (1980) concluded, "This is shocking when one realizes what a very, very small margin of stock price in any way relates to how well the individual company is doing in conventional terms—earnings, sales, and so forth" (p. 2). In this situation, numbers alone cannot provide a sufficient picture of a modern corporation; thus, enhanced disclosure is required.

Investors themselves realize this need for extensive disclosure and constantly demand more and more information. NIRI anticipates that investors are greatly expanding the scope of what they consider relevant information to include things such as human rights policies in distant lands, supply chain vulnerabilities, the company's commitments and disclosure on climate change, and so on.

The changes among investors themselves also add to the growing significance of the profession. Today, most of the stock is in the hands of large institutional investors. The Federal Reserve System Board of Governors reports that in 1950, only 6% of the stock belonged to institutions. In 2003, however, this number had increased to almost 60%. The rise in institutional ownership changed the practice of investor relations and raised the importance of the function for corporate success and survival. Institutional investors have great power in the boardroom and are quite capable of influencing the decision-making process of the top management. Large institutional investors often have a long-term view and want to promote long-term corporate growth. It is not a surprise that corporate governance initiatives were pioneered by large pension funds such as the California Public Employees' Retirement System (CalPERS) and the Teachers Insurance and Annuity Association, College Retirement Equities Fund (TIAA-CREF). This breed of investors sometimes wants to know even more about the company than what senior managers know themselves. They are often interested in maximizing their investment in the company by sharing their knowledge and expertise with the company's management and improving other aspects of corporate performance in environmental, social, ethical, or other areas. Their need for information is much greater and cannot be satisfied by financial statements alone. They want to listen to the management, but they also want to be heard. They require a constant dialogue with the company and expect management to pay close attention.

In addition, after suffering losses in Enron-like corporate scandals, investors want to know what stands behind the numbers on the income statement. They want to know how these numbers were generated. Investors want to know about the management team, the company strategy, research and development, and marketing campaigns.

Finally, the significance of investor relations is emphasized by the global nature of modern investor relations. New technologies of travel and communications made investing a truly international phenomenon. A corporation now competes for investment capital on a global scale in a 24/7 framework. New technologies make the information available globally, instantly, and to a wide range of publics—consumers, investors, suppliers, and so on. This cross-proliferation of information between various publics requires close cooperation of various communication functions within an organization and perhaps will lead to the merging of various communication functions such as public relations, investor relations, marketing, and others into one unified function in charge of all corporate communication efforts.

Investor Relations: Job Description

Investor relations today is based on a dialogue rather than monologue—two-way communication has become a key strategy in communicating with investors. Thus, investor relations officers have a double role in their work: They represent the company's management in front of the shareholders, and they also represent the shareholders in front of the company's management. For example, when a company is planning a merger, investor relations officers are involved in the deal from the start, representing and defending the interests of the shareholders if the merger is to go through. When the shareholders design a resolution to cut top-management bonuses, the investor relations officers are involved in talks with the shareholders, communicating the management's point of view and defending the company's interests.

It is not an easy role, but it is an important one. Making sure that parties hear and address each other's arguments is vital for building and maintaining a successful relationship. As one of public relations, specializations, investor relations is a relationship management function. The only difference is it manages relationships with highly specialized financial publics—investors, shareholders, financial analysts, prospective investors, stock exchanges, regulatory organizations, financial media, and others.

Investor relations is a management function rather than a communication function. Relationships cannot be built and maintained based on words alone; actions must follow words. Investor relations officers are involved in corporate decision making and in designing policies; they represent the interests of shareholders so as to protect the relationships between the company and its shareholders. After all, corporations should act in the best interests of the shareholders, and investor relations officers are there to ensure that this is the case.

Managing a corporation, however, is not an easy task—it involves a lot of complex decisions. Some of these decisions might make a company even lose money in the short term with the goal of making more money in the longer term. These complexities are not always obvious to all shareholders and investors—outsiders of the company.

Again, it becomes the job of the investor relations officers to communicate and explain the company's actions and policies and how they affect the shareholder value.

To be successful in this dual role, investor relations officers rely on formal and informal research. One of the key determinants of excellent public relations is being able "to recognize problems before they happen" (Heath & Coombs, 2006, p. 166). The same is true for investor relations. Investor relations officers must know their shareholders—who they are, why they own stock in the company, how long they plan on keeping the stock, and what they think about the company's actions. It is impossible to represent the interests of the shareholders without knowing first what these interests are. On the other hand, investor relations officers must also be knowledgeable about what is happening inside the organization and the industry—such as the launch of new products, changes in technology, the state of the management team, and so on. It is important to know and to understand what the corporation is doing and how it can influence the financial standings of the organization in areas such as cash flow, revenues, operating margin, and cost of capital. A survey of investor relations officers of Fortune 500 companies found that ownership research and analysis are among the most common activities performed by the investor relations professionals (Laskin, 2009).

The same survey also discovered that other common activities of investor relations officers are providing information to investors and shareholders as well as providing information to the top management of their organizations. Investor relations are often involved in road shows, conferences, presentations, private meetings, and negotiations. Among the least common activities are mass media communications and controlled media communications. Perhaps because mass media and controlled media communications are one-way communication channels, they are not as well equipped for the investor relations profession, where two-way flow of information is essential.

In modern corporations, investor relations is often housed in a dedicated investor relations department. This gives investor relations professionals necessary autonomy within the organizational structure. It is quite common for the investor relations officers to have two or more educational degrees with the most common combination being communication and finance. Many investor relations officers with undergraduate degrees in public relations, communication, or journalism later continue to pursue a graduate degree in business such as an MBA.

Thus, investor relations today is a management responsibility. Professionals have certain autonomy and decision-making power within the corporate structure. Investor relations officers are engaged in proactive two-way communications with the ultimate goal of having the interests of shareholders and management aligned.

Investor Relations: History

The first company that turned to investors to finance its growth is believed to be the Dutch East India Company, dating back to the 17th century. Some sources point to an even earlier period: The Stora Kopparberg mining company, dating back to the 13th century, issued its first share in 1288. However, these companies were more of an exception—the shareholders were small in numbers, and the issue of communicating with them did not command much attention of the executives until the middle of the 20th century.

The history of modern investor relations started after World War II. Investor relations as a specialization of public relations had certain similarities with public relations in its historic development. However, it also had certain differences in its time line—that is, in its specific periods and in the characteristics of these periods. In general, the historic development can be categorized into three large eras (presented in Table 43.1), similar to the four periods Grunig and Hunt (1984) described for the historic development of public relations.

Table 43.1 Historical Eras of Investor Relations and Their Characteristics

Characteristic	Communication Era (1945–1975)	Financial Era (1975–2002)	Synergy Era (2002–Now)
Comparison with public relations models	Press-agentry/publicity and public information	Two-way asymmetrical	Two-way symmetrical
Purpose	Promotion, dissemination of information	High valuation	Fair valuation
Direction of communication	From the company	Two-way	Two-way
Intended beneficiary	Organization	Organization	Both organization and investors
Practitioner's role	Communication technician	Accounting technician	Manager
Structural location	Public relations/corporate communications	Finance/treasury	Stand-alone investor relations department
Background of practitioners	Communication, journalism	Finance, accounting	Dual degree, graduate degree

The early era of investor relations is referred to as the "communication era" because of both who performed the function and what the function involved. This era was characterized by the domination of public relations or other communication professionals in investor relations who focused mostly on publicity.

The earliest mention of the investor relations function as such is traced back to Ralth Cordiner, a chairman of General Electric, who in 1953 created a department in charge of all shareholder communications. In the late 1950s and 1960s, investor relations departments started appearing at a number of large companies, and the consulting agencies first began offering investor relations services.

These developments did not happen in a vacuum but rather were a response to the changing economic and sociopolitical environments. The economic boom of the 1950s generated wealth for private Americans and, at the same time, encouraged business growth to satisfy the constantly increasing needs of consumers. The corporations needed money to finance this growth, while people needed a way to invest surplus income. In this situation, the meeting of the two worlds was inevitable.

At the beginning of the "stock" era, in 1950, only 6 million Americans owned stock. Since then, the number has grown exponentially. In 1997, this number became 160 million. The new kind of player on the financial market—a private shareholder—caused some changes in boardrooms across the country. The first corporations to strategically target private individuals were car companies, such as Ford, General Motors, and Chrysler. These companies realized that their consumers can also be their shareholders and vice versa. Indeed, shareholders were likely to purchase a car made by the company in which they owned stock rather than one made by its competitor. The companies accustomed to competing on the consumer markets brought similar strategies and tactics to their competition on the financial market.

In fact, shareholders' capital is a finite pool, and the companies have to compete for this resource. Thus, the investor relations function in its early years was charged with the task of grabbing investors' attention and selling them the company in a competition for shareholder capital with other corporations.

The variety of new private shareholders was quite a new experience for many corporations in the 1950s and created another incentive (along with the need to compete for capital) for the formation of investor relations departments. Indeed, before World War II, there were just a few wealthy stockholders who did not pay much attention to the company's management, did not attend annual meetings, and never complained. The new owners, however, were quite different. First of all, there were a lot of them, and they were constantly growing in numbers. They owned very small amounts of stock, but the sense of ownership among them was great. When they purchased stock they felt themselves as owners and demanded proper attention. At the very least, they wanted their voices to be heard and their questions answered. They demanded a steady stream of information from the company.

These were different types of publics Wall Street had to get used to:

> At the outset of the Bull market, a large chunk of the new money going into stocks came from those WWII-time savers who had little to spend their war industry wages on. These were not youth fresh from the field of the battle, but many who had suffered through the Depression and the cataclysmic closing of the banks in 1932. They were determined to keep a close eye on the funds they had entrusted to management and the stock markets, neither of which they really trusted. (Morrill, 1995, chap. 1)

These new shareholders craved information, yet because of their large numbers, it was difficult to communicate with all of them directly. The financial intermediaries who consolidate stock and transmit large amounts of financial information today were not well developed in the 1950s—most shares were owned directly by private shareholders. Thus, it was the private shareholder who caused changes in the way corporations were managed; it was the same private shareholder who was the target of the early investor relations communications.

These shareholders actively demanded communications, and the management needed to communicate with this group. At the same time, the management did not take private shareholders, often with very limited knowledge of finances and little understanding of corporate business models, seriously. So managers were looking for a way to communicate with these shareholders from a distance—that is, to give them information without meeting with them in person. In addition, they sought communications that did not require many efforts or resources.

This was a new experience for many corporations. Companies did not have internal expertise in investor relations; there were no investor relations agencies either. In this situation, management turned to the recognized experts in communication—that is, public relations.

In the 1950s, however, public relations was not a well-established practice itself. Only the largest companies had internal public relations staff, and the functions and roles of public relations were quite limited. It was not uncommon to view public relations as a simple adjunct to advertising to stimulate better sales. In other words, when corporations turned to public relations to manage their investor relations, public relations was not yet ready to take on this challenge.

At that time, public relations was still struggling for the right to strategically manage itself, as it was often a purely technical function of media relations. And this relatively new and not-well-established public relations function was suddenly charged with the additional duties of investor relations—a job for which most practitioners on the corporate or agency side were not prepared.

So they approached this new task in the same way they approached other public relations tasks—that is, relying on press-agentry and publicity. Most of the investor relations work focused on putting the word about organizations out and on attracting the attention of financial publics to the stock. Silver (2004) recalled that early investor relations focused on "the so-called dog and pony shows for sell-side analysts and retail investors" (p. 70).

One of the NIRI founders and a pioneer of investor relations, DeWitt Morrill (1995), reminisces: "In concrete terms, shareholder relations became transformed into publicity, promotion and pageants" (chap. 1). He provides several examples from the 1950s era:

- The annual reports suddenly blossomed as a 48-page, glossy sales brochure for the company's products. The financials were there, mandatorily, but the sell was in the sizzle, not the steak.
- The annual meeting became a huge, gala free-for-all. A large eastern railroad put together a special train for stockholders and carried them first class to a company-owned hotel in the southern Appalachians for the meeting.
- An international telecommunications company held a large gathering under two large tents in central New Jersey. A bountiful lunch was served, and there were several open bars. Members of the press were delivered in limousines from New York and returned the same way. Products were richly displayed. The chairman, himself a noted gourmet and bon vivant, addressed the gathering. Reactions were enthusiastic—but absolutely nothing of substance was done.
- Companies made gifts or gift boxes of products available to shareholders, sometimes free. Liquor companies also provided their products under advantageous purchase agreements. (chap. 1)

All these caused problems for investor relations. Shareholders invested their own money and wanted attention from the corporation: They needed to discuss the company's prospects for future growth instead of receiving gift baskets. Investors were interested in meeting with the CEO or CFO of the company—people who knew the strategy and the operations of the company—and instead had to communicate through a newspaper. In addition, public relations practitioners at the time rarely had any understanding of finance and accounting and lacked attention to details. This complicated things even more.

Public relations was set up to fail in investor relations—it just came too early. The new investor relations profession was looking for people who could understand the financials and at the same time could produce the required communication tactics, but such people were rare exceptions.

In addition, the corporations did not have any interest in listening to their shareholders—the focus was on a one-way stream of information from the company to the financial publics. The publicity and public information era of public relations contributed substantially to the development of many negative connotations that the term *public relations* has even today. Cutlip, Center, and Broom (2000) observed,

> As press agents grew in number and their exploits became more outrageous—albeit successful, more often than not—it was natural that they would arouse the hostility and suspicion of editors and inevitable that the practice and its practitioners would become tainted. This stigma remains as part of the heritage of public relations. (p. 107)

The same stigma tainted public relations in the financial world. Morrill (1995) concludes, "The word public relations became increasingly a pejorative on Wall Street" (chap. 1). Financial publics lost faith in public relations practitioners, in their ethics, in their integrity, or simply in their capabilities for handling investor relations. Investor relations engaged in significant efforts to distinguish itself from any public relations background.

As a result of this history, the investor relations profession in its early years was heavily dominated by communication and public relations expertise. However, it did not take much time to realize that success in investor relations requires expertise in financial matters. The pendulum started swinging the other way—that is, much of the communication expertise was disregarded as unnecessary in favor of financial and accounting expertise.

Changes in the economy also demanded changes in the way in which investor relations operates. The 1970s saw the shift from individual retail investors to institutional investors. The enormous growth of investment activities in the 1950s and 1960s put pressure on the financial markets infrastructure. As mentioned earlier, the growth in individual investments was exponentional in the years after World War II—in the early 1970s, every sixth American owned stock. The U.S. financial system was overwhelmed and could not handle any more transactions.

Another problem was the track record. The market was growing by leaps and bounds after World War II, and shareholders (especially individual shareholders) expected it to continue like this forever. People believed that the market could go only up. The expectations became too high for the reality to deliver. The system was destroying itself: Built on volume of transactions, it could no more handle that volume, and the customers were ready to quit.

In response, the U.S. stock market was becoming institutionalized. Large institutions started pooling the money of private shareholders together to decrease pressure on the financial markets while keeping the volume. For investor relations practitioners, it meant that instead of less than knowledgeable private shareholders, overqualified stock analysts and institutional investors had become the main persons of contact. These analysts could not be satisfied with gift baskets, tours of company headquarters, or beautiful glossy pictures—they demanded detailed information on the company's performance, strategy, and sales, sometimes even information the company's managers did not have themselves. Most of the investor relations practitioners at the time, however, were not capable of providing such information, nor were they speaking the same financial language as the analysts did.

Investor relations previously geared toward the private retail shareholder was becoming less and less relevant. Communications through mass media to reach the crowd of retail shareholders or conducting majestic special events to put the company's name out there were not appropriate tools of the trade anymore. The target audience of investor relations was changing, and the profession was not sure how to handle it. Public relations practitioners were losing their grip on investor relations, while the financial departments were engaging in talks with analysts and institutional investors more and more often.

As a result, the investor relations profession in the 1970s experienced a notable change. Investor relations moved away from the public relations of the 1950s and 1960s. First, there was no need anymore for mass-mediated communications to myriad private shareholders who moved off the market. Second, institutional investors demanded communication channels other than mass media. In addition, earlier publicity-based investor relations practices left a bad taste in the mouths of Wall Street professionals, and financial analysts rarely wanted to communicate with such a breed of investor relations personnel. Instead, institutional investors and analysts tried to talk with the top management of the company face-to-face. CEOs, however, avoided any direct contact, forwarding the analysts to their second in command—the CFOs.

As a result, new types of investor relations professionals were housed under the supervision of CFOs, often in treasury departments. They often were trained in finance or accounting. In addition, management often saw former financial analysts to be ideal for investor relations because they were expected to easily find a common language with the financial analysts bugging the company.

From mere providers of information, investor relations professionals had to turn into defenders of the decisions of top management: If investors had critiques for a company's actions, investor relations were expected to provide counterarguments to explain and protect the company's actions. Proactive investor relations practices called for anticipating shareholders' reactions and getting prepared to respond to them in advance. Shareholder research became a necessity. Other investor relations officers simply did not allow negative questions to be asked at conferences and annual meetings, tightly controlling the communication channels.

The focus for many professionals of that time was on persuasion and making the sell. Marcus and Wallace (1997) defined investor relations as "the process by which we inform and persuade investors" (p. xi). Ryan and Jacobs (2005), financial analysts turned investor relations consultants, suggested that the investor relations contribution is helping the management "to package their story for institutional buyers or sell-side analysts" (p. 69).

This financial era of investor relations history was focused on professional investors and financial analysts. For the tasks of defending the corporation in front of them, CEOs were hiring former financial analysts who became the new investor relations professionals. They lacked the public relations knowledge and skills, but they understood the numbers and knew the rules of Wall Street. CEOs decided that it was good enough, and they were quite happy to have these new employees between themselves and the professional investment community.

The shocking corporate failures of the early 21st century, including the collapse of dot-coms and accounting scandals at the largest companies, brought an end to this era of investor relations. In fact, the whole model of corporate America was put to a test. Pressure to package the results in a positive way and push the stock price up led to significant and constant overevaluations. Lack of communication between companies and their shareholders and an almost exclusive focus on financial results made understanding the nonfinancial aspects of business virtually impossible. The corporate failures became a wake-up call for the investor relations practice. They led to stiffer regulations from the Securities and Exchange Commission (SEC) and Congress. The unprecedented growth in the stock market was replaced by recession. The competition for capital got more intense. Investor relations became one of the key activities that could make or break a corporation; CEOs saw that investor relations was not an auxiliary function but a source of competitive advantage.

Investor relations today is not about the amount and accuracy of information provided. Rather, it is about understanding. Investor relations' task is to help investors understand the company and its business model. Finding the right investors, building trust and relationships with them, and developing long-term ownership patterns to combat volatility are the new goals for the professionals.

There is no point in arguing if investor relations is better left to public relations as was the case in the earliest era of investor relations history or if investor relations is better left to financial specialists as was the case in the second era. The profession must integrate both areas of expertise. Successful investor relations officers will need to gain proficiency in both areas as well through dual degrees, graduate degrees, or professional training. Thus, the modern period of investor relations, the third era in its history, can be referred to as the "synergy" era.

Investor Relations: Issues

Today, investor relations continues to evolve. Changes in laws, shareholder mix, and technology present new demands to the investor relations professionals. But not all are ready to meet new challenges. Investor relations practitioners with dual expertise in communication and finance are still a minority. Most of the corporate investor relations practitioners are educated in finance, while communication expertise dominates in investor relations agencies. Professional organizations such as NIRI and the Public Relations Society of America

(PRSA) are trying to improve the situation by providing training in finance and communications to investor relations professionals.

Although investor relations is often delegated to a stand-alone department, corporate practitioners are still more likely to report to a CFO than to a CEO. Such a chain of command combined with the financial background of practitioners creates a situation where the focus of disclosure is heavily shifted toward financial information. In his doctoral dissertation, Laskin (2008) observed that what nonfinancial information investors are looking for, such as corporate strategy, market position, research and development, and management team, may often be omitted from the disclosure. This makes understanding the company's business model and the company's fair value difficult, if not impossible.

Regulators work hard to improve the quantity and quality of information provided to investors. One of the key changes to the disclosure process is the implementation of eXtensible Business Reporting Language (XBRL). Imagine a press release where each word has an invisible tag. When a computer receives this press release, every word is automatically placed in the proper cell—a row for nouns, a row for pronouns, and a row for verbs. Now, imagine instead of a press release a quarterly financial report. And instead of every word, every number has an invisible tag. When a financial analyst receives this information, numbers are automatically placed into the proper cells in the financial analyst's Excel file, database, or financial model. This is XBRL in the simplest terms—eXtensible Business Reporting Language. The financial reporting becomes automated and computer processed—the data can be streamed from the company's database directly to investors' or financial analysts' databases.

Another regulatory change concerns social media communications. Today, the SEC encourages the use of electronic communications between companies and their shareholders by enacting a number of amendments about blogs, proxies, and electronic shareholder forums. Indeed, the Internet allows companies to disclose information to worldwide audiences within seconds. The electronic communication tools also allow companies to gain valuable information about their investors and to solicit feedback. At the same time, these tools also demand somebody who is very savvy in public relations because the cost of a mistake may be high.

References

Allen, C. E. (2002). Building mountains in a flat landscape: Investor relations in the post-Enron era. *Corporate Communications: An International Journal, 7*(4), 206–211.

Cutlip, S. M., Center, A. H., & Broom, G. M. (2000). *Effective public relations* (8th ed.). Upper Saddle River, NJ: Prentice Hall.

Grunig, J. E., & Hunt, T. (1984). *Managing public relations.* New York: Holt McDougal.

Heath, R. L., & Coombs, W. T. (2006). *Today's public relations: An introduction.* Thousand Oaks, CA: Sage.

Laskin, A. V. (2008). *Investor relations: A national study of the profession.* Unpublished doctoral dissertation, University of Florida, Gainesville.

Laskin, A. V. (2009). A descriptive account of the investor relations profession: National study. *Journal of Business Communication, 46*(2), 208–233.

Lev, B. (2004). Sharpening the intangibles edge. *Harvard Business Review, 82*(6), 109–116.

Marcus, B. W., & Wallace, S. L. (1997). *New dimensions in investor relations: Competing for capital in the 21st century.* Hoboken, NJ: Wiley.

Morrill, D. C. (1995). *Origins of NIRI.* Vienna, VA: National Investor Relations Institute. Retrieved March 1, 2009, from www.niri.org/FunctionalMenu/About/Origins.aspx

National Investor Relations Institute. (2003, March). *Mission and goals.* Retrieved March 1, 2009, from www.niri.org/about/mission.cfm

Ryan, T. M., & Jacobs, C. A. (2005). *Using investor relations to maximize equity valuation.* Hoboken, NJ: Wiley.

Seely, M. (1980). Myth and realities in investor relations. In A. R. Roalman (Ed.), *Investor relations that work* (pp. 1–4). New York: AMACOM.

Silver, D. (2004). The IR-PR nexus. In B. M. Cole (Ed.), *The new investor relations: Expert perspectives on the state of the art* (pp. 59–88). Princeton, NJ: Bloomberg Press.

CHAPTER 44

Public Relations Media

Kirk Hallahan

Throughout the 20th century, major changes took place in public relations communications—from initially relying on newspapers and magazines to later seeking exposure in theatrical newsreels, radio, television, and sponsored films as well as corporate video and multimedia productions. Most recently, Internet and mobile communications were added to the public relations media mix (Hallahan, 2010).

Although practitioners through the years recognized the potential of new communications technologies (Plank, 1983), and scholars periodically reviewed applications of new media (Pavlik, 2007), public relations theorists have devoted scant conceptual attention to media. Yet media choices play an increasing role in public relations strategy, and channel-related decisions are critical to the success of public relations efforts from practical and theoretical perspectives.

Public relations practitioners and theorists alike need to develop a deeper understanding of the similarities and differences between various media and how they influence public relations processes. As a starting point, *medium theory* posits that a particular medium possesses characteristics that make it physically, psychologically, and socially different from other media and from face-to-face interaction *regardless of the particular messages exchanged through them.*

Early medium theorists like Innis (1950, 1951) and McLuhan (1962, 1964) observed that the predominant media used in a society shaped social organization, favored particular modalities and sensory processes (based on oral vs. written vs. printed vs. broadcast communications), and shaped the nature of the experience and consciousness itself. More recently, Meyrowitz (1985, 1994, 1997) argued that media redefine social geography, while media use patterns among audiences shape group identities, socialization processes, and social hierarchies. Deibert (1997) similarly suggested that the advent of a new communications technology changes both the way in which information is distributed and social epistemology.

Recent Trends in Public Relations Media

For years, public relations media planning required little forethought. The goal during most of the 20th century was to obtain (favorable) coverage in newspapers, magazines, radio, and television. This strategy was supplemented with collateral materials or special events. Incremental expenditures of money or staff time to obtain additional exposure were small. Today, however, channels have exploded in number, requiring increased efforts to achieve comparable levels of exposure. Meanwhile,

- Commercialization of the World Wide Web, which began in 1994, drove much organizational communication online—through corporate Web sites and special-topic microsites, online newsrooms, social networking sites, Web conferencing, and the like. Organizational communication similarly became mobile with the nearly universal adoption of cell phones. Today, *messaging* is the generic term to describe the electronic distribution of announcements using Internet and mobile systems—and now includes e-mail, text, microblog, and instant messaging.

- Spending on the direct delivery of public relations messages, as a proportion of total campaign expenditures, is rising. Clients are increasingly willing to invest in the creation and production of information that can be shared directly with audiences and that circumvents traditional news media (Hallahan, 1994). Techniques include direct messaging, blogging, social networking pages, and video- and photo-sharing sites such as YouTube and Flickr.

- With the explosion in available media, audiences are spending more personal time engaged in media-related activities but have become increasingly fragmented. For example, only about half of the U.S. population reads a traditional newspaper and only half watch network television on a typical day. Meanwhile, public relations programs are targeting more and more narrowly defined consumer, business, trade, and community-based audience segments. These *micropublics* are highly involved and knowledgeable—and want specific, often technical, information personalized to them in formats they can customize for easy access.

- The expectations of publics about information access are greater. Technological advancements have taught audiences to *expect* immediate electronic access to organizations on demand. Many public relations units have become 24/7 purveyors of information that serve *glocalities* around the world. As a result, control over the timing of information delivery has shifted from message *producers* to *audiences.*

- Major public media continue to help create broad public awareness of topics, thus for setting the public agenda of discussion. But their gatekeeping function is under siege. Many traditional (or legacy) media struggle economically because of changing patterns of media use, competition from nontraditional information and entertainment sources, and declining advertising revenue.

- Distinctions between familiar media genres have become blurred with the advent of *hybrid messages* (Balasubramanian, 1991) and *stealth marketing* techniques (Goodman, 2006). Today's postmodern media environment is replete with ambiguous formats where the message's intent is not entirely clear to audiences. Examples include advertorials, docudramas, infomercials, infotainment/edutainment, video news releases, home shopping shows, product placements, and promotional events cosponsored by noncommercial entities (such as charities) and commercial enterprises that serve multiple purposes.

• Organizations are increasingly transparent; previous distinctions between external and internal communications are now irrelevant. Employees and members of organizations now routinely learn important news about organizations through public news media or electronic updates from other sources (including friends) because the speed of these external sources outstrips internal channels. Control of information once considered confidential or for use only within an organization is nearly impossible despite firewalls erected in today's networked world.

• Finally, demarcations that once separated public relations, advertising, and marketing are being dismantled with the rise of integrated marketing communication (IMC) programs (Hallahan, 2007). IMC provides two clear lessons: First, successful communication might demand using both paid (purchased) and unpaid (earned) media. Today, communicators readily recommend pay-per-click text- or display-based online advertising to drive traffic to a Web site. Second, neither public relations nor advertising can define themselves—nor delimit their activities—based on any particular tool or technique traditionally associated with either discipline.

An Integrated Public Relations Media Model

Whereas the primary emphasis in public relations strategy has been placed on developing compelling messages, public relations practitioners are increasingly concerned with making critical decisions about media. Yet the rationale for using particular media receives little conceptual attention (cf. Atkin, 1994; Salmon & Atkin, 2003; Pfau & Parrott, 1993; Schwartz & Glynn, 1989; Van Leuven, 1986). Public relations textbooks variously differentiate internal versus external media (Broom, 2009), news versus interactive media (Coombs & Holladay, 2010), or advertising versus publicity versus hybrids (Newsom, Turk, & Kruckeberg, 2007). Other texts discuss channels exclusively as mass media (Austin & Pinkleton, 2001; Ferguson, 1999) or merely list possible tactics with little rationale for choosing one over another (Kendall, 1996; Simmons, 1990). Three notable exceptions include Smith's (2009) four-part typology and Wilson and Ogden's (2008) three-cluster model based on whether various tactics are interactive and personalized. Alternatively, Heath and Coombs (2006) identify four circumstances in which media are deployed: (1) paid, (2) placed, (3) responsive, and (4) interactive.

The five-category model presented in this chapter has been refined and updated from the original in the 2001 version of this *Handbook* (Hallahan, 2001). The approach purposefully attempts to be both *comprehensive* (by incorporating mediated and nonmediated tools) and *parsimonious* (by grouping media and tools into the fewest possible categories). The rationale is that media planners must think about media *broadly* and *strategically* and must combine whatever channels or tactics are most appropriate in an integrated public relations program. In particular, media must overcome personal or client biases, and avoid "me-too" fads, where clients and communicators feel compelled to adopt the latest communication tool simply because it is fashionable. Such flawed thinking was evident in the widespread, but short-lived, adoption of corporate video in the 1980s and can be seen in the infatuation with Web sites, and later blogs, social networking, and microblogging.

The model categorizes media into five broad groups: (1) public media, (2) interactive media, (3) controlled media, (4) events/group communication, and (5) one-on-one communications. Table 44.1 provides an overview with examples of channels and vehicles found in each group. Table 44.2 contrasts key characteristics that distinguish each group. A brief description of each category follows.

Table 44.1 An Integrated Public Relations Media Model

← **Mass Communication** High-tech, Perceptually Based, Low Social Presence, Asynchronous				**Personalized Communication** → Low-tech, Experientially Based, High Social Presence, Synchronous
Public Media	**Controlled Media**	**Interactive Media**	**Events**	**One-on-One**
Key uses in a communication program				
Build awareness; enhance credibility	Promotion; provide detailed information	Respond to queries; exchange information; engage users	Motivate participants; reinforce existing beliefs, attitudes	Obtain commitments; negotiation, resolution of problems
Principal examples of media				
Publicity/ advertising/ advertorials/ product placements in • Newspapers • Magazines • Radio • Television Paid advertising in • Transit media • Out-of-home media (billboards, posters, electronic displays) • Directories • Venue signage • Movie theater trailers, advertising	Brochures Newsletters Sponsored magazines Annual reports Books Direct mail Exhibits and displays Point-of-purchase support DVDs/video brochures Statement inserts Other collateral or printed ephemera Advertising specialties	E-mail, instant, text, and microblog messages E-newsletters, e-zines Automated telephone call systems Web sites, blogs Vodcasts/podcasts Games Web conferences, Webinars, Webcasts Information kiosks Intranets and extranets Social networking sites Forums (chats, groups) Media sharing sites Paid text/display click-through advertising	Meetings/ conferences Speeches/ presentations Government or judicial testimony Trade shows, exhibitions Demonstrations/rallies Sponsored events Observances/ anniversaries Contests/ sweepstakes Recognition award programs (often supported with multimedia presentations)	Personal visits/lobbying Correspondence Telephone calls/Text Messages

Table 44.2 Comparison of the Five Major Media Groups

	Public Media	Controlled Media	Interactive Media	Events	One-on-One
Social presence, ties to others	Low	Low	Moderate	High	High
Basis for judgments	Perceptual	Perceptual	Perceptual and Experiential	Experiential	Experiential
Personalization of message	None	Limited	Moderate-high	Limited	High
Directionality of communication	One-way	One-way, with potential to include response mechanisms	Potentially two-way	Quasi two-way	Two-way
Synchronicity (real time vs. delayed)	Mostly asynchronous	Asynchronous	Synchronous	Synchronous	Synchronous
Technological sophistication	High	Moderate	High	Moderate	Low
Channel ownership/ control	Media organizations	Sponsor	Sponsor or third-party site operator	Event organizers	None
Message selection	Third-parties media editors/producers	Sponsor	Receiver	Presenters and event organizers	Participants
Audience engagement	Low	Low-moderate	Moderate-high	Moderate	High
Reach	High	Low-moderate	Low-moderate	Low	Low
Cost per impression	Extremely low	Moderate	Moderate	Moderate	High
Key challenges for use, effectiveness	Competition for attention, media clutter	Design, distribution	Availability, accessibility	Attendance, atmosphere	Empowerment of organization representative, personal dynamics

Public Media

Public media represent all channels owned by and operated by third-party media organizations, including major mass media and out-of-home advertising media. Public media are in the business of *creating audiences* and (with the exception of public broadcasters) serve as conduits for commercial message sponsors who want to reach potential purchasers of goods and services. Public media use news, information, and entertainment to create audiences; providing a link between exposure-seeking *information sponsors* (vs. commercial sponsors) is a secondary concern, at best.

Public media exposure can rely on news, entertainment, or advertising fare. Publicity, the longtime mainstay of public relations, involves obtaining coverage in the news or entertainment/editorial portions of public media. In their audience-building pursuits, producers of public media have become dependent on public relations sources for low-cost news and entertainment material deemed important or interesting to audiences. Public relations *information subsidies* essentially reduce the direct cost and staff time spent gathering news or producing programming (Gandy, 1982, 1992; Turk, 1986).

Entertainment programming is used with increased frequency for public relations purposes to heighten public consciousness of particular ideologies, issues, products, and personalities. Producers are willing to cooperate with information sponsors because they believe in the cause or become convinced that a topic will attract interest or endear them to audiences. Paid *product placements*, that is, the innocuous inclusion of products, venues, or locales in story lines or scenes, similarly have become direct ways to reduce production costs.

Finally, paid institutional, issue, financial, and event advertising are used with greater regularity by both for-profit and not-for-profit entities that previously avoided purchasing time or space. Advertising allows control over timing and content of strategically important messages and can provide for the repetition of messages—limitations inherent in publicity, donated public service announcements, and entertainment programming.

Key Challenge: Capturing Audience Attention. The primary challenge for practitioners in using public media is to capture the attention of audiences in a cluttered communication environment. Gaining attention in the public media arena involves infusing a client's story with either news or entertainment values (or both), thus making the story or idea attractive to media gatekeepers. Publicists must design public relations messages in ways that enhance the audience's motivation, ability, and opportunity to process them (Hallahan, 2000a).

Key Use: Building Awareness, Public Agenda Setting. From a strategic perspective, the primary value of public media lies in their ability to create broad public *awareness*, or a generalized knowledge, of organizations, causes, products, or people. This applies whether the message appears as news, entertainment, or advertising because there is little difference between the three approaches strategically, despite important differences between them (Hallahan, 1999a, 1999b). Alternatively, awareness leads to *agenda setting*, the degree to which people say that particular topics become important to them or they talk about them with others. Public media remain valuable to clients who must disseminate information during crises or who must reach extremely large audiences (such as the public at large) quickly or with a low cost per impression. Importantly, audiences are exposed to messages in public media through a process of *incidental exposure*, where audiences read newspapers, watch television, or drive past billboards as part of their daily routines. Attention to public media involves little special effort.

Controlled Media

Controlled media represent all categories of media that are physically produced and delivered to the recipient by the sponsor—any manufactured object that carries a client's name or message.

Unlike public media, information sponsors assume full responsibility for design, production, inventory, and distribution of controlled media (or often delegate specific tasks to outside suppliers). The message sponsor retains creative control over content. Sponsors are unfettered by creative or ideological restrictions imposed by third-party public media gatekeepers. Similarly, controlled media enable sponsors to control the timing, sequencing of presentation, and integrity (accuracy and completeness) of information.

Today, controlled media are often used in tandem with computerized databases that permit personalizing content and addressing communications directly to customers, prospects, employees, investors, contributors, community residents, or other constituents. Although controlled media can incorporate direct response mechanisms (such as bounce-back cards in brochures or reply forms in direct mail), reaction is often delayed and lacks spontaneity. Response rates are often very low.

Key Challenges: Distribution, Design. As they do with public media, audiences can encounter controlled media as part of their daily lives—by picking up a brochure in a doctor's office or receiving an invitation or solicitation in their daily mail, and so on. Nonetheless, access usually requires more deliberate effort than exposure to public media. Controlled media must be placed purposefully into the hands of targeted audiences in a timely, efficient manner—in person, via postal or package delivery services, through take-one racks or public displays, or in response to requests. Once audiences receive controlled media, the design of the material is critical. Engaging copy and presentational devices—graphics, photography, sound, video, and so on—are essential to lead audiences through the information, to highlight key ideas, and to prompt action.

Key Uses: Promotion, Providing Detailed Information. Controlled media are particularly well suited to communicate promotional messages as well as complex instructions or technical information. Messages can be as detailed as necessary because controlled media can provide greater message capacity and deliver more complex messages than are possible via public media, where time or space is limited.

Interactive Media

Interactive media include the growing array of communications options that allow people to communicate with organizations electronically using computers, telephones, and mobile devices. Audiences can use interactive media to receive updated information, make inquiries, perform routine tasks, share news with others, or exchange information with organizations electronically in real time. Instead of directly spending money in the production and distribution of materials, message sponsors must invest in either owning or obtaining access to the necessary software or systems.

Mobile communications, which are now used by nearly 50% of the world's population (80% in the United States and other developed countries), enable audiences to receive voice, e-mail, text, and microblog messages. Along with touch-tone landlines, mobile phones also enable individuals to also listen to audio-text recordings, leave voice messages, and conduct transactions with organizations using the device's keypad. Owners of "smart phones" similarly use a growing variety of sponsored "apps" (applications) that supply specific information ranging from the tracking of package shipments to obtaining sports scores.

Internet and Web-based communications, now used by 25% of the world's population (75% in the United States and other developed countries), today link networks of people around the world. Importantly, one in seven people in developed nations now access the World Wide Web using mobile devices—and that percentage is growing.

Other interactive media include personal digital assistants (such as Blackberry). MP3 players play an increasingly important role as listeners download blogs and sponsored music and videos at no charge from sources such as Apple's iTunes Store. E-readers are emerging as tools that will enable users to download books, newspapers, and magazines and eventually will provide access to organizational documents such as investment reports. Finally, interactive TV will allow audiences to use their remote controls to download sponsored content and interact with organizations in the same ways they can today with mobile communications and the Internet.

Interactive media blend characteristics of public and controlled media. Organizations can operate their own closed-access system for internal groups such as employees, members, or students (intranets), or for external or extended constituents such as suppliers/vendors and distributors/other resellers (extranets). They also can create visibility by supplying news and information to portal or news sites that publish proprietary information (such as AOL.com), by sponsoring their own Web sites (including blogs) on the public Internet, and by participating in third-party Web sites operated by others—forums, social networking sites, media-sharing sites, and wikis.

Audiences engage in interactive media in ways that are fundamentally different from public or controlled media. With the exception of electronic messaging (which relies on a more traditional *push strategy*), most interactive media involve a *pull strategy* where users must be attracted to information. Thus, users of interactive media usually *initiate* the process to fulfill some informational, entertainment, personal identity, or social need. They must sign on, or opt in (give permission), to be contacted via bulk e-mail or text messages or RSS (really simple syndication) updates from a blog or news source. As the name implies, various media allow users to interact with other people *or* with software systems that can supply information stored in databases without any human interface. This can include accessing information that has been recommended, rated, or bookmarked by others.

Key Challenges: Availability and Accessibility. In contrast to public media, but somewhat similar to controlled media, the key challenges of interactive media are to ensure that potential users are able to (a) *locate* and then (b) *access* information. The availability of telephone and Web site access must be actively promoted and made readily accessible via online or mobile directories or search engines. Online documents—ranging from Web sites and blogs to news releases and white papers—must be designed with *search engine optimization* (SEO) in mind. Once accessed, interactive media must be easy for audiences to use. Unlike sequentially organized messages commonly found in public or controlled media, online content is often parsed into fragments that are stored randomly and must be located by users. Message producers must guide users to information using intuitive keywords, voice prompts, or hypertext links.

Because users can access the same information via a variety of pathways, individual communications must be self-explanatory and avoid confusion by making no contextual assumptions about what users might have heard or seen previously.

Key Use: Handling Queries and Sharing Information. Compared with public media, interactive media are more limited in their ability to create public awareness quickly and broadly. Broad dissemination is delimited by the number of people who opt in and actually sign in at any given time, as well as by who might subsequently refer information (e.g., forward a message) to others. Yet interactive media are very powerful and low-cost ways for organizations to respond to queries and to provide routine and individualized information to users on demand. Similarly, interactive media can facilitate the sharing of information among organizations or among organizations and individuals. To take full advantage of the potential, organizations must fully anticipate the interests and concerns of possible users. They also must avoid overreliance on automation (such as autoreplies to e-mails) and be prepared to assign the staff necessary to respond to queries, participate in online conversations, monitor online discussions, and troubleshoot problems.

Events

Events involve direct, interpersonal communications between representatives of an organization and a group of people. A meeting among three or more persons is the simplest example. Events represent purposeful efforts by entities to communicate directly with the people in attendance (vs. spectacles, pseudo events, and stunts staged for media publicity purposes).

Possible venues for events can include a sponsor's premises, public streets and parks, or public event facilities (auditoria, stadia, hotels, convention centers, etc.). Events can involve interactive media that link remote participants through Web conferences, teleconferencing, or webinars.

In creating events, program planners assume responsibility for staging the activity but often cooperate with other organizations. Examples include a speech or presentation at another organization's meeting, conference, trade show, or exposition. Other examples include public meetings where organizational representatives give testimony or seek public input at government- or community-sponsored events as well as the growing number of fund-raising and lifestyle events staged by nonprofit organizations in partnership with other groups.

Key Challenges: Attendance, Atmosphere. For an event to be effective, an audience must be present. Recruiting an audience involves promotion using tools from all four of the other media groups. Once the targeted audience is at the event site, event organizers must create an inviting, conducive *atmosphere.* Although audiences can learn much by listening to speeches or watching presentations, event participants also gain insights and form impressions by monitoring the overall scene, by talking with other participants, and by observing their own actions. Events are primarily *experiential* media, and the success of an event is predicated on eliciting favorable *emotional responses*. Favorable audience reactions can be leveraged into a state of *emotional contagion* in response to the symbolic setting, festive staging, audiovisuals, entertainment, music, and food.

Key Uses: Motivation, Reinforcement of Existing Beliefs and Cultural Values. Although events are sometimes used for educational or information-sharing purposes, the real value of events lies in their unique ability to crystallize *already extant* beliefs or attitudes of attendees and to foster positive emotional responses. Events can motivate attendees to engage in particular behaviors—as witnessed in events such as college pep rallies and political demonstrations. Other events serve as ritualistic exercises that impart little new knowledge and encourage no change in behavior but can be highly effective to validate what attendees already feel or believe. Examples include installation ceremonies, anniversary observances, and award presentations that inspire and foster an affinity with the organization.

One-on-One Communication

The final group of public relations media includes all forms of *dyadic communication* that takes place *between* a single representative of an organization and an individual member of a public. Such interpersonal communications are often highly individualized, unstructured, spontaneous, and ephemeral in nature. As with events, the primary form of communication involves face-to-face contact using oral communication. However, interpersonal mediated technologies—telephones texting, and correspondence—also can be employed. Contexts in which one-on-one communications occur include fund-raising, lobbying, consumer/customer relations, and negotiation/bargaining.

Key Challenge: Empowerment, Personal Dynamics. Dealing effectively with individuals on a one-on-one basis requires organization representatives to be empowered with the *authority* to represent the organization and, as necessary, to make commitments or grant concessions. Success also is highly dependent on the *personal dynamics* that evolve between the parties. The organization's representative must be able to nurture positive rapport with the other party.

Key Use: Obtain Commitments, Problem Resolution. The deployment of one-on-one communications in public relations in programs generally is reserved for special situations involving *negotiations* that require highly interactive (and sometimes volatile) discussions between the organization and members of key publics. Sometimes, these negotiations involve seeking commitments from individuals or organizations in positions of power or influence, whether for fund-raising, lobbying, or endorsements of a cause. One-on-one communications also are used to resolve problems involving disgruntled customers, activists, employees, or other stakeholders based on perceived (or actual) shortcomings in an organization's performance. Often organizations must respond to individuals concerned about risks or uncertainties created in their lives and who confront organizations to demand resolution or restitution. Others merely seek acknowledgment of the legitimacy of their claim, cause, or concern.

Media Selection and Synergy

The model in Table 44.1 on page 626 provides a valuable framework for strategic media planning by focusing attention on fundamental differences between these five media groups. Each group is especially suited to meet specific communication objectives commonly found in public relations programs, but each group poses particular challenges.

The model suggests that an effective media strategy ought to begin by first considering an entity's communication objectives and then focusing on the groups of media best suited to attain those desired outcomes. Within each category, effective media planning entails picking particular *channels* (types of media, such as television), *vehicles* (specific media outlets, such as a specific newspaper), or *tactics* (tools or techniques, such as a printed brochure). Simply stated, objectives should drive media choice, not vice versa.

Obviously, no typology can be perfect. Considerable differences exist *within* each of these categories. Representative channels, vehicles, or tactics vary in the degree to which they exhibit each group's predominant characteristics. Table 44.3 summarizes two dozen secondary criteria that might guide choosing specific channels or tools within each group. Not all considerations apply in every decision; other considerations might also apply.

Six Principles of Media Planning

Further examination of the model suggests six key ideas or principles to guide media choices.

Hierarchy. The five groups in Table 44.1 represent a hierarchy of media tools that are best suited to creating *awareness* (left side) or to prompting *action* (right side). Interestingly, the media toward the left side of the continuum are highly dependent on sophisticated technology, provide few opportunities for social interaction, involve learning based primarily on perception from a distance (vs. the direct observance of personal experience), and involve *parasocial* rather than *actual* social relationships. In contrast, media toward the right side of the continuum are less technology dependent, offer greater opportunities for social interaction, involve learning by direct observation of personal experience, and depend on social relationships. Notably, interactive media—which have been praised for their ability to foster community and online relationships—fall squarely in the middle.

The array of media in the model—and the corresponding objectives they are best suited to achieve—correspond roughly to the stages or steps found in hierarchy-of-effects learning models

Table 44.3 Secondary Selection Criteria Within the Five Media Groups

Audience considerations • Geography • Timing • Segmentation • Reach • Precedence • Audience expectation/search *Message considerations* • Attention-getting ability/salience • Frequency • Agenda-setting capability/virality • Modality • Carrying capacity • Ease of understanding/decodability • Prestige	• Credibility • Believability/verisimilitude • Engagement • Effectiveness (ability to achieve outcome) *Production considerations* • Control/access over distribution • Deadlines • Personalization capability • Customization capability *Financial considerations* • Total cost • Cost per impression or response • Return on investment

(Lavidge & Steiner, 1961; Rogers, 2003; Strong, 1925) and related behavioral change models. Hierarchy of effects models suggest that when adopting an innovation, people progress from awareness and interest to higher-order steps such as desire, conviction, trial, and repeat behaviors. Media planners can benefit by choosing media in a program that corresponds closely to the progress of various audience segments in the adoption process and to attain desired outcomes.

Integration. Hierarchy also suggests the need for *integration* or the coordinated and synergistic use of a combination of media to achieve a desired result. Calls for media integration in public relations can be traced to the 1920s. This model provides a simple operational definition by suggesting that an integrated public realtions program combines media from at least two of the five media categories to achieve distinct, but interrelated communication objectives essential to achieving an overall program goal.

In keeping with the hierarchy of effects concept and everyday practice, the launch of a program often begins by concentrating on tools toward the left side of the continuum, such as publicity, and then advertising, in public media, basic collateral materials, and possibly a basic Web site. Other components then are often added over time to complement and build on the initial momentum. Additional tools include follow-on publicity, ramped-up levels of advertising, and more controlled media, interactive media, and events.

Engagement. Moving audiences along a continuum from mere awareness to action usually requires audiences to exert increasingly high levels of effort or message processing involvement—paying attention to a message, learning the message, retaining the message, seeking information, sharing information with others, and making judgments. Although media researchers have argued since the 1960s that public media audiences are "active" cognitive processors of messages (in the sense that they draw on their existing knowledge or experience to make sense of a message), public media consumption remains a comparatively passive activity.

As audience members progress along the hierarchy of media suggested in the model, audeinces participate in increasingly complex activities at each higher media level: playing a video brochure, searching the Web, attending events, or meeting with an organizational representative. Dual processing models of persuasion suggest that audiences with high topic-issue involvement process messages effortfully or systematically. However, individuals engaged in higher levels of information processing also are likely to learn by observing their own behavior during the process. This suggests that media planners must (a) recognize that varying levels of engagement are inherent in each media group and (b) make it easy and satisfying for audiences to engage in the activities associated with each successive level of engagement.

Referrals. The hierarchical and integrative nature of the model suggests that targeted audiences in a public relations program will obtain information from multiple sources. This underscores the importance of *referrals* or the inclusion of directions where audiences can obtain additional information or take action. Generally, this involves referring audiences up the hierarchy of media groups, but Figure 44.1 depicts varying patterns of referrals that actually occur. For example, messages in public media might refer audiences to any of the media groups higher up the continuum: controlled media, interactive media, events, or one-on-one communications with organizational representatives. Controlled media messages are likely to suggest visiting a Web site, attending an event, or contacting an organizational representative. In contrast, interactive media strive for audiences to use the same Internet or mobile device for queries or to take action, without involving any other media.

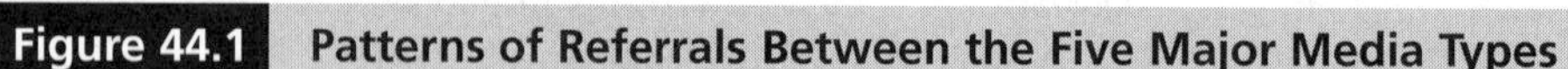

Figure 44.1 Patterns of Referrals Between the Five Major Media Types

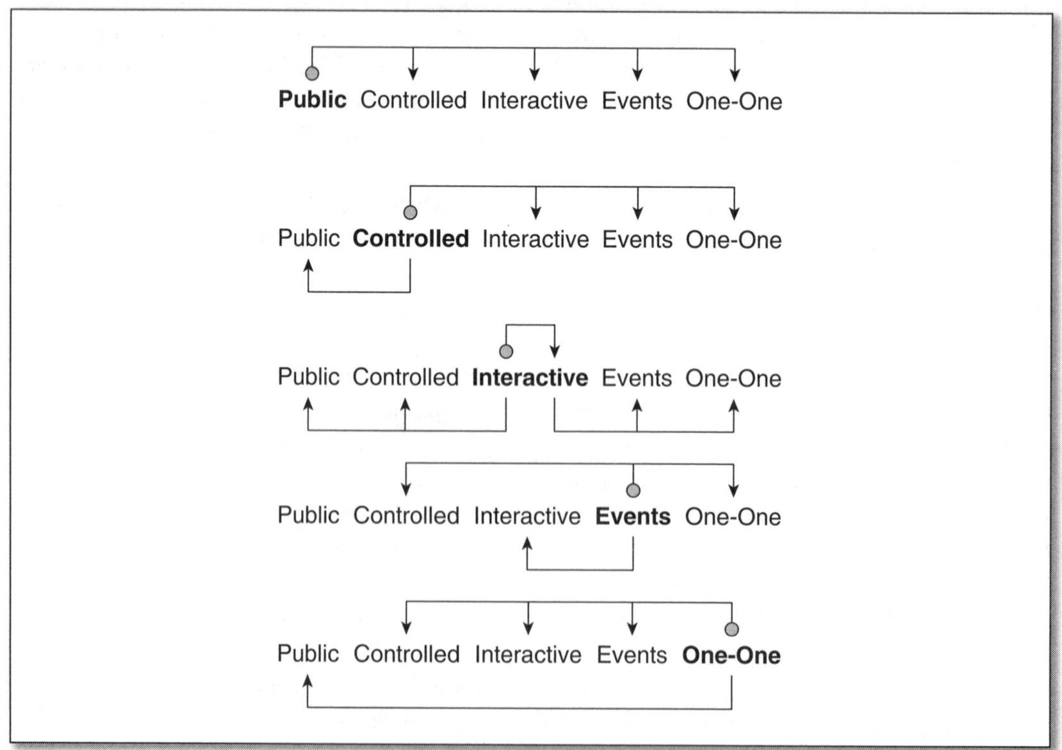

Note: Primary referral patterns are shown in bold on top, alternative or secondary referral patterns are shown below.

Audiences at events are generally referred to controlled media (brochures or pamphlets) or personnel available on the event site, while organizational representatives routinely provide controlled media as supplementary information tools when negotiating solutions or seeking commitments.

Effectiveness. Effectiveness entails deploying media vehicles and channels with sufficient power to attain the desired outcome—generating queries, creating conviction, prompting trial, or obtaining a commitment. Dilution of effectiveness occurs whenever lower-order media (toward the left side of the model) are employed to achieve higher-order objectives that require the use of more powerful tools. Evidence suggests that mere exposure in public media, viewing information on a Web site, or attendance at an event might not be sufficient if the decision has important consequences for an individual who requires advice or social support.

Efficiency. Separate from effectiveness, *efficiency* refers to obtaining a desired goal at the lowest possible cost, thus not wasting organizational resources. Dilution of efficiency occurs whenever higher-order media are used to achieve objectives when lower-order, more cost-efficient media would suffice. For example, one-on-one communication could be used to build awareness, respond to inquiries, provide detailed information, or reinforce existing beliefs or attitudes. However, such an approach could be extremely time-consuming and costly unless the target audience is extremely small. Efficient communication planning thus involves *trade-offs* between the two extremes suggested in the model and using a combination of tools efficiently. Thus, organizations have embraced public media, controlled media, and, most recently, automated interactive media as ways to reduce the high cost per contact associated with one-on-one communication. But in so doing, entities also run the risk of compromising effectiveness in the name of efficiency. The challenge is to balance or optimize the two.

Media: Implications for Public Relations Theory

The paradigm presented here suggests that all media are not created equal. Each of the five media groups has strengths to be exploited and weaknesses to be avoided. More needs to be understood about how these can be best used, both individually and in combination.

More broadly, media also raise important implications for public relations theory. Much public relations theory—including rhetoric, persuasion, relationships, risk and uncertainty, conflict, and negotiation—evolved from interpersonal communication and managerial communication and without regard to implications of media. Yet the emergence of today's dizzying array of new media forms makes clear the need for new perspectives. This concluding section identifies four important areas where public relations theory might be reexamined in the context of contemporary media.

Media and Relationships

Establishing and maintaining mutually beneficial, organizational-public relationships has been a major academic focus of public relations since the early 1950s (Cutlip & Center, 1952, p. 5). Beginning in the late 1990s, theorists have focused their attention in earnest on the relationship construct, yet theory has ignored contextual aspects of how relationships are formed.

Meyrowitz (1997) argued that media are important because they create the social structure or environment in which communication occurs. In so doing, media arguably provide the *social context* for organizational-public relationships. For many people, an organizational relationship might begin simply based on exposure to publicity or advertising in public media. Arguably, such relationships are the weakest types of relationships possible, and audiences might not even recognize their role as stakeholders or members of an inactive public important to the organization (Hallahan,

2000b). In contrast, many organizational-public relationships are complex and might involve multiple points of contact. For example, an employee might communicate directly with a supervisor, attend meetings, use an organization intranet or extranet, read organizational literature, follow organizational news, or monitor the organization's advertising in public media.

Thus, the nature, number, and variety of communication contacts can be an important predictor of the nature and depth of organization-public relationships. For comparatively uninvolved or unengaged publics, simple recognition, recall, or reputational assessments of an organization might be valid and reliable measures of the relationship (cf. Grunig, 1993). On the other hand, more multidimensional measures might be both appropriate and essential to assess more complex relationships (cf. Hon & Grunig, 1999). In the context of new media, the depth and quality of relationships is a continuing controversy, as critics charge that the quality of relationships in cyberspace, which are often based on limited and weak ties, cannot match those found in the offline environment (Hallahan, 2008).

Differences in media suggest that certain media lend themselves to the establishment and maintenance of relationships based on their inherent qualities. For example, *media richness theory* posits that *rich media* (which provide feedback, multiple verbal and nonverbal cues, language variety, and personal focus) are superior to *lean media* (which do not exhibit these qualities) when people confront uncertainty or equivocality (ambiguity) about a task to be accomplished. Accordingly, face-to-face meetings, telephone, and written addressed (personalized) documents are superior to unaddressed documents such as bulletins or standard reports in organizational communication (Daft & Lengel, 1986; Daft, Lengel, & Trevino, 1987; Trevino, Lengel, & Daft, 1987). This principle can be applied to the present model if public media and controlled media (especially print) are assumed to be lean—and interactive media, events, and one-on-one communications are assumed to be richer in terms of the message cues they provide.

In a similar vein, other theories related to media differences might inform understanding of relationships. *Social presence theory* (Rice, 1993; Short, Williams, & Christie, 1976) suggests that the greater the perception that another *person* is involved in the communication, the higher the sense of intimacy, immediacy, warmth, and interpersonal rapport that will be created. Greater social presence leads to greater social influence compared with a faceless organizational source. *Media naturalness theory* (Kock, 2001, 2004) argues that humans have evolved with face-to-face communication being their primary form of communication. Electronic media lend themselves to simple tasks but pose significant cognitive obstacles when humans undertake more complex tasks (such as forming a relationship). Finally, the *social identity of deindividuation model* (SIDE; Postmes, Spears, & Lea, 1999) posits that using new communications technologies does not lead to anonymity or loss of personal identity (which had been used to explain aggressive or out-of-character online behavior). Instead, SIDE posits that new communications technologies enable users to *selectively* communicate or enact particular aspects of their identity, while disguising others. This would explain possible differences in how individuals interact with organizations in new media versus face-to-face contexts.

Simply put, media can *bias* organizational-public relationship processes.

Media and Directionality of Communication

Public relations theorists have devoted considerable attention to the *directionality* of communication. The argument goes that public relations should be equally involved in listening to as well as talking at constituents. Prior to the advent of interactive media, events and one-on-one communications were the principal mechanisms through which organizations and their publics could engage in direct, spontaneous interactions. Otherwise, feedback required the use of a different medium, such as letters, telephone, or reply cards. However, today's interactive media enable exchanges (including actual conversations) to take place *between* organizations and their publics and *among* members of important publics using a single medium.

Figure 44.2 identifies five different models that might describe how public relations communications actually operate today. These include the traditional *monologic model* as well as the *monologic-with-feedback model*, which are rooted in the earliest models of communication that originated in the late 1940s. These provide the basis for the press-agentry/publicity, public information, and two-way asymmetrical models of public relations proposed by Grunig and Hunt (1984). Although arguably not ideal, such approaches continue to represent how many organizations disseminate information and analyze and incorporate responses in organizational decision making. In the context of the new interactive media, examples of one-way communication include bulk e-mails where replies are not permitted, microblogging, many Web sites designed as electronic brochures, and RSS feeds of news releases and blogs (Phillips, 2009).

More recently, *two-way* (Grunig, 2001) or *dialogic* (Kent & Taylor, 1998, 2002) approaches have been promoted as the ideal way to practice public relations. As represented in the dialogic model in Figure 44.2, today's interactive media enable organizations to engage in real-time exchanges and actual conversations with constituents. Examples include actual conversations enabled through e-mail exchanges, comments, and author's responses posted on blogs, chats, and threaded discussions in online forums. Yet the potential applications of new media extend far beyond simple dialogue. The *participatory interactive model* in Figure 44.2 suggests that interactive media

Figure 44.2 Five Patterns of Media Directionality and Interactivity

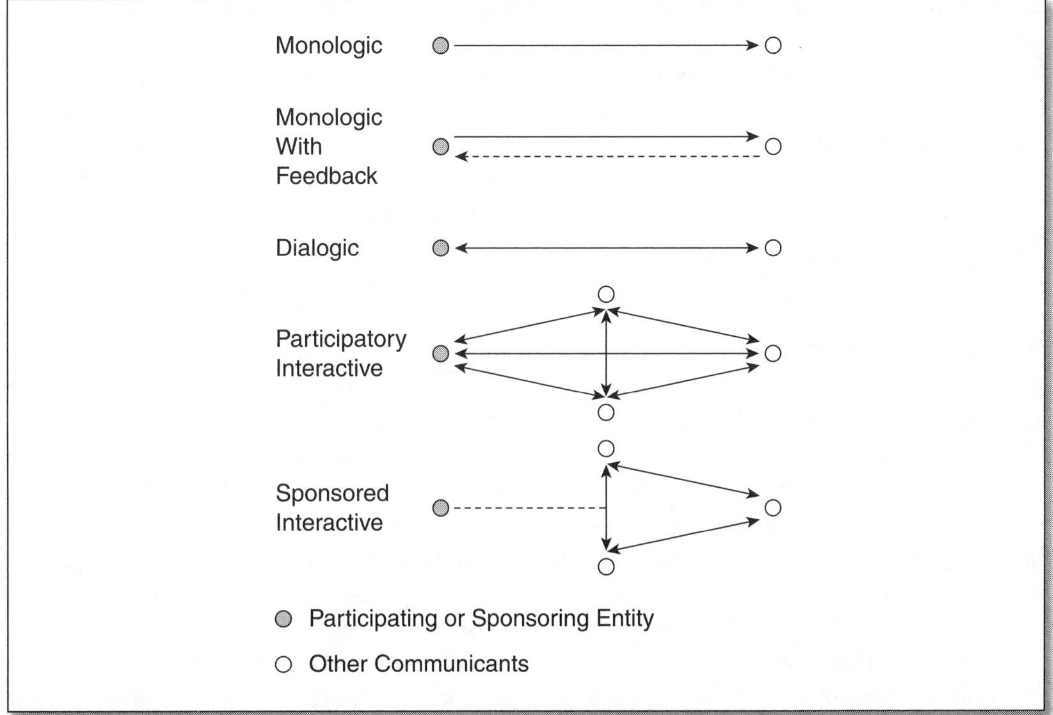

enable organizational representatives to participate in larger-scale online conversations in which the organization or organization-specific issues alone are not necessarily the focus of attention. Examples include public forums (chats, discussion groups, bulletin boards, etc.) that operate on stand-alone Web sites as well as social networking sites. Meanwhile, the *sponsored interactive model* suggests that organizations can underwrite the cost of social network sites, conversational sites (forums), and collaboration sites (wikis) on their own Web sites or microsites to bring publics together *without participating in conversations at all.* Benefits accrue to sponsoring organizations through (a) the goodwill created among members of key publics who are grateful to be brought together, (b) the resulting social capital that binds members of publics together, (c) insights gained from merely monitoring the discussions, and (d) the *conviviality* created as people take advantage of communications tools that help them fulfill their physical, emotional, and spiritual needs (Illich, 1973). In today's postmodern environment that emphasizes transparency, these alternative approaches to communication suggest the need to revisit assumptions about what constitutes effective public relations exchanges, including the necessity of the organization to control or even to be directly involved in the process (cf. Grunig, 2009).

Media and Empowerment of Publics

One of the important changes to take place in modern media is the redefinition of the role of audiences. Rosen (2006) observed that "the people formerly known as the audience" have been transformed into producers—not merely recipients—of mediated messages. He explained that audiences are "the formerly atomized listeners who with modest effort can connect with each other and gain the means to speak."

In the 1990s, public relations theorists recognized the potential of the internet to empower publics and to tilt the balance of power that favors large organizations in society (Badaracco, 1998; Coombs, 1998; Heath, 1998). Early case studies predicted the rise in online activism evident today. This power shift is consistent with Deibert's (1997) observation that the way in which information is stored, transmitted, and distributed at a given time inevitably favors certain social forces and ideas, and not others. In keeping with Darwinian theories of evolution, Deibert argued that new media evolve through processes of innovation and mutation and inevitably will alter the power dynamics in society.

Activism, as a process of social change, remains grounded in individuals and groups identifying conditions in society as problematic and then organizing to rectify them (Hallahan, 2000a). However, new media have transformed the methods for gaining public attention, recruiting supporters, and effecting public policy changes. Today, advocates enjoy direct, instantaneous electronic access to geographically dispersed communities with common interests (often around the world on a 24/7 basis at a very low cost). *Cyberactivism* and *cyberterrorism* are now commonplace, and issues managers and crisis communications professionals must be prepared to quickly respond (Hallahan, 2009, 2010).

The ability of media to empower publics raises important questions about assumptions regarding the role of symmetry in organizational-public relations. Although some social observers question whether symmetric relationships are possible in modern society (Coleman, 1982), the assumption in Excellence theory and elsewhere is that public relations is ideally practiced as two-way symmetrical communication (Grunig, 1992; Grunig & Hunt, 1984). Symmetrical communication suggests that organizations should give equal consideration to the interests of publics and that the two parties communicate openly and on an equal basis in terms of their knowledge and power. Excellence theory essentially argues that organizations should cede any power advantage to publics. However, the ability of media to enhance the power of publics so that it might actually exceed that of organizations suggests that the resolution of public relations problems might be pursued in at least three different situations: (1) where organizations exert more power than publics, (2) where the two parties exhibit equal power, and (3) where publics exceed the power of a particular organization based on their ability to sway public opinion and public policy. Symmetry thus is increasingly improbable, and calls for symmetry might be irrelevant.

In a similar vein, empowerment of audiences has altered crisis communication. Cyberspace has become a new venue where crises are vehicles through which organizations can communicate about risk and crisis topics (Hallahan, 2009, 2010). The advent of new media has enabled people to seek information directly (without relying on public media or others) and to share information with others at speeds and at levels not possible previously via tools such as message forwarding and hyperlinking.

Media and Complexity

The diversity of media and the channel options available today not only underscore the importance of understanding public relations media better but also suggest a high level of complexity. Instead of being a global village (McLuhan, 1964) or even a single network (Castells, 2000), the world today is composed of myriad loosely coupled human and electronic networks that will only grow in complexity in the future. Structuration theory contends that new media should not be viewed merely as conduits for communication or as rigid social structures. Instead, media are complex social systems that are continuously being created and enacted through the reproduced practices of their users. Online communities, such as those found in discussion groups or forums, are perpetually changing and can lead to the creation of new publics (Cozier & Witmer, 2001).

Qvortrup (2006) suggested that medium theory alone might not be sufficient to fully understand new digital media. He observed that media have always had a double effect of both *increasing* and *reducing* complexity—and do so in three ways: First, media make communication possible. Second, media increase social complexity by providing visibility and access to social acts worldwide. Finally, media can help manage social complexity by creating systems of internal complexity that can balance external complexity (Qvortrup, 2006). Thus, expanded forms of media will not only increase demand for public relations but also shape the nature of the practice itself.

References

Atkin, C. (1994). Designing persuasive health messages. In L. Sechrest, T. Backer, E. Rogers, T. Campbell, & M. Grady (Eds.), *Effective dissemination of clinical health information* (AHCPR Publication No. 95-0015, pp. 99–110). Rockville, MD: Public Health Service, Agency for Health Care Policy and Research.

Austin, E. W., & Pinkleton, B. E. (2001). *Strategic public relations management: Planning and managing effective communication programs.* Mahwah, NJ: Lawrence Erlbaum.

Badaracco, C. H. (1998). The transparent corporation and organized community. *Public Relations Review, 23*(3), 265–272.

Balasubramanian, S. K. (1991). *Beyond advertising and publicity: The domain of hybrid messages* (Report No. 91-131). Cambridge, MA: Marketing Science Institute.

Broom, G. M. (2009). *Cutlip & Center's effective public relations* (10th ed.). Upper Saddle River, NJ: Prentice Hall.

Castells, M. (2000). *The rise of the network society.* Malden, MA : Blackwell.

Coleman, J. S. (1982). *The asymmetric society.* Syracuse, NY: Syracuse University Press.

Coombs, W. T. (1998). The internet as potential equalizer: New leverage for confronting social irresponsibility. *Public Relations Review, 24*(3), 289–305.

Coombs, W. T., & Holladay, S. J. (2010). *PR strategy and application: Managing influence.* Malden, MA: Wiley-Blackwell.

Cozier, Z. R., & Witmer, D. F. (2001). The development of a structuration analysis of new publics in an electronic environment. In R. L. Heath (Ed.), *Handbook of public relations* (pp. 615–623). Thousand Oaks, CA: Sage.

Cutlip, S. M., & Center, A. H. (1952). *Effective public relations: Pathways to public favor.* Englewood Cliffs, NJ: Prentice Hall.

Daft, R. L., & Lengel, R. H. (1986). Organizational information requirements, media richness and structural design. *Management Science, 32*(5), 554–571.

Daft, R. L., Lengel, R. H., & Trevino, L. K. (1987). Message equivocality, media selection and manager performance implications for information systems. *MIS Quarterly, 11*(3), 355–366.

Deibert, R. J. (1997). *Parchment, printing and hypermedia.* New York: Columbia University Press.

Ferguson, S. D. (1999). *Communication planning: An integrated approach.* Thousand Oaks, CA: Sage.

Gandy, O. H., Jr. (1982). *Beyond agenda-setting: Information subsidies and public policy.* Norwood, NJ: Ablex.

Gandy, O. H., Jr. (1992). Public relations and public policy: The saturation of dominance in the information age. In E. L. Toth & R. L. Heath (Eds.), *Rhetorical and critical approaches to public relations* (pp. 131–164). Hillsdale, NJ: Lawrence Erlbaum.

Goodman, E. (2006). Stealth marketing and editorial integrity. *Texas Law Review, 85,* 83–152.

Grunig, J. E. (Ed.). (1992). *Excellence in public relations and communication management.* Hillsdale, NJ: Lawrence Erlbaum.

Grunig, J. E. (1993). Image and substance: From symbolic to behavioral relationships. *Public Relations Review, 19,* 121–193.

Grunig, J. E. (2001). Two-way symmetrical public relations: Past, present, and future. In R. L. Heath (Ed.), *Handbook of public relations* (pp. 11–30). Thousand Oaks, CA: Sage.

Grunig, J. E. (2009). Paradigms of global public relations in an age of digitalisation. *Prism, 6*(2). Retrieved March 22, 2010, from http://praxis.massey.ac.nz/prism_on-line_journ.html

Grunig, J. E., & Hunt, T. (1984). *Managing public relations.* New York: Holt, Rinehart & Winston.

Hallahan, K. (1994). Public relations and circumvention of the press. *Public Relations Quarterly, 39*(2), 17–19.

Hallahan, K. (1999a). Content class as a heuristic cue in the processing of news versus advertising. *Journal of Public Relations Research, 11*(4), 293–320.

Hallahan, K. (1999b). No, Virginia, it's not true what they say about publicity's third-party endorsement effect. *Public Relations Review, 25*(4), 331–350.

Hallahan, K. (2000a). Enhancing motivation, ability and opportunity to process public relations messages. *Public Relations Review, 26*(4), 463–480.

Hallahan, K. (2000b). Inactive publics: The forgotten publics in public relations. *Public Relations Review, 26*(4), 499–515.

Hallahan, K. (2001). Strategic media planning: Toward an integrated public relations media model. In R. L. Heath (Ed.), *Handbook of public relations* (pp. 461–470). Thousand Oaks, CA: Sage.

Hallahan, K. (2007). Integrated communication: Implications for and beyond public relations excellence. In E. L. Toth (Ed.), *The future of excellence in public relations and communication management: Challenges to the next generation* (pp. 299–337). Mahwah, NJ: Lawrence Erlbaum.

Hallahan, K. (2008). Organizational-public relationships in cyberspace. In T. Hansen-Horn & B. D. Neff (Eds.), *Public relations: From theory to practice* (pp. 46–73). Boston: Allyn & Bacon.

Hallahan, K. (2009). Crises and risk in cyberspace. In R. L. Heath & H. D. O'Hair (Eds.), *Handbook of risk and crisis communication* (pp. 415–448). New York: Routledge.

Hallahan, K. (2010). Online public relations. In H. Bidgoli (Ed.), *Handbook of technology management* (Vol. 2, pp. 497–517). Hoboken, NJ: Wiley.

Heath, R. L. (1998). New communication technologies: An issues management point of view. *Public Relations Review, 24*(3), 273–288.

Heath, R. L., & Coombs, W. T. (2006). *Today's public relations: An introduction.* Thousand Oaks, CA: Sage.

Hon, L., & Grunig, J. E. (1999). *Guidelines for measuring relationships in public relations.* Gainesville, FL: Institute for Public Relations.

Illich, I. (1973). *Tools for conviviality.* New York: Harper & Row.

Innis, H. (1950). *Empire and communication.* Oxford, UK: Clarendon Press.

Innis, H. (1951). *The bias of communication.* Toronto, Ontario, Canada: University of Toronto Press.

Kendall, R. (1996). *Public relations campaign strategies: Planning for implementation* (2nd ed.). Boston: Allyn & Bacon.

Kent, M. L., & Taylor, M. (1998). Building dialogic relationships through the World Wide Web. *Public Relations Review, 24*(3), 321–334.

Kent, M., & Taylor, M. (2002). Toward a dialogic theory of public relations. *Public Relations Review, 28*(1), 21–38.

Kock, N. (2001). The ape that used email: Understanding e-communication behavior through evolution theory. *Communications of the Association for Information Systems, 5*(3), 1–29.

Kock, N. (2004). The psychobiological model: Toward a new theory of computer-mediated communication based on Darwinian evolution. *Organization Science, 15*(3), 327–348.

Lavidge, R. J., & Steiner, G. A. (1961). A model for predictive measures of advertising effectiveness. *Journal of Marketing, 25*(October), 59–62.

McLuhan, M. (1962). *The Gutenberg galaxy: The making of typographic man.* Toronto, Ontario, Canada: University of Toronto Press.

McLuhan, M. (1964). *Understanding media: The extensions of man.* New York: McGraw-Hill.

Meyrowitz, J. (1985). *No sense of place: The impact of electronic media on social behavior.* New York: Oxford University Press.

Meyrowitz, J. (1994). Medium theory. In D. Crowley & D. Mithcell (Eds.), *Communication theory today* (pp. 50–77). Stanford, CA: Stanford University Press.

Meyrowitz, J. (1997). Shifting worlds of strangers: Medium theory and changes in "them" versus "us." *Sociological Inquiry, 67*(1), 59–72.

Newsom, D., Turk, J. V., & Kruckeberg, D. (2007). *This is PR: The realities of public relations* (9th ed.). Belmont, CA: Wadsworth.

Pavlik, J. (2007). *Mapping the consequences of technology on public relations.* Gainesville, FL: Institute for Public Relations. Retrieved March 22, 2010, from www.instituteforpr.org

Pfau, M., & Parrott, R. (1993). *Persuasive communication campaigns.* Boston: Allyn & Bacon.

Phillips, D. (2009, January 9). A Grunigian view of modern PR [LeverWealth Blog]. Retrieved from http://leverwealth.blogspot.com/2009/01/grunigian-view-of-modern-pr.html

Plank, B. A. (1983). The revolution in communication technology for public relations. *Public Relations Review, 9*(1), 3–10.

Postmes, T., Spears, R., & Lea, M. (1999). Social identity, group norms, and deindividuation: Lessons from computer-mediated communication for social influence in the group. In N. Ellemers, R. Spears, & B. Doosje (Eds.), *Social identity: Context, commitment, content* (pp. 164–183). Malden, MA: Blackwell.

Qvortrup, L. (2006). Understanding new digital media: Medium theory or complexity theory? *European Journal of Communication, 21*(3), 345–356.

Rice, R. E. (1993). Media appropriateness: Using social presence theory to compare traditional and new organizational media. *Human Communication Research, 19,* 451–484.

Rogers, E. M. (2003). *Diffusion of innovations* (5th ed.). New York: Free Press.

Rosen, J. (2006, June 27). The people formerly known as the audience [Press Think Blog]. Retrieved from http://journalism.nyu.edu/pubzone/weblogs/pressthink/2006/06/27/ppl_frmr.html

Salmon, C. T., & Atkin, C. (2003). Using media campaigns for health promotion. In T. L. Thompson, A. Dorsey, K. I. Miller, & R. Parrott (Eds.), *Handbook of health communication* (pp. 449–472). Mahwah, NJ: Lawrence Erlbaum.

Schwartz, D. F., & Glynn, C. J. (1989). Selecting channels for institutional public relations. *Public Relations Review, 15*(4), 24–36.

Short, J. A., Williams, E., & Christie, B. (1976). *The social psychology of telecommunications.* New York: Wiley.

Simmons, R. E. (1990). *Communication campaign management: A systems approach.* New York: Longman.

Smith, R. D. (2009). *Strategic planning for public relations* (3rd ed.). New York: Routledge.

Strong, E. K. (1925). *The psychology of selling.* New York: McGraw-Hill.

Trevino, L., Lengel, R., & Daft, R. (1987). Media symbolism, media richness and media choice in organizations. *Communication Research, 14*(5), 553–574.

Turk, J. V. (1986). Information subsidies and media content: A case study of public relations influence on the news. *Journalism Monographs, 100.*

Van Leuven, J. K. (1986, August). *A planning matrix for message design, channel selection and scheduling.* Paper presented at the annual meeting of the Association for Education in Journalism and Mass Communication, Norman, OK.

Wilson, L. J., & Ogden, J. D. (2008). *Strategic communications planning: For effective public relations and marketing* (5th ed.). Dubuque, IA: Kendall-Hunt.

CHAPTER 45

Directions in Social Media for Professionals and Scholars

Michael L. Kent

Anyone who has been teaching public relations for 5 to 10 years knows about the influence of technology. Indeed, if you have not taught one of the foundational courses like Introduction or Writing in a while you might have missed the changes. Incremental changes are easy to miss, and technology moves fast. When you look critically at your course notes from only a few years ago, you realize "Wow, news releases have completely changed," "the research process has changed," and "the skills that students are expected to have when they graduate have changed." Few journalists want printed news releases anymore (only about 2% still do), and more than 90% of journalists want to receive news releases via e-mail, organizational Web sites, or news wires (Bulldog Reporter, 2008). Layoffs and budget cuts in journalism have led to increased demand for free content from blogs, twitters, and organizational Web sites. Undergraduates are being asked what technology skills they have when they apply for internships and jobs because many of them will be required to watch, read, and write social media content.

When I recently turned to my own notes for Introduction to Public Relations from only 5 or 6 years ago, I ran across a list of "sample media channels" that included the following:

- Television
- Radio
- Newspapers
- Magazines
- Circulars
- Direct mail
- Point-of-purchase displays
- Posters
- Transit signs
- Public service announcements
- Advertisements
- Movie trailers
- Advertising specialties
- Pamphlets and booklets
- Meeting
- Speeches
- And computers (e-mail, www, Internet, electronic bulletin boards, etc.)

Ironically, computers were at the bottom of the list, "handheld devices" and blogs did not make the list, and Twitter had not been invented.

Over the past 20 years, technology has steadily advanced from Listservs in the late 1980s and early 1990s to modern technologies such as the World Wide Web, social media, and social networking in the past 15 years. But as McLuhan (1964/1999) pointed out in 1964, and Levinson in 1997, new technologies do not simply replace old ones. Old technologies persist, and new technologies fundamentally alter our relationship to the old ones. This chapter tries to avoid the mistake many researchers make when examining "new technologies" of assuming they are *new.*

Speaking of the Internet, which is more than 40 years old, or "social networking," which has been around for decades, as "new" is a mistake. Social media, for example, are often held up as a tool for social connectivity. However, Granovetter (1973), writing decades ago about the value of having large social networks among business professionals, argued that the success of individual messages and campaigns often depends on the experience and connections of the communicator constructing the messages. The current technology offers nothing genuinely new, only a new way to accomplish an old task.

To explain the complexities of social media, this chapter will be divided into five sections: The first section of the chapter will provide some definitions of key social media concepts as well as clarifying what is meant by social media from a public relations standpoint. The second section of the chapter will highlight important social media literature and issues. The third section of the chapter will discuss the direction of social media for public relations scholars. The fourth section of the chapter will describe the possible future of social media for communication professionals. And the fifth section of the chapter will conclude with some observations about new technology.

The chapter will define and analyze social media and highlight important issues for scholars and communication professionals. Topics such as moderation, interactivity, interchangeability, propinquity, responsiveness, spontaneity, and dialogue are examined, and theoretical and practical suggestions are made for improving our understanding of social media, how professionals use it, and how academics might study it.

Definitions

As suggested earlier, speaking about technology in public relations as "new technology" is a misnomer. Most of the "new" technologies that we now regularly use in public relations are well established as communication technologies, with the Internet introduced in the 1960s, e-mail in the 1970s, hypertext in the 1980s, the World Wide Web in 1993, and blogs in 1999. Even *concepts* such as "social media" are not new. Google now owns the Usenet archive (and still hosts thousands of groups), one of the first "social media." Usenet was started in 1981 and contains 500 million back-and-forth posts by tens of millions of people from more than 3.5 million groups.

Electronic mailing lists like the National Communication Association's list CRTNET (Communication, Research, and Theory Network), started in 1989 by Tom Benson at the Pennsylvania State University, have been hosting member dialogue for more than two decades. Internet Relay Chat (IRC), started in the early 1990s, is also still going strong, as are the infamous "chat rooms" where we occasionally hear about adolescents getting into trouble. Thus, calling our Internet communication technologies "new" makes people think that we do not already know a lot about them, which we do. Indeed, many of the early critiques of the Internet, of which we see very few in most literature reviews, were critical (cf. Elmer, 1997; Kent, 2001; Mitra, 1997; Warnick, 1998) and focused on understanding the medium rather than working out technical details.

In spite of the fact that there are decades of research, thousands of scholarly articles about "new communication technologies," and hundreds of articles just from communication and public relations sources, some scholars of new technology are actually turning to online (nonrefereed) sources like Wikipedia for definitions and proof for claims (cf. Terilli, Driscoll, & Stacks, 2008; Wright & Hinson, 2009a, 2009b). More important, when many scholars talk about new communication technologies, they take an implicit ontological stance about technology that assumes that dialogue, rhetoric, and persuasion are present, but completely ignore the actual use of the technology by public relations professionals, focusing on self-report data and content analyses.

What Are Social Media and Social Networking?

On the most basic level, any interactive communication channel that allows for two-way interaction and feedback could be called a social medium (Listservs, e-mail, radio call-in programs, etc.). Shortwave radio, Citizen's Band (CB) radio, and the telephone are probably the oldest broadcast media that allow for social interaction and networking.

Modern social networks are characterized by the potential for *real-time interaction*, *reduced anonymity* (with Facebook, MySpace, LinkedIn, etc., but not with blogs and lists), a sense of *propinquity* (brought on by the use of avatars, graphical interfaces, automated messages, etc.), *short response times* (often because of the number of users/members participating), and the ability to "time shift," or engage the social network whenever it suits each particular member. Thus, blogs, Twitter, Facebook, and MySpace are considered social media because of the responsiveness of participants and the vastness of networks, as are interactive Listservs, newsgroups, Usenet, and real-time chats like IRC.

More traditional forms of social media (personal letters, letters to the editor, videoconferencing, etc.) are not thought of the same way because they are often not capable of supporting interactions by people in vast social networks, because they do not take place in "real time," and, perhaps most important, because they do not allow time shifting. As few as five people would have difficulty holding a coherent, shared conversation via postal mail, while hundreds, sometimes thousands, regularly contribute to online blog posts or Facebook messages using "threaded dialogue." Social media have several other defining features: moderation, interactivity, interchangeability, propinquity, responsiveness, spontaneity, and dialogue.

Moderation. Moderation refers to editorial oversight rather than conservativeness. For example, successfully posting a message to the NCA's CRTNET Listserv requires that your message be read by the list moderator, who decides if the post is appropriate for distribution to the list. The same is true of many blogs. Other Listservs and blogs are completely open, allowing anyone (or anyone with an account) to upload posts responding to specific blog content or messages from fellow readers. Unmoderated blogs are uncommon because they are often flooded with advertisements for drugs, porn, and other inappropriate messages from bots and spammers.

However, not all social media sites are moderated in the same way. The blog SlashDot (SlashDot.org) enlists the help of its members to moderate the site, selecting hundreds of members each week and assigning them "moderator points" enabling them to raise or lower the score for particular posts. Because moderators have limited points, only inappropriate posts are scored down, and exceptional posts scored up. Subscribers to the blog are also allowed to select their threshold of content quality, reading only four- and five-star posts and ignoring the rest, reading everything, and so on. Many blog moderators filter only inappropriate content but allow all other posts through.

Moderation is a part of all social media, whether it is employed or not. Facebook, LinkedIn, and other social networking sites, for example, allow the site owner (moderator) to decide who will be granted access. Facebook and LinkedIn require the "moderator" to grant permission to others to join (when they receive a "friend request," etc.).

Ironically, moderating social media is *antisocial.* Social media create the illusion of knowing what someone is doing by seeing the posts by others on their social networking pages and reading the comments to their own posts. However, social media are not "social" in the sense of having your close friends over for drinks or tea. Rather, social media are like a party. Because "everyone" is there, few people pay much attention to anyone, even close friends. Everyone knows that their conversations might be overheard, so they do not really disclose too much, except if they are standing off in a corner (or sending a private message on a social networking site). As a result, being truly social cannot be done on a social networking site. Their public nature precludes intimateness, self-disclosure, and genuine sociality. Intimacy requires privacy.

Stories abound in the media of young people posting inappropriate content on their Facebook pages or not understanding the difference between public and private information and conversations (Bahney, 2006). Government employees, graduate students, business professionals, job applicants, interns, and high school and college students have gotten into trouble with social media.

Social media give the illusion of allowing people to pick their friends and colleagues and create an environment of freedom and democracy. In practice, however, professionals often feel pressured to grant entry to supervisors and colleagues for fear of suffering sometimes serious consequences. Thousands of people have been fired for blogging and posting comments about their employers, and people with active social networking sites need to spend a great deal of time posting and reading comments. As a result, many active social networkers maintain alternative social media sites for their "real friends." Thus, all social media require some level of maintenance and moderation.

Interactivity. Interactivity has long been a feature of social media going back to the early Listservs and professional "hotlines" (cf. CIOS: Communication Institute for Online Scholarship). However, the vast majority of people read blogs or monitor twitters, rather than post to them. In the early days of the Internet, these people were called "lurkers." Twenty years ago, active participants to lists would complain about people who just read the posts by others and never participated in the dialogue.

Modern social media such as Facebook, YouTube, and LinkedIn have actually institutionalized participation. For example, on Facebook, "friends" can give a "thumbs up" or "thumbs down" rating to the posts of others with very little effort. Little substantive discussion actually takes place publicly. Most people just post pictures of their outing with their kids at the lake or the results of their latest online IQ test or achievement in FarmVille. On most social networking sites, symbolic participation, or faux interaction, takes the place of genuine interaction (Kent, Harrison, & Taylor, 2006).

More conversational back-and-forth discussion takes place on blogs than on personal and professional social networking sites. On the one hand, substantive blog conversations make sense; blogs bring to readers and subscribers new information and topics of discussion. After all, how much can someone say about pictures of your nephew's picnic at the Jersey shore?—"Dude, that looked like it rocked!" However, a blog posting about a new health or technological innovation, or a political decision by the president, can spur heated commentary. Still, anyone who belongs to several social networking sites knows that most members are lurkers, and most sites receive the majority of their postings from a handful of active participants.

That most people are lurkers rather than discussants has a lot of implications. Again, as suggested above, social media turn out to be not all that social. Many, perhaps most, people use social networking sites to satisfy their socio-emotional needs of inclusion and acknowledgment. As Rogers (1957) suggested, humans have an innate need to be acknowledged and included. We are social beings. Although not everyone needs to be the center of attention as some bloggers do, everyone wants to feel a part of a social network. Interactivity both affords an opportunity to respond to others (sometimes anonymously, as a random blog poster, etc.) and initiates contact, giving a "shout out" to your "peeps" or uploading your own content or messages on Facebook, YouTube, or another social media site.

Interchangeability. Social networking participants are more or less interchangeable. Going back to the early days of social media, the IRCs and AOL chat rooms, we know that many people disguise their identities. Gender experimentation, where men pretend to be women and women pretend to be men, was (and still is) common on these lean, text-based, networks. Additionally, early social media were characterized by interaction among total strangers.

Many of the modern social media networks share this feature of linking anonymous strangers together. If I accept a friend's request on Facebook, for example, I am then offered the opportunity to select from among *his or her* friends, shopping for "friends" that both participants might have in common. Similarly, I am often sent requests by total strangers to join my own LinkedIn network. When I follow up on the background of the person sending me the request, I often discover that the stranger and I have absolutely nothing in common (bankers, real estate agents, etc.). The opportunity to create a network of anonymous friends and follow the antics of total strangers exists to a greater extent with Twitter, where I have lists of "followers" (people or organizations who are following me), and "following" (people and organizations who I am following). The opportunity to keep on top of Ashton Kutcher's dining habits or "Lindsay Lohan's Twitter trainwreck" is very compelling.

The point here is people on many social media sites are interchangeable. Sites are designed to build wide networks by sharing information among members. Apart from social networking with one's actual family and genuine "friends," everyone else is interchangeable. If Richard Edelman stopped blogging, I could follow some other blog. If I was interested in reaching key publics through an organizational blog, I could affiliate with new colleagues and professionals who share similar interests. With the exception of people whom we actually know and see regularly, everyone else might be computer generated. My Twitter "followers" are not necessarily who they say they are, and it is not necessary to blog, twitter, or Facebook to be professionally successful. Moreover, the time spent "social networking" (social media qua entertainment), rather than simply using social media like blogs for professional purposes (social media qua research) (cf. Kent, 2008a), is unlikely to result in any big professional dividends (Regan, 2007).

Finally, going back to an earlier point mentioned in "moderation," because people's "social networks" include friends, family, coworkers, colleagues, supervisors, and professionals from other organizations and industries, no candid or substantive advice or counsel is possible. An employee who negatively blogs about his or her employer is likely to be fired; thus, the blog needs to be "anonymous," diminishing its credibility and veracity. The same risk entails from posting to industry blogs, as well as posting candid comments on one's own social media sites. Thus, any "dialogue" that ensues—on order with pabulum and frequently just self-serving rants—in no way resembles what Granovetter (1973) described in "The Strength of Weak Ties":

> The overall social structural picture suggested by this argument can be seen by considering the situation of some arbitrarily selected individual—call him Ego. Ego will have a collection of close friends, most of whom are in touch with one another—a densely knit clump of social structure. Moreover, Ego will have a collection of acquaintances, few of whom know one another. Each of these acquaintances, however, is likely to have close friends in his own right and therefore to be enmeshed in a closely knit clump of social structure, but one different from Ego's. The weak tie between Ego and his acquaintance, therefore, becomes not merely a trivial acquaintance tie but rather a crucial bridge between the two densely knit clumps of close friends. To the extent that the assertion of the previous paragraph is correct, these clumps would not, in fact, be connected to one another at all were it not for the existence of weak ties. (p. 1363)

Social networking sites are not about "professional networking," as takes place at a conference, or with one's colleagues in the hall, but about "sociability." The friends, colleagues, blog, and Twitter sites followed are largely arbitrary, and an individual's participation in the network is as interchangeable as watching the nightly news on one channel rather than another.

Propinquity. Propinquity is often talked about as a feature of dialogue. Propinquity means closeness or proximity—nearness. We have the strongest relationships with those with whom we share physical space. As we know from the interpersonal communication literature, relationships are built over time and through shared interactions. Relationships are also built through self-disclosure and genuine contact. Being a member of the same professional association or social media site does not equate with friendship. As has been argued by Kent and Taylor (1998, 2002), Web sites, and by extension, social media sites, have the *potential* to function dialogically, as relationship building tools; however, actual intellectual contact is required for this to happen. Wikipedia, for example, has a lot of information on it, but it fosters no sense of closeness, since it is little more than a dictionary. Social media, on the other hand, have the "potential" to build relationships because of the shared sense of connection engendered by the media. But without devoting time and energy to interaction, social media fail.

Although the sense of propinquity fostered by social media sites is illusory, they do provide the ground for creating stronger professional relationships. Relationships, however, need to be nurtured. A professional interested in building a strong relationship with a fellow professional is likely to have more success and develop a stronger bond by spending time with the other person at a local event, a professional conference, or over lunch than via e-mail or a social networking site. Since strong relationships are premised on shared experience and understanding, social media provide an opportunity to create a sense of identification by unawareness (Burke, 1973) that is part of all true relationships.

Responsiveness. Responsiveness is a feature of most social media. As noted above, some social media sites like blogs do not allow all visitors to post comments, and many sites only allow comments by members (something that has been true since the early days of social media). Responsiveness gets played out in a number of ways. Probably, the most common way is through threaded dialogue. Threaded dialogue is conversation that emerges in response to news or conversational posts (or "threads"). Other forms of social media allow for responses to be posted by members and participants but are not threaded.

For example, recently on CRTNET (NATCOM.org), Richard Vatz posted a comment about whether NCA should be providing minority grants to graduate students. The original comment sparked substantial controversy, with dozens of members of the list posting lengthy comments over the course of several weeks. However, because NCA's list is moderated and has a time delay that varies from hours to a day or more, depending on when the list moderator is able to vet and upload member posts, having threaded conversations that refer to other posts and move back and forth between the comments of others is more difficult. Some of the content that someone might reference in a threaded context is being uploaded at the same time as yours, with the other five comments that came in between 5 p.m. and 8 a.m. A genuinely threaded context such as what is found on many blogs (e.g., SlashDot.org) has the potential to be more like genuine dialogue, with comments appearing in reverse chronological order, in real time, and with the ability to reference, incorporate, and interrogate the comments and insights of others. Completely open social media often attract "vandals" who use foul language, post inappropriate comments, insult members, and occasionally upload links to competing content. Thus, most social media sites for professionals are moderated. Responsiveness, then, is a feature of social media, but its implementation and value vary tremendously and affect the nature of the social experience.

Dialogue. Public relations and many other communication-oriented professions have been moving back toward rhetorical, relational, and dialogic communication models. Marketers are increasingly interested in "relationship building" (currently reified as brand loyalty, but increasingly more focused on building more tangible relationships of trust and commitment). Politicians have been showcasing their involvement in their communities by hosting "town halls" and providing online content. Public relations professionals have long recognized the power of relationships to foster trust and loyalty.

The principles of dialogue were first outlined by a number of interpersonal and relational scholars, professionals, and philosophers. Martin Buber (1923/1970) is generally considered the father of dialogue, but others, including Bahktin (1981), Laing (1969), and Rogers (1957), have contributed. In public relations, Ron Pearson (1989) as well as Kent and Taylor (1998, 2002) have also contributed.

Social media revolve around what is essentially a central tenet of dialogue: the value of the individual. One of the problems with the way that social media and dialogue interact, however, is that social media, as has been explained above, are not very social. When Martin Buber (1923/1970) wrote about dialogue almost a century ago, in 1923, he envisioned face-to-face interactions of genuineness, empathy, and compassion: There were no superstores, there were no cable TV networks, there were no cellular telephones, and there were no social networks that did not involve human beings interacting with each other face-to-face.

Some public relations professionals have argued that sometimes "we do not want a genuine interaction, we just want to get our groceries and go home." However, Buber's (1923/1970) dream and the dream of most dialogic scholars is a world where people have time, and a desire, to interact with their fellow human beings. Dialogue is an activity of patience and understanding. Thus, for social media to live up to the dialogic promise suggested by Buber (1923/1970) and Kent and Taylor (1998, 2002), they need to actually be capable of dealing with people, all people, as valued and trusted companions.

Many of the definitions of social media that are advanced by scholars limit themselves to description, never examining the assumptions behind their research or the appropriateness of their methodology for the phenomenon in question. There exists very little critical analysis of social media for scholars to draw on. For example, Waters, Burnett, Lamm, and Lucas (2009) wrote, "Relationships are the foundation for social networking sites" (p. 102) and "The purpose of this study is to examine how nonprofit organizations use Facebook to engage their stakeholders and foster relationship growth" (p. 103). Although the article provides some useful findings, there is a disconnect between what social networking sites are for "relationships," and what the authors study. The authors do not actually look at "how nonprofit organizations use Facebook to engage their stakeholders." They sent no messages to the nonprofits to see if they responded (responsiveness is something that previous researchers have shown to be very low among all types of organizations), posted no messages to their walls to see how the organization engaged them, nor content analyzed the quality and quantity of the comments that were posted. Yet Waters et al. concluded that nonprofit organizations "rarely provide information in forms other than external links to news stories, photographs, and discussion board posts" (p. 105).

Because this was a study of "social networking," and assumed that "relationships are the foundation," the authors really discovered that these types of organizations are not really doing *any* social networking. The conclusion seems to be that the organizations might be using social networking sites for marketing purposes, or to offer another Web presence, but not to actually engage people "socially." The problem with

Waters et al.'s study is not methodological or that their findings are flawed; the problem is that there is a contradiction between how we define and how we study social media.

Even more substantive essays on social networking such as Wright and Hinson's (2008), published in the *Public Relations Journal*, often proceed from flawed assumptions. Setting aside the fact that the article contains only two references to public relations books or articles (*Public Relations Tactics* and *PR Week*) and two references to conference papers (both by the authors), the remainder of the citations are to blogs, Web sites, business and marketing journals, and so on. No public relations body of literature is invoked in the essay to support the assumptions made by the authors or the conclusions drawn in the essay. Wright and Hinson (2008) wrote,

> David Meerman Scott, an online thought leadership and viral marketing strategist, says, "one of the coolest things about the Web is that when an idea takes off it can propel a brand or a company to seemingly instant fame and fortune".
>
> Scott also pointed out that although communicating via the Web usually is free—as opposed to purchasing space through traditional advertising—only a small number of public relations practitioners are effectively using blogs and other social media when communicating with their strategic publics. Scott claimed the challenge to public relations and marketing people "is to harness the amazing power of whatever you call it—viral, buzz, word-of-mouse, or word-of-blog—having other people tell your story drives action." (p. 1)

Wright and Hinson's (2008) article illustrates an important point because what they offer in their essay, "How Blogs and Social Media Are Changing Public Relations and the Way It Is Practiced," does not focus on public relations at all. Later in the essay the authors, under the heading "Blogging and Public Relations," wrote,

> Many aspects of technology recently have challenged how public relations is practiced. As Robert J. Key (2005) explains, "Public relations in the digital age requires understanding how your key constituents are gathering and sharing information and then influencing them at key points. Doing so requires strategies that embrace the digital age." (p. 3)

In spite of the title, there is no sense that the authors are interested in "social media" as a tool of relationship building, interactiveness, dialogue, or sociality at all. Rather, social media are examined as just another tool for organizational marketing initiatives and exploiting publics. Even Wikipedia's definition of social media (the grade school of scholarly thought) adequately describes social media as discussed here, suggesting social media are

> designed to be disseminated through social interaction. Social media supports the human need for social interaction, using Internet- and Web-based technologies to transform broadcast media monologues (one to many) into social media dialogues (many to many). It supports the democratization of knowledge and information, transforming people from content consumers into content producers. (en.wikipedia.org/wiki/Social_media)

Public relations professionals need to decide whether social media are useful *public relations tools* (and I believe that they are), or whether they are mere marketing tools. If the latter is true, that work should be published in another place and our focus should be on understanding how this new technology can be used to further public relations goals.

The question that we need to begin asking is "What exactly is being assumed when blogs and Twitters are examined?" Are we examining interpersonal influence, persuasion, pure information, social intercourse, professional discourse, power, ontological expressions of culture, postmodern conversations, psychic chatter, invitations to say more, what? All these and more are possibilities, depending on the nature of the interlocutors (or those just lurking from the sidelines). Which assumption scholars or professionals make about the technology will have a profound impact on how they view messages, how they interact with others, and the value that they place on the social network.

Important Social Media Issues and Literature

Although there are many articles on social media that are really more focused on marketing, advertising, promotion, or other activities than on public relations activities, a number of excellent articles have been written. Rather than try to review every article here, I will instead highlight several that treat social media in ways of value to public relations professionals and help focus discussion on what public relations professionals need to know to understand and use social media effectively.

Han and Zhang's (2009) essay "Starbucks Is Forbidden in the Forbidden City: Blog, Circuit of Culture and Informal Public Relations Campaign in China" poses a strategic question about how social media might be used by activist groups and organizations:

> Adopting the circuit of culture model, this study illustrates the intricate role of culture in international public relations within an Internet-based media context, as well as the tension surrounding the conflicting identities between Starbucks' global presence and the local sensitivity attached to the cultural heritage—the Forbidden City. (Abstract)

Han and Zhang's (2009) essay, although only a "research in brief" essay, deals with a real-world issue, examines how social media content was introduced into the mainstream media, subsequently resulting in a successful grassroots campaign, and most important, includes abundant scholarly support invoking public relations scholars and thinkers like Bourdieu, Curtin and Gaither, Hall, Heath, and others. The essay offers a valuable glimpse into the study of social media.

Other issues that have not received enough attention among scholars have been ethical issues related to social media. There have been a number of high-profile cases of social media being used unethically, including issues such as corporations unlawfully taking images from social media pages and using them in marketing and advertising campaigns without obtaining permission or paying for the use of the images (cf. Lyons, 2009; techdirt.com/articles/20070429/221551.shtml; www.wiredstrategies.com/lawsuit/release1.pdf; www.PDNPulse.com/2009/06/how-did-this-familys-facebook-picture-end-up-on-a-czech-poster.html). Another issue for several years now has been the use of social media pages by for-profit organizations and educational institutions (cf. Clark, 2006; Rubin, 2008; www.techdirt.com/articles/20060118/1056224.shtml) as a screening tool for job applicants or students.

More substantive issues that have been excluded include Edelman's flaunting of the ethical marketing guidelines of the Word of Mouth Marketing Association (WOMMA) that he helped write. Ironically, few public relations scholars have been willing to discuss the issue, instead accepting Edelman's weak apology. As Craig (2007) explained,

> The blog noted that it was sponsored by an organization called Working Families for Wal-Mart. But several other things were not disclosed:
>
> - Working Families for Wal-Mart was created by Edelman, the public relations firm, for Wal-Mart, in response to criticism of the company by union-supported groups such as Wal-Mart Watch. Nothing on the sponsor's "About Us" section on its Web site mentioned the organization's connection to Wal-Mart or Edelman.

- Working Families for Wal-Mart, which is funded by the company, paid for the trip—flying Laura and Jim to Las Vegas to start out, providing them an RV, paying for gas, setting up the blog, and paying Laura (freelance writer Laura St. Claire) for her blog entries.
- Jim Thresher, who shot photographs for the blog during his travels with Laura, was a staff photographer for *The Washington Post.*

Richard Edelman, after several days of silence about the matter on his blog, wrote on October 16:

> I want to acknowledge our error in failing to be transparent about the identity of the two bloggers from the outset. This is 100% our responsibility and our error, not the client's. . . . [in a later interview] Because we have people who are insufficiently experienced in this . . . I have to make sure people have the training in basics of PR and also in the morals of new media and that's what I'm totally focused on. (Craig, 2007, pp. 215–216)

The number of ethical lapses described by Craig (2007) here are numerous. Ironically, only journalists have paid much attention to the ethical issues here; public relations professionals have largely ignored the issue. Craig's commentary, along with others that appear in the same issue of the journal, explores a number of ethical lapses that have yet to be explored in the public relations literature. Through "the use of a front group, corrupting the channels of information, not acting with honesty and integrity, not serving the public interest, not identifying clients publicly," and so on, Edelman violated half of the PRSA's code of ethics clauses. To suggest that this was a lapse by inexperienced people who did not yet understand WOMMA's intent is unlikely.

Social media scholars need to *begin* by dealing with the ethical and definitional issues of the media before they move to studies of organizations' use of social media. "What *should* we be examining?" needs to be answered before random studies of social media.

A second essay is Kent's (2008a) "Critical Analysis of Blogging in Public Relations," which laid out a number of considerations about blogs and suggested that as professionals we should be aware that there are a number of different types of blogs and that how individuals think about blogs varies, depending on whether they are thinking about news blogs or a personal blog. Also, there are several types of blogs:

> The traditional or historic blog is written like a diary entry, or an op-ed page. By contrast, . . . the "news-blog," has emerged. News blogs are essentially clearinghouses of news headlines or abstracts that usually link readers to an actual news story. (p. 33)

Essays like Kent's (2008a), exploring the features of the various social media, are needed in every area of new technology. In the hands of public relations professionals, social media are much more than tools for marketers. When we allow our skills to be reduced to mere marketing assistance, our value as counselors disappears. Public relations professionals, as *communication* professionals, have insight into influence and persuasion, designing effective dialogic networks, responding to crises, apologizing for corporate misdeeds, and so on. Our value will diminish as long as we allow ourselves to be mere technical experts.

Using social media for "reaching publics" is not the same as "developing and maintaining the viability of corporate narratives," "strengthening organization-public relationships through identification and persuasion," and "adapting communication technologies to serve organizational goals rather than as replacements for more expensive broadcast media." That social media are inexpensive misses the point. News releases are inexpensive, but they are no replacement for advertising when it comes to publicity or promotion. But news releases are still a valuable tool in the professional communicator's box. Social media are also just a tool. When used effectively, social media have great potential and serve specific needs. When used simply as less costly replacements for advertising and marketing expenses, the other unique skills that public relations professionals bring are unnecessary. Let us send our students out to get marketing degrees if we have nothing to teach them.

Directions in Social Media for Scholars

As suggested above, social media are much more complex than we are giving credit for, and much of our research has naively studied "perceived" effects (how a technology makes you feel) rather than actual effects (how useful each technology is in distributing organizational messages and building and maintaining relationships with stakeholders). Several suggestions will help guide practitioners.

1. Rather than asking people whether they *feel* more powerful or connected after adopting social media tools, let us find out whether they actually are. Network analysis (Doerfel & Taylor, 2004; Taylor & Doerfel, 2003, 2005) is an excellent and underused research methodology in public relations and has the potential to reveal *more* than just whether people think social media tools are playing a major role in their success. Network analysis can reveal who the central players really are in a professional network and guide professionals to the people who likely have the best understanding of a professional milieu.

2. Marketers and advertisers have embraced analytical software like Google Analytics as a means of "driving sales" and increasing stickiness on Web sites; however, virtually no public relations professional has used the Web monitoring software to its fullest potential. Since social media are about dialogic goals, knowing how to bring visitors to Web sites into a discussion, as well as understanding their potential to actually engage, is crucial. In the parlance of blog posters, RTFA (Read the Fu Article) is used to mean, "If you haven't read the story, keep your mouth shut." The acronym is usually used to stifle debate; however, the underlying message is something that professional communicators should understand: Most people do not RTFA. Neither do they read long blog postings, background readings, and so on. Analytical and Web monitoring software has huge potential as a research tool to guide the development of effective networks, to focus professionals on issues of genuine interest, and to help professionals better understand the logic of Web navigation and maximize dialogic features on Web sites.

3. Social networking research has largely focused on studying outcomes and not strategies. On "What do visitors think?," "What do professionals believe?," "Do people like doing it?," and so on, rather than on how to improve on each strategy, how to gauge the effectiveness of social networking tools, and how to integrate the tools into more traditional media mixes. Scholars need to shift their focus from studying outcomes and effects—we already know enough about traditional media from prior technological revolutions to make fairly accurate predictions—and instead focus our attention on understanding how social networking technologies can best serve public relations professionals. Our assumption should not be that all technologies are beneficial; indeed, many technologies have not been. E-mail, for example, has not improved the quality of our communication with others, only the speed and convenience (Regan, 2007). Our assumptions need to be that each technology is likely to interact with the other technologies in predictable ways and that we should focus on understanding the nature of those interactions rather than simply what isolated effects each technology has.

4. We need more criticism and more theory. Criticism *extends, refines, and clarifies theory and practice.* Much of the research in our journals focuses on quantitative approaches to examining media, and not enough of our time is

spent considering the strengths, limitations, and directions of our media and our discipline. Kent and Taylor (2007) called for more emphasis on theory and research in "Beyond 'Excellence' in International Public Relations. . . . " The same move is called for with social media. The idea that there is one right way to do anything in public relations is absurd and ignores the needs of most public relations professionals to solve their own *unique* problems in their own *unique* organizational environment. So many other mediated tools exist for reaching publics—electronic portfolios, interactive Web sites, real-time chats, Web cameras, journalists-only sites, and knowledge networks—that the obsessive focus on social media ignores their place in the overall practice of public relations.

Directions in Social Media for Professionals

On the one hand, public relations professionals who have not embraced social media technologies wholeheartedly should understand that they are fine without them. Not every field needs a social media presence to succeed. On the other hand, the push for corporate social responsibility, sustainability, and dialogue (Kent, 2008b) is putting pressure on organizations to communicate more, and more openly. Nevertheless, "good organizations" are still capable of succeeding without constant communication with stakeholders and stake seekers.

The difference here, between embracing social media completely and understanding the role of social media, is a question of media literacy. Professionals need to understand the strengths and limitations of the media so that, when appropriate, they can use it.

However, when faced with a barrage of messages from professional associations about how professionals need to be twittering, blogging, and "embracing social media," remaining a technological agnostic becomes very difficult (Taylor & Kent, 2009). All professionals need to understand new media and social media so that they can make good decisions, but not all professionals actually need to *use* social media.

As suggested of scholars, they need to learn to ask better questions that will flesh out the boundaries of our new technologies rather than embracing them outright. As for the individuals who run our professional associations and practitioner journals, just because social media might be fun does not mean that they are essential. Consider these headlines from the front page of *PRSA Tactics* (February 2009): "Tweet and Low: Making the Most of 140 Characters," "Direct and Accurate: Increasing Social Media Success," as well as this recent advertisement from the PRSA and Ragan Communications e-mailed to members of the PRSA:

> You've heard all the buzzwords. Twitter, Facebook, blogs and podcasting. You've also heard how these tools will transform the way you do your job. But did you know that social media could save your organization time and money? That's because Web 2.0 tools are cheaper and easier than ever to use, and they can make your communications department run more efficiently and effectively. (February 9, 2009)

This sort of uncritical hype is inappropriate for our professional associations and part of the reason that many new practitioners see social media as essential.

A more important issue for public relations professionals is to appreciate the technician/manager split. Public relations professionals have historically started out as technicians, writing news releases, conducting research, and learning their craft from more experienced professionals. Once a professional has some experience, she or he will begin to look for more sophisticated work and try to move into a management position. Allowing the profession of public relations to be reduced to social media is an outgrowth of encroachment (Lauzen, 1991). By making the purview of public relations that of a toastmaster or cheerleader whose job is simply to talk up the organization and chat up its stakeholders, public relations professionals grow increasingly impotent and they require a smaller skill set. Far from helping the profession, social media are turning back the clock to a time when we were mere "journalists in residence," not strategic thinkers.

Conclusion

Some will argue that this chapter was not sufficiently objective, straying too far into editorializing and criticism and not simply describing the boundaries of the social media phenomenon. However, as someone who used the previous handbook to teach both undergraduate and graduate public relations classes, and someone who read almost every chapter in the book, I believe that the most valuable chapters were those that offered a new perspective and provided direction to readers. Social media have an important role to play in public relations, but not the only role. Students, professionals, and scholars also need to appreciate the role of rhetoric, including narrative, identification, and persuasion research, the importance of understanding crisis and issues management, and the importance of strategic planning and thinking.

Public relations academics and professionals need to spend some time coming to terms with the role of technology in public relations. We can no longer sit back passively and let our profession be defined as hospitality. The dream of dialogic public relations and of convivial technologies (Christians, 1990; Pearson, 1989) like social media was for public relations professionals to be actively involved in setting the organizational agenda, researching, understanding, and building relationships with key stakeholders and publics. Ten years ago, no one believed that public relations would eventually become "being responsible for updating the organization's Facebook page," or "tweeting about the latest product." Although this may sound trivial, social media *are* trivial. There are no research results or anecdotes about how an organization used social media to engage its publics and develop new mission or vision statements; neither are there articles about how to use social media to create a place of genuine dialogue and peace. We currently study "tweets" and not publics. We count blog posts and not solutions to problems. The future of social media and public relations is a future of stepping past the technologies as marketing and advertising tools and embracing them as tools capable of solving problems and engaging publics in real-world issues.

References

Bahktin, M. M. (1981). *The dialogic imagination* (C. Emerson & M. Holquist, Trans.). Austin: University of Texas Press.

Bahney, A. (2006, May 25). Interns? No bloggers need apply. *New York Times* (Late Edition—Final), p. G1.

Buber, M. (1970). *I and thou* (W. Kaufmann, Trans.). New York: Scribner. (Original work published 1923)

Bulldog Reporter. (2008). *Bulldog Reporter/Tekgroup International 2008 journalist survey on media relations practices: Executive summary.* Retrieved March 20, 2010, from www.bulldogreporter.com and www.tekgroup.com

Burke, K. (1973). The rhetorical situation. In L. Thayer (Ed.), *Communication: Ethical and moral issues* (pp. 263–275). London: Gordon & Breach.

Christians, C. G. (1990). Social responsibility: Ethics and new technologies. In R. L. Johannesen (Ed.), *Ethics in human communication* (pp. 265–278). Prospect Heights, IL: Waveland Press.

Clark, A. S. (2006, June 20). *Employers look at Facebook, too: Companies turn to online profiles to see what applicants are really like.* www.cbsnews.com/stories/2006/06/20/eveningnews/main1734920.shtml

Craig, D. A. (2007). Cases and commentaries. *Journal of Mass Media Ethics, 22*(2/3), 215–228.

Doerfel, M. L., & Taylor, M. (2004). Network dynamics of interorganizational cooperation: The Croatian civil society movement. *Communication Monographs, 71*(4), 373–394.

Elmer, G. (1997). Spaces of surveillance: Indexicality and solicitation on the Internet. *Critical Studies in Mass Communication, 14*(2), 182–191.

Granovetter, M. S. (1973). The strength of weak ties. *American Journal of Sociology, 78*(6), 1360–1380.

Han, G., & Zhang, A. (2009). Starbucks is forbidden in the Forbidden City: Blog, circuit of culture and informal public relations campaign in China. *Public Relations Review, 35*(4), 395–401.

Kent, M. L. (2001). Managerial rhetoric and the metaphor of the World Wide Web. *Critical Studies in Media Communication, 18*(3), 359–375.

Kent, M. L. (2008a). Critical analysis of blogging in public relations. *Public Relations Review, 34*(1), 32–40.

Kent, M. L. (2008b, November). *The dialogic turn in public relations: Toward a theory of dialogic practice.* Competitive paper presented at the annual meeting of the National Communication Association, Public Relations Division, San Diego, CA.

Kent, M. L., Harrison, T. R., & Taylor, M. (2006). A critique of Internet polls as symbolic representation and pseudo-events. *Communication Studies, 57*(3), 299–315.

Kent, M. L., & Taylor, M. (1998). Building dialogic relationships through the World Wide Web. *Public Relations Review, 24*(3), 321–334.

Kent, M. L., & Taylor, M. (2002). Toward a dialogic theory of public relations. *Public Relations Review, 28*(1), 21–37.

Kent, M. L., & Taylor, M. (2007). Beyond "excellence" in international public relations research: An examination of generic theory in Bosnian public relations. *Public Relations Review, 33*(1), 10–20.

Laing, R. D. (1969). *Self and others* (2nd ed.). New York: Pantheon Books.

Lauzen, M. M. (1991). Imperialism and encroachment in public relations. *Public Relations Review, 17*(3), 245–255.

Levinson, P. (1997). *The soft edge: A natural history and future of the information revolution.* New York: Routledge.

Lyons, C. (2009, July 24). Facebook can use your pictures for ads, no permission required. *Los Angeles Times.* from opinion.latimes.com/opinionla/2009/07/facebook-can-use-your-pictures-for-ads-no-permission-required.html

McLuhan, M. (1999/1964). *Understanding media: The extensions of man.* Cambridge: MIT Press.

Mitra, A. (1997). Diasporic Web sites: Ingroup and outgroup discourse. *Critical Studies in Mass Communication, 14*(2), 158–181.

Pearson, R. (1989). *A theory of public relations ethics.* Unpublished doctoral dissertation, Ohio University, Athens.

Regan, T. (2007, October 17). Maybe e-mail isn't such a great idea, after all. *Christian Science Monitor.* www.csmonitor.com/2007/1017/p16s01-stct.html

Rogers, C. (1957). The necessary and sufficient conditions of therapeutic personality change. *Journal of Consulting Psychology, 21*(27), 95–103.

Rubin, B. M. (2008, September 20). *Social-networking sites viewed by admissions officers: Survey shows some use Facebook, MySpace as another aspect to college application.* archives.chicagotribune.com/2008/sep/20/local/chi-facebook-college-20-sep20

Taylor, M., & Doerfel, M. L. (2003). Building interorganizational relationships that build nations. *Human Communication Research, 29*(2), 153–181.

Taylor, M., & Doerfel, M. L. (2005). Another dimension to explicating relationships: Network theory and method to measure inter-organizational linkages. *Public Relations Review, 31*(1), 121–129.

Taylor, M., & Kent, M. L. (2008). *Anticipatory socialization in the use of social media in public relations: A content analysis of PRSA's public relations tactics.* Competitive paper presented at the annual meeting of the Association for Journalism and Mass Communication (AEJMC), Chicago.

Terilli, S. A., Driscoll, P. D., & Stacks, D. W. (2008). Business blogging in the fog of law: Traditional agency liability principles and less-than-traditional. *Public Relations Journal, 2*(2), 1–22.

Warnick, B. (1998). Appearance or reality? Political parody on the Web in campaign '96. *Critical Studies in Mass Communication, 15*(3), 306–324.

Waters, R. D., Burnett, E., Lamm, A., & Lucas, J. (2009). Engaging stakeholders through social networking: How nonprofit organizations are using Facebook. *Public Relations Review, 35,* 102–106.

Wright, D. K., & Hinson, M. D. (2008). How blogs and social media are changing public relations and the way it is practiced. *Public Relations Journal, 2*(2), 1–21.

Wright, D. K., & Hinson, M. D. (2009a). Examining how public relations practitioners actually are using social media. *Public Relations Journal, 3*(3), 1–33.

Wright, D. K., & Hinson, M. D. (2009b). An updated look at the impact of social media on public relations practice. *Public Relations Journal, 3*(2), 1–27.

PART III

Public Relations as Globalicity

Robert L. Heath

Globalicity, and its variations, is too good a coinage not to use here. These terms occur in chapters in other parts, as well as this one. Through their use, researchers and theorists seek vocabulary to address what is increasingly a unique line of inquiry about public relations' role, practice, and value to society.

Many of the themes of research, theory, and context explored in previous parts of this book apply here. These chapters are interdependent with that body of discussion. The key, however, is to understand that the complexities and vicissitudes of local and even national public relations manifest themselves in manifold ways in a global society.

Whether global is the big picture might be debated. It is certainly "another picture." It adds a level of complexity and takes concepts such as control, power, change, meaning, discourse processes, and management to another level.

The chapters that constitute Part III are written by authors who not only reflect national cultures but have spent years analyzing complexities at this level. Their perspectives help us understand what we know and are wise to counsel and teach today. They also open us to new vistas of research, practice, and pedagogy.

CHAPTER 46

Why Culture Is Still Essential in Discussions About Global Public Relations

Robert I. Wakefield

This chapter addresses the relevance and impact of culture on public relations activities around the world. This perspective should be increasingly salient to public relations practitioners and scholars as corporations and other entities encounter ever more cultures in their international expansion and with the rapidly changing cultural compositions within many nations. The topic of culture is always "plagued with denotative ambiguity and diversity of meaning" (Ellingsworth, 1977, p. 101) but must not be ignored in public relations. As Curtin and Gaither (2007) asserted, "Cultural constructs don't affect public relations practice; they are the essence of public relations practice" (p. 12). Despite this awareness, "it is sad and alarming that the concept of culture is being treated almost as an afterthought in . . . public relations" (Sriramesh, 2007, pp. 521–522).

Early theories on public relations in the global arena emphasized culture as a major influence on the practice (Botan, 1992; Verčič, Grunig, & Grunig, 1996; Wakefield, 1995), but since those examinations, the world has changed dramatically. People are much more interconnected through the Internet (Micklethwait & Wooldridge, 2000), and societies seem more anxious to cooperate in resolving mutual problems such as climate change, biological pandemics, and poverty. Some authors claim that the world is becoming globalized around some form of universal (but not necessarily Western) capitalism (Friedman, 2006; Sirkin, Hemerling, & Bhattacharya, 2008), and that the postmodern era is reducing or eliminating the variances and impacts of culture on political and commercial affairs. Others counter that cultural roots and influences persist despite any illusions that global capitalism has overwhelmed these traditions (Inglehart & Baker, 2000). In fact, as many economic and technological aspects of the world converge, various cultures react strongly through government regulations, public demonstrations, boycotts, and even terrorism (Panzner, 2009). Tensions between globalization and culture have created perhaps more confusion, misunderstandings, and threats than ever before.

Public relations practices also seem to be shifting to accommodate globalization. As more corporations transcend their domestic confines, their public relations professionals encounter increased complexities (Verčič, 2003). Traditional challenges remain: regulatory variations, conflicting philosophies toward media and community participation, varying levels of technological development, time zone differences, and the like. Additional complexities have arisen from the expansion of social media, where blogs, videos, and tweets, often delivered anonymously, can have instantaneous global impact.

Communicators use these new tools as supposedly faster and better ways to reach global audiences. Stakeholder groups are also using social media to communicate with or pressure corporations, and this causes firms to rethink historical approaches to stakeholder relationships (Lim, 2010). At the same time, many nongovernmental organizations (NGOs) have upgraded the reach and sophistication of their own public relations; they serve as "prosocial" change agents. They participate in United Nations conferences and cooperate with corporations to deliver aid to needy societies.

As all this international activity occurs, public relations scholars have lagged behind (Curtin & Gaither, 2007), often exhibiting more confusion than clarification. It begins with fuzzy terminology—even the most fundamental definitions of public relations can differ greatly from one nation to another (Verčič, van Ruler, Butschi, & Flodin, 2001).[1] Beyond those basics, is there a proper term for the amorphous arena that spans national borders? Is it *global public relations* (Freitag & Stokes, 2009; Sriramesh & Verčič, 2009); *international public relations* (Curtin & Gaither, 2007); *multicultural public relations* (Banks, 1995); or all the above (or even something else)? And what about organizations served by the public relations industry: Are they *transnational corporations* (Verčič, 2003), *multinational corporations* (Lim, 2010), *transnational organizations* (Molleda & Laskin, 2005), or otherwise?

The scholarly disarray extends beyond terminology. Public relations literature once emphasized "mainstream organizations" such as corporations and governments; but what is a mainstream global entity? The literature used to espouse relationships between corporations and media, but many media today are global firms with their own public relations needs and programs. Are most public relations professionals now employed by global organizations, as Verčič (2003) claimed? Or do larger markets retain a majority of practitioners who focus on their home communities and don't think much about global matters (whether they should or not)? No wonder Curtin and Gaither (2007) proclaimed, "The discussion of international public relations [is] unpredictable, complex, and even illogical at times" (p. 3).

The term *culture*, with its iterations and ramifications, is no less ambiguous or unpredictable. For this and other reasons, culture is characterized as a misunderstood essential of public relations (Sriramesh, 2007). But public relations is not alone in this regard; even in the 1950s, there were almost 200 scholarly definitions of culture (Negandhi, 1983), and certainly hundreds have surfaced since. Curtin and Gaither (2007) noted that "culture forms the basis of a society's shared meaning system" and helps us make sense of our world (p. 36). Adler and Doktor (1986) identified culture by its main elements: It is shared by members of some social group; older members pass it down to younger generations; and it embraces the morals, laws, and customs that shape the group's behaviors or perceptions. Within this framework, it could be said that culture is infused into all aspects of public relations practice: public relations firms, their client organizations, targeted stakeholders, special interest groups, geographic communities, and virtually any other society or organization that exists. Thus, culture becomes so broadly framed as to render it close to impossible to categorize and explain.

The importance of culture in this chapter, though, is in how it influences public relations—especially considering the changes that have occurred as a result of our increasingly globalized world. Other scholars (Curtin & Gaither, 2007; Sriramesh, 2007) have thoughtfully addressed the topic of culture and public relations. It is hoped that this chapter will raise additional questions that need further clarification if public relations professionals are to enrich their cross-cultural activities in this era. If the chapter does not provide actual answers, at least it may offer more discussion around this subject. So three sets of questions will be addressed:

1. *Where is culture* in today's era of globalization, and is its location changing?
2. *Are the forces of globalization changing the influences of culture on public relations?* If so, are these influences being reduced, or are they greater?
3. If organizational response to the influences of culture is necessary, *how should entities respond?* Is needed response exclusive to the global arena, or are so-called domestic organizations also mandated to respond?

Where Is Culture, and Is It Changing?

The first of these questions, *where is culture*, may seem somewhat simplistic, with the obvious answer being that culture is everywhere. Culture is "the origin and basis of human behavior," noted Sahlins (1999, p. 400). "In all its dimensions . . . human existence is symbolically constituted, which is to say, culturally ordered" (p. 400). This being the case, culture is embodied in every human being (Ellingsworth, 1977). But when looking at culture as the basis for groups or societies, where these shared symbols and meanings occur (Adler & Doktor, 1986), the answer to where culture is found is much more complex.

Cultures are changing, mostly because they have done so since humanity began. Scholars acknowledge that most cultures are not isolated and rigid, bound forever by unalterable traditions and values. Rather, cultures continually evolve. In the United States, for example, people used to rely on horses and wagons for transportation to and from church, where they professed a belief in God. Today, many children have never seen a horse, and the targets of worship now are professional football games and celebrities. Furthermore, the various cultures of the world have regularly bumped against each other and assimilated the behavioral patterns of other cultures (Sahlins, 1999).

Despite the historical fluctuations of culture, until recently scholarly approaches to the concept were fairly rigid and superficial. Early examinations generally separated cultural groupings geographically and usually within national boundaries—in other words, equating culture and nation. Hofstede's (1980) groundbreaking cultural dimensions study, for example, categorized some 40 nations according to their supposed cultural similarities and differences. This study has been cited subsequently by numerous scholars, many of whom implicitly supported the nation-framing of culture (Pal & Dutta, 2008).

Today, the scholarly notion of single cultures rooted within nations is subject to widespread challenge—perhaps because the concept was incorrect from the outset. In the first place, most nations have long contained numerous cultures, served by their own languages, social and political leanings, and long-standing hostilities toward surrounding cultures. The African continent alone, for example, comprises some 50 nations and more than 1,000 languages—each of which is generally rooted within a certain culture (Curtin & Gaither, 2007). Even the United States, seen for decades as a "melting pot" of cultures, is now experiencing strong cultural variation and increasing calls not for *e pluribus unum* but for greater recognition and accommodation of diversity.

Appadurai (1990) and Kotkin (1993) also outlined the dispersion of ethnic groups from homelands to other nations, either through voluntary or forced migration, where they combine their shared origins, values, and traditions in their new abodes. These new cultural communities thrive because they retain strong bonds and means of mutual support. At the same time, they adapt well by assimilating many of the newly encountered cultural mores and behaviors (Kotkin, 1993). Many immigrants see this as a positive exchange, wherein "for giving up some of their cultural distinctiveness and assimilating into the dominant culture," they receive "promise of a better life" (Ogan, 2007, p. 312).

These cultural dispersions, or *diaspora* (Appadurai, 1990), have generated significant economic, political, and social impacts in societies throughout the world. Many of the dispersed groups have created their own media, resulting in more multicultural media content in many nations. In the United States, for example, some 10% of total media viewing time accesses Spanish-language media. Korean and Chinese soap operas have become popular in Japan (a former enemy and current economic competitor) and elsewhere in Asia, and Middle Eastern media have spread into Europe and the United States along with significant populations of Muslims (Tunstall, 2008).

Some scholars view instances such as these as evidence that cultures are changing under the weight of globalization. They point to convergence of economies and technologies as catalysts whereby isolated and distinct cultures are disappearing, replaced by a postmodern global conformity (Kramer & Ikeda, 2000). As the anthropologist Wade Davis pointed out, "When you and I were born there were 6,000 languages spoken on Earth. Now, fully half are . . . dead unless something changes. [So], by definition, half of humanity's cultural legacy is being lost in a single generation." What remains is "a blandly amorphous, generic world, as cultures disappear and life becomes more uniform" (Parsell, 2002, p. 1).

Other scholars are skeptical that global convergence is causing too much cultural assimilation (Kramer & Ikeda, 2000). Inglehart and Baker (2000) explained the dichotomy in the convergence and culture debate:

> One school emphasizes the *convergence* of values as a result of "modernization"—the overwhelming economic and political forces that drive cultural change. This school predicts the decline of traditional values and their replacement with "modern" values. The other school of thought emphasizes the *persistence* of traditional values despite economic and political changes. This school assumes that values are relatively independent of economic conditions. . . . It predicts that convergence around some set of "modern" values is unlikely and that traditional values will continue to exert an independent influence on the cultural changes caused by economic development. (p. 20)

Scholars in the traditional camp see changes of modernization as "overestimated" (Inglehart & Baker, 2000, p. 23). It seems apparent, for example, that when large populations of ethnic groups migrate from their homelands into new cities or nations, much of what these groups adopt in their new homes are the more superficial trappings of culture—a taste for at least some of the new food, clothing, and entertainment, and enjoyment of other aspects of the culture. However, Ogan (2007) argued that none of these groups ever really become totally assimilated. They often cling to the values and mores of home and many even retain their native language over a few generations. Only with several generations does any real melding of cultures occur. Even then, as Inglehart and Baker (2000) pointed out,

> The impression that we are moving toward a uniform "McWorld" is partly an illusion. . . . While it is obvious that young people around the world are wearing jeans and listening to [similar] pop music, the persistence of underlying value differences is less apparent. (pp. 22–23)

So it would seem that culture is indeed everywhere—and its overall effects will not go away soon. Myriad cultures exist within nations, and increasingly cultural groupings are crossing borders and extending into many different nations. The forces of global convergence seem to be tearing down cultural foundations. But if cultural assimilation is revealed mostly through artificial trappings while the deep-rooted values and traditions of culture endure, what does this current state of culture mean for public relations? Does culture still affect the field or not?

Does Culture Still Influence Public Relations?

Until 20 years ago, the concept of culture—if it ever showed up in public relations literature—was seen as affecting only those practices that crossed national borders. In the United States, practitioners were focused on domestic stakeholders (and usually ignoring all but "mainstream" Caucasians). Intercultural complexities were reserved for those few "international public relations specialists" whose programs were conducted "on the other side of the ocean" (Anderson, 1989; Wakefield, 1997).

In the late 1980s and early 1990s, early treatises on international public relations listed culture as an influential factor (Anderson, 1989; Booth, 1986). The thinking often was polarized over how to respond to culture in international strategy—what Pal and Dutta (2008) called a "dialectical tension between the local and the global" (p. 162). Authors such as Wouters (1991) advocated global standardization, and others believed that the variations in culture rendered standardization inadvisable (Traverse-Healy, 1991). The international business scholars Adler and Doktor (1986) and Tayeb (1988) referred to a standardized approach as *culture free*, which assumed that an organization could carry out global efficiencies while being "free" to ignore the cultures it faced. They called the opposite philosophy *culture-specific*, in which cultural variations encountered by a global entity should heavily influence decision making to the extent that decisions would be made and carried out in each local unit rather than headquarters.

As other scholars joined this early writing, intuition evolved into theory specific to international public relations. Meznar (1993), for example, focused on whether transnational organizations should engage in bridging or buffering strategies. Perhaps the first major attempt to mediate between centralization and localization was the generic/specific theory. The theorists believed that the solution to effective international public relations was not at the extremes but somewhere in the middle; that *both* central consistencies *and* local relationship building were needed (J. E. Grunig, 2006; Wakefield, 1995).

The generic/specific theory has been the basis for several subsequent examinations (Rhee, 2002; Sriramesh, 2003; Verčič et al., 1996; Wakefield, 2001); however, it was produced before the Internet was commercialized and as the effects of globalization were just surfacing. While subsequent studies have added insight into international public relations, they have left unexamined the effects of globalization and the Internet on the practice of public relations across borders. So what does all this mean in regard to culture? Is culture still relevant to the global public relations of today? Or have the impacts of globalization and the Internet become so pervasive that they are making the local disappear from international public relations practice?

There seems to be plenty of evidence for a globalized, integrated world of public relations that could reduce the impacts of culture. Instantaneous global communication now occurs through what Molleda (2000) called "integrative communication devices" like Web sites, cell phones, online video sharing, teleconferences, and such. The effects of this exchange can be dramatic. Social media have empowered individuals and groups in ways never imagined just a decade ago. One enterprising or enraged person can jump on a keyboard and engage entities anywhere in the world. Or likeminded activists can band together worldwide to pressure national governments and transnational corporations (Friedman, 2000). The firms themselves can cooperate toward universal codes of conduct and other global initiatives

(Lim, 2010). In such an environment, it seems easy to surmise that "all public relations is global or international" (L. A. Grunig, Grunig, & Dozier, 2002, p. 541). Observing this integration, Sriramesh (2003) questioned "whether there is such a thing as domestic public relations anymore because of the international outreach of organizations of all sizes and types" (p. xxv).

Certainly, local communities have been affected by this convergence. Even organizations that do not overtly operate in the global arena must respond to influences from outside their own communities. When international conferences on climate change or global health issues convene, the resulting treaties often affect those who rarely or never leave their homelands, as do international currency exchange rates and the price of oil. Business competition increasingly comes from external sources, and the dynamic cultural composition of most communities and nations is forcing public relations people to reexamine the targets and content of their communication programs. Both publics and issues are crossing national boundaries; as Pal and Dutta (2008) said, "The local is impacted by events that happen in the realm of the global, and simultaneously influences the processes that continue to take place globally" (p. 164).

However, the changes wrought by globalization should not be misconstrued to mean that the local has disappeared or is getting weaker; in fact, it is possible that local influences are becoming stronger. At a National Communication Association conference, the Ohio University scholar Kaustubh Nande (2009) said, "People are not global, it is the systems that are global—the interconnectedness is increasing, but large parts of the world are not interconnected." Therefore, despite convergence, the great preponderance of stakeholders encountered by public relations people remain and act solely in their own communities. Their values, attitudes, and behaviors still are rooted in their own cultures (Friedman, 2000). As one example, Tunstall (2008) countered the myth of a global media by citing reports that the world's citizens "prefer to be entertained by people who look the same, talk the same, joke the same, behave the same, play the same games, and have the same beliefs (and worldviews) as themselves" (p. xiv)—in other words, those who come from the same cultural backgrounds. To respond to these cultural communities, in the United States, at least, there are countless practitioners—those employed by state and local governments, by local health care facilities, those in community relations and in many other positions—whose focus on the purely domestic demands most of their time and attention.

Despite arguments to the contrary (Pal & Dutta, 2008), there still is reason to believe that cultural groups situated within nation-states affect public relations. Some scholars have argued convincingly that culture changes slowly (Inglehart & Baker, 2000; Kramer & Ikeda, 2000), and it therefore is unlikely that even globalization would have dramatically reduced local impacts in the past decade or two. After examining several studies on culture and public relations, Gower (2006) concluded that "cultural differences in the way public relations is practiced have been found in every country" (p. 180). If this is true, are these differences diminished just because the Internet exists and communication can occur across borders? Do all the values and perceptions of these geographically situated cultures disappear even though they may not be fully observed online? Logic alone would suggest otherwise.

Newsom, Turk, and Kruckeberg (2001) said, "Today's global environment demands a greater sensitivity to cultural nuances" (p. 650) because "culture and tradition impose a style of communication and result in certain types of behavior" (p. 652). These behaviors can be distinct within nation-states because "governments control what happens within their borders" (p. 654). Governments can have great impact on public relations by enforcing laws related to media ownership and communication tools such as telephones, computers, and the Internet; they can carve out or deny social benefits to citizens. They sometimes control citizens and organizations through their own military or police. Given nations may also differ from other nations because of their economic systems and the technological infrastructures that are available, the amount of activism that is culturally acceptable, the extent to which the citizens of the nation are congregated in urban areas or are spread into agricultural communities, the literacy rates, and other reasons.

Sometimes, the extent to which a given culture dominates a nation will determine the public relations program an organization will conduct in that nation. In many countries, for example, certain cultural communities will have cultural behaviors, communication styles, and perceptions or worldviews that differ from the majority culture. Culturally sensitive entities will implement outreach to these minority cultures, translate materials for better communication with them, and carry out other organizational responses toward the communities. But these public relations programs still would be much different from those carried out when a unit of a transnational entity exists within a country where the same cultural behaviors are emanating from the majority of the population than with minority groups.

One of the impacts of local culture that global entities must accommodate around the world is resistance or outright hostility toward outside influences that the entity represents. Part of this hostility comes as a cultural backlash against the forces of globalization that have been discussed here, forces that are seen as trampling over traditional values. As Martin and Nakayama (1999) asserted, "Culture is seen not as stable and orderly, but as a site of struggle for various meanings by competing groups" (p. 7). Kramer and Ikeda (2000) added,

> "Local" identity is being . . . attacked as "backward," "feudal," "obsolete," "an obstacle to progress," and ultimately as "impoverished" and "irrational." But the actual resides in the local [and] the genesis of meaning comes from diversity, difference. So as difference is extinguished in favor of global sameness, everyone's world is shrinking not just in terms of space and time but more importantly in terms of meaning. (p. 100)

Embedded within this sense of meaning are local perceptions related to the *haves* of the world versus the *have-nots*, *us versus them*, the globalized world versus local values and traditions, and many other perceptions and worldviews that arise against the forces of globalization, including the powerful transnational corporations that enter local communities and impose change (Micklethwait & Wooldridge, 2000).

While one may dismiss local resistance as desperate attempts to cling to cultural roots in the face of change, these local efforts have major implications for public relations. Underneath the resistance rests the genesis of international issues. While organizations engage publics to sell products, describe essential services, and build relationships, publics often try to communicate with organizations to express dissatisfaction or to pressure the entities to change (J. E. Grunig & Hunt, 1984). In the global arena, issues arise because publics believe that transnational corporations have societal obligations wherever they operate. When they see these entities as not fulfilling expectations, or worse, as exploiting local communities, the publics organize to do something about it (Nigh & Cochran, 1987). Morley (1998) explained that "the relentless rise of the multinational corporation [has] posed a series of threats, or, at least, perceived threats, to local communities" (pp. 30–31). Klein (2000) said that to reduce these threats from corporations, "counter-corporate activism" has formed around the world. "Dozens of brand-based campaigns have succeeded in rattling their corporate targets, in several cases pushing them to substantially alter their policies" (p. 366).

Regardless of where these issues begin, they can quickly have impact on organizations. Pal and Dutta (2008) outlined processes wherein "activist groups have emerged that mobilize locally, as well as globally, to shape global HIV/AIDS policies" (p. 165). Similar initiatives are at work throughout the world—some in cooperation with transnational corporations, some rallying against them. Whether perpetrated by traditional means of communication such as riots, boycotts, or negative media coverage or carried out through the global span of the Internet, many issues can harm organizational reputation, scuttle revenues, and divert resources toward resolving the problem. Sometimes transnational organizations are targeted simply because they serve as unwelcome icons of globalization, as when McDonald's outlets were destroyed by local insurgents during NATO (North Atlantic Treaty Organization) bombing in Belgrade just because the golden arches represented U.S. imperialism (Wakefield, 2000). At other times, corporations receive hostility because of their own arrogance, ignorance, or miscalculations in the various local communities where they operate. Recent history is littered with visible challenges to global entities such as Nike in Southeast Asia (Friedman, 2000), Disney in Hong Kong (Swann, 2008), or Coca Cola and Pepsi in India (Lim, 2010).

One area of potential tension that has received scant research is with the employees of transnational corporations—even the public relations staff members from various host nations. Artz (2007) suggested that host country employees can harbor viewpoints that align more closely with their own cultures than with their distant employer. "This transnational working class still lives primarily on a national level, politically constrained by national borders, laws, and state-enforced coercion, and socially susceptible to nationalism, patriotism, and localism" (p. 152). Even when employees desire to be loyal to their global corporations, they can be placed into positions of needing to explain to their employers the local cultures and their inherent ways of doing things—or to defend the behaviors of the transnational to their own family members and acquaintances. If this occurs too often, or if the transnational is insensitive to host country behaviors and needs, it can foster increasingly pent-up resentments among its staff members.

An example of this tension surfaced in an article recently reviewed by this author ("Public Relations," in press). The article summarized a study of public relations practitioners in Wales who were all employed by transnational corporations headquartered in London. Results showed the challenges for the practitioners in helping headquarters public relations professionals understand cultural differences between London and Wales:

> Striking the balance between the global and the local is as relevant . . . for organisations operating in the context of the U.K. as it is for multinational organisations operating on a worldwide scale. . . . Whilst respondents did not explicitly recognize culture as a key variable when explaining why organisations take a different approach in Wales, it is interesting that the importance of "local knowledge" (extending beyond the realm of politics) was noted by all. . . . Welsh practitioners seem to accept the concept that people in Wales "do things differently," or to use common social interpretative terminology, that Welsh publics have a collective system of meanings that is distinct. . . . The lack of understanding or recognition of sub-state diversities by some organisations and PR practitioners poses a particular challenge for Welsh or regional PR teams—both in-house and external. It is more important than ever that these practitioners continue to play an advisory role in order to move organisations further towards a localised approach that can accommodate Wales' distinctiveness. (pp. 12–13)

When employees draw their perspectives from the familiar parameters of local culture, certainly others within these societies will have no predilection for "outsider" transnational entities over their own cultural values and mores. Local employees can help their employers with intercultural facilitation, but if the entity ignores the cultural learning that can come from these employees, the employees can become resentful themselves—thus hurting productivity and creating more negative impacts on the entity's reputation in the given host country.

How Should Organizations Respond to Cultural Variations?

Sriramesh (2007) said that in our "rapidly globalizing world, our field will [still] ignore culture at its own peril" (p. 507). No matter how much transnational entities try to assimilate themselves into a certain culture, they will always be guests there. Those who accept that role and act like grateful guests will have gracious hosts. Those who instead act like commercial colonizers will turn skepticism into criticism.

All transnational organizations must work hard to build relationships with local cultures (using local employees as much as possible) and recognize that they can eventually face pressures of some kind from anywhere—from their own home communities, from far-off countries, or from the Internet. All these scenarios, good or bad, stem from cultural frameworks that will continue to be important for public relations practitioners to acknowledge, understand, and accommodate.

So how do transnational organizations respond favorably to the cultural influences on them? Below are a few suggestions:

1. Allocate sufficient attention and resources to international public relations. Practitioner Larry Foster (1998) said, "Of all the areas of public relations . . . the international sector is the most difficult to manage. It is more complex, more unpredictable, and generates more risk than most domestic-based public relations programs" (p. 1). Verčič (2003) added that because of these complexities, the best practices in public relations should be found in transnational corporations. Yet he added that "it is not uncommon for [transnational corporations] that have only a handful of public relations professionals in the headquarters being responsible for activities around the world. One may wonder how they succeed" (p. 485).

2. Build public relations strategies that preserve global consistencies without losing sight of local publics and potential local issues. Organizations that want effective international public relations programs should fashion and use horizontal teams comprising talented practitioners around the world. They should have central guidance, but not centralized control, and have enough flexibility to organize and initiate relationship-building efforts in each locale where the entity operates. They also should have constant sharing of internal communications so as to anticipate and be prepared to handle any contingency that arises anywhere in the world.

Most issues do not appear from nowhere; they fester somewhere or with someone, and then flare up out of those places or people. A corporation should have sensors in place *everywhere*—not just at headquarters, or in regional offices, or just in given geographic units, but everywhere—to reduce the risk of issues surprising the entity. An entity should seek and nurture long-term dialogic relationships and be responsible to their societal obligations, *everywhere*.

3. The public relations industry needs to improve its development programs around the world. One of the major tasks for finding qualified international practitioners is to seek intercultural understanding. Starck and Kruckeberg (2001) proposed, "The sine qua non of this . . . global community is intercultural communication. One of our major goals should be to promote intercultural literacy among present and future practitioners" (p. 58). Doorley and Garcia (2007) added that knowledge beyond the field is imperative: "To fully understand the practice of global corporate communication," they said, "one must not only understand the basic principles of public relations . . . but also draw upon a broad range of global society theories, cultural theories, management theories, and communication theories" (p. 243). Foster (1998) also explained that

> skilled international practitioners require a breadth of knowledge and a curiosity about the world. . . . Often they are proficient in several languages. But the one quality that marks the best of the international public relations professionals is the ability to recognize certain cross-cultural differences and be able to adjust to them. (p. 1)

Certainly other suggestions could be put forward here. However, even if just these suggestions were implemented, both in transnational public relations programs and in the public relations industry as a whole, transnational entities and their public relations practitioners would become better equipped to build relationships with publics in a variety of nations and cultural settings. This would allow for more transnational organizations to have long-term success in their efforts and reduce the consequences of skepticism and opposition that can exist in the international arena.

Conclusion

There should be little argument that the impact of culture on public relations is at least as strong today as it was at the conception of theories in international public relations two decades ago. Yet transnational entities still tend to ignore the reality that they exist in various communities only with permission from those societies—their existence there is a privilege rather than a right. Therefore, they are obligated, just like any other citizen, to be responsible to the societies and to give back in some way (Starck & Kruckeberg, 2001).

Public relations practitioners should be filling the inevitable gap between the entity's global imperatives (promoting the brand and generating revenue) and the expectations of their stakeholders and communities, wherever they are located. These gaps are filled through the careful cultivation of long-term relationships (Hung, 2007). Any farmer does everything possible to prepare for a successful harvest, but then he or she must petition nature to ensure that the harvest comes. Such is the nature of relationships, cultivated by a practitioner who understands the dynamic nature of people and the proper give-and-take that precludes genuine mutual benefits. As Heath (2001) noted, genuine community exists only through the cocultivation of "agreement and disagreement of many complementary and competing perspectives" (p. 7)—just one of which is the transnational organization housed in different cultures around the world.

Note

1. All the terms shown here actually have important distinct meanings, but addressing those specific differences is beyond the scope of this chapter. The terms are raised here simply to highlight the lack of clarity in the scholarly literature on worldwide public relations.

References

Adler, N., & Doktor, R. (1986). From the Atlantic to the Pacific century: Cross-cultural management reviewed. *Journal of Management, 12,* 295–318.

Anderson, G. (1989). A global look at public relations. In B. Cantor (Ed.), *Experts in action* (2nd ed., pp. 412–422). White Plains, NY: Longman.

Appadurai, A. (1990). Disjuncture and difference in the global cultural economy. In M. Featherstone (Ed.), *Global culture: Nationalism, globalization, and modernity* (pp. 295–310). London: Sage.

Artz, L. (2007). The corporate model from national to transnational. In L. Artz & Y. R. Kamalipour (Eds.), *The media globe: Trends in international mass media* (pp. 141–162). Lanham, MD: Rowan & Littlefield.

Banks, S. P. (1995). *Multi-cultural public relations: A social-interpretive approach.* Thousand Oaks, CA: Sage.

Booth, A. (1986, February). Going global. *Public Relations Journal, 42,* 22–26.

Botan, C. (1992). International public relations: Critique and reformulation. *Public Relations Review, 18*(2), 149–159.

Curtin, P. A., & Gaither, T. K. (2007). *International public relations: Negotiating culture, identity, and power.* Thousand Oaks, CA: Sage.

Doorley, J., & Garcia, H. F. (2007). *Reputation management: The key to successful public relations and corporate communications.* New York: Taylor & Francis.

Ellingsworth, H. W. (1977). Conceptualizing intercultural communication. In *Communication yearbook 1* (pp. 99–106). New Brunswick, NJ: Transaction Books.

Foster, L. (1998). *1998 Atlas award lecture on international public relations* (International Section Monograph No. 2). New York: Public Relations Society of America.

Freitag, A. R., & Stokes, A. Q. (2009). *Global public relations: Spanning borders, spanning cultures.* New York: Routledge.

Friedman, T. L. (2000). *The Lexus and the olive tree.* New York: Anchor Books.

Friedman, T. L. (2006). *The world is flat: A brief history of the twenty-first century.* New York: Farrar, Straus, & Giroux.

Gower, K. K. (2006). Public relations research at the crossroads. *Public Relations Research Journal, 18*(2), 177–190.

Grunig, J. E. (2006). Furnishing the edifice: Research on public relations as a strategic management function. *Journal of Public Relations Research, 18*(2), 151–176.

Grunig, J. E., & Hunt, T. (1984). *Managing public relations.* New York: Holt, Rinehart, & Winston.

Grunig, L. A., Grunig, J. E., & Dozier, D. M. (2002). *Excellent public relations and effective organizations: A study of communication management in three countries.* Mahwah, NJ: Lawrence Erlbaum.

Heath, R. L. (2001). Shifting foundations: Public relations as relationship building. In R. L. Heath (Ed.), *Handbook of public relations* (pp. 1–9). Thousand Oaks, CA: Sage.

Hofstede, G. (1980). *Culture's consequences.* Beverly Hills, CA: Sage.

Hung, C. J. F. (2007). Toward the theory of relationship management in public relations: How to cultivate quality relationships? In E. L. Toth (Ed.), *The future of excellence in public relations and communication management* (pp. 443–476). Mahwah, NJ: Lawrence Erlbaum.

Inglehart, R., & Baker, W. E. (2000). Modernization, cultural change, and the persistence of traditional values. *American Sociological Review, 65,* 19–51.

Klein, N. (2000). *No logo: Taking aim at the brand bullies.* London: Flamingo.

Kotkin, J. (1993). *Tribes: How race, religion, and identity determine success in the new global economy.* New York: Random House.

Kramer, E. M., & Ikeda, R. (2000). The changing faces of reality. *Keio Communication Review, 22,* 79–109.

Lim, J. S. (2010). Global integration or local responsiveness? Multinational corporations' public relations strategies and cases. In G. J. Golan, T. J. Johnson, & W. Wanta (Eds.), *International media communication in a global age* (pp. 299–318). New York: Taylor & Francis.

Martin, J. N., & Nakayama, T. K. (1999). Thinking dialectically about culture and communication. *Communication Theory, 9*(1), 1–25.

Meznar, M. B. (1993). *Public affairs management in multinational corporations: An empirical examination.* Unpublished doctoral dissertation, University of South Carolina, Columbia.

Micklethwait, J., & Wooldridge, A. (2000). *A future perfect: The challenge and hidden promise of globalization.* New York: Crown Business.

Molleda, J. C. (2000). *Integrative public relations in international business: The impact of administrative models and subsidiary roles.* Unpublished doctoral dissertation, University of South Carolina, Columbia.

Molleda, J. C., & Laskin, A. V. (2005). *Global, international, comparative, and regional public relations knowledge from 1990 to 2005: A quantitative content analysis of academic and trade publications.* Miami, FL: Institute for Public Relations.

Morley, M. (1998). *How to manage your global reputation: A guide to the dynamics of international public relations.* London: Macmillan.

Nande, K. (2009, November 15). *Exploring the relationship between globalization and public relations.* Panel presentation at the annual convention of the National Communications Association, Chicago, IL.

Negandhi, A. (1983). Cross-cultural management research: Trends and future directions. *Journal of International Business Studies, Fall,* 17–28.

Newsom, D., Turk, J. V., & Kruckeberg, D. (2001). International public relations: Focus on pedagogy. In R. L. Heath (Ed.), *Handbook of public relations* (pp. 649–658). Thousand Oaks, CA: Sage.

Nigh, D., & Cochran, P. (1987). Issues management and the multinational enterprise. *Management International Review, 27*(1), 4–12.

Ogan, C.L. (2007). Communication and culture. In Y. R. Kamalipour (Ed.), *Global communication* (2nd ed., pp. 293–318). Belmont, CA: Thomson Wadsworth.

Pal, M., & Dutta, M. J. (2008). Public relations in a global context: The relevance of critical modernism as a theoretical lens. *Journal of Public Relations Research, 20,* 159–179.

Panzner, M. J. (2009). *When giants fall: An economic roadmap for the end of the American era.* Hoboken, NJ: Wiley.

Parsell, D. (2002). *Explorer Wade Davis on vanishing cultures.* http://news.nationalgeographic. com/news/2002/06/0627_020628_wadedavis.html

Public relations in post-devolution Wales: A study of how U.K. organisations communicate and localise in Wales. (in press). *Contemporary Wales.*

Rhee, Y. (2002). Global public relations: A cross-cultural study of the excellence theory in South Korea. *Journal of Public Relations Research, 14*(3), 159–184.

Sahlins, M. (1999). Two or three things that I know about culture. *Journal of the Royal Anthropological Institute, 5,* 399–421.

Sirkin, H. L., Hemerling, J. W., & Bhattacharya, A. K. (2008). *Globality: Competing with everyone from everywhere for everything.* London: Headline.

Sriramesh, K. (2003). Introduction. In K. Sriramesh & D. Verčič (Eds.), *The global public relations handbook: Theory, research, and practice* (pp. xxv–xxxvi). Mahwah, NJ: Lawrence Erlbaum.

Sriramesh, K. (2007). The relationship between culture and public relations. In E.L. Toth (Ed.), *The future of excellence in public relations and communication management* (pp. 507–526). Mahwah, NJ: Lawrence Erlbaum.

Sriramesh, K., & Verčič, D. (2009). *The global public relations handbook: Theory, research, and practice.* New York: Routledge.

Starck, K., & Kruckeberg, D. (2001). Public relations and community: A reconstructed theory revisited. In R. L. Heath (Ed.), *Handbook of public relations* (pp. 51–60). Thousand Oaks, CA: Sage.

Swann, P. (2008). *Cases in public relations management.* Boston: McGraw-Hill.

Tayeb, M. H. (1988). *Organizations and national culture: A comparative analysis.* London: Sage.

Traverse-Healy, T. (1991). The corporate aspect. In M. Nally (Ed.), *International public relations in practice* (pp. 31–39). London: Kogan Page.

Tunstall, J. (2008). *The media were American: U.S. mass media in decline.* New York: Oxford University Press.

Verčič, D. (2003). Public relations of movers and shakers: Transnational corporations. In K. Sriramesh & D. Verčič (Eds.), *The global public relations handbook* (pp. 478–489). Mahwah, NJ: Lawrence Erlbaum.

Verčič, D., Grunig, L. A., & Grunig, J. (1996). Global and specific principles of public relations: Evidence from Slovenia. In H. Culbertson & N. Chen (Eds.), *International public relations: A comparative analysis* (pp. 31–66). Mahwah, NJ: Lawrence Erlbaum.

Verčič, D., van Ruler, B., Butschi, G., & Flodin, B. (2001). On the definition of public relations: A European view. *Public Relations Review, 27,* 373–387.

Wakefield, R. (1995, July). *Toward a theory on international public relations: Initial Delphi research supports generic/specific theory.* Paper presented at the second annual International Public Relations Research Symposium, Bled, Slovenia.

Wakefield, R. (1997). *International public relations: A theoretical approach to excellence based on a worldwide Delphi study.* Dissertation published by the University of Maryland–College Park.

Wakefield, R. (2000). World-class public relations: A model for effective public relations in the multinational. *Journal of Communication Management, 5*(1), 59–71.

Wakefield, R. (2001). Public relations in the multinational organization. In R. L. Heath (Ed.), *Handbook of public relations* (pp. 639–648). Thousand Oaks, CA: Sage.

Wouters, J. (1991). *International public relations: How to establish your company's product, service and images in foreign markets.* New York: AMACOM.

CHAPTER 47

The Local, National, and Global Challenges of Public Relations

A Call for an Anthropological Approach to Practicing Public Relations

Marina Vujnovic and Dean Kruckeberg

Public relations practitioners historically have not been fully aware—or particularly appreciative—of public relations' larger role in society, or of the greater potential of that enlarged role. The traditional understanding of public relations practice originates from a functionalist and organization-centric perspective in which the practice is seen as a managerial, strategic, and highly structuralized function that is easily quantifiable in its processes, albeit not so easily in the more elusive measurements of "effectiveness"—however this effectiveness may be conceptualized and operationalized. Such perspective has made the articulation of public relations' goals more acceptable to organizations' dominant coalitions that comprise those seeking outcome-oriented business models and to whom only numbers and dollar signs are most often the measures of success.

This narrow view of public relations' functions has been a pervasive paradigm, although less dominant paradigms have focused on the more-encompassing role of public relations in society. Today, the penalty of failure to understand public relations as a practice that is significantly different from that of the dominant paradigm has been exacerbated by the processes of globalization. Due to the complexity of the contemporary conceptualization of globalization and myriad interpretations of this phenomenon during the past two decades, we feature globalization as the "American-led global spread of markets and democracy," as defined by Chua (2004), who has observed that this process has "dramatically transformed the world" (p. 8).

The concept of globalism seems ubiquitous both in the recognition of its existence and largely in its acceptance as an irreversible phenomenon—an irreversibility that is undoubtedly true. Globalism is made possible through rapidly evolving communication technology that has become the most influential and powerful intervening variable that simultaneously permits and encourages a global society through the compression of time and space while paradoxically exacerbating social conflicts that are caused by the increased multiculturalism of globalization forces, in the world at large as well as in its regions, nations, and localities. Kruckeberg and Tsetsura (2009) noted that today's communication technology not only (a) is allowing and is encouraging the increasing compression of time and space and (b) is making global communication unprohibitively inexpensive both to send and to receive but also (c) has overwhelmed people with information and (d) has intermingled traditional vetted sources of information with user-generated content that may be suspect in its source credibility and non-transparent in its agenda.

This worldwide transformation assumes multiple shapes, and it affects most—if not all—of the aspects of contemporary life for much of the world's population. Here, we want to focus on the ways in which local, national, and global issues converge in societies throughout the world that ultimately shape and influence the practice of public relations worldwide. Because public relations is a practice that is embedded within the social structures of practitioners' organizations as well as these organizations' and their indigenous societies' cultures, public relations is practiced within the framework of identity.

The amorphous nature of this identity will be the focus of this chapter. Identity here is understood in terms of both public relations' identity as a professionalized practice and also the cultural identity of the societies in which public relations is practiced. Tomlinson (2003) argued that identity is a "considerable dimension of *institutionalized* social life in modernity" (p. 271). For public relations practitioners, both the knowledge of their own professional identity as it relates to the societies in which they practice and the process of changing the emerging cultural identities within these societies become prerogatives for successful and ethical practice. Collective identification has already become a neglected, if not ignored, aspect of globalization; as Chua (2004) argued, "Global spread of markets and democracy is a principal, aggravating cause of group hatred and ethnic violence throughout the non-Western world" (p. 9).

Furthermore, if we accept what Bekker and Prinsloo (1999) have argued, that "locality, globality and nationality, co-determine collective identification" (p. 12), the practice of public relations in the conditions of a globalized world becomes more a matter of understanding these processes than of upholding Western perspectives regarding how public relations practice is understood. Before we return to this discussion, however, we will review recent research that has examined public relations practice in different countries throughout the world that supports the thesis, which was proposed by L'Etang and Pieczka (2006), that today's public relations needs a more anthropological approach if we wish to fully understand its role within a global society.

Public Relations and Globalization: A Look at Recent Research

A global perspective on the practice of public relations has gained considerable attention in public relations theory and research (e.g., Molleda, 2008; Moss & De Santo, 2002; Sriramesh, 2004; Sriramesh & Verčič, 2003). One of the most recent perspectives in the understanding of the concept of global public relations is provided in Freitag and Stokes's book, *Global Public Relations: Spanning Borders, Spanning Cultures* (2009). This volume advanced the earlier work by Freitag (2002) on the importance of public relations practitioners' cultural competencies. His ascending cultural competence model argued for a rounded approach that included aspects such as acquiring knowledge of different cultures' politics, economies, and social rules to the more practical and obvious aspects such as learning foreign languages.

This preparative stage seems to be the key for the successful practice of public relations because it positively relates to global public relations curricula in higher education. According to Freitag (2002), students who have completed a course in public relations seem to be more willing to work in foreign and global environments and more easily adjust to different cultural environments. Freitag and Stokes (2009) suggested that the dimensions in which public relations practitioners work globally are so vast and diverse that the adjustment to different environments may take a considerable amount of time. Freitag and Stokes (2009) also suggested that multiple dimensions and complexities of global public relations not only challenge the public relations practitioners who work in foreign countries but also challenge our approach to a global public relations education curriculum.

The dominant model in global public relations research seems to be the global public relations theory that was first introduced by Verčič, Grunig, and Grunig (1996), which was advanced by Sriramesh and Verčič (2003, 2009) and which remains the most comprehensive view of the theory and research in global public relations. As most recently described in the expanded 2009 edition of *The Global Public Relations Handbook*, global public relations theory suggests an interrelationship of variables such as country's infrastructure, societal culture, and environment that together influence the practice of public relations (Sriramesh & Verčič, 2009).

Molleda (2008), in his study of public relations practitioners in Venezuela, used this theory as well as the concept of "coercive isomorphism." He suggested that the volatile socioeconomic and political dimensions of Venezuelan society as well as the cultural idiosyncrasies of that society both enable and constrain indigenous public relations practitioners. Scarce resources in the private and nonprofit sectors are juxtaposed on the public and government sectors that own most of the resources in Venezuela. One of Molleda's most heuristic findings is the emphasis on "contrasting socioeconomic realities" (p. 66), suggesting that within the national borders exist vast differences in locality between rural and urban centers. This makes the development of a universal theory or model of global public relations almost impossible and presents a formidable challenge to the global practice of public relations. Furthermore, the argument that a Western perspective on public relations practice doesn't consider some of the complexities of foreign countries' socioeconomic, political, and cultural aspects is well explicated in Molleda's (2008) study. Although "coercive isomorphism" considers these larger societal and cultural aspects as important variables in shaping public relations practice in different countries, the emphasis on the effect of different environments on an organization and its behavioral change narrows the possibilities of this model. Rather, the focus from the organization to the society at large could demonstrate how public relations as a practice could participate in assisting society in change rather than in imposing such change or in using an understanding of the larger context to the sole benefit of the organization itself.

This perspective extends community-building theory and the "organic model" of public relations that suggest that understanding the complex dynamics among the nonprofit sector, the governmental sector, and the media could not only help practitioners to adjust their organizational behavior as best suits the culture in which they are working but would best assist the indigenous society in needed transitions and change. Kent and Taylor (2007) observed that most researchers view international or global public relations through a lens of the normative "excellence theory" approach. We would agree—and, in fact, argue—that this very principal has been the most limiting aspect of global public relations theory and research. Although Sriramesh and Verčič's (2003, 2009) model has further recognized cultural complexities, as well as socioeconomic and political complexities, in which global public relations practice is contextualized, this model still appears to stem from the tradition of what we would like to call "organizational self-centeredness," as outlined in Verčič et al.'s (1996) generic principles that are based on the Excellence Study (Grunig, 1992), which we believe lacks the necessary outward look toward society. Kent and Taylor (2007) criticized this approach, arguing,

> To suggest that two-way symmetrical communication *à la* the U.S. is the most viable public relations model (ignoring other models such as dialogue, feminism, postmodernism, etc. which are only now receiving increased attention in public relations) misses the point of international public relations research. International public relations research should not be guided by efforts to prove that any single grand theory (or normative theory to use Verčič et al.'s terms) exists, but to understand the practice of public relations in other nations. (p. 13)

We agree with this assessment and, in addition, Kent and Taylor's (2007) finding in their study of public relations practice in Bosnia that "the more that one understands country/region specific communication imperatives, motivational issues, cultural events, hero/villains, etc., the more robust and thorough will be the understanding of a nation's public relations practices" (p. 18). Furthermore, as Kent and Taylor (2007) argued, this is not to say that the study of public relations should be culturally relativistic but rather that we must go back to the more cultural aspects of communication as Carey (1992), in his seminal work, argued, that is, for understanding communication as culture. Public relations is inherently communication practice and is not a strictly organizational practice as it has been theorized in the predominant "Excellence Project" and in the succeeding theoretical conceptualizations and research that have evolved from it. Testing how one model can be applied in different countries does not provide a heuristic understanding of public relations as a communicative practice.

In addition to this argument, Valentini (2007) argued that a cultural approach that is predicated on Zaharna's (2000, 2001) intercultural communication theories, rather than on the global model that has been advanced by Lee (2006, 2007), seems to result in better communicative practices with diverse publics. However, we would like to argue that the idea of global publics, rather than the global public as explicated by Lee (2006, 2007), should not be discounted, nor should the possibility be discounted of such publics that already exist in the forms of global activist organizations, feminist activist organizations, and environmental organizations. The problem in comprehending the possibility of coexistence of the microcultural differences and global identities in current communication and global public relations theory is only a problem if one looks at the world from a strictly organizational perspective, for example, how will my organization adjust to different cultures and still practice "excellent" public relations? From the perspective of society, coexisting are locality or local publics, nationality or national publics, and globality or global publics, and public relations practitioners should participate in all those spheres, whether these practitioners are trying to benefit their organizations or society at large.

First, public relations practitioners must recognize that their organizations will have an impact on the changing aspects of cultures in which they practice public relations, no matter what these practitioners do, simply by being present in this new, different environment. Second, practitioners' success will ultimately be tied to the level of success of society at large, and attempts to understand the intrinsic nature of culture and how it changes under the influence of globalization must be a primary goal of public relations practitioners in their role as communication professionals. To say it more bluntly, it is not the success of practitioners' organizations with which they should be primarily concerned but the success of the society in which they practice.

That said, public relations practitioners should also attempt to leave their Western mindsets behind and must understand that coercive methods of advancing their own goals may not result in organizational success; despite common assumptions of public relations practitioners who work for Western organizations, their role is not to bring tutorials on how to do business or to tell people worldwide how best to live their lives in their indigenous societies; rather, as "communicative professionals," practitioners must view their role and their professional identity as practitioners who can assist others in desired change within the realms and extensions of this change for which a society is prepared and which is determined locally.

Western practitioners and scholars alike will need to reexamine the plethora of historical assumptions and tired bromides about public relations to which they have been voluntarily held hostage, as well as the validity of concepts that they have been reticent to challenge because of Western practitioners' and scholars' smug confidence in an amazing number of flawed platitudes that have become embedded in the Western public relations literature and perceived "best practices." Examples include a needed reconciliation between the concept of "strategic communication," which is an attempt to collapse the roles of public relations, advertising, and marketing, but which semantically would appear to be the antithesis of symmetrical "relationship building" that is grounding much, if not most, contemporary public relations scholarship; or the concept of the "dominant coalition" to which practitioners ostensibly must seek entry, but which by its very definition suggests an asymmetrical relationship of dominance both within the organization and ostensibly within its societal environment; or the blatant attempts to "increase the bottom line," that is, to increase profits (which unquestionably is an honorable and requisite goal of for-profit organizations) as the primary (or only) reason for an organization's publicized altruism or the efforts to promote the ideological views of the organization under the guise of "corporate social responsibility"; or the self-centered umbrella of "branding" to encompass virtually all public relations' role and function.

Public relations literature and research agendas are replete with myriad examples of scholarship that does not sufficiently examine—and oftentimes unquestionably and benignly accepts—gross assumptions about public relations' role and function in global society, to the point for which new constructs may be required and for which theories of society (if even present and articulated) need to be reexamined and criticized.

An Anthropological Approach to Public Relations

Zaharna's (2000, 2001) work on a culture-specific understanding of public relations, which traces its origin to the work of anthropologists such as Margaret Mead and Clifford Geertz, is of importance here, but not because we want to argue that public relations practitioners should completely see culture as relative and must thereby abandon any possibility of a universal global practice; rather, Zaharna's perspective helps sensitize practitioners to the need to ponder that local and national aspects of culture coexist on the same level of the larger global culture that is rapidly taking shape. In fact, the proliferation of different cultural identities, as well as organizational identities, is a consequence of the globalization processes.

It is not a question of antagonism toward globalization or of any kind of global practices' tendency to destroy indigenous cultures' uniqueness or the proliferation of reemphasis of cultural identities (as evidenced in the resurgence of ethnic-identity movements and nation-building processes in many countries throughout the world); rather, it is a matter of practitioners' realization and ultimate acceptance that those two processes do coexist and certainly influence one another. We should not ignore people's power to resist any form of perceived oppression, whether it is manifest in the overflow of exported foreign consumer goods or in exported political ideologies, especially if the latter are presented and packaged as one normative, successful model, such as the Western model of democracy.

We see the role of public relations as key in raising an awareness of the differences that do exist in assisting diverse publics in their communication processes and in participating in providing a more thorough understanding of the actions and goals of diverse organizations and social groups, especially in communication among spheres of society where traditional antagonisms exist, for example, in nonprofit/profit communication and in governmental/nongovernmental communication. This gives rise to our interest in identity and in how the proliferation of different identities that are caused by processes of globalization, which, as Chua (2004) has argued, influence the role of public relations practitioners globally, including not only those practitioners who cross borders but also those who work within their indigenous societies who have a difficult task in communicating with diverse publics whose identities are shaped and reshaped as a result of the global exchange of goods, information, and people. As Tomlinson (2003) argued,

> This more complex, multidimensional conceptualization, which views globalization as operating simultaneously and interrelatedly in the economic, technological-communicational, political and cultural spheres of human life, is in fact relatively uncontentious—at least in principle—within academic discourses. But the cultural implication, rather less easily swallowed by some, is that globalization involves not the simple enforced distribution of a particular western (say, liberal, secular, possessive-individualist, capitalist-consumerist) lifestyle, but a more complicated dissemination of the entire range of institutional features of cultural modernity. (p. 272)

From that perspective, public relations practitioners should understand that their role is a part of those institutional features of cultural modernity. Organizations for which public relations practitioners work are part of the institutionalization of spheres of nation-states, or territorial spheres, as well as the more productivist spheres of the global capitalist economy, both of which influence cultural practices and a sense of community (Giddens, 1990; Tomlinson, 2003). These practices become delicate when cultural identity is properly understood as a political concept—in other words, when cultural identities are shaped around categories of difference such as class, race, gender, ethnicity, or nationality, all of which are easily inflected politically (Tomlinson, 2003). This becomes, in our belief, the biggest challenge for public relations practitioners in a globalized world; to invoke Tomlinson (2003) once again,

> In so far as globalization distributes the institutional features of modernity across all cultures, globalization produces "identity" where none existed—where before there were perhaps more particular, more inchoate, less socially policed belongings. This, rather than the sheer obliteration of identities, is the most significant cultural impact of globalization, an impact felt at the formal level of cultural experience. This impact might, on a narrow reading, be seen as "cultural imperialism"—in that this modern institutionalization of cultural attachments clearly arose first in the West. But, more interestingly, it can be understood as part of the cultural package, mixed in its blessings, that is global modernity. (p. 273)

In other words, public relations practitioners should stay fully aware of globalization through the prism of global modernity processes. These processes have made some aspects of modernity, such as a sense of national and ethnic belonging, ever more important and sometimes even radicalized (see Chua, 2004); aspects of globalization, such as the fragility of the world's interconnected economic capitalist system and market economy, are evidenced in the current economic depression. The argument that supports this view of globalization is supported by the fact that the most fragile economies are also the most politically unstable economies, and in these circumstances, public relations practitioners have an ever-increasing and critically important role as communication professionals who assist societies in transition in reaching the needed understandings among diverse publics. This understanding of complex transitions, of multiple identities that exist on different local, national, and global levels within which diverse publics connect, challenges public relations practice to its core.

Hence, we argue for a more anthropological approach to public relations that would acknowledge people as publics having changing natures, rituals, and cultures as well as having a rituality of their communication practices (Carey, 1992). At the same time, we must argue that shaping the global public that has its own cosmopolitan sensitivities cannot be ignored, and in fact, it presents a new challenge to global public relations practitioners to understand the ways in which this global public is influenced by diverse global issues, such as global economic dependency and environmental dependency. In addition, public relations practitioners must accept their primary role in communicating for and about governmental institutions that develop policies that have potential cross-border, that is, cross-national impact.

Within this global environment, Kruckeberg and Vujnovic (2006) argued that public relations scholars and practitioners must recognize the existence and primary importance of "non-publics" locally, nationally, and globally as well as of the "general public." They note that, without this recognition, public relations in both its theory and practice will continue to be asymmetrical, hypocritical in its attempts in relationship building, and inadequate in its efforts in community building. Lack of recognition of these publics, which not only exist but must be considered primary, only continues to allow and encourage societal inequities, for example, prejudices against those within society who do not have the benefit of productive and beneficial "strategic relationships" with others, especially with those possessing power in society, and thus are not deemed worthy of two-way symmetry "strategic relationships" and membership within the global community.

L'Etang and Pieczka (2006) argued that public relations as a practice is much more than a pragmatic, technical, rational, managerial, or promotional organizational function. In fact, their findings suggest that public relations comprises less-planned, less-strategic, and "less rational aspects." The rituality of communication, as they argued, suggests a more "anthropological approach" to an understanding of public relations as a practice that is embedded within society. Public relations is becoming such a prevalent function in society, as it is being performed by organizations worldwide, that the ritual of everyday practices can be best understood using anthropological methods. This means not only microethnographies of organizations that are situated within the context of cultures in which they exist, such as Sriramesh (1996) suggested, but, in addition, understanding the meaning of public relations in society and for society and how public relations relates to the changing nature of the cultural identities that we have tried to outline in this discussion.

References

Bekker, S., & Prinsloo, R. C. (Eds.). (1999). *Identity? Theory, politics, history.* Pretoria, South Africa: Human Sciences Research Council Press.

Carey, J. W. (1992). *Communication as culture.* Abingdon, UK: Routledge.

Chua, A. (2004). *World on fire: How exporting free market democracy breeds ethnic hatred and global instability.* New York: Anchor Books.

Freitag, A. R. (2002). Ascending cultural competence potential: An assessment and profile of U.S. public relations practitioners' preparation for international assignments. *Journal of Public Relations Research, 14*(3), 207–227.

Freitag, A., & Stokes, A. Q. (2009). *Global public relations: Spanning borders, spanning cultures.* Abingdon, UK: Routledge.

Giddens, A. (1990). *The consequences of modernity.* Cambridge, UK: Polity Press.

Grunig, J. E. (Ed.). (1992). *Excellence in public relations and communication management.* Hillsdale, NJ: Lawrence Erlbaum.

Kent, M., & Taylor, M. (2007, March). Beyond excellence: Extending the generic approach to international public relations: The case of Bosnia. *Public Relations Review, 33*(1), 10–20.

Kruckeberg, D., & Tsetsura, K. (2009, November). Keynote speech at the 20th anniversary celebration of the College of Journalism and Communications, University of Bucharest, Bucharest, Romania.

Kruckeberg, D., & Vujnovic, M. (2006, March). *Toward an "organic" model of public relations in public diplomacy.* Paper presented at the Ninth International Public Relations Research Conference, Miami, FL.

Lee, S. (2006). An analysis of other countries' international public relations in the U.S. *Public Relations Review, 32*(2), 97–103.

Lee, S. (2007). International public relations as a predictor of prominence of US news coverage. *Public Relations Review, 33*(2), 158–165.

L'Etang, J., & Pieczka, M. (2006). *Public relations: Critical debates and contemporary practice.* Mahwah, NJ: Lawrence Erlbaum.

Molleda, J. C. (2008). Contextualized qualitative research in Venezuela: Coercive isomorphic pressures of the socioeconomic and political environments on public relations practices. *Journal of Public Relations Research, 20*(1), 49–70.

Moss, D., & DeSanto, B. (Eds.). (2002). *Public relations cases: International perspectives.* New York: Routledge.

Sriramesh, K. (1996). Power distance and public relations: An ethnographic study of southern Indian organizations. In H. M. Culbertson & N. Chen (Eds.), *International public relations: A comparative analysis* (pp. 171–190). Mahwah, NJ: Lawrence Erlbaum.

Sriramesh, K. (2004). *Public relations in Asia: An anthology.* Singapore: Thomson Learning Asia.

Sriramesh, K., & Verčič, D. (2003). A theoretical framework for global public relations research and practice. In K. Sriramesh & D. Verčič (Eds.), *The global public relations handbook: Theory, research, and practice* (pp. 1–19). Mahwah, NJ: Lawrence Erlbaum.

Sriramesh, K., & Verčič, D. (Eds.). (2009). *The global public relations handbook: Theory, research, and practice.* New York: Routledge.

Tomlinson, J. (2003). Globalization and cultural identity. In A. G. McGrew & D. Held (Eds.), *The global transformations reader: An introduction to the globalization debate* (pp. 269–277). Cambridge, UK: Polity Press.

Valentini, C. (2007). Global versus cultural approaches in public relationship management: The case of the European Union. *Journal of Communication Management, 11*(2), 117–133.

Verčič, D., Grunig, L. A., & Grunig, J. E. (1996). Global and specific principles of public relations: Evidence from Slovenia. In H. M. Culbertson & N. Chen (Eds.), *International public relations: A comparative analysis* (pp. 31–66). Mahwah, NJ: Lawrence Erlbaum.

Zaharna, R. S. (2000). Intercultural communication and international public relations: Exploring parallels. *Communication Quarterly, 48*(1), 85–100.

Zaharna, R. S. (2001, Summer). Toward an in-awareness approach to international public relations. *Public Relations Review, 27*(2), 135–148.

CHAPTER 48

Cross-National Conflict Shifting

A Transnational Crisis Perspective in Global Public Relations

Juan-Carlos Molleda

A newsworthy event originates in one location and instantaneously flows through mainstream and emergent communication and media technologies in all directions worldwide. In addition to traditional mass-mediated channels, "YouTube and other social networks on the Internet have allowed individual users to be actors as social activists or citizen journalists" (Chang, 2010, p. 29). One could imagine this communication flow as a frenzied laser matrix over an infinite sky. Without delay, a news event will be published and discussed with great interest where it has some or high resonance.

From a U.S. perspective, a number of determinants predict international news coverage: instability, distance from the United States, U.S. investment, U.S. aid, religious diversity, military expenditure, and population (Golan, 2010). Despite the foreign character of a news event, domestic angles become a noteworthy component of the coverage and controlled strategic communication techniques and efforts through localization strategies and data, which appeals to audiences in specific national environments that should recognize rapidly its relevance and feel its impact for their familiar realities.

Transnational organizations (TNOs), including national governments and multilateral institutions, often are the subjects of the described phenomenon—that is, of the cross-national conflict shifts (CNCSs) or the transnational crises. The term *transnational* is used in this chapter as a strategic business mentality, in which

> diverse roles and dispersed operations must be held together by a management mindset that understands the need for multiple strategic capabilities, views problems and opportunities from both local and global perspectives, and is willing to interact with others openly and flexibly. (Bartlett & Ghoshal, 2002, p. 299)

Considering factors, including emerging demographics, environmental and natural resources, and global economic interconnectedness, is essential.

If TNOs, with their headquarters and subsidiaries, are not on top of the global flow of communication, media, and issues, it may be an enormous disadvantage to have their voices heard clearly and at appropriate volume when conflicting interests collide in the marketplace or in the cyberspace of ideas—that is, in the public sphere. The level of understanding of and preparedness for transnational crises or CNCSs would determine the efficiency and effectiveness of global public relations techniques and efforts in times of difficulties that cross multiple borders (J. S. Lim, 2010). Thus, "managers in most worldwide companies recognize the need for simultaneously achieving global efficiency, national responsiveness, and the ability to develop and exploit knowledge on a worldwide basis" (Bartlett & Ghoshal, 2002, p. 65).

To frame this discussion, we can recall a domestic product safety incident that became global news as it emerged from Central America in 2007. A Kuna Indian in Panama alerted the country's government and health authorities to the danger of a brand of toothpaste imported from China. His reading of the product's label, specifically an ingredient listed in the contents known to have detrimental physical impacts, caused concern for his health and the well-being of his fellow countrypeople. His actions and those eventually taken by government officials detonated a global hunt for and eventual multiple recalls of the tainted toothpastes manufactured in China. The crisis resulted in product recalls and health alerts in six continents, affecting approximately 34 countries. "People around the world had been putting an ingredient of antifreeze in their mouths, and until Panama blew the whistle, no one seemed to know it," reported Bogdanich and Koster (2007, p. A1). "A little butterfly in Panama beat her wings and created a storm in China" and other nations; a premise of chaos theory. This created a transnational crisis for many corporations, governments, and local businesses and retailers.

Transnational crises bear profound consequences for many countries, a host of organizations, and their associated publics, clients, and consumers in an era of world interdependence and interconnection. For instance, "The toothpaste scare helped galvanize global concerns about the general quality of China's exports, prompting the government . . . [in Panama] to promise to reform how food, medicine, and consumer products are regulated," explained Bogdanich and Koster (2007, p. A1). "And other countries are re-examining how well they monitor imported products."

Exploring this line of reasoning, this chapter conceptualizes CNCS as a theoretical perspective that explains the main challenges of global public relations education, research, and management. The chapter contributes to scholarship and specialized professional practice by using previous studies and original cases to illustrate the theory.

Conceptualizing CNCSs

CNCSs are crises or troublesome situations that TNOs face either at "home," where they have their headquarters, or in "host" countries, where they operate and engage in commercial and/or institutional activities. These situations not only resonate at home and in host locations, often simultaneously, but also where the organization is known or where its economic or political activities are felt or are relevant for the local environment. It does not matter where the conflicting situation happens because the "impact seems to be greater at the home country of the organization or organizations involved, which could be explained by the relevance and proximity of organization for the home publics"—that is, government, shareholders, employees, activist groups, concerned community, consumer protection groups, and traditional and emergent media (Molleda & Connolly-Ahern, 2002, p. 4). For instance, a French corporation facing a challenging or controversial situation in Morocco will be the object of media reports, French activist and Moroccan diasporas' pressures, and perhaps government inquiries and legal actions in France, where its top management resides and where global commands are formulated and dispatched. The headquarters is ultimately responsible for the performance and actions of branches worldwide (Wakefield, 1997, 2001).

Golan's (2010) study "results indicate that nations that are relevant to the home nation . . . were likely to receive coverage" (p. 142). Consequently, the TNOs' affairs in host nations would receive greater coverage in their home countries and other national environments where geographic proximity, trade activity with the involved nations, and foreign direct investment and international aid flows are significant. The author has registered dozens of CNCS cases in a personal database since 2000. They involved all kinds of TNOs and dealt with one or a combination of the following sets of organizational and contextual issues:

- *Employee treatment:* questionable corporate actions affecting the well-being of employees, including inhuman treatment, human rights abuses, discrimination practices based on ethnicity, and unequal opportunity and pay for women and various disadvantaged minorities
- *Workplace safety:* poor working environment, weak assessment and management of risk, and accidents and other operating or technical failures that may have harmed employees or neighboring communities
- *Corporate decisions, policies, and performance:* closing of economically viable plants in takeovers and mergers and poor financial performance of specific or regional subsidiaries or global headquarters
- *Living and natural ecosystems:* inhumane treatments of animals and company practices that threaten the balance of national environments
- *Community well-being:* actions or operations that may affect local communities, including threatening people's health and well-being
- *Cultural clash:* ethical practices that may not be permissible in the home country but are permissible in the host country
- *Strategic communications:* transnational products' or services' positioning in a host market against local competitors, including defective products, illegal advertising practices, unfair competition, advocating consumerism, creating environmentally unsound or wasteful products, and overpowering public relations and lobbying efforts
- *Home and host governments and legal systems:* conflicting regulatory requirements as seen by the host and home countries, keeping information from federal authorities intentionally in either home or host countries, acting in discordance to established contracts with host countries, offering and taking bribes and payoffs, and abusing power from host countries against corporate facilities, contracts, and practices
- *International relations:* economic or political impact of one country on another and, therefore, TNOs finding themselves in the middle of two or more nations' economic, political, territorial, or military disputes

These myriad incidents involving TNOs worldwide engage and affect interest groups and audiences because incidences and conflicts are not isolated to the country where they originated (Molleda & Connolly-Ahern, 2002). Decisions, behaviors, and operations of a TNO affect a variety of publics, including host publics in a foreign country, transnational publics in many locations, and home publics at its headquarters. This could tarnish an organization's reputation and result in negative financial and legal consequences at home and host locations.

An example comes to mind. Chiquita Brands International pleaded guilty for protection payoffs to paramilitary death squads—designated terrorist organizations—in Colombia and paid a $25 million fine to the U.S. Department of Justice in 2007 (Seper, 2007). Consequently, relatives of nearly 400 murdered and tortured Colombians filed a lawsuit in the Manhattan Federal Court against Chiquita for sponsoring terrorists who committed crimes and human rights abuses (Schapiro, 2007). Colombian officials threatened to consider the extradition of senior Chiquita's executives who may have been involved in the illegal payments to paramilitary groups ("Colombia May Extradite," 2007). This CNCS involved multiple active publics and, therefore, demanded multiple and carefully crafted responses and follow-ups to every aspect and location of the crisis.

Home, Host, and Transnational Stakeholders

Practicing public relations domestically entails engagements or public-organization relationship building and maintenance with internal and external stakeholders with various degrees of involvement and impact. Managing public relations across borders increases the number and complexity of involved and affected stakeholders. To be efficient and effective in engaging publics in various national and transnational environments,

> the effective public relations practitioner employed by a transnational will research and respond to a list of strategic constituencies that typically begins with any activist groups pressuring the organization, followed by shareholders and potential investors and, finally, labor unions or employees. The media, as a strategic public, would fall behind the organization's customers or clients; the community where it operates; its competitors or suppliers; and the local, regional or national government of the host country. (Grunig, 1992, p. 134)

The sequence of public-organization engagements may depend on where the CNCS originates and the number of countries involved, among other factors. Effective global public relations professionals should consider stakeholders at the home, host, and transnational levels (Molleda, Connolly-Ahern, & Quinn, 2005; Molleda & Quinn, 2004). Despite the access to emergent communication technology, such as social media, the publics in each geographical dimension would experience the TNO's actions in particular ways and may hold unique expectations and anticipate localized communications that place the conflicting situation into their perceived reality.

Home publics are in the country where the TNO has its headquarters. These publics will reside at the local, state, or national levels. Particular attention will be paid to government agencies in the country's capital that may rapidly become aware, assess, and demand rapid explanation of any incident involving national business or institutional interests in foreign nations. That is, a Dutch corporation found guilty of paying bribes to government officials in South Africa will be subjected also to the Netherlands' laws. Similarly, conflicting situations happening at home will be shifted to the global stage, affecting the organization abroad, especially in main host locations. The same Dutch corporation that may have been found guilty of cooking the books and owing a large amount of taxes may be seen with suspicion and also be a subject of investigation in South Africa and other nations where it too has significant operations.

Host publics inhabit the countries where the TNO operates or intervenes in domestic affairs. National governments and communities that are involved or affected are of primary importance. The number and level of involvement of host publics may be determined by where exactly the incident occurs—that is, in their country, in the region, in another host nation or nations, or in the corporate headquarters, such as the hypothetical case of the Dutch corporation. It is predicted that the closer the situation to the host country, the greater the impact, the number of publics, and the level of activist involvement of those publics. For instance, a large Brazilian construction corporation building a dam in Bolivia may be blamed by activist groups for design and construction defects that threaten indigenous communities. The accusations may follow extensive media coverage and government investigation that result in a substantial fine. This incident is likely to cause public reactions in Brazil and perhaps in other South American countries where the construction corporation also operates.

Transnational publics navigate cyberspace, newswires, and airways. International nongovernmental organizations, activist groups, and global media would be listed in this category. Their presence is felt everywhere in an interconnected and instantaneous fashion, often connecting and supporting local groups or using television or radio feeds from local broadcasters. They often identify and transmit the CNCS to where their influence is most felt or their audiences are more interested in the cause advocated, such as human rights or environmental protection. For example, the transnational activist organization CorpWatch seeks "to expose multinational corporations that profit from war, fraud, environmental, human rights, and other abuses, and to provide critical information to foster a more informed public and an effective democracy" (*Our Mission,* n.d., ¶ 2). In September 2007, they launched a Wiki project named Crocodyl.org, in partnership with the Center for Corporate Policy and the Corporate Research Project. The San Francisco–based CorpWatch has developed a global network of researchers and journalists to identify and report corporate wrongdoing wherever it happens. They offer reports and other publications aiming to empower governments and citizens in the fight against transnational corporate power.

In many cases, host and home publics are active and require close attention simultaneously. In 2004, Wal-Mart opened a subsidiary, "Bodega Aurrera," north of Mexico City at San Juan, Teotihuacán, which is 1.6 miles from the 2,000-year-old pyramids of Teotihuacán—UNESCO's World Heritage Site ("Pyramid Schemes," 2004). In Mexico, local and national politicians, artists, artisans, community groups, activist groups, media, and competitors were actively involved. The opposition alleged the commercial expansion of a U.S.-based corporation "to be an insult inflicted on the sacred site by a symbol of American consumerism" (Malkin, 2004, p. C6). In general, Mexican consumers and government officials were supportive of the new supermarket because it brought competitive prices, quality products and services, a convenient location, and sponsored social and cultural programs. Many communities in the United States used the international incident to strengthen their opposition to the expansion of the world's biggest retailer to their backyards. The argument based on Wal-Mart's alleged abuses of Mexican heritage was voiced by local media and at the city commission's sessions ("A Supercenter," 2004).

In the end, Wal-Mart succeeded in managing the transnational crisis with public relations techniques and efforts. They responded to home and host publics by proactively communicating the benefits of the supermarket to consumers and local communities, expressing timely clarifications in regard to the opponents' allegations, and including contextual information that addressed domestic concerns in both Mexico and various communities in the United States that seem to have a love-hate relationship with Wal-Mart. The retailer also posted updated and timely information on its Web site. Wal-Mart used global and local spokespeople and third-party supporters. The grand opening of Bodega Aurrera was a success, and the U.S. opposition stopped using the Mexican controversy as a valid argument to further oppose the corporation's expansion in their communities ("Wal-Mart Opens," 2004). Of course, the U.S.-based opposition continued to focus on home concerns and affect data.

There are CNCS cases that evolve with variations and diverse degrees of impact in different host locations. In September 2009, Pfizer paid the largest fine ever, $2.3 billion, to settle a marketing fraud case with the U.S. Department of Justice. The news about the world's largest drug company was in every newswire service and countless media outlets on every continent. Focusing on the contextual information contained in news reports, domestic coverage in many countries pointed out the large penalty involving "the New York–based" (Clark, 2009, p. 2) or a "U.S.-based" company (Hooi, 2009) in London and Singapore respectively. Specifically, Clark (2009) ended the news report with this contextual information:

> Pfizer employs 90,000 people around the world including 4,000 staff in Britain, where the company has a large research and development site at Sandwich, in Kent. Its top-selling products include the anti-cholesterol drug Lipitor, the arthritis drug Celebrex and the erectile dysfunction drug Viagra. (p. 2)

Similarly, Hooi (2009), writing for the *Business Times Singapore*, said that "the same year Bextra was withdrawn in the US, the Health Sciences Authority in Singapore had withdrawn Bextra, after reports from Canada and the US linked the drug to an increased risk of heart attacks and skin reactions" (¶ 4). Both news reporting examples put the U.S. settlement into their domestic contexts. However, the news story in Singapore included a greater amount of background details of the company, its performance, and products. Pfizer operates in Singapore, its "first large-scale active pharmaceutical ingredient manufacturing facility in Asia" (Hooi, 2009, ¶ 18). Other aspects contained in the Singaporean version of the news story were (a) domestic advertising regulations of prescription drugs; (b) names and uses of various medications produced and commercialized by the pharmaceutical company; (c) the company's brief history and performance in Asia and Singapore, including research and development and employment statistics and projections; and (d) quotes from global and local spokespeople, including Pfizer's senior vice president and general counsel.

Surprisingly, in some countries the news story seemed to be downplayed. Although NOTIMEX (Mexican news agency) reported on the settlement (*Negocios,* 2009), only small notes were found in major Mexican newspapers. Moreover, the news story was also reported in Spanish by the Spanish Agencia EFE and REUTERS. More important, Pfizer Mexico did not include any news release or pertinent information on its Web site (*Sala de prensa,* n.d.). In contrast, the information about the settlement was found easily on the U.S.-based company's Web site (*Recent Pfizer Press,* 2009). The common Mexican citizen may not have become aware of Pfizer's settlement through their national or domestic media; however, the Mexican elite and decision makers, including Mexican shareholders, would have learned about the multimillion-dollar fine through international media, including cable television networks such as CNN in English and Spanish and other online channels. Pfizer may have left the online void in Mexico consciously as a localized strategy to downplay a major legal incident with U.S. authorities. One Mexican colleague best summarized the potential causes for this strategic response:

1. In Mexico, the first few days of September are national holidays. The annual presidential address, similar to the U.S. State of the Union, was delivered and had a tremendous impact on the media before, during, and after the political event, resulting in the saturation of coverage. Pfizer's record settlement was announced in the United States on September 1, 2009.
2. The news about this event filtered in through international newswire agencies and not through other mass-mediated efforts. Only very few newspapers and radio stations briefly mentioned the event, but with no major impact. The Internet also had some impact but without surpassing the news coverage.
3. Additionally, the news media in Mexico dedicated to marketing and communication

only reported good industry news. There is no specialized media on marketing communication that includes news analysis and commentary.

4. Finally, for obvious reasons, Pfizer Mexico and its four public relations agencies must have tried to control the situation and not cause much commotion during those days so that people would not talk about the large settlement for illegal commercial practices (M. Herrera, personal online communication, September 28, 2009).

In addition to the above informal case studies to illustrate the main components of CNCSs, a research agenda offers evidence to further conceptualize and refine the developing theoretical perspective of global public relations.

Evolving Knowledge: Actions and Responses

Stakeholders' reactions and corporate responses to incidents involving public safety vary according to the cultural characteristics of the host environments. Taylor (2000) analyzed the Coca-Cola Company's response to an incident where its product allegedly caused Belgian children to become ill. "Given the high levels of uncertainty avoidance and power distance in Belgium, France, and Spain, it makes sense that those nations would respond quickly and severely to any threats to public safety," concluded Taylor (2000, p. 289). Home, host, and transnational publics actively engaged the organization. Their actions, specifically the brand boycott by publics in France and Spain, in addition to where the contamination happened, in Belgium, affected the stock value and its relationship with host stakeholders. This CNCS also served to identify the deficiencies of a highly centralized management in Coca-Cola's main office in Atlanta, which resulted in lack of flexibility and understanding of local conditions in the nations involved.

Freitag (2001) studied the cultural and international complexities and cross-national impact of the Ford-Firestone tire crisis, as portrayed by media outlets in Canada, Denmark, France, Germany, New Zealand, Poland, the United Kingdom, the United States, and Venezuela. The amount of national news coverage was predicted by the number of affected domestic consumers (in proximity and consequences), the place where the companies were headquartered, and the direct links between the companies and their countries of origin. Particularly in France, the large media coverage resulted from a tradition of activism in consumer and labor issues and the prominence of automobile and automotive manufacturing in the country. In contrast, the news coverage in East Africa focused on assuring consumers that faulty tires would not be dumped on African markets. According to Freitag (2001), cultural aspects determined the corporate responses to the transnational crisis—that is, it was difficult for a Japanese executive to accept the blame and offer an apology for fear of losing face, and Ford's U.S. executives were at fault because of arrogance.

Wang (2005) studied the DuPont Teflon crisis in China, which originated from the U.S. Environmental Protection Agency's administrative action against DuPont. The crisis shifted to China where it transformed into a consumer product safety crisis. The study found that DuPont, China, was unprepared for the crisis in terms of early signal detection and prompt initial response. DuPont subsequently implemented a series of active turnaround actions and multiple-response strategies. However, the damage to the company's reputation and the Chinese Teflon market due to its response lapses in the early stage of the crisis could have been hard to recover from in the short term. The findings also indicated that DuPont employed a strategy mix used to offer a competing narrative, considering the unfavorable perceptions held by its stakeholders, and redefined the alleged acts to ones of lesser offensiveness. According to Wang (2005), DuPont's combined strategies were found internally coherent and partially corroborated by the media coverage. Wang's study documented a case of reversed CNCS—that is, the conflict involving a TNO shifts from a home to a host country and results in greater impact in the host location. The study suggested interpreting such a phenomenon from three perspectives: (1) the *crisis management performance* of the involved TNO, (2) the *level of media interest* in the involved issue, and (3) the unique and complicated *social and cultural context* of the involved host country.

Kim and Molleda's study (2005) also combined CNCS with crisis management by analyzing Halliburton's bribery probe case in Nigeria. To advance the CNCS theory with in a more complex context, including political aspects, the authors offered three propositions dealing with (1) the prominence of the chief executive officer (CEO) or top-level management and how much more attention he or she would attract to the crisis, which may result in greater political repercussions and debates; (2) the way national conflicts are perceived differently by involved actors at home and host locations and framed differently by host and home media; and (3) how domestic conflicts of TNOs are sometimes combined with other related crises that negatively affect their reputation in home and host countries and, therefore, require more complex responses and public relations techniques and efforts until the conflicts resolve.

In 2004, Merck Sharp & Dohme announced a voluntary worldwide withdrawal of Vioxx, its arthritis and acute pain medication. Oliveira and Molleda (2008) documented the public relations effort of the withdrawal in Brazil. According to the authors, Merck's decision resulted in the development of the most elaborated and critical public relations campaign by the company in contemporary history. In Brazil, as in other world markets, the medication was a top seller, requiring prompt actions and responses to the concerns of the medical community, regulatory agencies, and consumers. The campaign aimed to ease any confusion the product withdrawal and the disclosed research may have caused, as well as to position the company as responsible and concerned for the well-being of patients and the reputation of physicians who prescribed the medication. The company announced the decision to each subsidiary around the world and offered common guidelines to keep the same institutional discourse. Merck Brazil created a crisis committee. They localized the global strategy by communicating the reasons for the product withdrawal with the use of domestic statistics and the company's compliance with national regulations. The domestic strategy also included the identification of influential and credible personalities to maximize the communication impact on targeted publics and assuring Brazilian consumers of secure reimbursements at drugstores and quality of the lines of products of Merck Brazil.

Molleda, Solaun, and Parmelee (2008) tested the CNCS theory with the analysis of international news agencies' coverage on lead-tainted Mattel toys manufactured in China and sold in the United States and other markets worldwide. They concluded that Mattel was effective in its crisis communication strategies, providing a transparent and timely response, which is a critical element of effective public relations and particularly critical in product recalls. However, from a global perspective, Mattel failed to fully integrate the needs of host, home, and transnational publics in its crisis communication approach. The Chinese government and manufacturing companies did not take a proactive approach in their crisis communication strategy. Defense of their actions was not communicated until late in the conflict, and once communicated, it likely escalated the conflict instead of assisting in resolving the issue for the various publics. Had Mattel and the Chinese government jointly approached the problem, acknowledging from the onset their shared roles and responsibility in resolving the global crisis, the intervention of activist groups might have been somewhat negated, and the crisis might not have taken such a grand scope.

H. Lim and Molleda (2009) analyzed the particular effects of a home crisis in host countries' consumers. The study showed that the type of crisis significantly affected potential customers' attitudes and behaviors in terms of purchase intention, recommending the company's product to a friend, and requesting more information about the company. A massive product recall produced more negative responses from potential consumers than a bribery scandal affecting a transnational automobile corporation. Prior attitude toward a TNO affected audiences' attitude formation and behavioral intentions.

Molleda and Quinn (2004) articulated a set of 10 CNCS propositions that were the basis of the summarized research agenda[1] and are now revisited and logically reorganized after a few years of systematic qualitative and quantitative research:

1. CNCSs are mainly related to corporate social performance issues, negative economic consequences of globalization, actions of home or host countries' governments, and diplomatic or trade conflicts among countries of the world where TNOs operate.
2. National conflicts shift to the international arena when primarily global NGOs or media report the situation to audiences in different world locations, as well as when common citizens creatively use emergent communication technologies to denounce the conflict situation. However, there will be occasions during which the TNO itself alerts home authorities to improper actions in which it is involved in other countries. Similarly, home authorities could uncover, prosecute, and punish TNOs for their businesses overseas.
3. CNCSs with a great human interest focus are likely to be shifted to be of interest to the international community and will attract greater attention of home, host, and transnational stakeholders.
4. Direct involvement of a TNO in a CNCS will produce greater consequences and demand a more comprehensive set of responses and public relations techniques and efforts than an organization that is embedded in a multi-industry consortium or business partnership or is indirectly related to the crisis.
5. TNOs that produce or commercialize tangible, boycottable products or are led by high-profile executives are more likely to receive attention by home, host, and transnational publics than those who produce and commercialize intangible services and whose top executives do not have a high-profile position outside the organization.
6. The magnitude of a CNCS will increase when it starts in an emergent or developing economy because of the greater pressure the TNO will face in both host and home countries and from the transnational activist community.
7. A greater number of involved parties will characterize a CNCS in which a developed nation's TNO is the principal participant of the crisis because they will be better known and have greater global impact than those organizations from emergent or developing economies progressively expanding to host locations.
8. The life of a conflict that occurs in developed nations, often where its headquarters are located, will be shorter and will produce low or no impact in host countries when the incident only involves home consumers and/or legal actions and the organization has been proactive in self-denouncing its wrongdoings or accepting blame. In contrast, the crisis will last longer when it involves corporate wrongdoing in host countries and is punished at home by regulatory authorities.
9. Therefore, a lower number of involved parties will characterize a CNCS in which a developing nation or emergent economy organization is the principal responsible for the crisis situation.

10. TNOs headquartered in developed nations that produce or are part of a conflict situation in host locations will attract significant attention from global NGOs, international regulatory bodies, national governments, organized citizen groups, and international newswire agencies and global media outlets.

Finally, Molleda and Laskin (2010) combined the original CNCS propositions and body of literature with studies from international business on coordination and control mechanisms. They articulated nine additional presuppositions concerning the intersection of the multidisciplinary theoretical perspectives and concluded that

> the strategies employed by a transnational organization to deal with CNCS depend on and are largely determined by the coordination and control structure of a TNO: centralization versus localization; subsidiary autonomy in marketing decisions; division of responsibilities; and the chain of command. (p. 337)

This concludes the up-to-date research agenda on CNCS, which implies some lessons learned for global public relations education, research, and practice.

Conclusion

The best TNOs may do is to avoid CNCSs by acting ethically and complying with home and host economic, political, social, and cultural norms. Nevertheless, CNCSs often are unavoidable because of the complexity of the world we are living in; therefore, they are likely to escape the control of TNOs. Thus, a close look at the management approach taken to develop global public relations techniques and efforts through functional departments and/or with the assistance of global agencies or independent indigenous professionals is necessary. We should ask if the availability of culturally appropriate spokespeople and the timely provision of information subsidies according to time zones and indigenous journalism or communication practices would result in a coordinated and consistent global public relations function. Moreover, does the efficient coordination and control of host and home responses and actions, as well as contextualization of information subsidies provision and controlled online communication use, increase the likelihood of a successful crisis-control program?

Today, those who nurture a transnational mentality (i.e., multinational responsiveness, global efficiency, and worldwide learning) may exert greater control over the crisis and effectively engage home, host, and transnational publics. In that regard, global public relations scholars and students must invest further efforts to research the evolution, effects, and management of transnational issues and crises. Professionals in TNOs and global and domestic agencies should maintain fluid channels of communication with the headquarters and other influential offices worldwide. The contribution of each part will make the whole greater. They must also be active observers of the reactions of local audiences to global events, particularly of their industries or sectors. The mastery of localization strategies and tactics will allow professionals and their organizations to meet domestic expectations of host publics, without leaving out the expectations and needs of home and transnational stakeholders.

Note

1. Taylor (2000) and Freitag (2001) did not base their research on the CNCS propositions; however, their work has always been cited and used to inform and develop the theory.

References

Bartlett, C. A., & Ghoshal, S. (2002). *Managing across borders: The transnational solution.* Boston: Harvard Business School Press.

Bogdanich, W., & Koster, R. M. (2007, October 1). The everyman who exposed tainted toothpaste. *New York Times*, p. A1.

Chang, T. K. (2010). Changing global media landscape, unchanging theories? International communication research and paradigm testing. In G. J. Golan, T. J. Johnson, & W. Wanta (Eds.), *International media communication in a global age* (pp. 8–35). New York: Routledge.

Clark, A. (2009, September 3). Pfizer drug breach ends in biggest US crime fine: Record lawsuit punishes misbranding of painkiller: Whistleblower told of "sales that risked lives." *Guardian*, p. 2.

Colombia may extradite Chiquita officials. (2007, March 19). *New York Times*, p. 3.

Freitag, A. (2001). International media coverage of the Firestone tyre recall. *Journal of Communication Management, 6*(3), 239–256.

Golan, G. J. (2010). Determinants of international news coverage. In G. J. Golan, T. J. Johnson, & W. Wanta (Eds.), *International media communication in a global age* (pp. 125–144). New York: Routledge.

Grunig, L. A. (1992). Strategic public relations constituencies on a global scale. *Public Relations Review, 18*(2), 127–136.

Hooi, J. (2009, September 4). Pfizer swallows a bitter US $2.3b pill: Pharma giant to pay record fine, penalty for illegal marketing. *Business Times Singapore* (n.p.). Retrieved September 24, 2009, from LexisNexis *Academic* database.

Kim, J. R., & Molleda, J. C. (2005, March). *Cross-national conflict shifting and crisis management: An analysis of Halliburton's bribery probe case in Nigeria.* Paper presented at the 8th International Public Relations Research Conference, Miami, FL.

Lim, H., & Molleda, J. C. (2009, May). *The influence of a cross-national conflict shift on a transnational corporation's host customers.* Paper presented at the International Communication Association 59th Annual Conference, Division of Public Relations, Chicago.

Lim, J. S. (2010). Global integration or local responsiveness? Multinational corporations' public relations strategies and cases. In G. J. Golan, T. J. Johnson, & W. Wanta (Eds.), *International media communication in a global age* (pp. 299–318). New York: Routledge.

Malkin, E. (2004, December 6). Mexico: More sales than its 3 top competitors combined. *New York Times*, p. C6.

Molleda, J. C., & Connolly-Ahern, C. (2002, August). *Cross-national conflict shifting: Conceptualization and expansion in an international public relations context.* Paper presented to the convention of the Association for Education in Journalism and Communication, Miami, FL.

Molleda, J. C., Connolly-Ahern, C., & Quinn, C. (2005). Cross-national conflict shifting: Expanding a theory of global public relations management through quantitative content analysis. *Journalism Studies, 6*(1), 87–102.

Molleda, J. C., & Laskin, A. (2010). Coordination and control of global public relations to manage cross-national conflict shifts: A multidisciplinary perspective for research and practice. In G. J. Golan, T. J. Johnson, & W. Wanta (Eds.), *International media communication in a global age* (pp. 319–344). New York: Routledge.

Molleda, J. C., & Quinn, C. (2004). Cross-national conflict shifting: A global public relations dynamic. *Public Relations Review, 30,* 1–9.

Molleda, J. C., Solaun, L., & Parmelee, K. (2008, October). *Advancing the theory of cross-national conflict shifting: An analysis of international news agencies' coverage of lead-tainted toys from China.* Paper presented at the InterAmericas Council Congress of the Americas II, cosponsored by ICA, Mexico City, New Mexico.

Negocios: Pagará Pfizer multa record de 2.3 mil mdd por promoción ilegal [Business: Pfizer will pay a record fine of 2.3 billion dollars for illegal promotion]. (2009, September 2). Agencia Mexicana de Noticias, NOTIMEX [Mexican Agency of News]. Retrieved April 1, 2010, from www.zocalo.com.mx/seccion/articulo/pagara-pfizer-multa-record-de-2.3-mil-mdd-por-promocion-ilegal/

Oliveira, T. M., & Molleda, J. C. (2008). Withdrawal of Vioxx in Brazil: Aligning the global mandate and local actions. In J. V. Turk & L. Scalan (Eds.), *The evolution of public relations: Case studies from countries in transition* (3rd ed., pp. 181–194). Retrieved August 26, 2008, from Institute for Public Relations Web site: www.instituteforpr.org/files/uploads/International_CB.pdf

Our mission. (n.d.). Retrieved September 28, 2009, from CorpWatch Web site: www.corpwatch.org/article.php?id=11314

Pyramid schemes: A Mexican shopping scandal. (2004, November 13). *The Economist* (U.S. Edition). Retrieved December 10, 2004, from LexisNexis *Academic* database.

Recent Pfizer press. (2009). Retrieved September 28, 2009, from Pfizer USA Web site: http://pfizer.com/news/press_releases/pfizer_press_releases.jsp#

Sala de prensa. (n.d.). Retrieved on September 28, 2009, from Pfizer Mexico Web site: http://pfizer.com.mx/index.asp?action=press.main&SectId=1376

Schapiro, R. (2007, November 15). *Daily News,* p. 18.

Seper, J. (2007, March 20). Chiquita pleads to protection payoffs. *Washington Times,* A06.

A supercenter among the ruins: Protesters, shoppers clash over Mexico store. (2004, November 7). *Gainesville Sun,* p. 13A.

Taylor, M. (2000). Cultural variance as a challenge to global public relations: A case study of the Coca-Cola scare in Europe. *Public Relations Review, 26,* 277–293.

Wakefield, R. I. (1997). *International public relations: A theoretical approach to excellence based on a worldwide Delphi study.* Unpublished doctoral dissertation, University of Maryland, College Park.

Wal-Mart opens amid pyramids. (2004, November 5). *Calgary Sun,* p. 40.

Wang, Y. (2005). *Cross-national conflict shifting: A case study of the DuPont Teflon crisis.* Unpublished master's thesis, University of Florida, Gainesville.

CHAPTER 49

Globalization and Public Relations

Opportunities for Growth and Reformulation

Krishnamurthy Sriramesh

Public relations practice is as old as the human race itself, contrary to assertions that it is a 19th- or 20th-century phenomenon. Through the millennia, members of the public have been kept informed through various channels. One of the oldest is cuneiform writing, used more than 4,000 years ago in ancient Iraq to educate farmers how to grow better crops (Al Badr, 2004). Another example is the use of rock and pillar inscriptions to educate citizens on civic matters during the reign of the Indian emperor Asoka, around 320 BCE. Ancient societies also have used different rhetorical strategies to influence public opinion (see Sriramesh, 2004; Sriramesh & Verčič, 2009a, for country-specific studies). Therefore, viewing public relations as a 20th-century practice as Pimlott (1951) did, and attributing its origins only to a couple of Western countries such as the United States and the United Kingdom, is open to serious challenge.

Origins of public relations scholarship are more easily traceable to the 20th century. Concerted efforts at conceptualizing public relations practice began in the mid-1970s, and the body of knowledge (BoK) has grown significantly from those humble beginnings as outlined by two BoK projects in the United States sponsored by the Public Relations Society of America (PRSA) and one in Europe in 2000. However, the glass is perhaps only half full and, as this chapter asserts, globalization has provided the opportunity and scope for significant development that should also enhance the synergies between practice and scholarship.

The current era of globalization has provided the opportunity for assessing how relevant the current BoK is for the demands of the 21st century. This chapter seeks to review the current BoK, juxtaposing it with globalization. It will present a brief review of the concept of globalization and then review concepts from the existing BoK and offer recommendations for future development of theorizing in this field. The primary theme of this chapter is that whereas globalization offers great opportunities for the growth of the public relations profession and scholarship, it also has exposed many deficiencies, most of which are attributable to ethnocentricity (Sriramesh, 2002). Scholars and practitioners need to find ways of overcoming this ethnocentricity to help public relations develop holistically to meet the demands of the 21st century. The challenge is to increase the relevance of public relations to societies around the world. Globalization affects, and is affected by, factors such as political ideology, economics, cultural values and traditions, and technological infrastructure (Croucher, 2004). As shall be apparent in the review offered in this chapter, these factors are very relevant to public relations as well. As we enter the second decade of this millennium, we should strive to harness the potential offered by this combination.

Globalization: A Brief Overview

The current era of globalization began in the 1990s, and the term has become the buzzword of the first decade of the 21st century. The term *globalization* can be defined in many ways, but in the 21st century, it is used primarily in an economic (some might contend "corporate") context to denote the removal of trade barriers facilitating the flow of goods, services, and labor across national borders. Communication has to form the underpinning of such economic and trade exchanges, and therefore the role of public relations becomes crucial. As attractive as *laissez-faire* trade may appear, globalization often produces uneven benefits; stronger economies usually gain much more than weaker ones (United Nations, 2002). Opposition to globalization stems from these inequities as well as adverse impacts on cultural values (homogenization of cultures) as a result of globalization. Among other things, robust communication and relationship building can help avoid activism by aligning the values and interests of diverse stakeholders with those of organizations. Therefore, the link between public relations and globalization is logical and important.

Globalization is not new to the 21st century. Depending on one's definition, one could contend that it has occurred in human history at various times, driven by factors such as military conquests, economic necessity, or political ambition. It is also erroneous to associate globalization with Westernization. Frank (1998) has contended that between 1400 and 1800 some Asian economies were just as large as the Atlantic or Euro-American ones, and India and China matched the population as well as output of Europe. In their study of sudden stops in the inflow of capital to developing countries, Bordo, Cavallo, and Meissner (2010) referred to the period between 1880 and 1913 as "the first era of globalization" (p. 227). Interestingly, these authors pointed out that "the determinants and output effects of sudden stops in emerging economies . . . shows that the pattern of events was remarkably similar to the experience of the 1990s and first years of the 21st century" (p. 238). For example, financial globalization during that "first era" made countries vulnerable to external capital inflows—a phenomenon that rings true exactly a century later with the global economic downturn in the past couple of years, the most recent example of which is the economic challenges being faced by Dubai. Globalization has been a recurring phenomenon in human history, although the causes and the scope of its manifestation may be different. Debeljak (2009) identified three eras of globalization: the *imperial* 16th century, the *colonial* 19th century, and the *corporate* 20th century. As the names suggest, each of these eras had its own version of globalism, including trade. Although there may be differences in the manifestation of globalization, two facts remain constant: It is not a phenomenon unique to the 21st century; and it brings about significant changes in its wake, not all of which are positive.

This chapter addresses the current era of globalization and its relationship with public relations. Three contributing factors make the current era distinctive, each of which is relevant to public relations. First, the present era follows the extensive democratization of the world during the 1900s, when 120 countries become democratic (by granting adult franchise), prompting Freedom House (2000) to label the 20th century "Democracy's Century." A parallel growth can be discerned in public relations, in its modern form, as it developed during the 20th century in most regions of the world, although scholars such as Bentele and Wehmeyer (2009) have contended that public relations as publicity existed in Germany in the mid-19th century.

Second, the 1990s heralded the formation of trading blocs through actions such as the signing of the Maastricht Treaty founding the European Union (EU), and the North American Free Trade Agreement (NAFTA), as well as the formation of the Asia Pacific Economic Council (APEC). Countries now trade as part of an economic bloc rather than as individual entities, offering greater bargaining power. Formation of trading blocs has certainly increased commercial interactions among countries of the world, leading to increased communication as well. Much of this communication is also multinational and multicultural, which is why public relations cannot afford to be ethnocentric. Demand for public relations in new markets has grown significantly in the 21st century, and making it holistic is bound to increase its stature as a practice and profession. An assessment of the global presence of the top 10 international public relations agencies indicated that the diffusion of these agencies, especially in Asia, grew significantly after the mid-1990s (Sriramesh & Verčič, 2004), primarily as a result of the liberalization of the economy of these countries resulting from globalization. We also observed that being corporations, these agencies logically followed the money trail, as a result of which they were conspicuous by their absence in much of Africa. Focusing almost exclusively on corporate communication at the expense of the work of nonprofits (e.g., the UN agencies that have done yeoman service against great odds in many developing countries for more than 60 years) and governments has stunted the growth of a holistic BoK (Figure 49.1).

Finally, the development of information and communication technologies (ICTs) has significantly altered the economic, trading, and communication map of the world. ICTs (also called "new media" or, more recently, "social media") have not only provided increased channels for communication but also increased avenues for people to communicate across political and cultural borders, thus increasing pressure on organizations to recognize global voices. In other words, in the contemporary era, there is no such thing as "domestic" or "local" public relations involving communication with monocultures.

The current era of globalization has provided significant growth opportunities for the public relations industry. Especially corporations, which are making a beeline to emerging markets such as Asia and Latin America, have been forced to communicate with diverse publics that are also multicultural. These corporations have relied on public relations communication practitioners to initiate at least some of this communication and later help maintain most of it. Anecdotal evidence suggests that practitioners have by and large coped with the challenges of communicating with multicultural audiences through trial and error or based on anecdotal evidence, as public relations scholarship has offered minimal empirical evidence that could help them predict outcomes based on empirical data.

Figure 49.1 The World Map of Public Relations Globalization

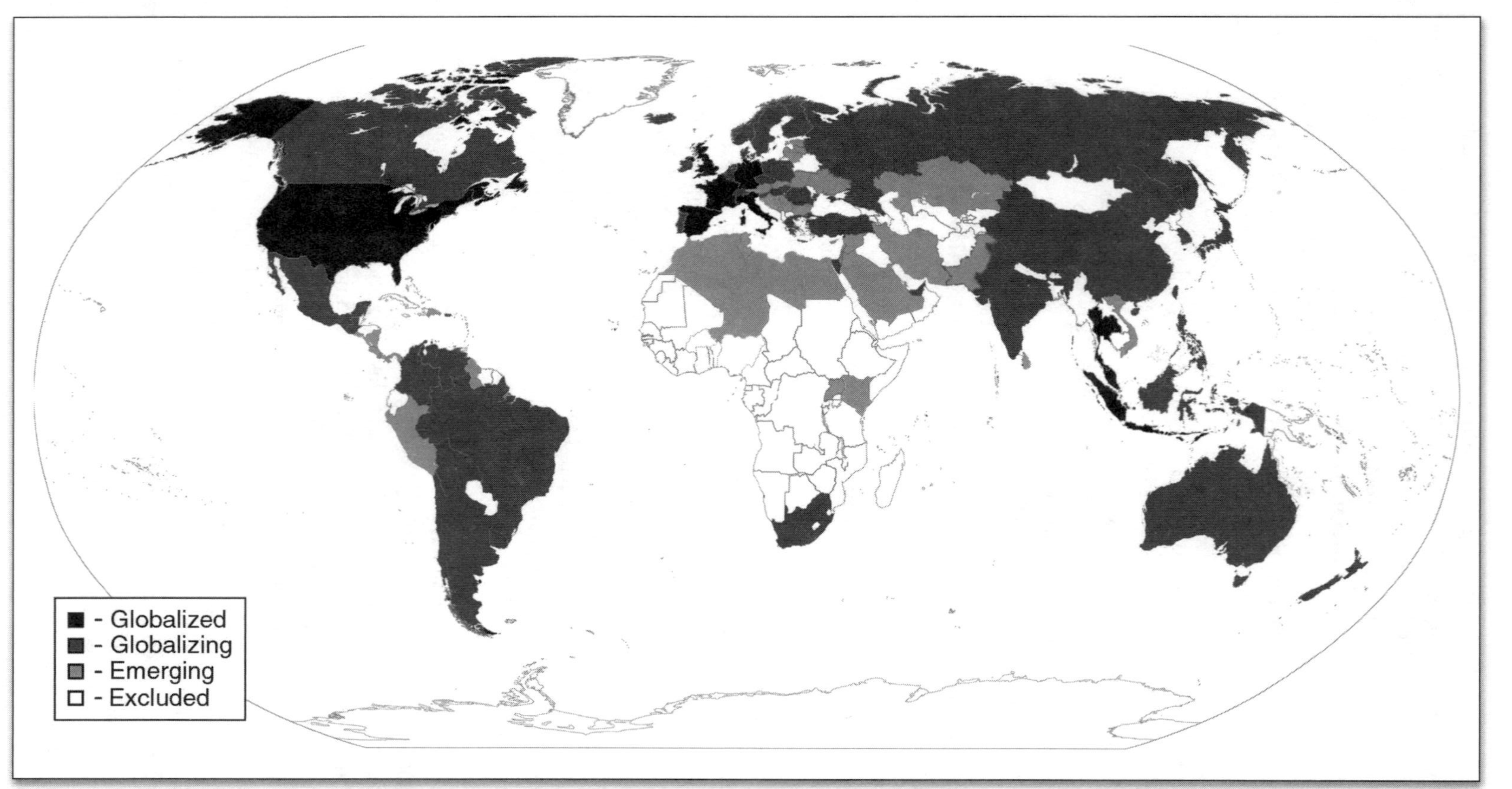

Source: Sriramesh and Verčič (2004).

Ethnocentricity and Public Relations

An introspective assessment of public relations scholarship leads to the conclusion that many deficiencies abound in the BoK, and it is not ready to help practitioners cope with the opportunities and challenges posed by globalization. Many of these deficiencies can be attributed to ethnocentricity. Although public relations scholarship began in earnest in the mid-1970s, until the early 1990s research predominantly focused on, and was built on empirical evidence from, the United States, the United Kingdom, and a few western European countries (Sriramesh, 2002). Although significant advances have occurred in the past 15 years, that development pales in comparison with the demands placed on the industry by globalization. Ethnocentricity can be discerned in research as well as in teaching and pedagogy. For example, the *Journal of Public Relations Research* published a special issue at the onset of the new millennium focusing on public relations *values* in the new millennium. The thoughtful articles in that issue discussed, among other things, rhetorical values, activist values, feminist values, and postmodern values. As illuminating and interesting as those articles were, the term *culture* appeared in the entire issue only once, which begs the question how one could discuss "values" devoid of culture given the innate relationship between the two concepts. Critiquing a manuscript that assessed the interplay between culture and consumer activism in an Asian country, the peer reviewer of a leading journal remarked 3 years ago, "How many more studies do we need from Asia?" If we do not recognize the problem (in this case ethnocentricity), how likely are we to find suitable solutions?

Ethnocentrism is evident in pedagogy as well. In 1999, the PRSA released the *Port of Entry* (PRSA, 1999) report with the aim of identifying "the knowledge and skills needed by practitioners in a technological, *multicultural and global society* [italics added]." The report also identified "recommended learning outcomes" with the explicitly stated purpose of preparing students to be effective communicators in the 21st century amidst globalization. The report listed six courses for the "ideal undergraduate major in public relations," of which not one had any multicultural elements in it (see Sriramesh, 2002, for a longer critique). The same was true of the graduate courses recommended by the report. The *Port of Entry* report was revised in 2006. Of late, the trend is to have a course on "international public relations" or "global public relations" as a way of countering criticisms of ethnocentricity in curricula. The impact of cultural differences should be integrated into all the courses (e.g., public relations campaigns, public relations research, public relations cases) to align curricula to the challenges of globalization rather than limiting culture only to a course such as "international public relations."

During a public debate about ethnocentricity in the public relations BoK, a leading practitioner from the United States remarked in defense of the *Port of Entry* report that it was intended for curricula in the United States and not for other parts of the world. One hopes that such an assertion is a minority opinion, because students in the United States are just as affected by globalization as those in the rest of the world. Until recently, public relations textbooks rarely contained a single example or case study from outside the United States or western Europe. Furthermore, the habit of translating textbooks published in the United States or United Kingdom verbatim with no cultural translations of the contents continues today, prompting one to wonder how relevant such wisdom is going to be to various local sociocultural conditions. Fortunately, in the past few years, there has been a noticeable shift away from this ethnocentrism in some textbooks, at least. However, to paraphrase Robert Frost, there are many "miles to go before we sleep" resting assured that the BoK is diverse enough to be able to make significant and meaningful contributions to prepare practitioners to operate in a globalizing environment. Obtaining the ability to be effective communicators across cultures will not only increase the profile (and reputation) of the public relations profession but also enhance the ability of public relations to find its place at the policy-making table. This begs the question, How can we reduce ethnocentricity in both practice and scholarship so that public relations can make meaningful contributions in this era of globalization?

When we discuss global public relations, a key factor to consider is whether one becomes a true cultural relativist and charts unique public relations strategies to suit every cultural environment—a Herculean task. The terms *globalocal* and *glocal*, combining the global with local, have been offered in the literature as a way of straddling the cultural relativism-ethnocentrism divide. British sociologist Roland Robertson is credited with popularizing the term *glocal* in English in the early 1990s. Theorizing emanating from the *Excellence Project* suggested that glocalization should be adopted by global public relations. Borrowing the idea of global strategies with local applications to "glocalize" public relations, Verčič, Grunig, and Grunig (1996) offered what they called *generic principles* of public relations that could be the foundation for public relations strategies in different sociocultural environments. In applying these principles, it was proposed that communication practitioners would have to make adjustments to suit the local *sociocultural environment.* This conceptual framework has been the foundation of the content of at least three books (Sriramesh, 2004; Sriramesh & Verčič, 2003, 2009a) to discuss public relations in about 50 countries. During the time that the Excellence Project was under way, Culbertson and Jeffers (1992) identified the relevance of "social, political and economic contexts (SPE)" to public relations. Building on that article, Culbertson, Jeffers, Stone, and Terrell (1993) wrote that their conceptualization of SPE was "still evolving" (p. 5). The next two sections will provide a brief overview of the *generic principles* and the *environmental variables.*

Generic Principles for Global Public Relations Strategies

One of the more obvious ways in which ethnocentricity has been evident in public relations practice in most parts of the world is in the application of public relations strategies and tactics imported from the West, often disregarding their applicability to the local culture. A key conclusion from the data of the Excellence Project was that there was a positive correlation between the value placed on communication by organizations and organizational effectiveness (L. A. Grunig, Grunig, & Dozier, 2002). That is, organizations performed better when they drafted organizational strategies based on inputs from the communication/public relations function.

By extension, the public relations function is empowered within the organizational hierarchy by being a part of the "dominant coalition" that makes policies, or by having a direct reporting relationship to the members of the dominant coalition. The first two generic principles state that no matter where in the world public relations is practiced, rich dividends can be expected when public relations is empowered in this way. Intuitively, these principles are logical, because in their boundary-spanning role, public relations practitioners are well placed to gather important inputs from key publics and transmit those to organizational leaders. One could reasonably contend that this principle should be applicable across a number of cultures, because evidence suggests that public relations practitioners currently do perform boundary-spanning roles across many cultures, albeit at a more technical level as opposed to a strategic one. We need more empirical evidence to support these largely conceptual linkages.

It is not uncommon to see several departments or divisions performing communications functions in an organization. Quite often, there is little coordination between these communications endeavors, leading to duplication and even contradictions in message delivery. Another generic principle recommends that organizations would be well served by having an "integrated public relations function," where a unified strategy drives the communication function of all the departments. Thus, even if management programs, such as human resources, investor relations, media relations, trade relations, and public affairs, are vested in separate departments for administrative or other reasons, it is efficacious for them to operate cohesively with one holistic communications strategy. A corollary to this principle is the prescription that as a management function, public relations should be separate from other functions such as marketing. Based on much of the available empirical evidence, in most instances when these functions are combined, public relations is relegated to a supporting technical function limited principally to publicity and media relations, negating the value that public relations can provide to strategic functions within the organization. Conceptually, this principle also appears to be applicable across a number of cultures, but we need empirical evidence to support the principle and also offer evidence on variations in such application.

The issue of the public relations practitioner as "manager" versus "technician" has been debated by scholars since the late 1970s. The generic principles, not unlike a significant section of the BoK, suggest that organizations benefit when public relations has a strategic managerial function and is not relegated merely to technical activities. The generic principles go beyond this mandate to also exhort public relations practitioners to endeavor to possess the education, professionalism, and knowledge level necessary to be able to contribute effectively to organizational policy making.

Until a couple of decades ago, most public relations practitioners around the world were "imports" from other disciplines such as journalism and English literature. This trend continues in parts of the world where public relations education has not yet permeated tertiary education or has done so only in the past few years. Sriramesh and Enxi (2004) found that in Shanghai, government agencies often promoted the person with most seniority to vacant posts regardless of professional background and job fit, resulting in steel mill workers and even chefs becoming public relations managers. With the recent development of public relations as a domain for study in institutions of higher education in many parts of the world, the pool of graduates trained in public relations will increase; these can be relied on to operate as communication strategists. Other principles have addressed the need to have symmetry in internal and external communication as well as ethics in public relations. Since the generic principles were offered, studies have gathered empirical evidence about the presence of some of the principles in countries such as South Korea (H. S. Kim, 2003; Rhee, 1999), Singapore (Lim, Goh, & Sriramesh, 2005), Bosnia (Kent & Taylor, 2007), and Kyrgyzstan (Turdubayeva & Sriramesh, 2010). A study is currently under way in Macedonia, but many more research studies are needed from all regions of the world to empirically test the reliability and validity of the generic principles across a number of countries and cultures to assess whether they can result in a robust theory of global public relations.

The 20th century was characterized by Western strategies and techniques of public relations regardless of their suitability to the local sociocultural environment. The ill-conceived interventions by Western allies in Afghanistan and Iraq are just two well-known, and continuing, examples of the results of trying to bring a total change in culture without understanding the local culture before getting involved. Replacing totalitarianism with democracy is a laudable goal, but merely because a goal is lofty does not mean it is achievable or pragmatic unless one understands the local culture and aligns the strategy with the values of the society. The next sections address factors that communication professionals ought to take into account when practicing public relations in a globalizing world.

Culture

Culture influences every human activity, including communication. Communication is central to public relations practice and scholarship; culture's relationship to public relations is incontrovertible. The reciprocal relationship between culture and communication has been more widely studied and chronicled than scholarship on the relationship between culture and public relations. Studies have attempted to link public relations with culture only in the past 15 years (see Sriramesh, 2009b, for a review of many of these studies). The relationship between culture and public relations is evident in three principal ways. First, culture can be seen as an antecedent for public relations practice. That is, culture (both societal and corporate) can be viewed as an "environmental variable" that influences public relations practice. In doing so, it is wise for public relations scholarship to also define *culture* more broadly by going beyond the term as studied by anthropologists and ethnographers and by including political, economic, media, and activist culture (Sriramesh, 2009a). Public relations is truly multidisciplinary.

A second intersection between culture and public relations is evident when one views public relations practice itself as a *culture*, thereby assessing, for example, how public relations as a domain differs from disciplines such as marketing or advertising that have their own cultures. It would be surprising if a discipline that is at least 100 to 150 years old (in its modern form) has not developed into a unique culture with its own idiosyncrasies, rites and rituals, and myths and stories. Viewing public relations as a culture has other important benefits such as helping distinguish public relations and its contributions from allied disciplines such as marketing and advertising.

Finally, the third nexus between culture and public relations relates to the *impact* that public relations has on the culture of a society and organization. Globalization has opened new markets that multinationals seek to enter, or in the eyes of some, *exploit*. Their entry has definitive impact on the local culture, which is why critics of the World Trade Organization (WTO) are so passionate in their opposition to globalization. Public relations practitioners often are at the forefront when a multinational enters a new market, causing them to be perceived as the purveyors of "cultural imperialism." Therefore, practitioners have a special tightrope to walk between serving the organizations that employ them and remaining socially responsible.

All the studies that have thus far attempted to link culture with public relations have viewed culture as an antecedent or "environment" for public relations practice and thereby belong to the first genre of research identified above (see Sriramesh, 2009b, for a review of these studies). The dimensions of culture that Hofstede (1991) identified (power distance, uncertainty avoidance, masculinity/femininity, individualism/collectivism, long-term orientation) have formed the foundation for much of that research. Although these studies have made significant contributions to the BoK, empirical evidence for much of this body of literature has emanated from a few countries in Asia. There is a dire need to expand the BoK by including evidence from countries in Latin America, Africa, and Central and West Asia.

Hofstede's seminal work is very useful, but restricting our analysis only to cultural idiosyncrasies that are common across several cultures, the primary focus of Hofstede's efforts, limits the utility of such conceptualization. We need to recognize that traits unique to a society are just as interesting for study and, more important, perhaps play a far greater role in communication and public relations. So far, only a few studies have attempted to assess the impact that idiosyncrasies unique to a culture have on public relations. For example, Sriramesh and Takasaki (2000) assessed how concepts such as *amae* (a desire to depend on the goodness of another), *wa* (harmony), *omote* (public, formal self), and *ura* (private, informal self) influenced communication and public relations in Japan. Huang (2000) studied the Chinese trait *guanxi* (relationship) and linked it to public relations. The paucity of studies linking public relations with cultural idiosyncrasies unique to a society is evidence of how much more work needs to be done in the next years in analyzing this important linkage.

Concerted efforts at linking culture with public relations are bound to yield significant returns not only for practice but for scholarship as well. Early in its conceptualization, the situational theory of publics (J. E. Grunig, 1997; J. E. Grunig & Ipes, 1983) consisted of four variables, including *referent criterion*. This fourth variable was dropped after some initial studies offered weak support to it. Scores of subsequent studies accepted this reconceptualization and repeatedly confirmed the theory with three independent and two dependent variables. Almost a quarter of a century after *referent criterion* was dropped, we found that culture played a key role in the propensity among consumer publics in Singapore to become activists when faced with poor customer service (Sriramesh, Saminathan, & Lim, 2007). After careful analysis of data from focus groups and a survey, the impact of culture on the variables of the situational theory was incontrovertible. If *referent criterion* had been retained as the fourth independent variable, there would have been an opportunity in the theory to include the impact of culture as a referent criterion that influences the information-seeking and -processing behaviors of publics.

Looking to the future, the above example denotes that much of the existing theorizing in public relations can be enhanced by assessing it within a cultural prism, defining *culture* broadly. There is a dire need for more studies that view culture as an antecedent for public relations (the first genre identified above). There also is a need to establish research programs to study public relations *as a culture* (the second genre of culture–public relations identified above) and the *impact of public relations on society* (the third genre).

Political System

The notion that influencing public opinion is the primary task of public relations practitioners has been popular in both practice and scholarship. Culbertson et al. (1993) explained the "political context" for public relations as "focusing on gaining support from officials—on power relationships having to do with clients and the public at large" (p. 5). The literature on issues management is a good example of the worldview that public opinion is paramount and that because public relations helps build public opinion, it is an important function for organizations. Early innovators of this topic, Jones and Chase (1979), reasoned that unlike citizens who can influence public policy by electing members of the legislative body in a democracy, corporations who have no such direct role resort to indirect means such as lobbying to influence legislators. Building on Jones and Chase's work, Crable and Vibbert (1985) offered five phases of an issue's "life cycle" that organizations could track and influence through various ways. Heath and Cousino (1990) reviewed the first decade of theorizing on the topic and offered further conceptualization by noting the four pillars of public relations: strategic business planning and management, issue monitoring, achieving high standards of corporate social responsibility, and engaging in communication regarding issues of fact, value, and policy.

Globalization, however, has forced public relations practitioners into operating in countries that do not have a pluralistic democratic environment as subsumed under existing issues management literature. Scholarship is only now beginning to recognize the need to conceptualize how public relations interacts with different political systems. As mentioned earlier, Freedom House called the 20th century "Democracy's Century," noting that there was not a single democratic country in 1900, but by 1999, there were 118 countries that were home to about 58% of the population of the world and that had democratic forms of government (Freedom House, 2000). Along with this democratization, one can trace a parallel growth in public relations, especially in the second half of the 20th century, as seen in countries such as Japan, South Korea, Sweden, and Germany following the end of World War II.

Freedom House also has noted that democracy is manifested in different forms across the world. For example, there are countries with "restricted democratic practices" where a single political party is in power and controls political, media, financial, and even electoral institutions and processes primarily to maintain the status quo. Other forms of government such as totalitarian regimes, colonial and imperial dependencies, monarchies, and protectorates show us that a pluralistic democratic system is not the only political philosophy present in the world, no matter how appropriate one may think it is for every society. Emerging democracies such as some members of the former Soviet bloc continue to face challenges that have restricted their transition to greater political pluralism. In a recent report, Freedom House (2009) lamented,

> Pivotal authoritarian regimes have adapted and modernized their repressive methods and are undermining democracy in updated, sophisticated, and well funded ways. The result is a disruptive and serious new challenge to the emergence of an international system based on the rule of law, human rights, and open expression.

In recent times one has witnessed a resurgence in theocratic political systems, whose influence has largely been ignored by public relations scholarship. The BoK of public relations has yet to integrate into scholarship and pedagogy how public relations practitioners can, and should, cope with the different political environments they encounter. Being able to make informed predictions on which public relations strategies and tactics work best given certain political conditions should be a key factor guiding public relations scholarship. Globalization has provided us the opportunity to move theorizing in this direction.

Economic System

The recent spurt in globalization has certainly stepped up economic activity in many countries—principally in Asia and Latin America. Most of the countries in these regions were hitherto recognized more for their poverty and social problems and often neglected in international discussions. However, as was evident in the environmental summit in Copenhagen in December 2009, developing countries such as India, China, Brazil, and South Africa have acquired significant bargaining power as a direct result of the interdependence of economies brought about by globalization. Whereas the barrel of a gun may have been paramount in the past, economic might has become a more subtle, and no less effective, weapon in the 21st century.

Economic activity and growth has a direct influence on the demand for public relations. Assessing the global presence of the top 10 public relations agencies, Sriramesh and Verčič (2004) found that being for-profit corporations, these agencies to a large extent had a very strong presence in the West. Only in the past decade or so have they increased their presence in countries such as China and India concomitant with the significant growth in economic activity brought on by globalization. Except for South Africa, Nigeria, and Egypt (countries with significant economic activity owing to natural resources or tourism), the 10 leading agencies barely had a presence in Africa. As will be discussed in the next section, there is an innate linkage between political system and economic system. The nature of the economy of any country is a direct result of the political philosophy of the government. Political ideology is affected by the economic system, and in most instances, economic growth leads to an increase in political pluralism.

Scholarship has yet to integrate the relationship between public relations and different economic systems into the BoK, instead focusing almost exclusively on Western capitalism. Liberal economic systems pose opportunities and challenges to the public relations practitioner that are quite different from ones posed by developing economies. The private sector versus public sector debate is very relevant in this context. Economic development increases the share of private sector enterprises inviting greater public relations activity in the corporate sector (Sriramesh & Verčič, 2004). Developing economies usually foster public relations aimed at national development and nation building, with government communication taking the bulk of the attention. In fact, the boundary between government communication and private sector communication is greatly blurred in such instances. Responding to the demands of globalization, then, public relations scholarship ought to spawn research programs that assess the nexus between different political systems and public relations. One hopes that the next decade will see the beginning of such expansion.

Political Economy

Political philosophy and economic systems are innately linked, and therefore, the concept of political economy is cogent to the discussion of the relationship between public relations and political philosophy and economic systems (see Duhe & Sriramesh, 2009). Although the concept of political economy dates to the 18th century, scholarly attempts to systematically link political economy with public relations have been sparse and muted. Duhe and Sriramesh stated that

> the study of political economy examines the inherent tensions, unintended consequences, and inevitable influences economic and political activities concurrently impart on society, as opposed to the study of economics, political science, or sociology, which examines these respective dimensions unilaterally. (p. 24)

In theories of political economy, the economic perspective often is the more dominant, and the focus is more on the market (which generates economic wealth), with political and social factors garnering secondary attention. However, as Gilpin (2001) stated,

> The ways in which the world economy functions are determined by both markets and the policies of nation-states, especially those of powerful states; markets and economic forces alone cannot account for the structure and functioning of the global economy. . . . The relationship of economics and politics is interactive. (p. 23)

Political economy helps us understand how organizations choose to respond (if at all) to change pressures created by issues. If we take environmentalism as an example, we can discern political (public policy), social (quality of life), and economic (cost/benefit) dimensions to the issue. A corporation operating in a political economy that values individual wealth creation (enhancing returns to the investor) may actively resist nongovernmental organization (NGO) pressures to adopt environmental care standards beyond those mandated by law. However, another that is operating in a political economy that places greater value on the collective good may proactively seek working partnerships with environmentalists as a normal course of business. As a philosophy, political economy stipulates the roles of, and relationships among, corporations, activist groups, and the government—as seen in corporativist countries. Although issues management scholars have addressed the relationships between these three groups, they have done so in a very limited manner, restricting their attention to corporation-oriented lobbying to seek favorable public policies.

Duhe and Sriramesh (2009) and Sriramesh and Duhe (2009) used the following three dimensions of political economy (proposed by Gilpin, 2001) to offer over a dozen recommendations on the linkage between the concept and public relations: (1) the primary purposes of the economic activity of the nation, (2) the role of the state in the economy, and (3) the structure of the corporate sector and private business practices. Although some of the recommendations may be implicit in current public relations theorizing, our discipline is yet to embark on a concerted program of research where these concepts are isolated and studied in depth based on empirical evidence prior to being linked with public relations. Globalization has made such an analysis inevitable, and unless public relations scholarship rises to the occasion, public relations practice will continue to be marginalized.

Media System

Public relations is often erroneously equated with media relations, probably because the typical public relations practitioner in many parts of the world tends to spend far more time interacting with journalists than with other stakeholders. Regardless of the merit in such comparisons, the fact remains that maintaining good relationships with the media is an important activity for public relations practitioners. Sallot and Johnson (2006) reviewed the relationship between journalists and public relations practitioners over a 15-year period and found that 44% of media content in the United States originated from public relations sources. The authors also found a 21st-century shift in journalists' perceptions of public relations practitioners as sources. Journalists interviewed between 2002 and 2004 were found to value public relations practitioners as news sources more than those interviewed between 1991 and 1996.

The nexus between mass media and public relations is important enough not to be viewed unidimensionally from an "information subsidy" perspective. Going beyond this, as Yoon (2005) suggested, to the "knowledge dimension" is necessary as well (see Sriramesh & Verčič, 2009a). Globalization has made it important for us to avoid unidimensionality in linking the mass media and public relations, recognizing the differences in mass media cultures evident around the world (Sriramesh, 2003). Over the course of almost four decades, scholars (e.g., Hachten, 1981; Martin & Chaudhary, 1983; Merrill & Lowenstein, 1971; Siebert, Peterson, & Schramm, 1956) developed normative theories of the mass media, offering us the first concerted stream of research on the differences in media environments in different regions of the world. Public relations scholarship has not adequately harnessed the wisdom from this stream of research to identify media relations strategies that are suitable to local media cultures (see Sriramesh & Verčič, 2009b).

Although many of the concepts of the normative theories of mass media are compelling, they are becoming less useful in a changing world, as evidenced by the Soviet media theory that is now obsolete. Public relations practitioners will find three factors pertinent in understanding the media environment in a different country. The first, media *control*, refers to media ownership in a country, and more important, who controls media content. The second, media *diffusion*, assesses which segments of the population consume different types of mass media—information that is key to any communicator. Illiteracy and poverty play a key role in mass media consumption. Finally, media *access* indicates which segments of the population in a country are able to place their content in the mass media for wider distribution. Anecdotal evidence suggests that public relations practitioners have certainly been paying attention to these three factors when they conduct media relations activities in different parts of the world (see Sriramesh & Verčič, 2009b, for a longer review). Such avenues offer scholarship the opportunity to link public relations with globalization.

Whereas normative theories of the mass media as well as concepts such as media control, media diffusion, and media access are useful in assessing the nexus between mass media and public relations, their utility is restricted to the print and broadcast media. The onset of new media technologies has changed the rules of the game, and while creating new opportunities as well as challenges to public relations practitioners, new media have certainly altered media relations activities in a globalizing world. A widely known example is the furor around the world as a result of the images of oppression in Tibet posted on the Internet in the months leading up to the 2008 Beijing Olympics. The successful campaign to unseat Joseph Estrada as president of the Philippines began with tens of thousands of text messages opposing his rule. Although there has been a significant increase in the number of studies that have attempted to link new media with public relations in the past decade, public relations scholarship has yet to study adequately the interplay between media and public relations in different regions of the world (see Sriramesh & Rivera, 2010). There is also a paucity of research on new media and their utility in emerging markets that are especially vulnerable to the effects of the digital divide. Empirical data also need to be gathered to help identify appropriate strategies for effective media relations localized to different media environments for print, broadcast, and new media. All these are fertile avenues for research in the next decades.

Activism

The current era of globalization appears to have generated much more concerted activism than previous ones. A variety of factors have contributed to this, including media technology that has made sharing information and views globally (at least among members of the "wired community" who are not affected by the digital divide) cheaper, easier, and almost instantaneous. A television anchor in China chose his personal blog rather than his television program to mount a popular and successful campaign demanding that the Starbucks outlet in the Forbidden City in Beijing be closed, as its presence was demeaning to the cultural heritage that this former imperial palace symbolized. Similarly, opponents of a chemical factory in the city of Xiamen mobilized a protest march of more than 10,000 people through text messages and through a concerted campaign often using new media, forcing suspension of construction. New media have changed the rules of the game and provided activists with a potent weapon against corporate (or government) excesses in general and the effects of globalization in particular.

Activists coalesce around problems caused by organizational activities and attempt to find resolution through various means, such as education through publicity campaigns, lobbying government for greater regulation, media relations, and sometimes even radical actions. In the early development of the BoK of public relations, activism had been recognized in issues management. Subsequently, the situational theory of publics (J. E. Grunig & Ipes, 1983) borrowed Dewey's definition of *public* and defined activists as those who face a problem based on an organization's activities, recognize the problem, and organize to resolve it. Taking a global perspective, J.-N. Kim and Sriramesh (2009) identified political, economic, media, cultural, and organizational contexts as antecedents to activism. They linked activism with 5 of the 10 generic principles. Few studies have assessed the linkage between public relations and activism in different parts of the world. Little, if any, evidence illuminates how the different environmental cultures discussed in this chapter affect activism. There is abundant potential for research programs on this topic as well (J.-N. Kim & Sriramesh, 2009).

Public Diplomacy and Public Relations

Globalization has inevitably increased interactions among countries of the world at the economic, political, and cultural levels. Public relations can play a crucial role in these interactions at all levels, which is why the linkage between public relations and the variables discussed in previous pages is so important. Political scientists have traditionally addressed exchanges between governments of nations under the terms *international relations* or *diplomatic relations*. The term *public diplomacy* has become an important addition to the parlance and conceptualization of relationships among peoples and governments of the world in the past few decades. Unfortunately, public relations scholarship has not really addressed the close relationship between public diplomacy and public relations save for a few articles on the subject. When a linkage between the two concepts is made, usually it is a negative one, as in the case of the equating of public diplomacy with advocacy of false propaganda conducted by public relations practitioners.

As with most terms and disciplines, there is no unanimity about the definition of the term *public diplomacy.* Cull (2009) distinguished between *diplomacy, traditional diplomacy,* and *public diplomacy* and defined *public diplomacy* as "an international actor's attempt to manage the international environment through engagement with a foreign public" (p. 12). He identified a shift in today's public diplomacy from its practice in the 20th century, and although he did not use the term, one could contend that *globalization* is the primary, if not the sole, reason for this shift. He identified seven characteristics of what he termed the *new* public diplomacy. Several of these characteristics have a direct relevance to public relations. He wrote that "actor-to-people Cold War era communication" (government to foreign audience) used in traditional public diplomacy has been replaced by "a new emphasis on people-to-people contact for mutual enlightenment" (p. 13) in new public diplomacy. Clearly, this is a direct reference to the notion of symmetry that has been discussed and debated by public relations scholars for over three decades, but we have yet to overlap the two concepts. Furthermore, Cull identified the shift from "top-down messaging" used in traditional diplomacy to "relationship building" (p. 13) in new public diplomacy. Given that in the past decade many public relations scholars have passionately advocated that public relations practitioners use symmetrical communication to build relationships among various publics, one sees a crucial role for public relations in the era of *new* public diplomacy, but such a role has yet to be fully articulated. It is pertinent to add here that *interactivity* (e.g., as offered by new media) should not automatically be equated with *symmetry* (Sriramesh & Rivera, 2006).

Cultural diplomacy is another allied area where public relations intersects with public diplomacy, but that linkage has yet to be integrated into the BoK of public relations. Schneider (2010) noted that "cultural diplomacy differs from its larger relative public diplomacy in that it is less closely aligned with policy (or promoting the acceptance of policies), and operates best as a two-way street" (p. 261). Governments are increasingly using cultural diplomacy as a complement to public diplomacy, as was evident during the 2008 Beijing Olympics. Ndlovu (2010) addressed how South Africa, which had been subjected, among other sanctions, to sports boycotts during the decades of apartheid, used sports and cultural diplomacy to win the rights to host the forthcoming FIFA World Cup in the country. Cultural diplomacy is not unlike the "soft power" (Nye, 2004) that has become so popular in recent years.

Public relations has often been criticized for not contributing meaningfully to organizations and society. At least some of this criticism is attributable to the fact that public relations has always been about "soft power" and therefore it is hard to measure its contributions. In its truest sense, public relations is about both *public* and *cultural* diplomacy. Both public and cultural diplomacy offer public relations the distinct opportunity for making significant contributions to international relations while also providing a way of enhancing the reputation of the practice. But first, public relations will have to shed its ethnocentricity and embrace culture in its broadest sense. The worldview that public relations is principally about corporate communication or that it can only be linked to government in a limited way through things such as political communication/campaigns or issues management has stunted the growth of the discipline. Public and cultural diplomacy offer avenues to overcome all these shortcomings. By extension, globalization has offered a golden opportunity for our field to grow out of this cocoon.

Conclusion

The current era of globalization offers significant challenges as well as opportunities to public relations as a practice and scholarly discipline. These opportunities have the potential to elevate public relations beyond its current restrictive parameters. However, ethnocentricity in both public relations practice and scholarship prevent the discipline from harnessing the potential that globalization offers. By defining culture broadly to include diversity in political ideology, socioeconomic systems, and media systems and integrating it into public relations practice, education, and scholarship, the field can flourish and rise to greater heights in the 21st century and make even more meaningful contributions to the global village. Globalization offers the rare opportunity to extend the horizons of public relations as a discipline. Scholars should accept this challenge and build an expansive research program that should prove useful to practitioners and the society at large, thereby enhancing the reputation of this domain.

References

Al Badr, H. (2004). Public relations in Saudi Arabia. In K. Sriramesh (Ed.), *Public relations in Asia: An anthology* (pp. 187–205). Singapore: Thomson.

Bentele, G., & Wehmeyer, S. (2009). From "literary bureaus" to a modern profession: The development and current structure of public relations in Germany. In K. Sriramesh (Ed.), *The global public relations handbook: Theory, research, and practice* (pp. 441–465). New York: Routledge.

Bordo, M. D., Cavallo, A. F., & Meissner, C. M. (2010). Sudden stops: Determinants and output effects in the first era of globalization, 1880–1913. *Journal of Development Economics, 91*(2), 227–241.

Crable, R. E., & Vibbert, S. L. (1985). Managing issues and influencing public policy. *Public Relations Review, 11*(2), 3–15.

Croucher, S. (2004). *Globalization and belonging: The politics of identity in a changing world.* Oxford, UK: Rowman & Littlefield.

Culbertson, H. M., & Jeffers, D. W. (1992). The social, political, and economic contexts: Keys in educating true public relations professionals. *Public Relations Review, 11,* 5–21.

Culbertson, H. M., Jeffers, D. W., Stone, D. B., & Terrell, M. (1993). *Social, political, and economic contexts in public relations: Theory and cases.* Hillsdale, NJ: Lawrence Erlbaum.

Cull, N. J. (2009). *Public diplomacy: Lessons from the past.* Los Angeles: Figueroa Press.

Debeljak, A. (2009, July). *In praise of hybridity: Globalization and the modern Western paradigm.* Paper presented at the 15th International Public Relations Symposium, Lake Bled, Slovenia.

Duhe, S., & Sriramesh, K. (2009). Political economy and global public relations research and practice. In K. Sriramesh & D. Verčič (Eds.), *The global public relations handbook* (Rev. ed., pp. 22–46). New York: Routledge.

Frank, A. G. (1998). *ReOrient: Global economy in the Asian age.* Berkeley: University of California Press.

Freedom House. (2000). *Democracy's century: A survey of global political change in the 20th century.* Retrieved March 25, 2010, from www.freedomhouse.org/reports/century.html

Freedom House. (2009). *Undermining democracy: 21st century authoritarians.* Retrieved December 23, 2009, from www.underminingdemocracy.org/execSummary.php

Gilpin, R. (2001). *Global political economy: Understanding the international economic order.* Princeton, NJ: Princeton University Press.

Grunig, J. E. (1997). A situational theory of publics: Conceptual history, recent challenges and new research. In D. Moss, T. MacManus, & D. Verčič (Eds.), *Public relations research: An international perspective* (pp. 3–46). London: International Thompson Business Press.

Grunig, J. E., & Ipes, D. A. (1983). The anatomy of a campaign against drunk driving. *Public Relations Review, 9*(2), 36–52.

Grunig, L. A., Grunig, J. E., & Dozier, D. M. (2002). *Excellent public relations and effective organizations: A study of communication management in three countries.* Mahwah, NJ: Lawrence Erlbaum.

Hachten, W. (1981). *The world news prism: Changing media, clashing ideologies.* Ames: Iowa State University Press.

Heath, R. L., & Cousino, K. R. (1990). Issues management: End of first decade progress report. *Public Relations Review, 16*(1), 6–18.

Hofstede, G. (1991). *Culture and organization: Software of the mind.* London: McGraw-Hill.

Huang, Y. H. (2000). The personal influence model and *gao guanxi* in Taiwan Chinese public relations. *Public Relations Review, 26,* 216–239.

Jones, B. L., & Chase, H. W. (1979). Managing public policy issues. *Public Relations Review, 2,* 3–23.

Kent, M. L., & Taylor, M. (2007). Beyond excellence: Extending the generic approach to international public relations: The case of Bosnia. *Public Relations Review, 33*(1), 10–20.

Kim, H. S. (2003). Exploring global public relations in a Korean multinational organization in the context of Confucian culture. *Asian Journal of Communication, 13*(2), 65–95.

Kim, J.-N., & Sriramesh, K. (2009). A descriptive model of activism in global public relations research and practice. In K. Sriramesh & D. Verčič (Eds.), *The global public relations handbook* (Rev. ed., pp. 79–97). New York: Routledge.

Lim, S., Goh, J., & Sriramesh, K. (2005). Applicability of the generic principles of excellent public relations in a different cultural context: The case study of Singapore. *Journal of Public Relations Research, 17*(4), 315–340.

Martin, L. J., & Chaudhary, A. G. (1983). *Comparative mass media systems.* White Plains, NY: Longman.

Merrill, J. C., & Lowenstein, R. L. (1971). *Media, messages, and men.* New York: Longman.

Ndlovu, S. M. (2010). Sports as cultural diplomacy: The 2010 FIFA World Cup in South Africa's foreign policy. *Soccer & Society, 11*(1), 144–153.

Nye, J. S. (2004). *Soft power: The means to success in world politics.* New York: Public Affairs.

Pimlott, J. A. (1951). *Public relations and American democracy.* Princeton, NJ: Princeton University Press.

Public Relations Society of America. (1999). *Public relations education for the 21st century: A port of entry.* New York: Author.

Rhee, Y. (1999). *Confucian culture and excellent public relations: A study of generic principles and specific applications in South Korean public relations practice.* Unpublished master's thesis submitted to the University of Maryland at College Park, MD.

Sallot, L. M., & Johnson, E. A. (2006). Investigating relationships between journalists and public relations practitioners: Working together to set, frame and build the public agenda, 1991–2004. *Public Relations Review, 32*(2), 51–59.

Schneider, C. P. (2010). The unrealized potential of cultural diplomacy: "Best practices" and what could be, if only . . . *Journal of Arts Management, Law & Society, 39*(4), 260–279.

Siebert, F. S., Peterson, T., & Schramm, W. (1956). *Four theories of the press.* Urbana: University of Illinois Press.

Sriramesh, K. (2002). The dire need for multiculturalism in public relations education: An Asian perspective. *Journal of Communication Management, 7*(1), 54–77.

Sriramesh, K. (2003). The mass media and public relations: A conceptual framework for effective media relations in Asia. *Asian Journal of Communication, 16*(3).

Sriramesh, K. (2004). *Public relations in Asia: An anthology.* Singapore: Thomson Learning.

Sriramesh, K. (2009a). Introduction. In K. Sriramesh & D. Verčič (Eds.), *The global public relations handbook* (Rev. ed., pp. xxxiii–xl). New York: Routledge.

Sriramesh, K. (2009b). The relationship between culture and public relations. In K. Sriramesh & D. Verčič (Eds.), *The global public relations handbook* (Rev. ed., pp. 47–61). New York: Routledge.

Sriramesh, K., & Duhe, S. (2009). Political economy and public relations: A blueprint for future research. *Public Relations Review, 35,* 368–375.

Sriramesh, K., & Enxi, L. (2004). Public relations practices and socio-economic factors: A case study of different organizational types in Shanghai. *Journal of Communication Studies, 3*(4), 44–76.

Sriramesh, K., & Rivera, M. (2006). Corporatism and communitarianism as environments for e-governance: The case of Singapore. *New Media & Society, 8*(5), 707–730.

Sriramesh, K., & Rivera, M. (2010, March). *Online public relations: Organizational Web sites and stakeholder relations.* Paper presented at the 13th International Public Relations Research Conference, Miami, FL.

Sriramesh, K., Saminathan, M., & Lim, D. (2007). The situational theory of publics in a different cultural setting: Consumer publics in Singapore. *Journal of Public Relations Research, 19*(4), 307–332.

Sriramesh, K., & Takasaki, M. (2000). The impact of culture on Japanese public relations. *Journal of Communication Management, 3*(4), 337–352.

Sriramesh, K., & Verčič, D. (2003). *The global public relations handbook: Theory, research, and practice.* Mahwah, NJ: Lawrence Erlbaum.

Sriramesh, K., & Verčič, D. (2004). The innovativeness-needs paradox and global public relations: Some propositions on the need for international public relations subsidies. *Media Asia, 31*(1), 3–13.

Sriramesh, K., & Verčič, D. (Eds.). (2009a). *The global public relations handbook: Theory, research, and practice.* New York: Routledge.

Sriramesh, K., & Verčič, D. (2009b). Mass media and public relations. In K. Sriramesh & D. Verčič (Eds.), *The global public relations handbook* (Rev. ed., pp. 62–78). New York: Routledge.

Turdubayeva, E., & Sriramesh, K. (2010, March 11). *Application of the generic principles in a different cultural setting: The case of Kyrgyzstan.* Paper presented at the 13th International Public Relations Conference, Miami, FL.

United Nations. (2002). *Annual review of developments in globalization and regional integration in the countries of the ESCWA region.* New York: Author.

Verčič, D., Grunig, L. A., & Grunig, J. E. (1996). Global and specific principles of public relations: Evidence from Slovenia. In H. Culbertson & N. Chen (Eds.), *International public relations: A comparative analysis* (pp. 31–66). Mahwah, NJ: Lawrence Erlbaum.

Yoon, Y. (2005). A scale for measuring media relations efforts. *Public Relations Review, 31,* 434–436.

Reflections and Concluding Thoughts

Robert L. Heath

From whence did we come and where are we going? In 1978, I first taught graduate courses in public relations; there was precious little literature to draw on. Having developed an interest in activist rhetoric, I began to explore public relations (and eventually issues management) as a response. In addition to examining other forms of public discourse, I thought blithely, let's examine public relations. Reading lists were pretty short and more often than not drawn from related areas of interest.

Public Relations Review was in its infancy. We had several texts. There were writings of icons like Edward L. Bernays and John W. Hill, but those were rarely if ever used in classrooms. We might adopt a text, but then we would be using for graduate courses the same ones that were popular at the undergraduate level. We might use *Public Relations Quarterly*, professional proprietary newsletter and reports, and *Public Relations Journal.* Today, in contrast, students at all levels of the discipline enjoy (or are frustrated by) several journals, tons of books, institute studies, and much more. What a variety of commodities, and even a feast, we have as we unload and ponder the contents of those "railroad cars."

The work shared in a volume such as this constitutes a festschrift–not to one honoree as such but to the academic aspects of a profession that in many ways is still in its infancy as a modern/postmodern practice shaped by theory and research. It is still derivative. It is still searching for its center. But it is searching. And the range of authors and disciplines being explored for implications increases rather than decreases. In this effort, some argue that we are attempting to consume and digest too much. Others say we continue to be too narrow.

This reflection leads to comments by Elizabeth Toth, one of the stalwarts of the field. Apart from working her own agenda of research, she has devoted many hours to editing works like this one that bring many voices together.

Reflections on the Field

Elizabeth L. Toth

In 2001, the first *Handbook of Public Relations*, edited by Heath, created a landmark compendium of definitional benchmarks, discussions of public relations practice issues, descriptions of best practices, and early introductory discussions of communication technologies and globalizing public relations as the new frontiers for scholarly consideration. This second *Handbook* promises to show how public relations scholarship is becoming even broader in scope, with an emphasis on evolving theoretical foundations and societal rationale. Some researchers have updated their previous 2001 chapters on public relations theory and research, marketing communication, crisis communication, discourse, publics, ethics, and globalization. New authors introduce topics such as risk communication, challenges of diversity, public participation, investor relations, and social media.

This closing chapter reflects on public relations as a field of academic endeavor or discipline and considers what is meant by a public relations discipline. Rather than assuming that the concept of a discipline has an agreed-on meaning, first, it provides a definition of a public relations discipline and implications for those of us who have chosen to be associated with it. Second, it considers various definitions of public relations and the few commonalities to be found in our discipline. Third, the numerous kinds of articles included in this volume suggest that we are still working in many different areas with differing assumptions and methodologies and thus are at home with no discipline. Previously, I have suggested at least three principle clusters of scholarship; but on reflection, I believe that we have many others that need naming, building, and supporting within our disciplinary focus.

What Is the Public Relations Discipline?

As an academic discipline, public relations is made up of university educators and scholars who read public relations texts and academic journals and belong to public relations interest groups in recognized academic organizations. This definition implies a loose confederation of academics who choose to belong to a group but don't necessarily subscribe to the same theoretical interests around the phenomena of public relations. This confederation includes scholars who have training in different theoretical areas, such as journalism and mass communication, communication studies, marketing, and business. These scholars might favor humanistic methodologies or social science quantitative or qualitative research methodologies. They may publish their work for a public relations academic audience or cross academic disciplines to publish in areas such as history, law, ethics, and mass communication. Some cross-disciplinary authors are encouraged by their academic units to place their work outside the public relations discipline. Fortunately, this loose confederation of academics continues to hold a strong clear focus on public relations.

To be a part of the public relations discipline suggests also that one teaches, but not necessarily, in the area of public relations, generally defined as "the management of communication between an organization and its publics" (J. E. Grunig & Hunt, 1984, p. 6), although there are many more definitions of public relations—with emphases on differing concepts and purpose statements. Heath and Coombs (2006) defined public relations with an emphasis on the programmatic activities of research, planning, and communication and with a purpose of building mutually beneficial relationships:

> The management function that entails planning, research, publicity, promotion, and collaborative decision making to help any organization's ability to listen to, appreciate, and respond appropriately to those persons or groups whose mutually beneficial relationships the organization needs to foster as it strives to achieve its mission and vision. (p. 7)

Another definition of public relations eliminates the concept of public relations as a professional activity, as in the case of Dozier and Lauzen (2000), who argued that public relations as an intellectual domain is "the study of action, communication, and relationships between organizations and publics, as well as the study of the intended and unintended consequences of those relationships for individuals and society as a whole" (p. 4). The public relations discipline then is a community of academic scholars and educators who share interests in the communication processes of organizations and groups that seek out purposeful relationships with one another.

The growth of public relations research and publication in the past 10 years is without question a major strength of the public relations academic discipline. It is not possible to discount the membership sizes of the public relations divisions of the Association for Education in Journalism and Mass Communication, the International Communication Association, the Public Relations Society of America's Educators Academy, and the National Communication Association. Each of these groups has at least 300 members. Informal assessments suggest, with the possible exception of the Educators Academy, that the public relations divisions of these national organizations are receiving easily more than 100 submissions for conference paper slots on an annual basis. The *Journal of Public Relations Research*, which received a mere 37 submissions per year during my editorship, between 1995 and 2000, is now receiving annually more than 150 submissions, according to the current editor Karen Russell (personal communication, December 23, 2009). Botan and Hazleton (2006) reported that public relations undergraduate enrollments "have skyrocketed" across the United States (p. 2); a first report on international undergraduate programs suggests that public relations is offered as a university degree all over the world (Toth, 2009b). Because the public relations industry continues generally to have jobs, students increasingly are drawn to public relations as an undergraduate course of study.

However, the growth of the public relations discipline has not necessarily meant that public relations theory and research are welcomed in any discipline's body of theory or knowledge, such as the communication discipline. Botan and Hazleton (2006) reported encouraging signs of public relations research being accepted in communication journals such as *Journalism and Mass Communication Quarterly*, *Journal of Applied Communication Research*, or the *Journal of*

Communication, "although," they wrote, "it is wise to check the policy of individual editors and the composition of editorial boards before submitting to non-PR journals" (p. 5). Informally, my colleagues and I have seen submissions returned by editors who believe that their communication journals "don't include public relations research."

An exception in the *Journal of Communication* was Botan and Taylor's (2004) invited "state of the field" piece in which they argued that public relations was a "subfield of communication with its own research and theory base as well as a professional practice" (p. 645). After reviewing a chronology of bibliometric studies of public relations research, beginning in 1987 with Pavlik's *What Research Tells Us* to the 2003 Sallot, Lyon, Acosta-Alzuru, and Jones analysis of public relations theory development, Botan and Taylor (2004) argued for a cocreationist perspective of meaning, interpretation, and goal collaboration that will even "situate public relations theory as a foundational member of the field of communication" (p. 659). To reinforce their position, they suggested that public relations issues management theory can contribute to other applied communication research areas such as health, risk, crisis, and political communication research (p. 654).

However, the public relations discipline has yet to be so embraced by the communication field. Phau (2008), writing about epistemological and disciplinary interactions, argued against communication disciplinary fragmentation and isolated "frog ponds" (p. 598). In those, he included public relations as a peripheral scholarship, which admittedly he engaged in but did not believe to be as valuable as the functional issues of the communication field, addressing questions about communication processes or end states: "I am engaged in peripheral scholarship when I address issues about political advertising, media uses in political campaigns, or public relations tactics" (p. 600). Phau's claim is that communication as an academic discipline should get at functional questions: "Functional issues are at the core of the study of communication" (p. 600).

One subdiscipline of communication that might be the most welcoming to public relations research is that of organizational communication. Partnerships are evident from the first *Handbook*'s chapters by organizational communication scholars Cheney and Christensen (2001), who rendered a second opinion about public relations, calling it a "contested disciplinary and interdisciplinary terrain" (p. 167). Everett (2001) contributed a chapter on public relations and the ecology of organizational change.

Public relations researchers have also not found publication traction in the management disciplines and organizational theory literature. Almost as neglected is the lack of management and business literature referenced in public relations research. A handful of public relations disciplinary efforts informing us of management literatures include The Excellence Study, drawing on its definition of organizational effectiveness from Robbins's (1990) landmark organizational theory text. The Excellence researchers adopted Robbins's four-part definition, identifying strategic constituencies and organizational values as critical to organizational effectiveness in achieving organizational goals, as were systems theory and management by objectives (J. E. Grunig & Grunig, 2000, p. 306).

Gower (2006) reminded us of the need to become up-to-date with a management literature that has embraced postmodernism, "leading to an evolution in thinking and strategy which we have failed to keep up with" (p. 185). Gower suggested the work of McKie (2001), who urged us to update public relations with "new science." Gower suggested also the work of Murphy (1996, 2000), who provides a postmodern view of complex organizations with their "characteristics of adaptivity, nonlinearity, coevolution, punctuated equilibria, and self-organization" (p. 185). Caywood (1997) and Hallahan (2007) have provided models and concepts from the business literature's work on integrated communication. Finally, the Arthur W. Page Society has provided white papers copublished with the Business Roundtable (Arthur W. Page Society, 2009) and venues to hear the faculty of business schools who publish in management journals about corporate communication, like Argenti (2006), Argenti, Howell, and Beck (2005), and Balmer and Greyser (2002).

Because the public relations discipline is only sometimes in the communication discipline and is less likely to be found in the management discipline, public relations is generally on its own in building a body of knowledge. Those who argue that public relations scholars are too insular (Broom, 2006; McKie, 2001), perhaps, have felt the need to create a disciplinary identity that will be included or recognized by more established disciplines. A clearer identity may lead us to accepting different disciplinary scholarship in our theory building.

Within the public relations discipline are found clusters of researchers who focus on specific concepts and methodologies to build knowledge. These clusters might be referred to as paradigms, although Botan and Hazleton (2006) considered the works of clusters of public relations scholars to be a disciplinary matrix, "defined by the practices and beliefs of a group of scholars who cooperate in the work of normal science within a paradigm" (p. 8). Botan and Hazleton (2006) claimed that the public relations discipline has only one dominating disciplinary matrix, the symmetrical excellence theory (pp. 8–9). This set of theoretical benchmarks represents successful public relations practice, including a two-way symmetrical communication, "that attempts to balance the interests of the organization and its publics, based on research and use of communication to management conflict with strategic publics" (J. E. Grunig, Grunig, & Dozier, 2006, p. 47).

Botan and Hazleton (2006) identified other alternative paradigms, such as a rhetorical based approach and the critically based approach (p. 11), as I have. However, Botan and Hazleton continue to describe the public relations discipline as one in a "struggle" between paradigms and to "celebrate the emergence of challenges to the dominant paradigm of the field" (p. 11).

I have previously taken the position that we need all paradigms because each one has different conceptual foci and contributes different knowledge to the understanding of public relations (Toth, 1992). I identified the rhetorical, critical, and systems paradigms as a means of comparing and contrasting the contributions of each. In 2009, I (Toth, 2009a) agreed with Botan and Hazleton (2006) that the three major paradigms were the excellence, rhetorical, and critical clusters of research and publication in the public relations discipline.

However, as I consider the breadth and record numbers of journal articles, books, and conference papers and this *Handbook*'s table of contents, my three-paradigm view looks overly simplistic. If a paradigm is defined as "a set of unquestioned presuppositions that provide an intellectual framework" (Botan & Hazleton, 2006, p. 8) or a disciplinary matrix is "defined by the practices and beliefs of groups of scholars who cooperate in the work of normal science within a paradigm" (Botan & Hazleton, 2006, p. 8), instead of three paradigms, there are many more operating in the public relations discipline. I can identify at least six, and I'm sure there are more to be seen in our public relations literature. In alphabetical order, so as not to suggest any hierarchy of paradigms, they are crisis communication, critical theory, feminist theory, rhetorical theory, strategic management theory, and tactical communication theories, including campaigns. Phrased another way by J. E. Grunig (2006), who called his general theory of the role of public relations in strategic management an edifice, "there are several edifices or structures being built to explain public relations. All can be useful for solving the same or different problems of public relations" (p. 152).

Crisis Communication Paradigm

At the 2008 National Communication Association conference, there were so many papers on crisis communication presented that the Public Relations Division members thought of renaming themselves the crisis communication division. *Public Relations Review* published six articles on crisis communication in its October 2002 issue. The *Journal of Public Relations Research* published a 2009 special issue on crisis communication, and *Public Relations Review*'s March 2009 issue had six articles on crisis communication. Coombs (2009) defined a crisis as "an event that threatens important stakeholder expectations about an organization and can significantly affect an organization's performance" (p. 238). Crisis communication, according to Coombs, is "actually a very broad concept encompassing any step in the crisis management process" (p. 238). Coombs also detailed several scholars' works in the crisis communication paradigm around corporate apologia (Hearit, 2006) and image restoration (Benoit, 1995), considered postcrisis response strategies on the part of organizations. The rhetoric of renewal after a crisis focused on more positive than defensive strategies (Ulmer, Sellnow, & Seeger, 2006). Coombs has worked for several years on crisis communication research, combining rhetorical and attribution theory to develop a method, called the situational crisis communication theory, for evaluating the reputational threat of a crisis and selecting the appropriate crisis response strategies (Coombs, 2006). Seeger (2002) addressed concepts of chaos theory as a general framework for describing organizational crisis and crisis communication.

Critical Theory Paradigm

The public relations scholars working within the critical theory paradigm are joined together by their questioning of the traditional search for theory, particularly through social science research methods. Critical theorists have sought to expose the ideologies buried within theory building. Dozier and Lauzen (2000) recommended critical theory to liberate the intellectual domain from the practice of public relations as a means of opening up different research questions, raising concerns, and employing different methodological approaches (p. 16). Critical theorists of public relations theory building have a worldview of organizations bent on dominating the less powerful, such as powerless publics or groups with irreconcilable differences. Finally, critical theorists reject any obligations to the practice of public relations or to build a fully functioning society but seek to disrupt beliefs and values.

Pal and Dutta (2008) described three variants of critical theory: critical theory, current postmodern, and critical modernism. Using Mumby's (1997) definition, Pal and Dutta stated that "critical theory emphasizes the social structures, political processes, economic interests and ideologies through which knowledge is articulated and practiced" (p. 160). For example, Motion and Weaver (2005) argued that "public relations practice uses particular political economy and discursive strategies to advance the hegemonic power of particular groups" (p. 50). They apply their perspective to the analysis of the Life Science Network campaign actors and texts, challenging public relations researchers to place "the issues of power and truth at the center of their inquiry in order to more fully understand the role of public relations in democratic decision-making processes" (p. 66). Pompper (2005) introduced critical race theory to public relations to expose and challenge the social nature of the social construction of race as it has appeared in public relations journals.

Postmodernism, according to Stroh (2007), "is considered a response to the failure or natural consequence of the shortcomings of modernism" (p. 204). Although there is not one postmodernism, it has a unifying focus of challenging rationalities and beliefs and values "held sacred" by societies and their organizations. The five characteristics of postmodernism include "an emphasis on individual realities rather than one; an ethically responsible society; accommodation of many diverse ideas and perspectives, including modernism; resistance to positivism; and a philosophy of the immediate rather than seeking the ideal state of society" (Holtzhausen, 2000, p. 96). An example of postmodernist work is the circuit of culture model presented by Curtin and Gaither (2005). This model positions public relations practitioners as "agents operating mainly within the sites of production and consumption to create meaning through the shaping and transfer of information" (p. 107). Boyd and VanSlette (2009) used the postmodern lens to make the case for how illegal activities and even Osama bin Laden's grainy videos belong within the public relations domain.

Pal and Dutta (2008) defined critical modernism as "aligning itself with postmodernism by approaching knowledge as socially constructed in the realms of social, economic, and political contexts and simultaneously takes up a critical stance by interrogating the deep-seated structures underlying the communication practices in a global context" (p. 160). They use this lens to consider issues of power, ideology, and hegemony as they play out in globalized theories of public relations.

Feminist Paradigm

Public relations practitioners are for the most part female. Numerous studies of public relations practitioners since 1995 have indicated that the percentage of women in public relations is between 60% and 70%, depending on the categories and samples that are reported (L. A. Grunig & Toth, 2006, p. 41). Toth, Aldoory, and Sha (2006) provided trend data on membership by gender of the Public Relations Society of America (PRSA), the largest professional association in the United States. In 1995, 63.5% of their randomly selected sample was female; in 2006, this percentage had risen to 75% (p. 22). Although the U.S. Bureau of Labor Statistics has dropped at times and changed public relations category labels, it is telling that in 2008, 60.3% of the public relations manager category was composed of women, 62.1% of the advertising and promotions managers were women, and 61.6% of the public relations specialists were women (Bureau of Labor Statistics, 2009). Most public relations educators would report that their classrooms are primarily made up of women. Although different studies report different percentages, it is no longer in dispute that the field of public relations is composed of a female majority.

The cluster of public relations scholars interested in the focal issue of whether the preponderance of women has influenced the practice of public relations have examined this issue from feminist perspectives. Like the many definitions of public relations, there are many definitions of feminism. A common understanding among these definitions, though, is the stance that both men and women are assigned gendered attributes by society. The organizations within society use these specific attributes to make decisions about hiring, promotion, assigning job roles, and setting workplace conditions. Applicable to public relations studies is Liao's (2006) definition of feminism: "Feminism grows out of social and political movements aiming to bring justice into society so the marginalized can choose their positions instead of being pushed into positions where they are" (p. 106). Feminist thought considers injustices to diverse groups, including men and women and racial and ethnic groups.

Contributors to building feminist theories of public relations have contested notions that women earn lower salaries because they have chosen lower paying jobs and it's merely a matter of time before women's salaries catch up with those of their male counterparts (Toth, 2001). Dozier, Sha, and Okura (2007) found gender differences in income, career interruption, and childbearing. Aldoory, Jiang, Toth, & Sha (2008) have exposed the organizational social structures that cause female and male public relations professionals to make disproportionate career sacrifices. Aldoory (2005) has urged scholars to consider how discourses themselves, made by public relations practitioners, reinforce gendered stereotypes.

Rhetorical Paradigm

The rhetorical paradigm considers "all of what each organization—as well as all of what each market, audience, and public—does and says—because of what meanings and interpretations people place on those actions and statements" (Heath, 2001, p. 32). Scholars working in the rhetorical paradigm consider the meanings—statements and counterstatements—to create decisions, organizations, and whole social movements. Scholars working in this paradigm have established knowledge about the rightness and wrongness of organizations "and publics" communication efforts. Rhetorical analysis of public relations messages—discourses—focuses on how points of dispute or rhetorical problems are resolved through strategic choices of arguments, ethics, and emotion (i.e., by logos, ethos, and pathos). Rhetorical analyses of public relations emphasize concepts such as social responsibility with a view of providing enlightened choices for publics. Using humanistic methods, rhetorical scholars examine the "marketplace of public relations ideas" in terms of ethics, character, zones of meaning, and the paradox of the positive. Authors have brought our attention to meanings of hypocrisy (Christensen & Langer, 2009), legitimacy (Boyd, 2009), and front groups' secret persuasion tactics (Palenchar & Fitzpatrick, 2009).

The two rhetorical theories proposed to advance understanding public relations are Heath's (2006) fully functioning society theory and Botan and Tayor's (2004) cocreational perspective. Heath (2006) argued that we need to be investigating whether and how public relations can add value to society (p. 95). He presented eight premises for public relations' contribution to a fully functioning society, resting on systems, rhetoric, and norms compliance to build relationships. His premises are as follows: (1) management of organizations must demonstrate the characteristics that foster legitimacy; (2) organizational legitimacy is based on sound principles of corporate responsibility; (3) management must be able to assess whether power is used for only narrow interests or the larger interests of society; (4) self-interests are an irrefutable part of the human experience; (5) relationships are symmetrical when they reflect the good of the whole community; (6) society is a complex of collectives engaged in variously constructive dialogues; (7) public discourses must make available evidence, facts, identifications, and policy choices; and (8) in addition to advocacy, rhetors may lead us to enlightened choices through shared narratives and identifications.

The cocreationist perspective sees "publics as co-creators of meaning and communication" (Botan & Taylor, 2004, p. 652) with organizations. "The major relationship of interest is between groups and organizations, and communication functions to negotiate changes in these relationships" (Botan & Taylor, 2004, p. 652). Botan and Taylor (2004) posited that this perspective places value on long-term relationships beyond achieving organizational goals, including organization-public relationships, community theory, coorientation theory, accommodation theory, dialogue theory, and symmetrical/excellence theory as examples of cocreationist research. This perspective suggests that relationships evolve and are shaped through socially constructed meanings agreed on by both parties. The focal interest in the cocreationist perspective is the discourses themselves.

Strategic Management Paradigm

J. E. Grunig (2006), primarily identified with the symmetric/excellence paradigm, has begun to address his work as a strategic management theory "that explains how the public relations function should be structured and managed to provide the greatest value to organizations, publics, and society" (p. 152). He described the strategic management paradigm as

> one that views public relations as a participant in organizational decision-making . . . a research based mechanism for organizational listening and learning. Its purpose is to help all management functions, including but not limited to marketing, to build relationships with their stakeholders through communication programmes that cultivate relationships with the publics that can be found within categories of stakeholders that are relevant to each management function. (J.E. Grunig, 2009, p. 4)

According to Sha (2007), "On the strategy side, four public relations dimensions reflect organizational approaches to problem-solving or organizational worldviews about the management of relationships with stakeholders" (p. 7): two-way communication, symmetrical communication, ethical communication, and conserving communication. J. E. Grunig (2006) identified focal concepts of "organizational decision-making processes, environmental scanning and publics, scenario building, empowerment of public relations, ethics, relationships, return on investment (ROI), evaluation, relationship cultivation strategies, and global strategy" (p. 151).

Contingency theory is a strategic management theory of public relations. Originally a matrix of 87 factors arranged on a continuum from accommodation to advocacy (Pang, Jin, & Cameron, 2007), contingency theory sought to describe how public relations practitioners made strategic choices to solve organizational communication problems. Contingency theory's focus described how public relations is practiced, how strategic choices are made, and what factors influence those choices. Contingency researchers have found that these predisposing factors influence a public relations strategic stance: the size of the organization, corporate culture, business exposure, public relations to dominant coalition, dominant coalition enlightenment, and characteristics of key individuals, such as the chief executive officer (CEO; Pang et al., 2007, p. 10). Situational factors influencing stance included urgency of the situation, characteristics of the other public, potential or obvious threats, and potential costs or benefits (Pang et al., 2007, p. 10). Contingency authors also identified proscriptive variables when accommodation was not possible at all. Over time, contingency theory's several factors have been collapsed into five thematic variables: external threats, external public characteristics, organizational characteristics, public relations department characteristics, and dominant coalition characteristics (Pang et al., 2007, p. 13). Contingency theory has been tested further to explain conflict and practice in an intra-organizational setting (Pang et al., 2007, p. 16), in the dynamism of stance movements where both advocacy and accommodation could be used at the same time (Pang et al., 2007, p. 17), and as applied to crisis communication, threat appraisal, and conflict positioning (Pang et al., 2007, p. 18).

Tactical Paradigm

The presence of a tactical paradigm, of clusters of researchers focused on "the concrete ways in which organizations might execute or support their strategies" (Sha, 2007, p. 9), has not resonated in articles about paradigms in public relations previously. Carroll, Lee, and Huang (2009) speculated that tactics are not well conceptualized because of a "managerial bias in our research" (p. 421). Sha (2007) proposed a tactical dimension to the understanding of public relations in her review of the four dimensions of public relations proposed by J. E. Grunig (2001) in the first *Handbook of Public Relations.* J. E. Grunig's dimensions were described as four continua: (1) one-way/two-way, (2) symmetrical/asymmetrical, (3) interpersonal/mediated, and (4) ethical/unethical (pp. 28–30). Sha (2007) has categorized the mediated/interpersonal dimension as "tactical, or the ways in which public relations strategies might be executed" (p. 9). Furthermore, based on her analysis and others, she separated mediated communication and interpersonal communication as independent measures of tactics and added a third measure called "social activities."

Sha's (2007) categorization of "tactics" helps describe more precisely the works of several scholars of media relations, media choices, and social media as tools. For example, Hallahan (2001) provided a much needed tactical scheme for media choices, from mass communication to interpersonal communication, providing comparisons of public media, interactive media, controlled media, events/group communication, and one-on-one communication.

Eyrich, Padman, and Sweetser (2008) provided the baseline data on public relations practitioners' adoption of online tools, such as blogs, intranets, podcasts, video sharing, photo sharing, social networks, wikis, gaming, virtual worlds, micro-blogging/presence applications, text messaging, videoconferences, personal digital assistants (PDAs), instant message, chat, social event/calendar systems, social bookmarking, news aggregation, and e-mail. Kelleher's (2009) observation of the "Internet as a potential tool for dialogue and two-way communication" (p. 172) locates his work in the tactical paradigm. His study examined the perceptions of conversational voice by people who had interacted with an organization through organizational blogs. He found that his study participants who reported the greatest exposure to the blogs in the study were more likely to perceive the organization as communicating with conversational voice and that conversational voice was correlated positively with relational outcomes (p. 172).

A grouping of articles on campaigns to be included in a tactical disciplinary matrix are works on political campaigns and public interest campaigns. Kiousis, Mitrook, Wu, and Seltzer (2006) used agenda-setting and agenda-building theory to look for linkages among candidate news releases, media coverage, and public opinion during the 2002 Florida gubernatorial election. Kiousis and Shields (2008) examined news releases, political speeches, and issue platform statements, continuing to examine the salience of issues and attributes in the 2004 presidential election, and identified intercandidate agenda-setting associations. Anderson (2009) reports on the efficacy of public service announcements for designing campaigns to prevent drunken driving.

Are There Commonalities?

Despite Dozier and Lauzen's (2000) provocative piece arguing to separate the intellectual domain of public relations from the practice, generally public relations disciplinary authors agree on public relations as an academic course of study and as a practice. Broom (2006) posited that "we owe the profession and the academy our best efforts to build theory that advances both the practice and our understanding of how it functions" (p. 142).

The general trend begun around 2000 has been to consider relationships as a focal concept for the discipline. Early on, Heath wrote in his 2001 *Handbook* preface that the discipline of public relations was shifting from a "revenue-generating paradigm" with its implications for examining public relations as the strategic communication function to achieve organizational goals to a "relationship development rationale" (Heath, 2001, p. 2). Heath (2001) summarized the definitions of public relations included in the first *Handbook* by stating that the position of authors like J. E. Grunig, Heath, Starck, and Kruckeberg; McKie, Leeper, Coombs, Vasquez, and Taylor; and Seger, Sellnow, and Ulmer suggest that public relations as an academic domain has shifted away from the organization's efforts to persuade others to a worldview of relationship construction and cultivation: "The underlying assumption is that public relations is a relationship-building professional activity that adds value to organizations because it increases the willingness of markets, audiences, and publics to support them rather than to oppose their efforts" (Heath, 2001, p. 8). Ten years later, although there are exceptions, the relationship worldview of public relations seems firmly established in scholarship, if not in practice.

The Future of the Field

Projections are not my forte. For most of my academic career, I have seen others attempt to project where the academic discipline of public relations is headed. Some have even predicted the loss of the term *public relations* for other concepts such as strategic communication, communication management, integrated communication, or organizational communication. Although public relations practitioners are similarly conflicted about the use of the term, it is still with us. We have yet to establish a distinct body of knowledge that is recognized and accepted by other disciplines. Our own disciplinary efforts, pulling ourselves up by our own bootstraps, have been attacked as too insular, as if quoting one another somehow weakens our disciplinary efforts. Some call on us to look to other research disciplines, either to improve our efforts to contribute to solving the problems of the public relations practice or to jar us loose from "functional thinking." Calling our academic discipline a "struggle" of paradigms against one another seems counterproductive. Our academic interests will be enhanced and refreshed as we look to the evolution of public relations itself.

The field of public relations has continued to evolve from its early-20th-century roots to today's interests in its role in democratic society and even to the global stage. I would not like to lose the practice connection, although I understand that this may be part of the evolution of educating scholars of the discipline who have not practiced public relations themselves. They are being trained in doctoral programs to build our public relations knowledge first and to forgo the public relations practice experience that universities required in the past. Our newer scholars are quite likely to pursue different research questions and perhaps with more objectivity than those who became academics after changing from long practitioner careers to academic ones. I like their energy and bet that their passion is a match for their advisers and the pathfinders of our field.

References

Aldoory, L. (2005). A (re)conceived feminist paradigm for public relations: A case for substantial improvement. *Journal of Communication, 55,* 668–684.

Aldoory, L., Jiang, H., Toth, E. L., & Sha, B.-L. (2008). Is it still just a women's issue? A study of work-life balance among men and women in public relations. *Public Relations Journal, 2,* 1–20.

Anderson, R. (2009). Comparison of indirect sources of efficacy information in pretesting messages for campaigns to prevent drunken driving. *Journal of Public Relations Research, 21,* 428–454.

Argenti, P. A. (2006). Communications and business value: Measuring the link. *Journal of Business Strategy, 27,* 29–40.

Argenti, P. A., Howell, R. A., & Beck, K. A. (2005). The strategic communication imperative. *MIT Sloan Management Review, 46,* 83–89.

Arthur W. Page Society & Business Roundtable Institute for Corporate Ethics. (2009). *The dynamics of public trust in business—emerging opportunities for leaders: A call to action to overcome the present crisis of trust in business.* Retrieved March 20, 2010, from www.awpagesociety.com/images/uploads/public trust_in_business.pdf

Balmer, J. M. T., & Greyser, S. (2002). Managing multiple identities in the corporation. *California Management Review, 44,* 72–86.

Benoit, W. L. (1995). *Accounts, excuses, and apologies: A theory of image restoration.* Albany: State University of New York Press.

Botan, C., & Hazleton, V. (2006). Public relations in a new age. In C. Botan & V. Hazleton (Eds.), *Public relations theory II* (pp. 1–18). Mahwah, NJ: Lawrence Erlbaum.

Botan, C., & Taylor, M. (2004). Public relations: State of the field. *Journal of Communication, 4,* 645–661.

Boyd, J. (2009). 756*: The legitimacy of a baseball number. In R. L. Heath, E. L. Toth, & D. Waymer (Eds.), *Rhetorical and critical approaches to public relations II* (pp. 154–169). New York: Routledge.

Boyd, J., & VanSlette, S. H. (2009). Outlaw discourse as postmodern public relations. In R. L. Heath, E. L. Toth, & D. Waymer (Eds.), *Rhetorical and critical approaches to public relations II* (pp. 328–342). New York: Routledge.

Broom, G. M. (2006). An open-system approach to building theory in public relations. *Journal of Public Relations Research, 18,* 141–150.

Bureau of Labor Statistics. (2009). *Labor force statistics from the current population survey.* Retrieved March 20, 2010, from www.bls.gov/cps/wlftable11 .htm

Carroll, C. E., Lee, S. Y., & Huang, N. C. L. (2009). The syntax of "tactic(s)" in public relations research. *Public Relations Review, 35,* 419–421.

Caywood, C. L. (1997). Twenty-first century public relations: The strategic stages of integrated communications. In C. L. Caywood (Ed.), *The handbook of strategic public relations and integrated communications* (pp. xi–xxvi). New York: McGraw-Hill.

Cheney, G., & Christensen, L. T. (2001). Public relations as contested terrain: A critical response. In R. L. Heath (Ed.), *Handbook of public relations* (pp. 167–203). Thousand Oaks, CA: Sage.

Christensen, L., & Langer, R. (2009). Public relations and the strategic use of transparency: Consistency, hypocrisy, and corporate image. In R. L. Heath, E. L. Toth, & D. Waymer (Eds.), *Rhetorical and critical approaches to public relations II* (pp. 129–153). New York: Routledge.

Coombs, T. W. (2006). Crisis management: A communicative approach. In C. H. Botan & V. Hazleton (Eds.), *Public relations theory II* (pp. 171–197). Mahwah, NJ: Lawrence Erlbaum.

Coombs, T. W. (2009). Crisis, crisis communication, reputation, and rhetoric. In R. L. Heath, E. L. Toth, & D. Waymer (Eds.), *Rhetorical and critical approaches to public relations II* (pp. 237–252). New York: Routledge.

Curtin, P. A., & Gaither, T. K. (2005). Privileging identity, difference, and power: The circuit of culture as a basis for public relations theory. *Journal of Public Relations Research, 17,* 91–116.

Dozier, D. M., & Lauzen, M. M. (2000). Liberating the intellectual domain from the practice: Public relations, activism, and the role of the scholar. *Journal of Public Relations Research, 23,* 3–22.

Dozier, D., Sha, B.-L., & Okura, M. (2007). How much does my baby cost? An analysis of gender differences in income, career interruption, and child bearing. *Public Relations Journal, 1,* 1–16.

Everett, J. (2001). Public relations and the ecology of organizational change. In R. L. Heath (Ed.), *Handbook of public relations* (pp. 311–320). Thousand Oaks, CA: Sage.

Eyrich, N., Padman, M. L., & Sweetser, K. D. (2008). PR practitioners' use of social media tools and communication technology. *Public Relations Review, 34,* 412–414.

Gower, K. K. (2006). Public relations research at the crossroads. *Journal of Public Relations Research, 18*(2), 177–190.

Grunig, J. E. (2001). Two-way symmetrical public relations: Past, present, and future. In R. L. Heath (Ed.), *Handbook of public relations* (pp. 11–30). Thousand Oaks, CA: Sage.

Grunig, J. E. (2006). Furnishing the edifice: Ongoing research on public relations as a strategic management function. *Journal of Public Relations Research, 18*(2), 151–176.

Grunig, J. E. (2009). Paradigms of global public relations in an age of digitalization. PRism 6(2): http://praxis.massey.ac.nz/prism_on_line_journ.html

Grunig, J. E., & Grunig, L. A. (2000). Public relations in strategic management and strategic management in public relations. *Journalism Studies, 1,* 303–321.

Grunig, J. E., Grunig, L. A., & Dozier, D. M. (2006). The excellence theory. In C. H. Botan & V. Hazleton (Eds.), *Public relations theory II* (pp. 21–63). Mahwah, NJ: Lawrence Erlbaum.

Grunig, J. E., & Hunt, T. (1984). *Managing public relations.* New York: Holt, Rinehart & Winston.

Grunig, L. A., & Toth, E. L. (2006). The ethics of communicating with and about difference in a changing society. In K. Fitzpatrick & C. Bronstein (Eds.), *Ethics in public relations: Responsible advocacy* (pp. 39–52). Thousand Oaks, CA: Sage.

Hallahan, K. (2001). Strategic media planning: Toward an integrated public relations model. In R. L. Heath (Ed.), *Handbook of public relations* (pp. 461–470). Thousand Oaks, CA: Sage.

Hallahan, K. (2007). Integrated communication: Implications for public relations beyond excellence. In E. L. Toth (Ed.), *The future of excellence in public relations and communication management: Challenges for the next generation* (pp. 299–336). Mahwah, NJ: Lawrence Erlbaum.

Hearit, K. M. (2006). *Crisis management by apology: Corporate response to allegations of wrongdoing.* Mahwah, NJ: Lawrence Erlbaum.

Heath, R. L. (2001). Shifting foundations: Public relations as relationship building. In R. L. Heath (Ed.), *Handbook of public relations* (pp. 1–9). Thousand Oaks, CA: Sage.

Heath, R. L. (2006). Onward into more fog: Thoughts on public relations research directions. *Journal of Public Relations Research, 18,* 93–114.

Heath, R. L., & Coombs, W. T. (2006). *Today's public relations: An introduction.* Thousand Oaks, CA: Sage.

Holtzhausen, D. R. (2000). Postmodern values in public relations. *Journal of Public Relations Research, 12,* 93–114.

Kelleher, T. (2009). Conversational voice, communicated commitment, and public relations outcomes in interactive communication. *Journal of Communication, 59,* 172–188.

Kiousis, S., Mitrook, M., Wu, X., & Seltzer, T. (2006). First- and second-level agenda-building and agenda-setting effects: Exploring and linkages among candidate news releases, media coverage, and public opinion during the 2002 Florida gubernatorial election. *Journal of Public Relations Research, 18,* 265–285.

Kiousis, S., & Shields, A. (2008). Intercandidate agenda-setting in presidential campaigns: Issue and attribute agendas in the 2004 campaign. *Public Relations Review, 24,* 325–330.

Liao, H. A. (2006). Toward an epistemology of participatory communication: A feminist perspective. *Howard Journal of Communication, 17,* 101–118.

McKie, D. (2001). Updating public relations: "New science," research paradigms, and uneven development. In R. L. Heath (Ed.), *Handbook of public relations* (pp. 75–91). Thousand Oaks, CA: Sage.

Motion, J., & Weaver, C. K. (2005). A discourse perspective for critical public relations research: Life sciences network and the battle for truth. *Journal of Public Relations Research, 17,* 49–67.

Mumby, D. K. (1997). Modernism, postmodernism, and communication studies: A rereading of an on-going debate. *Communication Theory, 7,* 1–28.

Murphy, P. (1996). Chaos theory as a model for managing issues and crises. *Public Relations Review, 22,* 95–113.

Murphy, P. (2000). Symmetry, contingency, complexity: Accommodating uncertainty in public relations theory. *Public Relations Review, 26,* 447–462.

Pal, M., & Dutta, M. J. (2008). Public relations in a global context: The relevance of critical modernism as a theoretical lens. *Journal of Public Relations Research, 20,* 159–179.

Palenchar, M., & Fitzpatrick, K. (2009). Secret persuaders: Ethical and rhetorical perspectives on the use of public relations front groups. In R. L. Heath, E. L. Toth, & D. Waymer (Eds.), *Rhetorical and critical approaches to public relations II* (pp. 272–289). New York: Routledge.

Pang, A., Jin, Y., & Cameron, G. (2007, May). *Contingency theory of strategic conflict management: A decade of theory development, discovery, and dialogue.* Paper presented at the International Communication Association Conference, Chicago.

Pavlik, J. (1987). *Public relations: What the research tells us* (The Sage CommText Series, Vol. 16). Newbury Park, CA: Sage.

Phau, M. (2008). Epistemological and disciplinary intersections. *Journal of Communication, 58,* 597–602.

Pompper, D. (2005). "Difference" in public relations research: A case for introducing critical race theory. *Journal of Public Relations Research, 17,* 139–169.

Robbins, S. P. (1990). *Organization theory: Structure, design, and applications* (3rd ed.). Englewood Cliffs, NJ: Prentice Hall.

Sallot, L., Lyon, L., Acosta-Alzuru, C., & Jones, K. (2003). From aardvark to zebra: A new millennium analysis of theory development in public relations academic journals. *Journal of Public Relations Research, 15,* 27–90.

Seeger, M. W. (2002). Chao and crisis: Propositions for a general theory of crisis communication. *Public Relations Review, 28,* 329–337.

Sha, B. L. (2007). Dimensions of public relations: Moving beyond traditional public relations models. In S. C. Duhe (Ed.), *New media and public relations* (pp. 3–26). New York: Peter Lang.

Stroh, U. (2007). An alternative postmodern approach to corporate communication strategy. In E. L. Toth (Ed.), *The future of excellence in public relations and communication management* (pp. 199–220). Mahwah, NJ: Lawrence Erlbaum.

Toth, E. L. (1992). The case for pluralistic studies of public relations: Rhetorical, critical, and systems perspectives. In E. L. Toth & R. L. Heath (Eds.), *Rhetorical and critical approaches to public relations* (pp. 3–15). Hillsdale, NJ: Lawrence Erlbaum.

Toth, E. L. (2001). How feminist theory advanced the practice of public relations. In R. L. Heath (Ed.), *Handbook of public relations* (pp. 237–246). Thousand Oaks, CA: Sage.

Toth, E. L. (2009a). The case for pluralistic studies of public relations: Rhetorical, critical and excellence perspectives. In R. L. Heath, E. L. Toth, & D. Waymer (Eds.), *Rhetorical and critical approaches to public relations II* (pp. 48–61). New York: Routledge.

Toth, E. L. (2009b). Global graduates: Examining PR education around the world. *Public Relations Tactics, October,* 21.

Toth, E. L., Aldoory, L., & Sha, B.-L. (2006, November). *Emerging trends: 24/7 PR mixes work and life.* Report of the committee on work, life and gender issues to the Public Relations Society of America, Salt Lake City, UT.

Ulmer, R. R., Sellnow, T. L., & Seeger, M. W. (2006). *Effective crisis communication: Moving from crisis to opportunity.* Thousand Oaks, CA: Sage.

Author Index

Subject Index

About the Editor

Robert L. Heath is Professor Emeritus, University of Houston. He has published 17 books, including *Handbook of Crisis and Risk Communication* (2009), *Strategic Issues Management* (2009, second edition), *Rhetorical and Critical Approaches to Public Relations II* (2009), *Terrorism: Communication and Rhetorical Perspectives* (2008), *Today's Public Relations* (2006), *Encyclopedia of Public Relations* (2005), *Responding to Crisis: A Rhetorical Approach to Crisis Communication* (2004), and *Handbook of Public Relations* (2001). He recently coedited *Communication and the Media* (2005), Volume 3 of the series *Community Preparedness and Response to Terrorism.* He has contributed hundreds of chapters, articles, and conference papers on issues management, public relations, crisis communication, risk communication, environmental communication, emergency management, rhetorical criticism, and communication theory. He has lectured nationally and internationally in academic settings and for companies, governmental agencies, professional associations, and NGOs (nongovernmental organizations). He has conducted company and community research, held research positions with public relations firms, and developed company and community response plans. He received his PhD from the University of Illinois.

About the Contributors

Günter Bentele is Professor of Public Relations at the University of Leipzig, Germany. He is author, coauthor, editor, and coeditor of about 40 books and more than 200 articles and book chapters in the fields of public relations, communication theory, journalism, and semiotics. He has advanced the field's understanding on topics such as trust and reputation, media relations and intereffication, and corporate media, as well as vocational and ethical challenges of public relations. He has served as the president of the European Public Relations Education and Research Association (EUPRERA) and the president of the German Association of Communication Science (DGPuK). He earned his two PhD degrees from Free University, Berlin.

Bruce K. Berger is Reese Phifer Professor of Advertising & Public Relations in the College of Communication & Information Sciences at the University of Alabama. His research interests include leadership in public relations practice and education, influence and power relations, and employee and organizational communications. He has coauthored a book about power relations in practice and published more than 40 articles and book chapters in academic and professional publications. He is a member of the Arthur W. Page Society and serves on the board of directors of the Plank Center for Leadership in Public Relations and the Institute for Public Relations. Previously, he was vice president of public relations for Whirlpool Corporation and president of the Whirlpool Foundation. He worked in international public relations for 20 years. He received his PhD from the University of Kentucky in 1999.

Pamela G. Bourland-Davis is Chair and Professor of the Department of Communication Arts at Georgia Southern University. She has presented papers and published in the areas of organizational culture, public relations firm-client relations, public relations and media theory pedagogy, internships, health communication, and activism. She has served as Chair of the public relations divisions of the Association for Education in Journalism and Mass Communication and Southern States Communication Association. She earned her PhD from the University of Georgia's Henry Grady College of Journalism and Mass Communication, her MS in journalism from Arkansas State University, and her BS in communication from Georgia Southern.

Shannon A. Bowen is Associate Professor in the S. I. Newhouse School of Public Communications at Syracuse University. She is the author of numerous journal articles and book chapters and is the Joint Editor of *Ethical Space: The International Journal of Communication Ethics.* She won the 2000–2002 International Communication Association's Public Relations Division *Outstanding Dissertation Award.* Her research interests include communication and media ethics, public relations ethics and theory, organizational communication, the strategic management of issues, and the ethical decisions involved in framing theory. She is a Kantian scholar, applying deontological moral philosophy to communication in media, public, and corporate contexts. She was an editorial adviser to the Sage *Encyclopedia of Public Relations* and was principal investigator on the International Association of Business Communicators (IABC) Research Foundation's study of communication ethics, *The Business of Truth: A Guide to Ethical Communication.* She received her PhD in 2000 from the University of Maryland.

F. Erik Brooks is Associate Professor of Political Science and Public Administration at Georgia Southern University. He has written and researched extensively in the areas of civil rights, African American politics, and public administration, authoring most recently *Defining Their Destiny: The Story of the Willow Hill School.* He earned his PhD from the L. Douglas Wilder School of Government at Virginia Commonwealth University. He holds three master's degrees: Counseling and Human Development from Troy State University; Public Administration from Auburn University, Montgomery; and Education from Alabama State University. He earned his BS in journalism and art from Troy State University.

Peggy Simcic Brønn is Associate Professor in the Norwegian School of Management's Department of Communication, Culture and Languages, and associate dean of the school's undergraduate public relations program. Her research interests are corporate branding, corporate social responsibility, and public relations and management perceptions. Her works are published in *European Journal of Marketing, Public Relations Review, Journal of Communication Management* (European editor), *Corporate Reputation Review* (editorial board), *Corporate Communications: An International Journal* (editorial board), *Journal of Business Ethics,* and *Business and Society Review,* among others. She is coeditor of *Corporate Communication: A Strategic Approach to Building Reputation* (second edition) and is coauthor of the first academic book on reputation in Norwegian. She is Norway's academic representative to the Reputation Institute and consults in the private, public, and nonprofit sectors in Norway. She holds a DBA (doctor of business administration) from Henley Management College in the United Kingdom.

Robert E. Brown is Professor of Communications at Salem State College, where he teaches up, down, and across the department's curriculum. He is faculty adviser to the PRSSA chapter and internship coordinator and manager of the department's assessment and program review. He is an editorial board member of the journal *Public Relations Review,* where his articles on public relations (PR) theory, history, and ethics appear. His explorations of the dramaturgy of political campaigns appear in the journal *American Behavioral Scientist.* He lectures on public affairs at Emerson College and teaches PR writing at Harvard University Extension School, where he received the Joanna Fussa prize for Distinguished Teaching in 2004. He has been a speechwriter and consultant. His byline appears occasionally in the *Boston Globe.* He received his PhD from the University of Rochester.

Glen T. Cameron is Gregory Chair in Journalism Research and Professor of Family and Community Medicine at the University of Missouri. He has authored more than 300 articles, chapters, conference papers, and books on public relations and health communication topics. His latest book, *Public Relations Today: Managing Competition and Conflict* (2008), focuses on strategic conflict management across the life cycle of public relations issues. His best-selling book *Public Relations: Strategies and Tactics* is adopted in more than

250 universities in the United States, with translations in Chinese, Spanish, Russian, Hindi, Romanian, Latvian, Serbian, and Greek. His Health Communication Research Center participates in more than $38 million in external funding, from sources such as the NIH, NCI, Missouri Foundation for Health, USDA, CDC, NIDR, the U.S. Department of Defense, and Monsanto. He received his PhD from the University of Texas.

W. Timothy Coombs is Professor in the Department of Communication Studies at University of Central Florida. He is the 2002 recipient of the Jackson, Jackson & Wagner Behavioral Science Prize from the Public Relations Society of America for his crisis research. His research has led to the development and testing of the situational crisis communication theory. He has published widely in the areas of crisis management, including articles in the *Journal of Public Relations Research*, *Public Relations Review*, *Journal of Public Affairs*, *Management Communication Quarterly*, *Journal of Business Communication*, *Journal of Communication Management*, and *Corporate Reputation Review*. His research includes the award-winning book *Ongoing Crisis Communication*. He has coauthored the award-winning books *It's Not Just Public Relations* with Sherry Holladay and *Today's Public Relations* with Robert Heath. He is also coeditor of *The Handbook of Crisis Communication*. He received his PhD in public affairs and issues management from Purdue University.

Jeffrey L. Courtright, Associate Professor of Communication at Illinois State University, studies public relations using rhetorical theory and criticism. His research specialty is the analysis of organizational rhetoric to understand how message design and the campaign messages that result relate to corporate reputation, audience adaptation, and societal and cultural values. He has published articles in *Corporate Reputation Review*, the *International Journal of Strategic Communication*, *Communication Studies*, the *Journal of Mass Media Ethics*, *Public Relations Journal*, and *Public Relations Review*. He also has contributed chapters to several books, including two National Communication Association PRide Award winners, and has presented 75 papers at professional conferences. He and Peter Smudde edited the book *Power and Public Relations*. He is coauthor with Smudde of a new book, *Inspiring Cooperation and Celebrating Organizations: Genres, Message Design, and Strategies in Public Relations*. He received his PhD from Purdue University in 1991.

Nigel M. de Bussy is Associate Professor, Public Relations Course Coordinator in the School of Marketing, Curtin University of Technology, Perth, Western Australia. He is a Fellow and past State President of the Public Relations Institute of Australia. Before joining Curtin, he spent more than a decade in public relations consultancy in the United Kingdom and Australia. His work has been published in *Public Relations Review*, *Journal of Communication Management*, *Journal of Marketing Communications*, and *Asia Pacific Public Relations Journal*, and has been presented at numerous international conferences. His current research interests include stakeholder engagement and the relationship between corporate social responsibility and corporate identity. He holds a PhD from Curtin Business School and an MA from The Queen's College, Oxford.

Marcia W. DiStaso is Assistant Professor in the College of Communications at Pennsylvania State University. Her research agendas focus on financial communication/investor relations and the use of social media in public relations. She is especially interested in research topics that help inform the practice of public relations. She received her PhD from the University of Miami in 2007.

Lee Edwards is Lecturer at Manchester Business School. She is interested in the function of power in and through public relations practice; the interface of public relations with the media and the subsequent effect on the public sphere; and discourses and experiences of difference and diversity in professional environments. She is a strong advocate of improving the theoretical basis of public relations scholarship, drawing on what

Bourdieu would call a "toolbox" of different theories and methods to improve our understanding of the practice. In particular, she uses the theoretical concepts in Bourdieu's work, in critical race theory, and in work on intersectionality, and she applies them to public relations to better understand the effect it has on the way we understand and interpret the world. She received her PhD from Leeds Metropolitan University in 2007.

Denise P. Ferguson is Chair and Associate Professor in the Division of Communication at Indiana Wesleyan University. In addition to teaching public relations introductory courses, writing, campaigns courses, research methods, and journalism courses, she has supervised nearly 100 campaigns and service-learning projects with nonprofit organizations and small businesses. Her research has been published in *Public Relations Review* and *Sociological Quarterly* and as chapters in edited volumes and has been presented at annual conferences of the International Communication Association, National Communication Association, and Public Relations Society of America, where she was awarded the 2008 Top Faculty Paper. Prior to joining Indiana Wesleyan University, Ferguson served on the faculty at Pepperdine University and the University of Indianapolis, and she has several years of experience in professional public relations and marketing communication in higher education, corporate, and nonprofit organizations. She is a member of the Commission on Public Relations Education and past chair of the Public Relations Division of the National Communication Association. She received her PhD from Purdue University.

Finn Frandsen is Professor of Corporate Communication and Director of the ASB Centre for Corporate Communication at Aarhus School of Business, Aarhus University (Denmark). His primary research interests are crisis communication and crisis management, environmental communication, public relations, marketing communication, corporate communication, organization and management theories, rhetoric, and discourse analysis. His research has appeared in *Corporate Communications: An International Journal, International Journal of Strategic Communication, Rhetorica Scandinavica, Hermes: Journal of Language and Communication Studies, LSP and Professional Communication, The Handbook of Crisis Communication* (2009), and *Handbook of Pragmatics* (2010), among others. He is the coauthor and coeditor of *International markedskommunikation i en postmoderne verden* (1997), *Den kommunikerende kommune* (2005), *Krisekommunikation* (2007), and *Intern kommunikation under forandring* (2009). He received his mag.art. degree from Aarhus University.

Dawn R. Gilpin is Assistant Professor of Public Relations at the Walter Cronkite School of Journalism and Mass Communication of Arizona State University in Phoenix, Arizona. Her research interests include crisis communication, issues management, social and new media, organizational identity, and reputation. She is particularly interested in using theories of complexity combined with network and narrative analysis to examine organizational relationships within a broad social, political, and economic context. Her work has appeared in *Public Relations Review* and the *Journal of Public Relations Research*, as well as in *Public Relations Theory II* and *The Handbook of Crisis Communication*. With Priscilla Murphy, she coauthored *Crisis Management in a Complex World* in 2008. She had more than 15 years of professional experience in public relations and international communication in Italy before embarking on an academic career. She received her PhD from Temple University.

Kirk Hallahan, Fellow PRSA (Public Relations Society of America), is Professor of Journalism and Technical Communication at Colorado State University. His research interests in recent years have focused on applications of technology to public relations and strategic communication. He received the PRSA Foundation's Jackson, Jackson & Wagner Behavioral Science Prize in 2001, the Institute for Public Relations' Pathfinder Award in 2007, and a suPRstar Award from AEJMC's Public Relations Division in 2009. He received his PhD from University of Wisconsin–Madison in 1995.

Julie K. Henderson, PhD, APR, is a tenured Professor of Journalism at the University of Wisconsin Oshkosh. In 2009, she began a 2-year term as the National Faculty Advisor for the Public Relations Student Society of America. She was named an American Society of Newspaper Editors Institute for Journalism Excellence fellow in 1998 and a University of Wisconsin System teaching fellow in 1999. She earned a Sweepstakes Award from the National Federation of Press Women communication competition in 1999. She was admitted into the Public Relations Society of America College of Fellows in 2004. She has had chapters included in PRSA's *Learning to Teach*, *Emerging Issues in Contemporary Journalism*, the *Handbook of Public Relations*, and *Mass Media in 2025*, plus articles in numerous public relations and mass communications journals. She serves on the editorial board of *Revista Romana de Marketing*, or the *Romanian Marketing Review*, published in Bucharest, Romania.

Susanne Holmström is Adjunct Professor in the Department of Communication, Business and IT at Roskilde University, Denmark. She has published in several international journals and books. From a basic position in sociology, she initiated the research program of "the reflective paradigm," which unfolds the interrelations between organizations and their social environment, and the legitimating notions mediating these interrelations as they change and differ according to society's constitution and challenges. This means studying these interrelations and legitimating notions partly in a historical, diachronic perspective as they change with society's evolution, partly in a cultural, sociopolitical, synchronic perspective as they differ in different types of societies today. She has a master's degree in social sciences. She received her PhD from Roskilde University, Denmark, in 2004.

James G. Hutton is Professor of Marketing and Communications at Fairleigh Dickinson University. Previously, Hutton was a manager of corporate and financial communications for three major multinational corporations. He has taught at seminars in Asia and Europe, served as a consultant to blue-chip organizations such as 3M and Financial Executives International, and authored numerous professional and academic publications, including *Marketing Communications: Integrated Theory, Strategy & Tactics* and *The Feel-Good Society: How the "Customer" Metaphor Is Undermining American Education, Religion, Media and Healthcare.* He received his PhD in marketing from the University of Texas at Austin, where he was a University Fellow and Dean's Doctoral Fellow.

Øyvind Ihlen is Professor of Communication and Management at BI Norwegian School of Management. He holds a second position at Hedmark University College. He has authored, coauthored, and coedited six books, including *Public Relations and Social Theory* (2009) and *Handbook of Communication and Corporate Social Responsibility* (2011). He has been vice chair of the Public Relations Division of the International Communication Association (ICA) and serves on the editorial board of seven international journals. He has published more than 40 journal articles and book chapters and earned the Pride Award for Best Article awarded by the Public Relations Division of the National Communication Association (NCA) in 2008. In 2009, he won the prize for best article in *Corporate Communications: An International Journal.* He received his PhD from the University of Oslo.

Thomas E. Isaacson is Assistant Professor of Corporate Communications and Public Relations in the Diederich College of Communication at Marquette University. His research interests include persuasive message development for campaigns related to sport public relations and health communication/physical fitness, and study abroad program design. He has taught at the American University of Rome, Michigan

State University, and Northern Michigan University, and his professional experience includes sport public relations work with the Chicago White Sox, Greensboro Bats, and Ferris State University. He is completing his PhD requirements in the College of Communication Arts and Sciences at Michigan State University.

Tony Jaques is Principal at Issue Outcomes Pty Limited, a specialist consultancy based in Melbourne, Australia, providing executive support in issue and crisis management and risk communication. He spent more than 20 years working across Asia-Pacific as regional Issue Manager for a multinational corporation and is a former Director of the Issue Management Council in Leesburg, Virginia, where he led an international project to develop Best Practice Principles. He is also a Senior Associate in the masters program of the School of Media and Communication at RMIT (Royal Melbourne Institute of Technology) University. He has been widely published in the academic and professional literature, with a strong focus on establishing issue management as a central function of proactive crisis prevention. He has also written and lectured extensively on bridging between academic research and improved practitioner standards. He completed his PhD at RMIT University.

Yan Jin is Assistant Professor of Public Relations at the School of Mass Communications, Virginia Commonwealth University. Her research interests include crisis communication, strategic conflict management, and how emotions influence public relations decision making and publics' responses. She has authored book chapters in *The Handbook of Crisis Communication* and *Public Relations: From Theory to Practice.* Her articles have been published in refereed journals such as *Communication Research, Journal of Public Relations Research, Public Relations Review, Journal of Contingency and Crisis Management,* and *Journal of International Communication.* She has won several top paper awards at the annual International Public Relations Research Conference, the annual conference of the Association for Education in Journalism and Mass Communication, and the annual conference of the National Communication Association. Her study on "Emotional Leadership as a Key Dimension of PR Leadership: A Strategic Conflict Management Perspective" was awarded a grant from the Plank Center for Leadership in Public Relations. She received her PhD from the University of Missouri.

Winni Johansen is Associate Professor at ASB Centre for Corporate Communication at Aarhus School of Business, Aarhus University (Denmark) and Director of the Executive Master's Program in Corporate Communication. Her research interests include crisis management and crisis communication, change communication, environmental communication, public relations, marketing communication, corporate communication, visual communication, and organizational culture. Her research has appeared in *Corporate Communications: An International Journal, International Journal of Strategic Communication, Rhetorica Scandinavica, Hermes: Journal of Language and Communication Studies, LSP and Professional Communication, The Handbook of Crisis Communication* (2009), and *Handbook of Pragmatics* (2010), among others. She is coauthor of *International markedskommunikation i en postmoderne verden* (1997), *Kultursignaler i tekst og billede* (1999), *Krisekommunikation* (2007), and *Intern kommunikation under forandring* (2009). She received her PhD from Aarhus School of Business, Denmark.

Michael L. Kent is Associate Professor of Public Relations at the University of Oklahoma's Gaylord College of Journalism and Mass Communication. He is an expert on public relations technology, dialogue, and mediated public relations. Kent has written dozens of articles and book chapters in public relations, including *Public Relations Review, Public Relations Quarterly, Gazette, Critical Studies in Media Communication,* and others, and has a forthcoming book on public relations writing. He was a Fulbright Scholar to Riga, Latvia, in 2006. Kent received his BA degree from the University of Alaska, his MS degree from the University of Oregon, and his PhD from Purdue University.

Jeong-Nam Kim is Assistant Professor of Public Relations in the Department of Communication at Purdue University. He "searches" and researches phenomena related to human communication and problem solving. He has developed the situational theory of problem solving (STOPS) and the communicative action in problem solving (CAPS) with James E. Grunig and Lan Ni. He is working on research projects applying CAPS and STOPS in the areas of public relations, digitalization and cyber-coping among members of publics, risk and health communication, public opinion, and sociological public diplomacy. He received his PhD from the University of Maryland, College Park.

Dean Kruckeberg, PhD, APR, Fellow PRSA, is Director of the Center for Global Public Relations and a professor at the University of North Carolina at Charlotte. He is coauthor of *Public Relations and Community: A Reconstructed Theory* and is coauthor of *This Is PR: The Realities of Public Relations.* He was the 1995 national "Outstanding Educator" of PRSA, was awarded the Jackson Jackson, & Wagner Behavioral Research Prize in 2006, and was the 1997 recipient of the Pathfinder Award. He is cochair of the Commission on Public Relations Education. He is a frequent lecturer worldwide.

Ruthann Weaver Lariscy is Professor in the Department of Advertising and Public Relations, College of Journalism and Mass Communication at the University of Georgia, Athens. Her research focuses on public relations and persuasive communication processes in health education campaigns and political processes. She received her PhD from the University of Missouri.

Alexander V. Laskin is Assistant Professor in the Department of Public Relations, Quinnipiac University. Most of his work experience has been in investor relations, international mergers and acquisitions, and marketing research. Today, his academic research focuses on investor relations, strategic corporate communications, social responsibility, and international business. His research on the value of investor relations was recognized by the Institute for Public Relations with the 2006 Ketchum Excellence in Public Relations Research Award. He received a degree in economic geography and English (1998) from the Moscow State Pedagogical University, an MA in communication studies (2003) from the University of Northern Iowa, an MA in international business (2008) from the University of Florida, and a PhD in mass communication (2008) from the University of Florida.

Shirley Leitch is Deputy Vice Chancellor Academic and Professor at Swinburne University of Technology in Melbourne, Australia. Her research focus on effecting change within corporate and societal discourses is interdisciplinary in character and has led to publications in the public relations, marketing, and management literatures, including *Organization Studies, Public Relations Review, Journal of Management Studies, Human Relations, Discourse Studies, European Journal of Marketing, Journal of Communication Management, International Studies in Management and Organisation, The Journal of Brand Management, Science and Public Policy,* and the *Australian Journal of Communication.*

Jacquie L'Etang is Senior Lecturer at the Stirling Media Research Institute (SMRI), University of Stirling, Scotland. Currently, she is pursuing interests in public relations (PR) anthropology. She has published 4 books and more than 40 articles and book chapters on a range of critical themes in PR, including history, ideology, ethics, rhetoric, the "professionalization" of PR, and its role in corporate social responsibility, propaganda, promotional culture, sport, and tourism and in public and cultural diplomacy. She received her PhD from the University of Stirling, Scotland.

Katherine A. McComas is Associate Professor in the Department of Communication at Cornell University, where she specializes in science, environmental, and health risk communication. She is particularly interested in public participation and community involvement in discussions, planning, and decision making about health and environmental risks. Much of her research focuses on the use of public meetings for risk communication and public participation, where she investigates the influence of procedural justice considerations on participants' judgments of trust, their satisfaction with the process, and their willingness to engage in future public participation activities. She received her PhD from Cornell University.

David McKie is Professor of Management Communication at Waikato Management School in Hamilton, New Zealand. He has authored or coauthored more than 50 articles, 22 book chapters, and 4 books. His latest book, cowritten with Vikram Murthy, on 21st-century leadership. was published in 2009, and he also cowrote with Debashish Munshi *Reconfiguring Public Relations: Ecology, Equity, and Enterprise*, which won the 2007 NCA PRIDE award. As CEO of RAM (Results by Action Management) International Consulting, he also works as a change, leadership, and strategic communication consultant. He has run leadership development programs as well as workshops for individuals and organizations in the private and public sectors in China, Europe, Korea, India, the Middle East, and the United States. He currently has one book proposal under review and is cowriting two more books: one on action research and another on complexity. He earned his PhD from the University of Stirling, Scotland.

Juan Meng is currently Assistant Professor in Public Relations in the Department of Communication at the University of Dayton. Her current research interests include the quantitative measurement of public relations leadership, the combined use of qualitative and quantitative methods to study participation in leadership development processes from an international perspective, and multinational firms' corporate reputation and knowledge management strategies in evolving markets. Her most recent publications appear in *Public Relations Review*, *Journal of World Business*, *The Social Science Journal*, and *China Media Research*. She teaches PR principles, PR writing, PR management, and case studies at the University of Dayton. She earned her MS and PhD (2009) from the University of Alabama.

Juan-Carlos Molleda is Associate Professor and Graduate Coordinator in the Department of Public Relations at the University of Florida (UF). He is an affiliated faculty of the UF Center for Latin American Studies and UF Paris Research Center. He is a founding member of the Institute for Public Relations' Commission on Global Public Relations Research. His research interests are in global corporate public relations management, including coordination and control mechanisms and transnational crises; public relations practices, regulations, professionalism, and social roles in Latin America; multisector partnerships creation and maintenance; and the interplay between authenticity and strategic communication practices. He received his BS in social communication in 1990 from Universidad del Zulia in Venezuela, his MS in corporate and professional communications in 1997 from Radford University in Virginia, and his PhD in journalism and mass communications with an emphasis on international public relations and international business in 2000 from the University of South Carolina.

Judy Motion is Professor of Communication at the University of New South Wales, Sydney, Australia. She has 25 years of experience as a communication scholar, and she is a specialist in public relations, public discourse, sustainability, and science-society engagement. Her work has been published in numerous journals, including *Organization Studies*, *Public Relations Review*, *Media, Culture & Society*, *Discourse Studies*, *Journal of Business Research*, *European Journal of Marketing*, *Journal of Communication Management*, *Political Communication*, and the *Australian Journal of Communication*. She has contributed chapters to the *Handbook of Public Relations*, the *Global Handbook of Public Relations*, *Public Relations and Social Theory: Key Figures and Concepts*, and the *Encyclopedia of Public Relations*. Funded research includes leadership of a project receiving a New Zealand $2.5 million Foundation for Research, Science and Technology (FRST) grant—"Socially and Culturally Sustainable Biotechnology" (2003–2008), and membership on a team receiving of a $1.6 million FRST grant—"Building Our Productivity: Understanding Sustainable Collective Productivity," as an international investigator (2008–2011).

Priscilla Murphy (PhD, Brown University) is Professor of Strategic and Organizational Communication at Temple University, Philadelphia, Pennsylvania. Her research interests include complexity and game theories, social and semantic networks, crisis communication, and reputation. Her work has appeared in the *Journal of Public Relations Research, Public Relations Review, Health Communication, Science, Technology & Human Values, Science Communication, Journal of Communication Management, Canadian Journal of Communication,* and *Journal of Applied Communication Research.* She is the coauthor, with Dawn Gilpin, of *Crisis Management in a Complex World* (2008), in which complexity theory is used to model the emergence and resolution of crises in corporations, government agencies, and NGOs. Prior to her academic career, she was Vice President of Public Relations for PaineWebber Group, Inc., in New York.

Bonita Dostal Neff is Associate Professor in the Department of Communication and head of the public relations major at Valparaiso University. Trained as a policy fellow in the Institute for Educational Leadership, she serves as the vice chair of the board of directors for Lakeshore Public Television and Radio (Indiana). She coedited *Public Relations: From Theory to Practice* (PRide Award 2008). She has published in *Public Relations Review, Handbook of Public Relations, Business Research Yearbook, Journal of International Business Disciplines, Encyclopedia of Public Relations, Infomatologia* (Croatian Communication Association), and *Strategist.* She was a member of the Commission on Public Relations Education contributing research to the final reports: *Port of Entry: Public Relations Education for the 21st Century* (1998) and *The Professional Bond* (2006). She founded the public relations divisions for the National Communication Association and Central States Communication Association. She cofounded the public relations divisions for the International Communication Association and International Public Relations Research Conference (Miami). She chairs the Public Relations/Corporate Communication track for the International Academy of Business Disciplines. She was selected as a National Teacher-Scholar by the National Communication Institute for Faculty Development in 2006. She was a visiting professor in Croatia (University of Zagreb & Kadar University) from 2002 to 2005 and South Korea (Sogang University) in 2005. She received her doctorate from the University of Michigan with a double major in broadcasting and group dynamics/rhetoric.

Lan Ni (PhD, University of Maryland, College Park) is Assistant Professor in the Jack J. Valenti School of Communication at the University of Houston. Her research focuses on strategic management of public relations, identification of publics, relationship management, intercultural public relations, and internal communication. She has published in journals such as *Journal of Public Relations Research, Journalism and Mass Communication Quarterly, Public Relations Review, Journal of Communication Management,* and *International Journal of Strategic Communication.*

Michael J. Palenchar is Associate Professor and Codirector of the Risk, Health and Crisis Communication Research Unit at the University of Tennessee and also holds a research affiliation with the National Center for Food Protection and Defense. His research interests include risk communication, issues management, and crisis communication, and he is also a research consultant for clients ranging from Fortune 500 companies to government and nongovernmental organizations. His research has been published in the *Journal of Public Relations Research,*

Public Relations Review, *Public Relations Journal*, *Environmental Communication*, and *Communication Research Reports*. He is coauthor (with Robert L. Heath) of *Strategic Issues Management* (second edition, 2008). He won the National Communication Association, Public Relations Division's Pride Award for top published article in the field of public relations in 2000 and 2007. He received his MA degree from the University of Houston and his PhD from the University of Florida.

Augustine Pang is Assistant Professor at the Division of Public and Promotional Communication, Wee Kim Wee School of Communication and Information, Nanyang Technological University, Singapore. His research interests include crisis management and communication, image management and repair, media relations, public relations, and media sociology and systems. Besides contributing book chapters to leading public relations and communication textbooks, he has published in *Corporate Communications: An International Journal*, *Public Relations Review*, *Journal of Contingency and Crisis Management*, *Copenhagen Journal of Asian Studies*, *Journal of Communication Management*, *Journal of International Communication*, *Asia Pacific Media Educator*, *Sphera Publica*, *Media Asia*, and the *International Encyclopedia of Communication*. He has won top paper awards at leading international conferences, including the Corporate Communications International Conference (2008, 2009), the Association of Educators in Journalism and Mass Communication conference (2007), and the International Public Relations Research Conference (2004, 2005, and 2009). He received his PhD from the University of Missouri.

Gayle M. Pohl is a faculty member at the University of Northern Iowa, teaching public relations on the graduate and undergraduate levels. She is an APR (Accredited Public Relations Practitioner) and an active member of PRSA (Public Relations Society of America), in addition to being a faculty adviser for PRSSA (Public Relations Student Society of America). She has also been a public relations practitioner, specializing in conflict management and negotiation, crisis communications, nonprofit, special events, health care, and entertainment public relations. Her research includes two books, titled *No Mulligans Allowed: Strategically Plotting Your Public Relations Course* (2nd edition) and *Public Relations: Designing Effective Communication*, articles on persuasive strategies used by home shopping networks, public relations strategies, fund-raising, and educational techniques used in teaching public relations. She has published in the *Journal of Communication*, *The Iowa Journal of Communication*, *The Journal of Promotion Management*, *Communication Reports*, *Advanced Interpersonal Communication*, and the *Handbook of Public Relations*. She received her doctorate in 1987 at the University of Kentucky.

Kimberly A. Schwartz, APR, MA, following her American Red Cross Public Relations career, became a public relations consultant while working toward a second career in education. She is currently Assistant Professor in the Communication Department of the University of Dubuque. In addition to her scholarly research, her contributions on American National Red Cross disaster relief response can be found in *Crisis Communications: What Every Executive Needs to Know*, by Devon Dougherty, and an American National Red Cross publication (ARC 4660), *Communication During a Crisis: A Guide to Effective Public Affairs*. She is a PhD candidate in the Educational Studies program at the University of Nebraska, Lincoln.

Matthew W. Seeger is Professor and Chair of the Department of Communication at Wayne State University. His work on communication and crisis management has appeared in *Journal of Health Communication*, *Journal of Organizational Change Management*, *The Encyclopedia of Public Relations*, *Communication Yearbook*, *Journal of Applied Communication Research*, *Communication Research Reports*, *Management Communication Quarterly*, *Journal of Business Communication*, and the *Journal of Business Ethics*, among others. His books include *Crisis Communication and the Public Health* (2007), *Effective Crisis Communication* (2006), and *Communication and Organizational*

Crisis (2003). His work has been supported by the Centers for Disease Control and Prevention, the Department of Homeland Security, and the National Science Foundation. He received his PhD from Indiana University in 1982.

Timothy L. Sellnow is Professor of Communication and Associate Dean for Graduate Programs in Communication at the University of Kentucky. His primary research and teaching focus is on risk and crisis communication. Much of his recent research focuses on strategic communication for mitigating the impact of and maintaining resilience in response to potential terrorist attacks on the United States. He has coauthored four books and published many refereed journal articles focusing on strategies for effective risk and crisis communication. He currently serves as theme leader for the risk communication research team at the National Center for Food Protection and Defense, a Center of Excellence sponsored by the Department of Homeland Security. He has also served on several occasions as a risk and crisis communication consultant for the Centers for Disease Control and Prevention. He received his PhD from Wayne State University.

Michael F. Smith teaches undergraduate and graduate courses in public relations, organizational communication, and conflict at La Salle University's campuses in Philadelphia, Athens, and Prague. He has worked with religious, athletic, cultural, and cause-related nonprofits and has supervised more than 100 service-learning projects, several of which earned national recognition. He is past chair of the National Communication Association's Public Relations Division, and his research interests include activism, place promotion, public relations pedagogy, and public relations and community building. In addition to several chapters in edited books, his work has appeared in the *Journal of Hospitality and Leisure Marketing* and *Destination Branding*. His views on various public relations issues have been quoted in *Public Relations Tactics*, *Public Relations News*, *U.S. News and World Report*, the *Los Angeles Times*, and the *Fort Worth Star-Telegram* and on CNBC. He received his PhD from Purdue University.

Peter M. Smudde is Assistant Professor of Public Relations at Illinois State University. After 16 years in industry, he moved to higher education in 2002. He is accredited in public relations (APR) through the Public Relations Society of America. His professional work has ranged from working in General Motors to consulting for family-owned companies. He also has won many industry awards. He researches public relations' synergy with corporate strategy, public relations discourse, and pedagogical approaches to public relations. He has published articles in *Corporate Reputation Review*, *International Journal of Strategic Communication*, *Public Relations Journal*, *Public Relations Quarterly*, *Review of Communication*, *Communication Teacher*, *Communication Quarterly*, *Visible Language*, and *Technical Communication*. He and Jeffrey Courtright published the book *Power and Public Relations*. He has also published two other books, *Public Relations as Dramatistic Organizing* and *Humanistic Critique of Education*. He is coauthor with Courtright of a new book, *Inspiring Cooperation and Celebrating Organizations: Genres, Message Design, and Strategies in Public Relations*. He received his PhD from Wayne State University in 2000.

Jeffrey K. Springston is Professor in the Department of Advertising and Public Relations, Grady College of Journalism and Mass Communication at the University of Georgia, Athens. His research focuses on public relations, health promotion, and tailored messaging using emerging communication technologies. He received his PhD from Ohio State University.

Krishnamurthy Sriramesh is Professor of Public Relations at the School of Business, Massey University in Wellington, New Zealand, and has taught at universities in four continents. His research has focused on global public relations, and he has been a leading advocate of holistic and culturally sensitive public relations practices and scholarship. He has edited or coedited four books and authored more than 60 book chapters and refereed journal articles. He also has presented more than 80 research papers, seminars, and talks in more than 25 countries. He serves as the associate editor of the *Journal of Communication Management* and is a member of the editorial board of several journals. He has won several teaching and research awards, including the prestigious Pathfinder Award from the Institute for Public Relations for "original scholarly research contributing to the public relations body of knowledge." He received a bachelor of arts degree majoring in economics, journalism, and criminology; a master's degree in mass communication from the University of Mysore, India; and a PhD in public communication from the University of Maryland.

Don W. Stacks is Professor of Public Relations and Associate Dean for Faculty Research and Creative Activity in the School of Communication at the University of Miami. His research agenda includes establishing which public relations outcomes best predict and affect return on investment. His latest work involves working on a better understanding of the social media and how it can be used to better predict specific outcomes associated with corporate communications practice (e.g., crisis trip-wires) and developing a common lexicon of social media and its measurement. He has received the Pathfinder Award for programmatic research from the Institute for Public Relations, the Jackson Jackson & Jackson and the Educator of the Year from the Public Relations Society of America, and elected a Distinguished Research Fellow and a Distinguished Teaching Fellow from the Eastern Communication Association and most recently as a 2010 Senior Fellow from the Society for New Communications Research. In addition he received the National Communication Association Public Relations Division's PRIDE Award for the Primer of Public Relations Research. He received his PhD from the University of Florida in 1978.

Maureen Taylor is Professor and Gaylord Family Chair of Strategic Communication in the Gaylord College of Journalism and Mass Communication at the University of Oklahoma. Her research interest is in international public relations, nation building and civil society campaigns, and new communication technologies. She has traveled extensively around the world and has conducted research in Malaysia, Taiwan, Bosnia, Croatia, Kosovo, Jordan, and Sudan. In 2001, she served as a Fulbright Scholar at the University of Sarajevo, Bosnia-Herzegovina. Her work has appeared in the *Journal of Public Relations Research*, *Public Relations Review*, *Communication Monographs*, *Human Communication Research*, *Journal of Communication*, *Management Communication Quarterly*, *Gazette*, and the *Atlantic Journal of Communication*. She earned a bachelor's degree in mass media and political science from Westfield State College. She earned a PhD in public affairs and issues management from Purdue University in 1996.

William Thompson, who retired from the University of Louisville after teaching public relations and communication theory for 23 years, maintained during his academic career an active practitioner role, often working with organized labor. His research and practical focus, after study at the universities of Missouri and Louisville in the United States, and Waikato in New Zealand, explores the role of power and identity in constructing messages and motivating consumer behavior. He is the former head of the public relations divisions of both the Association for Journalism and Mass Communication and the Southern States Communication Association. He has written a book on public relations, *Targeting the Message* (1996). He continues to speak at various conferences across the United States.

Natalie T. J. Tindall is Assistant Professor in the Department of Communication at Georgia State University, where she teaches undergraduate and graduate courses in public relations and journalism. The intersections of race, gender, ethnicity, and sexual orientation influence her primary research areas of diversity in the public relations profession and diversity among organizational publics. Her additional research interests include health, public relations, university and college fund-raising, philanthropy and the nonprofit sector, and Black fraternal organizations. She received her PhD in Communication from the University of Maryland, College Park.

Margalit Toledano is Senior Lecturer in the Management Communication Department of Waikato Management School in New Zealand. She studied public relations at Boston University on the Hubert H. Humphrey Fellowship Programme, became an accredited member of the Public Relations Society of America (PRSA) in 1985, served as president of the Israeli Public Relations Association (1993–1996), and became a Fellow of PRSA in 2007. As a practitioner in Israel, she served both the public and the private sectors and ran her own firm. Her PhD thesis, based on the evolution of public relations as a profession in Israel, was completed at Paris 8 University, France. She is a member of the editorial board of *Public Relations Review,* in which she has also published a number of articles. Her research focuses on public relations, social marketing, and ethics. She received her MA in Communication from the Hebrew University in Jerusalem.

Elizabeth L. Toth is Professor and Chair of the Department of Communication at the University of Maryland, College Park. She has coauthored *Women in Public Relations: How Gender Influences Practice* and *Public Relations: The Profession and the Practice.* She edited *The Future of Excellence in Public Relations and Communication Management: Challenges for the Next Generation* and coedited *The Gender Challenge to Media: Voices From the Field, Rhetorical and Critical Approaches to Public Relations,* and *Rhetorical and Critical Approaches to Public Relations II.* She has published numerous articles, book chapters, and convention papers on gender and public relations, and public affairs. Her work has received the Institute for Public Relations Pathfinder Award and the PRSA Jackson, Jackson & Wagner Award. Also, she has received the PRSA Outstanding Educator Award and PRSSA's Outstanding Faculty Advisory Award. She received her PhD from Purdue University.

Katerina Tsetsura is Associate Professor of Strategic Communication/Public Relations in the Gaylord College of Journalism and Mass Communication at the University of Oklahoma (United States). Her interests include social construction of public relations, global media and public relations ethics, media transparency, gender in public relations, and issues management in countries with transitional economies. Her research has appeared in internationally recognized books, such as the *Handbook of Global Public Relations* and Merrill's *Global Journalism,* annuals (e.g., *The Global Corruption Report 2005: Transparency International*), and journals (e.g., *Journal of Public Relations Research, Public Relations Journal, Public Relations Review, Asian Communication Research,* and *Russian Journal of Communication*) published in three continents. She has also presented papers at numerous research and professional communication conferences around the world, including in Germany, Mexico, Poland, Russia, United Arab Emirates, the United Kingdom, Ukraine, and the United States. She earned her PhD in communication from Purdue University in 2004.

Robert R. Ulmer is Professor and Chair of the Department of Speech Communication at the University of Arkansas at Little Rock. His research and teaching interests focus on risk and crisis communication. He has coauthored four books and numerous articles focusing on effective risk and crisis communication. His latest book, titled *Effective Crisis Communication: Moving From Crisis to Opportunity,* emphasizes how organizations can actually grow, prosper, and renew if they manage a crisis effectively. Beyond research and teaching, he often serves as an organizational consultant and research collaborator with public and private organizations, including the Department of Homeland Security, the National Center for Food Protection and Defense, the Arkansas Department of Health, and the Centers for Disease Control and Prevention.

Jennifer Vardeman-Winter is Assistant Professor at the University of Houston's (UH's) Jack J. Valenti School of Communication, where she teaches both undergraduate and graduate courses in public relations. She is also an affiliate faculty member in UH's Women's Studies Program. Her studies are concentrated in public relations campaigns, health communication, and multicultural feminist research. Previously, she worked for Lois Paul & Partners, a public relations firm focusing on the high-technology market. She also recently worked for ICF Macro, consulting for governmental agencies such as the CDC's Radiological Studies Branch and the Department of Homeland Security's Citizen Corps. She currently consults for Baylor College of Medicine's Teen Health Clinics, conducting communication research with teens from low-income communities of color to inform the development of informative Webisodes about safe sex. Her work has been published in *Health Communication* and *Media Report to Women*. She earned her PhD from the University of Maryland.

Marina Vujnovic, PhD, is Assistant Professor at Monmouth University in New Jersey. Her primary fields of research include participatory journalism and new media studies, media history and gender, critical political economy, and cultural studies. Her research interests focus on international communication and global flow of information; journalism studies; explorations of the historical, political-economic, and cultural impact on media; and gender, ethnicity, and media. Recently, she published a book titled *Forging the Bubikopf Nation: Journalism, Gender and Modernity in Interwar Yugoslavia*, and she is author of several research articles and book chapters.

Robert I. Wakefield is Associate Professor of Communication at Brigham Young University. He concentrates his research on stakeholder relations and reputation in transnational entities, examining the impacts of globalization, culture, activism, and other factors on these global practices of public relations. His publications include "Public Relations Contingencies in a Globalized World Where Even 'Glocalization' Is Not Sufficient," in *Public Relations Journal*; "World-Class Public Relations: A Model for Effective Public Relations in the Multinational," in *Journal of Communication Management*; and "Theory of International Public Relations, the Internet, and Activism," in *Journal of Public Relations Research*. Before becoming a full-time scholar, he practiced and consulted on strategic public relations in 25 nations between 1990 and 2005. He received his PhD from the University of Maryland in 1997.

Tom Watson PhD, FCIPR, FPRCA is Professor of Public Relations and Deputy Dean (Education) in The Media School at Bournemouth University in England. Before entering full-time academic life in 2003, his career covered journalism and public relations in Australia, the United Kingdom, and internationally. He ran a successful public relations consultancy for 18 years and was chair of the United Kingdom's Public Relations Consultants Association from 2000 to 2002. His research interests focus on measurement of public relations programs, reputation, corporate communication, and the history of public relations. With Paul Noble, he is author of *Evaluating Public Relations: A Best Practice Guide to Public Relations Planning, Research, and Evaluation*, published by Kogan Page. He is a member of the Commission on Public Relations Measurement and Evaluation. He was awarded his PhD in 1995 from Nottingham Trent University for research into models of evaluation in public relations.

Damion Waymer is Assistant Professor of Communication at Virginia Tech. His research uses issues management, public relations theory, and organizational rhetoric to shed light on issues of culture and diversity in general and issues of race, class, and gender specifically. Additionally, his research uses communication theories to explore some of the issues that marginalized or underrepresented publics can and do encounter, and what strategies are available to them to challenge these issues. His representative works have been published in outlets such as the *Journal of Applied Communication Research*, *Public Relations Review*, *Communication Quarterly*, and the *Journal of Communication Inquiry*. He received his PhD from Purdue University.

Brenda J. Wrigley, PhD, APR, is Associate Professor and Chair of the Department of Public Relations at the S.I. Newhouse School of Public Communications at Syracuse University. With 21 years of professional experience in broadcast journalism, advertising, and corporate public relations, she teaches theory, research, and management. A feminist scholar, her research interests include gender and diversity, as well as reputation management in the face of crises dealing with diversity and ethics. Her work has appeared in a variety of academic journals. She won the Meredith Teaching Recognition Award from Syracuse University in 2006. She holds an MS in public relations from Syracuse and a BJ from the University of Missouri/Columbia.